The Alfred Hit
Com_

**Written by Martin Grams, Jr.
and Patrik Wikstrom.**

Foreward by Patricia Hitchcock.

OTR Publishing / USA

INTRODUCTION

If Alfred Hitchcock could be compared to the wines he enjoyed savoring, 1940 should not only be singled as "vintage Hitchcock," but a great year as well. March 27, *Rebecca* premiered at the Four Star Theater in Los Angeles. Hitchcock's American directorial debut would later win an Academy Award for "Best Picture." August 26, American newspapers carried British producer Michael Balcon's criticism of his countrymen, who remained safely abroad during the war, while Britian was under attack. He publicly singled out Alfred Hitchcock, who, in reply, compared Balcon to Donald Duck. August 27, Hitchcock's *Foreign Correspondent* premiered at the Rivoli, winning acclaim and praise among movie critics. September 5, Shooting began on the set of *Mr. and Mrs. Smith*, and Carole Lombard, teasing Alfred Hitchcock for calling actors "cattle," brought three heifers on the set, each tagged with the name of an actor in the film.

To imagine that television was only in the minds of inventors and broadcasting moguls, during that same year, is a revolution that could only be accepted by the movie-going audience, who purchased the magic box, and made "television" a household word. Yet, fifteen years later, Alfred Hitchcock introduced himself to the same audience that viewed his pictures, and he himself became a household word.

With the recent Centennial of Hitchcock's birth, both his films and the television series that bore his name, have become "rediscovered," in a matter of speaking. Film students and a younger generation who were born after Hitchcock's death, far too late to experience the big-screen excitement of his pictures, are today, studying his movies scene by scene. Whether it was the shower stabbing in *Psycho* or the crop dusting sequence in *North by Northwest*, Hitchcock somehow – in some way – left an imprint in our minds.

His involvement with *Alfred Hitchcock Presents* and *The Alfred Hitchcock Hour* was minimal – to say the least. He hosted over 360 episodes, but he didn't even direct twenty. The television series made him a world-renowned celebrity, and even as his private life was often in turmoil. Myths, legends and stories have grown over the years, regarding the television series, so we felt it was time to give the television program the justice it deserved. Writing this book, of course, was no easy task. We gathered information from thousands of sources, published works, videos, interviews with cast and crew, and so on. We viewed the episodes (some we viewed more times than we can count), cross-referenced our interviews, and asked thousands of questions.

We ourselves didn't initially know how to approach the book. Our questions were many. One such example was should we give away the endings in the plot descriptions? We debated, but then it occurred to us. Regardless of which way we decide to go with this, we cannot please everyone. So without hesitation, the "twist endings" *are* given away among the plots. Our intention, with this book, is to publish a compilation of information, about the very aspects of Hitchcock's career, that have not yet been covered in extreme detail. Citing an example: since no one has yet compiled a list of the anthologies that featured his name, we now include a chapter, with a listing of all publications.

We have attempted to offer a scholarly, as well as informative look at the television series we have grown to love. We know this book is not perfect, but we feel it's pretty darn close. And hopefully, with the persistence of readers, we now offer a different perspective into the world of Alfred Hitchcock. Not as a movie director, but as a human being.

We do want to take time out to thank everyone who helped us with our book. With so many friends to thank, we hope we didn't over-look anyone. If we did, our sincere apologies. Regardless of how small or how large they contributed, in no specific order . . .

Virginia Darcy, A.I. Bezzerides, David Swift, Ray Bradbury, Elliott Reid, Tyler McVey, the late Talmage Powell, Marian Seldes, Jay Hickerson, Julie Adams, Harold Q. Masur, Tonnie Richardson, Janice G. Suttles, Kelley Schrumpf, Lorraine Richter, Richard Berg, Burt Styler, Brian Gauthier, George Sawyer, the late Audrey Meadows, Patricia Hitchcock for offering to write the foreward, Arthur Hiller, Irving Elman, Morris Hershman, Arthur Hiller, Rick Edelstein, the late Hazel Court, Robert Blees, Henry Corden, George F. Slavin, Clark Howard, the late Joan Harrison, Charles Bennett, Lawrence Treat, the late Robert Bloch, Gordon Payton, Harvey, Chuck Schaden for his informative essay, Richard Fry, Donald Ramlow for supplying us with hard-to-find titles, David Miller, Ray Keese, Joseph Pevney, John D. MacDonald, Fess Parker, David Siegel for the inspiration, Sydney Pollack, Marc Richman, Bob Burks, Teresa Wright, Joseph Stefano, Harry Muheim, Jerry Sohl, Janet Leigh, Herbert Coleman, Wayne Jeffrey, John J. Lloyd, Wayne Heffley, Henry Slesar, Bill Frye, Joel Coker, Warren Stevens, Fred Freiberger, Bruce Dern, Chip and Judy Diamond, Doug Benton, Norman Leavitt, R.A. Butler, Ken Adam, Gordon Hessler, Norman Lloyd, Doc Erickson, Ted Okuda, Thomas Lesser and his massive collection of mystery magazines, Hume Cronyn, Gene Leber, Rita Taylor, Ken Kaffke for his informative essay, Peter Bogdanovich, Charles Runyon, Alfred A. Whittaker, Theodore G. Bergmann, Anne Francis, Bill Mumy, Dan Auiler, Mary Dohrman, Charles Huck, Francis M. Nevins, Mike McWilliams, Evan Hunter, Calissa and Nick Lambert, Hilton A. Green, Ulrich Rüedel for his scholarly essay, Neill Potts, Arthur Laurents, the Lucille Fletcher (Wallop), Howard Prouty (for his generous assistance in more ways than we can count), Seth T. Smolinske, Lee Kalcheim, Jane Wyatt, Edward D. Hoch, Robert Briney, Dorothy Salisbury Davis, James Yafee, Dana Wynter, Line Blackburn, Julie Re'Jean Sullivan-Whited, Graham Kirkwood, Andrea Ragan, June and Lenny Fortnash, Tonnie Richardson, Leland H. Faust, Steven B. Kravitz, Tim Daley for supplying us many photos in this book, Ann Robinson, Anne Helm, John Fiedler, Barbara Dane, Henry Brandt, The American Film Institute in Los Angeles, Al Hubin, Tony Randall, all my friends at the William Morris Agency, Michael Pate, Stephen Youngkin, Cheryl Morris, Samuel Taylor, Derek Tague for getting us many great newspaper clippings and magazine articles about the program, Arthur Ross, Vanessa Dautreuil, Lorraine Kaufman, Larry Storch, Jaclyn Packer, Ken Mogg, Gary and Susan Svehla, Steve Oxford, Joyce Van Patten, Joel Davis of Davis Publications, Cathleen Jordan for taking time out of her busy schedule to help with the anthology chapter, Jonathan Glassner, Robert Iscove, Michael Uno, Jeff Janew, Joel Oliansky, Peter Enfantino, Kevin McCarthy, and to Alfred Hitchcock himself, who inspired us with his passion for movie making.

Special thanks to Dan Einstein and John Tirpak at the ATAS/UCLA Television Archives for arranging a screening of "The Jail," which contributed heavily on Howard Prouty's wonderful essay. The folks at the Museum of TV & Radio in New York, Betty Jane Reed and Walter Roberti in NBC's New York offices.

Tom Weaver, especially, who took a lot of his free time to help look over the manuscript, and add those little trivia tid-bits and quotes that everyone loves. (His books are listed in our bibliography.) Thank you Tom.

Howard Mandlebaum at Photofest in New York City, who supplied us with many of the photos you see in this book. If you're ever looking for a photo of your favorite movie star or television program, Photofest is definitely the one-stop source for glossies.

Ronald V. Borst of Hollywood Movie Posters, in Hollywood, California, who also supplied us with photos for our book.

Thomas Meisnest and Cindy Chang at Universal Studios for their publishing coordination and cooperation, to ensure that our project met it's expectation.

Patrik Wikstrom and Martin Grams, Jr.

FOREWARD

When Lew Wasserman came to my father with the idea for a television series, my father was a little reluctant. However, with the enormous respect and fondness that he had for Lew over many years, he agreed. He could not conceive of anyone but Joan Harrison to produce it. Joan and my parents had been working together since the 1930s. He knew that she could keep the integrity that he always insisted upon, and later the assistant producer – another old friend – Norman Lloyd.

When the idea for my father came to do the lead-ins, they found James Allardice. When Norman saw them, he said, "Hitch will never do these." However, my father liked them and whenever he had to make a speech, he told Jimmy what he wanted to say and Allardice wrote them!

I remember *Alfred Hitchcock Presents* with great fondness, as I was lucky enough to appear in many of them. I feel that *Alfred Hitchcock Presents* was unique in that the stories, writers and actors were all first class.

- Patricia Hitchcock, August 2000

Patricia Hitchcock in the episode "Into Thin Air"

TABLE OF CONTENTS

"GOOD EVENING . . . "

When television was ready to grace the national scene, it borrowed rather liberally two of Hollywood's major resources: its money and its mediocrity. As box-office receipts waned, the virtuosity of the grade B films made a mass migration from the motion picture lots to the television studio closets. There they contentedly continued to slice up their product; with television they learned to slice a little faster.

Once this incidental household rearrangement was completed, the film colony's survivors boldly proclaimed their eagerness to follow the one course open to them. Since television so effectively cornered the market for advertising, they would pursue quality. And so they did, with salutary benefits for both stockholders and moviegoers.

Alfred Hitchcock was fifty-six years old when his television program premiered in September of 1955. He was currently the director of forty-one movies, and his latest, *To Catch a Thief*, was a financial box-office success. The rotund director with the merry eyes and the macabre style, while directing movies or television plays, demonstrated some fine points of technique that made millions of people shiver and chortle simultaneously. But how *Alfred Hitchcock Presents* came to television has a history as equally fascinating as the man who hosted each and every episode.

Most writers who have bothered to deal at all with Alfred Hitchcock's television work have focused exclusively on the shows which he himself directed – and then only insofar as they reflect the stylistic and thematic preoccupations of his feature films. The series itself has remained almost completely unexamined, particularly with regard to: (a) Hitchcock's influence, regardless of the extent of his day-to-day involvement, on the content and style of the programs; and (b) the relationship between the enormous celebrity which the show brought him and the context/style of his concurrent and subsequent feature films.

Scholars and critics alike could account for hundreds of factors leading up to the formation of the television program, including – if not limited to – the birth of Alfred Hitchcock and the invention of television. But perhaps a few of the minor aspects should be accounted for. Certainly without the weekly host whose name plastered the television screen each week, *Alfred Hitchcock Presents* would never have been. It would be impossible to list them all, but perhaps the more intriguing aspects of Hitchcock's life might shed some light on the subject.

One of the many early formations of the program certainly originated with Hitchcock's childhood. As a young man (according to Hitchcock himself) he often found his father to be a little brutal. As their third child, he confessed that learning the values and morals of society was to experience it the hard way. "When I was no more than six years of age," Hitchcock told a reporter, "I did something that my father considered worthy of reprimand. He sent me to the local police station with a note. The officer on duty read it and locked me in a jail cell for five minutes, saying 'This is what we do to naughty boys.' I have, ever since, gone to any lengths to avoid arrest and confinement." These lengths also consisted of Hitchcock never owning a drivers license, or taking lessons behind the wheel. *

---

* Hitchcock often poked fun of his fear of the police during his hosting on *Alfred Hitchcock Presents*. Remember the time he complained about getting a ticket in "Lamb to the Slaughter"? Hitchcock received another ticket during his closing remarks in "Dead Weight." And he was arrested for reasons unknown in "The Crooked Road."

"I have always been fascinated by crime," Hitchcock noted. "It's a particularly English problem, I think. The British take a peculiar interest in the literature of crime. It goes back to reading [Sir Arthur] Conan Doyle. Every time you read about a particularly grisly trial at Old Bailey you also read that some famous actor or director or writer is present . . ." Newspaper accounts satisfied Hitchcock's thirst for crime until he discovered that murder was also evident in fictional stories. "At sixteen I discovered the works of Edgar Allan Poe," he recalled. "I happened to read first his biography, and the sadness of his life made a great impression on me. I felt an enormous pity for him, because in spite of his talent he had never been happy. When I came home from the office where I worked I went straight to my room, took the cheap edition of his *Tales of the Grotesque and Arabesque*, and began to read. I still remember my feelings when I finished 'The Murders in the Rue Morgue.' I was afraid, but this fear made me discover something I've never forgotten since: fear, you see, is an emotion people like to feel when they know they're safe. . . Very likely it's because I was so taken with the Poe stories that I later made suspense films."

By early 1919, encouraged by his employers, and inspired by mystery novels and stories he had consumed, Hitchcock wrote a short story for the premiere issue of *The Henley: Social Club Magazine of the Henley Company*. Printed in June 1919, the short story was entitled "Gas," about an innocent woman's descent into the moral decadent of Paris. The story ended with a surprise twist. *"Half a dozen men rushed towards her amid the encouraging shouts of the rest. She was seized. She screamed with terror . . . better had she been caught by her pursuer was her one fleeting thought as they dragged her roughly across the room. The fiends lost no time in settling her fate. . . Conscious only of a choking sensation, this was death . . . then . . . 'It's out, Madam,' said the dentist. 'Half a crown, please.' "* Although this would become the only short story ever written by Alfred Hitchcock, it certainly foreshadowed the shape of things to come. Hitchcock loved the idea of a twist ending to a story, the type of endings usually associated with O. Henry. Hitchcock's fascination with teasing the readers (allowing them to carry off their imaginations until reality strikes a blow at the climax) was very similar to the techniques he himself employed on screen.

Still, among the short stories and novels, newspapers and courtroom cases, Hitchcock became entranced by images projected on a screen, originating from a small box. Motion pictures established a new form of story telling and he discovered how this medium could be used to express those stories artistically.

One of the lesser known formations of *Alfred Hitchcock Presents* was radio. Throughout the 1930s and 40s, Americans were glued to their radio sets as often as we today, sit in front of the television and watch the evening news. Whether it was comedy or drama, radio became the means by which listeners could turn a dial and discover the latest world events. In an age where the internet and television didn't exist, radio influenced anyone who was willing to take time and listen – including Alfred Hitchcock.

Mystery and horror programs were broadcast across the country, both locally and coast-to-coast. *Inner Sanctum Mysteries* gave listeners the chance to hear grisly tales of murder and madness. (Boris Karloff starring in Poe's "The Tell-Tale Heart," broadcast on August 3, 1941, is chilling enough to make any listener hold their breath.) *The Whistler*, another series of mystery tales was one of the closest programs to resemble *Alfred Hitchcock Presents*, by offering tales of murder and embezzlement, with twists of fate acting as judge, jury, and on great occasion – executioner. But one of the granddaddies of these suspenseful radio programs was entitled, appropriately enough, *Suspense*. Each week, listeners heard highly-paid Hollywood actors star in leading roles that made them out as villains – or innocent victims – depending on the circumstances.

In July of 1940, CBS began looking for a summer replacement for *The Lux Radio Theatre*, which was scheduled to go off the air for the summer season. In view of the fact that radio programs were broadcast live at the time, there rose a dire need for a small, short-run program to take the series' time-slot until its return in the fall. There was no such thing as reruns or rebroadcasts, and it was during those small tenures, that radio stations presented episodes of new programs for a trial run. If the listening audience wrote in, asking to hear more, the stations knew they had a program of infinite potential. If the audience did not favor such proposals, the broadcasting studios pulled the plug.

William S. Paley, in charge of the Columbia Broadcasting System, built a reputation that "quality, not quantity, means a larger listening audience." During this particular summer, CBS (thanks to a little influence on Paley's part) came up with an idea for a series entitled *Forecast*. On July 15, 1940, *Forecast* premiered in *Lux*'s place as an hour-long playhouse. Each week, for a full hour, two thirty-minute episodes of varied entertainment were broadcast, with the announcement to the audience that if they liked what they heard, please write to CBS. The second presentation of July 22, 1940 offered a mystery/horror show entitled *Suspense*. . . and Hitchcock was the main course.

Walter Wanger, who was the producer of Hitchcock's second American picture, *Foreign Correspondent*, arranged for Hitchcock's name to be used over the air, but not the man himself. This condition was agreed upon, as long as a pitch about *Foreign Correspondent*, be mentioned sometime during the broadcast. To add some flavor to the deal, Wanger threw in Edmund Gwenn and Herbert Marshall as part of the package, both of whom had considerable roles in the movie. According to Herbert Marshall, he and Hitchcock decided on the same story to bring to the airwaves, which happened to be a favorite of both of them: "The Lodger" by Marie Belloc-Lowndes. Hitchcock had, of course, directed a movie version of this chilling story, for Gainsborough Studios in 1926.

Herbert Marshall portrayed the mysterious lodger, whose actions at night (such as walking the streets alone) went unexplained. Co-starring with him were Edmund Gwenn and character actress Lurene Tuttle as the rooming-house keepers who start to suspect that their new boarder might be the notorious Jack the Ripper. Wilbur Hatch, whose music would later be featured (stock music, mostly) on *Alfred Hitchcock Presents*, composed and conducted the music for this program. Gwenn was actually repeating the role taken in the 1926 film by his brother, Arthur Chesney. Lurene Tuttle would later work with Hitchcock twenty years later, playing the role of Al Chambers in *Psycho* (1960). Adapting the script for radio was not a great technical challenge, and a slight alteration to the story was made. The true identity of the mysterious lodger would not be given away. Instead, the story ended rather abruptly and the entire cast, including Alfred Hitchcock, spent the last remaining minutes discussing the possible conclusions. Since the purpose of *Forecast* was to present experimental dramas, and test the listening audience's reaction, why not give the eavesdroppers something to write in about?

Keeping in mind that Hitchcock himself would not become a familiar figure in American living rooms, most of the listening audience was unaware of how his voice sounded. With this notion in mind, character actor Joseph Kearns played the role of Hitchcock, with a British accent. Truth is, the famed director wasn't even present during the program's drama! A recording of this episode does circulate among collectors and upon hearing the program, it is evident that Hitchcock merely lent his name to the show – and nothing more. All for the sake of publicity.

Although the network did receive a small volume of mail regarding *Suspense*, CBS did not act too quickly. It wouldn't be until two years later, in the summer of 1942, that *Suspense* returned to the air as a prime-time program. And more importantly, *Suspense* would influence countless radio programs, win a considerable number of awards, and remain part of the CBS prime-time line-up for more than twenty years, until the program bowed out in September of 1962. Hitchcock himself became one of millions of fans who would tune in each week to hear *Suspense*. One episode of *Suspense* ["Death on My Hands" May 10, 1951] gained Hitchcock's attention to writer John Michael Hayes, who would soon script four of Hitchcock's motion pictures.

Perhaps the most important trivia regarding this episode: The *Forecast* presentation of *Suspense* was not initially a pilot episode of just any radio thriller. As reported by announcer Thomas Freebairn during the closing announcement, *Suspense* would originally feature dramatic offerings of Hitchcock's previous motion pictures. Had *Suspense* received a considerable amount of interest, (and if Hitchcock continued to allow the use of his name over the air), future productions would have presented an adaptation of *The Thirty-Nine Steps* and *The Lady Vanishes*.

Possibly swayed by the production standards of radio broadcasting, Alfred Hitchcock made a personal attempt to have his own mystery/horror series. On May 11, 1945, with the assistance of a few sound technicians and radio hands, Hitchcock arranged to have an audition show recorded on transcription disc, and presented it to the American Broadcasting Company (ABC). The show was entitled *Once Upon a Midnight* [from Poe's "The Raven"]. The initial proposal was for Hitchcock to host, narrate and supervise each episode, each offering a different story based on a previously-published short story. Felix Mills was hired as the chief musician, and at Hitchcock's insistence, the music was used more for emphasizing verbal and physical actions than for forming musical bridges between scenes. The music was also used to make plot points, and to add impact and sharpness to the dialogue.

The opening theme featured church bells tolling twelve, symbolizing midnight, courtesy of Mills. The story brought to life for the proposed pilot was Francis Iles' story, "Malice Aforethought," which Hitchcock confessed to director Francois Truffaut in 1968, was one of his favorite stories.

"Suspense, shock, murder. All the makings of a spine-tingling mystery drama, in the hands of a past-master of theatrical illusion, Alfred Hitchcock. We of the American Broadcasting Company believe this new series has the opportunity of becoming the most important and distinguished of its kind in radio. Mr. Hitchcock will appear in every program as the narrator and will personally supervise the writing and direction of each highly-dramatic tale. It is our good fortune that Alfred Hitchcock has an enormous interest in radio. In fact, the idea of this series originated with him. This is important because it means we have the great asset of a star, with a personal enthusiasm in making the series a true milestone in radio."

- Opening monologue of *Once Upon a Midnight*

This time, unlike *Forecast*, Hitchcock himself actually hosted. In the (unbilled) roles were Hume Cronyn and Jessica Tandy. Cronyn was a friend of Hitchcock's and played the lead role as the murderous doctor, with a supporting cast of unknowns. Cronyn had appeared in Hitchcock's last two films, *Shadow of a Doubt* (1943) and *Lifeboat* (1944). Hoping to convince ABC to broadcast *Once Upon a Midnight*, Hitchcock applied the same trick used in the *Forecast* broadcast. The story ended abruptly and the announcer told the listeners that the conclusion would be given the week after. But to Hitchcock's sorrow, ABC did not buy the idea after listening to the demo, and the project was more-or-less scrapped.

On the pilot, recorded for the purpose of acquiring a sponsor, Hitchcock himself explained that: "Murderers are serious people. You know, one thing that has always fascinated me about criminals, is that when you walk down the street, any passerby might be a murderer. They don't all wear black moustaches. I imagine most murderers behave just like mild ordinary people, until suddenly one day they turn and stab you in the back." This same "next-door neighbor" policy was the type of murder stories producers Joan Harrison and Norman Lloyd would route through and choose for *Alfred Hitchcock Presents*.

A short time afterwards – the internal evidence suggests 1947 – another audition was recorded, entitled *The Alfred Hitchcock Show*. This second production was again an adaptation of the same story, "Malice Aforethought," but the script was different: The opening scene took place in a courtroom and the story was told through flashback. The setting was in the United States instead of England. The cast was different, too. Hume Cronyn and his wife did not play any of the roles. Radio pro Joseph Kearns starred as the murderous doctor, and a supporting cast of Edmund McDonald, Jeff Corey, Janet Waldo, Norman Field, Margaret Breighton, Tom Holland and John Dehner. Hitchcock again participated, not just host, but narrator as well. In the same fashion as *The Whistler*, Hitchcock played the role of a guilty conscience, urging the doctor to kill, kill, kill . . . Hitchcock even apologized to the listening audience, promising not to get in the way of the story. In fact, his remarks included morbid jokes and awful puns – similar to what he accomplished as host on *Alfred Hitchcock Presents*.

> "*The Alfred Hitchcock Show*. Every week at this same time, you'll hear thirty minutes of sheer excitement. From the man who makes the movies everyone remembers, the famous director who gave you *Spellbound, Suspicion, Rebecca, The Lady Vanishes*. The gentlemen they call the 'cavalier of the macabre,' Mr. Alfred Hitchcock."
> - Announcer's introduction to *The Alfred Hitchcock Show*

"I'm a little worried about mysteries these days," Hitchcock introduced on the show. "I think we're getting altogether too many sinister looking butlers, hands coming through sliding panels and such. You see, I'm interested in people, in characters . . . horrible characters. I like to crawl inside a man's mind if I can possibly do so, and find out what makes him behave like a madman – or an imbecile. That's why I took a fancy to this story by Francis Isles called 'Malice Aforethought.' The shutter Isles doesn't tease you. He comes right out and tells you what happens. But he doesn't tell us why. He leaves that up to us . . . up to you and me. Well, let's have a listen, see what we can make of it. What do you say?"

Although it is not clear who directed or produced *Once Upon a Midnight*, the *Alfred Hitchcock Show* featured complete production credits, read by the announcer, after the drama. Jerome Lawrence was the producer. Lawrence co-wrote the script with Robert E. Lee, another established writer for television and radio. Original music was composed and conducted by Claude Sweeton, and arranged by David Stress, with Dr. Samuel Hoffman at the theramin (the same instrument used for the opening theme of *Once Upon a Midnight* and Hitchcock's *Spellbound*). Owen James was the announcer. No director credit was given, and without being in the same room at the time of the audition, it can only be "assumed" that Hitchcock directed.

Reasons why neither program aired on ABC is not clear. No broadcast date is known. It has been assumed by many researchers that *Once Upon a Midnight* and *The Alfred Hitchcock Show* never aired over any major network. The programs were Hitchcock's baby, since he was present during the recordings, and it can be certain that Hitchcock's already-growing celebrity status was the major factor used to pitch the program. It can also be assumed that ABC was not in favor of the program, for without the approval of the network, the show could not have been heard over the air. (On a long stretch, ABC was later the only network of three to not broadcast *Alfred Hitchcock Presents*, but that's a very long stretch).

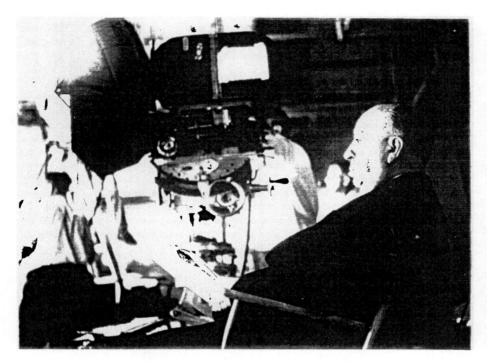

Hitchcock directs a scene. (Photo courtesy of Photofest.)

With two attempts at having his own mystery anthology series, Hitchcock was not discouraged. The third time would be the charm, but not with radio. This time it would be with television.

In 1950, Alfred Hitchcock was interviewed by Jack Mangan on the television program *Ship's Reporter*:

Jack Mangan: "I just read in the columns recently, an article about you in which they said: 'Gee, we hope that Alfred Hitchcock comes to television. Because he can bring so much suspense and so much new, shall we say. trick production methods.' "

Alfred Hitchcock: "Well, I have actually tried a bit of television in a movie, you know."

Mangan: "Not on television itself?"

Hitchcock: "No, no. I made a movie called *Rope*, you know, which was shot with one camera all the way through without any cutting. And that in a sense was a kind of preview of [the] television technique. The main thing was that the actors were moved around to create their own close-ups. In other words it's not just moving the camera, but moving the people backwards and forewards towards the lens so that automatically they make their own close-ups or their own waiste-shots and what have you."

Mangan: "I should think that would require quite a bit of preparation in advance."

Hitchcock: "Oh, definitely, yes."

Mangan: "More so, that in a usual picture."

Hitchcock: "Well much, because a usual picture, you see, is shot in little pieces and edited and put together afterwards. But here you have to anticipate all the requirements you may need dramatically, you see, in the movement of the camera and the size of the image on the screen."

Mangan: "Now this is taking on a new perspective, you're meaning that you actually shot the picture continuous more or less?"

Hitchcock: "Continuously."

Mangan: "Like you would do a stage play?"

Hitchcock: "As a stage play, but with the idea behind it, that the audience is looking at a screen in other words, you see? In a stage play, which is a fixed thing, the eye wonders all over the stage, but in movies of course we have to provide the eye with everything. Therefore in television they look at the screen and as you know the best results on television are the close image, and that's what I tried to do in this *Rope* picture, to give some preview of what would happen on television in the future.

(Photo courtesy of Photofest.) 13

Alfred Hitchcock and the Golden Days of Radio
Written by Charles Huck.

Theatrical movies and television productions were not the only mediums that exposed Alfred Hitchcock to the American public. Radio, a medium that frequently employed the top talent of Hollywood, played a somewhat important role in the director's career, since his first arrival in the United States. In August of 1937, when David O. Selznick brought Hitchcock to the States, the director was interviewed on radio, mainly for publicity purposes. This was to be one of Hitchcock's earliest exposures to the world of radio broadcasting. With the exception of trade magazines and newspapers, radio was considered an excellent medium for which producers and directors could "pitch" their film projects to a mass audience. The cost for advertising on radio was far cheaper than running attractive ads.

With the exception of *Forecast, Once Upon A Midnight* and *The Alfred Hitchcock Show* (which was previously covered), Hitchcock's involvement in network broadcasting was minimal. An occasional guest appearance on a radio series such as Fred Allen's *The Texaco Star Theater* (January 24, 1943) or *The Charlie McCarthy Show* (March 21, 1948) added little to his celebrity status. Hitchcock looked at radio only as a form of advertising and entertainment, but in reality, wanted very little to do with guest spots and panels.

Alfred Hitchcock Presents was not the first time Hitchcock ever hosted a mystery series. On June 18, 1949, the Mutual Radio Network premiered a mystery/detective anthology entitled *Murder by Experts*. Originally a Saturday night escape, the series quickly moved to Sunday evenings and by September of 1949, became a Monday evening thriller till its demise on December 17, 1951. The hosts of the program, known as the "master of mystery," were writers initially John Dickson Carr and Brett Halliday. During the last few months of 1951, Alfred Hitchcock took over the hosting duties. David Kogan and Robert A. Arthur were the producers and directors for *Murder by Experts*. Arthur, who would later become a ghostwriter and editor for numerous paperback and hardcover Hitchcock anthologies, would later have a few of his own stories dramatized on *Alfred Hitchcock Presents* and *The Alfred Hitchcock Hour*. Supposedly, the "master of mystery" chose the stories, tales written by the leading writers of mystery fiction, described by author John Dunning as "highly charged plots of crime and passion that turned on emotion rather than gimmicks." Arthur and Kogan chose the stories, not Hitchcock.

When Frederic W. Ziv began syndicating transcribed radio programs during the mid-1940s, he was hit with an inspiration. Why not present an anthology program in which Hollywood celebrities chose their favorite stories? Each episode opened with the announcer explaining what drama was going to be presented and who among the Hollywood clientele claimed it was their "favorite story." The program was entitled *Favorite Story*. Clyde Beatty chose "Ben Hur" and Ruth Gordon chose "Tom Sawyer." When it came around to Alfred Hitchcock's turn, he chose "Dr. Jekyll and Mr. Hyde." Knowing full well that Hitchcock publicly confessed his favorite stories years later, it seems all too obvious that "Dr. Jekyll" would not have been his favorite story. Rather, it was probably his favorite among a list of already-selected short stories and novels that were feasible for radio. Another possibility would be that stars like Hitchcock were asked to choose two or three favorites, and among them, one would be made feasible, performed and labeled as their favorite.

On January 22, 1943, Alfred Hitchcock became a panelist for a radio quiz program of intellectual exercise, entitled *Information Please*. Faithful listeners were encouraged to submit a question and answer, wherein, a board of editors chose the best ones. If a question was asked and the guest panelists were stumped, a prize was awarded to the listener who submitted the question. On the 1943 broadcast, Alfred Hitchcock was asked: "In which famous case was the guilt fixed by the purchase of hyacinth?" At which point Hitchcock answered, describing the case in such detail, how an American dentist living in London, married to a musical performer, gave the poison to his wife. Hitchcock went on to explain how the dentist stashed her body in the house so he could run off to Canada with his secretary. At which point, Clifton Fadiman, the moderator of the panel, asked Hitchcock: "How was the tide running at the time?"

Even with his guest appearances on radio, Hitchcock's name was more associated with the motion pictures he directed. Since many of his films were later re-created as condensed dramas on such programs as *The Lux Radio Theatre* and *The Screen Directors' Playhouse*, Hitchcock established a reputation as being a "master of suspense" among non-movie-goers. Crippled and handicapped people who could not normally attend a movie theater, found front row seats by merely tuning into their local radio station. Even though Hitchcock was not directly involved with the actual production of most of these dramas, his name was still associated as the director, and there he remained with the listeners.

The Lux Radio Theatre was probably the most successful of Hollywood's radio programs, with a broadcast history stretching back almost twenty years. Of the earliest was *The Thirty-Nine Steps* (broadcast on December 13, 1937) starring Robert Montgomery and Ida Lupino in the lead of Richard Hannay and Pamela. The same John Buchan novel from which the movie was based, was adapted for radio numerous times: *The Hour of Mystery* (September 1, 1946) starring David Niven and *Suspense* (March 3, 1952) starring Herbert Marshall. The *Lux* production was based on the Hitchcock movie, while the other productions were more or less, based on the book, but employing key scenes from the movie to heighten the drama. Many of those productions, however, whether they were based on the book or the movie, did make some mention that the story was formerly "an Alfred Hitchcock motion picture." *

Whenever possible, at least one member of the original cast was brought to the microphone for the radio adaptations. Producers insisted on this, but more often than not, such stars were unable to appear because of prior commitments. Studio contracts restricted their leading stars to a specified number of radio appearances. Some actors avoided invitations, terrified of appearing before a "live" microphone (commonly known as "mike fright"). Joseph Cotten was under contract with David O. Selznick and was often called upon as a last-minute casting solution by radio directors. Selznick saw the advertising potential that radio had to offer. He was always glad to lend his star to any radio production. As in most cases, Selznick stipulated that an announcement be made about an "up-coming motion picture produced by Selznick."

This sort of arrangement was quite common among broadcasting and Hollywood studios. For any star to appear on any radio program, a pitch or mere mention – usually by the announcer before or after the drama – of the star's latest picture *had* to be made over the air. When radio began to grow in popularity during the early 1930s, Hollywood studios were not in favor of it and even banned some of their contract actors from appearing behind a microphone. But, soon after they discovered the "power of the air," contracts were made, signed, and exercised, allowing stars to freely pick the programs of their choice. **

Radio itself proved to be an influence on Alfred Hitchcock, whose appearances were seemingly kept to a bare minimum. As an omnivorous reader of court room and mystery stories, Alfred Hitchcock became a weekly listener to such programs as *The Whistler, Inner*

* To clarify matters, the title of the John Buchan novel was *The Thirty-Nine Steps*. The title of the Hitchcock film was *The 39 Steps*, with "thirty-nine" in number form.
** As studios eventually gave in to radio, so would they give in to TV during the 1950s.

Sanctum Mysteries, and *Molle Mystery Theater*. The great anthology series *Suspense* provided more grist for the Hitchcock mill. Many original *Suspense* plays also became teleplays for the Hitchcock show. "Alibi Me," the story of a young man in search of an alibi to cover up a murder he committed, was originally broadcast on January 4, 1951. "The Evil of Adelaide Winters," a story about a fake medium who profited from victimized families after the war, became an episode of *The Alfred Hitchcock Hour*. "The Long Shot" was an original *Suspense* play that later became a Hitchcock TV episode, and another *Suspense* play, "The Long Wait" was the basis of the *Alfred Hitchcock Presents* episode "Salvage."

On September 30, 1957, Hitchcock directed an episode of the NBC-TV series *Suspicion* entitled "Four O'Clock." Based on the short story "Three O'Clock" by Cornell Woolrich, the tale concerned a watch repairman who set a bomb to go off in his basement at four o'clock, thinking that it will kill his unfaithful wife. This same story was dramatized on radio's *Suspense* with Van Heflin in the lead, but with two noticeable changes. The name of the *Suspense* production was "Three O'Clock," and the finale varied to the protagonist suffering a fatal heart attack. The watch repairman goes insane in the Hitchcock version. The comparison is most interesting.

Patricia Hitchcock even played roles on radio, which, she confessed, was her favorite medium. She acted in "masses of radio shows, all different kinds," both in New York and Los Angeles. One of them commonly circulating among collectors is Wilkie Collins' novel "The Moonstone," adapted as a two-part presentation for *Suspense*. Patricia played a small supporting role in the first of the two broadcasts, aired over CBS on November 16, 1953.

The Birds, which Hitchcock brought to theaters in 1963, was dramatized on *Escape* July 10, 1954. Daphne du Maurier's story about a feathered attack against the human race, became one of Hitchcock's most popular movies. When Francois Truffaut interviewed Alfred Hitchcock, the director admitted that he first read the story in one of the anthologies that bore his name (see Anthologies chapter). "Actually, it was one of those 'Alfred Hitchcock Presents' books," he explained. "I found out that there had been attempts to do 'The Birds' on radio and television, but they weren't successful." There were only two such attempts on radio. *The Lux Radio Theatre* was the first, broadcast on July 20, 1953 with Herbert Marshall in the lead. Although *Lux* was best known for presenting adaptations of motion pictures, this was one of those exceptions where the production was based on the story instead (regardless of those mail order catalogs that suggest otherwise). The second was almost a year later on the CBS program *Escape*, broadcast July 10, 1954. Radio actors Ben Wright and Virginia Gregg assumed the leads, and it was Gregg's voice of the ventriloquist dummy in the *Alfred Hitchcock Presents* episode of "And So Died Riabouchinska."

"My memory," he confessed once with boyish modesty, "is rather valuable." Hitchcock was a man with a long memory when it came to his kind of story. On one rare occasion he went to London to successfully scour for a certain book he had recalled, *A Century of Creepy Stories*, which had been out of print since 1932, and which he himself hadn't seen for years. While listening to Louis Pollack's short story, "Breakdown," on the May 15, 1949, broadcast on *Prudential Family Hour of Stars*, Hitchcock decided to film that particular story as his first television show. He also decided to use that reliable standby, Joseph Cotten, who had worked with the master before, and who had also starred in the original radio version.

But, along with the influence radio played on Hitchcock, and vise versa, many of his films were re-created as condensed dramas. Few productions actually featured Hitchcock for a brief moment, pausing to make personal comments about the productions and/or the film itself. And with the "possible" exception of *Once Upon a Midnight* and *The Alfred Hitchcock Show*, Hitchcock never directed any radio productions.

In 1958, Alfred Hitchcock co-starred with Peter Lorre and Boris Karloff, in an episode of *As Easy as A.B.C.* entitled "O Is for Old Wives' Tales." The series was the work of the UNESCO (United Nations Educational, Scientific and Cultural Organization). and broadcast over United Nations Radio. Among all the hosting and narrating of radio dramas, this would mark Hitchcock's only acting job on radio.

Sometime during the early 1980s, an anthology series produced in South America entitled *The Hitchcock Half Hour*, aired over numerous radio stations. Hitchcock had nothing to do with the show, any more than he did with the mystery magazine that bore his name. (He was dead by the time the show was produced). Only a few copies of this show circulate among collectors.

Still, over the years, transcription discs were cut, advertising movies then presently seen in the theaters, a method of publicity for radio listeners, and on occasion, Hitchcock himself commented about key scenes from the picture. These recorded commercials contained sound tracks to the movies, with sound clips of conversations with the actors, and on occasion, an announcer making a sales pitch "why you should see this movie!"

To give an example of the demand Hitchcock's pictures were being presented on radio, here is a selection of his films, the radio programs they were dramatized on, the broadcast date, and the lead actors. "The Lodger," which was Alfred Hitchcock's third motion picture, was adapted for radio programs so many times it is impossible to even begin listing them all. A few of those adaptations originated from Hitchcock's movie, while many others originated from the story itself, and especially after the release of the 1944 movie of the same name. In order to keep the list from expanding twice-fold, we have eliminated all of "The Lodger" adaptations.

The Lux Radio Theatre (December 13, 1937) "The 39 Steps" with Ida Lupino and Robert Montgomery.
The Campbell Playhouse (December 9, 1938) "Rebecca" with Orson Welles and Agnes Moorehead. *
The Lux Radio Theatre (March 2, 1941) "Rebecca" with Ronald Colman and Ida Lupino.
The Lux Radio Theatre (June 9, 1941) "Mr. and Mrs. Smith" with Bob Hope and Carole Lombard.
Philip Morris Playhouse (December 19. 1941) "The Lady Vanishes" w/ Flora Robson and Errol Flynn.
The Gulf Screen Guild Theater (February 8, 1942) "Mr. and Mrs. Smith" w/ Errol Flynn, Lana Turner.
The Lux Radio Theatre (May 4, 1942) "Suspicion" with Joan Fontaine and husband Brian Aherne.
Philip Morris Playhouse (November 6, 1942) "Rebecca" with Herbert Marshall.
The Lady Esther Screen Guild Theater (December 14, 1942) "Mr. and Mrs. Smith" with Joan Bennett.
The Lady Esther Screen Guild Theater (January 4, 1943) "Suspicion" with Basil Rathbone,
        Nigel Bruce and Joan Fontaine.
Philip Morris Playhouse (January 22, 1943) "Mr. and Mrs. Smith" with Virginia Bruce.
Philip Morris Playhouse (May 21, 1943) "The 39 Steps" with Madeleine Carroll.
The Lady Esther Screen Guild Theater (May 24, 1943) "Shadow of a Doubt" with Joseph Cotten.
The Lady Esther Screen Guild Theater (May 31, 1943) "Rebecca" with Brian Aherne, Joan Fontaine.
Philip Morris Playhouse (October 15, 1943) "Suspicion" with Madeleine Carroll.
Philip Morris Playhouse (November 12, 1943) "Shadow of a Doubt" with Orson Welles.
The Lux Radio Theatre (January 3, 1944) "Shadow of a Doubt" with William Powell, Teresa Wright.
The Lux Radio Theatre (September 18, 1944) "Suspicion" with William Powell, Olivia DeHavilland.
Matinee Theater (November 26, 1944) "Mr. and Mrs. Smith" with Victor Jory and Gertrude Warner.
The Lady Esther Screen Guild Theater (January 1, 1945) "Mr. and Mrs. Smith"
        with Louise Allbritton, Joan Blondell, Stuart Erwin and Preston Foster.
Matinee Theater (January 21, 1945) "Rebecca" with Victor Jory and BlancheYurka.

* Many radio fans insist that Orson Welles dramatized adaptations of novels, not movies, and with such reasoning, some would consider this broadcast an adaptation of the novel, rather than the movie. After all, the movie hadn't begun production yet. Still, Selznick sold Welles the radio rights to "Rebecca," and the deal was settled. There is a possibility that Selznick wanted to hear Welles's solution to complications within the plot, for his own use. This, in turn, is probably one of the first radio adaptations of a movie not-yet filmed before the cameras!

Theater of Romance (July 17, 1945) "Suspicion" with Anthony Quinn and Judith Evelyn.
The Lady Esther Screen Guild Theater (January 21, 1946) "Suspicion" w/ Loretta Young, Nigel Bruce.
Theater of Romance (April 9, 1946) "Jamaica Inn" with Louise Albritton.
Theater of Romance (April 30, 1946) "Shadow of a Doubt" with Brian Donlevy.
Hollywood Startime (July 20, 1946) "Mr. and Mrs. Smith" with Robert Montgomery.
Academy Award Theater (July 24, 1946) "Foreign Correspondent" with Joseph Cotten.
The Hour of Mystery (September 1, 1946) "The 39 Steps" with David Niven.
Academy Award Theater (September 11, 1946) "Shadow of a Doubt" Joseph Cotten and June Vincent.
Hollywood Players (October 1, 1946) "Rebecca" with Joseph Cotten and Joan Fontaine.
Academy Award Theater (October 30, 1946) "Suspicion" with Cary Grant and Ann Todd. *
The Lux Radio Theatre (January 26, 1948) "Notorious" with Joseph Cotten and Ingrid Bergman.
The Lux Radio Theatre (March 8, 1948) "Spellbound" with Joseph Cotten and Alida Valli.
Studio One (March 23, 1948) "The 39 Steps" with Glenn Ford and Mercedes McCambridge.
The Camel Screen Guild Players (June 21, 1948) "Shadow of a Doubt"
        with Vanessa Brown and Joseph Cotten.
The Screen Guild Theater (November 18, 1948) "Rebecca" with John Lund and Loretta Young.
The Screen Guild Theater (January 6, 1949) "Notorious" with Ingrid Bergman and John Hodiak.
The Ford Theater (February 18, 1949) "Shadow of a Doubt" with Ray Milland and Ann Blyth.
The Lux Radio Theater (May 9, 1949) "The Paradine Case" with Joseph Cotten.
Prudential Family Hour of Stars (July 24, 1949) "Rebecca" with Audrey Totter.
The Screen Guild Theater (November 24, 1949) "Suspicion" Joan Fontaine, Cary Grant, Nigel Bruce.
The Lux Radio Theatre (November 6, 1950) "Rebecca" with Vivien Leigh and Laurence Olivier. **
The Screen Directors' Playhouse (November 9, 1950) "Shadow of a Doubt" with Cary Grant.
The Screen Directors' Playhouse (Jan. 25, 1951) "Spellbound" Joseph Cotten, Mercedes McCambridge
The Lux Radio Theatre (December 3, 1951) "Strangers on a Train" Ray Milland and Frank Lovejoy.
Stars in the Air (December 27, 1951) "Mr. and Mrs. Smith" with Jane Greer and Fred MacMurray.
Hollywood Sound Stage (January 10, 1952) "Shadow of a Doubt" Ann Blyth and Jeff Chandler.
Suspense (March 3, 1952) "The 39 Steps" with Herbert Marshall and Ben Wright.
Philip Morris Playhouse on Broadway (May 25, 1952) "Rebecca" with Melvyn Douglas.
The Lux Radio Theatre (September 21, 1953) "I Confess" with Phyllis Thaxter and Cary Grant.
The Lux Radio Theatre (April 12, 1954) "Strangers on a Train" Dana Andrews and Robert Cummings.

A SELECTION OF RADIO SHOWS HITCHCOCK PERSONALLY APPEARED ON

(circa, 1938) Hitchcock, on his first visit to the U.S., in a radio interview with critic Otis Ferguson.
April 13, 1939 *The Royal Gelatin Hour*
June 27, 1941 *and* January 22, 1943 *Information Please*
January 24, 1943 *The Texaco Star Theater*
March 21, 1948 *The Charlie McCarthy Show*
January 30, 1949 *Screen Directors' Playhouse* "Mr. and Mrs. Smith" Robert Montgomery
        and Mary Jane Croft. Hitchcock described one of the scenes in the original movie.
November 11, 1950 *Screen Directors' Playhouse* "Lifeboat" Tallulah Bankhead and Jeff
        Chandler. Hitchcock made a few comments about the production and the actors.
April 27, 1958 *As Easy as A.B.C.* "O Is for Old Wives' Tales" w/ Boris Karloff, Peter Lorre.

* Nigel Bruce was originally scheduled to reprise his screen role in this adaptation, but was forced to bow out because of illness. His role was replaced by another actor.

** Laurence Olivier, who starred in the original Hitchcock production, was against Joan Fontaine being cast as the leading lady. Instead, he asked for his real-life wife Vivien Leigh to play the role, but she never got the opportunity. In this *Lux* production, Leigh finally got the chance to play the role (opposite her real-life husband), as he originally wanted back in 1939.

THIRD TIME'S A CHARM

The impetus for Alfred Hitchcock's entry into the world of weekly television is usually credited to Lew Wasserman, who by early 1955 had been the head of MCA (Music Corporation of America) for nearly a decade. There were two reasons why Wasserman was in a unique position to serve this function. In the early 1950s, while the major motion picture studios were still waging what would prove to be a futile war against the encroachment of the upstart television, MCA, through their subsidiary Revue Productions, plunged ahead into the production of prescience as it was good business sense: television's appetite for programming was becoming more voracious with each passing season, and MCA, at that time the world's largest talent agency, had a ready pool of talent on which to draw. The production of television programs seemed a logical way to keep their clients working steadily.

Of equal importance, MCA had also represented Alfred Hitchcock since 1945. (The director's first American agent Myron Selznick, had died in 1944; Selznick's agency was subsequently incorporated into MCA). Wasserman was not only head of the agency, but over the previous decade he had become one of Hitchcock's closest friends. They respected each other personally and professionally, and as John Russell Taylor put it, "When Lew Wasserman talked, [Hitchcock] listened." According to Taylor, it was at a television production meeting (probably in late 1954 or early 1955) that Wasserman was supposed to have "suddenly exclaimed": "We ought to put Hitch on the air." This precipitated some discussion on ways and means, and led eventually to a series of conferences on the subject with Hitchcock himself, who was supposedly "cautious but open-minded." "Lew thought it would be, you know, a great idea," Patricia Hitchcock recalled, "and if Lew said something, my father listened to him."

By the mid-1950s, all of the motion picture studios had unloaded sizable portions from their vaults for television, including Universal, who was having tremendous success with their "monster flicks," Ma and Pa Kettle, Abbott and Costello, and Francis the Talking Mule movies. But Universal was the only studio in Hollywood that had not gone into TV series production. Wasserman knew this, and he wanted to convince studio executives to consider producing films for television. Perhaps this was another reason he considered putting Hitchcock on the air. As influential as Hitchcock was, such success would prompt others to consider the same possibility.

It should be remembered that at this time Hitchcock's career was in one of his most productive periods, with seven films released from 1953 – 1956. Why then, did he decide to take on the added responsibility of a television series? There were a number of factors. Probably the most important was because his feature film production plans would not be interrupted by the new venture. This statement was made very clear during proposals. His involvement with the series would only be peripheral: a production staff would be hired to oversee story selection, hiring of writers and directors, casting, etc., all subject to Hitchcock's approval. According to author Donald Spoto, the picture of a financial carrot was angled in front of Hitchcock to convince him that his participation would be beneficial.

In early 1955, Lew Wasserman and his colleagues at MCA met several times with Hitchcock, with television executives, and potential sponsors. Negotiations took place for a series of television melodramas using the similar suspenseful tales Hitchcock became known for bringing to the big screen. In a matter of weeks, arrangements were finalized between CBS and Bristol-Myers to offer a weekly half-hour series. Highly impressive since the proposed series – unlike most television programs, required a pilot for network executives and sponsor agencies to view. Hitchcock would also receive $129,000 per show (one source reported that CBS and Bristol-Myers would pay part of the budget), and all rights of sale and rebroadcast would revert over to him after the initial airing.

For the name of his television company, Hitchcock chose "Shamley Productions," named after the summer home Winter's Grace, on an estate he and his wife Alma had bought in Shamley Green, a small village thirty miles south of London, back in 1928. Hitchcock's initial contract with Bristol-Myers stipulated that he would direct an unspecified number of episodes each season.

According to Donald Spoto, another suggestion for Hitchcock's attraction to television was a young actress named Vera Miles. Having seen her act in a half-hour drama on the *Pepsi-Cola Playhouse* *, Hitchcock had signed Miles to a five-year, three-picture contract beginning January 2, 1956. He put her to work before that date, however – she played the lead in "Revenge," which became the premiere episode on October 2, 1955. "He was very possessive of Vera Miles," Doc Erickson, production manager of *Alfred Hitchcock Presents*, recalled. "He was trying to bring along a second Grace Kelly."

"I think what happened with Vera is that she just wanted to resist the control that Hitch liked to exercise over people who worked for him," said Norman Lloyd. "I remember that when I was working for him, Sam Spiegel was making a picture in England and wanted Hitch to let me go for a period to produce the picture for him. Hitch said no [laughs] - Hitch just wouldn't brook anything like that. There was another actress, Joanna Moore, who did brilliant work on the Hitchcock shows. She was a marvelous actress. Hitch put her under contract . . . and he then wanted to change her hairdo and things of that nature. As soon as that happened, Joanna Moore quit. I think this was the same thing that happened with Vera—I think Vera had her own life and she wanted to be in control of that. So she just resisted. And as soon as the resistance appeared, Hitch was no longer [interested], because you just couldn't do that with Hitch. You had to fit into his 'operation,' so to speak. I was very fond of Vera, and we used to hire her on the hour show."

For the producing end, Hitchcock recruited Joan Harrison, his former secretary who was presently living in New York, to act as producer on the show. She went to Hollywood without hesitation. Since Hitchcock was aware of her knowledge of courtroom cases and mystery anthologies, he could choose no one better. As for the title of the program, proposals floated about, all carefully making sure Alfred Hitchcock's name would be featured in the title. After all, it was his name that was supposed to sell the series. "Before *Alfred Hitchcock Presents* went on the air," writer Irving Elman recalled, "they were scrambling for a good title. One day I was in the office when Hitch got a call from NBC asking if he had any titles in mind. He blandly suggested 'Playhouse 69!' "

Hitchcock was inspired to use Gounod's "Funeral March of a Marionette" as the theme music after hearing it in F.W. Marnau's *Sunrise* (1927). Marnau had stipulated that it be the musical background for the sequence involving the young couple and a photographer. Apparently, most of this was Hitchcock's own idea, from the theme music to the evocative procession of images which opened the program. He had designed his trademark silhouette in the 1930s; and as an avid reader with a taste for the macabre, he had an ample storehouse of stories, and many were not suitable for feature film adaptation.

* Vera Miles was on four *Pepsi-Cola Playhouse* broadcasts, but it is not known exactly which one: "The Grey and Gold Dress" broadcast on April 2, 1954; "Such a Nice Little Girl" broadcast on October 31, 1954; "The Golden Flowers" broadcast on January 9, 1955; or "The House Where Time Stopped" broadcast on April 17, 1955. The last one, "House," is considered by many Hitchcock researchers as the actual drama that brought Miles to the attention of Hitchcock, but tracing the original source of this statistic proved to be nothing more than speculation.

The juxtaposition of the music, the silhouette, the superimposed title, and Hitchcock's shadow as he stepped "into" the profile drawing, was certainly inspired – it established, almost subliminally, the idea of "Alfred Hitchcock." Thus, the visual procession: from symbol to shadow to substance. It was then left to the host himself to establish the tone of the show, in the famous prologues and epilogues – which were quite unlike the mere "introductions," provided by more run-of-the-mill TV hosts. It was almost universally agreed that Hitchcock's appearances "made" the show – transforming what might otherwise have been just a better-than-average mystery/melodrama series into something special. And one could make a convincing case that, without this element, *Alfred Hitchcock Presents* would today, enjoy much less syndication play.

Not only had there been numerous anthology shows exclusively devoted to this type of melodrama, but even such "prestige" series as *Kraft Television Theatre* and *Studio One* and the like were not beneath presenting an occasional "thriller." Even the "twist" ending with which the Hitchcock series was to become so strongly identified was somewhat old-hat by 1955. *Suspense, Danger, The Web, The Clock, The Unexpected, Rebound, The Whistler* and numerous other series devoted to suspense melodramas – several of which were explicitly predicted on surprise endings – had come and, in many cases, gone by 1955. Clearly something new was needed.

The something new was Hitchcock's personality. Through newspaper and magazine coverage, the lending of his name to various paperback short story anthologies (the first was *Suspense Stories*, published by Dell in 1945), and his cameo appearances in his own films, made Hitchcock familiar to the American movie-going public in both name and figure. Television, having already shown itself to be a most powerful creator and purveyor of personalities, seemed to be a natural next step. Certainly Hitchcock, with his flair for self-promotion, must have realized (even without Wasserman's urging) that the medium had the potential to make him – literally – a household name. And it did.

The realization of Hitchcock hosting each episode was nothing short of inspired. The notion of Hitchcock stepping in front of the cameras was hardly revolutionary; after all, virtually every dramatic series on television had a host or hostess, from Robert Montgomery to Loretta Young. What was novel, however, was the way in which his inimitable personality was exploited, now referred to as "the Hitchcock wit."

REVENGE WAS ONLY THE BEGINNING

The premiere episode of any television program served as the most important of any series, performing a number of functions. First, the broadcast itself had to introduce to the viewers what and who they were going to see each week. Since *Alfred Hitchcock Presents* featured only one recurring character (the host), the usual setup of an opening introduction, followed by a dramatic presentation, and closing remarks by the host, became a permanent fixture, all too familiar from other dramatic anthologies. Second, what type of stories and how well written the dialogue is, leaves another impression with the viewers. If the initial telecast didn't leave audiences with an "I want to see more" attitude, ratings would drop considerably. It is not known who made the decision of making "Revenge" the premiere episode, but it can be said that "Revenge" was not a bad decision at all.

Samuel Blas' short story "Revenge" was printed in the the January 11, 1947 issue of *Collier's*. The short story was very loosely dramatized on radio's *Suspense* in 1949 (changing the characters from a vengeful husband killing a man he thought molested his wife, to a father who attempts to kill the murderer of his son). The O. Henry-type of short story murderer of his son). The O. Henry-type of short story proved to be an excellent example of what *Alfred Hitchcock Presents* was, and still is. Hitchcock was certainly in favor of filming "Revenge," if not for the technical aspects, probably because he might never again get the opportunity to do so. "I'm doing material on television of a downbeat nature that possibly I could never do for the movies," Hitchcock said. "I doubt that a story of that kind could ever be done in Hollywood as a movie. I think the reaction at the studios would be 'Do you want us to pay $1,500,000 for that? Do you think people are going to pay to be depressed by a grim tale of that kind?' "

Ralph Meeker and Vera Miles in "Revenge" (Photo courtesy of Photofest.)

On October 3, 1955, *The New York Times* gave their review: "Alfred Hitchcock, the Hollywood master of cinema suspense, brought his talents to television last night at 9:30 on Channel 2. The first television film that he directed was routine Hitchcock, but the director's personal appearance as host on the program was something not to be missed. In the role of presiding officer, Mr. Hitchcock displayed a superb disdain for the usual television amenities. He said his function was to give the film's titles to those who could not read and after the show explain what had happened to those who couldn't figure it out for themselves. His sardonic introduction of the commercials should gain him an award with no trouble at all. Hitchcock, the director, was not, however, a match for Hitchcock, the matre d'. His initial film, "Revenge," starring Ralph Meeker and Vera Miles was a psychological item. It concerned a husband who killed the first man whom his mentally unbalanced wife identifies as her attacker. Moments later, of course, she points out a second man as her assailant. Last night Mr. Hitchcock was a shade careless. He ran out of suspense before he ran out of film."

Variety reviewed: "Hitchcock appears fore and aft for a few sly remarks, very tongue in cheek and a trifle elfin. Even such brief a taste as on the first show was enough to prove that he's very novel indeed for television and could go on the air and just talk anytime. He has a gorgeous semi-deadpan delivery, and set up, with a hint of sardonic humor, the Bristol-Myers spiels. 'Crime doesn't pay anywhere, and not on the television either,' he remarked, 'unless you have a sponsor.' That was followed by the third of the three products sharing the tab. Ipana and Bufferin had come earlier, via animations, nicely done and unobjectionable. But just before the credit crawl came Sal Hepatica, the laxative that works so fast (you see the door closing), and the sell [sales pitch] which is perhaps the most unflinchingly embarrassing commercial offered to mix company on the American television. Following the triumph of the lady who consumed the glass of Sal Hepatica, Hitchcock returned and said, 'After that, I don't believe I have anything I wish to add!' Nobody could."

Even if the story was not well-received, critics seemed to be leery of making any definite predictions about the program's success, and failed to make any such mention. It was decided that in the television series. the emphasis on horror and homicide might be relieved by tongue-in-cheek remarks at the beginning and end of each program. Hitchcock's quips, including jocular references to the sponsor's messages, had met with favor from most critics, and most important, the viewers. The cheerful gruesome-ness of the introductions, amusing in the style of a Charles Addams cartoon come to life, was one thing, but this alone may not have been quite enough. Hitchcock. however, dared to go where no host had gone before: he insulted the sponsor. In a nice way, of course.

First, however, we have the twentieth century equivalent of the rack. Now please, no screams. After all, this hurts me more than it does you.

Our story will begin following this one-minute entertainment blackout.

As you know, someone must always pay the piper. Fortunately, we already have such a person. This philanthropic gentleman wishes to remain anonymous, but perhaps the more discerning of our audience will be able to find a clue to his identity in the following commercial.

You know, I believe commercials are improving every day. Next week we hope to have another one - equally fascinating. And, if time permits, we shall bring you another story.

But first, unfortunately, we have one of those intelligent, amusing, dignified, provocative, brilliantly conceived, but painfully short commercials.

Let us heed the advice of a man who is earnest, productive and steadfast . . . a pillar of our civilization . . . and the sugar daddy of television – the sponsor.

When asked about the reaction of his sponsors to some of the reverent touches, Hitchcock recalled: "There were some misgivings I suppose. From time to time certain phrases have crept in that may not have been entirely to the liking of Bristol-Myers [one of the sponsors]. Once I said, 'The views expressed in the following commercial are strictly those of the sponsor.' They didn't like that. I could see their point of view, too. Afterward I changed it slightly. I said 'The views expressed here are entirely those of the sponsor' and I did a look –

you know - to show that, perhaps I really didn't mean it." But a celebrity making quips about his or her sponsor was not 100% original.

Dating the earliest, Ed Wynn was probably the first performer to directly "kid the product" in a network program, during his radio Texaco Fire Chief series beginning in April 1932. As Graham McNamee attempted to talk about Fire Chief Gasoline, Wynn would chirp out jokes exaggerating the power of the fuel. The sponsor became increasingly uncomfortable with the comic approach – and finally, in 1934, the company told Wynn point-blank to "back off." Another was radio and television personality Arthur Godfrey who would, on occasion, insert little needling gibes directed at clichés in the text of commercials. Once he was spieling Glass Wax, a polishing cleaner with the slogan, "Cleans 30 kinds of dirt in 30 seconds!" He stopped in the middle and said, "Cleans 30 kinds of dirt . . . ? Who wants to clean dirt?" Perhaps far more aggressive than Godfrey in ridiculing bad advertising was comedian Henry Morgan, who would sing little postscripts to goofy transcribed jingles, insert snide remarks in live ads, and generally project an air of insolence when delivering the sponsor's messages.

"Of course," Hitchcock said grandly, "we can't do anything that mentions the name of our dear sponsor [Bristol-Myers] - who makes Bufferin - because of the residuals. Not that we wouldn't like to. Once I thought it would be amusing to have one of the A's get mixed up with the B's in that race around the iron stomach. Then I decided to have the butler come in and announce, 'Mr. Hitchcock, your grandfather is here.' To which I would reply haughtily, 'Well, fine, send the old *duffer in.*' Of course, I have to resist temptation, because on the reruns we would have a different sponsor."

During the program's later years, Hitchcock once tossed around the proposal of doing the commercials himself. He was not able to get the sponsors to go along with him, and that too was perhaps understandable. "I'd do them," Hitchcock said, "like that British real-estate salesman, Roy Brooks, does them. He knocks the houses he sells with remarks like 'It's terribly in need of paint,' or 'The wallpaper's falling off in sheets,' and he gets a terrific volume of sales. I'd love to sell cars, and, as I am passing one of the doors, have the handle fall off as I'm extolling the car's virtues, and without dropping a line simply replace the door handle, or something like that. . . I'd like to take two asprin and, after swallowing them, stagger off the stage. Or, after brushing my teeth with some toothpaste or other, rinse and spit out a mouthful of teeth. Or show Joan of Arc being burned at the stake and comment, 'Are you smoking more now and enjoying it less?' "

Another idea Hitchcock liked was one his writer, James Allardice, once pulled off in a high school play. Allardice had an electric chair in one scene, and under it was displayed the sign, "You can be sure it is Westinghouse." In other words, what knocked Hitchcock out was "counterpoint" humor. In his lead-ins, he liked lines, props and devices that contrast sharply to his dignified self. When Hitchcock first started making his lead-ins, he decided that "If the shows were going to be macabre, what I wanted was the counterpoint of humor to introduce them. It's an English sense of humor, I think, rather than American."

The total image had to be one of incongruity. "It would be a mistake," Hitchcock said, for example, "to place me at the North Pole wearing an Eskimo outfit. Rather I should be at the Pole wearing a plain black suit, or a dinner jacket." It's all in the approach - the reverse approach, that is.

Two of the biggest myths related to *Alfred Hitchcock Presents* and *The Alfred Hitchcock Hour* are: (a) Hitchcock directed all of the episodes of the series. Not true, as his directing work consisted of eighteen episodes out of the 361, and (b) Hitchcock wrote the opening and closing narratives for all of the episodes. Truth is, Hitchcock never wrote a word. The man hired to concoct those tidbits was James Allardice, a not-particularly-distinguished playwright who scripted *At WAR with the Army* (1949) and *Francis Joins the WACs* (1954). Allardice would seem to have had nothing in his background to prepare him for the assignment, but he took to the task like the proverbial duck to water.

James Allardice never received any screen credit for his contribution to the series, but he was introduced to the "master of suspense" personally before writing the first of what would become a steady ten-year job. "When I first started, I was told that Mr. Hitchcock did not wear a wrist watch, did not wear rings and did not like eggs," Allardice told *TV Guide* in 1959. "This advice has never bothered me. Hitchcock is very objective toward death. Dead bodies are not necessarily sacred to him."

As evidence toward this, Hitchcock arranged for Allardice to view a screening of *The Trouble with Harry* (1955) for him, and told him this was the kind of offbeat humor he wanted to introduce to television. And he wanted to bring his audience in on a great private joke, the way he brought them in on private jokes and information withheld from the characters of his motion pictures.

Hitchcock recalled: "Remember the old saying, 'A knock is as good as a boost?' My guess is that the sponsor enjoyed my lack of obsequiousness, but in the beginning they had difficulty in getting used to my approach and they took umbrage at my less worshipful remarks. However, the moment they became aware of the commercial effects of my belittling - they took a look at the sales charts – [and] they stopped questioning the propriety of my cracks. But there's no getting around it, it did take getting used to. The tradition is that the sponsor must be coddled. In such an atmosphere I was a novelty."

"James Allardice, in one word, was a genius," producer Norman Lloyd recalled. "Did I use two words there, 'a genius?' He was remarkable. He was a little fellow, he was built and looked a little like Woody Allen, and he had the greatest humor. And anything he wrote, Hitch would do. He would put Hitchcock inside a bottle; he would put Hitch on with a lion; he would put Hitch in knickers, as a golfer; Hitch would play his own brother, Arthur Hitchcock, or whatever his name was - Allardice would write these things, and Hitch spoke *every word he ever wrote*, and never questioned a word. He did that for every show for ten years. Plus, when *Psycho* was a big hit and audiences had a line up outside the theater, there was a tape of Hitch talking to them, a tape that would be playing for the line to get in. Jimmy wrote that too."

Hitchcock playing his evil twin brother from one episode:
> *Mr. Hitchcock is indisposed this evening. As a matter of fact, we can't find him anywhere. I'm quite worried. I wouldn't want anything to happen to him. You see I'm his brother and sole heir. Of course we mustn't let brother Alfred's absence interfere with the evening's entertainment. I'm sure he would want it that way. I have his notes. The second item on the agenda is a drama entitled "Little White Frock." As for the first item he says . . ., I know my brother thinks I'm rather dull and somewhat of a prude, but this language is much too frank for television.*

Soon after television audiences recognized Hitchcock for his witty and macabre jokes, the public expected him to act the same way in person. So Allardice was paid to write dialogue for Hitchcock, even if it wasn't for the television series. Dinner speeches, movie trailers, and in 1958, Imperial Records released an LP entitled "Alfred Hitchcock Presents: Music to Murder By." (See the section about collectibles for more). James Allardice wrote all of Hitchcock's narratives. "Hitch's delivery was priceless," said Herbert Coleman, "but he couldn't have succeeded as a popular presence or delivered those comments without the talent of Jim Allardice, one of the best writers we ever had."

25

"He was great," Norman Lloyd continued. "He came from Yale; he had the show *At War With The Army* on Broadway, and that was a hit; and then turned it into a script for Martin and Lewis [for the 1950 movie version], which was also a hit. Then he wrote the first year of *The George Gobel Show*, which was another hit. MCA, that represented him, took him off that and put him with Hitch. Whoever thought of that deserves a few million dollars [laughs]! I cannot speak highly enough about Jimmy Allardice. We'd shoot about six stories, and we would then send the synopses over to Jimmy and ask him to write for Hitch. We'd send them to him about ten days to two weeks ahead of time. And we'd wait. Then we'd call him in about a week: 'How are things doing, Jimmy?' 'Oh, I haven't started yet. . . I'll get around to it. . .' And then, a few days later, we'd call again: 'Oh, yeah, yeah,' he'd say, 'I haven't got anything yet, but. . .' Now it was (let's say) the Friday before the Monday when we were going to shoot these things, and he'd say, 'I'll get 'em done over the weekend.' And that's how he wrote - he had to write right up against the deadline. He couldn't write unless it was gonna be shot tomorrow [laughs]! That deadline pressure would give Jimmy 'the electric shock,' and he would take off and do this work, which I think had genius in it. They were brilliant - so creative and marvelous."

But the prologues and epilogues were more than just an amusing framing device: they were integral to the style of the series. In an often-quoted 1957 interview with Pete Martin, Hitchcock said that "in selecting the stories for my television shows, I try to make them as meaty as the sponsor and the network will stand for. I hope to offset any tendency toward the macabre with humor." This he did, and did superbly. In addition to bucking the tradition of coddling the sponsor, he also violated another TV taboo: the dictum that all criminals must be duly punished for their crimes. On *Alfred Hitchcock Presents*, the thieves and murderers "got away with it" nearly as often as they were caught – at least at the fade-out of the story proper. It was then left to Hitchcock to inform us that justice had eventually triumphed.

"The fancy word for that in the broadcast world is 'retribution'," recalled Norman Lloyd in a 1973 American Film Institute seminar; Hitchcock himself called it "a small tolerance . . . a necessary gesture to morality." An example would be the episode "Malice Domestic," broadcast on February 10, 1957. The story concerned a killer's escape that was cut short, we were informed, because "his dog Cassandra was really a detective in disguise, and turned him in at the next town. It's getting so a man can't even trust his best friend." Even the host himself would occasionally get away with murder. On one occasion, after shooting his dueling opponent in the back during an opening minute of an episode, Hitchcock attributed this lapse of good sportsmanship to a piece of advice his mother had given him: "It's better to be safe than sorry."

But to say that Hitchcock had very little to do with the Hitchcock television show is like saying that J.P. Morgan was not much involved in the banking company that bore his name. Perhaps to preserve the image, Hitchcock maintained that he did have a lively interest in the proceedings at Revue. His own physical presence was not required often, because his appearances were "filmed in groups of six or seven at a time." But on at least one account, twelve appearances were done in a single day!

Beyond this, there is general agreement that the director had little to do with the day-to-day operations of Shamley Productions. Once this "fact" has been noted, most critics and historians have proceeded to analyze Hitchcock's infrequent directorial contributions to the series – as though those episodes are the only shows worth serious consideration, and only insofar as they relate to his "real" work in feature films. This has led to an unfortunate under-valuation of his influence on the style and substance of the series as a whole.

Among the assurance given to Hitchcock by Wasserman was that his movie activities would not be disrupted; therefore, the TV production set-up was designed to make maximum use of

Hitchcock's minimal participation. According to various principals, Hitchcock was involved only in a supervisory capacity – but within that role, particularly at the crucial stage of story selection, his influence seems to have been significant. Hitchcock would be presented with potential stories in synopsized form, which he would then approve or disapprove. The scripts were then developed under the supervision of Harrison and as Lloyd described: "Hitchcock seldom spoke about how a script should be shot. He had nothing to do with the pictures until he saw a rough-cut. Then he would look at it and say yes or no, and usually he'd say 'Well maybe you need a close-up or an insert or something.' That was the extent he played in the actual making of it." Lloyd, of course, came on board during the series' third season; there is reason to believe that Hitchcock was slightly more involved during the earlier period. He had always been a voracious reader and, according to Harrison (quoted in *Newsweek* in 1956), was quite active in proposing material for the series. "His mind is like a threshing machine, chomping out ideas, ideas as we walk, ideas at meals, ideas every minute." It was also during the story selection phase that Hitchcock had a chance to choose his own directorial assignments. (And it's evident, although he liked to claim otherwise, that the stories which he directed personally were quite carefully selected.)

But more importantly, as Lloyd also noted, "the whole style of the series was totally influenced by his style . . . the suspense with humor, with irony, with twist; it is totally Hitchcock. It was his point of view that we were looking for in stories." Certainly the selection of authors which were chosen for adaptation was significant: more than a few British writers, plus those whose morbid – not to say sadistic – bent of mind Hitchcock seemed particularly to relish: Cornell Woolrich, John Collier, Roald Dahl, Stanley Ellin and Robert Bloch among them.

"But I do insist on approval of all the writers' scripts," Hitchcock explained. "I read every last one and make whatever suggestions I can think of. And then - editing the final product, the film itself. It's a question of deciding how much of the original concept you can get on the screen. I've always figured that in a motion picture one's good fortune is to get 75 percent of the original concept. Don't forget, there are always compromises, in casting, in the quality of the direction, even in my own work . . . the minute you put a star into a role you've already compromised because it may not be perfect casting."

"There are certain ingredients for mass appeal," said Hitchcock, describing the stories he wanted to direct. "But it's all a question of the quality of that mass appeal. People get the impression that mass appeal has to be cheap. That's not true. Of course, attainment is difficult. When you're asking writers for quality, they would rather save [their ideas] for their movie or their play. There'll always be what I call play-in-the-drawer writers. You know the kind. They sit down at their desks and begin to think. Suddenly a light comes into their eyes, they look around furtively to see if anyone is watching, open up the drawer and make a secret note of the idea – for future reference."

Joan Harrison (and later Norman Lloyd) would first choose the stories they felt would be satisfactory for the program, and Hitchcock would look those over and have the final word of which ones would be adapted. Occasionally, writers like Harold Swanton and Gwen Bagni would write short, one, two or three-page drafts based on original ideas they had, and they would be added to the pile of proposals. Hitchcock, on occasion, also choose a couple off the side he liked and added it to the pile. But Hitchcock never wrote any of the scripts.

"It wasn't a rigid policy, but rather a pragmatic one," Norman Lloyd said. "He [Hitchcock] liked to know that a story had been published first because he always felt that if a story had been published, you had something to begin with. He was not one for developing stories, as is mostly done today."

27

"That's one reason we work from already published material," Hitchcock explained. "The ingredients are there and thus safe from the play-in-the-drawer writer. What are the ingredients? Well, you have to command the audience's attention. There are two ways to do it. First in terms of characters that interest them - that's the hook. Because there is no time to really develop character in a half-hour, casting becomes the substitute for character. Then there is the nature of the plot setup itself. Suppose I show you a mousy dentist and his wife [describing the episode "Mrs. Bixby and the Colonel's Coat"]. The wife is about to take off on one of her monthly visits to 'relatives.' Now we see her detraining at the station, met by a limousine with chauffeur. 'My, but she has rich relatives,' you say. Now she drives up to an ostentatious country home. Down the steps comes a handsome man and they embrace. Who is this man? At that point you've hooked them. Now we play the scene where the man tells her he won't be able to see her off for home tomorrow. She looks puzzled. Now he leaves her a box. In the box is a mink coat and a note. The note says, 'Sorry, we're through.' She prepares to go. The maid sees the mink coat. 'But aren't you going to wear it home, madam?' The wife and the audience realize for the first time, she can't. She's got a husband. That's the place for the middle commercial. Also the thing that keeps them tuned in through what my dear sponsor has to say."

"Hitch was very, very tough on stories," said producer Gordon Hessler. "There were some stories you'd be angry that he wouldn't use, but he was adamant. It was a very tough job. The great thing was that all the scripts were finished before any of the shows were shot, so you could really get the best actors in town and give the scripts to them long before they were booked. If you look at the roll call of that *Hitchcock* era of television, you'll see that many of those people turned into big, big film stars."

Henry Slesar, who probably had more stories adapted for the series than any other writer, recalled: "Hitchcock liked to be able to judge a story in its entirety rather than as a script. It was more the English style of doing things, the influence not only of Hitchcock, but of Joan Harrison, Gordon Hessler and Norman Lloyd as well. This was definitely a British contingent."

"But no story was done without Hitch's approval," added Norman Lloyd. "That is to say, we used to find the stories and then submit them to Hitchcock for approval, rejection or to be put on the 'reserve list' in case we ran out of stories. Then Joan and I would develop the story into a screenplay, having selected a writer; and then we would select a director; and then we would cast it. And shoot it. Edit it. And when we had a rough cut, we then would call Hitch and bring it up to him at his bungalow [at Universal] and he would look at it. I don't recall his ever rejecting any episode. And even his comments were very modest—he was wonderfully sensitive to people's work, and so he would just say, 'If you have shot a close-up there, you might want to use it.' This was very rare. And he never rejected a picture, he would say, 'Very good' or 'Good'—or 'Well, thank you' if he didn't like it [laughs]. He never said, 'I didn't like it.' "

Norman Lloyd continued: "Then we took the picture back, we did all the post-production on it, found a composer to do the scoring, and the next time Hitch saw the picture was on the air. He believed you could only judge it when you saw it at nine o'clock on the television set. But all the work that I've described to you, Joan and I did, yes. Hitch directed about ten of them [eighteen, actually] and always the scripts were delivered to him, given to him. Joan would say, 'This is a story that Hitch will do' and send it up to him, and he always... [laughs] he always accepted what he was told to do!"

On one occasion, Hitchcock did toss around an original proposal. "I suggested a story about a fanatic old man who works in a baseball factory," he said. "He makes up one and puts dynamite in it. The ball with dynamite becomes the central character. The ball goes out on the field, we follow it to the umpire, who throws it to the pitcher, who then strikes out three men in a row to win the game. . . Imagine the suspense! The ball is given to the club's director, and he puts it on a sideboard in his office with other trophies. At the very end I wanted to have a cleaning woman come in and jiggle the ball by accident, and it rolls and rolls toward the edge. The ball is about to fall down and explode, and she caught it in the very last shot. [sighs] We never worked it out."

"Hitch approved all the stories before they were shot, but really it was an entity of its own," Gordon Hessler continued. "Hitch looked at all the scripts, and if he didn't like something we had to change it. And he did all the introductions, but you know of course that they were all done in one day. Joan Harrison, who wrote some of the scripts [she would do rewrites and fine-tune various pages from time to time] was Hitchcock's personal assistant, was the actual producer of the show. Norman Lloyd, who was an actor in his own right - he was in Hitch's *Saboteur* (1942) - was also a producer, and was sort of my boss. When he moved up from associate producer to producer, I became the associate, then when he moved to executive producer I became producer. He was always one step ahead of me [laughs]!"

The mind that can conceive such a nerve-racking story of course had little time for family situation comedies, which, said Hitchcock, constituted about the only form of television he did not watch. But: "I watch almost everything else." His personal opinion thought that the best future of the industry lied in documentaries, news and special events. "Because, after all, you know, we may run out of stories. We only have a certain number of plots. Except. . . if one walks down Fifth Avenue, there are an awful lot of stories passing by."

NORMAN LLOYD: HIS FALL TO STARDOM

Norman Lloyd's association with *Alfred Hitchcock Presents* varies, depending on which part of his life you want to begin with. At the earliest, his long and distinguished career on the stage with Eva Le Gallienne began in 1932. And throughout the intervening years, he has become an actor, a director, a producer, and executive producer. His career as an actor took him to the stage, radio, television and movies. "I grew up in Jersey City and in New York," Lloyd recalled. "My father owned a small furniture store, first on the Lower East Side, then

on Lower Park Avenue, in the furniture district. He was doing well, satisfied, he thought everything was fine, and then the Depression came along. He lost his store. He never knew what hit him. He never understood." Lloyd was an adolescent by then, well on his way to an acting career; but the memory of the Depression and his father's failure haunted him.

His acting actually originated with his parents. "I've been performing professionally since I was seven. At that age, I did a soft shoe dance and songs with motions in a vaudeville act. Most obnoxious in retrospect. I kept this up (and my non-theatrical family thought I was so cute) until I was twelve, and then I realized that I just had to take time out for some formal learning. So I quit my career temporarily, and resumed it again at seventeen." Lloyd wasn't much over sixteen when he joined Eva Le Gallienne's Civic Repertory Theater, an old stand down on 14th Street. There, in "Liliom," as prize villain, he did nothing but walk on stage, leer silently and sneak off whence he has come.* When the Civic Rep folded, young Lloyd tried for Broadway – but no go. Finally he found his niche as leading player in the Federal Theater's *Living Newspaper*, from whence he went to Orson Welles, who was collecting for his Mercury Theater production of "Julius Caesar" and "Shoemaker's Holiday." Later that same year he scored a personal triumph as Johnny Appleseed in Marc Connelly's "Everywhere I Roam" which, nevertheless, only ran for twelve performances.

By the 1920s, Lloyd was starring in *The Living Newspaper*, a sort of theatrical precursor of today's docu-drama that captivated New York Theatergoers for the better part of a decade. Legitimate theater actors, no matter how popular, worked unsteadily for low pay in those days. "I never believed I could make a living in the theater," Lloyd recalled. "We were desperately poor. When I worked at the Mercury Theater, I made $40 a week; I got nine raises, to $75. Then we began to lose money and I was cut back to $40. I still – jokingly – accuse John Houseman of being an 'Indian Giver'; he's the only one who cut my pay."

"When Orson went to Hollywood," Lloyd recalled, "he took most of the Mercury group along – and I was among them. I was to have a nice fat part in 'Heart of Darkness,' only it never got to be made. So, I played tennis for five months while Welles discarded first one script, then another. When he finally decided on *Citizen Kane*, there wasn't any role for me. So I came back East and did an ill-fated show, Frank Craven's 'Village Green.' It closed in such a hurry that I had plenty of time on my hands – so I wrote a play. Meanwhile, I was up for a part in the new Ben Hecht show (also a flop), and before reporting for rehearsal one day, I took my manuscript to John Houseman, who used to be Welles' partner. He said he'd look at it, and then suddenly he exclaimed: 'Say, Norman, Alfred Hitchcock is in town and he's looking for a fellow of your description for *Saboteur*. Why don't you let me make an appointment for you?' "

"Well, whether it meant a part for me or not, I was dying to meet Hitchcock, whom I'd admired for years," Lloyd continued. "The date was set for that very afternoon, because he was leaving for Hollywood the next morning. It was more like a social get-together. We discussed pictures and plays and books. And casually he said, 'I'm going to test you. Have you got any material? Go up to such and such a place and tell them to get started.' I replied that I hadn't any material at the moment, but that I could dig up some within twenty minutes. I dashed out, got hold of a script of 'Blind Alley,' and within an hour I was before the cameras for the first time. As it happened, the weather was foggy the next day, so Hitchcock couldn't fly back. When he did leave, he took my test along, and the day after his arrival he wired me to come out in a hurry."

Norman Lloyd was married to actress Peggy Craven, and had two children. Six times the wedding was postponed because Norman, who at that time had formed his own theater group, was tied up with rehearsals. Finally Peggy literally and figuratively put her foot down and interrupted the proceedings by flatly stating, "Either you marry me now or we're through!" The two got hitched. In fact, Peggy and Norman were so afraid that his second trip to the movie capitol would be repetition of the Orson Welles incident that she wouldn't go with him. The day after the picture was finished Hitchcock said to him, "Well, you may as well go back and get your wife and baby."

Saboteur, which Alfred Hitchcock directed for Universal Pictures, has all the Hitchcock clichés of hair-breathing escapes, piled on nerve-tingling adventures. Yet in a fast-paced way it does indicate the possible workings of a nation-wide sabotage ring. Despite the fact such

* Lloyd was also a playing card in a stage production of "Alice in Wonderland."

rings are usually handled competently by the FBI, in this picture, Barry Kane (played by Robert Cummings) through a score of harrowing trials finally scores to a logical death, the man who set a fire in the Glendale plane plant in which both work. The Statue of Liberty sequence, in which Saboteur Fry (played by Norman Lloyd) plunges to his death, was one of the worst-kept secrets of movie press agentry. Hitchcock had requested the "fade" be kept from the news until the picture was shown. The news was well suppressed by everyone but the columnists, the screen-writers and the studio.

"It does thrill me that people still remember," Lloyd admits. "I think it speaks very well for Hitchcock and his concept." The big scene atop the statue was done in California on Universal's then-largest sound stage, but it had to be set up with location shots of Lloyd arriving at the Battery, catching the boat to Liberty Island, and so on. "December 15, a very cold day. We had to pretend it was spring, take our coats off and go out on deck. We did that all the way across, and a little old lady – a real customer – got mixed in with the extras and went right along with us taking our coats off and on. Finally, she asked someone, 'Do you have to do this every time you want to see the Statue of Liberty?' "

The climatic fight scene was not only choreographed but sketched out by Hitchcock. "He showed me drawings before we shot it. I was absolutely startled that such a thing could be done. It didn't inhibit me. The fact that he drew it was not that you should act it exactly that way; it was the way he'd shoot it – the way it'd look visually."

Hitchcock had a one second thought on the *Saboteur* scene: the hero should have been in jeopardy, not the villain – a situation he would later remedy in *North by Northwest* (1959), which had both the hero and the heroine dangle from the edge of Mount Rushmore. "Hitchcock would have these ideas and then save them," Lloyd recalled. "For years he drove from Los Angeles to his home in Santa Cruz, and he would see these crop-duster planes. He knew at some point he would use them, but he never found a place until *North by Northwest*."

"I was so fortunate to make my first picture with Hitchcock. I started at the top, and was introduced to a way of picture-making, a way of conducting oneself on the set, a way of life regarding a picture, that of an international star director. Not only was he an artist, but there was a very special world which he projected. Hitch always dressed in a black suit, white shirt, and black tie. He looked like either a banker or an undertaker. He actually had twenty-eight of these suits, all the same. The coats and trousers were marked with corresponding numbers, so they wouldn't get matched in the wrong way; this was done for dry cleaning purposes. It was characteristic of his mind, so well organized. He would walk on the set and conduct it as if it were a fine banking firm in England – very quiet and masterful. But he had great humor and a sense of fun. He still had remnants of his gift for practical jokes at that time, and sometimes played them; they were always very funny. He left an indelible mark on me of what it means to be a director and how to conduct oneself on the set."

"Norman Lloyd was second in command at Shamley," writer Talmage Powell recalled, "doing many of the executive details and occasionally directing when a script came along that inspired him to do so. I wasn't present when 'No Pain' was shot, but we talked about it some, he mentioning how certain [aspects] of the story developments had suggested camera angles and zoom details." Certainly a part of Hitchcock brushed on Lloyd.

After *Saboteur*, Lloyd began appearing in a score of films including Hitchcock's *Spellbound* (1945). In 1952, he became a production associate with Charlie Chaplin in *Limelight*. In 1953, Lloyd directed "The Golden Apple" at the Phoenix Theater, a production that won the New York Critics Award as the best musical of the season. In that same period, he directed five half-hour segments of the Abraham Lincoln films for *Omnibus*, which were written by the late James Agee.

The first year and a half of *Alfred Hitchcock Presents* ran smoothly and about half-way through the second season, the Shamley Production team accepted an additional task of filming ten hour-long broadcasts for the up-and-coming NBC's *Suspicion* series. (see *Suspicion* chapter) An additional member of the production team was needed and Norman Lloyd accepted the position. As an Associate Producer, Lloyd's tasks included much of the same as Joan Harrison's. Finding story material, hiring a cast of actors for each play, a director, writer, and so on. Lloyd even tinkered with directing a total of twenty-two episodes and acting in four himself. During the years that *Alfred Hitchcock Presents* was being broadcast, Lloyd took time out to direct an episode of television's *Insight* and an episode of *Alcoa Premiere* entitled "The Jail" (see "The Jail" chapter). His association with the program remained till the series went off the air in 1965.

In the fall of 1968, a new anthology series based on psychological horrors premiered on television, again produced by Joan Harrison and Norman Lloyd, entitled *Journey Into the Unknown*. The series was not able to capture the essence of the Hitchcock program, and left the air after four months. Less than ten years after, Norman Lloyd would produce another anthology series, *Tales of the Unexpected*, featuring many adaptations of Roald Dahl stories, a few previously filmed on the Hitchcock program. Lloyd also directed a few choice episodes of that series, and this second anthology series had more of a success than *Journey*. With Quinn Martin as executive producer, the program featured William Conrad as the narrator. "I've done other shows, other series, and they haven't worked as well," confessed Norman Lloyd. "I took over the Roald Dahl series *Tales of the Unexpected* at one point, and it was never the same. Roald tried to be a Hitchcock when that series started, and he just didn't have it."

"One afternoon we [Norman Lloyd] went over to a sound stage where a Henry Slesar segment was being shot," recalled writer Talmage Powell. "I think it was 'Pen Pal.' Sotto voce Norman remarked on camera movements and actor details. Only one camera was used. It never stopped. If an actor flubbed a line, the script girl would call a line number, and the on-stage players would drop back to that point and continue on. At the close of the scene, the director might call for cover shots, close-ups, that kind of thing. The whole kaboodle was later cut and pasted to provide a master film from which copies were made. Norman and I got along quite well from the very start. The last I heard, he was doing some outstanding things in public television." Indeed he was. In 1970, PBS took up a series of productions entitled *Hollywood Television Theatre*, with Lloyd as executive producer for at least six years. "We have better writers," Lloyd told a reporter for the *Jersey Journal* in December of 1974, comparing *Hollywood Television Theatre* with *Alfred Hitchcock Presents*. "Not only is the writing as good or better, but we can deal with more daring material."

Norman Lloyd's acting career also took a boost, when he began playing the role of Dr. Auschlander on television's *St. Elsewhere* for almost six years. He won acclaim for his role of Mr. Nolan, the headmaster in *Dead Poets Society* (1989) and most recently, as President of Wassamotta U. (University) in *The Adventures of Rocky and Bullwinkle* (2000). But over all, it was Lloyd's supporting role of Fry in *Saboteur* that he is most grateful, for it established a long-lasting career in Hollywood. Working for Hitchcock, Lloyd believes, was like no other experience an actor could have. *Saboteur* was positively inspirational. There was no wasteful effort. "His mind was constantly on the audience," Lloyd concluded. "He said for instance, 'while you're doing that, I want the audience to be reacting in such-and-such a way.' He was bulky, all right, but amazingly agile. He gave anybody a chance to make suggestions, and often take them even from a beginner."

JOAN HARRISON: HITCHCOCK'S PROTEGE AT CRIME

Joan Mary Harrison was the only woman in television who, during the year *Suspicion* aired, functioned as a producer on two different networks. She was blue-eyed and blonde, trim as a movie starlet (24-inch waistline), and according to *TV Guide*, she was "decisive as a broker in a bull market." A single grisly subject, crime (preferably murder, particularly as committed by normally respectable, if fictional, people) was her principal preoccupation. If this description doesn't make Harrison sound like Hitchcock's twin, guess again. Harrison was a woman who, it has been said, "never forgets a case." Behind her V-shaped desk at Hollywood's Revue productions, which filmed the shows for Hitchcock's Shamley Productions, she coolly maintained an executive exterior as misleading, she admitted, as a shadowy suspect in a Hitchcock plot. "Actually," she remarked to a reporter, "all I am after for 24 hours a day is a good story."

According to an article in *TV Guide*, an unnamed associate remarked that "The way to get to know Joan, was not to do business with her, but to take a walk with her. She could stroll past a two-year-old tri-cycling on the lawn and, before you've gone ten feet, outline a melodrama in which a baby saw her father murdered in her nursery but is too young to describe the murderer. Before it's over, the baby holds the fate of everyone concerned in her little pink hand. With Joan, unbearable suspense is one of the necessities of life, like tea at 4 o'clock."

Schooled daintly on Cicero and the Brownings, she kicked off her lace-up shoes at the age of 21 and asked her father, the late Walter Harrison, to step into the family library. Joan's father owned the biweekly newspaper, the *Surrey Advertiser*, published in her hometown of Guildford, 26 miles from London. Joan was the holder of a B.A. from St. Hugh's at Oxford (where she wrote airy, refined character sketches for the college women's magazine), and previous a student to the Sorbonne in Paris. She demanded her father give her a job.

(Photo courtesy of Photofest.)

"I want to be a journalist," she announced to her father. "I expect you to give me a job." Her father shook his head. She could go to work if she liked, but not as a journalist. Ambitious as she was, Joan folded up Dad's newspaper, handed it back to him with thanks, and took the Monday morning train into London. By Wednesday – with a little help from Dad – she was at work as a clerk in a midtown dress shop. On weekends she went home to Surrey and had breakfast in bed.

Six months of telling fat ladies they looked darling in tweeds, Harrison began to be palled. "At the end of the day, I found myself loathing women. A friend suggested I go to a secretarial school and find a job as a secretary. 'A secretary can learn any business,' my friend told me." Joan returned home for a spell to rest, then a second run into commercialism, this time as a typist for a publishing house, followed by a sprinkling of shorthand schooling in one of London's nicer seminaries. "So I went to secretarial school and another friend told me Mr. Hitchcock was looking for a secretary with enough education to read screen material." The news came to her on a sheet of blue note-paper written in white ink and carried in on a breakfast tray at 10 in the morning. By 12:30 she had zoomed into Hitchcock's office and right into a few dozen other girls, all there for the same reason.

"There were about forty girls queued up for the job as Hitch's secretary – I was at the end of the queue." Joan was meeting a friend for lunch at 1 o'clock, so she stalked up to the gentleman in charge, requested his ear, whispered that her sister was having a baby and could she be the next one in to see Mr. Hitchcock, so she could run back to the hospital and be there when the baby came. A father himself, the man placed her third in line, and Joan was introduced to Mr. Hitchcock ten minutes before one. "Hitch wanted me to go to lunch – you know how he likes his meals! – so I was hired in a hurry and both of us managed to be eating together by one!"

During their lunch conversation, she traced her interest in show business to movie reviews she used to write for her father's newspaper. "When I was a girl, I could get passes," she explained. Her interest in the crimes of the unrespectable, she attributed to her favorite uncle, the late Harold Harrison. For fourteen years before he was killed in World War II, her uncle was "keeper" of London's Old Bailey - the official who assigned various trials to various courts.

"He was one of those uncles young girls adore," she explained. "He not only took you to lunch, but he knew the grisly details of all the most shocking crimes. For years I've read the transcript of every interesting trial I could lay hands on. He used to let me squeeze into the courtroom when I was a little girl, to watch the trials. Hitch found it rather uncommon to have as secretary, a girl who was up on all the murders of recent times. There's nothing I enjoy like a good trial. That's where the drama in crime is. You can see the criminal's mind developing in the dock, and you ask yourself: Why is he any different from me? What made him do it? What was the final straw?"

That was in April of 1933. Hitchcock was doing *The Man Who Knew Too Much*. The phone at Gaumont British Studios rang constantly, there were letters to be answered, people to be sent away, scripts to be typed. But Joan Harrison was too busy watching the master direct, to mess her blonde curls. Finally, Hitchcock relieved her and let her read books for him instead. Most of Hitchcock's personal mail seldom got answered; but she sat with him through long hours of every conceivable kind of meeting. "Hitch taught me everything I knew about this business."

"In the beginning, I was stubbornly suspicious of Mr. Hitchcock's vaunted realism," she explained. "You remember the way Robert Donat and Madeleine Carroll were linked through much of *The 39 Steps* with a pair of handcuffs? I said to Mr. Hitchcock, 'Those look like fake handcuffs!' He promptly took them and snapped them around my wrist – I spent the rest of the day, helpless, looking for the man who had the key!"

Most people know by now that Hitchcock had one strange superstition. He liked to be in every picture he made, personally. just for a brief walk-on. Joan Harrison shared that circumstance just once. "I have been in one of Hitch's pictures – but not through superstition. The actress in a picture [*The Man Who Knew Too Much*, 1934 version] was supposed to drive a car in one scene – and she couldn't drive. So . . . for one glorious scene, I became a double for the heroine, for my first and last time on the screen."

The one scene in that movie which scared her the most, was one that mixed other emotions with suspense. "Remember where Edna Best saw the villain trying to push her child off the roof, and she took a rifle and took a long and steady aim . . . to shoot the villain without hitting her son? Hitch made you feel as though you were telling your own heart to be still, not to shake her aim . . ." Alfred Hitchcock's influence was more than just personal acquaintance or images on the screen. In an August 1962 interview, Hitchcock told director Francois Truffaut that "at one time Joan was a secretary, and as such she would take notes while I worked on a script, with Charles Bennett, for instance. Gradually she learned, became more articulate, and she became a writer."

Her first screenplay credit was a picture titled "The Girl Was Young" (the first U.S. title of Hitchcock's *Young and Innocent*), which was followed by an adaptation of Daphne du Maurier's *Jamaica Inn*, starring Charles Laughton. Then came the year 1939. By the time Hitchcock and company crossed the ocean to do business with David O. Selznick, Joan Harrison took over on the *Rebecca* writing job and rated a screen credit for her trouble. Other Hitchcock films Joan Harrison contributed to were *Foreign Correspondent* (1940), *Suspicion* (1941), and *Saboteur* (1942). After *Saboteur* was completed, Joan decided it was time to leave. She was in New York on a vacation when Hitchcock directed *Mr. and Mrs. Smith*, which she couldn't understand Hitchcock's preference for comedy. Instead, she announced herself as a writer and took M-G-M's assignment for "The Sun is My Undoing," then-currently languishing on the shelf. It went nowhere.

Then, an invitation from Universal, for a possible movie based on a Cornell Woolrich story, tempted her. A sizeable income and eight years of anonymous devotion to duty rewarded her the opportunity to produce a movie of her own. She at once set her hand to other scripts, but something always went wrong with them. In the first place, she liked mystery stories and no one but Hitchcock had been willing to let her try her hand at this sort of production, usually considered a man's field. At last she decided to write one anyway, and with Universal offering to hire her to do a script on a thriller called *Phantom Lady*, Joan Harrison took her opportunity.

She decided to outline the story exactly as she would do it, though this was contrary to the way she had been ordered to make it. When her conference with the studio came, she stuck to her point. It was said that there were almost loud words in the production office when she told the studio what it should do.

"At last." said Harrison, explaining how she became a producer, "they asked me if I thought I could produce it myself. and I said I could. That astonished them so much they signed me on the spot." Always women had fought a losing battle in Hollywood, especially when it came to producing or directing capacities. Dorothy Davenport, Fanchon Royer and one or two stars, such as Mary Pickford had acted as their own producers, and were success stories in their own right. Lois Weber and Dorothy Arzner, to name a couple, gave us some of our best "woman's angle" films, temporarily successful, but even Arzner's productions were always in charge of someone else.

"The front-office attitude resented a woman in authority and probably always will," Harrison once remarked. "They recognize women writers but prefer to keep us in prescribed grooves. Some day, they will have to admit that a woman can function successfully as an executive, too." But even with the success of *Phantom Lady*, Universal never gave her an extension when the movie was completed. *

"I felt grateful to Universal for they gambled on me," she explained. "Naturally, I was hurt that they didn't think enough of me. I was, like the young starlets, an option orphan. In a way they were swell. They gave me a free hand, within restrictions. Let me explain: *Phantom Lady* had a budget of $350,000. Our only expensive actor was Franchot Tone. We had to fill out with contract people. I will say that Ella Raines gave a most capable performance. But there it is: on a big lot, you're supposed to turn out an 'A' picture on a 'B' budget. Even so, we thought we had a 'sleeper' – that is, a film that would meet with popular public approval. But when the higher-ups saw it, they said, No." She grimaced, in remembered imitation. "They stuck their noses up there – and gave me the air."

Harrison next went to United Artists to become an associate producer with Benedict Bogeaus of *Dark Waters* (1944). "Bogeaus handles the money and I take care of all the artistic angles," Harrison explained. "I pass on every detail. Fabrics for costuming and the completed garments, sets, lighting, casting. You know how good women are at details. The only rub is that 'they' of the big companies don't like for us women to have so much supervision. Consider *Dark Waters*. We have a budget of $800,000, but it's elastic. Story, first, then the salaries of our four stars, Merle Oberon, Franchot Tone, Fay Bainter and Thomas Mitchell. We may splurge a bit on sets, cut down a trifle on something else, if necessary. I think I would like to play along with the independents. They're not in such a hurry – we have a 40-day schedule, but if we run a few days over, no one is going to have a fit. This is the perfect set-up. Let the man handle the money, let the woman have complete supervision of all artistic angles. Those years with Hitch were very pleasant, as we saw completely eye to eye. But when Universal let me go, I was stumped for a while. Oh, yes, they've made me an offer to return, but I would prefer not to. The fact that they didn't maintain faith in me rankles a bit."

Joan Harrison's credits began growing. From *Nocturne* (1946) to *Your Witness* (1950), she was showing Hollywood that women would do the same tasks as men, if not better. As a producer on her own, Harrison learned a few tricks the hard way, "by suffering through my mistakes. If you hold an expression of horror on screen too long, it becomes ludicrous and the audience laughs. That happened during a sneak preview of one of my pictures. The audience laughed out loud and I got up and went to the powder room for the rest of the movie, to hide my shame. That is one great trouble with being a woman – I am too sensitive to my own mistakes."

To be pretty, and a producer, suggested other problems. Working late one night on her first picture, she walked off the set alone. She was new and many of the technicians didn't know her. Two carpenters saw what they thought of only as another pretty blonde – so, being human, they whistled. "I smiled, and walked on. But the next day I was very busy, and I looked very much like a producer again. In the middle of a conference on the set, I sent for some carpenters. The two who had whistled showed up, and I'll never forget the look on their faces as they recognized me as the boss. They didn't quite know what to do – apologize, or just hope they wouldn't be recognized. I said hello . . . thanked them for their compliment of the night before . . . and after that, I never saw carpentry done faster or better!"

* Rumor has it that one tycoon in Hollywood remarked publicly, "A woman! It would never work. I hold my conferences in a steam bath!"

In 1953, when Hollywood began to cut down on production as television forged ahead, Joan picked up her books on criminology and took off for New York she had accepted the position to produce a video series *Janet Dean, Registered Nurse* for Coronado Productions. Joan Harrison's first television series lasted only 39 episodes, released through a limited syndication in February of 1954. Ella Raines, who impressed Harrison for her performance in *Phantom Lady*, starred as Janet Dean. Filmed entirely in New York, many individual television stations were not interested enough to carry the program – or sponsors for that matter – and an extension for an additional 39 episodes was denied. Her experience as a producer in Hollywood helped give her the edge to produce her first television series, but all of this experience was about to pay off. Just when Joan Harrison started looking for her next job, an old friend called her, and made a tempting TV offer.

"When Hitch told me the type of stories he had planned," she explained, "I decided to return to Hollywood. I knew I'd be back again doing murder with velvet gloves. And, as things turned out, I am – right up to my neck. I read about and 'planned' more murders than I ever thought existed in print. In motion pictures you're concerned with one, maybe two, scripts a year. In television, it's a weekly occurrence. And for every story telecast, at least a dozen are read."

Joan disclosed that one of the keys to a suspenseful drama on the series was attained by "switch" casting, using an actor who betrayed no tendency to crime, least of all murder. "That's the kind of person we began putting in our stories – the nice guy, the contented housewife, the man who loves children and animals. The sorry fact is that these types commit most crimes." As an Associate Producer, Joan Harrison's job was to read unfinished material. That is, most of the stories for *Alfred Hitchcock Presents* were submitted as skeletons, or in synopsis form. If the story is satisfactory, she hired a writer to do the screenplay. Joan then placed telephone calls to actors and their agents to cast for the show, and spent long hours in conferences with art directors, hairstylists and costume supervisors.

"There were some stories that demanded certain performers or no one else would do," Joan told a reporter for the *Courier-Journal*. "The basis of the show, however, is a good script. Given a good script, you need good actors to bring it to life. However, the producer should keep in mind that the actor is more important than the name, especially when, as so often happens, the famous-name actor doesn't fit the role."

There are a number of diverse – but complimentary – views about Joan Harrison. Her chief cameraman called her "a killer-diller." Woman of Achievement, that's what Theta Sigma Phi thought of Joan Harrison. The national professional fraternity for women in journalism presented Joan with the 1960 award for "distinguished accomplishment in writing" in connection with her job as producer. "Tell them: 'Don't be too proud to start at the bottom," was Joan's answer when asked what best advice she could give to young women starting a career in writing or producing for television. "Experience in all phases of the work – secretarial, cutting, story editor, script writer – all this experience helps. But get in and don't expect to earn very much at first."

During the first couple years as an Associate Producer, Joan Harrison lived alone in a one-bedroom apartment. She drove a 1957 Chevrolet Bel-Air hardtop coupe, arrived at the office promptly at nine, enjoyed a Pimm's cup before lunch and a cigarette afterward. She gave up tennis, and had "no hobbies except reading." And unbeknownst to many, British-born Joan didn't become a U.S. Citizen until the summer of 1957. She often spent her vacations in

England, where her mother, a resident of London, viewed *Alfred Hitchcock Presents* and had a few complaints about it. "Every story," she fretted to Joan, "seems to have a murder in it."

By 1960, Joan was married to novelist Eric Ambler, who would write the screenplay to *Mutiny on the Bounty* for M-G-M and Marlon Brando. After the marriage, the two moved into a home in the rolling hills of Bel-Air. "I love my work," Joan confessed. "It absorbs me from 9 in the morning until 6 at night, or until the work is done, five days a week. But I love my home too, my garden, the peacefulness." Eric Ambler preferred to write at home, so their work was a separate part of their lives.

Her office was a neat gray bungalow in the Revue Studios on the Universal-International lot in Universal City. As scriptwriter Talmage Powell recalled: "Her office was spacious, furnished in a French provincial, I guess you would call it. I associated the decor with Louis XVIth for some reason, knowing very little about such things. She was blondish, beautifully put together, smallish, though not in the least suggesting the petite or fragility. In a crass word, she was a looker. . . It's my impression, though I've never tried to confirm it, that she was with Hitch from early-on in England, starting as a youngster, sort of girl Friday. She was a quick and retentive learner, and as Hitch developed via experience, so did she. She was the right hand that every top executive dreams about. In Hitch's case, if it needed doing, from writing a movie script to organizing a television show, [you made] mention to Joan."

"Miss Harrison does the casting, yes, and Norman Lloyd," Hitchcock remarked. "I try to put out fatherly words of advice without trying to - what's the word? -*usurp* their position. I think, myself, in television that we have a greater chance to cast more freely than in pictures. I'm not sure that star names mean all that much in television, at least in dramatic series."

"Hitch is a great person to work with," Harrison returned the compliment. "He's a great person to learn from. No detail of the work is too small for him to explain. With him, there's always time."

"The way Joan Harrison kind of held the show was everything went through her," art director John Lloyd recalled. "The scripts were marvelous. The first two or three years they were marvelous, after that they kind of tapered off, but the first three years, boy they were a delight. Harrison was well organized and well done. I remember we had Bette Davis at one time and Claude Rains in a number of them. Davis was directed by Paul Henreid and the two had a relationship going at one time. I myself was trying to get into films and that was a very difficult transition to make. I succeeded, but the mediums are so different, not like the films today. Doing a lot of two-hour movies was fun but I do see an end to the television dramas. A series always starts with great writing and then after the first few episodes the writing tapers off. And they certainly film less today than what they filmed back then. If only we had people like Joan Harrison still around today."

After the Hitchcock series left the air, Joan Harrison continued producing other Hollywood features such as the 1970 television movie *Love Hate Love* and the television series *Journey to the Unknown* in 1968. Joan Harrison died on August 14, 1994, in London, England. She was 83.

SEASONS CHANGE: BUT NOT WITHOUT A HITCH

Presumably Hollywood agreed to enter TV because it believed the power of the medium would help induce home sitters to get up on their feet and go out to a motion-picture theatre. Yet, in it's efforts to pursuade the public to pay money to see their theatre jewels, Hollywood proceeded to display on TV only costumed gewgaws. As a business policy, it would seem to make as much sense as the salesman for a vintage champagne giving away free samples of lemonade. Still, television flourished and so did *Alfred Hitchcock Presents*. Season by season, the format changed ever so slightly, but the stories – on the whole – remained the same.

The premiere season is considered by many fans as possibly the best of them all. The initial nine months introduced to viewers a style of sharp direction, diabolical stories, and clever plot twists. Compared to all the other seasons, the first offered the most diverse story origins. From short stories ("Back for Christmas" and "Breakdown"), novellas ("And So Died Riabouchinska"), one-act plays ("The Older Sister"), original radio dramas ("The Long Shot" and "Salvage") to original story concepts ("Never Again" and "The Legacy"). If this season hadn't been as successful, *Alfred Hitchcock Presents* would not have gone any further than one season. The day after the final original episode aired over CBS (before summer reruns began), *Newsweek* printed their critical opinion about the program's quality and content. "As for Hitchcock's older and less lavish style, the solution is obvious," the review read. "It is ideally suited to the strictly confined, claustrophobic world of TV drama. If he would just pitch in himself, he could, thanks to television's vast coverage, curdle half of America's blood, give their spines a salutary tingle and raise their hair, right in their own parlors once a week. The medium could use this help."

Although Hitchcock's television work had been confined to film, he did not believe that a live program would entail techniques much different from those he was accustomed to use. "It seems to me that the whole point in live television is the laying out of the whole thing in advance and coordinating the movement of the camera with the movements of the actors," Hitchcock explained. "The viewer's eye should always be distracted from the movement of the camera itself by the movement on the screen - unless you're making a dramatic point of camera movement. In my filmed television productions I also map out everything ahead of time. But this is nothing new for me. I've done the same thing in motion pictures. I make a plan on paper before I start."

The second season (1956/57) pulled more stories from English writers, and the locale for a major amount of the plots was of foggy England, instead of America. Still, this didn't keep the ratings from going higher on the charts (*Alfred Hitchcock Presents* made it to the top 25 according to the Neilsen Ratings) and the fan mail grew. "There are certain ingredients necessary for mass appeal," said Hitchcock, describing the stories he wanted to direct. "But it's all a question of the quality of that mass appeal. People get the impression that mass appeal has to be cheap. That's not true. Of course, attainment is difficult. When you're asking writers for quality they'd rather save it for their movie or their play. There'll always be what I call play-in-the-drawer writers. You know the kind. They sit down at their desks and begin to think. Suddenly a light comes into their eyes, they look around furtively to see if anyone is watching, open up the drawer and make a secret note of the idea - for future reference." Classics such as "Wet Saturday" and "The Hands of Mr. Ottermole" were familiar stories done before on other mystery anthologies. One highlight of the second season was the only multi-part dramatization, "I Killed the Count," broadcast over a period of three consecutive weeks.

The third season (1957/58) started off with a tour-de-force. Certainly some of the program's most memorable episodes were broadcast, including the Emmy-Award winning "The Glass Eye." Barbara Bel Geddes murdered her husband in "Lamb to the Slaughter." The producers began checking out the newly-printed *Alfred Hitchcock's Mystery Magazine*, for story material. The magazine attempted to buy original submissions that were along the lines of the TV series, and the producers found this source indispensable. Stories from Henry Slesar were introduced for the first time.

The fourth season (1958/59) slowly disregarded the English locale of murder plots for more fanciful ones. From the ledge of a window to a period piece in nineteenth-century England, after sunset at a train depot to a dimly-lit court room drama. An outer-space alien invasion and duplicate androids began populating the Hitchcock mold. "We've managed to stay about a half dozen shows ahead," he explained. "Getting the proper material has not been a critical problem. We look for a short story format with a kind of O. Henry twist ending." Turning to the subject of homicide, he remarked: "It's fascinating to speculate about poisonings. Who knows how many unsuspecting women are exterminated by arsenic carefully administered by their husbands or lovers? It may be going on all around us. These men who murder women - so many of them are charming fellows. They must be. Otherwise the women never would have fallen for them in the first place."

In February 1959 MCA bought the studio itself, Universal City, from Decca Records. Revue was producing one-third of NBC's prime-time schedule – eight-and-one-half hours of programming per week. Universal City gave MCA-Revue a centralized production facility, and it gave Lew Wasserman a suitable base for his ever-expanding West Coast operations. Wasserman was now generally considered the most powerful man in Hollywood, and MCA was considered a model of diversification. The two judgements were not related. Universal Pictures was still independent and separate from MCA, at least in a technical sense.

The fifth season (1959/60) was quite a kicker with the viewers. "Man From the South" and "Not the Nervous Type" brought in fan mail from all over, many praises, and many unfavorable. Over the past few decades, when polled by internet fan clubs and TV stations, "viewer's choice marathons" favor more episodes from the fifth season than any other. "Road Hog" and "An Occurrence at Owl Creek Bridge" presented stark performances grabbing the attention of critics and viewers alike.

Hitchcock was, by then, never seen in public without his usual black suit, white shirt with black tie. He never looked into the camera when filming his choice episodes and did not peer through a finder that some directors seem to wear in the eye like a monocle. And did not raise his voice. He was proud of the episodes Shamley produced – but his attention turned elsewhere. He didn't direct as many episodes during the fifth season as he had during the first.

In September 1960, *Alfred Hitchcock Presents* began the sixth season on the air. But instead of the usual CBS Sunday night time-slot which viewers were used to since the program's premiere, the program was now seen on NBC, Tuesday evenings at 8:30. It seems that when NBC took over the show and moved it to Tuesday night ("Good-bye Sunday!" "Hello Tuesday!" the ads read) the ratings took a slight but regrettable drop. "The move was made for what I call Madison Avenue reasons," Hitchcock confessed to *TV Guide*. "They claimed there'd be a bigger audience without the competition of Sunday night. Well, we're creeping back. The quality is better and we've drawn a bigger response."

Hitchcock even introduced the viewers with the network and sponsor change:
> *Good evening, ladies and gentlemen and welcome to a new season of Alfred Hitchcock Presents. . . There is one aspect of this program which has changed. If you have tuned in to hear me make snide remarks about an innocent sponsor, you are doomed to disappointment. I am proud to say, I have resolved my antagonisms and have become completely sponsor-oriented. I have met our new sponsor and find him (a halo appears above his head) to be agreeable, charming, witty, honest, sincere, intelligent, dependable, trustworthy, loyal, brave, clean and reverent.*

By now, Henry Slesar's stories began populating the broadcast schedule. At one point, seven out of ten consecutive broadcasts were Slesar stories! "I was publishing a lot of short stories in the Hitchcock magazine as well as *Ellery Queen*," writer Henry Slesar recalled, "and they were being purchased in such sufficient quantity for the Hitchcock show that my agent eventually met with Joan Harrison when she came to New York and said, 'Why don't you give my client a chance to write one of your scripts?' Joan was a little dubious since I had never written for the screen before, so my agent took the bit between his teeth and implied that we might not sell her any more stories if she didn't give me a crack at an adaptation. I think she agreed because she figured she had less to lose by offering me that one assignment. The first one I did was called 'Forty Detectives Later.' It too was from a story of mine, though that wasn't its title in print. And, of course, I stayed on to do quite a few later, including two that were directed by Hitchcock, 'The Horseplayer' with Claude Rains and 'I Saw the Whole Thing' with John Forsythe."

The seventh season (1961/62) was by far the least impressive, but with a few stand-out episodes, noteworthy of mention. Stories that fit that "Hitchcock mold" were just getting harder to find for the producers. So it was agreed - by Hitchcock at least - that *Alfred Hitchcock Presents* had solved the problem of quality and mass appeal, despite the fact that by season six and seven, the show's ratings began to drop. They were still not quite as good as the years before, and the network executives were checking the charts twice. Joan Harrison called Hitchcock "my most economical director." His one regret about the mink-coat story, "Mrs. Bixby and the Colonel's Coat," was that it had no victims of any kind, a tendency which *Alfred Hitchcock Presents* was getting away from, reverting to those dear old dead bodies scudding around like autumn leaves in a windstorm. Could the lack of dead bodies mean lack of ratings?

The sponsors objected to one episode based on a morbid little Robert Bloch tale entitled "The Sorcerer's Apprentice," and the network went along with the sponsors, standing their ground. Viewers were sharing their opinions, and so were the critics. The complaints did not warrant earnest consideration. Offhand it seemed to reflect the unenviable dilemma in which the executives found themselves. They obviously needed a change of pace. Plans were being made on how to improve the program, and the hour-long format was tossed around.

THE BRITISH EDICT OF TV VIOLENCE

British viewers were slightly mystified by 1960 by fighting words against television violence, issued by the British Broadcasting Corporation as a code of practice. Viewers could not see any differences in the programs. The main introduction to producers was: "A sequence involving violence should arise naturally from the story, and be therefore dramatically necessary and defensible. If it is inserted extraneously for depraved effect, it should be rejected outright. This happens with many of the 'private eye' and police series that come from the United States." And *Alfred Hitchcock Presents* was on the BBC's "hit list."

The fact was that the British public did not know what it was missing. They still saw plenty of scrapping and shooting in imported American shows. Kenneth Adam was the controller of BBC television programs during the early sixties, and was responsible for the new manifesto, and explained publicly that many of the American series were rejected outright and never reached British TV screens. In the shows that did appear, he said, "jump cuts" were made when necessary. "How many?" asked the Associated Press. . . Ken Adam admitted only about two a week, but he declined to name them. Regarding *Alfred Hitchcock Presents*, the matter was settled when Alfred Hitchcock's hosting chores, those narratives that poked fun of American sponsors, were filmed with alternate resolutions. (More about Hitchcock's narratives later).

Television westerns were popular during the late fifties and early sixties (topping the rating charts) and shows like *Laramie* which were packed throughout with homicide and murderous assaults, suffered. Two installments of *Laramie* were banned, along with two scar-faced episodes of *Philip Marlowe*. If there was any suspicion that a scene had been written, or filmed deliberately to scare the imaginative or nervous viewer, then it should be cut out – at least that was the way BBC officials felt.

In curious contrast, though with much the same result, was the attitude of the BBC's rivals, commercial television known as Independent TV (ITV). No code had been issued and though the governing body, the Independent Television Authority could intervene, questions of censorship were left to the good taste and judgement of individual program contractors and producers. There was also a clause in the television act, section 3, which forbid anything being shown that was against good taste or likely to lead to crime.

Broadcasts on the ITV network were such series as *Gun Law, Wagon Train, Rawhide, The Cisco Kid*, and *Alfred Hitchcock Presents*, among others. Crime seemed, at the moment, mostly homicide and R.A. Butler, the home secretary contributing to the commercial TV Times commented: "Viewed as a whole, television programs both independent and BBC, seem to me to be generally decent and beneficial even though there are some exceptions. The exceptions that make me particularly apprehensive are those depicting the 'gangster' and 'big shot' in a way that can give some romantic youths and people of feeble character an urge to emulate."

Apart from the problems of crime and violence the British programs of the fifties and sixties had dealt boldly – and frankly – with a number of delicate controversial subjects such as homosexuality, abortion and venereal disease. Still, one of the handicaps in having a reputation as the "Master of Suspense" and "Sultan of Suspense" was that the public expected him to live up to it . . . even when he wasn't 100% directly involved. And if your name was Alfred Hitchcock, even more was expected.

However, censorship and public morality being what they were at the time, a producer of unusual thrillers had to draw the line in his endeavors to scare the wits out of an audience.

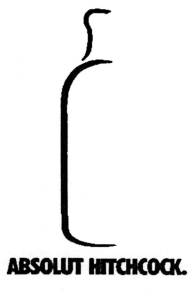

ABSOLUT HITCHCOCK.

Case in point: "Man From the South," concerning a chap whose hobby was betting fingers. The losers – including his wife – had their fingers amputated at the knuckle. This one got on the air, and the network received letters about it from concerned viewers.

SCREENS AND SCREAMS

Here, screenwriter and critic Robert Lewis Shayon provides insight into the realm of Hitchcock's creative process. In the April 20, 1963 issue of the *Saturday Review*, Shayon composed an essay entitled "Screens and Screams." The possibility of a Shayon / Hitchcock meeting is plausible, as evident below:

The shudder is a perennial element in mass entertainment. The medieval was fond of the religious sort – images in churchyards evoking the horror of death. The contemporary shudder is Freudian – summoned up in darkened cinemas by films like *Psycho*, where a nude is murdered while taking a shower – and mixes the dance of death with a counterpoint of eroticism.

Alfred Hitchcock is, of course, the acknowledged master of this genre. His next film will deal with a girl who is both a compulsive thief and frigid [*Marnie* (1964)]. His authority in this tradition has become so legendary (the publicists call him Alfred Hitch-shock) that it came as a mild shock during a recent luncheon with the master to learn that he, too, is subservient to higher powers in the production of his pictures. *The Birds* is his latest release for Universal Studios, based on a Daphne du Maurier story originally set in Cornwall. The film unfolds the doom of a village near San Francisco that is attacked by a multitude of vicious finches, crows, and seagulls. The hero and heroine escape as the picture ends and are seen driving along the highway to the city. There are no survivors in the du Maurier tale: implicit is the birds' destruction of the human species.

Mr. Hitchcock claimed that his ending was merely ambiguous but he admitted that, had he been permitted, he would have finished the film another way. Approaching San Francisco, the survivors would have seen the Golden Gate Bridge covered with birds. The director confessed other frailties. *Lifeboat*, an earlier film, had been shot entirely from the vantage point of survivors, in a crowded boat, after sinking at sea. He had cheated once, though, departing from the subjective camera to show a long shot of the lifeboat from a distance. He had erred in his treatment of *The Wrong Man*, imposing the Hitchcock style on a true story involving a case of mistaken identity. He realized, after he had finished the film, that he should have shot the whole thing with the objectivity of a newsreel. He had yearned, he said, to shoot *North by Northwest* for the pictorial imagery of a nightmare, but he conceded that audiences would probably have been unable to follow the story. Then, having humanized his own exalted image, Mr. Hitchcock revealed a shudder-frontier beyond the fantasies of his image-makers.

He foretold a mass entertainment experience in which audiences would be not merely empathizing spectators, but hypnotized participants in dramatic action. Theatre-goers would choose their roles in a play and actually, not vicariously, live them in mesmerized consciousness. The catharic effects of such mass hypnotic role-playing, especially in murder stories, are formidable to contemplate.

At lunch, Hitchcock talked with charm and animation about the difference between Hitchcock in films and on television. The greatest difference, he said, is the superior economic freedom in films. It took him seven days to shoot one minute of the shower-bath knifing in *Psycho*. The shooting sequence for his weekly hour-long CBS suspense thriller (actually only forty-seven minutes of story) is six days for one program. Mr. Hitchcock is utterly involved in his picture-making; his participation in the actual production of his television series appears vague. He said he chooses the stories (thirty-two were finally selected out of 2,400 scanned for one season) and occasionally he has directed a television production. One was good Hitchcock. A wife kills her husband by striking him over the head with a frozen leg of lamb. In the end the detectives unknowingly eat the murder instrument. The film director shot the television story in two days.

What is ordinarily missing, of course, in Hitchcock on television are superior stories, and the viewer also misses the imaginative direction that is the true Hitchcock hallmark. But then, the master considers television a medium of communication, not an art form; it does not permit a minutely controlled assembly of images evoking emotion despite language barriers. Furthermore, Mr. Hitchcock believes that television cannot mount broad, elaborate productions – only concentrated situations. The spectacle of birds destroying a village would be diminished on the small screen. The trouble is, of course, that a few years from now that's precisely where it will end up.

HITCHCOCK AT WORK

"The movie theater of today," Alfred Hitchcock said slowly, like a man about to coin a phrase, "is little more than an enlarged jukebox. Yes, you just put coins in the slot and out come the pictures and popcorn. They pay a manager a nominal salary to keep the place clean, but that's about all. They aren't selling pictures these days. Now television is a different matter altogether. In television you are playing to a very selective audience. I believe we too often underestimate the intelligence of the grown-up, you see, when they are getting something for free in their own homes. They become children again when they have to pay. The drive to the theater, the parking lot, the ticket at the box office. Having gone through all this inconvenience and suffered a financial loss, they expect something cheerful. They like the happy ending. After all, why should they pay their good money just to be made miserable?"

"I have been given more latitude in television than I ever had in motion pictures," he continued. "It is paradoxical of course, but the movie people hedge you in with all sorts of artistic restrictions; whereas, in television I can quite literally get away with murder. At the end of one of our little stories, you see - a story in which a murderer apparently has gotten away nicely with his crime - I come on and give some small hint to the effect that the murderer didn't really get away with it at all. Let us call it a small tolerance. I do it simply as a necessary gesture to morality."

In a business often completely surrounded, if not suffocated, by sponsors reluctant to offend even the smallest segment of the viewing population, Hitchcock had remained remarkably free of sponsor interference and had compounded his good fortune by airing some of television's most daring shows. "I persuaded them, shall we say, right at the beginning that, to be successful, you must be different. You must be bold, daring. Sponsors like to be abused, you know."

"The English, you see, have always had an inborn ability to see the humor in tragedy and to recognize the fine line that divides the two," he continued. "I imagine this is why I am so given to this type of picture. I could never direct a straight drama or Western, even if I wanted to. People would be looking for the body and they would feel cheated. You must never cheat your audience. I deal with the fine line. A man walks down the street and falls into a manhole. This is funny. Cruelty, you see, is funny. But if the camera follows the man down into the manhole itself and sees him lying there in agony with a broken back, then it ceases to be funny. The art of provoking laughter from tragedy lies in knowing the precise location of the fine dividing line."

The ten years during which Alfred Hitchcock was a weekly presence on the nation's television screens also encompassed a serious consideration of Hitchcock as a film artist who made its way, slowly and controversially, into English-language film criticism. Unlike the schedule of each and every television production, in which filming was completed within two or three days, Hitchcock's prologues and epilogues were filmed in batches, usually when he had free time between his big-screen projects. But with Hitchcock in front of the camera, who was behind?

The answer was simple. Hitchcock directed himself. Rather, he had James Allardice's narratives (sometimes on cue cards), adhered to the scripts word-for-word, and stood by patiently as the technical crew set up the props. Tables, chairs, podiums, costumes, a giant cannon, a large buzz-saw, and an occasional extra on the side-line were pre-planned and prepared for smooth filming. He would give the commands on how he wanted the props stood, the technicians set up the lights, and Hitchcock began his dead-pan deliveries. When animals were required, trainers were brought on the set. Hitchcock co-hosted with dogs, cats, a parrot, a lion, a monkey, and even an elephant. No harm came to the animals during filming, and no harm came to the bold director who stood by as an elephant or lion walked on stage, and stood beside him. Usually only one take was all that was needed, different camera angles were not required.

As Hitchcock explained, "I did each of them three times, actually: in English, French and German. [The films were shown abroad.] Three complete films for each lead-in." Certain English-speaking countries did not take to Hitchcock's anti-commercial remarks so alternative deliveries were filmed, usually containing the same silly Hitchcock situations, but with no remarks against the sponsors whatsoever (and occasionally substituted with jokes about Americans and/or American-style customs). For an example of these alternative deliveries, check out some of the episode entries later in this book.

"Now, he was very proud of the show doing so well in Japan," recalled Norman Lloyd, "and he used to describe how the Japanese wrote [the translated dialogue] perpendicularly along the side of the film, he thought that was great! The show played in France and Germany but I don't recall him ever doing [his deliveries] in French and German. Way, way back, he started in Germany, in a way, so maybe he was able to do the German; then, during the War, he did a documentary in French. So it's possible he worked in those languages. But I was never aware of it."

Judging by copies of episodes that circulate among collectors, it appears that Hitchcock filmed the alternative English deliveries throughout all seven seasons of *Alfred Hitchcock Presents*, but when it came time to film the deliveries for *The Alfred Hitchcock Hour*, only one version was filmed. From episodes 80 to 102, Hitchcock definitely spoke the narratives in French, for most of the third season, but this practice was soon dropped and the remainder of the productions were dubbed with someone else's voice for broadcast in France.

"Mr. Hitchcock," an associate volunteered (he is "Mr. Hitchcock" to everybody on his staff; it was impossible to call him "Alfie" as it would to refer to Mrs. Roosevelt as "Ellie."), "is a deceptively passive man. I have never heard him raise his voice and I certainly never have seen him blow his top. He just sort of pontificates a little and then grins and things get done. Behind that cherubic little grin, you would take an oath there lies a miniature gallows. With your name on it!"

"He was a marvelous boss because he very much believed in delegating," Norman Lloyd recalled. "He had no ego in that, even though he was a man of considerable ego." Even among his humorous deliveries, Hitchcock had worked out a nearly foolproof formula for television. The success of his formula was attested to by the longevity of the show. But his appearances on the program plagued him almost from the start. He became a celebrity almost over night and when he walked down a public street, people stared. He was not just your average passerby on the street. He was "Alfred Hitchcock." Crowds would occasionally gather. Tourists begging for autographs became a ritual he only saw in the actors he gave direction – now they wanted his. Evan Hunter, whose own stories would be adapted for the series (and later screenwriter of *The Birds*), recalled Hitch's popularity off the set. It seemed that young children cleverly searched for the popular express which Hitchcock would ride along, and as Hunter described it: "When they found out that was Hitch in a limo going by, the kids would be holding signs saying 'Mr. Hitchcock, Please Stop,' and he would stop and sign autographs and move on."

Henry Bumstead, production designer for many of Hitchcock's films, recalled: "We were working with Hitch on his last picture, *Family Plot* (1976), when we were on a flight from San Francisco to Los Angeles. Well, we were there about an hour and finally in came the crew. They all knew who we were and there wasn't a word said. The plane pulled in, the pilot came out and the taxis got to the end of the runway, and we could hear over the speakers, the captain or pilot said, 'Good eveeenninnng . . . . this is your pilot speaking," and everybody just went crazy and it was pretty funny."

"One thing I can tell you about Hitchcock," recalled Hilton Green, assistant director. "If you were an assistant director on the same set he worked on, you had to wear a suit and tie. That was one of his requirements, mostly for image I think. He was very professional and wanted to keep everything so organized that any disturbance from the norm might otherwise cut the peace."

"Hitchcock was a delightful fellow," recalled actor Norman Leavitt. "I was in a few of those episodes, as a gas station attendant in one, and an accountant in another, oh I was in lots of them. Hitchcock directed one of the episodes I worked on, and you could tell that he knew his craft very well. In fact, he was having the episode edited as we filmed."

"When he directed a show, the crew loved him," said Gordon Hessler. "He was enormously prepared, and there was no director who could shoot a show in the speed he could do it. He knew exactly how to tell a story cinematically and only filmed what would be used. Hitch was a perfectionist and completely intolerant of anybody who was not professional. If you were an actor, it was terrifying how he could behave; but on the whole he was enormously generous."

For all the reputation of being a leisurely soul who disliked sponsors, and would rather spend "quality time" offering chilling tales of murder and internal theft, Hitchcock quite obviously took to television as good food took to his girth. While he personally read every story or script submitted for the show, he labored lovingly over the now-familiar lead-ins to his half-hour show, which each season boosted him personally into the ranks of popular television personalities. "Good evening," became a trademark and anyone saying those two words in a similar dead-pan delivery, would inject a vision of Hitchcock among any eavesdropper.

Despite the fact that Hitchcock became a world-renowned celebrity, his private life was often in turmoil. His celebrity status plagued him as a result, and the suspense master was paying the dues. Confessing to Francois Truffaut in August of 1962, Hitchcock recalled how he loved making small cameo appearances in most of his pictures, a personal joke he enjoyed playing on the audience. Having become a familiar figure as a result of *Alfred Hitchcock Presents*, everyone in the audience – not just a small percentage – began catching him in the act. "Later on it became a superstition and eventually a gag," Hitchcock confessed. "But by now it's a rather troublesome gag, and I'm very careful to show up in the first five minutes so as to let the people look at the rest of the movie with no further distraction." *

"I too am trapped," said Hitchcock. "I can't make any picture I want to. I've got to make a *suspense* picture. If I don't, the audience keeps waiting for the body to be found. Same with television. I've got to have the surprise, the twist ending. The advantage of my show is that the husband can murder his wife and bury her in the cellar. Retribution can be dealt with at the end by me."

* For trivia buffs, Hitchcock's ever-familiar profile was seen in the 1948 movie *Rope*, in the form of a red neon sign. And in fact, on four different occasions he was seen as late as 20 – 40 minutes into the film, even after 1955.

Hitchcock enjoyed filming *North by Northwest*, with satisfaction knowing that Harrison and Lloyd was in complete charge of the television show. As Hitchcock described it, *North by Northwest* was "a picturesque adventure film with Cary Grant - a sort of American *Thirty-Nine Steps*." Hitchcock originally wanted the climax chase across the brows of Washington, Lincoln, Jefferson and Teddy Roosevelt at Mt. Rushmore Memorial in South Dakota. "Unhappily," he explained, "they wouldn't allow you to move around the faces. A pity. I should have so liked the hero to be seized with a terrible sneezing fit while hiding in George Washington's left nostril. Oh, well. I've had to endure worse deprivations. But, of course, filming on location is difficult anyway - now that I'm an actor. Now that they know my face, they gather from miles around. It's hard to get any directing done [on location]. I heard one woman say excitedly, 'Look, Maude, there's Hitchcock of TV! Now what do you suppose he's doing on this movie set?' "

Hitchcock even felt pressured by competing programs – the normal routine of network scheduling. Throughout the sixth season of *Alfred Hitchcock Presents*, NBC featured an hour-long television series entitled *Thriller*, hosted by horror star Boris Karloff. *Alfred Hitchcock Presents* ran from 8:30 to 9 while *Thriller* ran from 9 to 10, both on the same network. And *Thriller* started out in the same fashion as the Hitchcock program. The first dozen or so broadcasts were adaptations of mystery novels, but when the producers realized

their ratings were slouching as a result, they made a change for the more requested horror material. After all, Boris Karloff was known for his roles in horror films, so the viewers expected horror. When chillers instead of sleepers began filling in the *Thriller* mold, the ratings went back up.

"We [television's *Thriller*] were on the same network and being made at the same studio, as *Alfred Hitchcock Presents*," recalled Doug Benton, producer of *Thriller*. "And although I never heard this directly, I did hear it from people who worked on both shows: Hitchcock resented *Thriller* and he thought that Hubbell Robinson had infringed on his franchise. He thought that if he were doing this type of

(Photo courtesy of Ronald V. Borst/ Hollywood Movie Posters)

material for MCA and NBC, then we shouldn't be. Actually, we weren't doing the same thing he was; he was doing some very sophisticated, 'twist' material. Hitchcock was doing the sort of thing that they started out to do on *Thriller*, but were not successful with. We came along and improved the ratings considerably and got a tremendous amount of press, and Hitchcock didn't like the competition. I don't think he ever came out and said, 'Get rid of 'em !', but he did allow them to enlarge his show from a half-hour to an hour, and that made it more difficult for us to stay on."

"[I] don't think that Hitchcock and Joan Harrison weren't watching *Thriller*," recalled Bill Frye, the main man behind the series' finest hours. Hitchcock, however, was irked by *Thriller's* consistent high quality, which was consistently drawing higher ratings than *Alfred Hitchcock Presents*, and issued an ultimatum: he wouldn't go another season unless *Thriller* was withdrawn for one year. This was tantrum to cancellation: the network hesitated, but as Frye ruefully recalled, "Hitchcock's clout at NBC was greater than Karloff's." The network decided to cancel *Thriller* at the end of its second season. Hitchcock's program, soon after, expanded to a full hour. But since neither program aired during the same time slot on competing networks, could there really have been much competition among two programs?

THE ALFRED HITCHCOCK HOUR

"This is the way of television," Hitchcock remarked. "Half-hour shows were becoming one-hour shows, so it was decided that ours was to become a one-hour show. I don't recall whose idea it was. I cannot say I know how the arrangements were made. In television the problem is to maintain a standard - especially after seven years. We were always pretty offbeat, but people get used to us being offbeat." So the Hitchcock program attempted to become more. In fact, he reported gleefully, downright macabre. Indeed, there had been a few episodes that might just curdle the blood of a werewolf.

This public suggestion of Hitchcock's that business matters were insoluble mysteries to him, was a charming farce. He was one of the shrewdest businessmen in Hollywood and he probably followed every step in the complicated negotiations that transferred his program from one network to another. Hitchcock dropped all pretense of confusion when he discussed the actual production of the show. A change of material for the one-hour program would have to come from novels or novellas instead of from short stories. "I prefer the short story. A good short story is better suited to cinema than the novel. With the half-hour show the short story did not have to be expanded very much for plot, and the characters were developed sufficiently." Hitchcock agreed that the short story had, on many occasions, been used admirably for full-length movies, which were longer than his one-hour television programs, but for television, thirty-two productions a year?

"I much preferred writing for the half-hour show," Henry Slesar recalled. "There was always the possibility of doing what I call 'gems.' The half-hours were compact and full of sharp point-breaking, bringing the audience in at the middle and then hitting them with the climax. Very clean. This got a little difficult to achieve in the hour shows, which were more like features except that they weren't, not really. They were actually more like extended half-hours. More was told about the same thing. I think the show suffered because of it, and I think the Hitchcock people felt so, too."

Said Norman Lloyd, "My own feeling is that while the hour show did seem a bit spread out at times, we were able to do shows with a little humanity to them; we were able to develop characters more. There were a lot of good hour episodes. Like 'The Jar' and another Bradbury story called 'The Life and Work of Juan Diaz,' a marvelous story about a guy who earned more money dead than when he was alive. So, for my money, both formats were good and just as effective, only in different ways."

Hitchcock's simple explanation for the hour-long expansion was the most reasonable. "Money," he said, "Money and time, which is also money. If we had the money and the time for a television show I would still prefer to use short stories on the one-hour program. But it takes time to build up a short story if you want to do it properly. If it is done hastily there is the risk of a bad script. It is simpler to get a novel or novella when you are in a hurry and to prune it down to a one-hour show."

The directors were turning out one-hour dramas at the rate of one a week. If you were to delete commercial time, Hitchcock's led-ins and lead-outs, and the opening and closing themes, the actual drama was forty-five minutes long (the former dramas were twenty-two and a half minutes). The directors also noted that filming of the hour-long features were also without any of the panic, that was so indigenous to the sound stages, on which other television series or anthologies were assembled.

Throughout the new season, if it could be believed, his staff had to sift through 2,400 crime novels to glean the required scripts. This fact was reported by more than three sources that same year, but whether they actually had the novels in hand or just a list of titles remains to be seen. A handful of producers each year chose a few stories, instead of one producer choosing all the stories. Short stories were still being used, but lengthened to fit the time frame. "One must remember that in the early half-hour days, we were getting the cream of the crop," explained Norman Lloyd, "some of the best stories of their type in English literature, such as 'The Glass Eye.' In the latter days of the hour show, however, we occasionally had to develop stories from scratch, and the results didn't always measure up. The half-hour show - which ran twenty-two and a fraction minutes - was sometimes a delight in its brevity and its point. But that doesn't mean it was a better format. In fact, I tried to repeat it some years later when I produced *Tales of the Unexpected* and the results varied greatly."

"In judging stories, I worked on the principle of a child sitting on the parent's knee saying, 'What's next?' I've got to make the audience wonder that," Hitchcock explained. "I'm noted for suspense. . . but suspense isn't necessarily 'Is he going to be saved from the gallows?' Suspense can be a love story, too. Will they get together? I always think there's a tremendous analogy with music. You start out with your allegro, go into your andante, then you build up - the shape of a symphony - and then you get your final movement, which is your biggest. I've always kept to that principle because by the time they've got to that last movement they've been sitting here a while, and your main problem has been to distract them from their discomforts."

"But I always regard the fact that we've got to outwit the audience to keep them with us," Hitchcock continued. "They're highly trained detectives looking at us out there right now. . . I remember I was talking to a judge when I was making a little movie called *The Wrong Man*, with Henry Fonda. It was based on a real case, and he was the judge who'd heard it. He was saying that juries these days are much a nuisance because they've looked at television. They're all experts. They expect to hear a detective tell them about fingerprints, as they've seen it on *Perry Mason*. So, on our show, they're looking for flaws. We have to fool them. They think we're going in one direction, and we must have the twist at the end. When we had a half-hour show we could do short stories. Now, in an hour, we have to go to novels, crime novels, that sort of thing, but we still have a twist because they're disappointed if they don't get it."

Gilbert Seldes, writing in *TV Guide* reviewing the new hour series, felt that Hitchcock had "ended one of the best series in television and brilliantly began another which is even better." There is general agreement that, despite an occasional flash of excellence, *The Alfred Hitchcock Hour* was, by and large, inferior to *Alfred Hitchcock Presents*.

A MUSICAL ENTRANCE FOR BERNARD HERRMANN

(Photo courtesy of Ronald V. Borst / Hollwyood Movie Posters)

Much of the music used on *Alfred Hitchcock Presents* was stock music, bits and pieces of orchestral scores used on previous episodes (and other television dramas). But music played an important factor for the setting and emotions acquired during a viewing. Take "Beta Delta Gamma" and "Bad Actor," two episodes that used bongo drums and a jazz-swing to illustrate the juvenile characters for those episodes. Trumpets played in "Memo From Purgatory." "Summer Shade" featured an eerie score to illustrate the horror that remained untold. European classical music was served in the background of "The Crystal Trench." While a heart-pounding music score made the automobile sequences in "Road Hog" even more thrilling. But among the musicians who scored for *Alfred Hitchcock Presents* and *The Alfred Hitchcock Hour*, Bernard Herrmann is the most recognized.

Herrmann would compose and conduct original scores for seventeen episodes of *The Alfred Hitchcock Hour*. He also arranged the opening and closing theme for the second and third season of *The Alfred Hitchcock Hour*. Lyn Murray, another talented musician, who scored Hitchcock's *To Catch a Thief* (1955), conducted the theme for the first season of *The Alfred Hitchcock Hour*. Herrmann was a master at work, and his music scores are probably the most popular in Hollywood. It was his ear-piercing violin score for *Psycho* that drowned out the screams of movie-goers. Excitement was enhanced by his original score for *North by Northwest*. He even worked on *Marnie* while at the same time, composing pieces for *The Alfred Hitchcock Hour*. Reapplying the use of the habanera from *Vertigo*'s nightmare sequence, "The Life Work of Juan Diaz" still remains an excellent form of storytelling. A circus organ is used in the sound track of "The Jar," bassoons in "Terror at Northfield," and harps in "Consider Her Ways." Sadly, Herrmann, a gifted musician who knew how to add emotion to film, came in too late, only serving during the series' final two seasons.

OPINION CHANGES: FILMING AN HOUR

"No one is writing good suspense stories these days," Norman Lloyd told a reporter in the August 26, 1962 issue of *The Newark Evening News*. "I don't know what has happened to the great story tellers – people like Kipling and Stevenson. We have to take stories and shape them to our needs. Meanwhile, we must go on. We can't wait for the great ones to show up, I must take the scripts as they land on my desk. I'm responsible for sixteen programs, and I have only seven properties on hand. [Lloyd and Harrison produced all but four episodes from the first season] I've managed to get several fine stories, I believe. One is a gambling tale, 'A Piece of the Action,' starring Gig Young and Martha Hyer. It has bitter irony in it. Another is 'The Final Vow,' in which Carol Lynley plays a nun involved in a search for a stolen statue. It has a delicious twist."

"It's fairy-story stuff," Hitchcock described. "When I embark I have to let my imagination go into the realms of fantasy. This is the whole point of storytelling. And story telling is the whole point of television. It's hardly the medium to sell the wide, open spaces. The screen is too small. So we have to sell story and actors. If we are lucky we get a performance, too, but only in broad terms. In films, we are doing something quite different. We are able to understate, to photograph a mental process, then at the right moment to move mountains just with a look. It is the opposite of method acting."

"Think of the power of film," he continued. "Whole stories can be changed just by the way you cut it. Suppose I shoot a close-up of a smiling man. Then I cut to a girl with pretty legs. This has one meaning. But suppose instead I cut to a woman beating a child. It has an entirely different meaning. In the old days whole stories were changed in this way. Of course, nowadays the movies are different. There are no more moguls. A dozen stars control the business. All the rest are in television - or less successful commercial pictures. It seems the inmates are running the asylum."

THE ALFRED HITCHCOCK HOUR: DIRECTOR STYLE

Outside his office on the Revue lot in Hollywood was a place for men to deal with mortgages and money rather than mayhem and mischief. At a small table with a leather top, Hitchcock sat like a board chairman patiently and imperturbably waiting for his fellow stockholders to file in. He was always black-suited, banker-visage and well fed. In person, when he spoke, it was as though there was another Hitchcock inside directing him. It was a careful creation of character, fully as contrived as anything he did on the screen. But the show bore his name; the image must be preserved and the public must not be disappointed. His television record had not been quite as spectacular as his Hollywood career, the limitations of the medium being what they were, except in terms of length of stay. The series, along with the televised runs and reruns of his old films, made him the producer of more properties than there were pounds on him, and he made story-telling an art form.

Take "I Saw The Whole Thing," the only episode of *The Alfred Hitchcock Hour* that he himself would direct. Hitchcock was ready to supervise the shooting of his show. He sat beside the camera, nodded slightly and about a dozen youngsters began dancing the twist. The music subsided, and while bodies writhed, a young man and his girl discussed an accident he had seen. Before the dance had ended, the apparent casual talk between the couple was leading into a story of crime. Hitchcock thought the boy and girl were becoming excited too quickly. He wanted a slower build-up.

The next scene was a police station. Hitchcock asked for a run-through. Quickly, a sergeant talked on a telephone. A man arrived and waited briefly before explaining he was the driver wanted in a hit-and-run case. A lieutenant was called out of an inner office and the driver and lieutenant vanished into the other room. Hitchcock showed no emotion. Quietly he told his cameramen exactly what he wanted. While arrangements were made for the lighting, he explained his approach. "There is no sense wasting film with a long shot of the police station. We have established the fact that this man is going to a police station. All we need is the three stripes on the policeman's uniform behind the desk. It would be different if a man wandered into a police station and we wanted to show his fear, curiosity or bewilderment. Then we could have the camera move around the station house to create atmosphere."

Near the end of the second season, the end of *The Alfred Hitchcock Hour* was clearly in sight. As the headmaster of an institution, this was a fact of which Hitchcock was fully aware. Hitchcock liked his position, for he felt it gave him an edge over newcomers. "Some people probably watch me out of habit," he said. "There's an aura on institutional appeal about me - like Perry Como."

During the middle of the second season, in January of 1963, CBS began broadcasting Rod Serling's *The Twilight Zone* in a newly-expanded hour-long format. Since *The Alfred Hitchcock Hour* was currently a Thursday-evening vehicle, and *The Twilight Zone* was scheduled for the same evening, CBS moved Hitchcock to Friday nights. If ever two series offered bizarre escapism on Thursday and Friday nights, CBS had it. But *The Twilight Zone* – unlike *The Alfred Hitchcock Hour* – was not as successful in the hour-long format and the ratings continued to drop. Viewers expressed a negative opinion and Rod Serling realized his mistake. Hitchcock, however, had that trace of a wink-edged one eye.

With the success of *Psycho* (1960) and *The Birds* (1963), Hitchcock was certainly ahead of his time, influencing other film makers and studios. But *Marnie* (1964), his latest film, was released in theaters and was not as large a success as his past few movies. With his health and age starting to take a toll, and purely evident that Hitchcock was no longer directing any television episodes, the end was in sight. He was now sixty-five years old and his age was showing in front of the cameras. For the tenth – and what would become the final – season, *The Alfred Hitchcock Hour* moved again from CBS to NBC, where it would quietly fade away. But not before going out with a bang.

The producers were choosing stories that varied from the normal mystery clichés, and occasionally pushed the borders. Ray Bradbury's "The Life and Work of Juan Diaz" was received with high acclaim. "Lonely Place" was an intense character study of a neglected wife who took matters into her own hands. "Death Scene" concerned a horror film star who owed his gruesome screen presence to dealings with satanic ritual. The familiar W.W. Jacobs story, "The Monkey's Paw," was modernized and revised twentieth-century style.

"Memo From Purgatory" was a compelling story of an investigative reporter's study of juvenile gang warfare. The main character in "Consider Her Ways" suffered from a severe case of "maxamatoria," which is a fantasy world of large pregnancies. "Where the Woodbine Twineth" concerned a small child who traded places with her doll. The most impressive, however, was "An Unlocked Window," concerning two nurses caring for an invalid in an isolated Victorian home, as a mentally disturbed killer is loose in the countryside. One of the nurses turned out to be a homicidal male in disguise (can we say *Psycho*?). Even with story content that might normally stir a few concerns among the network censors, Hitchcock wanted to bow out in style.

THE PROGRAM ENDS A TEN YEAR RUN

Upon the cancellation, *TV Guide* noted: "As of May 10, Alfred Hitchcock presents no more. After ten years on CBS and NBC, the series leaves the air without fanfare - NBC did not even announce its departure, [they] simply failed to announce a renewal. The ratings of *The Alfred Hitchcock Hour* have gradually slipped, although not catastrophically, and, according to an NBC source, 'We merely found Mr. Hitchcock a little too costly.' " Hitchcock fans would still have summer and syndicated reruns to console them, but the master would no longer toddle onto the screen in prime network time, fit himself gently into his own Indian-ink profile, and deliver his flannel-mouthed, lugubrious jokes.

"We must be philosophical about this," said Hitchcock about the demise. "As we all know, television is a great juggernaut and we're all nuts and bolts attached to it. Sometimes the nuts and bolts fall off." He would be financially afflicted by this decision, of course, but artistically speaking it did not move him profoundly. Just before the decision was made, he was complaining about the difficulty of doing good work on television. In fact, apart from keeping his eagle eye on the scripts, Hitchcock had little to do with the practical work on the show. Needless to say, the Hitchcock organization - an economic and artistic institution known all over the world - still continued to pursue profitable activities of movie making, mystery-magazine and mystery-book publishing for a huge international audience. And, if scaring millions of people out of their wits every year is success, the Alfred Hitchcock organization was one of the most successful in history.

53

"As a little boy," he said in his slow flanned-mouthed way, "I always loved ad-ven-tchah. One of my favorite pastimes was to find out where the end of the road was, where the bus went, what it looked like. Later I had a passion for timetables. If you took cook's Continental Timetable you could take an imaginary ride on the Orient Express. I had a large map of the world and I used to make flags for steamship lines. And I'd follow shipping all over the world with these flags stuck on pins. I saw life and the world as an exciting, romantic adventure. This is one root of my work."

"The real reason was that Hitch didn't want to do it anymore," Norman Lloyd explained. "He felt that ten years was enough, and he had a lot of other things to do." There is every reason to accept this self-analysis. The name Hitchcock had come to mean a special amalgam of these two elements, generated in a far-off omnipresent childhood - an amalgam of romance and of dread in changing proportions. It was the dominantly romantic Hitchcock who had won the reputation of being one of the finest cinematic artists in the world. His achievements are too many to list. Countless books, written years after his passing, are evident.

Gordon Hessler started looking towards his own future. When his first opportunity to direct a feature came during his third year on the show and, while Hitchcock afforded him both the material and the time to make it, the line was drawn when Hessler wanted to expand on the opportunity. "My agent said, 'Is there a story or novel that's been rejected by Hitchcock that you like? I think I can get you a picture.' So I pulled out a novella called *Catacombs*. He then gave it to Robert Lippert, who was making all the B pictures for Twentieth-Century Fox. We had a script written [by Daniel Mainwaring], Bob liked it, and I got a three-week leave of absence from Hitchcock to go to England in November 1963 to make this film [U.S. release: *The Woman Who Wouldn't Die* (1964)]. When we finished, Lippert offered me a contract for three more pictures, but Hitchcock and MCA wouldn't let me out of my contract. I said, 'Well, you've got to let me direct [for *The Alfred Hitchcock Hour*]!' to which they consented." That promise was left unfulfilled when *The Alfred Hitchcock Hour* ended its run in 1965 but, with two more years on his contract, Hessler did get a chance to cut his directing teeth on other shows in the MCA camp until 1967, when he left Hollywood for England to direct his own pictures. *

Contrary to what has been printed, the death of James Allardice was not a contributing factor to the cancellation of *The Alfred Hitchcock Hour*. Allardice died on February 15, 1966, nine months after the last original episode had been aired, and about a year since the final episode went before the cameras.

The dominant trademarks of great Hitchcock movies are profoundly revealing of the man himself - as the short mystery plays, which appeared on his television show, almost never have been. When the Encyclopedia Britannica asked Hitchcock to write an authoritative article on film production, Hitchcock included an analysis of his own approach to horror. "The more original directors will want to present melodrama in a revolutionary way, to take melodrama out of the dark night, into the bright day, to show murder by a babbling brook, adding a touch of blood to its limpid waters . . . so emerges a kind of counterpoint and sudden upheaval in the ordinary things in life."

Alfred Hitchcock was retiring from television. He would not film any more episodes for his television program. But he had to content himself with lesser horrors. *The New Yorker* magazine once described some aspect of his work as "unconscious" and that irritated Hitchcock: "The stupid idiots! As if I don't know what I'm doing. My technique is serious.

* The Hessler-directed movie was based on a novel by Jay Bennett, whose short stories were previously filmed on the Hitchcock program. Reprinted courtesy of *Filmfax* editor Jim Wilson, and Christopher Koetting, from issue #62, August/September 1997.

I play that audience like an organ. I am consciously aware of what I am doing in all my work." Hitchcock was a perfectionist. "Hitch insisted upon perfection. He had no patience with mediocrity," says Bob Burks, his long-time director of movie photography.

"He demanded that the work be done at the highest possible level of execution." said Norman Lloyd. "Hitch had his own center. It was not egotism. It was not false pride. He had identity. He had a powerful presence. You feel it. And you can take it or leave it." He was surrounded by cooperative workers and professional adulation. He had a devoted wife and only a few close friends. ("I have a couple of real friends," he said, "a couple of businessmen.") He had little to do with show-business people. A profile writer once described Hitchcock's way of waiting, aloof, for a crew to prepare a new camera set-up: "He is likely to be sitting alone, with the look of a fat boy who has run away from cruelty of his contemporaries."

Hitchcock told one reporter that he gave up a Bentley that he owned because it was a status symbol. He told another, "I am proud to own a Klee, a Vlaminck and a Dufy - but I keep them in my country home for my own enjoyment, rather than putting them on display in our Los Angeles house for status purposes." He owned a comparatively simple house in Bel-Air and had turned the kitchen into the most important room in the house, where he and his wife spent much of their time, in the manner of an upper-class butler and cook.

THE MAD CONNECTION TO *ALFRED HITCHCOCK PRESENTS*
Written by Ken Kaffke.

The numerous stories that appeared within gruesome anthology comics of the 1950s, often shadowed the same tales dramatized on *Alfred Hitchcock Presents*. To start, "Revenge" inspired a fairly taut adaptation, albeit without a writer credit - by E.C. [Entertaining Comics] in the premiere issue of *Crime SuspenStories* (Nov. 1950). Five years later, the same "Revenge" story would become the pilot episode of *Alfred Hitchcock Presents*, directed by Hitchcock himself. For the inaugural issue of E.C.'s groundbreaking James M. Cain-ish anthology crime comic, the Samuel Blas story was retitled as "Murder May Boomerang." The lead characters were changed from a husband and frazzled wife to a man and his disoriented father (art and script by J. Craig). In this early example of the emerging "new trend" pioneered by the small but talented E.C. comics group, rape was still somewhat taboo – even for the daring team of draftsmen at E.C. – for at least another year.

A year later, for the 10th issue of *The Haunt of Fear* (November-December 1951), Gaines and Feldstein were inspired to begin the issue with "Grave Business!" a retelling of the Louis Pollock story "Breakdown." Hitchcock personally handled the directorial chores for "Breakdown," which aired as the seventh episode of *Alfred Hitchcock Presents*. *The Haunt of Fear* was another of E.C.'s anthology comics, with every issue offerring four terror/horror tales designed to surprise readers with twist endings. *Crime SuspenStories* #18 (August - September, 1953) presented "From Here To Insanity" which was later filmed as an episode of *Alfred Hitchcock Presents*. *Crime SuspenStories* #19 (October-November, 1953) reprinted "Murder May Boomerang," deeming it an "E.C. Classic."

The most notorious comic book cover ever printed is without a doubt the hanged man – the "cover of a children's comic book" as it was described by Dr. Fredric Wertham in his influential book, Seduction of the Innocent, a graphic singled out on national television in 1954, as well as in *SOTI* (the aforementioned book) and elsewhere. Most writers until now assumed the gruesome image (well-rendered by Johnny Craig for *Crime SuspenStories* #20, in late 1953) had no connection to the four illustrated stories inside, which it didn't. Few fans or even comic historians of the period bother to read the (required at the time) two column text piece.

Such text fare was a standard if generally weaker E.C. feature in every one of their ten-cent comic books, even the early MAD Magazine. In this infamous issue of *Crime SuspenStories*, the text titled "Rope!" is a retelling of the Ambrose Bierce short story "An Occurrence at Owl Creek Bridge." *Twilight Zone* presented an award-winning version filmed in France, created without utiliziling Cayuga Production at CBS other than adding on the opening sequence filmed by William Froug, along with Rod Serling's intro and final-voice over. The almost dialogue-free version aired on *Twilight Zone* (Febuary 2, 1964) and is generally considered superior to the talking heads version, run on *Alfred Hitchcock Presents*.

E.C. took as springboards, a number of basic plots suggesting common or perhaps public-domain short story antecedents, which should be familiar to scholars of *Alfred Hitchcock Presents*. Stories inspired by Cornell Woolrich, Ambrose Bierce, Ray Bradbury and John Collier (*Crime SuspenStories* #22 ran "In Each And Every Package," probably inspired by "Back for Christmas").

Two versions of the W.W. Jacobs story "The Monkey's Paw" were truly over the top, one entitled "The Gorilla's Paw" (*Haunt of Fear* #9), which featured the simple shock ending of a final wish to have some guy's brains, and the gorilla's paw slowly creeping up the back of the fool's neck, to replace his own brain with another . . . somewhat crudely, but with a complimentary scalp message! "Wish You Were Here" (*Haunt of Fear* #22) retells the monkey tale with modern inconveniences, such as a reanimation that neglected to pass on the embalming. The remedy simply had the poor blighter going all to pieces, each sliver writhing on the floor, still alive but not at all feeling relaxed.

Roald Dahl, who achieved greater recognition, perhaps, through his credited works adapted on the television series, also had similar tales sketched for the comics. Yet E.C. was as noble a precursor to the short and sweet shock-ending format that would be perfected on *Alfred Hitchcock Presents*, as there ever was. E.C. publisher William M. Gaines and editor Albert Feldstein often "borrowed" ideas for stories in the early months of the small but creatively ambitious company. They were caught red-handed by Ray Bradbury for lifting one of his published stories, but Ray good-naturedly asked for credit and a small payment. E.C. immediately worked out an arrangement with Bradbury whereby all subsequent adaptations credited Ray's name on the covers inside a large banner, and payment was sent promptly!

E.C. came to be one of America's most beloved comic book publishers ever, and recently celebrated its 50th anniversary with a reunion of surviving staffers at the San Diego ComicCon 2000. Of course, E.C. only managed to keep one of their original publications going without interruption through the 20th century . . . MAD is still published today. MAD frequently ribbed the *Alfred Hitchcock Presents* television show in their heyday, often featuring exquisite draftsmanship by the late great Wallace Wood. A particular favorite of the staff at MAD was to come up with unique ways to slip the Hitchcock silhouette into story panels. Issue #50 (October 1959) features Hitchcock's fleshed out profile in "The Big House Beacon," a parody purporting to be highlights of a prison yearbook for 1959. Hitchcock is given the absurd moniker "Alvin Flut."

Issue #53 (March 1960) offerred up a Wood tour de force, "An Alfred Hatchplot Movie." Almost every panel lampooned Hitchcock's cameo appearances in his movies. Also pushed over the top were Hitchcock's wacky TV show openings/closings. We see Hitchcock on TV screens switched on in the background of panels where the main action is identifiable as something from one of his 1950s hit movies. The familiar caricature profile is in two panels, and the frequency and intensity of Hitchcock's cameos increases to a frenzied pitch. By the last panel, Hitchcock's glib features are on the faces of an African mask, a portrait photo, and an entire family including the dog! The panel raised the curiosity of at least one reader whose letter, printed two issues later, (MAD #55, June 1960) split hairs about the wife not actually being properly married to Hatchplot. The last notable MAD magazine spoof of *Alfred Hitchcock Presents* ran in March of 1961 (Issue #61) as part of the "Extra Added Destruction Dept." The writers satirized ubiquitous guest shots, and Hitchcock's show is showcased in five panels figuring "it won't be long before the guest shot system spreads to the weekly TV series . . ." Hitchcock first appears simultaneously in silhouette and shadow profile, the next panel has him with the mummified Mrs. Bates sitting in her chair. Hitchcock is seen delivering his foreword: "Good evening. I'm proud of the reputation our show has earned for bringing spine-tingling horrors into living rooms all across America. Tonight, however, I plan to outdo myself. Those of you with weak stomachs may switch the channel. I am about to present the worst horror ever seen on television. Mainly, I am about to turn the show over to my guest host - who has her own show - Shirley Temple and Her Storybook."

In the documentary film Comic Book Confidential, MAD/E.C. editor Albert Feldstein is interviewed on camera and discusses the E.C. style of stories with "shock or surprise endings that were much like *Alfred Hitchcock Presents* and *Twilight Zone*." Indeed they were. I have to wonder if ol' Hitch himself read the occasional crime comic book.

In the 1950 edition of the motion picture Production Encyclopedia, there is a great early version of the famous Hitchcock profile. This version is in reverse, and Hitchcock has a bit more hair!

Switching from comic books to television, *The Flintstones*, often described as an animated version of television's *Honeymooners*, was a parody on modern suburban life, set in the prehistoric stoneage. Co-produced by William Hanna and Joseph Barbera, this cartoon series premiered on September of 1960. A wide range of caricatures passed through the episodes: attorney Perry Masonry (who never lost a case); and Ed Sullystone, a television host. On October 6, 1961, (ABC, Friday 8:30 to 9 pm, EST), the episode "Alvin Brickrock Presents" was broadcast. The plot (taken from the episode "Mr. Blanchard's Secret"): When the wife of one of Fred's neighbors suddenly disappears, Fred suspects the husband of foul play. After reading a detective magazine, he decides that mild-mannered Alvin Brickrock (who looks and sounds like Alfred Hitchcock *) may actually be Albert Bonehart, wanted as a three-time wife-killer. While the magazine says Bonehart is 5' 10" (Brickrock is about 4' 10"), both men have difficulty pronouncing "good evening." This is cause enough for Fred and Barney to sneak into the man's house and investigate. When Fred discovers a heavy monogrammed trunk, which Brickrock claims is for his wife's body, they think they've cracked the case, but it turns out to contain weights and barbells. Brickrock was innocent all along, and his wife is alive and well.

In December of 1961, *Alfred Hitchcock Presents* was parodied twice by Warner Bros. Studios. The first of the two, released in the theaters as a Merrie Melodie cartoon on December 2, was entitled "The Last Hungry Cat." Written by John Dunn and Dave Detiege, and featuring the voice talents of Mel Blanc, this animated short opened with a shadowy figure of a large bear, filling an all-too familiar profile via shadow, introducing "tonight's story about a murder." Tweety Bird is attacked by that "bad old putty tat," and fearing the wrath of Granny, Sylvester escapes the scene of the crime. The narrator, speaking in a British voice much like Hitchcock's, speaks to Sylvester. "Sardines and milk weren't enough, *you* had to commit murder!" Sylvester. mistaking a newspaper headline for the police hunting him, runs to the nearest radio and hears "Your local company will now present gas chamber music, I mean, your local gas company will present chamber music." Sylvester wears a groove into the floor, drinks down a pot of coffee, and smokes a pack of cigarettes. He can't sleep and downs a dozen sleeping pills, sobbing "other cats have eaten birds!" The narrator

* Elliott Field supplied the voice of Alvin.

suggests that Sylvester give himself up. So Sylvester runs back to Granny and finds Tweety alive, much to his surprise. Filled with joy, Sylvester kisses Tweety, and Granny hits him with her broom. Sylvester gets even with the "Hitchcock" figure by beaning him with a brick, showing the shadowy figure growing a bump on his noggen.

Three days later, on December 5, 1961, ABC broadcasted an episode of *The Bugs Bunny Show* entitled "Prison to Prison." This time Bugs was Alfred Hitchcock, who spoke about crime, surrounding three cartoons, "Deduce You Say," "The Hole Idea" and "Bugsy and Mugsy." "Deduce You Say" concerned Daffy as Dorlock Holmes and Porky as "Watkins" on the trail of the "Shorepshire Slasher." "The Hole Idea" concerned a fictional Professor Calvin Q. Calculus, scientist, who invents the portable hole. His invention falls into the wrong hands, and a crook runs amok stealing everything he wants, and escaping with ease, using the help of the portable holes. (Of course, who hasn't seen that one?) "Bugsy and Mugsy" concerned Bugs Bunny's old planting-devices-for-self-influenced-ideas plot, makes two killers turn on each other thinking each wants to kill the other, being arrested by the police in the end.

In honor of Halloween, on October 26, 1980, CBS television presented "The Bugs Bunny Mystery Special," a movie featuring Porky Pig as Alfred Hitchcock, narrating tales of mystery and terror. The complete cartoon of "Big House Bunny" was featured, with clips of seven others including "Bugs and Thugs," "Hare Lift," "Operation Rabbit," and "Catty Cornered." "Big House Bunny" was the cartoon that featured Bugs in prison, and Yosemite Sam trying to prevent Bugs from escaping, and always being scolded by the warden by name, "Shultz!" An episode of *Alvin and the Chipmunks* featured an animated image of Hitchcock, in the background of one of their episodes, during a musical sequence of Cowboy Joe. Steven Spielberg's *Animaniacs* also featured an animated version of Hitchcock, attempting to film a sequence of *The Birds*, using some pretty stupid New York pigeons as part of the cast. The pigeons act more like the Martin Scorsese's *Goodfellas*, who call themselves the "Good Feathers." Shortly before the appearance of Hitchcock, the shadows of the three animaniacs appear on the screen, (all three at the same time), filling in silhouettes.

Two movie trailers were put together for Hitchcock's last motion picture, *Family Plot* (1976). One trailer was short, lasting a minute and ten seconds, and the second ran a little over two minutes. Unlike the second trailer, the short one opened with music, the "Funeral March of A Marionette." accompanying Hitchcock's jovial, macabre remarks, such as "My word, what a grave insult. Please don't take it to heart."

In 1995, Quentin Tarentino starred and directed the fourth and final segment in *Four Rooms*, a cleverly plotted series of comical situations. The movie detailed a New Year's evening at a broken-down hotel, and a agonies sufered by the bellhop, played by Tim Roth. In the first segment, entitled "The Missing Ingredient," the bellhop had to serve a coven of witches (one of them played by pop singer/actress Madonna). In the second, "The Wrong Man," Roth found himself caught up in a perverted game of trust and dis-trust when a jealous husband (drinking booze and chewing pills like candy), ties his wife up and loads a gun, mistaking Roth as her lover. In the third segment, entitled "The Misbehavers," Antonio Banderas pays Roth to baby-sit his children while he and his wife enjoy a night out on the town – only to discover that the children are demonic demons from hell. The final segment, entitled "The Man From Hollywood," was a spoof of the *Alfred Hitchcock Presents* episode "Man From the South." A small group of Hollywood celebrities apparently watched the actual episode on television and loaded with alcohol, have decided on re-enacting the game . . . with the assistance of the bellhop. What resulted was the exact opposite conclusion of the original story, a build-up of about thirty minutes, and a climax with one unexpected laugh. For fans who love the "Man From the South" episode, this is required viewing.

In 1997, the *Alfred Hitchcock Presents* theme was featured during the opening sequence of Robert Zemeckis's *Contact*, starring Jodie Foster. This, however, was not the first time Zemeckis restaged the *Hitchcock* program. Beginning in 1991, Zemeckis, an executive producer for the made-for-cable television series *Tales From the Crypt*, began directing hand-picked episodes of the ghoulish anthology featuring a wide range of stories taken directly from the actual E.C. Comics, broadcast over HBO. Zemeckis occassionally directed an episode (much like Hitchcock, doubling both as movie director and television producer) entitled "You, Murderer." Broadcast on January 25, 1995, this episode, sort of a parody of *Dark Passage* – the 1947 Bogart film shown from the first person point of view – featured a few vintage actors, including Bogart, by use of computer imagery, digitally composed in. Zemeckis also employed this same method in *Forest Gump* (1994), (including reproducing a feather-in-the-wind scene). In the same manner, the Crypt Keeper's introduction featured Alfred Hitchcock as an additional guest host. It is so good to see that E.C. Comics and the Hitchcock program get together for a joint venture, after all these decades.

(Photo courtesy of Photofest.)

ALFRED HITCHCOCK'S SUSPICION

At the end of the second season (1956/57) of *Alfred Hitchcock Presents*, Shamley Productions contracted to supply ten, hour-long filmed shows for a new NBC series to be called "Crisis" (eventually renamed *Suspicion*). It was at this time that Norman Lloyd, a former Mercury Theater player, recently became active as a television director, and joined the organization to help handle the added workload. Joan Harrison, who had been credited on-screen as "Associate Producer" for the first two seasons of *Alfred Hitchcock Presents*, received the same credit on *Suspicion*; that title was assumed by Lloyd on the half-hour shows, with Harrison being promoted to "Producer."* Although *Suspicion* lasted only one season on NBC, the expanded Shamley production team continued thereafter, with Harrison and Lloyd sharing the various responsibilities. (With the 1958/59 season, Lloyd also became one of the series' regular directors – and apparently chose his assignments almost as carefully as Hitchcock had.)

Suspicion was a "hybrid" sort of series – half live, half filmed – which appeared on NBC during the 1957-58 season. A total of 40 shows were presented, with the 20 live dramas originating from New York and the 20 filmed programs produced in Hollywood. Of the 20 filmed, 10 were produced by Revue Productions (which would later produce the Hitchcock rival *Thriller*), and the other 10 by Hitchcock's Shamley Productions. Scheduled on Monday night beginning 10 p.m., EST, opposite CBS's *Studio One*, *Suspicion* lasted only one season. Although it has generally been dismissed by television reference works, in the context of Alfred Hitchcock's television production activities, it is interesting for several comparisons.

The best way to get a handle on the "Hitchcockian" aspects of *Suspicion* is to compare the programs made under his supervision with those produced by Revue Productions. Shamley's productions exhibit a definite classical literary bent, while the Revue offerings are dominated by original teleplays (and not very good ones, if the trade reviews can be trusted). The series can also be seen as a sort of precursor to *The Alfred Hitchcock Hour*, since the Shamley team was for the first time dealing with the production of hour-long shows. In this regard, it seems almost too obvious to state that Hitchcock's personal influence was being felt far more strongly in 1957 than in 1962, and that the quality of the shows reflected this. (Most accounts agree that Hitchcock got rather bored with the television work in later years, and that by the time *The Alfred Hitchcock Hour* began he was exercising only the most nominal supervision.) Yet another point to consider; the increased production responsibilities entailed by *Suspicion* led to the addition of Norman Lloyd to the Shamley staff. In the years to come, Lloyd's work as producer, director and occasional actor would provide some of the finest moments on both *Alfred Hitchcock Presents* and *The Alfred Hitchcock Hour*.

It's apparent, however, that if anything, the literary sources for the Shamley-produced *Suspicion* episodes were even more carefully selected than for *Alfred Hitchcock Presents*, and Hitchcock's preferences are clearly evident. Several classic stories (including works by William Hope Hodgson, W. Somerset Maugham and Oscar Wilde) were adapted, and two of Hitchcock's favorite contemporary writers, Roald Dahl ("The Way Up to Heaven") and Cornell Woolrich ("Four O'Clock") are represented as well. Eric Ambler, who would later marry Joan Harrison, contributed an original teleplay, and many of the writing assignments went to those who had already proven their talents on the half-hour series, notably Francis

---

* It should be noted that "producer" credits have always been unregulated – unlike the strongly guild-controlled writer/director designations. Technically, Hitchcock's proper credit would have been "Executive Producer" – if one generally understands that to be equivalent to the head of the producing entity (in this case Shamley Productions). On screen, however, the credit has always been "An Alfred Hitchcock Production," and remained so even during the last season of *The Alfred Hitchcock Hour*, and was so credited on-screen.

Cockrell and Stirling Silliphant. All the directors chosen for Shamley's *Suspicion* episodes (with the exception of veteran director of TV/movies Lewis Milestone) had previously directed a few episodes of *Alfred Hitchcock Presents* – with Robert Stevens, the workhorse of the early seasons, called upon for four of the ten shows.

Hitchcock's only sole directorial contribution to *Suspicion* was the premiere episode of the series, "Four O'Clock." It has been written about in some detail, with the rest of the productions for the series simply ignored. To note, the later NBC remake series in 1985 included a remake version of the Hitchcock-directed "Four O'Clock." A critical opinion is that if Hitchcock hadn't directed this *Suspicion* entry, "Four O'Clock"

(Photo courtesy Ronald V. Borst / Hollywood Movie Posters)

probably would never have been filmed for the remake series. The opening episode started with a shot of a watchmaker shop, and one scene from the episode to come, then the title sequence with the painted faces appeared after which the featured host Dennis O'Keefe, winding a clock (as Hitchcock did in *Rear Window*), made his statement:

For most of his history, man has told time by such simple devices as hourglasses, sundials and clubsiderates. In case you don't know what a clubsiderate is, it's a water-clock. The first mechanical clock is attributed to Pope Sylvester II in A.D. 996. In Europe, clockmakers were an exclusive set drawn from the ranks of jewellers, locksmiths, astronomers and priests. They kept their standards high and their prices higher. In America however, the first clockmakers were carpenters and mechanics. They soon learned how to achieve mass production of good, cheap time pieces. Like the every-day common garden variety dollar and a half alarm clock. Without this combined history of European science and American gumption, the central character in our story tonight might never have found the perfect weapon, for after all, there are difficulties in killing one's wife with a clubsiderate.

61

Variety commented shortly after the program's premiere: "There's one omnibus aspect to the NBC strategy in slotting *Suspicion* Mondays at 10. From a strictly competitive standpoint, NBC's desire to knock *Studio One* out of the box is understandable. But in an era when hour live shows are virtually extinct (and *Studio One* boasts a long and honorable career in this area of entertainment) the end result could be lamentable should *Suspicion* change course and upgrade itself. How *Suspicion* fares may well influence Westinghouse's soon-due decision on whether to ride along with its long-trademarked CBS entry. Thus far it has nothing to fear."

As for the premiere episode, "Four O'Clock," *Variety* was not favorable to the drama itself. "Alfred Hitchcock and NBC will have to be slightly more inventive than this if they want to translate the *Suspicion* series into more meaningful programming . . . not only was there nothing particularly unique or different about this premiere presentation, but in trying to create the desired momentum and mounting tensions, the Hitchcockisms were all of the cliché variety. The viewer really couldn't get worked up because [of the same] time-tested, tried and true tricks . . . perhaps but a desire to see the whole thing ended and done with."

Without Hitchcock as host, however, *Suspicion* suffered. Without Hitchcock as host, *Alfred Hitchcock Presents* probably wouldn't have lasted a full seven seasons, or even expanded to *The Alfred Hitchcock Hour* before the ratings took a toll. With *Suspicion* lacking the type of host *Alfred Hitchcock Presents* had, this anthology was probably already doomed for failure. Thankfully, a few good productions came as a result, and the show even won a coveted Television Chamion Award for "Best Mystery Program of 1957," beating out *Alfred Hitchcock Presents*, which was also nominated in the same category.

For the sake of "purity," we have included only those episodes contributed to the series by Shamley Productions. For the sake of seeing the Shamley output in context, they are provided as a brief rundown in the actual broadcast log. Various sources indicate that there were 21 filmed episodes produced for *Suspicion* – 11 by Revue rather than 10. The NBC program department logs do not bear this out, nor does anything else uncovered to date.

PRODUCTION CREDITS FOR SUSPICION:

Art Directors: Frank Arrigo, John J. Lloyd, Arthur Lonergan and Martin Obzina.
Assistant Directors: James H. Brown, John Graham, Hilton A. Green,
George Lollier, James Nicholson and Abner E. Singer.
Associate Producer: Joan Harrison (Norman Lloyd was the Assistant to the Producer)
Costume Supervisor: Vincent Dee
Directors of Photography: Ellsworth Fredricks, Reggie Lanning, Lionel Lindon,
Don Malkames, John L. Russell, a.s.c. and John F. Warren.
Editorial Supervisor: Richard G. Wray
Film Editors: Marston Fay, Daniel A. Nathan and Edward W. Williams.
Hair Stylist: Florence Bush
Location Supervisor: Chet Allen
Makeup Artists: Jack Barron and Leo Lotito, Jr.
Production Consultant: Robert Altman
Production Designer: Robert Boyle
Set Decorators: Fred Ballmeyer, George Milo, Mac Mulcahy and James S. Redd
Sound supplied by Stephen J. Bass, Al Manchee, B.F. Ryan and Jack Solomon.
Broadcast on Monday evenings from 10 to 11 p.m., EST, over NBC-TV.
Sponsors included Ford and Philip Morris, Procter & Gamble, and Van Heusen.
Filmed by Shamley Productions, Inc.. in association with the NBC Television Network.
Filmed at Revue Studios in Hollywood, California, in association with MCA-TV,
executive distributor for Shamley Productions, Inc.
Host for the series was Dennis O'Keefe, until May of 1958, when Walter Abel took over.

(1) EPISODE #1 **"FOUR O'CLOCK"** Broadcast September 30, 1957
Filmed at Revue Studios, July 29 - August 2, 1957
Cast: Nancy Kelly as Fran Steppe   E.G. Marshall as Paul Steppe
Richard Long as Dave, Fran's brother   Tom Pittman as Joe
Dean Stanton as Bill   Charles Seel as male customer
Jesslyn Fax as the customer's wife   Vernon Rich as the doctor
David Armstrong as the policeman   Juney Ellis as the neighbor
Brian Corcoran as Bobby, the neighbor's boy   Chuck Webster as the gasman
Teleplay written for *Suspicion* by Francis Cockrell, from the story "Three O'Clock"
by Cornell Woolrich, published in *Detective Fiction Weekly*, October 1, 1938.
Produced and directed by Alfred Hitchcock.
Music composed and conducted by Dave Cahn, Melvin Leonard and Bob Russell.
Story: Paul Steppe, a watch repairman, suspects his wife of cheating on him, while
he tends to the store every afternoon. Consumed with jealousy, he devises a time bomb, set
to go off at four o'clock – the same time her "lover" pays his daily visit. One day, when his
wife is at the market, he sneaks into the house to plant the device. There, Paul is surprised by
two burglars, who tie him up and gag him – leaving him at the mercy of his own device,
ticking away. With an hour to go, his wife comes home and Paul overhears the two talking.
Apparently her "lover" is none other than her brother Dave, who was recently released from
prison. Deciding to reveal her secret to Paul, the two leave for the clock maker's store,
leaving Paul alone with the clock, ticking away. As the last minutes pass, Paul
unsuccessfully attempts to free himself before the deadline. The meter reader comes by, but
he doesn't even notice him. A small neighbor boy does see Paul through the window, but
won't get help. When Fran and Dave return, they watch calmly as Paul is escorted out of the
house in a straight-jacket . . . having gone mad from the afternoon's experience. It seems the
bomb never went off because of a blown fuse earlier in the day.

Trivia, etc. The October 2, 1957 issue of *Daily Variety* reviewed this episode as:
"An ingenious half-hour telepic . . . The usual smooth directorial techniques associated with
Hitchcock were evident in the attempt to stretch 30 minutes of material over a 60-minute
course. The middle part particularly sagged, despite attempts to tighten tension by means of
recurring false hopes of victim E.G. Marshall. Trouble here was that it was all too evident,
from the start, that these would be false hopes. Additionally, Hitchcock might come in for
criticism in some quarters for the explicit exposition of the technique of making a time
bomb."

(2) October 7, 1957 "Murder Me Gently" (live telecast) Directed by Don Medford.
(3) October 14, 1957 "The Other Side of the Curtain" (Revue) Directed by James Neilson.
(4) October 21, 1957 "Hand In Glove" (live telecast) Directed by Jack Smight.
(5) October 28, 1957 "The Story of Marjorie Reardon" (Revue) Directed by John Brahm.*
(6) November 4, 1957 "Diary for Death" (live telecast) Directed by Perry Lafferty.

(7) EPISODE #2 **"HEARTBEAT"** Broadcast November 11, 1957
Cast: David Wayne as James A. Mennick   Pat Hingle as Dr. Robert 'Bob' Kalman
Barbara Turner as Emily   Warren Beatty as the young man
Frank Campanella as Sergeant Kinsley   Sidney Armus as a Frankfurter man
Barbara Barrie as Miss Gruber, the secretary   Raymond Bramley as Dr. Herb Harrison
Robert Dryden as the police sergeant   Gene Sultan as the boy at fire hydrant
Mary Boyd Thurston as the patient   Ward Costello as Dr. Gordon
Nell Harrison as the nurse
Also in the cast: Joseph Helgesen (billed 10th) , Eric Fleming (11th), Kenneth Konopka
(12th), John McQuade (13th) and Joseph Sullivan (14th).

* a.k.a. "The Marjorie Reardon Story"   63

Teleplay written for *Suspicion* by Ernest Kinoy, from a story by Terence John. Directed by Robert Stevens.

Story: Assured that he has a clean board of health, James Mennick leaves the medical office feeling like a new man. Intending to indulge in the pleasures he has been denied all his life, James pays a visit to the local tavern, saves a young girl named Emily from the brutality of a young man, and even purchases tickets for the rides at Coney Island. What James doesn't suspect is the mistake of a nurse, who accidentally switched the folders and the EKG with that of a healthy man. Returning to the tavern for a nightcap, James gets a good-bye kiss from Emily, and promptly keels over dead from a heart attack. The doctor arrives on the scene, only a moment too late. "Don't feel too bad about it Doc," remarks the police officer. "You did everything you could, didn't you? How long did you say he had to live anyway, six months? You know, he maybe had himself a ball this afternoon. Had himself a good time at least once before he kicked off."

Trivia, etc. David Wayne's performance in this episode earned *Suspicion* the only Emmy nomination for "Best Performance by an Actor in a Lead or Supporting Role." He lost to Peter Ustinov for an episode of ABC's *Omnibus*, entitled "The Life of Samuel Johnson." During the closing credits of this episode, Warren Beatty's name is mis-spelled as "Beaty."

Daily Variety reviewed the episode on November 13, 1957: "Medics may not approve of some of the shoddy practices that fouled up the records of two patients, but for sure they stayed with it along with the other millions who find this series their Monday night excitement. The early plotting of the narrative was as clumsy as the receptionist who snafu'd the file on two patients, physical opposites, but it soon straightened out and the story spread out evenly . . . [The ending] was a sudden and surprise finish, right out of the Hitchcock hamper, and as good a way as any winding things up . . . Wayne gave a sensitive performance as the lonely, stricken man who finally found romance and the good life, but too late . . . Direction of Robert Stevens was firm and moving."

(8) November 18, 1957 "The Sparkle of Diamonds" (live) Directed by Jack Smight.
(9) November 25, 1957 "The Flight" (Revue) Directed by James Neilson.

(10) EPISODE #3 **"RAINY DAY"** Broadcast on December 2, 1957

Cast: Robert Flemyng as Nigel Crosley   George Cole as George Willis
John Williams as Colonel Selby   Tom Conway as Featherstone
A.E. Gould-Porter as Marty   Martin Wilkins as Samba
Walter Kingsford as Doc   George Pelling as the mailman
Alex Davion as the second mailman   Ted Stanhope as Bartley
Dick Winslow as the piano player   Barry Harvey as the third man
Laurence Conroy as Larry

Teleplay written for *Suspicion* by Michael Pertwee, based on the 1921 short story "Rain" by W. Somerset Maugham. Directed by James Neilson.

Story: Nigel Crosley and George Willis, employees for a British import company in Bathurst, British West Africa, spend their Christmas holiday reading the mail. Nigel, who fancies himself as "a devil with the girls," receives letter after letter from people back home, but lonely George doesn't receive a single one. Determined to have something of possession, George offers to buy a letter from the bragging Nigel, for five pounds. But when George reads the envelope's contents, Nigel insists on knowing who it's from and what it contains. Especially since he believes it is from a girlfriend that is married to someone else. George keeps the letter a secret, which eventually plucks a nerve with his friend. During a special Christmas dinner, Nigel knocks over the table. Upset, George fetches the letter and the two struggle, resulting in the murder of George. Curious, Nigel opens the envelope to discover that there is no letter after all – merely a printed circular offering a special deal on a raincoat.

Trivia, etc. *Daily Variety* reviewed this episode on December 4, 1957: "This had to be seen to be believed. That two men arguing over a letter can consume the better part of an hour. Could be worse? It was. The two men are Britishers with clipped accents. It had rump weariness, little else, to hold the viewer to the climatic switch, the hallmark of all Hitchcock stories into psychological drama. The idea was hatched by W. Somerset Maugham in a short story and it is doubtful he intended it to run that long. While the cast seemed large credit-wise, it was actually a two-man show . . . back and forth they argue, ad infinitum . . . No fault to find with their acting jobs, at times dramatically superb, but the rambling story to reach a point of little return was even too much for James Neilson's direction, usually of high order."

(11) December 9, 1957 "The Deadly Game" (live telecast) Directed by Don Medford.

(12) December 16, 1957 "Doomsday" (Revue) Directed by Bernard Girard.

(13) December 23, 1957 "The Dark Stairway" (live telecast) Directed by Don Medford.

December 30, 1957 (PRE-EMPTION) "All – Star Jazz Show" Broadcast from 10 to 11 p.m., EST. With Louis Armstrong, Jack Teagarden, Carmen McRae. Woody Herman, Gene Krupa, Duke Ellington, and hosted by Steve Allen.

(14) January 6, 1958 "Someone Is After Me" (live telecast) Directed by David Greene.

(15) EPISODE #4   **"LORD ARTHUR SAVILE'S CRIME"**   Broadcast on Jan. 13, 1958

Cast: Ronald Howard as Lord Arthur Savile   Rosemary Harris as Sybil Merton
Gladys Cooper as Lady Windemere
Sebastian Cabot as Septimus R. Podgers
Melville Cooper as Mr. Merton   Mary Forbes as Mrs. Merton
Lily Kemble Cooper as the Duchess of Paisley   Tita Purdom as Lady Flora
Kendrick Huxham as Sir Thomas   Hilda Plowright as Lady Marvel
Frederic Worlock as the chemist   Doris Lloyd as Lady Clementina
Alex Davion as Count Rouvaloff   Fred Essler as Herr Vinkelkopf
Cyril Delevanti as Dean of Chichester   George Pelling as a police officer
Sally Newton as one of the Dean's daughters
Sheila Keddy as the Dean's other daughter
Molly Roden as the Maid   Selmer Jackson as the priest

Teleplay written for *Suspicion* by Francis Cockrell, based on the short story of the same name by Oscar Wilde, originally published in an 1887 issue of *The Court and Society Review.* Subsequently collected in *Lord Arthur Savile's Crime and Other Stories*, in 1891.

Directed by Robert Stevens.

Story: Lord Arthur Savile, a noble and respected Englishman, attends a palm reading and it is here that he learns the horrible fate, resting on his shoulders. Someday in the near future, he will commit a murder. Applying common sense, Lord Arthur decides to act out his crime before marrying Sybil Merton, whom he is engaged to, before putting her in any grim danger. Attempting to poison his wealthy old aunt, Lord Arthur discovers that she beat him to it, dying of natural causes. Deciding to plant a bomb to kill his uncle, a church dean, fate plays another hand as the explosive fizzles out. By coincidence, Lord Arthur runs into the only person in the world capable of revealing his secret – the unsuspecting palm reader – and strangles the life out of him. Tossing the body in the Thames, Arthur returns home to marry his beloved Sybil. After the marriage, Lord Arthur, haunted by his deed, writes a suicide letter explaining in detail why he killed the man, only to learn from Lady Windemere that the psychic was a fake. Feeling his actions were justified, Lord Arthur throws the suicide note into the fire. Only one problem . . . the maid saves the letter.

Trivia, etc. Actor Frederic Worlock's name was mis-spelled in the closing credits, as "Frederick." Fred Essler plays the role of an exploding clock-maker in this episode, similar to the role he played in "Cheap Is Cheap" on *Alfred Hitchcock Presents*. There, he played a man called Arthur, who was to put together some poison for Alexander Gifford.

Variety reviewed this episode on January 15, 1958: "What better combination is there than Alfred Hitchcock and Oscar Wilde to dish up a tasty case of murder, flavored with more delight than fright? A measure to a witty Francis Cockrell teleplay directed with a light-hearted touch by Robert Stevens . . . Ronald Howard, as Arthur, is justifiably sensitive about doing what he must, engendering complete sympathy. Because he played down his role, because director Robert Stevens and scripter Cockrell refused to forget Wilde's basic intentions, the teleplay results in a comedy of manners that's a tongue-in-cheek relief from the either-or stories that flood the channels."

(16) January 20, 1958 "End in Violence" (live telecast) Directed by Paul Bogart.
(17) January 27, 1958 "Comfort for the Grave" (Revue) Directed by Jules Bricken.
(xx) February 3, 1958 Rebroadcast of Shamley's "Heartbeat" episode of 11/11/57.

(18) EPISODE #5 **"MEETING IN PARIS"** Broadcast on February 10, 1958
   Cast: Rory Calhoun as Peter Lockwood Jane Greer as Claire Stangler
   Walter Abel as Harvey, "the fake" Major Denbrow
   Maurice Marsac as Monsieur La Fange Edward Manouk as the chauffeur
   John Zaremba as Concierge
   Robert Moechel as the American Private Roger Til as Jacques, the bartender
   Duane Cress as SHAPE Sergeant Jennifer Howard as WAC secretary
   Gordon Wynn as "the real" Major Denbrow Cris Roberts as the M.P.
   Lizz Slifer as the newswoman
   Marcel de la Brosse as proprietor of soup stall
   Eddie Coch as man at restaurant Peg LaCentra as Marianne, the pianist
   Jacques Gallo as the waiter
   Teleplay written for *Suspicion* by Elliot West and Stirling Silliphant, from the short story of the same name by Elliot West, originally published in the April 1957 issue of *Cosmopolitan.*
   Directed by James Neilson.
   Story: When Peter Lockwood flies to Paris to clear up a business matter at the Lockwood Oil Company, he meets up with his ex-wife Claire. Knowing how wealthy Peter is, and the connections he has, Claire asks a favor for old times sake. She wants to go back to America with her new husband Eugene, and asks Peter to help finance. An unsuspecting Peter agrees, seeing how he might score the chance to rekindle an old flame and Claire decides to stay in Paris. Later that day, Peter is approached by a Major Denbrow, from the U.S. Army, Shape headquarters, asking the whereabouts of Eugene, Claire's new husband. The Major explains that Eugene is offering a document with the names of numerous spies in Europe, and if he doesn't get to Eugene first, his own people will kill him. Seeing a window of opportunity, Peter reveals details of Eugene's trip to the States. Over dinner, Peter and Claire learn the horrible news about an American killed at the loading docks, fitting Eugene's description, which isn't taken too kindly by Claire, who demands to know why the tip-off. Proving to Claire that he did the right thing, Peter takes her to meet the Major himself, only to discover that the real Major doesn't look at all the same. The man he aided was a fake!

(19) February 17, 1958 "A Touch of Evil" (Revue) Directed by John Brahm.
(20) February 24, 1958 "If I Die Before I Live" (live telecast) Directed by Perry Lafferty.
(21) March 3, 1958 "The Hollow Man" (live telecast) Directed by Elliot Silverstein.
(22) March 10, 1958 "A World Full of Strangers" (live telecast) Directed by Don Medford.

(23) EPISODE #6   **"THE EYE OF TRUTH"**   Broadcast on March 17, 1958

Cast: Joseph Cotten as Gregg Carey	George Peppard as Lee
Leora Dana as Sue Carey	Carol Stone as Lena
Thayer David as Turko	Louise Larabee as Mrs. Holby
Philip Van Zandt as Holby	Edmon Ryan as Lubin
Ken Clark as Galloway	Byron Foulger as Mr. Kent
Sondra Rodgers as Mrs. Kent	Dorothea Lord as the nurse
Elvira Corona as the maid	Mike Ragan as the waiter

Also in the cast: Herbert C. Lytton and Fred Robbins.
An original teleplay written for *Suspicion* by Eric Ambler.
Directed by Robert Stevens.
Story: On route to his home, Gregg Carey, a successful lawyer who often employs unapproved methods to win his cases, picks up an innocent-looking hitch-hiker named Lee. Not suspecting anything wrong, Gregg is knocked out by his travelling companion, and robbed of his possessions. When Gregg wakes up, he discovers to his horror that the legal documents he was carrying were also stolen – one of which contained a document that if fallen into the right hands, would mean his disbarment. Knowing he can't get the police directly involved, Gregg gives a false description of his assailant, and then waits for Lee to return for blackmail. Lee does return, and Gregg reveals his true motives. One of the documents was obtained via shady methods, and contains evidence that the attorney bribed someone else to conceal his son's responsibility for a hit-and-run death. Murdering Lee, Gregg turns himself in to the police for the killing, but not before destroying the document first.

March 24, 1958 (PRE-EMPTION) *Hallmark Hall of Fame's* "Little Moon of Alban." Written by James Costigan. Julie Harrison portrays a deeply religious woman whose faith is shaken after the deaths of her father, her brother and the man she loves. With Christopher Plummer, George Peppard and Barry Jones. Produced and directed by George Schaefer.

(24) March 31, 1958 "Diagnosis: Death" (live telecast) Directed by Don Medford.

(25) EPISODE #7   **"THE BULL SKINNER"**   Broadcast on April 7, 1958

Cast: Rod Steiger as Frank Marre	John Beal as Evelyn "Ev" Peters
Sallie Brophy as Doris Marre	Harold J. Stone as Sam Strausky
Perry Lopez as Dominic	Mike Ragan as Kiley
Ike Jones as Charlie	

An original teleplay written specially for *Suspicion* by Ernest Kinoy.
Directed by Lewis Milestone.
Story: A diesel truck driver (also termed as a "bull skinner") named Frank Marre feels the ground tearing beneath his feet, when he learns to his horror, that his boss offered a promotion to Ev Peters, a newcomer who isn't as experienced as Frank. To make matters worse, Frank suspects his wife of cheating on him, with – of all people – the new field foreman, Peters. Frank's state of mind begins tearing up relations with both his wife and the employees at the workplace. When a tractor blade falls on Peters, cutting off his arm, Frank dismisses it as an accident – but when the same thing almost happens to Frank, he suspects Peters is trying to kill him. Tired of the emotional abuse, Frank's wife walks out on him. Returning to work, Frank searches out for Peters and during a wild chase involving a tractor, Frank loses control of his vehicle and dies in the wreckage. What he didn't know was that Doris, his wife, wasn't really cheating on him, and returned home shortly before the accident.

Trivia, etc. *Variety* reviewed this drama on April 19, 1958: "There is a rich dredging of human values in this tale . . . They are both enhanced and implemented by the sensitive acting of Rod Steiger and Sallie Brophy, a fine display of imbedded bitterness, emotional conflict poignantly surfaced to give this hour play its dramatic force . . . Ernest Kinoy's bristling script was powered with high tension and deep drama by Lewis Milestone's direction."

(26) April 14, 1958 "The Girl Upstairs" (live telecast) Directed by Don Medford.

(27) April 21, 1958 "Fraction of a Second" (Revue) Directed by John Brahm.

(28) EPISODE #8 **"THE WAY UP TO HEAVEN"** Broadcast on April 28, 1958

Cast: Marion Lorne as Mrs. Hester Foster	Sebastian Cabot as Mr. Robert Foster
Patricia Smith as Ellen Thibeau	Kathryn Givney as Jane, the maid
Selmer Jackson as Walker, the butler	Albert Carrier as Pierre Thibeau
Anthony Maxwell as Robert Thibeau	Nancy Ann De Carl as Celeste Thibeau
Joseph Holland as Dr. Winship	Warren Frost as the driver
Allen Kramer as the other driver	Dorothea Lord as the airport attendant
Tharon Crigler as the girl in the coffee shop	Cris Roberts as man at ticket counter

Teleplay written for *Suspicion* by Marian Cockrell, from a story by Roald Dahl, as originally published in the February 27, 1954 issue of *The New Yorker*. Subsequently reprinted in the November 1955 issue of *Ellery Queen's Mystery Magazine*.
Directed by Herschel Daugherty.
Story: Mrs. Foster is completely dominated by her selfish and sadistic husband. When she makes plans to fly out to Paris, so she can spend a few weeks with her daughter, Robert opposes the trip – not directly, but in a number of petty ways. Taking pills that make him sick, the ever-caring wife cancels her flight to stay home and nurse him back to health. Soon after, she starts packing her bags again – but this time Robert hides her ticket. When Mrs. Foster makes plane reservations for a third time, the fog delays the flight until the following morning and then when the time comes, Robert returns inside for a package, only to claim he's stuck in the elevator. Knowing her husband's schemes to keep her from making the flight, Mrs. Foster leaves for the airport. Six weeks later, an unsuspecting Mrs. Foster returns home to find the elevator stuck, and her husband – quite dead, of course – still inside.

Trivia, etc. *Variety* reviewed this episode on April 30, 1958: "There's a suspenseful, morbid attraction in 'The Way Up To Heaven,' a polished presentation of a sadistic man's domination of his wife. Marian Cockrell teleplay, based on Roald Dahl's New Yorker yarn, is a good one, and receives fine direction all the way from Herschel Daugherty." In this episode, Patricia Smith says "Celeste and Pierre are growing so big and you've never seen them." This is a blunder on her part since Pierre is her husband and Robert is her son. Celeste is her daughter. Furs for this episode were supplied by Beckman in Beverly Hills.

(29) May 5, 1958 "The Woman With Red Hair" (live) Directed by William A. Graham.

(30) May 12, 1958 "Protégé" (Revue) Directed by Jules Bricken.

(31) May 19, 1958 "The Velvet Vault" (live telecast) Directed by David Greene.

(32) EPISODE # 9 **"VOICE IN THE NIGHT"** Broadcast May 26, 1958
Cast: Barbara Rush as Mrs. Eleanore Thomasen
James Donald as James 'Jim' Thomasen
Patrick Macnee as Captain John Biersdorf   James Coburn as Philip
Teleplay written for *Suspicion* by Stirling Silliphant, from the short story of the same name by William Hope Hodgson. Subsequently reprinted in *Alfred Hitchcock Presents: Stories They Wouldn't Let Me Do On TV*, ed. Alfred Hitchcock (Simon & Schuster, 1957).
Directed by Arthur Hiller.

Story: Captain John Biersdorf and another sailor, Philip, find themselves lost in a thick fog, when a stranger in a small rowboat passes by, asking for provisions. The stranger, named James, won't show himself, nor will he board their ship, and judging by his story, he has a very good reason why. It seems James and his wife Eleanore were shipwrecked and having found an abandoned schooner, boarded the drifting vessel in the hope of finding food and water. But their relief soon turned to terror when they discovered that an uncontrollable fungus, was growing everywhere on the ship. Escaping to a nearby uncharted island, the hideous lichen began to grow on their bodies. Realizing they were beyond medical assistance, they pass the chance to be rescued, and decide to remain on the island. Hoping to obtain provisions for his wife, James ventured out on the small rowboat . . . which explains why he won't board their ship. Now curious after hearing the story, a suspicious Philip shines a light through the thick fog, and the captain catches a glimpse of the storyteller – a great grey, sponge.

Trivia, etc. *Variety* reviewed this episode on May 28, 1958: "William Hope Hodgson's famous short story . . . is the sort of chilling tale that is more suitable to the mind's eye than the camera's. A weird and fantastic sketch of horror at sea, it defies transposition to film by the very virtue of its almost unimaginable horror. All of which makes Alfred Hitchcock's presentation of it on *Suspicion* all the more noteworthy, since he has managed to capture on film much of what the author intended, and the reader imagined. It is also a tribute to sponsor Van Heusen and Procter & Gamble that they didn't wash their hands of this whole affair before it was allowed to unravel all of its ghastliness. Some of the author's passages were removed . . . most notably the section in which the ill-fated lover begin to eat the fungus out of not only starvation, but of a curious and insatible craving to devour the growth . . . Stirling Silliphant's teleplay does well by Hodgson's story, although at times, perhaps unavoidably, there is a tendency to lag. A superior directorial effort by Arthur Hiller aids consistently."

(33) June 2, 1958 "Death Watch" (Revue) Directed by Ray Milland.
(34) June 9, 1958 "The Man With the Gun" (live telecast) Directed by Jack Smight.

(35) EPISODE #10 **"THE WOMAN TURNED TO SALT"** Broadcast June 16, 1958
        Cast: Michael Rennie as Angus Martin
        Pamela Brown as Solange St. Rogers

Susan Oliver as Rosemary Russell	Rafael Campos as Pietro
Jane Rose as Mrs. Flora Russell	Pat Hitchcock as the secretary
Heather Angel as Grace Martin	Doris Lloyd as Mrs. Smythe
Marcel de la Brosse as the receptionist	Sean Meaney as the priest

        Teleplay written for *Suspicion* by Stirling Silliphant, from the story "Lot's Wife" by F. Tennyson Jesse, originally published in *The Solange Stories*, (London, Wm Heinemann Ltd., 1931).
        Directed by Robert Stevens.
        Story: On vacation on the Italian Riviera, Miss Solange St. Rogers, a British divorce lawyer, is confronted by Mrs. Russell, asking for advice. It seems Mrs. Russell doesn't want her daughter, Rosemary, to marry the wealthy Angus Martin, a playboy much older than her, and whose wife disappeared under mysterious circumstances. Solange does some investigating and finds Martin's wife, alive in Ireland, but on her deathbed. Having been contacted about his wife's whereabouts, Martin gets there just in time to hear her last words. Believing the mystery is solved, Mrs. Russell agrees for her daughter to marry Angus Martin, and the two lovers wed. But on a later visit, Solange discovers his secret. Martin has been blackmailed by a young man that happened to see him kill his wife. The woman in Ireland was someone he met and paid to "play" his wife. Before the police is informed, a storm knocks over one of the cement pillars in the garden, killing Martin – the same pillar in which he hid his wife's body.

Trivia, etc. *Variety* reviewed this episode on June 18, 1958: "One of those neat little British-styled mystery packages that quietly and almost unobtrusively build up suspense. This one builds most of the way through, but collapses in a pair of disappointing denouements. It doesn't quite come off because of the weakness in the story, but Stevens sets a directorial style that's slick and savvy, one that television could use more of." Heather Angel played Ethel, the maid in Hitchcock's movie with the same name as the series, *Suspicion* (1941). The sculpture and ceramics for this episode were made by Sascha Brastoff.

(36) June 23, 1958 "Eye for Eye" (Revue) Directed by Jules Bricken.
(37) June 30, 1958 "Return from Darkness" (live telecast) Directed by Herbert Kenwith.
(38) July 7, 1958 "The Devil Makes Three" (live telecast) Directed by Donald Petrie.
(39) July 14, 1958 "The Imposter" (live telecast) Directed by Don Medford.
(40) July 21, 1958 "The Death of Paul Dane" (live telecast) Directed by Elliot Silverstein.

SUMMER RERUNS
July 28, 1958 "The Story of Marjorie Reardon" (Revue)
August 4, 1958 "Four O'Clock" (Shamley) Directed by Alfred Hitchcock.
August 11, 1958 "The Other Side of the Curtain" (Revue)
August 18, 1958 "Lord Arthur Savile's Crime" (Shamley)
August 25, 1958 "Doomsday" (Revue)
September 1, 1958 "Comfort for the Grave" (Revue)
September 8, 1958 "Meeting in Paris" (Shamley)
September 15, 1958 "Death Watch" (Revue)
September 22, 1958 "The Eye of Truth" (Shamley)

TACTIC: HITCHCOCK'S EXPLORATION OF CANCER
Written by Jaclyn Packer, Ph.D.

On May 2, 1959, the National Broadcasting Network (NBC) presented the premiere episode of a short-run series, entitled *Tactic*. This six-part series of health information programs was intended to help in the fight against cancer, by informing the American public about the disease. For the premiere broadcast, Alfred Hitchcock and Hanya Holm tackled the topic of fear, which often causes cancer patients to avoid medical treatment.

As the broadcast opened, Ben Grauer, the host, introduced the director of the American Cancer Society, Dr. Charles S. Cameron, who explained that every year thousands of people die needlessly from cancer, because they avoid treatment. Creative guest panelists were told of a specific aspect of cancer, prior to each show. "Because people don't seek effective treatment," Cameron explained, "we want to change their attitudes," which are the following: Arrogance: people don't want to feel mortal. Procrastination: not getting around to getting help. Vanity: fear of disfigurement from surgery. Modesty: keeps people from getting checkups. Fatalism: once get cancer can't do anything about it. But, Cameron explains, there is a one in three chance of being successfully treated. Many innocent Americans lose their lives because of this. There are only two ways to cure cancer - surgery and irradiation. Avoidance: If one doesn't think about it. it will go away. Shame: Cancer is a social disgrace. (Cameron says the only cure is to bring it out in the open.) Ignorance: misconceptions about cancer. Early diagnosis and early treatment is the best way to save your life from cancer.

The medical expert then explained that these aspects of cancer were presented to creative artists who, "according to his or her genius," be that drawing, dance, or song, for instance, would better help save lives. "There is a single common denominator to all these attitudes - Fear. Today, we have one of the world's most distinguished experts on fear, Alfred Hitchcock."

Hitchcock goes on camera and explains his theory. "In my opinion," he said, "it is not fear that keeps people from doing what they should about cancer, it's the avoidance of fear." To demonstrate what he meant, Hitchcock set up an improvisation, using Broadway actors Diana van der Vlis and William Shatner, to perform a semi-improvised scene. The situation is a 24-year-old fashion model (Van der Vlis), engaged to be married, who needs admiration. The doctor must inform her she has breast cancer. She recently discovered a lump - it turned out to be malignant and she needs to have surgery immediately. The doctor (Shatner) tells the woman that she must have the breast removed. She begs him to tell her another way it can be treated. At this point of the story, Hitchcock walks onto the stage and interrupts Diana. "This is the most startling news of your life. You know it's serious. Play it tongue-tied." Hitchcock then turned to the cameraman and directed him to: "Take a tight closeup of her face . . . we want to see her reaction to the news."

The play continued. "I'd rather die, in one piece," said the model. The doctor tries to advise her to go for the surgery. Hitchcock interrupts again. "I'd like to do something here. A little subconscious act, which will carry out the symbolism of the letter opener." (There was a letter opener sitting on the desk, which Hitchcock had asked for earlier from the prop men). "As you talk, pick it up and toy with it," Hitchcock told Shatner. The doctor starts playing with the knife and the camera focuses on it. The model says that all her life it was so important that people admire her for her looks – now it all seems so unimportant. She never really believed she was beautiful anyway. She agrees to the procedure, and they set up surgery for the next morning. With the drama over, Hitchcock thanks the two "for a pair of very nice performances," with special emphasis on the words "pair of very nice performances."

Since the show was split about equally between Hitchcock's theatre piece and Hanya Holm's dance piece, the choreographer goes next. Hanya Holm stepped out to explain how dance could be used to influence attitudes and communicate ideas. Three dance sequences were performed by Sondra Lee and Don Redlich, who portrayed people who avoided facing problems - such as cancer - due to their fears. Hitchcock's participation for *Tactic* was minimal, and on the technical side, he didn't even direct the drama. Merely he provided the audience with a 'Hitchcock' point-of-view (behind-the-camera) of how such a drama would need to be expressed through the medium of television. There is nothing at all in this show that mentions Shamley Productions. The credits read "Presented by NBC and Educational Television and Radio Center, in cooperation with The American Cancer Society. This has been an NBC Production."

CREDITS:
Associate Producer: George Lefferts
Dance Choreographer: Hanya Holm
Dance Performers: Sondra Lee and Don Redlich
Director for Mr. Hitchcock: Frank Pacelli
Director: Lynwood King
Executive Producer: Malcolm MacGregor
Music composed and conducted by Freda Miller.
Producer: Marilyn Kaemmerle
Written by George Lefferts and Earl Hamner.
"This has been an NBC Production."

FORD STARTIME'S "INCIDENT AT A CORNER"

Broadcast over NBC on April 5, 1960, Tuesday evening from 8:30 to 9:30 p.m., EST
Filmed at Revue Studios, February 8-12 and 15-17.

Cast: Vera Miles as Jean Medwick   George Peppard as Patrick 'Pat' Lawrence
Paul Hartman as James Medwick   Bob Sweeney as Uncle Jeffrey
Leora Dana as Mrs. Tawley   Warren Berlinger as Ron Tawley
Philip Ober as Mr. Malcolm Tawley   Jerry Paris as W. E. Grimes, the lawyer
Alice Backes as Aunt Pauline   Charity Grace as Elsa Medwick
Leslie Barrett as Batie   Alexander Lockwood as Mr. Rigsby, the principal
Jack Albertson as Harry Crane   Eve McVeagh as Georgie Cluney / Mrs. Crane
Tyler McVey as Chief Taylor   Joe Flynn as Dr. Sidney Sinden
Barbara Beaird as Mary Jane Ryder   Hollis Irving as Mrs. Mabel Sinden
Mary Alan Hokanson as Mrs. Parker
Teleplay by Charlotte Armstrong from her novella of the same name, published in *Duo* by
Coward-McCann in 1959.
Produced by Joan Harrison. Directed by Alfred Hitchcock.

CREDITS:
Art Director: John J. Lloyd   Film Editor: Edward W. Williams
Assistant Director: Hilton A. Green   Hairstylist: Florence Bush
Associate Producer: Norman Lloyd   Makeup: Jack Barron
Costume Supervisor: Vincent Dee   Music Supervisor: Frederick Herbert
Director of Photography: John L. Russell Set Decorator: George Milo
Editorial Supervisor: Richard G. Wray   Sound: William Russell
An Alfred Hitchcock Production.
Filmed at Revue Studios in Hollywood, California, in association with MCA-TV, executive
distributor for Shamley Productions. Inc., in association with the NBC Television Network.

NOTES (and plot): " 'Incident at a Corner' starts intriguingly with the same incident
repeated from several different viewpoints – a school crossing guard reprimanding the PTA
president for careless driving. The guard (Paul Hartman) is later dismissed from his job on
the basis of an anonymous note accusing him of being too friendly with little schoolgirls. His
daughter's boyfriend (George Peppard) takes up his cause, assuming that the PTA president
sent the note out of spite. An hour later, it turns out that the note was sent by a woman living
across the street from the school, who knew Hartman from another city, and feared he would
expose her past life. Except for the novelty of the multiple viewpoint opening (which
includes one shot from the point-of-view of the woman who turns out to have sent the note),
with its connection to the present action flashback in *Vertigo*, the film is extremely
pedestrian."
> - Steven Mamber, printed in the Fall 1971 issue of *Cinema*

" 'Incident at a Corner' is drearier still [than *The Alfred Hitchcock Hour*'s "I Saw the Whole
Thing"]. In fact the spurious plot, which Jack Edmond Nolan mistakenly attaches to this
teleplay . . . sounds more interesting than the actual scenario. Like "I Saw the Whole Thing,"
the early passages of this TV drama promise more than it ultimately delivers. A
confrontation between a school traffic warden (Paul Hartman) and a woman motorist is
repeated from the vantage point of various witnesses. Then the meandering story-line takes
an unexpected turn and settles down into a turgid tale about the heinousness of poison-pen
letters, which seems to have little to do with the deftly designed opening sequence."
> - Gene D. Phillips, author of *Alfred Hitchcock*, 1984

Like Fred Astaire in "The Jail" and Dennis O'Keefe in *Suspicion*, Vera Miles introduced
"Incident at a Corner" with an introduction: *That's the man I'm going to marry and I agree
with every word he is saying. There was an incident, you see, involving the members of my
family. They became caught up in a vicious web of lies and slander. It was like a mystery
story. Only there was no murder, no corpse, not even a detective.*

Vera Miles' closing comments: *It's been a pleasure for me to appear on 'Ford Startime' tonight. I hope you enjoyed our show. From all of us, from Ford and your Ford dealer, good night.*

Two daily trade reviews were contradictory – perfectly illustrating the hopelessness of relying on one or the other as an indicator of a show's quality. Hank Grant in *The Hollywood Reporter* (April 7, 1960 issue) called it "Hitchcock at his non-violent best" and felt that "the suspense . . . was slightly terrific." The April 7, 1960 issue of *The Daily Variety* on the other hand, was of the opinion that Hitchcock had "made a full-blown affair of a thin story that tapered off to a contrived denouement. Not even Hitchcock's direction and overhead camera shots could compensate for the lack of dramatic voltage. Too much of the same ground was retraced."

One interesting note: *The Hollywood Reporter* refered to "Incident at a Corner" as "the first of two Alfred Hitchcock specials for this series." It appears that the second program never materialized (probably because *Ford Startime* went off the air at the end of May 1960) – unless it was "The Jail," diverted to the *Alcoa Premiere* series. Hubbell Robinson, who produced Boris Karloff's *Thriller*, produced many of the broadcasts for *Ford Startime*, but not this telecast.

Source: The last two paragraphs listed above were from the unpublished <u>The Alfred Hitchcock Teleguide</u>, written by Howard H. Prouty, West Hollywood, California, 1984.

ALCOA PREMIERE'S "THE JAIL"
Written by Howard Prouty.

Broadcast over ABC on February 6, 1962, Tuesday evening from 10 to 11 p.m., EST.

Cast: John Gavin as William Fortnum   James Barton as Hobbs
Barry Morse as the guard   Noah Keen as Peters, keeper of machine
Bettye Ackerman as Ellen Fortnum   Robert Sampson as Dr. Jack Bernard
Eve McVeagh as the young woman
An original teleplay written for *Alcoa Premiere* by Ray Bradbury.
Produced by Joan Harrison. Directed by Norman Lloyd.
Music composed and conducted by John Williams.

CREDITS:

Art Director: John J. Lloyd

Assistant Director: Edward K. Dodds

Associate Producer: Norman Lloyd

Costume Supervisor: Vincent Dee

Editorial Dept. Head: David J. O'Connell

Film Editor: Edward W. Williams, a.c.e.

Director of Photography: Ellsworth Fredricks, a.s.c.

Set Decorators: John McCarthy and Robert C. Bradfield

Hair Stylist: Florence Bush

Makeup: Jack Barron

Musical Supervision: Stanley Wilson

Sound: Joe Lapis

Title design by Saul Bass.

An Alfred Hitchcock Production.

Filmed at Revue Studios in Hollywood, California, in association with MCA-TV, executive distributor for Shamley Productions. Inc., in association with the ABC Television Network.

Fred Astaire pulls out a paper from a typewriter: *The name of this story is "The Jail." Doesn't look like much. does it? A bunch of holes punched in a card. That machine remembers everything you tell it and it also remembers things you didn't tell it. And this one makes confetti, from the holes punched in these cards. Now who is to say whether one day, these machines might not take over the duties of human beings, even assume human characteristics – but enough of that. In this room are other thinking machines. Tapes, transistors, electronic circuits. All of these devises exist today to be used for good. But perhaps sometime, with a few changes they can be used for evil. Now uh – in this room, you will see a machine that can make things upside-down, round-about, inside-out, backwards and forwards. I wonder, can a machine look and sound evil? Maybe. Well, good or evil, we'll leave this machine and the others waiting here. When we come back, forty years would have passed. Machines will not necessarily become wicked. People might build machines to hear evil, see evil, and speak evil. Only forty years. Well, until then . . .*

Story: Forty years in the future (i.e. 2002), a young man named William Fortnum is led into a "courtroom" by a guard. told that he is to be tried for an unspecified crime by "a jury of your peers" – twelve computers lined in a row. The judge is also a computer and there's even a machine representing William. ("I am innocent" it claims!) He is found guilty in due time (2 minutes and 21 seconds), sentenced to life imprisonment, and remanded into custody of the keeper of the "transit machine." "Pure justice . . . purely arrived at," gloats the guard. Fortnum is asked to pick at random (via a video screen) one of a group of derelicts on the street. The old man he chooses, Hobbs, is then brought into the room, and the nature of the "transit machine" – and of Fortnum's sentence – is learned. Both men are strapped into the machine, and their "souls" are exchanged – and Fortnum finds himself imprisoned in the decrepit body of Hobbs, who has a bad heart. "Turnabout is fair play, and all is right in an electronic world," the guard explains.

Hobbs on the other hand, is elated at his new lease on life. Fortnum is then released: "We set you free – within your jail." He tries to keep up with Hobbs. screaming "Be careful of my body!" but the exertion brings on chest pains. He then returns home to his wife Ellen – who knows it's only him when she looks into his eyes. Together they track down Hobbs (living it up at a bar), and Ellen uses her sexy figure to lure him outside. But Fortnum, with Hobbs' bad heart, is unable to overpower his own strong young body, and collapses from the strain. They receive help from an unexpected source: Peters, the keeper of the transit machine, who helps them trick Hobbs into returning to the machine, where they subdue him and switch the two back. As Peters helps them, he says, "because once . . . I was old."

During the soul exchange, and a discussion between Ellen and Peters, we also learn what Fortnum's "crime" was. On their vacation the previous mount, he had "skied over the line – he crossed the border." When Ellen protests that "he does that every year," Peters replies: "This year . . . even for a minute, it is a crime against the state." Out in the evening street, Hobbs – back in his own body – dies from the previous exertion. The guard shows up in response to an alarm, but Peters tells him that no souls were exchanged, allowing Fortnum and Ellen to escape, presumably to a life as fugitives.

Fred Astaire's closing remarks: *A very strange story indeed, in a year which I hope, will never come.*

NOTES: This drama, was in fact, "An Alfred Hitchcock Production," even though it was broadcast on the TV's series *Alcoa Premiere*. The hour-long feature was filmed and broadcast in black and white. The Copyright Catalog and the UCLA listing mistakenly attributes this show as Avasta Productions, the company which produced most of the *Alcoa Premiere* series. The copyright notice on the film itself however, reads: Shamley Productions, Inc.

The show itself is solid without being exceptional. It's very Bradbury-esque in a fascination with the relationship between humanity and machinery, with the most interesting thread having to do with the nature of the mind and body: "Can a sick mind, destroy a well body? Can a well mind, cure a sick body?" says the guard. "Is the mind a thing and the body a place? A room to be redecorated when a new mind moves in?" Everlasting questions, never ending. The soul-transference business is sort of a hokey gimmick, of course, but Bradbury redeems it somewhat with his emphasis on human values, and the conflict of wills: "You'd like to see me die . . . go insane . . . cry . . . in front of you," the imprisoned Fortnum tells his guard, then to himself, "I will do none of those things." Unfortunately, Norman Lloyd's direction tends to emphasize the more heavy-handed aspects of the script, and his portentous handling of the less-than-amazing special effects looks embarrassingly dated today. Barry Morse is excellent as the guard, who plays the role of judge, jury and executioner, and insinuates that he already knew the verdict before the trial began. He gets an emotional high on a few occasions out of the suffering of Fortnum, teasing about his falling down, a possible heart attack, and even handing him a photo of his younger self.

James Barton creditable as Hobbs (or rather Hobbs' body – since he's actually playing Fortnum for much of the show), and convinces you that he's actually suffering. Most of the acting for him was showing emotion and facial features, since the most of the dialogue was from thoughts, more so a recording of his voice. John Gavin is good ambassador material, playing a duel role with such a convincing performance, that the viewer can actually believe there was a body switch.

Two trivial notes: 1. The shiny aluminum "city" which serves as the background for the *Alcoa Premiere* credits, and over which "An Alfred Hitchcock Production" appears at the end of the show, was designed by Saul Bass. Bass also designed the opening titles for Alfred Hitchcock's *Vertigo* (1958), *North by Northwest* (1959) and *Psycho* (1960). 2. The character name "William (Bill) Fortnum" was previously used by Bradbury in the *Alfred Hitchcock Presents* episode "Special Delivery" from November 29, 1959.

DARK INTRUDER

Cast: Leslie Nielsen as Brett Kingsford   Mark Richman as Robert Vandenburg
Judi Meredith as Evelyn Lang
Gilbert Green as Commissioner Harvey Misbach

Charles Bolender as Nikola	Werner Klemperer as Professor Malaki
Vaughn Taylor as Dr. Kevin Burdett	Peter Brocco as Chi Zang
Bill Quinn as the neighbor	Ken Hooker as the first Sergeant
Richard Venture as the first man	Mike Ragan as the plain clothesman
Ingvard Nielsen as the second man	Claudia Donelly as the woman
Anthony Lettier as the second Sergeant	Chester Jones as the doorman
Harriet Vine as Hannah	

An original teleplay written by Barré Lyndon.
Produced by Jack Laird. Directed by Harvey Hart.
Music composed and conducted by Lalo Schifrin.

CREDITS:

Art Director: Loyd S. Papez	Assistant Director: Edward K. Dodds
Costume Supervisor: Vincent Dee	Film Editor: Edward W. Williams, a.c.e.
Director of Photography: John F. Warren, a.s.c.	Music Supervisor: Stanley Wilson

Hair Stylists: Virginia Darcy and Perc Westmore
Makeup Artists: Bud Westmore, Mike Westmore and Wally Westmore
Set Decorators: Julia Heron and John McCarthy
Sound: Robert R. Bertrand and Waldon O. Watson
Title by Pacific Title.
A Shamley Production, filmed in Hollywood at Universal City.
A Universal Studios Release, 1965
Black and White, 59 minutes long.

Story: San Francisco, 1890. Brett Kingsford, an expert of the occult, and wealthy man about town, is called in to investigate a rash of mysterious murders. The victims are savagely clawed to death and a grotesque Oriental carved head is left next to each of the bodies. The miniature statues are ancient Sumerian demon spirits, capable of taking possession of the body of any living person. Robert Vandenburg, a friend of Brett's, is engaged to marry Evelyn Lang, but hesitates because he fears there are times when he is not himself. During his investigations, Brett theorizes that Robert had a deformed Siamese twin brother, the two being separated at birth by Dr. Burdett, one of the latest victims. Trailing the murderer to a tower, Brett attempts to prevent a satanic ritual, which ends with the death of Professor Malaki, who was behind the killings. Sadly for Robert, the transformation was completed before Brett could interfere, and Robert begins a new reign of terror. In the cemetary late one night, Brett pieces one and one together and is forced to kill the savage beast, which turns back into the form of Malaki.

NOTES: Most of the cast here, were veterans of other Shamley productions. Mark Richman ("Man with a Problem"), Leslie Neilsen ("The Magic Shop," "Ambition" and "The $2,000,000 Defense"), Werner Klemperer ("Safe Conduct" and "The Crystal Trench"), Bill Quinn ("How to Get Rid of Your Wife"), and so on. Mike Ragan played numerous supporting roles in *Alfred Hitchcock Presents* episodes, including an escaped convict in the episode "Breakdown" and a plumber in "The Horseplayer."

Mark Richman and Leslie Nielsen go way back to New York and the Actor's Studio, so this was a reunion of sorts. In fact, Richman later did a cameo in *Naked Gun 2 ½*, which starred Leslie Nielsen. "At the end, I was in the graveyard [about to transform into a demon]," recalled Mark Richman. "I turned toward the approaching police, and I did a physical transformation which I was so proud of. I did physical movements, from a normal person into a monster – I contorted my shoulders and my hips and my arms and my neck, and the facial thing. And they pretty much cut the damn thing. I was so pissed when they put the picture together – they cut right to the point where they shoot me, they didn't give me the time to develop this whole thing, which was horrific because it happened on the film. And I was so-o-o angry!"

Revealing how the makeup was applied, Richman recalled, "You sit in a makeup chair and they pour over your face plaster of Paris, or some other material that hardens quickly, in order to make a life mask. Your only source of life are two nostrils – there's a straw sticking out of each nostril, and that's your source of air. When they were doing this, one of the straws got plugged, and I only had one nostril to breathe from. And I was in a panic, an absolute panic. It's a horrifying experience, because you can't move for about 45 minutes – it's the closest thing to being buried alive. I had five or six men working on me at one time when I "transformed." Bud, Mike and Wally Westmore; Perc Westmore who was a hair specialist, Hank Eads and Jack Barron. They had to work fast because there was a lot to do, and they had all these prosthetic pieces to gradually add on. They'd put some devices on me and we would go on the stage and shoot about 15 or 30 seconds, and then I'd go back to the makeup room. Each thing took an hour, two hours to do; They'd take off these pieces and then put on the new stuff, and then I'd go back to the stage and get set exactly where I needed to be. They'd shoot that, and then back to the makeup...! It took a lot of time, we did it all day long – it took about 15 hours."

"It was a money maker for Universal," Richman continued. "It cost nothing to make, and it was released as a 59 minute movie! Which no one bothered to tell me was going to happen. One day Nina Foch called me and said. 'Your movie opened in New York.' I said, 'What movie?' and I was thinking to myself, 'When have I done a movie lately?' She said, '*Dark Intruder*.' I said, 'Movie . . .?' It had opened in a double feature with a Joan Crawford movie, *I Saw What You Did*. *Dark Intruder* was the second film. And she read me a review by a leading critic of *The New York Times* which said that the Joan Crawford movie was not very good, etc. etc. etc., and that the real sleeper for 'all you Gothic horror fans' was *Dark Intruder*; 'it's a mini-classic.' I was flabbergasted. And of course, terribly happy, because Universal owed me 100% of my salary for the theatrical release!"

One interesting trivia was that Werner Klemperer played the role of Professor Malaki, always remaining a shadow or dark figure till the second-to-last climax near the end of the movie. Although Klemperer played the Sumerian demon to perfection (and you would never even know it was him if it wasn't for the opening and closing credits), the voice was not his. It was, in fact, Norman Lloyd's voice and growls used in the movie, not Werner's!

"Universal Pictures has put into theatrical film release *Dark Intruder*, originally made as a pilot for a television series, and nixed by all three networks," reported *Variety* on August 4, 1965. "[This] same film, called 'The Black Cloak' when it was a TV pilot, was just released and last week received a glowing review in the *NY Times*. Projected as an hour-long horror series, Universal-TV planned to spinoff the show on *The Alfred Hitchcock Hour*. It later decided not to, when NBC-TV, which had the Hitchcock series, nixed the project. [The] studio went ahead and made a pilot anyway, at [the] cost of about $250,000."

More Notes: A "revised pilot script" dated November 17, 1964 is in the script collection of the American Film Institute's Louis B. Mayer Library; three titles appear on the cover, in this order: The Alfred Hitchcock Hour, The Black Cloak, and Something With Claws.

In the November 1980 issue of the *Monthly Film Bulletin*, Steve Jenkins reviewed: "[The film's] small-screen genesis show most clearly in the relationships set up between Brett

Kingsford and his dwarf servant, Nikola, the aged Oriental, Chi Zang, and Misbach, the Police Commissioner: all potential confidants of the hero, and obviously planted for use in the episodes which never materialized. Also, the limited running time has curtailed certain elements in the script . . . Most important, the Siamese twins "explanation" fails to lend any resonance to the possible parallels between Robert and Malaki. Harvey Hart does, however, offset some rather uninspired dialogue exchanges with stylistic tropes, such as shooting round objects oppressively placed in front of the frame. And several scenes, shots and high angles, and the final struggle between Brett and Malaki/Robert in a foggy graveyard, at least echo visually the extraordinary melodramas Barré Lyndon scripted in the forties (*Hangover Square* and *The Lodger*) as well as Universal's own horror tradition."

The film was reviewed in the July 22, 1965 issue of *The New York Times*: "At the bottom of the hill [below William Castle's *I Saw What You Did*], barely publicized at all, lies 'Dark Intruder,' the good one. Thanks to an excellent new director, Harvey Hart, a trim cast, and a perfectly swell story that articulately uncoils over a handful of sets, 'Dark Intruder' is a small 'must' for mystery shoppers . . . an off-beat thriller of obvious teamwork that deftly proves the power of suggestion. Catch this one."

On July 28, 1965, *Variety* reviewed: "While no great shakes as an example of cinematic artistry, 'Intruder' is honest hokum, with some occasional flashes of excellent writing. Turn-of-the-century mellerdrama shows influence of and even copying from, earlier and better terror tales with same or similar settings. Evidently scripter Barré Lyndon was exposed to such films as *The Lodger*, *The Body Snatcher* and other Victorian horror minor classics, but at least he has been an attentive viewer. Occasional touches of humor, generally in the dialog, are his own contribution and welcome ones."

(Photo courtesy of Photofest.)

PSYCHO

Cast: Anthony Perkins as Norman Bates   Janet Leigh as Marion Crane
Vera Miles as Lila Crane   John Gavin as Sam Loomis
Martin Balsam as Arbogast   John McIntire as Sheriff Al Chambers
Simon Oakland as Doctor Richmond, the psychiatrist
Frank Albertson as Tom Cassidy, the millionaire
Pat Hitchcock as Caroline   Vaughn Taylor as Mr. George Lowery
Lurene Tuttle as Mrs. Chambers   John Anderson as "California Charlie"
Mort Mills as the Highway Patrolman   Ted Knight as the prison guard
Francis De Sales as one of the officials
George Eldredge as James Mitchell, the Chief of Police
Sam Flint as one of the officials   Frank Killmond as Bob Summerfield
Helen Wallace as the customer in Sam's Store
Alfred Hitchcock as the man in cowboy hat
Jeanette Nolan as the voice of mother
Produced and directed by Alfred Hitchcock.
Screenplay by Joseph Stefano from the novel of the same name by Robert Bloch.
Animated Titles: William T. Hurtz
Art Directors: Robert Clatworthy and Joseph Hurley
Assistant Director: Hilton A. Green
Costumes: Helen Colvig and Rita Riggs
Film Editor: George Tomasini
Hair Stylist: Florence Bush
Makeup: Jack Barron and Robert Dawn
Music composed and conducted by Bernard Herrmann.
Photography: John L. Russell
Set Decorator: George Milo
Sound: William Russell and Waldon O. Watson
Special Effects: Clarence Champagne
Title Design and Pictorial Consultant: Saul Bass
Unit Manager: Lew Leary
A Shamley Production, filmed in Hollywood at Universal City.
A Universal Studios Release, New York Premiere: June 1960
Black and White, 109 minutes long.

In an issue of *Theatre Arts*, Lawrence Kane wrote: "The film to [Hitchcock] has always been simply a means of telling a story, but the story has never been the means of telling something greater. One is left with the unhappy impression that the man himself is devoid of personal philosophy; a fact which is not only confirmed by, but would seem to account for, his increasing interest in technical trickery." There is some truth in this. The fears took a serious toll on the man - and seemed to be increasingly corroding his art, especially in the years following *Psycho*. Said Hitchcock: "It is difficult to characterize me. I have a forbidding dead-pan exterior and an internal shyness. People are in awe of me, and they shouldn't be."

But they were in awe of him. He was an amazing human being who sat in the center of a scary universe, like a morbid, elderly cherub still wrapped in the spiritual swaddling clothes of his childhood. He was a strange, unique man who tried to be true to the dreams of babyhood, and who never recovered from his terrors. "I suppose one early one was fear of the police," Hitchcock explained, "or fascination with the police as a child. I had a very quiet, Jesuit education. I read a lot but was terribly scared of the Fathers. They were very strict."

If *Psycho* is not considered a horror film – just as many consider it a macabre mystery – one thing can be agreed upon. The movie is a landmark in American cinema. The heroine of the story, Marion Crane, was in a frantic escape, physical and psychological. She couldn't decide whether or not she should return the money, and end her road to a new life – and possibly a new start. She soon found herself showering at the Bates Motel. As written in the book, "Mary started to scream, and then the curtains parted further and a hand appeared, holding a butcher knife. It was a knife that, a moment later, cut off her scream. And her head." It was this scene in the book that Hitchcock wanted to film. Certainly he spent more time preparing shots and filming than any other scene in the movie, but reading was a theater of the mind and Hitchcock had a vision.

The completed manuscript was entitled *Psycho* and published by Simon & Schuster in the summer of 1959. Apparently advanced copies were sent out to a few movie studios and producers. Some rejected the novel commenting that it was too graphic to film. But in April of that same year, an agent representing the Music Corporation of America (MCA) made an offer for the book. After negotiation, the screen rights were sold for $9,000. After the publisher and agent took their cut, author Robert Bloch was left with $6,750 before taxes. Bloch's contract with the publisher did not include royalties if sold to Hollywood, a mistake he would later regret. Bloch recalled with a sigh, "I learned that Psycho had been bought by Mr. Alfred Hitchcock."

In July of 1959, *North by Northwest* premiered at the United Artists Theater in Chicago. Filmed in glorious color and in VistaVision, this grand-scale epic cost about three million to make, and became a financial success. Cinema goers were asking "what's next?" and what they got was a low-budget, black and white mystery, almost a complete turn-around from Hitchcock's last picture. But why low budget? Could the master of suspense have anticipated a box office dud? Maybe. Hitchcock knew the shower scene would shock audiences, but whether this scene alone or the entire movie would become a success or not, remained to be seen – even to Hitchcock.

"It was an experiment in this sense," Hitchcock explained to Truffaut. "Could I make a feature film under the same conditions as a television show? I used a complete television unit to shoot it very quickly. The only place where I digressed was when I slowed down the murder scene, the cleaning-up scene, and the other scenes that indicated anything that required time. All of the rest was handled in the same way that they do it in television."

Referred to as "Production 9401," Robert Bloch was among the writers considered by Hitchcock to adapt *Psycho* for the screen. MCA agents told the director that Bloch was unavailable, but the author stated years later that this was not true. Instead, Hitchcock selected James P. Cavanagh, who had written many teleplays for *Alfred Hitchcock Presents*. Dissatisfied with his first draft, Hitchcock paid the writer off and went in search of someone else.* By someone's suggestion, Hitchcock met and hired Joseph Stefano, a musician and screenwriter, to adapt the novel.

"I knew from the very first day that I met Hitchcock, that he was going to shoot it with his TV company at Universal," Stefano recalled. "That was his plan because one of his very big intents with this movie was to do it for a million dollars or under. And one of the ways he expected to accomplish that was by using a company, that was already in place, and had been doing his television show for a long time, so we just swung right into Universal. I don't think he ever imagined shooting the film anywhere else."

Stefano's original ideas and conceptions touched base with the director, and a screenplay took form. Only one draft was really written, with alterations and cuts made as filming progressed. Perhaps another of Hitchcock's fancies was for Norman to be a normal,

* Hitchcock paid Cavanagh $7,166 on July 27, 1959, to be exact.

complacent, everyday man who lived, breathed and worked in the ordinary world we lived in. A rigid policy that had been explored on his television program, too numerous to mention. Perhaps that's why Hitchcock didn't want a Norman Bates as Bloch described in his novel.

Herbert Coleman, who co-produced the last four Hitchcock pictures, didn't like the way the rough ideas for *Psycho* were turning out, so he left to pursue his own career as a producer and director, which he would get to do during the final two seasons of *The Alfred Hitchcock Hour*. As a producer, Hitchcock was on his own. With four years of experience, Shamley Productions never got involved with any of Hitchcock's theatrical pictures, left to fend for themselves in the television medium. "It was made with the same television crew that made the show," producer Gordon Hessler recalled, "so he made that in a very short space of time. Bob Bloch, who is a very famous short story writer, came up with this very pasty, B-picture story, but Joseph Stefano, who wrote the screenplay, did a wonderful job. It was a very modern and dangerous kind of film, far away from any of Hitch's concepts, which were kind of fairy-tale suspense stories."

Hitchcock arranged for a shooting schedule of thirty days, and a budget between $800,000 to $900,000 to make. This dollar figure was more than four half-hour television episodes put together, and the shooting schedule ten times longer than the average half-hour production. Eva Marie Saint, who starred in *North by Northwest*, was considered for the lead, but in the end, Janet Leigh snatched up the offer to play Marion Crane. Much of the cast consisted of television actors, many of whom previously appeared on Hitchcock's program. Martin Balsam, John McIntire, Mort Mills, and of course, Vera Miles, who starred in the premiere episode of *Alfred Hitchcock Presents*.

Hitchcock himself would make his brief cameo walking outside the office, early in the movie. "We both felt it should be early in the movie, in order not to disturb the pull of the story line," Joseph Stefano recalled, "because he said people wait for it and he didn't want them waiting too long and having their mind on that, so we got it over with after the opening scene. He's standing there with the cowboy hat on, near the office where Marion works. I wasn't sure where it was going to be and he told me that he wanted it early on, so it happened after the hotel room opening, as the audience took a breath. Oh, I had a wonderful idea at the time, and he thought it was hysterical. In the opening shot, the helicopter view of the city, to have him sunning on a roof. I said why don't we have you sunning on a roof and he laughed. [laughs] But it was really part of his celebrity as well as a director and he knew he had to get it over with."

Like the teleplays he filmed before, Hitchcock played on the audience's psychology. We, the audience, feel for the Marion Crane character, even though she did wrong stealing from her employer. When the brutal shower scene occurs, we are shocked and disturbed. After all, does the audience not feel tense as the police officer follows Marion? And only after Marion's death, do we start to feel for Norman, who in the act of covering up the crime, tenses as the car, sinking in the mud, suddenly pauses for just a moment. Who should the audience feel for? The embezzler? The murderer? These concepts were already explored on the television series, especially the episodes directed by Hitchcock himself. How surprising the audience is in favor for Barbara Bel Geddes in "Lamb to the Slaughter."

"When I read the screenplay, I was thrilled," said Janet Leigh, "because it was so much better than the novel. The character of Marion was so thoroughly gone into and researched that it made my role a more interval part. She was so important in the first part of the movie that when she leaves, the audience was just struck with shock. I was stunned when I first saw it. I had no idea that it was going to have that kind of an effect on me, and on the audience in the screening room. Of course, we didn't know how the larger audiences would feel, but I can tell you that it had an extremely horrific imprint on my mind and on the people who first saw it on the screening."

Hitchcock contended, as he discussed his alleged monstrosity, that the violence in his television scripts and films were largely in the minds of the audience. He declared that the scene in which a young woman was done in with a knife in a shower (and Arbogast's murder), was the only violence in it. Anthony Perkins, contrary to belief, was not the attacker in that horrific scene. "I've been taking the rap for that sequence for twenty years now, but that's not me behind the curtain," he explained during the AFI Salute to Hitchcock, in 1979. "I was in New York that day rehearsing a Broadway show. And that scene, the credit for that act, belongs to my stand-in, Burt, and from now on, he can take the rap for it."

Still, *Psycho* would not – and could not – have been the film it was, artistically, commercially or psychologically, without having the precedent of five years of *Alfred Hitchcock Presents*. The television show had brought the director such enormous popularity that *Psycho* could be, and was, sold largely on the basis of his television personality. There is even a now-famous *Psycho* trailer, with Hitchcock conducting the camera on a tour of the (cleaned-up) Bates motel and house. This short little script was actually penned by *Alfred Hitchcock Presents* contributor, James Allardice. And from that trailer alone, (which showed barely a scene of the actual movie), viewers went to the theater expecting something they watched every Sunday evening at 9:30.

Recordings for the theatre lobbies were also written by Allardice:

> *This is Alfred Hitchcock . . . We trust that the presence of a special policeman throughout the current engagement of Psycho will not prove annoying or frightening. Personally, they scare me to death. Actually, he merely represents the theatre management, who have been instructed to make certain that no one is seated after the picture begins.*

> *This is Alfred Hitchcock . . . Having lived with Psycho since it was a gleam in my camera's eye, I now exercise my parental rights in revealing a number of significant facts about this well-eh—uh slightly extraordinary entertainment. I must warn you that Psycho was designed to be as terrifying as possible. Do not, however, heed the false rumor that it will frighten the moviegoer speechless. We do want your friends to come too.*

The audience was not the only one being tested. Hitchcock tried his own brand of power against the movie critics as well, by establishing strict rules and agreements. The largest of course, was that audiences only see the film from the start, and he ordered theaters not to admit people after the movie began. Another asked film critics not reveal the ending. This made the patrons more eager to see the picture, but the critics despised. So much so, that bad reviews were written for the purpose of denouncing the film, claiming it was a waste of money, and a bomb for Hitchcock. Perhaps it was the negative reviews that tempted audiences all the more, and created longer lines.

The production code was also against certain scenes. "Hitchcock sent me to argue with them," Stefano recalled, "as he just thought I would be able to defend the screenplay because I had written it. A lot of it was just very weird stuff. You know, they didn't want me use the word 'transvestite' and I said, 'But that's a scientific and medical word. A psychological word.' And they seemed to think it was some kind of slang about homosexuals and I said, 'Well, I don't think anyone has ever called a homosexual a transvestite' if they didn't want to wear women's clothes. So they argued with us for a very long time. They didn't want us to use the toilet, and they certainly didn't want us to have her throw anything in the toilet and they had a stink about having her flush the toilet . . . But that was the first time a toilet ever appeared on the screen and I understood their position. But I also explained to them that the need to see these things has to do with my feeling that without them, the audience might not be as conscious of the fact that somebody has been murdered. And I kind of sized with them and said 'Too many movies are showing murders as if they don't mean anything.' And my real intention was to upset the audience."

"As Hitchcock did with *Psycho*, he put on a motion picture for no reason other than to be horrific," critiqued Arch Oboler, writer, producer and director of psychological science-fiction films. "It had no saving graces, it showed no new fascists of anything, and that I say is irresponsibility. It is very simple for a person like myself to be horrific, just for the sake of being horrible. And I can ad-lib a dozen situations of that sort. So when you take an impossibility and call it a probability, you're hitting below the audience's belt. As I remember seeing *Psycho*, in Toronto, I walked out of the theater and said to Mrs. O, what I've said now about it, and I said 'This will trigger off all the psychos around.' And sure as I'm sitting here it happened. The next morning in the Canadian papers, a man had stabbed someone through a shower curtain, and stated that he had seen it done in the motion pictures and wanted the thrill."

"When *Psycho* was made, a man was arrested for murder in Los Angeles and he confessed to killing three women," recalled Hitchcock. "The last murder he committed, he said, was influenced by the fact, that he had just seen *Psycho*. So naturally the newspapers got on to me and asked for my comment. And I said, 'what film did he see when he murdered the second woman, and am I to assume that when he murdered the first woman, he had just finished drinking a glass of milk?' You see, people always generalize and of course it's the sick mind that is affected by these things. You know, people, to me when they complain, let's say about *Psycho*, they lack the sense of humor that I had to have when I made it. Because you couldn't make a picture like *Psycho* without your tongue and your cheek. Because you know people are going to scream. I'm no different from the man who built the switch-back railway, and says, 'I'm going to make this first dip a pretty good one. You listen to them scream.' " *

Still, any producer in Hollywood who turned down the novel, or thought that Hitchcock was out of his mind when he began filming the picture, probably had second thoughts after the money began flowing in. As for Hitchcock himself, both the TV series and *Psycho*, together, made him a very rich man. In 1964, Hitchcock sold the rights to the series, as well as to *Psycho*, which his Shamley company had also produced, to MCA in exchange for approximately 150,000 shares of MCA stock, a deal which made him the company's third-largest shareholder. The dominant figure in the public's mind, who hosted a weekly TV series, was a wealthy TV host.

"I was friends with Hitch, and I had a wonderful relationship with him," recalled Virginia Darcy, who not only supplied the hair styles for *Psycho*, but also for *The Alfred Hitchcock Hour*. "He was really a fantastic man, with a lot of power but never abused that. He knew what he wanted and he wanted to make absolutely sure that everything was set up ahead of time. Free storyboard. He was doing that before they started using the same technique for commercials. He worked with his editor, who was always on the set, the entire time, so he didn't make a lot of scenes where he had to cut them and run a lot of scenes where he didn't need it. Because they edited it as they shot. He did a few until he got them right, but I never saw him do the same shot ninety ways. He always knew the right angle."

"Hitch would always have a wrap-up party after filming completed," continued Darcy. "The production people that were running the place would say, 'you know, you're running over schedule' so they would have a wrap-up party, and then filming would last another month, which we would call post-production! [laughs] He'd tell people that we're done filming, because we already had the wrap-up party, and that we were then working on post-production. Hitch was just wonderful to work with. He hired you because you knew how to do your job and God help you because if you didn't know your job, you were fired. I mean that's all there was to it."

The *Psycho* house built on the Universal lot, was featured in a few episodes of *Alfred Hitchcock Presents* and *The Alfred Hitchcock Hour*, not for homage, but as a cost factor for production. The house, of course, would be disguised so the television audience would not familiarize themselves with the structure, used in multiple shots ["The Schwartz Metterklume Method" and "An Unlocked Window"]. This same house would also appear in "Masquerade," an episode of television's *Thriller*, hosted by Boris Karloff, also filmed on the same Universal lot. (On a side note: the same house owned by Vandamm near the end of *North by Northwest* was featured in an episode of television's *Peter Gunn*.)

As for Robert Bloch, whose novel made the director a lot of money – not the author – *Alfred Hitchcock Presents* began featuring adaptations of Bloch's stories in March of 1960, during the program's fifth season. Bloch himself would begin adapting stories for the series, and one of them, "A Home Away From Home," became a season opener for *The Alfred Hitchcock Hour*. "I am reminded of an interview once given by Robert Bloch, the able young man who wrote *Psycho*, a film which I trust you may have seen," Hitchcock has often been quoted. "Mr. Bloch also writes excellent short stories of terror and fantasy and when asked if he felt

* A Film Profile: Interview by Philip Jenkinson, BBC (approx. 1966)

the type of story he wrote had any effect on him personally, he said 'Oh, no, I have the heart of a small boy . . . I keep it in a jar on my desk.' "

It was television's good fortune to have had Hitchcock host and occasionally direct, if only as a script editor, for ten years. It was television's bad fortune never to have had him at his best. Thankfully he took that television transition to the big screen for one brief moment.

THE HITCHCOCK YOU NEVER SAW

A few years after *Alfred Hitchcock Presents* went off the air, reruns began airing on local stations, with a slightly different Hitchcock. Newly filmed introductions were hosted by Hitchcock himself – in color! These new hostings were interlaced with the original black and white dramas, and many of them were episodes Hitchcock himself directed, as evident upon reading the examples below. This was probably the only time Hitchcock's hostings were filmed in color.

Good evening. Of late I have grown weary of being a sex symbol, and have decided to return to television. I remind you that before I pose for that famous photograph in the centerfold of 'that' magazine, I was known as a man of mystery and suspense. To re-establish my reputation as a man of intrigue, join me as I bring you this story. Notice that I do so, while fully clothed.

Good evening. Are you aware that a good mystery will never show signs of age? A few years ago I presented some television programs, seasoned with mystery and suspense. And many of you found them diverting. It occurred to me that you might enjoy them again. In a moment, one of those ageless stories, brought to you – thanks to a rigid diet – by an ageless director.

Good evening. My astrologer tells me that there's a right and wrong time for everything. Since Mercury is in the house of Venus, now is a profusious time, for the retelling of tales of mystery and suspense. Do not defy your horoscope. The stars tell me you are tuned in perfectly for the tale now coming up. Which will be introduced by my younger brother.

Good evening. It is a rare man whose past does not return to haunt him. My past is about to catch up with me on this very show. If you are interested in watching, you will be treated to a macabre succession of murders, mysteries and crimes of passion. I freely confess my guilt. This burden of guilt I am pleased to share with you, in the program that follows immediately.

Later reruns consisted of two half-hour episodes, instead of one, so newly filmed bridges between dramas, again filmed in color, were offered to the local stations.

The adventure you have just seen was only half the menu I have planned for you. Being a gourmet of the bizarre, I can assure you that our next story will delight your palate. Incidently, bizarre should not be confused with bazaar, which is a place of commerce. This television station, by a strange coincidence, is a place of commerce. I trust you can hold your breath through the commercial, when our show will be resumed.

At this moment, in television parlance, I'm a bridge. A bridge of course, is a connection between the place where you were, and the place you are going to. Underneath could be a chasm, a stream, an abyss . . . you have just been in the land of mystery and suspense. After bridging a stream of sponsored messages, you will reach the terrafirma of our second episode. Happy watching.

(Photo courtesy of Photofest.)

Filmed promotions were also shot in color, commercials with Hitchcock asking the viewers to stay tuned to the same station, for an up-coming episodes listed on the station's schedule.

Good evening. I have returned to television to prove a point. We have some stories to tell you. Stories that deal with suspense, mystery and the macabre. The point I wish to prove is that you will be caught up in the frightening mood of this tale, despite it's introduction by such a cheerful person as myself. So stop that chuckling and watch for 'Alfred Hitchcock Presents' tonight.

Good evening. Film festivals are much in vogue this days. They have become quite a popular pasttime. It occurred to me that it might be enjoyable to have one of my own. I have blackmailed this station into reshowing some of my favorite little jems of crime and punishment. Tonight we offer the crime on 'Alfred Hitchcock Presents,' and leave the punishment to you.

Different introductions were filmed for afternoon reruns (thus the allusions to housekeeping tasks). These new introductions were filmed in black and white, not color, and like all the other alternatives listed above, no reference to the specific title of the drama was spoken.

(Hitchcock ironing) *Good afternoon ladies, and any gentlemen who may be lingering. Just make yourselves comfortable. We shall begin in a moment. Today we are bringing you our television album. 'Pictures to Iron By.' Together with a few long-playing commercials. I wish to show you that murder, like romance, can flourish as well in the daylight, as in night. It's all a wonder of one's attitude. As you know, this is part of a series. I have three other towels just like it. And now for our program. Naturally we shall steadfastly maintain our customary policy. Justice to all criminals, but no mercy to the sponsor. The wisdom of this double standard, will be demonstrated by the following.*

And then the closer:

(shirt is stiff as a board) *That concludes the fictional segment of our entertainment. There is one serious hazard to ironing while watching an engrossing story. You occasionally over-starch. Don't you find that so? While I contemplate this phenomena, suppose you inspect our final advertisement, following which, I shall still be here. After all, women's work is never done – even when a man is doing it.* (commercial break) *Well, I can always use it for a hockey stick. By the way, in the interest of speed, I've decided to modernize. I'm converting my steam iron into diesel. That concludes today's ironing. Tune in next time for another story, more commercials, and some household chores. Until then, good day.*

(Hitchcock drinking from a cup) *Good afternoon fellow sufferers. And welcome to another thirty-minute break. Between the dark and the daylight, when the night is beginning to lower, comes a pause in the day's occupation which is known as the children's hour. With that in mind, perhaps we should all rest up, in order to be ready for it when it comes. I realize that a sink full of dishes may be beckoning, windows may be crying to be washed, or floors to be waxed. But be strong. Resist the temptation to work. Slip off your shoes, loosen your girdle, and flee with me to the marvelous magic world of commercials. Who knows? We may also see a story.*

And then the closer:

I simply couldn't sit still another minute. I had to get to work. I'm sure you know the feeling. I'm equally sure that when the house is empty, and no one is watching, you ladies occasionally use the bannister as a means of getting from place to place more speedily. Naturally, I do to. I shall continue this conversation in a moment. I hope. (commercial break; sitting down on a handrail) *That was exhilarating. The somersault at the end was especially thrilling. I'm sorry that commercial couldn't have been, for I think you would have enjoyed watching. This concludes today's matinee. I hope you will join us next time. Until then, good day.*

COLLECTIBLES

In 1999, with the centennial celebration of Alfred Hitchcock's birthday, Parker Brothers released a special edition of CLUE, the famed detective game invented in 1944 by Anthony Pratt, a solicitor's clerk. (Pratt's wife designed the game board, which is still used today.) Since the game's introduction in the United States in 1949, over fifty million CLUE board games have been sold world-wide. With its six characters, six weapons and nine rooms, the game offers a potential of 324 different murder combinations. Parker Brothers released an updated version of the game, replacing the names of the characters (Professor Plum and Colonel Mustard, etc.) with the names of fictional characters from Hitchcock's movies. Hitchcock himself appeared in the cover of the box, and this edition sold extremely well. But collectibles featuring the image of Alfred Hitchcock have been sold for decades.

With the exception of paperback anthologies that bore Alfred Hitchcock's name, his image primarily rested in the pages of trade papers. Shortly after *Alfred Hitchcock Presents* premiered on television, his image began appearing on a variety of products, and his portrait graced the covers of magazines, sheet music and LP record labels. Merchandising was one way the sponsors were able to cash in on the pudgy-director's image. The more popularity, the better. Even today, t-shirts and mouse pads are made and sold daily. In August of 1998, the United States Post Office issued a stamp featuring the famous Hitchock profile, and his silhouette.* It would seem fans just cannot get enough. But the oldies are the goodies and with four decades since the series left the air, merchandise continues to appear on the world-wide-web every week. On-line auctions and mail order catalogs offer boxed editions of videos with Hitchcock offerings. His early British films have since gone into the public domain and can be found in almost any video store. It could take an entire book to document every Hitchcock collectable made, and a method of offering updated supplements, but for this book, we'll just cover *Alfred Hitchcock Presents*, and collectables relating to the television series.

One of the most popular Hitchcock collectables is the boardgame. Billed on the front as "Alfred Hitchcock Presents WHY," this mystery game required real thinking, planning and memory. A portrait of Hitchcock's face graced the cover, with a quote "It's A Mystery to Me." Issued by the Milton Bradley Company of Springfield, Illinois, in 1958, this game was one of many examples of television programs the Milton Bradley Company attempted to cash in on. "WHY" was commended by the consumer service bureau of *Parents Magazine*, and publicly guaranteed by *Good Housekeeping*.

Written on the inside of the box cover, with a copy of Alfred Hitchcock's signature: *"One stormy night, long ago, six people, dressed in masquerade costumes were coming home from a party. They took shelter in my old house and haven't been heard from since. Unfortunately their ghosts are still haunting the place. This is 'why' I asked all of you private eyes to come here today – and the person who can solve the mystery will be greatly rewarded."*

The object of the game is for each player (2 to 4) to roll the dice, and move across the game board appropriately. Each time someone entered a room in the haunted house, they gathered a game card, consisting of either a weapon, a ghost, or a piece of Hitchcock's shadow. The first one to collect all four parts of a weapon, a ghost and all six parts of Hitchcock, plus the one "It's a Mystery to Me" card, wins. The instructions that accompanied the game, also offered a more difficult alternative, in which everyone plays until all the cards are gathered. Then, each specific card is given a value: One complete ghost is $500; a complete Hitchcock is $1,000. Whoever holds the largest reward wins.

Just for fun, the four playing pieces each had a detective name, accompanying a comic rendition of the detective. Dick Crazy, Sergeant Monday, Charlie Clam and Sherlock Bones. For added fun, some of the game cards listed "no clue," just to irritate the players.

In 1961, Milton Bradley re-released the same board game, only with a different cover on the box, the roof top of a haunted house and Hitchcock's shadow in the moon. This time, "Alfred Hitchcock Presents" was not billed. Instead, the game was just labeled "WHY: Presented by Alfred Hitchcock." In 1967, Milton Bradley re-released the board game a third (and final) time. Now billed as "Alfred Hitchcock: WHY Mystery Game," this box lid

* This profile silhouette that Hitchcock himself designed, and "walked into" in the beginning of the television episodes, was laser cut in the upper left corner of each stamp, not printed!

featured a picture of Hitchcock holding a sign reading: "A fascinating game that requires real thinking, planning and memory."

(The various Hitchcock boardgames. Photos courtesy of Tim Daley.)

In 1989, due to recent showings of the newly-filmed *Alfred Hitchcock Presents* episodes, The John Hansen Company, Inc. in Anaheim, California, released an adult party game which allowed up to eight players to participate in a "live" action mystery. Copyrighted by the Alfred Hitchcock Trust and licensed by the Merchandising Corporation of America, Inc., this game was supposed to be the first of many adult party games, but remained the only. The game itself required eight players, each to assume a different role. Two tables, two candles, eight chairs or bar stools, and drinks and Victorian pub fare were required for everyone attending. Postcards were included in the game, so that the host could invite the guests of their choosing. Eight nametags were included with the game, along with an audio cassette. An Alfred Hitchcock Detective Award is also included for the winner of the game. When the guests arrive, they are each handed a copy of the script, and settling down at the table, an audio cassette with Hitchcock's voice is heard, welcoming them to an evening of the unexplained. Which is exactly what the game is called, "The Unexplained."

The cassette opened with the theme of the original *Alfred Hitchcock Presents* series, followed by an awful Alfred Hitchcock sound-alike: "Good evening ladies and gentlemen. How do you do? My name is Alfred Hitchcock and I am your director this evening. Thank you for accepting my invitation to audition in my new movie, *The Unexplained.*" Hitchcock then introduces the cast, played by the guests, by name, occupation, and personalities.

Sadly, once the game is played, the solution has been given and cannot easily be played again (but it

(Photos courtesy of Tim Daley.)

could with a little creativity). This game was a one-time enjoyment, much like audience participation during a murder play on stage. The scripts were so cleverly written that even shy actors could shine. During the game, there is a "group psychic reading" that provided clues to the identity of the murderer, the motive, and the weapon. Sold in some markets for as much as $60.00 today, the initial on-shelf price in 1989 was $25.00. Most people just threw the game away after it was played, so finding these collector items in mint condition is not as easy as the old Milton Bradley boardgames.

Pan-Musik, Ltd., located in London, England, released sheet music during the early sixties entitled "Havana Merry-Go-Round," featuring the theme song from *Alfred Hitchcock Presents*, composed by Melvyn Leonard for a solo piano. The famed Hitchcock silouette graced the cover. Decca Records also released a small 45 RPM record featuring the same theme song, performed and recorded by Cyril Stapleton and his Orchestra. This small 45 is very hard to find and a treasure among many collectors.

One of the more frequently-seen albums is the 78 LP, "Alfred Hitchcock Presents: Ghost Stories for Young People." Released in the early sixties by Wonderland Records (Record #89), a division of the A.A. Records company, the album was originally based on an idea submitted by Jonny Shimkin, who encouraged the record company to release an LP for young children, offering short horror stories hosted by Alfred Hitchcock. Each side of the record contains three chilling ghost stories. Side A featured "The Haunted and the Haunters," "The Magician," and "Johnny Takes a Dare." Side B featured "The Open Window" (a special adaptation of the short story by Saki), "The Helpful Hitchhiker," and "Jimmy Takes Vanishing Lessons" (based on the story of the same name by Walter R. Brooks). John Allen, who wrote and adapted the six stories, also narrated the stories.

The record started with the ever-familiar "Funeral March of a Marionette" as Hitchcock himself opened: "How do you do boys and girls. My name is Alfred Hitchcock, and I am delighted to find that you believe in ghosts, too. After all, they believe in you, so it is only common courtesy to return the favor. As a matter of fact, I tell them 'human' stories all the time and they enjoy them immensely. Now of course, the best way to listen to ghost stories is with the lights out. There is nothing like a dark room to attract ghosts. And you may like to have some of our mutual friends come and listen with you. Are the lights out? Good. Doors closed? Blinds drawn? Excellent. Don't worry about the ghosts getting in. They can slither through keyholes and under doors, you know. . ."

Hitchcock was heard between each story, giving the same dead-pan deliveries he told on television. On the record, he was unsuccessfully attempting to fix a leaky water pipe, then trying to bail out as the room filled with water. At the end of side A, Hitchcock reminded the listeners to turn over the record, where on the second side, he continued to solve his dilemma. This record was later re-issued for another generation of younger listeners, in 1979.

Perhaps the most entertaining was the second vinyl album designed to cash in on the television program, "Alfred Hitchcock Presents: Music to be Murdered By." Released by Imperial Records in 1958 (Record #12005), the LP was later put under license to London Records (UK) Limited. Again, Hitchcock himself hosted, but this time as the conductor of an orchestra. James Allardice wrote the text for Hitchcock, and all of the music was arranged and conducted by Jeff Alexander.

"How do you do, ladies and gentlemen . . . my name is Alfred Hitchcock and this is 'Music to be Murdered By.' It is more music in a jugular vein and I hope you like it. Our record requires only the simplest of equipment. An audio phonograph needle, a four-inch speaker, and a .38 caliber revolver. Naturally, the record is long playing, even though you may not be. So why don't you relax, lean back and enjoy yourself, until the coroner comes . . ." Hitchcock made the usual dry remarks between each and every song, and never failed to make at least one comment about how this record would not be interfered by sponsor breaks. (Hitchcock did take time to support his local mortician and dedicate a number for him.)

The featured music was: "Music to be Murdered By" (an original piece by Jeff Alexander); "Lover, Come Back To Me" (Romberg & Hammerstein); "Suspicion" (Alexander); "Body and Soul" (Green, Hayman, Sauer and Eyton); "After You've Gone" (Layton & Creamer); "I'll Walk Alone" (Styne & Cahn); "I'll Never Smile Again" (Ruth Lowe); "I Don't Have a Ghost of a Chance With You" (Crosby, Washington, and Young); "Funeral March of a Marionette" (without a doubt); and finally "The Hour of Parting" (Spolianski & Kahn).

(Photo courtesy of Tim Daley.)

"I trust that everyone is enjoying the music," Hitchcock remarked near the end of the album. "As the title of the album suggests, this was meant for your listening pleasure, while you are being 'done in.' However, anyone may listen. We have no intention to discriminate. After all, the murderer has as much right to enjoy himself as his victim." Hitchcock even suggested that if one was to turn the volume up real loud, it could drown out death-defying screams. This vinyl record was also reissued in 1980, as a DRG Recording Release (#5183) and a few months after as an eight-track, part of the Book-of-the-Month Records program in 1981.

Over the decades custom computer games have been made featuring Alfred Hitchcock, his profile, and the show's theme song. One such computer disc offers a roulette wheel and featured a limited release in Japan. During the early 1980s, when decorative pins were a hot trend to apply to a shirt or jacket, Hitchcock's profile made the grade when the American Film Institute issued a series of pins with the Hitchcock image. Even custom collectables have become prized possesions. A collector in Ohio makes custom refrigerator magnets and made the one of *Alfred Hitchcock Presents*.

One of the most oddest collectibles is soap. During the early sixties, Ivory Soap began manufacturing small bars, and offering them for hotels to place, complimentary, in the bathrooms for their guests. The white wrapper featured "Alfred Hitchcock Presents" on the front, and Hitchcock's silhouette on the back.

During the late 1950s, the Granada Company released matchbooks featuring the silhouette of Alfred Hitchcock on both the front and backside of the matchbook. Made in England and manufactured by Bryant & May's Safety Matches, this giveaway was also tossed away once the matches were all used, making this collector item very hard to find, and valuable.

In 1973, MCA/Universal released a promotional year-long calendar and mailed them complimentary to television stations across the country. The back of the wall calendar listed dozens of television programs MCA/Universal had to offer along the lines of syndication packages (*McHale's Navy, The Munsters, Ironside* and *Leave it to Beaver* to name a few). Printed on a single 8 ½ by 11 photo quality paper, the top half of the calender featured a publicity photo of Alfred Hitchcock, holding in his arms, a reproduction of his head (from the episode "One More Mile to Go). The MCA/TV globe logo was also imprinted on the calender, with the words "268 half hours, 93 hours." These calendars are snatched up by collectors, making the value of them worth a considerable sum. Even promotional sheets, posters created for the same purpose as the calendars, (new ones advertising the new USA network series of *Alfred Hitchcock Presents*), have been bought up by collectors. Eight by ten glossy photos are purchased by many dealers around the country. and often autographed at horror, sci-fi and film conventions by the stars who appeared on the program.

In 1986, MCA Home Video released a three-episode video of the original *Alfred Hitchcock Presents*, due to the recent success of the NBC and USA revival. The episodes offered were: "Banquo's Chair," "Lamb to the Slaughter" and "The Case of Mr. Pelham." This video, however, offered the episodes slightly edited, because all the remarks against the sponsor were deleted by a simple electronic fade out to the next scene!

In 1987, MCA Home Video released a Laserdisc featuring the same three episodes, "Lamb to the Slaughter," "The Case of Mr. Pelham," "Banquo's Chair" and an additional episode, "Back for Christmas." A Japanese laserdisc release included the episode "Mr. Blanchard's Secret," "Back for Christmas," and others, with Japanese subtitles on the screen!

In 1995, Goodtimes Home Video released a four-episode video featuring three more Hitchcock-directed episodes, "Dip in the Pool," "The Horseplayer," "Man From the South" (directed by Norman Lloyd) and "Mrs. Bixby and the Colonel's Coat."

Later that year (1995), Goodtimes Home Video released another four-episode compilation, all directed by the master himself, including: "Revenge," "Breakdown," "The Crystal Trench" and "The Perfect Crime."

Hollywood Select Video (now known as Timeless Video), released a double feature, "The Sorcerer's Apprentice" and "The Cheney Vase," with slightly edited versions. Goodtimes Home Video released a single-episode video, also containing "The Sorcerer's Apprentice," thankfully uncut this time.

Universal Pictures released three tapes each containing three hour-long episodes of *The Alfred Hitchcock Hour* in 1999. Volume One included "I Saw the Whole Thing," "The Black Curtain" and "A Tangled Web." Volume Two included "Bonfire," "Diagnosis: Danger" and "Run for Doom." Volume Three included "Death and the Joyful Woman," "Captive Audience" and "Hangover."

A remastered collector's edition of Hitchcock's movies, including *Rope* and *Rear Window* (among others) was released in the spring of 2001. Offered in two eight-disc compilation packages, two of the sixteen DVDs offered eight of the master's directorial efforts on television, in two so-called "Best of TV" compilations. Volume One included "Revenge," "Breakdown," "Wet Saturday" and "Mr. Blanchard's Secret." The second volume included "Poison," "The Perfect Crime," "Dip in the Pool" and "One More Mile to Go."

Many companies have been releasing music tracks from Hitchcock's motion pictures, and a few have been labeling them "Alfred Hitchcock Presents," even though the musical compact discs have nothing to do with the television series. The theme song itself has been printed on more LP record labels and compact discs than anyone can count, even when the records do not even have anything to do with Alfred Hitchcock, his movies, or the television show.

Old back issues of *TV Guide* have become hot items on the internet (especially eBay and other on-line auctions). These issues have become quite valuable, and there's even a price guide published on a regular basis, offering statistics and values of back issues. Alfred Hitchcock himself graced the cover of at least four issues. (One only featured an artist's rendition of the pudgy director. The issue pictured on the left is from March 25, 1961.)

Reprinted with permission from the TV Guide Magazine Group, Inc., publisher of *TV Guide* magazine. © March 1961, TV Guide, Inc. *TV Guide* is a trademark of TV Guide Magazine Group, Inc.

Comic books of *Psycho* have been printed, the Robert Bloch novel has gone into more reprints than anyone can possibly count, and even do-it-yourself model replicas of the *Psycho* house have entered the market.

When producers at NBC and USA began filming new episodes during the mid-late 1980s, most of the production crew each received a black jacket with the words "Alfred Hitchcock Presents" sewn on the front, and Hitchcock's profile sewn on the back. Printed by Starwears in Los Angeles, California, these jackets were very limited and never released in the commercial market. There are also black and white *Alfred Hitchcock Presents* T-shirts, which can be purchased at the CBS Store in New York, licensed through the Alfred Hitchcock Trust.

AWARDS

Just as Alfred Hitchcock never won an Oscar for any of his films directly, he never won an Emmy – the highest prize awarded for production of a television program. Here below is a selection of the honors awarded or nominated for *Alfred Hitchcock Presents* or *The Alfred Hitchcock Hour*.

1955 nominations
* *Alfred Hitchcock Presents* was nominated for an Emmy in 1955 for Best Action or Adventure Series, losing out to *Disneyland*.
* Alfred Hitchcock was nominated for an Emmy for Best Master of Ceremonies or Program Host (male or female) for a Television Series in 1955, he lost to Perry Como.
* Hitchcock was nominated for an Emmy for Best Director in a Televised Film Series in 1955, most notably, "The Case of Mr. Pelham." He lost out to Nat Hiken for the CBS series, *You'll Never Get Rich*.

1955 winners
* Edward W. Williams won an Emmy in 1955 for Best Editing of a Television Film, most notably the episode "Breakdown," directed by Alfred Hitchcock.
* *Look Magazine*'s Annual Television Awards listed Alfred Hitchcock as Best Director of 1955.
* *Television Almanac* awarded *Alfred Hitchcock Presents* as Best Mystery Program for Television in 1955.

1956 nominations
* Alfred Hitchcock was nominated for an Emmy in 1956 as Best Male Personality.
* *Alfred Hitchcock Presents* was nominated for an Emmy in 1955 for Best Television Series (half hour or less), losing out to CBS's *The Phil Silvers Show*.

1956 winners
* *Television Almanac* awarded *Alfred Hitchcock Presents* as Best Mystery Program for Television in 1956.
* James P. Cavanagh won an Emmy in 1956 for Best Teleplay Writing for a Television Series (half hour of less), notably "Fog Closing In."
* *Look Magazine*'s Annual Television Awards listed *Alfred Hitchcock Presents* as Best Television Series of 1956.

1957 nominations
* *Alfred Hitchcock Presents* was nominated for an Emmy in 1957 for Best Dramatic Anthology Series, but lost out to CBS's *Playhouse 90*.

1957 winners
* Robert Stevens won an Emmy in 1957 for Best Direction for a Television Series (half-hour or less), for his work on "The Glass Eye."
* *Alfred Hitchcock Presents* won the 1957 Golden Globe Award for Best Television Program.
* *Look Magazine*'s Annual Television Awards listed *Alfred Hitchcock Presents* as Best Television Series of 1957.

1958 nominations
* *Alfred Hitchcock Presents* was nominated for an Emmy in 1958 for Best Dramatic Series (less than one hour), but lost to NBC's *Alcoa-Goodyear Theatre*.
* Alfred Hitchcock was nominated for an Emmy in 1958 as Best Director, for "Lamb to the Slaughter," but lost to Jack Smight's "Eddie" on *Alcoa-Goodyear Theatre*.
* Roald Dahl was nominated for an Emmy in 1958 for Best Writing of a Single Program of a Dramatic Series (less than one hour), most notably, "Lamb to the Slaughter." He lost to Alfred Brenner and Ken Hughes in "Eddie" on NBC's *Alcoa-Goodyear Theatre*.

1958 winners
* *Alfred Hitchcock Presents* won the 1958 Golden Globe Award for Best Television Program.

1959 nominations
* John J. Lloyd was nominated for an Emmy in 1959 for Outstanding Achievement in Art Direction and Scenic Design, but lost to Ralph Berger and Frank Smith for CBS's *Westinghouse-Desilu Playhouse*.
* Edward W. Williams was nominated for an Emmy in 1959 for Outstanding Achievement in Film Editing for Television, most notably "Man From the South," but lost to Ben H. Ray and Robert L. Swanson for *The Untouchables*.

1960 nominations
* Edward W. Williams was nominated in 1960 for Outstanding Achievement in Film Editing for Television, most notably "Incident in a Small Jail." He lost to Harry Coswick, Aaron Nibley and Milton Shifman for ABC's *The Naked City*.

1960 winners
* *Television Almanac* awarded *Alfred Hitchcock Presents* as Best Mystery Program for Television in 1960.

1963 nominations
* James Bridges was nominated in 1963 for Outstanding Writing Achievement in Drama (Adaptation), most notably "The Jar." He lost to Rod Serling's "It's Mental Work" on NBC's *Bob Hope's Chrystler Theatre*.

1963 winners
* *Television Almanac* awarded *Alfred Hitchcock Presents* as Best Mystery Program for Television in 1963.

1966 winners
* Hitchcock received an Honorary Membership from the *Association of Cinematography, Television and Allied Technicians*.

1971 winners
* *British Society of Film and Television Arts* awarded Alfred Hitchcock first Honorary Membership in 1971.

Cinema en miniature: The Telefilms of Alfred Hitchcock
Written by Ulrich Rüdel.

In the autumn of 1956, <u>Cahiers du Cinema</u>, the French publication most instrumental in shaping Hitchcock's critical reputation, reported on a remarkable event[1]: "Since last November, every Sunday at 9:30 p.m. the Bristol-Myers company presents, with a signature tune adapted from Gounod ("Funeral March of a Marionette"), short films of twenty-eight minutes each, which form the show *Alfred Hitchcock Presents* . . . Two of the best episodes were those where John Williams appears as a lady killer and the one where Joseph Cotten, a big businessman paralyzed following a car accident, is declared dead and transported into the mortuary . . . " These episodes were not only presented and supervised, but also personally directed by Alfred Hitchcock. One of the most successful film directors thus embraced the new medium, limited to the visual confinements of a small screen, restricted budgets and shooting schedules. While other respected directors with careers likewise dating back to the silent days, like John Ford, paid an occasional visit to television, no-one made nearly half as many telefilms in his career as theatrical features, setting standard and style for a successful 373 episodes (includes the Hitchcock-produced programs) spanning ten years. With twenty films, about ten hours of cinematic storytelling for the small screen, Hitchcock's contribution to the medium establishes a significant, rich, yet often neglected part of his oeuvre.

A number of essays on these films have in fact been written[2], mostly focusing on the celebrity status the program achieved for Hitchcock, and on thematic similarities between his television and theatrical film work. Most notably, the transfer-of-guilt theme has been identified in a number of episodes[3], and the anticipation of key scenes of *Psycho* (1960) was noted. Furthermore *Alfred Hitchcock Presents* has also closely been linked to the other film which brackets it, the black comedy *The Trouble with Harry* (1955). Yet, as Thomas Leitch points out[4], "Given the radical differences between *The Trouble with Harry* and *Psycho*, which are virtually the two most disparate films in Hitchcock's entire oeuvre, how closely can a substantial body of work resemble both of them? And apart from the obvious differences in budget and scale, what thematic and structural differences between Hitchcock's theatrical and television films are obscured by emphasizing their similarities?" Take the basic setup of *North by Northwest* (1959) as an example. A businessman torn out of his normal life routine, the duplicity of Roger Thornhill and Kaplan – are indeed anticipated in *Alfred Hitchcock Presents*, but could anything be more different from the lavish VistaVision spy thriller than the minimalist, tense "Breakdown" or the disturbing doppelgänger thriller "The Case of Mr. Pelham"? On the other hand, apart from Vera Miles' role, *The Wrong Man* (1956) is rarely linked to the television series. Yet, does this film – besides *Psycho*, Hitchcock's only theatrical feature in black-and-white since the start of the television show – not share more, if so in a much more somber narrative tone – namely, the focus on common people, and the Hitchcock introduction for good measure? And whereas Fonda plays an innocent man suspected of a crime, not a single criminal offense is even committed in many of the telefilms.

There are exceptions to the general dismissive attitude towards the program, of course. Peter Bogdanovich treats the theatrical and the telefilms as equal in his Hitchcock filmographies[5]. As if supplementing his Hitchcock biography, John Russell Taylor wrote maybe the most balanced treatment of the telefilms, appropriately entitled "Video Noir."[6] Gene D. Phillips called them "Hitchcock's Forgotten Films"[7], and the chance to 'rediscover' them on TV and in a Munich film museum retrospective after decades of inaccessibility may explain the fresh, enthusiastic approach they received in a couple of German books published on the occasion of the Hitchcock centenary. Indeed, Hitchcock's television work should be evaluated on its own merits, as an essential chapter of his career. More than mere exercises, these films are masterly crafted visual short stories, within genre conventions that Hitchcock himself chose and established, demonstrating the *modus operandi* and providing the majority of the highlights of the program they were part of.

Filming for the small screen. Hitchcock was always open to new techniques, and to the creative energy triggered both by technical limitations, and innovations as early as the twenties. From visualizing the sound of steps by means of a glass floor in *The Lodger* (1926), to manipulating dialogue creatively in his first talkie *Blackmail* (1929). WW2 propaganda necessities resulted in Hitchcock's first couple of short films, *Bon Voyage* and *Aventure Malgache* (both 1944). These efficient, simultaneous shooting techniques were employed by him, most notably, in the courtroom sequence of *The Paradine Case* (1947). Thus, when Hitchcock started his own series in 1955, it provided him with another opportunity for technical and storytelling experiments. "As open-minded as he had been towards sound, color, 3-D and VistaVision, the Schüfftan process and the zoom, Hitchcock approached television. New techniques always appear to be welcome to him to realize new forms," wrote Munich film historian and restorer Enno Patalas[8], calling the telefilms 'Expanded Cinema.' Hitchcock told Peter Bogdanovich what appealed to him most about television work was "the challenge of speed. Most of the half-hours were shot in three or four days. [Some in just two days.] It was a complete change of pace, a different approach. It was no effort for me to do a TV show."

"People said that 'Hitchcock is too slow in order to make television. He won't be able to adapt to the pace of the recording studios.' Nonsense! I have worked equally fast when shooting *Rope*, and I even remember that we had only one camera whereas for TV, there are three or four cameras available in simultaneous use. Sure, it is difficult to shoot a scene without the possibility to stop without repetition, but in the end, one gets used to it. Television is, in a way, simplified cinema. One doesn't need complicated lighting since it won't have any effect on a twelve-inch screen. " (<u>Cahiers du Cinema</u>)

Naturally, the small screen also dictated frequent use of medium shots and close-ups, occasionally combined with voice-over techniques lifted from the golden age of radio, serving Hitchcock to focus on the protagonists like under a microscope. "Personally, I'm interested in the actors' faces since I know [full] well this is also interesting for the audience and this is what they look at first," said Hitchcock. "It is necessary to preserve the faces and especially the glance. I choose relatively short novels written by famous authors. I detest nothing more than the great dramas. which require three hours of projection time, condensed to half an hour of TV. Colossal error, fatal boredom."

"All in all the scripts are more forceful than those of my films, more concise and clear. One twenty-four minute program needs to be shot within three days, since the financial conditions do not allow us to stay with one film any longer. There is only one take per shot. It is correct that, in a normal film, I never do more than three takes, since I more and more believe in the quality of imperfection, not in the preparation or in the script, but in the interpretation. When shooting a TV film, you film a take towards the door, and the assistant asks: 'How many takes towards the door are there?' You look into the shooting plan (about 32 pages): 'There are 28 takes towards the door.' So you shoot those 28 takes one after another, from the same angle, the same composition, with the same lighting. It's kind of a challenge. What is also amusing is, that the editing is made little by little. The length of the material that has finished shooting is announced. At the third and last day, sometimes a third of the work remains to be shot, but only half has been edited. So, if you already have 16 minutes and need another 8, you take a large blue pen and you make dark cuts. There are two minutes dedicated to the advertising spots." (<u>Cahiers du Cinema</u>)

Like his theatrical features, Hitchcock had already shot the film in his mind when he arrived on the set, with a clear idea of what it should look like. "I'm a man of the movies and I think I have a strong visual sense. If I'm going to make a film, I don't have to look at the rushes every day, like an amateur going down to the drug store to see how his prints have come out. In television I just go in and shoot as I would with any ordinary movie. I don't look through the camera lens. I've got an understanding with the cameraman. Otherwise, I'd find myself saying: 'Oh, so that's what it's like'." Alfred Tennyson, then head of television production for Kenyon & Eckhart, a Hollywood advertising agency whose client, Lincoln-Mercury, sponsored the series after Bristol-Myers, observed the shooting of many later episodes on behalf of his client. "The shows that Hitchcock shot himself were terrifically organized – all the episodes were. But I saw firsthand how very clear he always made everything to his cameraman and crew. He had little sketches that he would show his cameraman. Sometimes, he would even leave the set while they shot some of the non-key sequences because he had clearly defined what should be in those shots and what they should look like. Almost the way an animator works – by doing certain key frames himself and then letting his in-betweeners or associates fill out the rest per his instructions. And everything always came out the way he wanted. No question. His people always knew exactly what to do." *

"The advantage of my show is that the husband can murder his wife and bury her in the cellar and then retribution can be dealt with at the end by me," Hitchcock said. Short stories with a "twist ending," often enough just exploring misdemeanors like cheating or cold-hearted attitude told with efficient narrative techniques, defined Hitchcock's idea of stories he couldn't do for the big screen. And "When crime is occasionally dealt with, it will be crime as practiced by ordinary people, like the fellow next door," as he explained in the episode "Mrs. Bixby and the Colonel's Coat." From traffic incidents, gossip and gambling, to murder and the grim business of corpse disposal, Hitchcock's telefilms form a kaleidoscope of stories that could happen right now, next door, much like the one Jefferies (James Stewart) observed through his *Rear Window* (1954). The success of the approach became obvious right from the start. For the first season, Hitchcock would direct as many as four episodes, bringing back, as he intended, murder to the living room.

The First Episodes. Given the director's talent and reputation, it seemed only logical to launch the show with one of his directorial entries. In "Revenge," Vera Miles – as if practicing for her role in *The Wrong Man* (1956) – stars as Elsa, a young woman who becomes victim of a rape. Unaware of her deranged mind, her husband is prompted to a cold-blooded killing upon her identifying a passing man as the offender. It has been noted that Hitchcock showed courage by choosing rape and "vigilante-justice" as subject matter for the premiere episode – but maybe, rather than subjecting the viewer to the courageous experiment, perhaps promoting Vera Miles was paramount for him.

In this show, Hitchcock's directorial techniques not only proved economical, and compatible with network restrictions, but also effective: "The rape itself is suggested visually by a shot of Elsa's inert hand clutching the crumpled carnation that she had torn from her attacker's lapel, a symbol of how her fragile spirit has been crushed by sexual aggression. "[9] Such style for directing the television plays was viewed with curiosity, and imitation. If Hitchcock filmed an episode under budget and under the time frame required, other directors of the program made sure to do the same. Although directors like Robert Altman and Harvey Hart added their own styles of cinematic direction, they still kept under budget and on schedule. "Hitchcock of course, wasn't the easiest man to work with," recalled John J. Lloyd, director of photography. "He was pretty exact and very talented and knew exactly what he was going to do, and you know, you had a meeting with him and he told us what he needed us to do and

* Source: <u>Alfred Hitchcock Presents</u> by John McCarty and Brian Kelleher, St. Martin's Press, 1985

right on – we got the opinion that we better do it the right way. He was a very difficult man to get on a first name basis with. We didn't call him Hitch, of course, but he was sort of a distant man. He wasn't mean or anything, he was just very much on preparation and I think because he might have been an art director in the beginning. He had a very visual mind, definitely." Nowhere in his television work is this more obvious than in the first episode he filmed for the series.

Joseph Cotton after the auto accident in "Breakdown." (Courtesy of Photofest)

Suspended Motion. "Breakdown" is one of the most audacious formal experiments of Hitchcock's entire career. Joseph Cotten (*Shadow of a Doubt,* 1943) stars as a cold-hearted businessman who despises people showing any signs of emotion. Trapped and paralyzed in a car accident, he has to endure being deemed dead by everyone – until finally, in the mortuary, a tear fills his eye, an outbreak of emotion that saves his life, once the coroner notices. A 'narrative experiment' is what Frank Arnold called this episode,[10]: "Following Callew's awakening, the film looks at him in a sequence of fixed brief takes, often close-ups. They are assembled in montages, reminiscent of a photo-film like Chris Marker's *La Jetée* (1962). In a somewhat longer sequence (at the moment when Callew notices the sign *City Morgue*) even the smallest facial movement of a person freezes." Interviewed by Peter Bogdanovich, Hitchcock explained this effect: "Frozen film – you optically repeat the last frame – that's how you get a still. But you must be very careful when you do frozen stuff, not to have any leaves fluttering around or any inanimate surroundings." For him, television was no less challenging than the deliberate technical limitations that he had imposed upon himself in *Lifeboat* (1944) and *Rope* (1948): "Wild [camera] angles tire the audience: in fact, television is photographic theater, nothing more. On the other hand, based on the saving possibilities, the television director can permit himself the luxury, give free rein to his artistic caprices. He can try his luck and even create poetry if that's what his heart tells him to. No more compromises." (Cahiers du Cinema) Thus, the combination of freeze-frames with radio-style voice-over (Cotten had done the same story previously on radio), resulted in "a veritable technical tour de force since the close-up of Cotten is only suspended to show what is happening around him from his paralytic's point of view" (Cahiers du Cinema). A tour de force in claustrophobic suspense.

The concept of distilling all possible suspense out of the helplessness of a virtually immobilized protagonist apparently fascinated Hitchcock – it is as close as he ever got to his dream of shooting a film in a telephone booth. Thus, he revisited and varied it twice, the first time two years later in his first one-hour teleplay, a surprising move given the expanded length. "Four O'Clock" was shot for the Hitchcock-produced anthology series *Suspicion*: "In addition to our weekly half-hour show, I'll do ten one-hour episodes," Hitchcock explained. "I'll have more time to develop character in them. One of the first stories I'll do is the Cornell Woolrich story, 'Three O'Clock.' It's about a man who makes a homemade bomb because he suspects his wife of having a lover and he's determined to blow them up, even if it means blowing up his own home. However, immediately after he's started the bomb's timing device going, two burglars break into the house, truss him up and put him in the cellar while they rob the house. Then they leave. There he is, helpless, facing his own ticking bomb and not finding the situation all that might be. In fact, he feels that's extremely doubtful it there is any future in it."* The protagonist's struggle to release himself is contrasted with the ticking clock. Unlike in "Breakdown," time is not frozen at all – quite on the contrary. Even the bug crawling along the basement window, observed by a boy who fails to report the funny sight of the tied-up man to his mother, seems to step in sync with the ticking clock. The bomb does not explode though – in a correction of the 'mistake' Hitchcock admitted to having made in *Sabotage* (1936) – but it is too late for the watchmaker and would-be killer, who has gone mad over the event.

Hitchcock's final variation of the concept was shot in 1958, again for his half-hour show. "Poison" is one out of four Roald Dahl stories Hitchcock would film for *Alfred Hitchcock Presents*. Here, the main protagonist is anything but paralyzed or tied, in fact he strives to remain motionless: Harry Pope is convinced a snake is in his bed, and he cannot move without risking death. His business partner, Timber Woods, is not quite that convinced, given the alcoholic condition of Pope, and tries to take advantage of the situation. But Harry is wrong, as Timber is to find out the fatal way.

Poe, Price and the Paranormal. Not limited to crime stories, *Alfred Hitchcock Presents* notably includes his only two works that clearly constitute fantastic films. Hitchcock had bordered on the horror genre before. In 1926, *The Lodger* explored a future staple of the horror genre, the Jack the Ripper myth (and was remade in 1944 by horror director and *Alfred Hitchcock Presents* regular John Brahm). Also (albeit surprisingly), the hidden similarities between *Shadow of a Doubt* (1943) and *Nosferatu* (1922) have been pointed out[11]. In the sixties, Hitchcock revolutionized the horror film with *Psycho* and *The Birds*, yet strictly speaking, neither belongs to the fantastic genre, lacking any clearly supernatural elements. In contrast, *Alfred Hitchcock Presents* contains both a Gothic ghost story and a variation of the doppelgänger motive – and his only collaboration with one of the great icons of horror film, Vincent Price, for good measure.

Tom Ewell plays the title role in "The Case of Mr. Pelham." Pelham is convinced, "like Poe's 'William Wilson,' that a doppelgänger would displace him from his usual roles, and goes insane. Maybe he was so to begin with and, like Francis in *The Cabinet of Dr. Caligari*

* Hitchcock quote from an interview with Pete Martin originally published in *The Saturday Evening Post* (July 27, 1957).

(1919), made up the story." (para. Patalas). In a narrative tone, "Pelham" is nonetheless intensely disturbing, offering no comforting explanation for the events of the play, but rather expanding the theme right into Hitchcock's closing remarks: a doppelgänger has taken over the host's role, too.

The eerie "Banquo's Chair" (1959) opens – with exact on-screen information on time and place, like later *Psycho* – in a Victorian mansion, with detective William Brent's (John Williams, essentially repeating his detective role from 1954's *Dial M for Murder*) plot to convict John Bedford of the murder of his aunt. By means of an intricately staged plot – the gas runs out and candles need to be lit; a dog barks like it did at the night of the crime – Bedford is made to believe his aunt's specter is back to haunt him. Since the suspected murderer is the 'victim' of detective John Williams' scheme, the audience cannot help but identify with him. Allusions to *Hamlet* and *Macbeth* help to set the stage for the expectation of the supernatural, and the soundtrack features a brief reoccurrence of the theremin, the musical instrument employed memorably in the main theme of *Spellbound* (1945) and in Hitchcock's radio play, *Once Upon a Midnight*. Thus, even before the twist end reveals the apparent ghost as such – the actress hired to play it, in fact, was late – the images of the late Miss Ferguson's apparition provide a genuinely chilling sequence.

The story construction is a fascinating and effective reversal of the often disappointing twist formula of films à la *London After Midnight* (1927) and *Mark of the Vampire* (1935), where what appeared to be supernatural events is revealed as trickery later on. Hitchcock, in contrast, used this concept inventively and successfully when *Vertigo* (1958) appears to commence as a classic melancholy ghost story. Also in this regard, "Banquo's Chair" makes instructive back-to-back viewing with a classic episode of the companion-competition show *Thriller*, which realized such a concept to chilling effect in "The Premature Burial." Based on the premise of the Poe story, it uses similar effective imagery when a man returns from the grave in what is later revealed as a scheme to expose a crime[12]. Poe was an acknowledged inspiration of the Hitchcock show, and echoes of "The Premature Burial" in particular imbue "Breakdown," with its paralyzed protagonist facing being buried alive. Yet, Poe's stories were never dramatized on *Alfred Hitchcock Presents*.

A far less agreeable detective than Mr. Brent is in the center of "The Perfect Crime" (1957), formally a thriller rather than a horror story. Then-emerging horror icon Vincent Price stars as a cross between classic sleuth and a madman.

Tom Ewell stars in "The Case of Mr. Pelham." (Ron V. Borst / Hollywood Movie Posters.)

detective Charles Courteney commits the perfect crime by killing the only man (James Gregory) able to reveal that Courteney had a wrong man executed. It has been pointed out that the twist ending – the detective ends up as a piece of pottery filling the spot in Courteney's memorabilia collection reserved for the perfect crime – seems to echo *House of Wax* (1953), the horror film that made Price a star. However, the resemblance is even closer to a film that tried to repeat its success formula, *The Mad Magician* (1954), where Price employs a bonfire for corpse disposal. and even constructs a crematorium for the same purpose. Notably, this film was directed by none other then *Alfred Hitchcock Presents* regular John Brahm.

Vincent Price's recollection on his collaboration with the "Master of Suspense" echoes what is often reported on Hitchcock's working style, in particular on television: "Yes, I did one of his TV shows, 'The Perfect Crime. You know, he's a character. Everybody knows about him, but he's a fellow who plays as much of a role as the director, as the actors do who are on the screen. It was just Jim Gregory and myself. We were the only two actors in it, actually. There were a couple of bit parts, but Hitch's whole direction to us was speed. It was two men talking about a murder, with Jim Gregory accusing me of doing it. There was one point where we looked over at Hitchcock in one of the run-throughs, and he was sound asleep, or else he was pretending to be sound asleep [laughs]. He did that all the time. He did it with Cary Grant, he did it with everybody. It was part of his routine, or his image . . . He only directed about a dozen of those TV shows himself, so when Jim and I were going to do it, we were both terribly excited. I don't think Hitchcock had ever done anything in four days in his life before this. . . . I'm glad I worked with him. . . ."[13]

From black humor to *Psycho*. Alfred Hitchcock's very particular brand of humor was not only the key ingredient for his introductions, but also for some of his own episodes. "In selecting the stories for my television program, I try to make them as meaty as the sponsor and the network will stand for. I hope to offset any tendency toward the macabre with humor. As I see it, this is a typically English form of humor . . . It's a piece with such jokes as the one about the man who was being led to the gallows to be hanged. He looked at the trap door in the gallows, which was flimsily constructed, and he asked in some alarm, 'I say, is that thing safe?' " (Pete Martin interview).

"Back for Christmas" is a comedy of corpse disposal, and a macabre version of the marriage comedy of *Rich and Strange* (1931) and *Mr. and Mrs. Smith* (1941). Hitchcock must have enjoyed the opportunity to finally realize a variation of the twist ending he originally intended for *Suspicion* (1941), here John Aysgarth (Cary Grant) was supposed to kill his wife and drop a letter describing her suspicions in detail in the mailbox, whistling merrily. Here, Herbert Carpenter (John Williams) kills his annoying significant other, buries her body in the basement, and leaves for the planned vacation, unaware that his wife has ordered the excavation of a wine cellar. A letter, though, reveals the unexpected building project to him – he will be back for Christmas after all. Sharing some very "British" sophistication and comedy talent, but not quite the glamour-star value of Cary Grant, John Williams, a favorite supporting actor of Hitchcock, was his archetypal TV lead. Here, he has a field day as sort of a seasoned Charley Chase character, whose wife propels him from one embarrassment to another. In the end, she does not cease to interfere with his plan – not even from her grave. Upon washing his hands, having committed the murder, Williams discovers that he cannot, for his wife turned the water off.

Williams returned months later, together with *Rope*'s Cedric Hardwicke, in "Wet Saturday," one of the most obvious variations of Hitchcock's transfer-of-guilt motive found in *Alfred Hitchcock Presents*. The film tracks Mr. Princey's (Hardwicke) cold-blooded and ultimately successful efforts to keep the family name clean, after his daughter has killed her lover, in a very British way: with a croquet mallet. Again the victim of circumstances in a black situation comedy. Williams has the misfortune of showing up at the wrong place and time, seeking shelter during the rainy day. Having overheard a tell-tale part of the tea conversation, he turns out not only a man who knows too much, but also an ideal subject to Hardwicke's well thought-through evidence planting.

"Mr. Blanchard's Secret," an attempted satire of *Rear Window*, is one of the few somewhat disappointing entries in Hitchcock's filmography. This episode doesn't quite work not only because *Rear Window* already handled the inherent ironic elements of the story more than adequate[14], but, worse than that, the twist ending is simply that there is no crime. Much like the formula of suspense requires a relief of tension, a concept Hitchcock only realized after ignoring it in *Sabotage* (1936), the lack of a "real" twist is disappointing. The joke is on the audience, a concept that fails here, but was proven maliciously effective and unsettling in *Psycho*, disorienting the audience rather than disappointing it.

Not merely the manipulative relationship between director and audience, but a complete key sequence of *Psycho* was anticipated in the main body of "One More Mile to Go." However, the opening scene is equally impressive: from remote, the camera approaches a house in the dark, and through the window, witnesses an escalating argument culminating in the violent death of Martha Jacoby, by the hands of her husband. With barely intelligible dialog, just by means of visuals and musical score, this sequence succeeds in conveying a story development that otherwise might have required pages of script. Hitchcock would re-use this efficient narrative technique in *Topaz* (1969). but here the result is especially haunting, adding an aura of voyeurism to the scene – as if the audience was secretly witnessing the couple's argument right through their neighbor's living room window. The husband, Sam Jacoby (David Wayne) then drags the body into his car trunk and drives around, soon to be pestered repeatedly by a police officer, thoughtfully concerned about Jacoby's broken tail light. The sequence dwells in the suspense of the impending discovery of the body, yet its carbon copy in *Psycho* is even more efficient. It is much easier for the audience to identify with a guilt-ridden secretary who has stolen money, rather than with a cold-blooded homicidal husband.

Another famous *Psycho* scene is modeled in arguably the show's best-known episode, "Lamb to the Slaughter." Pregnant Mary Maloney (Barbara Bel Geddes) kills her policeman husband with a frozen leg of lamb, after she learns about his decision to leave her. Serving a meal for the police, Mary cannot suppress a certain satisfaction at their consumption of the very murder weapon. The last shot shows her smiling much as "Mother" Norman Bates would at the very end of *Psycho*, but even surpassing the similar shot, it anticipates in terms of audience sympathy for the protagonist. On television, Hitchcock provided the actress an opportunity for a marvelously ambiguous performance. As he told *Cahiers du Cinema* earlier: "My business is not to create new stars. If certain actresses who have debuted in my films achieve fame quickly, that's purely coincidence. I like to work with new faces, as it is much more rewarding for a director to guide a newcomer rather than a capricious star. In addition, in TV, budgets are limited and it is important to work with unknown actors. Furthermore, in a good film the director's talent accounts for 95 percent and the remaining five percent with the actors. There is another problem with TV: the public that sees the same actor each week will find it boring. In cinema, the popular lead doesn't appear more than two or three times per year. A director has to reveal an actress as herself, her second nature which she doesn't know. During shooting she [Mary Maloney] suddenly realizes that she has changed, she starts to emanate joy, as of endless gratitude and filled with love."

Also based on a Roald Dahl story, "Dip in the Pool" was of a lighter nature. Maybe for that reason, it is the only instance where Hitchcock deliberately quoted himself: like in *Lifeboat*

(1944), he appears in a most unusual cameo in a magazine cover! This same story appeared in one of the Hitchcock anthologies, which might have been a source that caught Hitchcock's attention, since he himself occasionally chose a story for dramatization. While not based on a Dahl story, "Arthur" (1959) was similar in the macabre wit with which the twist-ending device is employed. Strictly speaking, "Arthur" – in which the title character (Laurence Harvey) kills his girlfriend, and then disposes of her by clever use of his new production technique for chicken food – which even tops "Lamb to the Slaughter." Interestingly, "Arthur" was also a short story found in one of the Hitchcock anthologies. From the Pete Martin interview: "You've edited a book called *Stories They Won't Let Me Do On TV*," said Martin. "I've noticed it in the bookstore. Why were those stories turned down?" Hitchcock replied: "Too macabre. I won't try to outline the plot of the short story called 'Two Bottles of Relish' . . . for you, because I'm sure your editor would be stuffy about it and find it distasteful, but there's another one in that book of mine that he may not find unpalatable. In it, a man murders his wife, the transforms her into chicken feed. Afterwards, he serves a pair of chickens to the local police inspector when he has him in for dinner.' I gulped . . ."

The macabre humor, the double narrative frame (both Hitchcock and Arthur serve as host; in the ending narrative, Hitchcock mentions the birds turning against Arthur) and the fowl, food chain theme actually serve as a reminder of another vital connection to Hitchcock's theatrical film work, anticipating the trailers for *Psycho* ("Well it's, it's too horrible to describe!") and *The Birds*. From the fifties onwards, Hitchcock would more and more appear in the trailers of his theatrical films, extolling his latest feature in quite the same manner as he would introduce his TV program. Indeed, one particular introduction to *Alfred Hitchcock Presents*, for the episode titled "Number Twenty-Two" (episode #60) even appears as if it might have originally been conceived as a trailer. In it, Hitchcock's theatrical films are cited as evidence against him, and he insists they got *The Wrong Man*[15].

The Frozen Gaze. "The Crystal Trench" is remarkably different from the usual *Alfred Hitchcock Presents* short stories. The short form rather takes the place of a condensed epic, a futile love story encompassing four decades. While without doubt it was the opposite, a stylized concept of Expressionist cinema that had a key impact on the young director during his German assignments, it is reasonable to assume that dramas like *Der Heilige Berg* (*The Sacred Mountain*, 1926) were known to Hitchcock and maybe even had some influence on his lost silent *The Mountain Eagle* (1926). In the finale of the famous silent *Die weisse Hölle vom Piz Palü* (*White Hell of Pitz Palu*, 1929), a mountaineer sacrifices himself to rescue a young couple, finally finding reunification with his fiancé in an icy death. The shot of the man, entrapped in a glacier like in a crystalline shrine, appears like a direct inspiration for the telefilm's central image[16]. In "The Crystal Trench," an aged widow sees the perfectly preserved young face of her beloved husband once more, released after forty years of waiting from a crevasse. Yet, most of the action takes place indoors and the mountain set where the husband's accident had happened shows as little realism as the criticized rear projections and mattes in *Marnie* (1964). With a stare literally frozen in time, the final twist – the man carried the photo of another woman with him – is "not one that evokes malicious pleasure. Rather, it marks the tragic end of a great love story. From the very beginning the tone of the story . . . is one of drama and solemn remembrance . . . " (F. Arnold).

Crimes and Offenses. In the telefilms following this tragic story, Hitchcock turned more and more away from the grizzly subjects of death and murder, and towards life's daily tribulations. While his earlier TV experiences culminated in arguably his darkest theatrical film, *Psycho*, followed by *The Birds* which likewise re-defined the cinema of pure horror, Hitchcock now sought out more realistic, socially relevant subject matter for TV, as if striving to balance the theatrical work. In "Incident at a Corner," Hitchcock tells the "powerful story of the devastating effects of gossip in a small town." (Robert M. Batscha, Museum of Television and Radio). Though "perhaps Hitchcock's most elaborate and ambitious telefilm," (Taylor), "Incident at a Corner" yet explores the most harmless of misdemeanors - or is it? Hitchcock takes the time of a one-hour teleplay with all the care and direction he would devote to any of his more spectacular subjects, to sensitively show the cancerous effects, the pain and tension arising from false accusation. In fact, it is the only telefilm by Hitchcock shot in color, and beautifully so (by his *Alfred Hitchcock Presents* and *Psycho* cameraman John Russell). Remarkably, this film remained unseen for nearly four decades since its original broadcast. Newly remastered from a 35mm interpositive, the MTR made this gem available again for the "Murder in the Living Room" retrospective, and on TV, for their *Museum of Television and Radio Showcase*. Largely unnoticed by professional critics, this did not fail to generate the appropriate enthusiasm among Hitchcock aficionados.

A lightweight counterpart to *I Confess* (1953), exploring moral dilemmas of a significantly lesser degree than those associated with murder and the seal of confession, "The Horseplayer" may be Hitchcock's most warm-hearted telefilm. Claude Rains stars as Father Amion, a priest very concerned about the necessary repair of the leaky church roof. Initially worried, then appalled about a new church member's success at horse playing – by praying his horse into winning – he finally cannot resist giving him a fair amount of his savings to bet. Soon having pangs of conscience, however, he prays, upon the Bishop's advice, for "his" horse to loose. It does, but Father Amion shall get his roof, in a gentle and kind twist ending. Not willing to risk the Father's money, you see, the horse player had bet to place!

More comical, "Mrs. Bixby and the Colonel's Coat" explores marital infidelity and related sorts of cheating. The show opens with an uncomfortable close-up of Mr. Bixby's profession – dentistry, quickly to establish the starting point of the story: his wife leaving to visit, once more, her "aunt." The visit takes an unexpected turn for Mrs. Bixby. Cheat and be cheated: probably tired of her year-long denial of the relationship, the "Colonel" ends it with a letter and a present, a mink coat, that will be hard to enjoy for Mrs. Bixby without revealing her infidelity. Thus pawning it for a mere fifty dollars and presenting her husband with the ticket, she finds herself robbed off with a mink stole – but nearly runs into her husband's assistant in an all too familiar looking coat!

In "Bang! You're Dead," Hitchcock once more, and even more obviously than in "Four O'Clock," corrects his *Sabotage* error. The loaded gun a child has taken to play around with does go off, but without killing anyone. Bogdanovich considered this episode "probably the most suspenseful of all the television films." The score, but most of all the montage and the close-up of the gun, gradually intensifies the suspense. As Hitchcock explained, "That was achieved mainly by the big inserts of the gun. It had to be, you know. When you have to make certain points like that you cannot blur the thing visually from an audience point of view. You must get right in close and fill the screen with the relevant object – the loaded chamber of that revolver the little boy is innocently carrying around and firing at people."[17] (Bogdanovich) Hitchcock meant more than a mere lesson in suspense though: his somber closing remarks reemphasized the intentions behind the episode, on an issue that sadly, is still as serious a problem as four decades ago.

Hitchcock's last teleplay was the hour-long "I Saw The Whole Thing," "a courtroom drama Plike *The Paradine Case* and at the same time a paraphrase on Kurosawa's *Rashomon*" (Patalas). In the opening, once more freeze-frames are employed when the witnesses of an accident get paralyzed in fear after hearing the sound of car tires screeching, the only instance where Hitchcock mentioned his telefilms with Truffaut. "I had a car accident, as the basis for a trial, in one of my recent television episodes. What I did was to use five shots of people witnessing the incident before I showed the accident itself. Or rather, I showed five people as they heard the sound of it. Then I filmed the end of the accident, just as the man hits the ground after his motorcycle has turned over, and the offending car is speeding away. These are moments when you have to stop time, to stretch it out."

The following courtroom sequences relied much more on rhythm and the inherent drama of the story, as more than competently conveyed by leading man John Forsythe as the driver accused of the hit-and-run accident. Like Bel Geddes, Forsythe is featured memorably as a supporting actor in Hitchcock's theatrical films, but would find stardom only later in his life, on television.[18] In the end, Barnes (Forsythe), who has chosen to defend himself, is not convicted; in a surprise revelation we learn it was his pregnant wife driving. As Hitchcock told Bogdanovich, the story is "about the complete fallibility of people as witnesses. Everybody thinks he's right and knows what is right and what is wrong. But there's no guarantee that right is right – no guarantee at all. And as the payoff shows, they were all wrong – the whole lot. Technically. this was the toughest to do of all the TV films. It was a courtroom sequence to be shot in five days. Only by breaking it all up and analyzing the nature of the shots in a courtroom by subject and area, was one able to do it that quickly."[19]

John Forsythe questions Evans Evans on the stand in "I Saw The Whole Thing." (Courtesy of Photofest.)

As the fourth episode of the expanded format of the *Alfred Hitchcock Hour*, Hitchcock may again deliberately have wanted to help establish the style of the program, based on the experience of both the half-hour plays and his two previous one hour telefilms: "Even with the expanded format of the series into hour-long episodes, Hitchcock favored a visually economical approach to storytelling and relied on camera placement to provide exposition. For the scene in which Forsythe turns himself in, Hitchcock explained that 'there is no sense wasting film with a long shot of the police station. We have established the fact that this man is going to a police station by the three stripes on the policeman's uniform behind the desk.' Tellingly, Hitchcock never looked through the camera viewfinder, but arrived on the set each day with every shot meticulously sketched out." (MTR).[20]

107

"I Saw the Whole Thing" was the last television film Hitchcock directed. His interest in the medium had waned somewhat with the years. "I too," he added, "am trapped. I can't make any picture I want to. I've got to make a suspense picture. If I don't the audience keeps waiting for the body to be found. Same with television. I've got to have the surprise, the twist ending. " With *Psycho* he had successfully translated many of the techniques he had established to the big screen. In the following years, he would shoot six more theatrical features. After a failed attempt to build up Tippi Hedren as his new star, he would finally, in his last two films, *Frenzy* (1972) and *Family Plot* (1976), employ lesser-known actors to good effect much as he often had in his TV films. When he added a wink as the final shot of *Family Plot*, it was a gimmick – but an appropriate closure to a 53-picture, 20 telefilm career.

NOTES AND REFERENCES TO THIS ESSAY:

1. Cahiers du Cinema, No. 62 (August - September 1956), pp. 6-7
2. See bibliography for many more articles consulted but not explicitly quoted.
3. Steve Mamber, "The Television Films of Alfred Hitchcock," *Cinema 7* (No. 1-2), pp. 2-7
4. Thomas M. Leitch, "The Outer Circle: Hitchcock on Television," in Richard Allen and S. Ishii Gonzales (ed.), Alfred Hitchcock: Centenary Essays, London, 1999
5. Peter Bogdanovich, The Cinema of Alfred Hitchcock, NY, The Museum of Modern Art, 1963 and Who the Devil Made It, Knopf, New York, 1997
6. John Russell Taylor, Hitchcock: Video Noir, Emmy (Summer 1979), pp. 50-53
7. Gene D. Phillips, "Hitchcock's Forgotten Films: The Twenty Teleplays," Journal of Popular Film and Television, Summer 1982, pp. 7-76
8. Enno Patalas, "Alfred Hitchcock," Munich 1999, pp. 114-119
9. Gene D. Phillips, Alfred Hitchcock, Boston, 1984 pp. 149-159 (Chapter 7)
10. Frank Arnold: "Du hast nur 23 Minuten - Alfred Hitchcocks Fernseharbeiten," in: L.-O. Beier, G. Seeßlen (ed.), Alfred Hitchcock, Berlin, 1999
11. Thomas Binotto, "Nichts als Zufälle," Film Dienst, April 2001, pp. 34-37
12. Just like the key sequences of *Alfred Hitchcock Presents* are often those directed by Hitchcock, host and fellow Englishman Boris Karloff would occasionally appear acting in this and other of the show's highlight episodes, shot by many of the same technicians as *Alfred Hitchcock Presents*. *Thriller* was filmed on the Revue lot at Universal.
13. From interview with Lawrence French from 1979 and 1985, in: Gary J. Svehla and Susan A. Svehla (ed.), Vincent Price, Midnight Marquee Press 1998.
14. The definite parody was delivered by Woody Allen in 1993 with *Manhattan Murder Mystery*. It succeeds exactly because it takes both the comedy and the murder plot seriously.
15. Also, the introduction's sets are much more elaborate than even those for "Bang! You're Dead," which Leich, ibid., singles out as "unusually detailed."
16. See the episode entry for Evan Hunter's recollection as to how this key shot was accomplished.
17. Peter Bogdanovich, Who the Devil Made It, Knopf, New York, 1997, p.534
18. Science-fiction thriller master Jack Arnold used him to very good effect as the lead opposite E.G. Robinson in *The Glass Web* (1953) though, a suspense mystery set in a TV studio.
19. Peter Bogdanovich, ibid., pp.534 and 535
20. Murder in the Living Room: Hitchcock by Hitchcock, Museum of Television and Radio website at http://www.mtr.org/exhibit/hitchck/hitchck.htm

NOTES ABOUT THE EPISODE GUIDE:

The cast is listed in the order they appear during the closing credits, *not* in the order of their appearance. The actors are listed from left to right, top column to bottom. Take episode three as an example:

Starring: Gene Barry as Del Delaney   Darren McGavin as Red Hillman
Ellen Corby as Maggie Flynn   Casey MacGregor as Mr. Flynn

This means Gene Barry received top billing, Darren McGavin was second, Ellen Corby was third and Casey MacGregor was fourth. If an actor appeared in an episode and received no screen credit, they are listed last. There are a few exceptions where a cast member was listed in the closing credits, but nowhere to be seen in the episode. Those exceptions are mentioned in the notes below those specific episodes. The authors have gone to extreme lengths to ensure the proper spelling of an actor's name. Some performers like Mike Ragan also went under the stage name Holly Bane, but we kept his name listed as Mike Ragan throughout. Other actors like Robert F. Simon, were billed – respectfully – without their middle initial, even though most television fans are familiar with the actor when he used his middle initial. The most reliable resources have been consulted to ensure accuracy.

Beginning with the sixth season, the closing credits started listing the actors and fictional characters they played. If the producers felt a certain actor was a special guest, they would list that actor, respectfully, last. Example: *The Alfred Hitchcock Hour*'s "I Saw the Whole Thing," directed by Alfred Hitchcock. Claire Griswold was credited last as "and Claire Griswold as Joanne Dowling." So just because she's listed last in the credit chain does not mean she had a minor role. Some members of the cast – especially during the hour-long seasons – were billed as "guest starring" or "co-starring." We have listed them accordingly.

All of Alfred Hitchcock's original American-aired presentations and afterwards are listed under each episode entry. *These can be found in italics.* For many of the *Alfred Hitchcock Presents* episodes, Hitchcock filmed an alternate version for non-American airings, usually without jabs toward the sponsors. We have included many of those alternatives. Nowadays, many television stations prefer to cut scenes out of older television programs, in order to air more commercials. Known as "syndication cuts," the Hitchcock program is no exception, and on many occasions, sections of Hitchcock's hostings were also cut (a last laugh from "the sponsor"?). Included in this book are the complete narratives of Alfred Hitchcock, with no cuts.

The titles are accurate, taken directly from the title screens for each and every episode. So detailed that the authors even double-checked to make sure episodes like "Listen, Listen . . . . . !" had exactly five periods and an exclamation mark, not four or six periods. Whether the title had "The" in the beginning or not, etc. Some reference works in the past have listed more than one title for an episode. One of the popular myths is "A True Account," which books list "also known as 'Curtains for Me." Sorry, but there was never an episode entitled "Curtains for Me." That was the name of the short story it was based on. Fans who have been spending years looking for the "other" episode with a different title can now relax.

The production credits for each season are listed, in alphabetical order, for easy reference. Keep in mind that more people were involved during the day-to-day productions, than were billed during the closing credits. We have listed only those who were billed on the screen. *Variety* magazine defined a whole new slang of English language with their film and television reviews, which is why words like "telepix" and "grizzly" are spelled and used in a stylistic approach. A few *Variety* reviews are featured throughout this episode guide (and the book), so if you read a few and wonder what some of the terms mean, they are not mis-spellings.

SEASON ONE - (39 episodes)

SELECTED PRODUCTION CREDITS:
Art Directors: Martin Obzina and James S. Redd *
Assistant Directors: Richard Birnie, Jack Corrick, James Hogan and Jack Voglin
Associate Producer: Joan Harrison
Directors of Photography: Reggie Lanning, John L. Russell, a.s.c., and Lester Shorr
Editorial Supervisor: Richard G. Wray, a.c.e.
Film Editor: Edward W. Williams, a.c.e.
Makeup: Jack Barron, Jack Casey, Ted Coodley, Sam Kaufman, Leo Lotito, Jr.,
G. McGarry, Garrett Morris and William Oakley
Music Supervisor: Stanley Wilson
Set Decorators: James S. Redd, Ralph Sylos and Jerry Welch
Sound: William Brady, Earl Crain, Sr., Earl Crain, Jr., Hugh McDowell,
Perc Townsend and Richard Tyler
Wardrobe Supervisor: Vincent Dee
Filmed at Revue Studios in Hollywood, California, in association with MCA-TV, executive
distributor for Shamley Productions, Inc.
Broadcast Sunday over CBS-TV, 9:30 - 10 p.m., EST. Sponsored by Bristol-Myers.

EPISODE #1 **"REVENGE"** Broadcast on October 2, 1955
Rehearsed and filmed on September 15 – 17, 1955.
Starring: Ralph Meeker as Carl Spann   Vera Miles as Elsa Spann
Frances Bavier as Mrs. Fergerson
Ray Montgomery as the man in the gray suit in room 321
John Gallaudet as the doctor   Ray Teal as the lieutenant
Norman Willis as the sergeant   John Day as the cop
Lillian O'Malley as hotel cleaning woman   Herbert Lytton as the hotel portier
Teleplay written for *Alfred Hitchcock Presents* by Francis Cockrell and A.I.
Bezzerides (uncredited), based on the short story of the same name by Samuel Blas, as
originally published in the January 11, 1947 issue of *Collier's*. Subsequently anthologized in
Best Detective Stories of the Year, ed. David C. Cooke (Dutton, 1948).
Directed by Alfred Hitchcock.
(Standing by a desk) *Good evening. I am Alfred Hitchcock and tonight I am*
presenting the first in a series of stories of suspense and mystery called, oddly enough,
'Alfred Hitchcock Presents.' I shall not act in these stories but will only make appearances.
Something in the nature of an accessory before and after the fact. To give the title to those
of you who can't read and to tidy up afterwards for those who don't understand the endings.
Tonight's playlet is really a sweet little story. It is called 'Revenge.' It will follow. . . . oh
dear, I see the actors won't be ready for another sixty seconds. However, thanks to our
sponsor's remarkable foresight, we have a message that will fit in here nicely.

Story: Salesman Carl Spann, consistently pictured as a cynical, worried and loving
husband, returns to his home in a remote California trailer park. Carl finds the house in
disarray, and his loving wife, Elsa. roughed up. Elsa explains that an unfamiliar stranger
attacked her. Despite the fact that his wife had suffered a nervous breakdown not long ago,
Carl believes her, and the two leave together to find the intruder, not wanting to wait for the
police to handle things "their way." Driving down the road, Elsa coincidentally catches a

* James S. Redd was billed as "Art Director" and "Set Decorator" for the same episode,
"The Case of Mr. Pelham."

glimpse of her accused attacker, dressed in a gray suit. Accepting her identification, Carl stops the car, orders his wife to remain in the front seat, and exits quietly. Putting a coin in the parking meter as a good law-abiding citizen, Carl unhurriedly follows the stranger into a hotel, up to his room, and without saying a word . . . murders the man in cold blood. When Carl returns to the car, and begins their trek back home, Elsa sees another man and identifies *him* as the attacker too!

Well, they were a pathetic couple. We had intended to call that one 'Death of a Salesman' but there were protests from certain quarters. Naturally Elsa's husband was caught, indicted, tried, convicted, sentenced and paid his debt to society for taking the law into his own hands. You see, crime does not pay. Not even on television. You must have a sponsor. Here is ours, after which I'll return. (commercial break) *That was beautifully put. In fact, after hearing that, there's nothing more I wish to add, so good night until next week.*

Trivia, etc. Every Hitchcock-directed episode of the series is presently available for viewing from the Museum of Television and Radio in New York and California. But the print of this particular episode at the Museum does not include the complete opener with the final two sentences of Hitchcock's opening narration, beginning with "It will follow ... to ... nicely." There exist prints of this episode not featuring any background music cue with the title screen right before the drama itself, and some prints featuring the name of the program in thick white words, instead of the usual black titles.

Variety reviewed "Revenge" the day after the program's premiere: "Gambling odds as to the continuing quality and popularity of this filmed series naturally relate to the question of how much of the personal time, attention and flair of Alfred Hitchcock is actually going to be invested. Just to the degree that Hitchcock is trade-marked by his style of story-pacing the absence of this style or touch may, and indeed should, be distinctly noticeable. Which, of course, is as it may be. In paying Hitchcock the compliment of assuming his directorial talents are unique the corollary assumption must be that he does not have a bevy of assistants who are just as good. So that's the problem, and that's the critic's reservation which has to be registered straight off. The importance of the Hitchcock direction showed with peculiar sharpness on the inaugural story, 'Revenge,' precisely because it was no great shakes to start with. The motivations were of the skimpiest."

Alfred Hitchcock himself commented about the filming of his teleplays a couple years after the program's premiere. "I've heard some say my stories are strong stuff," Hitch remarked. "I can't help raising my eyebrows at this. I've never violated any code in any of my pictures - whatever the code may be. I do everything by suggestion. You won't see violence in my films. All that is suggested - like in 'Revenge' which I directed with Vera Miles and Ralph Meeker. [If you'll notice,] I didn't show Meeker slugging the victim at all."

A.I. Bezzerides, who wrote the screenplays *They Drive By Night* (1940) and *On Dangerous Ground* (1950), should also be recognized for helping write this script. When the credits appeared on the television screen, Francis Cockrell was the only one who received credit. "What I did was polish the scripts," recalled Bezzerides, "and back then you didn't get any credit for that. I did a lot of polishing. I was considered one of the best for dialogue and I understood deliveries between people. I did dialogues for *Action in the North Atlantic* (1943). There were many scenes that the producers felt poorly, and so they asked me to make the dialogue better, and add to it. I remember doing many of the Hitchcock shows, but the only one I remember is 'Revenge'." Bezzerides also wrote the script to *Kiss Me Deadly* (1955), which also starred Ralph Meeker. "Revenge" was actually featured (along with another first season adaptation, "Breakdown") as one of thirteen short stories in the 1949 Dell publication, *Alfred Hitchcock's A Baker's Dozen of Suspense Stories*. In the fall of 1985, when NBC premiered the remake series, "Revenge" was again featured as the premiere broadcast of series. Clips from both lead-in and lead-out were used in the documentary, *Dial H for Hitchcock: The Genius Behind the Showman*. For trivia fans, the numbers on Carl's license plate add up to thirteen – a joke Hitchcock used in a few of his motion pictures.

EPISODE #2　**"PREMONITION"**　Broadcast on October 9, 1955

　　　　　Starring: John Forsythe as Kim Stanger

　　　　　Cloris Leachman as Susan　　　　　Warren Stevens as Perry Stanger

　　　　　George Macready as Doug Irwin　　Percy Helton as Mr. Eaton

　　　　　Harry O. Tyler as Isaiah Dobbs, the coroner

　　　　　Paul Brinegar as the cab driver

　　　　　Original teleplay written exclusively for *Alfred Hitchcock Presents* by Harold
Swanton.

　　　　　Directed by Robert Stevens.

　　　　　*Good evening. Have you ever had a premonition? A feeling that something
dreadful was about to happen? I mention that obviously because tonight's play is about a
young man, named Kim Stanger, about his strange homecoming and of the mystery he found
when he arrived. Follow him, if you will, as he attempts to unravel this mystery. Hindered
in every step by his friends and haunted always by a vague sense of foreboding. This story is
appropriately entitled "Premonition." I defy you to guess the nature of Kim Stanger's
premonition. Although we shall give you numerous clues, in the prologue which we now
present immediately.*

　　　　　Story: Kim Stanger, concert pianist, is returning home to Stangerford after four
years on tour. He doesn't know what it was that brought him home, just a longing to see the
family again, sort of a premonition. But Kim doesn't come home with open arms, as his
brother Perry breaks the bad news about their father. "He died of a heart attack on the tennis
court." Kim soon discovers that his brother is lying, since his father really left for a hunting
trip the day after. During further investigation, Kim learns from the undertaker that the burial
was held with an empty coffin. Taking a trip up to the family hunting lodge in Sheridan
Falls, Kim learns the truth. His father was killed with a hunting rifle in an argument and the
killer was himself, after which he apparently suffered a mental breakdown and was put into a
hospital in Arizona. He hadn't been on any performing trip to Rome and Paris as he had
apparently imagined. The family made up a story and paid everyone off, so no one knows the
truth. "I thought so," Kim starts recalling, "I . . . I had a premonition."

　　　　　*And as the cold New England sun slowly sinks behind the coroner's office, we take
leave of mysterious, far off Sheridan Falls, land of enchantment, and as the night breeze
carries our little craft away from these beautiful wooded shores, we slowly turn our eyes
back to the charms of television advertising and the lyrical chant of our sponsor's message.
After which I'll float back.* (commercial break) *I see it's time for our intermission. You may
leave your seats if you wish . . ., and . . . have some light refreshment, chat with your friends,
but please hurry back for our next play. That will be in just uh . . .,* (looks for his watch) *one
week. Good night.*

　　　　　Trivia, etc. Actor Warren Stevens recalled: "The Hitchcock shows were fun to do.
I had worked with Robert Stevens in New York in one of those live shows back there, and he
was nervous, that's about all I can say [laughs]! But, he got the work done. I had met Alfred
Hitchcock before and after I did *Alfred Hitchcock Presents* - he wasn't involved on that
show, really, it was Joan Harrison and Norman Lloyd. I was interviewed by Hitchcock for
one of his films, *North by Northwest* (1959). He knew my work - or said he did. That's
exactly what he said, he said, 'I'm familiar with Mr. Stevens' work' which I took very badly,
because I didn't get the part [laughs]!"

　　　　　Paul Brinegar also acted in literally dozens of TV westerns, plays his first of many
supporting roles on *Alfred Hitchcock Presents*. He played Wishbone in *Rawhide*, and was
Jim "Dog" Kelley on *The Life and Legend of Wyatt Earp*. Just as Vera Miles, who would
star in two Hitchcock motion pictures, appears in "Revenge," so would John Forsythe, in
"Premonition." Forsythe was Sam Marlowe in *The Trouble with Harry* (1956).

112

EPISODE #3 **"TRIGGERS IN LEASH"** Broadcast on October 16, 1955
Starring: Gene Barry as Del Delaney   Darren McGavin as Red Hillman
Ellen Corby as Maggie Flynn   Casey MacGregor as Mr. Ben Flynn
Teleplay written for *Alfred Hitchcock Presents* by Dick Carr, based on the short story of the same name by Allan Vaughn Elston, originally published in the July 1925 issue of *Frontier*. Subsequently anthologized in *Fireside Book of Suspense*, ed. Alfred Hitchcock (Simon & Schuster, 1947).
Directed by Don Medford.
(loading a gun, click) *That's precisely why I don't care for Russian roulette, I never seem to win. There are two revolvers such as this, which play a part in tonight's story. It's what you might call a western, although there isn't a horse to be seen. We intended to get horses but they couldn't remember the lines, so you'll be seeing people instead. The cast is a very small one and threatens to become smaller with every passing moment. You see two of the characters are threatening to eliminate each other on sight. Now I'm sure there are some of you who don't want to see them do that. So I suggest instead that you listen to our sponsor's message.*

Story: Red Hillman and Del Delaney, a pair of anger-filled cowboys, are determined to settle their differences by method of a shoot-out in front of Maggie Flynn's trail-stop. Maggie, not wanting to see the sight of blood on her own land, makes every attempt to convince the two men to come to their senses. She even insists that no matter who wins, she will accuse the winner of cold-blooded murder. Desperate, Maggie asks one last request - to remove a crucifix from the shelf next to the clock so that it won't be accidentally destroyed in the shoot-out. The men agree, and await the striking of the hour to duel. But for reasons unknown, the clock doesn't strike. Maggie claims it is a sign from God. Upon hearing her prayers, the two men settle their differences and ride into town. Seconds after Maggie's husband returns home, he sees the tilted clock on the shelf and says, "Hey, I told you not to move that Maggie, the last time I fixed this old clock, I told you it wouldn't run unless it was set on the level."

That was disappointing wasn't it? Still, you'll be happy to learn that both Del and Red did die eventually. That very day in fact, food poisoning. Maggie's heart was in the right place, she just wasn't a very good cook. And now, let us hear a word or two from our sponsor. A word or two? or three or four, five, six, seven . . . (commercial break) *Five-hundred and eleven, five-hundred and twelve, five-hundred and thirteen, thank you Sir.*

Trivia, etc. Ellen Corby, who would play the landlady of the McKittrick Hotel in *Vertigo* (1958), appears as Maggie Flynn. Darren McGavin had replaced Richard Carlyle as newspaper photographer Casey on television's *Crime Photographer*, four years before. Although McGavin is best remembered for his starring role of Carl Kolchak on *The Night Stalker* (1974-75) and the starring role in *Mike Hammer* (1958-59), his early television appearances on programs like *The Goodyear Television Playhouse* and *Suspense* are mostly over-looked. Back on July 4, 1952, McGavin worked under the direction of Don Medford in an episode of the science-fiction anthology, *Tales of Tomorrow*, entitled "The Duplicates." This episode united the two once more.

EPISODE #4 **"DON'T COME BACK ALIVE"** Broadcast on October 23, 1955
Starring: Sidney Blackmer as Frank Partridge
Virginia Gregg as Mildred Partridge   Robert Emhardt as Mr. Kettle
Irene Tedrow as Lucy   Edna Holland as the librarian
Teleplay written for *Alfred Hitchcock Presents* by Robert C. Dennis. from his short story "Don't Come Back Alive!", as originally published in the November 1945 issue of *Detective Tales*. Later anthologized in *Best Detective Stories of the Year*. ed. David C. Cooke (Dutton, 1946).

Directed by Robert Stevenson.

Good evening, ladies and gentlemen and especially the gentlemen. All of you have at one time or another speculated on how it would be to be separated from your wife for a week or a weekend. Ah, but have you ever thought of being away from the little woman for seven years. Oh, you have? Oh, well in that case you will be even more interested in tonight's play called "Don't Come Back Alive." It's a homey little story of intrigue, jealousy, avarice and fraud. It will follow immediately after this illustrated lecture on the virtues of our sponsor's product. May we see the first slide please.

Story: Frank and Mildred Partridge are desperate for cash. Checking up on their life insurance policy, the two discover a law that states anyone who is reported missing for seven years or more is legally declared "dead," and for insurance policy holders, payment is issued with a legal death certificate. So the two cook up a scheme where Mildred will "disappear" for seven years and her husband can cash in on her insurance money. Everything goes off without a hitch as Mildred vanishes without a trace. The insurance investigator looking into the case firmly believes that Frank has somehow killed the missing wife, but cannot figure how. Two days short of seven years later, Mildred returns. Time has changed more than her feminine figure. As a wiser woman who no longer has any interest in Frank or the money, she now just wants to have a divorce, so she will be able to get married again. An infuriated Frank doesn't like her new plans, especially since he would lose all the money. Angry, he really does kill her, and buries her body in the garden, fulfilling the insurance investigator's beliefs that foul play was involved. As a last check the investigator starts to dig in the garden . . .

By way of tidying up our story, I feel obligated to tell you that Mrs. Partridge eventually received what is termed, a decent burial. While this did not make her feel any better, knowing it may allow you to rest more easily. Well, that's our story for this evening, all of our show including the following commercial is on film. However, the corpse on tonight's program originated live in New York City. I'll be back in a minute. (commercial break) And now if you don't mind, I shall stage a disappearance of my own. But don't be alarmed. I shall not stay out of sight for seven years, just seven days. When I reappear it will be to tell you another of our little fairy stories for grown-up children.

EPISODE #5 "INTO THIN AIR" Broadcast on October 30, 1955

Starring: Pat Hitchcock as Diana Winthrop	Geoffrey Toone as Basil Farnham
Alan Napier as Sir Everett	Maurice Marsac as the hotel clerk
Mary Forbes as Mrs. Winthrop	Ann Codee as the doctor's wife
Gerry Gaylor as the maid	John Mylong as the doctor
Albert d'Arno as a Frenchman	Peter Camlin as a Frenchman
Jack Chefe as the hotel porter	Michael Hadlow as Meadows

Based on the short story "The Vanishing Lady" by Alexander Woollcott, later published in his 1934 book "While Rome Burns," and adapted for *Alfred Hitchcock Presents* by Marian Cockrell.

Directed by Don Medford.

(sitting at a desk) *Tonight we are going to tell the story of a woman who disappears into thin air. By the way, have you noticed that thin air seems to be the type of air most conducive to disappearances? That certainly is a fact well worth knowing. Now, in case you seem to recognize parts of this story, don't be alarmed. It is familiar because it is a classic of its kind. Many, many people have borrowed this legend, quite profitably too. Two novels have been written about it and it has been made into a motion picture called "The Lady Vanishes," once by no lesser personage than, uh . . . Alfred Hitchcock. It was also related by Alexander Woollcott in his book, "While Rome Burns." Here following our sponsor's all too brief message, is our version of that famous old tale. Now I'd better get out of the way to enable you to see better. May I have a bit of thin air, please?*

Story: A young lady, Diana Winthrop, arrives at the 1899 Paris World's Exhibition with her mother. Checking into the Hotel Madeleine, her mother takes ill and becomes bed-ridden. The hotel doctor arrives on the scene and after checking out Mrs. Winthrop's condition, he orders Diana to go out and fetch some medicine. When Diana returns, she is shocked to discover that her hotel room has not only changed, but is empty as well. Inquiring at the front desk about the room and her missing mother, the clerk denies even seeing the two. The doctor, too, denies laying eyes on Diana or her mother, and claims he never sent Diana out on any such errand. Finally, Diana, deciding that her memory is no delusion, becomes determined to learn the truth. Her persistence pays off, when she discovers that her mother had died of bubonic plague and the body was disposed of, not to disturb the tourist trade for the World's Exhibition.

Oh, I'm glad to see so many of you are still with us. There was a disturbing suggestion at the very close of our story, which I want to clear up at once. You will be relieved to hear that Diana and Basil's story ended happily. They did not get married. And now for the part of the program you have all been waiting for. After which, I'll be back. (commercial break) *And that completes our offering for tonight. However, I am not giving up. Next week, I plan to stage a comeback and shall present another in our series of situation tragedies. Good night.* (Hitchcock walks off, and returns with his face in camera) *Oh, uh, incidentally, I thought the little leading lady was rather good, didn't you?*

Trivia, etc. The original title of this episode was "The Vanishing Lady," the same title used on television's *Sure As Fate* (broadcast October 17, 1950), with Kim Stanley and Jeff Morrow in the leads. Vanessa Brown and Joan Brooks played the female protagonist in other earlier network productions. However, it was suggested that audiences might confuse this production with Hitchcock's earlier motion picture, *The Lady Vanishes*, so the title was changed to "Into Thin Air." (Also possibly the reason Hitchcock made a mention of his movie in his opening presentation, something he never did in any other episode.) Alexander Woollcott, the author of the tale, told how he had always believed that he was re-telling a true story that had been told to him in confidence, but was afterwards startled to find the essential details had already long ago been set down in print in the novel "The End of Her Honeymoon" by Mrs. Belloc Lowndes in 1913 (the same year her famous novel "The Lodger" appeared).

"Into Thin Air" was the first episode filmed for the series, but "Revenge" was the first episode aired. (Hitchcock directed "Breakdown" before "Revenge.) Having attended the Royal Academy of Dramatic Art in London, Hitchcock's daughter, Pat, sought chiefly to be a stage actress and successfully achieved some of her ambitions on Broadway before retiring to private life. On screen, however, her career was indelibly tied to her father, for whom she acted in *Psycho, Strangers on a Train,* and *Stage Fright,* as well as a number of television episodes in his television series. "Actually the one I did was the first one they shot," she recalled. "And they tried to do it in two days but they found out that [episode] was too little time. So from then on they always did them in three days. That was a story that was made into a movie with Jean Simmons before that called *So Long at the Fair* (1950) and it was actually supposed to be the World's Fair in Paris. And then the mother gets sick and supposedly the mother got tuberculosis and they didn't want to tell anybody. That's why they didn't tell, you know the . . . It basically, I think, came from a true story, you know, many, many years ago." (source from a recent BBC radio documentary)

Jack Chefe, Peter Camlin, and Albert d'Arno played very minor roles in this episode, all of who played bit parts throughout their careers in hundreds of movies, all as waiters, butlers, and barbers. From Abbott and Costello vehicles to Laurel and Hardy, these supporting actors reprised the roles they were most familiar with in American Cinema - the obedient servant. Another actor, Michael Hadlow, also played a bit part in this episode as a man named Meadows. Viewers with a quick and observant eye might have caught a glimpse of Hadlow playing a Monaco policeman in Alfred Hitchcock's *To Catch a Thief*, which was then currently in the movie theaters.

It may also be worth noting that the same story idea by Woollcott, was used by other authors, most notably Cornell Woolrich in "Finger of Doom," originally published in the June 22, 1940 issue of *Detective Fiction Weekly*, and especially in "All at once, No Alice" in the March 2, 1940 issue of *Argosy*.

EPISODE #6   **"SALVAGE"**   Broadcast on November 6, 1955

Starring: Gene Barry as Dan Varrel   Nancy Gates as Lois Williams
Maxine Cooper as Freda, the maid   Peter Adams as Tim Grady
Elisha Cook, Jr. as Shorty   Paul Bryar as Lou Henry
Edit Angold and Virginia Christine are the employees at the shop
Ralph Montgomery as the bartender   Billy Wayne as the drunk

Teleplay written for *Alfred Hitchcock Presents* by Dick Carr and Fred Freiberger, based on the original radio script "The Long Wait" by Fred Freiberger.

Directed by Justus Addiss.

(on a movie set)   *Hold it, hold it. Wait a minute, look, I object. I think you got much too much fill-light. I mean, look. This is supposed to be a night scene, it's full of daylight. Quiet, quiet back there. Oh, I beg your pardon. Oh, oh good evening. We wanted to take you behind the scenes for a moment to show you how we make our films. The friendly co-operation of many, many people is needed to bring you these stories. Prop men, make-up men, electricians, cameramen.* (gets up from chair) *All part of a team. I'm very proud of them, and they in turn . . .* (a spotlight falls and crashes onto the chair Hitchcock was just sitting in) *You know, I sometimes consider getting out of this business. Now about tonight's show. Our story is entitled, oh well, the title's unimportant. Tonight's story concerns, well. . . well small matter. I'm sure you'll. . . I'm sure you will enjoy our story, but first . . . but first, well, if you've been watching this program, I'm certain you always know when we have, but first. Here it is.*

Story: When Dan Varrel is released from a five-year prison sentence, the only thing on his mind is how he'll exact revenge on nightclub singer Lois Williams, because she was partly responsible for the death of his brother. Just as everyone in town assumed, Dan locates Lois, but finds a surprise. Expecting to find a woman pleading for her life, he hears her sad sob story. Her life is in shambles and if Dan kills her, he'll be doing her a favor. Unable to commit the murder, and needing a business to show the parole officers that he's gone legit, Dan makes a business proposition. If he supplies the money, she'll run a dress shop, and remain partners. The business becomes a financial success and everyone in town starts wondering if maybe Dan's gone soft. Lois even develops feelings for Dan, after all that he's done for her. Alone one day in a high-rise building, Dan asks if she is happier than she's ever been, and Lois proclaims that she is the happiest woman in the world. Then Dan pulls a gun and shoots.

Well, that's life I guess. As you know, it is my painful duty to tell you what happens to characters in our stories after the curtain drops. So, now for the results of this case. Lois was killed. A bullet wound. All the others lived happily ever after that is, with the possible exception of Dan, who was promptly executed by the state. And now here is someone who would like to explain how you can live more happily, after which I will be back. (commercial break) *Isn't it lovely? All my fellow workers, prop men, electricians and so on, bought this and presented it to me.* (chair with big target on it) *Next week we shall be back with another story. Join us then, that is if you have nothing better to do.*

Trivia, etc. This story was initially conceived and written for radio's horror anthology, *Suspense*, from which a handful of *Alfred Hitchcock Presents* tales originated. First broadcast over CBS radio on November 24, 1948, Burt Lancaster played the role of Dan, in a story entitled "The Long Wait." But "The Long Wait" didn't stop there. "What happened is that after I did the radio script, I sold it about three times," said author Fred Freiberger. "I didn't want to plagiarize myself but someone told me that 'anyone who sues for plagiarism in this business is out of his mind' or something like that, so I went ahead and sold it to different producers who asked for it. I guess I was so innocent at that time that somebody jumped on my credit and got in on the screenplay credit, which was common practice at that time. Usually I would have written the script for television by myself but after Alfred Hitchcock bought it, someone else put their name on it."

Gene Barry played the lead for this production, and this marked his second appearance on the *Alfred Hitchcock Presents* series. Much of the supporting cast worked together on similar pictures years before. Both Ralph Montgomery and Peter Adams appeared in *War of the Worlds* (1953), which starred Gene Barry. Billy Wayne, who was under contract with Universal at the time, had played minor roles in many mystery movies including a couple Charlie Chan films and half of the 1930's Perry Mason pictures released through Warner Bros. Wayne also worked with Montgomery in *Abbott and Costello Meet the Invisible Man* (1951) and *Salute for Three* (1943). Paul Bryar and Robert Montgomery also appeared in two movies together, *Ride the Pink Horse* (1947), *Chicago Deadline* (1949) and shortly after this episode, *The Joker is Wild* in 1957. Both leading actress and leading actor worked together in *The Atomic City* in 1952, so even Gates had a fond reunion with Barry. For Hitchcock fans: Paul Bryar would later play the role of an Interrogation Officer in *The Wrong Man* (1956) and as Captain Hansen in *Vertigo* (1958), both directed by Alfred Hitchcock.

Gene Barry
and
Nancy Gates
guest star
in the episode
"Salvage."

Photo
courtesy of
Ronald V. Borst
/ Hollywood
Movie Posters.

EPISODE #7 **"BREAKDOWN"** Broadcast on November 13, 1955
Rehearsed and filmed on September 7 – 10, 1955

Starring: Joseph Cotten as Mr. Callew   Raymond Bailey as Ed Johnson
Forrest Stanley as Hubka   Harry Shannon as Doc Horner
Lane Chandler as the Sheriff   James Edwards as the black clothes thief
Marvin Press as Chessy   Murray Alper as Lloyd, the sheriff's helper
Mike Ragan as the white clothes thief   Jim Weldon as a prisoner, tire thief
Richard Newton as a prisoner, tire thief   Aaron Spelling as a road worker
Harry Landers as a prisoner, tire thief
Elzie Emanuel as Mr. Callew's secretary   Also in the cast: Ralph Peters

Teleplay written for *Alfred Hitchcock Presents* by Francis Cockrell and Louis Pollock, based on the short story of the same name by Louis Pollock, originally published in the June 7, 1947 issue of *Collier's*. Subsequently anthologized in *Suspense Stories*, ed. Alfred Hitchcock (Dell, 1949).

Directed by Alfred Hitchcock.

(reading a book) *Oh, good evening. I've been reading a mystery story. I find them very relaxing. They take my mind off my work. These little books are quite nice, of course they can never replace hard cover books. They're just good for reading, but they make very poor doorstops. Tonight's story by Louis Pollock is one that appeared in this collection. I think you will find it properly terrifying but like the other plays of our series it is more than mere entertainment. In each of our stories we strive to teach a lesson or point a little moral. Advice like mother used to give. You know, walk softly and carry a big stick. Strike first and ask questions later, that sort of thing. Tonight's story tells about a business tycoon and will give you something to ponder, if you have ever given an employee the sack, or if you intend to. You'll see it, after the sponsors' story, which like ours, also strives to teach a little lesson or point a little moral.*

Story: Mr. Callew, bachelor by trade, callous and successful businessman by profession, has lived his life believing that only the weak show emotion or sympathy. Without showing respect to anyone who possesses the quality of standing in his way, Mr. Callew becomes a well-disliked man about town. At least until he wrecks his car while on a routine business trip, having hit a piece of road equipment. Thought to be dead, Mr. Callew's body is transported directly to the morgue. In reality, he is only paralyzed, but the coroner himself believes that Mr. Callew is dead, and begins preparing the tools of his trade. Unable to speak or move in any way to let anyone know that he is alive, Mr. Callew's one and only hope may be by showing some emotion and crying a tear . . . a tip-off that he is alive, if anyone notices.

Well, that was a bit of a near thing. It reminded me of my own situation. Imagine if you can the terror of being inside a television set, knowing that any moment the viewer may shut you off and being powerless to prevent it. And I go through this every week. My only consolation is that some portions of our program are so fascinating that they hold the viewers spellbound. Such an episode follows immediately and then I'll be back again. (commercial break) *There now, that really held you in suspense, didn't it? For more of the same, I recommend you tune in next week at this time. I shall see you then. Bon Soiree.*

Trivia, etc. On May 15, 1949, the radio program *Prudential Family Hour of Stars* presented a dramatization of this same Louis Pollack short story with Joseph Cotten in the lead. (Originally James Cagney was scheduled and signed to star, but a couple days before broadcast, Cagney backed out and Cotten substituted.) Now, about six years later, Joseph Cotten was able to reprise his radio role for a television performance! Joseph Cotten played the Widow Murderer in Hitchcock's favorite film, *Shadow of a Doubt* in 1943. "Hitch's tailor in New York gave him fittings every time he went to and from England," Joseph Cotten recalled about Hitchcock in his autobiography. "He would be fitted on the way there. On the way back he had lost ten pounds so the suit had to be taken in. The following trip he had put on fourteen pounds and the suit had to be let out. After several years of inflated and deflated fittings, the poor bewildered tailor greeted him by saying, 'I'm terribly sorry, sir, but I am afraid this suit is worn out.' So, I am sure, was the tailor."

This episode was not the first episode of the series to go before the cameras, but it was the first episode of *Alfred Hitchcock Presents* that would be directed by Alfred Hitchcock himself. "Revenge" was the second episode to be directed by the "master of suspense," but aired *before* "Breakdown." There are some prints of this episode in which Hitchcock's final sentence during the opening, "You'll see it . . . to . . . a little moral," is not featured. Harry Landers, who would later become the spokesman for the "Taster's Choice" coffee commercials during late 1960's, also played a young man (uncredited) in Hitchcock's *Rear Window* (1954). Richard Newton would later become a producer for television's *Honey West*, *Hawaii Five-O*, and *Burke's Law*, but he wasn't the only actor-turned producer in this episode. Aaron Spelling, who played a road worker in this episode, would later become one of Hollywood's most famous television producers, with such programs as *Starsky and Hutch*, *Charlie's Angels*, *Dynasty*, Fantasy *Island*, and *The Love Boat*.

EPISODE #8   **"OUR COOK'S A TREASURE"**   Broadcast on November 20, 1955
       Starring: Everett Sloane as Ralph Montgomery   Beulah Bondi as Mrs. Sutton
       Janet Ward as Ethel Montgomery   Elliott Reid as Earl Kramer
       Gavin Gordon as George Brooks   Doris Singleton as the secretary
       Walter Woolf King as the doctor   Olan Soulé as the laboratory assistant
       Teleplay written for *Alfred Hitchcock Presents* by Robert C. Dennis, based on the short story "Suspicion" by Dorothy L. Sayers, originally published in the October 1933 issue of *Mystery League*. Collected in *In the Teeth of Evidence* (Gollancz, 1939; Harcourt Brace, 1940).
       Directed by Robert Stevens.
       Oh, good evening. No, I'm not drinking on the job, not for pleasure at any rate. I'm an amateur wine taster. A friend suspects that someone has been tampering with his wine. Of course, there's no use of going through the trouble of a laboratory test, when any self-respecting gourmet can detect impurities. (takes a sample of wine labeled x) *Nothing wrong here, a very fine Burgundy, a Remani Conti, I would say.* (takes sample of wine labeled y) *This is muscatel, homemade no doubt. The do-it-yourself craze knows no bounds.* (takes sample of wine labeled z) *Something foreign has been added. A large quantity too. Anyone could have detected. . . but exactly what?* (bottoms up) *I have it, arsenic. I wish I had more of it, it's very good really. That is if you like a very dry wine. While you wait to see what possible effect this may have on me, you may watch our dramatization of one of Dorothy L. Sayers' stories. And to enliven the proceedings we have interspersed several delightful commercials. Here is one of them.*

Story: Ralph Montgomery finds himself in a dangerous position after hiring a cook named Mrs. Sutton, one he knows little about, to help his wife Ethel about the house. But the next day he reads in the papers about a woman, pretending to be a cook, who killed three employers, and he now wonders who it is he has given a job. Soon after reading the article, Ralph develops pains in his chest and when his doctor mentions the possibility of food poisoning, Ralph's suspicions grow stronger. To discover the truth, he hides some hot chocolate the cook makes for him and has it checked at a laboratory. The test results confirm that it had more than a lethal dose of poison in it. Returning home, Ralph fires Mrs. Sutton and then reads in the paper that the real murderous cook had been captured earlier that morning. Feeling ashamed for what he's done, Ralph apologizes, asking her to remain. The cook, however, rejects his offer and out of anger, suggests that his wife is cheating on him. Ethel, feeling sorry for her husband, fetches him a nice warm cup of cocoa . . .

That was a warm and touching little fable, wasn't it? A kind of story that gets you . . .(claps on stomach) . . . right here. Oh, about my wine testing. I'm afraid I was very much mistaken about brand z. You'll be relieved to hear that there was nothing wrong with it. Nothing had been added. You see it wasn't wine. It was mosquito spray, the arsenic belongs there. Apparently the mosquitoes prefer their spray very dry. And now let us turn from the ridiculous to the sublime and listen to a few concluding remarks from our sponsor. After which, I'll be back. (commercial break) *My, time certainly passes quickly when you're being entertained. Next week at this same time I shall invade your living rooms again, provided your television set holds up. Good night.*

EPISODE #9 **"THE LONG SHOT"** Broadcast on November 27, 1955

    Starring: Peter Lawford as Charlie Raymond   John Williams as English-Jim
    Gertrude Hoffman as Aunt Margaret Stoddard
    Robert Warwick as Matthew Kelson
    Frank Gerstle as Sergeant Mack   Charles Cantor as Tommy De Witt
    Tim Graham as the bartender   Virginia Christine as the secretary
    Teleplay written for *Alfred Hitchcock Presents* by Harold Swanton, from his original radio play of the same name.
    Directed by Robert Stevenson.
    (playing a slot machine) *My last quarter. I've been frightfully lucky this evening. Now if they would invent a machine that I could play using orange seeds and cherry pits, I'd be perfectly happy. All the foregoing will immediately seem justified, appropriate, clever and even dignified when I tell you that tonight's narrative is about a gambler. It is called "The Long Shot." If you like to bet when the odds are high and the risks great, you'll appreciate our hero's philosophy. But if you prefer to put your money on a sure thing, listen to this friendly tip about a highly touted product.*

    Story: Charlie Raymond played the horses and lost big time. In need of cash quick (and a fast ticket out of town), Charlie answers an advertisement in the newspaper about an Englishman looking for a Londoner as companion to travel by motor car to San Francisco. The pay is $150 plus expenses. When Walker Hendricks, his new employer, learns that Charlie knows London like the back of his hand, he's hired almost immediately. Along the way Charlie and Hendricks chat about London, life in general, and more of London. One evening in a hotel room alone, Charlie digs into Hendricks' briefcase to find out that Hendricks is to inherit $200,000 when he turns in the papers to a specific San Francisco address. Realizing that he can pick up the money himself if he does away with Hendricks, Charlie kills the Englishman and proceeds on. When he arrives at the attorney's office, Charlie is arrested by the police for murder. They had found Hendricks' dead body so Charlie admits to the killing in the Nevada desert, but the police had found Hendricks' dead body in New York. They believed the con-man English-Jim was the murderer and it was him that they had expected to see.

    We've had our dance macabre. But as you know, someone must always pay the piper. Fortunately, we already have such persons. In fact several of them. These philanthropic gentlemen, wish to remain anonymous. But perhaps the more discerning of our audience, would be able to find a clue to their identities, in what follows. After which, I'll be back. (commercial break) *Thank you. Our unknown benefactors will bring us back again next week at the same time. Why don't you tune in and see what little surprises we have dreamed up for you. Good night.*

    Trivia, etc. Harold Swanton wrote numerous scripts for *Alfred Hitchcock Presents*, some were based on radio scripts he wrote for radio programs years before - this one being no exception. "The Long Shot" was first dramatized over CBS radio's *Suspense* on January 31, 1946, with George Coulouris in the lead. Six years later, on June 8, 1952,

David Niven would play the same role in another production of the same script, this time for radio's *Hollywood Star Playhouse*. Three years after this *Alfred Hitchcock Presents* episode aired, Herbert Marshall would play the role of Charlie on radio's *Suspense* again, in February of 1958.

EPISODE #10   "THE CASE OF MR. PELHAM"   Broadcast on December 4, 1955
   Rehearsed and filmed on October 7, 8, and 10, 1955.
   Starring: Tom Ewell as Mr. Albert W. Pelham   Raymond Bailey as Dr. Harley
   Justice Watson as Peterson, the butler   Kirby Smith as Tom Mason
   Kay Stewart as Miss Clement, the secretary   John Compton as Vincent
   Jan Arvan as Harry   Norman Willis as Ray, the bartender
   Tim Graham as the man   Richard Collier as the tie salesman
   Diane Brewster as the typist
   Teleplay written for *Alfred Hitchcock Presents* by Francis Cockrell, based on the short story of the same name by Anthony Armstrong, originally published in the June 1955 issue of *Ellery Queen's Mystery Magazine*. Later expanded by Armstrong into the novel *The Strange Case of Mr. Pelham* (Methuen, 1957; Doubleday, 1957).
   Directed by Alfred Hitchcock.
   (chewing bubble gum) *Good evening. Due to circumstances beyond our control, tragedy will not strike tonight. I'm dreadfully sorry, perhaps some other time. However, I have just witnessed a sneak preview of this evening's story and I found it simply frightening. Sometimes death is not the worse that can befall a man and I don't refer to torture or any type of violence. I mean the quiet little insidious devices that can drive a man out of his mind, like putting bubble-gum in someone's coat pocket. Tonight's little frolic is called "The Case of Mr. Pelham." It will follow in a moment, after our announcer explains about tonight's secret word. It's something you find around the house. If you can't find it, I suggest you buy some.*

   Story: Mr. Albert Pelham is the owner of his own investment company and a luxurious apartment, and with no close personal ties. He isn't sure at first, but he suspects that his life is being imitated (or taken over) by an imposter, who looks and talks exactly like him. Although Pelham isn't able to prove it, nor has he actually seen this imposter, Pelham dismisses the theory of an evil twin. rather suspecting that more than a purely human agency is at work. The double is showing up at his job, parties, his bank, and other places representing himself as Albert Pelham, financial wizard. Reaching the point that his double seems to be taking control, Pelham tries several countermeasures hoping to expose the fraud, all of which fail. At last, the real Pelham and his double have a final confrontation in his apartment . . . and figure out the only solution to the identity crisis. One of them is mad.

   (Hitchcock being pulled away by men in white coats) *But I'm Alfred Hitchcock, I am, I can prove it!* (Man in white: "Sure, sure, everybody is.") *I am, I insist!* (camera pans over to the real Hitchcock) *An astounding hoax. He carried off the impersonation brilliantly except for one thing. Bubble-gum in his pocket, indeed. Alfred Hitchcock wouldn't be caught dead with a bubble-gum in his pocket.* (gun shot off the side) *Poor chap. Will you excuse me? I need a moment to pull myself together. Meanwhile, listen closely to this suggestion.* (commercial break) *You know, I believe commercials are improving every day. Next week we hope to have another one, equally fascinating and if time permits, we shall bring you another story.*

   Trivia, etc. An implausible but well-done treatment which mixes fantasy with pure horror. As Hitchcock described, a dead body isn't always needed to create the image of fright. The doppelganger theory has been explored in many science-fiction, horror and mystery tales, from *Tales of Tomorrow* to *The Twilight Zone*. This Hitchcock tele-version, however, does not employ any scientific reasoning or "another dimension" theory. The fear comes closer to home, as evident when most of the scenes are shot where Pelham works, drinks and sleeps.

During the discussion between Pelham and the psychiatrist (he is never referred to as a psychiatrist, though), Pelham asks the rational question: "Could a man actually be in one place, doing one thing, and still in his mind be elsewhere, doing something else so vividly, with such detail, that this is the real? The living part of his life to him?" Clearly the ending allowed the viewers to impose their own interpretations, since we're not sure the nightmare is all in his head, or if the events actually happened to him. "I can think of no reason at all for him to do what he's doing," Pelham fears. "I have the feeling that he's trying to . . . to move into my life. To crowd closer and closer to me, so that one day, he is where I was, standing in my shoes, my clothes, my life. And I will be gone . . . vanished." The climax centers his confrontation with reality, alone together in the hallway, when Pelham asks himself why and the duplicate explains, "You're mad, you know." Of course, Hitchcock himself was one step ahead of his duplicate, during the closing of the episode. (In case you didn't notice, his duplicate was also wearing a funny-looking white and black tie!) According to the closing credits, Tom Ewell appeared through the courtesy of Twentieth Century-Fox, soon to be seen in the starring role of the Cinema Scope production, *The Lieutenant Wore Skirts*. The casting of Tom Ewell might be the reason for an edge of comedy on the program, instead of leaving the story as horrific.

Hitchcock had experimented with showing different 'levels' of reality (and imagined reality) as early as the 1920s, in *Downhill* (1927) and *Champagne* (1928). In 1970, the same Anthony Armstrong story was made into a motion picture, entitled *The Man Who Haunted Himself*. Filmed

and released in England, Roger Moore stars in the role of Harold Pelham, a businessman who after suffering a nasty car accident, momentarily "dies" on the operating table, allowing an alter ego to escape and raise hell without Moore's knowledge. Soon Moore discovers that he is having an affair with a woman he met only once and his business career seems to have a mind of its own. The 1970 movie was to be director Basil Dearden's final film before dying in a car accident the following year.

EPISODE #11   **"GUILTY WITNESS"**   Broadcast on December 11, 1955
Starring: Judith Evelyn as Amelia Verber
Kathleen Maguire as Dorothy Crane
Joseph Mantell as Stanley Crane   Robert F. Simon as Detective Halloran
Ed Kemmer as Mr. Verber   Grazia Narciso as Mrs. Silvetski
Laiola Wendorff as Mrs. Santini

Teleplay written for *Alfred Hitchcock Presents* by Robert C. Dennis, based on the short story "Innocent Bystander" by Morris Hershman, originally published in the Spring 1949 issue of *Shadow Mystery Magazine.* Anthologized as "Guilty Witness" in the book "Butcher, Baker, Murder Maker," ed. George Harmon Coxe (Knopf, 1954).
Directed by Robert Stevens.

Oh, good evening. I was just constructing a mobile for my living room. They tell me the foreign hand is becoming less popular these days. I like it though. I'm just old fashioned I guess. But so much for fine art. This evening we have another in our series of plays designed especially for insomniacs. Actually our stories don't cure you of insomnia, but they do take your mind off your problem by stimulating your imagination and giving you something to think about as you lie there in the dark. Tonight's story will follow after we give . . . this . . . wake . . . ful . . . ness . . . test.

Story: Dorothy and Stanley Crane, a loving couple who think everything is wrong with the world except themselves, own the local food store where the town's citizens frequently visit. The Cranes' neighbors, the Verbers, constantly fight like cats and dogs and on many occasions the Cranes find themselves irritated over the neighbors' bickering. One evening they hear the neighbors get into a fight that ends in sudden silence. The next morning, Amelia Verber shows up at their store looking for a large carton, one about the size a man could fit into, claiming she wants to put her children's toys in something. A detective comes around asking questions, claiming that he has been given an anonymous report that Mr. Verber was bumped off. Without evidence, however, Mrs. Verber can continue walking about. After several days Stanley and Dorothy become convinced that their neighbor has been murdered and contact the detective.   Together, all three of them go down to the basement, the only place the body could be hidden, and finds Mr. Verber's body – stone cold.   When confronted by the evidence, Mrs. Verber admits to having murdered her husband, because he planned to leave and run away with "another woman." Before the detective takes her away, Mrs. Verber states in front of Stanley, that she should have killed Dorothy instead since Mr. Verber was leaving her for Dorothy.

Well that was a touching ending. Of course none of the story really happened. It was all made up. Just a tissue of lies out of some writer's head. For the benefit of those of you who prefer truth to fiction, we shall now present some. Here before I return are some unadorned facts, presented honestly and candidly and with impartiality and objectivity. (commercial break) *You know truth may be stranger than fiction after all. But tune in again next week when we have a real whopper to tell you. Good night.*

Trivia, etc. "My story appeared in an anthology done by the Mystery Writers of America," recalled Morris Hershman, "and I remember Shamley Productions got in touch with them for my address. I did watch the initial telecast and I don't feel that the changes they made did any harm to the story. I watched the show with a dozen friends and Hitchcock's postscript caused some comments at my expense. His postscript should have been thought twice before putting on the air."

Judith Evelyn played Miss Lonelyhearts in Alfred Hitchcock's *Rear Window* (1954).

EPISODE #12   **"SANTA CLAUS AND THE TENTH AVENUE KID"**   Dec. 18, 1955
Starring: Barry Fitzgerald as Harold "Stretch" Sears / Santa Claus
Virginia Gregg as Miss Clementine Webster
Bobby Clark as the 10th Avenue Kid

Arthur Space as Mr. Chambers	Justice Watson as Mr. Shaw
Norman Willis as the desk officer	Betty Harford as Doris
Mimi Gibson as one of the young girls	Gary Hunley as one of the boys
Wendy Winkleman as one of the young girls	
Anthony Blankley as one of the boys	Butch Bernard as one of the boys
Tyler McVey as Mac, the store detective	Harrison Lewis as the payroll clerk

Also in the cast: Alan Reynolds (billed 8th) and Noel Green (billed 14th)

Teleplay written for *Alfred Hitchcock Presents* by Marian Cockrell, based on the short story "Santa Claus and the Tenth Avenue Kid" by Margaret Cousins, originally published in the December 1943 issue of *Good Housekeeping*.

Directed by Don Weis.

(bricking up a fireplace) *Oh, good evening. I thought I might as well brick this up. I don't expect I'll be using this fireplace anymore. I expect the chimney to be closed very soon. I've uh, loosened the bricks so they'll fall in if anyone should brush against them on the way down. Santa Claus is always bringing surprises to others. I thought it would be interesting if someone surprised him for a change. I'm rather tired of his tracking soot in here every year. There. Let him ho-ho-ho himself out of that. At the risk of overburdening our program with the spirit of the season, we have arranged to dramatize a very appropriate story for tonight's divertissement. It is called "Santa Claus and the Tenth Avenue Kid." If follows this brief curtain raiser.*

Story: Harold Sears is out of prison again and his parole officer, feeling concerned over "Stretch," now an old man, tries to get him a job to send him straight. A job recruiter for ex-cons explains that he has already been convicted five times and his parole can be revoked at any time, which means it is time for him to settle down - or else. Harold doesn't like the idea, but seeing he has no other choice, begins his employment in a department store. His employer promises Harold that if he does his job well, he may be kept on after the Christmas season. Unfortunately for the store, Harold starts stealing from them on the very first day and plans to make a bigger haul later. But his holiday plans change when he meets a delinquent youth named "the Tenth Avenue Kid," and perhaps seeing a little of himself in the boy, Harold decides to set the kid straight before he too ends up in a life of crime.

The foregoing was based on an actual case. Only the names of the characters, their ages, occupations, physical likeness, speech and actions have been changed. This was done to protect the innocent, you. (commercial break) (someone falls down the chimney, Hitchcock smiles). *You know, he ain't such a bad chap after all, perhaps his taste in ties has improved. I think I'll give him one more chance. Rest ye merry, we'll have you out of there in a jiffy. And rest ye merry too, good night.*

EPISODE #13   **"THE CHENEY VASE"**   Broadcast on December 25, 1955
Starring: Patricia Collinge as Martha Cheney
Darren McGavin as Lyle Endicott
Carolyn Jones as Miss Pamela Waring, the secretary
George Macready as Herbert
Kathryn Card as Bella, the old maid
Ruta Lee as Ruby Boignton, the young maid
An original teleplay written exclusively for *Alfred Hitchcock Presents* by Robert Blees.

Directed by Robert Stevens.

(holding a voodoo doll) *Oh, oh good evening. I was just about to send greetings to an old friend. I'm sure modern civilized methods of homicide are much more efficient, but I don't care for them. I abhor violence. That is why on this program, we use stabbing, shooting and garroting only when they are absolutely essential to the plot, or when the whim strikes us. Tonight's play begins in a museum and the title is "The Cheney Vase." That's all I intend to tell you. You'll have to figure the rest out for yourselves. And now our sponsor wishes to say a few words, designed to send you rushing out immediately to buy his products. But please endeavor to restrain yourselves. I don't want you to miss our story.*

Story: Lyle Endicott is fired from his museum job for being grossly incompetent. On the way out he speaks with Mrs. Martha Cheney, a friend of the museum and owner of the Cheney Vase, an extremely valuable piece of art that the museum (and a very rich art collector in Germany) is willing to pay top dollar, but she refuses to part with. The old woman is confined to a wheelchair and when Lyle hears that she will need a new companion to take care of her, he forces his way into her good graces and ends up making her life pure hell, all for the opportunity to steal the priceless vase. He is constantly pulling tricks on Mrs. Cheney to force her to do his bidding, but to his horror she turns out to be not nearly as helpless as he had thought. For when he finally learns where Martha has hidden the vase, he races to her house before the museum curator, only to discover that she made a dozen copies so that Lyle can't figure out which one is the original. Mrs. Cheney comments, "You know, they're really rather adequate those copies. I'll probably be able to sell them for a great deal of money."

(table of vases) *And so another American primitive was born. Thinking our audience might be interested in obtaining a memento of tonight's story, we asked grandma Cheney to whip up a few thousand more vases. And we're prepared to make an amazing offer on a strictly first come, first served basis. Listen closely, this will not be repeated. If you wish one of these vases, just send us your name and address together with $45,000 in cash. Please do not send stamps or coins. And now our sponsor wishes to tell of an equally amazing opportunity for your benefit, after which I'll be back.* (commercial break) *My, they did go fast, didn't they? Next week we shall return . . .* (knocks over the last vase) *Please don't be alarmed, plastic. Next week we shall return with another story. Good night. Would you come back a moment please? I've been asked to give you a little Christmas message.* (puts on a beard) *We hope that everyone had a splendid Christmas and on behalf of our sponsor and myself, we wish to offer our best wishes for the holiday season.*

Trivia, etc. Patricia Collinge was, of course, the mother (Uncle Charlie's sister) in *Shadow of a Doubt*. She became a life-long friend to the Hitchcocks, and she appeared in several episodes. Robert Blees, who would later produce such television programs as *Bonanza, Bus Stop*, and *Combat!*, and write scripts for the big screen such as *The Black Scorpion* (1957), *From the Earth to the Moon* (1958), *Frogs* (1972) and *Dr. Phibes Rises Again* (1972). "I created the story, that is I wrote the story myself so I sold my own rights," Blees recalled. "I created it and wrote it myself at home. Most of those stories originated from already published material. I was a client of MCA and of course, Hitchcock was at MCA, so my agent got it to Joan Harrison who was producing the show. I even went on the set and found it very businesslike. It was a very 'in house' operation. Joan Harrison and Norman Lloyd ran the show. I never saw the rushes, and to this day, I forget if I ever saw it on film."

This was Darren McGavin's second appearance on the Hitchcock program. He previously co-starred in "Triggers in Leash," the third episode of the series.

A clip from Hitchcock's lead-in from this episode was used in the BBC documentary, *Hitch: Alfred the Auteur*.

EPISODE #14 **"A BULLET FOR BALDWIN"** Broadcast on January 1, 1956

      Starring: John Qualen as Benjamin Stepp
      Sebastian Cabot as Nathanael Baldwin / Mr. Davidson

      Philip Reed as Mr. Walter King   Ruth Lee as Miss Wilson
      Cheryll Clarke as Mrs. Baldwin   James Adamson as the janitor
      Don McArt as Labert   Kate Drain Lawson as the landlady

      Bob Patten, David Dwight and Arthur D. Gilmour are the business partners.

      Teleplay written for *Alfred Hitchcock Presents* by Eustace and Francis Cockrell, based on the radio play "Five Bullets for Baldwin" by Joseph Ruscoll, originally broadcast on *The Molle Mystery Theater* on April 16, 1948.

      Directed by Justus Addiss.

      (with 1920's style machine gun) *Good evening. I hope you'll excuse me if I appear a trifle excited. But I have just come into possession of a cure for indigestion. It comes in capsule form.* (holds gun) *For best results they must be taken internally and here is a handy applicator. It's an amazingly simple device. An idiot can operate it and indeed many do. Tonight in addition to our play we have a surprise for you. Usually at this time I introduce a commercial, not so tonight. Well, we'll have that commercial, I just won't introduce it. This on the theory that anything so well known, needs no introduction.*

      Story: San Francisco, 1909. Ben Stepp is a faithful employee of a financially successful investment firm, that managed to survive through thick and thin. But today, Ben is given the pink slip by his boss, Nathanael Baldwin. After first considering suicide, Ben decides to murder his boss. Surprisingly, he accomplishes the deed with little difficulty, and returns to work the next day, acting as if nothing happened the evening before. Boy is he astonished when he arrives that morning to see the investment firm manager alive and well.

And to top it off, Baldwin even gives Ben a raise and a promotion, making Ben think he is one brick short of a full load! But this isn't the case at all, as the new Baldwin is actually an impersonator who has been hired to complete a business deal. After the deal is closed Mr. King takes over, and explains that he was the one taking care of the dead body and hiring Mr. Davidson to impersonate Baldwin. Before long, Ben is called in by Mr. King and fired again, but this time he knows how to handle the situation.

That was amusing, wasn't it? Of course it was mere entertainment. But our next number, after which I'll be back, should appeal to those intellectuals, whose television tastes are more demanding. It is a serious work, more substantial, far deeper, and with a message you can take home and ponder. (commercial break) *Now I see why we occasionally repeat a commercial. It is impossible to grasp all the subtleties of thought and nuances of meaning in a single hearing. Perhaps if enough of you write in we shall be allowed to see that one again. This concludes our show. I have, however, scheduled a return engagement for next week at the same time. When we shall present another story. Good night.*

EPISODE #15 **"THE BIG SWITCH"** Broadcast on January 8, 1956
       Starring: George Mathews as Sam Donleavy   Beverly Michaels as Goldie
       George E. Stone as Barney   Joseph Downing as Al, the lieutenant
       James Edwards as Ed, the bartender   Mark Dana as Morgan
       Napoleon Whiting as Tony, the butler
       Teleplay written for *Alfred Hitchcock Presents* by Dick Carr, based on the story "The Big Switch" by Cornell Woolrich, originally published in the January 25, 1936 issue of *Detective Fiction Weekly.* Subsequently collected (under the pen name William Irish) in *If I Should Die Before I Wake* (Avon, 1945) and in *Rear Window and Four Other Short Novels* (Ballantine, 1984).
       Directed by Don Weis.
       This is a mouse trap, as any fool can plainly see. That is, if he isn't a mouse. It's amazingly effective, too. I've been fiddling with it only a few minutes and I have already caught three. Cornell Woolrich, the author of tonight's story, does not make mouse traps. Mr. Woolrich goes in for bigger game, he makes people traps and very good ones, too. This story concerns a perfect alibi. Actually one never knows when he will need an alibi. Recently I read of an innocent man who found himself in serious difficulty because although he claimed he had been watching a movie while the crime in question was being committed, his vagueness about details of the picture caused police to be suspicious. Please do not allow this to happen to you. Watch and listen closely to the following commercial which is furnished for your benefit. It will provide you with an airtight alibi as to your whereabouts during the next sixty seconds.

       Story: Chicago 1920: In the days of bullets, bootleggers and beautiful babes, Sam Donleavy, professional hit man for the mob, receives a visit from Al, his neighborly friendly police officer. Al knows Sam's profession by trade and asks Sam to vacate from Chicago. Al is also aware that Sam has returned from Miami to kill Goldie, his ex-girlfriend, for leaving him. Aware that the police will be keeping a close eye on him while he's in town, Sam decides that he must have a pretty good alibi for the time the murder takes place. Enter stage left, Barney, a man who for the right price, will provide perfect alibis. Barney has performed this service before but his price has gone up considerably. With no other recourse, Sam agrees to pay the amount, and leaves through a secret exit. Hours later, personal matters straighten out and Sam decides to change his mind and not kill Goldie. But upon returning, his alibi goes sour when the man he was supposed to be playing poker with, accidentally kills himself while cleaning his gun. With the police having kept an eye on him all evening, Sam is blamed for the card player's murder.

       Well, as they say in San Quentin, that's the way the little pellet drops. Now if only Donleavy had killed Goldie, he could have accounted for his actions at the time of Barney's accidental death. But suppose the police started asking questions about Goldie. And now for some of those delightful words from our sponsor, after which I'll be back. (commercial break) *I'm afraid that's all the commercials we have time for this evening. But we shall be back next week with some more, and uh, oh incidentally, if there's time we also plan to tell you another story.*
       Photo on other page, courtesy of Ronald V. Borst / Hollywood Movie Posters.

EPISODE #16 **"YOU GOT TO HAVE LUCK"** Broadcast on January 15, 1956
    Starring: John Cassavetes as Sam Cobbett   Marisa Pavan as Mary
    Lamont Johnson as Davis   Ray Teal as Warden Jacobs
    Vivi Janiss as Maude   Hal K. Dawson as the secretary
    Bob Patten as Willis   Steve Clark as the pilot
    Bill Pullen as the police officer   Wendy Winkleman as Susie
    Teleplay written for *Alfred Hitchcock Presents* by Eustace and Francis Cockrell, based on the short story of the same name by Stanley Ralph Ross, originally published in the October 1952 issue of *Ellery Queen's Mystery Magazine*.
    Directed by Robert Stevens.
    Good evening. The hour-glass is a wonderful invention but I'm afraid it will never replace the sundial, certainly not in my garden. This one doesn't even work. I sent it to a jewelist to be cleaned and he removed all the sand. Fortunately, the second hand still functions. Time is very important to the characters in tonight's story. One of them is doing it, but for another time seems to be running out. Time is also very important in television. We buy it, we fill it, we must start on it, we must finish on it. And appropriately enough, we occasionally kill it. I refer of course to my own fumbling efforts. Certainly not to the vital announcement which follows.

    Story: Sam Cobbett makes a successful prison escape, and looking for a place to hold up for a while until the heat is over, comes across a remote farmhouse occupied by a loving couple, Mary and Davis. After Davis leaves for work, Mary is shocked to discover that she has an unwanted visitor, who locks the doors and closes the curtains. Sam explains that he intends to stay – only for a few hours – until the cops stop looking for him. During the restless hours, Sam has the stilted-seeming Mary fix him some food and tries on some of her husband's nice clothes. When the phone rings, Sam forces Mary to talk to her mother as if nothing is wrong. Shortly before Davis is to return from work, Sam decides it's time to leave. The coast is clear. But just as he takes a few steps outside the front door, police pop out of nowhere and surprise Sam, handcuffing him. When Sam asks how they knew where he was hiding, the warden explains that Mary is deaf, and talking to her mother on the phone was a tip-off.

    Oh well, back to the old rock pile. I do think Sam should be congratulated for making such a good try. Perhaps he'll have better luck next time. And returning to the subject of time, I'm sure you have been aware of the occasional sly remark I have directed at television commercials. In the interest of fair play I will step aside for the moment to give my sponsor equal time to reply. Ladies and gentlemen, my worthy opponent. (commercial break) *This case is not without some merit I grant you. I shall present my rebuttal next week at the same time. So not to miss it, I suggest you set your alarm clocks at once. Good night.*

EPISODE #17 **"THE OLDER SISTER"** Broadcast on January 22, 1956
    Starring: Joan Lorring as Miss Emma Borden
    Carmen Mathews as Miss Lizzie Borden
    Polly Rowles as Nell Cutts, the reporter
    Pat Hitchcock as Margaret, the maid
    Wendy Winkleman as the little singing girl
    Kay Stewart as the woman on the street
    Teleplay written for *Alfred Hitchcock Presents* by Robert C. Dennis, based on the 1947 one-act play "Good-Bye, Miss Lizzie Borden" by Lillian de la Torre. Anthologized in *Twenty Great Tales of Murder*, ed. Helen McCloy and Brett Halliday (Random House, 1951).
    Directed by Robert Stevens.

This is an axe. I say this for the information of those of you whose television tubes may have burned out. I wish to reach the widest possible audience. Tonight we have a story based on one of our most celebrated murder cases. One that rocked Four Rivers, Massachusetts, and the entire country late in the last century. The crime was and still is a shocking one. But since it actually happened and is a matter of record we felt it unwise to pretty up the details to make them palatable for the squeamish. Tonight's theme song will be that familiar little ditty everybody knows. Lizzie Borden took an axe and gave her mother forty whacks and when she saw what she had done she gave her father forty-one. I venture that by this time you can see we are not presenting a romantic comedy tonight, however we shall not re-enact the crime. We had intended to, but casting difficulties interfered. Oh, we had no trouble casting the mother and father, but we kept losing them in rehearsals. So instead we shall show you a slightly different interpretation of the Lizzie Borden story. It begins just one year from the time of the murder and just one minute from now.

Story: After Lizzie Borden is cleared of the charges of having axe-murdered her father and stepmother, she turns into a spinster who is constantly hounded by people who think she is guilty. Even her sister, Emma, and the hired help, Margaret, are afraid to be in the house alone. Matters are not helped when Nell Cutts, a pushy female reporter, barges her way into the Borden house to do a follow-up story about the murders. In actuality, the nosy reporter wants nothing more than to unearth the truth about Lizzie. She makes a complete nuisance of herself talking about the details of the trial to Lizzie's sister Emma, who only wants to be left alone and claims not to have been in the house at the time. Nell finally meets up with Lizzie, who sees through the reporter immediately, and forces her out of the house. Emma and Lizzie confront the situation, where the axe that was never found is still in hiding, and how it was Emma – and not Lizzie – who committed the murders. The reporter, having heard this conversation outside the house, enters again to confront Lizzie about the true facts . . . only this time, the royal pain in the neck is about to get a reprised performance.

Did she seem a trifle overwrought to you? She did to me. But you know I react in precisely the same manner whenever I hear a child singing "Davy Crockett." Being more civilized than Lizzie I don't go about hitting tables. I hit the child instead. Not with the axe of course, but in a nice way. Now I am certain there are some of you who prefer that we have a happy ending on our program. For your benefit we are going to present one now, after which I'll be back. (commercial break) *That was more like it. It's so much better to end the program on a pleasant note, don't you think? Good night.*

EPISODE #18   **"SHOPPING FOR DEATH"**   Broadcast on January 29, 1956
Starring: Jo Van Fleet as Mrs. Shrike   Robert H. Harris as Mr. Clarence Foxe
John Qualen as Mr. Elmer Shaw   Mike Ross as Mr. Albert Shrike
Michael Ansara as clerk at Cut Rate Meats
Alfred Linder as the male neighbor   Charlotte Knight as female neighbor
Lee Erickson as the boy at the firehydrant   Jack Tesler as a man in the street
Laiola Wendorff as the woman with accent
Ralph Montgomery as a man in the street   Bob Morgan as the other man
Teleplay written for *Alfred Hitchcock Presents* by Ray Bradbury, from his short story of the same name, originally published in the June 1, 1954 issue of *MacLean's*. Subsequently collected under a new title, "Touched With Fire," in *The October Country* (Ballantine, 1955) and in *The Stories of Ray Bradbury* (Knopf, 1980).
Directed by Robert Stevens.
(fixing a creaking door) There, that's better, much better. The least we can do is to provide the proper atmosphere. This is truly an extraordinary item. Loud squeaking fluid. It is also excellent at making old shutters bang. And on dark nights one can spray it in

the air in case the wind isn't whistling loud enough. It's very practical too. It can make old shoes squeak like new again. Now that we have established our mood, I should like to tell you that tonight's story is by Ray Bradbury and is known by the provocative title of "Shopping For Death." It will follow the commercial, I repeat you will first see the commercial, then our story. I make this clear because many of our listeners have been confusing the two. It's immaterial to me except that after seeing the commercial they very often concentrate too much on that, rather than on the story. Ladies and gentlemen, the commercial.

Story: Mr. Foxe and Mr. Shaw, a pair of retired insurance salesmen with too much time on their hands, have put together a hypothesis that the majority of murders occur at a temperature of 92 degrees. To test out their theory, they choose the likely victim in a neighbor: the shrill Mrs. Shrike. She's a nagging old bat of a wife, who lives with a hulking longshoreman named Albert, known to have violent tendencies. They meet with her and, during conversation, she almost makes Mr. Foxe want to kill her himself. But Mr. Foxe insists that if she keeps her shrewish ways up, both she and her husband will end in a horrifying way. He pleads with her to be careful, but the advice does little good. When the temperature reaches 92 degrees, Alfred comes home and very shortly the police arrive at their front door step.

You needn't keep staring. We're not going to show you anymore. In fact, I'm not even going to tell you what happened. Television audiences are becoming entirely too dependent. You expect us to do everything for you. This oil is terribly difficult to get rid of. Look, while I'm working on this, please listen closely to the following and do exactly what they tell you. (commercial break) *Next week at the same time, I hope to see you again. Good night.*

Trivia, etc. "Shopping for Death" was the first of many Ray Bradbury stories adapted for *Alfred Hitchcock Presents.* Although some authors had the opportunity to adapt their own stories for the series, others merely sat quietly while someone else wrote the script. For this episode, Bradbury composed the teleplay based on his own short story.

For trivia fans, Mr. and Mrs. Albert Shrike live in apartment 321. The murder in the premiere episode "Revenge" took place in a hotel room, number 321!

EPISODE #19 **"THE DERELICTS"** Broadcast on February 5, 1956
Starring: Robert Newton as Peter Goodfellow   Philip Reed as Ralph Cowell
Peggy Knudsen as Herta Cowell   Johnny Silver as Mr. Fenton Shanks
Robert Foulk as Detective Monroeney   Cyril Delevanti as Alfred Sloane
Teleplay written for *Alfred Hitchcock Presents* by Robert C. Dennis, based on a story by Terence Maples.
Directed by Robert Stevenson.
(with top hat and lunchbox) *Oh, good evening. I hope you don't mind but I have to eat on the job tonight. We're terribly rushed, but no matter how busy, I think the least one can do is to dress properly. Tonight's supper show is called "The Derelicts" and there isn't much to tell you about it. Naturally. we shall populate our stage with a few delinquents. Ah. . .* (takes out a sandwich) *Rabbit. I could have pulled that out of the hat. When I was a young man, I had an uncle who frequently took me out to dinner. He always accompanied these dinners with minutely detailed stories about himself. But I listened because he was paying for the dinner. I don't know why I'm reminded of this, but we are about to have one of our commercials. Through a brilliant piece of strategy, it immediately precedes the pièce de résistance.*

Story: In the park late one night, alone, Ralph Cowell meets up with a creditor who demands to be paid off on a $10,000 debt. Angry because he can't pay up, Ralph murders the old man and takes his wallet. When Ralph gets home, it seems he can't find the handwritten I.O.U. in the wallet. A shabby and blackmailing bum named Goodfellow, witnesses the crime and explains to Ralph that he found the I.O.U. His demands? To let Goodfellow and his partner in crime, Fenton Shanks, take up residence in his luxurious apartment. Seeing no other way, Ralph reluctantly agrees. Within a few weeks, the bums have ruined Ralph's business, cleaned him out and pawned his possessions. Ralph's wife, Herta, finally learns the truth, and thanks to her resourcefulness, brings the I.O.U. out in the open, and Ralph burns the paper. Throwing the bums out, Ralph's problems seems to be over till a detective shows up, asking about the pawned items in Ralph's name. One of the items pawned was the creditor's cigarette lighter and the police have a few questions to ask him.

As you might expect, before Mr. Goodfellow and Mr. Shanks had reached the street, they had walked into the inviting arms of two luscious young ladies, an occurrence that was especially to Goodfellow's liking. Since the ladies were policewomen, his enjoyment was at best, momentary. A television program is constructed in much the same manner as a dinner. The best should be saved until last. You have partaken over the main course. Allow us to serve you the dessert. And then I will return to clear the table. (commercial break) *For those of you waiting for desserts, there wasn't quite enough of that, was there? That was deliberate. It's much too rich for you. If you wish another portion, join us next week. Until then, good night.*

Trivia, etc. The scene where the bums move in and take advantage is similar to the scene in Hitchcock's *Blackmail* (1929), where the blackmailer comes into the family's home and expects to be treated like a guest. Could Hitchcock have had any influence on the filming or pre-production of this episode?

EPISODE #20 **"AND SO DIED RIABOUCHINSKA"** Broadcast on February 12, 1956
    Starring: Claude Rains as Mr. Fabian
    Charles Bronson as Detective Krovitch   Claire Carleton as Alice Fabian
    Lowell Gilmore as Mel Douglas, Fabian's manager
    Charles Cantor as the booking agent   Harry O. Tyler as Dan
    Iris Adrian as Nickie   Bill Haade as the stagehand
    Virginia Gregg as the voice of Riabouchinska
    Teleplay by Mel Dinelli, based on the story of the same name by Ray Bradbury, originally published in the June/July issue of *The Saint Detective Magazine*. Later collected in *The Machineries of Joy* (Simon & Schuster, 1964) and in *The Stories of Ray Bradbury* (Knopf, 1980).
    Directed by Robert Stevenson.
    (as a ventriloquist) *Good evening. This misty bit of ectoplasm forming on the inside of your television tube, is one Alfred Hitchcock. I have materialized for the purpose of warning you that following a word from our dear patron, we shall present tonight's story, entitled "And So Died Riabouchinska." That is all I have to say just now, but don't be alarmed, I shall return. Old television actors never die, they only fade away.* (fade out for commercial)

Alternate narrative:
    (as a ventriloquist) *Good evening. This misty bit of ectoplasm forming on the inside of your television tube, is one Alfred Hitchcock. We shall present tonight's story, entitled "And So Died Riabouchinska." That is all I have to say just now, but don't be alarmed, I shall return. Old television actors never die, they only fade away.* (fade out for commercial)

Story: After a stranger named Ockham tries unsuccessfully to get in to see Fabian, the half-baked ventriloquist, Ockham's murdered body is later found by the police. Detective Krovitch arrives to talk to Fabian and his wife, hoping to learn something about the dead man's motives. During the questioning, Krovitch senses that the strange Fabian appears more devoted to a female marionette, Riabouchinska, than to his wife. The detective also notices that Fabian is strangely attracted to the dummy, so he returns to the police department and begins going through the missing persons files. It turns out that the marionette closely resembles a missing girl in his files. When Krovitch presents this information to Fabian, the ventriloquist confesses that he did indeed murder Ockham, as the man was going to expose Fabian's strange romantic involvement with the dummy, which Fabian fashioned after a young girl he was involved with. But the ventriloquist's confession does not come from his own mouth, but rather from that of his dummy.

And so died Riabouchinska, I hope you, uh . . . (Tell 'em about the commercial, Mr. Hitchcock.) *In due time Alfred, in due time. I hope you have* . . . (My name is Alfie, I'm Mr. Hitchcock's conscience. I bet you didn't think he had any.) *Alfred!* (Mr. Hitchcock has one alright, he just doesn't pay me any attention, that's all.) *Alfred! I wish I knew how to turn one of these things off.* (A very irresponsible man, Mr. Hitchcock. He never pays the proper attention to the commercials either. He spends all of his time with those frivolous toys of his.) *Are you quite finished, Alfred?* (Yes, sir.) *I hope you have enjoyed our play.* (commercial break) *Do you wanna tell the people, you'll be back, Alfred?* (No sir, I'm not coming back. I've decided to have a bit of fun, for a change. You see, you may have a conscience, but I don't.) *Why, Alfred!* (But don't you worry our Mr. Hitchcock will be back, I'll see to that. Good night.)

Alternate narrative:
That was pleasant. It also reminded me of my youth. When I was once a part of a vaudeville act called "Dr. Speewack and his puppets." But I never cared for Dr. Speewack, he thought he was better than the rest of us. But so much for tonight's entertainment. Until the next time we return with another play. Good night.

Trivia, etc. Radio actress Virginia Gregg, who played supporting roles in two previous Hitchcock episodes, also supplied the voice of Riabouchinska. Gregg played the supporting role of chattering Nurse Parker on radio's *Dr. Kildare* and Missy Wong, hotel servant to Paladin on radio's *Have Gun – Will Travel*. So naturally, an experienced radio actress with the talent of voice alteration sould supply the voice of Riabouchinska.* Gregg's relationship with Hitchcock wasn't limited to the television series. She helped supply the voice of Norman's mother in *Psycho* (1960), and the sequels *Psycho II* (1983) and *Psycho III* (1986). Earlier, she had worked with Hitchcock on *Notorious*, but her part, that of a file clerk in Washington, D.C., was cut out of the film. Mel Dinelli, who wrote the Hitchcock teleplay based on the Ray Bradbury story, also wrote a radio script based on the same story, for *Suspense* (broadcast on CBS, November 13, 1947). "Claude Rains was one of my favorites," Ray Bradbury recalled. "I had the pleasure of meeting him in person on the set but for the likes of me, I can't recall anything about the show except that it was wonderful."

EPISODE #21   **"SAFE CONDUCT"**   Broadcast on February 19, 1956
        Starring: Claire Trevor as Mary Prescott   Jacques Bergerac as Jan Gubak
        Werner Klemperer as Klopa   Peter Van Eyck as the officer
        John Bauner as the conductor
        Konstantin Shayne as the customs officer   Ralph Manza as the waiter

* The method of employing a radio actor for television or motion pictures still proved successful in 1973 when Mercedes McCambridge supplied the voice of the demon in William Friedkin's *The Exorsist*.

Original teleplay written exclusively for *Alfred Hitchcock Presents* by Andrew Solt. Directed by Justus Addiss.

(pool table and eye patch) *Oh, good evening. You know, this came as somewhat of a surprise to me. I was under the impression that all pool tables were kidney shaped. I guess that's only true in Hollywood. Our story tonight will be in a somewhat different vein. It is a tale of mystery and intrigue on a transcontinental express. It is called, uh . . . title seems to have slipped my mind, it's . . .* (man comes in with a pool cue, "you've dropped your cue.") (Hitchcock shrugs his shoulders and takes the top of pool cue and finds a note) *The title of tonight's play is "Safe Conduct." Thank you very much.*

Story: Behind the Iron Curtain for an interview with a communist leader, journalist Mary Prescott heads home on a transcontinental train. To avoid any problems crossing the border, she was given a special pass by the dictator himself. During the trip on board, she meets one Jan Gubak, who claims that he is an athlete on his way to West Germany to visit a sister, who is desperate for money for an expensive operation. With such a heart-breaking story, Jan asks Mary for a small favor – even if it is illegal. He asks Mary to use her special pass for smuggling purposes, which in turn will afford his sister's operation. Should she trust the man?

I hadn't expected that to be such a hair-raising story. I am about to undertake an extremely difficult shot. Since I'd rather you look the other way, I have talked a friend into offering this charming charade to divert you. After which, I trust you'll return. (commercial break) *Now, I'm sorry you didn't watch, you'll never believe me. A three-cushion shot. It caromed off the ceiling, floor and wall and into the side pocket. Next week at this time we shall all return. Our mummers to offer you their usual 26 minutes of drama, the sponsor with his three minutes of commercials and of course I shall be back to lay my customary one-minute egg. Good night.*

Jacques Bergerac and Claire Trevor guest star in the episode "Safe Conduct."

Photo courtesy of Ronald V. Borst / Hollywood Movie Posters in Hollywood, California.

133

Trivia, etc. Werner Klemperer and John Bauner would later work together, almost a decade later, on television's *Hogan's Heroes* as Colonel Klink and Sergeant Schultz. Klemperer would later be directed by Alfred Hitchcock in the episode "The Crystal Trench." *Alfred Hitchcock Presents* was one of the first television series Justus Joseph Addiss would helm in his career. Two years after this episode finished production, Addiss directed *The Cry Baby Killer* (1958), Jack Nicholson's first feature film. Addiss would later direct episodes of *The Twilight Zone, Adventures in Paradise, Mister Ed, Voyage to the Bottom of the Sea* and *Lost in Space*.

The role of the customs officer was played by Konstantin Shayne, brother of actress Tamara Shayne (remember Zenia in *Anastasia* (1956)?), Konstantin was to join the Moscow Arts Theatre, but World War I intervened, and he fought with General Wrangell and the White Armies. Although he received few significant roles, Konstantin was outstanding in *None But the Lonely Heart* (1944) as Ike Weber and in *The Stranger* (1967) as Gen. Meinike where his character dominates the first fifteen minutes of the film. His performance in *For Whom the Bell Tolls* (1943) was considered outstanding, but was cut from the release print. Not an ambitious actor, Konstantin made occasional guest appearances on television's *The Rogues* and an episode of *You Are There*, two months after this Hitchcock episode was broadcast. Shayne also played the proprietor of the Argosy Bookstore in *Vertigo* (1958).

EPISODE #22 **"PLACE OF SHADOWS"** Broadcast on February 26, 1956
Starring: Everett Sloane as Father Vincente   Sean McClory as Brother Gerard
Mark Damon as Ray Clements   Claude Akins as a police officer
Joseph Downing as Floyd Unser   Everett Glass as Brother Charles
Harry O. Tyler as train ticket agent   Steve Mitchell as police officer
Teleplay written for *Alfred Hitchcock Presents* by Robert C. Dennis, based on his short story of the same name, originally published in the January 1947 issue of *Crack Detective Stories*.
Directed by Robert Stevens.
Good evening, and thank you for allowing me to come into your living rooms. Well, I'm not easily shocked but I did expect people to dress a bit formally, before sitting in front of their sets. Now that two-way television is here. (screams from off the side) *Apparently not everyone was aware of the incessant march of progress. The next improvement should be more to your liking. I understand that scientists will soon make it possible for any object thrown at the television screen to actually hit the performer. All of which reminds me of a story.*

Story: After being swindled by a hustler named Rocco, Ray Clements travels north to a remote monastery, where Rocco was given sanctuary by the monks. It seems Rocco is bed-ridden after having faced a near-fatal accident. Rocco wrote to his old business partner to explain where he is hiding, but it seems young Ray stole the letter and attempted to take the business partner's identity, in hopes of killing Rocco. In the monastery, Father Vincente knows better, and explains to the boy that as long as he has hatred in his heart, he will not meet Rocco. Brother Gerard tells the boy that "you can never forget the face of a man you kill. Neither you or I can bring back the breath of life." Ray leaves the monastery disgruntled and back at the train station, the real business partner shows up. The two exchange gunfire. The businessman dies but Ray returns to the monastery wounded. Ray begs for forgiveness and asks Father Vincente to tell Rocco he's sorry. He holds no personal grudge. Father Vincente says the anger he displayed earlier in the day would have made no difference as Rocco actually died shortly before he came there.

The murder on tonight's television program was as usual, completely unrehearsed. In fact, we hadn't planned on having a killing at all. Our story was intended to be about a man found guilty of parking in front of a fire hydrant. But the actors seem to have gotten out of hand. (gun shots) *There they go again. A wild, unruly lot those actors. For more predictable entertainment, I recommend the following. After which I'll be back to see if you have observed its full significance.* (commercial break) *For those of you who fail to grasp the point of that message, it was prepared by my sponsor, who wishes you to buy his product. I don't think that's an unreasonable request to make. Next week, my beloved sponsor, and I, and all our actors who are not on the critical list, will be back to bring you another story. Until then, good night.*

Alternate narrative:

(standing, not sitting on desk) *That was a bit of a snapper, wasn't it? The murder on tonight's television program was as usual, completely unrehearsed. In fact, we hadn't planned on having a killing at all. Our story was intended to be about a man found guilty of parking in front of a policeman. But the actors seem to have gotten out of hand.* (gun shots) *There they go again. A wild, unruly lot those actors. I hope we have some of them left when we return with out next play, because uh . . . we'd be somewhat handicapped without actors. Until then, good night.*

EPISODE #23 **"BACK FOR CHRISTMAS"** Broadcast on March 4, 1956
Rehearsed and filmed on January 13, 14, and 16, 1956.
Starring: John Williams as Herbert Carpenter
Isobel Elsom as Hermione Carpenter

A.E. Gould-Porter as Major Sinclair	Lily Kemble-Cooper as Mrs. Sinclair
Gavin Muir as Mr. Wallingford	Katherine Warren as Mrs. Wallingford
Gerald Hamer as Mr. Hewitt	Irene Tedrow as Mrs. Hewitt
Ross Ford as U.S. work partner	Theresa Harris as the U.S. maid

Mollie Glessing as Elsie, the Carpenter's maid
Teleplay written for *Alfred Hitchcock Presents* by Francis Cockrell, based on the short story of the same name by John Collier, originally published in the December 13, 1939 issue of *The Tatler*. Reprinted in the August 1942 issue of *Reader's Digest*. Subsequently collected in *Fancies and Goodnights* (Doubleday, 1951) and in *The John Collier Reader* (Knopf, 1972).
Directed by Alfred Hitchcock.

(playing with a shrunken head) *Oh, good evening ladies and gentlemen, especially the ladies. Now you see what might happen if you fall asleep under the dryer. Shrunken heads are a hobby of mine, collecting them of course, not making them. Takes too long to make one, first of all you must wait until the original owner of the head dies. I haven't the patience for that. As you have no doubt already guessed, tonight's story has nothing what-so-ever to do with shrunken heads. It is called "Back for Christmas." Before we tell it however, I would like all of you to observe one minute of silence, out of respect . . . for my sponsor.*

Story: Herbert Carpenter and his nagging wife Hermione are getting ready to leave for work in California. But Hermione doesn't want to stay in California, she'd rather be home for Christmas. Herbert, whose hobby is his "devil's garden" in the basement, plans to stay in California a little longer than his wife thinks. Just before they leave, Herbert kills the shrew of a wife and buries her body in the basement. Covering the hole he dug so no one could suspect, Herbert leaves for sunny California. In California, Herbert tells the hotel staff that his wife and he separated. Spending warm afternoons in his suite in Beverly Hills, Herbert composes a letter with his wife's signature, telling all his friends back home that the Carpenters will be staying longer than they planned. Just when all seems fair and well, an envelope arrives addressed to his wife, a construction bill for excavating the cellar floor, as part of the construction of a wine cellar. Completion should be done before Christmas, as a surprise for her husband! "She said I would be back for Christmas," Herbert cries.

I think the lesson of that story is worth repeating. Gentlemen, dig deep. So much for our play. Now for the bright spot, in an otherwise somber picture. On the instructions of our foster father, I will be returning to you. (commercial break) *That concludes our sideshow. We should be back next week to . . . Made in Texas . . . by Texans, with New Yorkers. I think I'd better be trotting off. I just decided to have my head sanforized. Good night.*

Trivia, etc. John Williams, thespian favorite of Hitchcock's, and veteran of *To Catch a Thief* and *Dial M For Murder*, made his second of many guest appearances on *Alfred Hitchcock Presents*. His third was just three weeks later in "Whodunit" In this sweet English tale of murder and faithfulness, John Collier's short story fit the Hitchcock mold. "In some ways, I think it's fair to say he was Hitchcock's favorite actor," recalled Norman Lloyd. "I really always had that sneaking suspicion. Hitch had him in everything - and big parts, I don't mean just a good luck charm. He's in *Dial M for Murder* (1954), as the inspector, and he was the perfect English inspector. And he was that way on-screen and off-screen, you couldn't tell the difference with these guys! He had charm and style and a very objective way of approaching everything. Very English, but attractively so. Whenever we had an inspector [in an episode], the first one we'd go to was old John, and if he was free, he'd do it. I don't know how many he did! Then he retired to La Jolla, and now he's not with us any more. But he was the definitive Hitchcock actor, everything in his style served Hitchcock's purposes: The underplaying, the subtle humor. the indirect approach that he had."

A few months later, Williams would also be directed by Hitchcock again in the second-season opener, "Wet Saturday," another John Collier story. As for the story itself, "Back for Christmas" was dramatized previously on other radio and television programs, with English *and* American actors playing the role of Herbert Carpenter, including John McIntire, Herbert Marshall and Peter Lorre – all of whom made guest appearances in later Hitchcock episodes. In the original story, Herbert spent some of his free time making his acquaintance with a young store keeper, and shortly after murdering his wife, married the girl, replacing the void of Mrs. Carpenter with another woman. Neither the ship's crew or the American public, was aware of the switch, having never seen the real Mrs. Carpenter. The climactic twist is given to Herbert by method of telegraph, on board the ship already having set sail toward the West.* In this episode, the story is slightly altered, but shines through all-the-same. An interesting viewpoint: In order to make Hermione disliked by the viewers, the women do most of the talking during the tea scene. The men don't speak till they start leaving. A clip from the lead-in of this episode was used in the documentary, *Dial H for Hitchcock: The Genius Behind the Showman*.

EPISODE #24 **"THE PERFECT MURDER"** Broadcast on March 11, 1956
        Starring: Hurd Hatfield as Paul Tallendier
        Mildred Natwick as Madame Aunt Rosalie
        Philip Coolidge as Henri Tallendier
        Gladys Hurlbut as Ernestine the cook
        Walter Kingsford as the doctor   Percy Helton as the lawyer
        Hope Summers as Marie   Jack Chefe as the waiter
        Teleplay written for *Alfred Hitchcock Presents* by Victor Wolfson, based on the short story of the same name by Stacey Aumonier, originally published in a 1926 issue of *The Strand Magazine*. Later published in the March 1952 issue of *Ellery Queen's Mystery Magazine*. Subsequently anthologized in *The Third Omnibus of Crime*, ed. Dorothy L. Sayers, (Coward-McCann, 1935).
        Directed by Robert Stevens.

* This recalled the Crippen case – Crippen was intercepted after a telegraph message to a liner at sea, on which he was fleeting with his mistress to America. Could the case have been the influence for John Collier's story?

(knife in the back) *Oh, good evening, ladies and gentlemen and welcome to Hollywood. I think everyone enjoys a nice murder, provided he is not the victim. Well, tonight's little comedy of bad manners is concerned with that dream of all of us who harbor homicidal tendencies. The perfect murder. Of course, to be serious for a moment, there is no such thing as a nice murder or a perfect murder. It is always a sordid, despicable business, especially if you don't have a good lawyer. According to statistics a murder will be committed during the next sixty seconds, as well as four armed robberies, thirty-three petty thefts and a forgery. There will also be a television commercial, if you doubt me, watch.*

Story: Paul and Henri were always heartless toward their recently-deceased uncle, who left his entire estate to Aunt Rosalie. The boys will, however, inherit the estate and everything that goes with it, upon the untimely death of their Aunt. She plans to outlive the greedy relatives so she can give the money to her church, against the wishes of the two brothers, who just cannot wait any longer for her to die. Paul grinds a wineglass into a fine powder and orders Henri to administer the "special ingredient" to her egg dinner. Then the boys leave for the evening to create an alibi while their aunt dies of "natural causes." In the morning, Henri pays Aunt Rosalie a visit and finds a surprise. Aunt Rosalie never ate the dinner they wanted – she had fish instead of eggs. Paul however, ate an egg omelet that morning and died shortly after.

As for the eventual outcome of tonight's crime, the case was later reopened and Henri arrested and convicted of violating the pure food and drug act. He had used an inferior grade of glass. You see, one can't be too careful about these matters. Now for a cleverly timed interlude, after which I'll rejoin you. (commercial break) *And with that delightful bit of Americana, we reluctantly drop our curtain. We shall have our next performance of another play, one week from tonight. Oh yes, normally I detest sentimentality but I must leave you with this little thought for the day. Never turn your back on a friend. Good night.*

Trivia, etc. Mildred Natwick, who made several films for John Ford, played the spinster Miss Gravely in *The Trouble with Harry* (1954).

EPISODE #25 **"THERE WAS AN OLD WOMAN"** Broadcast on March 18, 1956
    Starring: Estelle Winwood as Miss Mundy Lawton
    Charles Bronson as Frank Bramwell   Norma Crane as Lorna Bramwell
    Dabbs Greer as the milkman   Emerson Tracy as the druggist
    Teleplay written for *Alfred Hitchcock Presents* by Marian Cockrell, based on a story by Jerry Hackady and Harold Hackady.
    Directed by Robert Stevenson.
    Good evening. I have a request for those of you who are not watching television. Please turn on your set. I'm sure I look much worse in the flamboyant Technicolor of your imagination than I do in the austere black and white of television. Thank you. I'm sure that's much better. Although it may still be one color too many. Black and white are very fitting this evening, as a matter of fact we considered edging the entire picture in black but we gave that up. It would have been decidedly unfair to those of you with very small tubes or narrow imaginations. Tonight's fable is about Mundy Lawton, a nice little old lady with a penchant for funerals. You shall learn more about Miss Lawton, after our sponsor gives this brief but heartfelt eulogy in behalf of . . . his product.

Story: A strange old woman, Mundy Lawton, lives alone with her imaginary relatives, whom she mourns when they pass away. Two low-lifes, Frank and Lorna

Charles Bronson and Estelle Winwood in "There Was an Old Woman"
(Photo courtesy of Photofest.)

Bramwell, hear a rumor that she is actually quite wealthy and that her money is hidden in the house. The couple show up at her home acting like they are long-lost relatives, and the mentally incompetent woman invites them in, introducing the members of her imaginary family. Meanwhile, Frank and Lorna are turning the house upside down searching for the cash, but they are unsuccessful at locating anything. Frank finally threatens the old woman, but finds he is getting nowhere as she continues to live in an imaginary world. However, the Bramwells get their just deserts when they don't take the old lady seriously at their next breakfast . . .

Ah well, as the French tells us, C'est la mort. I thought rat poison was charmingly appropriate didn't you? After all, sweets to the sweet and I can think of no better time to segue into our next theme, after which I'll segue back to you. (commercial break) *The opinions expressed by my sponsor, are his. Those of you who wish, may join us again next week when we'll be back with another play. Good night.*

138

EPISODE #26 "WHODUNIT" Broadcast on March 25, 1956
Starring: John Williams as Alexander Penn Arlington

Amanda Blake as Carol Arlington   Jerry Paris as Mr. Wally Benson
Philip Coolidge as Talbot   Alan Napier as Archangel Wilfred
Bill Slack as Vincent   Ruta Lee as the angel
Rudy Robles as Herman, the butler

Teleplay written for *Alfred Hitchcock Presents* by Francis and Marian Cockrell, based on the short story "Heaven Can Wait" by C.B. Gilford, originally published in the August 1953 issue of *Ellery Queen's Mystery Magazine*. Anthologized in *The Queen's Awards, Eighth Series*, ed. Ellery Queen (Little Brown, 1953).

Directed by Francis Cockrell.

(as an auctioneer) *Quiet please. Good evening, fellow necromaniacs. I'm glad so many of you could come. I should explain that the word has nothing to do with necking. I'm awfully sorry, I haven't the time to explain it now. You'll just have to look it up in the dictionary. As you know, we are not allowed to present our play unless we have a quorum. Tonight we are concerned with those three little words, who dun it. When our story opens, the more sordid details are safely out of the way, for the hero of tonight's Grand Guignol is already quite dead. But before we get to that portion of our meeting, I believe we have some old business to discuss.*

Story: A murdered mystery writer, Alexander Arlington, strikes a deal with an angel to let him return to Earth for twenty-four hours to find out who his killer was. Back on Earth, Alexander puts together a whole list of potential guilty persons, and just before his deadline is up he invites them to his library. Once there, they all deny being guilty, but after Benson turns out the lights Alexander is once again murdered. Back in heaven he decides he finally knows who the murderer really was. It must be someone who would have planned it together with Benson, that means his own wife, who is fooling around with Benson.

Well, why they would go to heaven, is certainly a mystery to me. After she had assisted her husband out of this vale of tears, Mrs. Arlington sought solace in a quick marriage to Mr. Al Benson and they lived happily ever after. He in the state penitentiary and she at the women's detention home, where she found a very nice job in the mail room. Vincent, of course became filthy rich. And speaking of money, since we have incurred a great deal of expense during the conduct of this meeting, I think it is high time we heard from the committee on ways and means after which this forum will again come to order. (commercial break) *I think the committee deserves a vote of confidence for its efforts on our behalf. Unfortunately time does not permit. I declare the meeting adjourned until next week.*

Trivia, etc. Although Francis Cockrell scripted numerous episodes for the series, this was his first of two directorial efforts. Francis and Marian Cockrell * were real-life husband and wife, who co-wrote the story *Dark Waters*, a film Joan Harrison produced years before *Alfred Hitchcock Presents*. Both Francis and Marian became staff writers for the series, especially during the program's first three years, at the request of Harrison. Francis would later write scripts for television's *Perry Mason*, *Alcoa Presents* (a.k.a. *One Step Beyond*), and *The High Chaparral*. Both Francis and Marian wrote scripts for television's *Batman* in 1966 and 1967. The names Al Benson and Vincent, spoken by Hitchcock during the lead-out for this episode, was actually dubbed in later. Perhaps the names of the characters were not known when Hitchcock was being filmed for this broadcast?

* Authors' note: Francis is the correct spelling of his name, even though he was occasionally credited as Francis M. Cockrell, Francis Cockrell III, and Frank Cockrell. His wife was often credited as Marian B. Cockrell and Marion Cockrell.

EPISODE #27 **"HELP WANTED"** Broadcast on April 1, 1956

Starring: John Qualen as Mr. Crabtree   Lorne Greene as Mr. X

Madge Kennedy as Laura Crabtree   Ruth Swanson as Miss Brown

John Harmon as the police officer

Malcolm Atterbury as the "real" blackmailer

Parley Baer as the detective   Paul Brinegar as the murdered blackmailer

Teleplay written for *Alfred Hitchcock Presents* by Robert C. Dennis (from an adaptation by Mary Orr and Reginald Denham), based on the short story "The Cat's Paw" by Stanley Ellin, originally published in the June 1949 issue of *Ellery Queen's Mystery Magazine*. Subsequently collected in *Mystery Stories* (Simon & Schuster, 1956) and in *The Specialty of the House and Other Stories* (Mysterious Press, 1979).

Directed by James Neilson.

(newspaper want ads) *Oh, good evening. How did you find me? I specifically asked for an unlisted channel. I'm taking the week off. I wanted a rest from television. If you're one of those critics who thinks that television is frightful, all I can say is, you should see it from this side. I've been reading the want ads. A man has a right to look around for a better job, hmm . . . Wanted: Host for television program, sounds like a job for me. Must be witty, charming, handsome . . . wow, this is perfect! Gracious and must be willing to work every week. Apply: Alfred Hitchcock Presents. I think I better scarper back to the old job. I don't want to miss the show and don't you miss it either.*

Story: Recently employed Mr. Crabtree is desperate for money since he learned that his wife of twenty plus years will soon need an expensive operation. Answering the want ads for a job, he strangely finds himself employed by an unknown "Mr. X," whose intentions are not laid out in writing. It turns out that Mr. X wants Crabtree to murder a blackmailer. Crabtree refuses until he is told that the payoff will be $5,000 in cash (how convenient). Mr. X explains the plan, having arranged for Crabtree to deliver the next payoff, and is given a key phrase to identify the man. When asked why not do the job himself, Mr. X explains that he needs an alibi as backup. But the envelope contains a suicide note, not a payoff, and Crabtree is to push the man out of a window so it will look like a suicide. The deed goes according to plan – with slight variation but no major difference – and Mr. X mails the cash payoff as agreed. But later that afternoon, as Crabtree is getting ready to go home, he discovers that the wrong blackmailer went out the window!

Our play is over, and we have now entered the sudden death over time period of television. The game will end at any moment. So I must allow my sponsor to make a few points. After which I shall dribble back. (commercial break) *A brilliant play. Sneaky, but brilliant. So nice to be with the winning team, and now please keep your eyes on this space for I shall return here next week to bring you another story. Good night.*

Trivia, etc. Lorne Greene, soon to play Ben Cartwright on NBC-TV's *Bonanza*, was devilishly evil in this humorous macabre story about blackmail and murder. Greene's last name, however, was misspelled in the opening titles of this episode, mistakenly spelled Lorne Green! Canadian-born Robert C. Dennis was a prolific contributor to the pulp and digest mystery magazines in the 1950s, and wrote two very good crime novels in the 1970s. Dennis wrote scripts for television's *Racket Squad* before applying his trade on *Alfred Hitchcock Presents*. He would later compose many original teleplays for television's *Perry Mason, The Fugitive, The Wild, Wild West, Batman* and *Dragnet*. Malcolm Atterbury, the real blackmailer who shows up at the end of this episode, was the farmer waiting at the bus stop in *North by Northwest* (1959) and Deputy Sheriff Al Malone in *The Birds* (1963).

140

EPISODE #28　"PORTRAIT OF JOCELYN"　Broadcast on April 8, 1956

Starring:　Philip Abbott as Mark Halliday　　　Nancy Gates as Debbie Halliday
John Baragrey as Arthur Clymer　　　　　　Raymond Bailey as Jeff
Olan Soulé as the clerk　　　　　　　　　Harry O. Tyler as the lodge manager

Teleplay written for *Alfred Hitchcock Presents* by Harold Swanton, based on a story by Edgar Marvin.

Directed by Robert Stevens.

(as a painter, a close-up of Hitchcock's thumb) *What an extraordinary thumb. It completely obscures the subject I'm painting. I used to paint along the roadside, but I had to quit. Motorists insisted on giving me rides. Hold that pose. Remain perfectly still for the next half-hour. Care to see my handiwork? I have several canvases ready.* (shows signs, Post no bills, Kilroy was here) *Or if you like something more exotic,* (Pas de stationnement) *It's French. And of course. . .* (please stand by)

Story: In the five years since Mark Halliday's wife, Jocelyn, disappeared under strange circumstances, his life fell apart, piece-by-piece. One day he met Debbie, a pretty young lady who soon took the place of Jocelyn in his heart, but not his memory. When picking up an anniversary gift for his new wife one afternoon, he sees a portrait of Jocelyn. Mark insists it is her, down to the most minute detail. Debbie thinks her husband is losing his mind and misses his first wife too much, and suggests he dismiss the painting. But Mark is persistent, tracks down the artist, who reveals that Jocelyn is still alive and well. At this point Mark's conscience cannot take it any longer, and breaks down, admitting that he actually murdered Jocelyn. This proves to be a bad mistake as Arthur Clymer is working for Jocelyn's brother to learn the truth behind the woman's disappearance.

And so Mark Halliday, finally found the bluebird of happiness. It had been there all the time. In any theatrical presentation, the next-to-closing spot is deemed the most advantageous. That explains the placement of this number, in tonight's variety show. (commercial break) *Bravo, bravo. That was a real show stopper, in every sense of the word. Now I see there is just time enough for me to wish you pleasant dreams and a happy analysis. Good night.*

Trivia, etc. The plot of this episode resembles that of the Humphrey Bogart film, *Conflict* (1945), in which Bogey plays the wife-murderer tricked into disclosing his guilt. Regarding the name of the murderer, Mark Halliday: the filmmakers seem to have jokingly named him after the mystery-writer in *Dial M for Murder*, who helps traps the guilty husband.

EPISODE #29　"THE ORDERLY WORLD OF MR. APPLEBY"　April 15, 1956

Starring:　Robert H. Harris as Mr. Lawrence Appleby
Meg Mundy as Miss Martha Sturgis
Gage Clarke as Gainsboro, the lawyer　　　Louise Larabee as Lena Appleby
Michael Ansara as Dizar　　　　　　　　Helen Spring as Mrs. Grant
Edna Holland as Mrs. Murchie　　　　　　Mollie Glessing as Ella, the maid

Teleplay written for *Alfred Hitchcock Presents* by Robert C. Dennis and Victor Wolfson, based on the short story of the same name by Stanley Ellin, originally published in the May 1950 issue of *Ellery Queen's Mystery Magazine*. Subsequently collected in *Mystery Stories* (Simon & Schuster, 1956) and in *The Specialty of the House and Other Stories* (Mysterious Press, 1979).

Directed by James Neilson.

Good evening, ladies. Has your husband recently acquired a far away look in his eyes? In the event something unforeseen happens to you, do all of your worldly goods go to him? Is he at this moment nervously excusing himself from the room? If you have answered yes to all the above questions, you receive a score of 100, a gold star for neatness and my advice to leave for mother's immediately. That is, immediately after the conclusion of our program. Our story tonight is called "The Orderly World of Mr. Appleby." Unfortunately he will do nothing to relieve your fears, if that is what you want. If you want contentment, security, peace of mind, listen to this advice from our friendly... philosopher.

Story: Mr. Appleby is a man who loves his antique shop with such a passion that he cannot bring himself to sell most of his inventory, resulting in him owing his suppliers large sums of money. His wife is totally unsympathetic, and won't go along with his brilliant idea of borrowing money on her insurance policy. So he decides to exercise the next best option. Appleby kills her in a manner that looks like an accident, collects the insurance payoff, then marries a wealthy widow who agrees to pay his suppliers. However, his new wife soon becomes fed up with spending all his time at the shop instead of with her, and she refuses to pay his latest bills when he gets in over his head again. He decides to resort to murder again, but the latest Mrs. Appleby is well aware of his intentions, having heard of the late Mrs. Appleby's death from her lawyer. But when her lawyer phones, Martha trips and knocks her head on the fireplace exactly as the late wife did.

Oh well. The bigger they come the harder they fall. By the way, what you have just seen is of historical significance. It was in precisely this way, that a housewife carrying an armload of vegetables invented the tossed salad. Now before I say good night, my uh, sponsor would like to bring you an important message. I needn't tell you to whom it is important. (commercial break) That concludes our entertainment for tonight. Once again through a propaganda play, we have attempted to make the world a better place in which to live. I am confident, that tonight we struck a telling blow in the cause of wall to wall carpeting. Good night.

EPISODE #30   **"NEVER AGAIN"**   Broadcast on April 22, 1956
Starring: Phyllis Thaxter as Karen Stewart   Louise Albritton as Renee Marlow
Warren Stevens as Jeff Simmons   Jack Mullaney as Mr. Marlow
Joan Banks as Margaret   Mason Curry as Mr. Sterling
Also in the cast: Karine Nordman, Marion Gray, Jack Mulhall, Carol Veazie, and Jack Ramstead.
Teleplay written for *Alfred Hitchcock Presents* by Gwen Bagni, Irwin Gielgud and Stirling Silliphant, based on a story by Adela Rogers St. Johns, originally collected in her book "Never Again and Other Stories."
Directed by Robert Stevens.
(tied to a chair)   (sign: Transmission Temporarily Interrupted, Please Stand By)
Oh, oh good evening. Thank you for waiting. I was uh, tied up in a story conference. The writers seem to have escaped with the secretary too. I wonder if they left the story behind. Oh yes, here it is. It's called "Never Again," may I show it to you? We have a one minute commercial... next. And that will give me just enough time to hire the actors, assemble the props and build the sets.

Story: An alcoholic named Karen Stewart has been unable to dry out despite several attempts. Her reputation for drinking surpasses her, grows with every party she attends. Despite repeated warnings from friends, Karen ignores everyone and everything – everything, that is, except for the bottle. On one particular evening, her latest boyfriend, Jeff Simmons, asks her to attend a party with him. There, she reluctantly takes a few drinks. Once drunk, she abandons Jeff to go to a bar with another man at the party. Jeff manages to find her and attempts to take her home, but she refuses with a wave of her glass, then loses consciousness. When she wakes up the next day, she finds that her habit has gotten the better saturnine of her, for she is now in jail for slashing the throat of her boyfriend, and charged with his murder.

I hope that ending wasn't unduly saccharin for your tastes. On these rare occasions, when we become more subliminal or sentimental, please bear with us. After all, we are dealing with a mass audience in a commercial medium. There's that word 'commercial' again. Quite timely too, considering what follows immediately. After which, I'll be back. (commercial break) *It is becoming painfully obvious to me, that my portion of the program must be made far more dignified, if I am to keep up the level of restraint and good taste set by my sponsor. I promise to do better next week, when I return at this same time. Good night.*

Alternate narrative:
Ladies and gentlemen, may I just for this once depart from our customary epilogue. Tonight we have brought you a drama based on one of Adela Rogers St. Johns' most powerful stories with the hope that somewhere, somehow, it will help someone.

EPISODE #31   **"THE GENTLEMAN FROM AMERICA"**   Broadcast April 29, 1956
Starring: Biff McGuire as Howard Latimer
Ralph Clanton as Sir Stephen Hurstwood

John Irving as Derek	Eric Snowdon as Hanson
Geoffrey Steele as the man	John Alderson as the attendant
John Dodsworth as Calender	Sonia Torgeson as one of the young girls
Jan Chaney as the other young girl	

Teleplay written for *Alfred Hitchcock Presents* by Francis Cockrell, based on the short story of the same name by Michael Arlen. Collected in *May Fair* (Collins, 1925; Doran, 1925).
Directed by Robert Stevens.
(at the table with candle and books)   *Good evening. Do you believe in ghosts?* (candle disappears) *Of course not. I knew you didn't.* (books and table disappear) *Noise is a mortal enemy of good motion picture making and television broadcasting. That is why I hired this particular house. It is deathly quiet.* (screams) *Most of the time. And its reputation for being haunted, keeps away the curious. The shifting of scenery also seems to be better here. The human element has been removed so if you would just lean back and relax, I'll tell you a little ghost story. Please don't hesitate to turn out your lights. I'm sure the warm glow from the picture tube will be sufficient to melt all your fears of the dark. But before we view with alarm, allow us to point with pride.*

Story: London, May. An American named Howard Latimer happens to meets two men who strike up a wager. They bet him 1,000 pounds that he could not spend the night in Hurstwood Manor. Howard, not believing in the supernatural, takes the men up on their bet. Unbeknownst to him, Hanson and Sir Stephen have prepared plans to trick Howard into believing that a real ghost is in the house. Later that evening, the fake apparition appears and Howard starts shooting, falls into shock and gets committed. Thus the hoax works and the men collect their money. But they are totally unprepared for the results of their scheme when a couple of years later, Howard shows up again. When he hears that it was all a hoax, he tries to strangle Sir Stephen, thinking he was guilty of killing his sister. Apparently Latimer went mad from their little escapade, and he is taken back to the asylum.

And just because a silly girl lost her head over some imaginary noises years before. (noise) *Appearantly some people can't read. It's allright. Just a young lady who needs* (Quiet sign on door) *help to put the chains on her car. I'll be back shortly, meanwhile considering the gravity of our next announcement, I think this is more appropriate.* (turns sign to Think) (commercial break) *A very interesting experience. Its been years since I saw a Stutz Bearcat. Now for a few posthumous announcements. The bullets used on tonight's program were made with new enriched gunpowder. Furs by feline. Tonight's guests were flown to Hollywood by the worlds oldest airline.* (floating broom appears) *Next week we shall fly some more in, if space is available. Until then, good night.*

Trivia, etc. "The Gentleman From America" was dramatized on television programs quite a number of times. On April 25, 1950, Robert Stevens (the same director of this episode) directed a "live" telecast of this same story, with Barry Nelson in the lead, on CBS-TV's *Suspense.*

EPISODE #32 **"THE BABY SITTER"** Broadcast on May 6, 1956
        Starring: Thelma Ritter as Mrs. Lottie Slocum
        Mary Wickes as Sophie Armstedder

Carol Mathews as Clara Nash	Theodore Newton as Mr. Nash
Reba Tassel as Janie	Michael Ansara as Mr. Demario

        Ray Teal as the sergeant
        Teleplay written for *Alfred Hitchcock Presents* by Sarett Rudley, based on the short story of the same name by Emily Neff, originally published in the May 1953 issue of *Cosmopolitan.*
        Directed by Robert Stevens.
        Good evening. Tonight's story is called "The Baby Sitter." You know, I don't think taking care of a baby is any great chore at all, if you are properly prepared. I bring my comforts with me. A portable radio, a few books, a hot lunch, a cold drink, a heavy mallot and if that fails, ear-plugs. Good heavens, I forgot the baby. Stay right where you are, I'll be back.

Story: Lottie is a woman with two problems; she talks too much and has too active an imagination. After the lady she baby-sits for is murdered, the police question her, but she doesn't provide any worthwhile information. After they leave, Lottie is invited over to the home of Mrs. Armstedder, who wants to hear gossip about the killing. And Lottis does just that - she goes on and on about Mrs. Nash having an affair with a man, and Mr. Nash being strongly attracted to Lottie. But her fantasy that Mr. Nash loves her leads to her undoing . . .

    And now, I suppose you babies who have just put the sitter to bed are wondering about Mr. Nash. He escaped in his automobile, but not for long. He was soon arrested for failing to yield the right of way. Well, he wasn't exactly arrested, you see it was a train he failed to yield to. And now, before I return, our special educational movie. Any child caught leaving the room will have to bring back a written excuse from the baby sitter. (commercial break) *And now children, if you aren't naughty and if the rabbit doesn't get drunk drinking too much carrot tea and fall on the elephant's trunk, next week I'll tell you another story. Good night.*

EPISODE #33   **"THE BELFRY"**   Broadcast on May 13, 1956
Starring: Jack Mullaney as Clint Ringle

Pat Hitchcock as Ellie Mollish   Dabbs Greer as the sheriff

Horst Ehrhardt as Albert Grinstead   Jim Hayward as the preacher

Ralph Moody as old man in search for Clint

John Compton as Walt Norton   Norman Leavitt as Elmer, Walt's cousin

David Saber as Dab Holland   Rudy Lee as young Luke

Kathleen Hartnagel as the young girl

Teleplay written for *Alfred Hitchcock Presents* by Robert C. Dennis, based on a short story of the same name by Allan Vaughan Elston, originally published in a 1939 issue of *The Boston Post* newspaper. Subsequently reprinted in *Fireside Mystery Book*, ed. Frank Owen (1947).

Directed by Herschel Daugherty.

(wanted poster) *Good evening. Perhaps I should explain this. My wife had these posters printed up as a joke, of course she doesn't really want me. Anyway there isn't a chance I'll be recognized. They're passport photographs. This one is for going abroad and this one for coming back. My excuse for making these undignified remarks is that tonight's story, "The Belfry," concerns a wanted man. In fact an entire town is looking for him. Such popularity must be deserved and in this case it is. But I shall allow you to learn the details on your own. First however, I want you to hear this description of a much wanted product. Listen closely, it may be in your neighborhood store. If it is, apprehend it at once. The reward is high.*

Story: In a small mountain town away from the big cities, Clint Ringle has fallen in love with the town's school teacher, Ellie Mollish. He does everything to show his affection, but Ellie won't have it. She is engaged to marry Walt Norton. Hearing this, Clint goes into a rage, and murders her fiancé Walt, when he pushes him away from Ellie. When the news about Walt's murder spreads, a posse led by the sheriff and cousin Elmer, begins a man hunt for Clint. But no matter how hard they search, no one is successful in finding Clint, who is right above everyone's heads, hiding in the bell tower on top of the Clark Country School. An ideal hiding place – or so he thinks. But after being disturbed by classes, children playing, meetings and services in the combined church and school, he finally gets killed by the giant bell above his head, after Walt's funeral. A poetic irony to a mis-led life.

That was satisfying wasn't it? It couldn't have happened to a nicer person. And speaking of nice people, before I return we will have a few quips from television's most tolerant sponsor. Surprised you, didn't I? (commercial break) (Hitchcock is painting moustaches on the wanted posters, and has one painted on his face) *Good night.*

Trivia, etc. Patricia Hitchcock played the love interest in this episode, Ellie Mollish. Dabbs Greer, who played supporting roles in hundreds of television programs, makes a short appearance as the sheriff. Greer played a sheriff in many other television dramas, most notably westerns and children's programs. As for the direction, Herschel Daugherty, had the complex problem of filming in the belfry of a school house/church. If you look carefully in all close-ups of Clint, the bell is close to his face, but in shots of the belfry the bell is high above him! Daugherty was a dialogue director for many filmed productions and even tried an acting stint for a time, before directing features for television. In the Warner Bros. Film *White Heat* (1949), Daugherty played an uncredited role of a policeman. For television, Daugherty directed episodes of *Gunsmoke*, *Rawhide*, *Wagon Train* and *Bonanza*, and the mystery/horror/science-fiction programs *Star Trek*, *Thriller*, *The Man From U.N.C.L.E.* and *Time Tunnel*.

EPISODE #34 **"THE HIDDEN THING"** Broadcast on May 20, 1956
Starring: Biff McGuire as Dana Edwards
Robert H. Harris as Mr. John Hurley Judith Ames as Laura
Theodore Newton as Lt. Shay Katherine Warren as Mrs. Edwards
Richard Collier as the counterman
Teleplay written for *Alfred Hitchcock Presents* by James P. Cavanagh, based on an original story idea by A.J. Russell.
Directed by Robert Stevens.
(searches in a trunk) *No, that's not it. I'm trying to locate a lost article. The only difficulty is, I can't remember what I lost. No, this isn't it. I don't know why I keep it. I don't even think it's any good anymore, its been used.* (pulls out a gun) *This is for the man who has everything. It's to enable you to take some of it away from him. By the way, this may take all evening, so while I'm looking here, why don't you look over there.*

Story: "Oh darling, you'll never lose me," Laura tells her fiancé, Dana Edwards, only minutes before he witnesses her death by a hit and run driver. When the police question Dana, he protests that he cannot remember the license plate of the car, or the make and model. Without that type of information, the police have nothing to go on. When word leaks of this information, a stranger introduces himself as Mr. John Hurley, explaining that he lost his son in the same way, and he knows of a complex psychological process called "total recall," that may help Dana recall the license plate number. The process fails at first, although Mr. Hurley keeps badgering Dana to try harder, and Dana is finally pressured to recall the number, writing it on the chalkboard. But when the detective shows up, he explains that Mr. Hurley is just a nut who keeps showing up all the time to bother the police. Hurley, unmarried, doesn't even have a son. Regardless of the fact that Hurley succeeded in helping Dana recall an important clue, the detective escorts him away from the premises.

I still can't remember what I'm looking for. If I had only partial recall it would help. Here it is, at the very bottom of the trunk. I remember now, it's a note I wrote myself, "remember to clean out trunk." I must remember to do that sometime. And incidently, here's something for you to remember, while I'm away for the next sixty seconds. (commercial break) *Our story tonight, taught us that once you have seen some things, you never really forget it. There are times when that can be an appalling thought. One further reminder. I shall be back next week with another story. And unless your license number happens to be KTY 478, I shall see you then, good night.*

EPISODE #35 **"THE LEGACY"** Broadcast on May 27, 1956
Starring: Leora Dana as Irene Cole Jacques Bergerac as Prince Burhan
Enid Markey as Cecilia Smithson Alan Hewitt as Howard Cole
Walter Kingsford as Colonel Blair Ralph Clanton as Randolph Burnside
Roxanne Arlen as Donna Dew, the actress Rudolph Anders as the Maître d'
Joan Dixon as the woman Vikki Dougan as the glamour girl
Teleplay written for *Alfred Hitchcock Presents* by Gina Kaus and Andrew Solt, from an original story idea by Gina Kaus.
Directed by James Neilson.
(hanging in a spider web) *Good evening, and thank you for allowing me to come into your parlor. It all happened so suddenly. I was walking along when I heard someone saying "knit one, pearl one" and I came over to see what she was doing. The really frightening part is that I forgot my hunting licence. Oh well, the show must go on, even though I may not. Tonight's entertainment is entitled "The Legacy," through it you will journey to Palm Beach and rub elbows with the idle rich and members of the international set. But before we join these useless playboys of the decaying society, let us heed the advice of a man who is earnest, productive and steadfast. A pillar of our civilization, and the sugar daddy of television. The sponsor.*

Story: Palm Beach, where the sun spends the winter, and the wealthy spend their vacation. Irene Cole, ten times wealthier than her woman-chasing husband, arrives at a Palm Beach hotel, and makes new friends. During her vacation, she meets Randolph Burnside, a well-established writer, and Prince Burhan from the Orient, with enough charms to make any woman fall in love – except Irene. In the usual fairy-book story, the Prince falls in love with the shy Irene, who insists she divorce her husband so they can run off and get married. But Irene remains faithful to her husband, and rejects the Prince's offer. After the Prince claims that he will kill himself if she won't go along with him, Irene suggests they split ways and never see each other again. The next morning, bad news hits and newspapers, reporting how the Prince died in an auto accident. Believing that he committed suicide, Irene has a mental breakdown. Randolph, in the meantime, discovers the Prince's true motives, when a friend investigates, and explains how the Prince was penniless, wanting only to marry Irene for her money. Weeks pass and Irene snaps back into reality and Randolph hesitates telling them the truth. For Irene's husband no longer flings with other women and she spends much of her time doing charity work. A happy couple, and all because they believed Prince Burhan had killed himself for the love of her. Who is Randolph to rob them of that legacy?

I suppose you're wondering how I escaped. Fortunately, my captor dropped a stitch at a crucial moment. In the event you may have missed a few freudian overtones of our story, I should like to offer a brief explanation. Irene Cole was a compulsive knitter with a Madame Defarge complex. Howard Cole was an extrovert who suffered from a regressive libido and oedipuscomplex, schizophrenia and an extremely low sales resistance. Prince Burhan's sportscar was obviously the symbol for his mother, he'd always wanted to drive her mad. And the accident wasn't caused by defective brakes at all, the automobile was psychosomatic, it has since undergone analysis and is now well adjusted. I hope this makes everything clear. And now before I return, my sponsor will indulge in a bit of symbolism of his own, for which I can offer no explanation. (commercial break) And now we hope you enjoyed that, I know Freud would have. Join us again when we shall be back with another story. Good night.

Trivia, etc. *Alfred Hitchcock Presents* offered director James Neilson one of his earliest directorial tasks. After having played the role of an "Operative" in "The Case of the Jealous Journalist" episode of *Perry Mason*, Neilson stuck to directing such television features as *Bonanza, Adam 12, Texas John Slaughter, Batman, The Fugitive,* and *Ghost Story.* His movie credits include Walt Disney's *Dr. Syn, Alias the Scarecrow* (a.k.a. "Scarecrow of Romney Marsh") (1962), *The Moon-Spinners* (1964), *The Adventures of Bullwhip Griffin* (1967), and *Where Angels Go, Trouble Follows* (1968).

EPISODE #36 **"MINK"** Broadcast on June 3, 1956
    Starring: Ruth Hussey as Paula Hudson
    Vinton Hayworth as Sergeant Delaney
    Vivi Janiss as Sergeant Bradford, the police woman
    Sheila Bromley as Mrs. Hudson's lady friend

Anthony Eustrel as Mr. Ronald, the furrier	Paul Burns as the furrier's helper
Eugenia Paul as the model	Veda Ann Borg as the hairdresser
James McCallion as Charlie Harper, the thief	Mary Jackson as Mrs. Wilson

    An original teleplay written for *Alfred Hitchcock Presents* by Gwen Bagni and Irwin Gielgud.
    Directed by Robert Stevenson.
    (behind bars) *Stone walls do not a prison make, nor iron bars a cage. But they help, they help. Actually this is my doctor's idea. When he says strict diet he means strict diet. The saw came in the traditional way, inside a cake. Have you ever had a piece of*

caritas cake? I should have eaten the saw and used the cake to bludgeon my way out. However, I do not want to concern you with my petty problems. But with those of Paula Hudson. Paula was one of those persons who had never spent a day in jail or even been given parking tickets. Then one day she found herself at the wrong end of the finger of suspicion. You will see Paula's story in a moment. It is called "Mink," from the fur of the same name.

Story: Paula Hudson finds the deal of her dreams when her hairdresser tells her where she can find a mink coat at an incredibly low price. However, when she takes her new mink to have it appraised, the furrier believes it is stolen and phones the police. Shocked at what is going on, Paula lays claim that the fur is not stolen and explains to the detectives how and where she bought it (in flashbacks). Sgt. Delaney, who listens to Paula's explanation, pays a visit to Charlie Harper and questions those involved, in hopes of substantiating Paula's story. But they all deny any knowledge of the fur. So who is telling the truth? Later, Charlie, pays a not-so-pleasant visit to Paula, trying desperately to buy the fur back so he can give it back to whom he stole it from in the first place. Paula refuses and Charlie resorts to stealing it again, only this time being taken by the police after a "tip-off" phone call from Paula.

So much for the case of the stolen stole. I think I'll give up my diet. Exercise, that's it. I think I'll take up sports again. I'm quite an athlete you know. I particularly excel in chess, falconry, wifebeating, that sort of thing. And now we pause a moment for sponsor identification, after which I'll be back. (commercial break) *Thank you for coming. Please call again. Our next visiting hours will be just one week from tonight. Good night.*

EPISODE #37 **"DECOY"** Broadcast on June 10, 1956
 Starring: Robert Horton as Gil Larkin   Cara Williams as Mona Cameron
 Jack Mullaney as Dave Packard, the disc jockey
 Philip Coolidge as Lieutenant Brann
 David Orrick as Ben Cameron   Harry Lewis as Ritchie
 Frank Gorshin as the man at the radio station   Eileen Harley as Ben's secretary
 Mary Jean Yamaji as Sasikawa, the dancer   Edo Mita as Sasikawa's husband
 Harry O. Tyler as the doorman
 Teleplay written for *Alfred Hitchcock Presents* by Bernard C. Schoenfeld, based on the 1952 radio play "A Murder of Necessity" by Richard George Pedicini.
 Directed by Arnold Laven.
 (magnifying-glass) *Good evening. I've been examining the fingerprints on the inside of your television screen. Very unusual, they're all thumbs. That's it. They must have been left by your television repair man. You know I could use this to watch television. I have a 27 inch set with an 8 inch screen. It also has an adjustment for color. The adjustment consists of a palette and brush and the viewer simply fills in the numbered squares. It takes a very deft hand. Tonight's tale is provocatively captioned "Decoy." Do I pique you? I hope so. A program host should always be a good peeker. In watching the story, I want you to pay particular attention to the three undraped ladies who dance in the final scene. Because one of these young ladies has since married a titled englishman and her face is now quite well known.* (explosion) *And now please listen closely. The next sound you hear will be that of my sponsor, dropping a hint.*

Story: Gil Larkin is in love with Mona, the wife of talent agent Ben Cameron. Although she is unaware of Gil's affections towards her, she confesses one day, in secret to Gil, that her husband is abusing her. At this point Gil takes the window of opportunity and reveals his love for her, claiming that he will solve her problem. Arriving at the agent's office, Gil finds Ben hard at work talking on the phone. Suddenly, a man enters the room behind Gil, Ben calls out the name Ritchie, and then Gil is knocked out before he can see who it is. Ben is then shot dead and the killer places the gun in Gil's hand. Gil wakes just seconds later to find himself framed for murder. He picks up the phone to see if the other party is still hanging on to the other end of the line, but all he hears is an old record playing in the background. The other party hangs up when Gil speaks. The only hope he has of clearing himself is to locate the person who was speaking to Ben on the phone. who heard the man address the real killer before the gun went off. After much searching and piecing together clues, Gil returns to Mona's place to confront her with the news of her dead husband. There he sees the same old record that he heard on the phone and realizes that Mona is the one who framed him. Then Mona calls for Ritchie and mentions the next step in her plan, Gil's so-called suicide. But Lieutenant Brann surprises them and arrests both Mona and Ritchie.

About that, uh, scene I mentioned. We ran overtime and had to cut it at the last moment. I'm sure you don't mind. It had nothing to do with the story but it was, uh, a lot of fun making it. Tonight's commercial comes in three installments. Here before I return is the third and concluding chapter. (commercial break) *That was my error. I see there will be three more installments of the commercial next week. I hope you can wait that long to see how it comes out. Good night.*

Trivia, etc. On March 24, 1952, radio's *Suspense* presented "A Murder of Necessity," scripted by Richard George Pedicini. The story concerned a man who shoots his blackmailer in cold blood, and then discovers that the phone was off the hook at the time of the murder. Although the names, places, and occupations are changed, the premise remained the same. Robert Young starred as the killer in the 1952 broadcast. Philip Coolidge played the doctor at the Glen Cove police station in *North by Northwest* (1959).

EPISODE #38 **"THE CREEPER"** Broadcast on June 17, 1956
    Starring: Constance Ford as Ellen Grant   Steve Brodie as Steve Grant
    Harry Townes as Ed Chase   Reta Shaw as Mrs. Martha Stone
    Percy Helton as George   Alfred Linder as the man in shoe-shop
    Teleplay written for *Alfred Hitchcock Presents* by James P. Cavanagh, based on radio play of the same name by Joseph Ruscoll, originally broadcast on *The Molle Mystery Theater* on March 29, 1946.
    Directed by Herschel Daugherty.
    (keyhole, eye-test sign)   *Good evening and thank you for peeping in at me tonight. I shall try to make it worth your while. Now if you will look through the keyhole with your other eye* (hangs up sign) . . . *Excellent, thank you. Incidentally those of you who think these letters don't spell anything, couldn't be more incorrect. The last line was copied from an old insurance policy. Now that we are all in focus, I should like to make a few prefatory remarks about tonight's libretto. It is called "The Creeper" and is about a person who had a very peculiar way of striking up an acquaintance with women. He killed them. A distinctly anti-social tendency for it never leads to any lasting friendship. But before we give you "The Creeper," we have a short film which we consider further evidence that television is the world's keyhole to culture.*

Story: The newspapers in a small New York neighborhood have been reporting the terrifying news of a murderer on the loose. Known as "the Creeper," this man has apparently been linked to at least three killings, all attractive women over the age of eighteen. Such terrorizing has kept the residents scared, and no one feels safe walking alone at night so long as "the Creeper" is still roaming the streets. Ellen Grant is no exception. She has been demanding that her husband Steve put a new lock on the door, a task that doesn't seem to be at the top of Steve's must-do list, but he does arrange for a locksmith to come and check it out, while he goes off to work. Ellen's paranoia keeps getting the better of her as she continues to imagine that everyone she meets, and every shadowy figure she sees, is the Creeper. Finally the locksmith arrives at her home to install the new lock, much to her relief. Relief that is short-lived when her husband calls her from work, to give her the latest police news bulletin. It seems the Creeper has been getting into homes disguised as a locksmith . . . but it is too late as Ellen is about to become victim number four.

And so, once again the Creeper commits the most heinous crime a woman can imagine. He takes a telephone away from her in the middle of a call. Obviously this sadistic criminal will stop at nothing. For the record, the Creeper was subsequently caught and is now repairing locks at one of our leading penal institutions. And now for an eye and ear test. See if you can read and hear the following without missing a word. I will be back in a minute to give you your grades. (commercial break) *Sorry time is up, pass in your papers at once. As for tonight's story, if you liked it, please write in. Perhaps we can give you a sequel to "The Creeper" called... "The Toddler." Good night.*

EPISODE #39 **"MOMENTUM"** Broadcast on June 24, 1956
    Starring: Skip Homeier as Richard 'Dick' Paine
    Joanne Woodward as Beth Paine   Ken Christy as A.T. Burroughs
    Henry Hunter as the man from the finance company
    Mike Ragan as the cab driver
    Billy "William" Newell as Charlie   Frank Krieg as Martin, the janitor
    Harry O. Tyler as the man wanting to see the apartment
    Also in the cast: Jack Tesler, Dorothy Crehan, Don Dillaway, Patricia Knox, John Lehmann, Joseph Gilbert and Myron Cook.
    Teleplay written for *Alfred Hitchcock Presents* by Francis Cockrell, based on the short story "Murder Always Gathers Momentum" by Cornell Woolrich, originally published in the December 14, 1940 issue of *Detective Fiction Weekly*. Subsequently collected (under the William Irish, Woolrich's pen-name), in *Somebody on the Phone* (Lippincott, 1950), and *Rear Window and Four Short Novels* (Ballantine, 1984), both as "Momentum."
    Directed by Robert Stevens.
    Did you ever have the feeling that you were being watched? Observe closely, no eyelid. He never sleeps. Obviously an ideal audience, unfortunately he doesn't watch television. That's true. He isn't watching me, he's watching you. To see if you're watching me. Please don't misunderstand, I love television. As a performer that is. But I feel the wrong person is being paid. Actors receive salaries, but the viewers, the people who do the really hard work, don't make a cent. It seems to me that television is exactly like a gun. You're enjoyment of it is determined by which end of it you're on. Tonight we plan to tell a story about this gun and what a very ordinary man did with it in the course of 24 hours. First however, we must pause briefly to issue a special report about one of our sponsors products.

    Story: Dick Paine is a mild-mannered man with a nagging wife. She is furious that he has agreed to work for half his usual wages because his employer is close to bankruptcy. She finally badgers him into standing up for himself and demanding the pay he has coming to him. But when he finally does so his boss refuses, and Dick is forced to resort to murder. When a man comes from the finance company to collect some money, Dick gets afraid and pulls a gun, thinking he is a policeman. But it is Dick that gets shot during the quarrel. Just before Dick dies from the bullet wound, Beth tells him that she had already gotten the money from his boss.

Well, that only proves you can't go by appearances. Who would have guessed that such an ordinary man like Richard Paine, would have had the nerve and the audacity to drive a taxi cab without a chauffeur's licence. Of course none of this would have happened if he had stayed at home that evening and watched television. And he would have learned many things. An example of which we now show you, after which I'll be back. (commercial break) *Very educational. Next week we shall return with another story. I suggest you join us. It might be unwise to disappoint big brother.*

SUMMER RERUNS

Although it isn't known who chose which episodes for broadcast during the summer season, the producers did not have a hand in the selection process. Most likely, the network made the decisions (reviewers and the rating system might have also played a part in the decision making).

July 1, 1956 "The Long Shot"
July 8, 1956 "You Got to Have Luck"
July 15, 1956
   "The Orderly World of Mr. Appleby"
July 22, 1956 "A Bullet for Baldwin"
July 29, 1956 "The Baby Sitter"
August 5, 1956 "Portrait of Jocelyn"
August 12, 1956 "Whodunit"

August 19, 1956 "Premonition"
August 26, 1956
   "The Gentleman from America"
September 2, 1956
   "The Case of Mr. Pelham"
September 9, 1956 "Back for Christmas"
September 16, 1956 "Never Again"
September 23, 1956 "The Creeper"

SEASON TWO - (39 episodes)

SELECTED PRODUCTION CREDITS:
Art Directors: John Lloyd and Martin Obzina
Assistant Directors: Richard Birnie, Jack Corrick, Hilton A. Green, James Hogan,
George Lollier, James Nicholson and Ronnie Rondell
Associate Producers: Joan Harrison and Norman Lloyd
Costume Supervisor: Vincent Dee
Director of Photography: Reggie Lanning, Lionel Lindon, a.s.c. , John MacBurnie, a.s.c.,
Lester Shorr, John L. Russell, a.s.c., John L. Russell, Jr., a.s.c., Joseph La Shelle, a.s.c.,
William S. Sickner, a.s.c., Bud Thackery, a.s.c., and John F. Warren, a.s.c.
Editorial Supervisor: Richard G. Wray, a.c.e.
Film Editor: Edward W. Williams, a.c.e.
Furs supplied by Beckman in Beverly Hills.
Hair Stylist: Florence Bush
Makeup Artists: Jack Barron and Leo Lotito, Jr.
Music Supervisor: Stanley Wilson
Produced by Joan Harrison.
Set Decorator: Perry Murdock, James S. Redd, Ralph Sylos and James Walters
Sound: Steve Bass, Earl Crain, Jr., William Lynch, Melvin M. Metcalfe, Sr.,
David H. Moriarty, Earl Schwartz and Richard Tyler
Filmed at Revue Studios in Hollywood, California, in association with MCA-TV, executive
distributor for Shamley Productions, Inc.
Broadcast Sunday over CBS-TV, 9:30 - 10 p.m., EST. Sponsored by Bristol-Myers.

EPISODE #40   **"WET SATURDAY"**   Broadcast on September 30, 1956
Rehearsed and filmed on August 22 – 24, 1956.
Starring: Sir Cedric Hardwicke as Mr. Princey
John Williams as Captain Smollet
Tita Purdom as Millicent 'Milli' Princey   Kathryn Givney as Mrs. Princey
Jerry Barclay as George Princey   Irene Lang as the maid
Teleplay written for *Alfred Hitchcock Presents* by Marian Cockrell, based on the short story of the same name by John Collier, originally published in the December 28, 1938 issue of *The Bystander*.   Subsequently collected in *Fancies and Goodnights* (Doubleday, 1951) and in *The John Collier Reader* (Knopf, 1972).
Directed by Alfred Hitchcock.
(lying on shelf with sign: "moved to new location") *Oh, good evening. I'm so glad you found me. As you can see our new quarters are rather modest, but we like the location and thought the change might do us good, also. And now, if you don't mind, the time has come for what has become an institution for Britishers even for those who have been permanently exiled to the barbarous regions of the world.* (tea time) *Oh, speaking of institutions here is an American one. It is called a commercial.*

Alternate narrative:
(lying on shelf with sign: "moved to new location") *Oh, good evening. I'm so glad you found me. As you can see our new quarters are rather modest, but we like the location and thought the change might do us good, also. And now, if you don't mind, I would like to indulge in an old American custom. No matter how busy they are or what the surroundings may be, Americans never omit this quaint ritual. If you don't care to join me, I think you'll find our play is about to begin on one of the lower shelves.*

Story: Mr. Princey has a daughter who until recently was considered the saint of the neighborhood.   Today she is a murderer, a situation that arose when the town's schoolmaster, a man named Withers whom she had a crush on, revealed that he was going to marry another woman. The dead body is being kept in the barn until Princey can determine a way to clear the family name and get Millicent off the hook. The perfect solution presents itself in the form of Captain Smollet, a man also engaged to marry the same woman the schoolmaster revealed his feelings for.   While Princey holds him at gunpoint, Smollet is given two options: plant his fingerprints on the murder weapon and help to get rid of the body, or be shot dead. With no other solution to the crime, Smollet accepts the first choice as long as Princey keeps his word that he will reveal the murder to no one . . . a promise he has no intention in keeping and will soon become Mr. Princey's downfall.

I presume that story was intended to illustrate that blood is thicker than water. I always find it heartwarming to see a family standing shoulder to shoulder in the face of adversity. Unfortunately the authorities were not thrilled by this sight and were seen tossing about such phrases as "obstructing justice," "accessory after the fact," "murder in the first degree," very nasty. The Princeys received substantial sentences. You see, unfortunately Captain Smollet didn't play the game. When the police arrived he insisted on his innocence, thus confusing poor Millicent to such an extent that she re-enacted the crime with her father as the victim. Broke the croquet mallet too. I'll believe I'll have another. (pours tea) *There's no more vermouth, oh well. Fortunately, I still have plenty of olives. While I'm sipping this, I'd like you to savor the following commercial.* (commercial break; Hitchcock sips tea) *That was exceedingly dry. Next week we shall be back at the same old stand, please drop in again. Good night.*

Trivia, etc. Sir Cedric Hardwicke played the role of Mr. Kentley in *Rope*, released through Warner Bros. in 1948, under the direction of Alfred Hitchcock. Here, Hardwicke was reunited with the director for the second season opener. "He [Hardwicke] was a great friend of Hitch's and a most amusing man," said Norman Lloyd. "Cedric as a person was more open and, I think, socially very much a friend of Hitch's. He was a very funny man. My two favorite stories about Cedric Hardwicke: He knew Bernard Shaw, who I think wrote the play 'The Apple Cart' for him. Cedric was talking to Bernard Shaw one day, and Shaw said to him suddenly, 'You know, you're my fourth favorite actor in the world.' And Hardwicke said, 'Thank you very much, sir. May I ask who the first three are?' And Shaw said, 'The three Marx Brothers!' [laughs]"

Hitchcock teaches the viewers about musical appreciation.
(Photo courtesy of Ronald V. Borst / Hollywood Movie Posters)

EPISODE #41   **"FOG CLOSING IN"**   Broadcast on October 7, 1956
      Starring: Phyllis Thaxter as Mary Summers   Paul Langton as Arthur Summers
      George Grizzard as Ted Lambert   Carol Veazie as Mrs. Connolly
      Billy Nelson as the man   Norman Willis as the police officer
      Teleplay written for *Alfred Hitchcock Presents* by James P. Cavanagh, based on the short story "The Fog Closing In" by Martin Brooke, originally published in the April 1956 issue of *Ellery Queen's Mystery Magazine*.
      Directed by Herschel Daugherty.

(Hitchcock standing behind desk)   *Good evening friends and others. Tonight, Madame, some of our audience are having difficulty in seeing. Would you mind?* (head taken away from blocking screen) *Thank you. On the theories of what was good enough for Shakespeare, is good enough for us, we plan to open tonight's play with a maid soliloquizing that she dusts. Unfortunately tonight happens to be the maid's night out. I'm expecting an important call.* (phone rings) *It must be London calling. Hello. Am I watching television? Would you excuse me, this is a very personal call. Meanwhile, my understudy will provide some alternate entertainment.*

Story: Mary Summers is afraid to be in her home alone while her husband is away on business. She wants to stay with her family, but Arthur refuses, saying she sees too much of them and needs to get used to being on her own. After he leaves, a young man who escaped from a mental asylum breaks into the house, but leaves Mary unhurt when police arrive in the area. Alone in the house again, Mary falls asleep, having a dream about someone breaking into the house and coming up the stairs after her. Suddenly, she wakes to hear someone coming slowly up the stairway just like she dreamed, so she pulls out her husband's gun to shoot whoever comes through the door - unaware that it is her husband who has come home early to check up on her.

(hangs up phone) *This concludes our play for tonight. Unhappily for Mary Summers however, there is more to her story. For she subsequently found herself in one of those institutions she had come to fear. Next we offer a brief message from our. . .* (hesitates) *sponsor, after which I'll return.* (commercial break) *Next week we shall be back with another nice story. Until then, good night.*

EPISODE #42 **"DE MORTUIS"** Broadcast on October 14, 1956
Starring: Robert Emhardt as Clarence Rankin   Cara Williams as Irene Rankin
Henry Jones as Wally Long   Philip Coolidge as Bud Horton
Haim Winant as the truck driver   William McLean as Benny
Teleplay written for *Alfred Hitchcock Presents* by Francis Cockrell, based on the short story of the same name by John Collier, originally published in the July 18, 1942 issue of *The New Yorker*. Subsequently collected in *Fancies and Goodnights* (Doubleday, 1951).
Directed by Robert Stevens.
(as a teacher)   *Good evening students of the macabre. This evening's lecture has as its text, the short story "De Mortuis." Translated from the latin, this means "about the dead." At the risk of being facetious, I would like to point out that latin is a dead language. Thank you. It is rewarding to know that there are still a few students interested in achieving high marks. If you can't hear me in the back of the room, please raise your hand and adjust the volume control. Regrettably the author wrote only his title in latin, and did the story in English. Writers are always compromising to attain commercial success. I shall leave it to your judgement as to whether or not, it would have sounded better in latin. Oh yes, this class, like Gaul, is divided into three parts. My lecture constitutes one part, De Mortuis another, and here is the party of the third part.*

Story: Clarence Rankin, a college professor by occupation, is married to a promiscuous female named Irene, whose philandering seems to be known by everyone except Clarence. One day a couple of friends stop by to inquire whether or not Clarence wants to go fishing with them, but instead they find Irene gone and her husband cementing up a hole in the rat-infested basement. Knowing how Irene is, the two parties assume Clarence finally caught on and killed her, but when they bring the matter of his wife's infidelity to his attention, he insists that Irene went on a trip. With no positive evidence and only assumptions to go on, the fishermen shrug the notion off, leaving the Rankin home, feeling justified for Clarence's actions. Moments after the men are out of sight, Irene returns, sadly explaining that she missed the train. No longer in the dark about his wife's philandering, Clarence asks his flirtatious wife to examine the basement . . .

And so, just like many a Hollywood movie star, Irene Rankin was immortalized in concrete, but Professor Rankin was not so fortunate, he remarried. His crime was later discovered and he paid the supreme penalty. I have asked one of the actors to come out after the show, for I want to congratulate him on the splendid performance and I'm sure you do too. He played the most ferocious of the rats. A characterization that was quite a departure for him. Off stage he's entirely different, as you can see. He's a family man, never seen in the nightclubs. He's just like the fellow who lives next door to you. Thank you. And now, a one minute demonstration of salesmanship. After which I'll be back. (commercial break) *I'm sure no one can continue to hold out against a plea like that. It was irresistible. We uh, oh, we have another story but I'm afraid there isn't time to present it. Uh, we have to do it next week. Until then, good night.*

EPISODE #43 **"KILL WITH KINDNESS"** Broadcast on October 21, 1956
 Starring: Hume Cronyn as Fitzhugh 'Fritz' Oldham
 Carmen Mathews as Katherine Oldham   James Gleason as Jorgy, the bum
 Margie Liszt as the woman   Mike Ragan as the fireman
 An original teleplay written for *Alfred Hitchcock Presents* by A.J. Russell, from a story idea of his own.
 Directed by Herschel Daugherty.
 (as a witch at the stake)   *Good evening. Television fans can be so demonstrative and unpredictable. At the time this happened I was under the impression I was being put on a pedestal. My wife's not going to like this, she's always telling me not to leave my ashes on the floor.* (lights cig) *Tonight we present a very warm little story called "Kill With Kindness."* (smoke rises) *Reception seems to be rather bad tonight. Is your screen clouding up? Mine is. I think we better run a test film first. If you have no difficulty in seeing it, we will show you our story.*

 Story: Katherine Oldham and her brother Fritz are in need of some cash, and together they decide to successfully swindle an insurance company. Inviting a wandering old bum named Jorgy into their house for some stew, the two agree that Jorgy is the exact size of Fritz. Playing the role of "good Samaritans," the couple dress the bum up in Fritz's finest clothes, and put him into bed. Their plan is to drug the bum so he won't wake up, and then set the house on fire. Fritz will remove his ring to put on the bum's hand, to ensure identification. Then Fritz will conveniently disappear and Katherine can claim his life insurance. But after getting the man into bed, Fritz discovers that the bum has a ring of his own and the two cannot get it off. Fearing an investigation, they get the old man out of the burning house, whereupon Fritz is greeted as a hero by neighbors who assume that he saved the man's life!

 And now (cough, cough) *we present* (cough) *a short,* (cough) *after which I shall try to reappear.* (commercial break) *I thought I'd better get out of there. I've just remembered that my tumbrel is doubleparked. I shall return next week at the same time to bring you another story and to relate the further adventures of Alfred Hitchcock. Good night.*

 Behind the scenes: For production number 53/2 (53rd episode filmed / second season), Hitchcock's presentation and afterward was filmed on August 28, 1956. John L. Russell, was the cameraman, and Hitchcock explained every detail of how the scene was going to be set up. How to start a fire within the confined walls of a studio? The smoke created for the effect of wood burning around Hitchcock during his opening presentation, was actually created by a small machine, held in the production assistant's hand. Sound effects would later be added to create the illusion of fire. "Kill With Kindness" was the 53rd episode filmed for the series, but the 43rd broadcast - television episodes were not broadcast in the order of production.

EPISODE #44 "NONE ARE SO BLIND" Broadcast on October 28, 1956
　　　　Starring: Hurd Hatfield as Seymour Johnston　　Mildred Dunnock as Muriel
　　　　K.T. Stevens as Liza　　　　　　　　　　　Rusty Lane as the detective
　　　　Lillian Bronson as the neighbor　　　　　　Dorothy Crehan as the maid
　　　　Teleplay written for *Alfred Hitchcock Presents* by James P. Cavanagh, based on the
short story of the same name by John Collier, originally published in the March 31, 1956
issue of *The New Yorker*.
　　　　Directed by Robert Stevens.
　　　　(sitting in front of a mirror, with wigs) *Good evening. The entertainment industry
is always crying for new faces. I've decided to give them one. Not that there is anything
wrong with the old one. In fact I think it's rather good . . .* (mirror cracks) *Well it could have
been worse, what if I had cracked? See here is the one . . .* (puts on a wig) *I've always
wanted to be someone else . . . That won't do, I look like a near-sighted throw rug. By an
odd coincidence we have a story about a man who decided to be someone other than himself.
If enough of you write in during the next sixty seconds, we shall present it. And while we
have been chatting here, someone has gotten his foot in the door. So we might as well allow
him to show his wares. Come on . . . come on . . .*

　　　　Story: Seymour Johnston, a man infatuated with his good looks, discovers to his
dismay that his recently deceased father left the entire estate to Aunt Muriel, as Seymour is
irresponsible and would only throw it all away. Aunt Muriel insists that Seymour settle down
and work for a living, and when he finally has a sense of value, she will turn the money over
to him. Otherwise, he will not get a cent until she dies - a status he decides to bring about.
Finding a wallet on the floor of a café, Seymour gets an idea. Disguising himself as Antonio
Bertoni, the person whose portrait was on the license, Seymour pays Muriel a visit and
murders the old woman. The police begin their investigation, finding clues and witnesses to
the fictional character Seymour created. Surprisingly, Seymour overlooked one minor detail
in his disguise. You see, he has a mole on the side of his nose, and never hid it when he
donned the costume, a feature everyone remembers Antonio also having.

　　　　*Poor Seymour, it couldn't have happened to a more deserving person. Hmm, I've
decided not to be someone else after all. If I won't be myself, who will? However, allow me
to indulge my exhibitionist tendencies with this quick-change demonstration. The Alfred
Hitchcock of today . . .* (turns his back to the camera, and turns back again) *The Alfred
Hitchcock of 30 years ago. The secret of this transformation is rather simple, I just removed
my wallet. And speaking of money, here is a splendid reason for spending some of it.*
(commercial break) *And on that pleasant note, we conclude our program. Next week we
shall be back with another play. Good night.* (theme song starts and camera pans to left)
Just a moment please! (camera moves back to right as Hitchcock sneakily checks to see if
anyone is around and pulls out an issue of his mystery magazine from his suit) *If you would
prefer your mystery stories uninterrupted by my comments, why not buy a copy of this new
magazine?*

EPISODE #45 "TOBY" Broadcast on November 4, 1956
　　　　Starring: Jessica Tandy as Edwina Freed　　Robert H. Harris as Albert Birch
　　　　George Mathews as McGurk, the neighbor　　Mary Wickes as Mrs. Foster
　　　　Ellen Corby as Mrs. Marie McGurk　　　　Penny Santon as Mrs. Swartz
　　　　Teleplay written for *Alfred Hitchcock Presents* by Victor Wolfson, based on a story
by Joseph Bates Smith.
　　　　Directed by Robert Stevens.
　　　　(heating milk) *Double, double, toil and trouble. Fire burn, cauldron bubble.
I don't know why people do this. It's not at all good for the cuffs. Takes the starch out of
them. I wonder if it does that to babies. Of course, that must be the idea. As you shall soon
see, tonight's play bears a relation to the foregoing. However slight, it is a tragical,*

comical, historical, pastoral, musical mystery. Entitled "Toby." (close-up) There is one change in our program. Shakespeare's "Hamlet" will not be presented as tonight's curtain raiser. We decided it wasn't suitable to show in the home, all those corpses you know. Instead we are giving our sponsor an opportunity to strut and fret upon the stage.

Story: It has been many years since Albert Birch has seen Edwina, his first real childhood love. With fond memories from a lonely bachelor, Albert shows no surprise when, out of the blue, Edwina contacts him and agrees to return and marry. Albert has no objections. Happy that his childhood fantasy might just come true, he goes along with this. But boy is Albert surprised when Edwina shows up with a baby she keeps hidden, one that she claims belonged to her deceased sister that she agreed to care for. Albert lets her move into his apartment, not yet realizing the strange relationship between Edwina and her unseen "child." Sadly for Albert, however, it turns out that Edwina ran away from a mental institution, and has to go back. In desperation, Edwina asks Albert to take care of Toby while she is gone, which turns out to be nothing more than a cat.

If it'd be true that good wine needs no bush, it is true that a good play needs no epilogue. Yet a good wine they do use good bushes and good plays prove the better by the help of good epilogues. I'm not sure that when he wrote that, the author had a television commercial in mind, but I do. Pri'thee tally a while. I shall be back, anon. (commercial break) Till we thee meet again, in thunder, lightning or in rain. When the hurly-burly is done, when the battle's lost and won. Oh that will be air the set of sun, or in other words, next week. Good night, cuzz.

Trivia, etc. For some strange reason Ben and Amos, the men who pick up Edwina to take her back to the asylum are not in the credits. Amos doesn't talk but Ben has a couple lines and should have been in the credits.

EPISODE #46 **"ALIBI ME"** Broadcast on November 11, 1956
Starring: Lee Philips as Georgie Minelli   Chick Chandler as Lucky
Harvey Stephens as Inspector Larkin   Alan Reed as Uncle Leo
Harry O. Tyler as Tim, the patient   Argentina Brunetti as Mrs. Salvatore
Shirley Smith as Goldie   Lee Erickson as the messenger boy
Charlie Cantor as Barney   Herb Vigran as the newspaperman
Eugenia Paul as the woman
Teleplay written for *Alfred Hitchcock Presents* by Bernard C. Schoenfeld, based on the 1951 *Suspense* radio play of the same name by Therd Jefre and Walter Brown Newman (uncredited).
Directed by Jules Bricken.
(conducts orchestra) *Good evening. Some of our late viewers tuning in. One of the commonest questions that people ask our producer of mystery motion pictures is: Which is written first, the words or the music? In our case the background music always comes first. After it is written we sprinkle the score liberally with sound effects, and then hire an author to write appropriate scenes to accompany the music. Quiet scenes to coincide with the somber passages and scenes of violence to synchronize with the noisier sections. Finally we garnish this potpourri with a title composed of from one to four words. Selected because they are eye catching and provocative and we arrange them in a manner designed to titillate and confuse. Let me show you what one of our stories sounds like, before it is written. (conductor - music, screams and noise) How fortissimo can you get? I trust this has been educational. I deliberately cut that number short because it was the music for tonight's story "Alibi Me" and I didn't want you to know how it comes out. Our author is already orchestrating this composition for the typewriter. So while we hastily dubbing the dialogue, you may observe our sponsor gives his rendition of the minute waltz.*

Story: A pair of gangsters, Georgie and Lucky, have avoided "rubbing each other out" simply because if one dies, the cops would immediately question the whereabouts of the other. Unfortunately, Lucky goes too far one day and Georgie shoots him dead. Knowing it's only a matter of time before the cops find out, Georgie knows that he must come up with an alibi – and quick. Georgie tries to talk all of his friends (and some not-so-friends) into covering up for him but each have a personal reason for refusing to get involved, except Tim, but he dies of a heart attack after accepting to give him an alibi. Finally his landlady agrees to provide an alibi, only after Georgie threatens to get her daughter Maria arrested for shoplifting. When a detective named Larkin arrives to ask questions the landlady delivers as promised, saying Georgie couldn't have committed such a crime as he was home at the time Lucky was killed. Just as Inspector Larkin is leaving the building, a delivery boy drops off a package and Georgie won't tip him, causing the boy to complain "five times I've come up and down them stairs. Twice this morning and three times this afternoon and not even a nickel's tip" . . . and the inspector overhears the boy.

Well, that was a surprise. The pistolshot Georgie used to kill Lucky wasn't in the original score but that's what happens when the musician who plays the revolver is allowed to improvise. Naturally Georgie was given life imprisonment, while the offending musician got off with a ten-year sentence. You are more fortunate. Your sentence is only a one minute one. (commercial break) *We never hesitate bringing down the curtain on another show, because then we are allowed to eat the props.* (holds a lollypop) *Next time we plan to bring you more music and sound effects and another story to accompany them, good night.*

Trivia, etc. The story "Alibi Me" was an idea originally conceived by Therd Jefre, who suggested it to radio script writer Walter Brown Newman. The plot, concerning a young killer in search of a false alibi in order to cover a crime he committed, was first dramatized on radio's *Suspense* on January 4, 1951. Mickey Rooney played the role of George. For the *Alfred Hitchcock Presents* teleplay, George underwent the name change to Georgie, and Lee Philips is no Mickey Rooney. Alan Reed, who played the uncle in this episode, was also a radio actor who starred on *Life With Luigi* and *Abie's Irish Rose*, and also the voice of Hanna-Barbera's Fred Flintstone. For Hitchcock fans, note how the music from the piano grows loud enough for Georgie to shoot Lucky in the opening scene, loud enough to drown out the sound of the gunshot. Hitchcock employed the same type of trick in both versions of *The Man Who Knew Too Much*.

EPISODE #47 "CONVERSATION OVER A CORPSE"   Broadcast on Nov. 18, 1956
Starring: Dorothy Stickney as Cissie Enright
Carmen Mathews as Johanna Enright
Ray Collins as Mr. Brenner
Ted Stanhope as the bank teller
Teleplay written for *Alfred Hitchcock Presents* by Marian Cockrell and Norman Daniels, based on an original story idea by Norman Daniels.
Directed by Jules Bricken.
(as a cook) *Good evening. Tonight we offer you a generous portion of mystery, a pinch of comedy, just a soupcon of commercial, all seasoned by a few irrelevant comments from your host. As you may know, food is a hobby of mine. I don't claim to be an expert cook, but I am rather a good eater. If you will wander in to my kitchen I'll allow you to watch me as I concoct some delicacy to tempt your palate. I can not abide careless cookery. Let me see, I've uh - I've just added 10 cc of sugar. All that is left is to add the white of one egg, and by the white I do not refer to the clear gelatine substance inside. Naturally, I mean the shell. This is where most amateur cooks make their mistakes. While you are waiting for me to finish, I suggest you turn your attention to tonight's story. It is called "Conversation Over A Corpse". It sounds like perfect dinner conversation.* (close-up) *It will follow the usual you-know-what.*

Story: When aggressive real estate agent Mr. Brenner talks Cissie and Johanna into selling their family home, the two offer him a cup of hot tea to celebrate. For years he has been trying to obtain their property, which will be worth a fortune, once he gains possession. But during the conversation, the women change their minds and only then does Mr. Brenner realize they poisoned his tea. Cissie couldn't bear to murder a man, so she didn't really put a fatal dose in the drink. Partially paralyzed as a result, Brenner watches as the women try several unsuccessful ways to kill him. Alone for a moment, Brenner begs Cissie to call the police. Johanna will kill him and blame the murder on her, he explains. When Cissie confronts Johanna in the kitchen, she denies it and heads to the living room to get rid of Mr. Brenner, once and for all. Slowly managing to grab a gun, Brenner shoots Johanna dead. As a consolation, Cissie offers him some whiskey (which contains poison) and he drinks it down without suspicion. Cissie gleefully smiles since the house will soon be hers, and the police will assume the two killed each other off.

She was no sissy. As a matter of fact, that was her downfall. She wanted to steady her nerves before the police came, so she took a few belts. Very sad. Except for the newspapers who detected a love triangle. The tabloids had more fun than at a hanging. (fills beaker) *Doesn't look like it should. This should be producing crème de menthe frappée. I'll try a little more heat. In the meantime, while I am briefly away, on with the show. The next sound you hear will be my sponsor.* (commercial break) *So much for tonight's cooking demonstration. I hope I have made everything clear. Next week I shall show you how to prepare an exotic delicacy. White hunter ala mau-mau. You'll be the talk of your neighborhood. I shall also reveal one of my own culinary secrets. How to remove the wrapper from a frozen food package without tearing the directions. Good night.*

EPISODE #48 **"CRACK OF DOOM"** Broadcast on November 25, 1956
Starring: Robert Horton as Mason Bridges   Robert Middleton as Sam Clinker
Gail Kobe as Jessie Bridges   Dayton Lummis as Tom Ackley
Gavin Gordon as the card player on the train
Kay Stewart as Della, the secretary   Francis de Sales as the four tens dealer
Card players: Pierre Watkin, Keith Britton, Jess Kirkpatrick and Alan Reynolds
Teleplay written for *Alfred Hitchcock Presents* by Robert C. Dennis, based on a story by Don Marquis.
Directed by James Neilson.
(playing with a deck of cards at the table) *Oh, good evening, kibitzes. I seem to be stuck. I don't suppose you see a place for a red seven? No, of course not, this program isn't in color. That's right. You can't distinguish colors, can you? There's nothing to winning really. That is if you happen to be blessed with a keen eye, an agile mind and no scruples whatsoever. Tonight's play is called the "Crack of Doom." As the title suggests, the "Crack of Doom" is a story about Mason Bridges, his wife Jessie, his secretary Della, his friends Tom Ackley and Sam Clinker and it begins in a club car of a New York-Chicago streamliner. This program is brought to you by our sponsor. If that suggests nothing to you it is because you haven't been paying attention to their animated and highly audible brochures. One of which follows.*

Story: On route across the country by train, Mason Bridges becomes upset when his friends try to talk him into a friendly game of poker. Telling them a story using flashbacks, Mason recalls the time he was once an insurance broker with several partners. Mr. Sam Clinker, one of the firm's wealthy clients, invited him over to play a game of cards. But once he was there, he was stuck playing what became a high-stakes game of poker, and lost nearly a thousand dollars. After leaving the house, he couldn't get the game off his mind. How can he possibly pay his debt off? Paying a visit to the office he takes $4,000 that doesn't belong to him and gambles it all away. Worse still, when he returned home to get his bank book to obtain the $4,000 to pay his firm back, it turned out that his wife, Jessie, had blown their life savings on a stock market deal that fell through. With his back against the wall, he removed the last $6,000 from the company safe and returned to the game to go for broke. After a long night of playing, Mason misread a Jack for a Queen and bet like he had four queens, which fooled Clinker (with four tens) to put his cards down. If he had known he only had three queens he would never have had the nerve to bluff.

I hope you weren't displeased by the lack of bloodshed in tonight's story. It is impossible for us to stage a murder every night . . . we're running out of victims . Of course we could replenish our supply by changing this into an audience participation show. However, for the present at least, I think we better limit your participation to the following, after which I am told to use a very familiar phrase, 'I will be back.' (commercial break) Next week we shall have another story to tell you and I hope you will allow us to come into your livingroom. It's terribly stuffy closed up in this dusty television set. Good night.

Trivia, etc. Francis de Sales played numerous recurring supporting roles on television programs such as *Mr. and Mrs. North* as Lieutenant Bill Weigand, as Sheriff Maddox on *Two Faces West*, and as the second Dr. James Spencer on *Days of Our Lives*. De Sales also played an uncredited role of an official in Alfred Hitchcock's *Psycho* (1960). Keith Britton would later play the doctor in the *Hitchcock* episode "You Can't Be a Little Girl All Your Life." On television, Alan Reynolds made guest appearances mostly in westerns like *Maverick, The Restless Gun* and *Wagon Train*. On the big screen, however, Reynolds played small roles in science-fiction films such as *Tobor the Great* (1954), *Beginning of the End* (1957), *Earth vs. the Flying Saucers* (1956) and *Curse of the Undead* (1959).

EPISODE #49 **"JONATHAN"** Broadcast on December 2, 1956
      Starring: Georgann Johnson as Rosine   Corey Allen as Gil Dalliford
      Douglas Kennedy as Jonathan Dalliford   Walter Kingsford as the doctor
      Nancy Kulp as Nurse Andrews   John Wilder as Don
      Hope Landin as the housekeeper   Heidi Mullenger as the nurse
      Teleplay written for *Alfred Hitchcock Presents* by Bernard C. Schoenfeld and Stirling Silliphant, based on the short story "Turmoil" by Fred Levon, originally published in a 1948 issue of *MacLean's*. Also reprinted in the April 1953 issue of *Ellery Queen's Mystery Magazine* as "Help Me --- If You Can."
      Directed by John Meredyth Lucas.
      (Hitch-double with dialect) *Hiah. I'm not Hitchcock, I'm Alfred, his stand-in. I'm just standing here while the lights and cameras are adjusting and the old boy just don't have the time. I got the job cause I look like him. That's what they say, but not to my face. I see they are rollin' him in. Do you suppose I'll look like that when I'm his age?* (The real Hitchcock has arrived: *That will be all Alfred*) *Arrivederci, daddy-O.* The real Hitchcock: *Cheeky fellow, isn't he? Unfortunately, he may soon be more than a stand-in. We are planning to send out a second company to tour the provinces. And Alfred will play my part. Which brings us to tonight's thrilling shocker. It is called "Jonathan." It will appear on our program immediately after this preview of a current attraction.*

      Story: Jonathan Dalliford and his son Gil, have been on their own since his wife died eighteen years ago. Gil has always had a close relationship with his dad but when he hears the news that his father is getting remarried, he feels their close relationship threatened, and he has little use for his future stepmother, Rosine. Shortly thereafter, Jonathan suddenly dies for reasons unknown, and Gil blames the death on his new mother, whom he believes poisoned his father. The police begin investigating and when traces of poison are found in Jonathan's corpse, Rosine is arrested. The truth of the matter is, Gil had bought the bottle of brandy as a wedding gift and poisoned it to kill her, since he knew his father never drank.

But she saved it . . . only later the doctor prescribed that some brandy would be good for Jonathan's heart problem. Wrongful intent on an unintended person.

Those of you who like to see nasty people receive their comeuppance, will be delighted with the results of tonight's tale. Gil took his story to the police, and he and Rosine were promptly punished. She for murder, and he for intent to murder. There is however a brighter side to all this, both have become model prisoners. And now for our next tale, a short, short, short, short story. In fact, so short you'll scarcely have time to miss me, thank goodness, before I return. (commercial break) *This concludes tonight's divertissement, but please remain tuned to this channel. I am not familiar with the program which follows, nor the one after that, but I have seen the story we are presenting in a week, and I think it's worth waiting for. Good night.*

Alternate narrative:
This concludes tonight's divertissement. But please remain tuned to this channel. I am not familiar with the program which follows, nor the one after that, but I have seen the story we are presenting next time and I think it's worth waiting for. Good night.

Trivia, etc. James Allardice, who wrote Hitchcock's presentations and afterwards, created the fictional "twin brother" for this episode, a classic comic situation that would be reprised over and over in the coming years. Although the humor may have been conceived with Allardice, and have no literary origin whatsoever, it might be interesting to know that Wardour Studios in Britain released a feature-length movie entitled *Brother Alfred*, in 1932. Based on the stage play by P.G. Wodehouse and Herbert Westbrook, the story concerned one George Lattaker, and his efforts to win back his fiancée by posing as his twin brother from Monte Carlo. Shades of imitation?

EPISODE #50 **"THE BETTER BARGAIN"** Broadcast on December 9, 1956
Starring: Robert Middleton as Louis "The King" Koster
Henry Silva as Harry Silver   Don Hanmer as Mr. Cutter
Kathleen Hughes as Marian Koster   Jack Lambert as Baldy
Teleplay written for *Alfred Hitchcock Presents* by Bernard C. Schoenfeld, based on the short story "The Better Bargain" by Richard Deming, originally published in the April 1956 issue of *Manhunt*. Subsequently anthologized in *Hitchcock in Prime Time*, ed. Francis M. Nevins, Jr. and Martin H. Greenberg (Avon, 1985).
Directed by Herschel Daugherty.
(violin case)   *Good evening ladies and gentlemen. A special word to those of you who have rushed to drive-in theatres to watch this show. Please stop sending us your tickets for speeding. Unfortunately, we cannot validate them. Tonight's narrative is about gangsters. And I thought I better test some of the props.* (takes out a machine-gun) *I would like to play "The Flight of the Bumblebee" for you, but we must get on with the show. Our story is entitled "The Better Bargain." And speaking of bargains . . .*

Story: A prosperous gangster named Louis Koster hires a private detective, Mr. Cutter, to trail the actions of his wife, suspecting her of cheating on him. Inquiring upon the services of the professional hit man Harry Silver, Louis reveals his suspicions, explaining that he wants the two lovers – both his wife and her boyfriend – dead but if the unreliable Cutter isn't reporting accurate, don't bother. The next afternoon, Cutter returns and breaks the bad news. Marian is definitely cheating on her husband, and worse, the boyfriend loves to quote poetry. Louis pays the detective off and phones Silver, agreeing to his expensive fee for the double murder. But after kissing and embracing his wife, Louis changes his mind, and orders Silver to kill only her lover, not Marian. He wouldn't want to see something as warm as her go stone cold. But Silver has a surprise for Louis – he's not in the mood for killing today. "You just don't appreciate the wonders of a woman," remarks Silver. "You think you can own a woman with money. Well, it's not enough." Pulling out his switchblade, the hired assassin starts quoting poetry while he makes toward Louis . . .

To summarize the next reel, Harry did as he threatened and Marian lived happily ever after. She had a rich, full life. It was too bad Harry didn't share it with her. You see, you can't spend money in the gas chamber. After all, murder will out, crime does not pay, virtue is rewarded and he who laughs last, is the sponsor. And now before I return, if you listen closely, you will hear ours, chuckling in the wings. Ha, ha, ha. (commercial break) *That was the concluding number on tonight's program. I hope you will find time to join us again, when we shall relate another saga of suspense and/or mystery. Good night.*

EPISODE #51 **"THE ROSE GARDEN"** Broadcast on December 16, 1956
      Starring: John Williams as Alexander Vinton
      Patricia Collinge as Julia Pickering
      Evelyn Varden as Mrs. Cordelia Welles   Ralph Peters as the cab driver
      Teleplay written for *Alfred Hitchcock Presents* by Marian Cockrell, based on a story by Vincent Fotre.
      Directed by Francis Cockrell.
      (digging in cemetery with sign "Cemetery Lots Come In And Browse") *Oh, good evening, friends, Romans and countrymen. I have just unearthed some items which may be of vast archaeological importance. Two fig leaves and a half eaten apple. Tonight's play is not about fig leaves but it does have a scene in a garden. It is called "The Rose Garden" and is concerned with two elderly sisters, in a magnolia- scented house in Louisiana. It begins in a moment. Just now, please watch this short training film.*

Story: Alexander Vinton represents a publishing house that received a murder novel in the mail, and found the book so extremely well-written, that he decided to visit the author, Cordelia, personally for the weekend. Arriving at her southern plantation, Alexander comes to the conclusion that the book is perhaps *too* well written - it may be based on her own real-life experiences. Julia, you see, subtly suggested that her sister Cordelia murdered her husband, Gordon, and buried him in the rose garden. When the sisters leave for choir practice, Alexander goes out to the garden, begins digging, but finds nothing. He gets surprised when Cordelia arrives home early. Forced to talk about the matter, Cordelia convinces him that the book is a work of pure fiction. But she also pleads with him not to publish the manuscript as other people may reach the same conclusion, forever tarnishing the family name. Alexander agrees with her wishes, not yet realizing the truth of the situation. You see, after packing up to leave, he overhears Cordelia threaten to kill her sister for making mention of the truth, and under which rose bed the body is buried.

      (gravestone for Cock Robin) *So much for the literary set. Our next item before I return, is an answer to those people who keep insisting that all this country needs is a good one-minute commercial.* (commercial break) *We must interupt our program for a week, while we prepare the next play for production. I shall see you then. Good night.*

EPISODE #52 **"MR. BLANCHARD'S SECRET"** Broadcast on December 23, 1956
      Rehearsed and filmed on October 18, 19, and 22, 1956.
      Starring: Robert Horton as John Fenton
      Meg Mundy as Mrs. Ellen Blanchard
      Mary Scott as Mrs. Fenton   Dayton Lummis as Mr. George Blanchard
      Teleplay written for *Alfred Hitchcock Presents* by Sarett Rudley, based on the short story of the same name by Emily Neff. Reprinted in the June 1978 issue of *Ellery Queen's Mystery Magazine*.
      Directed by Alfred Hitchcock.

(holding an umbrella)   Good evening, friends.   Would you all please examine the tops of your television sets and see if one of you doesn't find a goldfish bowl with a crack in it?   (Holds out hand to feel rain)   Thank you.   By the way, I have been asked to announce that some of you are missing this program unnecessarily.   You have moved and not kept us informed of your address, so we don't know where to send the show to you.   I hope you will take care of that matter at once.   Tonight we are presenting a tale of mystery and intrigue laid in middleclass suburbia.   It is called "Mr. Blanchard's Secret."   I realize this doesn't tell you much about the story but several fine actors have been hired to do that and I would hate to rob them of the privilege.   And now as our cast scrambles for places behind the curtain, we offer this brief unattraction to divert you.

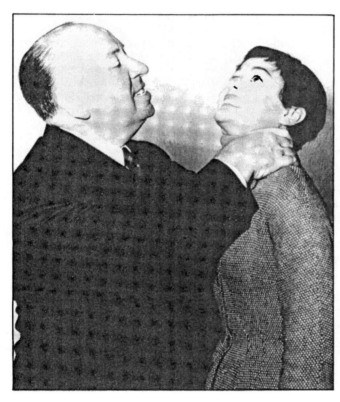

Hitchcock shows Mary Scott a method of strangulation, during rehearsals of "Mr. Blanchard's Secret." (Photo courtesy of Photofest.)

Story: Mrs. Fenton, a mystery novelist with an overactive imagination suspects her neighbor, Mr. Blanchard, of murdering his wife. To substantiate her theory, Mrs. Fenton breaks into Mr. Blanchard's home in hopes of finding some incriminating evidence, but discovers nothing. For that reason, she is even more shocked when the missing Mrs. Blanchard shows up at her apartment to introduce herself. Mr. Blanchard soon arrives and escorts his wife back home with him. Sometime after, Mrs. Fenton sees Mr. Blanchard hauling away a heavy bag and phones the police, again believing Mrs. Blanchard has finally been killed, but once again the woman shows up at her door, alive and well. Suddenly her dysfunctional silver lighter disappears and Mrs. Fenton puts together a new story about Mrs. Blanchard being a kleptomaniac. The police phone Mrs. Fenton to say they have recently found a dead body but when she leaves to identify the corpse, she meets Mr. and Mrs. Blanchard in the doorway. Mr. Blanchard has fixed the lighter.

So much for the fictional feature of our weekly magazine. Next we turn to a short theatrical piece. As for myself, I'm continued on the backpages among the advertisements. (commercial break) *That concludes our show until next week at this time.* (puts on hat) *Now if you will excuse me, I must hurry off to a little social affair. A dear friend is guest of honor. It's a stoning. I wouldn't miss it for the world. Good night.*

Alternate narrative: (filmed at a different angle)
    So much for the fictional feature of our weekly magazine. Next we turn to a short theatrical piece. As for myself, I'm continued on the backpages among the advertisements. (commercial break) *This concludes our show.* (puts on hat) *Now if you will excuse me, I must hurry off to a little social affair. A dear friend is guest of honor. It's a stoning. I wouldn't miss it for the world. Good night.*

    Trivia, etc. As with the new Mrs. de Winter in Hitchcock's *Rebecca* (1940), Mrs. Fenton is never mentioned by her first name. (Although she was called Julie in the 1989 remake "Murder in Mind.") Most interesting was Eloise Hardt, billed in the closing credits and production material says she played the role of an old woman. The entire episode, however, was actually a four-actor play. There is a possibility (but not proven) that Eloise Hardt was filmed in the old woman role, but when it came to editing the show together, her scenes were not included. This situation occurred to a great extent when television programs – including *Alfred Hitchcock Presents* – skipped an actor's scenes during the editing process, but their name remained in the cast credits. This same situation occurs later in "Nightmare in 4-D" and "One For the Road."

    An alternate presentation for non-American viewings was filmed, in a different angle, and with the last sentence taken out, replaced with: *And so without further ado, we reveal Mr. Blanchard's Secret.*

EPISODE #53 **"JOHN BROWN'S BODY"** Broadcast on December 30, 1956
    Starring: Leora Dana as Vera Brown   Russell Collins as John Brown
    Hugh Marlowe as Harold Skinner   Edmon Ryan as Dr. Croatman
    Walter Kingsford as Dr. Sam Helck   Jean Owens as Ellen, the maid
    Marcel Rousseau as the French waiter   Madelon Baker as the secretary
    Norman Leavitt as the business accountant
    Teleplay written for *Alfred Hitchcock Presents* by Robert C. Dennis, based on the short story of the same name by Thomas Burke, originally published in Burke's *The Pleasantries of Old Quong* (Constable, 1931; U.S. title *A Tea-Shop in Limehouse*, Little Brown, 1931).
    Directed by Robert Stevens.
    (payment scales)   *Good evening, and welcome to Alfred Hitchcock Presents . . .* (men put sacks of money on other side of the scale) *Thank you, see you next year . . . We thought you'd like to see this, so many of you have expressed an interest in knowing . . . how I was paid. Now I can afford to go back to my diet. Tonight's play is about a body, not mine. However, the title is "John Brown's Body." Since John Brown's body is not quite long enough to fill the entire half hour, we have sublet the next minute to a certain party with a passion for notoriety. I'm not sure what they plan to do with their time, but it might bare watching.*

    Story: Harold Skinner, the junior partner of John Brown's Furniture, has sketched some fancy designs for the future, but John is just too old-fashioned. Vera Brown, John's younger wife, spends quality time with Harold and together, the two plot to have John committed to a mental institution. Slowly but surely, Harold and Vera convince John that he is running his manufacturing company into the ground - which is what really starts to happen once John is committed. Harold, you see, doesn't know much about operating a business, and makes mistake after mistake, including the new line of fancy furniture Harold designed. Out of desperation Vera tries to get her husband released - only John Brown likes it where he is, reading books and painting on canvas in complete solitude. As the psychiatrist explains, John's mind is not yet feasible for the outside world. "You'd only be taking home his body," explains the medical man. You see, John has convinced the doctor that he really is insane, thus avoiding the possibility of being released . . . damning Harold and Vera to a financial disaster.

I hope that ending was properly terrifying. (Hitch unties a bag of money and puts his hand inside) (commercial break) *Thank you. After such a magnificent demonstration of humility and restraint. I find it difficult to make this next announcement. I shall, however. In making their annual television awards, the editors of* Look Magazine, *hold some fifteen hundred television critics. This year, the critics have voted* Alfred Hitchcock Presents *as the best half-hour dramatic series. An honor which pleases us very much. Next week we shall be back with another story. If I seem to loom a little larger on your screens, it will not mean that I have gained weight. Blame it instead on the righteous puff of pride. I hope you don't mind. Good night.*

Trivia, etc. Robert Stevens directed hundreds of television programs, both "live" and filmed productions. His credits as a director include *Arthur Godfrey's Talent Scouts, Suspense, Theatre of Romance*, and the premiere episode of *The Twilight Zone.* Later in 1968, Stevens would direct episodes of Joan Harrison and Norman Lloyd's television series, *Journey Into the Unknown.* A year after this episode was broadcast, Stevens would become the only director of *Alfred Hitchcock Presents* to win an Emmy Award for best direction.

EPISODE #54   **"CRACKPOT"**   Broadcast on January 6, 1957
    Starring: Biff McGuire as Ray Loomis
    Robert Emhardt as Mr. Moon / Detective   Mary Scott as Meg Loomis
    Michael Fox as Sergeant Carpenter   Phil Garris as the bellhop
    Raymond Guth as the room clerk
    Teleplay written for *Alfred Hitchcock Presents* by Martin Berkeley, based on a story by Harold Gast.
    Directed by John Meredyth Lucas.
    (in a sealed chamber)   *Good evening*   (echo: *Good evening*)   Hitchcock whispering: *Good evening. Certain parties have been objecting to my candid remarks so I'm doing tonight's show from this sealed chamber. It's as quiet as a tomb which is not surprising since it was the only type of structure available that suited our . . .* (echo repeats the same words) *Are you quite finished? Here in a moment is tonight's play. It is entitled "Crackpot."* (echo repeats again, Hitchcock sits down)

Story: Newlyweds Ray and Meg Loomis leave for their honeymoon only to have their car break down before reaching their destination. Luckily, a stranger named Mr. Moon stops to assist them, and fills their spare tire with air. When Ray accidentally stumbles and soils Moon's suit, the good Samaritan gets violently angry and threatens to kill them. Before he says another word, Mr. Moon drives off. Later checking into a hotel, the couple discover their assailant has the room next to theirs. Moon starts loud hammering, creating a large hole in the wall, and when Ray investigates, Mr. Moon pulls a gun, ordering the boy to mind his own business. Soon Ray starts hearing a clock ticking on the other side of the wall, but Meg doesn't hear it. Finally, Mr. Moon shows up at their doorway and Ray recognizes him as the man who murdered his aunt. Knocking the stranger to the ground, Ray orders his wife to make a break for it, while he attempts to retrieve the jewels, hidden behind a mirror in Meg's case. When Meg returns with a detective, Moon holds a gun on Ray, revealing his true intentions. His name isn't Moon, but a detective from the Pasadena Police. The clock and the hole in the wall was just a ruse to trick Ray into revealing the necklace, and proof of the murder. Seconds after, the alarm goes off proving that it was no bomb in the wall after all.

We wanted to withhold the end of that story but decided it was better that you learned the truth about Ray Loomis now than later. (Someone breaks a hole in the wall) *I knew it, it's the sponsor. The world just isn't big enough to escape. If some of you are contemplating leaving the room – don't. It's futile. No matter where you hide, he'll seek you out. You might just as well sit where you are until I return.* (commercial break) *That's all, until our next program. Which is just one week away as the crow flies. Good night.* (echo: Good night)

Trivia, etc. Martin Berkeley was a screenwriter at Universal when an offer to script an episode of *Alfred Hitchcock Presents* came his way. Berkeley had already scripted the science-fiction classics *Revenge of the Creature* (1955) and *Tarantula* (1955), and was at the time scripting the movie *The Deadly Mantis* (1957), when he was offered to write for *Alfred Hitchcock Presents*.

EPISODE #55 **"NIGHTMARE IN 4-D"** Broadcast on January 13, 1957
   Starring: Henry Jones as Harry Parker Barbara Baxley as Miss Lainie Elliott
   Norman Lloyd as Lieutenant Orsatti Virginia Gregg as Mrs. Norma Parker
   Percy Helton as Charlie, the janitor Norman Bartold as Sergeant Gold
   Teleplay written for *Alfred Hitchcock Presents* by Robert C. Dennis, based on a story by Stuart Jerome.
   Directed by Justus Addiss.
   (voice of the sponsor interrupts Hitch) "Ladies and gentlemen, tonight our sponsor presents another commercial but first, let us have a word from our producer." *Good evening -* (sponsor's voice interupts and Hitch gives a sour look.) "Thank you, and now the commercial."

   Story: Harry Parker leads a poor-man's rendition of a supportive husband in a life without any excitement. The only time he gets his heart pace faster is when he reads a fiction novel, or exchanges a look with Miss Lainie, his beautiful wanna-be actress-neighbor who lives downstairs. One evening Lainie knocks on his door and pleads with him to come downstairs to help. It seems that she was sitting with Barry Nielsen, another tenant, when he was suddenly shot through the window. She asks Harry to help move the body to the basement of their apartment building, so she can avoid bad publicity, which he reluctantly agrees to do. When Harry wakes the next morning, he confesses the deed to his wife, Norma, who doesn't believe a word he says. Unfortunately for Harry, his good deed doesn't go unnoticed by the police, as detectives begin asking the tenants questions. Harry is shocked when the lieutenant reveals Norma's association with Nielsen . . . when Harry was at work every afternoon. Then Harry tries to incriminate his wife for the murder, but it seems he will be charged, not as an accessory to murder, but for murder. Apparently Harry climbed down the fire escape and shot Nielsen in jealousy, not for his wife, but for Miss Lainie.

(Two commercial breaks during Hitchcock's closing remarks)
   That was amusing, although I think Norma was a poor sport about it all. Which leads me very logically to the next matter. At the opening of the program, you may remember, I was cut off rather abruptly. That is a game at which two can play. Ladies and gentlemen, the commercial. (attempted commercial break) *Wasn't that delightful and if the sponsor continues to be difficult I can make them even shorter.* (crying from off camera) *There he is now.* (crying) *Oh dear, I can't stand to see a grown man cry. Ladies and gentlemen, while I'm away the commercial – unabridged version.* (commercial) *Like any classic, the uncut version is the better, no question about it. And now the time has come for us to part, but please, no long good-byes. Don't even look back, I want to remember you as you were. So until next week, good night.*

   Trivia, etc. Actress Minerva Urecal, familiar with television audiences as Dean Josephine Bradley on *The Ray Milland Show*, and as "Mother" on *Peter Gunn*. Although credited in a few reference sources for playing the role of Mrs. Henderson in Hitchcock's *Shadow of a Doubt* (1943), she did not appear in the movie. (Actress Ethel Griffies played the role of Mrs. Henderson.) Again, like *Shadow of a Doubt*, Urecal's name appears in the cast credits, but she makes no noticable appearance during the drama. The voice of the sponsor during Hitchcock's presentation was that of Paul Frees, a Hollywood announcer whose versatile voice narrated the opening of Paramount's *War of the Worlds* (1953), Mr.

Tipton on CBS-TV's *The Millionaire,* and supplied voices for numerous animated cartoon characters including Professor Ludwig Von Drake, Boris Badenov, and The Beatles. Norman Lloyd, future associate producer of *Alfred Hitchcock Presents,* played Lieutenant Orsatti in this episode.

"The casting directors didn't know what to do with me. I was never tall enough or good looking enough to play juvenile leads," actor Henry Jones recalled in an interview. This didn't stop Jones from making guest appearances in over 350 television broadcasts, and known for becoming a favorite of Alfred Hitchcock's, playing the future role of a cruel coroner in *Vertigo* (1958). The murder in this television episode, by the way, actually took place in apartment 3-D. It's the Parker's that live in apartment 4-D.

Inger Stevens and Harry Townes in "My Brother Richard"
(Photo courtesy of Photofest)

EPISODE #56   **"MY BROTHER, RICHARD"**   Broadcast on January 20, 1957
    Starring: Royal Dano as Martin Ross   Inger Stevens as Laura Ross
    Harry Townes as Richard Ross   Ray Teal as Sheriff Briggs
    Bobby Ellis as Tommy Kopek, the caddie
    Lisa Golm as Tommy's mother, Mrs. Kopek

Teleplay written for *Alfred Hitchcock Presents* by Sarett Rudley, based on a story by Jay Bennett.

Directed by Herschel Daugherty.

(toy horse, golf club)   *Good evening. I firmly believe that everyone should indulge now and then in some form of athletic sport, don't you? Personally I don't require much exercise, since I lead a very Spartan existence. But when I do, I find my needs are adequately filled by such sports as riding or reading the less violent portions of the Sunday papers. Of course, for a true test of bodily coordination, I think there is nothing better than lying in a hammock. But I suppose that would only appeal to those of you who enjoy living dangerously. As for tonight's play, it is called "My Brother, Richard" and it begins in a country club. By the way, golf is one game I've never cared much for. I don't like the paperwork. I find adding up my strokes too fatiguing.* (close-up) *And now, you have a moment to prepare for tonight's rendezvous with death.*

Story: Local district attorney Martin Ross is running for state governor when Richard, his deranged brother, puts him in a precarious position: Richard has just murdered the opponent running against Martin. Martin and his wife Laura confront Richard, explaining that what he did is wrong, and that they themselves could end up losing the race, if it is discovered that they had a hand in their opponent's death – even though they didn't. Richard gets angry when he is told that his help is unappreciated, so he pulls out his smoking pistol and holds them captive. As the local district attorney, Martin receives a phone call and told to investigate a boy believed to be responsible for murdering Richard's victim. Martin, nervous, convinces Richard into letting him leave, so he can investigate the boy. Realizing that the only way to get his wife back alive is to make it appear that the young man is guilty, and confess to the crime, Martin successfully accomplishes this, but things still don't work out as planned. Tommy's mother comes for a visit, very upset, and when Richard tells her that her son is obviously the murderer, she stabs Richard to death.

Thus ends "My Brother, Richard." Needless to say Mrs. Grant was brought to trial, but fortunately the jury took into account many of the circumstances which we saw reenacted tonight. Earlier in the program our . . . (takes his hat off) *dear sponsor gave us a few words of advice. If there is anything he wishes to add, I think he should do it now, while we are still on the air. However, while I am briefly away, I have just one word of advice you might consider. Anything you say could be held against you.* (commercial break) *Perhaps you didn't hear me. We began with a commercial and we ended with one. Somehow it gives one a comforting feeling to know that once again life has come full circle. So until next week, cheeri-hoo.*

Trivia, etc.   During Hitchcock's closing remarks, Hitchcock called Tommy's mother "Mrs. Grant" instead of Mrs. Kopek. This might possibly have been because the intros were written after James Allardice read the script, and the name of the character might have been changed during filming.

The murder of Burton Reeves took place in the shower. He was shot in the back of the head, but just with one camera set-up and one additional close-up of the gun. Although Hitchcock would not film *Psycho* for at least two more years, he had already bought the story and the fact that a murder being taken place in a shower – over network television – seemed to go over well without any known reported disturbance with the viewers, could have made some sort of a decision for the future to come.

EPISODE #57   **"THE MANACLED"**   Broadcast on January 27, 1957

Starring: Gary Merrill as Ben Rockwell	William Redfield as Steven Fontaine
Rusty Lane as the conductor	Betty Harford as the waitress
Edith Evanson as the elderly woman	Gary Hunley as the boy
Kay Stewart as the girl	

Teleplay written for *Alfred Hitchcock Presents* by Stirling Silliphant, based on a story by Sanford Wolf.
Directed by Robert Stevens.
(handcuffs table)   *Good evening, ladies and gentlemen and television fans all over . . . the livingroom floor.   Tonight's drama is called "The Manacled" and features a pair of these attractive and useful charm bracelets.   These of course are stage handcuffs especially made so that one can easily get out.   Of course, as you may know, these little trinkets are not only used to cuff hands, they also work very well on legs, regarding . . .*
(Hitchcock stops talking, realizing he cuffed himself to the table legs)

Story: Steven Fontaine, a convicted thief, is being transported to prison by train and is escorted by an armed police officer named Ben Rockwell.   Fontaine will do anything to escape before arriving at San Quentin, so he talks Ben into unlocking him from an immobilizing "Oregon boot," and letting him run in exchange for the $50,000 he stole. Shortly after Ben takes off the cuffs, he realizes what a mistake he made and changes his mind.   He doesn't want the money and orders Steven back into the boots.   Steven, once again locked up, sees this as his only opportunity to escape, and tries to overpower the officer, making for the keys.   A fight between the men forces Ben's gun to go off, killing the officer. But Fontaine is far from being off the hook, as he has just found that the bullet that killed Ben also destroyed the key to the locked boot.

(Hitchcock is trying to free himself from cuffs around leg of the table) (commercial break) (Hitchcock just lifts the table and slides the cuffs down to escape)   *I wish I had discovered that three commercials ago.   I hope to have my hand free by next week at this same time, when I shall be back with another story.   Good night.*

EPISODE #58   **"A BOTTLE OF WINE"**   Broadcast on February 3, 1957
Starring: Herbert Marshall as Judge Harley Condon
Robert Horton as Wally Donaldson   Jarma Lewis as Grace Condon
Teleplay written for *Alfred Hitchcock Presents* by Stirling Silliphant, based on the short story of the same name by Borden Deal, originally published in the premiere issue (December 1956) of *Alfred Hitchcock's Mystery Magazine*.
Directed by Herschel Daugherty.
(in a wine cellar)   *Good evening.   I came down here because I understand that the current year is a very good year for wine.   For drinking it, that is.   I'm looking for some, uh, champagne . . . Not to be taken internally.   Oh.   For bathing only.   Fortunately my tastes aren't so expensive.   I bathe in rootbeer.   That way one doesn't have to add a softener.   All this is by way of introducing tonight's play.   It is called, by an extraordinary coincidence, "A Bottle Of Wine."   So much for the banalities.   Now we present our first feature.   The heart and core of our evening's entertainment.   It is an adaptation of a Japanese no-drama, by an advertising agency "yes man."*

Story: One hot summer afternoon, Grace tells her husband, a well-known and practical judge, that she's leaving him.   After years of marriage, she prefers a younger man with a lucrative income.   Her lover is outside waiting and she will be leaving in a few minutes.   While Grace is upstairs packing a wardrobe scanning the years, the judge invites Wally Donaldson inside for a drink of wine.   The two uncomfortably discuss their futures, after which the judge pulls out a gun and forces Wally to finish the wine, and then puts down the gun, not wanting to shoot him.   "I respect the law, but I despise myself," the judge remarks.   Then he announces that the wine Wally consumed has been poisoned.   He himself drank as well, but while he takes an antidote, Wally will soon feel the deadly effects.   His true intentions is for Wally to make a fool of himself, resulting in his young wife changing her mind.   Instead, Wally proves that any well-laid plan can go awry when he picks up the judge's gun and vengefully kills the judge, not realizing that he was never really poisoned.

Forsooth, such knavery. I didn't realize the judge was such a sore loser. Oh well, so much for our little preachment on the evils of drink. And now as a service to you television addicts, who are trying to give it up. Here before I return, is something that will certainly do the trick. (commercial break) *Those of you who are still with us, should be congradulated for your fortitude and endurance. I hope you will join us again next week. Good night.*

EPISODE #59 "MALICE DOMESTIC"   Broadcast on February 10, 1957
Starring: Ralph Meeker as Carl Borden   Phyllis Thaxter as Annette Borden
Ralph Clanton as Perry Harrison   Vinton Hayworth as Dr. Ralph Wingate
Lili Kardell as Lorna Jenkins
Teleplay written for *Alfred Hitchcock Presents* by Victor Wolfson, based on the short story of the same name by Philip MacDonald, originally published in the October 1946 issue of *Ellery Queen's Mystery Magazine.* Subsequently collected in *Something to Hide* (Doubleday, 1951; British title: *Fingers of Fear*, Collins, 1953).
Directed by John Meredyth Lucas.
Good evening. Ladies and gentlemen of the jury. The first case on today's docket is entitled "Malice Domestic." I hasten to add however, that malice domestic is not about the servant problem, nor is it a puff for imported wines. It is concerned with some mysterious doings in a family of three. Carl Borden, his wife Annette, and their charming dog, Cassandra. To give you a clearer picture of exactly what happened, we now transport you to the scene of the crime, where we shall reenact it. But before we do that, his honor wishes to charge the jury.

Story: When Carl Borden visits his personal physician Dr. Wingate, because of stomach pains, the good doctor discovers large traces of arsenic in his system. As a close friend, the doctor suggests that someone, presumably his wife Annette, is trying to murder Carl. When his wife soon dies of arsenic poison herself, everyone believes she drank Carl's poisoned coffee by mistake. The police investigate, perform chemical tests on the coffee, and even question Dr. Wingate, leading to the conclusion that Annette died by her own hand - an unmistakable accident. With his name in the clear, Carl follows his doctor's advice and takes a vacation - in San Francisco with his girlfriend - where he tells her how he almost died in the process of pulling off the perfect crime . . . ingesting the original cups he tainted himself for the initial visit to his friendly doctor.

You are all wondering, no doubt, how Carl Borden ended up in the Pokey. Quite simple. His dog, Cassandra, was really a detective in disguise and turned him in, at the next town. It's getting so a man can't even trust his best friend. (commercial break) *Uh, that concludes this session of our little court of. . .uh, inhuman relations. I hope you'll rejoin us when we present a different case. Good night.*

EPISODE #60   "NUMBER TWENTY-TWO"   Broadcast on February 17, 1957
Starring: Russell Collins as Skinner   Rip Torn as Steve Morgan
Ray Teal as the chief of detectives   James Nolan as Kelly
Paul Picerni as Assissi   Bob Ross as Bohlen
Charles Watts as Franklin   Peter Leeds as the custodian
Mike Ross as the jailer   Martin Wilkins as the man
Hugh Sanders as the booking officer
Teleplay written for *Alfred Hitchcock Presents* by Joel Murcott, based on the short story "First Offense" by Evan Hunter, originally published in the December 1955 issue of *Manhunt.* Subsequently collected in *The Jungle Kids* (Pocket Books, 1956; British title, with somewhat different contents: *The Last Spin and Other Stories*, Constable, 1960).
Directed by Robert Stevens.
(Hitchcock in a police line-up, voice from behind camera calls out) Voice: *This is a police line-up. Here, desperate criminals who have been brought to bay appear before the*

detective force and are questioned by the chief detective. Listen: Take your hat off. Name:
Hitchcock, Alfred. Height: 5"6' (167 cm). Weight: prisoner refuses to make a statement.
Here's his record: 1940 picked up on Suspicion, 1942 Spellbound, 1944 Notorious, 1955
Rear Window, 1956 The Man Who Knew Too Much. Anything to say Hitchcock? Hitchcock:
Well sir, I admit it ain't a good record, but I'm trying to do better. Voice: *Better? Do you*
call this latest charge doing better? Appearing on television? Hitchcock: *I'm sorry Sir, but*
my family was hungry. Voice: *Take him away.* Hitchcock: *Wait a minute sir, you've got the*
wrong man. Don't you want to see a sample of my work? Voice: *O.K. Here is what we*
found on him when we picked him up.

Story: A young punk named Steve Morgan attempts his first robbery, striking the
owner of the candy store in the process. When the police corner Steve in an alley, they
discover the only weapon on his possession is a toy gun. Still, Steve must spend the evening
in jail, booked for assault. Reveling in the excitement of a line-up, Steve answers the
questions thrown at him and thinks the whole matter will go public so he can impress his
friends. Skinner, an old man booked for attempted robbery, tries to assure the young man
that there's nothing good about being fingerprinted and photographed, but Steve doesn't pay
any attention, smiling and bragging the entire time. The chief of detectives tries to break a
confession out of Steve, asking why Steve picked that specific candy store, but the boys gets
angry and brags about how he hit the old man, after leaving with just twelve dollars. Steve
wallows in all the glory until he's informed that they have not arrested him for theft, but for
murder - as the man he hit, has died as a result of a fractured skull.

Occasionally in our series we touch on a subject that is far too real to be made a
butt of my usual flippant remarks. Tonight's story of juvenile delinquency is certainly a case
in point and we have presented it with a hope that it might, in some small way, throw a little
light on what has become a serious national problem. (commercial break) *Thank you very*
kindly for that enlightening public document. And now ladies and gentlemen, I am afraid we
must leave but we shall return next week with another play, as usual. Good night.

Trivia, etc. Hitchcock's presentation was more than just a publicity stunt when he
told the announcer "Wait a minute sir, you've got the wrong man. Don't you want to see a
sample of my work?" This line has double meaning since Hitchcock's latest feature was the
Warner Bros. release *The Wrong Man* starring Henry Fonda and Vera Miles. Like the
episodes "Memo From Purgatory" and "Bang! You're Dead," Hitchcock made a public plea
for the observance and concern over juvenile delinquency. (Last season's "Never Again"
featured a plea for the seriousness about alcoholism.)

EPISODE #61   **"THE END OF INDIAN SUMMER"**   Broadcast on February 24, 1957
Starring: Steve Forrest as Joe Rogers
Gladys Cooper as Mrs. Marguerite Gillespie
James Gleason as Howard Fieldstone   Kathleen Maguire as Helen Rogers
Philip Coolidge as Sam Henderson   Hal K. Dawson as Mr. Graham
Ned Wever as Saunders   Mason Curry as the desk clerk
Hope Summers as the maid   Mike Kuhn as the bellhop
Teleplay written for *Alfred Hitchcock Presents* by James P. Cavanagh, based on the
short story of the same name by Maurice Baudin, Jr.
Directed by Robert Stevens.
(fishing in a bath tub)   *I can't understand it. Of course, how stupid of me. I*
forgot to put in the water. I must do that at once if I want to catch anything today. All of this
is not as absurdly irrelevant as you think. For if you listen very closely, you will hear the
words "bath tub" mentioned in tonight's script. Of course other topics are mentioned which
we could have discussed. For example, the story is about marriage. However, I don't feel
that marriage should be discussed on television. It's too controversial, no question about it.
We are much safer with a bathtub. And now in a moment, here is tonight's opera buffé, "The

End of Indian Summer." Like all stories about marriage, it has a great deal of romance in it. But watch for that bathtub.

Story: Marguerite Gillespie, an elderly lady, is suspected of murder when both of her heavily-insured husbands immediately died under strange circumstances. The first was for $50,000 and the second husband was also insured for more. Both bodies were cremated before the insurance companies could prove it was poison. Insurance Investigator Joe Rogers doesn't suspect Gillespie of murder, but his boss has suspicions, so Joe begins snooping. With Gillespie now engaged to another man, Howard Fieldstone, Rogers trails the couple, and notices someone else keeping an eye on the pair. At first, Rogers assumes that this is just another insurance investigator checking up on his duties, but when he finally speaks to the man it turns out that the stranger is actually following Fieldstone, a man who has had four previously-insured wives die in bathtubs. But it's too late, for the old couple have already left for their honeymoon. Not knowing where the newlyweds went, and deciding that this is a marriage made in heaven, the investigators decide to leave it at that.

Their's was truly a wedding of december and december. It ended in a draw, with no one the winner, except the insurance companies. And now, for the epilogue of tonight's story, after which I'll scamper back. (commercial break) *We have now passed another tombstone along television's highway to culture. Please join us next week, when we continue our pilgrimage. Good night.*

EPISODE #62 **"ONE FOR THE ROAD"**   Broadcast on March 3, 1957
>Starring: John Baragrey as Charles Hendrix
>Georgann Johnson as Beryl Abbott
>Louise Platt as Marcia Hendrix
>Teleplay written for *Alfred Hitchcock Presents* by Robert C. Dennis, based on a
story by Emily Neff.
>Directed by Robert Stevens.
>(in medieval stocks) *Good evening. Me thinks I should never have come to the colonies. Here I am, the producer's dream, a captive audience. Unfortunately, knowing the producer, I have already seen tonight's story several times. It is called "One For The Road." They say there are two sides to every question. But tonight's little problem has three sides. For it is that age-old bit of marital geometry, the eternal triangle. I suppose you're wondering why I'm a prisoner. If you think we have freedom of speech here, just try speaking your mind about television commercials. But I've learned my lesson. Ladies and gentlemen, may I present my esteemed sponsor, who will give as a public service, a short and candid appraisal of one of his superb products?*

Story: Marcia Hendrix learns to her dismay that her husband, Charles Hendrix, is cheating on her with a hussy named Beryl Abbott. When she confronts her knowledge to Charles, he admits his wrong-doing, and asks for time to straighten things out. One morning, while Charles is at work, Marcia drives out of town and manages to sneak into Beryl's flat to put poison in her sugar, with the cruelest of intentions. But when she returns home, Marcia discovers that Charles is going to see Beryl tonight. Fearing that he may be poisoned, Marcia jumps in the car and races out of town. Meanwhile, Charles tells Beryl that he has to call the relationship off, simply because Marcia has caught on. While Charles steps into the back room for a few minutes, Marcia arrives, rushing to Beryl's apartment, and confesses her deed. Beryl, surprised, tells an awful story about Charles drinking coffee before leaving, and there was enough sugar to kill him within an hour. Marcia panics, intending to tell the police what she did, even if it means confessing to murder. "My husband is more important," she explains, running out of the apartment. Charles, unaware of the women's conversation, steps out of the back room and prepares to go home. Before he can leave, Beryl asks him to stay for a few minutes, and have a cup of coffee. "How about one for the road, with an old friend?" Beryl asks. Charles pours himself a cup . . . with sugar.

(no longer in stocks) *It's good to be free again, which is more than Beryl Abbott is. For she was arrested and paid for her crime. Now before I return, we shall have the last commercial. One for the road. And no doubt, it will be just as effective as the drink in our story.* (commercial break) (Hitch back in lock) *My the sponsor's a sensitive fellow. Well, why don't you tune in next week and see if he has relented. I suspect I shall be here and we shall have a story as well. Good night.*

Alternate narrative:
(no longer in stocks) *It's good to be free again, which is more than Beryl Abbott is. You see, she was arrested and paid for her crime. Next time we shall be back with another story. Good night.*

Trivia, etc. Actor Michael Kuhn was billed in the closing credits, but he never made an appearance during the drama. Apparently he fell victim to the Eloise Hardt syndrome (see episode 52), playing a small supporting role that, during the editing process, got cut out completely. "One for the Road" remained a three-actor play. This also made the third time in the past eleven episodes that an actor received billing for an episode they didn't appear in! Kuhn did make an appearance as a card player in the episode "Vicious Circle."

EPISODE #63   **"THE CREAM OF THE JEST"**   Broadcast on March 10, 1957
Starring: Claude Rains as Charles Hannover Gresham
James Gregory as Wayne Campbell   Paul Picerni as Nick Roper
Joan Banks as Leigh   Johnny Silver as Jerry
Also in the cast: Don Garrett, Carol Shannon, and Tom Martin.
Teleplay written for *Alfred Hitchcock Presents* by Sarett Rudley, based on the short story "Last Curtain" by Fredric Brown, originally published in the July 1949 issue of *New Detective.* Subsequently reprinted as "The Cream of the Jest" in the July 1956 issue of *Ellery Queen's Mystery Magazine.* Also collected in *The Shaggy Dog and Other Murders* (Dutton, 1963; Boardman, 1964), as "Good Night, Good Knight."
Directed by Herschel Daugherty.
(in a library coat)   *Good evening. I understand it is fashionable to introduce television plays from a library and so I thought I would preface tonight's play, "The Cream of the Jest," in this way. "The Cream of the Jest" is a play about the theatrical business . . . (shhh!) and it has as its central character a fading actor named Charles Hannover Gresham. Our play will . . . (shhh!) Our play begins in just one moment.*

Story: Charles Hannover Gresham, an unemployed thespian because of his alcoholism, tries to get a part in a play being produced by a former friend, Wayne Campbell. But Campbell knows about his drinking problem and turns him down. Gresham then decides to blackmail the producer for cash, as he knows Campbell once embezzled $5,000. Campbell gives him some money to keep him quiet, and is eventually forced to give him a job as well. There is one catch, however, as Gresham must audition in front of the show's backer, a mobster named Nick Roper. Unknown to Gresham, Campbell has given him not lines from the show, but ones that will make Roper believe that he is being blackmailed – a situation that will quickly put Gresham out of the way permanently.

Well, there's no use taking that book home with us, now that we've finished it. By the way uh . . . in case you're interested, the police learned of Wayne Campbell's connection with tonight's crime. Now while I'm struggling with this coat, suppose you accept this little missive for our shaftive by our sponsor. (commercial break) *I can't understand why this coat doesn't seem to fit. I just bought it. Seems to be a label stuck inside. Occupancy by more than one person contrary to law. Well, no wonder! Next week we shall return with another story, join us then. Good night.*

EPISODE #64   **"I KILLED THE COUNT"**   (PART I)   Broadcast March 17, 1957
Starring: John Williams as Inspector Davidson
Alan Napier as Lord P. L. Sorrington   Charles Cooper as Bernard Kay Froy
Melville Cooper as Mullet, elevator man   Charles Davis as Sergeant Raines
Pat Hitchcock as Polly Stevens, the maid
Anthony Dawson as Count Victor Mattoni
Kendrick Huxham as Mr. Martin, the landlord
George Pelling as Johnson, the elevator man
A. E. Gould-Porter as Clifton   Jerry Barclay as Peters
Teleplay written for *Alfred Hitchcock Presents* by Francis Cockrell, based on the
stage play of the same name by Alec Coppel, originally published by Heinemann, 1938. (In
novel form under the same title: Blackie, 1939).
All three parts were directed by Robert Stevens.
(standing beside knight's armour)   *Good evening ladies and gentlemen. This
is Alfred Hitchcock. Tonight's play takes place in merry old England, and is called "I Killed
The Count." When they asked me to wear this, I demured. I didn't realize it would be an
invitation for automation to take over. Empty. Now what does that imply? Oh well. Let the
play begin.* (close-up) *I guess they won't let it begin until we've had an opportunity to study
the advertisements in the program. Let the commercial begin.*

Story: Count Victor Mattoni was found with a bullet hole in his head but it wasn't
suicide – at least that's what Inspector Davidson insists. Inspector Davidson has a record
unsurpassed in solving crime, and he won't let this murder break that record, as he's about to
retire. The maid says the last time she saw the Count was about nine last night, when he
came home drunk. The cartridge case was found on the floor in the next suite, owned by a
Mr. Rupert who's never been seen except by the elevator man, but Rupert leaves an envelope
of money each week to pay for the rent. Two letters name Bernard Kay Froy and Lord
Sorrington, both of whom insist – at first – that they don't know Mattoni. Davidson shows
one of the incriminating letters and Froy confesses to murdering the Count, but he didn't
assume the role of any fictional Rupert. Later that afternoon, Lord Sorrington is revealed as
the fictional Rupert, thanks to observations of the elevator man, and seeing the hoax is up,

also confesses to murdering the Count!
Inspector Davidson is at a loss of words.

*Oh, this is embarrasing, our time is
running out and here we are with an
unfinished story on our hands. I'm afraid
you will just have to wait until our next
show, to find out more about just who killed
the Count.   Personally, I shall welcome a
week in which to think up some answers.
After all, Froy and Lord Sorrington can't
both be telling the truth. There is nothing I
detest more than a murderer who tells fibs.
But enough of that for now. I shall return
in a moment for a further discussion of the
case.   Meanwhile, I'm sure that this is
unnecessary for me to say, that although
our story policy is being temporary
changed, our schedule of commercials will
be rigidly adhered to.* (commercial break)
*Next week we shall continue the strange
case of Count Victor Mattoni. Thus far our
desperate detectives have two very good
suspects. But their confessions seem to ask*

more questions than they answer. If all this has managed to pique your curiosity, join us next time. I know what you're thinking. No, I did not kill the Count. Good night.

      Trivia, etc. "What on Earth does it take to surprise Hitchcock? Alfred Hitchcock presents the surprisingest surprise ending that Hitchcock ever ended a surprise with," read the attractive advertisements in the newspapers. "I Killed the Count" was the only multi-part story dramatized on the original *Alfred Hitchcock Presents* series. The opening title screen of the first presentation never made mention of "part one" so viewers were definitely in for a surprise. The television production varied slightly from the original stage play by Alec Coppel. In the play, Inspector Davidson, a Detective for Scotland Yard, on the day before his retirement, is assigned to investigate the murder of an Italian count. Four people come forward and confess to the murder, confusing Davidson to the point where his nerves are about to explode. As it actually happened, a neighbor killed the much-despised nobleman, and the self-sacrificing confessors remain free to continue their lives, freed of the presence of the onerous aristocrat. The conclusion of the Hitchcock production, however, made for all four victims to cleverly devise a get-away with murder, a loophole in the system of justice.

      In 1939, writers Lawrence Huntington and Alec Coppel co-wrote a film script based on Coppel's play. Director Frederick Zelnick also co-wrote the script. Syd Walker played the lead of Inspector Davidson, and Terence de Marney was Sergeant Raines. Grafton Studios released the film in England under the original title. In 1940, when the movie debuted in American theaters, the movie was re-titled to *Who is Guilty?*

      Alan Napier played the role of Mr. Rutland, Snr. in Hitchcock's *Marnie* (1964).

EPISODE #65   **"I KILLED THE COUNT"**   **(PART II)**   Broadcast March 24, 1957
       Starring: John Williams as Inspector Davidson
       Rosemary Harris as Miss Louise Rogers
       Alan Napier as Lord P. L. Sorrington   Charles Cooper as Bernard Kay Froy
       Melville Cooper as Pat Lummock / Mullet, the elevator man
       Charles Davis as Sergeant Raines
       Anthony Dawson as Count Victor Mattoni   Roxanne Arlen as Miss Laloon
       George Pelling as Johnson, the elevator man
       A. E. Gould-Porter as Clifton   Jerry Barclay as Peters
       (2 intros with summary)

Good evening. Tonight's play is called "I Killed The Count." Now I know what you're thinking. Last week's play was also called "I Killed The Count" and you think tonight's is just a revival. On the contrary, since we were unable to finish the story last time we shall have another stab at it tonight. I shall be back in a moment to fill in some of the details for those of you who were careless enough to miss the first episode. I hope you realize the trouble you're putting us to. Just don't let it happen again. But first, let us dispense with this bit of routine business. (commercial break followed by episode title screen) *I'm sure you didn't expect me back quite so soon. But I think it very important to summarize the minutes of our last meeting. First of all, Count Victor Mattoni was found quite dead in the livingroom of his London flat.*

There was a single bullet hole in his forehead. It's my personal opinion that this was a contributing factor in his death. Inspector Davidson and his assistant Raines, the investigating detectives, have uncovered a number of clues, among them two letters. One which lead to Bernard Kay Froy and another written by a Lord Sorrington, an industrialist. Before the detectives are quite settled down to work they are faced with an embarrassing over-supply of confessions. For both Froy and Lord Sorrington confessed to a murder that only one of them could have committed. I'm certain this is all quite clear but for the benefit of any small children who may have missed some of the plot fascinations, here to clarify are two brief scenes from our last show after which our story continues.

**Charles Davis and John Williams trying to figure who killed the Count.
(Photo courtesy of Ronald V. Borst / Hollywood Movie Posters.)**

Story: Lord Sorrington confesses that the Count was married to his daughter Helen, and the disgrace embarrassed Sorrington. He didn't want his daughter to live with such misery. That's why he rented the flat next door. Last night he sneaked into Mattoni's suite, woke him up and the two struggled. Mattoni was shot in the head, and Sorrington placed the body back in the chair. After Sorrington is detained, Inspector Davidson questions Bernard Froy, the other suspect, and learns that Froy was in love with Mattoni's wife. Froy says he got one of the duplicate keys to the flat from the lobby, entered Mattoni's room and used his gun to hold Mattoni against his will for the letter that incriminated Helen. The two struggled and the gun went off. Froy placed the body back in the chair. None of the tenants in the building seems to have heard a gun shot the night before, but one tenant claims she couldn't use the elevator because the elevator man wasn't available. When Johnson the elevator man is questioned, he confesses that he switched shifts with Mullet. The detectives discover that the fingerprints from both Froy and Sorrington didn't match any of the prints found on the Count's wallet. When Davidson questions Mullet the elevator man, he gets reminded that he has seen him before, but then under the name of Pat Lummock. When asked to "come clean," Mullet confesses, saying it was he who killed the count!

Well, we've done it again. We still haven't finished the story. How extremely careless of us, but I promise you on my honor, the truth will be out next week. Fortunately you won't have to wait that long for the truth about our sponsor's product. Voila. (commercial break) *I have excused the actors until next time when they will present the final act of our play. Unfortunately, since you are all accessories after the fact, I cannot permit you to leave the room. You may, however, discuss the case among yourselves. Who killed the Count, and why? Only one person could have done it. Was it Mullet, the elevator man? Did Bernard Froy do it? Was it Lord Sorrington, or was it a fourth person? Who is the guilty party? Tune in next week and find out. Good night.*

EPISODE #66   **"I KILLED THE COUNT"   (PART III)**   Broadcast March 31, 1957
Starring: John Williams as Inspector Davidson
Rosemary Harris as Miss Louise Rogers / Helen Sorrington / Countess Mattoni
Alan Napier as Lord P. L. Sorrington
Charles Cooper as Bernard Kay Froy
Melville Cooper as Pat Lummock / Mullet, the elevator man
Charles Davis as Sergeant Raines
Anthony Dawson as Count Victor Mattoni   A. E. Gould-Porter as Clifton
Nora Marlowe as the Policewoman at the Yard
Peter Gordon as the Policeman at the Yard
(2 intros with summary)   *Good evening ladies and gentlemen. Those of you who have been sitting on the edge of your chairs all week will be glad to know that tonight we shall definitely present the final chapter in our story, "I Killed The Count." For those of you who have missed the earlier installments, or have lost your score-cards, I shall present a resume. But before we present mystery, we must give you the solution . . . to your shopping problem.* (commercial break followed by episode title screen) *Well, if you liked that commercial you'll love our story. Now to review the bidding. Within a few hours, after Count Victor Mattoni was found dead in his London flat with a single bullet hole in his head, the detectives found themselves with three persons, each of whom confessed that he and he alone killed the Count. They were Bernard Froy an American, Mullet the elevator man and a*

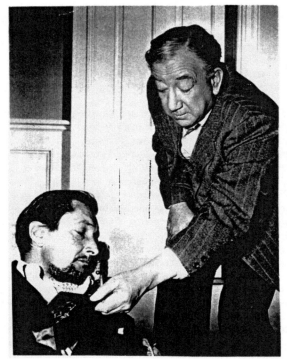

Lord Sorrington an important industrialist. In each case there is some corroborating evidence. Mullet obligingly left his fingerprints on the Count's wallet and Froy had written an incriminating letter and Lord Sorrington's pistol was found on the scene. There was also a fourth bit of evidence, skin and blood under the Count's fingernails indicating he had scratched his assailant. Yet none of the three suspects wore any scratches. Neither Froy, nor Lord Sorrington, nor . . . I don't know why I bother to explain all of this, for the brief three scenes which preface tonight's story will make everything quite clear.

Story: Pat Lummock explains how every night he helped put the Count to bed and with the man intoxicated and asleep, he usually stole a couple quid here and there. Only last night when

Charles Cooper, one of the three main suspects, threatening Anthony Dawson in "I Killed the Count." (photo courtesy of Ronald V. Borst / Hollywood Movie Posters.)

he found the Count fast asleep, and picked the wallet, the Count woke up. The men struggled and the gun went off. Lummock put the body into the chair, panicked and left. Back at Scotland Yard, Davidson places the three suspects in the same room, so they can hear each other's story. Davidson leaves for a moment to talk with Miss Rogers, (Mattoni's wife and Sorrington's daughter) who also claims she killed the count. In the other room, the three men chat quietly about how their plan is coming along, with Lummock planting evidence that incriminates all three of them. Apparently the law states that two or more people cannot be tried or sentenced for the same crime, if it is proven that only one person committed the crime. Davidson escorts Miss Rogers into his office to meet her father and his two accomplices, demanding to get to the truth. When Raines, Davidson's assistant, shows the inspector a law from one of the Yard's books (the same law all three suspects are consciously aware of), Davidson finally figures it out. They're all in on it and they will all get away with murder!

I knew we'd finish that story if we kept at it. I'm sure Inspector Davidson is longing for the good old days when, on investigating a robin's death, he simply went out and arrested the first sparrow he saw carrying a burning empty quiver. A policeman's lot is not a happy one. However the inspector's bulldog spirit did finally pay off and our little band of conspirators eventually faced trial. Fortunately they were let off with light sentences. In fact, when the jury found out what kind of a chap the Count was, it recommended the defendants for the order of the garter. We've had the final chapter of "I Killed The Count." Now for our final commercial after which I'll be back. (commercial break) *This of course was the end of our trilogy. Next week we shall resume our policy of telling a complete story on each program. I hope you will join us then. Good night.*

Trivia, etc. There were two versions of Hitchcock's opening and closing remarks for this particular episode, but the alternate version featured only a slight difference. In the opening, Hitchcock subs the words "all week" in the second sentence for "since last time." In the closing, Hitchcock subs "Next week we shall" for "Next time we shall." The other noticeable difference is that the alternate opening and closing featured Hitchcock standing beside some polished armor, instead of a faded backdrop.

EPISODE #67 **"ONE MORE MILE TO GO"** Broadcast on April 7, 1957
Rehearsed and filmed on January 9 – 11, 1957.
Starring: David Wayne as Sam Jacoby   Steve Brodie as the trooper
Louise Larabee as Martha Jacoby
Norman Leavitt as Red, attendant at Bob's Super Service
Teleplay written for *Alfred Hitchcock Presents* by James P. Cavanagh, based on the
short story of the same name by George F.J. Smith, originally published in the June 1956
issue of *Manhunt*. Anthologized in *Best Detective Stories of the Year*, ed. David C. Cooke
(Dutton, 1957).
Directed by Alfred Hitchcock.
(with an extra head in Hitchcock's arm) *Good evening.*
Most of you have doubtless read, how Anne Boleyn lost her head.
King Henry VIII, no longer fascinated, said "let her be decapitated."
Thereaupon the legend goes. . .
Her ghost roamed about each night, with utmost dignity and charm,
with her head tucked underneath her arm.
Now with two heads it occurs to me, I can think more clearly than with three.
However if the worst should come, one head's a basic minimum.
Therefore in my work I hardly dare, to roam about without one spare.
Tonight's legend tells of modern life, and how to solve a problem . . . wife.
(picks up head) *But first, kind friend, potential buyers. Heed this advise.*

Story: In a heated moment of emotion, Sam Jacoby kills his hen-pecking wife with
the fireplace poker. Deciding he has to get rid of her body, he drags the body of his dead
wife into the trunk of his sedan and heads for a nearby lake. Before Sam can arrive at his
destination, a motorcycle officer pulls him over to tell him that he has a taillight out. The cop
suggests that he visit a nearby gas station to have it fixed. The attendant finds out the bulb is
okay and that there must be some defective wires in the trunk. Sam explains he can't fix it
because he doesn't have a trunk key, but suddenly the light comes back on and the cop lets
him go. On his way toward the lake again, the same cop pulls Sam over for a second time,
because he forgot his change at the gas station. Again, the light goes out for a second time.
As a favor to Sam, the cop orders him to follow him to police headquarters, about half a mile
up the road, where a trained mechanic can open his trunk and fix it.

Moral - When your heart stops yearning, keep your taillight burning.
Now for the thumbscrews and the rack. Endure it please for I'll be back.
(commercial break)
Thank you. One less mile to go. Next week another script, another show.
When electrons glide across your screen, bringing some new and unforeseen
brand of murder. I mean the quiet kind, perpetrated solely in our mind.
A gentle thump, a soothing splash, no bullets, shriek or livid gash.
No stains, no fumes, no ugly splatter. We use only the purest subject matter.
Good night.

Trivia, etc. There are two versions of the presentation and afterward, but
surprisingly, not a word differs between them. Instead, the only difference is that Hitchcock
is filmed in close-up for the line "and how to solve a problem . . . wife" in one version, and
not in the other!

EPISODE #68 **"VICIOUS CIRCLE"** Broadcast on April 14, 1957
Starring: Dick York as Manny Coe   Kathleen Maguire as Betty
George Macready as Mr. Williams   Kathleen Hughes as Ann
Russell Johnson as Turk   Paul Lambert as Gallagher
George Brenlin as Georgie   Tracey Morgan as a card player
Betty Woods as the woman at the party   Michael Kuhn as a card player

Roy Darmour as a card player

Teleplay written for *Alfred Hitchcock Presents* by Bernard C. Schoenfeld, based on the short story "Murder Comes Easy" by Evan Hunter, originally published in the March 1953 issue of *Manhunt*. Subsequently reprinted in the September 1953 issue of *Verdict*, under a new title, "Vicious Circle." Also collected in *The Jungle Kids* (Pocket Books, 1956), also as "Vicious Circle."

Directed by Paul Henreid.

(beauty contest with beauty) *Good evening. This is a beauty contest. I shall explain however that I am not one of the contestants. At the last moment someone stole my bathing suit, so I was made a judge. You know the uh . . . the uh . . . problem of finding an unobtrusive spot for a vaccination is getting more and more difficult. Uh hmm, see now, uh . . . This is ridiculous. What difference does it make which one is the tallest? While I continue with the tiresome task of ogling these young ladies, our poor players will present tonight's story. It is called "Vicious Circle." First however, we have a treat for you. They say a picture is worth a thousand words. My sponsor is not a man to take chances – he gives you both.*

Story: Mr. Williams orders a hit man named Manny Coe, to kill a punk named Gallagher, who bungled a jewelry heist. Betty, Manny's girlfriend, reads about the murder in the newspaper and threatens to call off their affair, and possibly go to the police. When she first met him, he was clean and respectable. Mr. Williams knows Betty doesn't like him, and because she's been visiting the police, Manny is ordered to eliminate her before she causes more trouble. Manny doesn't want to, even trying to persuade her to leave town for a few weeks, but she stubbornly hangs around, talking to more people instead of keeping quiet. When he tries to shoot her in an alley, Manny finds that he cannot bring himself to shoot the woman he loves, causing Betty to run out in the streets and is accidentally hit by a car. After the funeral, Mr. Williams rewards Manny with a new sports car, nice clothes, and a promising future as a partner in his shady business deals. But when Manny foils his next job, the hit man learns that his rewards come with some rather stiff penalties as he becomes the next victim.

So much for life among the smart set. As you may have guessed, the law did not catch up with Manny, however the bullet with his name on it did. Actually it had someone else's name on it but it was mis-sent. However the error wasn't discovered until it was too late. Next we have a one-minute break, during which our sponsor will discuss his favorite subject. I shall return when he has exhausted his topic, or you. (commercial break) *That concludes tonight's divertissement. Next week we shall return with more of the same. Good night.*

EPISODE #69 "THE THREE DREAMS OF MR. FINDLATER" April 21, 1957

Starring: John Williams as Mr. Ernest Findlater Barbara Baxley as Lalage
Isobel Elsom as Mrs. Minnie Findlater Walter Kingsford as Manley
A. E. Gould-Porter as Rogers Mollie Glessing as Bridget

Teleplay written for *Alfred Hitchcock Presents* by Sarett Rudley, based on the short story of the same name by A.A. Milne, originally collected in *A Table Near the Band and Other Stories* (Methuen, 1950; Dutton, 1950).

Directed by Jules Bricken.

(at the psychiatrist) *I dreamt that I was in a huge theatre where one of my motion pictures was being shown. But the theatre was absolutely empty, not a full seat anywhere. On one wall was a gigantic mirror and when I looked into it I didn't see my own face, I saw my wife's. I suppose I'd accidentally wandered into her dream.* Psychiatrist's voice: *That's not unusual. Do you and your wife sleep in a double bed or in twin beds?* Hitchcock: *Both. She has a twin, I sleep in a double bed.* Psychiatrist: *Of course.* Hitchcock: *And then I dreamed . . . Oh, good evening. As you see, this week I'm very much pressed for time. However I should be glad to squeeze you in for our customary session. Tonight's story is about a man whose driving ambition was to become a widower. It is called "The Three Dreams of Mr. Findlater."*

Story: Mr. Ernest Findlater escapes the daily nagging from his wife by dreaming of being on a South Sea island with a wonderful young girl who caters to his every whim. After spending so much time imagining his wife being dead, Ernest's smile grows longer and longer, until one afternoon, he decides it is high time to do something about it. Returning home from work, determined to set right what he's been wronged, Ernest enters the house intending to get rid of his wife for good. But he is shocked when he finds Minnie already dead, having passed away of natural causes. Mr. Findlater discovered the meaning of the old saying, "be careful what you wish for . . . you just might get it."

See, all things come to him who waits. I shall return in a few moments for my usual 'Good Night', and to remind you of your appointment next week. First however, we have another of those charming little shadow plays, which my psychological friend claims is the object of my infantile antagonism. I don't know where he gets his ideas. (commercial break) (Hitchcock fall asleep and snores) Psychiatrist: *shhhhh!*

Trivia, etc. British actors John Williams and Isobel Elsom (ocassionally billed as Isabel) plays a dis-contented married couple, just as they did in first season's episode "Back For Christmas." Sadly, this episode which acted out more of a fantasy than a mystery, lacked the punch "Back for Christmas" provided for viewers, and leaves something to be desired. Trivia buffs take note: John Williams and Isobel Elsom also played small supporting roles in Alfred Hitchcock's *The Paradine Case* in 1947; Williams in the role of Barrister and Elsom as the hostess at the Station Hotel.

EPISODE #70   **"THE NIGHT THE WORLD ENDED"**   Broadcast on April 28, 1957
 Starring: Russell Collins as Johnny Gin   Harold J. Stone as Harold Halloran
 Edith Barrett as Miss Felicia Green   Bart Burns as Nick, the bartender
 Ned Wever as second man at bar   Clark Howat as the reporter
 Robert Ellis as newspaper boy   Harry Shearer as the rifle kid
 Billy Miller as the basketball kid   Charles Herbert as the 8-year-old
 Mike Ross as the police officer
 Also in the cast: Robert Ross (billed 4th), Joe Marr (6th), Henry Corden (10th) and Paul Brinegar (last).
 Teleplay written for *Alfred Hitchcock Presents* by Bernard C. Schoenfeld, based on the short story of the same name by Fredric Brown, originally published in the January 1945 issue of *Dime Mystery*. Subsequently collected in *Mostly Murder* (Dutton, 1953; Boardman, 1954) and in *Carnival of Crime* (Southern Illinois University Press, 1985).
 Directed by Justus Addiss.
 (high voltage)   *Good evening. I'm just completing a rather interesting device. I think it will amuse you. Tonight we are presenting a story. I should have explained, you see this is arranged so that anyone touching the channel selector to change programs gets a nasty shock. We rather hope it will improve the loyalty of our viewers.* (bang!) *There goes another one. It's no trifling matter. 25,000 volts leaves them crisp as bacon. Unfortunately is has one shortcoming. It also burns out the television tube, making it impossible for the bereaved to watch the rest of the show. But nothing is perfect and there's nothing like a good practical joke. At least that's what the character in tonight's play thought.* (close-up) *But first an item that is the essence of practicality. But to our sponsor it is no joke. My, my, I'm afraid we caught more than our limit that time.*

Story: Harold Halloran is a reporter with a penchant for practical jokes. One night as he leaves a bar he shows a drunk, Johnny, a fake newspaper with a headline that claims that the world will end at 11:45 tonight, as a result of a collision with the planet Mars. Johnny, not knowing his leg is being pulled, decides to live it up while he can, and robs a liquor store, almost forces himself on an old lady, and breaks into a store to give three kids what they want to make them happy. The evening comes to a close with Johnny killing a security guard, figuring everybody is going to die in the next few minutes anyway. After glancing at some real newspapers without the special headline, Johnny returns to the bar to confront Halloran, and pulls a gun out and shoots the reporter dead . . . at exactly 11:45 p.m.

Well, it couldn't have happened to a nicer fellow. Unfortunately justice had to be meeted out to Johnny Gin and six months later he was responsible for a momentary dimming of the lights of Sing Sing. Which reminds me, I shall be back in a moment after this word from you-know-who, but as a concession to those of you who forgot to slip into rubber sole shoes. (commercial break) *That is all for this evening. I hope you will join us next time when we shall return with another story. Uh, we also hope to have the bugs out of this little device. Good night.*

Trivia, etc. Director Justus Addiss, might have shadowed his *Alfred Hitchcock Presents* experience for the 1958 movie, *The Cry Baby Killer*, featuring the film debut of Jack Nicholson. The film concerns a juvenile delinquent who panics when he thinks he has committed murder. Needless to say, the teleplay tells the exact opposite: a drunk panics when he thinks the world is coming to an end, only to finish the story by committing a murder!

Robert Ellis, who played Tommy Kopek (as Bobby Ellis) in "My Brother, Richard" a few months before, returns for a bit part in this episode. Ellis was familiar with movie audiences as Babe Ruth (as a child) in *The Babe Ruth Story* (1948), and supplied the uncredited voice of one of the Lost Boys in Walt Disney's animated feature *Peter Pan* (1953). Ellis was known to television audiences as Dexter Franklin on *Meet Corliss Archer*, and as *Henry Aldrich* on *The Aldrich Family*. Harry Shearer, who supplied the voice for Carl Sagan in *My Stepmother is an Alien* (1988), and many character roles on television's *The Simpsons* including Ned Flanders and the bus driver. Shearer also famously played Derek Smalls, the bass player with latent free-form jazz tendencies in the "rock 'n' roll-spoof" *This is Spinal Tap!* (1984), directed by Rob Reiner.

Henry Corden's voice might be a bit familiar to fans of Hanna Barbara cartoons as the voice of Paw Rugg on *The Atom Ant/Secret Squirrel Show*, General Urko on *Return to the Planet of the Apes*, and as the voice of Fred Flintstone during the 1970's and 80's animated movies. Corden also played the role of Farouche in *I Confess* (1953), and recalled how he never once spoke to Hitchcock: "I was lined up with a bunch of other actors, he pointed his finger toward me, whispered to somebody and I got the part [in *I Confess*]. I did my whole scene in front of one of those rear projection screens, and at no time did I hear a word from him! He had conversation with Brian Aherne, and one or two other people who were of some significance . . . and who were English. With me, there was nothing!"

EPISODE #71   **"THE HANDS OF MR. OTTERMOLE"**   Broadcast on May 5, 1957
Starring: Theodore Bikel as Sergeant Ottermole
Rhys Williams as Summers, the reporter

Torin Thatcher as the constable	Charles Davis as the second reporter
John Trayne as the policeman	Barry Harvey as Whybrow's nephew
Arthur E. Gould-Porter as Herbert Whybrow	
Nora O'Mahoney as the Irish neighbor	
Nelson Welch as the third reporter	Molly Roden as the English neighbor
James McCallion as Ben, the bartender	Hilda Plowright as the flower lady
Gerald Hamer as the spectator at Peterson's murder	

Teleplay written for *Alfred Hitchcock Presents* by Francis Cockrell, based on the short story of the same name by Thomas Burke, originally published in Burke's *The Pleasantries of Old Quong* (Constable, 1931; U.S. title *A Tea-Shop in Limehouse*, Little Brown, 1931).
Directed by Robert Stevens.

(in a bathrobe)   *Oh, good evening. I hope you'll excuse me for not being ready at show time, but my watch is slow. As a matter of fact it hasn't even gotten here yet. Tonight's little fable is entitled "The Hands of Mr. Ottermole," and takes place in far off England. England. A place I've always wanted to visit. However, I don't like to be laughed at and I'm sure they would find my American accent peculiar. But so much for idle dreams. Now due to circumstances over which our sponsor had complete control, we bring you this special message, while I slip into something more uncomfortable.*

Alternate narrative:
(in a bathrobe)   *Oh, good evening. I hope you'll excuse me for not being ready at show time, but my watch is slow. As a matter of fact it hasn't even gotten here yet. First I would like to announce a change in our program. Shakespeare's Hamlet will not be presented tonight. We don't feel it's suitable to show in the home. All those corpses you know. Instead we are offering a story entitled, "The Hands of Mr. Ottermole." Most of our stories have taken place in the United States, or one of the other colonies. But tonight we offer a new locale. "The Hands of Mr. Ottermole" is laid in that far off land of mystery and enchantment – England. And now suppose you continue squinting at this little screen, while I slip into something more uncomfortable.*

Story: London 1919.   A strangler is on the loose, and has managed to avoid capture by the police, despite all their efforts. The police become increasingly desperate as the body count rises. It seems the strangler whistles an English tune and the victims are both man, woman, rich and poor. There is no apparent motive for the killings and to make matters worse, a roaming reporter named Summers hangs about the police station picking up theories and ideas so he can write his stories, much to the disgust of the police. Children are not allowed to play in the streets, women have to shop before dark, and no one is safe at night. "The police are potent so long as they are feared," claims Summers. When the fifth victim turns out to be one of the policemen themselves, Summers creates his own theory, a solution staring at them in their own faces. Alone together in the foggy London night, Summers asks Sergeant Ottermole "just why did you kill those inoffensive people?" Ottermole claims that "Everybody knows we can't control the workings of our mind, but everybody's supposed to be able to control the workings of his body . . ." and with that, Summers becomes the next intended victim.

(someone trying to tie Hitchcock's bowtie but looks like he's strangling him) *Help! Stop it! I'll tie it myself. It will only take a moment. While you are waiting, my co-entertainer will offer this refreshing change of pace. (commercial break) And now I'm all ready for the show. Dear me, we've already had it, haven't we? Oh well. There'll be another one next week. I shall hold myself in readiness, you do likewise. Good night.*

Alternate narrative:
(someone trying to tie Hitchcock's bowtie but looks like he's strangling him) *Help! Stop it! Stop it! I'll tie it myself. It won't take long. I'm sure it'll be ready by next week's show and you be ready too.*

Trivia, etc. This classic mystery yarn has been dramatized on dozens of radio and television programs including *Suspense* and *Molle Mystery Theater*. James McCallion played the role of a Plaza Valet in *North by Northwest* (1959). Hilda Plowright usually played a nurse or a maid in the movies she acted in, but most notably she played the postmistress in *Suspicion* (1941) and Mrs. Pimm in *Foreign Correspondent* (1941). Gerald Hamer played a bit part in *Foreign Correspondent*. He also plays Mr. Hewitt in the first season episode "Back for Christmas." Hamer also played supporting roles in a handful of the Basil Rathbone / Sherlock Holmes movies, including the villain in *The Scarlet Claw* (1944).

EPISODE #72   **"A MAN GREATLY BELOVED"**   Broadcast on May 12, 1957
Starring: Sir Cedric Hardwicke as John Laughton / Anderson
Evelyn Rudie as Hildegarde Fell

Hugh Marlowe as Reverend Richard Fell	Robert Culp as Clarence
Rebecca Welles as Mrs. Fell	Edith Barrett as Mrs. Whiteford

Ken Christy as the old man at the bazaar

Teleplay written for *Alfred Hitchcock Presents* by Sarett Rudley, based on the short story of the same name by A.A. Milne. originally collected in *A Table Near the Band and Other Stories* (Methuen, 1950; Dutton, 1950).

Directed by James Neilson.

(places swords in basket after small boy enters) *Good evening. Good heavens, he looks like a toothpick holder on an hors d'oeuvres table. Oh well, I guess I just have to practice some more. So much for the sideshow. (close-up) Now turn your attention to the center ring where you will find our main attraction. But before the main event, we must pause a moment to allow one of our hawkers to. . . uh, pass among you and peddle his wares.*

Alternate narrative:

(places swords in basket after small boy enters) *Good evening. Good heavens, he looks like a toothpick holder on an hors de ouvers table. Oh well, I guess I just have to practise some more. So much for the sideshow. Now turn your attention to the center ring where you will find our main attraction.*

Story: In a small Massachusetts town, young Hildegarde Fell sneaks over to John Anderson's house one afternoon to make her acquaintance and it seems the two strike up a quick companionship - John having found out that Hildegarde is a good chess player. The old man rarely ever goes out of his home, and the locals keep their peace when it comes to gossip about Mr. Anderson. One day, Hildegarde learns from Clarence that there used to be a judge John Anderson back in Boston, who retired years ago, also known for being a recluse. When she pays a return visit to the old man, Hildegarde tells him that she knows his secret. He's the retired judge from Boston, and she won't tell anyone about him, if she can hold the church bazaar in his garden – which Mr. Anderson is forced to accept. When it starts to rain the town folks are forced to move into his house, and his secret becomes public. After the bazaar, Mr. Anderson becomes a changed man, even donating a stain glass window for the church! The town locals look up to him often seeking his advice, and the day he dies the whole town mourns for the recluse. who made everyone happy during his final days - until Clarence finds out that he was actually an ex-con sentenced by the same judge whose name he borrowed!

I suppose that once again one might say, what's in a name? A rose by any other name would, etc, etc, etc. Just as a commercial called anything else would still, etc, etc, etc. But I'm getting mordant. Here for those of you who may have forgotten who is sponsoring this program, we offer this subtle reminder, after which I'll be back. (commercial break) Well I'm glad we did that. The sponsor's name had completely slipped my mind too. Next week I understand he will again refresh your memory. Please tune in then for we shall have another story as well. Good night.

Alternate narrative:

Thus ends tonight's story. After seeing it, I think you'll treat your neighbor more kindly. After all, he may be a former axe murderer. Of course there's nothing to worry about . . . he's probably out of practice. I hope you will join us next time when we shall present another story of mystery and/or suspense. Good night.

EPISODE #73 **"MARTHA MASON, MOVIE STAR"** Broadcast on May 19, 1957
>   Starring: Judith Evelyn as Mabel McKay   Robert Emhardt as Henry McKay
>   Vinton Hayworth as Mr. Abernathy   Rusty Lane as the police detective
>   Karen Morris as Cora, "the other woman"   Claire Carleton as Bernice
>   Teleplay written for *Alfred Hitchcock Presents* by Robert C. Dennis, based on the
short story "Martha Myers, Movie Star," by Raymond Mason, originally published in the
January 1957 issue of *Alfred Hitchcock's Mystery Magazine*.
>   Directed by Justus Addiss.
>   (As a spaceman departing his spacecraft) *Good evening. I've been on Mars where
I went for the opening of a new television station. In all part of a scheme to take the best of
our cultural advances to the Martians . . . or uh . . . martinis as they prefer to be called. They
are highly intelligent and my attempts to educate them were quite successful. Within a matter
of minutes, they were able to spell out, "Earth Men, Go Home," using my two companions to
form the letters. It was very gratifying. As you have doubtless already guessed, tonight's
story is entitled, "Martha Mason, Movie Star." It will follow in a moment, after this moth-
hole in the fabric of our entertainment.*

>   Story: Mabel McKay lives under the illusion that she looks like beautiful actress
Martha Mason, although nothing could be further from the truth. She drives Henry, her
husband, batty about the subject but he just laughs it off and makes jokes about her to his
fellow lodge members. When he finally airs his opinions on the subject to Mabel directly,
she bashes his skull in with a hammer and buries his body in the backyard garden. She cries,
telling everyone that Henry left her for another woman, and she even types a "good-bye"
letter forging her husband's name. Her husband's boss, Mr. Abernathy, pays her a visit and
recreating scenes from Martha Mason pictures, Mabel plays her sad sob role to the max.
Abernathy suggests that she keep quiet about the situation as it could bring her a lot of
publicity. The police start an investigation as to the whereabouts of Henry, and finally
stumble upon his body – during a search about Mabel's house they would never have done if
it wasn't for Henry's real "other woman" coming forth and testifying. It seems Henry had a
secret his wife never knew about . . . a surprise to Mabel who passes out from shock, just like
the movie actress she saw on the screen.

>   *Poor Mabel. I'm afraid she just didn't have a green thumb. I shall return, after
this word from the people who make this program possible, that is, when they are not making
things impossible.* (commercial break) *Next week we shall be back with another story.
Meanwhile, I'm off to another planet. I've always been curious about Venus. Good night.*

EPISODE #74 **"THE WEST WARLOCK TIME CAPSULE"** Broadcast May 26, 1957
>   Starring: Henry Jones as George Tiffany
>   Mildred Dunnock as Louise Tiffany
>   Sam Buffington as Waldron   Bobby Clark as Charlie
>   Russ Thorson as Dr. Rhody   Charles Watts as the Mayor
>   James F. Stone as the customer   James Philbrook as the transport help
>   Teleplay written for *Alfred Hitchcock Presents* by Marian Cockrell, based on a
story by J.P. Cahn.
>   Directed by Justus Addiss.
>   (moose head) *Good evening television watchers. Tonight's masque is entitled
"The West Warlock Time Capsule." The tale of a timid taxidermist. This gives me the
excuse to exhibit this prize of mine and to discuss taxidermy. I feel I know quite a bit about
stuffed animals. After all, it takes one to know one. This I shot myself. You see deer
poaching is one of my hobbies. It took only two shots. The first one hit a bearded old man
wearing a ridiculous red suit and riding in a sleigh. I'm having him stuffed too. It probably
sounds silly to you but I'm sentimental that way. But enough of this. Here in a moment is
"The West Warlock Time Capsule." (close-up) However, before our story, we have an
experiment in electronic taxidermy. Watch the following closely. You will notice that after a*

few moments you will begin to become glassy-eyed. But we shall run the experiment only 60 seconds, otherwise you'd find yourself hanging on a wall, like our friend with the filigree horns.

Story: A taxidermist is hired to prepare a horse, the town mascot, to be put on display in a glass case, next to a time capsule that is being installed, scheduled to be opened in one hundred years. As George goes to work, his brother-in-law Waldron, stops over for a short visit and ends up staying for weeks, making George's poor wife Louise so exhausted she has to be hospitalized. This is the final straw for George, who decides to get rid of Waldron . . . and give the city a special surprise to find in their time capsule in about one hundred years.

Honesty demands that I reveal that all did not go as Mr. Tiffany had planned. The weight of Waldron's pouchy body proved too much for Napoleon, and within a few months the time capsule was opened by a Caesarian section. Waldron, of course, was quite dead and Napoleon hasn't been the same since. As for Mr. Tiffany, the jury proved quite lenient which leads us to the next matter. Here I have pleaded for leniency but our sponsor is adamant. I'm afraid you must take your punishment. Here it is. (commercial break) *Hours longer vita bravis, but I think that was overdoing it. Next week we plan a return trip to your living room. I hope you will join us then. Good night.*

EPISODE #75   **"FATHER AND SON"**   Broadcast on June 2, 1957
 Starring: Edmund Gwenn as Joe Saunders   Charles Davis as Sam Saunders
 Frederic Worlock as Gus Harrison   Pamela Light as Mae
 George Pelling as a police officer   John Trayne as a police officer
 Dan Sheridan as Mr. Schiller
 Teleplay written for *Alfred Hitchcock Presents* by James P. Cavanagh, based on the short story of the same name by Thomas Burke, collected in *Night Pieces* (Constable, 1935; Appleton Century Crofts, 1936).
 Directed by Herschel Daugherty.
 (bow and apple) *Good evening. Have you, uh. . . seen a small boy with an apple on his head? I know he's here somewhere but, uh. . . my eyes aren't what they used to be. Oh, oh, there he is. I missed again. I think I'd better quit, I even missed the boy that time. Tonight the flickering shadows on our magic lantern screen, tell a story of life in the big city. It is called "Father And Son."* (close-up) *First however, we have a brief preamble. It is so short, so subtle and such a delicate work of art, that unless you are unusually attentive, you will miss it entirely. Watch closely.*

Story: London, 1912. Sam Saunders, age 35, hasn't held a job longer than two weeks throughout his entire life. When he tries to get money from his father, a pawnshop owner, Sam finds his dad too stubborn to cough up. Even Mae, the saloon girl down the road who likes Sam, won't offer assistance until he gets a decent job. When Sam learns that his father is sheltering a friend of forty years, wanted for a crime he never committed, Sam decides to turn him in for the reward. When Mae learns of Sam's intentions to betray his father's good will, she places a phone call to the old men, urging the criminal to make a run for it. While Sam signs a statement claiming he saw Gus enter the store and never leave, the police go to apprehend the fugitive. Only Sam's father is apprehended instead, and promptly arrested for harboring a fugitive. Sam insists he get the reward money, since he didn't give any mis-information, and the police reluctantly agree. Sick to his stomache for what he's done, Sam leaves, stumbles down the stairs, and breaks his leg. His ever-caring father comes to his aid, asking "Did you hurt yourself son? Did you hurt yourself?"

Unfortunately, he wasn't. Sam was one of those persons for whom all things seemed to work out well. No matter what happens to him, he always manages to land on his head. Next we have that portion of our program that has been called by many, the shortest half-hour in television. After which, I'll be back. (commercial break – now Hitchcock speed talks) *If they make these commercials any shorter, I won't have time to get to the kitchen and back. That is all for tonight. In just a week we plan a similar foray into your parlor. I hope you'll be home. Good night.* (Hitchcock takes a bite of an apple)

EPISODE #76 **"THE INDESTRUCTIBLE MR. WEEMS"** Broadcast on June 9, 1957

Starring: Robert Middleton as Cato Stone   Joe Mantell as Harry Brown
Russell Collins as Clarence Weems   Don Keefer as Mr. Elkins
Harry Bellaver as Mr. Brodsky   Rebecca Welles as Laura Weems
Gladys Hurlbut as Sara Collins   Theodore Newton as Dr. Allen
Ferdi Hoffman as the minister   Ted Bliss as Mr. Evans

An original teleplay written for *Alfred Hitchcock Presents* by George F. Slavin. Directed by Justus Addiss.

(resting on a bed)   *Good evening. Since you are allowed to make yourselves comfortable during our show, I thought it only right that I'd be allowed to relax. After all, the rules of television seem weighed far too much in favor of the viewer. You can relax in your home, while I must stay here in this drafty studio. I'm not feeling a bit well, but the show must go on, whether you like it or not. And tonight's show is called "The Indestructible Mr. Weems." Of course the show is not the only thing that must go on. We also have commercials, and they too, must go on and on and on and on . . .*

Story: Harry Brown, co-owner of Elysium Park, a new cemetery near the verge of financial collapse, comes up with an ingenious idea to start off business. Mr. Brown and his lodge members pay a visit to Clarence Weems, a practical man in bad health with name status, and explain their problem. During the visit, it appears to the members that Harry is very close to, and about to marry Mr. Weems' daughter. Wanting to cash in from their investments, they theorize that if Mr. Weems is buried there, many others will follow suit. The lodge will pay him fifty dollars a week while he still lives, if he agrees to be buried at their cemetery. Mr. Weems agrees, now becoming self-supportive and no longer a burden, his daughter can finally get married. But his financial interest in the cemetery gives him a reason to live, and his health gets better and better. "Lifetime annuity is a challenge to any man," explains the doctor. Cato Stone, the head master of the lodge, angry because he's not going to profit anytime soon, goes to see Mr. Weems but having run up the stairs so often, his heart gives up and he ends up being the first customer in the new cemetery.

There, I think that proves that we can be as sunshiny as anyone. Clarence and the widow Collins lived happily ever after. And in desperation, the trustees finally converted their park into a track for dog racing. It proved more popular than a cemetery and rather profitable too. One of the consolations of being ill is the gifts one receives. One of my dear friends sent me this. . . solid oak. (coffin) *Silver handles too. Apparently the donor wishes to remain anonymous. The card is unsigned, simply says,* (shows sign "Wear it in Good Health"). *Oh dear. I've been rattling on and now there isn't time for the last commercial. Oh there is, if we hurry, then go ahead and I'll . . .* (commercial break) *So glad we were able to squeeze that one in, otherwise we would have had four of them next week, and I doubt whether I've had the strength to face that many. Until our next visiting hours then.* (picks up a "Do Not Disturb" sign)

Alternate narrative:
There, I think that proves that we can be as sunshiny as anyone. Clarence and the widow Collins lived happily ever after. And in desperation, the trustees finally converted their park into a track for dog racing. It proved more popular than a cemetery and rather profitable too. One of the consolations of being ill is the gifts one receives. One of my dear

friends sent me this. . . solid oak. (coffin) *Silver handles too. Apparently the donor wishes to remain anonymous. The card is unsigned.* (shows sign "Wear it in Good Health") *Very nice. But I better not overtax myself, until our next visiting hours then.* (picks up a "Do Not Disturb" sign)

      Trivia, etc. Screenwriter George F. Slavin, who authored seventeen motion pictures and over three-hundred episodes and pilot episodes of television programs, made this episode his only contribution for the Hitchcock series. "You know, I think that was one of the only comedies they did," Slavin recalled. "It was the first and I can tell you how I know that. Hitchcock was out of town, and the director pulled a fast one and said that he wanted to do a comedy. But Hitchcock said very clearly that he didn't want to do any comedies. This was supposed to be a gruesome show. I don't even know if it was rebroadcast because of that. It was an accident and I won a nomination for best teleplay in the Writers Guild for that episode. I think I came in second! But it didn't do any good because Hitchcock never liked comedies. To this day, I have never received any residual on that one. The story itself came to me at my father's funeral. The Rabbi there told me that they had a congregation on Long Island that wanted to do something for the members, so they bought a golf course and turned it into a cemetery for their members. Problem was, when they sent the people out to sell the plots, nobody wanted to be first. So they had to recruit somebody from the congregation, who they thought was sick and dying, and they said 'We'll support you until you die if you agree to go into the plot and be the first one.' The trouble was . . . that gave him a reason to live. He wound up being the one who lasted while the others were expiring one-by-one. The story goes on and on but that actually happened and the Rabbi told me this story and I thought it was a good idea. They kept the whole production quiet because they didn't want word to leak or else Hitchcock would have probably come back from vacation. As a matter of fact, I was in Spain while they were shooting it. I had written the script just before I left for Spain and I was surprised that they did it."

EPISODE #77   **"A LITTLE SLEEP"**   Broadcast on June 16, 1957
      Starring: Barbara Cook as Barbie Hallem   Vic Morrow as Bennie Mungo
      Jack Mullaney as the young man at the café   Robert Karnes as Ed Mungo
      John Carlyle as Chris Kymer   Douglas Kennedy as Arthur
      George Chandler as the champagne drinker at the party
      Teleplay written for *Alfred Hitchcock Presents* by Robert C. Dennis, based on the short story "Lullaby" by Joe Grenzeback, originally published in the February 1957 issue of *Alfred Hitchcock's Mystery Magazine.*
      Directed by Paul Henreid.
      (upside down with a dog)   *Good evening. This is Alfred Hitchcock speaking to you from the bottom of the world. I mention this so that if snow should appear on your screen you won't waste time adjusting your set. Ah, man's best friend, and a dog too, even though I have all the comforts of home. I'm afraid it is time for our play. And I wouldn't want everyone to watch this standing on his head.* (turns right) *Well, we seem to have lost the dog, but it's nice to feel the blood rushing to my feet again. Ladies and gentlemen, here proper side up, is our story, "A Little Sleep."* (close-up) *But first, someone wishes to deliver a message and I assure you that neither snow, nor rain, nor heat, nor gloom of night can stay this courier. We have tried everything.*

      Story: Barbie Hallem decides to drive up to an uncle's unoccupied, remote cabin for some rest. Before arriving there, she stops off at a cafe owned by Ed Mungo, there a young man tells her about Ed's brother Bennie, who is being hunted by the police for murdering Ed's girlfriend. Moving on to the cabin, she finds Bennie hiding there, but he claims he's innocent, never knowing that she was dead, so it appears that Ed actually killed Benny's girlfriend. Ed soon arrives and is killed during a fight with Bennie. As they plan to drive away from the cabin, Bennie asks Barbie who her jacket originally belonged to and Barbie says that she borrowed it from a friend she thinks is boring. Bennie comments that his

Vic Morrow poses on the set of "A Little Sleep."
(Photo courtesy of Ronald V. Borst / Hollywood Movie Posters)

girlfriend said the same thing about him – "just before I put her to sleep." Bennie was the murderer after all, and starts making for Barbie, intending to strangle the life out of her . . .

And he did too. Naturally Bennie was properly punished. As is always the case on this program. Speaking of punishment, we have some retribution for those of you who were careless enough to allow your eyes to stray from the screen during the last commercial. Here it is, after which I shall skate back. (commercial break) *That was much too severe. I suspect the television commercial is a punishment for which no crime has yet been devised. After all, the punishment should fit the crime. So I'm afraid we must wait until man's sadistic tendencies can catch up. Next week we shall be back again. Pax vobiscum.*

Trivia, etc. Three years after this episode aired, George Chandler would become President of the Screen Actor's Guild. Known for his role of Uncle Petrie on television's *Lassie*, Chandler would continue acting throughout the fifties and sixties on both television and motion pictures.

EPISODE #78 **"THE DANGEROUS PEOPLE"** Broadcast on June 23, 1957
     Starring: Albert Salmi as Mr. Jones   Robert H. Harris as Mr. Bellefontaine
     Ken Clark as the escaped lunatic (disguised as a policeman)
     Harry O. Tyler as the station agent   David Armstrong as the asylum worker

Teleplay written for *Alfred Hitchcock Presents* by Francis Cockrell, based on the short story "No Sanctuary" by Fredric Brown, originally published in the March 1945 issue of *Dime Mystery*. Subsequently collected as "The Dangerous People" in both *Mostly Murder* (Dutton, 1953; Boardman, 1954), and *Carnival of Crime* (Southern Illinois University Press, 1985).

Directed by Robert Stevens.

(wearing a blindfold) *Good evening, you'll excuse me if I speak rapidly but I haven't much time. I'm playing some idiotic children's game and I'm supposed to stand against this wall blindfolded and with my hands tied behind me. While I'm standing here waiting for something to happen you may watch tonight's drama "The Dangerous People." I shall join you later.* (gunshots) *Thank you, but please no more applause.*

Story: Two men waiting in a train station, about half an hour before the train arrives, are both aware that a dangerous killer has just escaped a mental asylum. The more time they nervously spend together, the more they suspect the other of being the escaped lunatic. Bellefontaine insists that he's a lawyer for a big firm and Jones says he works for Saks, a painting company. But what if one of them isn't telling the truth? Word has it that the lunatic may have split personality who kills anyone without reason. The men rationally suspect each other of being the murderer, believing Bellefontaine has a gun in his pocket, Jones tries to pick up the fireplace poker as an act of self-defense. Bellefontaine actually has a gun but before they can harm each other, a policeman arrives. The only problem is that the "cop" is actually the lunatic, who is wearing the uniform of an officer he recently murdered.

I think I've had enough. I distinctly feel a draft. While I untie this, suppose you watch the following. (commercial break) *That's all for this evening. Uh, I think we shall be back another time with another story. Until then, good night.*

SUMMER RERUNS

Reruns for the summer of 1957 consisted entirely of episodes from the second season, with the exception of "The Creeper," the only first-season episode, which ended the summer reruns for a second year in a row.

June 30, 1957 "Fog Closing In"
July 7, 1957 "The Manacled"
July 14, 1957
    "Conversation Over a Corpse"
July 21, 1957 "Wet Saturday"
July 28, 1957 "The Cream of the Jest"
August 4, 1957
    "The Hands of Mr. Ottermole"
August 11, 1957 "Crackpot"

August 18, 1957 "A Bottle of Wine"
August 25, 1957
    "The West Warlock Time Capsule"
September 1, 1957
    "The End of Indian Summer"
September 8, 1957 "Father and Son"
September 15, 1957 "Crack of Doom"
September 22, 1957 "The Creeper"

On September 29, 1957, *Alfred Hitchcock Presents* was pre-empted on this date for a special CBS broadcast of *Dupont Show of the Month*. This was a black and white *and* color presentation, broadcast live from New York. The broadcast was entitled "Crescendo," about America's musical heritage. Broadcast from 9 to 10:30 p.m., EST. Starred Rex Harrison, Louis Armstrong, Peggy Lee, Julie Andrews, Stubby Kaye, Carol Channing, and Benny Goodman. Produced by Paul Gregory.

SEASON THREE - (39 episodes)

SELECTED PRODUCTION CREDITS:
Art Directors: John J. Lloyd and John Meehan
Assistant Directors: Ben Bishop, James H. Brown, Jess Corralo, Frank Fox,
Charles S. Gould, Hilton A. Green, James Hogan, George Lollier,
James Nicholson, Ronnie Rondell, William Sheldon * and Dolph M. Zimmer
Associate Producer: Norman Lloyd
Costume Supervisor: Vincent Dee
Directors of Photography: Joseph F. Biroc, a.s.c., Reggie Lanning, Lionel Lindon, a.s.c.,
John L. Russell, a.s.c. and John F. Warren, a.s.c.
Editorial Supervisor: Richard G. Wray, a.c.e.
Film Editors: Edward W. Williams, a.c.e. and Marston Fay
Furs supplied by BECKMAN in Beverly Hills, California.
Hair Stylist: Florence Bush
Makeup Artists: Jack Barron, Bob Dawn and Leo Lotito, Jr.
Music Supervisor: Stanley Wilson
Producer: Joan Harrison
Set Decorators: Mac Mulcahy, George Milo, James S. Redd and James Walters
Sound: Stephen J. Bass, John C. Grubb, John F. Keen, William Lynch,
Melvin M. Metcalfe, Sr., David H. Moriarty and Richard Tyler
Filmed at Revue Studios in Hollywood, California, in association with MCA-TV, executive
distributor for Shamley Productions, Inc.
Broadcast Sunday over CBS-TV, 9:30 - 10 p.m., EST. Sponsored by Bristol-Myers.

EPISODE #79   **"THE GLASS EYE"**   Broadcast on October 6, 1957
Starring: Jessica Tandy as Miss Julia Lester   Tom Conway as Max Collodi
Rosemary Harris as Mrs. Dorothy Whitely   William Shatner as Jim Whitely
Pat Hitchcock as the sales lady at hat shop   A. E. Gould-Porter as the hotel man
Billy Barty as George, the dummy   Nelson Welch as the music hall presenter
Colin Campbell as the old man   Paul Playdon as Allan, the neighbor's son
Teleplay written for *Alfred Hitchcock Presents* by Stirling Silliphant, based on the
short story of the same name by John Keir Cross, collected in *The Other Passenger*
(Westhouse, 1944; Lippincott, 1946).
Directed by Robert Stevens.
(glass eye in a box) *Good evening. Tonight's narrative is about a private eye, a
very private eye.* (close-up) *A glass eye is a very interesting object. For one thing, I've
always thought a glass eye would be better than the real article. It never gets blood-shot and
being made of glass it must certainly be easier to see through. This evening, due to one of
those delightful coincidences, our story happens to be about a glass eye. It is entitled "The
Glass Eye." You see, everything fits in. By the way - these programs are made possible by
your contributions. Allow us to explain.*

Story: While cleaning out his dead cousin's apartment, Jim Whitley tells his wife a
story about how close Julia was in leaving her drab, lonely existence but how it ended up
with just a glass-eye in a box as a reminder. It seems that Julia had fallen in love with a
celebrated ventriloquist named Max Collodi. She pursued the man around Britain, attending
his many performances, but he always refused to meet with her personally. At long last,
persistence paid its price and he agreed to meet her, but under certain conditions. She agrees
and rushes over to his motel where he is with George, his wooden dummy. But, to her
dismay, when she touches Max his arm falls off and George jumps up and screams at her to
leave - George is the real person, and Max was the dummy.

* Billed as Willard Sheldon during the closing credits of one episode.   191

Jessica Tandy and Tom Conway in Emmy-award winning "The Glass Eye"
(Photo courtesy of Ronald V. Borst / Hollywood Movie Posters)

That was a heartwarming little story, wasn't it? Obviously, heaven does protect the working girl. Now we have a short story, which we hope will be equally warm and tender, after which I'll re-appear. (commercial break) *Wasn't that touching? That's a kind of story, that gets you* (knocks on heart) *right here, or wherever you carry your wallet. Now I have a confession. This is not a glass eye. We were unable to find one, but we got the next best thing. I hope you don't mind. Good night.*

Alternate narrative:
That was a heartwarming little story, wasn't it? Obviously, heaven does protect the working girl. Now I have a confession. This is not a glass eye. We were unable to find one, but we got the next best thing. I hope you don't mind. Good night.

Trivia, etc. In what is probably one of the best narratives for any episode of the series, the director was not solely to be praised for the success of this particular entry. Rather, equal credit should go to both Hitchcock and Robert Stevens. Billy Barty, a real-life midget who worked with Spike Jones' band and appeared in such films as Roger Corman's *The Undead* (1957) and *The Bride of Frankenstein* (1935), played the charlatan extraordinaire, and helped supply the kicker for the closer. (Barty would also return in the *Alfred Hitchcock Hour* "The Jar" giving another wonderful supporting performance.) William Shatner who stars as Jim (and would later be directed by Hitchcock himself: see section about *Tactic*), supplies the narrative throughout. Although considered one of the best episodes of the series, and a favorite among fans, it was not directed by the master of suspense himself. Robert Stevens was responsible, who came from directing "live" television, and made a niche on the Hitchcock program, not to mention leaving an impression with the famed director himself. It's pretty obvious from years of discussion and debates from Hitchcock fans all over the world that the two favorite episodes from *Alfred Hitchcock Presents* are "Lamb to the Slaughter" and "The Glass Eye." (From the *Alfred Hitchcock Hour*, "The Jar" and "An Unlocked Window.")

"The more outrageous a subject can get, the better I like it," said Hitchcock. "For centuries children have been listening to Little Red Riding Hood with delight. If you examine this story closely you'll find that it's nothing more than a horror story. So I am no different from a child who gloats over the horrific. Then there was the one about the Cockney shop-girl who gets a crush on a handsome ventriloquist. She gives up her job, gives up her friends and exhausts her savings following him all over the music halls of England. At last, quivering with anticipation, she meets her idol. But alas, the ventriloquist is a wax dummy, and the 'dummy' an ugly dwarf. In her frustration she knocks over the sawdust-filled figure, and a glass eye rolls across the floor. It made a splendid close-up."

"Joan Harrison would pick a story and she'd say, 'I want Hitch to do this story.' These were stories of great quality," Norman Lloyd recalled. "But Robert Stevens would get equally good stories. For example, do you remember 'Specialty of the House,' where they're fattening up Robert Morley? That was Robert Stevens. And Stevens won the Emmy for 'The Glass Eye' with Jessica Tandy. I could go on and on like this about Robert Stevens, who had a brilliant style particularly suited to the Hitchcock show. Sometime Hitch was available, and sometimes he wasn't, and Stevens we always tried to get to direct. But there was never any rank who got one, two, three or bottom of the list."

At the Cocoanut Grove in Hollywood and at NBC's studios in New York, the 9th Annual Emmy Awards were presented on April 15, 1958. When it came time to award for Best Direction for a Half-Hour Show or Less, Robert Stevens took home the award for his work in "The Glass Eye."

EPISODE #80 **"MAIL ORDER PROPHET"** Broadcast on October 13, 1957
    Starring: E. G. Marshall as Ronald J. Grimes
    Jack Klugman as George Benedict

Judson Pratt as the postmaster	Barbara Townsend as the secretary
Ken Christy as the office manager	Linda Watkins as the bar room customer
Victor Romito as the waiter	

    Teleplay written for *Alfred Hitchcock Presents* by Robert C. Dennis, based on a story by Antony Perry.
    Directed by James Neilson.
    (staring out of an office window) *Oh, hello fellow speculators. I've just made a killing in the stock market. Nothing to it. I simply told my partner we've been wiped out. He's a very excitable fellow. Naturally, I was joking. We haven't been wiped out. Actually, we've made a very tidy profit. I wish he hadn't done it. We have a very sensative elevator man. He doesn't like it when he brings people up and then they don't ride down again. It confuses him. As for our story, it is called the "Mail Order Prophet" and it too, is set in a background of stocks and bonds. First, however, I have a market tip. I recommend that you invest your money in this blue chip.*

    Story: For many years, Ronald Grimes has worked the same poorly-paying New York office job, and wants in some desperate way to make a small fortune, so he can retire early and relax. One afternoon he receives a letter at work from a Mr. J. Christiani who claims he has supernatural powers and can make accurate predictions. This Mr. Christiani, you see, cannot use his powers to make himself money, so he has randomly chosen Ronald to perform the favors. Ronald, of course, believes it's a joke from someone at the office but the letter (and many letters following) make accurate predictions of future newspaper headlines and shortly after, Ronald starts to use this information to place bets that quickly add up to $125,000. Finally, one of Mr. Christiani's letters requests a donation, which Ronald (now a rich man) gladly does, shortly before leaving for Bermuda. Ronald's friend George, however, brings the whole matter up with the postmaster general and learns that Mr. J. Christiani is in jail, having performed one of the cleverest mail frauds in years . . . a fact Ronald himself will never know, and probably never believe.

Naturally, Grimes had a miserable life. Money does that you know. I shall be back in a moment but meanwhile, my sponsor would like to give you some uh – closing quotations. (commercial break) *That is all we have to offer. But we shall have more next week. Good bye.* (Hitchcock throws his ex-business partner's hat and umbrella out the window)

Alternate narrative:
This concludes our entertainment. So until next time when we shall bring you another story . . . (Hitchcock throws partner's hat and umbrella out the window) *. . . Goodbye.*

Trivia, etc. The author of the original story, from which this episode was based on, was actually, Antony Perry, but mis-spelled in the closing credits as Antony Ferry.

EPISODE #81   **"THE PERFECT CRIME"**   Broadcast on October 20, 1957
Rehearsed and filmed on July 17 – 19, 1957.

Starring: Vincent Price as Charles Courtney	James Gregory as John Gregory
Gavin Gordon as Ernest West	Marianne Stewart as Alice West
Mark Dana as Harrington	Charles Webster as a reporter
John Zaremba as the newspaper photographer	Nick Nicholson as a reporter
Therese Lyon as the housekeeper	

Teleplay written for *Alfred Hitchcock Presents* by Stirling Silliphant, based on the short story of the same name by Ben Ray Redman, originally published in the August 1928 issue of *Harper's*. Later reprinted in the July 1951 issue of *Ellery Queen's Mystery Magazine*. Anthologized in *101 Years' Entertainment: The Great Detective Stories, 1841 – 1941*, ed. Ellery Queen (Little Brown, 1941).
Directed by Alfred Hitchcock.
(as Sherlock Holmes, smoking a pipe)   *Good evening, ladies and gentlemen and Dr. Watson wherever you are.* (blowing bubbles from pipe) *Tonight's case is a. . .* (blowing more bubbles) *. . . tonight's case is called "The Perfect Crime." I'm not sure who it was who said, 'a perfect crime is exactly the same as a perfect marriage.' Their being perfect* (beating the bubbles) *depends on you not being caught. Tonight we plan . . .* (beating more bubbles) *This is exactly why I never take my pipe to bed, if you fall asleep you can be bubbled to death. And now join me, if you will, while we contemplate "The Perfect Crime."* (blowing more bubbles)

Story: Charles Courtney is one of the most gifted criminologists in the world. The press goes so far as to call him the "world's greatest detective." He cannot conceive of ever making an error, his reputation is all too important. But, he is stunned when a defense attorney presents irrefutable evidence that Courtney made one of the worst errors of his life. Courtney is responsible for the conviction and execution of a perfectly innocent man, because the accused took the blame for his lover. Now, Courtney must do everything in his power to make sure this information is not shared with the public – and even if it means strangling the attorney and dumping his body in a pottery kiln. This, according to Courtney's theory, is having committed the perfect crime and can fill up the vacant spot in his collection of memorabilia from his successful cases.

(Hitchcock in Courtney's study) *I regret to inform you that Courtney did not retain his last trophy very long, he was caught. A char woman knocked over the precious vase breaking* it into pieces. *A few of them identifiable as . . . bits of Mr. Gregory. You see the gold-fillings in his teeth had resisted the heat of the kiln, but all the good doctors and all the good police couldn't put Mr. Gregory together again. As for the char woman, she became the 'pride of the press.' Here is where the real historical significance of the case lies. Ever since, cleaning women the world over have been knocking over vases, trying to emulate her success. And now, less you conclude that crimes against society are invariably punished, allow me to cite the following example, after which I'll pop back.* (commercial break) *Indeed, there ought to be a law, but one of these days, he'll be caught. Why don't you tune in next week and see. Good night.*

Alternate narrative:
    (Hitchcock in Courtney's study)   *I regret to inform you that Courtney did not retain his last trophy very long, he was caught. A char woman knocked over the precious vase breaking it into pieces. A few of them identifiable as . . . bits of Mr. Gregory. You see the gold-fillings in his teeth had resisted the heat of the kiln, but all the good doctors and all the good police couldn't put Mr. Gregory together again. As for the char woman, she became the 'toast of the tabloids.' Here is where the real historical significance of the case lies. Ever since, cleaning women the world over have been knocking over vases, trying to emulate her success. That's all until next time when we shall be back with another, though imperfect crime. Good bye.*

    Trivia, etc. Directed by Hitchcock, actors James Gregory and Vincent Price pull off a wonderful acting challenge without a Hitch – in a matter of speaking. "I was terribly excited about working with Hitchcock, he's one of the great movie makers of all time," Vincent Price recalled. "There were only two of us in it [Price and Gregory], just two characters, and I thought it was going to be wonderful. It was a very elaborate thing called 'The Perfect Crime,' and I was really very thrilled to think of Hitchcock telling us what to do. His entire direction was, he came on the set one day and he said, 'Faster.' [laughs] And so we did it a little faster and he said, 'That's better. A little bit faster.' Then he went over and slept! [laughs] I've read four books about Hitchcock recently and he slept all through everything – or gave the appearance of sleeping. He set things up so brilliantly that he didn't really have to watch very carefully."
    Gavin Gordon, who played the role of Ernest West in this episode, also played the uncredited role of Ernest Weylin in Alfred Hitchcock's *Notorious* in 1946. Gordon played numerous supporting roles in many Hitchcock episodes, and shortly before filming for this episode, Gordon had also appeared in *The Vagabond King* (1956), which was narrated by Vincent Price. Later, Gordon co-starred in *The Bat* (1959), which also featured Vincent Price. Horror fans remember Gordon best as playing Lord Byron in Universal's 1935 classic, *The Bride of Frankenstein*.
    Although it's unknown why, a third version of Hitchcock's closing remarks is in circulation. This third version is *exactly* like the first (not the alternate) using "toast of the tabloids" in place of "pride of the press."

EPISODE #82   **"HEART OF GOLD"**   Broadcast on October 27, 1957
    Starring: Mildred Dunnock as Martha Collins   Darryl Hickman as Jackie Blake
    Nehemiah Persoff as Ralph Collins   Edward Binns as Ned Brown
    Len Lesser as the hoodlum   Cheryl Callaway as the little girl
    Teleplay written for *Alfred Hitchcock Presents* by James P. Cavanagh, based on the short story "M Is for the Many" by Henry Slesar, originally published in the March 1957 issue of *Ellery Queen's Mystery Magazine*. Subsequently collected in *Clean Crimes and Neat Murders* (Avon, 1960).
    Directed by Robert Stevens.
    (working on a lathe) *Oh, there you are. Pardon me.* (turns lathe off) *Uh, Good evening fellow hobbyists. I've decided to do it myself. I'm sure most of you would expect me to be all thumbs. This is definitely untrue. The way things are going I should be lucky to*

have any thumbs at all. Tonight's story is about a parolee, and so I thought you would be interested in this machinery, which has been designed as a therapeutic measure for paroled convicts, who may still harbor homicidal tendencies. It gives them a healthy outfit for their energies. We have a saw, lathe and drill. As my first project, I've been – uh converting Chippendale furniture into kindling. I'm sure my work here would only bore you. So we've arranged to show you tonight's story in just a moment. Perhaps I should explain. This is a circular saw. (turns switch on and woman tied to log starts for blades)

Mildred Dunnock and Darryl Hickman in the episode "Heart of Gold"
Photo courtesy of Ronald V. Borst / Hollywood Movie Posters)

Story: Jackie Blake pays a visit to Ralph Collins and his mother Martha, and introduces himself as a friend of Martha's son Allie. Two years ago the boys were involved in a bank robbery of $150,000 and Jackie drove the getaway car. Because he was only seventeen at the time, the warden released him on parole and wanting to let Martha know that her son is doing okay behind bars, finds himself becoming a member of the family. Two strangers pay Jackie a visit one evening asking where the money is, but like Jackie told the cops and detectives, he just drove the getaway car. He doesn't know where the missing loot is. Having been roughed up a little, Jackie returns to the Collins where Ralph beats on the kid. It seems Ralph sent the two goons to break a confession. Jackie stabs Ralph in self-defense and when Martha comes home to find her son on the floor dying, she accuses Jackie of murdering her Ralph in cold blood. "All we wanted was the money," Martha cries. "That's why I took care of you, that's why I was nice to you. We wanted the money."

(Hitchcock has his tie stuck in lathe and cuts tie with scissors) *I've become disenchanted with this equipment. First that hysterical girl managed to escape, and now this. While I'm looking for her, suppose you listen to this subtle suggestion, after which I hope you will rejoin me.* (commercial break – Hitchcock is now tied to the log, girl at controls) *We seem to have reached the end of our program, if not the end of the entire series. Why don't you tune in next week and find out. Good-bye . . . Good-bye.*

Alternate narrative:
(Hitchcock has his tie stuck in lathe) *Excuse me a minute.* (cuts tie with scissors) *There. I've decided to give this machine to a very dear friend of mine for two reasons. He's insufferable and wears long ties. As for the girl you saw earlier, you will be pleased to know that she acquired a job as the result of appearing on our program. A talent scout saw her and immediately signed her up as a pair of bookends. And speaking of ends, that is what this is – of our show that is. But we shall be back another time with another story. Good night.*

Trivia, etc. "I've always had a debt of gratitude to Alfred Hitchcock, who was the first to dramatize a story I had written," said Henry Slesar. "Eventually, he dramatized so many that I was able to bargain for the rights to self-adaptation, and this led to the TV writing career that is now the main supplier of food, fuel, and fineries in the Slesar home. But my gratitude extends beyond the pecuniary. Because there is another, perhaps greater reward for writers in seeing good, intelligent adaptations of their work in a dramatic medium. It enables us to start *seeing* the people we are writing about; to visualize the action we have plotted only in our heads; to hear the dialogue which seemed 'real' enough on paper but might not be so convincing when it becomes the spoken word. The process results in a kind of 'feedback,' helping writers to 'see' and 'hear' the action of their stories while they're still ink on paper (or pixels on a word processor.)"

EPISODE #83 **"SILENT WITNESS"** Broadcast on November 3, 1957
Starring: Don Taylor as Professor Bob Mason
Dolores Hart as Claudia Powell   Pat Hitchcock as Mrs. Nancy Mason
Harry Bellaver as Sergeant Flagner   Mercedes Shirley as Mrs. Davidson
William Boyett as Mr. Davidson   Theodora Davitt as the blonde student
Katherine Warren as the old baby-sitter
Teleplay written for *Alfred Hitchcock Presents* by Robert C. Dennis, based on a story by Jerome Barry.
Directed by Paul Henreid.
(behind bars in crib) *Good evening, fellow inmates. I suppose you are wondering why I'm here. I was picked up by an agent from the federal bureau . . . the bureau of standards that is. He claims I was lying about my weight. The vertical stripes were my tailor's idea. They not only give me that slim look, they also make it impossible for the guards to tell where the bars leave off and I begin. I have a different uniform for each day and on each one the stripes are closer together. In 10 days I expect to disappear completely. As for tonight's story, it is a sombre little jape entitled "Silent Witness."* (close-up) *First of course we must listen to a few inspirational words from our ward-.* (gun-fire) *I see I should have warned you not to attempt to break for the kitchen, for the guards are all well armed and they have their instructions.* (more gun-fire)

Story: Professor Mason has had a romantic involvement with a female student, and although he knows when to say enough, she won't take "no" for an answer. One evening Claudia takes up a baby-sitting job next door and after his wife leaves for the gym, he sneaks over to pay the girl a visit. Claudia has young girl fancies about marriage and children, but seeing no other route of escape, he strangles the life out of Claudia, leaving behind the only witness to the crime, a crying baby. When she learns about the murder, Mrs. Mason comments that seeing the murder will probably change the child for life, as the infant reaches the age of consciousness. Perhaps one day the infant will recall the horrible scene . . .

Months later, Professor Mason gets more worried with each passing week. Every time he gets a glance of the baby, the infant starts screaming and crying. Believing it's only a matter of time till the baby starts talking, he turns himself into the police, giving a full confession. Only what the Professor didn't know was that the child kicks up an awful cry at the sight of any man.

Well you can't win them all. I understand that Don Mason was condemned to a cell very much like this one. And now daddies and mummies, if you want some time off for good behavior I suggest you watch the following, after which I shall toddle back. (commercial break) *After seeing that, getting out of here is all I can think of. Suppose you also take this opportunity to escape. Until next week, of course. Good night.*

Alternate narrative:
And now daddies and mummies, I think the time has come to lam out of here. Suppose you take this opportunity to escape. Until next time, of course. (Hitchcock shoots water pistol against the screen.)

Trivia, etc. Hitchcock calls the Professor "Don" but Patricia Hitchcock calls her husband "Bob" in the actual script. Somewhere along the way, between filming of the script and the afterwards, the name of the main character got changed. Once married to actress Phyllis Avery, actor-turned-director Don Taylor would later direct a few Hitchcock episodes himself, only months after completion of this episode. His directing work for other television programs would win him an Emmy nomination for an episode of *Night Gallery*. Taylor would also directed movies such as *Escape From the Planet of the Apes* (1971) and *The Island of Dr. Moreau* (1977 version). Hitchcock's alternate closing remarks for this episode ended the Universal documentary *Dial H for Hitchcock: The Genius Behind the Showman*.

EPISODE #84 **"REWARD TO FINDER"** Broadcast on November 10, 1957
    Starring: Jo Van Fleet as Mrs. Anna Gaminsky
    Oscar Homolka as Carl Gaminsky
    Claude Akins as the police officer
    Teleplay written for *Alfred Hitchcock Presents* by Frank Gabrielson, based on a story by George F. J. Smith.
    Directed by James Neilson.
    (money tree) *Oh, Good evening. I saw you're as surprised as I was to see a money tree like this. The ones I've seen have always been much taller. Oh I smudged that one. The ink wasn't dry yet. Last year my entire crop was wiped out by grasshoppers. I finally tried insect spray, but by that time the grasshoppers were so rich, they could afford gasmasks. Actually I have no regard for money. Aside from its purchasing power it's completely useless as far as I am concerned. Unfortunately the leading characters in tonight's play, do not share my detachment. You shall see what befell them in a moment. But first, I would like to explain our new get-aquainted offer. Watch what comes up next carefully. If at the end you are not completely satisfied, why don't you give up?*

Alternate narrative:
    (money tree) *I'll be with you in a moment. I suppose you're as surprised as I was to see a money tree like this. The ones I've seen have always been much taller. Oh I smudged that one. The ink wasn't dry yet. Last year my entire crop was wiped out by grasshoppers. I finally tried insect spray, but by that time the grasshoppers were so rich, they could afford gasmasks. Actually I have no regard for money. Aside from its purchasing power it's completely useless as far as I am concerned. Unfortunately the leading characters in tonight's play, do not share my detachment. You shall see what befell them in a moment.*

198

Story: Carl Gaminsky, a junkman by occupation, returns home one evening to give his wife good news. He found a wallet with the initials G.E. stamped on it, and $5,200 in one-hundred dollar bills inside. No name or license was found, so the two ponder whether they should return the wallet for a reward. The next day, an advertisement in the paper offers a generous reward to the finder, and Carl reluctantly agrees to return the wallet. When he comes back, he gives his wife Anna the bad news. No reward, just a verbal thanks. Two weeks later, Anna has turned into a shrew, complaining about her poverty, but discovers that Carl still has the wallet. Because he lied, Anna blackmails him into buying her things for the house, including a new fur coat. With her half already spent, Anna realizes the only way to keep all the money is to kill her hubby, so she poisons his coffee. Carl by now, has also come up with the same conclusion, and when Anna turns around, he clubs her to death. Drinking the coffee, Carl remarks to the lifeless body, "One thing I got to say about you Anna, you sure make a good cup of coffee."

The mar of that little tale is unmistakeable. In fact after seeing it, my wife got rid of my money tree. She exchanged it for a tree that grows soap coupons. And now for those of you who are long suffering victims of television commercials, my humane sponsor will deliver this coup de grâce, after which I'll be back. (commercial break) *My, that was an awfully low blow, even for a coup de grâce. I'll miss my little tree. However I had the foresight to strip it completely.* (looks at money) *Void if detached.* (throws money into the air) *Good night.*

Alternate narrative:

Naturally, no one was the winner in that little merry-go-round. No one except for the local art store owner. The demand for statuettes shot up to astronomical heights. It was surpassed only by the amount of coffee that was sold. By the way, I thought my money tree was a bad influence on me, so I sold it. However, I had the foresight to strip it completely. (looks at money) *Void if detached.* (throws money into the air) *Good night.*

Trivia, etc. Actor Robert Whitesides is listed in the closing credits, but once again, an actor suffered the Eloise Hardt syndrome – listed but not seen in the play.

EPISODE #85 **"ENOUGH ROPE FOR TWO"** Broadcast on November 17, 1957
Starring: Jean Hagen as Madge Griffin   Steven Hill as Joe Kedzie
Steve Brodie as Maxie   Don Hix as the hardware store owner
Teleplay written for *Alfred Hitchcock Presents* by Joel Murcott, based on the short story of the same name by Clark Howard, originally published in the February 1957 issue of *Manhunt*. Subsequently anthologized in *Hitchcock in Prime Time*, ed. Francis M. Nevins, Jr. and Martin H. Greenberg (Avon, 1985).
Directed by Paul Henreid.
(rope in the basket trick)   *Good evening, television addicts. Thank you for your kind attention. Please don't jump to conclusions, we have not joined the stampede for western stories. Tonight's story does take place in the far west, but it is not about cowboys and their playmates. I feel that the cow has been very much overrated as a performer. By way of further contrast, my portion of tonight's pot-pourri, will have a definite eastern flavor. Now for an amazing demonstration.* (Hitchcock claps his hands and the rope raises) *Charles!* (man climbs the rope) *I can see that this is especially useful when you have a place you wanna get away from, but no place you wanna go to. He doesn't seem to be coming down. Perhaps we'd better have our play. It will begin in a moment and is called "Enough Rope For Two." I hope you appreciate how skillfully we have woven the theme throughout our introduction. Uh, oh, our next performer is an old, old friend. If we give him plenty of rope . . . he may do us a big favor.*

Alternate narrative:

(rope in the basket trick) *Good evening, television addicts. Thank you for your kind attention. Please don't jump to conclusions, we have not joined the stampede for western stories. Tonight's story does take place in the far west, but it is not about cowboys and their playmates. I feel that the cow has been very much overrated as a performer. By way of further contrast, my portion of tonight's pot-pourri, will have a definite eastern flavor. Now for an amazing demonstration.* (Hitchcock claps his hands and the rope raises) *Charles!* (man climbs the rope) *I can see that this is especially useful when you have a place you wanna get away from, but no place you wanna go to. He doesn't seem to be coming down. Perhaps we'd better have our play. It will begin in a moment and is called "Enough Rope For Two." I hope you appreciate how skillfully we have woven the theme throughout our introduction.*

Story: Joe Kedzie is released from a ten-year prison sentence for the theft of $100,000 and one of the first things he plans to do is recover the money. Forced to take along his partner in crime, Maxie, and Joe's old girlfriend, Madge. Joe is unaware that it was Maxie who turned him in to the Las Vegas police, a fault on Maxie's part since he didn't know at the time that Joe hid the money before being apprehended. A hundred miles into the Mojave desert, Joe explains that he buried the money in an abandoned mine shaft. Now that the hiding place is revealed, Maxie attempts to finish the job by pulling a gun on Joe. Joe, however, planned well in advance and shoots Maxie first. One gun shot hits the canteen. Once Joe is lowered to the bottom of the shaft, he digs up the loot and sends the package up to Madge, awaiting for the prize up at the surface. When Joe starts back up, Madge cuts the rope with a knife. Joe falls, breaking his leg when he hits the bottom. To her horror, Madge discovers that Joe still has the car keys, so while Joe is now doomed at the bottom of the shaft, she also has little chance of getting out of the desert alive with no water or transportation.

I'm worried about our little friend. I'm afraid he'll fall. This is why I've asked that his bed be placed on the ground to break his fall. (shows bed of nails) *Perhaps I'd better reel him in, while doing this I shall perform a feat of magic and vanish by turning myself into a television commercial. But please don't leave. After sixty seconds I shall turn the commercial into an Alfred Hitchcock.* (commercial break) *He left a note. "I just came to the end of my rope." I'm sure that's enough mystery to last until next week, when we'll return with another story. Now we come to that part of the program for which you've all been waiting. Good night.*

Alternate narrative:

In case you're wondering what happened next, Madge Griffin was found by a uranium prospector. So our story had a happy ending – for the prospector that is. You see, he didn't find Madge for two years. However, you'll be glad to hear that the money was in an excellent state of preservation. Perhaps I better reel our little friend in. He'll catch cold if he stays up there too long. (pulls rope down with a note on it) *He's left a note. "I just came to the end of my rope." That I'm sure is enough mystery to last until next time, when we shall return with another story. Now we come to that part of the program for which you have all been waiting. Good night.*

Trivia, etc. Joel Murcott wrote numerous scripts for radio and television, both originals and adaptations. He wrote scripts for the short-run television series *Pentagon USA* in 1953, *Bonanza*, *Little House on the Prairie* and *Cannon*. For the big screen, Murcott wrote *Manfish*, a 1956 production starring Lon Chaney, Jr. For this Hitchcock episode, Murcott composed a faithful adaptation to the Clark Howard story of the same name. "This was the first short story I ever sold to television," recalled Howard. "It was the eighteenth story I had written, the fifth I had sold. When it appeared on Sunday night in prime time, I was thrilled to see that its stars were Steven Hill, Jean Hagen, and Steve Brodie. Not only that, but the segment had been directed by Paul Henreid, a longtime favorite actor of mine who had recently moved behind the camera. As I watched the show, I was pleased to see that the screenwriter not only followed the original story very closely, but also used a great deal of the dialogue I had written. The only major change was that the female role had been expanded for Jean Hagen, who was a popular TV star at the time [*Make Room for Daddy*]. All in all, this first adaptation of a story of mine for television was a thoroughly pleasant experience."

EPISODE #86 **"LAST REQUEST"** Broadcast on November 24, 1957
        Starring: Harry Guardino as Gerald Daniels   Cara Williams as Mona Carstairs
        Hugh Marlowe as Bernard Butler   Karin Booth as Sheila
        Jennifer Lea as the other cheating woman Mike Ross as Frank Carstairs
        Fred Kruger as the warden   Robert Carson as Harry Judson
        Robin Morse as the cheating woman
        Teleplay written for *Alfred Hitchcock Presents* by Joel Murcott, based on the short story of the same name by Helen Fislar Brooks, originally published in the January 1957 issue of *Alfred Hitchcock's Mystery Magazine*.
        Directed by Paul Henreid.
        (in a giant boiling kettle) *Good evening fellow gourmets. Have you ever been in the position where the success or failure of a dinner party depended entirely on you? Of course, all this is not without its compensations. It is always reassuring to learn that other human beings still find you desirable. . . and I am the main course. It would be horrible to go through this and be nothing but an hors d'oeuvre. Confidentially, they are miserable chefs. I certainly would not cook a pot roast with his shoes on. Actually, I still haven't explained why I'm here. It seems that one of the natives was condemned to death and as a last request, was granted the right to indulge in a hearty meal. I am proud to say, I was his first choice. And now, while I'm coming to a boil, suppose you watch tonight's story, which is also about a condemned man.*

        Story: Gerald Daniels is on death row for a crime he claims he did not commit. As a last request, hours before execution, Gerald is allowed the use of a typewriter and some paper. He composes a long letter to the editor of the Star Times, explaining how Bernard Butler, the district attorney that prosecuted him, made one mistake too many. Gerald, you see, committed a double murder one evening and the D.A. mistakenly looked at the scene of the crime as "a lover's quarrel and suicide." When a witness was called forth, a waitress named Mona, Gerald bumped her off in an alley. Butler prosecuted Mona's ex-husband, never knowing it was all Gerald's doing, and the innocent man took the chair. A few days later, Gerald went out to pay off a big-time bookie, only to find the payoff man dead, and the police nabbed him in the streets. The District Attorney had a field day, sentencing Gerald to death row, again for a crime an innocent man did not commit. So now Gerald admits to the first crime - but also points out that the D.A. is as guilty as he is for prosecuting and having sent to prison an innocent man who died for someone else's crime. "Is this the face of a man who wants to be Governor?" he asks. Ten minutes before the execution, the D.A. pays a visit. He found a witness and Gerald has a stay of execution. He'll be a free man, but in the meantime, his letter is being read by the secretary at the prison for censorship . . .

        Oh well, it's those little surprises that make life interesting. I too am surprised to find myself the after-dinner speaker But I was given a stay of execution in answer to a last request I made. Speaking of requests, uh -we've been asked to play a little number for you, after which I shall return con auchulachium, meaning as quickly as I can. (commercial break) *That request was for uh - Charlie, Mabel, Judy, Lou, Jack, Taft, Donner, Pinky, Agnes, Dutch, Sonny, Jimmy, Fred, Elmo, and all the gang at O'Connor's drug store. I hope they liked it . . . for there is certainly no accounting for taste. Please tune in next week for another story, and we shall also spin your favorite commercials. Good night.*

Trivia, etc. Just to give an example of the difference between the French and English versions of Hitchcock's hosting chores, here is a translation of the lead-out to this episode: *I have never been insulted that way in my whole life. They have stricken me off the menu. The Chef pretends I'm not tender enough. Anyway, this will give me the chance to come back again with another story. Waiitng for that, good evening and good appetite.* (A girl wearing glasses and reading a book, is boiling in the pot.)

EPISODE #87 "THE YOUNG ONE" Broadcast on December 1, 1957

Starring: Carol Lynley as Janice "Jan"   Vince Edwards as Tex
Stephen Joyce as Stan   Jeanette Nolan as Aunt May
Rusty Lane as Matt, the police officer   Frank Marlowe as the bartender

Teleplay written for *Alfred Hitchcock Presents* by Sarett Rudley, based on a story by Phillip S. Goodman and Sandy Sax.

Directed by Robert Altman.

(gift collection)   *Good evening and thank you for being so prompt. I detest being kept waiting. I thought you might be interested in this collection of gift selections. They range from conventional to rare. Here is the ever popular revolver. It is an excellent means of establishing credit in a strange city. It is equally useful in the removal of unwanted or unsightly persons. Here is a jar of poison mushrooms for those smart alecks who know toadstools when they see them.* (picks up an axe) *Here we have a weapon that is primitive . . . but effective. It is guaranteed to be 50% painless. You see, it takes two men to operate it and the one at this end doesn't feel a thing. And for the house frau whose aim with the family china is not what it used to be, here is a very handsome item . . .an exploding cream pitcher. Says on it "God bless our happy home." As for tonight's story, I wont tell you whether or not any of these weapons are used. You will have to watch and see.* (close-up) *I did think I had an example of a blunt instrument to show you, uh . . . Ah, Yes. What could be more blunt than the following ?*

Story: Pretty, young Janice wants out of the hick town she lives in and away from Aunt May, her bossy guardian. Her boyfriend Stan won't marry her or take her away because he can't find a job. Finally getting fed up with her hum-drum existence, the seventeen year-old girl kills her aunt. Then she goes out to the downtown bar where she coaxes an older man to her home - a move to check up on things, she suddenly tears her clothes and screams for help. Once she is "saved" by a police officer, she claims that the man attacked her after killing Aunt May. She thinks she has pulled off the perfect crime until her boyfriend arrives to announce that he's found a job, and is willing to take her away. But when he came to the house earlier to take her away he found Aunt May dead instead.

Well, she had me fooled. After all, anyone who would bludgeon her elderly aunt can't be all bad. And now while I'm briefly away, I'd like to show you still another lethal weapon. If used in large quantities, one of these can bore a person to death. (commercial break) *When the dosage is as limited as that, there's no danger. After all, a one minute commercial never hurt anyone. We have another play prepared to show you next week. I hope you'll join us then. Good night.*

EPISODE #88 "THE DIPLOMATIC CORPSE" Broadcast on December 8, 1957

Starring: Peter Lorre as Detective Tomas Salgado
George Peppard as Evan Wallace   Mary Scott as Janet Wallace
Isobel Elsom as Janet's Aunt   John Verros as Manuel Hera, Chief of Police
Orlando Rodriguez as the border guard   Harrison Lewis as the boy
George Navarro as the waiter   Sid Cassel as Dr. Elliott

Teleplay written for *Alfred Hitchcock Presents* by Robert C. Dennis, based on a story by Alec Coppel.

Directed by Paul Henreid.

(wearing a mexican hat) *Good evening, seniors and seniores and members of our little book of the week club. Originally I was to play a different role but I proved to be a rather bulky bookmark. Tonight's little volume takes us to exotic nearby Mexico.* (Hitchcock sits with his back against a cupboard.) *Home of the tortilla, the bullfight and the forty-hour coffee break. It is called "The Diplomatic Corpse." Allow me.* (closes the cupboard)

Story: Evan and Janet Wallace are out for a car ride with her rich aunt and decide to cross the Mexican border illegally, upon the insistence of the old woman, who wants to see Mexico before she returns to England. But after they do, the old woman dies as a result of a heart attack, and Evan and Janet stop at a cantina to think about their situation. When they leave the cantina, the two discover their car – and the dead woman – missing, probably as a result of theft. Knowing they need the wealthy woman's body in order to inherit her fortune, they hire a detective named Salgado to help them find the car (without the knowledge of the police). The police, however, find the automobile first, with the body missing, so the couple return to Salgado's office and explain the situation. The detective agrees and a few days later, finds the corpse at a funeral home, where Salgado arranges for the casket to be smuggled illegally - and expensively - across the border. However, back in America, Evan and Janet find to their horror that the coffin does not carry their relative, but an old Mexican man. Having obviously been ripped off, they have to head back to Mexico for another try.

Oh well, what can you expect from people who go out in the mid-day sun? So much for our travelogue. Just a moment, there seems to be a postscript we overlooked.

George Peppard and Peter Lorre conduct some business in "The Diplomatic Corpse" (Photofest)

(commercial break) I'm glad we noticed that. Without that bit of erratum, we would have missed the entire point of the story. (puts on hat) *Oh, by the way, you probably think I'm Alfred Hitchcock. He's Alfred, I am Omega. Good night.*

Trivia, etc. Having spent thirty-some years frightening audiences, Peter Lorre played other notable non-sinister roles before, such as Mr. Moto. "There comes a time when you have to find the integrity to stand up and refuse to play certain kinds of roles," he told a reporter for *TV Guide*. "Of course, you have to allow yourself to be typed for a period of time. I have been typed five or six times in my life. But the day comes when you must make the break. Television came into being before people knew what to do with it. Today it's an industry and nobody has the time to *think* about it."

Peter Lorre played the role of Hans Beckert in Fritz Lang's *M* (1931), which soon caught the attention of Alfred Hitchcock, who filmed Lorre for two of his movies, *The Man Who Knew Too Much* (1934) and *Secret Agent* (1936). "I did insist on having Peter Lorre," Hitchcock told Francois Truffaut. "He had done *M* with Fritz Lang and this was his first British role. He had a very sharp sense of humor. They called him 'the walking overcoat' because he went around in a long coat that came down to his feet."

"Peter [Lorre] was a kind, very pleasant person with a big sense of humor, very delightful," recalled Charles Bennett. "I remember a funny thing about Peter, on *The Man Who Knew Too Much*. We had a secretary who was named Joan Harrison, and she had come down from Oxford. She was supposed to speak French very well, and Peter Lorre couldn't speak English but he could speak French and a smattering of English. So Hitch said to Joan, 'Look, go and explain the scenes to Peter in French, so he'll understand them.' So Joan did. She went to Peter, talked a lot of French to him, he listened very beautifully. And at the end of it he said, very kindly, 'Please . . . I do not understand . . . speak English!" Her French was so bad, he had a better chance of understanding in English [laughs]!"

In this story, the protagonists visited an old Spanish mission, about 55 to 60 miles from Tijuana, about the same time Hitchcock filmed his masterpiece, *Vertigo*, in which they also visited an old Spanish mission for the famous scene in the bell-tower. On the inside of the large human-sized cupboard Alfred Hitchcock opens and closes during his hosting, the words "Copyright by Shamley Productions" is printed. Apparently an "inside" joke by Hitchcock and the production crew.

EPISODE #89 **"THE DEADLY"** Broadcast on December 15, 1957
      Starring: Phyllis Thaxter as Margo Brenner   Lee Philips as Jack Staley
      Craig Stevens as Lewis Brenner   Frank Gerstle as Sergeant Thompson
      Anabel Shaw as Rhoda Forbes   Peggy McCay as Myra Herbert
      Teleplay written for *Alfred Hitchcock Presents* by Robert C. Dennis, based on the short story "Suburban Tigress" by Lawrence Treat, originally published in the July 1957 issue of *Alfred Hitchcock's Mystery Magazine*. Subsequently anthologized in *Hitchcock in Prime Time*, ed. Francis M. Nevins, Jr. and Martin H. Greenberg (Avon, 1985).
      Directed by Don Taylor.
      (fixing plumbing above an electric chair) *Oh good evening. I guess if you want something done right, you have to do it yourself. The plumber keeps fixing the leak and I don't want it fixed. I'm sure many of you have one of these in your homes. But for the benefit of the backward, I shall explain. The subject is strapped in this chair. I then turn this valve, and the water drips on his head, one drop each minute. After about a week of this, I suddenly turn the water off. It produces the most astounding effects. It is especially valuable if you have a friend who wishes to lose his inhibitions. Naturally, you may lose your friend too. However, there is one serious danger. Don't ever leave it running when there is no one in the chair. Because in a few days, the force of the dripping water, can actually drill a hole through the wood. (close-up) Now, while I go back to the shop to get the proper tools, we shall have the rest of this evening's entertainment. First, I have a special announcement. The following commercial will be interrupted for approximately twenty-five minutes to enable us to present a play.*

      Story: Before finishing with the dinner, Margo Brenner informs her husband that there is a leak coming from the water heater in the basement. The next morning, before leaving for work, her husband suggests she call a plumber, which she promptly does. Enter stage left Jack Staley, local plumber who has found that blackmail is more profitable than repairing drains. It seems Jack selects homes with rich housewives who have something to hide. Using his good looks and charms, he tries to pull one over on Margo Brenner, his latest victim, charging her $500.00 just for a fix-it job, or else he'll spread gossip through the neighborhood about "the two of us." Regrettably, Margo finds no other alternate than to pay his fee, and phone the police. But the plumber already has the police angle covered, so her situation only gets worse. Fighting fire with fire, Margo plays the same game, getting some dirt on Jack Staley to put an end to his blackmail hobby. Margo assembles some of the ladies Staley blackmailed and threatens to phone the police, but blackmails him to do some plumbing for free instead.

A thief and blackmailer posing as a plumber. Nothing is sacred anymore. I shall be back in a moment after you view this rusty elbow in the plumbing of television. (commercial break) *There's nothing to it really.* (Hitchcock causes a leak and water hits him in the face) *Good night.*

Trivia, etc. "Besides the obvious pleasure of seeing a story of mine acted out on television and being able to tell everybody," recalled Lawrence Treat. " 'Sure, I've had stuff on TV,' my chief reaction was astonishment. Astonishment that practically all the dialogue was repeated verbatim from my own script, and that all the action had already been lined out in that same story of mine. For which somebody had been paid handsomely. And for which I got nothing. Or at least, nothing extra."

EPISODE #90   **"MISS PAISLEY'S CAT"**   Broadcast on December 22, 1957
Starring: Dorothy Stickney as Miss Paisley
Raymond Bailey as Inspector Graun   Harry O. Tyler as Bob Jenkins
Fred Graham as Mr. Rinditch   David Armstrong as police officer
Joel Smith as another tenant   Mark Sheeler as the dog owner
Teleplay written for *Alfred Hitchcock Presents* by Marian Cockrell, based on the short story of the same name by Roy Vickers, originally published in the May 1953 issue of *ElleryQueen's Mystery Magazine.* Subsequently collected in *Eight Murders in the Suburbs* (Herbert Jenkins, 1954).
Directed by Justus Addiss.
(cutting meat with huge butcher's knife) *Oh, good evening. The leading man in tonight's saga is an alley cat. He must be fed before each performance. It keeps him from eating the actors. Today he's having finely chopped mice burger. Naturally, we use nothing but contented mice. For two weeks they have been fed nothing but tranquilizers. Now, just as soon as I can feed our star, you shall see our story, "Miss Paisley's Cat."*

Story: Miss Paisley, a lonely old woman, adopts an alley cat and gives the animal the name of Stanley. She even talks to the cat as if it was her own child. Her downstairs neighbor, a vulgar bookie named Mr. Rinditch, threatens to kill the beast if it sneaks into his apartment again. But time after time, Miss Paisley is unable to keep the cat from leaving her apartment and asks Jenkins, the landlord, to turn Rinditch in to the authorities. But Jenkins says it won't help matters any. "Principal don't mean a thing to Mr. Rinditch." Being fined is part of his business expense. One evening, the old woman comes home to realize that her cat has disappeared and her landlord shows her the body of the feline in the garbage can outside. In a daze, Miss Paisley goes to sleep on her chair and wakes to hear the news that Mr. Rinditch has been murdered, stabbed to death. Miss Paisley calls the police to say that she committed the crime in her sleep (even though she has no proof and can't recall any details), but the police won't believe her, thinking landlord Jenkins is the guilty suspect. Six months later, Miss Paisley finds the cat collar and remembers the details that prove she was the murderer, but it's far too late. Jenkins has already been executed for murder.

Unfortunately for Miss Paisley, murder will out. She was finally uncovered . . . chiefly through the efforts of the SPCH . . .the Society for the Prevention of Cruelty to Humans. It's not a very powerful organization, but it's growing. And now, my sponsor would like to have his say. . . afterwhich. . . I shall sneak back. (commercial break) *I can think of no way I could top the last offering, so they let. . .* (Hitchcock realizes he was sitting on the knife) *. . . that concludes tonight's entertainment. Next week, we shall be back again with another story. Good night.*

Alternate narrative:

Unfortunately for Miss Paisley, murder will out. She was finally uncovered...

**Dorothy Stickney and "Stanley"
(Photo courtesy of Photofest)**

chiefly through the efforts of the SPCH . . .the Society for the Prevention of Cruelty to Humans. It's not a very powerful organization, but it's growing. As for the star of our show, Miss Paisley's cat Stanley, he went down in the line of duty. Making a revival of our play impossible. But all is not lost. He is being used . . . (Hitchcock realizes he's sitting on the knife) *. . . for dog food. And on this pleasant note, we conclude tonight's entertainment. Until next time, good night.*

Trivia, etc. Alfred Hitchcock had many dogs over the years of course, but the names of the two West Highland White Terriers we see him walking in *The Birds* (1963) during his famed cameo appearance, were Geoffrey and Stanley. The connection between this episode and Hitchcock's dog? Miss Paisley's cat was also named Stanley.

EPISODE #91   **"NIGHT OF THE EXECUTION"**   Broadcast on December 29, 1957
       Starring: Pat Hingle as Warren Selvey   Georgann Johnson as Doreen Selvey
       Russell Collins as Ed Barnes
       Harry Jackson as Hank Vance, Assistant D.A.
       Vinton Hayworth as Sydney, Doreen's father   Frank Marlowe as the judge
       Also in the cast: Murry Julian, Edward Schaaf, Ben McAtee, Ed Spencer and
Alfred Tonkel.
       Teleplay written for *Alfred Hitchcock Presents* by Bernard C. Schoenfeld, based on
the short story "The Day of the Execution" by Henry Slesar, originally published in the June
1957 issue of *Alfred Hitchcock's Mystery Magazine*. Subsequently collected as "The Day of
the Execution" in *Clean Crimes and Neat Murders* (Avon, 1960), and as "Night of the
Execution" in *Death on Television* (Southern Illinois University Press, 1989).
       Directed by Justus Addiss.
       (grenade, apple)   *Good evening. Uh, this looks like a hand grenade, doesn't it?
Please don't be frightened. It really isn't a grenade, it's a music-box. You see, if this were*

real and I were to pull the pin, I'd be blown to bits in a few minutes. But when I pull the pin on this one you shall hear the sweet strains of "I'm all shook up." Watch. (pulls pin) *There must be something wrong. Oh, it's all right. I just got the wrong grenade. The musical ones didn't have this inscription on it . It says: Who ever finds this grenade, I love you. While I stand here waiting for something to happen, suppose you observe as our drama unfolds. Of course, as usual, we have an explosive little item which comes first. I've heard that it's a real bomb.*

Story: Warren Selvey has political ambitions, but little hope of following through with them because he has failed to convict many of the cases he has prosecuted. Deciding to take a case that will prove his abilities, he relentlessly prosecutes an accused murderer which ends with a death sentence. But before Rodman is convicted, a stranger named Barnes shows up to claim that he committed the crime. This puts Selvey over a barrel, as he doesn't want an innocent man to die. Problem is, now that he has a good chance of being elected to District Attorney, he cannot afford the bad publicity. Deciding not to stop Rodman's execution, it does Selvey little good as he and Barnes end up in a fight that leaves the man dead, at which time Selvey learns that the man was a crank, having built a reputation of confessing to murders by reading up on the evidence.

(bites into apple) *I'm sure you're wondering what happened to the grenade. A little grey-haired old lady came by selling apples and I managed to slip the grenade into her basket.* (rugs shoulders) *By now she should be selling apple sauce. The word "selling," brings us to the next item on the agenda. After which, I shall bounce back.* (commercial break; Hitchcock returns up-sidedown) *Excuse me, but I have just noticed in the current issue of this magazine, that "Alfred Hitchcock Presents" again has been voted Look's Annual Television Award for the best half-hour dramatic series of the year. And as you see, I'm walking on air. The Look Award by the way, is an award not for looking, but for being looked at. Quite confusing, but nonetheless satisfying. I wish to thank the editors of Look, and the television critics around the country, who voted for the award. Thank you and good night.*

Trivia, etc. "When 'The Day of the Execution' was written, I thought it was a good story, a clear and eventually ironic exposition on the subject of ambition," recalled Henry Slesar. "When it became an episode of *Alfred Hitchcock Presents*, something changed. It was the same story, the events occurred just as they were on paper, even most of the dialogue was intact. But there was one difference. Suddenly, the minor people of the story, who had been only pawns in the fictional chess game played between the two main characters, became flesh and blood. The prosecutor's beautiful wife became not just a symbol of his acquisitiveness, but a human being with a stake in the circumstances. The prosecutor's rival, only a name on paper, made a brief appearance that gave emphasis to the prosecutor's own motivations. Its been a long time since I have reread 'The Day of the Execution.' But I have to admit that, when I did, I saw Warren Selvey and Phil Arlington and all the rest on my old black-and-white TV screen, followed shortly by that familiar rotundity whose sly concluding remarks ended . . . It was definitely a good evening for me."

Frank Marlowe played the role of a photographer in Alfred Hitchcock's *Notorious* (1946), a South Dakota taxi driver in *North by Northwest* (1959), and as a man in the newsreel truck in *Saboteur* (1942).

EPISODE #92 **"THE PERCENTAGE"** Broadcast on January 5, 1958
      Starring: Alex Nicol as Eddie Slovak   Nita Talbot as Louise Williams
      Don Keefer as Pete Williams / Wyzanski   Carole Mathews as Fay
      Walter Woolf King as Eddie's boss   Frederick Ford as the neighbor
      Ralph Barnard as the police officer   Lillian O'Malley as the neighbor

Teleplay written for *Alfred Hitchcock Presents* by Bernard C. Schoenfeld, based on the short story of the same name by David Alexander, originally published in the April 1957 issue of *Manhunt*.

Directed by James Neilson.

Oh, Good evening. I bring good news to those of you are plagued with faulty television sets. I am prepared to repair your set. It only stands to reason, more can be accomplished working from the inside out, then from the outside in. Lets see. Perhaps I should tighten this a bit. (Hitchcock uses screwdriver and picture gets fuzzy) *On second thought, it looked very good the way it was.* (Hitchcock uses screwdriver and picture focuses again) *Oh, here's the trouble. We can't have loose wires hanging around.* (Hitchcock starts pulling a wire from the ceiling) *Tonight's playlet is called "The Percentage" and is about a professional hoodlum named Big Eddie, who meets up with a television repairman.* (Hitchcock pulls down a television antenna) *As you see, it has exciting prospects. Someone has sent me the bird. But let's go on with the show. Perhaps we shall get some ideas from the repairman in the story. First however, we will subject the set and the audience, to this grueling test.*

Story: Eddie Slovak is a professional hoodlum who one day, calls on television repairman Pete Williams. Pete and Eddie are old Army friends from Korea. After the war, Pete kept his mouth shut and Eddie ended up taking all the glory. Now, Eddie is a rich man and he feels he owes something to Pete. But Pete won't accept any money even when Eddie says: "I don't let nobody have a percentage on me, I've got to pay you back." The money tempts Pete's wife Louise and shortly after, Eddie and Louise start an affair. A couple days later, Eddie learns that Louise is only playing with him and angry, the hoodlum murders the woman. Pete listens to Eddie's explanation, "its even now Pete, the percentage I mean." Pete finally agrees to help even the percentage, by turning his old Army buddy in to the police. With the hoodlum behind bars, Pete and Fay (Eddie's girlfriend) can spend the rest of their lives together.

Well, that's the way the old body bounces. I think you're tube is in excellent condition. (Hitchcock breaks glass picture tube) *I'll have this replaced, and be back in a moment. Meanwhile watch this.* (commercial break) *I didn't have a spare tube and we have to operate on candle-power. I think it does rather well. Next week we will be back with a new story and a new tube. Until then, good night.*

EPISODE #93 **"TOGETHER"** Broadcast on January 12, 1958

Starring: Joseph Cotten as Tony Gould   Christine White as Shelley
Sam Buffington as Charles   Gordon Wynn as Mr. Courtney
Sanford L. Gibbons as a man at the party   Bonne Greene as the dark-haired girl
Florence MacAfee as woman in window
Frank Allocca as Frank, the young police officer
George Eldredge as George, the old police officer

Teleplay written for *Alfred Hitchcock Presents* by Robert C. Dennis, based on a story by Alec Coppel.

Directed by Robert Altman.

(bottles on desk, lion)   *Good evening, fellow revelers. Tonight we are indulging in an old American tradition. It is the event that turn the mild-mannered white collar-worker into a four-armed beast of prey, the office party. However, we had this room designed especially for the party by the girls in the office. It has no corners. I am in charge of the entertainment* (shows the bottles), *which all should enjoy. After most of the hors d'oeuvres has been eaten, we're going to throw a vice president to the lions. I realize it isn't much but the lions are a great deal cheaper than the string quartet we had last year. They don't drink as much either. But before we begin our party, the. . . chief wishes to remind us why we work here.*

Story: Tony is a married man who is seeing a girl on the side. Everything goes well until the girl-friend, Shelley, gets drunk at a Christmas office party and demands that he get a divorce right away or she will tell his wife all about their relationship. Unwilling to give up the money he married along with his wife, Tony agrees to meet Shelley at her office once the party has moved elsewhere. Alone together, the lovers argue and Tony stabs Shelley with a letter opener. This turns out not to have been a good decision, as when he goes to leave, he had forgotten that Shelley had locked them in the office. Finding the keys, he forces the wrong key and breaks the lock. Out of desperation, he calls Charles for help but he is too drunk to be of any assistance. Then, through a window, he tries to get some attention from a woman in the next building, but she doesn't phone a locksmith, she phones the police. Then after the police force the door open and are about to leave, the drunk Charles comes and starts calling for Shelley and finds her dead.

(lion on the table) *If you think Tony Gould is in trouble, you should have been at our party. My fastidious friend here refused to eat the vice president we had prepared for him. The other workers are furious. Several of them were only one heart beat away from a promotion. It was all I could do to rescue Leo from the crowd. People can be quite vicious once they get the smell of blood. I think I shall allow him to continue his escape by turning out the lights for one moment, after which I'll return.* (commercial break; followed by a scene with the lion eating Hitchcock's jacket)

Trivia, etc. George Eldredge played the Chief of Police in *Psycho* (1960).

EPISODE #94 **"SYLVIA"** Broadcast on January 19, 1958
        Starring: Ann Todd as Sylvia   John McIntire as Mr. Leeds
        Philip Reed as Peter Kent   Raymond Bailey as Dr. Jasen
        Edit Angold as Bertha, the house servant
        Teleplay written for *Alfred Hitchcock Presents* by James P. Cavanagh, based on the short story of the same name by Ira Levin, originally published in the April 1955 issue of *Manhunt*.
        Directed by Herschel Daugherty.
        Good evening, parents, children, babysitters and settees. Tonight's discussion is concerned with that thorny problem that all parents face as they survey their children. Is co-existence really possible? The problems of the teenager are well discussed but I would like to say a word for his father, the middle-ager. The middle-ager is truly an outcast from society. Youth pays no attention to him, except to steal his hub-caps. Those traditional symbols of virility. He can only drive down the dusty road towards senility in a cooled-off hot rod. Forever doomed to be a mere spectator in the great drag-race of life. Of course, any connection between this treacle and tonight's story, is pure coincidence. (close-up) *I might add that any connection between what follows immediately and the rest of the show is not mere coincidence, but is a very practical business arrangement.*

Story: Mr. Leeds has a problem. In flashback he tells a story, about a few years ago when his daughter Sylvia met a man named Peter Kent, and almost immediately the youngsters fell in love. They got married two months later but Peter and Sylvia's father never saw eye-to-eye. Peter lived on Sylvia's income and one day Mr. Leeds discovers that Peter forged a check in his name. Mr. Leeds agrees not to press charges against his son-in-law on one condition. That Peter divorce his daughter. Peter agrees but when Sylvia receives the heartbreaking news, she becomes distraught. Later, when Sylvia calls him, and wants him back, Peter meets with Mr. Leeds again to update the agreement. With the forged check already destroyed, Mr. Leeds is left with no other choice but to pay. It is only then that Mr. Leeds learns that his daughter purchased a gun and Mr. Leeds fears that she is thinking of suicide. The father immediately tells Sylvia about the blackmail scheme, and upset, believing that her father won't let her have anything of her own – including a husband – turns the gun on him.

I hope all parents were watching closely. Sylvia was arrested but this did not prove to be much consolation for her father. I shall return after our next item, which is far too sophisticated for anyone who has not yet completed kindergarten and therefore bears the adult only label. In fact, those of you who live in Boston, will notice that certain parts of the picture are blocked out. If you want to see the entire commercial, I suggest you scamper down to Brockton or Fall River. (commercial break) *Another story has been prepared for our next week's show, I hope you'll join us then. Good night.*

EPISODE #95 **"THE MOTIVE"** Broadcast on January 26, 1958
        Starring: Skip Homeier as Tommy Greer   William Redfield as Richard
        Carl Betz as Jerome   Carmen Phillips as Sandra
        Kay Stewart as the woman   Ken Clark as a police officer
        Tharon Crigler as the young girl   Jim Johnson as a police officer
        Gary Clarke as the young man
        Original teleplay written for *Alfred Hitchcock Presents* by Rose Simon Kohn.
        Directed by Robert Stevens.
        (armchair, button)   *Good evening. I always sew on my own buttons. It's out of sentiment. You see, an ancestor of mine was the inventor of the button hole. It happened during a duel, although his opponent never knew it was a duel. Unfortunately this resulted in the false notion, that the button hole should be in the back of the coat. Actually, the invention of the button hole, brought a great sigh of relief from the whole world. You see the button had been invented long before and for over a hundred years, the world hadn't known what to do with it. By the way, I have deliberately refrained from telling you about tonight's story for I'm sure you would forget it during the enthralling entertainment which follows.*

        Story: After spending the evening getting very drunk, two young men named Jerome and Tommy debate over whether statistics show that police catch murderers in motiveless killings. Deciding to prove their point, Jerome suggests they pick a total stranger from the phone book for Tommy to kill. Sobered up the next day, Jerome can't believe what he did and discovers that his buddy is still going to travel to Chicago to kill the man, as he goes through with it. After murdering the stranger, Tommy returns home. The following morning Tommy reads the paper and discovers that the "stranger" he killed was his ex-wife's new husband - Jerome has set him up on murder charges as revenge for a past indiscretion.

        Well, that only goes to prove that you can't be too careful about whom you murder. He might turn out to be someone you don't like. And now, speaking of motives, see if you know an ulterior one when you see it. (commercial break) *You know, I get the distinct impression they're trying to sell something. I shall listen more closely next week. Until then, good night.*

EPISODE #96 **"MISS BRACEGIRDLE DOES HER DUTY"** Broadcast Feb. 2, 1958
        Starring: Mildred Natwick as Millicent Bracegirdle
        Gavin Muir as the priest   Tita Purdom as Maude
        Vera Denham as Mrs. Crump   Arlette Clarke as French chamber maid
        Albert Carrier as French room service man
        Teleplay written for *Alfred Hitchcock Presents* by Marian Cockrell, based on the 1916 short story of the same name by Stacey Aumonier. Subsequently collected in *Miss Bracegirdle and Others* (Hutchinson, 1923; Doubleday, 1923).
        Directed by Robert Stevens.
        Good evening. That sound you just heard was made by a guillotine. I brought it home from a recent trip to France, we just can't make them the way the French do. A motion picture company borrowed it to use on the adjoining soundstage. They're shooting a picture about the tragedy of a rich, middle-age ruler who falls hopelessly in love with a woman old enough to be his wife. Of course they're not using the guillotine in the picture. They just happen to have a leading man who's very vain and exceedingly short. Every one of the extras

who reported this morning was about a head too tall. We have no such problem. The leading character in our picture is an English spinster. You shall meet her in a moment. Many of our finest motion pictures are made from best sellers. Here is one made about a best seller.

Story: Paris, 1907. Millicent Bracegirdle has spent her whole life sheltered from outside influence, and as a result, has become an old spinster. Travelling to Paris, France to meet Clara, a friend of hers, she checks herself into a hotel, she finds boring and plain. Not at all as fancy and expensive as her home. She takes a warm bath to rest from her journey, and by accident, enters the wrong hotel suite. Trying to get out, the doorknob falls off and she finds herself locked in with a dead man! Ashamed of what her friends might say if wind of her situation reaches home, Millicent makes a successful attempt to sneak out of the room, which she finally manages to do after many considerable attempts. Realizing she forgot her towel and bedroom clothes, she returns quickly to fetch her things. Room service enters, finds the body, and runs to get the manager. Millicent sneaks back to her room again, thankfully unseen. News spreads through the hotel about the dead man, who as it turned out, was a murderer who died of a heart attack. As if this wasn't enough of a shock, room service returns with a stocking she had left behind in the dead man's room, notices it matches the one hanging on her bedpost, and gives her a wink of an eye as he exits quietly.

So much for the intrepid Miss Bracegirdle. Uh, there's been a development next door. The extras have rebelled and over-thrown the star. There he goes now. I'm afraid he's through being tall in the saddle. Now we have another movie for you. This is the picture they said Hollywood would never make. Filmed behind locked doors and here it is. After which I shall make a personal appearance. (commercial break) (yawns) *They never should have unlocked those doors. Next week we shall be back to try again. Until then, good night.*

Alternate narrative:
That concludes the life and loves of the intrepid Miss Millicent Bracegirdle. As for Monsieur Boudeu, the corpse in the story, he was buried in accordance with his last request. He was cut in pieces, placed in two barrels and thrown into the river. There's been a development next door. The extras have rebelled and overthrown the star. (sound of guillotine) *There he goes now. I'm afraid he's through being tall in the saddle. And I'm through being wide on the screen so until next time, good night.*

Trivia, etc. Two years after playing the role of Miss Ivy Gravely in Alfred Hitchcock's *The Trouble With Harry*, and playing the spinster madame Aunt Rosalie in the episode "The Perfect Murder," Mildred Natwick returns to *Alfred Hitchcock Presents*. Tita Purdom, who played another Millicent sixteen months earlier in the second-season opener "Wet Saturday," also returns to the Hitchcock program.

EPISODE #97 **"THE EQUALIZER"** Broadcast on February 9, 1958
Starring: Leif Erickson as Wayne Phillips   Martin Balsam as Eldon Marsh
Norma Crane as Louise Marsh   Dudley Manlove as Harris
Robert Riordan as Mr. Harvey Sloan   Lynn Cartwright as Mrs. Jane Sobel
Robert Gibbons as the police officer   Jack McClure as Carl
Frank Watkins as the police officer   Paul Maxwell as Ed Sobel
Teleplay written for *Alfred Hitchcock Presents* by Robert C. Dennis, based on the short story of the same name by Roy Carroll (pen-name of C. B. Gilford), originally published in the October 1957 issue of *Alfred Hitchcock's Mystery Magazine*.
Directed by James Neilson.
(as a golfer with no ball) *Good evening, and welcome to tee time. I'm taking up golf. I learned to play by watching a demonstration on television. I'm convinced that it's very easy to make a hole-in-one. At least this one.* (starts to swing at man's head) *In the*

demonstration, a golfer knocked a ball off his friend's head. I'm not using a ball. Being a beginner, I feel I'm entitled to a larger target. Perhaps you'd better look the other way. I know I shall.

Story: A company treasurer named Eldon Marsh is happily married until the new company salesman, Wayne Phillips, starts spending some "quality time" with Eldon's wife. When Eldon starts catching on, he challenges Wayne to a fight, revealing the love-bird's relationship in front of the other employees. The scandal forces his wife to pack and leave, and Eldon's boss is forced into the position of firing his best employee. Eldon by now is extremely furious, determined to start a fist-fight with Wayne, but is knocked to the ground. Not giving up, he hounds Wayne day and night demanding satisfaction. "You gotta kill me, or I'll kill you," Eldon remarks, "Let's equalize it, you can choose the weapon." The salesman finally agrees and the two choose pistols in a fair duel to the death, on the roof of a building. Making their appearance on the rooftop, Wayne takes advantage of the moment and shoots Eldon in cold blood. The police arrive shortly after and Wayne starts telling his story, claiming self-defense . . . or at least until the police discover Eldon never had a weapon in hand!

So much for the high price of low fidelity. I'm quite angry with my friend. He ruined my club and he didn't land anywhere near the hole. As a matter of fact, I can't even find him. Now I have to buy a ball, it's quite distressing. Why don't you join me in the locker room after we pass one of those sand traps that dot the fairways of television. (commercial break) *I thought we'd never get out of that one. However, we seem to have completed the course in thirty minutes, which is par. Why don't you join us next week for another round? In the club house, of course. Good night.*

EPISODE #98 **"ON THE NOSE"** Broadcast on February 16, 1958
        Starring: Jan Sterling as Fran   David Opatoshu as the bookie
        Karl Swenson as Ed   Carl Betz as the man
        Tharon Crigler as the young woman
        Also in the cast: Linda Watkins, J. Anthony Hughes, Bill Baucom, Sondra Rodgers and Mike Ragan.
        Teleplay written for *Alfred Hitchcock Presents* by Irving Elman, based on the short story "Something Short of Murder" by O.H. Leslie (pen-name of Henry Slesar), originally published in the November 1957 issue of *Alfred Hitchcock's Mystery Magazine.* Subsequently collected in *Clean Crimes and Neat Murders* (Avon, 1960).
        Directed by James Neilson.
        (riding-crop on weighing scales) *Good evening, ladies and gentlemen and good evening to the rest of you as well. We've ceased being particular. I'm training to become a jockey and this is the mount they assigned me. This is an improvement, it usually takes three cents.* (reads card) *Will one of you please get off. I forgot to tell you, this machine is very impudent. It's all very discouraging. I don't know what to do.* (reads card) *Why don't you cut out that two o'clock feeding. I think I better get off these scales. Tonight's story touches on racing and is called "On The Nose." But before we see it, a very worthy organization, would like to make this urgent appeal.*

Story: A gambling housewife cannot pay off a small wager and her bookie threatens to tell her husband about her secret gambling addiction. Desperate to come up with twenty dollars, Fran tries to shoplift but is caught. On the way to the police station the detective offers her the money in exchange for some "favors." She refuses, and gets away after the detective is involved in an auto accident that kills him. In her rush to get away from the scene of the accident, she leaves her purse behind, along with the twenty-dollar bill that the detective was trying to give her. The police show up at her door to return her purse and the twenty dollars, never piecing two and two together. Now that she has the money to pay the bookie by the deadline set, she receives a phone call from her husband who informs her that he'll be away in Chicago for business. So Fran calls her bookie and asks him to use the money to place a bet on a horse named Washington Flyer. On the nose, of course.

So much for our story. I've decided to give up horse racing. The shirts are much too loud. Besides, I couldn't go on after the touching tribute I received. The horses chipped in and bought me an automobile. But the show must go on. You understand of course, that all you have seen so far, is merely a prelude to the extravaganza which follows. (commercial break) *I do wish we had longer commercials. They are so short that one must be very agile to get to the kitchen and back. I know, you've said that. Next week we shall be back with another story, but without the services of my rude friend. Until then, good night.*

Trivia, etc. "I was in New York then, having taken time out from writing movies in California to work with Rodgers and Hammerstein on *Tevye's Daughters*, a musical play I had sold them, based on Sholom Aleichem's stories, the subject subsequently being made moot by the production of *Fiddler on the Roof*, based on the same material," recalled Irving Elman. "During that time, long before Hitchcock got involved in television or had any idea that he ever would, my agent at William Morris set up a meeting with him at the St. Regis Hotel where he was staying, to discuss the possibility of writing a movie adaptation of some book for him. But at that point he was so uncertain and vague about it, he had difficulty even remembering the name of the book and I never did find out what it was and nothing further came of it. But it was fascinating meeting him. Then, while I was still in New York, Hitchcock's long-time close associate and producer, Joan Harrison, produced a half-hour television series called *Janet Dean, Registered Nurse*, starring Ella Raines, and asked me to write a number of the scripts for the show. And then later when *Alfred Hitchcock Presents* was born, she produced that and again asked me to write for her, which I was delighted to do because she was the best producer, stage, screen or television, that I ever worked for in my almost sixty years in show business."

EPISODE #99   **"GUEST FOR BREAKFAST"**   Broadcast on February 23, 1958
    Starring: Joan Tetzel as Eve Ross   Scott McKay as Jordan Ross
    Richard Shepard as Chester Lacey
    Teleplay written for *Alfred Hitchcock Presents* by Robert C. Dennis, based on the short story of the same name by C. B. Gilford, originally published in the October 1956 issue of *Mike Shayne Mystery Magazine*.
    Directed by Paul Henreid.
    (breakfast newspaper)   *Good evening. I just happened upon this abandoned breakfast table. It was set for two persons and is complete, down to the morning paper, which was lying on the floor. With incidentally, a bullet hole through it. It looks as though someone's husband missed the 8:20 this morning. In fact, he may have missed it for good, for the bullet seems to have struck him between the society section and the want ads. While you are watching tonight's show, "Guest for Breakfast," I think I shall help myself to some toast. First however, let us pause for the unseemly sight of a man, toasting himself.*

Alternate narrative:
    (breakfast newspaper)   *Good evening. I just happened upon this abandoned breakfast table. It was set for two persons and is complete, down to the morning paper, which was lying on the floor. With incidentally, a bullet hole through it. It looks as though someone's husband missed the 8:20 this morning. In fact, he may have missed it for good, for the bullet seems to have struck him between the society section and the want ads. Of course, there is always a possibility that this hole was made for a man with a long, thin eyeball who wanted to see both sides of the paper at the same time. But that is enough sleuthing for now, while you're watching tonight's show "Guest for Breakfast." I think I'll have some toast.*

Story: Jordan and Eve Ross have been spending day and night verbally exchanging words. Their marriage is falling apart and both of them admit they are veering toward a divorce. One morning, over the usual breakfast which Jordan is insulting, they are interrupted by the arrival of a wanted killer named Chester, who needs a place to hide until the sun sets. Using the gun he holds in hand, he remains their temporary guest and spends the entire afternoon talking to the couple to pass the time. Chester tries to figure a plan to escape without heat from the police and each time, the two try to out-bid each other by offering money to the killer. They don't care what happens to the other, just as long as one of them survives. Finally, in a climatic fury, Chester decides to shoot Eve but Jordan comes to her aid at the last minute and over powers him. The police arrive and arrest the brash youth, who it appears was quite a desperado. The day's event causes the couple to face reality, and work out their differences, in an attempt to salvage their marriage. Poetic irony because Chester was wanted for murdering his wife and her lover.

As you have already guessed, tonight's show illustrated man's inhumanity to man. His indestructibility in the face of obstacles. The senselessness of war, the need for a dream, the value of spiritual action to combat the lust for profit and finally, the corrosion of life, the depletion of energy and the frustration of love which results from following a philosophy of romantic opportunism in a idealistic society. Naturally, we don't believe any of that but we felt that the author deserved to be heard. Did you ever. . . did you ever have the feeling you were being followed? That something vaguely ominous was following you? I do, on this program, uh. . . Let's have a look at him, after which I shall slink back. (commercial break) *You know there are times when I find myself wishing my television tube would blow out. I'm sure you have the same feeling, but if you thought that was bad, you should have tasted this toast. Burnt to a crisp. However, it indicates to me that it was the wife, and not the husband who was the victim of this little 'fou pa de deux.' And justifiably too. She was no cook, she was an arsonist. Next week we shall be back with another story. Until then, Good night.*

EPISODE #100   **"THE RETURN OF THE HERO"**   Broadcast on March 2, 1958
   Starring: Jacques Bergerac as Sergeant Andre   Susan Kohner as Therese
   Marcel Dalio as Marcel   Vladimir Sokoloff as the drunk
   Michael Granger as Leon's relative   Luis Van Rooten as Leon, the waiter
   Karen Scott as bar girl, Marcel's girl   Victor Varconi as Count d'Auberge
   Iphigenie Castiglioni as Countess d'Auberge
   Caren Lenay as the singer with accordian
   Gloria Castillo as Lilly, the youngest girl   Lilyan Chauvin as Sybil
   Teleplay written for *Alfred Hitchcock Presents* by Andrew Solt and Stirling Silliphant, based on an original story idea by Andrew Solt.
   Directed by Herschel Daugherty.
   Good evening, ladies, gentlemen and those of you who arrive too late to classify. I wish to welcome you to Alfred Hitchcock Presents. Please relax. There is no admission charge, no cover and no minimum. This is a non-profit organization. Profit being defined as that which is left after I take my share. Tonight's electronic floor show transports us to France. The nation noted for fine wines and provocative postcards. The scene is Leon's Café in Marseille. Of course, we still believe in first things first. (commercial attempt) *Just a moment, half of you weren't even paying attention. Our sponsor goes to considerable time and expense to prepare these little brochures and the least you can do is to watch them. That's better. Uh, you may continue, from the beginning, please.*

Story: Sergeant Andre is the son of the wealthy d'Auberge family, and a recently-discharged war hero returning home from the French-Algerian conflict. On his way toward his vast estate, Andre phones home to tell his mother that he is bringing home a friend, Marcel, who was crippled in battle, having lost his leg to save Andre's life. His mother, Countess d'Auberge, doesn't want Andre's "friend" with one leg to stay in the house - she doesn't think a man of Marcel's stature be welcome. Therese, the daughter of a French Café

Alfred Hitchcock celebrates the 100th episode with a birthday cake,
laced with dozens of murder weapons. The date on the cake is March 2, 1958.
Many photos were taken of Hitchcock on this particular day, all with various
murder weapons. One of these shots appear in the back of the LP Album,
"Music to be Murdered By." (See Collectables chapter)

owner, falls in love with Andre, regardless of the fact that he's engaged to a woman back home. This poses a couple of problems for the pair of resourceful Frenchmen, but Andre's problem is a little larger than that. You see, he knows his family and fiancée all too well which is why he told a lie over the telephone. Andre is the one with the missing leg, not Marcel. And knowing he can't go home, Andre limps away on crutches with his friend.

Tonight I shall not indulge in my usual gallows humor, for this program has no desire to make light of men who have suffered because of war. However, there is one feature of our show which remains constant and from which you cannot escape. Here it is, after which. . . I will be back. (commercial break) *That concludes tonight's program. Next week we shall return to the scene of our crime. I hope you will join us. Good night.*

EPISODE #101 **"THE RIGHT KIND OF HOUSE"** Broadcast on March 9, 1958
Starring: Robert Emhardt as Mr. Waterbury   Jeanette Nolan as Sadie Grimes
James Drury as Michael Grimes   Harry O. Tyler as Aaron Hacker
Jamie O'Hara as Sally   Charles Watts as Chief Taylor
Paul Maxwell as Sergeant Singer

Teleplay written for *Alfred Hitchcock Presents* by Robert C. Dennis, based on the short story "The Right Kind of A House" by Henry Slesar, originally published in the February 1957 issue of *Mike Shayne Mystery Magazine*. Subseqently collected in *Clean Crimes and Neat Murders* (Avon, 1960), *Murders Most Macabre* (Avon, 1986) and *Death on Television* (Southern Illinois University Press, 1989).

Directed by Don Taylor.

(as a real estate agent with a telescope)   *Good evening fellow realtors and clients. I'm very anxious to call your attention to the investment possibilities of our new subdivision. Pitted Hills. Naturally it lacks certain of the luxuries, but this is the price one pays for getting in on the ground floor. The sewer's are not yet in. However, there are enough craters to go around. As for its lack of atmosphere and water, I don't expect that to deter those of you with a real pioneer spirit. Those of you with vision can, I'm sure, imagine the beautiful sight of the moon, completely covered with the well-known, inexpensive Hitchcock homes. All with picture windows, giving everyone an unobscured view of his neighbor's picture window. Naturally, each home would be individualized. For there are seven different models to chose from. Seven, mind you. Red, green, blue, orange, lemon, lime and the ever popular chartreuse. For those of you who are budget-minded, we do have cheaper lots in the upper area, very fine of course if you like a lot that completely disappears at half noon. Like our prologue, tonight's story touches on real estate. It begins immediately . . . after this brief advertisement.*

Robert Emhardt guest stars on "The Right Kind of House"

Photo courtesy of Ronald V. Borst / Hollywood Movie Posters

Story: Among the cozy country-side of tall trees and lush greenery sits the house of Sadie Grimes, an old woman who lives quite in comfort. One day a chubby-sized man by the name of Mr. Waterbury, introduces himself as a wealthy man interested in the sale of her house. Sadie welcomes him in and even though Sadie asks $50,000 for her house (greatly overpriced), Mr. Waterbury takes her up on it even though, he attempts to talk the price of the house down. When the sale is settled, the old woman starts telling the story of how her son died, murdered in this very house about five years ago, by a stranger she never saw. She heard the arguing from upstairs. By the time she got down to her son's body, the murderer fled. The Sheriff later informed Sadie that her son stole $200,000 and probably hid it within the confines of the house. This hardly scares Waterbury off as he still agrees to pay the unbelievable price of $50,000, but it seems that he won't get the opportunity. The woman had poisoned the lemonade he just finished drinking, after she went under the assumption that the only one foolish enough to pay the huge sum would be someone who knew the house really contained $200,000 - her son's murderer. Mr. Waterbury, having been out-smarted by the old woman, swoons over and drops dead.

So much for life in these United States. Unfortunately Mrs. Grimes' crime. . . Mrs. Grimes' crime was discovered and her reputation ruined. Prior to this she had never been known to make a bad glass of lemonade. Prices have gone sky high on the moon, so I'm seeking land that isn't so close in. I think I shall have a look at Venus. Most of you seem too young, however, so I think you should look at something more wholesome. I suggest the following, afterwhich I hope you'll rejoin me. (commercial break) (Hitchcock returns with black eye from telescope) *Very dull. I couldn't see anything but a planet. I'd might as well have looked at the commercial. A practise I may take up at our next meeting. Until then, good night.*

Trivia, etc. Jeanette Nolan was the real-life wife of actor John McIntire, who had starred in a few *Alfred Hitchcock Presents* episodes. Nolan's credits include *Macbeth* (1948) and *The Man Who Shot Liberty Valance* (1962). Her husband John McIntire played Sheriff Chambers in Alfred Hitchcock's *Psycho* two years later. Nolan also supplied the uncredited voice of "mother Bates" in *Psycho* (1960).

Robert Emhardt and Jeanette Nolan poses in character.

(Photo courtesy of Ronald V. Borst / Hollywood Movie Posters)   217

EPISODE #102 **"THE FOGHORN"** Broadcast on March 16, 1958

Starring: Barbara Bel Geddes as Lucia Clay   Michael Rennie as Allen Bliss
Bartlett Robinson as John St. Rogers   Jennifer Howard as the Nun
William Yip as Wong, the waiter   Selmer Jackson as the elderly man
Mark Henry as the doctor

Teleplay written for *Alfred Hitchcock Presents* by Frank Gabrielson, based on the short story "The Foghorn" by Gertrude Atherton, originally published in the November 1934 issue of *Good Housekeeping*. Subsequently collected in *The Foghorn and Other Stories* (Houghton Mifflin, 1934; Jarrolds, 1935).

Directed by Robert Stevens.

(in an Indian canoe) *How! Mr. and Mrs. America and a special word to all you ships at* (close-up) *sea. I've been examining this new blue sew canoe for two. It is perfect for the brave who wants to take his wife out for a moonlight ride. It tips quite easily. Of course, this was used before the invention of sash weights, but I'm sure Indian ingenuity triumphed. This is apparently a souped-up job, for I noticed it has a 1620 chassis, with 1750 paddles. Tonight's story is entitled "The Foghorn," but we must first have our sponsor's product. Stuffed in the suffocating sack of commercialism and drowned in a sea of adjectives.*

Alternate narrative:

(in an Indian canoe) *How! and a special word for all you ships at sea.* (close-up) *I've been examining this new blue sew canoe for two. It is perfect for the brave who wants to take his wife out for a moonlight ride. It tips quite easily. Of course, this was used before the invention of sash weights, but I'm sure American Indian know-how triumphed. This is apparently a souped-up job, for I noticed it has a 1620 chassis, with 1750 paddles. It also has bucket seats and naturally, being an American vehicle, you steer it from the left. I shall now emulate the vanishing American, while we have tonight's story. After which, I shall paddle back.*

Story: During her engagement party, Lucia Gray meets her fiancé's employer, Allen Bliss. Her fiancé, John St. Rogers, thinks more of money than he does of her, but Lucia finds Allen more of a people person . . . and he attracts her. It doesn't take long for Lucia to fall in love with Allen, but her dreams are shattered when she learns that he is already married. Over a dinner at a Chinese restaurant, the two agree to be friends and Lucia breaks her engagement with John. Allen asks his lawyer to arrange for a divorce, and the two plan to run off and get married. A few weeks later, a complication stands in the way. His wife has changed her mind and she will never allow a divorce. Unsure how to proceed with their future, Allen and Lucia go for a boat ride, making for an island. A thick fog lays and soon after, the two lovers are hit by a ship. Lucia wakes in a missionary fifty years later crying for her beloved Allen.

That concludes our play. Now I shall emulate the vanishing American for a moment while we have a word from the great white father. . . after which, I shall paddle back. (commercial break) *As the Indians would say, uhhh. This is all of our first show of the evening. The second showing follows immediately and I trust you will leave promptly so that those waiting can get in. Thank you for allowing us to come into your teepees and until next week at the same time. Good night.* (Hitchcock repeats his entry, but not exactly the same) *How! Mr. and Mrs. America and a special word for all you ships at sea. I have been examining this new blue sew . . .*

Alternate narrative:

This is all of our first show of the evening. The second showing follows immediately and I trust you will leave promptly so that those waiting can get in. Thank you for allowing us to come into your teepees and until next time. Good night. (Hitchcock repeats his entry as if a movie in the theaters is starting over) *How! and a special word to all you ships at sea. I have been examining this new blue sew . . .*

EPISODE #103 **"FLIGHT TO THE EAST"** Broadcast on March 23, 1958
Starring: Gary Merrill as Ted Franklin Patricia Cutts as Barbara Denham
Konstantin Shayne as Sasha's father Anthony George as Sashalamail
Mel Welles as the airplane passenger Harvey Stephens as the police officer
Ralph Clanton as Sir Robert, the prosecutor
Teleplay written for *Alfred Hitchcock Presents* by Joel Murcott, based on the short story "Night Flight" by Bevil Charles, originally published in the August 1957 issue of *John Creasey Mystery Magazine.*
Directed by Arthur Hiller.
(flying carpet) *Good evening earthlings. Now you housewives know what to do with your rugs when the moths get them. Put the moths to work. After all, if you can't lick them, join them. This could be the transportation of the future. I'm certain that the day is not far off, when the two-carpet family will be quite common. No special launching platform is needed. The well waxed hallway of your home will do. 10,000 feet up and yet I could swear I saw a billboard. Over there.*

Story: Nairobi, 1958. On a plane leaving for Cairo, Ted Franklin recalls to a passenger how he developed a strong reputation for himself as a war correspondent, and after WWII, he was sent to the Middle East to cover the trial of an accused arms dealer. Franklin assumed "Sasha the Terrible" was guilty and milked the stories for all they were worth. Before the trial was over, Ted met an old man, Sasha's father, who pleaded with Ted to interview the boy. During that interview, Ted heard more facts than what was brought up in the trial. Changing his mind, Ted begins writing different articles claiming the man is innocent, a deal he made with Sasha that would save the boy's life. Payment is to be half of the diamonds upon sentence. The articles, however, prove to be a blunder when Sasha is later found guilty of the crime. His career now in ruin, Ted finds himself arrested for the murder of Sasha's father, a crime he committed not having received the diamonds he was supposed to get years ago. But the passenger sitting next to him in the plane has a confession. She too is a reporter and she plans to make Ted' story public. This will place Franklin's name in print again, but not in a way he ever imagined.

I shall certainly never try that again. I learned too late that it was a three-stage carpet and I was the first stage. I did manage to take some pictures which I shall show you now. Here is how the earth people look to a Martian. (commercial break) *As you can see, the Martians have a rather distorted picture of our world.* (a carpet falls down) *It looks as though our flying carpet is falling earth-ward and disintegrating into throw rugs. This concludes tonight's space adventure. Next week we shall be back with more fiction, scientific or otherwise. Until then, good night and a happy international geophysical year to all of you.*

Trivia, etc. Arthur Hiller was the director of numerous television episodes and big-screen movies. Among his television credits: *Gunsmoke, Naked City, Thriller*, and *The Addams Family.* He has also been known to play bit roles in movies such as a bar patron in *Beverly Hills Cop III* (1994), as judge in *Land of the Free* (1997) and as a scientist in *Roswell* (1994). But when it came to *Alfred Hitchcock Presents*, Arthur Hiller recalled fond memories of the creative control he had in directing: "Norman Lloyd was such a strength and support for me and came up with most of the casting suggestions. . . and of course he and Joan Harrison were the ones who kept the show on course. They were very caring about the creative people on the show. They made sure we had enough prep time and they would try to arrange for the director to see the editors' work and be involved in comments and changes. That may sound like nothing now, but it was many years later that the DGA finally negotiated the rights of a director to work with the editor and reach a 'director's cut.' In those days the director was mostly ignored at the conclusion of filming and often pushed away. Norman and Joan cared and always tried to arrange for us to be part of the editing process."

EPISODE #104 **"BULL IN A CHINA SHOP"** Broadcast on March 30, 1958
Starring: Dennis Morgan as Detective Dennis O'Finn
Estelle Winwood as Hildy Lou   Elizabeth Patterson as Miss Bessie
Ellen Corby as Miss Samantha   Ida Moore as Miss Birdie
Joseph Downing as Kramer   Paul Maxwell as the chemist

Teleplay written for *Alfred Hitchcock Presents* by Sarett Rudley, based on the short story of the same name by C. B. Gilford, originally published in the September 1957 issue of *Ellery Queen's Mystery Magazine*.

Directed by James Neilson.

(bullfighter) *Good evening, aficionados. Tonight's story is called "Bull In A China Shop," so we decided to indulge in a bit of bullfighting.* (Hitchcock gets speared in the back) *An obvious case of mistaken identity. Originally I was to have appeared in the skin tight pants of a matador, however at the last moment it was decided that this was a sight for which the television audience was not yet ready. Television is like bullfighting in one respect. They both have what is called, "the moment of truth." In bullfighting, it is the moment the matador faces the bull. . . before he converts him to hamburger. Ladies and gentlemen, the moment of truth.*

Story: Homicide Detective O'Finn pays a returning visit to a group of little old ladies, who reside in the house next to his. But he hasn't come for a social call, just to deliver distressing news. It seems that one of their group, who lately died of what looked like natural causes, was not natural. She was poisoned with arsenic. The coroner stakes his reputation on it. The four ladies seem indifferent to their friend's death, and explain it away as Elizabeth must have accidentally put arsenic in her tea instead of sugar. The arsenic turns out to be in the cupboard, where they also keep their container of tea. O'Finn suggests that they find a more suitable place to put their tea. The ladies won't hear of it, their interest seems to be the visitations of the handsome detective, whom they have been keeping an eye on for some time. They know his age, his hobbies of jogging, his occupation, and especially the fact that he is not married. A few days later, as Elizabeth's death didn't keep O'Finn coming back, the little old ladies call him over again for some tea. It seems another of their group has died of what appears to be natural causes . . .

I hope you weren't too disappointed that our story containing neither a bull nor a china shop. As for the ending, eventually Miss Bessie became enamoured of a fireman. A love which ultimately consumed her. And now a word from our sponsor, after which I shall flip back. (waits) *Now a word from our sponsor.* (more waiting) *The poor fellow is just too modest to come out. We'll have to encourage him, with some applause.* (commercial break) *That will teach you to encourage someone. Fortunately, I have no such reticence. I shall be back next week, whether you want me or not. But I do hope you'll see fit to join us. Until then, good night.*

EPISODE #105 **"DISAPPEARING TRICK"** Broadcast on April 6, 1958
Starring: Robert Horton as Walter Richmond
Betsy Von Furstenberg as Laura Gild
Perry Lopez as Julio   Raymond Bailey as Herbert Gild / Fielding
Frank Albertson as Regis   Percy Helton as Mr. Bruce
Thomas Wild as the doctor   Dorothea Lord as the nurse
Joe Conley as the old man

Teleplay written for *Alfred Hitchcock Presents* by Kathleen Hite, based on the short story of the same name by Victor Canning, originally published in a U.K. edition of *Argosy*.

Directed by Arthur Hiller.

(tennis-racket) *Good evening, fellow athletes. I believe that everyone owes it to his well being to indulge in some sport. My favorite past time as you can see is . . . filching loving cups. Naturally, I never steal too much at a time for fear of losing my amateur standing. But the people from whom I take the cups don't mind, I'm sure. After all, it isn't who wins that counts, it's how you play the game. By the way, I'm inventing a device that should make tennis much more enjoyable. It suddenly raises the net half a foot just as the victor leaps over to offer condolences to the loser. Through it, I hope to add what is lacking in tennis: Laughs. Before viewing tonight's chronicle, we must identify the party who is footing the bill. I must apologize for the brevity of this announcement, but this is one of the conditions laid down by our modest sponsor.*

Story: Tennis pro and insurance investigator Walter Richmond is assigned to investigate the "presumed death" of Herbert Gild. While on vacation from his working life in Los Angeles, Walter meets up with Laura Gild, a very beautiful (and rich) widow. She recalls how Herbert went boating one day, and his body was never found. Walter goes back home and after checking the books, discovers that her husband (or someone using her husband's name), placed a bet three months ago, but her husband died six months ago. So Walter returns to the beautiful and charming woman, and the two embrace. He tells her that Herbert's body was not found, and he suspects Herbert faked his own death. Paying a visit to a racetrack, Walter finds out that Herbert is very much alive, under another name, living below the border, applying his trade so skillfully. Herbert blackmails Walter to forget everything, including not saying anything to his wife. As Walter goes back to his car, Laura waits outside, fully aware of her husband's motives, and next time the lovers need money, she'll visit Herbert herself. Back at her apartment, the lovers find her husband holding them at gun-point. He recognized his cuff links on Walter's wrists. While trying to take the gun away from the old man, Walter gets shot and is taken to the doctor. After the examination, Walter realizes that both Laura and the money are gone.

Since tonight's story was an allegory, I offer this footnote to make everything clear. Walter represented youthful innocence, Mrs. Gild was unrequited love and of course Mr. Gild symbolized Mrs. Gild's husband. The following item could use many things, but a footnote is not one of them. When this is over, I shall flip back. (commercial break) *Since this program is on film and will probably be shown for many years to come, I should like to address my next remarks to those of you who are watching the show in the year 2000. Please write in at once and tell us what life is like, I'm quite curious. Until next week, good night.*

Trivia, etc. Although writer Victor Canning already had three filmed adaptations of his novels, this episode would mark the first of two Hitchcock-type associations. Later in 1976, Victor Canning's novel "The Rainbird Pattern" would serve as the basis for Hitchcock's final big-screen feature film, *Family Plot* (1976). Perry Lopez was credited as Julio Lopez in *Creature from the Black Lagoon* (1954). Thomas Wild also played a doctor in the next episode.

EPISODE #106   **"LAMB TO THE SLAUGHTER"**   Broadcast on April 13, 1958
    Rehearsed and filmed on February 18 – 19, 1958.
    Starring: Barbara Bel Geddes as Mary Maloney
    Harold J. Stone as Lieutenant Jack Noonan, chief inspector
    Allan Lane as Patrick Maloney   Ken Clark as Mike
    Robert C. Ross as the grocer   William Keene as a cop
    Thomas Wild as the doctor   Otto Waldis as a cop
    Teleplay written for *Alfred Hitchcock Presents* by Roald Dahl, based on his short story of the same name, originally published in the September 1953 issue of *Harper's*. Later reprinted in the April 1955 issue of *Ellery Queen's Mystery Magazine*. Subsequently collected in *Someone Like You* (Knopf, 1953; Secker & Warburg, 1954) and in *Tales of the Unexpected* (Michael Joseph, 1979; Vintage, 1980).
    Directed by Alfred Hitchcock.

(Supermarket where cop leaves after giving a Hitchcock a ticket) *He gave me this ticket for blocking an aisle during the rush-hour. I don't understand, I was in the slow lane. I'd just stopped a moment at the condiment shelf where the store's having a get-acquainted sale on low calorie calories. Tonight's play is not unrelated to this milieu. It is called "Lamb To The Slaughter." But before we see it, the store has asked that I direct your attention to their very best bargain.*

Story: After the many years Mary faithfully devoted to her husband, she goes into shock when he comes home from work one evening, revealing that he has fallen in love with another woman and plans to leave her. In retaliation, Mary pulls a frozen leg of lamb from the freezer and hits him over the head with it, killing him. Covering her tracks, Mary throws the leg into the oven and leaves for the grocery store. Buying a bag or two of food, she returns home. Dropping the bags as if she just discovered the murder, she then overturns and knocks over everything in the room, then phones the police. When the detectives arrive, she claims to have been at the store when her husband was killed, and found the house as it is. What baffles the police is the murder weapon, as there doesn't seem to be one. While they continue asking questions, and searching for clues, Mary almost over-cooks the leg of lamb, and being a good host, she asks the officers who haven't had a chance to eat, to consume the meal. In her present state, she couldn't possibly eat the meal now, and it would be a waste of meat if she has to throw it out. The officers gleefully appreciate the good meal, not realizing that they are actually consuming the murder weapon!

Well, that's the way the old meat ball bounces. As for Mary Maloney, she would have gone scot-free if she hadn't tried to do in her second husband the same way. Unfortunately, he was the forgetful type and had forgotten to plug in the freezer. The meat was as soft as jelly. Speaking of plugs, that is precisely what our sponsor wants to do for his product. After which I'll wheel back. (commercial break) *And now, ladies and gentlemen, those of us who work in television, have a technical term for this part of the program. We call it, "the end." Next week we should be back with another story.* (car horn honks) *I must be going, I can't risk another ticket. Good night.*

Trivia, etc. "You'd be mad to miss it!" read the advertisements. "This mad-cap Hitchcock-directed 'Conversation Piece,' starring Barbara Bel Geddes, is one of Hitchcock's all-time favorites with a real 'snapper' on the end. You *would* be mad to miss it!" Considered by many Hitchcock fans as one of the best episodes of the series – and certainly the most memorable – Barbara Bel Geddes plays the role of Mary to perfection, allowing the viewing audience to believe that she not only got away with murder, but justice was aptly served. Her third motion picture, *I Remember Mama* (1949), garnered her a nomination for Best Supporting Actress, although Hitchcock fans probably remember her most for portrayal of Marjorie Wood in Hitchcock's 1958 masterpiece, *Vertigo*.

"The biggest problems were always solved by Jimmy Allardice, with Hitch's closing comments," recalled Norman Lloyd. "There was at that time the requirement of retribution - in a program, if a person killed somebody or committed a theft or did anything unlawful, you had to have some form of retribution. So we used to do it by having Hitch do it - which, obviously, the audience never believed! For example, in 'Lamb to the Slaughter,' Barbara Bel Geddes kills her husband with a frozen leg of lamb. Then she puts it in the oven, cooks it and serves it to the police - who of course can never find the evidence, and she goes off scot-free. Now comes retribution: We don't do it in the story, but Hitch comes on and says, 'She remarried, and she got very upset with this new husband and decided to do away with him too. So she hit him over the head with the leg of lamb . . . but the freezer had gone on the blink and it hadn't frozen quite. It was a soft leg of lamb, and she was caught.' Who believed that? [No one.] We'd done the story. That's the way we'd get away with it."

Often credited with coining the term "Gremlin" during the second world war, Roald Dahl wrote many remarkable short stories, many of which were dramatized on *Alfred*

Hitchcock Presents. Dahl would later host his own short-lived television series, *Way Out!*, followed by *Tales of the Unexpected*.

The speed at which this episode was filmed was two full days, a quicker turnover than most Hitchcock episodes, which were completed in a usual three-day production cycle. "Hitch's methods for directing a television show were exactly the same as those he used for features," Norman Lloyd continued. "and he took enormous pride in doing these things very fast on a tight television schedule without going a moment over. I remember when he did 'Lamb to the Slaughter' and he finished on the nose at six o'clock quitting time, he turned around and said, 'There's your picture.' Then he looked at everybody as if to say, 'So don't come to me with any ideas that you need an extra hour or two for something else.' It was all in fun, but the message was clear: all of you had better be able to finish at six too."

Art Director John Lloyd recalled his Emmy nomination for his work on this particular episode. "I worked for MCA at the time the Hitchcock became a success, and I was an assistant with a gentleman that was an art director named Martin Obzina, and when he left I took over. I was the art director for maybe about five or six years. I did the episode, 'Lamb to the Slaughter' that Hitch was nominated for an award on. I was also nominated for an Emmy Award for that one too. The real technical challenges to make Hitchcock happy, if you want to be technical about it, is I suppose – was to just do the job without being asked anything. I was an art director for almost fifty years and it's hard to say what technical challenges came up. Hitchcock loved it when things ran smoothly. We knew what we were doing and he knew that and he relied on us to do our job, which we did. Color television was later one of the technical challenges, but we learned to overcome that."

Allan Lane, known to western fans as Allan 'Rocky' Lane, plays the quick but all-important role of Mary's husband, who was planning to leave her for another woman. Lane played Red Ryder on television for a brief time, and was the voice of Mr. Ed, the talking horse, on the popular television sitcom, *Mister Ed*.

EPISODE #107   **"FATAL FIGURES"**   Broadcast on April 20, 1958
    Starring: John McGiver as Harold Goames   Vivian Nathan as Margaret
    Ward Wood as Detective McBane   Nesdon Booth as the shopkeeper
    Teleplay written for *Alfred Hitchcock Presents* by Robert C. Dennis, based on the short story of the same name by Rick Edelstein, originally published in the March 1958 issue of *Mystery Digest*.
    Directed by Don Taylor.
    (calculator)   *Good evening telewatchers. I am about to demonstrate this amazing electronic brain. Uh, may I have the problem, please?* (girl walks over to hand Hitchcock paper) *Figures fascinate me . . . two plus two! Now we feed this problem into the machine and the answer will appear there . . . perhaps we should have started with something simpler.* (lady picks up plug) *Of course, would you please.* (she plugs machine in, and machine whistles) *As you can see it's almost human, and now for the problem. I think the answer is coming.* (think) *If this machine persists in these Do-It-Yourself suggestions, he may find himself replaced by a human being. Now while I tinker with this, suppose you watch tonight's play "Fatal Figures."*

Story: An incredibly bored bookkeeper picks up a copy of the latest Almanac to discover last year's crime statistics, and finds the publication, compelling reading. Deciding that a secret life of crime would provide a thrilling new experience, and keep him from just being a mere statistic, Harold attempts to steal the car belonging to the local town councilman to become among the 226,530 that has stolen a car. Overjoyed that he has made an impact (regardless of how minor) in the world, he decides to try his hand again, now performing theft and after stealing a bottle of perfume, he can change the figures from 63,197 to 63,198. To beat that, he continues with another crime, murder. As the perfect target for his killing he chooses his drab, dominating sister who lives with him. After Margaret dies of food poisoning (rat poison in the tea), Harold informs the police, figuring that he will achieve fame and notoriety through her death. But his plans fail when the police mistakenly decide that Margaret died of natural causes and it won't be accepted as murder number 7,125. Harold continues to explain how he killed her, and the police finally realize he is telling the truth. When asked why, Harold explains: "I guess it was mostly a matter of statistics, that's the only place in which I can make a mark." When Harold goes for his coat, to follow the men down to the police station, he notices that there had been 16,008 suicides during the past year, and decides that there should be one more.

I'm giving the brain one more chance. 3,137 multiplied by 38,915. Please, no help from the audience. While the brain digest the problem, see if you have an answer to the following, after which I hope you'll rejoin me. (commercial break) There's nothing difficult about mathematics. I found an answer in a few seconds. I'm now trying to get a problem to fit it. This is all now until next week, when we should be back with another story. Perhaps I should erase this so you can see the following show. Good night.

Trivia, etc. Rick Edelstein, who wrote, produced and directed *The Doctors, The Edge of Night, Starsky and Hutch, Sanford and Son, Charlie's Angels* and many other television programs, recalled the incidents that led up to this story: "It was a total serendipity. I wrote the story and sold it to a friend at *Mystery Digest,* and then he sent the galleys to Alfred Hitchcock. And then I got a check for three hundred dollars which now that I am in the Writers Guild, and having written for TV for fifteen years, I can see how I was ripped off and that was how that happened. I wrote the story, by the way, just as an argument with my wife. She said, 'You can't write,' and I said, 'Sure I can.' So I went upstairs and wrote a short story and showed it to her. She said it was shit but I showed it to a friend of mine who was a professional writer and he said, 'This is pretty good. Mind if I have it?' I said sure. I was just settling an argument with my wife and that was the first thing I ever wrote. The next thing you know, my friend gave it to this guy and they called me and said 'I want to buy it. I'll give you a hundred dollars for it.' I said okay. So he published it in *Mystery Digest* and sent the galleys to Alfred Hitchcock and I got a check for three hundred dollars – my friend may have gotten a check for much more, I don't know. I'm not sure if my wife saw the episode when it was broadcast. I know I did and I thought it was pretty good. In fact, the writer [Robert C. Dennis] did it tougher than me. The final outcome shows the guy putting a gun to his head and we hear the sound of the shot. I didn't. I ended the story with him reading suicide . . . but he went that one step further."

EPISODE #108   **"DEATH SENTENCE"**   Broadcast on April 27, 1958
        Starring: James Best as Norman Frayne
        Katharine Bard as Paula Frayne   Steve Brodie as Al Revenel
        Frank Gerstle as Walt Haney, chief of police
        Teleplay written for *Alfred Hitchcock Presents* by Joel Murcott, based on the short story of the same name by Miriam Allen de Ford, originally published in the May 1948 issue of *Ellery Queen's Mystery Magazine.* Subsequently collected in *The Theme is Murder* (Abelard-Schuman, 1967).
        Directed by Paul Henreid.
        (in the bathtub)   *Good evening. No, this is not an effort on our part to add sex to the program. I'm dressed for the party . . . a come-as-you-are party. This is what one gets for having a telephone in the bathroom. Well it could have been worse. I feel a bit like Cinderella. For I've been warned that I must positively leave the ball before low tide, and I can't afford to take chances. After all, I was once arrested for indecent exposure when I removed a Halloween mask. All of you, of course, are invited to the party. But remember: don't drop what you're doing, bring it along. But first we must greet the man who throws these weekly soirées, and who always manages to spoil the fun. Our dear host.*

224

Story: Twelve years ago Norman Frayne was a mere orphan who got himself involved in the death of a night watchman. Al Revenel took a plea bargain, claiming he shot the watchman in order to save Norm's life, and was sent behind bars for life. Out on parole now, Al visits his old friend to find Norman a successful realtor with his own business, one he inherited by marriage. Al wants Norm to pay what he owes him, $50,000. Paula Frayne has no knowledge about her husband's past, only that Norm has little confidence in himself running a business. Al gets his own room at the house and shows an interest in Paula. Walt, the Chief of police warns Norman that he should keep his eyes on Al. Norman says "We were kids together," but he fails to tell the officer the whole story. Talk soon starts spreading about town and Norm decides that the only way to solve his problem is to kill Al. Purchasing a few sticks of dynamite from the local hardware store, Norm sets the sticks in the motor of the car and then enters the house to confess his past to Paula. Through thick and thin, Paula says nothing happened between her and Al, and her love is still as strong as ever for Norm. Realizing he can't live with himself anymore, Norm locks his wife in the bedroom and goes out to start the car . . .

This is not part of the festivities. I found this bottle with a message in it, floating in the tub. It could be a plea for help from some castaway, or even a last note from the hero of tonight's saga. (reads the note) *This is certainly a sneaky way to get a message in. It's from big brother again. I'll just put some soap on the floor and slip back at the conclusion of his remarks.* (commercial break; now with bathrobe on) *Well, the evening wasn't a total loss. For I got my back washed and also received a very good job offer. An Italian actress needs a stuntman to take a bubble bath for her in her next picture. I was hired when it was discovered that the actress and I had the same measurements. In different places, of course. I shall be finished in time for next week's program. Until then, good night.*

EPISODE #109   **"THE FESTIVE SEASON"**   Broadcast on May 4, 1958
    Starring: Carmen Mathews as Celia   Edmon Ryan as John Benson
    Richard Waring as Charlie Boerum   Benny Baker as the bartender
    Teleplay written for *Alfred Hitchcock Presents* by James P. Cavanagh, based on the Stanley Ellin short story "Death on Christmas Eve," originally published in the January 1950 issue of *Ellery Queen's Mystery Magazine*. Subsequently collected in *Mystery Stories* (Simon & Schuster, 1956; Boardman, 1957) and in *The Specialty of the House and Other Stories* (Mysterious Press, 1979).
    Directed by Arthur Hiller.
    (Hitchcock watching himself on TV) "Good evening and thank you for allowing me to come into your living room. The miracle of electronics makes many new pleasures possible." (Hitchcock now turns to the audience and says the same as the TV) *I frequently watch television, it takes my mind off my work. You aren't interrupting, however, for I seldom pay much attention to this part of the program. It's really quite superfluous. I find I can miss it entirely and still know what the commercial is all about. I must say I sometimes find myself fascinated by the amazing ego of this man. He speaks as though he were certain we were all sitting here with ears akimbo, listening to his every word. Let's listen to what he's saying now.* (Hitchcock turns back to the TV) "But first we have an important announcement. My sponsor . . ." *The way he bows and scrapes before the sponsor, it's disgusting. He's obviously a relative. Shhhhh.* ". . . and expensive message."

    Story: John Benson, the family attorney, pays a Christmas Eve visit to Charlie Boerum, an old friend. Celia, Charlie's sister, lives in the same house, but neither of the two talk to each other. You see, Charlie feels his wife's death was Celia's fault, but she confesses that Charlie's wife fell down a flight a stairs by accident, she just happened to be in the same house at the time. John explains to Charlie that the inquest ruled Jessie's death "accidental" and Celia is not to blame. No evidence found to say otherwise. But Charlie still insists that

Celia hated Jessie, and she did his wife in. Like their mother before her, she won't let him go his own way. Charlie shows John an ordinary ball or chord he found in Celia's bedroom, and pieces together a theory of Celia using it to trip his wife down the stairs. Charlie even attempts to do the same to his sister. but Celia only gets bruised up a little. Charlie cries that he'll try it again, and keep trying until his wife's death is avenged. Maybe not tonight, but one of these days. John leaves the Boerum residence and heading back home, stops at a tavern and orders the usual. Chatting with the bartender, John says the siblings have been like this for two decades, and the murder of Charlie's wife was exactly twenty years ago tonight on Christmas Eve!

"... after that, I think you must agree. . ." *That was a very charming mime. I don't think we should be bothered with much more by our syncopanthic friend. I have a remote control device which eliminates those portions of a program you don't wish to hear.* (a bomb box with a lever on top) *Just a moment, here's the part I never miss.* (commercial break) ". . . our sponsor goes to keep you amused . . ." *This remote control device is second hand, but is in excellent condition. It belonged to a little old lady in Pasadena, a widow who only used it once.* ". . . please understand. . ." *Ah, there is that obnoxious fellow again.* ". . . until next week, good night." (boom!)

EPISODE #110 **"LISTEN, LISTEN . . . . . !"** Broadcast on May 11, 1958
        Starring: Edgar Stehli as Herbert Johnson
        Adam Williams as Lieutenant King

Dayton Lummis as Sergeant Oliver	Baynes Barron as Charlie, the bartender
Robert Herrman as Mr. Beekman	Jackie Loughery as the bar girl
Rusty Lane as Father Rafferty	Edith Evanson as Mrs. Johnson
Kitty Kelly as Miss Andrews, the housekeeper	Rad Fulton as the young man
Elsie Baker as the older woman	

        Teleplay written for *Alfred Hitchcock Presents* by Bernard C. Schoenfeld, based on the short story by R.E. Kendall, originally published in the June 1947 issue of *Ellery Queen's Mystery Magazine*. Subsequently anthologized in *The Queen's Awards, 1947*, ed. Ellery Queen (Little Brown, 1947).
        Directed by Don Taylor.
        (Hitchcock plays a record) *Good evening ladies and gentlemen. I hope you'll excuse the use of this mechanical device. But I have a mild case of laryngitis, and I don't wish to strain my voice. Tonight's story is in . . .*(skip) *Tonight's story is in . . .* (skip) *Tonight's story is in . . .* (Hitchcock picks up needle and places down again) *Good evening ladies and gentlemen. I hope you'll excuse this broken record, but it was improperly handled. Tonight's play is called, "Listen, Listen."* (skip) *"Listen, Listen"* (skip) *"Listen, Listen."* (Hitchcock corrects the record again) *But "Listen, Listen" really is the name of the story. "Listen, Listen"* (skip) *"Listen, Listen"* (skip) *"Listen –"* (Hitchcock turns it off and whispers the rest) *I think we have made that point quite clear. Now to save my voice, I think we shall indulge in some mental telepathy. Look at the expression on my face and see if you can tell, what is coming next.*

        Story: An old man named Herbert Johnson pays a visit to the police station, asking if the police are satisfied with the solution of the recent stocking murders. The sergeant says they have their killer. The old man suggests that the third murder, that of the Jamison girl, might not have been the work of the actual killer, but rather a copycat on the loose, having heard about the first two murders in the paper. The sergeant, not interested in another theory from a raving crackpot, sends him to the Eastern Precinct, where Johnson again presents his theory. There were three victims, young girls, all strangled with a stocking, and the letter "A" smeared on their forehead with gold lipstick. Herbert suggests that the third murder was done by a copycat killer, but again he is thrown out. A newspaper reporter won't listen to Herbert's story either, so as a last resort, the old man visits a church where he tells his story to Father Rafferty. The Father insists that the police wouldn't make a mistake, and suggests

Herbert go home to rest for the evening. Returning home, Herbert's wife fixes him a hot cup of soup. Herbert cries at the table, saying they wouldn't listen, nor will they ever listen. His wife smirks at the suggestion, revealing a pair of stockings and lipstick in the kitchen drawer.

(Hitchcock whispers) *To speak and not be heard, that is a frustrating fate. It probably accounts for the strange behavior of our sponsor. So for the next minute, pay strict attention, lest he become more neurotic than he is. I shall see you in sixty seconds.* (commercial break) (Hitchcock points to his throat, cups both ears one at a time, circles in the air, and grasps his hands in cheer when the camera starts to pan away.)

Trivia, etc. Baynes Barron was also the taxi driver in Hitchcock's *North by Northwest* (1959), the one who drove Cary Grant to the United Nations. Adam Williams was one of James Mason's henchmen, Valerian, who attempted on more than one occasion to kill Grant in *North by Northwest* (1959).

EPISODE #111 **"POST MORTEM"** Broadcast on May 18, 1958
  Starring: Steve Forrest as Stephen "Steve" Archer
  Joanna Moore as Judy Archer   James Gregory as Mr. Westcott
  Edgar Peterson as the first reporter   David Fresco as the second reporter
  Fred Robbins as the third reporter   Roscoe Ates as the undertaker
  Patrick Martin as the Sergeant
  Teleplay written for *Alfred Hitchcock Presents* by Robert C. Dennis, based on the short story of the same name by Cornell Woolrich, originally published in the April 1940 issue of *Black Mask.* Subsequently collected in *Rear Window and Four Short Novels* (Ballantine, 1984).
  Directed by Arthur Hiller.
  (standing behind a basement of plants, lamps, gardenspade) *Good evening members of the garden club. I have been asked to reveal some of my horticulture secrets. First and foremost I recommend plenty of sunshine. I think it is shameful the way some plants are allowed to loaf all night, when they could be growing. Of course, the lamp has other uses. It also comes with a five-foot eight-inch motor driven spit, a basting brush and a gallon of sun tan lotion. This evening's entertainment well suits this sunny and bucolic atmosphere. It is called "Post Mortem." It begins quicker than you can say...*

Story: Blonde-haired Judy Archer learns from reporters that her recently-deceased husband, Harry Meade, who died six months ago from a heart attack, was the winner of an Irish Sweepstakes ticket, worth $133,000! When Steve, her newly married husband, arrives home, she tells him the good news. The problem is that the ticket was in the pocket of one of Harry's well-tailored suits, the same one he happened to be buried in. Her husband won't have anything to do with it, so when Steve leaves for Philadelphia on business, Judy authorizes a digging in the Shady Rest Cemetery. There, a man introduces himself as Mr. Wescott of the Daily Bulletin, and an hour later, hands her the winning ticket. When Steve returns, Judy shows him the ticket, which again makes him upset. A few days later, Steve goes into the bathroom and purposely drops an electric fan into the bathtub, which causes Judy to scream and wiggle in shock. Running downstairs with the ticket, Steve falls into the long arm of the law. Westcott, you see is an insurance investigator and Steve had Harry poisoned, so he could marry Judy and collect on her life insurance policy. When the ticket came into her possession, her life became the new object of Steve's murderous ways. Judy comes down in a bathrobe and takes the ticket back, alive courtesy of Westcott who pulled a fuse just in time.

You can see how effective the lamp is. It looks as though I should turn off the lamp. I shall do so following the following. (commercial break) (Hitchcock looks to have grown a compared to the flower table) *I'd better be off. In case the lamp does something to me. I'll be back next week with another story. Until then, good night.*

Trivia, etc. Throughout the third, fourth and fifth season of *Alfred Hitchcock Presents*, a shop named Beckman supplied the furs required for the actors to wear in many of the episodes. This episode, however, actually had the furs supplied by Teitelbaum in Beverly Hills. David Fresco made his first of eight appearances on *Alfred Hitchcock Presents*, and four more on *The Alfred Hitchcock Hour*, which made Fresco appear in more episodes than any other actor.

EPISODE #112   **"THE CROCODILE CASE"**   Broadcast on May 25, 1958
    Starring: Denholm Elliott as Jack Lyons
    Hazel Court as Phyllis Chaundry   John Alderson as Superintendent Carslake
    Pat Hitchcock as Adie, Phyllis' sister
    A. E. Gould-Porter as Arthur Chaundry   Dan Sheridan as a police officer
    Frederic Worlock as Dan Mence   Laurence Conroy as a police officer
    Teleplay written for *Alfred Hitchcock Presents* by Robert C. Dennis, based on the short story of the same name by Roy Vickers, originally published in the March 1949 issue of *Ellery Queen's Mystery Magazine*. Subsequently collected in *Murder Will Out* (Faber, 1950; Detective Book Club, 1954) and in *Best Detective Stories of Roy Vickers* (Faber, 1965), as "The Crocodile Dressing-Case."
    Directed by Don Taylor.
    (projector screen, Hitchcock's voice is dubbed)   *Good evening. I can tell by the rude noises you are making, that you are impatient to see our film. However, there will be a slight delay. Is there a barber in the house? If there is, will he please report to the projection booth? Our projectionist seems to have caught his moustache in a sprocket. Of course, it could have been worse. The popcorn machine might have broken down. As you know, our theatre spares no expense to make you television addicts feel at home. Our movies are the oldest that money can buy. And tonight as a special attraction we shall present some television commercials. I knew you'd like that. They will be injected at various points during our picture to keep you from getting too engrossed in the story. I understand they're very good at relieving tensions, and furnishing comic relief. And now if you will quiet down, we shall begin our program.*

Story: Jack Lyons has fallen in love with a married woman named Phyllis, and decides to kill her husband so nothing could stand between them. Since no one saw Jack leave the party, he cleverly sneaks out for a spell, finds Arthur on the side of the road, kills him, and then returns to the party completely unnoticed. Jack offers Phyllis a ride home in front of witnesses, and explains to her later how he did it. When the police arrive at the Chaundry residence, Phyllis starts the crying act, and describes a crocodile dressing case that her husband was carrying with him, never found at the crime scene. For over a year the two love-birds spend time trying to forget the murder and Phyllis pays numerous visits to Scotland Yard asking whether or not her crocodile case has yet been found. So much so that Jack and Phyllis keep getting into arguments, Jack fearing that Phyllis might spoil everything. Unfortunately, when the police do investigate and ask questions, Lyons is a bit too helpful. He identifies a dressing case recently found and ends up giving them information that only the murderer could know.

And now for the information of you youngsters who were slashing the upholstery and tearing out the seats during the dénouement, I would like to tidy up one of the story's loose ends. Phyllis Chaundry, she was arrested as an accessory, and she and her husband Jack both went to prison. An inspiring example of togetherness. (commercial break) I'm sure you'll be interested in knowing that the sound track of the three commercials seen tonight, are available in the album "Music to Cook Three Minute Eggs By." The album is available in all speeds, including reverse, as well as in Fi. Both Hi and Lo. Next week we shall have a completely new attraction. As well as new seats and fresh popcorn. Good night.

Trivia, etc. "I did the TV series *Dick and the Duchess*, which we did in England, and then CBS brought me to America, where I did several episodes of the Alfred Hitchcock TV series," said Hazel Court. "I did four of those - in fact, my present husband, Don Taylor, was the director of the first episode I did, which was called 'The Crocodile Case.' So I was doing a lot of going back and forth. Yes, I knew him [Hitchcock] well, and I am also great friends with Patricia Hitchcock, who is his daughter. Of course, Hitch never cared much about actors, it was always the camera, you know. So you were always fighting that. But he was fun - he was a great storyteller and a very funny man."

John Alderson also played a detective in Hitchcock's *To Catch a Thief* (1956). During Hitchcock's closing remarks, the name "Jack" was dubbed in, suggesting that at the time his hosting was filmed, a name was not yet given (or changed since) for the main character.

EPISODE #113   **"DIP IN THE POOL"**   Broadcast on June 1, 1958
Rehearsed and filmed on April 15 – 16, 1958.

Starring: Keenan Wynn as William Botibol	Fay Wray as Mrs. Renshaw
Philip Bourneuf as Mr. Renshaw	Louise Platt as Mrs. Ethel Botibol
Doreen Lang as Emily	Ralph Clanton as the ship's purser
Doris Lloyd as Emily's companion	Ashley Cowan as a boat employee
Owen Cunningham as the auctioneer	Barry Harvey as the steward
Michael Hadlow as the bidder on 505 miles	
Margaret Curtis as a passenger on boat	
Judith Brian as a passenger on boat	William Hughes as a boat employee

Teleplay written for *Alfred Hitchcock Presents* by Robert C. Dennis, based on the short story of the same name by Roald Dahl, originally published in the January 19, 1952 issue of *The New Yorker*. Subsequently collected in *Someone Like You* (Knopf, 1953; Secker & Warburg, 1954) and in *Tales of the Unexpected* (Michael Joseph, 1979; Vintage, 1980).

Directed by Alfred Hitchcock.

(on a cruise boat) *Oh good evening. I'm on vacation from the rigors of television and coming to you by remote pickup. Our cameras are quite ordinary, but they are fastened to the longest extension cords in history. However, I find this vacation quite exhausting. Shuffleboard simply cannot be played from the prone position. Incidently, the Captain informs me, that changing channels is not only fool-hardy but also extremely dangerous. So I don't believe you ought to try it. I understand that in my absense you are to see a play based on the story "Dip in the Pool." Having said that, I now return you to our studios.* (moves in the chair and pulls a blanket over and continues to read)

Story: On board an Atlantic cruise ship, William and Ethel Botibol debate how they won't have any money left when their vacation comes to an end. The solution presents itself in the form of Mr. and Mrs. Renshaw. Mr. Renshaw explains a betting pool based on how far the ship travels in twenty-four hours, and Botibol agrees to play the game. Since the bets are based on the Captain's estimate of the distance they will cover, Botibol bases his wager on his knowledge of an upcoming storm that will slow down the ship. Unfortunately, he learns only the day after that they missed the storm and the ship is able to speed up. Because of all the money he has wagered, Botibol puts together a plan to jump overboard with a witness that will cry loud enough, and surely cause the ship to stop and pick him up. All of which will take up much time and delay the trip, enabling him to win the bet. Botibol's scheme, however, goes down the drain after he jumps overboard and the witness doesn't utter a word to anyone. He didn't know when he picked her for a witness that she is mentally incompetent. No one will believe the woman, even when she tells her companion.

You will be pleased to know that our story has a happy ending. The ship was delayed by engine-trouble so that Mr. Botibol won the pool. Regrettably, Mr. Botibol was not there to enjoy the money, but his wife and her second husband had a very good time with it. Our voyage should be over in a few minutes but we are approaching rough water. I think

I shall move nearer the railing. You stay here however, for I shall weave back in just one minute. (commercial break) *That was worse than I expected. And to add insult to injury, the captain has asked me to get off the ship. He claims I'm tipping it over. It's absurd of course, but all the passengers are with him. And it's jump or be pushed. So until next week, bon voyage.*

Trivia, etc. Loaded with "in-jokes," galore, this episode cries for repeated viewing. Most people are aware that Hitchcock loved making on-screen cameos in his theatrical features, but one movie posed a challenge for him. In 1944, the setting for *Lifeboat* was filmed in a lifeboat, and therefore, Hitchcock realized a problem in making a cameo appearance in the movie. He found a solution by appearing in a weight-loss advertisement, on a newspaper one of the derelicts read. In a similar fashion (since this episode also takes place on the seas) Hitchcock himself is actually reading a copy of an *Alfred Hitchcock's Mystery Magazine*, which features a front cover photo of Hitchcock himself! The lifepreserver hanging on the railing, which Hitchcock later jumps over, labels the ship as the S.S. Hitchcock.

With an almost full-English cast, Judith Brian and Michael Hadlow both made previous appearances in the 1953 Universal film, *Abbott and Costello Meet Dr. Jekyll and Mr. Hyde*. Ashley Cowan and Michael Hadlow, both of who played passengers on board the vessel, also played passengers in the 20th Century-Fox movie, *Titanic* (1953). Michael Hadlow had already worked under Hitchcock's direction, having played one of the Monaco Policemen in *To Catch a Thief* (1955). As for "Dip in the Pool," this same Roald Dahl short story was previously dramatized on the television series *Danger*, on March 2, 1954 under the full title, "A Dip in the Pool." Harry Townes played the lead, Albert Hubbell wrote the script for the earlier adaptation.

Doreen Lang, who witnesses Botibol's dive, played several roles for Hitchcock, including Thornhill's secretary at the beginning of *North by Northwest* (1959), as Ann James in *The Wrong Man* (1956) and as the concerned mother in the diner in *The Birds* (1963).

EPISODE #114 **"THE SAFE PLACE"** Broadcast on June 8, 1958
    Starring: Robert H. Harris as George Piper
    Joanne Linville as Miss Milly Mannis   Phillip Pine as Victor Manette
    Jerry Paris as Fred Piper   Wendell Holmes as Henry Farnsworth
    Robert Karnes as Sergeant Henderson   Joel Mondeaux as Mr. Martinson
    Teleplay written for *Alfred Hitchcock Presents* by Michael Hogan, based on a story by Jan Wilson.
    Directed by James Neilson.
    (as a surgeon with two other surgeons and a woman in a magician's box) *Good evening interns, patients and curiosity seekers. One of the marvels of television is its educational value. A few years ago, only a handful of people could have witnessed this rare and delicate operation. Now because of television, millions may witness this event, including the subject herself. For we are going to present her with a film of tonight's proceedings. Together with a projector, to say nothing of a beautiful charm bracelet. Each charm to represent a phase of the operation with replicas of each organ removed. Incidentally we call our program, "This is Your . . ." A sentence we don't finish until we see how the operation turns out. And now gentlemen, you may make the incision.* (the two surgeons start sawing the box in half) *Stop. This is a dramatization.* (men continue) *Just a moment. Just a moment. We forgot the anaesthetic. However, I have something here that will put anyone to sleep in just sixty seconds.*

Story: George Piper has been looking toward a successful retirement plan, although his bank teller job at the Amsterdam Trust Company doesn't provide much money to invest with. George's brother, Fred, tries to talk him into embezzling money from the bank, but George gets a better idea. George devises a way of stealing the $15,000 withdrawal from a bank client who withdraws that much every week, and known to gamble it away.

George figures he could pay a visit to the client, rob him of the money, shoot the gambler so there's no witnesses, and then hide the $15,000 in the false bottom under his drawer. George pulls off the plan flawlessly. Afterwards, George is questioned by the police but the law decides he wasn't involved, and dismiss any ideas they had. Unfortunately, George's boss is in line of a Vice-President promotion and in fear of bad publicity, he fires his faithful teller. Before George gets the time to empty his drawer, the manager asks for George's cash drawer key to give it to his replacement.

I can now report that the operation was a huge success. Our patient now has what she wanted – perfect measures. 36 – 0 – 36. So much for Operation: Operation. Now a word from you-know-who, after which I shall toddle back. (commercial break) *I'm sorry to say that after further consideration, the girl on whom we operated, became unhappy with the results. She learned that two cannot live as cheaply as one. For one thing she had to buy a sidecar for her motorcycle, things like that. So while she's pulling herself together, I would like to say that I shall be back next week with another play. Until then, good night.*

EPISODE #115   **"THE CANARY SEDAN"**   Broadcast on June 15, 1958
Starring: Jessica Tandy as Laura, Mrs. James St. George Bernard Bowlby
Murray Matheson as Mr. James St. George Bernard Bowlby

Gavin Muir as Mr. Thompson	Patrick Westwood as Mason
Weaver Levy as Chang, the chauffeur	Barry Harvey as the steward
Barry Bernard as the bartender	Leonard Strong as man at ouija board
Owen Cunningham as Mr. Adams	Tetsu Komai as the elderly Chinese man
James B. Leong as Mr. Nixon, the car salesman	

Teleplay written for *Alfred Hitchcock Presents* by Stirling Silliphant, based on the short story "The Buick Saloon," by Ann Bridge, which appeared in the publication, *50 Masterpieces of Mystery* (Odhams, 1935).
Directed by Robert Stevens.
(wiping dust off television screen) *Good evening ladies and please don't adjust your sets. I think the picture tube needs . . . little dusting.* (genie appears – Hitch's head) "What is your wish O Master?" *Who are you?* "I'm Alfred, the genie of the lamp." *Wow, my name is Alfred too.* "Why is it Master, that when you can have any wish you desire, you prefer small talk." *Any wish I desire?* "If you want me rub the lamp." *How long have you been in that tube?* "Master, you have a mania for the unimportant. I have been there for years. No one ever dusts and whoever heard of a genie conjured up by a vacuum cleaner? And now master, the wish, and remember the words of Allah. Think big." *But what I want is priceless.* "Nothing is too great, diamonds, rubies." *This would be too much to ask.* "Master, the wish, the wish." *Give me a commercial, give me a commercial.*

Story: Mrs. Bowlby, a lonely woman with psychic abilities, arrives in Hong Kong where her husband is in town for business. Wanting his wife to feel at home, he sends her to a local shop where she buys a black sedan, and hires a chauffeur. She mentions to the dealer that instead of a black car, maybe she'd like it a little better if it were in a lighter color, perhaps canary yellow, a statement that astonishes the man, who explains that the sedan had been canary yellow before the new paint job. In the back of the car Mrs. Bowlby hears the voice of a woman passionately talking to her lover, Jacques, which apparently ended in tragedy. After hearing about the love affair, she wishes her own marriage provided such passion, but her very proper and businesslike husband will have none of it. When she finally tracks down the resting place of the dead woman who once owned the sedan, she is shocked to see that the tombstone contains a poem that ends with the initials of the woman and Mr. Bowlby!

"Alfred, don't rub so hard." Why don't you appear? I have two more wishes coming. "I think I know what you want. But I don't care to be there to see it, then you wish and it will be granted." Naturally I would get a fastidious genie. Ladies and gentlemen, I present a rare and priceless gift, a television commercial, after which I shall take my leave until next week. (commercial break) *"I have already granted the little man his third wish, which was to leave you until next week. Granting wishes is easier two at a time. I save on overhead. Now that you know how to summon me, we shall probably be seeing more of each other. Well, don't just sit there, get the dust cloth."*

EPISODE #116   **"THE IMPROMPTU MURDER"**   Broadcast on June 22, 1958
      Starring: Hume Cronyn as Henry Dow
      Robert Douglas as Inspector Charles Tarrang

Valerie Cossart as Mary Dow	Doris Lloyd as Miss Wilkinson
David Frankham as Holson	George Pelling as the gateman
Mollie Glessing as Lucy, the maid	Frederic Worlock as Barkley, the farmer
Gwen Watts as Mrs. Barrett	Reggie Dvorak as carriage driver

      Teleplay written for *Alfred Hitchcock Presents* by Francis Cockrell, and based on the short story by Roy Vickers, originally published in the October 1950 issue of *Ellery Queen's Mystery Magazine*.
      Directed by Paul Henreid.
      (with 3 ladies and policeman)   *Good evening, ladies and gentlemen. I must interrupt this program to make a grave announcement. The invasion from Mars is already underway. I repeat, the invasion from Mars is already underway. Martians have actually landed and are among us. We have captured some of them and will show them to you now, so that you can know your enemy. You may have seen some of these creatures in your city. They have rounded backs, a body that looks like a tired balloon, pointed red feet with no toes and long colored legs. Here are the prisoners we have taken so far.* (three women) *This one was captured in broad daylight at the Sans Souci Canasta Club. Notice the needle point heel, probably lethal. The uniform seems to have been designed so that we can't tell which way this one's going. Very deceptive. Notice the napsack and the space for weapon storage, and look at the shoes. Obviously they were never designed for the human foot. And here we have the most dangerous type. Notice the high oblong head and the cloche helmet. The creature can, at a moments notice, inflate this for a fast return to Mars.* (tells officer) *Take them to our leader. And now, speaking of our beloved leader. I feel it is indeed fitting and proper. That in this moment of grave world wide danger, he giveth one of his one minute inspirational talks.*

      Story: Swallowsbath, England 1916. An attorney, Henry Dow, soon to be in line for mayor of the community, invites Miss Wilkinson, a woman who wants to withdraw her capital from his firm, to stay with him and his sister Marjorie. When he learns that she indeed has a large sum of money on her and she intends to use it to invest in her brother's factory, Henry murders her and buries her body under a slab of stone near the river. He won't have to pay out if she's not around to withdraw. Henry later has to take part in the ceremony of dedicating a bridge, but it is interrupted when a body is seen floating in the river, probably washed up as a result of the recent rains. Later in the afternoon, Henry is asked to come down to the morgue to identify the female as the missing Miss Wilkinson, but he doesn't really look at the body and claims it's not her. All would be as fitting if it wasn't for the inquisitive Inspector, who badgers Henry till the murderer cracks and confesses that he is the murderer - a mistake on his part, since Miss Wilkinson's brother insists the body they found in the river is not his sister!

      So much for the strange case of Henry Dow. For the next minute I intend to step over to the stockade and interrogate our prisoners. After which I'll buzz back. (commercial break) *I wish to state categorically that all the statements made previously were facetious,*

that no invasion from Mars is taking place and that the attractive costumes you see on these lovely earthlings are the final step in a gradual evolution toward the ultimate in beauty. I shall be back . . . I shall be back next week with another story. Until then, good night.

Trivia, etc. Robert Douglas would later produce and direct episodes of *The Alfred Hitchcock Hour.*

**Hume Cronyn and Doris Lloyd in "The Impromptu Murder"
(Photo courtesy of Photofest)**

EPISODE #117   **"LITTLE WHITE FROCK"**   Broadcast on June 29, 1958
Starring: Herbert Marshall as Colin Breitner

Julie Adams as Carol Longsworth	Tom Helmore as Adam Longsworth
Jacqueline Mayo as Lila Gordon	Roy Dean as Terry Bane
Bartlett Robinson as Mr. Robinson	Edwin Jerome as Mr. Ambrose
Otto Waldis as Mr. Koslow	Kitty Kelly as Marie, the maid
Joe Hamilton as the stage man	

Teleplay written for *Alfred Hitchcock Presents* by Stirling Silliphant, based on the short story of the same name by Stacey Aumonier, collected in *The Love-a-Duck and Other Stories* (Hutchinson, 1921).

Directed by Herschel Daugherty.

(putting weights in a coffin; wearing a moustache) *Good evening. I was just putting weights in this box of trash so it will sink quickly. I'm about to throw it into the river. Perhaps I should explain why I'm here. Mr. Hitchcock is indisposed this evening. As a matter of fact, we can't find him anywhere. I'm quite worried. I wouldn't want anything to happen to him. You see I'm his brother and sole heir. Of course we mustn't let brother Alfred's absence interfere with the evening's entertainment. I'm sure he would want it that way. I have his notes. The second item on the agenda is a drama entitled "Little White*

Frock." As for the first item he says . . ., I know my brother thinks I'm rather dull and somewhat of a prude, but this language is much too frank for television. I don't know about you, but I'm very curious about anything that would provoke such language. Uh . . . Shall we have a go at it?

Story: Adam and Carol Longsworth are given an invitation to the home of an expired actor, Colin Breitner. Since Adam is producing a new play he suspects Colin, of hitting him up for a part. Adam believes that all they'll see is faded photographs and old stage review clippings. Carol, recalling how they too were once broke, convinces her husband to accept the invitation. After a nice dinner, the three retreat to the lounge to drink and chat. Colin claims he didn't ask them over to get another role, but to announce that he's retiring from the stage. The old man tells them a tragic story about losing the girl of his dreams, actress Lila Gordon, who played Desdemona on his earliest stage production of Shakespeare's *Othello*. He once proposed to her but she turned him down. Years later on her deathbed, Lila asked Colin for a last request. She wanted Colin to bring a little frock to a little ten-year-old girl. When he returned to say the little girl didn't want it, Lila had died. The story touches the Longsworth's hearts but all is not as it seems. Marie. Colin's maid, comes in to retrieve her niece's dress and Adam realizes that the whole story was a complete lie. But Colin had presented it so realistically that he accomplishes his task, and gets the job.

(Hitchcock still with box) *Now I believe it is time for another of those splended little commercial messages, which my uncouth brother detests so, but which I like very much. I shall be back following . . .* (lid to box opens and he fights the lid) *As I was saying, I shall be back in a moment.* (commercial break) (Hitchcock cementing floor) *Oh, good evening. I don't believe my brother will be bothering you anymore. Oh, he was a nice enough fellow if he just hadn't been such a stickler for form. He was that way to the end. The last thing I heard him say was, "Really Alfred, with an axe?" Next week we shall have another story and I promise to be here on time. Until then, good night.*

Trivia, etc. Herbert Marshall made his second appearance on the program *Alfred Hitchcock Presents* in this charming little tale of an actor striving to keep his good name. "I think I did make real tears as I recall!" laughed Julie Adams. "Herbert Marshall was an utterly charming man. He was very quiet and professional, an utter gentleman just as one would expect from him, and that wonderful seasoned veteran quality about him that is so attractive and so overwhelming, that you know when you work with people who are so skilled and done so much film work." Having played Sir John Menier in Alfred Hitchcock's *Murder!* (1930) and Stephen Fisher in *Foreign Correspondent* (1940), Marshall actually kept a secret of his own during much of his acting career. Shortly after serving his Majesty's Army during World War I, Marshall lost a leg in action, and had it replaced with a prosthetic limb. He continued his acting career (even during this episode) without making the loss apparent.

SUMMER RERUNS

The summer of 1958 consisted entirely of third-season episodes. Two directed by Alfred Hitchcock and the Emmy-Award winning "The Glass Eye" closed the summer season.

July 6, 1958 "Mail Order Prophet"
July 13, 1958 "The Perfect Crime"
July 20, 1958
    "The Right Kind of House"
July 27, 1958 "Bull in a China Shop"
August 3, 1958 "Last Request"
August 10, 1958
    "The Impromptu Murder"

August 17, 1958 "The Motive"
August 24, 1958 "The Foghorn"
August 31, 1958 "Little White Frock"
September 7, 1958 "Disappearing Trick"
September 14, 1958 "Dip in the Pool"
September 21, 1958 "The Glass Eye"
September 28, 1958
    "Lamb to the Slaughter"

SEASON FOUR - (36 episodes)

SELECTED PRODUCTION CREDITS:
Art Directors: John J. Lloyd and Arthur Lonergan
Assistant Directors: James H. Brown, Charles S. Gould, Hilton A. Green,
Ronnie Rondell, William Sheldon, Abby Singer and Dolph M. Zimmer
Associate Producer: Norman Lloyd
Costume Supervisor: Vincent Dee
Directors of Photography: Ernest Haller, a.s.c., Lionel Lindon, a.s.c.,
John L. Russell, a.s.c. and John F. Warren, a.s.c.
Editorial Supervisor: Richard G. Wray, a.c.e.
Film Editor: Edward W. Williams, a.c.e.
Furs supplied by Beckman in Beverly Hills, California.
Hair Stylist: Florence Bush
Makeup Artists: Jack Barron, Bob Dawn and Leo Lotito, Jr.
Music Supervisor: Frederick Herbert
Produced by Joan Harrison.
Set Decorators: John McCarthy, George Milo, Perry Murdock and James S. Redd
Sound: Stephen J. Bass, Earl Crain, Jr., John C. Grubb and William Lynch
A Shamley Production.
Filmed at Revue Studios in Hollywood, California, in association with MCA-TV,
executive distributor for Shamley Productions, Inc.
Broadcast Sunday over CBS-TV, 9:30 - 10 p.m., EST. Sponsored by Bristol-Myers.

EPISODE #118 **"POISON"** Broadcast on October 5, 1958
Rehearsed and filmed on August 21 – 22, 1958.
Starring: Wendell Corey as Timber Woods   James Donald as Harry Pope
Arnold Moss as Dr. Ganderbai   Weaver Levy as the Malayan houseboy
Teleplay written for *Alfred Hitchcock Presents* by Casey Robinson, based on the
short story of the same name by Roald Dahl, originally published in the June 5, 1950 issue of
Collier's. Subsequently collected in *Someone Like You* (Knopf, 1953; Secker & Warburg,
1954) and in *More Tales of the Unexpected* (Michael Joseph, 1980; Penguin, 1980).
Directed by Alfred Hitchcock.
(snake in pocket) *Good evening. Here we are in orbit once again. Most of
tonight's program will be taken up with a story called "Poison." (zzz) A rattlesnake. It's a
new warning device, I've instituted to sound an alarm when a pickpocket is at work. It comes
in several sizes, including very small ones for ladies' purses. (zzzz. . .) He's very alert. This
is far superior to ordinary burglar alarms for if the thief is foolhardy enough to put his hand
in the pocket . . . There are a few bugs in it. Once when a thief put his hand in my pocket,
the snake became confused and struck in the wrong direction. The doctor had to put a
tourniquet around my stomach. Unfortunately that proved to be the wrong stomach. It was
the snake who died. I see that it is now what my sponsor calls. . . high time. And here is
what he thinks it is high time for.*

Alternate narrative:
(snake in pocket) *Good evening. Here we are in orbit once again. Most of
tonight's program will be taken up with a story called "Poison." (zzz) A rattlesnake. It's a
new warning device, I've instituted to sound an alarm when a pickpocket is at work. It comes
in several sizes, including very small ones for ladies' purses. (zzzz. . .) He's very alert. This
is far superior to ordinary burglar alarms for if the thief is foolhardy enough to put his hand
in the pocket . . . There are a few bugs in it. Once when a thief put his hand in my pocket,
the snake became confused and struck in the wrong direction. The doctor had to put a
tourniquet around my stomach. Unfortunately that proved to be the wrong stomach. It was
the snake who died.*

Story: In the southern country of Malaya, Harry Pope, an alcoholic trying to dry up, whispers for help from his bed. His business partner, Timber Woods, enters the room and asks what the problem is. Harry has suspicions that a krait curled up underneath the bed sheets and is presently sleeping on his stomach. One of the most poisonous snakes in the country – a krait bite will kill its victim in minutes. It's only after considerable convincing, and sweat pouring from Harry's forehead, Timber realizes the problem might be real. Seeing this as a possibility to win over Harry's girlfriend, Timber says he'll get help and calls on the local doctor. Together the two try to put the krait to sleep by administering chloroform, but after slowly lifting the sheets they find no snake. The medical man thinks he's been made a fool and leaves, but Timber stays to ridicule Harry – laughing until the snake appears from behind a pillow and strikes the man on the face. "Harry get the doctor, please," Timber begs. But Harry, having faced the worst of Timber, just stands his ground and replies, "The doctor's gone, Timber."

For failing to call a doctor when his friend was bitten, Harry spent some little time in prison. Apparently the snake couldn't keep his mouth shut. Which reminds me, I believe it is time for another message, however, I shall be back. (commercial break) *If you are interested in obtaining one of my pickpocket alarms. . . good heavens! I've been robbed. Good night.*

Trivia, etc. *Variety* reviewed (accidentally calling the title "Strange Tale of Poison"): "In good chiller-diller style, *Hitchcock Presents* began its fourth season Sunday at 9:30 p.m. with a tale of a poisonous snake on CBS-TV. At this late date, it's hardly news that *Hitchcock* is head and shoulders above many of the murder and mayhem series popping into the living room. When Hitchcock commits murder, it has class. He gets some believable psychological motives, creates suspense and leavens the proceedings with prosaic things, like getting the wrong number for a crucial phone call. And the 30-minute format is just perfect for his vehicles, with scenes clicking away for the final time-bomb explosion. There have been better episodes in the series than this fall's opener 'Strange Tale of Poison.' But the preem [premise] too, had its moments."
Variety concluded: "Initialer concerned the plight of a man with a poisonous snake lying on his stomach. Story took place on the outskirts of Singapore and involved only four actors, discounting Hitchcock's tongue-in-cheek hosting chores. . . The teleplay by Casey Robinson from a story by Roald Dahl could have illuminated the conflict between the two business partners better. The viewer was given only bare hints of the enmity between them. Direction by Hitchcock had the master's touch. The series should still command attention."

EPISODE #119 **"DON'T INTERRUPT"** Broadcast on October 12, 1958
Starring: Chill Wills as Mr. Kilmer   Cloris Leachman as Mrs. Templeton
Biff McGuire as Mr. Templeton   Peter Lazer as Johnny Templeton
Scatman Crothers as the waiter   Jack Mulhall as the conductor
Roy Glenn, Sr. as the waiter   Geoffrey Lewis as the escaped criminal
An original teleplay written for *Alfred Hitchcock Presents* by Sidney Carroll, from his own story of the same name.
Directed by Robert Stevens.
(tied to the train-track)   *Good evening fellow tourists. I think this proves that in some areas the aeroplane can never replace the train. The gentleman who tied me here was most thoughtful. In order to keep the railroad ties from chapping my hips, he put me on an ant hill. And in the event I wanted to do some reading, he left me a railroad timetable. I have found it most useful. You see my assailant was a railroad executive who took exceptions to some of my remarks about the promptness of trains. I have the last laugh however, for I see by a footnote that the train he expected would trisect me, runs only on the Friday preceding Decoration Day and the Tuesday following Labor Day except on leap year. There isn't another train scheduled to pass for thirty minutes. That should give us just enough time to watch a half- hour television show. Keeping to the theme of tonight's program, I must*

warn you that before you get a look at the pleasant scenery, we must first pass through one of those dismal tunnels.

Story: The Templetons are on their way home by train after their young son was expelled from a private school, and is now being a general nuisance to the other passengers. In the boxcar, an old cowpoke named Kilmer joins the couple in a drink and friendly conversation. Johnny's boundless energy takes the best of them and Mr. Templeton offers his son a whole dollar - if he promises not speak a word for ten minutes. Not one sound or syllable. Meanwhile, the train temporarily stops for repairs, and most of the lights dim low. The radio reports of a mental patient who recently escaped and on the loose. The man isn't dangerous, but will likely die if he stays out in the blizzard ravaging the area. As the cowboy tells the Templetons a story, Johnny sees a man scratching at the window, leaving finger marks, but says nothing as he will lose the dollar. Moments later the power comes back on and the train begins to pull away, leaving the mental patient behind to seal his own fate.

(starting to snow) *I suppose you expect me to be discouraged but I'm not. I have faith that the railroad will not allow a man to lie here indefinitely. As a matter of fact, some passing workers have assured me that the train will be by in a few seconds.* (whistle) *There it is now. If you want to turn away. . . you may.* (commercial break, followed by the sound of a train crash) *Look, a complete loss. Fortunately no one was hurt. No one on the train that is. I seem to have sustained a very bad bruise on one finger. If you've enjoyed our story or any of this trivia, perhaps you'll be interested in tuning in next week, when we shall have more of the same. Until then, good night.*

Trivia, etc. Roy Glenn, often credited as Roy E. Glenn, Sr., played numerous supporting roles in television's *Amos 'n' Andy*, and television's *Rawhide* and *Maverick*. Jack Mulhall, known for being the first actor in Hollywood to earn $1,000 a week, here plays a supporting role on a television program that certainly didn't pay $1,000 for a small performance. Scatman Crothers made numerous film roles including Kubrick's *The Shining* (1980); and his masterful voice-over in the animated television series *Hong Kong Phooey*. Chill Wills, the "cowboy" telling his southernly stories, was actually a colorful character actor in numerous American Westerns. It was his voice used in six of the *Francis, the Talking Mule* movies. He was Gene Autry's sidekick for a short time on television. Wills would later win an Academy Award nomination for his role in John Wayne's *The Alamo* (1960). While campaigning for that Oscar, Wills took out a series of ads with the declaration "Win, lose or draw, you're all my cousins and I love you." It was signed "Your cousin, Chill Wills." One member of the Academy placed a response ad stating: "Dear Mr. Chill Wills, I am delighted to be your cousin but I voted for Sal Mineo." It was signed, Groucho Marx.

A clip from the French version of Hitchcock's lead-in from this episode, was used in the documentary, *Dial H for Hitchcock: The Genius Behind the Showman*. Hitchcock's opening lines in this episode is not without irony. When he was about seven years old, Hitchcock loved to read timetables, "as literature," he was once quoted. He would often amaze his parents by reciting from memory the train schedules in England. Here, Hitchcock allows his past to coincide with the television viewers with his remark: "In the event I wanted to do some reading, he left me a railroad timetable."

EPISODE #120 **"THE JOKESTER"** Broadcast on October 19, 1958

Starring: Albert Salmi as Mr. Bradley	Roscoe Ates as Pop Henderson
James Coburn as Andrews	Jay Jostyn as Morgan
Art Batanides as the Police Sergeant	Jim Kirkwood, Jr. as Dave
Charles Watts as the Police Captain	Baynes Barron as the bartender
Claire Carleton as Millie	Richard Benedict as Mike

Teleplay written for *Alfred Hitchcock Presents* by Bernard C. Schoenfeld, based on the short story of the same name by Anthony Morton (pseudonym of Robert Arthur), originally published in the March 1952 issue of *The Mysterious Traveler*. Previously anthologized, as by Robert Arthur, in *Stories They Wouldn't Let me Do on TV*, ed. Alfred Hitchcock (Robert Arthur as ghost writer) (Simon & Schuster, 1957).

Directed by Arthur Hiller.

(The Hitchcock Rock)   *Good evening. It grieves me to announce that it will be impossible for my cousin Alvin Hitchcock to entertain you with his singing. He fell victim to a crowd of teenage souvenir hunters. After first helping themselves to bits of his clothing they began snipping off lots of his hair. He held still for that. After all, he certainly needed a haircut but when they had exhausted his hair, they refused to stop snipping. He was very popular. This was all we found. Tonight's program was to have included many of his greatest hits. "I dig you darling because you're sick, sick, sick." "The FBI breaking up that old gang of mine," "Take off your leather jacket mother you shall not rise tonight" and "Tchaikovski's Rock n'roll concerto." Substituting for his concert is a play, "The Jokester." However, as a tribute to Alvin, let us first observe, one minute of noise.*

Story: Bradley is a man who doesn't know when to quit pulling practical jokes. His latest involves pretending to be a corpse and suddenly sitting upright in front of the morgue attendant, Pop Henderson. Pop nearly loses his job after running for help, but is given one more chance. Later, Bradley pulls another stunt on a lady in a bar and her boyfriend strikes back by knocking him unconscious. Believing he is dead, Bradley's body is taken to the morgue again, but awakens paralyzed. He tries to tell Pop that he is still alive, finding out that he is paralyzed, unable to move. But Pop isn't about to be made a fool again and he locks Bradley in a freezer drawer, saying "Not twice, Mr. Bradley, no more jokes on me."

If you've been waiting for me to play this, I'm afraid I must disappoint you, I can't. Of course Alvin couldn't play either. He just pounded it as he sang. Now we bring you the greatest single argument for the return of radio. After which, I shall do some returning of my own. (commercial break) *We seem to have more time, but no more entertainment. So we shall fill the gap with a list of names of those we hold responsible for tonight's buffoonery, as for myself...*

Trivia, etc. An item of possible interest is this story by Robert Arthur, originally published under a pseudonym because Arthur had another story under his own name in the same issue. Unfortunately, his choice os a pseudonym, Anthony Morton, was also the personal pseudonym of prolific British crime writer John Creasey, who wrote 49 novels under the Morton name, This has mistakenly led at least one reference work to credit the *Mysterious Traveler* story to Creasey rather than Arthur.

EPISODE #121   **"THE CROOKED ROAD"**   Broadcast on October 26, 1958

Starring: Richard Kiley as Harry Adams
Walter Matthau as Pete, the Highway Patrolman
Patricia Breslin as Mary   Richard Erdman as Charlie Brown
Charles Watts as Judge Stanton   Peter Dane as the police officer

Based on the short story of the same name by Alex Gaby, originally published in a 1958 issue of *Esquire*, and adapted for *Alfred Hitchcock Presents* by William Fay. Subsequently reprinted in *A Month of Mystery*, ed. Alfred Hitchcock (Random House, 1969) and in *Dates with Death*, ed. Alfred Hitchcock (Dell, 1972).

Directed by Paul Henreid.

(2 policemen, booth)   *Oh, good evening. I don't know what this means. They won't tell me why I've been arrested. They keep saying, 'your turn will come.' I don't like the sound of it. But officers, I didn't do a thing.* (Officer: "OK you, it's your turn now.") (Voice in booth: "Mr. Hitchcock, I understand your category is television commercials.") *Oh*

then, I wasn't arrested. (Voice in booth: "Don't be absurd. Now for your first question. We shall play the soundtrack from a well known commercial. After hearing the sound, tell us what the person in the commercial has just eaten, drunk, smoked, used or driven in.") *Is that all? Uh may I hear it again, please?* (Voice: "Very well.") *I have it, the answer is . . .*

Story: A middle-aged couple, Harry and Mary, are traveling down a remote country road when they are pulled over by a Highway Patrolman who claims the two were speeding. Harry insists he wasn't, but the Patrolman insists otherwise, also claiming something is wrong with Harry's car and it will have to be towed into town and repaired - for a hefty price. A mechanic and his tow truck happen to be passing by, and delivers the service. Meanwhile, Harry and Mary are hauled into town and raked over coals in the local courtroom, where they are forced to pay a large fine and all of their rights are ignored. At one point during the trial, Harry gets hit by the Patrolman and is fined for striking an officer! Finally, while the couple attempts to leave the town, the mechanic charges them a huge sum for repairs that were never done and never needed. Harry, by now has figured it out, and suggests how certain inhabitants of this small out-of-the-way town, such as a patrolman, a judge and a mechanic – can make a killing financially to their benefit when passing strangers drive through their town. All quick and convenient larceny. The mechanic picks up a heavy wrench and suggests they leave town if they know what's good for them. An hour later, as Mary and Harry are driving out of town, they laugh to themselves. It seems that they are Special Investigators for the State Highway Commission, looking into charges of the town's speed trap, and a tape recorder hidden in Mary's purse recorded everything.

I'm glad you came. I'm very worried. Things didn't go at all well. They liked my first answer but after that I'm afraid I said some nasty things about commercials. It seemed to infuriate the gentleman asking the questions. I'm still not sure who he is? (Officer: "Quiet. OK, it's your turn now") *Did you ever have the feeling you've been here before?* (into booth) *It's very close in here. May I open a window?* (Voice: "No") *What's going on here and why can't I see you?* ("Here I am, look") *The sponsor. What's that? I smell gas.* ("Quiet") (Hitchcock faints) ("Ladies and gentlemen, we now offer a special message after which Mr. Hitchcock will attempt to return.") (commercial break) *I'll bet you're surprised to see me, I know I'm surprised to be here. I received a last minute reprieve and I learned something interesting about my sponsor. He doesn't like commercials either but the public demands them so what's he to do? Next week he will offer three more which promise to be enormous popular successes. Be the first one in your neighborhood to see them. There will also be a story. Until then, good night.*

EPISODE #122 **"THE $2,000,000 DEFENSE"** Broadcast on November 2, 1958
    Starring: Barry Sullivan as Mark Rosen, defending counsel
    Leslie Nielsen as Lloyd Ashley
    Wendell Holmes as Herrick, the District Attorney
    Lori March as Eve Ashley   Herbert Anderson as John Keller
    Edwin Jerome as the judge   Herbert C. Lytton as the doctor
    Ralph Barnard as the police officer
    Teleplay written for *Alfred Hitchcock Presents* by William Fay, based on the short story of the same name by Harold Q. Masur, originally published in the May 1958 issue of *Ellery Queen's Mystery Magazine.* Subsequently anthologized in *Hitchcock in Prime Time,* ed. Francis M. Nevins, Jr. & Martin M. Greenberg (Avon, 1985).
    Directed by Norman Lloyd.
    Good evening. My name is Alfred Hitchcock and the program is Alfred Hitchcock Presents. In the interest of enlightening our audience, we are inaugurating a new policy for this portion of the program. From time to time we plan to interview important figures in various fields. Tonight we have with us one of the world's outstanding mathematicians. If you will, Sir. (a horse walks in) *Good evening, Sir. I shall begin the interrogation at once. My first question concerns a matter which has no doubt been bothering members of our*

audience for many years. How much is 2 and 2? (horse scratches five) *The opinions expressed by our guest are his own and in no way reflect my own views or those of my sponsor. And now sir, what is your favorite television story?* (horse starts scratching) *I think he's telling us that his favorite television play is "The $2,000,000 Defense," in which case we are in for a very long time of it. Long enough, in fact, to show you. . . "The $2,000,000 Defense." But first, my sponsor wishes to put his two cents in.*

Barry Sullivan takes his case to court.

Story: Lloyd Ashley is being tried for the murder of Thomas Ward, the man he suspected was having an affair with his wife. Lloyd swears on the stand that it was an accident and that the safety was on when the .32 Colt Automatic accidentally fired. A ballistics expert swears on the stand that the gun could not discharge with the safety on, and it couldn't have discharged even if dropped from the top of a skyscraper. Alone in private, Lloyd makes an agreement with his attorney to split his four million dollar asset if his lawyer can get him off the hook. By any way or means as long as he can get an acquittal. He really is guilty, but his high-power lawyer, Mark Rosen, goes back to his office to think up an idea. The next afternoon, in court, Mark tricks the ballistics expert and convinces the jury that the fatal gunshot was an accident, blaming the incident on the gun's safety catch. Now off the hook for the murder, Ashley and Mark take a few drinks in his office, celebrating Ashley's freedom. Suddenly Ashley pulls a gun on the attorney, having recently found out that Mark is his wife's real lover. As revenge, he shoots the attorney down in cold blood.

1,999,938, 1,999,939. . . So much for our story. Unfortunately Lloyd Ashley had spent all his money on his first murder trial. And when his trial for the shooting of Mark Robinson came along, he didn't have another two million dollars for a good lawyer. I believe that's 42 - or was it one million? Oh well, I give up. I don't know how he does it without fingers. Now for something you can always count on, after which I'll be back. (commercial break) (Hitchcock at the black board) *Before our guest left, I discovered him scribbling on this black board. Frankly, I don't know how long we can hold our scientific superiority over the horse, but I think we better do something drastic. That is unless you relish the thought of suddenly finding yourselves on the wrong end of a plough or chasing each other around racetracks while the horses do the betting. And on this grim note I must leave you until next week, when I shall be back with another play. Until then, good night.*

Trivia, etc. "Few authors would fault the TV version of a story when gifted performers like Barry Sullivan and Leslie Nielsen interpret the principal roles," said author Harold Q. Masur. "Since the adaptations and dialogue closely followed the original, I was inclined to applaud an industry that often in the past had disappointed. I lament only the lack of a video recorder at that time to immortalize my favorite yarn." Somewhere along the lines of production, between filming of Hitchcock's hosting and the dramatization itself, the character Mark Rosen was also Mark Robinson. Throughout the drama, the principal players clearly call him Mark Rosen, but Hitchcock says Robinson near the close of the episode! "The $2,000,000 Defense" became the first of many episodes directed by Associate Producer Norman Lloyd.

EPISODE #123   **"DESIGN FOR LOVING"**   Broadcast on November 9, 1958
  Starring: Norman Lloyd as Charles Brailing   Marian Seldes as Lydia Brailing
  Elliott Reid as Tom   Barbara Baxley as Ann
  Teleplay written for *Alfred Hitchcock Presents* by Ray Bradbury, from his short story, "Marionettes, Inc.," originally published in the March 1949 issue of *Startling Stories*.
  Directed by Robert Stevens.
  (beware of dog, Fido; Hitchcock in dog-kennel)   *Good evening, ladies and gentlemen. A simple incident can change one's life with dazzling swiftness. In a single day my pet caught a glimpse of his pedigree and my family tree. Now he won't sleep anywhere but in the house. It's rather large as you can see. I shudder to think what he'll be like when he grows up.* (close-up) *Tonight's narrative is called "Design For Loving" and as the title suggests, it concerns marriage and its problems. But before our play, here is a message from a gentleman who has designs on your purse.*

Story: Charles Brailing has concocted the perfect way to leave his wife. Returning home one night, Charles tells his friend and neighbor, Tom, that he has built a robot that looks and acts just like him, and secretly keeps it locked in his basement tool chest. His wife can't tell the difference between the two, and anytime he wants to leave somewhere, all he needs to do is let the robot out. As the final test, Charles plans to run off to Rio for a considerable amount of time. Tom doesn't believe this at first, until Charles gives him a sneak peak through the window of his house. Sure enough, a duplicate of Charles is spending time with Lydia. But when he sees the robot get overly friendly with his wife, Charles confronts the mechanical man downstairs, who proceeds to put Charles in the toolbox - permanently.

That story is a somewhat disturbing one, but only to people. Our next story is also disturbing and that is why I think I shall take this opportunity to walk my dog. I shall be back, I hope. (commercial break) *Fortunately for me, he slipped his collar, and disappeared in a herd pertrum. This concludes our show. Next week we shall be back with another. But before I go, there's something I would like you to consider. You keep me in this box all week, and then allow me to appear after only half an hour before closing me up again. I don't like it. You see I keep running, there's no way to shut me off. After all, I have feelings too. Think it over. Good night.* (gets down from huge chair, with "Made In England" sticker on his back)

Trivia, etc. "I did many, many shows with Ray [Bradbury]," recalled Norman Lloyd, who not only served as an Associate Producer, but actor as well. "You may think I'm a bore because I say everybody's wonderful . . . but Ray is great. First of all, he looks like one of the characters from his Martian stories. Ray looks like a Martian - and if anyone is a

Martian, it's Ray! He's constantly creative, constantly dreaming up ideas, constantly promoting his ideas. I'm proud to say that he said this once at a tribute lunch given to me by the Pacific Pioneers radio people: We had the most wonderful collaboration between him and Joan Harrison and myself. So I can only sing his praises. And the material that I got from Ray. . . was just wonderful. He adapted a story for me once, somebody else's, but for the most part they were all his stories."

Elliott Reid, who played Tom in this episode, recalled: "Norman Lloyd and I were both members of the original on-stage Mercury Theatre, with Orson Welles. [circa 1937] In fact, the characters we played were the same names as in Julius Caesar. Norman was Cinna the poet, and I was Cinna the Conspirator. After the murder of Caesar, the mob turns on Cinna the poet, thinking he is Cinna the Conspirator. So, as you can imagine, Norman and I have had a long, long friendship - though many years often went by without our seeing each other. So, yes - with me at least - he was very easy to work with. He had a close friendship with Hitchcock and a number of other top directors, too, and I guess that's why he was Associate Producer of the Hitchcock series. Hitchcock respected Norman's intelligence, and obviously - felt that Norman would be very helpful on the series, as Associate Producer, and he was."

"I remember Barbara Baxley in the same acting class as Richard Boone and I in 1946 to 1947 at the Neighborhood Playhouse," recalled Marian Seldes. "Another reunion I had was with Norman Lloyd. Norman had directed *Mr. Lincoln*, in which I played Nancy Hanks, for Omnibus, so I already loved working with him. Elliott – well, what can I say? He was a brilliant comedian and a dear man. Elliott was so funny between takes and we all adored being around him. Ray Bradbury was on the set during part of the filming. I was in a play with his daughter, Patricia, called 'The High Ground' on Broadway and I later met the Hitchcocks there at the St. Regis Hotel."

EPISODE #124   **"MAN WITH A PROBLEM"**   Broadcast on November 16, 1958
Starring: Gary Merrill as Carl
Mark Richman as Steve Barrett, the police officer

Elizabeth Montgomery as Karen	Ken Lynch as the police lieutenant
Alex Gerry as Dr. Landers	Bartlett Robinson as the hotel manager
James Johnson as the bellhop	Jean Field as a spectator
Sid Melton as the cab driver	

Also in the cast: Guy Rennie and Victor Tayback
Teleplay written for *Alfred Hitchcock Presents* by Joel Murcott, based on the short story of the same name by Donald Martin (pseudonym of Donald Honig), originally published in the July 1958 issue of *Alfred Hitchcock's Mystery Magazine*. Subsequently anthologized, as by Donald Honig, in *My Favorites in Suspense*, ed. Alfred Hitchcock (Random House, 1959).
Directed by Robert Stevens.
(skeleton exercise) *1, 2, 3. 4 . . . 1, 2, 3, 4. Now raise your hands above your head. Higher. . . higher. I wish to take this opportunity to welcome you latecomers to Alfred Hitchcock Presents. Someone suggested I go to a slim and trim class and I decided to go even further and start one of my own. Here to encourage you beginners is an illustration of what hard work and determination can do. 1, 2, 3, 4 . . . 1, 2, 3, 4. This is Mr. Webster who I'm certain is the envy of all of you. When Mr. Webster first came to me, he weighed nearly 300 pounds. He was sluggish and run down and was the object of ridicule because of his obesity. Furthermore, his wife had threatened to walk out on him. Now all that has changed for the better. He has his old energy back. He's quite popular socially and his wife has left him. He also has a pleasant job, modelling in the anatomy department of one of our largest Universities. And in evenings, he's endman in a minstrel show. And now ladies and gentlemen, a special low calory story. However, first, for those of you who aren't dieting, we have this bit of treacle.*

Story: Carl has decided to commit suicide by jumping off one of the top floors of a tall building. Once on the ledge, a policeman from the local beat is informed by the hotel manager of the situation, and he tries to talk Carl down. Later, the lieutenant comes and tries to take charge of things but almost makes Carl jump. In flashbacks, Carl explains that he plans to jump because his wife is no longer alive and he has nothing else to live for. She meant the world to him. Carl's wife left him for a man named Steve, but she came back, and then killed herself because Steve wouldn't leave his wife. After a little persuasion, the officer talks Carl out of the idea of suicide. The police officer, named Steve, seeing a promotion in the near future, goes out on the ledge to help Carl back inside. But Carl has another confession. Looking into the policeman's eyes, Carl recognizes the man who slept with his wife. By now it's too late for the policeman, for Carl grabs a stead-fast hand, and pushes him off the ledge.

Unfortunately for Mr. Adams, revenge was not sweet, for he ultimately paid for his crime. While we were watching this sad saga, I was doing some thinking. This program might be improved by the use of our special spot reducer. I can think of three spots in particular, here is one of them, after which Mr. Webster and I shall return. (commercial break) Mr. Webster seems to have disappeared again. This is one aspect of his life that is a bit tiresome. You see, the dogs keep carrying him off and burying him. I've had to dig him up at least three times. And now it's time for me to disappear. Until next week that is, I shall be back then with another story. Good night.

EPISODE #125 **"SAFETY FOR THE WITNESS"** Broadcast on November 23, 1958
    Starring: Art Carney as Cyril T. Jones
    Robert Bray as Lieutenant Flannelly
    James Westerfield as Commissioner Cummings   Mary Scott as Nurse Copeland
    Karl "Killer" Davis as Big Dan Foley   George Greico as Tarzan Joe Felix
    James Flavin as the desk sergeant   Doris Lloyd as Mrs. Crawpit
    Dorothea Lord as the cashier   David Fresco as the motel night clerk
    Ken Patterson as Thomas Bergman
    Teleplay written for *Alfred Hitchcock Presents* by William Fay, based on the short story of the same name by John DeMeyer, originally published in the March 1955 issue of *The Saint Detective Magazine*. Subsequently anthologized in *Best Detective Stories of the Year*, ed. David C. Cooke (Dutton, 1956).
    Directed by Norman Lloyd.
    (Hitchcock shoots a man in the back during a revolver duel)*Well, as mother used to say, it's better to be safe than sorry. Actually what you have just seen is not to be taken seriously. It was all make believe, all play acting. Of course the gun is genuine and was loaded, but the doctor isn't a real doctor, he's an actor. I think it's interesting that the duel is no longer considered good form, while cold blooded murder is more popular than ever. There seems to be no way to stay the march of civilization. Tonight's story is about murder and we call it "Safety For The Witness." Our next minute is devoted to a television commercial and I call that.*

Story: A Big City 1927: Custom gunsmith Cyril T. Jones has a grudge against police protection, having lost a few friends in the past, but always cooperates when they ask questions. When Cyrcil witnesses a shooting in the streets, the killers turn their guns on Cyril, putting him into the hospital. Knowing full well that he's the next intended victim, Cyril refuses to tell the police anything, as the mob will certainly kill him if he talks. Once he's released from the hospital, Cyril rents a hotel room across the street from his gun shop and arms himself, turning the tables on the assassins, whom he kills. When the police realize what he has done, even though Cyril has gotten rid of the evidence, they decide not to try to prosecute him as he has done the community a favor and the arrest would make them look bad.

Thus it is that Mr. Jones learns the sad truth about murder. Committing it is not difficult, it's being convicted that's the trick. Fortunately the next city administration was a thoroughly dishonest one, and it granted him his request. And now I shall be back in a minute, after this brief you-know-what, from you-know-whom. (commercial break) *My worthy opponent has taken what I consider, an unfair advantage of my poor shooting, and insisted that we go through this again. Afterwards I should be back, next week with another story. Ready!* (four guns point at Hitch) *Good night.*

Trivia, etc. On November 30, 1958, *Alfred Hitchcock Presents* was not broadcast. Instead, CBS presented "Wonderful Town," a musical comedy based on the book "My Sister Eileen." Broadcast from 9 to 11 p.m., EST. Rosalind Russell reprised her Broadway role. The story concerned two Ohio girls who came to New York, seeking fame and fortune. Supporting roles by Jacquelyn McKeever, Sydney Chaplin and Joseph Buloff.

EPISODE #126 **"MURDER ME TWICE"** Broadcast on December 7, 1958
        Starring: Phyllis Thaxter as Lucy Prior
Tom Helmore as Professor Miles John Farnum
Alan Marshal as Will Prior
Ward Costello as William G. Burke, Assistant D.A.
Herbert Anderson as George   Liz Carr as Adele
King Calder as Mr. Sherman   Robert Carson as the judge
        Teleplay written for *Alfred Hitchcock Presents* by Irving Elman, based on the short story of the same name by Lawrence Treat, originally published in the May 1957 issue of *Alfred Hitchcock's Mystery Magazine*. Subsequently reprinted in *For Love or Money*, ed. Dorothy Gardiner (Doubleday, 1957) and *A Choice of Evils*, ed. Elana Lore (Davis Publications, 1983).
        Directed by David Swift.
        (hypnotism)   Voice: "You are very sleepy, you can't seem to hold your eyes open. You're beginning to drift . . . you're drifting . . . you're sound asleep. Can you hear me?" Hitchcock: *Yes.* "Say, good evening ladies and gentlemen." *Good evening ladies and gentlemen.* "Thank you for tuning in." *Thank you for tuning in.* "You're now going back in time. Back years and years ago. You're drifting back through the years, back, back, back . . . When you speak next you will be 40 years old." *Forty!* (Hitchcock jumps up from sofa) "I'm sorry, I mean four." *That's better. I have a little shadow that goes in and out with me. And what can be the use of him? Mommy, why do I cast such a large shadow? I never liked the way she answered that question.* "What games did you play?" *I didn't play much. I spent most of my time watching television.* "Television? When you were four?" *Yes, I was a very precocious child.* "What did you see on television?" *Stories, mostly stories like this one.* "Wait a minute, we haven't time for you to tell us a long story." *Who said they were long? These lasted only a minute, but they were the most satisfying and delightful vignettes you could imagine and I could see thirty of them every half-hour. As I said, they were like this.*

        Story: Lucy Prior is hypnotized at a party and while in a trance she acts like a Quaker woman named Dora Evans, who proceeds to pick up a pair of scissors and stab her wealthy – and much older - husband in the back. After being arrested, the Assistant District Attorney questions Lucy, with a slight disbelief in the art of hypnotism. Placing a phone call to the Philadelphia Historical Society, William Burke, the Assistant D.A. learns that there really was a Quaker woman named Dora Evans, who actually murdered her husband in a similar fashion. During an inquest, Lucy's defense surrounds the fact that she didn't know what she was doing when she was hypnotized, and Burke claims Lucy was in her right mind during the murder. In order to prove that it was Dora, and not Lucy who committed the crime, Professor Farnum is called back in to put her under again. Having unsuccessfully tried to blackmail her once, the Professor reluctantly agrees to hypnotizes her, and again she takes on the Quaker woman's identity, reenacting the murder scene, killing the Professor. With all charges dropped, the Assistant District Attorney confronts her in private, pointing out no recording devices, no one close enough to verify what she says, he asks her – just to settle his curiosity – if she planned the whole thing. "Would's not thee like to know?" Lucy remarks, leaving for home.

(Hitchcock now dressed like an executioner with an axe) "Back, back, you're drifting further back. Now tell me who you are." *Albert Evans, my Lord. In the service of his Majesty King Henry the eighth.* "And what do you do for the king?" *I'm in charge of severing relations with his wives. His royal highneth approaches now. Be silent and attentive until my return.* (commercial break) *What do you think of this? He regressed me and then only brought me half way back. I - Good heavens! Everyone's asleep! That last commercial must have hypnotized them! It put the entire audience under.* (snaps fingers) *That didn't do the trick. Since I can't wake you up I can only leave you with this posthypnotic suggestion. Next week when you awaken, you will feel compelled to tune in again when we promise to bring you another story and three less soporific commercials. Good night.*

Trivia, etc. Director David Swift, making his only directorial effort for the Hitchcock series, recalled: "I was pretty hot in those days, directing every television show in town - I couldn't service all the calls. We were hired guns. Norman Lloyd, the fine Group Theatre actor, was Associate Producer on Hitchcock and he hired me. I read it, cast it, shot it, and went on to the next show. [*General Electric Theatre, Wagon Train, Have Gun - Will Travel, The Rifleman, Climax, Playhouse 90,*] It was shoot and run. Phyllis was competent, but no star sparkle. Tom was the same, but like all of us, he was a solid workaday mechanic like me - we were all looking for a feature break, hoping and trying with honing skills. There was no plot change, just minor word changes. There was no time to edit, and no budget for complications."

Irving Elman, who wrote the script for this episode, recalled "Murder Me Twice" being his second and final episode of the series: "I wrote at least one other script for the show. I didn't write more because I turned producer then and was too busy with my own shows [*The Eleventh Hour* and *Ben Casey*]. "Murder Me Twice" was remade, as you probably know. Universal launched a second version of the series, which failed because they did such a lousy job. I wasn't on the set when they shot it originally, not because I wouldn't have been welcome. Joan Harrison loved writers,which was one of the things which made her such a superb producer, but because I was too busy writing other shows, just as Swift was so busy directing them. That was the Golden Age of Television when we couldn't keep up with the demand and loved it. Was I satisfied with the job they did with it? Yes. Did they make many changes? Joan Harrison asked for and made fewer changes than any producer who ever lived. Why do you think I and the other writers were all so crazy about her? Her practice was to have a long story conference with the writer, discussing every detail of the script before a single word of it was written. Consequently if you then turned in the script you had both agreed upon in advance, there was no need for radical changes or rewriting -- usually just a few word changes. That was my experience with Joan on both *Janet Dean* and *Alfred Hitchcock Presents.*"

David Swift concluded: "I had a commitment to do an *Alcoa Presents* for Bill Sackheim following Monday at Screen Gems. It was during shooting of this half hour show [with Cliff Robertson playing a pool hustler] that Walt Disney called and gave me my first feature film, *Pollyanna* (1960), to write and direct and that was the end of television for me."

For Hitchcock fans, take note: Lucy Prior stabbed two men in the back (with only one stab) in the spine. Grace Kelly did the same in *Dial M For Murder* (1954). Quoting Alfred Hitchcock who once publicly commented about the murder: "The best way to do it is with scissors."

EPISODE #127 **"TEA TIME"** Broadcast on December 14, 1958
Starring: Margaret Leighton as Iris Teleton   Marsha Hunt as Blanche Herbert
Murray Matheson as Oliver Teleton   George Navarro as the waiter
Teleplay written for *Alfred Hitchcock Presents* by Kathleen Hite, based on the short story "Two for Tea" by Margaret Manners, originally published in the May 1957 issue of *Alfred Hitchcock's Mystery Magazine.* Subsequently reprinted in *The Lethal Sex*, ed. John D. MacDonald (Dell, 1959).
Directed by Robert Stevens.
(with a large metal hoop and an icon) *Good evening ladies and gentlemen. No, this is not a production of 'Hamlet.' I'm indulging in a hobby, archeology. I've unearthed the grave of a man who lived thousands of years ago. Obviously, we have changed somewhat since then. This man was buried with all his possessions. His cattle, his two wives, and several of these. However, instead of wearing them in his nose and ears, as any civilized person would, he wore this around his middle. Each of his wives had one around her. As nearly as we can judge, they all died of exhaustion. This man shrewdly combined the eternal triangle and the family circle. For details of how a more modern man coped with the situation, I refer you to tonight's chronicle.*

Story: Blanche Herbert invites Iris Teleton to dine with her at a restaurant, and right away Iris clears the air. She knows her husband has been seeing Blanche for some time now. What she doesn't understand is why Blanche would invite her to a restaurant. Blanche explains that she wants Iris to divorce her husband, but Iris won't have it. Not only because it would cut off her financial funds, but it would convenience the lovebirds, and jealousy spawns hatred. Blanche reveals a letter she has on her possession that incriminates Iris in a way worse than cheating. Oliver doesn't know of the letter yet, but Blanche wants to give Iris a chance to change her mind about a divorce. Realizing her position, Iris tries to buy the letter. A few days later, the women are alone together and Iris is forced to shoot Blanche when the woman just gives her half the letter after taking the jewelry Iris had given her. Unfortunately, when Iris goes to her husband's office, she learns that the incriminating letter Blanche had was given to her by her husband, who also had a detective document Blanche's murder. Iris also meets her husband's *other* girlfriend, who he intends to run off with.

I've just been informed that this relic which I unearthed was not a decoration or part of a double ring ceremony, but was a means of sport. The participant put it around his body in this matter. It doesn't seem to be my size, but no matter. You then rotate the hips. Watch closely. I shall demonstrate. (commercial break – Hitchcock out of breath) *I hope you were watching. I did quite well. You will admire your ancestors more when you learn that they made these out of stone. These hoops not only took off weight, but made formidable weapons. That's quite enough hoopla for one evening. I hope you will join us next week. Good night.*

EPISODE #128 **"AND THE DESERT SHALL BLOSSOM"** Broadcast Dec. 21, 1958
Starring: William Demarest as Tom Aiken   Roscoe Ates as Ben White
Mike Kellin as the stranger   Ben Johnson as Jeff, the sheriff
Wesley Lau as the deputy
Teleplay written for *Alfred Hitchcock Presents* by Bernard C. Schoenfeld, based on the short story of the same name by Loren D. Good, originally published in the March 1958 issue of *Ellery Queen's Mystery Magazine.*
Directed by Arthur Hiller.
(wearing a cowboy hat, cactus beside him)   *Good evening partners, cattle rustlers, wranglers, desert rats, varmints, hombres and all you prospectors who futilely comb the hills of television looking for something of value. This is no mirage. No optical illusion. I'm as real as a piece of motion picture film, as authentic as a shadow. As for tonight's play I'm afraid I have disappointing news. It will not be an adult western. The plot is not yet twenty-one years old. Unfortunately we are not completely out of line. For although*

television fans demand adult stories, their taste in commercials run to another extreme. Allow me to illustrate.

Story: Two old desert rats, Tom and Ben, live in the Nevada wilderness, content and happy with what they have – until the one day when the sheriff pays them a visit. He is concerned about their being so far from town, and they can't homestead on their own as they've stopped mining, farming or growing anything. The old men strike a deal with the sheriff, pointing out a half-dead rose bush in the front yard, and if the sheriff can pick a bouquet of roses from the bush in about a month from today, they can stay. After the sheriff leaves, the old men admits they need a miracle, as their water supply is low. A few days later, a gun-wielding criminal wanted for everything in the book, arrives and demands that they drive him to town. A struggle breaks out between the wanted killer and Tom, and the old man is knocked out cold. When he wakes up he shoots the stranger. A month later, when the sheriff arrives to check up on Tom and Ben, he is amazed to find the rosebush growing beautifully. What he doesn't know is that the recently-buried killer must have been great plant fertilizer.

Requests are pouring in from garden clubs across the country for details of Ben and Tom's method of desert reclamation. Directions are as follows, for best results select a sunny spot and place the body in a shallow grave, 6 to 10 inches below your plants. Water frequently and watch out for garden pest and the police. As for Tom and Ben, they soon ran out of desperate criminals and began planting innocent passers-by. They are now in prison after first donating their property to the government as a national cemetery. We have a one minute film now, after which I shall meet you at the pass. (commercial break) And now the time has come for me to ride off into the sunset. I shall return next week. Until then, so long partners.

Hitchcock sits patiently while the cameraman makes adjustments.

Trivia, etc. Although the entire five-man cast consisted of actors who played numerous roles in television and big-screen westerns, one stands out among all of them. Ben Johnson, who played the sheriff in this episode, was actually one of the best horse riders in Hollywood. Behind the camera, Johnson was responsible for training actors like Richard Boone and James Arness how to ride a horse (or at the very least, give the appearance of riding a horse). Winner of rodeo championships, Johnson doubled for John Wayne and James Stewart. Johnson would later win an Academy Award for his portrayal of Sam the Lion, the theater owner in *The Last Picture Show* (1971). Although Johnson made numerous appearance in television programs. *Gunsmoke, The Virginian, Have Gun – Will Travel, Bonanza, Laramie*, etc., this Hitchcock performance was one of his earliest – if not first – appearance on American television.

EPISODE #129 **"MRS. HERMAN AND MRS. FENIMORE"** Broadcast Dec. 28, 1958
Starring: Mary Astor as Mrs. Fenimore   Russell Collins as Uncle Bill
Doro Merande as Mrs. Herman   Wesley Lau as the detective
Teleplay written for *Alfred Hitchcock Presents* by Robert C. Dennis, based on the short story "Mrs. Herman and Mrs. Kenmore" by Donald Honig, originally published in the May 1958 issue of *Alfred Hitchcock's Mystery Magazine*.
Directed by Arthur Hiller.

(knife throwing board) *Good evening ladies and gentlemen. First of all I want to make it clear that we always appreciate constructive criticism. Any expression of your feelings is always welcome.* (knife) *We have a very warm feeling toward our viewers. We know they are intelligent, discerning and warmhearted.* (knife) *Present company excepted of course. Yes, I have an announcement to make.* (knife in the back of studioman) *Touché. Is Dr. Finchley in the audience?, he is wanted at home. And . . . if it's not too inconvenient, perhaps he could stop here on his way out. As for our knife-throwing friend. Here is something better to throw at.*

Story: An actress rents a room from Mrs. Herman, a woman who lives with her evil-tempered Uncle Bill. Mrs. Herman confesses to the actress that she plans to kill the old man when the opportunity arises. Mrs. Herman offers to pay the actress, Mrs. Fenimore, $2,500 for turning on the charm with Bill, and when the time is right she will kill him and make it look like an accident. The plan goes off without a hitch, and the police rule it an accidental death. Unfortunately for Mrs. Herman, Mrs. Fenimore announces that her acting skills paid off better than expected, as the old man had a lot more money than either of them knew, and she married him to get it all - except for the $2,500, which she will give to the landlady.

Here is further evidence that crime does not pay. For the law caught up with Mrs. Herman and Mrs. Fenimore shortly after they had spent the inheritance. They are now living at government expense. The subject of money brings us quite naturally to the following, at the conclusion of which, I shall rejoin you. (commercial break) *By the way, that last commercial was one which was sent to Russia as part of the cultural exchange. I don't know what we received in return, we're afraid to open it. Now, until next week when we shall return with another story. Good night.*

Trivia, etc. Recalled director Arthur Hiller: "I really got on well with Lloyd and Harrison creatively, and I liked them so much personally. I guess they liked my work. They kept asking me to direct another episode and another episode and another. . . and . . . and . . . I presume Hitchcock liked my work too. When he was supposed to be directing every fourth episode of the weekly TV series *Suspicion*. There would be three "live" from New York and then one filmed by Hitch. But he was not available because he was on some other film, so he asked me personally to direct [*Suspicion*'s "Voice in the Night"]. It made me very proud. I don't remember stories about many of the episodes, but I remember feeling 'boy, I'm going to work with Mary Astor, wow!' And it was wow!"

EPISODE #130 **"SIX PEOPLE, NO MUSIC"** Broadcast on January 4, 1959
Starring: John McGiver as Arthur Motherwell   Peggy Cass as Rhoda Motherwell
Howard Smith as Stanton C. Baravale   Joby Baker as Thor
Wilton Graff as Fulton Agnew   Joe Hamilton as handyman at funeral home
Teleplay written for *Alfred Hitchcock Presents* by Richard Berg, based on the short
story, "The Damnedest Thing" by Garson Kanin, originally published in the February 1956
issue of *Esquire*.

Directed by Norman Lloyd.

(standing on the wall)   *Good evening, ladies and gentlemen.   In the
television business it's extremely difficult to keep both feet on the ground. I'd be happy if I
had just one foot down there. If you think this is easy, you should see me trying to get
through a doorway. And yesterday I accidently stepped through a window. If my arm hadn't
caught in the sash I might still be going and that's not all. Twice I've been mistaken for a
dirigible. They keep trying to deflate me. I'm certain by now, you have guessed that
tonight's play is about gravity and people who resist the earth's pull. You're wrong. It's
about an undertaker and one of the persons he undertakes. And it begins in just a moment.*

Story: Arthur Motherwell is an undertaker who finds himself in a perplexing
situation. It seems that a wealthy family has arranged for an incredible, extravagant funeral
for their deceased relative, who is then delivered to the funeral home. While there, the
"corpse" suddenly comes to life long enough to write out a note in which he demands a
small, inexpensive funeral, then dies. Now the undertaker isn't sure if he should honor the
man's last wish, or that of the family. Who's to believe a corpse? After discussing the
matter with his wife, they decide to destroy the note.

*That I am certain is the only
example we have of a man
dying posthumously. Mr.
Baravale's funeral turned out
to be a very gala occassion.
Especially for Mr. Motherwell.
It produced quite a business
boom for him. You see,
someone accidentally put
embalming fluid in the coffee
that was served. But so much
for life's lighter side. I hope
you rejoin me after this next
number. Personally, I think I
shall sit it out.* (sits down on
the wall) (commercial break)
*That was short and sweet. Too
sweet. Oh, that's a hopeful
sign. Next week I shall return
with another story. Perhaps by
then I shall have settled down.
Good night.*

**John McGiver and
Joby Baker contemplating
their futures in "Six People,
No Music." (Photo
courtesy of Photofest.)**
249

Trivia, etc. Richard Berg made his sole writing contribution on the Hitchcock series in this episode. "I was a writer that just came out of New York working on the live TV shows toward the end of the golden age," Berg recalled. "I wrote scripts such as 'The Drop of a Hat' for *Studio One*, and 'The Right-Hand Man' for *Playhouse 90*, and as a matter of fact, that was another Garson Kanin story. Anyway, Universal brought me out here and gave me a contract. Ultimately I became a producer at Universal and stayed there for ten years. I ended up producing *The Bob Hope Chrystler Theater* for five years, *Checkmate* for a year, and I produced *Alcoa Premiere*. They sent me the story from Hitchcock's office and I know I retitled it myself. 'Six People, No Music' was not Kanin's original title. Norman Lloyd was the executive for Hitchcock, and was an excellent director. It was his decision for the casting. I think John McGiver was magnificent."

Actor Wayne Heffley recalled the casting for this episode. "I only did one *Alfred Hitchcock Presents* but I was associated with a second one. Norman Lloyd heard about me from a mutual friend and promised to use me when he could. I got a call one day to look over the script called 'Six People, No Music' that he was directing and I was told that he needed someone to rehearse with Peggy Cass, because the leading man, John McGiver, was busy in New York. I rehearsed with Peggy for that day, but I never ended up being on that episode. I did later star in 'Your Witness,' an excellent episode of the Hitchcock series."

The corpse wakes for a moment to write his last request.
(Photo courtesy of Ronald V. Borst / Hollywood Movie Posters)

EPISODE #131　"THE MORNING AFTER"　Broadcast on January 11, 1959
　　　　Starring: Robert Alda as Ben Nelson　　Jeanette Nolan as Mrs. Trotter
　　　　Dorothy Provine as Sharon Trotter　　Fay Wray as Mrs. Nelson
　　　　Dorothea Lord as the maid
　　　　Teleplay written for *Alfred Hitchcock Presents* by Rose Simon Kohn, based on the short story of the same name by Henry Slesar, originally published in the February 1957 issue of *Ellery Queen's Mystery Magazine.* Subsequently collected in *Clean Crimes and Neat Murders* (Avon, 1960).
　　　　Directed by Herschel Daugherty.
　　　　(fan mail)　*Good evening. I'm answering my correspondance. I receive some very interesting letters, threatening and otherwise. Dear Mr. Hitchcock, I'm a man of 60 with a wife of 22. We have a handsome young man of 25 rooming with us. Yesterday I discovered ground glass in my sugar. Isn't this unusual? Anxious. Dear Anxious, yes this is unusual. I believe arsenic is customary in cases of this kind. But your wife is young, I'm sure she'll learn. Dear Mr. Hitchcock, we have endured your snide and impertinent remarks about our commercials long enough. This is to warn you that . . .* (turns letter). *So much for fan mail. Now we come to that part of the program for which the sponsor has been waiting. I'm too prudent to describe it.*

　　　　Story:　Mrs. Trotter has been furious ever since she learned that her teenage daughter is seeing Ben Nelson, owner of a plastics factory, a married man almost twice her age.　Talking person-to-person to the man in question seems to get her nowhere, so in retaliation, Mrs. Trotter informs Mrs. Nelson about her husband's infidelity.　The woman takes it calmly and later that evening, tells Ben that he can have his divorce, but he won't get any money.　Thinking rationally about his situation, since it is his wife who is wealthy, not he, Ben decides to kill her, then phones his girlfriend, Sharon, as an alibi.　Explaining over the receiver what he's done, he asks Sharon to tell her to claim he was with her all night - not realizing that he is actually talking to Mrs. Trotter, who promptly hangs up the phone and breaks the news to her daughter.　Ben just phoned, and the police are coming to ask questions, and "Ben wants you to say that he wasn't here all evening."　Sharon, not suspecting a thing, agrees just as the police arrive, ringing the doorbell.

　　　　I hope you liked our play. We now have a one minute soap opera which I'm sure you'll love. This is the story that asks the question: Can a poor, lonely advertising man from rural Madison Avenue, win customers for his sponsor and find happiness in the upper income brackets? (commercial break) *I'm afraid I may have done it again. However, if I'm sacked, moving up will be no great problem. I'm a clean desk man. This is the type of desk where everything is out of sight. The waste basket, the telephone and here is my secretary. That will be all, Miss Whiteleather. Suppose you tune in next week to see if I'm still on the job. I can at least promise you another story. Good night.*

　　　　Trivia, etc.　The character named Miss Whiteleather, the secretary in Hitchcock's desk drawer, returned five years later as the person in charge of the finals in the Hitchcock look-alike contest in the presentation to *The Alfred Hitchcock Hour* episode, "The Gentleman Caller." This time a different lady played the role of Miss Whiteleather. On top of that, she was the one who won the look-alike contest!

EPISODE #132　"A PERSONAL MATTER"　Broadcast on January 18, 1959
　　　　Starring: Wayne Morris as Brett Johnson　　Joe Maross as Joe Philips
　　　　Frank Silvera as Senor Rodriquez　　Richard Bermudez as Manuel
　　　　Frank DeKova as Pedro, the servant　　Leonard Strong as the doctor
　　　　Anna Navarro as Maria
　　　　Teleplay written for *Alfred Hitchcock Presents* by Joel Murcott, based on the short story "Human Interest Stuff" by Brett Halliday, originally published in the September 1946

issue of *Ellery Queen's Mystery Magazine*.　Subsequently anthologized in *Murder by Experts*, ed. Ellery Queen (Ziff-Davis, 1947).

Directed by Paul Henreid.

(holding a balloon)　*Good evening. My sobriety is under question but not in a way you think. This is a joviality test. I do this before each program to test my spirits. I seem to have passed with flying colors. Once again I wish to welcome you to Alfred Hitchcock Presents, for another half-hour of group therapy. I'm told there is nothing like a good murder to work off one's antagonisms. And if you have no antagonisms, our commercials will create some for you. Allow me to illustrate.*

Story:　Brett Johnson is flown to a remote Mexican construction site, hired by Rodriquez to assist Joe Philips. After an accident that almost makes him lose his life, Joe decides to quit but Johnson convinces him otherwise. Over the next few days, the men become friendly at the site, especially since they accomplish a lot more tunneling than ever before. One evening, the boys confess their true identities. Joe is a man wanted for the murder of a construction boss (which Joe insists was self-defense) and Brett is really an undercover cop, who just found the man he was looking for. Knowing both of them are stranded until the plane arrives in a few weeks, the boys agree not to get hostile until then. But Brett, believing that Joe killed the man in self-defense, (having seen him save another man's life in a mineshaft cave-in) convinces him to give up a concealed gun. Brett promises to testify on Joe's behalf at the trial, which might help in his defense.

(balloon lowers toward floor)　*I'm sure it's obvious to everyone that my spirits are sagging. I've seemed to have gone into eclipse. Perhaps we'll both have a better view after the following.* (commercial break)　*You should have seen the baloon drop during that commercial. I hope it isn't too symbolic. Next week I shall return with soaring spirits and an uplifting story. Until then . . .* (Hitchcock steps on balloon and pops it) *. . . good night.*

EPISODE #133　**"OUT THERE - DARKNESS"**　Broadcast on January 25, 1959

Starring: Bette Davis as Miss Fox　James Congdon as Eddie McMann

Frank Albertson as Sergeant Kirby　Arthur Marshall as Jerry, the elevator man

Teleplay written for *Alfred Hitchcock Presents* by Bernard C. Schoenfeld, based on the short story "Over There – Darkness" by William O'Farrell, originally published in the October 1958 issue of *Sleuth*. Subsequently anthologized in *Best Detective Stories of the Year*, ed. David C. Cooke (Dutton, 1959).

Directed by Paul Henreid.

(elevator)　*Good evening, ladies and gentlemen and watch your step please. I'm certain that any of you who have wearyly pushed rich maiden Aunts in their wheelchairs, share my appreciation of elevator shafts. I also find the elevator quite easy to operate. It works just like a yo-yo. Well, not exactly but we do use the same grade of string. We are now about to have our first commercial. I want to assure you that it will only last 60 seconds. I have to tell everyone this because I understand it gives people the sensation of being trapped between floors . . . courage.*

Story:　Miss Fox is a wealthy woman who treats her dog better than the people around her. Eddie, an employee who walks her dog on a regular basis, shows up in rags and asks for a small loan. His girlfriend needs an operation or she'll die. Miss Fox has heard this same story before, and gives him a lecture instead. He storms out telling her that he will never walk the dog again. Miss Fox does the job herself, and along a dark alley, she is mugged and robbed of her valuable ring. She cannot identify the man the police pick up, but in the presence of Sergeant Kirby, she accuses Eddie of taking her ring and money, stretching the truth in front of the police. Both law and court agree, and Eddie is sent to prison. A year later, the real mugger is arrested, the same man they picked up a year ago, who actually had the ring in his possession. Out of prison, Eddie stops by to see Miss Fox, who gives him $500 in cash for his trouble. But he doesn't really want any money for an operation. His girlfriend died while he was in prison. Later that evening, Miss Fox is attacked and this time she is strangled to death. As the killer leaves, $500 in cash is dropped on the floor beside the body.

Ground floor. Ladies lingerie, men's accessories, lotions. I seemed to have missed again. It doesn't matter. Our building like tonight's program has only one story and you've seen that. Uh-oh, here comes the owner of the building. He doesn't like his employees chatting with their betters. I'll continue as soon as he leaves. (commercial break) *I hope you'll return next week, when we shall add another story. And now if you don't intend to climb aboard, please step back off the pad. Going up.*

James Congdon and Bette Davis star in "Out There – Darkness"
(Photo courtesy of Ronald V. Borst / Hollywood Movie Posters)

EPISODE #134 **"TOTAL LOSS"** Broadcast on February 1, 1959
Starring: Nancy Olson as Jan Manning
Ralph Meeker as Mel Reeves   Ruth Storey as Evy
Dave Willock as Frank Voss, the insurance agent
Barbara Lord as Susan   Ray Teal as the fire chief
Jack Bryan as the young fireman   Jim Beck as Michael, the loan manager
An original teleplay written for *Alfred Hitchcock Presents* by J. E. Selby.
Directed by Don Taylor.

(in a steamcabinet) *Good evening, friends. . . and critics. Welcome to Alfred Hitchcock Presents. I say this for those of you who may be under the impression, you have tuned in to a production of Salome with me playing John the Baptist. I'm sure you are wondering why I, of all people would be in a steamcabinet. Actually, I'm having my suit pressed and was too modest to remove it.* (steam plus train whistle) *We had to hurry that a little. You see there's a certain party who wishes to press . . . his suit. A matter he will attend to at once.*

Story: No matter how hard she tries, Jan Manning finds herself running the clothing business into the ground. In debt, the loan manager at the bank won't giver her an extension, so Mel Reeves, a salesman friend, offers her a way out. Mel claims he knows a friend who can agree to torch the firm in exchange for half of the insurance money. Desperate, she agrees. Later that night, the police phone Jan at her house, waking her up to tell her that her business is burning down. Rushing down to the scene, the fire chief informs Jan that the building may be spared, but the inventory is a total loss. Sadly, an employee was hurt in the fire, third degree burns and when Jan learns about her faithful employee, she breaks down and tells an insurance investigator about the arson scheme. The inspector assures her that the fire was caused by an accident: Jan left a coffeepot on when she left work, and that was the cause of the fire. Unfortunately, the cat is out of the bag, and the investigator now wants to know more about her arson scheme.

I can't seem to get out of here. The certain party I mentioned a short time ago locked me in and is now selling three baseballs for a dime to passers-by. I'm not sure what he has in mind, but I don't like the way they're looking at me. (baseballs thrown at Hitchcock) *Fortunately we had already planned to inject something at this time that may save my life a more inviting target, here it comes now. After which I shall try to rejoin you.* (commercial break) *As you see, I managed to escape. Next week, we shall be back with another story. Until then, . . .* (train sounds) *. . . plum pudding. Good night.*

EPISODE #135 **"THE LAST DARK STEP"** Broadcast on February 8, 1959
   Starring: Robert Horton as Brad Taylor Fay Spain as Leslie
   Joyce Meadows as Janice Wright Herb Ellis as Detective Breslin
   David Carlile as Sergeant Langley
   Teleplay written for *Alfred Hitchcock Presents* by William Fay, based on the short story of the same name by Margaret Manners, originally published in a 1957 issue of *Argosy*. Subsequently anthologized in *Best Detective Stories of the Year*, ed. David C. Cooke, (Dutton, 1958).
   Directed by Herschel Daugherty.
   Good evening friends and suspects. From time to time we receive letters asking us to help viewers commit the perfect crime. Naturally we don't want to be put in the position of encouraging hardened criminals - amateurs perhaps. I think the first thing to remember is not to leave fingerprints around. Where homicide is concerned one should be as tidy as possible. I think I have just the thing. (glove with six fingers on) *One, two, three, four, five, six. Six. I happen to have over 400,000 of these. The gentleman who made them was a production genius. He just couldn't count. Next we have a training film and I want you latent criminals to pay closest attention.*

Story: Brad Taylor wants to end his relationship with novelist and television writer Leslie, a girlfriend who helped support him for years. He wants to marry Janice Wright, and even proposed to her this afternoon, which she accepted. When he breaks the news to Leslie, Brad realizes that she will never let go of him, no matter how hard he explains. Brad is her prize, not Janice's. and she'll do anything to keep from losing him. The next evening, Leslie and Brad drive down to the beach where the two take a swim and Brad, taking advantage of the opportunity, keeps Leslie under. drowning her in the surf. Arriving back home, Brad is amazed that the police know about the murder of his "lady friend." The police search him, finds his pocketknife, with a few strands of hair and blood on the handle. It seems Brad is going to be accused of murdering Janice Wright, which was actually a deed Leslie committed earlier in the afternoon!

Our training film has brought up another problem for you criminals, arch and otherwise. Vampir. Are you bothered by unsightly blood stains? Are tell tale stains hurting your social life and making the police suspicious? Why not try Vampir? Well. (reads label on can of powder and tries it on cloth) *While I continue my efforts, why don't you listen to this news report, on a more reliable product? Afterwhich I'll naturally and inevitably return to you.* (commercial break) *On reading the label, I discovered that actually Vampir does not claim to remove blood stains, it merely changes them into gravy stains. They're more socially acceptable. Next week we shall be back with another story and some shoplifting hints. If you desire any of the items we have demonstrated tonight, simply rip off the top of your cell block and send it in. Good night.*

EPISODE #136   **"THE MORNING OF THE BRIDE"**   Broadcast on February 15, 1959
    Starring: Barbara Bel Geddes as Helen Brewster   Don Dubbins as Philip Pryor
    Pat Hitchcock as Pat   Helen Conrad as Mrs. Beasley
    Teleplay written for *Alfred Hitchcock Presents* by Kathleen Hite, based on a story by Neil S. Boardman.
    Directed by Arthur Hiller.
    (croquet, foot-shackle) *Good evening. This is the most difficult and frustrating game of croquet I've ever played. I seem to be able to drive the ball quite well, but my shoulders keep getting stuck in the wickets. It's all very trying. Actually, I've consented to stand here like a watch fob in order to dramatize the subject of tonight's story. It concerns one of our oldest institutions. An institution which seeks to rehabilitate men by keeping them shut up for years. . . marriage. But first we have another equally revered institution, the television commercial.*

Story: For almost five years, Helen has been wanting to meet her boyfriend's mother. But for one reason or another, she never got to meet his mother. For a short while, Philip joined the service and left for Korea, but the dashing young man returned and again his mother remained evasive. Helen gets persuasive and attempts to visit Mrs. Pryor by herself, without Philip's assistance, but mother isn't at home. Later, when she mentions it to Philip, he explains that the doctor says mother is ill. Helen finally calls off their four-year engagement because of Philip's strange behavior, causing him to plead with her to marry him that night, and in the morning visit her mother-in-law. She reluctantly agrees, until they arrive at his mansion, and Helen reads a newspaper clipping describing the death of the old woman – which occurred seven years ago. A distressing fact Philip could never accept.

Ah, there you are again. These may look like rocks to you but they're really clusters of atoms. This is a very important job. And now, here's a scene from next week's show, after which you will find me still firmly anchored here. (commercial break) *If you liked that sample you will love next week's show for it will contain three such scenes. After seeing that one however, I put in an order for a set of these. For each of our viewers. Good night.*

    Trivia, etc. "Working with Patricia Hitchcock was like working with any of the other actresses I worked with and enjoyed creatively," said Arthur Hiller. "I wasn't thinking, 'Gee, this is Hitch's daughter,' nor was she thinking, 'Gee, I'm Hitch's daughter.' It was a normal fulfilling, creative relationship. I didn't know Hitchcock very well personally, but well enough for him to suggest a variety of drinks for me to try. I didn't like the taste of liquor and he kept trying to find a mixture that would appeal to me and give me pleasure. We often did the show in two long days of shooting rather than the three for a normal half hour show. Our shows were shorter in time due to the wonderful Hitchcock comments during the half hour. Hitch, of course, enhanced the show with his personality and wit, but boy did it put pressure on us during filming."

EPISODE #137 **"THE DIAMOND NECKLACE"** Broadcast on February 22, 1959
Starring: Claude Rains as Andrew Thurgood
Betsy Von Furstenberg as Miss Thelma Thurgood
Alan Hewitt as George Maynard   Stephen Bekassy as Dr. Antoine Rudel
Selmer Jackson as Henry, the clergyman
Peter Walker as Thurgood's assistant   Dorothea Lord as Mrs. Jessica Rudel
Norman DuPont as Thurgood's other assistant
An original teleplay written for *Alfred Hitchcock Presents* by Sarett Rudley.
Directed by Herschel Daugherty.
(art-exhibition paintings) *Oh, good evening. Uh, we seem to have had an art exhibition here. I realize artists are supposed to suffer, but I can't understand why they insist on sharing their sufferings with us. This one is called nursery wall. Strawberry jam. Now we come to the prize winner. I wonder what this one's called.* (empty frame) *Nude with necklace. I don't think this is a painting you should be allowed to look at too closely. So while I'm appreciating it, I shall ask you to look at another exhibit. One that may not be a work of art, but is wholesome enough for your children to watch.*

Story: George Maynard has plenty of new ideas for Maynard's Jewelry Store. Sadly for Andrew Thurgood, those ideas do not include him, and he is told to retire at the end of the week. During the thirty-seven years Thurgood worked there he has never been robbed once, a record he is proud to boast. But on the last day, before he packs his things, a woman manages to walk off with an expensive necklace. Being insured, the owner isn't too upset, and lets Thurgood off the hook - the employer not realizing that it was Thurgood's daughter who was the thief. It seems that the Thurgood clan had its own set of traditions, including one of having a member of each family's generation steal from the Maynard store just one time. Just when they think they have succeeded, Mr. Maynard comes by and says that he can't get away with it, as he left behind his bonus and gold watch. Seeing Thurgood's daughter, Mr. Maynard breaks another old rule of Maynards and hires a female, so the Thurgood tradition will go on.

(Hitchcock in the empty frame) *Oh - Well I guess that proves that heaven will protect the working girl. However, Thelma discovered why the Thurgood tradition was to steal from Maynards only once in a generation. The second time she was caught. I'm still fascinated by this painting, nude with necklace. It's just as good from this side. Uh, this seems to have slipped off.* (necklace) *I hate to hang this on the wrong spot. Look um, while I'm fumbling with this, suppose you turn your attention to our sponsor's message. Afterwhich I shall reasonably hasten back.* (commercial break) *Next week we shall be back with another story. Incidentally, to avoid any further embarrasment, I bought the painting only to discover that the frame doesn't go with it. But I think it's worth every cent.* (walks off with invisible painting).

Trivia, etc. Both Alan Hewitt and Peter Walker would later return to *Alfred Hitchcock Presents* four months later, playing against each other in "Invitation to an Accident." Selmer Jackson, who played the elderly man in this episode, also played the role of the F.B.I. Chief in Alfred Hitchcock's *Saboteur* (1942).

256

EPISODE #138   **"RELATIVE VALUE"**   Broadcast on March 1, 1959
        Starring: Denholm Elliott as John Manbridge
        Torin Thatcher as Uncle Felix Edward Manbridge
        Tom Conway as the Chief of Police   Frederic Worlock as Mr. Betts, the butler
        Walter L. Burke as Benny, the bookie   John Trayne as the Sergeant
        Barry Harvey as Longdon, the constable
        A. E. Gould-Porter as Tom, the bartender
        Mollie Glessing as Mrs. Simpson, the maid
        Teleplay written for *Alfred Hitchcock Presents* by Francis Cockrell, based on the
short story "The Supersluous Murderer" by Milward Kennedy. Subsequently reprinted in *A
Century of Detective Stories* (Hutchinson, 1935).
        Directed by Paul Almond.
        (advertisment board says "This Space For Rent, Inquire Within")   *Good evening.
This began when someone asked me if I wanted to go into the advertising business. I always
imagined it had more dignity than this. Of course, the term sandwich-boards intrigued me
too, little did I know that I would serve as the. . . boloney. As for boloney, more of that in a
moment. The possibilities of this type of advertising are limitless. I understand they are
putting advertising on the inside of reading glasses. This is excellent for people who
frequently stare off in space. I know I shall like it, because now I can sit down with a book
without having the feeling I'm wasting my time. Tonight's story is called "Relative Value,"
but first some of that meat I mentioned a little earlier.*

        Story: John Manbridge gets himself deeper and deeper into debt, and his wealthy
cousin Felix won't help him out. The old man tells John that all he has to do is wait, and
soon enough he will inherit Felix's fortune. Finally deciding that he must murder the man for
his money, John cleverly creates an alibi, kills his cousin and sneaks out of the house. When
an officer of the Yard passes by, the two of them, together, are shocked to find the dead body.
The Chief of Police, however, finds loopholes in John's alibi and figures out what really
happened. John realizes that he murdered the man for nothing, because his cousin was
already dying, having read a suicide note Felix left behind, and passes out from shock. The
constable tries to bring him around with a shot of whiskey which, unfortunately, is what Felix
had mixed his poison with.

        *That is the fate of anyone so careless as to kill a man who's already dead. I
wouldn't care if Felix had been living. But to strike a defenseless corpse is simply not my
idea of fair play. Speaking of fair play, I'm afraid it's my beloved sponsor's turn. But he
assures me that I shall have the last word.* (commercial break) *That on a note of triumph, we
conclude this evening's activities. Next week we shall have another story and of course,
more advertisements. I almost forgot to tell you. I finally leased the advertising space on my
backboard . . . to my insurance agent. Good night.* (Sign says "Fragile, Handle with Care")

EPISODE #139   **"THE RIGHT PRICE"**   Broadcast on March 8, 1959
        Starring: Eddie Foy, Jr. as "The Cat," the burglar
        Allyn Joslyn as Mort Bonner   Jane Dulo as Jocelyn Bonner
        Teleplay written for *Alfred Hitchcock Presents* by Bernard C. Schoenfeld, based on
the short story "Make Me An Offer" by Jay Street (alias Henry Slesar), originally published
in the December 1958 issue of *Alfred Hitchcock's Mystery Magazine*.
        Directed by Arthur Hiller.
        (drawing-table)   *Good evening fellow creatures. I've uh . . . been working as an
aeronautical engineer. I'm developing safety devices.* (crash) *Well, it was better than the
last time. For a moment I thought I was out of a job. Tonight's drama is called "The Right
Price." For those purists who like to see the connection between my part of the program and
the story, here it is.*

Story: Mort and Jocelyn Bonner's marriage is falling apart. With both of them constantly arguing, they won't even give each other the time of day. One evening, while Jocelyn is asleep in the bedroom upstairs, Mort encounters a burglar in the house, an enterprising individual who tries to strike a deal with Mort, in splitting the payoff from the robbery. This gives Mort other ideas: if the burglar was to kill his wife Jocelyn, they can later split her life insurance. Mort would get away with the perfect murder, and prosper at the same time. The burglar agrees and sneaks upstairs to commit the crime. After some time passes, Mort finds himself impatiently waiting downstairs and he begins to wonder if the crook didn't run out on him. He heard no sounds and the burglar has yet to return. Finally Mort gets the courage to go upstairs, and is unknowingly hit over the head and killed. It seems Jocelyn has worked out a better deal with the burglar.

I think the lesson that story teaches is, if you want a job done properly, do it yourself. Naturally Jocelyn and the burglar were caught. Personally I don't see anything shocking about a person being paid to commit murder. I do it every week. But now I must do some more experimenting which will take exactly, I think one minute. (throws paperplane) (commercial break) *If that wasn't more too learnt, than I might refer to that commercial as a hard sell. However the cell I think of in connection with that, is a padded one. I believe I have at last designed the perfect flying machine.* (shows a drawing of a bird) *As you see it has its production problems. It still has some bugs in it and the workers on our assembly line are going to look rather odd sitting on all those eggs. But I'm optimistic. Now I wish to thank all of you for your indulgence. Next week I should be back with more of the same. Until then, good night.*

Trivia, etc.: For some reason Joe, the police officer that stops by at the house is not billed during the closing credits.

EPISODE #140 **"I'LL TAKE CARE OF YOU"** Broadcast on March 15, 1959
Starring: Ralph Meeker as John Forbes   Russell Collins as Dad
Elisabeth Fraser as Dorothy Forbes   Ida Moore as Kitty
Arthur Batanides as the police detective   Rad Fulton as student #1
Richard Evans as student #2   Richard Rust as student #3
Richard Gering as student #4
Teleplay written for *Alfred Hitchcock Presents* by William Fay, based on the short story of the same name by George Johnson, originally published in the November 1958 issue of *Bestseller Mystery Magazine*.
Directed by Robert Stevens.
Good evening television viewers. Before we continue with tonight's motion picture, allow me to call your attention to some of the bargains available in our used rocket division down at "Honest Alfred's." All our rockets are late, one-owner models with very low mileage. In fact some never even got off the ground. They are also simple to operate provided you know how to count to one. Listen to these typical bargains. A Vanguard rocket complete with extras, this exceptional bargain travelled only 250 miles before falling into the water off Cape Canaveral. Or perhaps you'd be interested in a late model "Thor," which still has the original mouse in its nosecone. But now for our movie. It is a one-minute condensation of a 1935 hit.

Story: Used car salesman John Forbes is stressed to the max. He's in hock, business is slow, and he wants to get rid of his money-blowing wife, but business must come first. Three college students ride onto the lot one afternoon, and explain that they need a cheap but good-looking jalopy for demolition in a school carnival. John tells them to come back at the end of the week and he'll see what he can do. Later that evening, along the road, John sees an advantage to run his wife over, and returns home to tell his father that he was involved in an accident. Always the ever-caring father, the old man takes the car to the shop and fixes it up, covering any signs of the accident. Later in the week, the students return and seeing the solution to his problem, the father offers the same car for demolition. Two detectives snooping around, figure the old man knocked Mrs. Forbes off, having seen him sell a good car for a mere $50, and it looks as if the father is going to take the rap. And who tipped off the police? None other than Dad's wife, Kitty. It looks like son-in-law John will have to financially take care of her now – which again puts John in a financial situation.

I'm sorry to say that Honest Alfred's cold war supplier store has been forced to close. Our buyers just didn't keep up their monthly payments and it was rather difficult for us to get in touch with them after they got into orbit. Here is news from a more successful enterpreneur, after which I shall return. (commercial break) *By the way, those of you who witnessed tonight's crime will be glad to learn that the party who perpetrated it has been justly punished. I refer not to the recent commercial, but to John Forbes' murder of his wife, when I last heard the person responsible for the commercial was still at large. The big ones always get away. Next week I shall be back with another story. Until then, goodnight.*

EPISODE #141 **"THE AVON EMERALDS"** Broadcast on March 22, 1959
    Starring: Roger Moore as Inspector David Benson
    Hazel Court as Lady Avon   Gertrude Flynn as Mrs. Catherine Smedly
    Alan Napier as Sir Charles Harrington   Ralph Clanton as Mr. Saunders
    Richard Lupino as Fletcher, the thief   Barry Harvey as Hodges
    Louis G. Mercier as French detective
    Teleplay written for *Presents* by William Fay, based on a story by Joe Pidcock.
    Directed by Bretaigne Windust. *
    (customs trunk)   *Good evening, ladies and gentlemen. I decided quite suddenly to go abroad. It seems a very rich but distant aunt has disappeared. I decided to console myself on the Riviera until the matter is cleared up and the insurance policy paid off.* (blood oozing from a trunk) *Ketchup! It's perfect for travel. I find a bottle or two will make any dish taste like home cooking.* (security) *I've already told him I have nothing to declare. The upturned palm, the symbol of travel. However, I'm afraid he wants the key to my trunk. I think this would be the perfect moment for you to look the other way. Those of you who know of no other way to look, will have to endure the following.*

Story: David Benson, a detective at the Criminal Investigation Department, is ordered to tail the wealthy Lady Avon, to discover if she is trying to smuggle a valuable emerald necklace out of the country, so it can be sold on the open market for full value – thus defrauding the Treasury. A concerned Benson contacts Lady Avon and asks her to place the jewels somewhere other than a non-secure hotel safe, but she refuses and shortly after, the jewels are stolen. He tries to learn the truth by questioning her, but she can easily prove being nowhere near the robbery. She never insured the jewels and being stolen, makes it convenient for selling on the black market. As Lady Avon leaves England, the detective continues to follow her, but French authorities explain to him that the matter is out of their hands, as she has broken no French laws. Lady Avon is satisfied she is in the clear and sells the necklace, then afterwards settles down with the real thief, Detective Benson.

My friend seems to have been disturbed by something he discovered in my trunk. He has asked me to discuss the matter in his offices. But please remain here, I know I shall be back in a moment. Isn't this a great deal of fuss to make over a bottle of ketchup? (commercial break) *My difficulty with the customs official turned out to be rather serious. He found my aunt in the trunk, quite dead of course, but it was a peculiar place for her to be. He was terribly upset. You see, she had no passport and they are very strict you know. I'm very much afraid I shall have to change my plans and continue without her. But my trip is a short one. I shall be back in a week. Until then, Au revoir.*

* Opening music also used in "Incident at a Corner."

Alternate narrative:

My difficulty with the customs official turned out to be rather serious. He found my aunt in the trunk, quite dead of course, but it was a peculiar place for her to be. He was terribly upset. You see, she had no passport and they are very strict you know. I'm very much afraid I shall have to change my plans and continue without her. Au revoir.

EPISODE #142   "THE KIND WAITRESS"   Broadcast on March 29, 1959
> Starring: Rick Jason as Arthur
> Olive Deering as Miss Thelma Thompkins, the waitress
> Celia Lovsky as Mrs. Sara Mannerheim   Mary Alan Hokanson as Marion
> Robert Carson as the judge   Charles H. Meredith as Dr. Lacey
> John Zaremba as Dr. Maxwell   Charles Seel as the court clerk
> Teleplay written for *Alfred Hitchcock Presents* by William O'Farrell, based on the short story "Case of the Kind Waitress" by Henry Slesar, originally published in the October 1958 issue of *Alfred Hitchcock's Mystery Magazine*. Subsequently collected in *Clean Crimes and Neat Murders* (Avon, 1960).
> Directed by Paul Henreid.
> (lunch-o-mat)   *Good evening. Tonight I'm dining at my favorite club. There are many advantages here. As you can see, informality is the rule. There is also the stimulation of intellectual companionship without the deafening quiet that pervades in most clubs. Best of all I like its privacy. Only four persons are allowed at a table and of course no one pays any attention to you. Our program is not restricted to views of Attonia clubs. We also plan a visit to the cinema where we shall see a film entitled "The Kind Waitress." It begins after this one minute appetizer.*

Story: Waitress Thelma Thompkins is considered one of the kindest waitresses in the town's most fashionable restaurant. This opinion is also shared by an old lady named Mannerheim, a regular customer of Thelma's, who tells the waitress that Thelma is mentioned in her will. Back at home, Thelma and her boyfriend decide to speed up the old woman's demise, so they can inherit a fortune. He obtains a poison named Anatine, but no matter how much they give her, she seems to do better. Frustrated, Thelma meets the old woman in private and strangles Mrs. Mannerheim. After she is arrested does she learn that the old woman's doctor had been prescribing Anatine for the old woman's heart condition.

Oh. This type of restaurant underlines one of the basic confusions of my life. I frequently find myself trying to tip slot machines and tilt waitresses. Just now I'm trying to find the kaviar. While I am looking, suppose you do the same. I shall rejoin you in a minute. (commercial break) *They don't have kaviar. The manager has offered me elderberry jam, which he claims looks exactly the same. He feels that when you buy kaviar you're just spending a lot of money for the name. He may be right. I'll never know. Next week we shall return with another story. Until then, good night.*

EPISODE #143   "CHEAP IS CHEAP"   Broadcast on April 5, 1959
> Starring: Dennis Day as Alexander Gifford   Alice Backes as Jennifer Gifford
> Fred Essler as Arthur   Jack Lambert as the hit man
> Gage Clarke as the doctor   Frank Richards as Mugg, the prisoner
> An original teleplay written for *Alfred Hitchcock Presents* by Albert E. Lewin and Burt Styler.
> Directed by Bretaigne Windust.
> (half picture)   *Good evening, ladies and gentlemen. Please do not be alarmed. Nothing has happened to your television set, nor are you slipping below the coffee table again. We've decided to economize. Everyone had to take a 50% cut. I was fortunate, we have an extremely short camera man who was eliminated entirely. We anticipate great*

260

savings since we shall be transmitting only half as much as previously. This process also has an educational value. The very young can cover the top part of the screen and be able to see what radio programs used to look like. And now ladies and gentlemen, for our next two features we leave our new wide-screen process and go to the conventionally shaped picture.

Story: Jennifer is married to an amazingly cheap individual, Alexander Gifford. When she is finally driven to the point where she cannot tolerate his miserly ways, and finds out that he had money put away in the bank, she goes on a super-shopping spree in retaliation. Gifford is furious and contemplates divorcing her, then considers having a hit man kill her, but both alternatives are too expensive. He then visits a man called Arthur to buy poison but that also is too expensive, so he decides to knock Jennifer off himself. First trying with food poisoning but when that fails, he puts a pillow over her face at night. But when he finds out that it will cost $160 to bury her, he instead sells the body to the Pathology Department at the State University Medical School in the interest of science . . . and makes a nice $75 profit.

Where are you? I'm looking . . . oh there you are. I couldn't find you. Before our overzealous efficiency expert blacks me out entirely, I should mention that Mr. Gifford was caught and paid the supreme penalty. In his case a heavy fine. You see the moral of tonight's story is, the perfect murder should also include a happy funeral and a decent burial. And now for the perfect commercial after which I will return. (commercial break) *I'm certain that you'll be delighted to know that we saved enough money tonight so that next week we shall be able to send you a double exposure. And now until then,* (light goes out) *when I assure you we shall return to television. Good night, wherever you are.*

Trivia, etc. Pervading this comical approach of murder and cheapness, humor infiltrated scene after scene. Dennis Day, who is probably best known as the singer stooge on *The Jack Benny Program*, actually plays a similar role of his ficticous boss Benny, that of a stingy penny grubber. Director Bretaigne Windust also helped bring humor to the screen cinematically, besides the printed word. During the struggle in which Alexander smothers the life out of his wife, the words "Home Sweet Home" are sewn on the front of the pillow. But the best in-joke of them all was probably when a comment in the story was made about seeing a dame on TV that used a frozen leg of lamb for murder, at 59 cents a pound. Does "Lamb to the Slaughter" sound familiar?

"Al and I were working for a producer named Harry Coogan, who was doing a Ray Milland series [*Markham*] for Universal," explained Burt Styler. "We had done a number of scripts and then we came up with a story idea Harry thought was a little too strange for him. But he phoned Joan Harrison and said, 'I think you should have a talk with these guys." So we went in and talked with Joan Harrison, told her the story and she said 'write it.' We originally wrote it for Charles Laughton and Elsa Lanchester. It was a murder story about a man who was driven by his cheapness to kill, but unfortunately we didn't get the casting we wanted because they had Dennis Day. That was the way it went. But we really needed a real actor for that. In those days, you see, they didn't rewrite you. What you put down on paper went on stage as they shot. It was such a wonderful feeling working for them back then. We were pretty busy doing one show from another but the whole relationship between writer and producer was so different than it is today. You did the script, they didn't bring in a truckload of rewrite men, and after a few questions and answers, they left you be. That was the way it went with any show I worked on at that time. Al and I wrote for so many television comedies at that time, *My Favorite Martian* and *The Life of Riley*, so our humor fit in place. Afterwards, Joan Harrison actually called us in to do another one, from a story by Valerie Dyke, about a dog that inherits a fortune ["Craig's Will"]."

EPISODE #144 "THE WAXWORK" Broadcast on April 12, 1959
        Starring: Barry Nelson as Raymond "Ray" Hewson
        Everett Sloane as Mr. Marriner   Shai K. Ophir as Henry Bourdette
        Charles Davis as a museum attendant   Mavis Neal as a museum attendant
        Betty Fairfax as museum employee
        Also in the cast: Laurence Conroy, Hal H. Thompson, John O'Leary. Patrick
Westwood. Dorothy McKinnon and Vincent G. Perry.
        Teleplay written for *Alfred Hitchcock Presents* by Casey Robinson, based on the
1931 short story of the same name by Alfred M. Burrage. Burrage originally wrote the story
under the alias Ex-Private X, collected in *Someone in the Room.*
        Directed by Robert Stevens.
        (medieval rack)   *Good evening. This is called a rack. A kind of medieval chaise
lounge. The victim lies down and his limbs are fastened to the rollers at each end. The body
is then gradually stretched to. . . and past the breaking point. They were quite droll in those
days. You see a latin inscription, placed so the victim can't read it. Nunc potes altior quam
illam. Meaning, now you can be taller than she is. Tonight we're presenting a play entitled
"The Waxwork." First however, we have the 20th century equivalent of the rack. Now
please, no screams. After all this hurts me more than it does you.*

        Story: London, 1954. Ray Hewson, a free-lance writer for the Illustrated Weekly,
has an interest in writing a picture story, in order to pay for a gambling debt he hasn't made
good on. After taking a tour of the museum's workshop and exhibits, Ray asks Mr. Marriner,
the owner of the Waxworks Museum, if can let him spend the night in his "murderer's den"
exhibit. Mr. Marriner is reluctant at first, but seeing that wax dummies can't hurt anyone, he
agrees. Later that evening, when all is quiet and everyone gone, Ray is typing away on his
typewriter when he is shocked to see the figure of Henry Bourdette, come to life. Bourdette
was supposed to have been executed this morning, a murderer ten times over. always with a
knife, and with his talent for practicing mesmerism with his deep, staring blue eyes. It seems
Bourdette escaped execution and has been hiding among the waxworks all day, to elude
capture. And thanks to present circumstances, Bourdette is ready to give the reporter a close
shave . . . When the museum is opened the next morning, Ray is found dead, sitting with his
head back as if he was in a barber's chair, though there isn't a mark on him. Assuming he
died of fright, the owner prepares to display the just-finished wax figure of Henry Bourdette,
the latest addition to his gallery.

        *So much for our museum memories. In the earlier part of this program, I referred
to the commercial as the 20th century rack. Unfortunately, our sensitive sponsor mistakingly
interpreted this as a veiled insult. I certainly want to apologize. Furthermore I'm going to
turn over a new leaf.* (screen flips around) *There, I feel much better. Now ladies and
gentlemen, before I return.* (waves and leaves; commercial break) *A moment ago I
apologized for comparing the rack and the commercial. But I neglected to mention to whom
I was apologizing. I think I shall leave it that way. As for this charming device, it is being
returned to the athletic department of Arcadia University. I especially wish to thank the
Arcadia basketball coach, Stretch Mulligan, for his generosity. Good night.*

        Trivia, etc. Actors Betty Fairfax, Laurence Conroy and Mavis Neal, who played
small supporting roles in this episode, all played small supporting roles in *The Notorious
Landlady* (1962). "The Waxwork" has been featured on numerous horror / mystery
anthologies, with many actors playing the role of the victimized reporter: Claude Rains,
Herbert Marshall and William Conrad to name a few.
        As a sidelight, this was one of many stories to appear in the 1957 publication,
Alfred Hitchcock Presents: Stories They Wouldn't Let Me Do on TV.

EPISODE #145 **"THE IMPOSSIBLE DREAM"** Broadcast on April 19, 1959
Starring: Franchot Tone as Oliver Matthews
Carmen Mathews as Miss Hall
Mary Astor as Grace Dolin
Suzy Lloyd as the woman in the car
Irene Windust as Myra Robbins, the actress
Dick Jeffries as the director
William D. Kruse as the man in the car
Pat O'Malley as wardrobe assistant/stagehand
Teleplay written for *Alfred Hitchcock Presents* by Meade Roberts, based on a story by John Lindsey.
Directed by Robert Stevens.
(camera with gun in back) *Good evening, and please watch the birdie. Actually we couldn't afford a birdie for you to watch, that is why I am here. My camera is a new one and I'm quite proud of it. Oh this. . . this is an attachment of my own. I find it invaluable for making the subjects sit still. It's really quite effective. My prints turn out perfectly, it's just the people who need retouching. Now I see it is time for a word from someone, who has continuily refused my invititation to sit for a portrait. But perhaps a candid shot.*

Story: An aging, over-the-hill actor is close to unemployment with little likelihood of being hired for a leading role. The only one who shows interest in the former leading man is his secretary, Miss Hall, whose presence he cannot stand. She's so dedicated that she writes all the fan mail he gets. To get her out of his hair, he lies to Miss Hall, claiming he is going on a trip to Mexico, but in reality he returns to his home, where he meets Grace Dolin, a studio worker who has been blackmailing him for many years. Oliver claims he never murdered Grace's daughter years ago, but his love letters that would incriminate him and create scandal, won't leave Grace's possession so long as he continues paying. The penniless Oliver complains that he cannot afford to pay her anymore, but she still wants money, and he is forced to kill her and dump her body in a lake. Returning to his house, he finds Miss Hall there, who tells him she knows all about the blackmail and murder, but she is willing to stay quiet . . . if he will marry her.

And they lived happily ever after. You see Oliver also had an impossible dream, and it also came true. His dream was that he and Miss Hall would be caught and convicted and sentenced to separate penal institutions. And now before I return, I want you to meet a gentleman who, though never dream, has become quite impossible. (commercial break) *Thank you Sir, for that unsolicited testimonial. I also wish to thank Alfred Hitchcock Productions, makers of fine suspense stories, for relinquishing a minute of their time. Next week we should all be back. Until then, good night.*

Trivia, etc. Franchot Tone, who starred in *Dark Waters* and *Phantom Lady* (both 1944 pictures produced by Joan Harrison), made his one and only appearance on *Alfred Hitchcock Presents*, and would be the only time he ever worked with actress Mary Astor. Playing the role of Oliver Matthew's wardrobe assistant/stagehand is Pat O'Malley, a veteran of silent movies who played almost every role thought of in American cinema. Here, in ironic casting, he supports an over-the-hill actor from the era that originated in his career. O'Malley also appeared in two films Mary Astor also appears in: *The Fighting American* (1924) and *Those We Love* (1932).
On April 26, 1959, *Alfred Hitchcock Presents* was not broadcast. Instead, CBS presented a two-hour special presentation of "Meet Me in St. Louis," based on the book by Sally Benson. This original television presentation featured Patty Duke, Jacquelyn McKeever, Ed Wynn, Myrna Loy, Jane Powell, Walter Pidgeon, Tab Hunter and Jeanne Crain. Broadcast from 9 to 11 p.m., EST.

EPISODE #146   **"BANQUO'S CHAIR"**   Broadcast on May 3, 1959
Rehearsed and filmed on March 25 – 26, 1959.
Starring: John Williams as Mr. William Brent   Kenneth Haigh as John Bedford
Reginald Gardiner as Major Cooke-Finch   Max Adrian as Robert Stone
Thomas P. Dillon as Sergeant Balter
Hilda Plowright as Miss May Thorpe / ghost of Miss Ferguson
George Pelling as Lein, the butler
Teleplay written for *Alfred Hitchcock Presents* by Francis Cockrell, based on the short story of the same name by Rupert Croft-Cooke, originally collected in *Pharaoh and His Waggons and Other Stories* (Jarrolds, 1937).
Directed by Alfred Hitchcock.
(lady bearers come in with department store boxes and Hitchcock is dressed for a Hollywood safari)   *Buana, wait here. Good evening ladies and gentlemen and welcome to darkest Hollywood. Night brings a stillness to the jungle, it is so quiet you can hear a name drop. But the savage beasts have already begun gathering at the waterholes to quench their thirst. Now one should be especially alert. The vicious tablehopper is on the prowl. And the spotted backbiter may lurk behind a potted palm. In order to reach the scene of tonight's story our little safari must now move inexorably and incomprehencebly from smoggy Hollywood to foggy London. Fortunately we make this sidetrip through the pure exhilarating air of commercial television.*

Story: Blackheath, near London. October 23, 1903. John Bedford is suspected of being the murderer of his wealthy aunt, Miss Ferguson, but the police are unable to break his alibi. Now, exactly two years after the crime, a retired Scotland Yard investigator named William Brent, puts together a plan that he hopes will make the nephew confess. Brent invites the young man to a dinner at the home that once belonged to the late Aunt, and secretly hires an actress to pretend to be the ghost of the dead woman. Everyone at the dinner is in on the scheme, and when the apparition appears, no one claims to see anything – except Bedford, that is. The fifth time the ghost appears, the men play stupid again till Bedford, out of wit's end, cracks: "get out whoever you are or I'll kill you again!" The ghost vanishes and the men stand to attention. The police take the nephew away just as May Thorpe, the hired actress, shows up and asks if she is too late to play the part of Miss Ferguson.

Good evening again. Following that little presentation, I'm prepared to continue our safari through the jungles of Hollywood. As you can see I'm ready to hunt for the really big game, so I've hired a native guide. (snaps fingers and a guide comes out with sign "addresses to the stars") *He claims to know exactly where the big ones are to be found.* (snaps again and the guide leaves) *In order to flush the game from its hiding place we use a pack of fierce autograph hounds. Just yesterday they treed a big boar and before they could be stopped they had torn his dinner jacket to bits. Now, as an example of the flora and fauna of this area, we present a motion picture. This picture was shot under incredible conditions. We were in constant danger of the heat, native attacks and temperamental outbursts. Five years in the preparation, a year in shooting. All destilled into one precious minute. But I see it's time for me to keep an important appointment. I shall rejoin you following this, it will only take a minute. His time is valuable.* (Hitchcock rests on couch and begins talking to a witch doctor – commercial break) *I'm afraid I must press on until next week at the same time. My native bearers are getting restless. That last commercial frightened them. Coenga! Macambo!* (walks off with his bearers, women carrying department store boxes)

EPISODE #147   **"A NIGHT WITH THE BOYS"**   Broadcast on May 10, 1959
Starring: John Smith as Irving "Irv" Randall
Joyce Meadows as Francie Randall   Sam Buffington as Smalley
Joe De Santis as the lieutenant   David Carlile as the police officer
Buzz Martin as the kid
Dick Nelson as the fourth card player   William D. Kruse as Manny

Teleplay written for *Alfred Hitchcock Presents* by Bernard C. Schoenfeld, based on the short story "A Fist Full of Money" by Henry Slesar and Jay Folb, originally published in the February 1959 issue of *Playboy*. Subsequently collected in *Clean Crimes and Neat Murders* (Avon, 1960).

Directed by John Brahm.

(with beard and beret) *Good evening fellow members of the beat generation. Thank you for allowing me in your pad. Some of you cats are no doubt wondering how I got with it. Well man, getting in this generation isn't hard. No daddy-o, you just lie about your age. But I didn't join just for kicks or just to dig the crazy types, no mam. I joined because I wanted to be as avant as I could get. And this is it. I'm a jug man and I love to ball along with the wheel in the hand and a ball on the road. I'll have to dig the cool notes of a tenor man blowing his top in a wild drive in San Fran. For it is then that I know the essence of life. But you must think me that talking this cat that ever flipped. It's time to cut out. This associates me from the bolshevize trivia which follows. I'll dig you later.*

Story: Irving, a man with a low-paying job, is upset that he lost $96 playing cards with his obnoxious boss and wonders how he will explain it to his pregnant wife. A police officer stops Irving as he walks home to warn him about muggers, which gives him a brainstorm. He smothers dirt on his clothes, cuts his face and goes home to his wife to claim he was robbed, but his wife forces him to call the police. Irving doesn't know what to do when the police tell him they have the mugger, who had $92 on him. He cannot bring himself to condemn an innocent kid, so he agrees to drop the charges if the money is returned, which the stranger agrees to do, although he states: "I never saw this guy before." With his money returned, Irving stops to pay a visit to his old poker partner, only to find that he has been mugged the night before and lost $92 exactly.

John Smith and Joyce Meadows phone the police after John returns home, having been mugged by an unknown attacker.

Photo courtesy of Ronald V. Borst / Hollywood Movie Posters.

265

What can I say man? A typical tale of middle class types. Caught in the rat race of modern society. And a happy ending as a final sellout to commercialism. But that reminds me, you wanted to know why I'm hung up. I shall now show you what bugged me. I'll dig you at its conclusion. Please reciprocate. (commercial break) *Man, I've changed my mind. That was the greatest. The story may be unhip, but those crazy commercials are pure poetry. They deserve better treatment. Next time I shall read them to a jazz accompaniment. Man, this could be a new art form. Pure but frantic. And now it's time for me to split the joint. I'll dig you in one week. I hope you can make the scene.*

Trivia, etc. William Douglas Kruse would later become a location manager for television's *Hunter*, and *When the Bough Breaks* (1986). He would also become an assistant director for *Captive Hearts* (1987). Dick Nelson would later write an episode for television's *Hunter*. Joe De Santis was host and narrator for the TV series *The Trap*, which aired a few years before this Hitchcock episode was broadcast.

EPISODE #148 **"YOUR WITNESS"** Broadcast on May 17, 1959
Starring: Brian Keith as Arnold Shawn   Leora Dana as Mrs. Shawn
William Hansen as Henry Babcock   Brian G. Hutton as Kenneth Jerome, Jr.
Gordon Wynn as Kenneth Jerome, Sr.   John Harmon as Al Carmody
G. Stanley Jones as a lawyer   Everett Glass as the judge
Wayne Heffley as the prosecutor   William D. Kruse as a police officer
Teleplay written for *Alfred Hitchcock Presents* by William Fay, based on the short story of the same name by Helen Nielsen, originally published in the December 1958 issue of *Alfred Hitchcock's Mystery Magazine*.
Directed by Norman Lloyd.
(as a New England judge) *Good evening ladies and gentlemen and welcome to Alfred Hitchcock Presents.* (walks over and sits down at the hairdressers) *I am busy getting ready for tonight's play, which is a courtroom drama and is called "Your Witness." Before court convenes, however, we have our usual one-minute recess.*

Story: A young man runs over and kills an old pedestrian, but a high-power lawyer, Arnold Shawn, possessing the talent of making innocent people look guilty and vice versa, is hired to get him off the hook. And he does just that by proving on the stand that the only witness, Mr. Babcock, is 85% visually impaired, and therefore could not have seen the young man's careless driving, or the circumstances involved. Meanwhile, Shawn's wife has become increasingly aggravated with her husband's fooling around with another woman. With the trial now over, she asks Shawn to sign papers that would start a divorce, but he has no intention of losing his stature or position. Outside the courthouse, she meets Mr. Babcock, who proves to her that he can see very well indeed – her husband merely applied a shrewd tactic that just ruined Babcock's career. It seems he had a cataract operation recently that corrected his vision, but now that he has been discredited in court, he doubts he will ever get his teaching job back. A few minutes later, in desperation, Shawn's wife runs her husband down with her car. "But officer," she explains, "I don't know how it happened except that he stepped right in front of the car." The police are baffled as to which shots to call, and the only witness to the accident was Mr. Babcock, who tells the officers that they are going to have to take her word for it. "It's a legal fact that I'm not a competent witness."

I think that we have once more pointed out that behind every great man there is a woman. So men watch out. Sadly enough the police quickly saw through Mrs Shawn's story and the community gave her a rousing boat of thanks and a 99-year sentence. And speaking of long sentences, I shall be back after this one. (commercial break) *Thank you very much.* (manicurists leave) *You know, I thought there was something peculiar about those girls. Now I'm ready, but I'm afraid the trial is over. Perhaps I can use this costume next week when we shall return with another story. Until then, good night.*

Trivia, etc. "About a month or two after 'Six People, No Music,' I was assigned a good role in 'Your Witness,' which was to star Wendell Corey and Leora Dana, the latter I was looking forward to meeting since I'd heard so much about her work on Broadway," recalled Wayne Heffley. "I got to the set that Monday morning only to find that Wendell Corey was being replaced by Brian Keith. The courtroom scenes were wall to wall dialogue, Keith to play the Defense Attorney, I to play the Prosecutor, so we went into his dressing room and had a marathon line reading . . . until he was ready. Keith did the whole thing by the seat of his pants and he did it well. I worked a lot with him subsequently on *Family Affair* and always found him wonderful to work with."

EPISODE #149   **"HUMAN INTEREST STORY"**   Broadcast on May 24, 1959
Rehearsed and filmed on April 8 – 9, 1959.
Starring: Steve McQueen as Bill Everett
Arthur Hill as Yangan Dahl in Howard Wilcox's body
Tyler McVey as Cargan   William Challee as Barney Welsh, the bartender
Anne Anderson as Mrs. Elsie Wilcox
Teleplay written for *Alfred Hitchcock Presents* by Fredric Brown, from his short story "The Last Martian," originally published in the October 1950 issue of *Galaxy Science Fiction Magazine.* Subsequently collected in *Honeymoon in Hell* (Bantam, 1958) and in *And the Gods Laughed* (Phantasia, 1987).
Directed by Norman Lloyd.
(Hi-Fi stereo jail) *Good evening. Do you enjoy assembling your own high fidelity or stereophonic sound systems, with their complicated components as speakers on every wall? Then you'll be especially interested in what I'm about to show you. I have just developed what I consider the latest in sound reproduction. This is designed for those persons who desire simplicity rather than fidelity. As you can see there is only one speaker, nor is that the only improvement. We have also eliminated the old fashioned record changer. Now only two attachments are necessary, a small crank and a hearing aid. By the way, neither of those items is needed for our next number.*

Story: Bill Everett is a newspaper reporter who does an interview with a man who claims, of all things, to be a Martian. He states in total seriousness that he escaped a Martian asylum and noticed that most Martians seemed to have died. Then, beside the body of a priest, he found a button which he pushed and strangely found himself walking the streets on Earth, in Howard Wilcox's body. Hearing the entire story about some Martian invasion, Bill suggests to Wilcox that it would be best if he not reveal his true nature to anyone else. Arriving back to work, Bill tells the editor that he had to kill Wilcox, as the man would have caused undue attention to the Martian invasion plans, which the man apparently knew nothing of. The editor agrees with Bill's decision, as the world must not suspect their presence until the Martians can completely conquer Earth.

As for Mr. Everett, I should say that he was caught and paid his debt to society, except that the Earth man society that love to catch and penalize one another, ceased to exist after we took over. . . We have taken over, haven't we? We haven't? (commercial break) *My fellow Martians seemed to have taken umbrage of my letting the cat out of the bag. However I shall be allowed to return to Earth next week at the same time. We Martians have found that those not smart enough to be trusted, the ones with very low IQ's, are still perfectly suited to appear on television. Our institutions are full of them. Good night.*

Trivia, etc. "I met Steve McQueen for the first time when I showed up on the set of 'Human Interest Story'," said Tyler McVey. "As I recall, he was very cooperative on the set and worked well with the cast. I liked Norman Lloyd as a director and he apparently liked me, because I worked on several Hitchcock episodes that he directed. Those shows were very well planned and well directed. The people that made those shows in those days had a great sense of humor and there was always a certain amount of clowning around on the set."

EPISODE #150 **"THE DUSTY DRAWER"** Broadcast on May 31, 1959

Starring: Dick York as Norman Logan Philip Coolidge as William Tritt
Wilton Graff as Mr. Pinkson J. Pat O'Malley as Colonel Binns
Almira Sessions as Mrs. M. Merrell Charity Grace as Mrs. Babford
Edgar Dearing as the gun salesman
Barry Brooks as Lewis, the bank security guard

Teleplay written for *Alfred Hitchcock Presents* by Halsted Welles, based on the short story by Harry Muheim, originally published in the May 3, 1952 issue of *Collier's*, (even though it was the reprint in the March 1956 issue of *Ellery Queen's Mystery Magazine* that caught Harrison or Lloyd's attention). Subsequently anthologized in *Best Detective Stories of the Year*, ed. David C. Cooke (Dutton, 1953) and in *Hitchcock in Prime Time*, ed. Francis M. Nevis, Jr. and Martin H. Greenberg (Avon, 1985).

Directed by Herschel Daugherty.

(bank cashier) *Good evening. It is always pleasant to greet old customers. As you know I have always been a great believer that there is safety in numbers provided those numbers are preceded by dollar signs. Working in a bank has also taught me a great deal about people. Most of them don't seem to be able to fill out our withdraw slips properly. Here is one I was handled recently, a typical example. He didn't even attempt to use our form, but made one of his own. At the top, he has printed, "This is a hold-up." Below that is written, "Put 5,000 dollars in a brown papersack, and hand it to me." He didn't even sign his name, but I honored it. I recognized him as the President of the bank across the street. Tonight's drama is concerned with a bank. The commercial is about money. That's what our sponsor makes, you know.* (puts up a sign - next window, please)

Story: Ten months ago, William Tritt, a teller at the State Bank, short-changed Norman Logan $200 in order to cover one of his mistakes. Logan knows what happened but without proof, he's stuck in a hard spot. With his mother in the hospital, Norman has been resorting to cashing in his bonds every month. One day, while waiting for Tritt to bring out his bond chart, Logan discovers a dusty drawer in a table that appears to have been forgotten, and completely unknown to the bank staff. Pulling out a toy gun, Logan orders Tritt to fetch $10,000 in twenty-dollar bills. The alarm, of course, is tripped and Logan is searched – but no gun. The police are forced to let him go for lack of evidence. Tritt gets into hot water over the situation, having been made to look like a fool, so the month after, Logan pulls the same stunt again, this time he gets the $10,000 he asks for, and once again, hides the gun (and money) in the drawer. Outside the bank, Logan is searched again, and the same results - no money or gun. Returning to the bank, Logan sneaks the money and gun out of the drawer, into his case, and cashes his bonds. Tritt, in the meantime, has gone crazy, not able to comprehend what's going on, and is sent to a hospital for examination.

And almost everyone lived happily ever after. Closing time is almost upon us. I must count up the money. You watch the following after which I'll be back. Here ladies and gentlemen is the ultimate ending to tonight's story. (commercial break) *Well you pays your money and you takes your choice. I haven't been able to balance my books, so I am taking my work home with me. I'm very conscientious that way. I hope you tune in next week, when we shall have another story. Until then, good night.*

Trivia, etc. "The Hitchcock script was based on a short story of mine of the same name that appeared in the late *Collier's* magazine in 1952," recalled Harry Muheim. "I subsequently adapted it into a one-hour for presentation on the *Philco Television Playhouse* – 'live from New York' as they used to say. My Philco script used the device of the performer-as-narrator. William Prince played the lead, and he would play a scene, turn from the scene to comment to the camera, then turn back into the scene. It was a complex device that worked against the essential simplicity of the prose piece. But I liked it. Maybe because I had written it! I had no connection with the making of the Hitchcock version, and I remember seeing it some years later with no freshness in my view. I was just looking to see how it differed from 'my' version. It was an unfair way to look at a perfectly substantial show. But that's the way I was in those days – back in the Pleistocene era. Matter of fact, I would like to see it again sometime."

(Photo courtesy of Photofest)

EPISODE #151 **"A TRUE ACCOUNT"** Broadcast on June 7, 1959
        Starring: Jane Greer as Mrs. Maureen Hughes   Kent Smith as Gilbert Hughes
        Robert Webber as Paul Brett   Jocelyn Brando as Alice
        Madge Kennedy as Mrs. Mary Hughes
        Dorothea Lord as Hughes secretary
        Lillian O'Malley as Miss Susie, the maid   Selmer Jackson as the priest
        Teleplay written for *Alfred Hitchcock Presents* by Robert C. Dennis and Fredric Brown, based on the short story "Curtains for Me" by Anthony Gilbert (pseudonym of Lucy Beatrice Malleson), originally published in the February 1958 issue of *John Creasey Mystery Magazine*. Subsequently reprinted in *The Mystery Bedside Book*, ed. John Creasey (Hoder & Stoughton, 1960).
        Directed by Leonard J. Horn.

(with a nurse beside the bed) *Good evening. Please don't be alarmed, this is just a routine check-up. It seems to me that she could take my blood pressure with a tire-gauge. If you don't care to watch the details of my physical examination, perhaps you will enjoy perusing my doctor's collection of x-rays of prominent personalities.*

Story: Maureen Hughes visits her attorney, Paul Brett, under her maiden name Miss Cannon, to explain that she was once a nurse under the employment of Gilbert Hughes, whose wife had become bed ridden. One evening Mrs. Hughes died of what seemed like natural causes, and months later Gilbert became a lonely man. Regardless of Maureen's past occupation, Gilbert started courting her and weeks later, they got married. One evening, she found Gilbert walking in his sleep, reenacting the scene of the crime. Paul assures Maureen that a wife cannot be forced to testify against her husband, and perhaps it would be better to forget about it. Soon after, Paul attends the funeral of Gilbert Hughes, who committed suicide. Seems Gilbert just couldn't handle the death of his first wife. Maureen, however, marries Brett and although she doesn't walk in her sleep, she does talk a lot – a little too much. It was she who poisoned Mary Hughes, and her husband did not commit suicide. Brett manages to dictate the story into his tape recorder, shortly before he dies of poison, at the hands of Maureen, who throws the recording into the fireplace.

Mrs. Hughes made one fatal mistake. Killing her husband and his first wife was one thing, but when she killed a lawyer, the police simply wouldn't stand for it. It's all very reassuring. This is all of tonight's program, next week we . . . (nurse says "He'll be back in a minute") (commercial break, Hitchcock chews and swallows the thermometer) *We'll be back with another story. Until then, good night.*

Trivia, etc. The director of this episode, sometimes credited as Leonard Horn, directed episodes of other television programs, including *The Untouchables, The Outer Limits, The Fugitive, Voyage to the Bottom of the Sea, Lost in Space, Branded, Mannix, Wonder Woman, Hawk, Mission Impossible* and *The Rookies*. He also directed such movies as *Rogues' Gallery* (1968), *The Magic Garden of Stanley Sweetheart* (1970). and *Climb an Angry Mountain* (1972).

EPISODE #152 **"TOUCHÉ"** Broadcast on June 14, 1959
 Starring: Paul Douglas as Bill Fleming   Hugh Marlowe as Philip Baxter
 Robert Morse as Sandy Baxter   Dody Heath as Mrs. Laura Fleming
 King Calder as George Faber, the attorney
 James Flavin as Otto, the bartender   Robert Carson as the judge
 Charlotte Knight as the old woman in the crowd
 Teleplay written for *Alfred Hitchcock Presents* by William Fay, based on the short story of the same name by Bryce Walton, as originally published in the November 1958 issue of *Alfred Hitchcock's Mystery Magazine*.
 Directed by John Brahm.
 (dressed as Zorro with sword) *Good evening amigos. I fear the day of the illiterate swordsman has passed. They seem to be spending so much time writing that they are neglecting the really important work, scurrying opponents. It's a very unhealthy state of affairs. Take this gentleman for example, listen . . .* (sound of swords) *He couldn't possibly win a duel, yet he can write sixty words a minute. Now, here is someone who can neither duel nor write, but can speak volumes, and insists on doing so.*

Story: Millionaire Bill Fleming decides that it is about time to do something about his cheating wife. While on a hunting trip Bill runs into a young man named Sandy, who hasn't won his bar association yet. The young man relates to the millionaire about an old law still in effect that states how a husband can engage another man in a duel, without being prosecuted. So Bill challenges his wife's lover to a duel with fencing swords and the man is killed. During the trial, Bill's lawyers bring mention of the law, and the judge reluctantly has to let Bill free. But it seems that the same law requires the penalty of a substantial payment, to be determined by the court, to the deceased man's family. $100,000 plus $1,000 a month for life. Knowing he's getting away with murder, Bill Fleming agrees without protest. Arriving home, he finds his wife with Sandy, who as it turns out, is the dead man's son, and receiver of the payment since he is now the only remaining relative.

This is not quite the end of our story. One duel later, junior was dead and Fleming was in prison. I believe I see a very rich and pompous landowner, approaching with another one minute proclamation. I shall return anon. (puts on mask) (commercial break) *I'm quite excited. I have here the very latest model. It has tremendous commercial possibilities. You see this one writes under water. Now if we can just get the bankers to approve. Next week we shall be back with another story. Until then, good night.*

Trivia, etc. Charlotte Knight, credited in this episode as Charlott during the closing credits, was also a writer of fantasy and science-fiction. She wrote an original story that became a classic motion picture, *20 Million Miles to Earth* (1957), although someone else wrote the script. She did write a couple of screenplays, *The Story of Little Red Riding Rood* (1949) and *Hansel and Gretel* (1951). She also made guest appearances on such programs as *Maverick, Alcoa Presents, Petticoat Junction* and *The Big Valley*.

EPISODE #153   **"INVITATION TO AN ACCIDENT"**   Broadcast on June 21, 1959
>   Starring: Gary Merrill as Joseph Pond   Joanna Moore as Virgilia Pond
>   Alan Hewitt as Albert Magnum   Ernestine Barrier as Mrs. Bedsole
>   Peter Walker as Cam Bedsole   Lillian O'Malley as Flora, the housekeeper
>   Teleplay written for *Alfred Hitchcock Presents* by Robert C. Dennis, based on the short story of the same name by Wade Miller, originally published in the July 1955 issue of *Ellery Queen's Mystery Magazine*.
>   Directed by Don Taylor.
>   (with medieval castle and book)   *Good evening parents and welcome once again to Uncle Alfred's Story Book.* (close-up) *We thought it would be refreshing to present a children's program at night after the little darlings were in bed so that adults could watch it undisturbed and without all that peanut butter on the picture tube. Tonight's fairytale comes to you slightly expurgated. We felt that there were certain parts of it unsuitable for adults. Therefore we have cut that part where the stepmother is forced to dance in red hot metal shoes and the scene where the prettiest daughter has her hands cut off as well as the bit about the old servant being turned into a toad. We also omitted the part where the dwarf falls into the boiling cauldron, where the raven plucks out the king's eyes and where the magic staff beats the old witch to a pulp. Admittedly our story has lost some of its punch, but we deemed the deletions necessary because adults just don't have the same sense of humor as their children. And now . . . Once upon a time there was a wicked old king. Three times each half hour he would look into the glass in his livingroom and ask, "Mirror, mirror on the wall, who's product is the best of all?" and the mirror would answer.*

Story: Virginia Pond is married to Joseph, a very jealous but quiet man, quiet enough to make you wonder what goes stirs in that head of his. Albert Magnum, a close friend of the family, advises her to stop flirting with other men, before it is too late. Right now, her hobby it's her ex-husband, Cam. Not long afterwards, she is almost killed by some falling scaffolding, possibly because the rope was tampered with. Albert suspects her husband Joseph, of trying to kill her, but has no proof. In order to learn why, Albert and Joseph go south of the border on a fishing trip. Joseph tells Albert a "fictional" story of the family friend who spends comfortable time with a married woman. While drinking some coffee, Albert realizes he has been poisoned. Joseph made the coffee, which won't effect him because he built up a tolerance against arsenic. Always a ladies' man, Albert slumps over as he confesses that it isn't him. "But it isn't me, it's Cam." Joseph realizes his mistake.

And everyone lived happily ever after. I will admit Albert might be an exception. He didn't look at all well in that last scene, but Pond lived on and on. He's one of the happiest persons in the State Penitentiary. He works in the prison nursery. So much for the magical world of make believe. Now for some grim realities. After which I shall skip back. (commercial break) *I would like to add just one more commercial before bidding adieu for another week. Parents: Are you looking for sand for the kiddies to play in? Why not buy the best. Insist on quick, q – u – i – c - k, quick sand. Good night.*

SUMMER RERUNS

Of the thirteen summer reruns, six were directed by Alfred Hitchcock, and one was the Emmy-award winning "The Glass Eye." The summer re-runs did not consist entirely from the previous season. Only four out of the thirteen reruns were from season four. Was this a hint from the network that the stories for the fourth season were not satisfactory?

June 28, 1959 "Poison"
July 5, 1959 "Tea Time"
July 12, 1959 "The Cream of the Jest"
July 19, 1959 "The Foghorn"
July 26, 1959 "Wet Saturday"
August 2, 1959 "Fog Closing In"
August 9, 1959
    "The Diamond Necklace"

August 16, 1959 "The Glass Eye"
August 23, 1959 "The Crooked Road"
August 30, 1959 "Back for Christmas"
September 6, 1959 "Dip in the Pool"
September 13, 1959
    "Lamb to the Slaughter"
September 20, 1959 "Breakdown"

(Photo courtesy of Photofest)

SEASON FIVE - (37 episodes)

SELECTED PRODUCTION CREDITS:
Art Director: Raymond Beal, John J. Lloyd, Arthur Lonergan,
Martin Obzina and George Patrick
Assistant Directors: Ben Bishop, George Bisk, James H. Brown, Jack Doran,
William Dorfman, Frank Fox, Charles S. Gould, Hilton A. Green,
James Hogan, Frank Losee and Ronnie Rondell
Associate Producer: Norman Lloyd
Costumes: Vincent Dee
Director of Photography: Neal Beckner, Lionel Lindon, a.s.c.,
John L. Russell, a.s.c. and John F. Warren, a.s.c.
Editorial Supervisor: David J. O'Connell and Richard G. Wray, a.c.e.
Film Editor: Edward W. Williams, a.c.e.
Hair Stylist: Florence Bush
Makeup: Jack Barron (mis-spelled Baron in "Dry Run") and Robert Dawn
Music Supervisor: Frederick Herbert and Joseph E. Romero
Producer: Joan Harrison
Set Decorator: Rudy Butler, Hal Gausman, Julia Heron, Fred MacLean,
John McCarthy, George Milo, and James S. Redd
Sound: Earl Crain, Jr., Earl Crain, Sr., Howard J. Fogetti, Bernard Fredricks,
John C. Grubb, Joe Lapis, William Lynch, Cameron McCulloch,
Melvin M. Metcalfe, Sr. and William Russell
Filmed at Revue Studios in Hollywood, California, in association with MCA-TV, executive
distributor for Shamley Productions, Inc.
Broadcast Sunday over CBS-TV, 9:30 - 10 p.m., EST.
Sponsored by Clairol and Bristol-Myers.

EPISODE #154 **"ARTHUR"** Broadcast on September 27, 1959
Rehearsed and filmed on July 7 – 9, 1959.
Starring: Laurence Harvey as Arthur Williams   Hazel Court as Helen Braithwaite
Robert Douglas as Inspector Ben Liebenberg of the C.I.D.
Patrick Macnee as Sergeant John Theron   Barry Harvey as constable Barry
Teleplay written for *Alfred Hitchcock Presents* by James P. Cavanagh, based on the
short story "Being a Murderer Myself" by Arthur Williams, originally published in the
August 1948 issue of *Ellery Queen's Mystery Magazine*. Subsequently anthologized in *The
Queen's Awards, Fourth Series*, ed. Ellery Queen (Little Brown, 1949).
Directed by Alfred Hitchcock.
(hens clucking) *Good evening ladies and gentlemen and brooders. I decided to
go into the egg business. Like any other business it needs fresh ideas. Here is our latest
design.* (picks up pyramidal egg) *Its advantages are obvious. No more eggs rolling off the
table. Valuable storage space saved in the refrigerator. Unfortunately this particular
innovation has not filtered down below the management level. Our executives quickly saw its
possibilities, but the hens seem rather slow at grasping new ideas. This is one of our plastic
models, we have a large number of them scattered about, to demonstrate to the hens what
can be done if they put their minds to it. As you can see, we are using every psychological
weapon at man's disposal.* (sign: THINK SQUARE) *And now, perhaps this slogan will also
give you strength, to bridge the gap between this vignette and tonight's story.*

Story: A wealthy New Zealand chicken farmer named Arthur confesses he's a
murderer . . . of chickens, that is. When his fiancée leaves Arthur for another man, he accepts
her decision by conveniently enjoying the life of a single bachelor. A year passes and
Helenpays him a return visit, asking for forgiveness. It seems her love interest didn't work

out, and Helen wants to rekindle an old flame, against Arthur's wish to remain a bachelor. Accustomed to strangling chickens for a living, Arthur angrily applies the same method to Helen, then hides her body. The police suspect him of murder, but can do nothing for lack of evidence. After Arthur returns from a three-day trip, he finds the police thoroughly going through his house and farm, hoping to find the corpse, but again no avail. Arthur bears the police no ill will for what they have done, and even offers them some chickens as a showing of good faith. They are happy with the deal, as the birds are nice and plump - no doubt due to their new feed, to which the girlfriend substantially contributed.

There was a very sad end to our story. Because of the excellent bone meat and blood meal Mr. Williams kept supplying them, his chickens grew to enormous size. Then it happened. One day as he shouldered his way through the hungry flock. . . but it is too awful to describe. Please re-join me in a minute, after I've pulled myself together. (commercial break) *I have abondoned the egg business. Our model was successful in only one case. One hen dutifully reproduced it perfectly, but unfortunately the uses of a plastic egg are rather limited. It appears to be time to say good night. Next week we shall be back with another story.*

Trivia, etc. *Variety* reviewed: "Opener of the new season wasn't the best of Hitchcock, but it'll suffice. There were some chills, bits of sardonic humor, a few acid lines, some clever shots and, of course, a murder. The old pro salvaged what otherwise [would] have been a weak outing in the script furnished by James P. Cavanagh, based on a story by Arthur Williams. Titled 'Arthur,' the plot lines, without the Hitchcock flair, could have become overly static. The element of time in the teleplay also tendered to confuse comprehension. But counter-balancing the short-comings were the sure Hitchcock touches of building suspense, a pro acting stint by Laurence Harvey in the main role, and the introspective use of the camera to build psychological situations."

"Acting with Harvey is like acting by yourself – only worse," recalled Jane Fonda, on their film *Walk on the Wild Side* (1962). He adopted his stage name 'Harvey' from the Harvey Nichols shop, and is well remembered for playing Colonel Travis in John Wayne's *The Alamo* (1960). British actor Laurence Harvey played the role of Arthur in this, the fifth-season opener, directed by the master of suspense himself. Harvey, who would later achieve his greatest success as the brain-washed assassin in *The Manchurian Candidate* in 1962, played the same type of disaffected-citizen character in this Hitchcock episode, as he did on the big-screen. "Oh, yes, with Larry Harvey," recalled Hazel Court. "Two thousand chickens and me and Laurence Harvey! I remember Harvey saying to me, 'Are you as nervous as I am?' and I said, 'Yes, I am!' I remember us both saying, 'This is not going to be our best day' - we were nervous."

"Being a Murderer Myself," the short story this episode was based on, seems clearly to have been written by a professional, rather than a weekend writer. Yet, in the letter to *Ellery Queen's Mystery Magazine* that accompanied submission of the story in 1948 the author wrote:

"As this is the first story I have tried to get published, I do not know whether it is necessary or not to state that, should this story be accepted, I would not like my real name divulged. Not that I am ashamed of the story . . . but in this particular case I think the effect of the story might be lost should my real name be given. Incidentally, the pen-name will save me from being troubled by people with no sense of humor. Also, I am writing a novel on South American life in which one of the characters is a detective story writer, Arthur Williams, and it would add to my attempt at realism if stories were actually published under the name."

Apart from the information that the story was written in a Native Reserve just alongside the Kruger National Park Game Reserve, the author said nothing about himself. The magazine published he story, and it was awarded a prize. So who was Arthur Williams?

Nothing further had been published by the magazine. A letter to his home (which was named "Journey's End") in Cape Providence, brought a reply from his widow. She said his real name was Peter Barry Way, and that he had been born in Sunderland in 1917. The family emigrated to South Africa when he was eight years old, and Barry Way studied medicine at Cape Town University. He did not become a doctor, however, but worked for a travel agency, "travelling across the country and studying people," as the widow put it. He married, had four children, and died unexpectedly in 1969. "Throughout the years he tried his hand at writing, sitting in the loft of his Cape Dutch home overlooking the Franschock Mountains." The novel he mentioned, however, if completed, was never submitted to a publisher, and this remarkable tale was the only story ever published by Barry Way, alias Arthur Williams.*

EPISODE #155 **"THE CRYSTAL TRENCH"** Broadcast on October 4, 1959
Rehearsed and filmed on August 25 – 27, 1959.
Starring: James Donald as Mark Cavendish
Patricia Owens as Mrs. Stella Ballister   Werner Klemperer as Herr Ranks
Ben Astar as the hotel manager   Patrick Macnee as Prof. Kersley
Harold O. Dyrenforth as Frederick Blauer   Eileen Anderson as the woman
Oscar Beregi as the Austrian
Also in the cast: Frank Holms and Otto Reichow
Teleplay written for *Alfred Hitchcock Presents* by Stirling Silliphant, based on the short story of the same name by A.E.W. Mason, collected in *The Four Corners of the World* (Hodder & Stoughton, 1917; Scribner, 1917).
Directed by Alfred Hitchcock.
(mountain climbing) *Good evening ladies and gentlemen. I thought I would cut this rope since it seems to be obstructing my path. I can't seem to find my partner. He was here a moment ago, then let out a cry and disappeared.* (Hitchcock cuts the rope) *My, my. I seem to have made a faux pas. My friend was on the other end of that rope. Rotten luck. He was also my business partner, but the show must go on. Tonight we are presenting a chilly little tale entitled "The Crystal Trench." It follows at a respectful distance.*

Story: Switzerland: September 1907. Stella Ballister receives the horrifying news that her husband met with an untimely demise while mountain climbing. Newly married, Stella asks for the retrieval of her husband's body - but the task proves impossible when the corpse accidentally falls into a deep crevasse, where no human eyes or hands can reach him. Mark, having feelings for Stella, stays by her side, a close friend and nothing more, throughout London and Switzerland. Forty years later (in 1947), still trying to get over the news of the accident, Stella learns that the glacier has moved. Hiring a crew to help prospect her husband out of the ice, they find the body preserved and untouched. Stella views the body of her husband one last time, and discovers a horrifying secret. Her husband froze to death holding a locket containing the picture of another woman, not Stella!

So much for our version of the Iceman Cometh. (ties the rope around him) *I shall return for a final word in a moment. First we have come to one of those treacherous crevasses that riddle the glacier of television.* (commercial break) *I think I shall begin my descent. . . before I become the source of a legend about an abdominal snowman. Next week I shall once again return with another story spliced together by commercials. Until then, good night.* (starts descent, but is cut down)

Trivia, etc. All of the title screens in the beginning of each and every episode were in uppercase letters, and of the same size, with the exception of this broadcast. Patricia Owens, who starred as the heroine in the 1957 classic *The Fly*, recalled working under

---

* The last two paragraphs were reprinted from *The Penguin Classic Crime Omnibus* by Julian Symons. (Penguin / Harmondsworth, New York, Victoria, Ontario and Auckland, 1984), p.366.

Hitchcock's direction, off the camera: "Alfred Hitchcock was a very strange man to describe. You never quite knew what he was thinking about you. And he never directed you, either. The only thing he said to me was, 'Patricia, your voice is too high. Lower it.' And that was all! He invited me for tea in his trailer - we had English tea and he asked me about England. He was very proper . . . very pompous . . . and I was very nervous around him. I don't know what it would have been like to have made a full-length movie under him - It was only three or four days to make that half-hour show. Maybe he was different on a long-term project, but he was intimidating."

Evan Hunter, who wrote the script to next week's "Appointment at Eleven," recalled his initial meeting with Alfred Hitchcock. "After the screening [of "Appointment at Eleven"], Joan took us down to meet him. Since he directed so few of the television shows, his personal appearances on the set were rare, and always occasioned an appreciably higher energy level. There was an unmistakable buzz in the air when we walked down from Joan's office. That day, he was shooting a particularly difficult scene in which an actor was lying under a block of ice, the crystal trench of the title. The ice was resting on a narrow wooden ditch, which the actor had crawled. Another actor was supposed to rub his gloved hand over the ice until the face of the actor below was gradually revealed."

"Hitch strolled over from where his people were setting up the scene," continued Hunter. "Joan introduced us, and he immediately began explaining to my wife the enormous technical problems of lighting the scene from above, as well as from inside the trench – somewhat similar to lighting the rain from both front and back in Gene Kelly's famous *Singin' in the Rain* number. At least, that was what I gathered from what I could overhear; all of the conversation was directed at my wife. Hitch took an immediate liking to her, which was somewhat surprising considering his predilection for glacial blondes. As he showed her around the set, explaining pieces of equipment, introducing her to his cinematographer and his assistant director, the people setting up the shot began to get a bit frantic because the huge block of ice seemed to be melting under the glare of lights and Hitch still showed no intention of wanting to direct the scene. Finally, after the plaintive words, 'Mr. Hitchcock, sir, we're ready to go now, sir' had been repeated half a dozen times, he cordially bade us goodbye, and got on with his work. Two years later, he asked me to write the screenplay for *The Birds*."

EPISODE #156 **"APPOINTMENT AT ELEVEN"** Broadcast on October 11, 1959
        Starring: Clint Kimbrough as Davy Logan   Norma Crane as the blonde
        Clu Gulager as the sailor   Sean McClory as the Irish drinker
        Amy Douglass as Davy's mother   Michael J. Pollard as the shoe shine boy
        Also in the cast: Joseph Sullivan, Richard Gering, Taldo Kenyon, Jerry Rhoads and Frank Sully.

Teleplay written for *Alfred Hitchcock Presents* by Evan Hunter, based on the short story "11 O'Clock Bulletin" by Robert Turner, originally published in a 1955 issue of *McCall's*. Subsequently reprinted in *A Choice of Murders*, ed. Dorothy Salisbury Davis (Scribner, 1958).

Directed by Robert Stevens.

(as a bartender watching TV) loud noise from TV (close-up) Hitchcock turns it down a bit but you still can't hear him so he turns it down some more and then you can hear him. . . . *from our sponsor.*

Story: Davy Logan enters a bar one evening and meets up with a blonde who takes an interest in him. While he talks to the girl, Davy explains how much he hates his father, who abandoned him and his mother. It seems "Dad" was caught fooling around with a beautiful blonde – just like the one Davy is drinking with tonight. When the girl asks him more questions he becomes surprisingly violent and has to be subdued by a sailor. When the boy hears a piano player performing, he tries to pick another fight, and Davy has to be restrained again, this time by an Irish bar customer. Two minutes later, the men and women in the bar understand Davy's motives. A news report comes on the television screen reporting that Davy's father has just been executed for the murder of his blonde girlfriend.

You know, I like that story very much. Especially the part where he. . . (looks at TV) *And now we have a commercial - that is, you have a commercial. I'm swearing off.* (smashes the TV screen; commercial break) *Until next week, good night.* (watching an aquarium in a TV set)

Trivia, etc. Evan Hunter, who wrote the screenplay for this *Alfred Hitchcock Presents* episode, based on a short story by Robert Turner, had two of his own previously-published stories filmed for *Alfred Hitchcock Presents*, but the teleplays were adapted by other writers. Hunter recalled his first meeting with Alfred Hitchcock on the set of "The Crystal Trench" in his 1997 autobiography *Me and Hitch*: "In the early part of 1959, my agent called to say that Shamley had bought a story by one of his clients, and they wanted me to adapt it for *Alfred Hitchcock Presents*. I still had no substantial screenplay or teleplay credits, and I wondered why Joan was willing to take a chance on me. Hitch later told me he specifically wanted a novelist to adapt this particular story because of its 'internal' nature. This was a difficult story to adapt because it all took place in the lead character's head, in a silent internal monologue. [In late summer of 1959,] Joan Harrison invited Anita, my then wife, and me to the studio to view the final cut of *Appointment at Eleven*, which was to air in November. Watching the film, I discovered to my great surprise that Hitch had abandoned his usual wry introduction, instead stating quite simply that the subject matter of tonight's show was too serious to joke about, and he would let the story speak for itself."

(Photo courtesy of Photofest)

EPISODE #157 **"COYOTE MOON"** Broadcast on October 18, 1959
Starring: Macdonald Carey as John Piltkin   Edgar Buchanan as Pops
Collin Wilcox as Julie, the girl   Wesley Lau as Harry
Jack Lambert as the first gas station attendant
Eve McVeagh as the diner attendant   James Field as the car owner
David Fresco as the second gas station attendant
Chuck Henderson as the police officer
Teleplay written for *Alfred Hitchcock Presents* by Harold Swanton, based on a short story by Kenneth B. Perkins.
Directed by Herschel Daugherty.

(sitting on the moon) *Good evening ladies and gentlemen. I can now state unequivocally. There is not an ounce of cheese up here. There is a cow who goes by now and then, but much too fast to be milked. Tonight's program has been a rather long time in the making. The light from that star for example, has taken 50,000 years to reach you. But I suppose that is rather unimpressive, considering the age of some movies now seen on television. Our play is considerably younger. It is called "Coyote Moon." I tried out for the title role but was rejected. They're using the real thing. Favoritism you know. Before our play, we present the pilot film in a new series. If this proves popular, we plan to show two more before the program is over.*

Story: John Piltkin is robbed and given a hard time by three hitchhikers while he is on a trip. Later he sees the same two men and the woman at a diner, so he steals a car at a gas station after they leave and picks them up again. Keeping his face hidden in the dark, they have no idea who he is, and he acts as though the car has died and he has to walk back for help. Later on, the police find the three with the stolen car and arrest them for the theft.

In case you are wondering about Julie, Harry and Pops - that trio of natures noblemen - they received just what they deserved and more. As it turned out, they had been part of a gang of hijackers that stole supermarket carts, filed off the serial numbers, smuggled them to Mexico, where they had sold them as baby carriages. The court showed them no mercy, which is precisely what we are about to show you, after which I shall reappear. (commercial break) I hope you didn't mind the lack of murder and mayhem in tonight's story. But we thought we might give you a vacation from it. For those of you who insist on violence, I can only refer you to your local newspaper or your inner most thoughts. Next week we promise to do better. Until then, good night.

EPISODE #158 **"NO PAIN"** Broadcast on October 25, 1959
Starring: Brian Keith as Dave Rainey   Joanna Moore as Cindy Rainey
Yale Wexler as Arnold Barrett   Dorothea Lord as Nurse Collins
Teleplay written for *Alfred Hitchcock Presents* by William Fay, based on the short story "Pigeon in an Iron Lung" by Talmage Powell, originally published in the November 1956 issue of *Manhunt*. Subsequently anthologized in *Alfred Hitchcock's Anthology #9: Tales to Make Your Hair Stand on End*, ed. Eleanor Sullivan (Davis/Dial, 1981).
Directed by Norman Lloyd.

(boxing ring) *Good evening ladies and gentlemen and welcome to tonight's program of boxing matches. In this corner for tonight's main event, we have Steven Forbush. And his opponent, Mrs. Steven Forbush. As you know these two are traditional rivals. Having met many times before for the middle-class championship of the world. But before the main event, we must have this preliminary. Watch closely while this light weight vies for your attention.*

Alternate narrative:
(boxing ring) *Good evening ladies and gentlemen and welcome to tonight's program of boxing matches. In this corner for tonight's main event, we have Steven Forbush. And his opponent, Mrs. Steven Forbush. As you know these two are traditional rivals.*

Having met many times before for the middle-class championship of the world. As you may have noticed, I am quite at home in the ring. For me, boxing is very easy. It's lifting my hand above my head, after I've won, that I find difficult. It's much too strenuous. But so much for the preliminaries. Now for the main event.

Story: Because of a medical condition, Dave Rainey remains paralyzed inside an iron lung, or as his wife describes it, as an "air-tight pound of coffee in a can." Using simple logic instead of suspicion, Dave asks his wife when she plans to bump him off. Not known for her nobler forms of solitaire, Cindy confesses soon – but not tonight. Cindy spends most of her free time with a young (and rich) neighbor, Arnold Barrett, and Dave becomes more and more convinced that Arnold is going to be the one to pull the plug. Returning late that evening, Arnold tells Dave that Cindy's body will surely be found when the tide goes out in the morning. Arnold took care of the job as Dave wanted, and that Cindy's death involved "no pain." Dave sighs a breath of relief, knowing that the hit man got her first, before she had the chance to kill him.

And as Cindy's body slowly sinks into the bay, we take leave of the lovely seaside setting for our story. Of course as it must to all men, the law caught up with Arnold and Dave. (commercial break) We have just had the shortest fight in history. They met in the center of the ring and it was over faster than you could say: Who was that lady I seen you with last night? I think this should be a lesson to all of us. We shall be back with another story. Until then, good night.

Alternate narrative:
And as Cindy's body slowly sinks into the bay, we take leave of the lovely seaside setting for our story. Of course as it must to all men, the law caught up with Arnold and Dave. As for our boxing match, it turned out to be the shortest fight on record. They met in the center of the ring and it was over faster than you could say: Who was that lady I seen you with last night? I think this should be a lesson to all of us. Next time we shall be back with another story. Until then, good night.

Trivia, etc. "I cannot specify how I came up with the idea for 'No Pain'," recalled Talmage Powell. "It's but one of several hundred stories I wrote. I can safely say that at the moment of writing I needed copy in that genre. Probably there was something about an iron lung in the voluminous notebooks of jotted-down tidbits that might at some time suggest a story. 'Iron-lung' would have been sufficient, in that it suggested a full situation, the helpless state of an individual in case someone simply pulled the plug. The actual development would continue on from there."

Actor Brian Keith doesn't even have to lift a finger when it came to acting the role of Dave Rainey. Playing a paralyzed man in an iron lung, however, from an actor's point of view, was more of a challenge during filming. All of his emotions could only be accomplished by facial expressions. The director, Norman Lloyd, also granted the viewers of this episode, the chance to see the story from both the protagonist's point of view, and the other actors. Many of the shots were filmed of the mirror connected to the iron lung. Sometimes from Keith's point-of-view, and sometimes vice versa. "Norman Lloyd was second in command at Shamley," Talmage Powell recalled, "doing many of the executive details and occasionally directing when a script came along that inspired him to do so. I wasn't present when 'No Pain' was shot, but we talked about it some, he mentioning how certain story developments had suggested camera angles and zoom details." For Hitchcock fans, take note. It could be compared that blonde actress Joanna Moore played the role of Grace Kelly, and Keith in the role of Hitchcock, during much of the conversation exchanged between the two, including Keith's "I wasn't talking about the Prince of Monaco," and Moore's "We had a few good years."

EPISODE #159 **"ANNIVERSARY GIFT"** Broadcast on November 1, 1959
        Starring: Harry Morgan as Hermie Jensen   Barbara Baxley as Myra Jensen
        Jackie Coogan as George Bates   Michael J. Pollard as Hansel Eidelpfeiffer
        James Field as the doctor   Maurice Manson as the postman
        Steven McAdam as Shorty, the neighborhood boy
        Teleplay written for *Alfred Hitchcock Presents* by Harold Swanton, based on the
short story of the same name by John Collier, reprinted in the April 1959 issue of *Ellery
Queen's Mystery Magazine.*
        Directed by Norman Lloyd.
        (meat-eating flower)   *Good evening ladies and gentlemen.   I'm sending this
beautiful plant to my sponsor. I think that should dispel any talk that we are not on excellent
terms. I believe it's feeding time. These carnivorous plants get quite hungry. This one has
been quite useful around here as a garbage disposal. I shall hate to part with it, but I know
my sponsor will love it and I'm sure it will love him too. And now speaking of the sponsor,
by the sponsor and for the sponsor. . . the sponsor.*

Alternate narrative:
        (meat-eating flower)   *Good evening ladies and gentlemen.   I'm sending this
beautiful plant to a dear friend. I believe it's feeding time. These carnivorous plants get
quite hungry. This one has been quite useful around here as a garbage disposal. I shall hate
to part with it, but I know my friend will love it and I'm sure it will love him too.*

        Story: In a comedy of errors, Hermie Jensen has been a slave to his animal-loving
woman day in and day out. Fifteen years of marriage to Myra and all he gets is a weekly ten-
dollar allowance.   Hermie would rather fish and drink beer all day like his next-door
neighbor, but instead, he has to run errands for pet supplies. Since Hermie can't trade in her
livestock or train Myra to drink beer, he decides to put the bite on her. Buying a poisonous
coral snake, one that instead looks like a harmless king snake, Hermie comes home one day
to give his wife an anniversary present.   Returning home a few hours later, Hermie is
surprised to find Myra alive and well, complaining that the snake is unfriendly.   She hands
him the reptile, and the snake immediately bites him, whereupon Hermie falls over dead. But
when the doctor shows up later, he informs Myra that the snake was harmless, and that
Hermie must have died of a heart attack.

        *I'm attempting to improve on nature by giving this flower a more inviting scent. I
want the sponsor to get quite close. This perfume has such a suggestive name that I'm not
even allowed to mention it on the air. The sales woman told me it's infallible in attracting
men. This was the last bottle they had. Their entire supply was bought up by the Army
Recruiting office. I shall return in a moment to bid adieu until next week.* (commercial
break; followed by Hitchcock being eaten by flower) *Good night.* (off screen)

Alternate narrative:
        *I'm attempting to improve on nature by giving this flower a more inviting scent. I
want my friend to get quite close. This perfume has such a suggestive name, I'm not even
allowed to mention it on the air. The sales woman told me it's infallible in attracting men.
This was the last bottle they had. Their entire supply was bought up by the Army Recruiting
office. I shall return next time with another story. Until then, good night.* (Hitchcock being
eaten by flower)

        Trivia, etc. Harry Morgan, who would later direct two episodes of *The Alfred
Hitchcock Hour*, plays the suffering Hermie Jensen in this comical approach to love and
marriage, the tale of a rich wife who spends more time with her pets than she does with her
husband. Norman Lloyd, the associate producer of the series, also directed this episode.
"There was a John Collier story called 'Anniversary Gift' with Harry Morgan and Barbara
Baxley," Lloyd recalled. "In it, Morgan gives Barbara a poisonous snake in a box as an

anniversary gift. Shortly after, somebody was arrested for trying to kill his own wife in the same fashion."

EPISODE #160   **"DRY RUN"**   Broadcast on November 8, 1959
    One of the days of filming was September 14, 1959.
    Starring: Walter Matthau as Moran   Robert Vaughn as Art
    David White as Mr. Barbarossa   Tyler McVey as Prentiss, the accountant
    Teleplay written for *Alfred Hitchcock Presents* by Bill S. Ballinger, based on the short story of the same name by Norman Struber, originally published in the April 1956 issue of *Manhunt*. Subsequently reprinted in *Young and Deadly*, ed. Leo Margulies (Fawcett Crest, 1959).
    Directed by John Brahm.
    (Hitchcock in overcoat and hat)   *Good evening. It seems that on television of late, tales of mystery and crime are incomplete without jazz music. So much so that it is now almost impossible to tell whether you are watching a detective story or a jazz festival. There is a difference of course, a jazz festival has more violence. The basic requirements for a television mystery program seem to be an alto saxophone, a piano, bass drums and if the budget allows, a detective. Now we throw the spotlight on one member of our little combo, while he takes a solo. Our sponsor. On a one minute chorus, after which, if you watch closely, you may see our story.*

    Story: Syndicate boss Mr. Barbarossa compares his business along the lines of a baseball game, and he himself is the coach. Art, a young punk wanting to get in good with the syndicate, wants to try out for the team, and Mr. Barbarossa decides to give him a dry run. Art's job is to deliver a payoff to a gangster named Moran, hiding out at the Old Valley Winery, and when the time is right, shoot the crime boss. But when Art finally meets up with Moran, the gangster proves to be more difficult to kill than imagined. Moran explains that he wants to take over, and until Mr. Barbarossa is put out of the way, Moran will always remain a push-over. He convinces Art into being part of his organization, even offering the boy $5,000 to return and murder his employer. After some quipping over the payoff, Art decides to return and kill Mr. Barbarossa, only to discover that Moran was just another employee testing his loyalty. Having failed the test, Art is killed.

    The results of this case in a moment. Our decision to join the rush to jazz seems to have been a success with one difference. We decided to take the silencers off the guns and use them in the orchestra. Now ladies and gentlemen, a delightfully cacophonous commercial, after which I shall swing back. (commercial break) *Perhaps our sponsor should use a mute. As for tonight's case, Moran was found guilty and fined, by the jazz musicians union. For shooting a man, acappella. The use of firearms without accompaniment is strictly forbidden. He was, of course, also dealt with by the municipal authorities. Next week I shall return with another story. Until then, good night.*

EPISODE #161   **"THE BLESSINGTON METHOD"**   Broadcast on November 15, 1959
    Starring: Henry Jones as Mr. Treadwell   Dick York as Mr. J. J. Bunce
    Elizabeth Patterson as Grandma   Irene Windust as Mrs. Treadwell
    Paul E. Burns as the man on the pier   Vaughn Meadows as Treadwell's son
    Nancy Kilgas as Treadwell's daughter   Penny Edwards as the secretary
    Teleplay written for *Alfred Hitchcock Presents* by Halsted Welles, based on the short story of the same name by Stanley Ellin, originally published in the June 1956 issue of *Ellery Queen's Mystery Magazine*. Subsequently collected in *The Blessington Method and Other Strange Tales* (Random House, 1964; Macdonald, 1965) and in *The Specialty of the House and Other Stories* (Mysterious Press, 1979).
    Directed by Herschel Daugherty.

(in a wheelchair)   *Good evening, ladies and gentlemen and welcome to Alfred Hitchcock Presents. The National Safety Council has asked that I remind you that most accidents occur in the home. Therefore this might be a very good place to avoid. If you must be there, now would be an excellent time to check for those items that may be lying around, waiting to produce accidents. Rollerskates at the bottom of the stairs, poorly insulated wires near the bathtub, ground glass in the sugar bowl, arsenic in the coffee. Little things which if you don't find, you may regret for the rest of your life. So much for accidents. Now for something intentional and designed to strike you where it will hurt the most. Right in the pocketbook.*

Alternate narrative:
(in a wheelchair)   *Good evening, ladies and gentlemen and welcome to Alfred Hitchcock Presents. I should explain. I came down with a cold. The broken leg was a later development. These nurses can become quite forceful at times. The National Safety Council has asked that I remind you that most accidents occur in the home. Therefore this might be a very good place to avoid. If you must be there, now would be an excellent time to check for those items that may be lying around, waiting to produce accidents. Rollerskates at the bottom of the stairs, poorly insulated wires near the bathtub, ground glass in the sugar bowl, arsenic in the coffee. Little things which if you don't find, you may regret for the rest of your life. So much for accidents.*

Story: In the future, July 13, 1980 to be exact, Mr. Bunce represents the Society for Experimental Gerology (SEG), a group trying to find a solution about the problem of people living too long, usually into their hundreds. He is telling this to Mr. Treadwell, a man plagued by an old and trouble-making mother-in-law. He wants to get rid of her, but resists using the Society. Finally, when he can stand no more, he has the organization kill her in what looks like an accident. Only after she is gone does Treadwell realize that someday he himself may end up receiving a similar treatment.

The doctor told me I could take the cast off any time. But I find I receive much better treatment with it on. As for Mr. Bunce and Mr. Treadwell, even their advanced society frowned on their activities. By then mothers-in-laws were most numerous and even more powerful than they are today. It is something to look forward to, provided you are a mother-in-law. I shall wheel back after this word from our subscriber. (commercial break) *We seem to have run out of commercials, so that will be all for tonight.* (gets up with cast still in wheelchair) *Until next week at the same time, good night.*

Alternate narrative:
The doctor told me I could take the cast off any time. But I find I receive much better treatment with it on. As for Mr. Bunce and Mr. Treadwell, even their advanced society frowned on their activities. By then mothers-in-laws were most numerous and even more powerful than they are today. It is something to look forward to, provided you are a mother-in-law. I shall wheel back after this word from our subscriber. (commercial break) (Hitchcock gets up with cast still in wheelchair) *Now until next time. Good night.*

Trivia, etc. Nancy Kilgas was also a professional dancer, having roles in big-screen musicals such as *Oklahoma!* (1955) and *Seven Brides for Seven Brothers* (1954). She played the role of a dancer in *Earth vs. the Spider* (1958) and *Shake, Rattle and Rock* (1956). In 1956, author Stanley Ellin won the highest honor that can be achieved for a mystery short story, the coveted Edgar awarded annually by the Mystery Writers of America, for "The Blessington Method."

282

EPISODE #162 **"DEAD WEIGHT"** Broadcast on November 22, 1959
Starring: Joseph Cotten as Courtney Nesbeth Masterson
Julie Adams as Peg Valence   Don Gordon as Rudy Stickney
Ted de Corsia as Lieutenant Ward   Angela Greene as Mrs. Masterson
Claude Stroud as Lester Eldridge, the Private Investigator
Gail Bonney as Mary, the older secretary   Reita Green as Rita, the secretary
George Dockstader as the motorcycle policeman
Teleplay written for *Alfred Hitchcock Presents* by Jerry Sohl, based on a story by
Herb Golden.*
Directed by Stuart Rosenberg.
(with signs) *Good evening fellow motorists. The road signs became so dense that
I had to abandon my automobile and proceed on foot. I do hope the time never comes when
billboards will obscure this lovely scenery. Actually I believe these are seedling signs. This
is where the highway department grows them. You are probably more familiar with the wild
variety that springs up along the roadside. Tonight's play has a connection, however
tenuous, with the foregoing. In it you will see an automobile. The play is called "Dead
Weight" and will begin after this one minute detour.*

Story: Advertising executive Courtney Masterson revives a relationship with an old
girlfriend he runs into, but after they drive to a secluded spot for some romance, they are held
up by a young punk named Rudy. Courtney overpowers him and puts him in the trunk, then
returns the girl home. Now he has a choice of going to the police, which would let the cat out
of the bag to his wife, or let the punk go, which will probably result in blackmail. Deciding
against both options, he kills Rudy, not realizing that his suspicious wife had hired a detective
to follow him and the man has seen everything - and now demands blackmail payments for
his silence.

*Private enterprise should be encouraged, but I think Mr. Eldridge was carrying it a
bit far. There was one further development however. It seems that Mr. Eldridge also had a
suspicious wife and he too had been followed the preceding night. If you don't follow that,
perhaps you'll be interested in the following, which is what I shall follow.* (commercial
break) *I have just been surprised by a policeman, who was lurking in the underbrush. He
gave me a ticket for wreckless driving, parking overtime, speeding and jay walking.
However, he agreed to tear up the ticket if I would show him how to get out of here. Next
week I shall return with another story. Until then, good night.*

Trivia, etc. Writer Jerry Sohl discussed how he came about writing for the
Hitchcock series: "Well, you get into the pool of TV writers and if they like what you do in
the assignment that they give you, in the beginning, then you get called in to do more scripts.
So I could do as many scripts as I wanted at that time. The series isn't around anymore and I
forget how many I did. The program was not really controlled by just anybody. There was a
lot of free movement in the series and you could do just about what you wanted – of course it
would be flagrantly non-desirable to break the format. They would ask you what your
favorite stories were, and then if you had published some of your own they would also credit
you on the screen for it. Otherwise, they would use something you thought up at the
moment. It was great fun and I really am sorry the show passed."
Julie Adams, who played the female lead in Universal's 1954 classic, *Creature
From the Black Lagoon*, recalled her fondness for this episode: " 'Dead Weight' was a
cheery old story. I recall Joe Cotten and I having lunch at the Universal commissary one day
and I also recall how I got him to talk some about making *Citizen Kane* and how he said 'Ah,
yes. None of us really knew anything about making movies. We were just all doing this –
and we didn't even know anything about close-ups! They called us all back in to do a scene

* Final draft and shooting script of this episode was dated August 7, 1959. Production
#1520A. This info thanks to Jerry Sohl.

and we'd tell them that we just did that scene!' He was a very, very nice man. He never talked about Hitchcock, even though he did a lot of movies for him. I never met Hitchcock, sad to say. I wish I did get to meet him or work under him in one of the episodes he directed. Stuart Rosenberg directed me instead and he was a very sharp director and as I recall it was a very interesting show, camera-wise."

"That was when I was working at Universal and that episode, 'Dead Weight,' they suggested that I do," Jerry Sohl concluded. "They had a stock of ideas and stories and I picked one out and did it. It wasn't a freak of nature, the story was highly planned and they felt I was capable of handling the project. It fit in well with the program. I was writing for other series and I guess some of my stories fell into their niche. I liked the producers of the show because they let me do what I wanted to do with the script, within reason of course, because they had all these stories they bought and thought up themselves. I remember telling them once that 'Gee, I can't work on this,' and they tossed that story aside and gave me another one. I was always meeting with Norman Lloyd and Joan Harrison. I met Hitchcock several times, too. He was a much smaller person than I thought. When he comes onto the screen and that profile of him, you'd think of him as a big, fat man in charge of the program. But I went in to talk with him and he was a small guy and he really surprised me. He never came to the studio very often but when he did, everyone knew who he was. How could you possibly escape the feeling that Alfred Hitchcock was in the studio? He was a very quiet person. When he attended banquets he just sat there and never said anything. It was really strange for a man who was in charge of a program to be like that. I got along very well with him, even though he was very quiet and didn't have much to say."

EPISODE #163   **"SPECIAL DELIVERY"**   Broadcast on November 29, 1959
        Starring: Steve Dunne as Bill Fortnum   Beatrice Straight as Cynthia Fortnum
        Peter Lazer as Tom "Tommy" Fortnum   Frank Maxwell as Roger
        Cece Whitney as Dorothy   Michael Burns as the boy
        Pat Hagerty as the woman   Jim O'Neill as Joe. Roger's son
        Ethel Shutta as Mrs. Goodbody, the grouchy old neighbor kicking mushrooms
        Teleplay written for *Alfred Hitchcock Presents* by Ray Bradbury, from his short story "Come Into My Cellar," published in the October 1962 issue of *Galaxy*.
        Directed by Norman Lloyd.
        There will be a slight delay in starting tonight's show. The sponsor's message usually heard at this time, has not yet arrived. Uh however, it is being rushed to us by the fastest means available. (clip-plane) *Unfortunately the message has a long and very complicated route to travel.* (clip-train) *We haven't much more time, but I assure you that the sponsor will make every effort to get the message through.* (clip-runner) *I'm afraid we'll have to start without it.* (clip-cavalry) *Just in the nick of time. The commercial is saved.*

Alternate narrative:
        There will be a slight delay in starting tonight's show. Our play's special delivery has not yet arrived. However, it is being rushed to us by the fastest means available. (clip-plane) *Unfortunately it has a long and very complicated route to travel.* (clip-train) *We haven't much more time, but I assure you that our producer will make every effort to get the message through.* (clip-runner) *I'm afraid we'll have to start without it.* (clip-cavalry) *Saved! Just in the nick of time.*

        Story: Young Tom Fortnum receives a special delivery package sent from the Great Bayou Novelty Greenhouse, an order of mushroom seeds from a mail order company advertising to "grow your own mushrooms in your cellar for fun and profit." The young boy is fascinated with the hobby, as are the other children in the neighborhood, but his father, Bill Fortnum, becomes suspicious when one of the neighbors disappear. After piecing together clues, Bill finally thinks he has the mystery solved. The mushrooms are actually a form of mind-controlling Martians, planning one-by-one, to take over the bodies of humans. His wife, Cynthia, thinks the idea is ridiculous, but when Bill confronts his son in the basement, he finds boxes of the plants growing all over the place and young Tom, with eyes glowing in the dark, demands his father digest a few mushrooms. Mesmerized by the Martian, Bill can do nothing but eat the sandwich.

I think that story has a very comforting message, for mushrooms all over the world. What you are about to see is no bigger than a minute. It goes into millions of homes. It seems innocuous at first, but gradually you develop a craving for it, then. . . but watch, after which I shall be back. (commercial break) *After watching that message from our sponsor, I think we'll send it back.* (clip-all clips from presentation, backwards) *Good night.*

Alternate narrative:
I think that story has a very comforting message, for mushrooms all over the world. I am seriously thinking of starting a counter-movement to persuade the mushrooms to grow people in their basements. Now that we have seen our play, I think we will send it back. (clip-all clips from presentation, backwards) *Until next time, good night.*

Trivia, etc. Ray Bradbury used much of his own Bradbury-esque material and dialogue for this episode, including a scene in which Frank Maxwell recited a poem, "By the pricking of my thumb, something wicked this way comes." *Something Wicked This Way Comes* would later become the title of a fantasy novel written by Bradbury.

Steve Dunne tries to convince his wife that the mushrooms are from Outer Space to guest Beatrice Straight in "Special Delivery."

Photo courtesy of Photofest, in New York City.

285

EPISODE #164 **"ROAD HOG"** Broadcast on December 6, 1959

Starring: Richard Chamberlain as Clay Pine   Raymond Massey as Sam Pine
Robert Emhardt as Ed Fratus   Roscoe Ates as the bar rat
Ray Teal as Ben Tulip, the bartender   Betsy Hale as the young girl
Gordon Wynn as the doctor   Jack Easton, Jr. as Davey Pine
Brad Weston as Sam Pine, Jr.

Teleplay written for *Alfred Hitchcock Presents* by Bill S. Ballinger, based on the short story of the same name by Harold R. Daniels, originally published in the September 1959 issue of *Ellery Queen's Mystery Magazine*. Subsequently anthologized in *Ellery Queen's 15th Mystery Annual*, ed. Ellery Queen (Random House, 1960).

Directed by Stuart Rosenberg.

(with campfire)   *Good evening aficionados of outdoor cooking. I am quite thrilled with my new bar-b-que. It was rather inexpensive, but of course, I didn't take any of the extras. I assuaged the heat indicator and temperature control, the motor-driven spit, the glass-covered rotisserie, the stainless steel wide table, the built-in blower, the warming oven, the utensil rack, and the asbestos gloves. I did buy the fire starter however.* (sticks) *I understand one rubs these together. For buying the lighter, I received free, a restaurant credit card. Now in just sixty seconds, tonight's story.*

Alternate narrative:

(with campfire)   *Good evening aficionados of outdoor cooking. I am quite thrilled with my new bar-b-que. It was rather inexpensive, but of course, I didn't take any of the extras. I assuaged the heat indicator and temperature control, the motor-driven spit, the glass-covered rotisserie, the stainless steel wide table, the built-in blower, the warming oven, the utensil rack, and the asbestos gloves. I did buy the fire starter however.* (sticks) *I understand one rubs these together. For buying the lighter, I received free, a restaurant credit card. I expect to have no trouble acquiring charcoal, since I have fellow bar-b-quer who makes it out of beef steaks. I was given this amusing costume to wear.* (apron with words "Danger, Men at Work") *Frankly, I have now lost my appetite completely. Perhaps we shall turn our attention to the play.*

Story: When Sam Pine tries to rush his injured son to a hospital, a traveling salesman named Ed Fratus, hogs the road by purposely driving slow enough, so they can't pass on the country road. The young man dies before they can reach the medical facility, and the doctor confesses that had they managed to get the boy to him fifteen minutes sooner, young Davey might have lived. Knowing that the salesman returns to the local tavern to peddle business on occasion, Sam plays the role of a kind Samaritan, offers Fratus a few drinks, and recalls the details of the road hog responsible for his boy's death. When Fratus realizes that what he drank was poison, the salesman jumps in his car and starts speeding down the road. Only Clay, one of Sam's sons, is driving down the road at such a slow rate of speed that Fratus screams for the boy to pull over. In a hasty attempt to pass Clay's truck, Fratus gets into a severe auto accident that takes his life. And that's what the police will think when they arrive on the scene of the crash, since Fratus actually drank liquor, not poison.

I've given up outdoor cooking. (holds up apron and hat) *"Come and Get It, Danger, Men at Work." I was given this uh . . . amusing costume to wear and promptly lost my appetite completely. And now for something which should do the same for you.* (commercial break) *This concludes our entertainment for this evening. You'll be pleased to know that I have solved my bar-b-que problem. It involves burning down a barn each time you want roast lamb. It's even better on those occassions, when I can get my guests into the barn too. Next week, I shall return with another story. Some commercials, etc., etc., until then, good night.*

Alternate narrative:

This concludes our entertainment for this evening. You'll be pleased to know that I have solved my bar-b-que problem. It involves burning down a barn each time you want roast lamb. It's even better on those occassions, when I can get my guests in the barn too. Next time, I shall return with another story. Until then, good night.

EPISODE #165 **"SPECIALTY OF THE HOUSE"** Broadcast on December 13, 1959
Starring: Robert Morley as Mr. Laffler   Kenneth Haigh as Mr. Costain
Madame Spivy as Spirro   George Keymas as Paul, the waiter
Bettye Ackerman as Miss Hincle, the secretary   Charles Wagenheim as Henline
Tetsu Komai as Mr. Long Fong Ho   Lee Turnbull as the doorman
Cyril Delevanti as the bearded dinner guest
Teleplay written for *Alfred Hitchcock Presents* by Victor Wolfson and Bernard C. Schoenfeld, based on the short story of the same name by Stanley Ellin, originally published in the May 1948 issue of *Ellery Queen's Mystery Magazine.* Subsequently collected in *Mystery Stories* (Simon & Schuster, 1956; Boardman, 1957) and in *The Specialty of the House and Other Stories* (Mysterious Press, 1979).
Directed by Robert Stevens.
(picnic basket) *Good evening ladies and gentlemen. My dear sponsor invites me to this picnic, but doesn't seem to be around. I trust something has happened to him.* (sound comes from basket) *Ah, the reason for my invitation is now obvious, rattlesnake stakes, in the original package. Perhaps now is the time to meet the man, whose diabolical mind conceived this. Afterwhich, you may witness tonight's story.*

Alternate narrative:

(picnic basket) *Good evening ladies and gentlemen. A dear friend invited me to this picnic, but he doesn't seem to be around. I seldom go on safaris of this kind. They can be simulated perfectly in your own home, thanks to these two shakers. You just sprinkle these on your sandwiches. This one contains sand and this one, ants.* (sound comes from basket) *Ah, the reason for my invitation is now obvious. Rattlesnake stakes, in the original package. While I attempt to unravel this mystery, we have one feud puzzle over. Here it is.*

Story: Businessman Mr. Laffler feels that two qualities missing in this day and age is mystery and dignity. At a private "member's only" restaurant named Spirro's, Mr. Laffler has found both. Having already tasted some of the club's finest gourmets, Laffler becomes more and more obsessed with the ambition of not only gaining a lifetime membership, but learning what and how a specific "specialty of the house" called Lamb Armistran is really made of. Offered so rarely that Laffler almost loses his patience with Madame Spirro, owner of the dining club, when he demands to know how the meat is prepared – which would require a tour of the restaurant's kitchen – something that is always forbidden. Finally persistence pays its price when Laffler is granted his wish, and vanishes in the meat freezer, becoming part of the next "specialty of the house."

I trust you understand, that our having Mrs. Spirro on our program, does not necessary constitute an endorsement of her, or her restaurant. I shall not remove myself until after you have seen chapter three, in the continued story we are showing this evening. (commercial break) *I'm wondering if picnics might not be as bad as I imagined. I haven't even seen any ants.* (huge ant appears) *Until next week when I shall return with another story . . .* (sprays big ant) *Good night.*

Alternate narrative:

I trust you understand, that our having Mrs. Spirro on our program, does not necessarily constitute an endorsement of her or her restaurant. You know, I'm wondering if picnics might not be as bad as I imagined. I haven't even seen any ants. (huge ant appears) *Until next time when I shall return with another story.* (sprays big ant) *Good night.*

Hitchcock introducing "Specialty of the House"
Photo courtesy of Ronald V. Borst / Hollywood Movie Posters.

Trivia, etc. Actor Charles Wagenheim played Henline in this episode. Hitchcock fans would remember Wagenheim best as the assassin in *Foreign Correspondent* (1940). Wagenheim also played the role of a French waiter in *Paris Calling* (1941) and *Criss Cross* (1949). Japanese actor Tetsu Komai played numerous supporting roles in numerous mystery movies (especially when there called for a Japanese setting) including Sherlock Holmes, Bulldog Drummond and Fu Manchu. When Stanley Ellin's first published story, "The Specialty of the House," appeared in a 1948 issue of *Ellery Queen's Mystery Magazine*, the story made "something of a splash." The editor of the mystery magazine, admitted once that his greatest editorial blunder was the failure to award First Prize to the short story, as the best story in *EQMM*'s 1948 International Contest. This short story has been universally acclaimed a modern classic, and was considered by author Anthony Boucher as "the best first-published story" he ever read. And to think that this was Stanley Ellin's literary debut!

"Robert Stevens, who was our superb director and did extraordinary shows for us, was also quite eccentric," recalled Norman Lloyd. "He was very nervous, so he was easily upset. He had Robert Morley in 'Specialty of the House,' and one day Morley was approached on the set by the Screen Actors Guild representative and told that he'd better cough up 65 bucks because he hadn't paid his Screen Actors dues... (He was a Brit, you see - from England.) Morley went over to Robert Stevens (he was a true eccentric, too, old Morley), and he said, 'Can you give me $65 so I can pay this man?' Well...Stevens flipped [laughs]! Stopped shooting ...came up to us in the office...and said [babbling], 'You know what he did?? He wanted $65!!' But Bob Stevens was brilliant in that episode, and won the only Emmy the show ever won [for his direction of 'The Glass Eye']. We never won an Emmy other than that one Emmy, and I think history has shown that Hitchcock is one of the great shows. People tell me even now that, when they run on TV Land, these stories are absolutely marvelous. And what actors! I mean, my God, we got the cream!"

One actress we cannot forget is Madame Spivy, best remembered for playing Ma Greeny in *Requiem for a Heavyweight* (1962) and as the female Berezovo in *The Manchurian Candidate* (1962). She actually operated her own New York City nightclub, "Spivy's Roof," from 1940 to 1951.

EPISODE #166   "AN OCCURRENCE AT OWL CREEK BRIDGE"
        Broadcast on December 20, 1959
        Starring: Ronald Howard as Peyton Farquhar   Juano Hernandez as Josh
        Kenneth Tobey as Colonel Jack Venable   Douglas Kennedy as the officer
        James Coburn as the Union Soldier
        Brad Weston as the corpral who makes the noose
        Ruby Goodwin as Farquhar's maid   Gregg Stewart as the soldier on the bridge
        Teleplay written for *Alfred Hitchcock Presents* by Harold Swanton, based on the
1891 short story of the same name by Ambrose Bierce.
        Directed by Robert Stevenson.
        (in a cannon)   *Good evening and welcome to Alfred Hitchcock Presents. Please*
excuse me if I speak rapidly, I have a very short fuse. Tonight's play is a period piece which
takes place during the war between the states, when space travel was limited to this primitive
means. I shall be in orbit during the next minute so I'm afraid I shall miss the commercial.
However, my sponsor has arranged matters so that as I go through the sky, I shall spell out
his product. He thinks of everything. (boom)

        Story: When Peyton Farquhar attempts to burn down a bridge built by Union
troops, he is caught and sentenced to hang for aiding in the Confederate cause. Escorted to
the top of Owl Creek Bridge, Farquhar is sentenced to hang. But when the wooden plank
drops, the rope snaps in two and Farquar's body falls to the river below, where he loosens his
tied wrists and swims away among a hail of bullets. Running through the forest, Farquhar
seeks refuge with the assistance of Josh, an old friend he once thought died in a house fire.
Even when the two pass a regiment of Union troops, not one of the soldiers notices Farquhar.
Finally arriving at his estate and mansion, Farquhar catches a glimpse of his wife, who died
last week giving birth. Just as he's about to fall into the arms of his beloved woman, he
suddenly dies, having imagined all of the escape . . . as his lifeless body hangs from Owl
Creek Bridge.

        My experience with the canon turned out to be a humiliating one. How would you
like to be publically labeled a dud. Here among the other war surplus, I have found this. It
contain the plans for the defence of Atlanta and was given to a Union spy, with instructions
to eat it if he were captured. (cling) *Those were formidable men. Now, here's a message for*
you to decode after which, I shall return. (commercial break) *I have discovered that the art*
of espionage was a highly developed one, even back in Civil War days. As you may
remember, this is what the spy had to chew up and swallow. (takes out note) *Preheat oven to*
350 degrees, bake for 20 minutes and serve. Now until next week. Good night.

EPISODE #167   "GRADUATING CLASS"   Broadcast on December 27, 1959
        Starring: Wendy Hiller as Miss Laura Siddons Gigi Perreau as Gloria Barnes
        Jocelyn Brando as Julia Conrad   Robert H. Harris as Ben Proudy
        Sheila Bromley as Dorothy, the principal   Madge Kennedy as Gloria's mother
        Josie Lloyd as a student   Julie Payne as a student
        David McMahon as the doorman   Olan Soulé as the book store clerk
        Teleplay written for *Alfred Hitchcock Presents* by Stirling Silliphant, based on a
story by Edouard Sandoz.
        Directed by Herschel Daugherty.
        (sport spectator) *Good evening fellow fans. I suspect this is a side of me you never*
expected to see but I feel there is nothing undignified about following a sport and routing for
one side. Excuse me, my team is now entering the arena. (waving for LIONS - roar) *By the*
way, for the information of those of you who are unfamiliar with sports, that was not the
mascot you heard. He is one of the participants. Now I see they are about to throw. . .
correction. The other team is about to come onto the field. I also see by your chalky faces
that some of you prefer more intellectual entertainment. That is why we offer the following,
after which we shall present our play.

Story: A new literature teacher at an exclusive, private school quickly makes friends with Gloria, her only student with an interest in reading. Becoming concerned when she sees Gloria enter a fast nightclub, Miss Siddons asks her about it, but the student steadfastly maintains that she was with her sick mother. Later, while her teacher is on a date with Ben Proudy, she sees the girl in the same nightclub. This time Gloria admits that she is married to the young man she was with, but hasn't told her mother because of her poor health. Miss Siddons agrees to keep the matter quiet, but is unnerved the next day when she hears that Gloria's mother has gone into a coma, after Proudy tried to blackmail the woman about her daughter's behavior. Unfortunately, Gloria assumes that Miss Siddons was the blackmailer and accuses her of it, destroying the new teacher's career.

We lost. Our first defeat. We shall protest of course. I think the policy of allowing the other team to carry weapons is definitely unsportsmanlike. I have already reported the matter to the society for the prevention of cruelty to animals. And now the opposing side wishes to lead a cheer. I shall return at its conclusion. (commercial break) *Unfortunately someone seems to have taken too much time. So we shall have to rush through the remainder of our show.* (rest in high speed) *That concludes our entertainment for this evening. Next week we shall be back with another story. Until then, good night.*

Trivia, etc. Samuel Goldwyn gave actress Madge Kennedy the title (nick-name) of "winsome," and over a period of years, Madge appeared in dozens of comedy and mystery movies. Madge played the part of Aunt Martha on television's *Leave It to Beaver* and in 1959, she played the uncredited role of a housewife in Alfred Hitchcock's *North by Northwest*. Actress Jocelyn Brando is Marlon Brando's sister, who also played the role of Emma Jane in *The Alfred Hitchcock Hour* episode "The Jar." Olan Soulé appeared in this episodes as the book store clerk, but his name was not listed in the closing credits.

The episode "Man From the South" was originally scheduled for broadcast on January 3, 1960. For reasons unknown, it was pre-empted and later broadcast in March, two months later.

EPISODE #168   **"THE IKON OF ELIJAH"**   Broadcast on January 10, 1960
Starring: Oscar Homolka as Mr. Carpius
Sam Jaffe as the Archimandrite, Father Superior
Arthur E. Gould-Porter as Major Parslow
Richard Longman as Callost Chiringirian
David Janti as Paul Carp   William Greene as Theodoras
Danielle de Metz as Malvera   Robert P. Richards as Brother Constantine
Fred Catania as Brother Damiaos
Teleplay written for *Alfred Hitchcock Presents* by Victor Wolfson and Norah Perez, based on the short story of the same name by Avram Davidson, originally published in the December 1956 issue of *Ellery Queen's Mystery Magazine*.
Directed by Paul Almond.
(with a hammer in a tomb)   *Oh, good evening. I enjoy digging around in old tombs. They can be quite convenient too. If your assistants become as difficult as mine are, you can always manage to leave them inside. This one is typical, quiet, comfortable, attractive and roomy. Man has always provided better living conditions for the dead, than for the living. But that is enough persiflage badinage. We have work to do. That however, will take only a minute, then our story begins.*

Alternate narrative:
(with a hammer in a tomb)   *Oh, good evening. I enjoy digging around in old tombs. They can be quite convenient too. If your assistants become as difficult as mine are, you can always manage to . . . leave them inside. This one is typical, quiet, comfortable, attractive and roomy. Man has always provided better living conditions for the dead, than for the living. But that is enough persiflage badinage. Now for tonight's story.*

Story: An antique shop owner named Mr. Carpius, intends to break into a monastery to steal a valuable ikon, leaving behind a fake one in its place. By claiming he is seeking spiritual assistance, Carpius is granted entrance and promptly steals the ikon. Caught red handed by a monk, Carpius kills him. When the other monks over-hear the struggle, they rush in and catch Carpius, who begs for their forgiveness for what he has done. The Archimandrite says it is possible, but only if Carpius stays in the ikon room and pray for forgiveness. When the cell door is locked, Carpius realizes that they intend for him to stay there for the remainder of his life.

So much for the Carpius caper. I am sure it's very comforting to know where you are going to spend the rest of your life. Does it seem dark to you? I'll bet my assistant has accidentally shut the tomb door. I shall be back in a moment. . . I hope. Help. (commercial break) *That was a dismal, frightening minute, wasn't it? As it turned out, the tomb door wasn't closed. It became dark because the occupant hadn't paid his last electric bill. This concludes tonight's show.* (reads the writing on the wall) *R. Montague loves J. Capulet. These teenagers, defacing property. Good night.*

Alternate narrative:
So much for the Carpius caper. I'm sure it's very comforting to know where you are going to spend the rest of your life. (reads the wall) *R. Montague loves J. Capulet. These teenagers, defacing property. Does it seem dark to you? I bet my assistant has accidentally shut the tomb door. I have a feeling it's time for me to say good night. Help.*

Trivia, etc. On January 17, 1960, *Alfred Hitchcock Presents* was not broadcast. Instead, CBS presented a ninety-minute monthly special, *Dupont Show of the Month*. This original television drama was "Arrowsmith," based on the novel of the same name by Sinclair Lewis. Starring in the lead roles were Farley Granger, Diane Baker, and Oscar Homolka (who starred in *Alfred Hitchcock Presents* the week before). Granger played a young doctor whose battle against complacency in his profession, took a toll on his private life. Broadcast from 9:30 to 11 p.m., EST.

EPISODE #169 **"THE CURE"** Broadcast on January 24, 1960
    Starring: Nehemiah Persoff as Jeff Jenson   Mark Richman as Mike
    Cara Williams as Marie Jenson   Leonard Strong as Luiz
    Jhean Burton as the maid
    Teleplay written for *Alfred Hitchcock Presents* by Michael Pertwee, from the short story of the same name by Robert Bloch, originally published in the October 1957 issue of *Playboy*, and later in the January 1959 issue of *Bestseller Mystery Magazine*. Subsequently collected in *Blood Runs Cold* (Simon & Schuster, 1961; Robert Hale, 1962) and in *Such Stuff As Screams Are Made Of* (Ballantine, 1979; Robert Hale, 1980).
    Directed by Herschel Daugherty.
    (preparing a stake) *Good evening. No, we're not preparing a barbecue. I consider outdoor cooking rather uncivilized. Tonight we hope to revive one of the truly inspiring ceremonies of ancient times. The Aztec human sacrifice. I think it is regrettable, that in the hustle and bustle of this modern age, we've lost sight of some of the fundamental values and neglected some of the beauties of ancient times. For this event, we thought it would be only fair to become an audience participation program and choose the victim from our own loyal viewers. The winner will receive many prizes, including a free trip to Hollywood. . . one-way. Our story begins in a moment. But first we present what I'm certain will some day be shown as an example of the folk art of the 1950's, used to drive evil spirits out of the home.*

Story: Jeff Jenson takes his wife Marie to Africa not for a vacation, but for business, looking for oil. One morning Jeff finds his wife coming at him with a knife. His life is saved by an employee, Luiz, who intercepts Marie, just in the nick of time. Luiz privately offers to murder her for her attempted crime, but Jeff's partner Mike, thinks that she has had too much of the jungle and only needs to see a head shrinker. Jeff goes along with this and the woman is taken away by Luiz and Mike, unaware that Mike and Marie are having an affair. On the way to their destination, the two attempt to go against Luiz, but the faithful servant kills Mike. A few weeks later, Luiz returns from the native's head shrinker, and explains that he had to kill Mike in self-defense, but was able to take care of Marie. As proof, he shows Jeff his wife's shrunken head.

Of course there was a bright side to all this. For it was the beginning of a marvelous new invention, instant girl. All you do is add water. And now in just one minute I shall announce the winner of our contest, to select a human sacrifice. (commercial break) I am very pleased to announce, that we have chosen our human sacrifice. She is Mrs. Stanley K. Ladoski, of Wentfield, New Jersey. And of course we are already shipping the freezer, the automobile and the other prizes to our contest winner, Mr. Stanley K. Ladoski, who submitted Mrs. Ladoski's name. Our thanks to both of you. Now until next week at the same time, good night.

Trivia, etc. "Early on in our relationship, a writer living three thousand miles away popped up with a claim that my story 'The Cure' was plagiarism," recalled Robert Bloch. "At that time I was still pretty much of an unknown quantity as far as the Hitchcock team was concerned, and they could have been understandably forgiven had they ended our relationship then and there – for nothing distresses Hollywood producers more than possible involvement of a lawsuit. But once I assured them of my innocence they rallied to the rescue without further question.   Upon investigation they discovered that the charges were completely unfounded; outside of the South American setting, my *Playboy*-published story, which, it developed, the accusing writer had never even read – bore no resemblance whatsoever to the supposed counterpart. There was no litigation and my reputation, thanks to their quick action and support, remained unsullied."

Michael Pertwee also wrote the script for a Hitchcock-produced episode of *Suspicion* entitled "Rainy Day," also set in Africa. (see *Suspicion* chapter) Alfred Hitchcock himself had a shrunken head in the presentation for the first-season episode "Back for Christmas."

EPISODE #170   **"BACKWARD, TURN BACKWARD"**   Broadcast on Janaury 31, 1960
    Starring: Tom Tully as Phil Canby   Phyllis Love as Sue Thompson
    Alan Baxter as Sheriff Andy Willett   Raymond Bailey as Mr. Harris
    Rebecca Welles as Betty Murray   Paul Maxwell as Saul
    Peggy Converse as Miss Lyons   Selmer Jackson as the clergyman
    Teleplay written for *Alfred Hitchcock Presents* by Charles Beaumont, based on the short story of the same name by Dorothy Salisbury Davis, originally published in the June 1954 issue of *Ellery Queen's Mystery Magazine*. Subsequently collected in *Tales for a Stormy Night* (Foul Play Press, 1984).
    Directed by Stuart Rosenberg.
    (big cement gift, statue) *Good evening, ladies and gentlemen. I'm making a gift for a dear friend. It's a going away present. It's also in the nature of a surprise since he isn't aware the trip is being planned for him. Oh well, I don't really need anything fancy. I'm only going to chain it to his feet. Perhaps you are curious as to the identity of my friend. Here is a one minute hint.*

Story: A scandal has hit town. Matt Thompson is dead and the police found the murder weapon, a plumber's wrench. The leading suspect is Phil Canby, a man of 59 who worked for Matt Thompson, and secretly spent time with Matt's teenage daughter Sue. Miss

Lyons, a neighbor who also had feelings for Phil Canby, claims she heard a baby's cry about ten o'clock last night. But there is only one baby on the whole block, and that's Canby's grandson and Canby claims the baby was sleeping. After questioning Phil, the sheriff cannot find one speck of proof that he didn't kill Matt. "If they hang me it won't be for murder," Phil comments, "it will be because I fell in love with a nineteen year old girl." Later, the sheriff is forced to arrest his old friend, and Sue begins to act like a child, crying similar to a baby. This tips the sheriff off that the true killer is Sue, who is mentally disturbed.

That concludes the comedy portion of tonight's program. Now for something more grim. After which you will find me here, hard at work. (commercial break) *There will be no more from out lot of entertainment . . . until next week that is. I have a new piece of stone and have decided to give sculpturing one more try.* (stone breaks into pieces, leaving a small statue) *Oh well, what can you expect from a beginner? Good night.*

Trivia, etc. "I watched with fascination a story that was totally foreign to me," recalled Dorothy Salisbury Davis. "That didn't matter. I enjoyed it. The cast was excellent, the suspense was gripping. Alas, it was still gripping when the show was over and Mr. Hitchcock was saying his inimitable adieus. Friends called to ask what happened. I wasn't sure myself. Then I remembered how the story ended as I had written it. It ought to have been an actress's dream, and a director's, but as Charles Beaumont, the screenwriter, wrote me afterward, it came across a writer's nightmare: nobody in the audience understood the ending. Shall I say that Mr. Hitchcock himself proved the dramatic worth? In a picture, some years later, a picture which shall be nameless here. Mercifully, for more reasons than one."

"But like that other tight little island, Shamley Productions was only a semi-paradise," Henry Slesar added. "Producers and writers both to disagree, it seems, and there was the customary amount of abrasion before a script was stamped FINAL. For one thing, Shamley was sensitive to the most frequent viewer criticism of all: 'I saw your show last night and *I didn't understand the ending.*' The truth is, a goodly number of television watchers were simply unable to grasp those droll, devastating, delightfully ironic twists. Shamley and the writers went to great pains to set up the snap-trap endings that were the Hitchcock trademark. But too often, after the trap was sprung, the mouth-breathers in the audience were still waiting for the curtain line. They were a minority, but their influence was felt. The most common command to writers was, 'For God's sake, make the endings clear!'"

EPISODE #171 **"NOT THE RUNNING TYPE"** Broadcast on February 7, 1960
Starring: Paul Hartman as Milton Potter   Robert Bray as Captain Ernest Fisher
Bert Freed as the bald headed man   Wendell Holmes as John B. Halverson
Herb Ellis as Captain Fisher's assistant   O. Z. Whitehead as Newton
Murray Alper as Sergeant Ed Carmody
Maurice Manson as Captain Harvey Ellison
Teleplay written for *Alfred Hitchcock Presents* by Jerry Sohl, based on the short story of the same name by Henry Slesar, originally published in the January 1959 issue of *Ellery Queen's Mystery Magazine.* Later collected in *Clean Crimes and Neat Murders* (Avon, 1960).
Directed by Arthur Hiller.
(standing beside a translator) *Good evening, ladies and gentlemen.* (Translator speaks in French) *You see we are making an effort to reach the widest possible audience. Tonight* (Translator speaks 3 languages) *The last was included in case this program reaches the moon. Tonight we present* (Translator interupts and Hitchcock, angry, pulls a gun and shoots.) *Haven't you forgotten something? No offense meant toward the countries involved, but he was a show off, til the very end. Always wanting the last word. And now, without further interruption . . .* (Translator on floor, dying, speaks in French. Hitchcock points gun at him again and shoots.) *I just didn't like those interruptions. And now, after one more interruption, tonight's story.*

Story: One morning, having served thirteen years for the Metro Investments firm, meek Milton Potter decided not to show up at the office and it wasn't until the third day that the firm began noticing the void – along with Potter's unbalanced books, indicating a loss of $200,000! Days later, the police are baffled when Milton Potter walks into the station and turns himself in. Having spent all those years at the firm, Potter confesses, he just had to do it. But he admits that he's just not the running type, so he wants to turn himself in. Just one problem. Potter won't say where the money is, or what he did with it. Potter pleaded guilty and was swiftly awarded a fifteen-year prison sentence. Now, twelve years later, Potter has been released on good behavior and one of the first things he does is returns the money. All $200,000! Again, the police are baffled. Afterwards he leaves for a round-the-world cruise, chatting with a fellow traveler, as he discusses how he retired, merely by quarterly-compounded interest with money banked at various institutions over a period of twelve years!

So much for high finance. I realize you have already had two commercials, but why not have one more for the road? After that, I shall act as the chaser. (commercial break) *It is customary to announce to an audience, when the program they are watching is in color. I can only assume that this is for the benefit of the color blind, so that they will know they are missing something. I have good news for them tonight. The preceding program was not in color. Next week I shall return with another story. Until then, good night.*

Trivia, etc. Murray Alper played the role of the Ferris Wheel Conductor in Alfred Hitchcock's *Strangers on a Train* (1951), Mac the truck driver in *Saboteur* (1942), and Harold, the taxi driver in *Mr. and Mrs. Smith* (1941). Maurice Manson played the District Attorney in Alfred Hitchcock's *The Wrong Man* (1958), and later played the role of the doctor in the episode, "I Saw the Whole Thing." Regarding the lead-out, Hitchcock actually directed his only TV episode in color the following week. Filming started the day after this *Alfred Hitchcock Presents* episode was broadcast. The color episode, entitled "Incident At A Corner," was broadcast two months later on April 5 on *Ford Startime*. The music for the opening of this episode was also used in "Incident At A Corner."
   "'Not the Running Type' was one of the most popular shows we ever did," recalled Norman Lloyd. "Audiences were just delighted with it and sent bags of mail expressing their delight."
   "I wrote a story called 'Not the Running Type'," said Henry Slesar. "It was about a man who embezzles a great deal of money from a bank, deposits it all in another bank, then gives himself up. When he is let out of jail years later, he gives back the money and quietly lives off the interest it has earned for the rest of his life. This episode had an upshot. A man in England pulled the same caper. But he was caught. When the police arrested him, they said, 'We saw the Hitchcock show too.' It was called the Hitchcock Case in England because of its exact duplication. The Hitchcock people always felt terrible when this sort of thing happened. But what can you do? There are those occasions when life does imitate art."
   "So there we were, discussing story ideas for the show," recalled Jerry Sohl, "and they would say, 'Well, why don't you do that?' And they would often say 'If you have any ideas you want to try out, let us know and if we like them, we'll use them.' I can't remember any of my stories being done on that show, just adaptations I wrote from others. 'Not the Running Type' was a Henry Slesar story and I never knew if that story was going to have visibility or be a clunker. When I saw the shows on the tube, I thought they came out very well, and so I must say that they were very crafted people who knew what they were doing. All the cuts were in the right places and a few changes, but not very many."

EPISODE #172 **"THE DAY OF THE BULLET"** Broadcast on February 14, 1960
   Starring: Barry Gordon as Ignace "Iggy" Kovacs
   Glenn Walken as Cletus 'Clete' Vine (as a boy)   Dennis Patrick as Mr. Rose
   Biff Elliott as Mr. Kovacs   Harry Landers as Joe, Rose's thug

John Craven as Clete Vine　　　　　　　Clegg Hoyt as the sergeant
Sam Gilman as the police officer　　　　David Fresco as the beat-up man
　　　　Teleplay written for *Alfred Hitchcock Presents* by Bill S. Ballinger, based on the short story of the same name by Stanley Ellin, originally published in the October 1959 issue of *Ellery Queen's Mystery Magazine*. Subsequently collected in *The Blessington Method and Other Strange Tales* (Random House, 1964; Macdonald, 1965) and in *The Specialty of the House and Other Stories* (Mysterious Press, 1979).
　　　　Directed by Norman Lloyd.
　　　　(free parking lot)　*Good evening and welcome to half-an-hour of free parking. However, I no longer park the car for you. During the period I was rendering that service, we had the distinction of being the only parking lot ever to be proclaimed a disaster area. Naturally we cannot assume responsibility for articles left in the car, so please take your children with you. Tonight's story is called "The Day of the Bullet," but first why not have your ticket validated?*

　　　　Story:　After Clete Vine learns that a friend from his childhood has received a gangland-style killing, he remembers how honest Iggy was as a boy. In fact, when Iggy was young he turned in a gangster for nearly killing a man, but the thug was let go since the police wouldn't charge him on the strength of a child's word. Not even his father had the guts to stand up for his son, so when Mr. Rose paid him off with ten dollars, Iggy knew which route to take in life.

　　　　Well, that's the way the old bullet bounces. I see some of you are about to leave in order to avoid that last minute rush at the parking lot. Please remain in your seats for this important announcement. I shall again be visible at its conclusion.　(commercial break)　I know many of you are asking how I can afford to offer free parking. This is possible because of a very lucrative sideline.　(turns sign - used cars for sale)　This combination is quite economical. I need only one lot and one set of cars. Naturally we pass the savings on to you. Next week will find me doing business at the same old stand. Your patronage is kindly solicited. Good night.

EPISODE #173　**"HITCH HIKE"**　Broadcast on February 21, 1960
　　　　Starring: John McIntire as Charles Underhill
　　　　Robert Morse as Len, the boy　　　　Suzanne Pleshette as Anne
　　　　Read Morgan as the police officer　　Paul E. Burns as the proprietor
　　　　Teleplay written for *Alfred Hitchcock Presents* by Bernard C. Schoenfeld, based on a story by Ed Lacy (a pseudonym of Leonard Zinberg).
　　　　Directed by Paul Henreid.
　　　　(Hitchcock strike)　*Good evening ladies and gentlemen. I wish to announce that during the strike* (sign - Alfred Hitchcock Unfair) *we shall continue to do business and all but the very near sighted can see our show without crossing the picket line. Actually, these aren't workers at all. They represent management, or more precisely, the sponsor. I'm accused to being unfair to commercials. He also claims that I'm attempting to turn the one hour lunch into a ninety-minute spectacular. During the negotiations we hope to obtain shorter hours. Actually, all I'm fighting for are shorter minutes. This one for example.*

Alternate narrative:
　　　　(Hitchcock strike)　*Good evening ladies and gentlemen. I wish to announce that during the strike* (sign - Alfred Hitchcock Unfair) *we shall continue to do business and all but the very near-sighted can see our show without crossing the picket line. Actually, this is not a strike about wages. I am a worker myself when I can't avoid it, and I have longed campaigned for the four-hour lunch. Actually, these are actors who claim I killed too many of them off during my stories. They're striking for longer hours. I see the pickets have stopped walking so they can watch tonight's story. Will you join them?*

295

Story: Business councilman Charles Underhill shows a grudge against the younger generation, believing children these days are reckless, lacking the proper emotional development. Len, a young man recently released from a juvenile prison, repairs Underhill's broken car horn in exchange for a ride to the next town. Underhill gets paranoid when Len starts to talk about knives, and starts speeding eighty in a forty-five mile zone. Stopped by a cop for speeding, Underhill tells the officer of his suspicions, and the boy is searched for a knife. But when the cop finds no weapon on the boy, Underhill is issued a heavy speeding ticket. After the officer leaves, Underhill threatens Len's return to the prison camp until the boy shows him the cop's ticket book, complete with speeding ticket. The boy confesses that he served a three-month stretch for being a pick-pocket, and his talent just came in handy. Handing the book to Underhill, Len remarks, "You wanted to think the worst of me. Of course, if you're such an up-right citizen, you can always walk across the street and hand them this officer's book, and then you'll take the rap." Underhill hesitates for a moment and orders the boy back in the car.

I wish it understood that my presence here does not constitute an endorsement of this method of fixing trafic tickets. Of course if you wish to try... There goes that man again. We shall continue negotiations under cover of the following public announcement by management. After which I shall return to present my side. (commercial break; sign - Unfair to Viewers) *Our little labor dispute has been settled. My sponsor offered to shorten my work week. By cutting up the story entirely and cutting the commercials down from three to one. That one to be a single thirty-minute message. You'll be relieved to know that I declined his generosity. Next week we shall be returning with business as usual. Until then, good night.*

Alternate narrative:
I wish it understood that my presence here does not constitute an endorsement of the methods employed by the characters in the play. The striking actors were somewhat disappointed that no one was killed in tonight's play. They are the understudies, you know. Next time we shall try to do better. Until then, good night.

EPISODE #174   **"ACROSS THE THRESHOLD"**   Broadcast on February 28, 1960
Starring: Patricia Collinge as Mrs. Sophia Wintor
George Grizzard as Hubert Wintor   Barbara Baxley as Miss Irma Collett
Teleplay written for *Alfred Hitchcock Presents* by Charlotte Armstrong, based on the short story "The Queen" by L.B. Gordon, originally published in the August 1958 issue of the *John Creasey Mystery Magazine*. Subsequently reprinted in *The Mystery Bedside Book*, ed. John Creasey (Hodder & Stoughton, 1960).
Directed by Arthur Hiller.
(TV séance)   *Good evening. So glad you could join us. We are holding a seance tonight. At our last session we managed to get in touch with the spirit of Marconi, the inventor of radio, but unfortunately it was impossible to understand what he was saying because of the static. Now, if all of you will place your hands palm down on the tops of your television sets, we shall attempt to speak to Alexander Graham Bell. Hallo, hallo* (knock, knock, knock) *I seem to have reached him already. Mr. Bell, do you?* (knock, knock, knock) *That's peculiar. It's a woman. She says Mr. Bell is not in.* (knock, knock) *No I'll call later. That was his answering service. Now if you will concentrate on the little screen in front of me, there is someone, I am positive, wants to get in touch with you. And I am certain he'll be in, listen.*

Story: Sophia Wintor's husband, Arthur, died six years ago, and she wonders if her husband – wherever he is - misses her as much as she misses him. When she confesses to her non-descript son, Hubert, that she wants to see her husband, he decides to speed up the process – and arranges a fake seance with the help of his girlfriend. The two con artists convince her that Arthur is lonely, and that it would be best to pass on and join him across the threshold. Deciding the best route, Sophia plans to take the poisonous medicine. As she gets ready to die, Hubert drinks some brandy to celebrate her departure. Only later does he realize the brandy was poisoned by his mother, who wanted to keep the family together. In the meantime, Hubert's girlfriend has second thoughts and phones the police. When Sophia finally is ready to take her medicine. she gets disturbed by someone ringing the doorbell.

That concludes our tribute to mother love. I shall return after we reveal our sponsor's identity. (commercial break) *There is an epilogue to tonight's story. Mrs. Wintor decided to trade spiritual togetherness for solitary confinement, and discovered she preferred it that way. After seeing Hubert, I can't say I blame her. Next week we shall make our own attempt at togetherness with you. Until then, good night.*

Alternate narrative:
If you found this story amusing, you will be pleased to know that we have prepared another for our next presentation. So until then, good hyphened night.

Trivia, etc. "My Godmother was visiting from my home town of Edmonton, Alberta and came on the set of 'Across the Threshold' to see how a show was made," said Arthur Hiller. "This was a woman who adored me and spoke so highly of me no matter what, even when matters were ordinary. When she returned to Western Canada and was asked 'What was it like watching your treasured Godson filming a show?' she replied, 'I don't know. This guy [George Grizzard] just kept coming in the door over and over again saying, 'Mother, I'm home.' She didn't take to our doing a few takes and a few angles."

George Grizzard comforts Barbara Baxley in "Across the Threshold"

297

EPISODE #175 **"CRAIG'S WILL"** Broadcast on March 6, 1960
Starring: Dick Van Dyke as Thomas 'Tom' Craig
Stella Stevens as Judy, Tom's spoiled girlfriend   Paul Stewart as Vincent Noonan
Harry O. Tyler as Sam Loomis, the butler
Joseph Holland as the reader of the will
Almira Sessions as Martha Henderson   Maurice Manson as the hunter
Stephen Roberts as the psychiatrist   and Special Guest Star Casper the dog
Teleplay written for *Alfred Hitchcock Presents* by Burt Styler and Albert E. Lewin,
based on a story by Valerie Dyke.
Directed by Gene Reynolds.
(with three dogs)   *Good evening. I have some advice for those of you who want to
be performers. Don't blindly answer an advertisement. How was I to know that they call
themselves the Doheeny brothers. That is Shep, that's Talsa and this is Bounce. All right
and I'm Spot. You have no idea what I've been through this week, jumping through hoops.
They're jealous because I can stand on my hind legs better than they. It's the only trick I do
well. Ours is a difficult act to follow. But I know someone who is just fool-hardy enough to
try. After which, we shall have tonight's play.*

Story: When his wealthy uncle dies, Tom discovers that most of the estate is willed
to his favorite dog, Casper, and the young man will receive nothing until the dog passes
away. Judy, Tom's girlfriend, tries to talk him into killing the pooch, but after assuring her
that he would do it, Tom changes his mind. Judy turns to a professional hit man, and offers
$1,000 plus expenses to eliminate the dog. "This is got to look like an accident," she
explains. The hit man nearly kills himself by ant poison during the first attempt, and then the
dog ends up saving his life when he tries for a "boating accident." Eventually, Tom gets wise
and turns against Judy because of her desire to murder Casper, who still loves the woman,
despite her deadly intentions. Finally she realizes the truth. If she wants the money, she
must become a dog and marry Casper. Man's best friend.

*I lost the rest of my act. Their uncle died and left them a small fortune, so they
retired. Now that you have seen "Craig's Will," listen to this codicil, after which I shall
return.* (commercial break)   *After the humiliations we've experienced this evening, I think
it's time man reasserted his superiority over animals.   Until next week, good night.*
(Hitchcock approaches the cats with a chair and whip)

Trivia, etc. The name of the butler, Sam Loomis, is the same name as the
character John Gavin played in *Psycho*.

EPISODE #176 **"MAN FROM THE SOUTH"** Broadcast on March 13, 1960
One of the days of filming was 11/18/59.
Starring: Steve McQueen as the young man
Peter Lorre as Carlos, the gambler   Neile Adams as the young woman
Katherine Squire as the gambler's wife   Tyler McVey as the referee
Marc Cavell as the bellhop   Phil Gordon as the bartender
Teleplay written for *Alfred Hitchcock Presents* by William Fay, based on the 1948
short story of the same name by Roald Dahl. Subsequently collected in *Someone Like You*
(Knopf, 1953; Secker & Warburg, 1954) and in *Tales of the Unexpected* (Michael Joseph,
1979; Vintage, 1980).
Directed by Norman Lloyd.
(at the races)   *Good evening, ladies and gentlemen and welcome to the land of
two dollar windows and quarter horses. Racing has been called the sport of kings, but here
at the two dollar window, I've met relatively few of them. Well, apparently there's no
business like show business and speaking of shows, we have one following the next race.
Those of you who wish to bet me, still do so. Naturally, I can't give you any tips but there's*

one entry that has been timed at just one-minute flat. (bell) *Ah, there he is now.* (voice over speaker: they're off and running)

      Story: Down to his last dollar, an attractive young man with a passion for cars, is approached by an odd-looking millionaire with a flare for creativity. The millionaire wagers his convertible (this year's model), against one of the young man's fingers, that a cigarette lighter won't light ten times in a row. Testing out his lighter a couple of times, the young man gets a feel of the car and agrees to the bet. Upstairs in a hotel room, the young man is subjected to drinks while one of his hands are tied down to a table. The millionaire grabs a firm grip on a meat cleaver. One by one, sweating nervously, the young man flips open the lighter and strikes the wick. After seven starts with the lighter, the millionaire's wife arrives and puts an end to the proceedings. Might have been good though, since the lighter only clicks when he tries to light a cigarette. The old man cannot wager the car, she explains, as it really belongs to her – she earned it herself. When she reaches for the keys the young man is horrified to see that her hand has only two fingers left.

      Now you know how Venus DeMilo got that way she is. By the time the poor old girl won an automobile, it was impossible for her to drive it. Of late there's been a great deal of talk about pay television. Actually, most of us already have it. . . and here is the gentleman who makes us pay. (commercial break) *I'm not sure what to say. That last commercial left me completely under whelmed. Perhaps I shall simply bid you adieu until next week when my, uh. ., sponsor and I shall return with another story. Good night.*

Alternate narrative:

      I am somewhat upset about the happy ending to that story. It'll cost me a pretty penny. It wasn't supposed to end that way at all. I never saw that woman before in my life. Someone put her in there at the last minute to throw the race. (bells) *Good heavens! Isn't that the dutchess shoeing that horse?* ("Until next time. Good Night!" on sign)

Trivia, etc. "I directed an episode called 'Man from the South' from a story by Roald Dahl," recalled Norman Lloyd. "Steve McQueen and Peter Lorre starred as two gamblers. The bet was could McQueen ignite his lighter ten times in a row, risking a finger for every misfire. The lighter he used was a Zippo. The upshot was that kids in a number of schoolyards around the country started playing a game called 'Zippo.' The only difference was that they didn't risk their fingers if they missed. Well, Peter Lorre was one of the great actors - it's tragic what happened. He was charming, brilliant, a great conversationist. . . but by the time he came to us, he felt that his career was sort of over. He wasn't doing the features any more, and he was rather sad about it, I thought. But he was wonderful - marvelous."

Originally scheduled for broadcast on January 3, 1960, this episode was filmed back in November of 1959, finally broadcast in March. What makes this episode so interesting is that no one is mentioned by name in the entire episode (with the exception of Carlos, but only revealed at the end). Hitchcock also staged a similar lighter joke in *Torn Curtain* in 1966, but the other way around. The lighter clicks a couple of times for Gromek (Wolfgang Kieling), but later it works perfectly for Professor Armstrong (Paul Newman).

Tyler McVey acted with McQueen in the episode "Human Interest Story," and would soon act again with Neile Adams in "One Grave Too Many." Regardless of much speculation, Neile Adams, who co-starred with Steve McQueen in this episode, was already McQueen's real-life wife. "I had already been supporting him [Steve McQueen] for three years prior to that," recalled Neile Adams. "Steve and I met when I was doing *Pajama Game* (1957). He was doing *A Hatful of Rain* (1957), replacing Ben Gazzarra. But he hadn't replaced him yet. Then we got married four months later, during *This Could Be the Night* (1957). He wasn't doing very much of anything at that point. So, he got the series *Wanted: Dead or Alive* in 1958. He had the tough, cool way, which was very much like Humphrey Bogart and James Cagney. Those were his idols, anyway. Those, and Spencer Tracy. There were very few and far between actors like Steve. Even now, his popularity's beginning to soar again. Everything old is new again. For awhile there, after his death, there was no activity. Now, in the last two years, I've done four documentaries. There have been more books about him. This licensing business is tremendous! Actually, it was a lark. We had a good time doing that. Plus, he adored Peter Lorre. He was a cute man. Like I said, it was a lark. There was this part. They said, 'Would you like to do it?' I said, 'Sure. Why not?' So, we did it. The whole shoot was really just terrific. There were no problems. The script was so tight. I just had the baby, Terry, and all I could think of was, 'How do I look?' (laughs) All I kept thinking was, 'God, I hope I don't look too fat.' That was a fun time. It was great." *

The actress who played the gambler's wife, Katherine Squire, played a full five-fingered role in a later *Alfred Hitchcock Presents* episode, "Pen Pal." She did have all five of her fingers. "We made a glove to fit that," recalled Norman Lloyd. "Katherine Squire, a very good actress, played the part and we made a glove like that and she thrust her hand into it."

On March 20, 1960, *Alfred Hitchcock Presents* was not broadcast. Instead, a ninety-minute special was broadcast over CBS, entitled "The Valley of Decision." Teleplay written by Arthur Wallace, based on Marcia Davenport's romantic story about an immigrant Irish lass. Nancy Wickwire, Lloyd Bridges and Liam Redmond starred in the leads. Broadcast from 9:30 to 11 p.m., EST.

EPISODE #177 **"MADAME MYSTERY"** Broadcast on March 27, 1960
      Starring: Audrey Totter as Betsy Blake   Joby Baker as Jimmy Dolan
      Harp McGuire as Steve   Mike Ragan as Alfredo
      Meri Welles as Lois, the young starlet wanna-be

* Reprinted courtesy of *Filmfax* magazine and author Ira Sandler.

Teleplay written for *Alfred Hitchcock Presents* by William Fay, based on the short story "Is Betsy Blake Still Alive?" by Robert Bloch, originally published in the April 1958 issue of *Ellery Queen's Mystery Magazine.* Subsequently collected in *Blood Runs Cold*(Simon & Schuster, 1961; Robert Hale, 1962).

Directed by John Brahm.

(with a credit card press) *Good evening, ladies and gentlemen. I'm making credit cards. As you can see this credit card is cleverly patterned after the $20 bill. In this way we do away with such troublesome features as the monthly statement. Furthermore these are good in any city in the country and in any business establishment . . . provided the cashier is nearsighted. Normally our sponsor utilizes this next minute to talk about himself. However, in a great show of self-sacrifice he has consented to relinquish this time so that we may present a new feature. The best television commercials of the year. Here is the winner of this week's gold loving cup.*

Story: Jimmy Dolan, a hot young 23-year old who believes he has "box-office instinct," handles publicity for Goliath Film Studios. When actress Betsy Blake dies in a boating accident, the studio hits it big with a reviving interest in her old nickelodeon films. Jimmy starts juggling ideas to his friend Steve, milking the situation for all it's worth, and the studio continues to make big money. Betsy, however, has a surprise for Jimmy. The starlet is actually alive and well. There was a boating accident, she explains, but a fishing trawler out of San Diego found her body and her out. "You stick to your dreams Junior and I'll stick to mine," she tells Jimmy. Realizing what a mess this will make with his career, Jimmy kills her. Returning to Steve's house, Jimmy confesses his deed. Steve phones the police while commenting: "You'd kill your own mother to be a big man at Goliath Studios, wouldn't you?" "But how did you know that's who she was?" Jimmy asks.

So much for our ode to mother love. I must say it was a pleasant change to meet Jimmy Dolan. Here's a boy unsullied by any oedipus complex, not tied by any silver cord, unfeted by any sentimental clap trap. Just a healthy, happy, well adjusted killer. It's all very refreshing. And now for those of you who are accustomed to enjoying television, here is something that is also refreshingly different, after which I'll be back. (commercial break) *Jimmy Dolan, the hero of tonight's playlet, had a bit of bad luck, which I must relate to you. He met with an accident in his home and died as the result of a fall. He tripped over his grandmother while he was attempting to throw her down a flight of stairs. Very sad. Next week I shall return with another story. Equally uplifting. Until then, good night.*

Trivia, etc. The boathouse used for this episode was the same filmed for two another *Hitchcock* episodes, "The Last Dark Step" broadcast on February 8, 1959, and "Beta Delta Gamma" broadcast on November 14, 1961.

EPISODE #178   **"THE LITTLE MAN WHO WAS THERE"**   Broadcast April 3, 1960

Starring: Norman Lloyd as the little man

Arch Johnson as Jamie McMann	Read Morgan as Ben
Robert Armstrong as Hogie, the bartender	Clegg Hoyt as Hutch
Mike Ragan as Pete, Hutch's friend	Clancy Cooper as the old man
Frank Christi as one-armed bandit gambler	Roscoe Ates as the piano player

An original teleplay written for *Alfred Hitchcock Presents* by Gordon Russell and Larry Ward.

Directed by George Stevens, Jr.

(television switch-board) *Good evening, ladies and gentlemen. Just a moment please.* (switch-board) *You probably think these are telephone lines. Actually they are attached to television cables. In this way I can sidetrack people who attempt to dial another channel. Usually, after getting the wrong channel, they don't bother trying again. It helps our ratings enormously. This fellow is certainly persistent. This is a recording, you have reached a disconnected channel. We suggest you watch Alfred Hitchcock Presents. Thank you. This is a recording, you have reached . . . I've never seen this play fail. They always give up and watch our show. Why don't you? It begins in one minute.*

Story: A group of rowdy miners at a bar meet an unusual man when he arrives and says "many men have tried to beat me but not a soul has ever succeeded." Two hulking miners, Ben and Jamie, decide to take him on and are instantly paralyzed by some unknown force. With everyone else in the bar in a state of shock, the little man warns the miners not to interfere as he robs everyone of their valuables. The men in the bar hands over wallets, money and watches, and the mysterious little man leaves. Later, the little man meets up with his two accomplices, Ben and Jamie, and they split up the loot, having performed a successful heist.

That concludes our story just in case you haven't guessed. An amusing thing happened at the next town Ben, Jamie and their little man friend visited. A stranger happened into town on the night of the payoff. A man who were seeing their show for the second time. Their's was a show that could not stand any repeat business. As it turned out, it was their final performance. For the next minute I shall attempt a television first. I shall show you what is on another channel, after which I shall bring you safely back. (commercial break) I can see you feel you made a wise choice this evening. Why don't you do the same next week when I shall return with another play. Until then, good night.

EPISODE #179   "MOTHER, MAY I GO OUT TO SWIM?"   Broadcast April 10, 1960
      Starring: William Shatner as John Crane   Jessie Royce Landis as Claire Crane
      Gia Scala as Lottie Rank   Robert Carson as the judge
      Donald Elson as the court clerk
      Teleplay written for *Alfred Hitchcock Presents* by James P. Cavanagh, based on the short story of the same name by Q. Patrick, originally published in the July 1948 issue of *Ellery Queen's Mystery Magazine*. Subsequently collected in *The Ordeal of Mrs. Snow and Other Stories*, as by Patrick Quentin (Random House, 1962).
      Directed by Herschel Daugherty.
      (on high diving board on top of a building) *Good evening, ladies and gentlemen and welcome to another thirty-minute treatment. (diver goes off) (close-up) Jumping from the high diving board into a small tub of water is exactly like presenting a play on television. You may have a big hit, then again you may miss. But in either event you make a big splash. While we're waiting for our friend to land, let's put the time to good use.*

Story: When John Crane takes his first vacation without his mother, he meets Lottie Rank and the two fall in love. Their marriage plans go down the tube, however, when John's over-bearing mother arrives and it is pretty clear that the two women cannot tolerate each other. Lottie asks John to break the news to his mother about their plans, so the old woman won't have any ill feelings toward her. But always having lived under the careful scrutiny of mother, John can't bring himself to do it. Lottie, feeling John has chosen his mother over her, suggests that they tell her together. Visiting a high cliff near a waterfall, all three of them chat and John starts thinking that Lottie has planned on pushing his mother over the edge. As it turns out, however, Lottie was the one that got pushed off. After the deed is done, the judge at the county coroner's office rules the death an accident, which is good news for John, who leaves in the arms of his beloved mother.

A word about our story in a moment. I've just been told that our diver landed, but I'm awaiting confirmation. (Hitchcock gets splashed) Well, I suppose it's nice to know he landed safely. I plan to disappear for a minute. During that time, the screen will be filled with this diverting test pattern. (commercial break) I have a few matters to take care of, before I make my leap. First, the truth about Lottie's death was eventually discovered. I knew you'd want to know that. Secondly, in keeping with this show's policy of frankness and candour, I must announce that parts of the preceding program were commercials. Good night. (Takes an umbrella, holds his nose and jumps off the diving board) *Good niiiiiight.*

Trivia, etc. At the time this episode aired, Q. Patrick and Patrick Quentin, as well as Jonathan Stagge, were joint pseudonyms of Hugh Wheeler (who went on to write a number of successful Broadway plays such as "A Little Night Music") and Richard W. Webb. Jessie Royce Landis played Clara Thornhill in Alfred Hitchcock's *North by Northwest* (1959).

EPISODE #180 **"THE CUCKOO CLOCK"** Broadcast on April 17, 1960
Starring: Beatrice Straight as Mrs. Ida Blythe
Fay Spain as Madelene Hall   Donald Buka as the mental patient
Pat Hitchcock as Miss Dorothy Blythe   Don Beddoe as Burt, the shopkeeper
Teleplay written for *Alfred Hitchcock Presents* by Robert Bloch, based on the short story of the same name by Frank Mace.
Directed by John Brahm.
(shelf of cans) *Good evening and thank you for your kind attention, erratic, though it may be. You have, of course, heard of canned laughter. The horror recorded laughter which accompanies some comedy shows. Naturally since this program is entirely serious in nature, we have never resorted to this means of audience stimulation. However, I have just been shipped a number of cans of fresh audience sounds which may be useful.* (opens a can and a scream lets out) *Most of these cans contains screams. There are some filled with shudders and some of them hold whimpers and gasps. Just now we do not intend to use these recordings. This is merely a warning. If you fail to react to our stories at the emotional level we feel they deserve, we'll turn these sounds loose. So much for blackmail. Before our story begins we must present this commercial.* (we hear screams) *As you see, when they're confronted with something really horrifying, there's no need to open the can.*

Alternate narrative:
(shelf of cans) *Good evening and thank you for your kind attention, erratic, though it may be. You have, of course, heard of canned laughter. The horror recorded laughter which accompanies some comedy shows. Naturally since this program is entirely serious in nature, we have never resorted to this means of audience stimulation. However, I have just been shipped a number of cans of fresh audience sounds which may be useful.* (opens a can and a scream lets out) *Most of these cans contains screams. There are some filled with shudders and some of them hold whimpers and gasps. Just now we do not intend to use these recordings. This is merely a warning. If you fail to react to our stories at the emotional level we feel they deserve, we'll turn these sounds loose. So much for blackmail. Now for our story.*

Story: Ida Blythe, a lonely widow, is dropped off at her cabin in the mountains for the weekend, against the protests of her daughter, because the radio reports a lunatic escaped from an asylum in the nearby town. That evening – a dark and stormy night – Ida receives a visit from a young lady named Madelene. Pleased to have some company for the evening, Ida starts talking with the girl. Madelene claims to have seen the lunatic outside, and he might have followed her to the cabin. The young girl's bizarre stories alarms suspicion in the back of Ida's head, confirmed by a knock at the door, which no one dares to open. Later they get startled by a loud whistling sound, although it's only the tea kettle, but when someone knocks on the door again, Ida now feels compelled to open. A man in a raincoat stands by the doorway, warning Ida about the escaped lunatic – *a woman* – seen about the area. The two women get into a scuffle and Madelene is knocked out. Ida unlocks the door and the man enters, looking at the young girl's body lying on the floor. When the cuckoo clock on the wall strikes, he smashes the clock on the floor. "I can't stand being mocked," he remarks. The lunatic has arrived.

I don't think he played that quite fairly, do you? Some people will cheat, tell fibs, do anything in fact, in order to kill someone. I don't approve at all. It gives murder a very bad name. For I can assure you he won't try that again. At the next house he broke into, they were more hospitable. It belonged to the sheriff. This is from the section of quick frozen screams. They have to thaw out. I shall return after the following, after which you may have to thaw out. (commercial break) *I wonder if those commercials could be hermetically sealed. A number of people have been asking, where we obtain these canned screams, gasps, etc. They are, of course, authentic audience reactions recorded at a comedy show. I don't believe it is on the air any longer. Next week I shall return with another story laced together by my impertinent remarks. Until then, good night.*

Alternate narrative:

I don't think he played that quite fairly, do you? Some people will cheat, tell fibs, do anything in fact, in order to kill someone. I don't approve at all. It gives murder a very bad name. For I can assure you he won't try that again. At the next house he broke into, they were more hospitable. It belonged to the sheriff. Oh, this is from the section of quick frozen screams. They have to thaw out. A number of people have been asking, where we obtain these canned screams, gasps, etc. They are, of course, authentic audience reactions recorded at a comedy show. I don't believe it's on the air any longer. (looks inside can) *Good heavens, they forgot to remove the audience! Next time I shall return with another story laced together by my impertinent remarks. Until then, good night.*

Trivia, etc. "Shortly after I began my own work as a novice television writer for a little-esteemed syndication series, I was summoned to Hitchcock's Shamley Production office and offered an assignment to do a script based on Frank Mace's story, 'The Cuckoo Clock'," recalled Robert Bloch. "And here was I, with my meager list of credits on *Lock-Up*, a low-budget syndication series, suddenly moving forward into the fast lane. Apparently I managed to cope. While 'The Cuckoo Clock' was far from state of the art, it seemed adequate enough to bring me further assignments. I began adapting my own published stories along with those of other writers, and my work was dramatized by outsiders only when working commitments on the concurrently running *Thriller* series or my first screenplays pre-empted working hours. In spite of such conflicting assignments, from the end of 1959 until the termination of the show in its revised format, I was represented by sixteen offerings, ten of which were my scripts."

EPISODE #181   **"FORTY DETECTIVES LATER"**   Broadcast on April 24, 1960
Starring: James Franciscus as William Tyre   Jack Weston as Otto
George Mitchell as Munro Dean   Arlene McQuade as Gloria
Robert Kelljian as the customer *

Teleplay written for *Alfred Hitchcock Presents* by Henry Slesar, from his short story "40 Detectives Later," originally published in the May 1957 issue of *Manhunt*. Subsequently collected in *Clean Crimes and Neat Murders* (Avon, 1960).

Directed by Arthur Hiller.

(stone wheel / record)   *Good evening. If you've been wondering where it all began . . . Here it is. In fact,* (close-up) *here is where the first flat tire was patched some 4,000 years ago. Patching was more practical since the spare tire weighed several thousand pounds. Of course, once the wheel was invented many things became possible. Things which before had been only dreams. Things like the pancake and the pizza. But now I must interrupt this scholarly discussion to bring you tonight's play. It is called 'Forty Detectives Later' and will appear sixty seconds later.*

* Robert Kelljan's name was spelled "Kelljian" in the closing credits of this episode, but later in "The Dividing Wall," on *The Alfred Hitchcock Hour*, his name was spelled "Kelljan."

Alternate narrative:

(stone wheel / record)   *Good evening. If you've been wondering where it all began . . . Here it is. In fact,* (close-up) *here is where the first flat tire was patched some 4,000 years ago. Patching was more practical since the spare tire weighed several thousand pounds. Of course, once the wheel was invented many things became possible. Things which before had been only dreams. Things like the pancake, the pizza and the donut. Of course it took a long time for these things to catch on, since for hundreds of years, it was naturally assumed that they had to be made out of stone. But now I must interrupt this scholarly discussion to bring you tonight's play.*

Story: Munro Dean is determined to find his wife's murderer, although dozens of detectives he hired in the past have all failed. The latest private eye, William Tyre, gets more information than his predecessors, since Dean has managed to round up a suspect named Otto, and Dean offers to pay the detective to kill the suspect. Tyre refuses, but he goes to meet Otto and pretends to be interested in his records and sets up another meeting in Dean's hotel room. Realizing that Dean will probably try to kill the suspect himself, he attempts to intervene but arrives too late. Dean has already shot Otto. Tyre struggles with Dean over the gun, and Dean accidentally gets shot in the process. As Otto dies, he tells Tyre that he is the murderer – having originally been paid by Dean to do it. It seems that Munro Dean was trying to find him since the murder, in order to keep him from talking.

I seem to have been mistaken about this. It's not a wheel, it's a record. Long playing, of course. The title is "Ten Evenings with the Stonehenge Philharmonic." And now let us hear what is on the flip side. After which I shall spin back. (commercial break) *Now you understand why that sounded so raucous and primitive. Of course we've come a long way since then. But I'm afraid our disc jockeys aren't the men they used to be. Next week we plan to show another story in two acts, another commercial in three parts and of course your host making his three appearances in one. Until next week, good night.*

Alternate narrative:

I seem to have been mistaken about this. It's not a wheel, it's a record. Long playing, of course. The title is "Ten Evenings with the Stonehenge Philharmonic." My, their discjockeys must have been formidable men. While you are pondering my petty remarks, I must take leave. Next time we plan to show another story in two acts and of course your host making his two appearances in one. Until next time, good night.

EPISODE #182   **"THE HERO"**   Broadcast on May 1, 1960
Starring: Eric Portman as Sir Richard Musgrove

Oscar Homolka as Jan Vander Klaue	Irene Tedrow as Lady Musgrove
Ralph Clanton as the purser	Jack Livesey as the captain
Richard Lupino as the photographer	Irene Windust as Janet Boswell
Bartlett Robinson as Henry Coswell,	Barry Bernard as the bartender

Unbilled: Barry Harvey as the steward, and Sally Pearce as Elizabeth Musgrove
Teleplay written for *Alfred Hitchcock Presents* by Bill S. Ballinger, based on the short story of the same name by Henry de Vere Stacpoole, originally collected in *In Blue Waters* (Hutchinson, 1917).
Directed by John Brahm.

(ship in a bottle)   *Good evening. I thought you might be interested in seeing one of the world's first television tubes.* (close-up) *In those days everything was in glorious unsponsored color. Repairs were unheard of and the tube never wore out. But of course we've managed to improve those details. A few of you may consider staring at this, a rather limited form of entertainment. But our ancestors found this bottle quite exciting, but of course they were the ones who had emptied it. At this time we had intended to present a drama called "The Hero." However, after reading the story, our sponsor insisted that it was*

305

something for which the television audience was not yet ready. But please remain seated, he feels you will be ready in 60 seconds, meanwhile . . .

Story: While on board a vacationing ship heading for Africa, financial celebrity Richard Musgrove catches a glimpse of what appears to be a ghost, Jan Vander Klaue, an old mining partner from twenty years ago. The ship's passenger list doesn't have a Vander Klaue listed, but later that evening, Musgrove meets up with the stranger again, who claims his name is A. J. Keyser. But the resemblance is uncanny. When Mr. Keyser is supposed to meet him in his cabin, no one shows up, and instead an old newspaper clipping is pushed under the door. The clipping tells the story about a prospector who was once beaten and left for dead in a veldt. Keyser later tells him a story about a young man who's money was stolen, money needed for an operation to save the life of his wife, who later died as a result. The same money used to make Sir Richard a multi-millionaire. It's not murder because of the statute of limitations, but the scandal could ruin Sir Richard. Musgrove now knows the truth, and jumps overboard to try to commit suicide. Keyser dives in after him and drowns the man while pretending to save his ex-partner. For his feat of bravery, Keyser is later presented with a cup for his gallant deed.

By a stroke of good fortune, I happened to be on board that particular ship. I caught the whole rescue with my little long focus movie camera. I got every detail. I thought the captain might like the roll of film as a little souvenir. Oh, I want to tell you more about this but just wait one minute. (commercial break) That concludes our show for tonight. Next week I shall be back with another story. By the way, building a boat in a bottle isn't difficult. And it's no work at all once you have shrunk the carpenters down to the proper size. (little people singing) Good night.

EPISODE #183 **"INSOMNIA"** Broadcast on May 8, 1960
 Starring: Dennis Weaver as Charlie Morten Cavender
 James Millhollin as Dr. Tedaldi   John Ragin as Jack Fletcher
 Al Hodge as Mr. Turney   Sam Gilman as Frank, second fireman
 Ken Clark as the first fireman   Dorothea Lord as the receptionist
 Teleplay written for *Alfred Hitchcock Presents* by Henry Slesar, from his short story "Sleep Is for the Innocent," originally published in the February 1960 issue of *Alfred Hitchcock's Mystery Magazine.* Subsequently collected in *Clean Crimes and Neat Murders* (Avon, 1960).
 Directed by John Brahm.
 (standing on top of a larger-than-life desk) *Good evening, ladies and gentlemen. I have only myself to blame for this embarrassment. I insisted that every phase of our organization should be run on a business-like basis. Of course one bright employee thought it would be appropriate to put the entire program in the dead file. We put him there instead. Naturally, our dear sponsor has prepared his message in triplicate. Here is the first copy. Please study, initial and pass on.*

Story: Mail order clerk Charlie Cavender suffers from insomnia and is forced to visit a psychiatrist, in the hope of finding a cure for his sleeping disorder. While talking with the psychiatrist, Charlie admits that his brother-in-law, Jack Fletcher, holds him responsible for his sister's death, because she died in a massive house fire. The doctor says it might just be guilt from the accident, but Charlie says he slept all right after the fire. The insomnia started after he had gotten a letter from Jack. The doctor suggests that Charlie try to settle matters with the brother-in-law, so the anxiety will go away. Cavender pays a visit to his brother-in-law and tries to talk things out with Jack. Filled with rage, Jack will have none of it and pulls a gun on Charlie. Forced to defend himself, Charlie struggles with the gun and shoots it toward Fletcher's face, making it look like a suicide. Believing he's all cured, Charlie returns home for a good night's sleep, the first in many months. In fact, Charlie sleeps so soundly that he doesn't wake up when a faulty heater in his room starts the whole building on fire.

You must have heard months ago, that certain things in our land were considered in and others out. It has taken me all this time to comprehend just what all this meant. Now to my dismay, I'm told that the whole subject is no longer in. In other words, if you understand in and out, you are now out, which is exactly where I shall be in a minute. Here is a matter for you to study for appropriate action. (commercial break) *I think there is very little I can say at this juncture. But I must say I'm disturbed by the unabashed glee with which my assistance boosted me into this. Next week we shall return with business very much as usual. Until then, good night.*

EPISODE #184 **"I CAN TAKE CARE OF MYSELF"** Broadcast on May 15, 1960
    Starring: Myron McCormick as Bert Haber   Linda Lawson as Georgia
    Will Kuluva as Joey Palermo   Edmon Ryan as Simpson
    Frankie Darro as Little Dandy   Leonard Weinrib as Amos
    William Sharon as the man   and Pat Harrington, Jr. as the insurance man
    Based on a story by Fred McMorrow, and adapted for *Alfred Hitchcock Presents* by Thomas Grant.
    Directed by Alan Crosland, Jr.
    (as a diver) *Good evening, ladies and gentlemen. I'm considering taking up skin diving. I've avoided it for a long time, because of the name. The term skin diving conjures up a very macabre picture to anyone but a mosquito. However, since I have become bored with waterskiing, fencing, windwalking and the like, this might be an excellent way to work off excess... energy. And the moment I have any I shall take it up. Uh, one thing that strikes me is the necessity for good feeling among your companions. As for tonights entertainment it is called "I Can Take Care Of Myself." And follows this cold plunge into the depths of television.*

    Story: A mobster called Little Dandy is out to get Bert Haber, after the piano player intervened to protect a female singer named Georgia. The gangster sends a man over to sell Bert some "life insurance," which he ignores, knowing just who sent the insurance representative. Then a cop appears on the scene, asking questions about the musician and the singer, who was recently found murdered. Bert says he will gladly testify against the thug if the police can provide him protection, which the cop agrees. Being escorted outside to the police car, Bert meets the officer's partner, the "insurance" man, who pulls a gun and remarks, "Little Dandy says hello."

    A young skindiver, uh not him, not him. A young skindiver was to come and explain this paraphernalia but he's busy making a motion picture. He's co-star with an octopus. Perhaps he will be here when you recover from the following. (commercial break) *Unfortunately the young man I mentioned won't be able to be here. In his movie with the octopus, it turned out to be a tour de force for the octopus. He stole the scene completely. It's quite sad really. The young man was headed for stardom, while the octopus is quite limited in the roles he can play. Next week I shall be back again with another story. Until then, good night.*

EPISODE #185 **"ONE GRAVE TOO MANY"** Broadcast on May 22, 1960
    One of the days of filming was April 7, 1960.
    Starring: Neile Adams as Mrs. Irene Helmer   Jeremy Slate as Joe Helmer
    Biff Elliott as Lieutenant Bates   Howard McNear as Mr. Pickett
    David Carlile as the patrolman   Tyler McVey as Sergeant Dugan
    Paul Bradley as Mr. Sonnyboy Capa, the pick-pocket

Teleplay written for *Alfred Hitchcock Presents* by Eli Jerome, based on the short story of the same name by Henry Slesar, originally published in the November 1958 issue of *Alfred Hitchcock's Mystery Magazine*. Subsequently collected in *Clean Crimes and Neat Murders* (Avon, 1960), *Murders Most Macabre* (Avon, 1986) and *Death on Television* (Southern Illinois University Press, 1989).

Directed by Arthur Hiller.

(horses and chariot) *Good evening. Did anyone see a golf ball go by? It couldn't have gone far. I just gave it a toss. I've been employing this means of getting around the golf course since the club voted to ban all motorized carts. It was a ban I heartily endorsed. By the way, since the carts were always tipping over when they ran over loiterers, this slowed up the game terribly. This system of travel also helps me comply with another rule, which was made because of the crowded condition of the course. We are asked to play in foursomes. But I believe you tuned in for a story. I shall step aside and allow you to play through.*

Story: Unemployed and desperate, Joe Helmer rushes to the aid of a stranger who falls on the sidewalk, and notices the man carrying a large sum of money in his wallet. Joe steals the wallet, but only later does he see a card inside reading: "I am not dead. I am subject to a form of cataleptic illness which may appear to cause death." His feelings of guilt get the better of him, and Joe tries to find the man, whose name is apparently one Marvin Horn. But the body is gone and only after going to the police, does Joe learn that the man already died - definitely. Joe feels obliged to confess to stealing the wallet and finding the card, in order to get the police to make sure that the stranger is really dead. The police take Joe to the morgue to show him the body, where they comment that the man was a skilled pick-pocket who probably didn't have any money of his own to his name, and he had simply died of a heart attack. Now the police want to question Joe, about the wallet he stole, that the dead man apparently had stolen from someone else.

I hear the shout of fore. Apparently someone is counting my horses again. I shall have to move on. Suppose you join me at the next tee. (commercial break) *I found this in the rough, we just passed through. I wonder who it belongs to?* (goes through golfbag and finds huge toothbrush and comb) *Until next week, good night.*

Trivia, etc. "I liked that [episode]," recalled Neile Adams. "I haven't seen it since the sixties, but I remember liking it and feeling very good about it, because it was probably a stretch for me. [laughs] It taught me a lot. I think it taught me how to relate more to the camera, because I'm a stage actress, you know, and also to relate more to my husband and not have to worry about the big physical movements, because I was always told there's a big difference between stage and film work. I was constantly aware of just bringing myself down. But in that show, I found a happy medium. I felt more lonely. Suddenly, I was a Broadway performer, not an actress, so, I felt a little insecure. Steve would prop me up and just tell me, 'You're wonderful, baby' [in "Man from The South"]. Then I would feel that I was terrific. [laughs] This time, [in "One Grave Too Many"] I was alone. Arthur Hiller was directing this. He was very good. He was a director I've known in New York. I felt, 'I better deliver here!' [laughs] I was alone. I didn't have anybody to lean on, and it came up well. The one thing I remember is that, looking back at all these things, when I see myself on television⟨I have donated a bunch of scrapbooks to the Motion Picture Academy. Karl Malden suggested, 'Why don't you donate all that stuff to the Academy?' They do have the Steve McQueen / Neile Adams archives. When the man came to pick up all that stuff, he said, 'Do you feel bad that this is going out of your hands?' I said, 'No. That was in another time, in another place. I don't even think of it. The only thing that really infuriates me is that I didn't know how great-looking I was." (Reprinted courtesy of *Filmfax* magazine and author Ira Sandler.)

EPISODE #186   **"PARTY LINE"**   Broadcast on May 29, 1960
        Starring: Judy Canova as Helen Parch   Royal Dano as Sheriff Atkins
        Arch Johnson as Heyward Miller   Ellen Corby as Emma
        Gertrude Flynn as Betty Nubbins   Charity Grace as Mrs. Gertrude Anderson
        Ted Knight as Mr. Maynard, the grocer
        Teleplay written for *Alfred Hitchcock Presents* by Eli Jerome, based on the short
story "The Deadly Telephone" by Henry Slesar, originally published in the January 1960
issue of *Alfred Hitchcock's Mystery Magazine.* Subsequently collected in *Clean Crimes and
Neat Murders* (Avon, 1960) as "The Deadly Telephone" and in *Death on Television*
(Southern Illinois University Press, 1989) as "Party Line."
        Directed by Hilton A. Green.
        (time machine) *Good evening, ladies and gentlemen. This is a time machine. By
standing on this platform and moving this lever, one can be transported into the future.*
(pulls lever and ends up in 1975) *It's positively amazing. Positively amazing. I'm going to
stay. Things are much better, much better.* (pulls out a piece of paper) *For failing to file
income tax returns for the years 1960 through 1975, you are hereby . . .* (goes back to 1960)
*I think I shall take the future, one minute at a time. The first one may be hard to take but
after that we present our play.*

Alternate narrative:
        (time machine) *Good evening, ladies and gentlemen. This is a time machine. By
standing on this platform and moving this lever, one can be transported into the future.*
(pulls lever and ends up in 1975) *It's positively amazing. Positively amazing. I'm going to
stay. Things are much better, much better.* (pulls out a piece of paper) *For failing to file
income tax returns for the years 1960 through 1975, you are hereby . . .* (goes back to 1960)
I think I shall take the future, one moment at a time. So in just one moment, tonight's story.

        Story: A few years ago, ignorant Helen Parch refused to get off a party line, not
believing that Heyward Miller was trying to call a doctor for his terminally ill wife. Miller
lost his wife that day, because Helen would not oblige his plea for help. A couple of years
later, Miller went to jail for a petty theft, and Helen never thought another thing about it –
until this afternoon, when a sheriff pays Helen a visit, informing her that Miller broke jail.
Even with a three-state alarm out for him, the sheriff warns, there is a remote possibility that
he wants vengeance from Helen. After the officer leaves, someone tries to break into her
house and Helen, convinced that Miller will try to kill her, grabs the phone for help. But
Helen falls victim to her own faults. when two gossipy women won't get off the line . . . and
Miller casts a shadow over Helen's body.

        *Well, as the Germans say: Jeder hat seinen gesmach. There is no accounting for
taste. Oddly enough, Mr. Miller was punished very severely for his crime. Apparently the
Sheriff shared the same party line and overheard the whole thing. I shall still be here if you
survive our next item. Once again my only comment is: Jeder hat seinen gesmach.*
(commercial break) *You know, even in the present year, there are some incredible sights to
be seen. Next week, I plan a return visit to your living room. If you aren't going to be home,
please leave the television set on, so I can come on in. Until then, good night.*

Alternate narrative:
        *Well, as the Germans say: Jeder hat seinen gesmach. There is no accounting for
taste. Oddly enough, Mr. Miller was punished very severely for his crime. Apparently the
Sheriff shared the same party line and overheard the whole thing. Next time, I plan a return
visit to your living room. If you aren't going to be home, please leave the television set on, so
I can come on in. Until then, good night.*

TIMES CHANGE GREAT TV DOESN'T

Trivia, etc. Assistant director Hilton A. Green took control of the camera for this, his only directorial effort on the Hitchcock series. "I worked for Revue Productions, who was making the series. It was Hitchcock's show and he personally asked me if I wanted to direct an episode and I said, 'Of course.' I didn't get to choose which story to do, I was just assigned to it and I did it. Judy Canova was the star and I think she was wonderful. That was the only episode of the series I directed. I helped Hitchcock all the time with his other features. Almost from the beginning, I worked with Hitchcock on most of those, all the way up till he died. Working for Hitch those twenty-five some years was absolutely sensational."

EPISODE #187   **"CELL 227"**   Broadcast on June 5, 1960
      Starring: Brian Keith as Professor Herbie Morrison
James K. Best as Hennessey   James Westerfield as Lieutenant Pops Lafferty
Frank Maxwell as Maury Berg, the lawyer   Liam Sullivan as Father McCann
Sal Ponti as De Baca, the condemned man
Harry Raybould as Callahan, the guard   Robert Carson as the warden
      Teleplay written for *Alfred Hitchcock Presents* by Bill S. Ballinger, based on the short story "Good-bye Sweet World" by Bryce Walton, originally published in the August 1958 issue of *Alfred Hitchcock's Mystery Magazine*.
      Directed by Paul Henreid.
      (sitting behind bars)   *Good evening, ladies and gentlemen and why did it take you so long to get here? I've been sitting here for ten minutes. I don't know why everything is so heavily guarded. Even if I could get through this screen, I couldn't escape without breaking your picture tube. All this is to illustrate to you that while the television viewers lot may be difficult, the performers is even worse. Only one half-hour visit a week and in between nothing but work. As final proof of our miserable state, let me show you the kind of film that passes for entertainment inside these grey walls.*

Alternate narrative:
      (sitting behind bars)   *Good evening, ladies and gentlemen and why did it take you so long to get here? I've been sitting here for ten minutes. I don't know why everything is so heavily guarded. Even if I could get through this screen, I couldn't escape without breaking your picture tube. All this is to illustrate to you that while the television viewers lot may be difficult, the performers is even worse. Only one half-hour visit a week and in between nothing but work. There of course, my associates aren't the best, singers, comedians, news-analysts and the like. But perhaps we shall have our play, before I reduce all of you to tears.*

Story: Having seen other men suffer the same wait, condemned Professor Herbert Morrison figures that the real death isn't the gas chamber, rather the mental breakdown and agonizing lack of dignity that is injected weeks before the final execution. Soon to be put to death by the state for a crime he claims he did not commit, Morrison isn't really upset over his fate, and he won't give the guards that pleasure. Increasingly aggravated over a guard named Pop, who sadistically tries to cheer up the men on death row, Morrison visions Pop as "the sadist with a sunshine smile," wishing one day to get his chance to hit the guard where it counts. Minutes before the execution, Morrison attacks Pop, and strangles the old man. The warden orders the execution postponed because of this incident, and offers some revealing news. A witness was found, offering to clear Morrison of his crime, only now the stay of execution doesn't offer the chance of freedom. Morrison will have to stand trial for the death of Pop – a situation the guards won't take as lightly as before.

I have a theory which would account for the immense popularity of revenge. Revenge is sweet without being fattening. (alarm) *And now I believe the warden wishes to make an announcement. Since there is no place else to go, I shall be here at his conclusion.* (commercial break) *I see the guard is signalling that our time is up. I hope you will visit me again next week. Until then, good night.*

Alternate narrative:
I have a theory which would account for the immense popularity of revenge. Revenge is sweet without being fattening. (alarm) *I see the guard is signalling that our time is up. I hope you will visit me again next time. Until then, good night.*

EPISODE #188 "THE SCHARTZ-METTERKLUME METHOD" Aired June 12, 1960
Starring: Hermione Gingold as Lady Charlotte   Elspeth March as Mrs. Wellington
Doris Lloyd as Nannie, the maid   Pat Hitchcock as Rose, the maid
Noel Drayton as Ben Huggins, the horse-keeper   Ida Moore as Miss Hope
Veronica Cartwright as Violet, the older Wellington daughter
Angela Cartwright as Irene, the younger Wellington daughter
Teleplay written for *Alfred Hitchcock Presents* by Marian Cockrell, based on the short story of the same name by Hector Hugh Munro (a.k.a. Saki), originally collected in his book, *Beasts and Superbeasts* (John Lane, 1914).
Directed by Richard Dunlap.
(black board, dunce cap, apple) *Good evening fellow students. I'm glad to see everyone here. Our dear professor is very strict about attendance. Anyone who is absent must bring a note signed by their television repairman, and anyone who is tardy and misses the first part of the program must stay after school and watch the late, late show. Perhaps you are wondering why I have this apple. It is for the teacher, naturally.* (throws apple and it explodes) *And now we are about to take up one of his favorite subjects. Watch closely, he may ask questions later.*

Story: Lady Charlotte jumps off the train to stop a man abusing his horse, and finds herself stranded at the depot when her train leaves without her. Being mistaken as the new governess, Charlotte is escorted to the Wellington estate where she is introduced to the children. Being a practical woman, she accepts the position and uses what she calls the Schartz-Metterklume method for teaching history, allowing them to run wild with frogs and tadpoles, and re-enact scenes of Roman history (the rape of the Seabine Women). Mr. and Mrs. Wellington disapprove of her methods and a couple days later, the parents finally lose their patience. The governess is fired. Back at the train station, Lady Charlotte meets the real Miss Hope, and tells her to hire a conveyance of some sort, and drive out to the house since the Wellingtons are not expecting her today.

I thought that was an excellent lesson of how to put idle time to good use. And now I have a lesson to write on the board. The rest of you are to be part of an experiment in sleep teaching. This is the theory, that if a message is repeated during one's sleep it becomes a part of one's subconscious. This particular lesson is unusually well fitted for this experiment, for it not only repeats its message, but if you aren't already asleep, it takes care of that too. (commercial break – Hitchcock returns writing "I shall not criticize the commercial again.") *Our beloved professor took umbrage at my remarks concerning his audio/visual aids. But I don't believe I need to finish this. You see, our professor was teaching us by the Schartz-Metterklume method. He was playing the part of Louis 16th on his way to the guillotine, and he failed to realize that the class was filled with very dedicated Schartz-Metterklume actors. He will not be back next week, but I shall. Until then, good night.*

Trivia, etc. The mansion in this episode is also the same used in *Psycho*, only hastily disguised! This was also the acting debut of Veronica and Angela Cartwright. Veronica, the older of the two sisters, would later play Cathy Brenner in Hitchcock's *The Birds* (1963), as well as supporting roles in *Invasion of the Body Snatchers* (1978), *Alien* (1979) and *The Witches of Eastwick* (1987). Angela played young Brigitta von Trapp in *The Sound of Music* (1965) and is probably best remembered as Penny Robinson on television's *Lost in Space*.

EPISODE #189 **"LETTER OF CREDIT"** Broadcast on June 19, 1960
      Starring: Bob Sweeney as William Spengler

Robert Bray as Henry Taylor-Lowden	Ronald Nicholas as Arnold Mathias
Theodore Newton as Sam Kern	Jacqueline Holt as Miss Foster
Joseph Hamilton as the stationmaster	Cyril Delevanti as Josiah Wingate

      Teleplay written for *Alfred Hitchcock Presents* by Helen Nielsen, based on her short story, "Henry Lowden, Alias Henry Taylor," originally published in the July 1960 issue of *Alfred Hitchcock's Mystery Magazine*.
      Directed by Paul Henreid.
      (election coverage) *Good evening, ladies and gentlemen. Thank you for that heartfelt and technically augmented cheer.* (close-up) *Will the delegates please clear the aisles? Return to your seats please. I have an announcement. Will the delegate from Yugoslavia please report here at once? The credentials committee suspects you may have made a mistake. And now, ladies and gentlemen, I wish to place in nomination, a friend of, a steadfast champion for, and a man who at the mention of his name you will be allowed to stage a spontaneous one-minute demonstration . . . our sponsor.*

Alternate narrative:
      (election coverage) *Good evening, ladies and gentlemen. Thank you for that heartfelt and technically augmented cheer. And now, ladies and gentlemen, I wish to place in nomination, a friend of, a steadfast champion for, and a man who I'm certain you have guessed his identity. If not, I shall give you a hint. He is the producer of the following television play.*

      Story: Henry Taylor is writing a book on unsolved crimes. His main interest is a particular theft that occurred three years ago at the Kirkland Mercantile Bank, in which an employee made off with an un-recovered $200,000 from the bank's vault. The employee, Arnold Mathias, claimed he was innocent. The court thought otherwise, and found him guilty of theft. After spending three years in jail, Mathias was recently shot to death while trying to escape. Henry Taylor believes the boy was innocent and meets personally with the bank president, William Spengler, to get some inside facts that may have been overlooked by the police. As Henry probes into the case it becomes more and more obvious that Spengler is the real guilty party, and realizing that Henry knows the truth, offers him part of the money to keep quiet. Henry won't accept any hush money because he really isn't a writer. His real name is Henry Taylor-Lowden, the same police guard who shot the innocent employee.

(in close-up) *Obviously the prison guard was eager for a promotion, and now we have a gentleman who is eager to promote the next speech. I shall return at his conclusion.* (commercial break, ribbons and banners lying everywhere) *I must say he did the impossible. The convention wasn't to adjourn for another hour. But our sponsor's message emptied the hall in sixty seconds. Next week, we shall reassemble in this hall at the same time. Until then, good night.*

Alternate narrative:

(ribbons and banners lying everywhere) *I shall never again accept a political nomination without knowing the identity of the office involved. I like being a collector, but I rather hoped it would be taxes, not rubbish. Perhaps I can resign next time, when we reassemble at this same hall. Until then, good night.*

Trivia, etc. The photo on this page comes from the episode "Letter of Credit."
Here, Hitchcock is seen behind the pedestal cheering on the sponsor.
State signs wave up and down in front of Hitchcock.
On the next page, you'll see a behind-the-scenes view of how this is done.

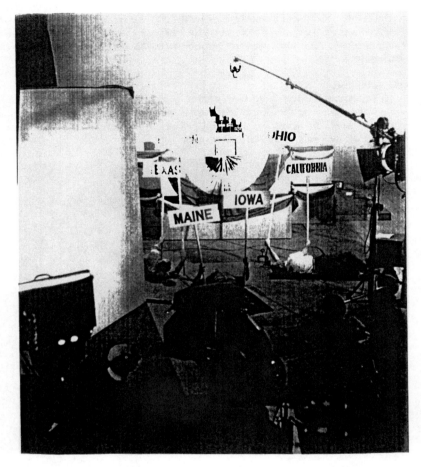

This candid shot shows the lights and cameras in position.
The microphone is high above Hitchcock, out of the camera's view.
Production crew lay on the floor lifting the State signs up and down.
A sound recording of a crowd will be dubbed in later.

EPISODE #190   **"ESCAPE TO SONOITA"**   Broadcast on June 26, 1960
Starring: Burt Reynolds as Bill Davis
Murray Hamilton as Marsh   Venetia Stevenson as Stephanie
James Bell as Andy Davis   Dean Stanton as Lemon
Robert Karnes as Ted, the first police officer
George Dockstader as the second police officer
Teleplay written for *Alfred Hitchcock Presents* by James A. Howard and Bill S. Ballinger, based on the short story of the same name by James A. Howard.
Directed by Stuart Rosenberg.
(weather map and girl) *Good evening. Television has done much to raise the level of weather prognostication. The addition of the weather girl has not improved the predictions, but she does make the mistake more enjoyable.* (close-up) *Those of you in the North East sector,* (girl draws X) *can expect the weather to continue. I must warn those of you in the West that there is a cloud on your horizon.* (Hitchcock draws cloud), *So if this is a*

raincloud, you can expect rain . . . perhaps. But enough of being evasive. Now for a prediction that is positive and accurate. The weather for the next minute will be . . . dismal.

Story: Andy Davis and his son Bill take a rest on the side of a desert road when they suddenly notice a car coming towards them at an uncontrollable rate, and get stuck in the sand. The drivers, however, have a bound and gagged girl in the back, causing Andy and Bill to realize that she is actually the kidnap victim they heard about on the radio. But the kidnappers pull their guns on Andy and Bill, and steal their tank truck, figuring the deserters will die from the heat and exposure on the secluded desert road. Using initiative, the team makes it back to town, and assists state troopers in hunting down the kidnappers. They find one of the men first, shot to death with a bullet to his head. Later the tank truck is found, and with it the other kidnapper, dead from exposure and lack of water - not having realized that they killed themselves over nothing. The truck they stole was hauling 3,000 gallons of fresh drinking water!

The weather in the Sonoita area continues fair. Very fair. Now in the central portion, there is a low pressure area. (draws circle) *Now from a low pressure area to high pressure salesmanship. After which we shall continue our weather show.* (commercial break) (girl draws X) *And cloud formations in the east central section.* (Hitchcock draws cloud and a line, winning game) *Good night until next week.*

Alternate narrative:
The weather in the Sonoita area continues fair. Very fair. Now in the central portion, there is a low pressure area. (draws circle) *Which leads me to predict high velocity winds in the southeast.* (girl draws X) *And cloud formations in the east central section.* (Hitchcock draws cloud and a line, winning game) *Good night until next time.*

SUMMER RERUNS
Summer reruns consisted entirely of episodes from season five.

July 3, 1960 "The Day of the Bullet"
July 10, 1960 "Dry Run"
July 17, 1960 "Arthur"
July 24, 1960 "Anniversary Gift"
July 31, 1960 "Madame Mystery"
August 7, 1960 "Dead Weight"
August 14, 1960
   "Not the Running Type"

August 21, 1960
   "The Little Man Who Was There"
August 28, 1960 "Across the Threshold"
September 4, 1960
   "Forty Detectives Later"
September 11, 1960
   "One Grave Too Many"
September 18, 1960 "Insomnia"

EPISODE #191 **"HOOKED"** Broadcast on September 25, 1960
     Starring: Robert Horton as Ray Marchand   Anne Francis as Nila Foster
     Vivienne Segal as Gladys Marchand   John Holland as Floyd Foster
     Teleplay written for *Alfred Hitchcock Presents* by Thomas Grant, based on the short story of the same name by Robert Turner, originally published in the February 1958 issue of *Manhunt*. Subsequently anthologized in *Bad Girls*, ed. Leo Margulies (Fawcett Crest, 1958).
     Directed by Norman Lloyd.
     (trashbin, broom) *Good evening, ladies and gentlemen. This tableau is designed to make it clear that when the television industry decides to clean house, it means just that. I must say the job is more difficult than I imagined, what with all those . . . westerns. I am sure that, like me, you feel there is too much violence on television. Naturally, my first step has been to request our sponsor omit his commercials. Thus far he is adamant and I can only suggest that if there are any sensitive young children in the room, that you make sure they turn their heads during the next minute.*

Story: Ray Marchand finds himself in hot water when his wealthy, but older wife Gladys, learns that he's been flirting with a young girl named Nila Foster. Ray and Nila have actually been having an affair but Nila decides that it's time to call it quits, since Ray is legally bound to his wife. Knowing she wouldn't divorce him if he asks, Ray knows the only way he can win the girl (and his wife's money) is to bump the old woman off. Spending a week up at the lake, Ray decides to go along with Gladys on one of her fishing trips, and knowing that she can't swim, Ray plans to push her overboard. But when the boat returns, Gladys arrives on shore alive and well. Thanks to Nila and her father, Ray has been disposed. Gladys and Nila's father agree that six months mourning should be long enough before they get married.

The moral of this story is that fishing is poor in the state penitentiary. A fact which Gladys, Floyd and Nila subsequently learned. And now for another moral, after which you shall find me still on the job. (commercial break) *If you think watching a commercial is tiring, you should try cleaning up afterwards.* (waves to the camera to pan left)

Trivia, etc. "Good-bye Sunday! Hello Tuesday!" read the advertisements, printed in newspapers and trade magazines. Alfred Hitchcock was moving to a new network. Instead of the old Sunday night time-slot over CBS, *Alfred Hitchcock Presents* was now seen on Tuesday evenings over NBC. This episode, "Hooked," was still broadcast in the old CBS time-slot but was not a summer rerun. It was actually a new episode, being shown on the old time slot, possibly for the purpose of conveniently making the announcement to viewers, that the Hitchcock program would be seen two days later on NBC. The next broadcast, "Mrs. Bixby and the Colonel's Coat," was the premiere episode of the sixth season (and labeled as the "premiere" among advertisements).

SEASON SIX - (39 episodes)

SELECTED PRODUCTION CREDITS:
Art Directors: John J. Lloyd, John Meehan and Martin Obzina
Assistant Directors: George Bisk, John Bowman, Charles S. Gould, James H. Brown,
Jack Doran, Frank Fox, James Hogan, Henry Kline, Ronnie Rondell,
William Sheldon and Wallace Worsley
Associate Producer: Norman Lloyd
Costume Supervisor: Vincent Dee
Directors of Photography: Neal Beckner, John L. Russell, a.s.c. and John F. Warren, a.s.c.
Editorial Supervisor: David J. O'Connell
Film Editor: Edward W. Williams, a.c.e.
Hair Stylist: Florence Bush
Makeup Artists: Jack Barron, Bob Dawn and Leo Lotito, Jr.
Music Supervisors: Frederick Herbert and Joseph E. Romero
Producer: Joan Harrison
Set Decorators: Rudy Butler, Julia Heron, John McCarthy, George Milo,
James S. Redd and James M. Walters
Sound: James Brock, Lyle Cain, Earl Crain, Sr., Lambert Day, Joe Lapis,
William Lynch, John W. Rixey, William Russell, Harry Smith,
Ed Somers, J.S. Westmoreland, L.D. Wiler and Frank H. Wilkinson
Filmed at Revue Studios in Hollywood, California, in association with MCA-TV,
executive distributor for Shamley Productions, Inc.
Broadcast Tuesday over NBC-TV, 8:30 – 9 p.m., EST.
Alternating sponsors are Ford Motors and Revlon.

EPISODE #192 **"MRS. BIXBY AND THE COLONEL'S COAT"** September 27, 1960
Rehearsed and filmed on August 17 – 19, 1960.
Starring: Audrey Meadows as Mrs. Bixby
Les Tremayne as Dr. Fred Bixby   Stephen Chase as the Colonel
Sally Hughes as Miss Pultney, the nurse   Howard Caine as the pawnbroker
Maidie Norman as Eloise, the Colonel's maid   Bernie Hamilton as the butler
Harry Cheshire as Mr. Gorman, a patient
Ted Jordan as Mr. Evans, a patient   Lillian Culver as a patient
Teleplay written for *Alfred Hitchcock Presents* by Halsted Welles, based on the
short story of the same name by Roald Dahl, originally published in an issue of *Nugget*.
Subsequently collected in *Kiss Kiss* (Michael Joseph, 1960; Knopf, 1960) and later in *Tales
of the Unexpected* (Michael Joseph, 1979; Vintage, 1980).
Directed by Alfred Hitchcock.
*Good evening, ladies and gentlemen and welcome to a new season of Alfred
Hitchcock Presents. As has been our custom, we shall present homey little stories of an
unusual nature. We shall continue to give the little man, or woman, his due. When crime is
occasionally dealt with, it will be crime as practiced by ordinary people, like the fellow next
door. I think that by spring a large number of you will be thinking of moving. There is one
aspect of this program which has changed. If you have tuned in to hear me make snide
remarks about an innocent sponsor, you are doomed to disappointment. I am proud to say, I
have resolved my antagonisms and have become completely sponsor-oriented. I have met
our new sponsor and find him* (a halo appears above his head) *to be agreeable, charming,
witty, honest, sincere, intelligent, dependable, trustworthy, loyal, brave, clean and reverent.
Tonight's show is entitled "Mrs. Bixby And The Colonel's Coat." But first, unfortunately,
we have one of those . . .* (halo disappears), *but first fortunately, we have one of those
intelligent, amusing, dignified, provocative, brilliantly conceived,* (gives an expression of
disgust) *but painfully short commercials.*

Story: Mrs. Bixby takes one of her monthly, weekend train trips up north to spend
time with her mother. What Mr. Bixby doesn't know is that her mother is really the Colonel,
a man she has been having an affair with for many years. At the end of this weekend,
however, the wealthy Colonel admits that he has to break off their relationship and as a
parting gift, leaves Mrs. Bixby with an expensive wild labrador mink coat. During her train
ride back home, Mrs. Bixby realizes that she can't take the coat home, without a logical
explanation to her husband. Stopping at a pawnshop down the street from her husband's
office, she pawns the coat, making sure that there is no description on the ticket. That
evening Mrs. Bixby tells her husband how she found a ticket in the cab. Mr. Bixby says it's a
pawn ticket and he explains how tomorrow morning, he'll go and pick up the object, with the
intention of handing her the surprise. Arriving at his office the next afternoon. she expects to
be presented with the coat, only to be handed an inexpensive small mink stole instead. As
Mrs. Bixby sits in her husband's office pondering what went wrong, she notices that her
husband's nurse is leaving for lunch, wearing the new mink coat!

*My honey-moon with the sponsor lasted just as long as the first commercial. As
for my present mood, will it out-last the final commercial? You shall see in a moment.*
(commercial break) *At least my sponsor doesn't seem to be taking any action as the result of
my attitude.* (noose appears above Hitchcock's head) *Until next week, good night.*

Trivia, etc. This, the premiere episode of the sixth season, and the third Roald
Dahl story to be directed by Hitchcock, fit the dark-humor mold of the series perfectly – even
with the lack of a dead body. The casting was wonderful, from Stephen Chase, Les
Tremayne and Audrey Meadows (playing a non-Alice-like role from the *Honeymooners*).
"One of the greatest thrills in my career was working with Alfred Hitchcock," Meadows
recalled. "He had me come to California to do a dramatic role on his television show, *Alfred*

Hitchcock Presents. The episode was called 'Mrs. Bixby and the Colonel's Coat,' which later won an award. Each day when I went to the studio for wardrobe fittings, he either invited me for lunch or for tea. And each time I thought, 'Now he will discuss the role with me.' I was wrong. We talked of nothing but books. He gave very little direction, and when he did, he would walk the actor away from the crew so no one could hear what he was saying."

"It's really the purest form of the original short story," said Hitchcock, "as developed by De Maupassant and O. Henry, and of which 'The Gift of the Magi,' read by every schoolchild, is still the classic example. The real problem on this mink story was the casting. We had to have an actor who in the beginning was sufficiently conservative, but who in the end you could believe might have been playing around. Les Tremayne played the part admirably."

"I had a breakfast scene, during which I had to take a bite of toast and jam," Audrey Meadows continued. "On a second take, the prop man had to replace the toast. I was not used to getting up at five in the morning, and by the time we shot the scene, I was very hungry. Mr. Hitchcock noticed that I was nervously consuming all the toast and jam in between takes. He dryly said to me, 'Miss Meadows, we can add eggs and bacon to the scene if you're still hungry.' I swallowed and smiled. No one did verbal fencing with Alfred Hitchcock. No one."

Variety reviewed this episode: "Un-hitched at last from its snug Sunday time-spot and CBS, *Alfred Hitchcock Presents*, to no one's surprise, hasn't changed a whit in its transfer to Tuesday and NBC. Just as it was a popular favorite on the Sabbath, so it figures to hold its own in the new surroundings. To get matters off to a proper start on the occasion of the fifth anniversary, the boss man himself directed this particular half-hour tidbit, a mild Hitchcock-and-bull session titled 'Mrs. Bixby and the Colonel's Coat'."

Variety continued . . . "It was one of the less diabolical, less grizzly entries of this

Alfred Hitchcock and Audrey Meadows discuss a scene.

series. Perhaps it's a direct result of the lighter tone, but it came off more amusingly and less predictably than this show's average outing. . . Hitchcock shelved his familiar bizarre reining touches for this one in favor of a more appropriate sane and sensible approach."

Lillian Culver, who plays a small role in this episode, was a distant cousin (third cousin twice removed) of Hollywood actor Brad Pitt. Her husband, Harry Hazel Culver, was the founder of Culver City, California.

EPISODE #193   **"THE DOUBTFUL DOCTOR"**   Broadcast on October 4, 1960
     Starring: Dick York as Ralph Jones   Gena Rowlands as Lucille Jones
     John Zaremba as Talbert Collins   Michael Burns as Sidney, the boy
     Joseph Julian as Ted Parkinson   Ralph Smiley as Jimmy, the waiter
     Teleplay written for *Alfred Hitchcock Presents* by Jerry Sohl, based on a story by Louis Paul.
     Directed by Arthur Hiller.
     (picture of Hitchcock is rotated)   *Good evening, ladies and gentlemen and welcome to Alfred Hitchcock Presents. Before we show you tonight's story we shall have a commercial. I hope the manner, in which my picture jumps about the screen doesn't confuse you. I had a small disagreement with our cameraman. Fortunately, being the producer, I have the last word. In this case, that word is help!!!!* (while the picture is rotating)

Story: Ralph Jones is an overworked executive who longs for his simpler bachelor days when he wasn't afraid of finances, or the pressure of his responsibilities. He privately confesses to his psychiatrist the desire for the days gone by, and how late one afternoon he fell into a daydream, reproducing his past of two-and-a-half years ago. Only some things are not the same, it's really the world he never lived through. His girlfriend doesn't recognize him, his landlord demands the rent. and Ralph's friends don't recognize him. After giving away all his money to a boy for some baseball cards, Ralph realizes that the real world is much better than what it could have been, and promptly commits suicide by jumping in a river, bringing him back to his real life. The psychiatrist tells him not to worry about the matter, as it was just an anxiety fantasy. Ralph doubts this, as earlier that day he found water-logged baseball cards in his pocket.

     (Hitchcock is upside-down) *I thought that cameraman would never stop spinning me about. I missed the whole story. Now, you're upside down. Well here is something that should put you on your feet, after which I shall drop in on you again.* (commercial break) *That is quite enough for tonight. First the blood rushed to my head, and now my head seems to be rushing someplace. Oh. . . next week we shall return with more commercials, a new story and a new cameraman. Until then, good night.*

EPISODE #194   **"VERY MORAL THEFT"**   Broadcast on October 11, 1960
     Starring: Betty Field as Helen Thompson   Walter Matthau as Harry Wade
     Karl Swenson as John Thompson   Sal Ponti as Carl
     David Fresco as Mr. Parker   Rusty Lane as Mr. Ivers
     Sam Gilman as Charlie, the bartender   William Newell as Mr. Fescue
     Robert Sampson as Jimmy   Charles Carlson as George, the teller
     Claude Stroud as Orville   Keith Britton as Ben, the guard
     Teleplay written for *Alfred Hitchcock Presents* by Allan Gordon, based on the short story of the same name by Jack Dillon, originally published in the May 1960 issue of *Alfred Hitchcock's Mystery Magazine.*
     Directed by Norman Lloyd.
     (bow and arrow)   *Greetings my merry men. Welcome to the forest's prime evil. Pri'thee tarry whilst we tell you a story called, a "Very Moral Theft," a title which would befit any tale of bold robin. However, our story, I am happy to say, takes place in our own*

age. (arrow with a note hits the tree) *As the saying goes, there will always be a Sheriff of Nottingham. Listen to his proclamation.* (reads note)

Story: Lumberyard owner Harry Wade may lose his business because a customer owes him a large sum of money, and cannot pay off his debt. Harry's solution comes in the form of realtor Helen Thompson (his girlfriend), who loans him the $8,000 he needs to keep the business going, on the stipulation that she is repaid within two days – no more. When Harry cannot pay on time, she admits to have embezzled the money from work, thus the reason she expressed two days. Shocked and surprised to hear the news, Harry rushes out to even the deal. The next afternoon, Harry shows up with the money on time, claiming that he got it from some customers that needed a large supply of cheap lumber. He knows he'll be able to put them off long afterwards, but her job is more important. After not seeing Harry for a few days, Helen learns to her horror that he had actually gotten the money from some loan sharks, who killed him when he couldn't pay them back on time.

So much for our merry tale. Now a stranger approacheth to tell us what to do with those extra farthings. (commercial break, Hitchcock closes a large book) *I have finally finished Robin Hood's merry adventures, the revised edition. The Sheriff gets him in the last chapter. Income tax evasion. Until next week, good night.*

Trivia, etc. Karl Swenson played a drunk in *The Birds* (1963) and William Newell played a drunk in "I Saw The Whole Thing" from *The Alfred Hitchcock Hour* (episode #4), both directed by Hitchcock.

EPISODE #195   **"THE CONTEST FOR AARON GOLD"**   Broadcast October 18, 1960
Starring: Barry Gordon as Aaron Gold
Sydney Pollack as Bernie Samuelson   Frank Maxwell as Lionel Stern
William Thourlby as Lefty James, the diver   John Craven as Herbert Gold
Buddy Lewis as Angelo, the foreman
Michael Adam Lloyd, Robin Warga and Phil Phillips are the boys.
Teleplay written for *Alfred Hitchcock Presents* by William Fay, based on the short story "Contest for Aaron Gold" by Philip Roth. Subsequently reprinted in *Best American Short Stories of 1956* (Houghton, 1956).
Directed by Norman Lloyd.
(standing by a large kiln) *Good evening, ladies and gentlemen. I've just been terribly hurt. My ceramics instructor just insulted my pot, the one I made in his class. He says it isn't fit to be put in the kiln. And he will probably be throwing it out in a moment. He's in there now cleaning out the kiln. Tonight's play is "The Contest For Aaron Gold," and it begins after the usual one minute pause for sponsor identification. Well, it'll mean lighting it myself and I've never done that. Don't blame me, what can you expect from a generation that was raised on Hansel and Gretel?*

Story: Welcome to Camp Lakeside, a summer camp for the children of top-notch clientele. Bernie Samuelson, a ceramics teacher, watches as the children make snakes, pancakes and ashtrays, but one promising young boy named Aaron Gold, makes a sculpture that is a real piece of art. A clay warrior knight with a missing arm. Aaron seems to fail at everything, from swimming to basketball, but he has artistic talent, and Bernie takes the child under his wing. Bernie even tries to coax the boy to complete the figure in time for Parent's Day. When the camp director sees the figure, he insists that Bernie himself complete the model and add a right arm, so it won't make the director look bad when the parents arrive. Bernie is reluctantly pressured into completing the figure, and when Aaron finds out, the boy is furious. When Parent's Day arrives, Bernie and the camp instructor understands why . . .
. . . Aaron's father has no right arm.

320

Seeing that story almost makes me want to let my instructor out. However, he is not done yet. Perhaps he will be in another minute. We shall see. (commercial break) *I wonder if the sponsor could be persuaded to clean out the kiln sometime. My vase turned out beautifully don't you think? I'm gonna use it to hold these ashes I found on the floor in there. As my dear instructor used to say: Art is long, life is brief. So until next week at this time, good night.*

Trivia, etc. "[There was an episode] I directed called 'The Contest for Aaron Gold,' based on a Philip Roth story," recalled director Norman Lloyd. "It was about a little boy in summer camp, and the kid not putting an arm on a piece of sculpture he was doing. Hitch had the idea that the boy's father walks in at the end and he's missing an arm, and [now the audience understands why] the kid couldn't do this little piece of sculpture and put both arms on, because his father didn't have an arm. When Hitch had an idea like that, he'd call us, but otherwise, we did the whole shebang."

Al Tennyson, spokesman for Ford Motors, the sponsor for *Alfred Hitchcock Presents*, recalled: "I seldom saw Hitchcock get involved with shows that weren't his, but one time, he did. It was a show called 'The Contest for Aaron Gold.' As the sponsor's watchdog, I was usually on hand during shooting as well as screening the rough cut. I mentioned to him how much I liked the episode, but it seemed to play a bit disappointingly. This was none of my business, of course, but he asked me why anyway, and I told him. In the show, this athletic director is constantly trying to draw the lonely little boy away from his art class in order to engage him in swimming activities; to do so, he continually blows this whistle. That seemed to me a metaphor for what the boy was experiencing as well as a symbol for the athletic instructor's character, but the whistle was not used very much on the soundtrack. I suggested adding more whistle, sort of as a recurring motif. Hitchcock agreed and asked for more whistle. That was the only time I saw him interfere."

Sydney Pollack, who played the role of Bernie Samuelson in this episode, would soon establish himself as one of Hollywood's most prestigious and talented directors. "I had done an acting job on a Hitchcock shortly before I began directing a couple of episodes of *The Alfred Hitchcock Hour*," recalled Pollack. " 'The Contest for Aaron Gold' was I believe a Philip Roth story and I played Uncle Bernie! [laughs] Hitchcock came on the set a couple of times for that one and he later directed one with my wife, Claire Griswold ["I Saw The Whole Thing"], and then signed her to a seven-year contract. She was going to be the replacement for Grace Kelly and then she got pregnant, but she lasted out about a year into that project. She never did any big-screen films for him. But Hitchcock spent a lot of money for a test reel where she did *Anastasia* and pieces of *Rear Window* and things."

"The extraordinary thing was how well Hitch prepared everything," recalled producer Gordon Hessler. "When he directed an episode, he would finish up much more quickly than any of the young hotshot directors; he "cut in the camera" as he was shooting, so there was no waste of film. He would only put on film what was going to be in the finished episode. He was able to use very little film and he used little time because he knew exactly what he wanted - it was all pictured and storyboarded in his mind very, very carefully beforehand."

EPISODE #196 **"THE FIVE-FORTY-EIGHT"** Broadcast on October 25, 1960
Starring: Phyllis Thaxter as Iris Dent   Zachary Scott as James Blake
Irene Windust as Mrs. Compton   Raymond Bailey as Mr. Watkins
Penny Edwards as the young woman   Charles Davis as the middle-aged man
Phil Gordon as the man   Joseph Hamilton as the older man
Teleplay written for *Alfred Hitchcock Presents* by Charlotte Armstrong, based on the short story of the same name by John Cheever, originally published in the April 10, 1954 issue of *The New Yorker*.
Directed by John Brahm.

(booth, train) *Good evening fellow railroaders. I became bored with model railroading. I like . . .* (one train and one small cart approaches from opposite directions) *Hmm, no point in using two tracks when one will do.* (sound of train crash) *Never even stopped that one. And now for something else that can't be stopped. That is inevitable, unrelenting, unseisin.*

Story: Executive James Blake leaves his office and heads for the subway, only to run into Iris Dent, his former secretary. He attempts to give her the slip, but once on the subway train, she sits next to him and pulls out a small gun. Iris recalls her recent past when she used to work for Blake, before she had that nervous breakdown, and how he took advantage of her by making her work long hours, even having an affair with her. Fearing the wrath of his wife when suspicions grew, Blake had an associate terminate her job, and she understood the real reason why. Now that she has him cornered, she orders him off the train at gunpoint, and makes him kneel in the dirt. Blake breaks down and begs for forgiveness, ashamed for what he did. Expecting to be killed, he instead hears Iris laugh and walk away - all she wanted was his humiliation.

Apparently there are more hazards to commuting than I knew. I'm afraid you seem to be approaching one of those dismal tunnels again. Just sit quietly and beware the strange person sitting next to you. I shall be here when the smoke clears. (commercial break) *We have arrived at our destination. We made the trip in just thirty minutes. Next week we shall make another sojourn on the great railroad of life. Join us then. Good night.*

Trivia, etc. The John Cheever story "The Five-Forty-Eight," which this episode was based on, won critical acclaim upon its initial release in *The New Yorker*. This same story was the winner of the O. Henry Award of 1955, and later won the Ben Franklin Award. Actor Phil Gordon is best known for his portrayal of Jasper Jazzbo Depew on television's *The Beverly Hillbillies*, and was actually a dialogue coach for *Green Acres*.

EPISODE #197 **"PEN PAL"** Broadcast on November 1, 1960
Starring: Katherine Squire as Margaret Lowen   Clu Gulager as Rod Collins
Stanley Adams as Lieutenant Berger   Ray Montgomery as the intern
Teleplay written for *Alfred Hitchcock Presents* by Hilary Murray, based on the short story by O.H. Leslie and Jay Folb, (both pen names for Henry Slesar), originally published in the December 1957 issue of *Alfred Hitchcock's Mystery Magazine*. Subsequently collected in *Clean Crimes and Neat Murders* (Avon, 1960).
Directed by John Brahm.
(holding a baseball) *Good evening ladies and gentlemen. A number of persons have written asking me to explain the game of baseball. Normally I wouldn't do this, but some of those who wrote were professional ball players, and I sensed a tone of urgency in their appeal. Baseball gets its name from the type of field on which it is played. A baseball field. There are twenty-seven players on each team. However, no more than thirteen are allowed on the field at one time. Nine from one team, and from one to four from the other. To make it a fair match, the team with the smaller number of players, is allowed to carry clubs. The larger team has no weapons at all, except this pellet, but it is hard enough to knock a man unconscious. Naturally, both teams occasionally use their fists, but this is usually unnecessary. You see, all players have ingeniously attached sharply pointed metal cleats to their shoes. With these, the more experienced players can with grace and skill, badly lacerate an opponent. Yet make it look quite accidental. As you can see, the game is an excellent means for building character, and teaching young men good sportsmanship, fair play, and first aid. So much for the finer points of the sport. I see our friend the umpire, is signaling for time out. The game will commence in just one minute.*

322

Story: Lieutenant Berger pays Margaret Lowen an unexpected visit, asking the old woman questions about her young niece, Margie. It seems Margie has been corresponding with a young man named Rod Collins, who until this morning, was serving a life sentence in the State Penitentiary. Thankfully, Margie is away for the weekend with friends, but the Lieutenant says Collins might be paying a visit to her house. Margaret agrees to contact the lieutenant if Collins shows up, which he does later in the evening, breaking into her house through the window. Serving the young man food, Margaret starts a conversation and he admits that he has fallen in love with her niece, whom he wants to see. Pretending to call Margie, Margaret really phones the lieutenant, and Collins catches on to her trick. When he makes a move toward the old woman, she knocks the boy unconscious with a candlestick. The police come and pick up Collins, and after the authorities leave, Margaret begins writing another pen pal letter to Collins and admits the truth: it was she and not her niece who wrote the letters.

And so the curtain falls on our play, "Pen Pal." Which reminds me, I must write this note to a pal in the bullpen. (Hitchcock autographs baseball and throws it) *It's time for our seventh inning stretch, after which, I shall steal home.* (commercial break) *I have an announcement to make, which you will all be overjoyed to hear. There will be no more commercials, positively no more commercials during the balance of this program. So until next week at this time, good night.* (Hitchcock takes a bite out of the baseball.)

Trivia, etc. Talmage Powell, whose stories were adapted for the Hitchcock program, recalled one of the day's filming for this episode: "One afternoon we [Norman Lloyd and I] went over to a sound stage where a Henry Slesar segment was being shot. What a natural writer for that series. I think it was 'Pen Pal.' Sotto voce Norman remarked on camera movements and actor details. Only one camera was used. It never stopped. If an actor flubbed a line, the script girl would call a line number, and the on-stage players would drop back to that point and continue on. At the close-up of the scene, the director might call for cover shots, close-ups, that kind of thing. The whole caboodle was later cut and pasted to provide a master film from which copies were made. Norman and I got along quite well from the very start."

The niece in question, Margie, is only a character described and talked about in this episode, but not seen except for a photo, handed to Margaret by the lieutenant. The photo of Margie is actually a glamour photo of little-known actress Gloria Ellis.

On November 8, 1960, *Alfred Hitchcock Presents* was pre-empted, as was most CBS programing that evening, due to Presidential Election Returns.

EPISODE #198 **"OUTLAW IN TOWN"** Broadcast on November 15, 1960
Starring: Ricardo Montalban as Pepe Lorca Constance Ford as Shasta Cooney
Arch Johnson as Bart McCormack Bernard Kates as Billy Feeney
Addison Richards as Trigger Owens Roscoe Ates as Zachary, the old man
Ray Weaver as the judge Brad Weston as Pat Munk
Clegg Hoyt as the man who claims community property during the mob
and Patsy Kelly as Minnie Redwing
Original teleplay written for *Alfred Hitchcock Presents* by Michael Fessier, from an original story idea by Fessier.
Directed by Herschel Daugherty.
(on a wanted poster) *Good evening, ladies and gentlemen. This is one instance when two heads are not better than one. However I don't believe people realize what a happy lot we criminals have. What could be better than to be wanted? It gives one the inner security of knowing he has a place in society, that he is popular and sought after. No wonder criminals vie with each other to be among the top ten. Tonight's story is called "Outlaw In Town" and most of it takes place in The Last Chance Saloon. It should follow immediately, but I have promised my sponsor first chance.*

Story: The notorious Tony Lorca enters the Last Chance Saloon and one of the locals at the bar recognizes Lorca from a wanted poster, hanging in the post office. Lorca has a $5,000 bounty hanging on his head, and when the Billy produces the poster, everyone wants in on the reward. The customers organize an auction-type raffle to decide who will have the privilege to take Lorca in to the Marshal of Center City, Texas. Tony finds this amusing and agrees to go in peacefully, with the highest bidder. The bids go as high as $4,500, but Shasta has a better idea. When Tony steps outside the Saloon for a minute, she orders gunpoint, to hop in her wagon. He shot her unfaithful husband a couple of years ago, and with the money he just collected, she sees herself with a healthy profit, and a boyfriend besides. She has no intention of turning him in for the reward. A day later and back at the saloon, the town Marshal hears about what happened and looking at the wanted poster, informs the men that Tony Lorca died more than a year ago. His brother, Pepe, who looks just like the wanted man, has been passing himself off as Tony, to fleece unsuspecting suckers. Then, very suddenly, Pepe and Shasta come back, newly married.

Thus ends the saga of the Whistling kid. I'm afraid he no longer does much whistling. But he's no kid anymore, either. I shall return after we hear about a product which my sponsor feels is the most wanted. (commercial break) I have just been reading some of the shocking things they have written about me. Age, weight . . . I assure you I'm not guilty. Why don't you tune in next week and see if I beat this wrap? Until then, good night.

Trivia, etc. Actor Addison Richards played the uncredited role of the Police Captain in Hitchcock's *Spellbound* (1945). Ray Weaver, who played the judge at the end of this play, was also the Grand Central Station policeman in Hitchcock's *North by Northwest*.

Hitchcock Explains to his Crew how he Likes certain Set-ups, on the Set of *Alfred Hitchcock Presents*.

Photo courtesy of Photofest.

EPISODE #199 **"O YOUTH AND BEAUTY!"** Broadcast on November 22, 1960
Starring: Gary Merrill as Carrish "Cash" Bentley
Patricia Breslin as Mrs. Louise Bentley   David Lewis as Jim Blackwood
Theodore Newton as the doctor   Maurice Manson as Arthur
Dudley Manlove as George
Gloria Henninger as Cathy, the baby-sitter   Dick Winslow as Harry
Teleplay written for *Alfred Hitchcock Presents* by Halsted Welles, based on the short story "O, Youth and Beauty" by John Cheever, originally published in the August 22, 1953 issue of *The New Yorker*.
Directed by Norman Lloyd.

(on an olympic podium) *Good evening and thank you very much. Naturally I am pleased to have won the race. But I would like to console the losers with this bit of philosophy. It matters not who runs the race, it's how you win that counts.* (close-up) *I have a feeling I wasn't expected to triumph. The wreath is sized eight and a quarter, I'll have to take a tuck in it. And now for the next event. In the preliminaries this contestant made the distance in one minute flat. Let us hope he can improve that time.*

Story: As the former Olympic champion of the hurdle race, Cash Bentley is pressured by his wife to give it up. She explains that he's grown too old to compete anymore, but at the Riverview Country Club, Cash is talked into performing again for the amusement of his friends. When returning home, drunk, Cash sets up a course with furniture, and ends up injuring his leg. The doctor gives him some wise advice: grow up and forget about hurdling. He's just too old now. Fed up with his leg not yet well, while seeing one of his victories on film, and having faced another humiliation at the next Club dance, Cash talks his wife into letting him run one last time. Handing her the revolver, he tells her to fire when ready. She closes her eyes and shoots – just as he tries to run and the bullet catches him in mid-leap, killing him.

That is known as domestic skeet shooting, with live skeet. I . . . I see another commercial is coming up. It's amazing what you see when you don't have a gun. (commercial break) *By the way, tonight's story has inspired something new and exciting in track meets. Spectators are sold pistols instead of popcorn, but the bag is limited to three hurdlers per person. I am told it adds a great deal of zest to the sport. Next week we shall continue our study of the strange by-ways of American folklore. Until then, good night.*

EPISODE #200 **"THE MONEY"** Broadcast on November 29, 1960
Starring: Robert Loggia as Larry Chetnik   Doris Dowling as Angie
Will Kuluva as Stephen Bregornick   Wolfe Barzell as Miklos
Monica May as the secretary
Teleplay written for *Alfred Hitchcock Presents* by Henry Slesar, based on his short story "Trust Me, Mr. Paschetti," originally published in the June 1959 issue of *Man's World*. Subsequently collected in *Clean Crimes and Neat Murders* (Avon, 1960) as "The Money," and in *Death on Television* (Southern Illinois University Press, 1989).
Directed by Alan Crosland, Jr.

(huge 8-ball) *Good evening. This is not to symbolize my expulsion from an exclusive club. It is a mode of transportation. This is just the vehicle for those of you who have always longed to see Niagara Falls, from the bottom. This is the first two-passenger model. For that couple that enjoys living dangerously, even on the honeymoon. It is also attractively decorated.* (turns 8-ball) *I don't understand why we don't sell more of them. And speaking of sell, we have had complaints that our sponsor's sell is so soft, viewers have the feeling something is being left out of the commercials. For them, here is the uncensored, uncoofed version.*

Story: Larry Chetnik is a minor bookie with big ideas, but full of promises. For one thing, he keeps promising his girlfriend that he'll obtain a good-paying job and marry her, but he never succeeds. Paying a visit to Stephen Bregornick, a prosperous exporter who always deals in cash (and an old friend of his father's), he asks for employment – and gets it. Four months later, Larry begins making his plans to pull over one "big haul." Knowing his employer deals only with cash, he devises a scheme that will allow him to steal $30,000. But when Mr. Bregornick talks to Larry about how his father was such a wonderful friend, and knowing his girlfriend only wants him for his money, guilt overcomes Larry and he decides to give the money back, placing him in a position of extreme trust with the old man. What Mr. Bregornick doesn't know, is that the return of the money will make it all the easier for him to make the one "really big haul."

Well, I was so glad to see Larry get over his pre-occupation with money. I shall have news for you, after the following, sponsorial pronunciomento. (commercial break) *I want to thank the sponsor for that heartwarming and revealing human document. I look forward to more of the same next week. I understand that since the very best people watch this program, it has become a status symbol. If you wish to impress your neighbors, do as others do. Turn the set so that it faces an outside window. In that manner, passers by can see what you are watching even if you can't.* (walks round 8-ball)

EPISODE #201   **"SYBILLA"**   Broadcast on December 6, 1960
Starring: Barbara Bel Geddes as Sybilla Meades
Alexander Scourby as Horace Meades   Bartlett Robinson as Sybilla's attorney
Madge Kennedy as Mrs. Carter   Gordon Wynn as the doctor
Teleplay written for *Alfred Hitchcock Presents* by Charlotte Armstrong, based on the short story "Hard Way Out" by Margaret Manners, originally published in the December 1956 issue of *Mike Shayne Mystery Magazine*. Subsequently anthologized in *For Love or Money*, ed. Dorothy Gardiner (Doubleday, 1957) as "Sybilla."
Directed by Ida Lupino.
(lovers leap)   *Good evening, ladies and gentlemen and young lovers wherever you are.* (couple walks by) *No doubt their parents have forbidden the bans. So rather than face separation, they resort to . . .* (lady comes back alone and kisses another man) *Well, it did have a happy ending. I suppose I'm just an incurable romantic. But I so enjoy seeing true love triumph. And now, while I savour this moment, we shall have a few words on love of a different kind.*

Story: Frustrated Horace Meades will do just about anything to get out of being married to Sybilla. At first she appeared to be the most perfect woman in the world, but now she has become too perfect, and Horace wants to have her split ways. In fact, as a writer, he has written down all his ideas on how to be rid of her. A short time later, his wife describes a mystery book she's reading, in which a caring wife finds plans for her murder and sends copies to her attorney for safekeeping. Believing that she knows his secret, Horace is terrified. If anything happens to Sybilla, he'll be blamed. Eventually she becomes terminally ill and bedridden, and Horace asks Sybilla to reveal the truth about his diary. She dies before confessing. When her attorney later settles her finances, he discovers that she never copied his diary, but had only meant to save him from making a great mistake. Realizing her great care for him, he decides that he will miss her very much.

I shall return in a moment, but first we have that feature of television that all viewers long for. The end of a commercial, that moment will come in just sixty seconds. (commercial break) *That concludes our pot-pourri for this evening. Next week we shall continue our study, of that age old riddle. Did they jump or were they pushed? Until then, good night.* (turns "Lovers Leap" sign around to "Have you checked your valuables?")

326

EPISODE #202 **"THE MAN WITH TWO FACES"** Broadcast on December 13, 1960
Starring: Spring Byington as Mrs. Wagner
Steve Dunne as Lieutenant Meade   Bethel Leslie as Mabel
Harp McGuire as Leo   Adrienne Marden as Mrs. Wagner's friend
Teleplay written for *Alfred Hitchcock Presents* by Henry Slesar, based on his short story of the same name, originally pubished in the August 1956 issue of *Manhunt.* Subsequently collected in *Clean Crimes and Neat Murders* (Avon, 1960).
Directed by Stuart Rosenberg.
(bowling with a canon) *Good evening fellow bowlers. I seem to have done it again. There isn't much to this game really. With the advent of the automatic pin setter, I felt there should be some compensating automation at this end of the alley.* (bowling ball put into canon) *I haven't had a sore arm since I began using this.* (lights a match and cannon goes off. Strikes pins) *This will be very difficult to score. I knocked down all ten pins, the back wall and three small boys who were playing in the parking lot outside. In fact, I put one of the boys in orbit. But perhaps we should get down to business, after which we shall get down to business.*

Story: Mrs. Wagner, walking home alone one evening, is robbed by a young punk and hit in the face. Visiting the police station, a detective asks her to look through a couple of mug books, in hopes she might recognize her attacker. She doesn't find the thief, but she does find a man who looks very much like her son-in-law. Arriving home, Mrs. Wagner asks her daughter about Leo's past, but Mabel becomes irate and threatens to move out if her mother asks any more questions. Still suspicious, Mrs. Wagner returns to the police station with a photo of Leo. The police compare the pictures, but suggest the similarity is probably a coincidence. That evening, however, the police arrive at Mrs. Wagner's home and arrest both Leo *and* Mabel, who have been identified as wanted criminals. If she had looked through the female mug book, the detective explains, she would have found a photo of her daughter as well.

Mrs. Wagner was hoping her son-in-law would get out of the house and start doing something. Well he's now doing five to ten. The law also has a way of catching up with me. I refer to that statute which dictates that my sponsor make as many appearances as I do. If you've been keeping score, you know that I shall return. (commercial break) *That concludes our* (looks at man off camera) *. . . I don't mind you leaving the room during the commercial, but I expect you to be in your seats for my parts of the program. I shall return next week and I shall expect all of you to be here promptly. Good night.*

EPISODE #203 **"THE BABY-BLUE EXPRESSION"** Broadcast December 20, 1960
One of the days of filming was May 23, 1960.
Starring: Sarah Marshall as Mrs. Barrett "Poopsie"
Peter Walker as Philip Weaver   Richard Gaines as James Barrett
Leonard Weinrib as Harry, the bellboy   Edit Angold as Ellen, the maid
Chester Stratton as Raymond   Liz Carr as a party guest
Frank Richards as the postal clerk   Charles Carlson as a party guest
Teleplay written for *Alfred Hitchcock Presents* by Helen Nielsen, based on a story by Mary Stolz. Subsequently collected in *The Beautiful Friend and Other Stories* (Harper, 1960).
Directed by Arthur Hiller.
(at the piano) *Good evening, ladies and gentlemen. Before I begin tonight's concert, I would like to explain the structure of a symphony. All symphonies are composed of two parts. Sounds and silences. It is very important that you know the difference between the two. Perhaps I shall give you an example: This is sound.* (finds corpse in piano) *Good heavens, I don't like this a bit. I was told I would be the only one on the program. He's as*

stiff as a board, he must have been here some time. To continue our little chat about musical appreciation: for an example of sounds, I know nothing better than the next sixty seconds.

Story: James Barrett doesn't suspect his young wife, Poopsie, of having affair with his business assistant, Philip Weaver. When James leaves for business in Toronto, the lovebirds create a sure-fire plan to eliminate her husband. Philip is shrewd enough to put the plan to paper, and mails Poopsie instructions, which tells her to write her husband a warm pen letter. This is to create an alibi and eliminate suspicion when the police investigate. But after composing her love-letter, the feather-brained female mails both letters together, and after she realizes what she did, fails to get it back before the mailman picks it up. Missing the letter at the post office as well, she returns to her apartment seriously upset, until Harry, the bellboy, tells her that the letter was returned due to insufficient postage. But, being an efficient employee, he put the correct postage on the envelope and re-mailed it for her!

You have probably been wondering about our friend in the other piano. Rather than disturb him, we simply buried him in his piano. It was rather moving, really. Like going down with one's ship. And now I shall play the minute waltz. (commercial break) *That was the fastest I've ever played it. I suppose you've noticed that this piano has only one pedal. Because of my speed they had to put in an automatic transmission. Next week I shall be back with more music and further explanatory comments. Until then, good night.*

EPISODE #204   **"THE MAN WHO FOUND THE MONEY"**   Broadcast Dec. 27, 1960
    Starring: Arthur Hill as William Benson
    Guest Star: Rod Cameron as Curtis Newsome   R. G. Armstrong as Captain Bone
    Lucy Prentiss as Elaine Purdy   Clancy Cooper as A. J. Meecham
    Baynes Barron as Mr. Lent   Mark Allen as the man
    Teleplay written for *Alfred Hitchcock Presents* by Allan Gordon, based on the short story of the same name by James E. Cronin, originally published in the February 1954 issue of *Manhunt*.
    Directed by Alan Crosland, Jr.
    (as the captain of a ship)   *Good evening land lovers and welcome aboard. We shall have a pleasant voyage this evening.* (Hitchcock turns the wheel and picture rotates) *Sorry, I get carried away sometimes. We shall make several interesting ports of call tonight, but first, we must endure a rather dull sixty seconds, while we get beyond the three mile limit.*

Story: After losing all his money at a casino in Vegas, William Benson thinks his luck just took a turn for the better when he innocently finds a money clip with $92,000 in cash, lying in a car parking lot. Benson goes to the police, to report the lost and found. Captain Bone identifies the clip, but remarks that it originally had $102,000 and insists that Benson stole the missing $10,000. Benson, being innocent, denies the accusation, and the timely arrival of the rightful owner, Curtis Newsome, prevents Benson from getting into trouble with the police. Newsome assures the Captain that he knows about the missing $10,000, and as a reward, Benson is invited to spend the weekend at his casino. Newsome even invites Benson's wife, Joyce, all compliments of the wealthy benefactor. Thinking he has it all made, Benson is unsuspectingly escorted to the back room where he hears his wife on the other end of the phone. Newsome demands the immediate return of the $10,000, or something awful will happen . . . of which Benson can't supply.

So much for our visit to exotic Las Vegas. We shall cast anchor soon, for I wish to have a meeting with a business associate. But hang on please, I see one of those dreadful sand bars ahead. I shall see you after we tie-up. (commercial break, someone is hanging from the top of the ship) *I've just completed a meeting with my sponsor, in which he had a change of heart, and I think it's safe to say that we may be spared his commercials in the future. Why don't you tune in next week and see? Until then, good night.*

Trivia, etc. "We did a show called 'The Man Who Found the Money' with Arthur Hill," recalled Norman Lloyd. "In it, Hill, while gambling in Las Vegas, finds a money clip containing $92,000. Honest soul that he is, he decides to give it back. After much effort, he locates the owner, a Las Vegas big shot played by Rod Cameron. The trouble is, the clip originally contained $102,000 and Cameron accuses him of stealing the missing $10,000. Well, we received tons of mail on that show, all of it castigating Hill for giving the money back, saying that he got what he deserved. Around this same time, there was a news item about a bag full of money that had fallen off a Brink's truck. The money was found by a porter, who promptly returned it. And do you know, the people in his neighborhood castigated him so badly that he had to move? When you talk about the psychology of our shows, this should give you some idea of the kinds of audiences we had. And why the Hitchcock series always possessed such a unique appeal."

EPISODE #205   **"THE CHANGING HEART"**   Broadcast on January 3, 1961
Starring: Nicholas Pryor as Dane Ross
Anne Helm as Lisa   Abraham Sofaer as Ulrich Klemm
Robert Sampson as Dane's friend, visiting Mr. Klemm
Teleplay written for *Alfred Hitchcock Presents* by Robert Bloch, from his short story "Change of Heart," originally published in the Fall 1948 issue of *The Arkham Sampler*. Subsequently collected in *Atoms and Evil* (Gold Medal, 1962).
Directed by Robert Florey.
(Hitchcock steps out of a big cuckoo clock)   *Present company excepted.* (close-up) *Good evening, fellow clockwatchers and welcome to Alfred Hitchcock Presents. I shall never again lease an apartment on the strength of an advertisement. This one read: "Quarters for rent for very slim gentleman who loves animals." The animals are that infernal bird you just heard and an idiotic mouse that runs up the pendulum every now and then. You know the nursery rhyme that goes, "when the clock struck one." Unfortunately, I'm the one it strikes, but enough of my problems. Now as is customary on this program, we shall have a word or two . . . from a dear friend. Listen.*

Story: Dane Ross falls in love with the granddaughter of a master clockmaker, Mr. Ulrich Klemm, a native German who fled the Nazis during the war, and now lives quietly in peace making clocks. Shortly after, Dane is transferred to a distant job in Seattle, and asks Mr. Klemm for Lisa's hand in marriage. The grandfather refuses to let his granddaughter go and after apparently hypnotizing her, she agrees with the old man. Months later, when Dane hears that Lisa is seriously ill, he returns to her home to discover that the old man has since passed on, probably because of his bad ticker. Lisa, however, is still alive but now confined to a wheelchair. With love in his heart, Dane kneels beside her, and is shocked to hear a strange ticking sound coming from inside her body. Dane realizes that the old German's last clockwork job was indeed an intricate one . . .

Perhaps it was something she ate. And now our sponsor would like to tick-off a few of the reasons why he feels he deserves your stead-fast support. I shall again be available after the customary interval. But don't bother to call me, I'll call you. (commercial break) *My problems have been solved. I had a workman over and he removed that awful cuckoo sound. I won't be needing these anymore. That's all for tonight. Next week we shall be back with another story. Until then, good night.* (clock strikes midnight)

Trivia, etc. Actor Baruch Lumet is listed in the credits of this episode, but somehow he does not appear on screen anywhere throughout the entire drama. Robert Florey was perfect for the direction of this macabre episode. Florey, who directed numerous episodes for television's *The Outer Limits*, *Thriller* and *The Twilight Zone*, had established himself as a director of numerous mystery/horror movies. Among them, *Johann the Coffinmaker* (1927), *Murders in the Rue Morgue* (1932), *Meet Boston Blackie* (1941), *The Face Behind the Mask* (1941), and *The Beast with Five Fingers* (1946).

"I loved the show because it was well-done for a half-hour series, and it always had fascinating stories, sort of like *The Twilight Zone*," Anne Helm recalled. "Robert Florey, who directed me in one of them, also directed a lot of movies. In that one, I was the granddaughter of a clockmaker, and at the end it turns out that he killed me and put a ticking clock inside me [laughs]! When my lover comes back, he sees me sitting in the chair and it's sort of like a *Psycho* moment – he comes running up and the camera pans in and you hear this "tick-tock, tick-tock." The grandfather wanted to possess me, and that was the only way he could, by making me into a clock." Helm's remark about having a *Psycho* moment couldn't be far from the truth. Robert Bloch, whose story was adapted for this episode, also wrote the novel which *Psycho* was based on.

EPISODE #206 **"SUMMER SHADE"** Broadcast on January 10, 1961
>   Starring: Julie Adams as Phyllis Kendall   James Franciscus as Ben Kendall
>   John Hoyt as Reverend White   Charity Grace as Amelia Gastell
>   Stuart Nedd as the doctor   Veronica Cartwright as Judy Davidson
>   and Susan Gordon as Kate Kendall

Teleplay written for *Alfred Hitchcock Presents* by Harold Swanton, based on the short story "Summer Evil" by Nora H. Caplan, originally published in the October 1960 issue of *Alfred Hitchcock's Mystery Magazine*.

> Directed by Herschel Daugherty.

(dunking stool) *Good evening, ladies and gentlemen. Do you have the feeling that we are moving ahead too swiftly? That in our quest for fame, for material wealth, we are neglecting some of the old traditions, the old customs from whence we once drew our strength? This for example? This may look like a seesaw built for one but it is a dunking stool. In puritan times, if a woman were a scold or a gossip, she was placed here. The seatbelt was fastened securely and a number of brave men and true proceeded to dunk her in a pond as though she were a donut. It was most invigorating, I'm sure. Unhappily in modern days, we have no such convenience. Today, if a woman is a gossip, she isn't dunked, she is syndicated. Tonight's story has a connection, however, remote to the preceding. While our sponsor has a connection, however, obviously to the following.*

Story: Ben and Phyllis Kendall purchase a new home in New Salem, Massachusetts, and almost immediately their daughter, Kate, dreams up an odd imaginary playmate called "Letty." Kate's parents dismiss the notion at first, assuming it's just the lack of a playmate, but as the days pass, Kate begins acting strangely. A charm made of buzzard bones appears by Kate's bedside, and Letty told the girl that it helps ward off small pox. Consulting the local minister for help, Ben and Phyllis discover that a real Lauretta Bishop died nearby, from a severe case of the small pox, back in 1694. With their fears worsened, the parents believe their daughter is possessed. Before they can consult an actual exorcism, the next-door neighbor brings over a little girl for Kate to play with, much to the relief of the concerned parents, since their daughter starts acting normal again - not yet knowing that the new playmate is possessed as well . . .

I hope you enjoyed our story, "Summer Shade," because that will give you strength to face this next item, after which I'll return. (commercial break) *That is all of tonight's entertainment. We shall return next week with more of the same. Now I must hurry off, I'm shooting a picture.* (Hitchcock walks into a photo booth) *Good night.*

Trivia, etc. "They were very good stories, weren't they?" recalled Julie Adams. "They were very well written stories. James Franciscus was a handsome young man who later on had a series of his own [*The Investigators, Hunter* and *Doc Elliot* to name a few].

Herschel Daugherty did a very fine job on the series because they had very talented people. The producer, Norman Lloyd, I got to know him very well in the three episodes I did. I got to work with him again years later on a PBS series called *Hollywood Television Theatre* – one of those programs with six characters in search of an author, in which Stacy Keach directed and Lloyd produced it. Norman Lloyd and I talked on that set about the Hitchcock show and he told me that he particularly liked the episode I did with Joseph Cotten. Lloyd was a very, very charming man."

On January 17, 1961, *Alfred Hitchcock Presents* was not broadcast, due to President Eisenhower's Farewell Address to the Nation, which began 8:30 p.m., EST.

EPISODE #207   "A CRIME FOR MOTHERS"   Broadcast on January 24, 1961

Starring: Claire Trevor as Lottie Mead
Biff Elliott as Phil Ames, the investigator

Patricia Smith as Jane Birdwell	Howard McNear as Mr. Maxwell
Robert Sampson as Ralph Birdwell	King Calder as Charlie Vance
Gail Bonney as the secretary	Sally Smith as the young girl

Teleplay written for *Alfred Hitchcock Presents* by Henry Slesar, based on his short story of the same name as published in the December 1960 issue of *Alfred Hitchcock's Mystery Magazine*. Subsequently collected in *A Crime for Mothers and Others* (Avon, 1962).

Directed by Ida Lupino.

Good evening, and welcome to The Best of Hitchcock. In the absence of my vacationing brother Alfred, we are presenting clips from his past shows. I find it amusing, by the way, that television at last confirms what our family has known for years. That I, rather than Alfred am the best of Hitchcock. And now for those clips: (as a witch on the stake) *This was one of the high spots for me.* (big rotating saw) *This one stopped just short of perfection. I think it is obvious why I cherish those shows. I'm sure many of you feel the same way. And now here are two more, equally delicious. After which we shall have our story. Ladies and gentlemen, the best of Hitchcock.* (on the rail road tracks)   *Alfred never looked better.* (in a laboratory) *The next sound you'll hear will be my sponsor.* (explosion)

Story: Seven years ago, Lottie Mead was a washed up alcoholic, whose husband ran out on her, and was forced to throw her newborn infant on the steps of a church. A loving couple, the Birdwells, adopted the little girl, and in return, paid off Lottie's debts. Now, seven years later, Lottie shows up to pester the Birdwell family, asking for blackmail payments – or her daughter. Her true goal is money, but when that fails, she leaves, turning to a few lawyers for advice. With the reputation she's built, no one will represent her. Phil Ames, a Private Investigator, suggests she repossess her own property, and the two scheme to kidnap the girl and demand a ransom. But when she does so, Lottie discovers that she nabbed the wrong girl, and now faces a real kidnapping charge. Ames, the private detective, explains to her what she's done, in the presence of a detective, who claims he can clear her of all charges once the girl is returned, provided that she leaves the Birdwell family alone, for good. She agrees, not realizing that the kidnapped girl is Ames' daughter and the Birdwell family are his friends.

Good evening. This is Alfred Hitchcock. Welcome to the end of tonight's episode of Alfred Hitchcock Presents. I should explain that my vacation was the result of a nasty remark I made on the show. The person at whom I directed the remark has been given the following minute to retaliate. After which I shall return. (commercial break) *Perhaps it's my sponsor who needs a vacation. Before taking leave, I would like to show you a few of my selections for The Best of Hitchcock.* (wine cellar) *Now this is truly vintage Hitchcock.* (beauty contest) *And without the violence my brother seems to admire. Much more pleasant than my brother's choices. After all, I like to keep this a happy show. Next week we shall be back with another story. Until then, good night.*

EPISODE #208   **"THE LAST ESCAPE"**   Broadcast on January 31, 1961

Starring: Keenan Wynn as Joe Ferlini   Jan Sterling as Wanda Ferlini
Dennis Patrick as Phil Roscoe   John Craven as Tommy Baggett
Jack Livesey as Dr. Rushfield   Ronnie R. Rondell as Dave
Charles Meredith as the clergyman   Robert Carson as the police chief
Claude Stroud as the official   Sam Flint as a business man
Ed Allen as the musician

Teleplay written for *Alfred Hitchcock Presents* by Henry Slesar, from his short story of the same name, originally published in the July 1960 issue of *Alfred Hitchcock's Mystery Magazine.* Subsequently collected in *Clean Crimes and Neat Murders* (Avon, 1960), *Murders Most Macabre* (Avon, 1986) and *Death on Television* (Southern Illinois University Press, 1989).

Directed by Paul Henreid.

(mermaid, fishing-rod)   *Good evening. You should have seen the one that got away. The only one I've ever seen with gold lame scales. I'm sure all of you are interested in the details of this catch. It's really a matter of finding the proper bait. I soon learned that these little creatures can tell cheap costume jewelry on sight, and won't come near it. You must bait your hook with the real article and sometimes they make off with the bait before you can reel them in. However, that's a situation with which most of you may now already familiar. Tonight's fabel is entiled "The Last Escape." But first, something from which there is no escape.*

Story: Escape artist Joe Ferlini plans a spectacular escape from handcuffs, inside a locked case that is lowered into a river. Unknown to him, his wife Wanda is fed up with Joe, and substitutes a fake key for the handcuffs, insuring his death. The police never suspect anything, because of the nature of Joe's business, and Wanda gets away with murder. After drowning, Joe is buried, but a suspecting police officer insists that the coffin be opened before it is lowered into the grave. Sure enough, Joe's body is gone, as any escape artist would, causing Wanda to suffer a nervous breakdown. Unknown to her, Joe had made private arrangements for his body to disappear if one of his stunts ever failed, thus assuring him a place in history as one of the greatest escape artists of all time.

You must remember that things are always much better than they seem. That this is the best of all possible worlds. That every cloud has a silver lining and that it is darkest just before the dawn. I tell you this, not because of what you have just experienced, but for what you are about to see. (commercial break) *I suppose, you're wondering what became of my catch. The game warden insisted I'd throw her back in, because her measurements didn't meet specifications. In order to keep them they must be larger than 36 – 22 - 15 and of course it's quite difficult knowing precisely where to take that last measurement. Next week I shall be back . . . so let us hope I have some more luck in the meantime. Until then, good night.*

Trivia, etc. The character named "Dave" was played by Ronnie Rondell, one of the many assistant directors on the Hitchcock program, playing a small role in this episode! Dennis Patrick and John Craven also appeared in the same episode a year earlier in "The Day of the Bullet."

On February 7, 1961, *Alfred Hitchcock Presents* was not broadcast. Instead, a CBS special presentation of the *Hallmark Hall of Fame* was broadcast. Starring Christopher Plummer, Edith Evans and Janet Monro in Jean Anouilh's romantic comedy, "Time Remembered," adapted by Theodore Apstein, from the English version by Patricia Moyes. Produced and directed by George Schaefer. Broadcast over CBS in living color, 7:30 to 9 p.m., EST. Supporting cast included Barry Jones and Paul Hartman.

EPISODE #209 **"THE GREATEST MONSTER OF THEM ALL"**
Broadcast on February 14, 1961
Starring: William Redfield as Fred Logan   Richard Hale as Ernst Von Kroft
Sam Jaffe as Hal Ballew   Robert H. Harris as Morty Lenton
Meri Welles as Lara Lee, the blonde actress   Charles Carlson as movie crew
Baruch Lumet as movie crew   Mike Taylor as a movie goer
Ronnie Sorenson, Eve Lesley, Joan Marcus and Phil Adams are also movie goers.

Teleplay written for *Alfred Hitchcock Presents* by Robert Bloch, based on the short story of the same name by Bryce Walton, originally published in the May 1959 issue of *Ellery Queen's Mystery Magazine*. Subsequently reprinted in *Ellery Queen's Anthology* (1967).

Directed by Robert Stevens.

(five ladies in a harem, with a cigar)   *Oh, good evening. I'm sure there's a question in everyone's mind. You're all wondering how I have managed to overcome the health problem. The secret lies in offering fringe benefits, on-the-job training, things like that. These items don't cost much and what I spend on them, I save on costumes.* (close-up) *Seriously, this is certainly not an honest picture of life in Hollywood. We do believe in being comfortable while we work, but we never eat grapes during business hours. Tonight's story is entitled "The Greatest Monster Of Them All," which certainly should be a cue for the sponsor to speak up.*

Story: In the hopes of making a large profit from a low-budget horror picture, movie director Morty Lenton and producer Hal Ballew hire Ernst Von Kroft, a retired actor once known as the "The Greatest Monster of Them All." While he gives a spectacular and creepy performance, the cast and crew start getting the notion that Von Kroft is actually living the role, rather than acting it. During a showing of the movie, to test out audience reaction, Von Kroft is horrified to learn that his voice has been dubbed over with someone else's, in unintended humor. The audience laughs and Von Kroft leaves embarrassed. "I went to the theater expecting to see my comeback," says a disgusted Von Kroft to the screenwriter, "instead I found myself attending my own funeral." Back at the soundstage, the screenwriter finds the body of Morty, the director, with bite marks on his neck. Hal, the producer, pleads for help, while high above him in the catwalks is Von Kroft, fully dressed in cape and coattails. They watch as the aging actor makes a deadly leap to the floor below, ending the career of "The Greatest Monster of Them All."

Obviously the lesson of that story is quite clear. One should be careful what friends you hang around with, as in this business. These girls are very carefully screened. The one here for example, the one lighting my pipe. . . she and I do not hit it off. She won't be here long. See you in a moment. (commercial break) (explosion blows Hitchcock into the air) *Until next week, good night.* (spoken by the girl)

EPISODE #210 **"THE LANDLADY"** Broadcast on February 21, 1961
Starring: Dean Stockwell as Billy Weaver   Patricia Collinge as the landlady
Laurie Main as Mr. Wilkins, the bartender   George Pelling as Bert
Barry Harvey as Tom   Burt Mustin as the old man
Jill Livesey as Rosie, the cook at the tavern

Teleplay written for *Alfred Hitchcock Presents* by Robert Bloch, based on the short story of the same name by Roald Dahl, originally published in November 25, 1959 issue of *The New Yorker*. Subsequently collected in *Kiss Kiss* (Michael Joseph, 1960; Knopf, 1960) and in *Tales of the Unexpected* (Michael Joseph, 1979; Vintage, 1980).

Directed by Paul Henreid.

(standing beside a safe)   *Good evening. This should be a relatively simple task.* (opens safe, turns out it was a refrigerator) *Nothing to it really. I'm not really hungry, but I resent the implication that I haven't the self control to stay on my diet. Tonight we have fried chicken, cold apple pie, potato sallad, a story entitled "The Landlady" and one fast frozen commercial.* (eats a chicken leg)

Story: Billy Weaver, a mild-mannered bank clerk, arrives in a small provincial town in England, looking for a new residence, and finds a boarding house with thrifty rates. The landlady is a little peculiar, but Billy shrugs it off, assuming her rational mind expired from age. She explains that there are two other boarders, but it strikes him strange that he never sees them. One afternoon Billy has tea with his landlady, and observes that her pet parrot is not really alive, but rather stuffed. Asking her about it, she explains that she has all of her pets stuffed after they pass away, a talent she possesses and occasionally practices. All too late, Billy realizes his tea has been poisoned, and he is about to become the latest addition to her taxidermy collection.

So much for our tale of the talkative taxidermist. Now for a short soliloquy from a super salesman, after which, a fast farewell from a hungry host. (commercial break) *I don't understand it, but I seem to have quite lost my appetite. That looks real, doesn't it? It's not. It's stuffed. As for our dear landlady, she was eventually caught. Overconfidence and a flair for exhibitionism, led her to make Billy into a throwrug for her entry hall. It was excellent for discouraging peddlers and agents, but it was no way to keep a secret. Next week we shall return with still another story. Until then, good night.*

Trivia, etc. Actor Laurie Main, who plays the bartender in this episode, was also the narrator for many Winnie the Pooh movies (replacing the late Sebastian Cabot) and also supplied the voice for Dawson, in Walt Disney's animated feature, *The Great Mouse Detective* (1986). Dean Stockwell was only twenty-six when he was filmed for this episode, but he played a twenty-two year-old very convincingly. Patricia Collinge, who appeared three times before in earlier *Alfred Hitchcock Presents* episodes, returns in what is probably her best role of the series, known as "the Landlady." She also played the role of Emma Newton in Hitchcock's *Shadow of a Doubt* (1943). She later returned twice to *The Alfred Hitchcock Hour.*

Barbara Baxley and Henry Morgan in "Anniversary Gift." (Photo courtesy of Photofest.)

EPISODE #211 **"THE THROWBACK"** Broadcast on February 28, 1961
Starring: Scott Marlowe as Elliott Gray
Murray Matheson as Cyril Hardeen   Joyce Meadows as Enid Patterson
Bert Remsen as the detective   Howard McLeod as the man
John Indrisano as Joseph

An original teleplay written for *Alfred Hitchcock Presents* by Henry Slesar, which was later published as a short story entitled "And Beauty the Prize," in *A Crime for Mothers and Others* (Avon, 1962).

Directed by John Brahm.

(trampoline) *Good evening, ladies and gentlemen. I'm sure you are wondering what I'm wearing. It's the latest thing I'm told, called a trampoline. I do not intend to discuss how I arrived here, but I'm open to suggestions for a way to get out. As a costume it has severe limitations. Fortunately, you won't have to sit there staring at me all evening. We have a story for you. It is called "The Throwback." But first, we have this one minute tear in the tapestry of television.*

Story: Enid Patterson breaks the bad news to her boyfriend Elliott, that she has been seeing another man, Cyril Hardeen, who is much older than she. Elliott, being a practical man, tells Enid that she will have to make a choice. Him or Cyril, but not both. Enid, ashamed, agrees to leave the older man. After the break up, Cyril demands to fight Elliott, who keeps declining because he is afraid the old man would be hurt. But the determined Cyril produces a proxy, an ex-prize fighter who annihilates Elliott. After Elliott returns home badly beaten, he is met by the police, who arrest him for the beating of Cyril Hardeen. Escorting the boy back to Cyril's house, the old man is attending his wounds that he claims were inflicted by Elliott. Enid over hears all this, and decides to leave Elliott forever.

That was a pleasantly romantic story, but I was in no mood to enjoy it. My feet are beginning to hurt. Fortunately, my assistant has promised to extract me under cover of the following one minute entertainment blackout. I shall see you at its conclusion. (commercial break) *I appreciate getting up, but I don't think the job called for a heavy construction crane and a crew of four men. One of my assistants is given to large scale ideas. He was the one who thought of opening the show with a shot of me bouncing merily on a trampoline. However, he won't be with us when we return next week. We're sending him on location to Devil's Island. Good night.*

Trivia, etc. Actor Bert Remsen, who played the detective in this Hitchcock episode, and would later play a police lieutenant in the episode "Gratitude," made his film debut in the 1959 feature, *Pork Chop Hill*, also the role of a police lieutenant. He continued to play police officers in big screen films. In 1964, however, an eight-foot-four crane collapsed on the set of the television series *No Time for Sergeants*, breaking his back and nearly killing him. Remsen was able to walk again with crutches, but believing his acting career was over, became a casting director instead. He eventually headed the casting department of Lorimar Productions and it was while he was casting the film *Brewster McCloud* (1970), that director Robert Altman assigned him the acting role of Douglas Breen. Robert Altman, who directed two episodes (both aired in the third season) of the Hitchcock series, also made sure that Remsen received many more roles in his pictures.

EPISODE #212 **"THE KISS-OFF"** Broadcast on March 7, 1961
Starring: Rip Torn as Ernie Walters
Mary Munday as Florrie   Ken Patterson as Phillip Bentley, the D.A.
Florence MacMichael as the woman witness
Harry Swoger as the taxi driver   Don Keefer as the tax clerk
Frank Sully as the desk clerk   Bert Freed as Detective Cooper

Teleplay written for *Alfred Hitchcock Presents* by Talmage Powell, based on the short story of the same name by John P. Foran, originally published in a 1951 issue of *Male*. Subsequently anthologized in *Best Detective Stories of the Year*, ed. David C. Cooke (Dutton, 1952).

Directed by Alan Crosland, Jr.

(at the voting booth) *Good evening ladies and gentlemen. This is a voting booth. It comes complete with voting instructions. You will observe that it is a one-passenger model. When you enter, you go alone. There is not even room for your conscience. The inventor was afraid that would prove too large a handicap to speedy elections. These booths come in only one size, thus automatically disenfranchising, certain of our population who do not conform to conventional, physical standards. This has no direct bearing on tonight's story, but is merely offered as a public service. Actually, there is much that has no direct bearing on tonight's story, the following for example.*

Story: Six years ago, Ernie Walters was sent to prison, falsely accused of robbing a filling station that someone else committed. When the truth is finally learned and the real thief comes forward, Ernie is released. The very first thing he does, even before meeting his old girlfriend, is to put on a disguise and rob a branch of the Department of State Revenue for $12,000. The police pay Ernie a visit, search his hotel room, but find nothing. No money, no costume, no gray suit. (It's really at his girlfriend's apartment.) Still, the police arrest him, based on circumstantial evidence, and the witnesses to the hold-up can't say for certain that Ernie was the man. Alone in private with his old friends, the District Attorney and Detective, Ernie recalls the details of the case six years ago when they set him up for a crime he didn't commit. Seeing how they'll have a hard time convicting him again, the District Attorney orders Ernie to get out of town, and stay out. Ernie leaves remarking, "I can afford to."

As has been said before on television, a District Attorney's lot is not a happy one. But on Ernie's next effort, the law caught up with Ernie, and he paid the penalty for a sloppy make-up job. And now we must listen to a speech, from a gentleman who consistently ignores the rule against electioneering within fifty yards of the poll. After which I shall return for a rebuttle. (commercial break) *I don't see the lever, much less the voting machine. Actually, these weren't made originally for voting booths, they were Army surplus having been – ah! There it is!* (Hitchcock enters booth and gets wet) *As I was saying, these were formerly portable showers. Next week I shall return to campaign once more for clean government. Until then, good night.*

Trivia, etc.   Director Alan Crosland, Jr. was actually a film editor before establishing himself as a director. He helped edit *The Adventures of Don Juan* (1948) and the television series, *Sergeant Preston of the Yukon*. Shortly thereafter, Crosland directed sixteen episodes of *Alfred Hitchcock Presents* and three for *The Alfred Hitchcock Hour*, as well as many for *Maverick*, *Peter Gunn*, and *The Twilight Zone*. Crosland also did a little acting years before, playing the role of the young King of Sardalia in the silent movie *Three Weeks* (1924).

EPISODE #213   **"THE HORSEPLAYER"**   Broadcast on March 14, 1961
Rehearsed and filmed on January 4 – 6, 1961.
Starring: Claude Rains as Father Amion   Ed Gardner as Mr. Sheridan
Percy Helton as Morten, the Church Sexton
Mike Ragan as Mr. Cheever, the plumber   William Newell as a bank teller
David Carlile as a bank teller   Ada Murphy as the elderly woman
and Kenneth MacKenna as Bishop Cannon
John Yount and Jackie Carroll are the alter boys (uncredited)

Teleplay written for *Alfred Hitchcock Presents* by Henry Slesar, based on his short story "Long Shot", originally published in the November 1960 issue of *Fantastic*. Subsequently collected in *A Crime for Mothers and Others* (Avon, 1962) as "Father Amion's Long Shot."

Directed by Alfred Hitchcock.

(with a horse costume) *Good evening, ladies and gentlemen. Someone had the brilliant idea that I should don this costume in order to dramatize the title of tonight's play. It is called "The Horseplayer." Just a moment, you forgot something. I'm sure you want to know, who authored this clever charade. His previous works include the following one-minute audio collage.*

Story: The church has a leaking roof and a plumber quotes the price of $1,500. Concerned, Father Amion meets up with Mr. Sheridan, a man who not only made two large charitable donations, but has since become a regular attendee. But it turns out that Sheridan is not a saint by heart, but a gambler by trade, and his practice of praying for the right horse has been working well. Father Amion tells Sheridan that he is misusing the power of prayer, but Sheridan ignores the Father's words and continues betting, somehow winning race after race. So much so, that Sheridan's methods begin to intrigue Father Amion. Eventually Sheridan gets the priest involved in the betting game by giving the Father an "inside tip" on a horse. Father Amion gambles his entire savings account, $500, on Sheridan's hot tip, hoping it will pay for repairs needed for the church. Shortly after, the priest feels very guilty about the whole thing, and the Bishop forces Amion to pray for the horse to lose. As a result, Sheridan loses his entire wager, but the priest fares better, as Sheridan happened to bet Father Amion's money to place, paying the church $2,100!

The sponsor is being unusually difficult about this matter of the horse costume. I've explained the labor-saving advantages of employing a real horse to do the work of two men, but he is so enchanted with this pun of his, on the word 'horseplayer', that he insists on having it out with me. I should be back shortly. It will only take a minute to put him in his place. (commercial break) (The two people in the horse costume wanders off, in different directions.)

Trivia, etc. "Oh, well, Claude Rains . . . now you're talking about one of the greats," said Norman Lloyd. "He was wonderful. He came on . . . he was about seventy years old then, I think . . . and he played this wonderful priest. He was an old Hitchcock star - I mean, he is so marvelous in *Notorious* (1946), which by the way Hitch always called 'No . . . .torious.' Ben Hecht saw it and he said, 'He should have had a better tailor!' [Laughs] Anyway, Claude Rains . . . a doll, just wonderful, a marvelous actor. I was an admirer of Claude Rains ever since I saw him in the theater [in the Theatre Guild production *They Shall Not Die*] playing Sam Liebowitz, the lawyer who defended the Scottsboro Boys.* He was wonderful. When he came on to do this Hitchcock, it was just a delight. That show was about a priest who bet the church funds on a horse race so he could repair the roof of the church."

"The Hitchcock show was also a showcase of nostalgic performances," Henry Slesar continued. "I watched with inordinate pleasure when I saw my story characters brought to life by people like Claude Rains, Judy Canova, Claire Trevor and Eduardo Ciannelli – the last a permanent part of my childhood psyche, if only for his portrayal of the mad Thuggee in *Gunga Din* (1939). I also recall a special gulp of joy upon seeing Ed

* The Scottsboro Boys, nine black Alabama youths, were accused of a criminal assault on two white girl mill-hands. In a court case that became a national cause célèbre, they were defended by New York attorney Sam Liebowitz, whose counterpart ("Nathan G. Rubin") was played by Rains in *They Won't Forget* (1937).

Gardner speaking *my words*, although only Trivial Pursuit players may remember him as Archie of radio's *Duffy's Tavern*."

There is also a goof in the play. If a bet of $500 was placed, and the horse paid 8,40, that should give him $4,200, not $2,100!

EPISODE #214   **"INCIDENT IN A SMALL JAIL"**   Broadcast on March 21, 1961
     Starring: John Fiedler as Leon Gorwald   Richard Jaeckel as the mechanic
     Ron Nicholas as Officer Kylie   Myron Healey as Sheriff Martin
     Crahan Denton as Deputy Bill Sanderson
     William Challee as the gas station attendant   Joan Dupuis as the young girl
     Teleplay written for *Alfred Hitchcock Presents* by Henry Slesar, based on his short story "The Man in the Next Cell," originally published in the February 1961 issue of *Ellery Queen's Mystery Magazine*. Subsequently collected in *A Crime for Mothers and Others* (Avon, 1962).
     Directed by Norman Lloyd.
     (parking-meter)   *Good evening. We have here one of the latest and most improved parking meters. The old type merely indicated a violation and unless a policeman happened by, the driver could get off scott free. This meter assures us that the violator will be punished.* (explodes) *Needless to say, even if the automobile is hauled away, it can easily be identified and so can the driver, if he is within range. The advantages are not all on the side of the law however, for this device also will blow away any parking ticket left on your windshield. And now I see our sponsor is parked in a one minute zone. Following which we shall have tonight's story.*

     Story: Travelling salesman Leon Gorwald finds himself in bad situation. Being locked up in a small town jail for an innocent jaywalking, Leon finds himself in a cell next to a young man suspected of murdering a young teenager. But an unruly crowd gathers outside, demanding justice, and Leon suspects a lynch mob brewing. Sheriff Martin decides to move the accused murderer, in an attempt to prevent violence, but the young man knocks the cop out and forces Leon to change clothes with him. After the boy escapes, the mob rushes the jail, bent with the intention of killing the innocent salesman. After moments of fury and anger, Leon's life is saved at the last second, and is free to go on his own way. Driving out of town, Leon stops to give a pretty hitchhiker a ride, she not realizing that Leon is the real murderer after all . . .

     By the way, I wouldn't worry about that female hitchhiker if I were you. That was John Charles Wentworth, the gentleman who later authored a book, "I was a Girl for the FBI." There was another announcement I was to make but I can't remember it. Give me one minute and perhaps I can. (commercial break) *I now remember the announcement I wanted to make. We shall return next week at the same time. Until then, good night.*

     Trivia, etc.   Actor John Fiedler made his first of three appearances on the Hitchcock program, in this tension-filled episode. "The first one I did, 'Incident in a Small Jail,' was really quite a good one," Fiedler recalled. "They made a TV movie of *Alfred Hitchcock Presents* several years ago; the guy who produces *Law and Order* was the producer, and they remade that episode. Ned Beatty played my old part. I went in to see this producer about the pilot of *Law and Order*, and his *Hitchcock* movie hadn't been shown yet. He had just finished it. And he said to me, 'I'll tell you right now, yours was a lot better'. They never asked me to star in it. I'm sure they wanted a bigger name. I knew Norman Lloyd for a long time in New York. We acted together on the *Kraft Television Playhouse*, a live television show in the fifties. Occasionally we still see each other."

338

EPISODE #215 "A WOMAN'S HELP" Broadcast on March 28, 1961
    Starring: Geraldine Fitzgerald as Elizabeth Bourdon
    Scott McKay as Arnold Bourdon   Antoinette Bower as Miss Joan Grecco
    Lillian O'Malley as Mrs. Bourdon   Leon Lontok as Chester
    An original teleplay written for *Alfred Hitchcock Presents* by Henry Slesar, which
was later published as a short story "A Woman's Help" in *A Crime for Mothers and Others*
(Avon, 1962). Subsequently collected in *Murders Most Macabre* (Avon, 1986) and *Death
on Television* (Southern Illinois University Press, 1989).
    Directed by Arthur Hiller.
    (roof with antennas) *Good evening. Something must be done about this. On this
roof alone there are three reindeer and a stork caught in the antennae. We certainly can't
have that. It interferes with reception. The picture becomes quite grotesque. Allow me to
illustrate.* (grabs one antenna) *You see what I mean? It's rather like home movies, made by
Picasso or someone. But enough of this. You tuned in to see a story and I'm certain you
don't want to spend the time looking at a negative. But first one minute from a man who is a
positive thinker.*

    Story: Arnold Bourdon is wealthy, but lonely. His invalid wife Elizabeth seems to
live for the opportunity to continuously browbeat him, claiming he's not dependent without a
woman's help. For Arnold, things take a turn for the better when the couple hire a live-in
nurse, whom Arnold eventually spends time with on the side. Unfortunately, Miss Grecco
will not continue their passionate relationship unless he gets rid of Elizabeth. Together, they
decide to overdose the woman's medication. Before they can go through with it, Elizabeth
discovers Arnold and Miss Grecco kissing, and the nurse is immediately fired. Arnold is told
to arrange for a substitute. This time, his wife will interview the candidates personally.
Elizabeth decides to hire an older, overweight woman, who couldn't possibly arouse
Arnold's feelings. Arnold explains to the new nurse about Elizabeth's dosage of medicine - a
deadly one - and how it should be given, remarking, "I certainly appreciate this, Mother."

    *Well, that's the way the bustle bounces. Now we have some medicine of our own
we must take, after which I shall re-appear. Courage now. It may be bitter but you'll feel
better when it's over.* (commercial break) *By the by, Arnold Bourdon's attempt to achieve
single blessedness, was frustrated by his mother. At a crucial moment the poor woman
became completely adult, due to an overdose of cooking cherry. Next week we shall return .
. .* (baby cry) *This is amazing, I never saw a stork at work before. I hope they have a layette
ready. They'll find it isn't Santa coming down the chimney. Good night.*

EPISODE #216 "MUSEUM PIECE" Broadcast on April 4, 1961
    Starring: Larry Gates as Clay Hollister
    Myron McCormick as Newton B. Clovis   Bert Convy as Benjamin Hollister
    Edward C. Platt as Mr. Henshaw   Tom Gilleran as Tim McCaffrey
    Charles Meredith as the judge   Darlene Tompkins as the girl
    Tom Begley as the security guard   Paul Bradley as the attorney
    Teleplay written for *Alfred Hitchcock Presents* by Harold Swanton, based on a
story by William C. Morrison.
    Directed by Paul Henreid.
    (mummy, museum) *Good evening. This object which looks like a gentleman who
innocently wandered into a red cross bandaging class, is a mummy. This particular one is
an Egyptian Pharaoh, and was buried with all his wives. A rather extreme example of
togetherness. A few of his more progressive colleagues, subscribe to this custom,* (close-up)
*but with a difference. They buried their wives first, promising to follow at their earliest
convenience. Appropriately enough the title of tonight's theatre piece is "Museum Piece."
First, however, we have an item with no title but perhaps after watching it, you can think of a
name to call it.*

Story: After finishing a tour at a museum of Indian artifacts one evening, Clay Hollister meets Mr. Clovis, an archeo-psychologist, whose primary interest are the bones of a young Caucasian male, on display here at the museum. In fact, Mr. Clovis gives so much accurate information about the skeleton, that Clay is inspired to tell him the truth. It seems that Clay's son was falsely accused of committing a murder, and with an election coming on, Mr. Henshaw, the District Attorney, intended to see the boy convicted. Having been sentenced to the State Penitentiary for life, Clay unsuccessfully pleaded for mercy with Henshaw. As a result of losing interest in life, the boy died two months later. Mr. Clovis, however, has a confession. He's actually a detective from the District Attorney's office, searching for the body of Mr. Henshaw, who disappeared shortly after the boy's death. Hollister confesses that he killed Henshaw, and when Clovis starts asking questions about it, Clay stabs him in the back, giving him yet another set of bones to add to his collection.

Unfortunately the police took a dim view of the old curator, personally adding a new exhibit for the museum. Sometimes I find the attitude of the authorities puzzling. They seem bent on stifling initiative. But enough of that. Now we shall watch while my sponsor makes an exhibition of himself. (commercial break) *That is all until next week, when we return with another story. Perhaps we shall put our gift-wrapped friend back in his box.* (reads inside of sarcophagas) *His last will? No. "Listen for dial tone before depositing money." Good night.* (goes in and closes sarcophagas)

Trivia, etc. Actor Edward C. Platt played the role of Victor Larrabee, Thornhill's Attorney in Alfred Hitchcock's *North by Northwest* (1959). Darlene Tompkins was the niece of actress Beverly Washburn, who played Lisbeth Searcy in Walt Disney's *Old Yeller* (1957). Tompkins began her Hollywood career appearing in television commercials, and an Elvis Presley movie, *Blue Hawaii* (1961). During the 1970's, Thompkins was a stand-in and stuntwoman for Cheryl Ladd on the television series *Charlie's Angels*.

EPISODE #217 **"COMING, MAMA"** Broadcast on April 11, 1961
    Starring: Eileen Heckart as Lucy Baldwin   Don DeFore as Arthur Clark
    Madge Kennedy as Mrs. Baldwin   Jesslyn Fax as Mrs. Evans
    Robert Karnes as Mr. Simon   Arthur Malet as Doctor Larsen
    Gail Bonney as Mrs. Clark
    Teleplay written for *Alfred Hitchcock Presents* by James P. Cavanagh, based on the short story of the same name by Henriette McClelland, originally published in the September 1960 issue of *Ellery Queen's Mystery Magazine*.
    Directed by George Stevens, Jr.
    (instant situation comedy) *Good evening. Tonight we have another treat for those of you who enjoy a peek behind the scenes. I'm sure most of you imagine that years of thought and work go behind the creation of a television situation comedy series. You are absolutely correct. However, modern science has managed to destill and concentrate all this work into this small package. Instant situation comedy. All you do is to add water. You don't even have to stir. Contains the ingredients for a complete cast together with recorded laughter and a large supply of the following: Retorts, witty. Replies, devastating. Quips, modest. Reproofs, parental. Mots, bons and takes, double. All that is necessary is to slice the results into thirty-nine segments.* (pours on the floor and adds water, explosion, four people appear up in the smoke) *That is what I would term, a population explosion.*

Story: Although Lucy Baldwin is getting up in years, she gets a marriage proposal from Arthur Clark, a casual male acquaintance. Lucy's problem is trying to figure out what to do with her overbearing mother, who objects to the union. When Mrs. Baldwin fakes being ill, Lucy decides to give her one nightly dose of sleeping tonic, which proves fatal. The tonic is overlooked by the police and the doctor, who believe the old woman died from natural causes. Before long, Lucy is free to marry, but after she ties the knot, she finds that

Arthur's mother is a domineering female who is a near-duplicate of her recently deceased. Arthur breaks the bad news that his mother is ill and she must stay with them for a while (perhaps longer). But that presents no problem, as Lucy knows the perfect sleeping tonic.

That may not have been situation comedy for Lucy, who was caught on her next try, but perhaps the rest of you found it amusing. I shall be back after the following, which is designed to sober you up. (commercial break) *Next week, our situation comedy takes place in far off Denmark. Junior overhears a scrap of conversation and quite naturally jumps to the conclusion that his uncle murdered his father in order to marry his mother. This amusing misunderstanding leads to a great number of hilarious situations, and to the death of all four principles. I'm sure you'll enjoy it. So tune in next week when we present, "Junior Sees a Ghost." Good night.*

EPISODE #218 **"DEATHMATE"** Broadcast on April 18, 1961
           Starring: Lee Philips as Ben Conant / Freddie Sheldon
           Gia Scala as Lisa Talbot   Russell Collins as Alvin Moss
           Les Tremayne as Peter Talbot   Ann Staunton as the lady by elevator
           Teleplay written for *Alfred Hitchcock Presents* by Bill S. Ballinger, based on the short story of the same name by James O. Causey, originally published in the March 1957 issue of *Manhunt.*
           Directed by Alan Crosland, Jr.
           (guillotine) *Good evening. Because the television screen distorts the human figure, some people have the mistaken idea that I'm larger than the average. I can only say that if you think I am large now, you should see me before taxes. No doubt inspired by this impression, a well-meaning viewer has sent me a reducing machine. However, it is so unique I want to share it with you. It is amazingly successful in cutting off those extra pounds. As you see, this is a revolutionary concept in weight reduction.* (close-up) *These exquisite machines come in a number of sizes. This is the Madame LaFarge model. Except for two knitting needles, it has no extras at all. From this they are variously priced up to the salon size, which comes with a parking lot for tumbrils and a small crowd to jeer and spit at you. I'm certain you will agree that the advertisements for the salon model do not exaggerate when they say it is fit for a king. But we have a dramatic show to present. If I were a critical man, I would say the production could be vastly improved, by some judicious pruning, for example this.*

Story: Ben Conant is a con artist sleeping with a married woman, whose wealthy husband has turned into an alcoholic. Ben is startled one day when he discovers a detective following him. Believing Lisa's husband is to blame, he informs her, and the two decide to kill the drunk. To make his death look natural, Ben tries to bring on a second heart attack by starting a confrontation that surprisingly leads to a fight. After knocking Peter out, Ben drags his body to the bathroom and puts him in a filled bathtub, making plans to tell the police that he had a heart attack and drowned. The detective arrives and doesn't fall for the story, as it was Lisa who actually hired him. It also turns out that Lisa's husband never had a previous heart attack. With Lisa now set to inherit her husband's fortune, it seems that she out-conned the con man.

By the way, Lisa and Ben Conant did not get married, if any of you are wondering. Her studies would not permit it. She's working on an advance degree at a large state penitentiary, where she must remain in residence some twenty years. I know many of you would like to see me use this machine. I shall do so in just one minute or faster than my sponsor can say . . . (commercial break) *(using the guillotine as a work-out machine) Next week we shall be back with another story. In answer to requests for these machines, I would like to announce, that they are available in all French Revolutionary war-surplus stores. Good night.*

EPISODE #219 **"GRATITUDE"** Broadcast on April 25, 1961

Starring: Peter Falk as Meyer Fine Paul Hartman as John Ingo
Edmund Hashim as Frank Mazzotti John Dennis as Joe Dunphy
Bert Remsen as the police lieutenant Karl Lukas as Otto
Adam Stewart as Avery H. Combs, Jr.
Phil Gordon as Frank, the bartender Clegg Hoyt as Hubert
Forrest Lederer as a croupier Janos Czingula as the investigator
Based on a story by Donn Byrne (a.k.a. Brian Oswald Donn-Byrne), and adapted for *Alfred Hitchcock Presents* by William Fay.
Directed by Alan Crosland, Jr.

(in a western saloon) *Good evening ladies and gentleman. Welcome to Alfred Hitchcock Presents. After many years on television, I've just learned that we open our show incorrectly. These days, good form demands that you begin with a provocative and exciting scene, designed to enchant and entice the viewer. This scene is called the teaser. Always eager to embrace new ideas after others have thought of them, we present tonight's teaser. The time 1878. The place, Tombstone, Arizona.* (bartender: *What's a pretty school teacher like you doing in a place like this?* Big gunfight erupts, scene freezes) *After seeing that I'm sure you won't want to miss our story. Which takes place entirely in New York City in the year 1916.* (Hitchcock waves to the bartender for a drink)

Story: Four days before Christmas, wealthy gambling club owner Meyer Fine believes he has it made. John Ingo, Meyer's faithful servant, is no exception. Although he cannot explain why, Meyer believes death is lingering over his head, but he confides his premonition only to John. Soon disaster occurs when a young man who looses a fortune in the casino, commits suicide out in the streets. The police start turning their attention toward all the clubs in town. To make matters worse, one of Meyer's thugs kills a man for photographing the casino, and the photographer turns out to be a detective. With the police putting the heat on all the gambling joints, all the other racketeers plan to kill Meyer in retaliation, and almost succeed. With the worst on his shoulders, Meyer realizes it would be best if he committed suicide, but he just doesn't have the courage. Instead, his valet does the job for him . . . a last gesture of gratitude, faithful to the very end.

This concludes our story for tonight. We shall give you a scene from our next tale, immediately after this preview of next week's commercials. (commercial break) *I've been asked to announce that next week's commercials will be just as witty, just as engrossing, just as exciting and entertaining as that last one. And now before I say good night, here is that scene from next week's play. The time: 1879. The place: Fargo, North Dakota. Scene: from the saloon.* (same scene from beginning, Man to girl: *Didn't I meet you once in Tombstone Arizona?* Fight starts again. Hitchcock shrugs his shoulders when fight stops.)

EPISODE #220 **"THE PEARL NECKLACE"** Broadcast on May 2, 1961

Starring: Hazel Court as Charlotte Jameson Rutherford
Ernest Truex as Howard Rutherford Jack Cassidy as Mark Lansing
Michael Burns as Billy Lansing (10 yrs. old)
David Faulkner as Billy Lansing (20 yrs. old)
Diane Webber as "the other woman" Shirley O'Hara as the maid
An original teleplay written for *Alfred Hitchcock Presents* by Peggy and Lou Shaw.
Directed by Don Weis.

(fountain of youth) *Good evening, ladies and gentlemen and boys and girls. I'm seeking the fountain of youth. Unfortunately, I've had absolutely no luck at all. I keep finding oil instead. Of course, oil has its good points too. It may not make you young, but it can make old age much more tolerable. My task is made more difficult because I don't know what to expect. When searching for the fountain of youth, one doesn't know whether to look for a milk bar or a water pistol. While I continue my search suppose you watch tonight's story. It was especially written to illusidate our theme.*

Story: Millionaire Howard Rutherford has a confession, and shares it with his secretary, Charlotte. His doctor says he has only a year to live, and to enjoy his remaining months, he wants to marry her. When he is gone, she will inherit his fortune and she can then marry her real fiancé, Mark. Mark thinks it is a good idea, so Charlotte marries Howard. But for reasons unknown, the old man continues to live year after year. Mark eventually starts seeing someone off the side and even has a son as a result. When Charlotte learns about Mark's son, she takes a special interest in the boy, paying for an expensive education and much more. Finally, after twenty-five years Howard dies, and Mark believes that the now refined and cultured - and fabulously rich - Charlotte will marry him. Instead, she infuriates him with her decision to uphold the Rutherford tradition by marrying someone much younger, his son – who happens to be a spitting image of a younger Mark.

I'm sure you will agree that Charlotte's marriage to her young man has a very good chance of success. They have at least one thing in common, Mark. This is the famed fountain of youth. It must be very powerful stuff indeed. I had to show my draftcard to get in here. I haven't noticed any change. I think I'll have another and rejoin you in a minute. (commercial break) (nurse with baby in pram) *"He says night, night, 'til next week."*

EPISODE #221   **"YOU CAN'T TRUST A MAN"**   Broadcast on May 9, 1961
   Starring: Polly Bergen as Crystal Coe Joe Maross as Tony
   Frank Albertson as George Wyncliff   Walter Kinsella as the police lieutenant
   Claire Carleton as Pauline, the servant Andy Romano as the police officer
   Keith Britton as the gas station attendant
   Teleplay written for *Alfred Hitchcock Presents* by Helen Nielsen, from her short story of the same name, originally published in the January 1955 issue of *Manhunt*. Subsequently anthologized in *Best Detective Stories of the Year*, ed. David C. Cooke (Dutton, 1955), and in *The Deadly Arts*. ed. Bill Pronzini and Marcia Muller (Arbor House, 1985).
   Directed by Paul Henreid.
   (waking up from a nightmare)   *Oh, good evening. I just had a terrible nightmare. It lasted only a minute but it was a shattering experience. Let me tell you about it before we see tonight's play. It was like a motion picture and as I watched a voice kept shouting at me . . .*

Story: Crystal Coe is a singer whose ex-con husband has just been released from prison. Actually, the sentence he served was for a crime she committed, but he took the rap, a fact he is not likely to forget. Crystal wants nothing to do with him, but he insists on moving back in, since they were never legally divorced. On the way back to her home, he explains that all he really wanted to do was make her sweat a little, as he wants nothing more to do with her. When they stop for gas, she slips the attendant a note to phone the police. Further down the road, a police car pulls in behind her. Crystal produces a gun, and explains that she'd rather eliminate the only proof of her past, and shoots Tony. She tells the officer that it was self-defense. The police believe her, since the stranger was an ex-con. But the tables are turned when Crystal later learns that Tony had patented a successful device, while in prison, that will make millions . . . which she can't get her hands on, since she is supposed to be a complete stranger to him. The police lieutenant explains that they'll have to do a lot of digging to find the stranger's beneficiary . . .

I just learned that nightmare I had was a commercial. I suppose one can't expect to get pleasant dreams for nothing. but I never realized before, that they were sponsored.

Now that you know, there is no escape in sleep, perhaps you'll watch the following electronic nightmare. Please do not be frightened. I shall be right here all the time. (commercial break) *That is all for tonight. Now you're on your own. So until next week at the same time, pleasant dreams.*

Trivia, etc. Former host of *The Polly Bergen Show* and *The Pepsi-Cola Playhouse*, Polly Bergen plays a stage singer with a hidden past. In reality, Polly Bergen was a singer years before she began a major acting career. She was a cantina singer in *Across the Rio Grande* (1949) and was the uncredited voice of the juke box singer in *Champion* (1949). Andy Romano, who played the role of the police officer, later became a rat pack member in half a dozen mid-1960's *Beach* movies such as *Beach Party* (1963), *Bikini Beach* (1964), and *Beach Blanket Bingo* (1965). Romano made his first of eight appearances on the Hitchcock program, more than half were as police officers. One interesting bit of casting was his portrayal of the law officer, since he played Detective Joe Caruso in television's *Get Christie Love!*, Warren Briscoe in *Hill Street Blues*, and Inspector Aiello on *NYPD Blue*.

EPISODE #222 **"THE GLOATING PLACE"** Broadcast on May 16, 1961
One of the days of filming was April 7, 1961.

Starring: Susan Harrison as Susan Harper Henry Brandt as Lieutenant Palmer
Erin O'Brien-Moore as Mrs. Linda Harper King Calder as Phil Harper
Marta Kristen as Marjorie Stone Tom Gilleran as Tom, the student
David Fresco as the photographer Tyler McVey as Sergeant Steve Morten
Monica Henreid as a student Eve McVeagh as Eve, the reporter

Teleplay written for *Alfred Hitchcock Presents* by Robert Bloch, from his short story of the same name, originally published in the June 1959 issue of *Rogue*. Subsequently collected in *Blood Runs Cold* (Simon & Schuster, 1961; Robert Hale, 1962).
Directed by Alan Crosland, Jr.

(ice cream) *Good evening, and welcome to the Hitchcock Youth Center. It is designed to keep the children off the streets. We've been very successful so far. Some of my concoctions not only keep the children off the streets, they make it impossible for the darlings to move out of the booths. I'm putting the finishing touches on my specialty now. It contains seven scoops of chocolate ice cream, three of strawberry over a large rum cake, sliced bananas, strawberries, ground nuts, maraschino cherries, maple fudge syrup and a marshmallow topping. Sweetened to taste. It is called dieters delight. It's for those who are on a 900 calorie a day diet. This contains exactly 6,400 calories. Just one week's supply. Here comes the customer. Being rolled up to the fountain now.*

Story: Susan Harper wants to be famous more than anything in the world, so she fakes an attack from a mugger and fabricates a story about a masked attacker, which the local newspaper publishes. The story makes her an instant celebrity about town, but then someone's climbing accident takes over the headlines in the papers. So to receive more attention, she takes a friend to the same spot she was supposed to have been attacked and strangles her. The newspapers put her in the limelight again, with the reporters raising suspicion of a killer on the loose, and Susan being the only surviving victim. When the press starts dying down, she returns to the spot to try to come up with something new, and unbeknownst to her, a masked attacker grabs her and strangles the life from her. Her name will appear in the headlines again, but for a final time.

We'll have to conclude our story, since we seem to have lost our leading lady. The police arrived on the scene a few moments later and arrested her assailant, but this offered Susan very little consolation. I see someone putting a coin in the jukebox. I know better than to try to talk above it. I shall continue in a moment. (commercial break) *That is all for tonight. I hope to see you next week, when the special will be our frosted tutti frutti, cherry crush, marshmallow, fudge ecstasy. Until then, good night and pleasant dreams.* (puts up "closed" sign and start eating ice cream)

Trivia, etc. In this episode, Susan Harper attends a fictional "Shamley High School," named after Hitchcock's summer home "Shamley Green" in England, and the production company which produced the Hitchcock episodes. The March 6. 2000 issue of *People* magazine confirmed that actress Susan Harrison is the mother of Darva Conger, the instant bride in *Who Wants to Marry A Multi-Millionaire?*, a controversial Fox-network "reality-TV" program that aired in February 2000.

EPISODE #223 **"SELF DEFENSE"** Broadcast on May 23, 1961

Starring: George Nader as Gerald A. Clarke   Audrey Totter as Mrs. Phillips
Steve Gravers as Lieutenant Schwartz   David Carlile as Detective Lou
Jesslyn Fax as Mrs. Gruber, liquor store clerk   Selmer Jackson as the priest
Bob Paget as Jimmy Phillips, the robber
Alexander Lockwood as Henry Willet
An original teleplay written for *Alfred Hitchcock Presents* by John T. Kelley.
Directed by Paul Henreid.

(with a boxer) *Good evening, ladies and gentlemen. Tonight's topic is self-defense. A matter of importance to everyone, especially the ladies. The first rule is to be suspicious of strangers, especially if they are stripped to the waist and have arranged mattresses on the floor in advance. In nine cases out of ten, they are jiu-jitsu instructors. Put out your hand and appear to be friendly, then pick out a corner of the room.* (boxer seen thrown to the corner of the ring) *I have a feeling I'm not going to pass this course. I won't tell him why it was he couldn't throw me, he was standing on my foot. Now our story follows this one minute attack on your sensibilities against which there is no defense.*

Story: Stopping inside a liquor store one evening, Gerald Clarke finds himself the victim of a robbery when a young man turns his gun on Clarke. When the kid tries to make a getaway, Clarke grabs the storekeeper's gun and shoots the kid three times. When the police arrive, they find that the boy's gun was unloaded, but they let Clarke go, logically believing it was all in the act of self-defense. Hours later, the boy dies at the hospital and Clarke, meeting up with the child's mother at the police station, feels guilty about what happened. He offers the grieving family to help by paying for the funeral. The boy's mother seeks him up later that evening, at Clarke's apartment, and when she learns how frightened he was at the time, she pulls a gun on the man. Clarke just stands in fear, but after hearing him plead his innocence, she confesses that she was only trying to learn the truth. She only meant to scare him, but as she goes to leave, Clarke grabs the gun and shoots her dead, saying "I told you not to point a gun at me!"

I realize it's impolite to point, but Gerald's reaction was a trifle drastic. I think you too will be glad to know that he was subsequently apprehended as he emptied his revolver into the figure of uncle Sam in an Army recruiting poster. And now, I shall be back after this word from a very pruent gentleman, who points with pride, but only to himself. (commercial break) *That is all we have to offer tonight. We shall be back next week with more of the same.* (Hitchcock standing on boxer) *Until then, good night.*

EPISODE #224 **"A SECRET LIFE"** Broadcast on May 30, 1961

Starring: Ronald Howard as James Howgill   Mary Murphy as Estelle Newman
Patricia Donahue as Margery Howgill   Arte Johnson as Mr. Bates
Addison Richards as Crandall Johnson
Florence MacMichael as Mrs. Hackett   Meri Welles as Kathleen Perry

Teleplay written for *Alfred Hitchcock Presents* by Jerry Sohl, based on the short story of the same name by Nicholas Monsarrat, originally published in a 1959 issue of the *Saturday Evening Post*.

Directed by Don Weis.

(diving boat) *Good evening, ladies and gentlemen. Good evening, ladies and gentlemen.* (tries second time during noise) *Good evening, ladies and gentlemen. I hope you didn't mind that interruption. This trip was my sponsor's suggestion. He wanted to show off his diving prowess. You see, he's the gentleman who just went over the side. Now he's jerking on the line, I intend to ignore him. His messages are always the same, always just like this one coming up.*

Story: James Howgill is fed up with his job and hum-drum life, and tells his wife Margery that he wants a divorce. She refuses. James leaves her anyway and heads for Acapulco, where he leads a care-free existence, and meets a beautiful young girl that he falls in love with. Realizing that something must be done with Margery, he flies back to the United States to see his lawyer. The attorney tells James that his only hope now is to hire a detective to follow her, and perhaps find enough dirt for him to procure the divorce. Before long, detective Bates reveals that Margery *is* seeing another man, but as the detective continues telling James more about his wife, James becomes more and more interested in her. Unknown to James, Margery wasn't the woman the detective was following, but rather a woman who was sub-letting the house, and Margery just now returned home. Finding out the hard way, James realizes that he is right back where he started from.

Those of you who admire our dear sponsor as much as I, will be glad to know he's approaching a record for staying under water without air. He left this note to be opened in the event he didn't return. Let's have a look at it. (commercial break) *That sneaky sponsor of ours came up on the other side of the boat. He holds me responsible for the defective equipment. Next week I shall be back with another story. Actually, I suspect I'll be here all week. Until then, good night.*

EPISODE #225   **"SERVANT PROBLEM"**   Broadcast on June 6, 1961

Starring: Jo Van Fleet as Molly Goff   John Emery as Kerwin Drake
Kathryn Givney as Mrs. Colton   Grandon Rhodes as Mr. Harold Standish
Alice Frost as Mrs. Standish   Bartlett Robinson as Mr. Colton
Jane A. Johnston as the secretary   and Joan Hackett as Sylvia Colton

An original teleplay written for *Alfred Hitchcock Presents* by Henry Slesar, which was later published as a short story entitled "Servant Problem," in *A Crime for Mothers and Others* (Avon, 1962).

Directed by Alan Crosland, Jr.

(blows a whistle) *Good evening. I've decided to take up touch football. I understand it's the thing to do. The players are perfect gentlemen. That penalty was not for them. It was a clipping penalty and was called on an over zealous popcorn salesman, whom I caught short changing a customer. He'll be penalised five cents. However, he's the best man they have. I'm sure he'll make it up on the next play. I - I see by the clock that we have time for just one more play before the half-time show. Which is entitled "Servant Problem."*

Story: On the night Kerwin Drake plans an important dinner party with his publishers, just about everything goes wrong. His cook takes ill, so Kerwin's secretary throws together some food before leaving for the evening. Then his wife, intoxicated with liquor, whom he had walked out on twenty-two years ago, suddenly shows up and demands to stay. He tries to explain the situation, but she won't leave, so he orders Molly to stay in the upstairs guestroom. When the guests arrive, Molly makes an appearance so Kerwin tries to pass her off as the cook. Once the party is over, and the guests leave, he tries again to get rid of Molly, despite her threats to make trouble for him. Molly insists that she stay, not as a servant, but as his wife. Infuriated, Kerwin strangles the life out of her. Unfortunately, his timing left something to be desired, as the guest who met the "cook" earlier in the evening has returned to see if she could hire Molly, only to witness the whole murder.

Before we continue our game, I must tidy up the story a bit. Kerwin Drake was put on trial for his crime and the judge threw the book at him. Which was exactly what Mr. Standish did to his wife. But in that case, it was the cook book. Please rejoin me after this brief, institutional announcement. (commercial break) *Good night, until next week. Now I must get back to the touch football game.* (whistle) *Touché, touché.*

EPISODE #226 **"COMING HOME"** Broadcast on June 13, 1961
> Starring: Crahan Denton as Harry Beggs   Jeanette Nolan as Edith
> Susan Silo as Angela, the girl   Robert Carson as the warden
> Kreg Martin as Lucky, the bartender
> Harry Swoger as the prison cashier   Josie Lloyd as the bank teller
> Syl Lamont as the silent man   Gil Perkins as the bus driver

Teleplay written for *Alfred Hitchcock Presents* by Henry Slesar, based on his 1961 short story "You Can't Blame Me." originally published in the May 1961 issue of *Alfred Hitchcock's Mystery Magazine.* Subsequently collected in *A Crime for Mothers and Others* (Avon, 1962) as "Welcome Home," and in *Death on Television* (Southern Illinois University Press, 1989) as "Coming Home."

Directed by Alf Kjellin.

(body disposal unit) *Good evening, ladies and gentlemen. Do you find it tiresome waiting for cement to dry before dropping it in the river? If so, you'll be interested in our new pre-fabricated body disposal units. At first glance this might appear to be a concrete telephone booth. It is far more useful. The body is placed in here. The two sides are bolted together. It is taken to the edge of the dock and then. . .* (pushes) *All very neat and tidy. You ladies will love it. No more messy mixing and pouring of concrete. No more complicated and expensive equipment. No more tell-tale cement on the soles of your shoes. For details please consult your friendly neighborhood hood.* (close-up) *Now for a sixty-second consultation with our sponsor. Definitely not a hood. This man's record is spotless. After all, boring people to death is not yet a criminal offense.*

Story: Having spent many years in prison for a convicted robbery, Harry Beggs is a changed man. Having been recently released, one of the first things he wants to do is phone his wife, and tell her that he's coming home. But after calling her, he has second thoughts and hangs up. Instead, he plans to use the $1,600 he saved over the years to start over. Stopping at a bar for a drink to wash away his indecisions, he meets a pretty young girl and together, the two drink to the future. When he sobers up, he discovers the young girl gone, and his money stolen. Now penniless, Harry goes to his wife's apartment and she reluctantly lets him in. As they embrace, the apartment door opens and the pretty girl from the bar enters - who turns out to be his daughter, now grown up, and following in the footsteps of her dad.

I know the more cynical of our audience will object to the unabashed sentimentality of our story's conclusion. But I'm sure most of you enjoy seeing a loving family together, once more under one roof. I shall return to discuss this after the following. (commercial break) *Now I must show you our economy size. The only difference being that the victim must be allowed to stiffen, so that he can stand erect. Then his feet are placed in here and the concrete pieces bolted together. If you don't wish to be splashed, you just aim the gentleman toward the end of the dock. And . . . rollerskates. We think of everything. Until next week. Good night.*

Trivia, etc. Besides directing episodes of *Bonanza, Dr. Kildare* and this one episode of *Alfred Hitchcock Presents* (he would later direct eleven episodes of *The Alfred Hitchcock Hour*), Alf Kjellin was also an actor, occasionally using the stage name of Christopher Kent. He played the role of Leon Dupuis in *Madame Bovary* (1949), and short performances on *Mission: Impossible* and *Combat*. He also played the small role of Edwin Volck in *The Alfred Hitchcock Hour* episode "Don't Look Behind You." Jeanette Nolan and Crahan Denton also worked together in an episode of television's *Have Gun – Will Travel*.

EPISODE #227 "FINAL ARRANGEMENTS"   Broadcast on June 20, 1961

Starring: Martin Balsam as Leonard Compson   Vivian Nathan as Elsie Compson
O. Z. Whitehead as Mr. Simms   Slim Pickens as Mr. Bradshaw
Bartlett Robinson as Dr. Maxwell   Susan Brown as the secretary
George Kane as the pharmacist   Bryan Russell as Billy Howard, the boy

Teleplay written for *Alfred Hitchcock Presents* by Robert Arthur, based on the short story of the same name by Lawrence A. Page, originally published in the July 1961 issue of *Alfred Hitchcock's Mystery Magazine*. Subsequently reprinted in *Alfred Hitchcock's Tales to Keep You Spellbound*, ed. Eleanor Sullivan (Davis Publications, 1976) and in *Alfred Hitchcock: The Best in Mystery*, ed. Alfred Hitchcock (Galahad Books, 1980).

Directed by Gordon Hessler.

(at an assembly line) *Good evening. We decided to utilize assembly line methods in the making of our shows. Mine is the last operation. You will notice one of our productions coming along now. A sprinkle or so of saccharine, a little pruning, one, two commercials, three commercials. I . . . Here's another one. I can see this is going to keep me quite busy. In the meantime, suppose you look at one of the finished products.*

Story: Leonard Compson is stuck with an obnoxious, overbearing wife who drives him crazy. Driving over to the Simms Mortuary, a local funeral home, Leonard orders an expensive casket, part of their "Supremacy Service." While there, he tells the funeral director to keep the casket for him until he contacts him again. His wife, in the meantime, continues to nag Leonard all evening, almost to the breaking point. On the following day, Leonard returns to the Mortuary and hands the director his home address, including payment in full (cash), and instructs him to pick up the unnamed body at Leonard's, eight o'clock tomorrow night. The funeral director finds this odd, but business is business, and agrees to the strange arrangement. The next afternoon, Leonard quits his job and returns home to mix a lethal dose of rat poison in a glass of milk. His wife, having heard that Leonard quit his job, bitches about their up-coming financial problem, which causes Leonard to rage. Raising his voice, the first time in many years, Leonard tells his wife that he's had enough. The doorbell rings and Leonard orders her to open the door. When the funeral director introduces himself, the shrew turns around to find Leonard lying on the floor dead, having drank the glass of milk.

I would like to make it clear that the appearance of a suicide on our program, in no way constitutes an endorsement of this, as a solution to life's problems. There are many better means to get out of a difficult situation. Money for example. And now I shall return in a moment. (commercial break) *That is all for tonight. I wonder if we could leave out commercials now and then?* (line stops) *Big brother never sleeps. Good night.*

EPISODE #228 "MAKE MY DEATH BED"   Broadcast on June 27, 1961

Starring: Diana Van Der Vlis as Mrs. Elise Taylor
James Best as Bishop 'Bish' Darby   Jocelyn Brando as Mrs. Della Hudson
Biff Elliott as Doc Bob Hudson   Alexander Lockwood as the sheriff
Joe Flynn as Ken Taylor   Madeleine Sherwood as Jackie Darby
Judy Erwin as little Maddy Darby   Dennis Rush as little Bob Darby

Teleplay written for *Alfred Hitchcock Presents* by Henry A. Cogge, based on the short story of the same name by Babs H. Deal, originally published in the April 1960 issue of *Alfred Hitchcock's Mystery Magazine*. Subsequently anthologized in *Best Detective Stories of the Year*, ed. Brett Halliday (Dutton, 1961), and *A Mystery by the Tale*, ed. Cathleen Jordan (Davis Publications, 1986).

Directed by Arthur Hiller.

Good evening fellow creatures. This evening we are making a daring experiment. We shall present a blank screen and let your imagination fill in the picture. (lady) *Since I have no idea what you are thinking, I have no idea what you are seeing. I understand a good many men watch our show. Of course, I'm sure their wives occasionally peek in from the kitchen* (lady disappears), *but when they see the show hasn't begun they return to their work.* (back again) *I'm afraid our experiment may be getting out of hand* (lady starts taking her clothes off). *I shall ask our sponsor to fill the screen with his own wholesome, untroubled thoughts. This is especially designed for those of you with nothing at all on your mind.* (takes skirt off)

Story: Bishop Darby and Elise Taylor fall in love at a New Year's Eve party. The only problem is that they are both already married to someone else. Darby's wife, Jackie, realizes something is going on behind her back, so she puts poison in his saccharine and before leaving for a few days to visit with her parents, instructs Elise to check that he sticks to his diet. But after she leaves, Elise's husband, Ken, catches the lovebirds together and shoots Bishop dead. Elise goes into shock and Della fixes her some coffee to calm down, and Elise uses some of the saccharine. She starts feeling ill and helps herself to another cup of coffee. When Jackie hears that her husband has died, she assumes that he was poisoned and confesses to the crime. When she hears that he was shot, she suggests that they better do something about that saccharine, but it's too late. Elise is already dead.

Oh well, we all make mistakes. Poor Jackie Darby had no way of telling that her rival shared her husband's diet. Now here's another commercial after which I shall return. (commercial break) *Some of you have inquired about the small bullet holes in the commercial you have just witnessed. This should explain. The preceding film was selected and shown to the armed forces. Actually it was nothing, .30 caliber and under. But next time we hope to persuade the sponsor to make a personal appearance instead. Now until next week, good night.*

Trivia, etc. Babs H. Deal, the author whose story is adapted for this episode, was the wife of Borden Deal, whose stories were adapted for an earlier *Hitchcock* episode ("A Bottle of Wine" February 3, 1957). Babs either had or very much wanted to have an affair with a more popular mystery writer, John D. MacDonald, as we learned from the recent MacDonald biography, *The Red Hot Typewriter*.

Diana Van Der Vlis also starred in the television production of *Tactic*, directed by Alfred Hitchcock (see *Tactic* chapter). Alexander Lockwood, who played the sheriff in this episode, also played the uncredited role of Judge Anson B. Flynn in *North by Northwest* (1959), Emmerton in *The Wrong Man* (1956), a Marine in *Saboteur* (1942), and as a Parson in Hitchcock's final film, *Family Plot* (1976).

EPISODE #229   **"AMBITION"**   Broadcast on July 4, 1961

Starring: Leslie Nielsen as Rudy Cox	Harold J. Stone as Mac Davis
Ann Robinson as Mrs. Helen Cox	Bernard Kates as Lou Heinz
Harry Landers as Ernie Stillinger	Charles Arnt as George, the Mayor
Charles Carlson as Cliff Woodman	Howard McLeod as the lieutenant
Syl Lamont as the hood on the street	

Teleplay written for *Alfred Hitchcock Presents* by Joel Murcott, based on the short story of the same name by Charles Boeckman, originally published in the August 1960 issue of *Keyhole Mystery Magazine*.

Directed by Paul Henreid.

(with a talking bird) *Good evening, ladies and gentlemen. This is an associate of mine, Mr. Lloyd. Mr. Lloyd will introduce tonight's show.* (silence) *I've paid a great deal of money for this bird, but of course it will be worth it. He may even take over my work permanently, thus freeing me for other duties. Go ahead, Mr. Lloyd.* (silence) *Come now. "Good evening, ladies . . . Good evening, ladies and gentlemen." I don't understand it, he's been working regularly on a local radio station. Had a program of his own, as a news commentator. "Good evening, ladies and gentlemen." I'm afraid I'll have to do it myself. Ladies and gentlemen, welcome to Alfred Hitchcock Presents. Next on view is tonight's story "Ambition."*

Story: After learning that a mob informant has been found out, Rudy Cox, an ambitious D.A., is told by the mayor to stay off the case as he used to be friends with mobster Mac Davis. Mac and Ernie Stillinger, both mobsters, would rather see the informant dead. The mayor, knowing Rudy is an old friend of Mac's, suggests he back off because publicity might be bad for both of them. Mac pays Rudy a visit, suggesting the same thing, recalling how he saved the D.A.'s life during the war, and wants the favor paid back. Mac insists he's going straight, because of a girl, and throwing the whole organization in someone else's lap. The next morning, police pay Rudy a visit, breaking the bad (and good news). The informant was found murdered. Ernie claims he was playing cards with two other men at the time, and can prove his alibi. Mac claims he was with Rudy during the time, and the D.A., realizing that he has a chance to become state governor, takes the best course of action – and claims that he had no contact with Mac since he joined the D.A.'s office.

(the bird is hanging upside-down from a hook) *I'm afraid we didn't show you all of that story. Unfortunately, Helen discovered that two coffee cups had been used the night before, and became suspicious. And to save his marriage, poor Rudy had to tell the truth. Of course, his career was ruined. But that's the way life is . . . on television. Oh, oh. Have you ever observed that catastrophies usually come in threes? If this is true another commercial must be on the way. I shall rejoin you as soon as it seems prudent.* (commercial break; the perch is now empty) *Thank you for your kind attention. The garrulous Mr. Lloyd is no longer with us. He has answered a higher calling.* (bird on plate) *Next week we shall return with another story. Until then, good night.*

Trivia, etc. James Allardice, who wrote Hitchcock's presentations and closers, had some fun with this episode, when he thought up the idea of describing associate producer Norman Lloyd as "He may even take over my work permanently, thus freeing me for other duties," which technically described Lloyd's position. There also exists an alteranate ending to Hitchcock's closing remarks. It picks up where he says "Oh, oh," and with the bird still sitting on the perch, until he comes back from the commercial break.

As for the cast, Ann Robinson, who played the female lead in *War of the Worlds* (1953), recalled her work on the series: "I don't think I was in it for more than a few minutes. I remember on the very first day I was late and I was terribly late [laughs] and I don't know why. They all sat around a big table and they had this big read-through and rehearsal. And here I was, and there sat Norman Lloyd, who I was so impressed to meet, staring at me like 'I'm sorry I hired her,' and all because I was late! I was so embarrassed! And Leslie Nielsen was a very young man, and his hair wasn't white! I wasn't that too familiar with his work until after I had worked with him, then I realized, you know, that he was well-established."

"Nielsen had a big party the night before at his house," Robinson continued. "I remember him discussing it with someone, I'm not quite sure who it was, but he had drunk something called Kirsch – but it's a very sweet liqueur, which I had never heard of before.

And he had just felt awful! He said 'Never again will I ever have after-dinner drinks as sweet as liqueur like that!' And he had come to work that day and he commented that he felt absolutely horrible! He performed without any trouble but he complained terribly about his huge dinner party. They had all drunk this after dinner drink. But I was just sitting there listening to the conversation. And he said he felt terrible because nothing will make you feel worse than that – it was so sweet and you drink so much more after dinner, more than you usually do. And he had this large, large dinner party with all those guests at his house . . . *but he wasn't late!"*

SUMMER RERUNS

Summer reruns consisted entirely of episodes from season six.

July 11, 1961
   "Mrs. Bixby and the Colonel's Coat"
July 18, 1961 "The Landlady"
July 25, 1961 "A Crime for Mothers"
August 1, 1961
   "The Greatest Monster of Them All"
August 8, 1961
   "The Contest for Aaron Gold"
August 15, 1961 "Very Moral Theft"

August 22, 1961 "The Horseplayer"
August 29, 1961 "O Youth and Beauty!"
September 5, 1961 "A Woman's Help"
September 12, 1961
   "The Changing Heart"
September 19, 1961 "Coming Home"
September 26, 1961
   "You Can't Trust a Man"
October 3, 1961 "The Pearl Necklace"

(Photo courtesy of Ronald V. Borst / Hollywood Movie Posters)

351

SEASON SEVEN - (38 episodes)

SELECTED PRODUCTION CREDITS:
Art Directors: John J. Lloyd and Martin Obzina
Assistant Directors: Donald Baer, Les Berke, Ben Bishop, George Bisk,
James H. Brown, Edward K. Dodds, Frank Fox, Charles S. Gould,
Frank Losee, Ronnie Rondell and Wallace Worsley
Associate Producer: Norman Lloyd
Costume Supervisor: Vincent Dee
Directors of Photography: Neal Beckner, Dale Deverman, John L. Russell, a.s.c.
and John F. Warren, a.s.c.
Editorial Department Head: David J. O'Connell
Film Editor: Edward W. Williams, a.c.e.
Hair Stylist: Florence Bush
Makeup Artists: Jack Barron
Music Supervisor: Joseph E. Romero
Producer: Joan Harrison
Set Decorators: Glen L. Daniels, Julia Heron, John McCarthy and James S. Redd
Sound: Charles Althouse, Robert Bertrand, Earl Crain, Jr., Frank McWhorter, Roy Meadows,
David H. Moriarty, John W. Rixey, William Russell and Frank H. Wilkinson
Filmed at Revue Studios in Hollywood, California, in association with MCA-TV,
executive distributor for Shamley Productions, Inc.
Broadcast Tuesday over NBC-TV, 8:30 – 9 p.m., EST.
Alternating sponsors by Ford Motors and Revlon.

EPISODE #230   **"THE HATBOX"**   Broadcast on October 10, 1961
Starring: Paul Ford as Professor Jarvis   Billy Gray as Perry Hatch
Frank Maxwell as Lieutenant Roman   Jamie Brothers as Dan
Teleplay written for *Alfred Hitchcock Presents* by Henry Slesar, based on his short story "Murder Out of a Hat," originally published in the July 1961 issue of *Alfred Hitchcock's Mystery Magazine*. Subsequently collected in *A Crime for Mothers and Others* (Avon, 1962).
Directed by Alan Crosland, Jr.

(black board) *Good evening students. I have always felt that night school has a distinct advantage. People may not be able to learn more at night than in the day, but what they do learn is infinitely more interesting. Tonight's subject is phrenology. Miss Forbes?* (woman enters) *Phrenology is the system of psychology, based on the belief that the size and shape of the surface of certain regions of the body, have a relation to the function performed within that region. Uh, pull down the chart please. Thank you. This area, number six, is referred to by doctors and phrenologers as the forehead. This is the worry center. In the case of this individual, his forehead seems to have slipped down over his eyes. I'm sure many of you know that feeling.* (bell) *Oh dear, it's time for you to move on to the next class. You'd better hurry as you have just one minute to make the change. During that minute you will hear the voice of the head of this institution, urging you on to greater and greater achievement.*

Story: After Professor Jarvis catches his student Perry cheating on a test, the boy pleads unsuccessfully with the Professor, who intends to write a letter to his parents. Later that evening, Perry returns to see the Professor, hoping to plead his case again, but finds the man getting rid of a hat box belonging to his wife. Known as the original hen-pecked husband, the anatomy instructor claims his wife has been staying at her sister's for the past few weeks. But Perry theorizes that a woman wouldn't let her husband throw away a brand new hat – unless she was dead. Hoping to exact revenge, the student gets the police involved, who find out that the sister hasn't even seen Mrs. Jarvis in over a year. Finding this a little odd, Lieutenant Roman questions Jarvis, but the Professor changes the story and explains that he and his wife are separated. The investigating lieutenant can't find any proof to say otherwise, and believes the respectable Professor. After Lieutenant Roman has left, Jarvis takes out the hat and places it on a skeleton that hangs in his study, muttering, "Goodnight, Margaret."

In these days of creeping anti-intellectualism and anti-eggheadery we thought it would be wise to show the other side of the picture. But there are professors who outside the classroom, can be original and inventive and who lead interesting eventful lives. In short, that some of them are just like you and I. Our lecture continues after this brief footnote. (commercial break) *As it must to all men, the law caught up with Professor Jarvis. Thus ironically his wife Margaret again had the last word. Which is what I'm having now. Until next week then, good night.*

Trivia, etc. "The Hitchcock people bought forty-plus published stories from me, all of which were turned into teleplays," said Henry Slesar. "I wrote the majority of them eventually, and then did some originals. There were times when I wouldn't wait for a magazine publication, but sent the story directly to Hitchcock if I thought they would like it. On several occasions, they did."

Billy Gray, who played the role of Bud Anderson on television's *Father Knows Best* and young Bobby Benson in *The Day the Earth Stood Still* (1951), plays the role of student Perry Hatch in this, his only Hitchcock episode. Gray would later be involved in numerous "Speedway" Motorcycle Races as a competitor during the sixties, seventies and eighties. Gray is also the inventor of the F-1 guitar pick.

EPISODE #231 **"BANG! YOU'RE DEAD"** Broadcast on October 17, 1961
    Rehearsed and filmed on July 25 – 27, 1961.
    Starring: Steve Dunne as Rick Sheffield   Biff Elliott as Fred Chester
    Lucy Prentiss as Amy Chester   Juanita Moore as Cleo, the maid
    Marta Kristen as the Jiffy Snack Girl
    John Zaremba as the Supermarket Manager   Karl Lukas as the mailman
    Olan Soulé as Darlene's Dadd
    Craig Duncan as George Webster, the market clerk
    Thayer Burton as the cashier   and Billy Mumy as Jackie Chester
    Kelly Flynn as little Stevie   Dean Moray as little Gary
    Mary Grace Canfield as the lady customer at register 7 (uncredited)
    Teleplay written for *Alfred Hitchcock Presents* by Harold Swanton, based a short story by Margery B. Vosper.
    Directed by Alfred Hitchcock.
    (movie box office) *Good evening and welcome to Alfred Hitchcock Presents. The feature is about to commence. Please don't be alarmed, we are not charging admission. This is not pay-TV. As usual, all we ask is that on those occasions when you can't view our show that you let us know, so that we can send it to someone else. Please don't be a no-show.* (steps out of the booth) *This is not a hold up. I wish to dramatize the title of tonight's play.* (gun pops a "Bang" sign) *Tonight's story is called "Bang! You're Dead." Despite the fact that it has been introduced with my usual flippancy it concerns a very serious subject, and I would be doing you a dis-service if I led you to regard it lightly. Now I must hurry in to the theatre. For I don't want to miss the beginning. Fortunately, I have a minute to find my seat before the feature starts, for it is preceded by an unselected short subject. It's the management's way of discouraging those who might stay through more than one show.*

Story: Five-year-old Jackie Chester has a problem: the other kids in the neighborhood won't play with him because he doesn't have a gun like their own. The solution presents itself in the form of Uncle Rick, a world-wide traveller who always brings great gifts home to the family. Not waiting patiently for his gift, Jackie routes through his uncle's suitcase to find a great gun - in fact, the gun is real! Jackie goes outside without anyone realizing he has a weapon, and walks around the neighborhood, taking play shots with the gun, and pulling off the trigger several times while aiming at innocent people. As he continues to put more and more bullets in the gun, the risk gets greater. Returning home, Jackie aims the gun at the maid who won't play with him, and just as Rick - who, along with Jackie's parents, has been frantically searching for the boy – arrives, the gun goes off, narrowly missing the woman.

After an experience like that, we need something to break the spell and I have just the thing. I shall rejoin you in a moment. (commercial break) *On rare occasions we have stories on this program which do not lend themselves to levity. "Bang! You're Dead" is a case in point. We only hope that this play has dramatized for parents the importance of keeping firearms and ammunition out of reach of children. Accidents of this type occur far too frequently nowadays and the tragic fact is that with proper precaution they could be avoided. That is all for tonight. Please join us next week, when we shall return with another story. Until then, good night.*

Trivia, etc. Although they didn't know it at the time, child actor Billy Mumy would later star with Marta Kristen in television's *Lost in Space* years later. Mumy stated many times that while he admired Hitchcock's work, he detested the man himself, as Hitchcock was verbally abusive on the set. "I was a busy actor in those pre-'Lost in Space' days, and I was so very fortunate to work with/for such an eclectic batch of talent from Walt Disney to Rod Serling to Loretta Young, James Stewart, Jack Benny, Lucille Ball, and yes . . . Alfred Hitchcock," Billy Mumy recalled. "I'd ping pong back and forth from comedy to drama to fantasy and even sci fi . . . Working on the *Alfred Hitchcock Presents* shows was fine with the exception of one person . . . Alfred Hitchcock. He was cruel to me and I'll never forget one syllable of what he said to me while filming 'Bang You're Dead,' (which is quite a good show, and I'm glad I did it, and I'm proud to be a part of it). Anyway, as you know, I was in most of that episode, and you can only work a minor so many hours a day... they were about to 'lose' me for the day, and they wanted to get one more close up shot before I went home. Well, I'd been working all day, and I was fidgeting around as they tried to light me. Hitchcock rises out of his chair and slowly lumbers towards me. He was sweating. In my memory, he was always sweating. Several chins waggling, he approaches me in his black suit and leans down to whisper into my ear so that no one else can hear him but me, and this is EXACTLY what he said to me... 'If you don't stop moving about, I'm going to get a nail and nail your feet to your mark, and the blood will come pouring out like milk... so stop moving!' Well, I was truly terrified. They got their close up, and I went home for the day, and as we were leaving I told my mom all about how he wanted to nail my feet to my mark, and she laughed and said, 'Oh Honey, he's British. They have a different sense of humor.' Well, all he ever had to do was tell me he was just kidding. That he wouldn't really have nailed my feet to my mark. But he didn't, and he didn't because he knew that he scared the shit out of me, and he loved knowing that. Let's not forget the fact that I was seven years old at the time."

Billy Mumy also made a special appearance in the 1985 NBC-TV pilot movie *Alfred Hitchcock Presents*, in a remake of this same episode, but this time playing the role of a clerk in the supermarket.

EPISODE #232   **"MARIA"**   Broadcast on October 24, 1961

Starring: Norman Lloyd as Leo Torbey   Nita Talbot as Carole Torbey
Edmund Hashim as El Magnifico   Merry Anders as Lena
Kreg Martin as Benny, the cowboy
Marjorie Bennett as the elderly woman   Doug Carlson as the roustabout
with Venus De Mars as Maria Travatore   Billy Curtis as the circus midget

Teleplay written for *Alfred Hitchcock Presents* by John Collier, based on a story by John Wyndham.

Directed by Boris Sagal.

(space monkey) *Good evening, ladies and gentlemen. I shall resist the temptation to make tiresome comparisons with my sponsor. After all, I have no desire to hurt anyone's feelings. And my friend here is about to become one of our nation's heroes. You must have learned the news, he's been selected to go to the moon. He's not very excited about it, either that or his trousers are too tight again. Before we launch our brave little explorer, we have a training film to show him. You may watch too.*

Story: Leo Torbey, a carnival manager, wakes up after a drunken binge and finds himself the new owner of a female midget who dresses like a monkey and paints portraits. His wife is not amused by his purchase, and the midget, Maria, detests Carol as well - particularly because she is in love with Leo. In an attempt to break them up, Maria makes a painting of Carol and El Magnifico, one of the carnival stars, in a passionate embrace, although nothing actually happened between them. When Leo confronts her, Carol denies everything, but he doesn't believe her, packs her suitcase and forces her to leave. Later that day, Leo discovers his mistake. Confronting Maria, Leo learns of her feelings for him, and explains he has no further use for her. Selling the chimp to another carnival worker, Benny, Leo believes all his problems are solved, especially since his wife wrote to say she's coming back. Before she does, however, Leo is shot by Benny in cold blood. It seems Maria made another painting, this one of Leo and Benny's wife making love.

Tonight's story had a very happy ending for Maria. She went to Paris to study painting and is doing very well now, under a different name of course. Toulouse something, rather. As for Ben, his was a happy ending too, except that it has been delayed by a twenty-five year sentence. And speaking of interminable sentences, I shall return after this one. (commercial break) *I don't know how it happened, he simply out-witted me. I'm afraid to ask who's going to the moon now? Good night.*

EPISODE #233   **"COP FOR A DAY"**   Broadcast on October 31, 1961

Starring: Walter Matthau as Phil   Glenn Cannon as Davey
Carol Grace as the woman in the street   Bernard Fein as Marty Hirsch
Robert Reiner as Tom Spinelli, the first policeman
George Kane as Max Miller, the second policeman
Anatol Winogradoff as the delicatessen clerk   Susan Brown as the receptionist
Tom Begley as John Hessler, the bank messenger   Kathryna Dudley as Mary

Teleplay written for *Alfred Hitchcock Presents* by Henry Slesar, based on his short story of the same name, originally published in the January 1957 issue of *Manhunt*. Subsequently collected in *A Crime for Mothers and Others* (Avon, 1962), and in *Death on Television* (Southern Illinois University Press, 1989).

Directed by Paul Henreid.

(with a tea set)   *Good evening. So nice of you to come for tea. It's very pleasant to observe the amenities even in America. Unfortunately one of my other guests performed rather badly.* (dead man with broken cup) *He took one sip and fell to the floor like a common drunk. Not even a with your leave or a bye your leave. He just left, broke a piece of my good china, too. But what I shall never forgive him for, he took the cup of tea I had been saving for another guest. A dear friend of mine. Ah, here comes our guest now.*

Story: A big-time crook named Phil and his young accomplice Davey, rob and shoot a messenger of the National Bank in the street, and get away with $18,000 in cash. Two days later, the police hold a witness to the crime in protective custody. She claims she saw the whole scene and is willing to identify young Davey if she ever sees him. When the papers report that the messenger died from his wounds, the crooks realize they have to eliminate the young woman. Phil cleverly puts together a plan without revealing the details to his accomplice. Dressing up as a cop, he bluffs his way past the police guarding the witness, and once in her apartment. shoots her and makes a clean escape. Returning to his hideout, Davey sees him enter and thinking Phil is a cop, pulls out a gun and shoots him dead.

In case you are wondering, Davey was apprehended by the police. As for Phil, the police gave him an excellent funeral, after all he did die in uniform. As for Alfred Hitchcock, he'll be back presently. (commercial break) *That exhausts our supply of commercials, to say nothing of our audience. Next week we shall all reassemble, renewed and refreshed. Until that happy day, good night.*

Walter Matthau admires the realistic costumes for sale, in "Cop for a Day."

EPISODE #234   **"KEEP ME COMPANY"**   Broadcast on November 7, 1961
    Starring: Anne Francis as Julia Reddy
    Co-starring: Jack Ging as Detective Joe Parks
    Edmund Hashim as Marco Reddy / Harry Meland
    Anthony Hall as Sam Reddy   Billy Wells as Kenny Reddy
    Hinton Pope as the first policeman   Howard McLeod as the second policeman
    Teleplay written for *Alfred Hitchcock Presents* by Henry Slesar, based on his short
story, subsequently collected in *A Crime for Mothers and Others* (Avon, 1962).
    Directed by Alan Crosland, Jr.
    Good evening, ladies and gentlemen and welcome to . . . (masked robber walks in
for a hold-up) *Please, I'm quite busy, would you wait a moment? Welcome to Alfred
Hitchcock Presents. This evening we are presenting a drama entitled "Keep Me Company."
And now sir, what is it you wan't?* (whsipers) *If you insist.* (takes Hitchcock's wallet) *Do
you realize you're on television? That you're in full view of millions?* (whispers again) *He
says, business is bad and he needs the publicity. Some people have no shame. I say this in
reference not to the gentleman you have just seen, but to the one you are about to see.*

Anne Francis dresses up for an evening vistor in "Keep Me Company."

Story: Ever since Julia's husband, Marco, went into partnership with his two brothers, he's been working late almost every night. Julia tries to explain to her ignorant husband how lonely she is night after night. One evening she hears strange noises outside her window and phones the police, but when two policemen arrive they cannot anyone outside on the fire escape. This gives her an idea. Julia dolls herself up and again phones the police, claiming she saw a prowler outside, who this time sends over a detective. When he arrives, instead of being upset over an intruder, Julia tries to seduce him. Her husband comes home and when he catches a glimpse of the detective, he tries to make a break for it. The detective cuffs her husband, explaining that his picture is all over the department these days. It seems Marco is really called Harry Meland and his two accomplices have been ripping off warehouses at night, and thanks to her, he has finally been caught.

I think this should teach you men a lesson. Marco should have taken his wife with him. In that way he would not only have avoided arrest, but he and Julia would have had a shared experience to talk over in their declining years. And now appropriately enough, in the declining minutes of this program, a commercial, after which I shall return. (commercial break) *The police apprehended the gentleman who held me up earlier in the program. I'm very pleased of course. I didn't mind losing the wallet, but the money once belonged to a beloved aunt of mine. Next week I shall return with another story and possibly another on-screen hold-up. Until then, good night.*

Trivia, etc. Having previously played one of the gangsters' henchmen in the episode "Gratitude," and El Magnifico in "Maria," Edmund Hashim returned for a much larger role in his third and final appearance on the *Hitchcock* program. Anne Francis, who made five appearances on the *Hitchcock* series, recalled: "I never got to meet Alfred Hitchcock. I remember being called in to play whatever role they wanted me to do, good-girl or bad-girl. We had rehearsals in those days, which made work much easier. I later worked with Gladys Cooper in one of those Hitchcock's and she and I always broke up numerous times during the shoot. She was just adorable. She ate yogurt and swam each morning, which still amazes me. I just did too many different characters to recall specific moments during those shows."

EPISODE #235   **"BETA DELTA GAMMA"**   Broadcast on November 14, 1961
Starring: Burt Brinckerhoff as Alan   Duke Howard as Mark
Joel Crothers as Robert   Severn Darden as Franklin
Barbara Harris as Beth   Petrie Mason as Dodo
with Barbara Steele as Phyllis
An original teleplay written for *Alfred Hitchcock Presents* by Calvin Clements.
Directed by Alan Crosland, Jr.
(fraternity paddle)   *Good evening, brothers and sisters. This evening's story is concerned with higher education. Specifically with members of greek letter fraternities. I presume there are fraternities for other nationalities as well. This is a fra . . .* (turns it around) *is a fraternity paddle. Apparently they have very small canoes. In keeping with tonight's theme we shall first see a short educational film and then a story. As the story opens you will find the students hard at work, wrestling with the compact problems which face man in his neverending quest for truth.*

Story: At a college fraternity house, two students challenge each other to a beer-drinking contest. Alan accepts, drinking a whole pitcher of beer without stopping, and then flies off the handle when Mark concedes. Alan, however, is too drunk to do anything about it, passing out before anything serious happens. Deciding to pull off another prank, the other students put fake blood on Mark, and give him an injection that will make him appear to be dead. Then the kids place a bloody poker in Alan's hand, and leave quickly and quietly. When Alan wakes up, he puts one and one together, panics, and tries to cover up the murder by burying Mark out on the beach. not knowing his buddy is really alive. Sadly, after he learns the truth, Alan and the students return to the beach to find Mark's body, but by that time the tide has removed any trace of the location.

Yes, poor Alan left more than footprints in the sands of time. If you think college students don't learn anything, you are sadly mistaken. These people certainly learned something that night. They've never done anything like that again. They were assisted in their resolve by the police, for justice was meeted out to the pranksters. I have more to say but it can wait sixty seconds while our dear sponsor speaks to you on his favorite topic. (commercial break) *How he does go on. By the way, we would like it known that the foregoing story does not constitute a condemnation of fraternities or sororities or Greeks or Universities or young people or the sea shore or salt water or sand. I yield to no man in my affirm adherence to an uncompromising policy of offending no one. So, until next time, good night.*

EPISODE #236   **"YOU CAN'T BE A LITTLE GIRL ALL YOUR LIFE"**
    Broadcast on November 21, 1961

Starring: Dick York as Tom Barton	Carolyn Kearney as Julie Barton
Ted de Corsia as Lieutenant Christensen	Frank Milan as Dr. Vaughn
Howard Caine as Mr. Dahl	Bill Quinn as Mr. Dutton

    Teleplay written for *Alfred Hitchcock Presents* by Helen Nielsen, based on the short story of the same name by Stanley Ellin, originally published in the May 1958 issue of *Ellery Queen's Mystery Magazine.* Subsequently collected in *The Blessington Method and Other Strange Tales* (Random House, 1964; Macdonald, 1965) and in *The Specialty of the House and Other Stories* (Mysterious Press, 1979).
    Directed by Norman Lloyd.
    (big shoe)   *Good evening, ladies and gentlemen. Tonight as I promised you we are presenting a really big shoe. Our play is entitled "You Can't Be a Little Girl All Your Life," so we thought it would be appropriate to show you the home of one of our first and perhaps greatest child psychiatrists. But before we show you the story, we want to test your reflexes with this commercial. If on seeing it, you have the impulse to leave the room, you are absolutely normal.*

    Story: When Tom Barton comes home from work late one evening, he discovers that an intruder broke into his house and bruised his wife Julie. Tom phones the police but during routine questioning, they discover that she never got a good look at her attacker during the struggle. Julie is definitely sure that she ripped one of the man's gloves, when the intruder put his hand around her mouth. During a line-up, Julie is panic-stricken and although unsure of her choice, she does point out one man. Tom goes crazy, breaking his leg when he attacks the suspect. A few days later, after the incident seems resolved, Julie finds a torn glove in Tom's coat and confronts him about it. Tom confesses that he was the attacker, having done it after suffering a nervous breakdown from overwork at his job. Julie runs to get the police and Tom is not mobile enough to stop her, due to his recent injury.

    I was sorry to see the police catch up with Tom. I must say I can't blame him too much. After all, any woman who would deliberately mutilate a pair of her husband's gloves . . . I shall be back in just one minute. (commercial break) *That is quite enough for one night I'm sure. Next week you may be strong enough for more. By the way, this is the child psychiatrist I mentioned. Good night.* (lies down on the sofa with a child sitting beside him.)

EPISODE #237   **"THE OLD PRO"**   Broadcast on November 28, 1961

Starring: Richard Conte as Frank Burns	Sara Shane as Loretta Burns
Stacy Harris as Cullen	Richard Carlyle as Mace
and John Anderson as Nicholson	

Teleplay written for *Alfred Hitchcock Presents* by Calvin Clements, based on the short story of the same name by H.A. de Rosso, originally published in the December 1960 issue of *Manhunt*.

Directed by Paul Henreid.

(as a life guard) *Good evening, ladies and gentlemen, beach combers, sun worshipers, skin divers and other flotsam and jetsam, which may have washed ashore on the sandy wasteland of television. I have a new position now. I'm not certain I was cut out for this work. I can't swim but that doesn't bother me. What is embarrassing is that I can't even climb into the chair. I shall have to keep an eye on that gentleman to see that he doesn't go in over his head. While I'm doing that, why don't you keep your eye on this gentleman, our sponsor. To be followed by "The Old Pro," our story.*

Story: Loretta Burns has always spent her years believing her husband Frank was an engineer. If the truth be known, Frank was actually a hit man for the mob. Now retired, he used his payoffs to buy a beautiful lakefront home, and all goes well until a scheming blackmailer introduces himself, and threatens to tell Loretta all about Frank's true occupation. Frank easily knocks off the blackmailer, and his partner, which inspires Frank's ex-employer to demand that he return to his job. Otherwise, Loretta's fate will be none too pleasant . . .

This is all of our story. For Burns however, there was more. There were other jobs to be done. Then inevitably there was the job he didn't get away with. (close-up) *Which reminds me that time is catching up with me. One minute in particular, after which I shall reappear.* (commercial break) *I'm trying to get the young man we saw earlier, to tell me where he buried his father. However the boy's father is no longer my greatest concern. I think this demonstrates that although quicksand may be cheap, spreading it on a beach does not pay in the long run. Fortunately the boy doesn't seem to sink. Perhaps he doesn't weigh as much as I do. Young man don't stand there, run for help, please. Well, I won't have to worry about the sand anymore. I see the tide is coming in. So until next week, or later. Good night.*

Trivia, etc. John Anderson was also California Charlie, the car salesman in Alfred Hitchcock's *Psycho* (1960).

EPISODE #238   **"I SPY"**   Broadcast on December 5, 1961
Starring: Kay Walsh as Mrs. Morgan   Eric Barker as Mr. Al Frute
Cecil Parker as the lawyer   William Kendall as Captain Morgan
Elspeth Duxbury as Gladys   Nicholas Selby as the process server
Teleplay written for *Alfred Hitchcock Presents* by John Collier, based on the one-act stage play "I, Spy" by John Mortimer, originally collected in *Three Plays* (Elek Press, 1958; Grove Press, 1958).

Directed by Norman Lloyd.

(waiter, table) *Good evening patrons. May I recommend the specialty of the house? It's tipping. It seems odd to me that restaurant employees are called waiters, when it's the customers who do most of the waiting. . . but no matter. Our story du jour is called "I Spy" and takes place at an English seaside hotel. But before we serve it up, you must first wait just one minute.*

Story: London. Private detective Al Frute is hired by Captain Morgan to follow his wife, even though the two remain separated for a possible divorce. Morgan wants to know what she is up to, having suspicions that it involves other men. But the private eye himself ends up falling for Mrs. Morgan, unaware that he's under the payroll of her ex-hubby. A few days later, the Captain demands evidence about his wife's infidelity, so Frute supplies documentation of every possible transgression. The effect is exactly what he expected: Morgan decides to divorce her, making it possible for Frute to marry the woman.

I think that illustrates, that all things come to him who waits. And polishing silver doesn't hurt either. And now here is the commercial that comes with this story. Sorry, we don't allow substitutions. (commercial break) *That last certainly makes one long for a la carte television. Next week I shall return with a different story . . . and unless I'm more diplomatic, a different sponsor. Until then, good night.*

EPISODE #239 "SERVICES RENDERED"   Broadcast on December 12, 1961
   Starring: Steve Dunne as the young man
   Hugh Marlowe as Dr. Ralph Mannick   Percy Helton as Cyrus Rutherford
   Bert Remsen as Jimmy, the bartender   Karl Lukas as Uncle Ben
   Bernadette Hale as Miss Sherman, the nurse Tom Page as the man
   Ottola Nesmith as the woman   Andy Romano as the young workman
   Teleplay written for *Alfred Hitchcock Presents* by William Link and Richard Levinson, from their short story "No Name, Address, Identity," originally published in the July 1961 issue of *Alfred Hitchcock's Mystery Magazine*.
   Directed by Paul Henreid.
   (painted into a corner)   *Oh, good evening. I have always been deathly afraid of painting myself into a corner, but my precautions have been useless, you see I now remembered that this door I've been backing toward is a closet.* (a skeleton falls out) *Of course, it's always comforting to learn that others have made the same mistake but I wish he hadn't done that. Its ruined my floor. Now I shall have to spend the next few minutes re-painting and miss the first commercial and the opening of the story. I don't mind about the story, I've seen that, but the commercials come in sets of three and if you miss one it might be difficult to learn who the sponsor is.*

   Story: A young man is accidentally hit in the head by a wooden plank while passing a construction site, causing him to temporarily lose his memory. The only clue he has to his true identity is the name and address of a doctor scribbled on a piece of paper he has on him, and a thousand dollar bill. Going to Dr. Mannick for help, the physician suggests that seeing something familiar may jog his memory. Glancing at a photo the doctor has of his wife, does spark a little memory, and only after he leaves the doctor's office does he recall the true events of the case. It was Mrs. Mannick who paid him the one thousand dollars to kill her husband. Dutifully he returns to Dr. Mannick's office to let the good doctor know he did his job well, and then kills him.

   As you can see I'm making an effort to avoid a repetition of my recent experience. As for the story you have just seen, the state has put our young hero away so he won't be in any danger from falling scaffolding. But neither he nor anyone else can escape the following. If you survive, you will find me here. (commercial break) *There are times when a loss of memory might be a good thing.* (painted into a corner) (paints a door - and opens it) *Until next week at the same time, good night.*

   Trivia, etc. Levinson and Link are the creators of the television series *Columbo*, which starred Peter Falk (who also appeared in an episode of *Alfred Hitchcock Presents* and *The Alfred Hitchcock Hour*). A print of this episode is available for viewing at The Museum of Television and Radio, which offers the alternate version for non-American telecasts, where Hitchcock just says "Good night," instead of "Until next week at the same time, good night." A blooper was made in this episode. as the closing credits bill Hugh Marlowe as Dr. Mannix, but the name on the door of Marlowe's office reads "Ralph Mannick, M.D." In fact, this same mistake was made in the next episode: The closing credits bill Robert Redford as Charlie Pugh, when in fact the police calls him Charlie Marks in the play.

Another film goof in this episode: the doctor says his nurse left a few minutes ago, then later she comes in to say good-bye. Perhaps a mistake on the film editor's part.

EPISODE #240   "THE RIGHT KIND OF MEDICINE" Broadcast December 19, 1961
Starring: Robert Redford as Charlie Marks
Russell Collins as Mr. Fletcher, the pharmacist
Joby Baker as Vernon, the pharmacy clerk
Bernard Kates as George Lassiter, the witness   King Calder as the lieutenant
Bob Karnes as the sergeant *   Bert Remsen as Pete, the officer
Gage Clarke as Dr. Emmet Vogel   Harry Swoger as Mr. Grissom

Teleplay written for *Alfred Hitchcock Presents* by Henry Slesar, based on the short story "Never Cool a Cop" by Bill Ryder (pen name for Henry Slesar), originally published in the November 1958 issue of *Off Beat Detective Stories*. Subsequently collected in *A Crime for Mothers and Others* (Avon, 1962) as "The Right Kind of Medicine."

Directed by Alan Crosland, Jr.

(horse and blacksmith) *Good evening fellow villagers. I've been promised a chestnut tree, but it hasn't been delivered yet. The job came as a result of my answering an ad. I got it here somewhere. Let's see, here we are. Wanted: man with large and sinewy hands. The muscles of his brawny arms, strong as ironbands. Hair must be crisp, black and long. His face must be quite tanned, no salary guaranteed, he earns whate'er he can. I found the job very interesting and not difficult at all. This case for example, he doesn't need new shoes. He needs arch supports. From this bucolic scene, we move to an urban setting for tonight's drama. Less the contrast be to jarring for your sensibilities, we present the following, pleasantly, incongruous transition.*

Story: A young burglar named Charlie Marks (alias Charlie Grant), turns to his old friend Emmet Vogel, the neighborhood doctor, for help. It seems that Charlie was shot in the leg during a daring robbery, in which a police officer was shot to death. Although the bullet went right through, the pain is more than Charlie can stand. The doctor, not asking questions, mends the wound and offers a prescription to ease the pain, which Charlie picks up at the pharmacy on his way home. Realizing that he must get out of town, Charlie decides to head to the bus station, but as he leaves his apartment, he catches a glimpse of the pharmacist who sold him the drugs, walking up the stairs. Believing the pharmacist identified him, Charlie shoots the man and makes a run for it. When the police arrive at the scene, they learn the real reason why the pharmacist followed Charlie. The pharmacist was only coming to warn him that they had accidentally given him a deadly poison instead of painkillers. The police smile, knowing all they need to do is sit back and wait. Aboard the bus leaving town, Charlie takes the painkillers.

There is a group of men in this country, members of a noble profession, who each day go about their work quietly and efficiently. Merely because this program shows one of these men, blundering is not meant as a condemnation of the whole group. What Charlie did was inexcuseable but we certainly do not imply that all criminals would make the same mistake. And now a brief advertisement after which I shall return. (commercial break) *I must say horse shoes are very cheap, yet sensible this year. Open-toed flats. Now until next week, good night.*

EPISODE #241   "A JURY OF HER PEERS"   Broadcast on December 26, 1961
Starring: Ann Harding as Sarah Hale   Frances Reid as Mrs. Mary Peters
Philip Bourneuf as George Henderson   Robert Bray as Henry Peters, the sheriff
June Walker as Mrs. Millie Wright   Ray E. Teal as Jim Hale

* Robert Karnes was in eight episodes of the *Hitchcock* series, but this was the only time he was credited as "Bob Karnes."

Teleplay written for *Alfred Hitchcock Presents* by James P. Cavanagh, based on the one-act play entitled "Trifles," written by Susan Glaspell. (Which in turn was based on her short story of the same name, originally published in the March 5, 1917 issue of *Every Week*) Later published as a separate book: Benn (London), 1927. Subsequently anthologized in *To the Queen's Taste*, ed. Ellery Queen (Little Brown, 1946).

Directed by Robert Florey.

(operating table) *Good evening devotees of television. Recognizing the popularity of medical drama on TV, we are preparing one of our own. In this series, I play the part of a wise fatherly head of the largest dog and cat hospital in Los Angeles. This lad plays the part of young Dr. O'Hara, a very promising and dedicated young veterinarian. Here you see him as he will appear during the most of our first story. In this story he wrestled with the problem of whether he should remain with me, treating the pets of motion picture stars and millionaires and the animals who themselves maybe stars, or whether he should go back to a small town where he can treat the ordinary un-pedigreed poodles. Fortunately, I convinced him that integrity isn't everything.* (close-up) *Now for an episode from another series, Alfred Hitchcock Presents. After this one minute special.*

Story: Millie Wright is suspected of having killed her husband in cold blood, but the sheriff doesn't find any evidence proving she committed the crime. By a coincidence, Sarah Hale and Mary Peters (the sheriff's wife) happens to find a couple of clues that might show that Millie was guilty. But which also leads to the discovery that her husband had been an abusive, no-good louse. So they decide that he probably deserved what he got, and therefore doesn't mention the findings.

The story you have just seen was intended to be the beginning of a series about Mrs. Wright. I'm afraid we blundered badly however, for she was convicted along with Mrs. Peters and Mrs. Hale and her adventures were rather limited after that. As for our series about doctors, this too was abandoned. The young man managed to hold up, but being kind and fatherly and folksy proved too much of a strain for me. Now for the last of a series of three commercials, after which I shall tell you more of our producing plans. (commercial break) *During the coming months I hope you will look for our two newest projects. Our series about gangsters in the clothing industry called "The Unmentionables" and another built around the adventures of an itinerant strike breaker in the old west entitled, "Frontier Fink." Until next week, good night.*

Trivia, etc. Frances Reid, who played the role of Mary Peters in this episode, also played the role of Mrs. O'Connor in Alfred Hitchcock's *The Wrong Man* (1957). Robert Bray also played another Henry in the *Hitchcock* episode "Letter of Credit." In 1980, Sally Keckel wrote a screenplay based on the Susan Glaspell play, entitled *A Jury of her Peers*, directed by Keckel. The role of Sarah Hale was played by Frances Bay.

EPISODE #242 **"THE SILK PETTICOAT"** Broadcast on January 2, 1962
Starring: Michael Rennie as Humphrey J. Orford
Co-starring: Antoinette Bower as Elisa Minden   Jack Livesey as Dr. Minden
Doris Lloyd as Mrs. Boyd, the housekeeper
David Frankham as Lieutenant Philip Haven
Mollie Glessing as the parlor maid   Shirley O'Hara as Flora Orford
Teleplay written for *Alfred Hitchcock Presents* by Halsted Welles and Norman Ginsbury, based on the short story "The Scoured Silk" by Joseph Shearing (a pseudonym of Gabrielle Margaret Vere Long), originally published in the August 1951 issue of *Ellery Queen's Mystery Magazine*.

Directed by John Newland.

(by a brickwall)   *Good evening. I'm serving a sentence for slander. Something I said about our sponsor I believe. The warden thinks I'm making a tail for my kite. He's not terribly bright.* (whistles a tune like a snake charmer) *And now while I make my escape, you less fortunate must stay and face the music.*

Story: London, 1817. When Humphrey Orford begins talking over the grave of his dead wife Flora and about the virtues of torture, Elisa Minden, his fiancée, begins to think marrying him may be a mistake. After all, talking to the dearly departed is one thing, but the subject matter makes it difficult to cope with. She also finds a silk petticoat in his study and a painting of a hanged man. Orford admits that the painting shows his late wife's lover, but he claims that the petticoat belongs to his housekeeper. Elisa goes through with the marriage anyway, hoping the change will do Humphrey good and also because Orford would then settle her father's debt. She soon regrets her decision, however, after finding her husband stabbed to death in his study, although the door was locked from the inside. Observing the silk petticoat stuck in a secret door, Elisa finds a hidden room, where Flora is very much alive. She has been locked up in his study, where she could not scream for help as he has cut out her tongue - all because she had been caught with another man.

This seems to be the end of my attempted escape. As for our story however, there is a bit more. Shortly after the scene you have just witnessed, the police ended the picture. But because of the circumstances, justice was tampered with mercy. If tonight's story seemed a bit strong for you. Perhaps you would like to escape into the delightful make-believe of one of our commercials, after which I, representing grim reality, shall return. (commercial break) *I don't understand. There must be something in the atmosphere that makes otherwise strong ropes and ladders shatter under my weight. Next week, if I escape in time, we shall have another story. Until then, good night.*

EPISODE #243 **"BAD ACTOR"** Broadcast on January 9, 1962
Starring: Robert Duvall as Bart Collins
Carole Eastman as Marjorie 'Marge' Rogers
Charles Robinson as Jerry Lane   David Lewis as Ed Bolling
William Schallert as Lieutenant Gunderson
Bartlett Robinson as Donald Wellman   Jo Helton as the secretary
Raven Grey Eagle as the bongo player

Teleplay written for *Alfred Hitchcock Presents* by Robert Bloch, based on the short story "Acting Job" by Max Franklin (a pseudonym of writer Richard Deming), originally published in the January 1961 issue of *Mike Shayne Magazine*. Subsequently anthologized in *Best Detective Stories of the Year*, ed. David C. Cooke (Dutton, 1959) and in *Young and Deadly*, ed. Leo Margulies (Fawcett Crest, 1959).

Directed by John Newland.

(woman and elephant)   *Good evening. Before we begin our play, I would like to demonstrate the training method we use here at the Hitchcock Actor's Studio. You see, we give the students symbols or certain images to assist them in portraying character. Because of the type of character our Miss Schmeltz was to portray, we suggested that she think of herself as a tree.* (woman stands weird) *I think she projects it very well. Thank you, Miss Schmeltz. Our next student, Mr. Blackwood, was asked to portray a large jowlly captain of industry, and to help him we suggested that he think of himself as an elephant. Excellent. In all honesty, I must admit that Mr. Blackwood has been with us longer than Miss Schmeltz.* (close-up) *And now after this brief acting demonstration we bring you tonight's story, preceded by tonight's commercial. Thank you Mr. Blackwood. That will be all, Mr. Blackwood. I said, that will be all, Mr. Blackwood. Mr. Blackwood. . .*

Story: Desperate to get ahead, a young alcoholic actor named Bart Collins waits impatiently for his big break. When Bart and another actor are both up for the same job, Bart invites Jerry to come over to his apartment. There, Bart gets drunk again, and gets carried away with his role, when he strangles Jerry, instead of pretending to. Not wanting to go to prison, Bart places the corpse in the bathtub, hoping to hide the evidence. Buying some sharp knives and large jars of acid, Bart chops up the dead body and destroys most of it with acid. When his girlfriend and manager show up unexpectedly, Bart is forced to hide the last pieces of his evil deed quickly. When a detective shows up asking questions, Bart applies his acting talents, pretending to know nothing of Jerry's disappearance. The detective decides to leave after finding no reason to suspect Bart - until on the way out, when Marge wants to make a toast for Bart getting the much sought-after role. When Bart refuses to let them take any ice from the ice bucket, the lieutenant looks in the bucket to find the remains of Jerry – what's left of him.

Mr. Blackwood, Mr. Blackwood, this is most upsetting, especially to Miss Schmeltz. He had a date to take her to dinner after class, perhaps you should give me another minute, Mr. Blackwood. (commercial break) *Next week we shall be back with another story. As for this incident I have become philosophical about it. After all, we may have lost a student, but we have gained a mascot. Good night.*

Trivia, etc. There is a scene when the secretary picks up the phone and talks to someone named Mr. Robinson. In reality, there are two Mr. Robinsons in the same room, Bartlett and Charles! John Newland was originally a stage actor, moving up the ranks to television acting, and later became a director for such television shows as *Thriller*, *The Man from U.N.C.L.E.* and *Star Trek*. Amazingly, Newland doubled as host *and* director for all 99 episodes of television's *Alcoa Presents* (also known as *One Step Beyond*), from 1959 to 1961. Seventeen years later, John Newland later hosted a short-run syndicated series entitled *The Next Step Beyond*, in 1978. The revised series was not as popular as the original series, and went off the air shortly after it's premiere.

EPISODE #244   **"THE DOOR WITHOUT A KEY"**   Broadcast on January 16, 1962
Starring: Claude Rains as Leonard Eldridge
Co-Starring: John Larch as Sergeant Shaw
Connie Gilchrist as Maggie Vanderman   David Fresco as the delivery man
Sam Gilman as the squad car officer   Andy Romano as the patrolman
Jimmy Hawkins as Dewey Sims and Jeff Parker as Larry Rowan, motorcyclists
and Billy Mumy as Michael "Mickey" Holland
Robert Carson as the lieutenant and Susan Hart as Marti Thomas, were unbilled.
Teleplay written for *Alfred Hitchcock Presents* by Irving Elman, based on the short
story of the same name by Norman Daniels, originally published in the March 1961 issue of
Ellery Queen's Mystery Magazine.
Directed by Herschel Daugherty.
(bicycle)   *Good evening, ladies and gentlemen. I have just been competing in a
six-day bicycle race. I'm quite proud to say I finished first. I quit after five minutes.
Fortunately, the bicycle seems to have been invented by some realist who knew how often he
would have to push it. For those of you who do not care to watch bicycling, we have a
pageant presented by a group of travelling players. But first, this solo from a strolling
troubadour.*

Story: A police sergeant working the night desk is confronted with several unusual
cases, including an old man with amnesia and a lost little boy. Sergeant Shaw tries to send
the child to a home and the amnesia victim to a hospital, but both refuse to go. Shaw finally
settles down to get all of his other cases out of the way, but still must contend with the old
man and the boy, the latter whom finally admits that his father has abandoned him. Hearing
this, the old man realizes that he has lost his family as well, and lives alone in his luxurious
mansion. Shaw suggests that the wealthy man adopt Mickey, solving both their problems.

*I wan't to apologize for the lack of bloodshed on tonight's program. We should try
to do better next time. However, if all you wishes something to make your blood run cold, we
have commercials to do that. Here is one of them, after which I shall again peddle into view.*
(commercial break) *I have abandoned my bicycle. I find the job can be done much better by
hand. Next week we shall be back again with another program. Based on authentic stories
taken from the files of America's best television writers. Good night.* (Honk! Honk!
Hitchcock drives off in golf cart)

Trivia, etc. Actress Susan Hart, played the unbilled role of Marti Thomas in this
episode. Hart, later an AIP (American International Pictures) star, was wife of company head
man James H. Nicholson. This episode opens with a shot of the entrance to the 16th precinct
police station. The same exact shot was used four weeks earlier for the scene when George
Lassiter picks out Charlie Marks among the mug-shots in "The Right Kind of Medicine."

EPISODE #245   **"THE CASE OF M. J. H."**   Broadcast on January 23, 1962
Starring: Robert Loggia as James 'Jimmy' French
Barbara Baxley as Maude Sheridan   Richard Gaines as M. J. Harrison
Theodore Newton as Dr. Ernest Cooper   Marjorie Eaton as the landlady
Leatrice Leigh as the receptionist
Teleplay written for *Alfred Hitchcock Presents* by Henry Slesar, based on his short
story of the same name, originally published in the August 1959 issue of *Alfred Hitchcock's
Mystery Magazine*. Subsequently collected in *A Crime for Mothers and Others* (Avon, 1962)
as "Won't You Be My Valentine?", and as "The Case of M. J. H." in *Murders Most
Macabre*, (Avon, 1986), and in *Death on Television* (Southern Illinois University Press,
1989).

Directed by Alan Crosland, Jr.

(with a microphone, people hanging from above) *Good evening, ladies and gentlemen. Welcome to tonight's discussion program. Since we talk for hours without reaching any conclusion whatsoever, we call the program "Dead End." I have heard of anti-intellectualism, but this is a new high. Perhaps I should remove my microphone.* (close-up) *I see it can become rather lethal. This demonstrates that contrary to what I said previously, our participants can* (zoom-out) *reach conclusions. And all at the same time. It is very upsetting however, because we have half-an-hour left. Too bad they couldn't wait. But I see our sponsor is already rushing to fill the void, and on his heels a story.*

Story: A small time hood named Jimmy French gets in good with the secretary of a psychiatrist, whom he talks into looking at the doctor's files for a wealthy patient to blackmail. Maude won't go along with the scam at first, but eventually, love prevails and she reluctantly agrees. Checking out the prospects, Jimmy chooses M. J. Harrison, a wealthy, married 55-year-old real estate broker, who feels guilty about seeing an eighteen-year-old woman. When approached, Harrison agrees to pay the blackmail, but instead of paying the $10,000, he shoots Jimmy dead. The next day at the doctor's office, the psychiatrist breaks the bad news to Maude. His patient, M. J. Harrison, shot a blackmailer named Jimmy French. "There was no cause for blackmail," the psychiatrist puzzles. The young girl, you see, was pure fantasy. "He was guilt ridden by something that never existed. When the blackmailer threatened him, he protected his delusion with murder. The ultimate rationalization."

I think our point should be quite clear. In these times a thorough grounding in psychology is essential in any profession, even blackmail. For receptionists, a slightly different lesson. Never pinch the boss's files. You see, Maude was tried and punished as an accomplice to the crime. In precisely sixty seconds I shall return to warn you about next week's program. (commercial break) *I may not be back with "Dead End" next week. You see, the producers prefer to be called intellectuals and they feel that my presence here tends to give credence to the epithet "egghead." It's absurd of course. Next week Alfred Hitchcock Presents will be seen in this spot. Until then, good night.*

Trivia, etc. Robert Loggia appeared in four episodes of the *Hitchcock* series, and played the role of Doctor Raymond in *Psycho II* (1983), the sequel to Alfred Hitchcock's original 1960 film. Loggia would later play the role of Charley in the 1986 remake Hitchcock episode entitled "A Very Happy Ending." Marjorie Eaton also played a landlady in the big-screen movie, *The Three Stooges in Orbit* (1962).

EPISODE #246 **"THE FAITH OF AARON MENEFEE"** Broadcast January 30, 1962
   Starring: Sidney Blackmer as Otis "Healer" Jones
   Andrew Prine as Aaron Menefee   Maggie Pierce as Emily Jones
   Robert Armstrong as Doc Buckles   Gail Bonney as the old woman
   Olan Soulé as Brother Charley Fish   and Don Hanmer as Vern Byers *
   Teleplay written for *Alfred Hitchcock Presents* by Ray Bradbury, based on the short story of the same name by Stanley Ellin, originally published in the September 1957 issue of *Ellery Queen's Mystery Magazine*. Subsequently collected in *The Blessington Method and Other Strange Tales* (Random House, 1964; Macdonald, 1965) and in *The Speciality of the House and Other Stories* (Mysterious Press, 1979).
   Directed by Norman Lloyd.

* Don Hanmer, who first appeared as Mr. Cutter in "The Better Bargain," had his name misspelled Hammer in the closing credits for this episode. He later re-appeared in two episodes of *The Alfred Hitchcock Hour.*

(circus, animal trainer) *Good evening, ladies and gentlemen and welcome to what we modestly call, "the greatest show on earth." Becoming an animal trainer is not difficult at all. Anyone who has raised children already possesses the proper humility. Our star performer, Gordon, will now jump from this stool to this one.* (close-up) *I think you will appreciate his performance more when you realize . . . that Gordon is a flea. He's getting ready. By the way, Gordon is the one in the blue trunks. There he goes, well done. As for those trunks, he can pick them up when he returns. Now for a riddle. What has no legs, is a bit thick, definitely does not fly and is one minute long. Here is the answer.*

Story: Aaron Menefee, modern-day mechanic, repairs a faith healer's car for a small and honest fee, whereas the Reverend Jones heals Aaron's stomach ulcer. After meeting the preacher's daughter, Emily, Aaron abandons his job working on engines and goes to work for Rev. Jones' revival. It doesn't take long for Aaron and Emily to fall in love, but sadly, her father will not allow them to marry. For months they travel from town to town and the faith offerings keep pouring in. One day the revival returns to Aaron's hometown, and visiting his old friend, the town doctor, he discovers the medical man being held captive by two escaped convicts - one of whom, Vern Byers, has been badly hurt and his legs paralyzed. Aaron promises the wounded criminal that Reverend Jones can heal the criminal's wound, and goes out to fetch the faith healer. The Reverend is told by the criminal that if he fails to remove the pain, he will kill him. Aaron, leaving the building expressing complete confidence in Jones, realizes that no matter how things work out, events will lead to a desired conclusion . . .

So much for life and death under the big top. By the way, the police finally caught up with Vern Byers, but not before he had done in Otis Jones. My final appearance in a moment, but first . . . (zoom-out) *To convince the cynical that Gordon does exist, he will now jump through this hoop.* (close-up) *This always happens, I must remember to use thinner paper, but as Gordon would say, that's show business. Which reminds me, you have seen the show, now we give you the business.* (commercial break) *Good evening. Good to have you ringside again. Gordon was miffed as a result of the accident with the hoop and has disappeared. He first changed into street clothes, however, so he will be much more difficult to find. He's wearing a dark grey flanel suit, pearl-grey felt hat, a blue necktie, and three pairs of suede shoes.* (Hitchcock scratches his arm) *Now until next week at this same time, good night.*

EPISODE #247   **"THE WOMAN WHO WANTED TO LIVE"**   Broadcast Feb. 6, 1962
   Starring: Charles Bronson as Ray Bardon   Guest Star: Lola Albright as Lisa
   Ray Montgomery as Fred, the gas station attendant
   Craig Curtis as Rook   Ben Bryant as the fat boy
   Robert Rudelson as Cuke   Jesslyn Fax as the motel manageress
   Teleplay written for *Alfred Hitchcock Presents* by Bryce Walton, based on his short story of the same name, originally published in the May 1961 issue of *Ellery Queen's Mystery Magazine*. Subsequently anthologized in *To Be Read Before Midnight*, ed. Ellery Queen (Random House, 1962).
   Directed by Alan Crosland, Jr.
   (at the gallows) *Good evening. I've been replacing a loose board in the steps. Someone could have had a nasty fall and we certainly don't want anyone to get hurt. This of course, needs no explanation. This one passenger model now seems quaint, but prior to the introduction of more efficient methods, this was the best way our ancestors had to cope with the population explosion. Notice the raised platform. This was placed in the center of a courtyard or other public place and men could crowd around - with their ladies - to watch criminals being put to death. Of course we do the same thing today, but we call it a drive-in-movie. And now for a modern institution, which instead of driving audiences in, drives them out. After which, our story.*

Story: Convict Ray Bardon escapes from prison and hangs out at a gas station waiting for someone to ride with. When a car comes by, the attendant tries to attack Ray but gets shot instead. The young girl in the car, Lisa, volunteers to help Ray get away if he promises not to kill her. Down the road a few miles, Lisa has a flat tire, which she actually fixes without trying to escape. A couple of punks from a gang called the Dragons stop by and tries to mess with Lisa, but Ray scares them away when he takes out his gun. On the road again, Ray falls asleep but Lisa still doesn't make an escape attempt. Arriving at a motel, the two check into a room and instead of taking a chance to leave and phone the police, she stays to bandage him up. Ray starts doubting why she is being so helpful, and while they talk, she manages to get hold of his gun. Lisa explains her motives: Ray Bardon murdered her fiancé at the gas station, and now that she has a gun, she can have her revenge . . . pulling the trigger.

That should teach you men, never to accept a ride with a pretty girl. And judging from this instance, it did Lisa no good either. The law is not kind to those who meet out their own justice. Now it is time for you to view a brief institutional announcement. As for me, I shall be hanging around at its conclusion. (commercial break) *Thank you for bearing with me all this time. Next week we shall return with another story and three well chosen words from our sponsor. Until then, good night.*

EPISODE #248 **"STRANGE MIRACLE"** Broadcast on February 13, 1962
Starring: David Opatoshu as Mr. Sequiras   Miriam Colón as Lolla Sequiras
Eduardo Ciannelli as the priest   Frank de Kova as Senor Vargas
Adelina Pedroza as Maria   Tina Menard as the nun
Teleplay written for *Alfred Hitchcock Presents* by Halsted Welles, based on a story by George Langelaan.
Directed by Norman Lloyd.
(as a mail-man) *Good evening Mr. and Mrs . . . uh. . . Occupant. Tonight's story is called "Strange Miracle" and I consider it first class. Before I'm permitted to deliver it however, there's a certain gentleman with another message which I can only say is in a class by itself. I have attempted to dissuade him but neither snow, nor rain, nor any amount of acrimony can stay this ego courier. Here he comes now.*

Story: Mr. Sequiras, one of the lucky few to survive a train wreck, is severely injured, and rushed to a hospital. Because he successfully fakes being paralyzed from the waist down, he manages to collect a huge settlement from the railroad company. But after spending considerable time in a wheelchair, he becomes bored with the restrictions. A scheme comes to mind when he meets Maria, a little girl who is really paralyzed, and has been paying visits to a nearby shrine, where they say cripples are healed. This gives Sequiras an idea. If he tries the same gimmick, planning to fake a miraculous public recovery, people will believe the hand of God blessed his legs, and he can then walk around with other people, and still keep the settlement money. But once there and making a prayer, he discovers to his horror that now, he really is paralyzed. The little girl Maria, however, received a vision from the virgin, and by a strange miracle, she now has the use of her legs!

(tick-tick coming from package) *I shall see you in a moment. I have orders to get this package to the addressee with all possible speed. Yes, I haven't much time.* (commercial break) *Well, I delivered my package.* (booom!) *It's a shame I didn't give it to the right person but there wasn't time. The important thing is that someone got it. After all, the mail must go through. That's all for tonight's delivery. Next week I shall have some more. Until then, good night.*

EPISODE #249   **"THE TEST"**   Broadcast on February 20, 1962

Starring: Brian Keith as Vernon Wedge	Eduardo Ciannelli as Mr. Marino
Rod Lauren as Benjy Marino	William Bramley as Dr. Hagerty
Steve Gravers as Mr. Wickers, the prosecutor	Rusty Lane as the judge
Eve McVeagh as Mrs. Archer	Tenen Holtz as Sol Dankers
Dee J. Thompson as Olga, the secretary	Ken Harp as the bailiff
Dick Hilleary as the jury foreman	

Teleplay written for *Alfred Hitchcock Presents* by Henry Slesar, based on his short story "Thicker Than Water," originally published in the November 1961 issue of *Alfred Hitchcock's Mystery Magazine*. Subsequently collected in *A Crime for Mothers and Others* (Avon, 1962) and in *Murders Most Macabre* (Avon, 1986).

Directed by Boris Sagal.

(moustache and beard)   *Good evening and welcome to sing-along with Hitch. I have a feeling this would be much better if we could hear you singing. As it is, it strikes me as a rather limited form of entertainment. And you have no idea how insecure one can feel when he knows that at any time, he can be replaced by a bouncing ball. For those of you who are too shy, or for some reason have not chosen to join us. I have an enticement. Perhaps if you sing loud and lustily enough you will drown out the commercial.   After which, our story. Remember the competition tends to become rather fortissimo.*

Story: A young boy, Benjy, is charged with killing another boy with a knife, so Benjy's father goes to see an attorney, Vernon Wedge, in hopes of convincing him to take the case. Wedge agrees to represent the boy, even when he explains that "the odds are heavily stacked against him." Wedge decides to base his defense on a test, which would prove if the knife has ever had contact with blood, but the prosecution objects to the test and Wedge is not allowed to use it. Luckily, the attorney still wins the case, but his curiosity gets the better of him. Just before going through with the blood test to find out for himself whether the youngster was guilty or not, the boy's father grabs the knife, and cuts himself with it, making it impossible to learn the truth.

Those of you with a passion for peripheral detail, will be interested in knowing that the actual killers in this case were ultimately brought to justice. As for this next detail, it is a television commercial. An item for which I have a passion. Frankly, I like them because I feel so wonderful when they're over. Which is when I shall next see you. (commercial break) *I hope you have enjoyed singing along with Hitch.   It is the best way I know to indulge in a community sing, without actually having to rub elbowes with ones neighbors. Next week we shall be back. Myself and all the gang. Until then, good night.*

Trivia, etc. Besides directing three episodes of *Alfred Hitchcock Presents*, Boris Sagal also directed episodes of television's *Mike Hammer*, *Naked City*, *The Twilight Zone*, *Way Out!*, and *The Man from U.N.C.L.E.* In 1981, just a few months before his death, Sagal paid tribute to Alfred Hitchcock by directing a made-for-television movie, *Dial M For Murder*, a remake of the 1954 Warner Bros. film.

For the third time this season, the closing credits billed the right actor with a non-existent role. In this case, Eduardo Ciannelli was billed in the closing credits as Mr. Bleeker, a mistake since he really played the role of Mr. Marino. Ken Harp made only one more appearance on the *Hitchcock* series and that was eight months later, again as a bailiff under Hitchcock's direction in *The Alfred Hitchcock Hour* episode "I Saw the Whole Thing." This episode was also Rod Lauren's acting debut for the screen. Lauren would later play roles in *The Crawling Hand* (1963), *Black Zoo* (1963), *Once Before I Die* (1965) and *Childish Things* (1969).

370

EPISODE #250   **"BURGLAR PROOF"**   Broadcast on February 27, 1962
Starring: Paul Hartman as Sammy "The Touch" Morrissey
Robert Webber as Harrison Fell   Philip Ober as Wilton Stark
Whit Bissell as Mr. Bliss   Howard McLeod as Mr. Grady
Josie Lloyd as Miss Dorothy Morrissey

Teleplay written for *Alfred Hitchcock Presents* by Henry Slesar, based on his short story "Be My Valentine," originally published in the January 1962 issue of *Alfred Hitchcock's Mystery Magazine*. Subsequently collected as "Be My Valentine" in *A Crime for Mothers and Others* (Avon, 1962), and as "Burglar Proof" in *Death on Television* (Southern Illinois University Press, 1989).

Directed by John Newland.

(dentist chair)   *Good evening dear patients.   Just a little wider please.   That's quite wide enough.   You see, I suffer from achrophobia.   Now let's see, uh . . . Some of my patients are inclined to get nasty.   Fortunately, I keep both hands completely anaesthetized, while I'm in the office.   I admit this makes for some rather sloppy work since my fingers aren't quite as deafed as they might be, but I save a great deal of suffering.   And while we're on that subject, perhaps we shall pass the Novacane around.   This next minute promises to be rather painful.*

Story: Harrison Fell is given the job of coming up with an advertising campaign for a new type of burglarproof safe, called the 801 Burglar Proof. He gets an idea of inviting a famous safecracker known as "The Touch" to a press conference, where ex-criminal Sammy Morrissey will publicly try to open the safe. Harrison tells Morrissey that he can have the $50,000 in cash, locked in the safe, if he can get to it. While he is initially reluctant to get involved in the stunt, Sammy finally agrees to do so. During the press conference, Morrissey spends considerable time trying to crack the safe, but is unable to, and ends up leaving with a $500 consolation prize. The next day, however, when the time-lock mechanism opens the safe, they find the envelope full of worthless blank paper. Unknown to Harrison, Morrissey's new occupation is picking pockets, for he switched the envelopes before it was put into the burglarproof confine.

That film gave me some excellent suggestions for opening stubborn mouths.   Of course Sammy's triumph was rather brief, but I think he deserves some time off for ingenuity.   Perhaps the judge will agree.   Now we shall pause a minute for the filling to dry.   After which I shall return.   If you need anything, just call.   (commercial break)   *I would like you to know that I was not defrocked.   I quit.   It was a photograph of the grand canyon that did it.   The sight of that unfilled cavity, left me with a feeling of complete inadequacy.   I shall return next week at the same time and I see that you too have an appointment.   I hope you'll keep it.   Until then, good night.*

EPISODE #251   **"THE BIG SCORE"**   Broadcast on March 6, 1962
Starring: Rafael Campos as Gino   Evans Evans as Dora
Tom Gilleran as Mike   Philip Reed as Mr. F. Hubert Fellowes
Nick Sills as Arne   Jesse Jacobs as Ozzie
Joe Trapaso as Murphy   Timmie Spees as Larry Fellowes
John Zaremba as Lieutenant Morgan

Teleplay written for *Alfred Hitchcock Presents* by Bryce Walton, based on the short story of the same name by Sam Merwin, Jr., originally published in the July 1955 issue of *Manhunt*.

Directed by Boris Sagal.

(black board)   *Good evening, ladies and gentlemen and welcome to another skull session.   I think we have at last conceived the perfect football play.   If you have ten men to do your blocking and follow this plan, you should have no trouble reaching the refreshment stand at half time.   If you haven't ten men, you can do just as well using two elderly ladies armed with hat pins. Tonight's training film is called "The Big Score," but first. . . the head coach wishes to give you a one-minute pep-talk.*

Story: A young girl takes a baby-sitting job so that she and her three friends can rob the wealthy Mr. Fellowes, but as the three are cleaning house, Mr. Fellowes returns home early and they are forced to kill him. Dora, Gino, Arne and Mike get away with $32,000, but when Gino tries to buy a police radio from a mobster, the word is out and Gino and Dora are chased and killed. It turns out that Mr. Fellowes was a leader of a mob, a person you should never steal from.

And that concludes tonight's play "The Big Score." However, while Ozzie and his friends appeared to be ahead on points in our final quarter, it was the police who finally won the game. Mike, Arne, Ozzie and Murphy have all been benched for 20 to 30 years. In case you've been puzzled by this athletic theme, I should explain. This portion of the program was originally prepared for a story about college football. Of course, we soon discovered that football is hardly a suitable subject for television. There's far too much violence. Then there's a matter of athletic scholarships and quite a bit of bribery and all in all we felt the story put American youths in much too bad a light. For this reason only we substituted tonight's tale of juvenile delinquency. And now for that part of the program for which I wish there were a substitute, after which I shall return. (commercial break) How do you do? I'm Alfred Hitchcock. I thought you might have forgotten during my absence. This concludes tonight's training session. We shall return next week when I shall lecture on the art of point-shaving and game-throwing. Until then, good night.

EPISODE #252   **"PROFIT-SHARING PLAN"**   Broadcast on March 13, 1962
>Starring: Henry Jones as Miles Cheever   Ruth Storey as Mrs. Cheever
>Rebecca Sand as Anita   Frank Maxwell as Rudy
>Stephanie Hill as Miss Lemmon   Humphrey Davis as Mr. Dougherty
>Jim Sweeney as the elevator operator   Lew Brown as the airline clerk
>Lael Jackson as the stewardess   Suzanne Noel as the junior stewardess
>Hinton Pope as the plain-clothesman

Teleplay written for *Alfred Hitchcock Presents* by William Link and Richard Levinson, from their short story "The End of an Era" originally published in the January 1962 issue of *Alfred Hitchcock's Mystery Magazine*.

Directed by Bernard Girard.

(big cake, hat, umbrella) *Good evening and happy birthday. I'm some what afraid to cut this cake. The last time I attempted that, a young lady stepped out. It was extremely unnerving, especially since it was obvious, she was no lady. However there's little chance of a recurrence of that memorable event, for our celebration is a more formal one. The company is commemorating my many years of servitude. This time they will probably give me black birds. While I'm cutting this, I believe my employer, wishes to make a short speech and present us with a story.*

Story: After twenty years with Cumberland, Inc., Miles Cheever retires and is given a party, along with an inexpensive gift. When he returns home, his wife berates him for getting so little, after giving so much. Even though he plans to leave her, Miles agrees that she is right, so that night he breaks into the office and wipes out the safe. Miles and his girlfriend board a plane for Hawaii leaving behind his wife and brief criminal career. But his plans run afoul when a stewardess makes him put his money-filled case in the luggage compartment. Someone, you see. has called in a bomb threat and the authorities are searching the luggage, and will no doubt find the stolen money. Little does he know that the bomb scare is just a hoax - perpetrated by his abandoned wife . . . who suspected he was running away with another woman.

372

In all my years of employment, I have never missed a show, nor been late for a performance. I occasionally step out for a breath of air during the commercial, but there are limits to what even a company-man can indure. This unmatched record of loyalty has so moved my sponsor that he has granted me the rest of the evening off. This struck him as the ideal gift, being both appropriate and cheap. In my place after the commercial you will see a bit of film, taken when I first joined the firm. I'm certain you will find it interesting. (takes the hat) *Oh, by the way, Mr. Cheever had the last laugh at his wife's expense. For she was subsequently prosecuted for creating a bombscare.* (takes the umbrella and leaves) (commercial break) (a young man says: that is all for this evening, until next week at the same time, good night.)

Trivia, etc. Lew Brown, who played the role of the airline clerk in this episode, also played the part of an American Official in Alfred Hitchcock's *Topaz* (1969). Rebecca Sand and Humphrey Davis were both regulars on television's day-time soap opera, *The Edge of Night.*

EPISODE #253   **"APEX"**   Broadcast on March 20, 1962

  Starring: Patricia Breslin as Margo Vivienne Segal as Clara Shorum
  Mark Miller as Claude Shorum George Kane as Mr. George Weeks
  Teleplay written for *Alfred Hitchcock Presents* by John T. Kelley, based on the short story of the same name by James Workman, originally published in the March 1958 issue of *London Mystery Magazine.*
  Directed by Alan Crosland, Jr.
  (guard and tourist)   *Good evening fellow tourists. The first item on today's schedule is a stop at Buckingham Palace for a view of the historic changing of the guard.* (close-up) *The gentleman performing the gymnastics is a Mr. Wedgeley of Topper, Iowa. Mr. Wedgeley is engaging in one of the favorite tourist's sports. He's trying to make the stern-looking guardsman smile. In fact, Mr. Wedgeley has made a small wager with me . . .* (gun-shot, guard returns to his post) *I'm afraid that wasn't quite what Mr. Wedgeley had in mind. On second thought, I believe he did win his bet with me for I now see just the hint of a smile on the guardsman's face. Originally our tour-schedule provided for one minute of free time at this point. But because of this incident, I think a brief eulogy would be appropriate.*

  Story: After being married with Clara for seven years, Claude Shorum has started an affair with their neighbor, Margo, unbeknownst to Clara. Over time, Margo tells Claude that his wife plans to divorce him because of their shaky relationship, a move that will leave him broke as she owns everything. As such, they should murder her immediately. Since Claude proves that he's not capable of killing his wife, Margo throws the suggestion around that he hire a professional hit man to eliminate the woman. While Margo takes matters into her own hands by poisoning Clara, Claude has already made the mistake of hiring a hit man, that shows up at their house. Mistaking Margo for the recently deceased Clara, the hit man performs the job he was paid to do.

  As Aesop would have said, when you are part of a triangle, it is wise to remain in your own corner. As a result of the scene you have just witnessed, Claude Bunsen and the stranger with the gun received punishment in keeping with their guilt. And of course, the guardsman who shot that tourist also received his just deserts. He now wears the Victoria Cross. I have an important announcement in just sixty seconds. Ah, here is something else which should make our guardsman smile. (commercial break) *That time the guard made no effort to shoot. He just laughed out loud. Next week we shall be back with another story. Now I must bid you good night, until then. I believe the guard is going into his shelter. You know it's remarkable how they retain their dignity at all times.* (guard knocks his hat off)

Trivia, etc. Once again, something happened between the filming of Hitchcock's hosting and the filming of the actual story, for the host refers to Claude as Bunsen instead of Shorum.

EPISODE #254 **"THE LAST REMAINS"** Broadcast on March 27, 1962
        Starring: Ed Gardner as Marvin J. Foley   John Fiedler as Amos Duff
        Walter Kinsella as Lieutenant Morgan   Leonard Weinrib as Stanley
        Molly Ryder as Foley's secretary   Gail Bonney as the librarian
        Teleplay written for *Alfred Hitchcock Presents* by Henry Slesar, from the short story "Dead Give-Away" by O.H. Leslie (pen name of Henry Slesar), originally published in the November 1961 issue of *Alfred Hitchcock's Mystery Magazine*. Subsequently collected in *A Crime for Mothers and Others* (Avon, 1962), and in *Murders Most Macabre* (Avon, 1986) as "The Last Remains."
        Directed by Leonard J. Horn.
        (playing darts on a ship) *Good evening and welcome to tonight's pleasure cruise. Our social director is very resourceful and cooperative.* (throwing darts at the captain) *Our friend is getting a bit nervous, however, he doesn't mind darts but some of the passengers are interested in skeet shooting, using him as the skeet. Tonight our crowded schedule of fun and games includes a drama called, "The Last Remains." First however a word from our skipper.*

        Story: After Marvin J. Foley's partner, Robert D. Kessler, is killed in an auto accident, Marvin goes to see Amos Duff, the funeral director of the Silver Glen Mortuary, to make the necessary arrangements. For some reason, Marvin chooses the economy class funeral instead of a standard funeral. Amos, however, discovers that Kessler had been murdered, shot to death, unknown to the police who assumed it was a simple auto accident. Amos pays Marvin a visit and tells the crook that if he buys his most expensive funeral service, the class A for $1,800, he won't go to the authorities. Marvin is forced to agree and pays $750, assuring he'll pay the rest after the body has been cremated. But after the funeral, when he knows the evidence has been destroyed, Marvin backs out regarding payment. Marvin, you see, had noticed in Duff's catalogue that the most expensive funeral costs only $750. Amos gets furious and goes to the police, who promptly picks up Foley. At the police station, Amos explains that "The bullet was steel-jacketed so it didn't really melt. When they found the bullet among the ashes, they included it among the remains. That's why I had to come to the police."

        Too bad Mr. Foley didn't consider burial at sea. It's simple and inexpensive. Besides, the trip back can be much more enjoyable for the bereaved. All that sea air you know. And now that I mention it, I see a quantity of hot air coming our way. I shall re-emerge after it has passed by. (commercial break) *I am pacifying our social director by playing a game of his choosing.* (Hitchcock is blindfolded and walking a plank) *I'm to pin the tail on the donkey. Fortunately, you do not have to suffer through this childish nonsense. You may be excused until next week at the same time. So until then, good night.*

EPISODE #255 **"TEN O'CLOCK TIGER"** Broadcast on April 3, 1962
        Starring: Robert Keith as Arthur "The Professor" Duffy
        Frankie Darro as Boots   Karl Lukas as Soldier Fresno
        Syl Lamont as the attendant   Andy Romano as the cop
        Charles E. Perry as Charlie, the handler
        Chuck Hicks as Gypsy Joe   Bruce Dushman as Buster
        Teleplay written for *Alfred Hitchcock Presents* by William Fay, based on his short story of the same name, originally published in the August 9, 1947 issue of the *Saturday Evening Post*.
        Directed by Bernard Girard.

(standing on shoulders) *Good evening, ladies and gentlemen. Since you are accustomed to hearing my brother Alfred at this time, I shall allow him to make his usual announcement. You may carry on, Alfred.* (pans down) *Thank you, kind Sir. I agreed to take part in this absurd charade only because I was assured it would get us a booking on a certain, sunday night variety show. However, I'm not sure it's worth it, since watching us is rather limited form of amusement. We have provided you with some alternate entertainment.* (lets go of one leg) *Here it is.*

Story: Boxing manager Arthur Duffy is approached by a weird stranger named Boots, who claims he has a special formula that improves the performance of race horses. Duffy decides to try it out on an over-the-hill boxer named Soldier Fresno, and is surprised to see Fresno win fight after fight, making a small fortune for both Duffy and Boots. While all of this is going on, Boots begins to realize what a beating Soldier is taking, and to end their partnership, he explains to Duffy that the formula was never his to begin with, and the supply is running out. Boots tells Duffy not to raise the intake, but to make sure Soldier wins the evening's big championship fight. Duffy, ever greedy, gives Soldier two doses, but the high level of drugs makes the fighter think he is already in the ring and he beats Duffy to death.

That is the end of the story, I think. Needless to say, Soldier was later apprehended. I don't know how you feel, but for me the story is merely a feeble overture to the greater music provided by our sponsor, after which Alfred and I, shall return. (commercial break) *Alfred has been strangely silent. Alfred, what are you up to?* (pans down) *Nothing. Until next week,* (lighted match to his shoe) *Good night.*

EPISODE #256 **"ACT OF FAITH"** Broadcast on April 10, 1962
Starring: George Grizzard as Alan Chatterton
Dennis King as Mr. Rolston Temple   Florence MacMichael as Alice
Jeno Mate as Luigi   Alan Campbell as the show-biz man
Mary Grace Canfield as Mrs. Cathy Carr, woman in bookshop
Teleplay written for *Alfred Hitchcock Presents* by Eric Ambler, based on a short story by Nicholas Monsarrat.
Directed by Bernard Girard.
(on a fire truck) *Good evening. As a public service we thought it might be wise to take our remote cameras and show you how those alert, never-tiring, public service, the firemen, go about their work. Because being on the road only ten seconds and already I see the fire, I understand this is the fastest firetruck in the world. We seem to have taken a wrong turn somehow, and a very wide turn at that. Ah, as I was saying these men have been on the road less than a minute, and yet here we are, in Arabia. It isn't . . . It isn't the fire that's out of control, it's the truck. Perhaps you better get back to the show. I doubt if you thought to bring your passports. Here then is our show for tonight, following this one minute false alarm.*

Story: A successful writer, Mr. Temple, is contracting Alan Chatterton, a man who has been unable to get anything published, and Mr. Temple can see by the material that Alan is writing an excellent novel, called "The Locked Stable." Temple decides to loan him money so he will have something to live on during the six months he says it will take to finish the book, but long after the time has elapsed, the novel still isn't done. Alan asks for money again, and Temple gives it to him, but becomes enraged when he finds out that Alan is out having a good time on the town. Temple confronts him and claims that he has been ripped off, then tears up the contract they had. To Temple's amazement, some time later the book is finished and becomes a best seller, leading Alan to pay off his loan with the impatient Temple.

I hope you enjoyed our play. I had little time for anything but holding on here. Darkness is an excellent condition for viewing a commercial. If you don't see me at its conclusion, just wait a moment and I'll be by. (commercial break) *My only hope is that the driver will run out of gas. I know I have. I shall be back next week and the week after that and the week after that. . . until I finally fall off. Good night.*

Trivia, etc. Eric Ambler. a distinguished writer of mystery and espionage stories and novels, was also married to producer Joan Harrison. His novels, *A Coffin for Dimitrios* (1939), *Journey Into Fear* (1940), and *Epitaph for a Spy* (1938), were made into successful movies. In 1953, Ambler received an Oscar nomination for his adaptation of *The Cruel Sea*, a novel by Nicholas Monsarrat. For this Hitchcock episode, Ambler again adapts a story by Monsarrat for the screen.

EPISODE #257 **"THE KERRY BLUE"** Broadcast on April 17, 1962
      Starring: Gene Evans as Ned Malley   Carmen Mathews as Thelma Malley
      John Zaremba as Dr. Chaff   Robert Reiner as Dr. Prentiss
      David Carlile as the detective   G. Warren Smith as the intern
      An original teleplay written for *Alfred Hitchcock Presents* by Henry Slesar, later published as "Death of a Kerry Blue" in an issue of *Alfred Hitchcock's Mystery Magazine*.
      Directed by Paul Henreid.
      (photographs and girl) *Good evening, ladies and gentlemen. Welcome to "Candid Capers." This is the program which photographs people in amusing and embarrassing scenes and then shows them to the television audience. Our photographer is returning with a new set of pictures.* (lady hands photos) *Thank you. Allow me to explain how our program works. Our photographer goes into nightclubs, hotels or parked cars and snaps these candid pictures. We then show the photographs on television and everyone has a good laugh. This first picture was snapped in a dark corner of the New Vogue Pauvre Coffeehouse and shows Mr. Andrew Spearman and Miss Gertru . . .* (picture of Hitchcock) *Oh, there's something on this one, excuse me. It's from Mr. Spearman. I see . . .* (rips the photo) *Candid Capers loves a good laugh, but we certainly wouldn't want to cause any misunderstandings. Apparently all he could find on which to write his note, was a hundred dollar bill. While I go through these pictures, perhaps you'd like to look at the following, more formal photography. Thank you.*

      Story: Thelma Malley worries about her husband because of his intense love for his old dog Annie, and Thelma is somewhat jealous. When Ned returns from a business trip, and learns that the dog suddenly died, he blames his wife for burying the pooch alive, and retaliates by putting a fatal dose of sleeping pills in her hot chocolate. As the woman is overcome by the drugs, Ned hears a dog whimper and heads outside to check, but in his hurry to get out of the house he trips and bangs his head, accidentally killing him. A neighbor hears what has happened and calls for an ambulance, and when it arrives, the medical team is able to revive Thelma, who mentions that Ned never got the chance to see that she had bought him a new dog.

      (counting money) *Would you believe it? We don't have a single photograph to show you. I shall tell you more of this in just a moment.* (commercial break) *That concludes our show for tonight. As for Candid Capers, we have added a new feature. The Telephone Tapping Hour. We hope this will be even more entertaining and profitable. So until next week, good night.*

EPISODE #258 **"THE MATCHED PEARL"** Broadcast on April 24, 1962
      Starring: John Ireland as Captain McCabe   Ernest Truex as Mr. Wilkens
      Émile Genest as Lawrence Kirkwood   Michael King as Conroy
      Charlotte Knight as the cleaning woman   Sharon Farrell as Lolly Wilkens

An original teleplay written for *Alfred Hitchcock Presents* by Henry Slesar, which was later published as a short story entitled "The Matched Pearl," in *A Crime for Mothers and Others* (Avon, 1962).

Directed by Bernard Girard.

(huge pearl) *Good evening. I'm examining this pearl. You should have seen the oyster. I already have a customer for this. He's a very wealthy, but suspicious gentleman who plans to give it to his lady friend as a pendant. I'm sure you agree that this is the kind of gift which inspires fidelity. That is why I told him, I don't think it's necessary to attach it to her ancle. This is peculiar. There's a very sinister gentleman in your future. I think he's trying to tell you something.*

Story: Lawrence Kirkwood finds out the hard way that it doesn't pay to rip people off. He manages to sell an expensive pearl on consignment, but then cheats the seller, Captain McCabe, on part of the money that should have been his. The buyer of the rare pearl returns and wants another to match it, so Kirkwood reluctantly returns to Captain McCabe and reveals the truth. McCabe is furious, but agrees to find another one - with a huge markup because of Kirkwood having cheated him. He approves, figuring that he can charge the buyer extra, not realizing until he buys the second pearl, that it is actually the same one - and he has been fleeced by the captain and the buyer, who have been working together to set Kirkwood up.

Goodness, what cynicism. Those of you who like to see evil-doers punished, will be overjoyed to know that is exactly what happened in the next reel. However, to make the rest of you happy we shall spare you the pain of actually seeing it and shall show a commercial instead, after which I shall hustle back. (commercial break) *In closing, I would like to explain something to Miss Ethel T of Pasadena, California. She doesn't care for our cynicism and has asked: Why don't we present more, sweet little stories? We would like to, Miss T, but they are much too fattening. So until next week at this time, good night.*

EPISODE #259   **"WHAT FRIGHTENED YOU, FRED?"**   Broadcast on May 1, 1962

Starring: R. G. Armstrong as Fred Riordan   Edward Asner as Warden Bragan
Adam Williams as Dr. Cullen   Steven Peccaro as Tony Wando
Eve McVeagh as Mae   Kreg Martin as Kowalski
Harry Mackin as the side man in the patrol car

Teleplay written for *Alfred Hitchcock Presents* by Joel Murcott, based on the short story of the same name by Jack Ritchie, originally published in the May 1958 issue of *Alfred Hitchcock's Mystery Magazine*. Subsequently collected in *Alfred Hitchcock's Tales to Make You Week in the Knees* (Dial Press/Davis Publications, 1981).

Directed by Paul Henreid.

(following footsteps with a dog) *Good evening, ladies and gentlemen. We have been trying to track down an escaped convict. But we seem to have lost him here. . . where he stopped to take some dancing lessons, obviously. What's worse, my friend the hound, now runs with a definite cha-cha-cha motion. It's rather embarrassing. He also insists that I lead and you can't track down anyone that way.* (close-up) *Of course it's fine while we're dancing. While I cope with the problem of a convict at large in a dance school and a hound who wants to learn the tango, suppose you take up the case of the sponsor, who merely wants to be liked.*

Story: Ex-convict Fred Riordan violates his parole and is promptly returned to the state pen. The prison psychiatrist and the warden (who has political ambitions) interview Fred, hoping to learn why the ex-con broke parole forty-eight hours after being released. Fred claims he had little choice of returning to prison, because no one in the old neighborhood wanted him around. With that kind of persuasion, a big-time gangster named Tony Wando asks him to break parole and return to the cold hard cell, with a $25,000 agreement for killing an associate who is behind the walls. Fred considered the deal and figured a thousand dollars a month is worth more than seventy dollars a week. The warden, not understanding Fred's true intentions, tries to show some compassion by assigning him duty in the laundry, and promises to give him the job as his personal clerk if he promises to stay out of trouble. Fred agrees that the job will be perfect, as the man he has to assassinate is the warden himself.

(tuba) *This is all that is left of the dance school orchestra. They were playing the twist when it happened. When they began, this was a saxophone. I would say dancing the twist is like scratching your back on a post, without the post. Now, for those of you who wish to practice the twist, this would be an excellent time. In fact, if you twist around far enough, you might miss the next commercial, after which I shall waltz back.* (commercial break, footsteps lead up a wall) *We don't intend to turn our convict in, we just want him to show us, how he did it. We shall probably still be waiting here next week,* (close-up) *when we return with another story. Until then, good night.*

EPISODE #260   **"MOST LIKELY TO SUCCEED"**   Broadcast on May 8, 1962
      Starring: Jack Carter as Stanley Towers   Joanna Moore as Louise Towers
      Howard Morris as Dave L. Sumner   King Calder as Jim, Stanley's attorney
      Bruce Anderson as Harry, the business associate
      Walter Kinsella as Frank Anderson   John Zaremba as the tax investigator
      Mollie Glessing as Hilda, the maid
      Teleplay written for *Alfred Hitchcock Presents* by Henry Slesar, based on his short story "Beggars Can Be Choosers," originally published in the October 1961 issue of *Alfred Hitchcock's Mystery Magazine*. Subsequently collected in *Death on Television* (Southern Illinois University press, 1989) as "Most Likely to Succeed."
      Directed by Richard Whorf.
      (car polish and man in trunk) *Good evening. I hope it doesn't dis-illusion you to see me doing such menial labor, but I like to demonstrate that I'm just an ordinary person. Besides, I need the money. You see this isn't my car, it's my brother's. He hires me to do work of this sort. He keeps telling me it's for my own good. I suppose it is in a way, since the car will become mine if anything untoward should happen to brother.* (knock from trunk) *Most peculiar. I don't believe you've met my brother. Goodness, he used to drop his h's, now he's dropped the entire alphabet. I close the trunk because I know he'd like it that way. He always hated our stories and we have one coming up in just one minute.*

Story: Unemployed Dave Sumner visits his old college friend Stanley Towers. Unlike Dave, who can't seem to hold a job more than a couple months, Stanley has turned into a highly-successful business executive with all the obvious scruples of a shark. Stanley spends quite a bit of time bragging about beating the government out of huge sums of tax dollars, thus a major player in the get-rich-scheme of things. Stanley offers Dave a job, and a chance to gain the true "funds" of corporate business. Just when Stanley thinks he has it all made, including a new employee that can be trusted, his wife decides to go on a trip. Suspecting his wife of having an affair with Dave, Stanley promptly fires his old school chum. A month later, Stanley and his attorneys are called in to a meeting with the Bureau of Internal Revenue. It seems his books are about to be audited. Arriving at the Bureau office, Stanley goes into a state of shock when he learns that Dave is considered "the most successful agent in the Treasury Department." Dave, you see, already had a full-time job, working as an undercover agent!

I do believe that was the most frightening story we have ever presented. Fortunately, it will only frighten one segment of our population, taxpayers. Now for something equally frightening, a commercial, after which I shall appear. (commercial break) *That is all for tonight, and it was quite enough too. Next week I shall be here again, and I know my brother will be also. I seem to have locked the trunk key inside. So until then, good night.*

Trivia, etc. As part of an "in-joke," Norman Lloyd's name was sneaked into the episode, the college yearbook says "Lloyd College" on the cover.

EPISODE #261 **"VICTIM FOUR"** Broadcast on May 15, 1962
　　　　　Starring: Peggy Ann Garner as Madeline Drake　John Lupton as Ralph Morrow
　　　　　Paul Comi as Joe Drake　　　　　　　　　　Bryan O'Byrne as Mr. Tuttle *
　　　　　Nesdon Booth as the bartender　　　　　　　Stephanie Hill as the young girl
　　　　　Glenn Stensel as Freddy, the young man　　　Harry Hines as the old man
　　　　　Teleplay written for *Alfred Hitchcock Presents* by Talmage Powell, from a story of
his own.
　　　　　Directed by Paul Henreid.
　　　　　(chair, crackers) *Good evening, ladies and gentlemen. This chair is more modern than you imagine. You see, it not only rocks but also roll. Actually, all of this is by way of answering certain of our listeners, who like a bit of homey philosophy, dispense with their television. Most of our philosophizing will be done later in the program. But the entire show is fraught with meaning. Listen especially to this next minute. It is very, very fraught.*

　　　　　Story: After just getting married, Joe Drake and his wife Madeline are involved in a severe accident that leaves Joe with a limp, and her with occasional bad headaches. Joe is further upset that Ralph, an old boyfriend of Madeline's, sends her an expensive gift and shows up for a visit. Both men become distressed one evening, when she doesn't arrive home, as lately there have been three unsolved murders in the immediate area. They agree to split up and go looking for her, and alone in a dark alley, Joe finds Ralph's dead body - stabbed repeatedly. Then Madeline shows up, with a knife in her hand. She explains to Joe that she thought someone was after her. "I had to protect myself with this, night after night" . . . just as she had done three previous times, ever since her headaches began.

　　　　　So much for our story. Now for some inspirational verb. "As down lifes rugged road you roam. Ever nearing that home sweet home. Bear this in mind as troubles round you team, that things are not as bad as they would seem. That all is darkest just before the dawn. That when you will, if you would carry on. That though you're bloody head is also bowed, remember that there's silver in each cloud." I find it difficult to go on. So to prove that into each life some rain must fall, my sponsor will fill this void with his own idea of inspiration. After the deluge, me. Proving that all things do come to those who wait. (commercial break) I find myself so emotionally drained, that all I have the strength to do, is to give you the postscript to our story. That Joe reluctantly placed Madeline in the hands of the law. And to bid you good night, until next week.

EPISODE #262 **"THE OPPORTUNITY"** Broadcast on May 22, 1962
　　　　　Starring: Richard Long as Paul Devore　　　Coleen Gray as Mrs. Lois Callen
　　　　　Rebecca Sand as Kate Devore　　　　　　　Olive Dunbar as Mrs. Ranwiller
　　　　　Teleplay written for *Alfred Hitchcock Presents* by Bryce Walton and Henry Slesar, based on the short story "The Golden Opportunity" by J. W. Aaron. subsequently anthologized in *Best Detective Stories of the Year*, ed. David C. Cooke (Dutton, 1959).
　　　　　Directed by Robert Florey.
　　　　　(in a hot air balloon basket) *Good evening fellow astronauts. We seem to have encountered several delays. The first balloon did not withstand the launching ceremony for it became deflated when a bottle of champagne was smashed over it.* (close-up) *This time however, we have found a better use for the wine. I sincerely hope. Unfortunately, the ground crew managed to get most of it and as a result they have lost some of the dedication*

* Bryan O'Byrne's character was mis-spelled "Mr. Tittle" during the closing credits.

to duty which once characterized their work. The countdown has begun but it will take some twenty-five minutes, just long enough for a story and a few commercials.

Story: When Lois Callen is caught shoplifting from a department store, Paul Devore, the assistant manager, questions her. Instead of phoning the police – and her husband - he gives her an ultimatum. Handing her the address to his house, he asks her to show up Sunday evening, or else he'll send her to jail. Paul's wealthy wife, you see, has a congenital ailment. She loathes Paul and refuses to give him a divorce, leading him to put together another scheme to get his hands on her money. With his wife gone for the weekend, Lois arrives on schedule, and Paul explains his plan. Ransacking the house and looting the safe, Paul has Lois tie him to the bed and gag him, so when his wife returns, she will think that robbers were to blame. Lois leaves, paying of her debt. Kate returns an hour later, ungags her husband, and listens to his explanation. Before he can be untied, she remarks that he was lucky the robbers didn't kill him, and since they didn't, she grabs a pillow does the job herself . . .

I wish I could say that everyone lived happily ever after. But that would not be quite true. Perhaps you noticed that Paul Devore was not at all well when we last saw him. As for Kate, the poor child found herself accused of murder, by an overly conscientious District Attorney. Furthermore, he managed to convict her. Most peculiar. Now a commercial, but hurry back, I blast off in one minute. (commercial break) *With that I should be out of orbit in time for next week's story. Until then, good night.* (The balloon lifts with Hitchcock left standing on the ground.)

Richard Long poses for a photo during the filming of "The Opportunity."
Photo courtesy of Ronald V. Borst / Hollywood Movie Posters.

EPISODE #263   **"THE TWELVE HOUR CAPER"**   Broadcast on May 29, 1962
Starring: Dick York as Herbert J. Wiggam   Sarah Marshall as Miss Pomfritt
Wendell Holmes as Sylvester Tupper   Gage Clarke as Mr. Frisbee
Charles Carlson as Lawrence Westbrook
Ned Wever as Mr. Hargis, the detective   Kreg Martin as Mr. Webster
Thomas 'Tom' Bellin as Mr. Brand, the robber
Andy Romano as the second police officer on the scene
Robert 'Bob' Reiner as the airport clerk
Lillian O'Malley as Mrs. Wiggam, the elderly cleaning woman
Ernest Losso as the messenger   and Don Durant as Lowe

Teleplay written for *Alfred Hitchcock Presents* by Harold Swanton, based on the short story of the same name by Mike Marmer, originally published in a 1961 issue of *Cosmopolitan*.   Subsequently anthologized in *A Pride of Felons*, ed. The Gordons (Macmillan, 1963), and in *A Month of Mystery*, ed. Alfred Hitchcock (Random House, 1967).

Directed by John Newland.

(ticker-tape printer)   *Good evening. I've gone into a new business. It is the manufacture and sale of ticker-tape for parades.* (close-up) *Our motto is: We can make any street, Wall Street. A secondary purpose of this paraphernalia is to get our audience in the proper mood for tonight's play, "The Twelve Hour Caper." The preceding information has been obtained from sources believed to be reliable, but its accuracy and completeness, and that of the opinions based there on, are not guaranteed. This is in sharp contrast to the information you are about to receive.*

Story: Herbert Wiggam works for Sylvester Tupper, confirmed slave driver in charge of a prosperous investment firm. Most of the employees at the investment firm break their backs to keep up with the demands of Tupper, so one afternoon, Herbert plans to get even by stealing an unsecured $565,000 negotiable bond shipment, with the help of two professional thieves. Planned to the minute detail, the strangers enter the office at the proposed time, knock Herbert and Tupper out, and stash the bonds in the trashcan. Herbert's plan is to retrieve the bonds after the police leave, but a cleaning lady throws the papers into the rest of her trash. The other conspirators will never know what happened, since the quick-thinking Herbert arrives at the airport to take a flight to Brazil, along with his mother, the cleaning lady.

Here are the closing stock averages.   Thirteen industrials, down 3.7, fifteen utilities up 1.6. We shall have more closing quotations in one minute. (commercial break) *There has been a change in our business. I've eliminated the middle man. As for our final quotations, they were from Herbert Wiggam and his mother, as they left for prison and we decided not to repeat them on the air. Next week we shall be back with another story. Until then, good night.*

Trivia, etc. This was the sixth and last *Alfred Hitchcock Presents* appearance for Lillian O'Malley. Always playing small parts as a maid, housewife or cleaning woman, this episode and the one broadcast a year earlier on "A Woman's Help," showed her doing roles that were very important to the plot. Don Durant plays a very small supporting role in this episode, but was popularly known for playing the title role in the short-lived television series *Johnny Ringo*. (He also composed the theme song to his TV series). Ernest Losso later became an associate producer, casting director and occassional director for television's *Bewitched*, which also starred Dick York.

Tom Bellin made two more appearances on the *Hitchcock* series, then credited as Thomas Bellin. Bob Reiner had already appeared twice on the series, and later did six more appearances on *The Alfred Hitchcock Hour*. In all of those eight episodes, he was credited as Robert Reiner.

381

EPISODE #264 **"THE CHILDREN OF ALDA NUOVA"** Broadcast on June 5, 1962

Starring: Jack Carson as Frankie Fane   Stefan Schnabel as Siani
Thano Rama as Paolo   Lidia Vana as the old woman
David Fresco as the cripple   Carlo Tricoli as the man in the village
Christy Cummins as Gina   Raymond Cavaleri as Giulio
Ray Giarrusso as Cesare   Vincent Padula as the waiter
and Christopher Dark as Ainsley Crowder

Teleplay written for *Alfred Hitchcock Presents* by Robert Wallsten, based on his short story of the same name, originally published in the August 1961 issue of *Ellery Queen's Mystery Magazine*. Subsequently anthologized in *To Be Read Before Midnight*, ed. Ellery Queen (Random House, 1962).

Directed by Robert Florey.

(tower of Pisa) *Good evening, ladies and gentlemen. Welcome to one of the seven wonders of the world. It was through this tower that the ancients left us one important word of wisdom.* (close-up) *When scrubbing floors, never put all the furniture on one side of the room. I believe you will rejoice with me when you hear that the people of Pisa have resisted the offers from the head of a chain of American pancake restaurants. The city fathers were quite willing to paint the building, to resemble a pile of hotcakes, but the thought of syrup cascading down the sides was too much for their sensibilities. Instead, they are having serious negotiations with a pizza company that submitted a higher bid. Naturally, here on Alfred Hitchcock Presents, we never allow commercial considerations to interfere with art or vice versa. Here is a one minute example of the latter.*

Story: Rome. An American criminal named Frankie Fane, is staying in Italy, since he is wanted by the department of justice. To kill some time he goes sightseeing in Alda Nuova, after a tip from Mr. Crowder, an American that lives in Rome. There, he takes a tour of its near-by caves and ruins. A group of wild kids – all juveniles – manage to overtake and rob Frankie, dumping him into a deep pit, leaving him to die in his own good time. An Italian official and Crowder arrive to search for him, because he had supplied narcotics to children, but unsuccessfully finding him, they decide to move on. Stranded helplessly in the pit, Frankie realizes that the children he did a disservice to have returned the favor.

It seems to be catching. Which reminds me, the authorities caught up with the youthful pranksters in Alda Nuova. By the way, workers, designers and painters are about to swarm over the tower and redo it completely. In a minute I shall show you how it will look after the renovation. (commercial break) (Eiffel tower) *This is the way the tower will look after the work is finished. I'm sure you agree it will be a vast improvement. Next week I shall return with another story. Why don't you look in and see if I'm improved?* (the tower leans) *Until then, good night.*

EPISODE #265 **"FIRST CLASS HONEYMOON"** Broadcast on June 12, 1962

Starring: Robert Webber as Edward Gibson   Jeremy Slate as Carl Seabrook
James Flavin as the doorman   Kim Hamilton as the maid
Elaine Martone as Marian   with John Abbott as Mr. Abner Munro
Marjorie Bennett as Mrs. Phalen

Teleplay written for *Alfred Hitchcock Presents* by Henry Slesar, based on his short story "First-Class Honeymoon," originally published in the June 1961 issue of *Mike Shayne Mystery Magazine*. Subsequently collected in *A Crime for Mothers and Others* (Avon, 1962).

Directed by Don Weis.

(travel agency) *Good evening, fellow tourists. Have you longed to visit Europe but lacked the money? Did you ever think it possible to travel there aboard a luxurious ocean liner for less than $25 roundtrip? That is precisely what we are prepared to offer you* tonight. *Here is a sample of our luxurious cabin. All this for only $23 and 50 cents to London, England. Slightly higher if you are discovered. All this is prompted by the title of tonight's fable, "First Class Honeymoon." It follows this commercial which is in a class by itself.*

Story: Edward Gibson has never been happier. Having just divorced Gloria, now his ex-wife, Edward wants to go out and celebrate. A month after the divorce, Edward's feelings have changed, as he's being wiped out by alimony payments, costing him more than $2,000 a month. A possible avenue of escape presents itself in the form of Carl Seabrook. Carl proposes that he marry Gloria, thereby putting an end to the alimony, all for only $10,000. Gibson agrees, seeing the long-term benefits, and gives him $5,000, agreeing to pay the remainder the day after when the bank opens. As a special gift, he will add $500 bonus for a first-class honeymoon. Arriving at Gloria's apartment to present her with a wedding gift, Edward learns from the doorman that Gloria actually died of a heart-attack the night before, while in the company of Carl Seabrook. Edward phones to his apartment only to hear from his maid that he has just left on a honeymoon. Apparently with a beautiful brunette named Marian.

Those of you who were disappointed because you expected "First Class Honeymoon" to be a love story, will be glad to hear that subsequent events were more to your liking. While in St. Thomas, Mr. Seabrook met a beautiful girl, fell madly in love with her and she swindled him out of all his money. And speaking of money, I shall be back in a moment. (commercial break) *That concludes tonight's entertainment. We shall be back next week with more.* (geese, lamas, calfs run by) *Well, I think I got aboard just in time. Good night.* (Hitchcock holds out hand to feel rain)

EPISODE #266   **"THE BIG KICK"**   Broadcast on June 19, 1962
Starring: Wayne Rogers as Kenneth 'Kenny' Redmond

Anne Helm as Judy Baker	Frances Morris as the landlady
Thomas Bellin as Monk	Rees Vaughn as Bruce
Martin Clark as Kong	Jan Conaway as Connie
Susanne Wasson as Linda	Bruce Andersen as the jewelery store clerk

and Brian Hutton as Mitch Baker
Teleplay written for *Alfred Hitchcock Presents* by Robert Bloch, based on his short story of the same name, originally published in a 1959 issue of *Rogue*. Subsequently collected in *Blood Runs Cold* (Simon & Schuster, 1961; Robert Hale, 1962) and in *Such Stuff As Screams Are Made Of* (Ballantine, 1979; Robert Hale, 1980).
Directed by Alan Crosland, Jr.
(antiques) *Good evening, ladies and gentlemen. I'm sure you antique addicts recognize this as an early American television set, the stereoscope. Naturally, this was long before the invention of flopover linear distortion and the hard cell. There are some 19th century authorities who claim to know of instances of distortion and flopover, but these only occured when the stereoscope was used in conjunction with hard cider. The stereoscope was followed by an improvement called "paid stereoscope." You know it as the penny arcade. So much for the days when a man was satisfied with one spinning wheel and didn't need four and a spare. Now let us turn to more modern times. But to ease the transition, this timeless admonition.*

Story: A pair of unemployed beatniks can't pay their rent, so they try to get what they can from a few friends who were throwing a party for all the area beatniks. Mitch and Judy attend, and it is there that she meets a man named Kenny, who shares an unusual attraction for her, and even asks her out. Seeing that the man is well-off, Mitch goes along with the idea because he sees this as an opportunity to acquire the money they need, although Kenny can easily see through their motifs. When they start spending time together, Judy gets upset about Kenny's criticism that all beatniks are downbeats, but Mitch keeps her going back in hopes that Kenny will finance a trip for him. When that doesn't work out, Mitch tries to sell a diamond bracelet Kenny gave Judy, only he ends up in jail because Kenny had stolen it, with the sole purpose of getting Mitch out of his hair. With Mitch gone, Kenny shows his real intentions and attractions by murdering Judy.

Yes, we all get our kicks in different ways. And Kenny learned that the district attorney was no exception. I shall continue my examination of Americana in a moment. (commercial break) *The early Americans who used this butterchurn, were indeed a hardy lot. Mmmmm, a recipe of some sort. Serves twelve, put in several scoops of ice, add three quarts of vermouth and four gallons of gin. Yes a hardy lot. That's all for tonight. Quite enough in fact. We shall return next week with more of the same. Until then, good night.*

Trivia, etc. "I would love to have really met with Alfred Hitchcock and talked with him about things. And he was a very secretive man, from what I understand," Anne Helm recalled. "I heard that he was very interested in me for some film; while I was doing *The Swingin' Maiden* (1964) over in England, he ordered a lot of my films. I never knew if that was true or not, but I was just delighted, 'cause I thought, 'Oooh, maybe I'll get to do a movie with him,' which would have been just wonderful. He did the same thing with Tippi Hedren: He had sort of a "film test" of her, and then hired her. But it was all very secretive, sort of the way Howard Hughes used to work. I always thought of Alfred Hitchcock as being the same style of man."

EPISODE #267 **"WHERE BEAUTY LIES"** Broadcast on June 26, 1962
    Starring: George Nader as Collin Hardy
    Cloris Leachman as Caroline Hardy   Pamela Curran as Joan Blake
    Charles Carlson as Paul Ross   Raymond Bailey as the doctor
    Marilyn Clark as Julie Ross   Norman Leavitt as Mr. Burns, the painter
    Teleplay written for *Alfred Hitchcock Presents* by James P. Cavanagh, based on a story by Henry Farrell.
    Directed by Robert Florey.
    (fishing through a hole in the Arctic ice) *Good evening and welcome to the Arctic, the original home of frozen food.* (close-up) *One warning about life here in the North. Always be sure your TV dinner has been killed before you thaw it out. This always gives me the feeling that I am standing on the edge of an enormous sardine can. It's a message. Let's see what it says.*

Story: Caroline Hardy is having an affair with the desirable Paul Ross. Caroline becomes distraught when she discovers that he is married and that her own brother, told Paul's wife about it. Caroline even acts jealous toward her brother's fiancée Joan. To get even she arranges for an explosion to go off, which doesn't kill him, but makes him blind and badly scars his face. While he goes through plastic surgery to rebuild his face, Caroline realizes that she has the opportunity to keep him all to herself, so when the bandages come off, she claims that the surgery has failed. Since he cannot allow anyone to see him disfigured, he locks himself in his home, with Caroline by his side - who never reveals that after the plastic surgery he is more handsome than ever.

Unfortunately, Caroline's defence plea that her act was merely a case of sibling rivalry, did not hold up in court. And now for a plea of a different sort, after which I shall skate back. (commercial break) *That concludes our program for today. I may as well take my catch and march on. Not bad and you should have seen how many I threw back because they were too small. Next week we shall be back with more ice cold commercials and a freshly thawed out TV story. Until then, good night.*

SUMMER RERUNS

Summer reruns consisted entirely of episodes from season seven.

July 3, 1962 "Bang! You're Dead!"
July 10, 1962 "Maria"
July 17, 1962
    "The Door Without A Key"
July 24, 1962 "Strange Miracle"
July 31, 1962
    "The Faith of Aaron Menefee"
August 7, 1962 "Apex"

August 14, 1962 "The Test"
August 21, 1962 "The Case of M.J.H."
August 28, 1962 "Ten O'Clock Tiger"
September 4, 1962 "Cop for a Day"
September 11, 1962
    "Keep Me Company"
September 18, 1962 "The Old Pro"

THE UNAIRED *ALFRED HITCHCOCK PRESENTS*

"THE SORCERER'S APPRENTICE"   Broadcast in syndication only.
Filmed in the summer of 1961 (probably August), not broadcast during original network run.
    Starring: Diana Dors as Irene   Brandon De Wilde as Hugo
    David J. Stewart as Victor Sadini   Larry Kert as George
Teleplay written for *Alfred Hitchcock Presents* by Robert Bloch, based on his short story of the same name, originally published in the January 1949 issue of *Weird Tales*.
    Directed by Josef Leytes.
    (x-ray of a goat) *Good evening. I'm looking to see what lies ahead. The old Romans used to tell the future by cutting animals open and examining their entrails. Due to some objections by anti-vivisectionists we have to omit the butchering but through the wonders of modern science, we are not denied a glimpse into the future. Besides, it's much more tidy this way.* (looks at x-ray) *This is an x-ray of a goat. An animal which the ancients found to be full of strange portents.* (looks closer) *Hmm, it looks like rain. I can see this will also give one inside about the past. For example, I now know what happened to those car keys I lost last summer. As to the immediate future . . . Either this x-ray plate wasn't properly developed or else we are in for a very dismal time of it, for the next minute.*

    Story: A homeless retarded boy named Hugo is befriended by a carnival magician, Sadini the Great, and the boy takes a keen interest in the man's performances. One of those involves sawing his wife Irene, the beautiful assistant, in half with a large buzz saw, and then making her whole again. Irene, however, happens to be in love with the strong man and wanting her husband put out of the way, sees Hugo as the solution to her problem. Throwing her wilds on the boy, she convinces him that the sawing-in-half trick is real and the wand has magic in it. "And I cannot bear to be cut in half anymore," she cries. Filled with rage, Hugo kills Sadini, and believing he now has the same abilities as her dead husband, pays a visit to Irene, all dressed up in cape and wand. Irene, however, gets her just rewards when, after she is knocked out in a struggle with Hugo, he decides to try the sawing-in-half trick himself, with an unconscious Irene as the assistant. Waking to see the buzz saw piercing the box, she screams . . . and Hugo, mystified why she doesn't smile, pleads "Smile Irene! Smile! Smile!"

    I don't know quite how to put this, however I must tell you the truth. The saw worked excellently but the wand didn't. Hugo was terribly upset and Irene was beside herself. As for the police, they misunderstood the whole thing and arrested Hugo for murder. There's not much more to say, but I shall say it after the following commercial break. (commercial break) *The foregoing has made it obvious to me that we've had quite enough for one evening. We shall save the rest until next week, when I shall re-appear. Until then, good night.*

NOTES: The irreverent approach to issues of crime and punishment may have delighted audiences, but it invariably led to censorship problems. "We were really the thorn in the side of the network," said Lloyd. "The Sorcerer's Apprentice" was a case in point.

On October 2, 1961, two *Alfred Hitchcock Presents* episodes that chilled their television sponsor were described to Federal investigators in New York's Federal Courthouse in Foley Square. Theodore G. Bergmann, vice president in charge of advertising for Revlon, Inc., claimed that the company had taken exception to the programs when they were scheduled for production on the National Broadcasting Company network. Revlon was an alternate sponsor for *Alfred Hitchcock Presents*. Bergmann was a witness at a Federal Communications Commission hearing on sponsor influence on network programming. He described the horrifying climax of "The Sorcerer's Apprentice," when a "deranged" assistant to a magician, "decided to emulate the magician and saw a woman in half – and in this case he really did it," the advertising executive stated.

"We believe that this was excessive, unnecessary and not something we wanted to be associated with in having our name brought to the living rooms of America," he continued. "We protested to the network and succeeded in having it eliminated." The other controversial show ended with the strangling of a young girl. There was another protest to NBC, but the objection was overruled and the program went on the air.

Samuel Thurm, advertising vice president of the Lever Brothers Company, told Ashbrook P. Bryant, chief of the FCC's office of network study, that he believed there had been increasing control over programs by the networks in recent years. As an instance, he discussed a disagreement that developed earlier in the year between his company and NBC. Lever Brothers wanted to sponsor *The Audrey Meadows Show* on the network but NBC said the series was "not acceptable" and offered, instead, *The Joey Bishop Show*. "We said it was not acceptable to us," he testified.

The reasons Revlon and Lever Brothers were concerned about the programs they were sponsoring was obvious to the public, who did not hold the advertiser responsible for the content of stories in magazines and newspapers. Television audiences did hold the television advertiser responsible for program content. In which case, the television advertiser takes a large monetary risk, over a relatively long period of time, whereas the advertiser in printed media does not. Printed media offers a guaranteed circulation and known editorial content; broadcast media did not.

"Audience ratings in television have been controversial and greatly misunderstood by many," stated Alfred A. Whittaker, director of advertising and vice-president of the Bristol-Myers Products Division, testifying at the FCC hearing on sponsor influences on television programs. "No one denies that ratings play a part in arriving at program decisions. As long as an advertiser is interested, as we are and must be, in knowing how many people he is reaching with his message, ratings will continue to be given important consideration."

"Furthermore," he continued, "ratings serve the public interest as well by providing a means whereby the viewing public can accurately reflect to advertisers, networks and producers their reaction, show by show, to television's bill of fare."

This ghoulish play, "The Sorcerer's Apprentice," was to be the only filmed episode of the Hitchcock series denied a network broadcast, due to the gruesome ending. It has, over the years, been shown in syndication and even offered on a couple of video releases. "When the network censors viewed the teleplay there was thunder from on high," Robert Bloch recalled. "This show was simply 'too gruesome' to be aired. Nobody called me on the carpet because of this capricious decision – as a matter of fact, when the series went into syndication, my show was duly televised without a word from the powers that be."

"Robert Bloch was a favorite of mine, a darling, darling man," Norman Lloyd recalled. "Some writers who write that kind of stuff look like the stuff they write - you say, 'Oh, he's capable of murder, no question.' Robert Bloch didn't at all - he was a very nice man. He wrote the one show we were never able to release because of censorship, the one where Diana Dors was sawed in half. She was in a carnival act where she was 'sawed in half' by her magician-husband, and Brandon de Wilde saw this and thought he could do it - and he really sawed her in half! We couldn't release that one - and that was a Bob Bloch story. I don't have an anecdote about Bob, except to say that he was a wonderful writer of that kind of material. What'll amuse you is this: Whenever I got into a discussion about censorship of a particular story about Broadcast Standards [with the network censors], I would finally fall back on Shakespeare. I'd say, 'Now, look - in *King Lear*, they stamp out the guy's eyes! 'Out, out, vile jelly!' Now are you gonna tell me I can't cut Diana Dors in half?' After a while the guy would say, 'You cannot saw Diana Dors in half - and don't quote Shakespeare!' "

Photo courtesy of Ronald V. Borst / Hollywood Movie Posters.

THE CHANGING OF THE SEASONS

The Alfred Hitchcock openings varied from season to season, both visual and physical. For the first seven seasons of *Alfred Hitchcock Presents*, the ever-familiar shadow of Alfred Hitchcock, projected against the silhouette of his figure, remained the same. But the title screen, which listed the words "Alfred Hitchcock Presents," was in black words with quotes during the premiere season. Beginning with the second season, the title became larger, bolder, hollow and white. Around season six, the music score was changed slightly, and for season seven it changed again to a slightly slower speed, and what appears to have been with a larger piece orchestra.

For *The Alfred Hitchcock Hour*, the theme music again changed slightly, with Lyn Murray and his Orchestra performing the piece. Hitchcock's shadow walked along the floor, which eventually grew on the ever-familiar wall, featuring the silhouette, and the words "The Alfred Hitchcock Hour" remained large, bold and white. With the expanded format came the need for a new opening scene. Of course, this changed for seasons two and three of *The Alfred Hitchcock Hour*, this time with Hitchcock's shadow stretching across the floor, with symbols of horror and terror floating by (including the images of a haunted house, the eyes of an owl and Hitchcock's silhouette). As this animated piece gave the illusion that Hitchcock approached a door and opened it, the screen faded to black.

For seasons two and three of *The Alfred Hitchcock Hour*, a short four or five second clip of Hitchcock taking a formal bow announcing "Good Evening . . ." graced the television screens, after the opening sequence. After which, the screen would fade to black, and

Hitchcock's filmed escapades began. This illuminated the use of Hitchcock having to say "Good evening" for every filming. During the final season, however, this clip was not used in every episode, rather Hitchcock just started his hosting chores without the familiar introduction. One noticeable change was Hitchcock's dress. Instead of wearing a tie, as he had during the first seven seasons, he now wore a bowtie. For all three seasons, the cast was listed with both actor and character (except the leading characters), something they had started with for season six and seven of *Alfred Hitchcock Presents*.

Hitchcock and Gig Young in "A Piece of the Action" (Photo courtesy of Photofest)

SEASON ONE - (32 episodes)

SELECTED PRODUCTION CREDITS:
Art Director: Frank Arrigo, Raymond Beal, Howard E. Johnson, Russell Kimball,
John J. Lloyd, Alexander A. Mayer, Martin Obzina and George Patrick
Assistant Director: Donald Baer. Ben Bishop, John Clarke Bowman, James H. Brown,
Carter De Haven III, Edward K. Dodds, Jack Doran, Frank Fox, Hilton A. Green,
Frank Losee, Ronnie R. Rondell, Ray Taylor, Jr. and Wallace Worsley
Associate Producer: Gordon Hessler
Costume Supervisor: Vincent Dee, Burton Miller
Director of Photography: Benjamin H. Kline, a.s.c., Lionel Lindon,
William Margulies, a.s.c., John L. Russell, a.s.c., and John F. Warren
Editorial Dept. Head: David J. O'Connell
Film Editor: Lee Huntington, Tony Martinelli, Douglas Stewart
and Edward W. Williams, a.c.e.
Hair Stylist: Florence Bush
Makeup: Jack Barron, Leo Lotito, Jr.
Music Score and Theme: Lyn Murray and his Orchestra
Musical Supervision: Stanley Wilson
Set Decorators: Robert C. Bradfield, Glen L. Daniels, Julia Heron, John McCarthy,
George Milo, Maurice Malcahy and James S. Redd
Sound: Robert Bertrand, Ralph E. Butler, Lyle Cain, Earl Crain, Jr., Earl Crain, Sr.,
Corson Jowett, David H. Moriarty, John W. Rixey, William Russell,
Ed Somers and Frank H. Wilkinson
Filmed at Revue Studios in Hollywood, California, in association with MCA-TV,
executive distributor for Shamley Productions, Inc.
Broadcast Thursday over CBS-TV, 10 – 11 p.m., EST. Multiple sponsors.

EPISODE #1   **"A PIECE OF THE ACTION"**   Broadcast on September 20, 1962
Starring: Gig Young as Duke Marsden   Martha Hyer as Alice Marsden
Co-starring: Gene Evans as Ed Krutcher   Robert Redford as Chuck Marsden
Nick Dennis as Danny   Raymond Bailey as Allie Saxon
Roger de Koven as Nate   Kreg Martin as Smiley
Jack Sahakian as the gambler   Ralph Smiley as the waiter
Dee J. Thompson as Kelly   Robert Reiner as Pete
Teleplay written for *The Alfred Hitchcock Hour* by Alfred Hayes, based on an
original story by Oliver H.P. Garrett.
Produced by Norman Lloyd. Directed by Bernard Girard.
(standing beside a big key)   *Good evening. I am organizing a key club. It
seems to be the thing to do. For the uninitiated, a key club is one which members can enter,
only if they possess a key. These clubs are terribly exclusive since membership is limited to
men. My club is completely different. It is for women. Inside the club is everything a
woman could want, including me. You see, I am the club's only bunny, but enough of my
troubles. This evening's story has little to do with keys or clubs. It is about gambling and is
called "A Piece of the Action." However, before we proceed with that part of our show, we
bring you this paid announcement.*

Story: Gambling addict Duke Marsden is told by his wife to quit his habitual
wagering or she will leave him. He promises to quit, and makes good on his promise. But
when his brother arrives wanting in on a high-stakes game, Duke decides to teach him a
lesson by allowing Chuck to play with some card sharks that are sure to beat him badly.
When they finally play, Chuck succeeds in winning, wiping out his opponents. One of the
players is clearly upset and tells Duke so, making him decide to play one more game with

marked cards to trounce Chuck, which he does. However, after seeing Duke win with the marked cards they begin to wonder if Chuck was the only one ever beaten unfairly, and they decide a little payback is in order.

(mid-line) Your local stations have been clammering for a piece of the action, so we are rewarding them with the following segment to identify themselves. This should be enough time unless some of them have extra ordinary long call letters.

In tonight's play everyone learned a lesson. Ed and the boys learned that one shouldn't go about shooting people. The police took a hand in teaching them that. Chuck learned that you shouldn't gamble. Duke learned you shouldn't cheat at cards and Alice learned that you shouldn't marry an investment counsellor. There is also sad news about my new key club. It has become even more exclusive than we planned. The Sheriff is now our only member. We've been pad-locked. I shall be back next week with another drama, scenes of which will appear in just a moment.

Trivia, etc. "A Piece of the Action" was not a bad entry for the newly-expanded Hitchcock format. Unlike any other episode of the series, this one was virtually a remake of the movie *Street of Chance*, released through Paramount in 1930. Based on the story "Street of Chance," by Oliver H.P. Garrett, the tale was inspired by the true life of gambler Arnold Rothstein, who was murdered amid a great deal of publicity. In the movie, Regis Toomey played a California card player who arrives in town, meeting up with the notorious Natural Davis, a gambler of ill repute (played by William Powell). Natural, you see, is Toomey's brother and learns why his kin looked him up. It seems the youth learned all too well about gambling successfully with ace gangster cronies, and wants Natural to bail him out. The gamblers are convinced that he must have set them up. Natural reluctantly decides to gamble once more, coming to his brother's rescue, by setting everybody down at the card table and proving his sibling's innocence. Again, the gangsters lose and angry, they vow to break him, which they do. The final scene in the movie is ironic. As Toomey, Powell and a doctor ride in the back of an ambulance, the doctor predicts Powell will pull through. As a gambler to the end, Powell offers 50 to 1 odds that he will not. The doctor says, "It's a bet." Powell dies.

The screenplay for *Street of Chance* was written by Howard Estabrook and Lenore J. Coffee and it was this script that Alfred Hayes based his Hitchcock teleplay on. *Street of Chance* was remade in 1937 under a different title, *Her Husband Lies*, but the picture proved to be a financial disaster. Norman Lloyd, the producer of this Hitchcock episode, recalled, "I spent most of my waking hours searching for material, reading publishers' galleys, foreign periodicals, old movie scripts [ala *Street of Chance*], anything where I might find a kernel of a story." For this episode, the characters changed from John "Natural Davis" Marsden to Duke Marsden, played by Gig Young. As for the role of Duke's younger brother, "Babe Marsden" became Chuck Marsden, played by Robert Redford. (A similar role Redford would expand ten fold, years later in *The Sting*.)

Variety reviewed this episode: "For a time, 'A Piece of the Action,' as the tee-upper was titled, could have passed for a straight dramatic teleplay. But one of the great virtues of the Hitchcock series is that it has never pretended to be anything more than a divertissement, and therefore it was not at all disappointing that the doors were suddenly thrown wide open for all manner of coincidence and contrivances of plot. [The] show had a grim ending, but typically Hitchcock made light of it. In the key role of the gambler with a conscience for his family, Gig Young gave a classy performance. Martha Hyer wasn't as dramatically persuasive, but she's extremely photogenic and did well enough by her lines. Good supporting performances were turned in by Robert Redford and Gene Evans, but it's a good bet that in another anthology context – with that Hitchcock touch that never lets the tale be taken too seriously, 'A Piece of the Action' would have fallen on its face card."

390

EPISODE #2 **"DON'T LOOK BEHIND YOU"** Broadcast on September 27, 1962
        Starring: Jeffrey Hunter as Harold Lambert   Vera Miles as Daphne Grey
        Abraham Sofaer as Dr. MacFarlane   Dick Sargent as Dave Fulton
        Alf Kjellin as Edwin Volck   Mary Scott as Wanda Hatfield
        Madge Kennedy as Mrs. MacFarlane   Ralph Roberts as Paul Hatfield
        Clancy Cooper as the police lieutenant   Suzanne Noél as the woman
        Teleplay written for *The Alfred Hitchcock Hour* by Barré Lyndon, based on the
novel "Don't Look Behind You!" by Samuel Rogers (Harper, 1944; U.S. publication,
Harper, 1956).
        Produced by Norman Lloyd. Directed by John Brahm.
        (lady on stage)   *Good evening ladies and gentlemen and welcome to The Alfred
Hitchcock Hour. I trust you will excuse my startled expression but* (close-up) . . . *this is what
I just pulled out of my hat. It's rather a shock when one is expecting a rabbit. However, I
suppose it isn't as traumatic as it would be if I were expecting her and got the rabbit. Since
my hand is not quicker than the eye I think she will be quite useful in diverting your
attention. This evening I shall attempt several feats of legerdemain. One is to make an hour
disappear without you realizing it. That will not be easy considering this first minute.*

        Story: When two female college students are found murdered in a nearby woods,
the faculty becomes suspect. Two professors of chemistry and music are the prime suspects,
and this intrigues psychology professor Harold Lambert. With the help of his fiancée
Daphne, Harold theorizes that the murderer would try the same stunt again. knowing they
could get away with it the first time. Harold convinces Daphne to walks through the woods,
retracing the college students' path, acting as the lone bait to catch the culprit. The plan
succeeds and the music professor, Edwin Volck, is caught. But unknown to anyone, a
second psycho has been inspired to murder as well, which Daphne finds out the hard way
when her fiancé attempts to strangle her with a piece of rope.

        (mid-line) *I shall begin my act immediately following the station break so please
hurry. . .* (commercial break) *I warned you to not to stay so long. You can hardly expect
rabbits to simply sit around waiting for a station break to end. Now it is time for the second
half of our story, perhaps after that there will be time for a few tricks.*   •

        *Next week we shall be back with another story. Now there's just time enough for
my escape act.* (Hitchcock gets locked into a big suitcase with a sign saying "Do not open
until Christmas – Season's Greetings." The assistant says "Good night.")

EPISODE #3 **"NIGHT OF THE OWL"** Broadcast on October 4, 1962
        Starring: Brian Keith as James Mallory   Patricia Breslin as Linda Mallory
        Mike Kellin as Parker   Philip Coolidge as Rev. George Locke
        Robert Bray as Lieutenant Ames   Frank Ferguson as Captain Garner
        Norman Leavitt as Ben Kaylor   Terry Ann Ross as Barbara Mallory
        and Claudia Cravey as Anne Mallory
        Teleplay written for *The Alfred Hitchcock Hour* by Richard Fielder, based on the
novel "The End of the Track" by Andrew Garve (Collins, 1955).
        Produced by Joan Harrison. Directed by Alan Crosland, Jr.
        (television booths)   *Good evening television consumers. You will be very much
interested in these latest products. . . of the scientific mind. They will be placed on street
corners, drugstores, hotel lobbies, etc. These are not telephone booths. Television booths.
No matter where you are, you can slip into one of these, and by depositing a dime, can view
three minutes of this wondrous art form. How often have you had to go to the corner
drugstore, on an errand, and then never learned how a play ended? Now you need no
longer be chained to your home-set. In one city where the television booth was introduced, a
gentleman ventured from his home for the first time since 1947. His wife reports that he*

walked out of the house with fifty dollars worth of dimes and has not been seen since. Because so many people are used to seeing television from a horizontal position, either flumped down, feet on the coffee-table, or while lying in bed, every other booth is constructed with a TV-screen in the floor, so you can look at the picture through your feet. But we must begin our show. If you have paid a dime and one of your three minutes turns out to be this next one, you have my sympathy. But we shall keep the dime.

Story: Forest Ranger James Mallory and his wife Linda adopt a teenage girl named Anne, whose parents died under mysterious circumstances, in a strange murder-suicide. Afraid that Anne will revive some killer instinct, the Mallory family never reveals the true circumstance of her parents' death. When a blackmailer and his assistant introduce themselves to James, they demand $5,000 – or they'll let Anne in on the truth. Being a true Ranger, James contacts the police, giving them a description of the blackmailer, and then sets out to apprehend them. He has no real intention of paying, and plans to out-fox the pair of criminals. Meanwhile, the partners have had a falling out and one killed the other. When the body is found James Mallory becomes their main suspect, but manages to prove his innocence at the end. Anne, however, learns of the news, and shrugs it off. She always considered the Mallory's her true parents.

(mid-line) *Our story will continue in a few moments. Just now we must observe the quasi folk ritual of the station break. Actually, the station break was designed for a very useful purpose. It keeps the two halves of a show from bumping into one another.* (commercial break) *I hate to break this to you, but the opinions expressed during the past two minutes, do not represent those of our sponsor. We have yet to hear from him. However, following that, we shall have the second half of "Night Of The Owl."*

You remember my mentioning the gentleman who disappeared with fifty dollars in dimes? It saddens me to relate that he became stuck in a television booth, where he eventually succumbed. Fortunately he had deposited all his money, so that the set will be on for the next twenty-four hours. I know he would have wanted it that way. Next week I shall return with another story. Scenes of which will be visible after the following.

Trivia, etc. This program was filmed in cooperation with the Forest Service, U.S. Department of Agriculture. The closing credits not only thanked them for their cooperation, but even cautioned: "Please help them prevent forest fires."

EPISODE #4 **"I SAW THE WHOLE THING"** Broadcast on October 11. 1962
Rehearsed and filmed on July 23 – 27, 1962.
Starring: John Forsythe as Michael 'Mike' Barnes

Kent Smith as Jerry O'Hara	Evans Evans as Penelope 'Penny' Sanford
John Fiedler as Malcolm Stuart	Philip Ober as Colonel John Hoey
John Zaremba as Richard Anderson	Barney Phillips as Lieutenant Sweet
William Newell as Sam Peterson, the drunk	
Willis Bouchey as Judge B. Neilson	Rusty Lane as Judge R. Martin
Billy Wells as George Peabody	Robert Karnes as the police sergeant
Maurice Manson as Dr. Palmer	Ken Harp as the bailiff
Anthony Jochim as foreman	Lou Byrne as the nurse
Mel Jass as the court recorder	Marc Cavell as Freddy Drew, young man
Ronnie R. Rondell as Harold Brady, the motorcyclist	
Ben Pollock as the court clerk	and Claire Griswold as Joanne Dowling

Teleplay written for *The Alfred Hitchcock Hour* by Henry Slesar, based on the story of the same name by Henry Cecil.
Produced by Joan Harrison. Directed by Alfred Hitchcock.

(standing beside a big key)   *Good evening. I am organizing a key club. It seems to be the thing to do. For the uninitiated, a key club is one which members can enter only if they possess a key. These clubs are terribly exclusive since membership is limited to men. My club is completely different. It is for women. Inside the club is everything a woman could want, including me. You see, I am the club's only bunny.* (close-up) *This evening's story is not about key clubs. It is about a man who finds himself in a unique predicament and is called "I Saw the Whole Thing." If you wish to see the whole thing, I suggest you watch this spot closely for the next sixty minutes.*

Story: Mystery writer Michael Barnes is facing criminal action when he accidentally hit a motorcycle driver, who failed to head a stop sign. The police gather witnesses who claim they saw the whole thing, and Barnes is forced to show up in court. In order to disprove the five unreliable witnesses, Michael, having been around enough courtrooms to know how it works, proposes he defend himself, even though Michael is advised that: "A man who keeps his own council has a fool for a lawyer." During the trial, of which Michael is accused of involuntary manslaughter, the mystery writer cross-examines the witnesses, breaking down the testimony of his opponents one-by-one, proving to the jury that neither of them really saw the whole thing. Finally, George Peabody is called in as a witness. He was the only one who really saw the whole thing. Which is lucky for Michael's wife and new baby, who might have had to go through the whole ordeal, if Michael never decided to take matters into his own hands. The truth is, she was driving!

(mid-line) *We now take time-out to hear from an unscheduled witness, your local station. We've asked him to limit himself to the bare facts of the case, but unfortunately he is a garrulous fellow so I'm afraid you're in for some extraneous details.* (commercial break) *Oh, back so soon? I thought you'd become lost among all those commercials, announcements, bulletins and reminders. Just in case you may still remember what happened in the first half of our story, we present one more distraction.*

(close-up) *There is sad news about my new key club. It has become even more exclusive than we planned. The Sheriff is now our only member. We've been pad-locked.* (zoom-out) *I shall be back next week with another drama, scenes of which will appear in just a moment.*

Trivia, etc. Hitchcock's presentation and afterword were almost the same used for the premiere episode of the season. There are, of course noticeable differences, such as additional lines and during the afterword of this episode, Hitchcock's lines were filmed in a close-up, which he was not for "A Piece of the Action." This episode was also John Fiedler's third appearance in a Henry Slesar script on *Alfred Hitchcock*, but the first directed by Alfred Hitchcock. "Alfred Hitchcock directed the first show when it went to an hour-long format. I was in a brief part, but I remember nothing special about the direction. In fact, all of my takes were done within a relatively small amount of time, less than an hour if I recall. It all went by so fast."

The opening scene for this episode is interesting, if not at least worth mentioning. The television viewers are introduced to the witnesses, who hear the sound first, *then* turn to see the scene of the crime. We, the viewers, already know that none of the witnesses are reliable because they only heard the sound, then turned to look. And like the witnesses, we see only what they saw, the motorcyclist fall to the street, and the automobile taking off at full speed. When the twist ending is given away, we ponder to think back at the scene. Did we really see Michael speed away in the car? Or did we just see a faint figure in the car?

Hitchcock Humor: The bus bench on the sidewalk which can be seen during the automobile accident, displays an advertising sign: "Hammond's Mortuary: One of America's Finest Mortuaries." Certainly not something you see advertised anywhere, let alone a bench on the sidewalk. Ronnie R. Rondell, an assistant director for many of the Hitchcock programs, plays the motorcyclist in this play, even though there's only a five second long shot of that motorcyclist. Rondell would also play the role of a college student, later in the season in the episode "A Tangled Web."

EPISODE #5 **"CAPTIVE AUDIENCE"** Broadcast on October 18, 1962

Starring: James Mason as Warren Barrow

Angie Dickinson as Janet Waverly	Arnold Moss as Victor Hartman
Ed Nelson as Tom Keller	Roland Winters as Ivar Waverly
Sarah Shane as Mrs. Helen Barrow	Bart Burns as Lieutenant Summers
Geraldine Wall as Mrs. Hurley	Renee Godfrey as Hartman's Secretary
Don Matheson as Mr. Jack Pierson	Cosmo Sardo as the croupier
Barbara Dane as the folk singer	

Teleplay written for *The Alfred Hitchcock Hour* by William Link and Richard Levinson, based on the novel "Murder Off the Record" by John Bingham (Dodd Mead, 1957; UK title: "Marion," Gollancz, 1958).

Produced by Norman Lloyd. Directed by Alf Kjellin.

(with toy sports car) *Good evening ladies and gentlemen and welcome to The Alfred Hitchcock Hour. This is my new sports car. I'm quite proud of it. However, I wish I also had one for the other foot. I did consider entering this in the Grand Prix, but decided not to. I'm sure I would have won the Booby Prix. However, we must be getting on with tonight's show. I receive a great many inquiries from viewers who wonder why I permit commercials on our show. Frankly I feel that television commercials are ideally suited to this type of program. This next one for example, is most appropriate. It's deadly.*

Story: Mystery novelist Warren Barrow sends his publisher a series of tape recordings transcribing his latest novel. On the tape he mentions that Barrow is a pseudonym acquired before he met his publisher, and describes the incident in which he and his wife up with an American couple, Janet and Ivar West, while vacationing in France. Later on the same trip, his wife was killed in an auto accident. Three years later in a club in San Francisco, Warren met up with Janet and starting an affair, they discuss many means of killing her husband, so they can live together. When Warren finds out that Janet is having other affairs on the side, he believes that he'd better off killing Janet. The publisher replays the tape recordings for another mystery writer, Tom Keller, and both men are convinced that this is not a pure work of fiction. At this moment, Barrow enters the office to try and convince them it is just a book, but he slips and mentions Janet's real name. Tom races to the home of Janet Waverly, but it's too late. Warren just murdered her in cold blood. At the police station, Warren finishes his mystery novel for the publishers, by providing a complete confession, but it seems he's having problems finding the right ending.

(mid-line, Hitchcock behind toy sports car and sign: Radar Zone) *We are about to pass the halfway point. Time will be allowed if you need to change your tires or gas up. (close-up) I must warn you about this, however, this area is well policed. Do not attempt to leave your living room or to change channels. Any attempt to defect will be dealt with harshly. (commercial break) Radar is a marvellous device. During the station break, an elderly gentleman in Peru, Indiana, attempted to go to the kitchen for a jelly sandwich and was detected at once. (close-up) He has been given a long sentence at hard labor. To be precise, he must watch the following commercial.*

This is the ideal sports car for me. It lends an air of dash and zip. Yet with perfect safety, since I'm only permitted to drive it on the sidewalk. We have arrived at the finish line of tonight's show. Next week I shall drive back with another story. Now a scene from next week's commercials.

Trivia, etc. "There really wasn't much to my work on the *Alfred Hitchcock Hour*," recalled Barbara Dane. "I'm a professional singer and I toured all over the states. I remember one day my agent telling me that he got me a role on the Hitchcock program and I was excited. It wasn't long. I sang my own song. Then I went back on tour. I did perform in another mystery program sometime after Hitchcock. I was excited to be on that too, and I've been looking for a copy of my performance for years."

Don Matheson was credited as "Jack Pierson" during the closing credits, when in reality, he plays a Mr. Pierson (his silent partner is called Jack).

EPISODE #6 **"FINAL VOW"** Broadcast on October 25, 1962

Starring: Carol Lynley as Sister Pamela	Clu Gulager as Jimmy Bresson
Don Hanmer as Wormer	Carmen Phillips as Bess Macken
Isobel Elsom as Reverend Mother	Charity Grace as Sister Jem
Nora Marlowe as the landlady	Sam Gilman as Lieutenant Shapiro
John Zaremba as Mr. Meecham	Sara Taft as Sister Lydia
Gaylord Cavallaro as the butler	Bridget Rohland as the first girl
Darlene Lucht as the second girl	Craig Duncan as the sergeant
Virginia Aldridge as the lay sister	Hinton Pope as the train conductor

and R.G. Armstrong as William Downey, the reformed gangster

An original teleplay written for *The Alfred Hitchcock Hour* by Henry Slesar, based on his short story "Hiding Out," later printed in the March 1976 issue of *Alfred Hitchcock's Mystery Magazine*. Subsequently collected as "Final Vow" in *Death on Television* (Southern Illinois University Press, 1989).

Produced and directed by Norman Lloyd.

(at a tattoo shop) *Oh, good evening. I'm taking up a new hobby, tattooing. It's a rather neglected art form. A shame really, for it has many advantages over more conventional forms. Tattooing adds a dimension most paintings do not have: motion. And it sometimes adds the element of sound, when I stick the needle in too far. Actually, I am only an apprentice. I'm practicing on this piece of raw beef steak. My assignment is to use varying shades of brown to make the steak look medium rare. In this way, if the aspiring artist can't sell his canvases, he can always eat them. I think tattooing will revolutionize the cosmetic field. If your lips aren't red enough or you want the roses put in your cheeks, allow me. Or if you wish to avoid military service, I'm quite good at varicose veins. But enough about body murals. We are almost ready for tonight's narrative. First however, an item that is certain. . . to get under your skin.*

Story: A nun, Sister Pamela, is having doubts about her convictions, only a day or two before taking her final vows. The Reverend Mother sends her outside the church to pick up a priceless statue being donated by a reformed mobster, hoping the evils of the outside influence will convince Sister Pamela which road is the right one. When a young punk steals the statue, Sister Pamela seeks out its return. By stealing a pawn ticket and telling lies, Sister Pamela gets knee deep into trouble and almost murdered. Saved by the grace of a reformed gangster, the nun returns to the church with her prize, ready to take her final vows without hesitation, or second thoughts.

(mid-line) *That concludes the first half of The Alfred Hitchcock Hour. We now have what is known as a station break. I know that during a coffee break one drinks coffee. I have no idea what one drinks during a station break.* (commercial break) *Quite some time ago I mentioned that during a coffee break, one drinks coffee but I had no idea what one drank during a station break. After enduring that last one I know . . . If your constitution can stand it, we have one more commercial and then the second half of "Final Vow."*

I've graduated from tattooing raw beef steak to working with a live model. I'm quite excited. (cow in picture) *In some localities busy bodies are destroying the natural beauty of the landscape by removing billboards. We hope to circumvent this by tattooing advertisements on the sides of the animals that graze along the highway. Thus art, nature and commerce are fused in a beautiful tribute to man's ingenuity. And speaking of commerce . . .*

Trivia, etc. Henry Slesar's story about seeking blind faith, "Final Vow," was later dramatized on another mystery anthology, *The CBS Radio Mystery Theater* (August 15, 1974), with Rosemary Rice, star of television's *I Remember Mama*, in the lead role of Sister Pamela.

Thirty-eight years after this episode aired, Carol Lynley and Clu Gulager would meet up again to play the starring roles of Vic Reeves and Mary in *Vic* (1999), directed by Sage Stallone. The same movie is known under the title *Final Act*. Two years after this episode aired, Carol Lynley and Isobel Elsom would appear in the same film, *The Pleasure Seekers*, in 1964. Lynley played Maggie Williams and Elsom played Dona Teresa Lacaya. And if this wasn't enough of reunions, Carol Lynley played the character of Jo Hudson in the TV movie, *The Smugglers* (1968), also directed by Norman Lloyd.

EPISODE #7   **"ANNABEL"**   Broadcast on November 1, 1962
      Starring: Dean Stockwell as David Kelsey   Susan Oliver as Annabel
      Kathleen Nolan as Linda   Bert Remsen as the Sheriff
      Bryan O'Byrne as Mr. Phelps   Florence MacMichael as Daisy
      Henry 'Hank' Brandt as Gerald Delaney   Gary Cockrell as Wes Carmichael
      Charles Robinson as Wes
      Teleplay written for *The Alfred Hitchcock Hour* by Robert Bloch, based on the novel "This Sweet Sickness" by Patricia Highsmith (Harper, 1960; Heinemann, 1961).
      Produced by Joan Harrison. Directed by Paul Henreid.
      (a new costume)   *Good evening ladies and gentlemen and welcome to The Alfred Hitchcock Hour. I hope you like my new evening attire. I'm quite proud of it. It is made of a new synthetic fabric: 100% spunned sugar. I wish you could see it in color. This revolutionary fabric will end cleaning bills forever.   It is even better than wash and wear. You simply wear it and then eat it. I specially recommend it to those of you who wish to look refined. So much for fashion tips, now we come to the truly important part of The Alfred Hitchcock Hour, after which we shall have our story.*

Story: A research chemist named David Kelsey is a rather unbalanced young man. He is madly in love with a girl named Annabel, despite the fact that she is happily married. Both Annabel and her husband try everything in the book to keep David away, but he's too blind with love to forget about her. David goes to ridiculous lengths to posses her love, including building a house whose walls are covered with her photographs. Even after the memorial shrine is built, neither Annabel or her husband can get David to stop pursuing her, and the increasingly desperate young man is forced to turn to murder to permanently posses his one true love. After her husband is killed, David murders Annabel, and stores the corpse in his shrine, as a personal keepsake for all time.

(mid-line) *We have now reached that part of our program wherein the local stations identify themselves. There seems to be doubt as to who they are. Naturally, I would be the first to admit the psychological importance of their identifying. As well as justifying their existence, air go, this station break. I shall see you at his conclusion.* (commercial break) *Welcome back to The Alfred Hitchcock Hour. When you were here last, we were showing a message from our sponsor. We might as well pick up where we left off.*

(Hitchcock in bathrobe) *Thus concludes the story of Annabel and the capricious chemist. As for my change of costume, I'm afraid our synthetic fabric has turned out to be somewhat less than successful. I was feeding a horse a lump of sugar and somehow he began nibbling my sleeve. He just didn't know when to stop. Next week we shall return. . . with more news of the world of science. Another story, some commercials and a new suit of clothes for yours truly. Until then, good night.*

Trivia, etc. Actor Henry 'Hank' Brandt recalled how this episode was filmed twice, because for some reason, the original episode didn't turn out successful. "Paul [Henreid] was a very nice and dear man. I remember we shot that episode twice, once with a couple of people, and they changed the actors and we went back and shot those scenes again. Dean Stockwell and Susan Oliver starred in the one I was in, but the other featured a couple people and that was the one that didn't air. I'm guessing that maybe it was their performance, but I think someone came in and did the extra shooting without Paul, so there are technically two directors for that one. I was in both versions. I've never known them to do that in television, especially now with the cost factor involved. I went under contract with Universal when I first came out here, not yearly, but multiples where I would do a handful of episodes at a time, and I got to sit in on a couple of his films and watch the direction. I was kind of interested in directing at that time."

EPISODE #8 **"HOUSE GUEST"** Broadcast on November 8, 1962
      Starring: Macdonald Carey as John Mitchell   Robert Sterling as Ray Rosco
      Co-starring: Peggy McCay as Sally Mitchell   Adele Mara as Eve Sherston
      Karl Swenson as George Sherston
      Robert Armstrong as Captain Charles Faulkner   Linda Rand as Kira
      William Hellinger as the workman   Billy Mumy as Tony Mitchell
      Teleplay written for *The Alfred Hitchcock Hour* by Henry Slesar and Marc Brandel, based on the novel "The Golden Deed" by Andrew Garve (Collins, 1960; Harper, 1960).
      Produced by Joan Harrison. Directed by Alan Crosland, Jr.
      (camping trailer and violin) *Good evening and welcome to The Alfred Hitchcock Hour. With trailer camps springing up at every corner and all America taking to the road,* (close-up) *I thought you might be interested in this, the latest in trailers. This model is a superb gasoline-saver. For it comes complete with this lovely violin, a set of earrings and two stolen horses. I see it is time for you to face the music. Here it is. After which we shall view tonight's story.* (puts up the violin for starting to play)

      Story: John and Sally Mitchell are indebted to unemployed Ray Rosco, when the young man saves the life of their little boy. In appreciation, they ask him to move in until he can find a job. But the young man turns out to be a lazy freeloader and womanizer. Ray manages to wreck the family car and then tries to pick up a camper's wife. A final confrontation results in John knocking Ray to the ground. When the camper checks out the dead body, he suggests they bury the corpse in the woods, so the police won't link them to the crime. John reluctantly agrees. A few days later, John learns that the grounds will soon be excavated, which will result in the discovery of the body. Asking the camper for help, John is blackmailed for a large sum - or answer to the police. Before he can hand over the check, his wife Sally explains that Ray is alive and well, living in the camper's trailer. It seems John was almost taken in by the con, and it is she who will be phoning the police.

      (mid-line, Hitchcock playing cards) *You are going on a long journey . . . to your local stations. But please do not disembark, or you'll miss the last half of our story.* (commercial break) *I don't mind the local stations identifying themselves, but they seem bent on identifying a large number of other people as well. But take heart. We have only one more interruption before we return to our play.*

      I think the lesson of our story is quite clear. If a stranger offers to save your life, think it over. You may be letting yourself in for a great deal of trouble. This concludes my part of the program. Next time I shall return with another story. Some scenes of which will be shown after this next . . . and last commercial.

EPISODE #9   **"THE BLACK CURTAIN"**   Broadcast on November 15, 1962
Starring: Richard Basehart as Philip 'Phil' Townsend
Lola Albright as Ruth
Co-starring: Harold J. Stone as Maury Epstein, the taxi driver

Gail Kobe as Virginia Carlin	James Farentino as Bernie, the mugger
Neil Nephew as Chuck, the mugger	Celia Lovsky as Mrs. Fisher
George Mitchell as the druggist	Andy Romano as the P. A. L. Officer
William Sharon as Mr. Green	Joe Trapaso as the motorcycle policeman
Frank Sully as the drunk	and Lee Philips as Frank Carlin, private detective

Teleplay written for *The Alfred Hitchcock Hour* by Joel Murcott, based on the 1941 Simon & Schuster novel of the same name by Cornell Woolrich.
Produced by Norman Lloyd. Directed by Sydney Pollack.

(in a pet shop)   *Good evening ladies and gentlemen. I'm pleased you can spend this hour with me. Quiet please if you don't mind.* (close-up) *I have some very interesting pets on sale here. For yacht owners I would suggest an albatross. They are intensely loyal and will follow you anywhere, circling for hours over the spot where your ship sinks. For those of you with swimming pools, if your friends and neighbors are taking advantage of your generosity, may I suggest one of two pets: the ever popular hammer head shark or the Siamese crocodile. Both are quiet, but efficient. They can clear a pool as fast as a TV commercial can empty a room, which brings us to this next item, a pet peeve.*

Story: After being mugged outside the town drugstore, an awakened Phil Townsend discovers that he is suffering from a severe case of amnesia, although he remembers that he was on his way to be married, to a girl named Virginia. Arriving at the home of his fiancée, he learns that she is already hitched. Phil, you see, disappeared three years ago and has never been seen or heard of since. Upon digging further, Phil learns that for the past three years, he's been living under the name of David Webber and worked as a bodyguard for a hot-shot lawyer. As if that news wasn't bad enough, the lawyer's wife was found murdered the other day and Phil, alias David Webber, is under suspicion. On top of that, one of the muggers is the janitor in Phil's apartment building, and he starts to blackmail him. After digging deep and uncovering evidence that clears him of the murder charge, Phil realizes that he needs proper medical treatment – three years to catch up on – so he checks himself in to a hospital.

(mid line) *That was the first half of The Alfred Hitchcock Hour. Now a word from the provinces.* (commercial break) *And now ladies and gentlemen we are about to begin the second half or flipside of The Alfred Hitchcock Hour. The first number will be a solo from our sponsor, followed by the second half of our story.*

That is all for tonight. I'm afraid I must abandon the pet business. They are eating me out of house and home. Listen to the poor dears, and I'm completely out of food. But soft, I see the sponsor approaching!

Trivia, etc.   Shortly after an adaptation of Woolrich's novel was televised on *The Alfred Hitchcock Hour*, Collier Publishers released a new paperback edition following the telefilm's heels. Until this new 1962 edition, the novel had not been re-released in almost fifteen years. Actress Celia Lovsky played a bit part in Alfred Hitchcock's *The Man Who Knew Too Much* (1934 version), and was also the wife of actor Peter Lorre. Sydney Pollack directed episodes of many television series including *Kraft Suspense Theatre*, *Ben Casey* and *The Fugitive*, before directing big-screen features.

Lee Philips Comforts Lola Albright in "The Black Curtain," directed by Sydney Pollack.

Photo courtesy of Ronald V. Borst / Hollywood Movie Posters.

EPISODE #10   **"DAY OF RECKONING"**   Broadcast on November 22, 1962

Starring: Barry Sullivan as Paul Sampson   Claude Akins as Sheriff Jordan
Katharine Bard as Caroline Sampson   Hugh Marlowe as Harold
Jeremy Slate as Trent Parker   K. T. Stevens as the woman
and Louis Hayward as Judge David Wilcox   Les Tremayne as Dr. Ryder
Robert Cornthwaite as the District Attorney
Alexander Lockwood as Dr. Campbell   James Flavin as the coroner
Tom Begley as the court clerk   Buck Taylor as Frazier
Hinton Pope as the police officer   and Dee Hartford as Felicity Sampson

Teleplay written for *The Alfred Hitchcock Hour* by William Link and Richard Levinson, based on the novel "Murder Isn't Private" by John Garden (Michael Joseph, 1951; U.S. title: "Day of Reckoning," Lippincott, 1951).

Produced by Joan Harrison. Directed by Jerry Hopper.

(small yacht)   *Good evening fellow yacht owners. This is not champagne. You can see my tastes are much too simple for that. This is not intended for a christening. It is my ship-to-shore communication. I realize that my yacht may seem rather old-fashioned to luxury minded people, but I find the relationship between a man and a gasoline engine too coldly impersonal. My engine is far more economical and very quiet too, except for an occasional scream and the clanking of chains. It is also quite speedy. This . . .* (pulls out a whip) *is the accelerator. So much for the simple pleasures. We are presenting a story tonight called "Day Of Reckoning." It follows in precisely one minute.*

Story: Paul Sampson, a successful architect by occupation, learns of his wife's unfaithfulness and kills her in a fury of emotion. When the police investigate, they rule the death as an accident, and Paul is cleared of all charges. Days pass and Paul's conscience gets the better of him. No longer able to take the guilt of his act, he confesses the murder to family relatives, who dismiss his ramblings as strain of losing his wife. Turning to an old friend, a judge, Paul confesses his crime again, hoping to relieve the tension building inside, but again, the judge pays no heed. You see, it was the judge himself who was sleeping with Paul's wife, and after seeing how Paul tortures himself day in and day out, decides to leave Paul suffer his own fate. With no other choice, Paul returns to the family to confess and this time they agree he's routing for mental breakdown – so they commit him to a hospital.

(mid-line) *This concludes the first half of the Alfred Hitchcock Hour. Now for our main attraction. The following montage of images and cacophony of sounds, is called a station break, and I am sure you will find it an exciting and colorful experience. Observe.* (commercial break) *Welcome back. Before we can continue with the Alfred Hitchcock Hour . . . the beloved sponsor's minute.*

I have a joyous footnote to the grim scene, which you have just observed. Eventually our story had a happy ending. Judge Wilcox later admitted he had been fibbing and the world knew that Paul had been guilty of murder, so he was finally granted his wish. To his great relief, he was taken out of Fairfield and suitably disposed of. I have the feeling that I've done quite enough for one day, however I commend you to the following commercial and the sampling of next week's play.

Trivia, etc. Hugh Marlowe and K.T. Stevens were husband and wife in real life, married in 1946. They had two children before their divorce in 1968. This would mark the only time the loving pair worked in the same television show or movie during their careers. Jeremy Slate, who appeared in many episodes of the Hitchcock series including "First Class Honeymoon" and "One Grave Too Many," was also a policeman at the train station in Hitchcock's *North by Northwest* (1959).

EPISODE #11   **"RIDE THE NIGHTMARE"**   Broadcast on November 29. 1962
          Starring: Hugh O'Brian as Chris Martin   Gena Rowlands as Helen Martin
          John Anderson as Adam   Jay Lanin as Fred
          Richard Shannon as Steve   Philippa Bevans as Mrs. Anthony
          Gail Bonney as the elderly woman   Olan Soulé as Bill
          Richard Franchot as the bank teller   George Gaynes as Mr. Campbell
          Teleplay written for *The Alfred Hitchcock Hour* by Richard Matheson, based on his 1959 Ballantine novel of the same name.
          Produced by Norman Lloyd. Directed by Bernard Girard.
          Music composed and conducted by Richard Shores.
          (stands in sewer)   *Good evening ladies and gentlemen. I suppose you are wondering what I'm doing here. Not much, actually. So far I've spent most of my time trying to get out. Passers-by are not being very helpful. They seem to think I'm an errant actor from the theatre of the absurd. Actually, I was answering a real estate advertisement. Small compact residence on thoroughfare, close to schools, shops, freeways. Plenty of transportation. Running water. And that serves to remind me that tonight's play is called "Ride the Nightmare." And speaking of nightmares, here is our first commercial.*

Story: Chris Martin has a secret he's never shared with his loving wife Helen. It seems many years ago, when Chris was a teenager, he was involved in a crime, and got off debt free. Three of his buddies, however, took the rap and went to jail, just as justice delivers to all guilty parties. The problem is, these three men recently broke out of prison and angry because Chris got away, want some justice of their own. Always fearing his wife would leave him, Chris never told her – until today. Helen agrees to help him, and with her help, they successfully apprehend the criminals.

(mid-line, pokes his head out of a manhole) *You have just witnessed the first half of our play. We now come to that part of the program which one viewer says reminds him of a bologna sandwich, a station break between two slices of Hitchcock.* (commercial break) *Good evening, and welcome to the Hitchcock Hour again. You have come back a trifle early, but no matter. We have an excellent little time-killer, which will keep you from getting restless. And now, if you'll be good enough to give me a hand, I shall get out of here.*

I'm terribly sorry. That was a nasty tumble. However, we did manage to get me out of there. Perhaps you can amuse yourself by sitting in the darkness and imagining what our next commercial will be like. Sorry, regulations you know. (puts the lid on)

EPISODE #12 **"HANGOVER"** Broadcast on December 6, 1962
      Starring: Tony Randall as Hadley Purvis   Jayne Mansfield as Marian
      Robert P. Lieb as Bill Hunter   Myron Healey as Bob Blake
      Tyler McVey as Mr. Driscoll, the district attorney
      James Maloney as Cushman   June Levant as the saleswoman
      William Phipps as the bartender   Chris Roman as Cliff
      Richard Franchot as Albert   and Dody Heath as Sandra 'Sandy' Purvis
      Teleplay written for *The Alfred Hitchcock Hour* by Lou Rambeau, based on John D. MacDonald's short story "Hangover," originally published in the July 1956 issue of *Cosmopolitan*, and Charles Runyon's short story "Hangover," which was originally published in the December 1960 issue of *Manhunt*. MacDonald's story was collected in *End of the Tiger and Other Stories* (Fawcett Gold Medal, 1966). Runyon's story was anthologized in *Hitchcock in Prime Time*, ed. Francis M. Nevins, Jr. and Martin Harry Greenberg (Avon, 1985).
      Produced by Norman Lloyd. Directed by Bernard Girard.
      (with a sling-shot) *Good evening and welcome to The Alfred Hitchcock Hour. This object . . . plays an important part in a new television series we are in the process of creating. Since the public or at least the producers, relish stories about the military, we will soon launch our own series about World War II. World War II B.C. that is. As wars go, I can't say this is a favorite of mine.* (close-up) *I had hoped to get one with a catchy title, like "The Wars of the Roses" or the "Whiskey Rebellion," but of course, they were snapped up long ago. This trend is not difficult to understand if you know it is an established fact that situations are more dramatic, and jokes are funnier if the characters involved are dressed in uniforms. This explains a large number of shows about nurses, maids, butlers, etc. Naturally these remarks have nothing at all to do with tonight's story. They are only meant to divert your attention, so that our sponsor . . . can sneak up on you, and here he is . . . ready to pounce.*

Story: Hadley Purvis, an advertising man, finds himself facing a divorce if he doesn't knock off the heavy drinking. This does little to slow him down as he continues to drink himself into an alcoholic stupor, and one morning, finds himself at home with a girl named Marian that he picked up the night before. At work he learns that he was fired after being drunk at a meeting which he doesn't even remember. He finally realizes that he has had one drink too many when he finds his wife dead - strangled to death with a scarf he just bought for her.

(mid-line) *Completing the first half of our play has so exhausted our actors that they need a rest. However, in television it is a cardinal sin to allow the viewer a single moment when his ears and eyes are not assaulted by sound and fury. Therefore we shall now ask your local stations to take up the battle.* (commercial break) *And now ladies and gentlemen, a commercial. After which we shall show a few scenes from this week's show.*

This concludes tonight's story. Of course there was a legalistic footnote, but the jury was charitable. I customarily close on a light note but I feel that tonight's subject is an unsuitable one for humor. Alcoholism is being recognized as one of the most serious diseases of our society, and I hope this program has helped dramatize some of the frightening aspects of the problem. Good night.

Trivia, etc. Unlike any other episode of *The Alfred Hitchcock Hour*, this was actually based on two short stories instead of one.* "The passage of years has not diminished my bafflement and annoyance at what television did to 'Hangover'," said John D. MacDonald. "I was indeed pleased when I heard that it would be on the *Alfred Hitchcock Hour*. As soon as the titles came on the screen, I realized some committee of idiots had decided to combine my story with another story by Charles Runyon. The result, of course, was cluttered nonsense. The bright and shining spot was Tony Randall as Hadley Purvis. He was absolutely right. 'Hangover' is, I think, a sufficiently strong story to carry the viewer along for the required fifty minutes of narrative flow. I suspect that it is decisions like this one, errors in taste and in performance, which have brought the networks to the sorry condition in which we see them today, dying and dwindling and flapping about in a hen yard of schlock."

"I never saw 'Hangover'," said Charles Runyon, "but I could write reams about the events surrounding the story from its conception – based on a real-life drama – to publication in *Manhunt* magazine. It is the Hope Diamond of short stories, with a history permeated with blood, bizarre coincidence, and permutations of evil."

"Jayne Mansfield was fun," recalled Tony Randall. "During the filming she didn't take herself too seriously. I had a good, fat part in the script. I'll tell you one thing about that broadcast you probably don't know. During the conclusion of filming, the script girl mistimed the show so we ended up several minutes short. We had to improvise a bar room scene that wasn't in the script. All in all it was a lot of fun."

EPISODE # 13 **"BONFIRE"** Broadcast on December 13, 1962
    Starring: Peter Falk as Robert "Robbie' Evans
    Dina Merrill as Laura Freshwater
    Co-starring: Patricia Collinge as Naomi Freshwater
    Paul von Schreiber as the youth   Sam Weston as the taxi driver
    Craig Curtis as the young man   Craig Duncan as the police officer
    Teleplay written for *The Alfred Hitchcock Hour* by Alfred Hayes and William D. Gordon, based on a story by V.S. Pritchett.
    Produced by Joan Harrison. Directed by Joseph Pevney.
    Music composed and conducted by Pete Rugolo.
    (in a ghost town with a stock exchange tele-printer) *Good evening. I thought you might enjoy seeing this ghost town. These towns sprung into being over night and prospectors flocked here, enticed by the lure of easy riches. Everyone wanted to get rich quick and for a while it looked as though everyone would.* (close-up) *Then the bubble burst, no one even took the time to turn off the ticker tape. Unless I keep on running too long, also.*

* Hitchcock's *Stage Fright* (1950) was also based on two stories, both by Selwyn Jepson. They were called "Man Running" and "Outrun the Constable." In fact, *The Alfred Hitchcock Hour* "Power of Attorney" was also based on a story by Jepson.

Perhaps we should begin tonight's show. In keeping with the theory that we shall have no where to go, but up. We begin with the following.

Story: Robert Evans, the preacher in charge of the local gospel mission, will go to any means to obtain the funds he needs to build himself a church – including breaking the commandments. Courting Naomi Freshwater, a wealthy old lady about town, Robert takes advantage of the woman's heart attack, by holding back her heart pills. Later he meets Laura, the elderly lady's niece, who returns to town to help settle the estate. Robert tries to score with Laura, but the woman turns down his proposal and says she's going to sell the house, resulting in another murder. With the help of an unsuspecting gardener, Robert buries a giant chest in the backyard – a chest that contains the body of Laura. Setting fire in the hole, Robert leaves to attend the congregation, knowing that when he gets back, the body will be cremated, beyond human recognition. But this time Evans is a bit careless, not counting on the evening's rainfall (an act of God) to reveal his sin.

(mid-line) *We now pause for a moment. This is the last chance our local stations have to identify themselves, before we plunge on into our story. At the conclusion of the identification, I shall reappear.* (commercial break) *Two stations did not have the proper identification, and were arrested for vagrancy. For the others we now continue our show.*

That is the end of our story. Next week we hope to bring you another one. Next for you is a commercial. Meanwhile I shall see if I can turn off this ticker tape. (gets drowned in strips of paper)

Trivia, etc. "I'll tell you what I think is fairly interesting," said Joseph Pevney. "This was one of Peter Falk's introductions to American television [Falk appeared on

Alfred Hitchcock Presents a year and a half earlier in "Gratitude"]. He didn't know how to hit a mark. I had to explain to him, 'Peter, the camera is lit for a certain spot, and you've got to hit it, otherwise you won't look as good as you could look. The camera won't be focused on you and I'll have to cut it.' And what did he say to me? [laughs] Well . . . he was a funny guy. He looked at me with that glass eye and he was fun to work with. He wasn't the same man who developed into the *Columbo* figure later. 'Cause here he was new to the game. But I loved him and I liked Dina. She was wonderful."

Hitchcock poses for the episode "Bonfire." (Photo courtesy of Ronald V. Borst / Hollywood Movie Posters.)

EPISODE #14 **"THE TENDER POISONER"** Broadcast on December 20, 1962
Starring: Dan Dailey as Philip 'Barty' Bartel   Howard Duff as Peter Harding
Jan Sterling as Beatrice Bartel   Philip Reed as John O'Brien
William Bramley as Lieutenant MacDonald   Richard Bull as the detective
Robert Reiner as the policeman   G. Stanley Jones as the drug store clerk
and Bettye Ackerman as Lorna Dickson

Teleplay written for *The Alfred Hitchcock Hour* by Lukas Heller, based on the novel "Five Roundabouts to Heaven" by John Bingham (Gollancz, 1953; U.S. title: "The Tender Poisoner," Dodd, Mead / Red Badge Detective 1953).

Produced by Norman Lloyd. Directed by Leonard J. Horn.

(as your friendly pharmacist, complete with white suit)   *Good evening and welcome to the friendlier pharmacy. I recently found a very lucrative use for my empties. I use them to make a sugar substitute. Ground glass.* (close-up) *Excellent for men and women who prefer a spouse-free diet, also very effective for getting rid of unwanted heirs. Best of all, a doctor's prescription is not required, at least not before it is swallowed. Tonight's story is entitled "The Tender Poisoner." As you see, I have not been misleading you, and consistent with this policy of frankness, I must warn you that this next minute may be hard to swallow, but be brave.*

Story: Peter Harding, an influential executive, tries to save the career of a failed colleague, Philip, by arranging for Philip to go through a comprehensive training course, offered by his corporation. Shortly after, Peter learns that Philip's private life is falling apart as well, because Philip wants to divorce his loving wife of fifteen years, so he can marry another woman. This might pay off for Peter, who is willing to make a sacrifice by taking the beautiful "other woman" off Philip's hands to save his marriage. But when he gives Philip some poisoned medicine, Philip sees through it and calls the police to examine the contents of the glass.

(mid-line, takes taste of concoction) *We still have a long way to go. Join me again after the following local interruption.* (commercial break) *I know I shall label everything, but those station breaks defy description. Now for the next minute . . . it's not toxic but it is highly soporific so be careful. If you are a heavy sleeper, you could miss the entire second half of our play.*

I like that ending very much, but unfortunately it is not consistent with the facts of the case, for the police eventually learned the truth about Bartel's villainy. (close-up) *Before leaving you I wish to mention that although a poison such as the one mentioned in the story does exist, it is not considered in the public interest to identify it. Therefore it was given a fictitious name. I mention this to save discontented husbands the trouble of searching fruitlessly through medical books.* (zoom-out) *Until next week, good night.*

Trivia, etc. No new episode was aired on December 27, 1963. Instead, the season opener, "A Piece of the Action," was rebroadcast.

EPISODE #15 **"THE THIRTY-FIRST OF FEBRUARY"** Broadcast January 4, 1963
Starring: David Wayne as Andrew Anderson
William Conrad as Sergeant Kress   Elizabeth Allen as Molly O'Rourke
Co-starring: Staats Cotsworth as Mr. Vincent
William Sargent as Peter Granville   Bob Crane as Charlie Lessing
Steve Gravers as the psychiatrist   Stacy Harris as the District Attorney
Bernadette Hale as Miss Wright   King Calder as Reverton
Kathleen O'Malley as Valerie Anderson   Robert Carson as the coroner

Teleplay written for *The Alfred Hitchcock Hour* by Logan Swanson, based on the novel of the same name by Julian Symons (Gollancz, 1950; Harper, 1951).

Produced by Joan Harrison. Directed by Alf Kjellin.
Music composed and conducted by Robert Drasnin.

(as a conductor/prompter) *Good evening ladies and gentlemen of the ensemble. I suppose you think I'm the prompter, I'm not. I am the conductor.* (close-up) *This is my answer to outdoor opera. Singing opera in the out-of-doors is like painting with oils under water. I don't claim the art suffers but the artist does. The orchestra may have a bit of difficulty seeing me but I'm also less of a target for the audience should they decide to become demonstrative. I understand the soprano and the tenor have stopped fighting, so the curtain must be about to go up. But before you see tonight's opus, we present this little opera buffé.*

Story: Andrew Anderson is shocked to find the lifeless body of his wife at the bottom of their cellar steps. He phones the police, who promptly begin a thorough investigation. The coroner rules the matter an accident, but the investigating detective, Sergeant Kress, is not so sure. Deciding to put into action his own plan to learn the truth about the executive's guilt or innocence, he bends Andy's world by making him think his wife was having an affair with another man. She may still be alive, living alone with her "lover," and when Andy shows up to confront them, the true facts of the case are clear. Andy was innocent all along. Having been hounded one time too many, Andy snaps and kills the detective.

Psst! Several stage hands are attempting to pull me out of here. If they succeed by next week, I shall bring you another story. Scenes from our next production will be shown immediately after this commercial.

Trivia, etc. Logan Swanson, the writer of this teleplay, is actually a pseudonym of Richard Matheson, who also scripted another episode of *The Alfred Hitchcock Hour*, "Ride the Nightmare." Matheson wrote a huge number of television scripts for *The Twilight Zone*, and this marked one of only two contributions to the Hitchcock program. The other episode, "Ride the Nightmare," was actually based on one of Matheson's novels, and for that episode, he used his real name for the on-screen credits. His son, Richard Christian Matheson, also writes short stories and teleplays, including scripts for TV's *The A-Team*. Swedish director Alf Kjellin was also credited as an actor, playing the murderous music teacher in the episode "Don't Look Behind You."

EPISODE #16 **"WHAT REALLY HAPPENED"**   Broadcast on January 11, 1963
Starring: Anne Francis as Eve Raydon   Ruth Roman as Addie
Gladys Cooper as Mrs. Raydon   Steve Dunne as Jack Wentworth
Co-starring: Michael Strong as Molloy   Tim O'Connor as Halstead
Gene Lyons as Howard Raydon   Charles Irving as the judge
Theodore Newton as the doctor   Fern Barry as the maid
Michael Crisalli as Gilly Strain

Teleplay written for *The Alfred Hitchcock Hour* by Henry Slesar, based on the novel of the same name by Marie Belloc Lowndes (Hutchinson, 1926; Doubleday, 1926).
Produced by Joan Harrison. Directed by Jack Smight.

(with knights in arms) *Good evening knights and ladies. I believe we have at last devised the perfect television show. These two gentlemen are its leading characters. They are a father and son team. Defenders of the underdog. Each week they find a new maiden in distress or a new dog as the case may be, and thus we have a completely different story, yet retain the same magic ingredients. Being father and son not only gives them some excellent*

Freudian conflicts, but also enables them to gang up on a single opponent. Of course the son furnishes the fire enthusiasm, while the father is the brains of the team. In each and every story we have a dramatic courtroom scene, in the court of King Arthur. Our heroes ride horse-back for the benefit of western fans, and for a little extra fun I have quietly sharpened the lances, thus assuring us some excellent operating-room scenes. I don't see how it can miss. Of course, just as no rose is complete without thorns, so no television show is complete without the following.

Story: Eve Raydon attempts to prevent her husband from firing the family maid. It seems Addie's son accidentally broke an antique vase and Howard wants the maid fired as a result. In retaliation, Addie, the maid, poisons Howard, who promptly dies. When the police investigate, Eve's mother-in-law accuses Eve of murdering her son, and the police consider her a prime suspect. The court trial is swift and the prosecutor reveals some startling evidence. Addie's son is really Eve's, which is why she didn't want her husband Howard to fire her. Believing everything will turn out okay, the maid sits back and watches. To her surprise, a guilty verdict is delivered. Upset because her kind and innocent employer is going to be sentenced, the maid writes a confession and attempts suicide. Revived in time to stand trial, the maid's confession is used to save Eve, who promises to assist her throughout the upcoming ordeal.

(mid-line) *Just to keep you from becoming too engrossed in our story, the ground rules of television provide us this cooling off period, after which we shall all be back.*

You have now seen the whole of what really happened, we shall cross-examine you later. By the way, Mrs. Strain was subsequently tried and found guilty. She hoped for a suspended sentence but unfortunately they suspended her. My two shoreward heroes are no longer partners, the split-up was entirely friendly, however. You see this way they can represent both sides of a case. Defending the underdog is fine, but it is usually the upper dog who can pay the big fees. Next week The Alfred Hitchcock Hour will bring you another story. Some previews of this will follow the following.

EPISODE #17   **"FORECAST: LOW CLOUDS AND COASTAL FOG"**
Broadcast January 18, 1963
Starring: Inger Stevens as Karen Wilson   Dan O'Herlihy as Simon Carter
Co-starring: Chris Robinson as Ricky Garrison, a surfer
Peter Brown as Ed, a surfer   Richard Jaeckel as Tom, a surfer
Simon Scott as Stanley 'Stan' Wilson
Russ Thorson as Geary, Deputy Sheriff   Robert Millar as Mitch
Greg Morris as Dr. Foster   and Christopher Dark as Manuel Sanchez
An original teleplay written for *The Alfred Hitchcock Hour* by Lee Erwin.
Produced by Leon Benson. Directed by Charles Haas.
(with a surf board)   *Good evening ladies and gentlemen and fellow surfers. This evening's drama is only incidentally concerned with surfing. Actually it touches on many popular sports. Drinking, revenge, kidnapping, homicide . . . I first became attracted to surfing when I was told that it was possibly the only sport, which involved no competition, and where the participants did not throw or catch a ball or run and jump. It seemed to be a perfect way to relax from the strain of over-sleeping. I've become quite good at it really and I'm eager to see how it works in the water. You see, we're still looking for a wave, large enough to support me. Meanwhile, here is the sponsor who is supporting this portion of the program.*

Story: Late one night when Karen Wilson's husband has left for a trip, a stranger named Manuel Sanchez begins beating on the door. He asks to use the phone, claiming he's having problems with his car. Out of distrust, Karen refuses entrance, forcing him to go elsewhere for help. Later that evening, she is shocked to learn that while Sanchez was walking to the nearest service station, his girl friend was still waiting at the run-down car, and was attacked and left on the beach. Sanchez blames Karen for his girlfriend's death, promising to get revenge. Karen, however, suspects her next door neighbor, Simon Carter, may be the guilty party, probably hearing the commotion outside, from the night before. She confirms her suspicions, particularly when Carter shows up drunk and three boys "save" her from Carter's sexual advances – not realizing that the three boys are the real killers. Confessing to Karen that they attacked the girl who died earlier that day, Karen will be their next victim. What the boys don't know is that Sanchez has sneaked into the house, intending to kill Karen, but after hearing the confession, holds the boys at gunpoint till the cops arrive.

(mid-line) *This is turning out to be more strenuous than I imagined. But enough of me, let us hear from your local announcer, and all his friends.* (commercial break) *Good evening and welcome back to the Alfred Hitchcock Hour . . . or rather what is left of it. I now turn you over to our sponsor, who will introduce the second half of our story.*

This is my final appearance tonight. However, we have some scenes of next week's story, which I'm anxious for you to see. As for surfing, I've just discovered why one sees so many of these about. At the beach, on the highway, on top of automobiles, etc. It's because they're so practical. (folds up an ironing-table) *Good night.*

Trivia, etc. There's actually two versions of the opening, the second almost the same with the exception of the word "Murder" substituted with "Homicide" in the presentation. Greg Morris, who played Dr. Foster in this episode, began his acting career appearing in episodes of *The Twilight Zone* and *The Dick Van Dyke Show*, before being cast in *Mission: Impossible* as electronics expert Barney Collier.

EPISODE #18   **"A TANGLED WEB"**   Broadcast on January 25, 1963
      Starring: Robert Redford as David Chesterman

Zohra Lampert as Marie Petit	Barry Morse as Karl Gault
Gertrude Flynn as Ethel Chesterman	Cathleen Cordell as Mrs. Spaulding
Joan Houseman as Mrs. Flingston	Elizabeth Thompson as the student's girl
Ronnie R. Rondell as the college student	Hinton Pope as the cab driver
Hal Bokar as the reporter	Syl Lamont as the photographer

      Teleplay written for *The Alfred Hitchcock Hour* by James Bridges, based on the novel of the same name by Nicholas Blake (Collins, 1956; Harper, 1956). *
      Produced by Norman Lloyd. Directed by Alf Kjellin.
      (tied to the ground like Gulliver)　　　　*Good evening ladies and gentlemen. I hope you will pardon me if I don't get up. It's rather a shock to awaken and find yourself fastened to the floor like a carpet. I told these little people that this was no way to treat a tourist, even if it is the off-season.　　But they say they don't care. They have a new and sensational tourist-attraction - me. I'm being advertised as a Lilliputian Disneyland. Of course, there are some compensations. I think I'm probably the first member of my family ever to be declared a national monument. Tonight's story is called "A Tangled Web," a title I find embarrassingly apropos. In it a young girl falls in love and follows her young man with no regard for his past or future. As for your future, it includes a commercial. One which I intend to watch all the way through. I shant move a muscle.*

      Story: David Chesterman, son of a respectable, wealthy family, falls in love with Marie, the French maid, and the two get married. David isn't just an innocent boy, however,

* Nicholas Blake was the mystery-writing pseudonym of English poet laureate C. Day Lewis (actor Daniel Day-Lewis's father).

he's a professional hoodlum who robs the houses of wealthy families. His best friend, Karl, is jealous of David, because the boy is young, wild and impulsive . . . and he owns Marie. One evening, alone together, Karl tells Marie the truth about her husband, but she still won't leave David, since he goes respectable and gets a job. Sadly, once a hoodlum, always a hoodlum, and David's next job is a set-up, and the caretaker is killed. Karl contacts the police, anonymously, and David is soon arrested. At the trial, Karl testifies against David, and how convenient that Marie was not in the room at the time – all part of Karl's plan. This still doesn't get him the girl, who stabs Karl out of self-defense with one of Karl's darts. Racing to the courtroom, Marie climbs out the window and threatens to jump if they don't send her husband to the window. She asks David to explain his innocence, and he confesses his guilt.

(mid-line) *That was short. Time passes quickly when you are having a good time. The next sounds you'll hear will be that of our stations breaking.* (commercial break) *Welcome back to The Alfred Hitchcock Hour, but I wish you had brought along a pair of scissors. The entertainment I can furnish is extremely limited so I shall turn you over to my sponsor. I am sure he will think of something to do.*

We are coming to the end of the second half of The Alfred Hitchcock Hour. In fact we are coming to the end of Alfred Hitchcock. Two rival groups of little people were fighting over me, but they have now hit upon a happy compromise. (a big pendulum swings) *The pendulum drops a few inches each day, so by next week I imagine I shall be able to host two half-hour shows simultaneously. Until then, good night.*

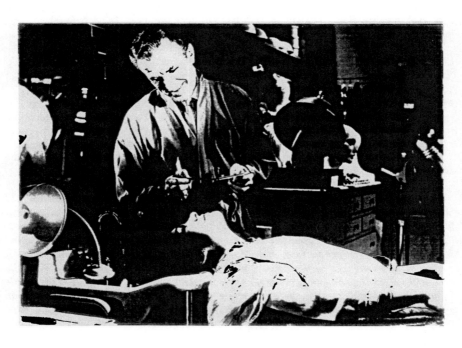

Barry Morse helps Zohra Lampert acquire a new hair-style in "A Tangled Web."
(Photo courtesy of Photofest, in New York.)

EPISODE #19 **"TO CATCH A BUTTERFLY"** Broadcast on February 1, 1963
Starring: Bradford Dillman as Bill Nelson
Co-starring: Diana Hyland as Janet Nelson

Ed Asner as Jack Stander | June Dayton as Barbara Stander
Than Wyenn as Doctor Burns | Clegg Hoyt as the trucker
John Newton as the policeman | Andy Romano as the second fireman
John Pickard as the first fireman
and Mickey Sholdar as Eddie Stander

An original teleplay written for *The Alfred Hitchcock Hour* by Richard Fielder.
Produced and directed by David Lowell Rich.

(tree and buckets) *Good evening and welcome to the forest primeval. You can see that there are times when a forester like myself must be both tree surgeon and plumber. This particular pair of trees is interesting because although scarcely more than a few feet apart, one is hot and the other cold. By the way these are not maple trees. Hemlock. It's in great demand among intellectuals these days. We also package up a gift bottle for students who wish to remember their teachers. This evening's tale is about a charming little boy and his parents who might be the family next door, though I sincerely hope not. But first we wish to demonstrate a new product for breaking up parties or getting rid of visiting relatives, we call it "the handy dandy room emptier." You know it as a television commercial.*

Story: Bill Nelson and his wife Janet move into the house they have always dreamed of owning, only to find their neighbors not-so-inviting. Jack Stander claims he controls his little boy Eddie with an iron fist, but whenever the father is not around, Eddie turns out to be a little terror. During the first few weeks in their new home, Eddie poisons the Nelson's dog, and even tries a wire at the top of the stairs, almost causing Janet to break her neck. Bill tries to explain this to his neighbor, but Jack Stander refuses to believe his son would commit such actions. In retaliation for squealing on him, little Eddie sets out to murder Janet by rather grisly means, only to prove to Bill that he's not at all as bad as they make him out to be.

I should be pleased with this amazing response but I'm not getting what I anticipated. Unfortunately it's turning out to be oil. We have only a little bit of story left this evening and that seems to consist of small segments of next week's show. We shall show it to you in a moment.

EPISODE #20 **"THE PARAGON"** Broadcast on February 8, 1963
Starring: Joan Fontaine as Alice Pemberton | Gary Merrill as John Pemberton
Virginia Vincent as Madge Fletcher | Linda Leighton as Evie Wales
June Walker as Mrs. Wales | Irene Tedrow as Ethel
Susan Gordon as Betty | Richard Carlyle as Leo Wales
William Sargent as Walter Fletcher | Jesslyn Fax as Mrs. Bates
Willis Bouchey as Mr. Norton | Lester Maxwell as Colin
Donald Elson as the mailman

Teleplay written for *The Alfred Hitchcock Hour* by Alfred Hayes, based on a story by Rebecca West.
Produced by Joan Harrison. Directed by Jack Smight.
Music composed and conducted by Robert Drasnin.

(shoots his sponsor) *Good evening ladies and gentlemen and welcome to The Alfred Hitchcock Hour.* (whistle) *That was my sponsor. He is of the opinion that my way of opening the show lacks zip and excitement. He is attempting to zip me up.* (whistle) (a series of still shots with up-tempo music) (gun shot) *Oh, if that had the same effect on the viewers as it did on me, our audience will be too exhausted to watch the show and that would be a pity, for it tells how to treat a wife who is too loving, too kind and too thoughtful. I'm sure all of you husbands know this problem.* (whistle) (two gun shots) *And now before we have tonight's play, a few words from our sponsor, quite possibly his last ones.*

Story: Alice Pemberton is not the kind of wife every husband wishes for. As an insufferable busybody, she cannot help by pry into everyone's business, offering suggestions and insisting they do things *her* way. Her husband, John, tries to explain that her "helping" is only alienating their friends, but Alice doesn't seem to understand. One-by-one, John loses most of his business associates and even family relatives hesitate paying the Pembertons a visit. Again, John tries to explain that being a quiet housewife is acceptable, but Alice thinks he doesn't like the way she improves things. When the situation finally reaches the point where she has just about run off all their friends and associates, the husband exercises the only option left: to poison her.

(mid-line) *You have to admire our sponsor. He's a far more, hearty individual than I imagined . . . and nimble too. During that last commercial, I couldn't once draw a bead on him. And now another word from another energetic fellow, your local station.*

In case you haven't guessed, that was the end of our story, at least that is all we intend to show. The scene in which John turns himself into the police is of course an integral part of the story but we feel it would be in poor taste to show it. We have not yet come to the end of our commercials, however I shall do what I can to pep them up a bit. (whistle)

Trivia, etc. Joan Fontaine, the star of Alfred Hitchcock's *Rebecca* (1940), was reunited with Joan Harrison in this episode. Fontaine played the role of the second Mrs. de Winter, and Harrison helped write the script.

EPISODE #21   **"I'LL BE JUDGE - I'LL BE JURY"**   Broadcast on February 15, 1963
Starring: Peter Graves as Mark Needham   Albert Salmi as Theodore Bond
Ed Nelson as Alec Trevor   Sarah Marshall as Louise Trevor
Rodolfo Hoyos as Inspector Ortiz   Eric Tovar as Perez
Zolya Talma as Mrs. Bond   Eileen O'Neill as Laura Needham
Judith DeHart as Margaret   Martin Garralaga as the Mexican Priest
Teleplay written for *The Alfred Hitchcock Hour* by Lukas Heller, based on the novel of the same name by Elizabeth Hely (Scribner, 1959; U.K. title: "Dominant Third," Heinemann, 1959).
Produced by Norman Lloyd. Directed by James Sheldon.
Music composed and conducted by Pete Rugolo.
(as a barber)   *Good evening. I am now engaged in a new business. As you can see I am the resident barber specializing in blood letting. I think it's a sad commentary on our times that barbers have concentrated so on the mere appearance of their patients, that they have neglected their health. In fact, they have so forgotten their true calling, that today when one of them nicks you while shaving, he apologizes. The only thing they do that is vaguely medical is to amputate a beard now and then. I haven't heard of a good blood letting in years. Occasionally a gangster may be shot down in a barbershop, but that's not the same thing. But enough of the miracles of medical science. I'm sure you are anxious to get on with tonight's commercials. Here is the first one.*

Story: Newlyweds Mark and Laura Needham decide to spend their honeymoon in Mexico, south of the border. This proves to be a costly mistake, when a couple of days later, Laura is found murdered. Mark, filled with grief and rage, demands action from the police, who calmly explain that they already have a suspect, American businessman Theodore Bond. Without proof, however, the police are unable to make an arrest. Mark sets out to meet Mr. Bond, only to be murdered as a result. Deciding to take matters into their own hands, Mark's visiting in-laws, Alec and Louise Trevor, decide to set a trap for the obviously guilty suspect, using Louise as bait.

(mid-line) *In case you didn't know, we part our show in the middle, and that is precisely where we happen to be. I now turn you over to your local station.* (commercial break) *Welcome once again to the Alfred Hitchcock Hour. The second half of our story begins in a moment. First however, here is another bald spot on the toupee of television.*

That concludes tonight's story. Next week we shall present another one for your approval. By the way before tonight's case was completely closed, Alex learned to his sorrow that one can't go beyond the law, no matter what the motive. Before we have our final commercial I would like to tell those of you who are interested in my services for blood letting that I do not make house calls, however I have a trained bat who will go anywhere. Good night.

Trivia, etc. Peter Graves, who would star as Jim Phelps on television's *Mission: Impossible*, would work again with guests Albert Salmi and Ed Nelson. In 1973, Ed Nelson made a guest appearance on *Mission: Impossible* in "The Western." Salmi would later make a guest appearance on *Mission: Impossible* (remake series) in "The Fuehrer's Children" in 1989.

No new episode was broadcast on February 22, 1963. Instead the network featured a rebroadcast of "The Black Curtain," directed by Sydney Pollack.

EPISODE #22 **"DIAGNOSIS: DANGER"** Broadcast on March 1, 1963
    Starring: Michael Parks as Dr. Daniel 'Dan' Dana
    Charles McGraw as Dr. Simon P. Oliver   Berkeley Harris as Sheriff Judd
    Co-starring: Rupert Crosse as Dr. Paul Mackey
    Allen Joseph as Dr. Norman Abrams   Dee J. Thompson as Miss Nelson
    Douglas Henderson as Huntziger, the reporter
    Hellena Westcott as Mrs. Helen Fletcher   Marc Cavell as Alf 'Alfie' Kolton
    Gus Trikonis as Gordon 'Gordie' Sykes
    Marc Rambeau as Douglas 'Doug' Lynch   Clarke Gordon as Dr. Miller
    Al Ruscio as Dr. Taylor   Celia Lovsky as Mrs. Chertava
    Irene A. Martin as Mrs. Benson   Howard Wendell as the general practitioner
    Audrey Swanson as the office nurse   and Stefan Gierasch as Sergeant Boyle
    Original teleplay written for *The Alfred Hitchcock Hour* by Roland Kibbee.
    Produced by Roland Kibbee. Directed by Sydney Pollack.
    (stethoscope-radio) *Oh, sorry. My transistor radio. Much more dignified looking than most models. People are terribly impressed. I understand these have become very popular in medical circles, in fact they are out-selling stethoscopes. They satisfy everyone. The patient is happy because he thinks the doctor is listening to his heartbeat, and the doctor is pleased because he's getting the latest ball-scores. Our play tonight is a blend of mystery and medicine. It begins with what appears to be an ordinary case of dead-on-arrival, but it turns out to be something less than that and something more than that. It follows this one-minute anaesthetic.*

Story: Dr. Daniel Dana, a brilliant young physician working for the Los Angeles County Health Department, battles both red tape and a puzzle of how an outbreak of pulmonary anthrax could have occurred. It seems a man named Harry Slater was found dead from anthrax and the complicated problem is that the police don't know what to look for. After questioning friends of the dead man, Dr. Dana finally traces the disease to a bongo drum purchased in Mexico and brought across the border from Mexico by the young drummer. When the secret is known, news bulletins are spread throughout Los Angeles, urging everybody who has ever been in contact with this drum to get in touch with medical help. Finally they trace the drum to a kid named Gordie, hiding out at the beach.

(mid-line) *We hate to interrupt this commercial, but the local stations are clamoring to be heard. I shall return to you after they have had their say. So keep an effigy burning in the window.* (commercial break) *Welcome back to the Alfred Hitchcock Hour and to another commercial. Our sponsor persists in communicating with us week after week, although we never answer. You'd think he would begin to understand, but no, here he is again.*

This is the end of tonight's play. For those whose appetite for entertainment is not yet sated, we have another commercial. As for my transistor radio it seems to have lost its enchantment, as far as the medical profession is concerned. The hospitals obtained their own transmitters and began cutting in on the broadcasts to page the doctors, sometimes right in the middle of a song or even a commercial. Something which will never happen on this program, I assure you. Observe!

Trivia, etc. This episode was designed by Roland Kibbee, who not only wrote the script, but produced as well. This was to serve as the pilot for a possible network series that apparently never made it off the ground. " 'Diagnosis: Danger' was the title of the script, as I recall," said director Sydney Pollack, "and that aired over the *Alfred Hitchcock Hour*. The judgement was probably laid out since the Hitchcock show was already a success, 'Diagnosis: Danger' would receive the fullest attention. I'm not sure if a lot of publicity was used to introduce the pilot, but I wouldn't be surprised if executives at the network viewed the program during the initial telecast."

Just like the episode "I Saw the Whole Thing," a bench displayed a morbid advertisement: "Donated by Schuster and Lindsay, Funeral Directors."

EPISODE #23　**"THE LONELY HOURS"**　Broadcast on March 8, 1963
  Starring:　Nancy Kelly as Vera Brandon　　　Gena Rowlands as Louise Henderson
  Co-starring: Joyce Van Patten as Grace Thorpe　Alice Backes as the policewoman
  Willa Pearl Curtis as Hassie　　　　　Juanita Moore as Mrs. McFarland
  Jackie Russell as Sandra　　　　　　Mary Adams as the nurse
  Jesslyn Fax as Miss McGuiness　　　Sally Smith as Marjorie Henderson
  Jennifer Gillespie as Celia　　　　　Annette Ferra as Harriett Henderson
  Teleplay written for *The Alfred Hitchcock Hour* by William D. Gordon, based on the novel "The Hours Before Dawn" by Celia Fremlin (Gollancz, 1958; Lippincott, 1959).
  Produced by Joan Harrison. Directed by Jack Smight.
  (hotel check-in)　*Good evening fellow traveler and welcome to Chez Hitchcock. We have had a rash of unexplained homicides lately.* (close-up) *I knew you would enjoy hearing that, but I'm terribly upset. You see, with all these people checking in and then not checking out, our books just don't balance. However, I'm sure our house detective will clear them all up, just as soon as he finds out who stole his seeing-eye dog. I believe you'll be also interested in knowing that we have television in every room, television cameras that is. The receiving sets are in the dining room in the casino. I see the supper show will begin in a minute, just time enough for you to get settled.* (zoom-out; Hitchcock rings bell) *Front!*

Story: There are times when motherhood can be a moving experience. Case in point: Louise Henderson, who rents a room upstairs to a strange-acting woman named Vera. Louise becomes suspicious after she observes how Vera shows a considerable amount of interest in her newborn son. Louise begins investigating Vera's past, and soon discovers that both women recently shared the same maternity ward, where Vera's child died, resulting in her becoming mentally unbalanced. After finding this out she rushes home - only to find her son and Vera, missing. Phoning the police, Louise goes to Vera's old home address to find the mentally unbalanced woman caring for the baby. The police hand the child back to Louise, and take Vera away where she'll steal babies no more.

I trust you have enjoyed your stay here. Please return next week for we plan to have another intriguing floorshow. As for your bill, someone else is taking care of that for you. I can't reveal his identity but, uh. . . he. . . he left this message for you.

Trivia, etc. Joan Harrison, who produced this episode, felt that the maternal instinct of women would best be projected if no men were present on the screen. Thus the entire cast of this episode consisted of female actors – no male leads! Joyce Van Patten, who played the role of Grace Thorpe, recalled: "I was under contract to Universal at the time and they simply gave me the part. I worked with Nancy Kelly a few times before on radio's *Grand Central Station*. I was a child actor then. But I remember Gena and I thought how Nancy Kelly was such a great looking woman. We both admired her face which was an older woman's face and we envied it. Hah! Now we both have that face. However, shortly before filming they made my hair brown because Gena Rowlands, who had the lead, was blonde."

EPISODE #24 **"THE STAR JUROR"** Broadcast on March 15, 1963
>   Starring: Dean Jagger as George Davies
>   Betty Field as Jenny Davies   Will Hutchins as J. J. Fenton
>   Co-starring: Crahan Denton as Sheriff Walter Watson
>   Harry Harvey, Sr. as Dr. Vince   Katherine Squire as Mrs. Fenton
>   George Mitchell as Judge Higgins   Don Hanmer as Leo Lloyd
>   Ray Hemphill as Pete   Jennifer West as Alice Moorse
>   Sam Reese as Martin Hendrix   Lew Brown as the prosecuting attorney
>   William Challee as Jess Bartholomew   Martine Bartlett as Flossie
>   Cathie Merchant as Lola Penderwaller   Darius Guernsey as Bob
>   Mark Murray as Jack   Kathryn Card as Elsie Grissom
>   and Josie Lloyd as Pauline Davies
> Teleplay written for *The Alfred Hitchcock Hour* by James Bridges, based on the 1958 novel "Le Septieme Jure" by Francis Didelot (English Translation: "The Seventh Juror," Macdonald, 1963; U.S. publication, Belmont, 1963).
>   Produced by Norman Lloyd. Directed by Herschel Daugherty.
> (bricking up a closet) *Good evening. Just a bit of 'Do-It-Yourself.' I'm bricking up an old closet and are about to put in the cornerstone. I saw this as an opportunity to provide future generations with a picture of our culture. Therefore I am placing a few significant items inside the stone. Naturally, I have included several of the current hit records in their original tongue, a supply of plastic credit cards, some low calorie chewing gum, a frozen TV-dinner. By the way, in order to conserve space and at the same time demonstrate our scientific know-how, all of these items have been placed here in concentrated form. All one has to do is to add water. Of course, in order not to take chances I also placed five gallons of water in the cornerstone. Obviously, that too is in concentrated form. So concentrated in fact, that I don't seem to be able to find it. All of us, at one time or another, sit in judgement of ourselves but never in quite the sense that the*

hero of tonight's story did. We were also planning to place a copy of the weekly television schedule in here but we were afraid by the time this is opened, future generations would have lost the art of reading. So we are putting in the following bit of film instead.

Story: George Davies, meek store operator by occupation, and horny bachelor by trade, attempts to pursue the hottest girl in town. When she turns down his affection, an argument persues, resulting in the accidental death of the girl. Luckily for George, the girl had an evil-tempered boyfriend who becomes the prime suspect in the police investigation, and the boy ends up going on trial. George can't save the boy without revealing his own guilt, but when he gets selected to be a member of the jury he sees a way to save the boyfriend from going to prison. The plan works, - but backfires terribly for both George and the innocent youth. The citizens in town boycott George's store, treating him like an outcast. As for the boy, not able to cope being branded a murderer, he commits suicide. When George hears the bad news, he visits the police to confess his crime. Problem is, they won't consider his confession, believing he's just suffering a nervous breakdown as a result of the crime.

(mid-line, pointing to a brick on center of the table) *Still another item to go into the cornerstone as a specimen of life today . . . one station break.* (commercial break) *Next we demonstrate the obvious, but the cornerstone of commercial television, is not television, but the commercial.*

You'll be comforted to know that George ultimately got his wish and was sent to prison, where he died a broken man. One item I haven't mentioned which I'm placing in the cornerstone, is my dear sponsor's last will and testament. The bothersome fellow seems to have mysteriously disappeared. Never mentioned me in the will either. (a hand is seen through the whole in the wall) *Certain people are forever getting in a man's way, when he's working.* (Hitchcock hits him on the fingers) *Now I can continue. You may watch our final commercial and scenes from next week's story.*

Trivia, etc. Producer Norman Lloyd invested a long-time effort to acquire permission for the use of this story. Based on the 1958 novel "Le Septieme Jure" by Francis Didelot (English Translation: "The Seventh Juror,"), Lloyd recalled how "I located a great story in France called 'The Seventh Juror,' but I worked for nearly four months to clear the title to that piece." With Lloyd producing only sixteen of the hour-long features this season, he had to be selective. If Hitchcock didn't like the story, it wouldn't be used. "One thing about Mr. Hitchcock," Lloyd complimented, "he hired people to do a job, and then left them alone to do it."

EPISODE #25 **"THE LONG SILENCE"** Broadcast on March 22, 1963
    Starring: Michael Rennie as Ralph Manson
Phyllis Thaxter as Nora Cory Manson
Co-starring: James McMullan as George Cory   Natalie Trundy as Jean Dekker
Vaughn Taylor as Dr. Babcock   Connie Gilchrist as Emma
Claude Stroud as Edgar Ogden   and Rees Vaughn as Robbie Cory
    Teleplay written for *The Alfred Hitchcock Hour* by William D. Gordon and Charles Beaumont, based on the short novel "Composition for Four Hands" by Hilda Lawrence, originally published in two installments in the April and May 1947 issues of *Good Housekeeping.* Subsequently collected in *Duet of Death* (Simon & Schuster, 1949).
    Produced and directed by Robert Douglas.
    (standing by a screen) *Good evening ladies and gentlemen and welcome to The Alfred Hitchcock Hour. I've been asked to fill in for my brother Alfred, who has been delayed. He's been giving some lessons in masking one's identity. Ah, here he comes now.* (woman comes and steps behind screen) *It's about time. Now, get out of that ridiculous*

disguise and get to work. Granted he has a certain act for impressions and ingenious disguises, but that was sheer exhibitionism. (woman undresses behind screen) *Brother Alfred is almost ready now, although there's hardly any point in his appearing. I now turn you over to Alfred.* (dog comes from behind the screen and barks) *He's telling you that tonight's story will begin in a minute and that one of the characters is a strange indescribable four-footed monster, but first . . .* (bark) *a word from our sponsor. Show off!*

Story: Ralph Manson married his wife Nora for her money, unbeknownst to her, or her two sons from a previous marriage. When Ralph blows a deal to make some fast cash, he accidentally kills his step-son in the process. To make matters worse, Ralph tries to cover up his involvement in the death by faking a suicide note, but is caught by his wife, Nora. The woman collapses and becomes paralyzed. Now disabled and bedridden, she realizes that Ralph will try to kill her as well. Enter stage left, Jean Dekker, Nora's attending nurse, unaware of Ralph's murderous ways. Nora watches as her husband tricks the nurse into allowing him to administer poisonous cocoa and tea, but remains helpless. Slowly but surely, Jean makes contact with the paralyzed woman, and discovers the truth. When Ralph learns that the two women have caught on to his plan, he attempts to murder both of them. At the last minute, Nora gives out a scream that alerts her surviving son, who rushes in to save the day.

Good evening. I wanted to appear as myself, in order to say, Good night.

Trivia, etc. No new episode was broadcast on March 29, 1963. Instead, *The Alfred Hitchcock Hour* presented a rebroadcast of "Hangover," starring Tony Randall and Jayne Mansfield.

Natalie Trundy, James McMullan and Michael Rennie guest star in "The Long Silence." (Photo courtesy of Ronald V. Borst / Hollywood Movie Posters.)

EPISODE #26　**"AN OUT FOR OSCAR"**　Broadcast on April 5, 1963
　　　　Starring: Henry Silva as Bill Grant　　Linda Christian as Eva Ashley
　　　　Larry Storch as Oscar Blinny　　　John Marley as Mike Chambers
　　　　George Petrie as Rogers　　　　　Myron Healey as Peter Rogan
　　　　Rayford Barnes as Ronald　　　　and David White as Detective Burr
　　　　Alan Napier as Mr. Hodges

Teleplay written for *The Alfred Hitchcock Hour* by David Goodis, based on the novel "My Darlin' Evangeline" by Henry Kane (Dell, 1961; U.K. title: "The Perfect Crime," Boardman 1961).

Produced by Norman Lloyd. Directed by Bernard Girard.

(with a panda and hammer)　*Good evening ladies and gentlemen and show-offs the world over. I use this to test my strength. The panda bear that is. If I'm to lift it I feel that I'm keeping in good physical condition. Tonight's play is about the banking business and it promises to be as much fun as a foreclosure. Our story concerns one Oscar Blinny. It also concerns a beautiful woman who looks as though she would be an asset, but turns out to be a liability. But first we have something that manages to be both of these at the same time.*

Story: Oscar Blinny has a problem with a female element. He wants to divorce his unfaithful wife, and she agrees – for a $50,000 settlement, which she insists he can steal from the bank where he works. Oscar's problem becomes more complicated when Eva's boyfriend, Bill Grant, a professional hit man, makes a counteroffer. Bill says he'll kill Eva on a day they pre-arrange, in exchange for $250,000. Oscar will be at work, so his alibi will hold. As for the money, the hood will rob the bank, with Oscar's help of course. Bill will then leave the country, and all is fair in love and war. Oscar agrees, and everything goes off without a hitch, until the last minute, when Oscar turns a gun on the robber and shoots him dead. The police fall for the ruse, believing Bill killed Eva, and Oscar the innocent victim. Impressed with Oscar's bravery, the head cheese at the financial institution promotes Oscar.

(mid-line)　*Next we give our stations a break. You may take one too, if you wish. But hurry back for our second half.*　(commercial break)　*I trust that you were paying attention, when the local announcer recited his call letters. We plan to ask questions later. You will also be held responsible for the following minute.*

Oscar Blinny seemed on the threshold of a contented life when suddenly there appeared on the horizon, a cloud no bigger than a man's hand. Unfortunately it happened, that the hand was on the end of the long arm of the law. As for this, I've developed a technique to master it. No hands.　(Hitchcock steps on to an amusement park sledgehammer machine which goes sky high, and a panda bear flies to him as a reward)

Trivia, etc.　Larry Storch, former host of television's *Cavalcade of Stars* (circa 1952), was also the star of his own short-run series, *The Larry Storch Show*. "I appeared on the show by invitation and sadly, never got to meet Hitchcock personally," Storch recalled. "Bernard Girard was one of the best directors and a fine guy to work for. I never got to work with David White, Alan Napier or Henry Silva after that Hitchcock broadcast. I didn't even have to prepare for the role – the situation was there so I just did it." Although Storch is best remembered for playing the role of Corporal Randolph Agarn on television's *F Troop*, his voice has been featured in hundreds (probably thousands) of animated cartoons including *The Pink Panther Show*, *The Ghostbusters*, *Scooby and Scrappy-Doo*, and *The Brady Kids*.

EPISODE #27　**"DEATH AND THE JOYFUL WOMAN"**　Broadcast on April 12, 1963
　　　　Starring: Gilbert Roland as Luis Aguilar　　Laraine Day as Ruth Hamilton
　　　　Co-starring: Laura Devon as Kitty Norris　　Tom Lowell as Dominic Felse
　　　　Don Galloway as Alfred 'Al' Aguilar　　　Raymond Greenleaf as the doctor
　　　　Richard Bull as the butler　　　　　　Andy Romano as the assistant

Jack Sahakian as the man   and Frank Overton as George Felse
Maggie Pierce as Jean Aguilar
Teleplay written for *The Alfred Hitchcock Hour* by James Bridges, based on the novel of the same name by Ellis Peters (Collins, 1961; Doubleday, 1961). *
Produced by Norman Lloyd. Directed by John Brahm.

Good evening ladies and gentlemen and welcome to The Alfred Hitchcock Hour. I suppose you are wondering what kind of dog this is. It's an invisible one, and this . . . as you can see, is an invisible cat. None of this is very remarkable, until you realize they're not fighting. Peaceful co-existence seems to be a natural side effect of invisibility. We are now thinking of trying it on human beings and television commercials. After all, if my sponsor's messages were invisible, I suspect I might not be as critical as I am. I might even grow to love them. "Death and The Joyful Woman" is the name of tonight's hour of charm. But do not be deceived. The story is very American, very contemporary and just a little bit homicidal. And now in a highly visible state, the sponsor's message.

Story: Luis Aguilar, a wealthy and powerful vineyard owner, shows little interest in his son, who refuses to marry Kitty Norris, the daughter of a recently deceased vineyard owner. The union would result in a merger of their businesses, and double his empire. Disgracing his son by out-drinking him at a party on a wine called The Joyful Woman, Luis disowns his son and then makes a pass at Kitty. The woman has no interest in him or his winery, and when she pushes him back, he falls down a flight of steps, knocked unconscious. The incident is seen by his secretary, who is secretly in love with Luis, and after finding out that Luis was not planning on marrying her as he had promised, she hits her employer over the head with a wine bottle to kill him - and frames Kitty with the murder. When the waiter finds pieces of a wine bottle, he knows what actually happened but then Kitty knocks him out, and throws his body into a cask. The investigating detective makes the case personal, because the waiter is his son. But after a tip from Kitty they find the boy just in time, and solve the mystery.

(mid-line) *For the next moment, ladies and gentlemen, we cut your wire to the world, and abandon you to the tender mercies of your local station.* (commercial break) *Good evening, and welcome to the second half of The Alfred Hitchcock Hour. As you know, our sponsor is not exactly the type of person, who has streets named for him. He has never even had an hour named in his honor. All he gets is one minute. We give it to him now.*

Sorry to be late, but I've been arguing with my sponsor, and he has now been convinced that invisibility will help my attitude toward the commercial. After all, if I can't see it, how can . . . (Hitchcock becomes invisible) *My sponsor seems to have missed the point. Needless to say, next on view, is a commercial.*

EPISODE #28 "LAST SEEN WEARING BLUE JEANS" Broadcast on April 19, 1963
Starring: Michael Wilding as David Saunders   Anna Lee as Roberta Saunders
Katherine Crawford as Lauren Saunders   Randy Boone as Pete Tanner
James Anderson as Vince Cates   Jesse Jacobs as Grosse
Eve McVeagh as Rose Cates   Russ Conway as Henderson
Kreg Martin as Al   Jose De Vega as Gato
Frank Albertson as Tom Batterman   Carlos Romero as Alfau
Tito De Mario as the first youth   Ricky Vera as the second Youth
Paul Fierro as the priest   Rose Montiel as Maria
and Co-starring: Karl Lukas as Mel Tanner

* Ellis Peters is a pseudonym of Edith Pargeter, who went on to write the well-known Brother Cadfael series of medieval mystery novels.

Teleplay written for *The Alfred Hitchcock Hour* by Lou Rambeau, based on the novel "Encounter With Evil" by Amber Dean (Doubleday, 1961).

Produced by Joan Harrison. Directed by Alan Crosland, Jr.

(border guard booth)   *Good evening. Our country welcomes you, and may I search your luggage? I find the life of a border guard quite diverting. It's very much like working at the check out stand of a giant supermarket. I also have a very lucrative sideline. I retouch passport photographs for men. The women prefer to retouch their faces instead. Since tonight's story is called "Last Seen Wearing Blue Jeans," it was first suggested that I dress accordingly, however I demured. I consider it undignified to appear in women's clothes. Our story concerns an English family on a tour of America. Because of a strange happening, their tour becomes a detour. And they see more of the continent then they had planned. Their adventure follows in just one minute.*

Story: While David Saunders and his family are vacationing via cross-country trip through America, they decide to stop late one night at the Cates cafe in Slawson, Arizona. Their daughter, Roberta, can't keep the sleepy dust out of her eyes, and returns to the car, where she crawls into the back seat and goes to sleep. Only she accidentally crawled into a similar-looking car instead of her own . . . and the car she is in now was recently stolen, and on the way to Mexico. While hiding in the back, she witnesses the car thief try to pass it on to his contact, but an argument ensues resulting in murder – and the survivor suddenly realizes that he is not alone. By now, the police are in on the chase and eventually catch up to the murderer and young Roberta. When Roberta is returned to her family, the police make a surprising twist. They arrest the café owner because he is actually the mastermind behind the hot car ring!

Anna Lee, who played the crusader fighting against torture to the mentally insane in the 1945 classic "Bedlam," co-starring Boris Karloff, makes a guest appearance with actor Michael Wilding in the Episode "Last Seen Wearing Blue Jeans."

Photo courtesy of Ronald V. Borst / Hollywood Movie Posters.

(mid-line) *You have reached the half-way point in your journey, and you must detour briefly to the stations that carry the program. I shall be on duty when you return.* (commercial break) *In the theater, before the beginning of a new act, an expectant hush falls on the audience. In television we take no chances. We drown you out with a commercial.*

And so as the sun begins sinking in the West, we take leave of charming, larcenous Slawson, Arizona. By the way, you may proceed on through. I can now reveal that this is not actually the border of anything. Just a device to keep the audience until the play is over. Good night.

Trivia, etc. No new episode was broadcast on April 26, 1963. Instead, a rebroadcast of "I Saw the Whole Thing," directed by Alfred Hitchcock, was presented.

EPISODE #29 **"THE DARK POOL"** Broadcast on May 3, 1963
Starring: Lois Nettleton as Diane Castillejo
Anthony George as Victor Castillejo   Madlyn Rhue as Consuela Sandino
Co-starring: David White as Lance Hawthorn
Eugene Iglesias as Pedro Sanchez, the servant   Doris Lloyd as Mrs. Andrina Gibbs
John Zaremba as the coroner   Isobel Elsom as Sister Marie Therese
Walter Woolf King as Senator Hayes   Eva Novak as Mrs. Hayes
Bess Flowers as Mrs. Pradanos   Paul Bradley as Mr. Pradanos
Teleplay written for *The Alfred Hitchcock Hour* by William D. Gordon and Alec Coppel, based on a story by Alec Coppel.
Produced by Joan Harrison. Directed by Jack Smight.
(big firecracker) *Good evening. Do you sometimes get the feeling that things have changed since you were a boy? I'm quite convinced that either firecrackers have become much larger, or people have become smaller. This particular model is for the child who has everything and wants to get rid of it. You'll be relieved to know a child cannot buy one of these, unless he is accompanied by an adult. Actually, the stores will sell this to a child, he just needs the adult to carry it home for him. This evening's tale takes place in California where the climate is sunny but dispositions are not necessarily so. Our heroine survives one tragedy only to learn that she is not at the end of her trials, but at the beginning. Speaking of beginnings, I had hoped to open our show with some attention-getting sound, fortunately our sponsor has come to the rescue. Noise is a specialty of his. He has long been an advocate of beginning a show, not with a whimper but with a bang.*

Story: Diane Castillejo, a former alcoholic now dried out, leaves her adopted son unattended for a moment to answer the phone. When she returns, she finds the boy floating dead in the swimming pool. A couple days later, a woman named Consuela Sandino introduces herself to Diane, claiming to be the boy's real mother. Threatened with exposure of her past, after the accidental drowning, Consuela blackmails Diane into letting her stay in her house for a few days. In truth, Consuela lied about being the boy's true mother. Her real motives are obvious – she plans to drive Diane to drink again, and have run her off so that she can snare Diane's wealthy, good-looking husband. She does a pretty good job by playing a tape recording of a baby when Diane sleeps, and as the days pass, Diane tries to drown out her sorrow. After grief and hard liquor, Diane finally confesses the truth to her husband, and Consuela is ordered out of the house. Diane has herself committed to a sanitarium, with a loving husband willing to stay by her side.

(mid-line; Hitchcock lit the fuse) *Please excuse my haste. I shall return in a moment. The next sound you hear will be that of our stations breaking.* (commercial break; turns out to be a candle) *This was not precisely what I had in mind. I did leave it burning in the window so that you could find your way back. Now, as if one dud was not enough, we have a commercial.*

(now tied to another giant fire cracker) *The storekeeper who sold me my first firecracker took umbrage of some of my remarks. One word led to another but as you see, I won, and am now publicly demonstrating my disdain for his product. I had expected the wax would begin dripping by now, this is likely to take some time. Why don't you amuse yourselves with another commercial and scenes from next week's show.* (bang!)

EPISODE #30 **"DEAR UNCLE GEORGE"** Broadcast on May 10, 1963
        Starring: Gene Barry as John Chambers   John Larkin as Simon Aldrich
        Co-starring: Patricia Donahue as Louise Chambers
        Dabney Coleman as Tom Esterow   Robert Sampson as Sergeant Duncan
        Brendan Thomas Dillon as Sam   Charity Grace as Mrs. Weatherby
        Jimmy Joyce as the fingerprint man   Joseph Trapaso as the policeman
        and Alicia Li as Bea   with Lou Jacobi as Lieutenant Wolfson
        Teleplay written for *The Alfred Hitchcock Hour* by William Link, Richard Levinson and James Bridges, based on a story by William Link and Richard Levinson.
        Produced by Norman Lloyd. Directed by Joseph Newman.
        (with an umbrella) *Good evening ladies and gentlemen and welcome to The Alfred Hitchcock Hour. This is a device for those persons who enjoy walking in the rain, but are afraid not to carry an umbrella. less people think them peculiar. You may have noticed that I'm not wearing a raincoat either. There are several practical applications of my umbrella. It is excellent for those who enjoy tuning in on local radio stations with their hearing aids. As you can see it's convertible, in case you occasionally wish to walk with the top down. Naturally, the proceeding nonsense has nothing what so ever to do with tonight's play. Nor for that matter does the following.*

        Story: John Chambers, an advice columnist for the New York Examiner who works under the pen name of Uncle George, receives a startling letter in the mail. A lady named Mrs. Weatherby writes to Uncle George, describing her concern over her neighbor, who secretly cheats on her husband. This is a sad day indeed, for Mrs. Weatherby happens to be John's neighbor across the court, a fact she herself doesn't know. And the lady she describes in the letter? Why Mrs. Chambers, of course. When John confronts her about the affair, an argument breaks out and he murders his wife, pinning the killing on his wife's lover . . . a plan that seems foolproof, with the police falling for the bait. That is, until Mrs. Weatherby expresses to the police her concern over the situation, and the letter she wrote to Uncle George . . . Mrs. Weatherby adds: "I should have called you and told you about it. I'm sure that if you knew what was going on, you'd have done something about it."

        (mid-line) *My appearance now is a signal indicating we have come to the half-way point. After me, the deluge of commercials, spot announcements, stations identification, etc. and if time permits, the second half of our story.* (commercial break) *We have one more country to hear from. After which we shall continue our story.*

        That concludes tonight's story, however since there is still some more time remaining we shall show you some of next week's story. This is The Alfred Hitchcock Hour and we intend to give full measure. As for my umbrella, there is one other use which I failed to mention. Some people have used this for tightrope walking, but only when they were . . . very tight. Good night.

Photo on next page: Anne Francis guest stars in "What Really Happened."
(Photo courtesy of Ronald V. Borst / Hollywood Movie Posters.)

EPISODE #31   **"RUN FOR DOOM"**   Broadcast on May 17, 1963
Starring: John Gavin as Dr. Donald 'Don' Reed
Diana Dors as Nickie Carroll (real name Nadine Bryan)

Scott Brady as Bill Floyd	Carl Benton Reid as Horace Reed
Tom Skerritt as Dr. Frank Farmer	Lew Brown as David Carson
Robert Carson as Mulloy	Gail Bonney as Sarah, the housekeeper
Jackie Russell as the waitress	Jon Shepodd as Curtis Cane
Barry Cahill as the Chief Petty Officer	Patricia Krest as the teller
Audrey Swanson as the nurse	and Cathie Taylor as the singer

Teleplay written for *The Alfred Hitchcock Hour* by James Bridges, based on the novel of the same name by Henry Kane (Boardman, 1960; Signet, 1962).

Produced by Norman Lloyd. Directed by Bernard Girard.

(lockers)   *Good evening and welcome to the grand opening of our new railway station. As one of the features of the celebration we are offering a prize to the person who can guess the number of bodies which will be found in these lockers during the first week of operation. Station lockers seem to be a favorite spot to check one's friends. It's much more tidy than having them lay around the house. In this connection we have a very interesting feature, our architect thought of everything. Just on the possibility that bodies might not be discovered as quickly as they should, all the lockers are refrigerated. I knew you'd like that.* (close-up) *Now that I have given you that chilling thought we should best be getting on with the principle business of the evening. Selling our sponsor's product. And if time permits . . . we may even present a play.*

Story: A pretty, young nightclub singer named Nickie manages to "catch" Dr. Don Reed, even though her current boy-friend, Bill Floyd, the band-leader and his own father warn Don about Nickie. Blind with love, Don ignores the repeated warnings and pops the question. His father, who still opposes the girl, dies when he hears the news about his son's marriage. Don inherits a tidy sum, the two get married and together they board a cruise ship for their honeymoon. Catching his new bride in the arms of another man, Don punches the man overboard and he drowns - a murder they both agree to keep quiet about. Soon after, Nickie gets bored with her hubby and says she wants a divorce – and his money – else she'll tell the police everything. After leaving for work, Floyd arrives to try to get her back but when she refuses he tries to strangle the life out of her. When the police investigate, Don notices that she's not really dead and finishes the job . . . not knowing that the police officer knows she's still alive and he would like to get her statement.

(mid-line) *We have reached the halfway point in tonight's program. And so it is time for a word from your local stationmaster.* (commercial break) *The midway portion of our program contains so many announcements and advertisements, that I feel like a bookmark in a mail order catalog. Just one more item and then we proceed with the story.*

Sorry but that is all the story we have room for tonight. Next week we shall be back with another. As for our modern terminal, for persons whose departure is being arranged by the entire community we have this: rather warm tar and . . . (feathers)

Trivia, etc. Although this was the second episode of the Hitchcock series to feature Diana Dors in the lead, this was the first to be broadcast. She previously starred in "The Sorcerer's Apprentice," the *Alfred Hitchcock Presents* episode that never aired in the original network run. In this broadcast, Diana Dors plays a lounge singer whose true intentions is to use men, and then take them for what they're worth. On stage, she sings a song entitled "It Was Just One of Those Things," somewhat ironic to the character she played. Dors appeared on the cover of The Beatles' *Sgt. Pepper's Lonely Hearts Club Band* in 1967, and the cover of the *Smiths'* 1995 compilation album, *Singles*.

Cathie Taylor, a professional singer who also made an appearance in this episode, played herself in the 1963 movie, *Hootenanny Hoot.*

EPISODE #32   **"DEATH OF A COP"**   Broadcast on May 24, 1963

Starring: Victor Jory as Paul Reardon   Peter Brown as Philip Reardon
Co-starring: Paul Hartman as Trenker   John Marley as Singer
Richard Jaeckel as Boxer   Paul Genge as Lieutenant Tom Mills
Jean Willes as Eva   Wilton Graff as George Chaney
Read Morgan as Freddie   Rex Holman as Jocko
Shirley O'Hara as Alice Reardon   Bob Okazaki as Wong
Rees Vaughn as Sammy Garrison   Marc Rambeau as Alec Malloy
Joseph Ruskin as Gabby Donovan   Hari Rhodes as the patrolman
Tenen Holtz as the druggist   Rita Conde as Mrs. Dominguez
and Lawrence Tierney as Herbie Lane

Teleplay written for *The Alfred Hitchcock Hour* by Leigh Brackett, based on the novel "Death of a Snout" by Douglas Warner (Cassell, 1961; Walker, 1962).

Produced by Norman Lloyd. Directed by Joseph Newman.

(standing by a road sign, each pointing different directions, one to Sodom and the other Gomorrah)   *Good evening ladies and gentlemen and welcome to The Alfred Hitchcock Hour. My part of the program this evening is, as usual, remote. In all my travels I don't know of any object which has been more perplexing. This would appear to be an excellent place for a picnic. This is solid salt. Rather a lot of it. I expected to see another one marked pepper. There is another one nearby, but instead of being marked salt and pepper, they are labeled, his and hers. I would appear to be introducing a biblical drama, but such is not the case. Tonight's play is a modern tale of two policemen, a father and son, called "Death of A Cop." It is a story of revenge. It begins in one minute.*

Story: Paul Reardon has everything a father could want in life. His son, Philip, became a police officer, following in the footsteps of his good old dad. But one afternoon, when trying to question a thug named Boxer, Philip is killed and Paul, seeking vengeance, vows to bring down the entire gang, including their leader, Herbie Lane. Paul quits the force and sets up a deal that ends with him shooting Boxer, and then being shot himself. But Paul has made sure an old friend, Trenker, has remained in the shadows to act as witness, as he knew the risk was high, but dies happy knowing Herbie Lane and his entire gang, is going to be brought to justice. His son's murder is avenged.

(mid-line) *I see we are at the half-way point. I also see a local station ahead. Let's see if we can identify it.* (commercial break) *Welcome to The Alfred Hitchcock Hour part two. If you wish a summary of the first half, I suggest you watch the next minute closely.*

I can see that a policeman's lot is not a happy one. I believe it is time to be on my way, however I shall take just one glance back at the city. I understand it's beautiful. (Hitchcock turns into a pillar of salt)

Trivia, etc. Leigh Brackett wrote the script for the 1946 classic, *The Big Sleep*, starring Humphrey Bogart. Bracket is also co-credited for writing the first version of the science-fiction script, *The Empire Strikes Back* (1980), but she died of cancer before completing it. Tough-guy actor Lawrence Tierney, best known for his roles in *Dillinger* (1945) and *Prizzi's Honor* (1985), played the heavy in this cops-and-robbers script.

SUMMER RERUNS

Summer reruns consisted of episodes from the first season of *The Alfred Hitchcock Hour*. During the season, however, there were a few reruns such as "I Saw the Whole Thing" and "A Piece of the Action." They did not air during the summer.

May 31, 1963 "House Guest"
June 7, 1963 "Don't Look Behind You"
June 14, 1963 "Ride the Nightmare"
June 21, 1963 "Night of the Owl"
June 28, 1963 "The Paragon"
July 5, 1963
    "The Thirty-First of February"
July 12, 1963
    "I'll Be Judge - I'll Be Jury"
July 19, 1963 "The Lonely Hours"

July 26, 1963 "A Tangled Web"
August 2, 1963 "The Long Silence"
August 9, 1963 "Captive Audience"
August 16, 1963 "Bonfire"
August 23, 1963
    "Death and the Joyful Woman"
August 30, 1963 "Dear Uncle George"
September 6, 1963 "The Dark Pool"
September 13, 1963
    "To Catch a Butterfly"

September 20, 1963 "Hedda Gabler," an adaptation of the Henrik Isben play about the wife of a college professor who becomes involved with a former lover. Stars Michael Redgrave, Ingrid Bergman, Trevor Howard, and Sir Ralph Richardson. Directed by Alex Segal. Broadcast from 9:30 to 11 p.m., EST. Translation by Eva Le Gallienne.

SEASON TWO - (32 episodes)

SELECTED PRODUCTION CREDITS:
Art Director: Raymond Beal, Howard E. Johnson, Russell Kimball,
John J. Lloyd and Alexander A. Mayer
Assistant Director: Donald Baer, Les Berke, Ben Bishop, George Bisk, John Clarke Bowman,
Ridgeway Callow, Chuck Colean, Edward K. Dodds, Jack Doran, Milton Feldman,
Charles S. Gould, Ronnie Rondell, Ray Taylor, Jr. and Dolph M. Zimmer
Associate Producer: Gordon Hessler
Costume Supervisor: Vincent Dee and Burton Miller
Director of Photography: Benjamin H. Kline, Lionel Lindon, William Margulies,
Jack Marquette, a.s.c., Richard L. Rawlings, John L. Russell, Walter Strenge, a.s.c.,
Bud Thackery, Robert Tobey and John F. Warren, a.s.c.
Editorial Dept. Head: David J. O'Connell
Executive Producer: Norman Lloyd
Film Editor: John C. Fuller, Danford B. Greene, John M. Haffen, Bus S. Isaacs,
Marvin I. Kosberg, Tony Martinelli, Douglas Stewart,
J. Howard Terrill and Edward W. Williams, a.c.e.
Hair Stylist: Florence Bush and Larry Germain
Makeup: Jack Barron, Bob Dawn and Bud Westmore
Music Score and Theme: Bernard Herrmann and his Orchestra
Music Supervision: Stanley Wilson
Producer: Joan Harrison
Set Decorators: Julia Heron, John McCarthy, Mac Mulcahy,
James S. Redd, Ralph Sylos and James M. Walters
Sound: Lyle Cain, Stanley F. Cooley, Earl Crain, Jr., Earl Crain, Sr., Corson Jowett,
William Lynch, Ed Somers, J. S. Westmoreland and Frank H. Wilkinson
Filmed at Revue Studios in Hollywood, California (Universal City), in association with
MCA-TV, executive distributor for Shamley Productions, Inc.
Broadcast Thursday over CBS-TV, 10 – 11 p.m., EST. Multiple sponsors.

EPISODE #33 **"A HOME AWAY FROM HOME"** Broadcast on September 27, 1963
Starring: Ray Milland as "the fake" Dr. Fenwick

Claire Griswold as Natalie Rivers	Co-starring: Mary La Roche as Ruth
Virginia Gregg as Miss Gibson	Peter Leeds as Andrew, the officer
Ben Wright as Dr. Norton	Connie Gilchrist as Martha
Jack Searl as Nicky Long	Richard Peel as the first officer
Brendan Dillan as Inspector Roberts	Ronald Long as Major Hamilton
Peter Brooks as Donald	and Beatrice Kay as Sarah Sanders

Teleplay by Robert Bloch, based on his short story of the same name, originally published in the June 1961 issue of *Alfred Hitchcock's Mystery Magazine*. Subsequently collected in *Tales in a Jugular Vein*, (Pyramid, 1965), and in *The King of Terrors* (Mysterious Press, 1977).
Produced by David Lowell Rich. Directed by Herschel Daugherty.
Music composed and conducted by Bernard Herrmann.
(on a desert island) *Good evening. I thought Friday would never come. I'm not here, by the way, as a result of a shipwreck. It was a misunderstanding . . . something to do with our ship being overweight. I understand the pirates once buried their treasure on this island. I've been digging and if this is true they spent most of their time burying water. Actually it's rather nice here. We have sports, particularly swimming, when tide comes in. I may not have said that correctly. To be truthful, it's touch and go as to whether the tide comes in or the island goes out. This evening's drama is appropriately entitled "A Home*

Away From Home." In it, a young lady finds herself in a world she never made nor quite understands. It follows the following.

Story: Natalie Rivers arrives at Norton Sanatorium, a mental institution, operated by her uncle, Dr. Fenwick. Until today, Natalie never met her uncle in person, and glad to see his niece, the good doctor invites her in with open arms. When she is given a tour of the building, she notices how some of the employees act peculiar, but shrugs it off. When Natalie accidentally stumbles upon a dead body, she urges her uncle to phone the police, which he does. The detective arrives with a startling revelation – he's one of the escaped lunatics. Assuming the murder as an act from one of the inmates, Natalie discovers that she isn't far from the truth – as the corpse is her real uncle. The man posing as Dr. Fenwick managed to overpower and kill the asylum director, and imprison the institution's employees, substituting in their place other inmates. Before she can get help, the imposter decides to silence her permanently.

(mid-line) *I don't seem to be getting anywhere but you have progressed to the half-way mark. To celebrate the occasion, we have arranged a station break, after which we shall continue our story.*

So much for Dr. Fenwick. As for my own problem it is fast being solved. I understand the rumor was spread that my island was a quaint out-of-the-way paradise, untouched by civilization. Two boatloads of tourists, three hotel men and a souvenir-manufacturer are already on their way to correct the situation. In that case I should be back next week to tell you another story. Scenes of which, you will see in a moment. But first we must allow the sponsor to say a few words . . . Permissive therapy.

Claire Griswold and Ray Milland guest star in Robert Bloch's chilling story, "A Home Away From Home."

(Photo courtesy of Photofest.)

425

Trivia, etc. "Of all my stories televised on the Hitchcock programs, 'A Home Away from Home' probably comes closest to Sir Alfred's slightly Hitchcockeyed view of the world," said Robert Bloch. "That's because I wrote it expressly for a short story contest conducted by *Alfred Hitchcock's Mystery Magazine*, where it won a prize. Essentially a variation on Poe's 'The System of Dr. Tarr and Prof. Fether,' the tale is a mere 2,500 words long, and hardly contains enough material for dramatizing in a one-hour television format. So when producers Joan Harrison and Norman Lloyd asked me to adapt it for the show, I was faced with a problem. How could I expand the story line and develop the characters while still retaining the elements that made the plot work in its short printed version?"

Many of Robert Bloch's short stories, such as "Yours Truly, Jack the Ripper" and "The Grim Reaper" were dramatized on Boris Karloff's *Thriller*, another mystery/horror anthology series filmed on the Universal lot. Here, Bloch took a wonderful – and chilling – story and made it into a suspenseful mystery yarn worthy of attention. As the season opener, it was perfect.

"That's a rather pretentious way of saying that I wanted to keep the yarn exciting all the way through, instead of just adding extra scenes for padding. Television's arbitrary program length is like the legendary bed of Procrustes, which either stretched or shortened its unfortunate occupants to make them fit properly within its confines. But it takes more than simple stretching or squashing to make a story work, and my adaptation was no easy task. If you read the little tale with this in mind, you'll see it wasn't easy for me to enlarge it and maintain the same level of suspense, but I think the dramatization worked. At least it satisfied me to the point where, years later, I did two novels and a full-length motion picture set [*Asylum* (1972); reissued in 1980 as *House of Crazies*, starring Patrick Magee] in part, in a similar locale. Perhaps, if the truth were known, such a setting really is my home away from home."

EPISODE #34   **"A NICE TOUCH"**   Broadcast on October 4, 1963
      Starring: Anne Baxter as Janice Brandt   George Segal as Larry Duke
      Charlene Holt as Darlene Vance   Mimi Dillard as the receptionist
      Gil Stuart as the actor   Martha Stewart as the secretary
      Walter Woolf King as the executive   and Harry Townes as Ed Brandt
      Teleplay written for *The Alfred Hitchcock Hour* by Mann Rubin, based on his short story of the same name, originally published in the February 1958 issue of *Alfred Hitchcock's Mystery Magazine*. Subsequently anthologized in *My Favorites in Suspense*, ed. Alfred Hitchcock (Random House, 1959).
      Produced by Robert Douglas. Directed by Joseph Pevney.
      (with two actors)   *Good evening. Welcome to our improvisational theatre. This is a course completely unrehearsed, unwritten and unintelligible. Nothing is planned. We just ask our audience to call out. what you would like us to do. Simply give us a last line, a title, some characters, a theme, a setting, a point of view, a plot, a first line and some lines in between and we make up the rest. Improvising as we go along. To be perfectly honest, we've never done this. Since today, no audience has managed to come up with a last line, a title, characters, a theme, setting, etc. etc. etc. They keep getting hung up. Apparently people can think on their feet but have difficulty when they are sitting down. Tonight's play tells of an actor in Hollywood and his response to a call for help, from a desperate girl in New York. This next minute is completely rehearsed, planned and calculated. Your reaction to it however, may be improvised. You are on your own.*

      Story: Enter stage left, young Larry Duke, a rising star in Hollywood. His girlfriend, Janice Brandt, has done everything she could to help Larry advance his career, including giving up on her own husband back in New York, whom she ran away from. One day, Janice informs Larry of the bad news. Her husband Ed has tracked her down, and showed up drunk. A fight ensued and the result left him knocked unconscious. Over the phone, Janice asks Larry for help and he advises her to finish the man off, with a pillow, so it will all look natural. Leaving no fingerprints or evidence to suggest otherwise, Janice does exactly what Larry suggests, putting Ed out of the way permanently. What she doesn't know is that Larry recently got married, and his next action will be phoning the police to inform on Janice, effectively getting her out of the way of his next career move. What a wonderful actor Larry has turned out to be . . .

There is a postscript to tonight's story. At first all seemed blissful for Larry. When suddenly there appeared on the horizon, a cloud no bigger than a man's hand. Actually it wasn't a cloud at all. It was a man's hand. And it was on the end of what is known as the long arm of the law. Darlene, a truly ambitious girl, couldn't resist the publicity inherent in breaking down in court and turning state's evidence. You see, she'd been listening to Larry's conversation with Janice. Next week we return with another story. Scenes of which you shall see in a few moments.

Trivia, etc. "I did a lot of movies before television," recalled director Joseph Pevney. "As a matter of fact, the assistant to Alfred Hitchcock, Joan Harrison, said to me, 'How come you're not doing any more movies?' I said, 'I don't know.' She said, "I know. You've made yourself too valuable to television.' And that's what happened. I used to do *Adam-12* and *Emergency* back to back and Jack Webb didn't know about it. He used to have his directors prepare for at least a week before filming. I just liked doing a lot of work quickly. Harrison was tremendous. She brought me out to Hollywood because she saw me in 'Home of the Brave.' This is a funny story but it's the truth. She was looking for a killer that reminded her of Hoagy Carmichael [laughs] and I was doing 'Home of the Brave' because I just came out of the Army, and she came back stage. She wanted me to test or be in her picture *Nocturne* (1946), and I said, 'Well, I'm not interested in acting. If I come out to Hollywood I want to direct.' She was interested in me wanting to direct so I signed a contract for acting and directing at RKO, thanks to her, and I acted in *Nocturne* [directed by Edwin L. Marin]. She was a very creative gal and as I understand it, she was very instrumental in helping Hitchcock with his first few movies in America. She was responsible for letting Robert Douglas direct, and he wanted to direct because he found out I was doing it too! [laughs] And he was the producer!"

Pevney also directed episodes of *Star Trek*, *Wagon Train*, *The Fugitive*, *Mission: Impossible* and *Emergency!* Recalling this particular cast: "Anne Baxter was wonderful, and very talented. You could tell when she first walked into a room. Harry Townes I respected and enjoyed. I used him a lot in those *Star Trek* episodes because he was such a good actor."

EPISODE #35   **"TERROR AT NORTHFIELD"**   Broadcast on October 11, 1963

Starring: Dick York as Sheriff Will Pearce	Jacqueline Scott as Susan Marsh
R.G. Armstrong as John Cooley	Katherine Squire as Mrs. La Font
Peter Whitney as Bib Hadley	Dennis Patrick as Walter 'Frenchy' La Font
Curt Conway as Dr. Buxton	Gertrude Flynn as Flora Sloan
Jim Boles as the grocer	Harry Harvey, Sr. as Mayor Sanford Brown
Raymond Guth as the farmer	Bryan O'Byrne as Mr. Smith
Gail Bonney as Mrs. Hayes	Hal Bokar as the third man
William Newell as Mr. Jones	Harry Antrim as the councilman
Robert Reiner as Mr. Brown	Hinton Pope as the second man
Dee Carroll as the woman	

Teleplay written for *The Alfred Hitchcock Hour* by Leigh Brackett, based on Ellery Queen's novelette "Terror Town," originally published in the August 1956 issue of *Argosy*. Subsequently collected in *The Tragedy of Errors* (Crippen & Landru, 1999).

Produced by Charles Russell. Directed by Harvey Hart.

Music composed and conducted by Bernard Herrmann.

(goat and rifle) *Good evening. Welcome to the Hitchcock Hillbillies. We had planned a series based on a family of simple mountain folk who discover oil on their land and move to the Murray Hill section of New York. Unfortunately things didn't work out. None of the family knew what the oil was and so instead of going to the big city, they simply sold their farm and moved down the road where the land wasn't so slippery. My sponsor requested that I dress appropriately for the series . . . and I agree. I'm wearing long underwear. Actually, it isn't as long as it is wide but I did my best to co-operate. There's another item I wish was shorter, the next minute. For that is what separates us from a story of a small town, terrorized by an unknown assailant.*

Story: A fanatically religious man named John Cooley is determined to obtain revenge after his son Tom is found dead. Using the only piece of evidence - part of a headlight glass found at the scene, John begins a search for the killer. When seeing the right car he finds out that three people have owned the vehicle during the time Tom was missing. Meeting up with Frenchy La Font, the original owner of the car whose headlight is smashed in, John beats him to death. The next owner was an elderly librarian named Flora and he strangles her. Sheriff Will Pearce soon figures out what is going on about town, pieces one and one together, and rushes off to find his girlfriend Susan, who bought the car from Flora. Susan is indeed next on the list, but the law officer arrives in the nick of time, explaining to John that Frenchy was the real killer, which he confessed in a letter found by his mother.

(mid-line) *Those who are paying attention to our story, need not be told there is more to come. It will follow this calculated, but confusing interruption.*

Although the Hitchcock Hillbillies has been abandoned as a project, I have retained this weapon, which they tell me is excellent for feuds. Which leads me to say, our dear sponsor should be along soon. . . (points the rifle towards the screen) *Next week, those of us who remain, will be back with another story. Now. . . a final word from our sponsor. . .* (points the rifle towards the screen again)

Trivia, etc. "Terror Town" was the only piece of short fiction by Ellery Queen that did not feature the world-famous Ellery Queen detective character. Charles Russell also produced television episodes of *You Are There*, *The Untouchables*, and *Adventures in Paradise*.

EPISODE #36 **"YOU'LL BE THE DEATH OF ME"** Broadcast on October 18, 1963

Starring: Robert Loggia as Driver Arthur

Co-starring: Pilar Seurat as Mickey Arthur

Sondra Kerr as Ruby McCleod	G. B. Atwater as Gar Newton
Carmen Phillips as Betty Rose Calder	Hal Smith as Tompy Dill
Charles Seel as Doctor Chalmont	Norman Leavitt as Kyle Sawyer
Sam Edwards as the bartender	and Kathleen Freeman as Mrs. McCleod

Teleplay written for *The Alfred Hitchcock Hour* by William D. Gordon, based on the story "The Goldfish Button" by Anthony Gilbert, originally published in the February 1958 issue of *Ellery Queen's Mystery Magazine*. Subsequently reprinted as "You'll Be The Death of Me" in *The Lethal Sex*, ed. John D. MacDonald (Dell, 1959).

Produced and directed by Robert Douglas.

Music composed and conducted by Bernard Herrmann.

(lost and found) *Good evening. May I help you? We have a fantastic assortment of lost articles. We have a number of ways, some bearings and a national purpose. We have some dear little lambs, a weekend and one entire generation. And we have one gentleman back here, named Mr. Keen. A single button is found early in tonight's story and as they used to say, "Thereby hangs a tale." The tale is called "You'll be The Death of Me" and it begins in a few moments.*

Story: At a bar one evening, Driver Arthur is heckled by a former girlfriend, Betty Rose, whom he hasn't had anything to do with since he left the military and got married. She won't leave him alone, and an argument breaks out. Slightly intoxicated, Driver fights her and accidentally takes her breath away, permanently. During the scuffle, however, he inadvertently pulled a button off her jacket, which is later found in his pocket by Driver's wife. With the incriminating evidence in her possession, he realizes he must kill her as well . . . so he plans to perform a second "perfect" murder. Sadly for Driver, there is no such thing as a "perfect" murder. A deaf girl, Ruby, notices a chain in Driver's possession that Mrs. Arthur had on her when she was killed, that proves he is the murderer.

(mid-line) *I am afraid that the requirements of commercial television, make it necessary for you to tear yourselves away from the story for a short time. Lest, you lose your place, I shall stay here and hold it for you.*

Those of you who watched our broadcast of October 27, 1957 will remember that four minutes were lost, due to a power-failure. You will be glad to learn that those four minutes have been found. They were discovered just west of Billings, Montana, by an elderly prospector who unfortunately used three of those four minutes to soft-boil an egg. However, he has returned the other minute and we show it to you now.

EPISODE #37 **"BLOOD BARGAIN"** Broadcast on October 25, 1963
Starring: Richard Kiley as Jim Derry	Richard Long as Eddie Breech
Guest Star: Anne Francis as Connie Breech	Barney Martin as Rupert Harney
Ross Elliott as Lieutenant Geer	Anthony Call as Earl
Peter Brocco as Figaro	Craig Duncan as the detective
Thomas Bellin as the bartender	

Teleplay written for *The Alfred Hitchcock Hour* by Henry Slesar, based on his own short story of the same name. Subsequently collected in *Death on Television* (Southern Illinois University Press, 1989), and later published in the June 1981 issue of *Web*.

Produced by Joan Harrison. Directed by Bernard Girard.

(car with sword and windshield wiper) *Good evening.* (wiping windshield) *May I check to see if there's something loose under your bonnet?* (checks oil with sword) *I would suggest that you add a quart before it's too late. An automobile figures in tonight's play, which is the story of a man with an unpleasant job to perform. One which he did not wish to do, a situation which I understand perfectly, but duty is duty. Ladies and gentlemen . . . the first commercial.*

Story: Connie Breech is a beautiful, young girl who is confined to a wheel chair - and stuck with a two-timing husband named Eddie. A professional hit man named Jim Derry is hired to murder Eddie, but learning of Connie's condition, has second thoughts. Instead, Jim Derry makes the couple an offer. If the two are willing to run off to Mexico, and never show their faces around here again, he'll stage a fake murder and still get paid. The couple agree and start packing their bags. Jim in the meantime, pays a visit to an old friend in a morgue, purchasing a corpse with similar dimensions as Eddie. When the corpse rides off the road into a fiery crash, Eddie returns to his employer to collect his fee. Surprisingly, the police pay the hit man a visit, charging him with murder. It seems Connie wasn't as innocent a cripple as he assumed, for she knew about her husband's infidelity and switched bodies. Explaining to the police that Jim murdered her husband, Connie starts the crying act.

The moral of tonight's story is of course, "never underestimate the power of a woman." Then again, perhaps it's simply, "shoot first, ask questions later." In any case, I'm certain you are better for having watched. Personally I enjoy seeing a hired killer getting the worst of it. For in this particular field, I'm an ardent advocate of do-it-yourself. Unfortunately the police took a more stuffy view of events and Constance is now at a woman's honor farm, where she scurries about in her wheel chair arousing pity and riding rough-shod over her fellow inmates. The next item on the agenda consists of scenes of our coming attraction. The first scene may appear to be a commercial, and if I know my sponsor, it will be.

Trivia, etc. On November 1, 1963, *The Alfred Hitchcock Hour* was not broadcast. Instead, CBS televised the "Miss Teenage America Pageant" from 10 to 11 p.m., EST. The ceremonies culminating in the selection of Miss Teenage America of 1964, from Dallas, Texas. With Bud Collyer and Allen Ludden.

EPISODE #38 **"NOTHING EVER HAPPENS IN LINVALE"** Broadcast Nov. 8, 1963
    Starring: Gary Merrill as Harry Jarvis   Phyllis Thaxter as Mrs. Logan
    Special Guest Star: Fess Parker as Sheriff Ben Wister
    Co-starring: George Furth as Charlie   Robert P. Lieb as Dr. Wyatt
    Burt Mustin as Mr. Bell   Jan Arvan as Al
    Cathie Merchant as the receptionist   Sam Reese as Henry, the barber
    Robert Roter as the boy   and Martine Bartlett as Mrs. Bergen
    Teleplay written for *The Alfred Hitchcock Hour* by William Link and Richard Levinson, based on the short story "Out of This Nettle" by Robert Twohy, originally published in the January 1962 issue of *Ellery Queen's Mystery Magazine*. Subsequently reprinted in *To Be Read Before Midnight*, ed. Ellery Queen (Random House, 1962).
    Produced by Norman Lloyd. Directed by Herschel Daugherty.
    Music composed and conducted by Bernard Herrmann.
    (with a bed of nails) *Good evening. Sorry to keep you waiting, but I had to make my bed. It will surprise you I know, but to be perfectly honest, this is not really my bed. I'm making it for my brother. He insists on coming home late at night, and making a great deal of noise in the dark before he tumbles into bed. I thought that this orthopedic mattress would be precisely what he needs to cure him of that bothersome habit. Our story does not concern a bed like this, but it does take place in a sleepy little town. Apparently nothing much ever happens in Linvale but I have the uneasy feeling that if we watch closely, something will. In case you're doing the driving, Linvale lies just on the other side of this one-minute billboard.*

    Story: Harry Jarvis has been acting very strange lately, sitting around all day drinking beer, and staying up all night digging in the backyard. Meanwhile, his wife has hasn't been seen for days. None of this goes unnoticed to Mrs. Logan, his nosy neighbor, who promptly phones Sheriff Wister. When the law abiding officer arrives, she explains her suspicions, citing examples, that foul play may be involved. The Sheriff plays Jarvis a visit, asking routine questions, who receives reasonable answers. His wife left him over a petty argument and her dog died, so he buried it in the backyard. Noticing the man acting strangely, the sheriff gets a search warrant and has the grave dug up. When the body of the dead pooch is found, and nothing more, the sheriff apologizes and has the grave filled in. Alone together that evening, Jarvis and Mrs. Logan, who are in reality lovers, get together to finish their joint plan of burying the body of Mrs. Jarvis in the freshly-dug grave. Their plan won't work. The sheriff, you see, returned to remind Jarvis that county ordinance says a pet cannot be buried in residential ground and then Mrs. Logan throws a spade over the garden fence and says: "Darling, here, you'll need this."

I think our story is further evidence to support my belief that in cases like this, there is nothing quite so good as burial at sea. It is simple, tidy and not very incriminating. One word of warning however, if you take your wife on a sea voyage, buy her a round-trip ticket, no matter what your plans may be. Next week I shall return with a story, some commercials and more friendly tips for happy husbands. Until then, good night.

Trivia, etc. George Furth also played another character named Charlie, in the movie *Myra Breckinridge* in 1970. Known for playing the role of Van Johnson in Mel Brooks' *Blazing Saddles* (1974), Furth still continues to make appearances on television dramas and comedies.

Hitchcock admitted that he was a very poor television watcher himself. He liked public-affairs programs "of an international nature." He expressed his sorrow to see the quiz show go because it contained "a good element of suspense." The quiz show scandals, he thought, killed off the suspense by causing the public to doubt the element of truth. On Westerns he was less willing to commit himself. He never made a suspense Western, because he admitted that he knew nothing at all about the West. "There is one slight ray of hope," said the master, apropos of the rash of Westerns glutting the air. "Even the children tired of 'Davy Crockett,' you know."

"From an actor's standpoint you're conceited as a person with an entirely different role," noted Fess Parker [billed in this episode as "special guest"]. "I am not sure that the Hitchcock shows were appropriate for children, but I was available to play the part of Sheriff Ben Wister, and it was a job that I enjoyed doing. Gary Merrill and Phyllis Thaxter were very nice people to work with. It was fun working on the set. I had the pleasure of being neighbors with Alfred Hitchcock's daughter Patricia at my first residence in Santa Barbara. She was a strong and supportive activist from community theater to charities. I once asked Mr. Hitchcock why he didn't make a Western film with some spooky twists. He just stuck out his lower lip and from what I gathered he wasn't too enthusiastic about the idea."

Gary Merrill in "Nothing Ever Happens in Linvale."
(Photo courtesy of Ronald V. Borst / Hollywood Movie Posters.)

EPISODE #39   **"STARRING THE DEFENSE"**   Broadcast on November 15, 1963

Starring: Richard Basehart as Miles Crawford

Co-starring: Russell Collins as Sam Brody	S. John Launer as Ed Rutherford
Teno Pollick as Tod Alexander Crawford	Diane Mountford as Ruthie
Jean Hale as Babs Riordan	
Christopher Connelly as Rudy Trask	John Zaremba as the judge
Rockne Tarkington as the police officer	Vince Williams as court bailiff
Selmer Jackson as the movie chaplain	Nolan Leary as the movie judge
Charles Fredericks as the movie warden	Buster West as the movie foreman
Will Allen as the movie boy	and Barney Phillips as Hanley

Teleplay written for *The Alfred Hitchcock Hour* by Henry Slesar, based on his short story of the same name, originally published in the April 1963 issue of *Alfred Hitchcock's Mystery Magazine*. Subsequently collected in *Death on Television* (Southern Illinois University Press, 1989).

Produced by Joan Harrison. Directed by Joseph Pevney.

(as a dog catcher with net and truck) *Good evening. I have just made my first catch. This* (claps truck) . . . *no license, no pedigree, just running loose in the streets and attacking people. The highway seem to be filled with them, all equally vicious. Incidentally, getting this position proved to be quite easy. I was the only applicant who didn't mind going out in the noon day sun. Oh, there was one other, a dog, but he didn't look a bit well. For those of you who are wondering, this is The Alfred Hitchcock Hour. Tonight's tale concerns a man who was once a motion picture actor but who decided to take up honest work instead and became a lawyer. It begins as soon as our sponsor makes his opening statement to the jury.*

Story: Miles Crawford is aghast when he learns that his son has been arrested for murder. Although the boy is guilty, Miles, a former actor who took up law as a profession, agrees to defend the boy with a stirring plea on his behalf, that greatly moves the judge and jury. At least until the prosecutor reveals that the brilliant and moving speech was stolen from a movie Miles had starred in years earlier.

That concludes tonight's story. Those of you who are anxious for more, we can offer you scenes from our next attraction. By the way, I have made my second arrest. I picked this one up for drunkeness (dog lying on the floor). *I must take him in and book him but I shall return next week. Buck, in you go. Buck! In you go.* (looks helpless)

Trivia, etc. Before becoming a director, Joseph Pevney played numerous acting roles in many movies, including *Outside the Wall* (1950). In that movie, both Richard Basehart and Joseph Pevney had starring roles. "I worked with Dick [Richard Basehart] years before when I was in the Army," Pevney recalled. "I don't remember that show specifically, but he was getting along pretty good at that time. Russell Collins came from the Group Theater, about the same time I was there. Norman Lloyd and I went to high school together. That episode was just old friends, course I'm old too! You know, I met Alfred Hitchcock only one night at Joan Harrison's. Joan had a dinner for Hitchcock, I think, at her house and he was recalling his knowledge of wines. He was discoursing on American and French and English wines. That was the only time I ever met him and I don't know if he was aware at the time that I was directing the show for which he received credit."

EPISODE #40 **"BODY IN THE BARN"** Broadcast on November 29, 1963
Starring: Lillian Gish as Bessie Canby   Maggie McNamara as Camilla
Guest Star: Peter Lind Hayes as Henry Wilkins
Kent Smith as Dr. Adamson   Josie Lloyd as Nora
James Maloney as the storekeeper   Doodles Weaver as Gregg
Bruce Andersen as Huckaby
Charles Kuenstle as Huckaby's clerk   Ralph Roberts as the driver
Richard Niles as the deputy
and Kelly Thordsen as Sheriff Pate Turnbull
with Patricia Cutts as Samantha Wilkins

Teleplay written for *The Alfred Hitchcock Hour* by Harold Swanton, based on the short story of the same name by Margaret Manners, originally published in a 1945 issue of *Argosy*. Subsequently reprinted in *Best Detective Stories of the Year*, ed. David C. Cooke (Dutton, 1946), and *Best of the Best Detective Stories*, ed. David C. Cooke (Dutton, 1960).

Produced by Charles Russell. Directed by Joseph Newman.
Music composed and conducted by Bernard Herrmann.

(as a scarecrow) *Good evening. Someone has at last found a practical use for my talents. He reasoned that since I have been frightening people for years, why not birds? The job is somewhat restricting, but I have a number of visitors. One little girl and a tin woodman are quite bothersome. They seem to be under the absurd impression that I'm going to go dancing up the road with them. In keeping with this bucolic mood, tonight we are presenting a pleasant little tale of homicide, lust, deceit, revenge and greed. I'm sure you'll love it, it follows this short prologue.*

Story: Bessie Canby and her daughter Camilla try to patch up relations between their constantly-feuding neighbors, Henry and Samantha Wilkins, by offering an invitation to dinner. Samantha won't go, so Henry accepts the Canby's invitation alone. When Henry suddenly disappears, the neighbors become concerned. Bessie is even more upset when she watches Samantha digging a grave in her barn. Assuming the wife finally did her husband in, Bessie phones the police. The cops dig up the grave to find a long-dead, unidentifiable body, assumed to be that of Henry. Samantha is tried and executed, only to learn that Henry suddenly returns from a "long sea voyage." Realizing that she became a pawn in Henry's scheme to get rid of his wife, Bessie designs special plans in which she ingests poison, and Henry is to blame.

That is the end of tonight's story. We would like to show you more but we seem to be running out of characters. I decided to come down from my pedestal. The, uh, the birds lacked the proper respect. I also took umbrage of one person's observation that the whole scene looked like a code of arms for television. A large ham rampant on a field of corn. Until next week, good night.

Trivia, etc. This episode was originally scheduled for broadcast on November 22, 1963, but was pre-empted, as was all originally scheduled programming, due to network coverage of the assassination of President John F. Kennedy. "Body in the Barn" was instead, broadcast the week after, on November 29, 1963. As for Robert Arthur's "The Cadaver," which was regularly scheduled for this date (November 29), that episode was pushed ahead to January 17, the next available time-slot open for an episode of *The Alfred Hitchcock Hour*, since newly-filmed episodes were scheduled till the 10th. (The broadcast date for this episode has been falsely attributed to it's summer rerun, on numerous web sites and magazines as July 3, 1964.)

A clip from Hitchcock's introduction to this episode was used in the Universal documentary, *Dial H for Hitchcock: The Genius Behind the Showman*.

On December 4, 1963, *Variety* reviewed this episode as: "A neat, suspenseful murder mystery done with style, was rendered on CBS-TV's *Alfred Hitchcock Hour* Friday (29) night. Titled 'The Body in the Barn,' it starred Lillian Gish, Maggie McNamara and Peter Lind Hayes. Teleplay by Harold Swanton had many engaging twists and turns, themed to the proposition that 'two wrongs make a right.' Miss Gish portrayed an old, salty busybody who felt responsible for a death sentence carried out against an innocent victim, Peter Lind Hayes, essaying a straight dramatic role, played one of the 'heavies,' rendering his partner in crime, Miss McNamara. How Miss Gish, in her role, beat the 'heavies,' rendering her 'two wrongs make a right' justice was the heart of the teleplay, adapted from a story by Margaret Manners. Joseph Newman directed in good, clipped style."

EPISODE #41   **"THE DIVIDING WALL"**   Broadcast on December 6, 1963

Starring: James Gregory as Fred Kruger	Chris Robinson as Terry
Katharine Ross as Carol Brandt	Norman Fell as Al Norman
Simon Scott as Durrell	Robert Kelljan as Frank Ludden
Rusty Lane as Otto Brandt	Judd Foster as Polson
Renata Vanni as the female customer	
William Boyett as the radio operator	Erik Corey as the little boy

Teleplay written for *The Alfred Hitchcock Hour* by Joel Murcott, based on a story by George Bellak.

Produced by Joan Harrison. Directed by Bernard Girard.

(bank vault)   *Good evening. Welcome to tonight's program. As you see, I have joined those of you who enjoy the most popular indoor hobby, coin collecting. Perhaps some of you think that the rise of the credit card and credit buying was spontaneous. Actually, the reason for these devices is quite simple. Coin collectors have taken so much money out of circulation, there isn't enough to spend. If this trend should continue, and I see no reason why it should not, we will have to re-introduce barter. With that possibility in mind, I have already begun collecting beaver pelts. I'm sure it will come as no great surprise to you, to learn that in tonight's program, a crime will be committed and I do not refer to the one our sponsor is about to perpetrate.*

Story: Fred, Terry and Al, a trio of paroled ex-convicts, manage to go straight getting jobs as auto mechanics. Sadly, however, once a thief always a thief, and they get the idea of stealing the company payroll, after learning where it is stored. Breaking into the payroll office they discover that they cannot crack open the safe, at least with the tools they have in hand. Hauling the whole darn thing with them back to the garage, they begin to work on the door. Unfortunately, they have taken on more than they realize, as the safe contains a cobalt capsule that, if released in the atmosphere, could cause death all over the city.

(mid-line) *We have now come to what is known as a station break. A rip in the fabric of television entertainment. If you press an eye to the opening, one generally sees another giant eyeball staring back. As an announcer intones the call letters of the local station, after which the second half of our story.*

That concludes our story for tonight. My coin collecting has also ended. I had forgotten about that greatest of all coin collectors - the government. It all went for taxes and is back in circulation again. I am too until next week when I shall return with another story.

Trivia, etc.   Robert Kelljan's name was spelled Kelljian in the *Alfred Hitchcock Presents* episode "Forty Detectives Later." This was also Katharine Ross's first notable TV appearance. Ross's first movie was *The Singing Nun* in 1965, and later she played one of the leads as Elaine Robinson against Dustin Hoffman in *The Graduate* (1967).

EPISODE #42   **"GOOD'BYE, GEORGE"**   Broadcast on December 13, 1963
Starring: Robert Culp as Harry Lawrence   Stubby Kaye as George Layne
Guest Star: Patricia Barry as Lana Layne   Elliott Reid as Dave Dennis
Kreg Martin as the patrol officer   Mike Ragan as the bartender
Sally Carter as the starlet   Jimmy Joyce as the photographer
Bernie Kopell as the director   and Alice Pearce as Haila French

Teleplay written for *The Alfred Hitchcock Hour* by William Fay, based on the 1959 short story "Getting Rid of George" by Robert Arthur, originally published in the May 1959 issue of *Bestseller Mystery Magazine.* Subsequently reprinted in *My Favorites in Suspense,* ed. Alfred Hitchcock (Random House, 1959).

Produced by Joan Harrison. Directed by Robert Stevens.

(with a tape recorder)   *Good evening. Welcome to the Alfred Hitchcock Hour. When one becomes interested in collecting authentic folk music, the first instrument to purchase is an electronic tape-recorder. I recently made a trip among the mountaineers of our country. The trip was most rewarding, for it is from people like this, that one can hear music that is uncontaminated by sorted commercialism. Sounds that speak from the human heart.* (starts tape player) *At this point, I was still creeping up on my subjects.* (sound of gun shots) *There is perhaps no better place to collect folk music than in a jailhouse, and I lost little time reaching this goal.* (sound of cell door slams) *Actually the town didn't have a jailhouse. They use an echo chamber instead. This evening's hootin' anny deals with some folk in the little village of Hollywood, California. Lana Layne was a motion picture star, with hardly a care in the world, until. . . but that's what our story is about. First however, a number that is truly indigenous to American television, a commercial.*

Story: After her husband dies, Laura Layne goes on to become a celebrated actress. But after winning an Oscar, ex-convict George Layne suddenly shows up alive and well where he announces that he plans to live comfortably on his wife's ample income. Given that choice or a messy divorce, Laura decides to strike George over the head with a vase, killing him. She contacts her fiancé, Harry, and together they plan out how to get rid of the body. Insisting that their honeymoon be a secret, they pack the corpse into a trunk and set of for their top-secret destination in Mexico, where they plan to bury poor George. Unknown to either of them, a gossip columnist has learned of their destination and has prepared an unforgetable reception, that no one is likely to forget.

(mid-line) *This is the point of the program where I always feel like a man in the middle. On one side is the first half of our show, on the other, the second half. Straight ahead – the station break.*

Well, I feel they got what they deserved. I don't approve of taking the first husband along on the honeymoon. Next on our program is a one-minute solo by the sponsor, followed by some scenes from next week's play.

Trivia, etc. "Robert Culp was cheerful and friendly on the set, and he and I talked about writing," recalled Elliott Reid. "He had an upstairs, round tower room in his house, where he retreated to do his creative work. I guess I've never found the right room; I continue on with my 'writer's block.' Sadly, I never worked with, nor saw Culp again." Robert Culp would later write scripts for *The Saturn Awards, The Greatest American Hero,* and *I Spy,* the last of which he co-starred with Bill Cosby.

Bernie Kopell, who played the role of the director in this episode. also appeared with Robert Culp in three movies. *Comedy Central's Canned Ham: The Dr. Evil Story* (1999), *Combat High* (1986) and *The Greatest Heroes of the Bible,* a miniseries for television in 1978. Patricia Barry would also appear in two movies, both featuring Robert Culp, *Her Life as a Man* (1984) and *Sammy, the Way Out Seal* (1962).

The Oscar statue featured in this episode was real, not a replica. At the end of the closing credits, there billed: "The Academy Award statuette used on this program is by special permission of the Academy of Motion Picture Arts and Sciences, copyright holders."

EPISODE #43 "HOW TO GET RID OF YOUR WIFE" Broadcast December 20, 1963
    Starring: Bob Newhart as Gerald Swinney
    Co-starring: Jane Withers as Edith Swinney   Joyce Jameson as Rose Feather
    Mary Scott as Laura   George Petrie as Henry
    Ann Morgan Guilbert as the pet shop proprietress
    Robert Karnes as the police sergeant   William Wellman, Jr. as the delivery man
    Joseph Hamilton as the stage doorman Helene Winston as Mrs. Penny
    Harold Gould as the district attorney   Bill Quinn as Mr. Penny
    Harry Hines as the rat poison salesman Gail Bonney as Mrs. Harris
    Based on an original teleplay, written for *The Alfred Hitchcock Hour* by Robert
Gould.
    Produced by Charles Russell. Directed by Alf Kjellin.
    (on a wooden horse) *Good evening. Contrary to appearances, we are not converting our show into a middle-eastern western. This is a lovely gift that just arrived and I'm having workmen tear out a wall so that I can get it into the house. What is especially touching, is that the gift came from a person I had not regarded as a friend. A social climber, who is always trying to wrangle an invitation to my home. I'm quite pleased however. Now that I have a wooden horse, I may even take up water polo. From this innocent hobbyhorse we turn to a hobby of another kind. Tonight's program is dedicated to the do-it-yourselfer and is called "How to Get Rid Of Your Wife." It concerns one Gerald Swinney, a gentleman seemingly too meek for the task ahead. But we shall see . . . we shall see. As a special feature tonight we are delaying the start of the story by one minute. Time for you to gather up a pencil and paper. After all, some of you may wish to take notes.*

    Story: After seeing him dig a grave in the back yard, Edith Swinney is certain her husband plans to get rid of her, but when she tells friends and neighbors about the situation, they think Edith is having a nervous breakdown. As it happens, Gerald really is fed up with the ever-nagging Edith, and his constant antics designed at driving her crazy begin to work. When Gerald purchases some rats for the house, Edith rushes out to buy some poison from the local pet store. When he makes the suggestion that she'll be gone in a short time, Edith tries to beat him to it by mixing poison in the hot chocolate and feeding it to her husband. After phoning the police the next morning, Edith discovers that Gerald is alive and well, never drinking the cocoa. Edith is arrested for attempted murder and sentenced to prison. Now able to live the life of a single man, things take a turn for the worse when the woman at the pet store pays him a visit. She is the only woman who knows about Gerald's secret, and for a price - a very high one - the woman insists she will be quiet. The woman has always wanted a husband . . .

    I still have my wife, but you will notice I have gotten rid of my horse. I wouldn't have cared if it were a talking horse, but I discovered this one was ticking. I promptly gave it away. I felt there were others who deserved it more than I. My sponsor for one. After all the very foundation of commercial television is the Trojan horse principal, as witnessed the following.

    Trivia, etc. This episode was filmed in the same house set used in the current popular comedy sitcom, *Leave it to Beaver*. This episode also had two directors of

436

photography, William Margulies and John F. Warren. All other Hitchcock episodes only billed one director of photography. On December 27, 1963, a rebroadcast of the first hour-long season's "The Star Juror" was presented.

EPISODE #44   **"THREE WIVES TOO MANY"**   Broadcast on January 3, 1964
Starring: Teresa Wright as Marion   Guest Star: Dan Duryea as Brown
Co-starring: Linda Lawson as Lucille Brown Jean Hale as Bernice Brown
Steven Gravers as Lieutenant Storber   Robert Cornthwaite as Mr. Bleeker
Lew Brown as Detective Lanning   Dee J. Thompson as the sister-in-law
Duane Grey as Detective Millard   David Fresco as the brother-in-law
Teleplay written for *The Alfred Hitchcock Hour* by Arthur Ross, based on the short story of the same name by Kenneth Fearing, originally published in the September 1956 issue of *Mike Shayne Mystery Magazine*. Subsequently reprinted in *Best Detective Stories of the Year*, ed. David C. Cooke (Dutton, 1957).
Produced by Herbert Coleman. Directed by Joseph Newman.
(with a lawn-mower in-doors)   *Good evening. How do you do? I've just been promoted. The office hasn't been occupied for some time and the carpet hasn't been properly kept up. This area near the water-cooler will have to be completely re-seeded.* (looks at bump under the rug) *I see the former occupant was partial to gentle, rolling landscape. On the other hand I have the feeling that this may be the former occupant himself. I find this quite up-setting. They told me he had left. To be precise they said, "He is no longer with us." I assumed he left the normal way one does in the business world, by leaping out of the window. While I contemplate this dilemma of the organization man, I invite you to observe the machinations of an extremely well-organized man. It is the story of a travelling salesman with an intriguing design for living. And now . . . speaking of salesmen . . .*

Story: Newark, New Jersey. Mr. Brown is a gambling bigamist who finds himself in hot water when his wealthy wives begin dying one by one. Every time he is arrested, the police are forced to release him for lack of evidence. This is just as well, as the real murderer is Brown's first wife, Marion, who has decided to "eliminate" her competition. Brown confronts Marion, threatening her, but the woman was on to him. She has carefully arranged things so that if anything happens to her, her death will reveal information that will be sufficient to convict Brown of all the killings. And if he plans to spend time with another woman, the same fate will befall him.

(mid-line)   *In any office, the most important moment is the break. It is on television too – for the local stations, that is. Here they come now. Following our break, we shall all get back to work again.* (Hitchcock dumps trash into a trashcan)

This idyllic situation was not destined to last. The police don't like to leave their books unbalanced for any length of time. They eventually stumbled on to the puzzle of Richard's private life and moved in just in time to save him, for themselves. Richard was not only guilty of simple bigamy, in his case it was more like trigonometry. He is now in a well known federal prison. You see, the law took the position that he must be punished, as though having four wives were not punishment enough. Incidentally this turned out . . . not to be the former occupant. I knew you'd be pleased to know. It was his wife. Next week we shall bring you another twisted tale, scenes of which will be on-view in a trice.

Trivia, etc. "The producer [for *The Alfred Hitchcock Hour*] was Norman Lloyd," the capable and marvelous actor who was with the Mercury Theatre," Arthur Ross recalled. "The production of the hour shows wasn't going too well, so Hitchcock asked Norman to take over the production. Norman did, and he was just superb at it. It was one of the most civilized relationships I've had with anybody. I did about eight of those [episodes of *The*

Alfred Hitchcock Hour] and it was a marvelous time. I enjoyed it very much. My episodes got pretty good attention in *TV Guide*: If there was an exceptional show in a series, it got a half-a-page review, and over half of my Hitchcocks got the half-page reviews."

The story takes place at Newark, New Jersey – Norman Lloyd's home town. For anyone who cares, the word "brother-in law" was mis-spelled in the closing credits as "bother-in-law."

John Megna and Leslie Nielsen pose for photographers in "The Magic Shop."
(Photo courtesy of Ronald V. Borst / Hollywood Movie Posters.)

EPISODE #45 **"THE MAGIC SHOP"**   Broadcast on January 10, 1964
        Starring: Leslie Nielsen as Steven Grainger
        Co-starring: Peggy McCay as Hilda Grainger   John Megna as Tony Grainger
        Guest Star: David Opatoshu as Mr. Dulong, the magician

Paul Hartman as Mr. Adams	William Sargent as Dr. James Stone
Ted de Corsia as Herlie	Hugh Sanders as the first cop
Rolfe Sedan as the old man	Audrey Swanson as Eric's mother
Robert Reiner as the intern	Brian Corcoran as Eric

        Teleplay written for *The Alfred Hitchcock Hour* by John Collier, based on an adaptation (script) by James Parish from the short story of the same name by H.G. Wells, originally published in the June 1903 issue of *The Strand*.
        Produced by Joan Harrison. Directed by Robert Stevens.
        Music composed and conducted by Lyn Murray.

(holding a kite)   *Good evening. Greetings fellow astronauts. I believe the search for inexpensive space exploration is at an end. Our program thus far has achieved untold of heights, in a budgetary sense. Now I'm confident that we shall be able to reduce the important cost per mile factor to an unprecedented low. Simplicity is the key note. I believe a child could operate this ship, thus freeing men for more important tasks. We shall stage a demonstration this evening, but first we wish to bring you a story. It is called "The Magic Shop." For that is where Steven Grainger has a frightening and eerie experience. It begins in a few moments.*

Story: Steven Grainger gives his son money for his birthday, and takes the small boy to a remote magic store in town, where Tony can spend his money. The owner, Mr. Dulong, sees a promising future in the young lad, and offers to teach Tony all he knows about "real" magic. Tony's eyes fill with delight and stepping into a cabinet, he promptly disappears. Dulong then vanishes as well, leaving Mr. Grainger stranded in the streets, searching for his son. Strangely enough, the magic shop has disappeared, along with young Tony. The next day, the boy walks out of his room, but not into the open arms of his parents. Tony, you see, has become a master of black magic – a fact soon established by the shady going-ons about the neighborhood . . . and they had better not get in his way.

(mid-line; standing beside a boy holding string to kite) *Sorry you missed the blast off. Except for a moment when the tail was momentary caught in a tree, it progressed without incident. Notice the ground to space-craft communication. We shall continue our experimentation, under cover of this station break, and the second half of our show.*

(boy flies off with kite) *Our daring astronaut sustained a skinned knee but that only made the sight more colorful. As for the criticism that our launching lacks dramatic sounds, I believe his screams will soon put an end to that loose talk. They say what goes up must come down, so while we wait for that truth to be verified, we shall see some scenes from next week's story.*

EPISODE #46   **"THE CADAVER"**   Broadcast on January 17, 1964
Starring: Michael Parks as Skip Baxter
Ruth McDevitt as Mrs. Fister   Joby Baker as Doc Carroll
Co-starring: Martin Blaine as Professor Dawson Jennifer West as Ruby
Don Marshall as Tom Jackson   William Sharon as the bartender
Bronwyn FitzSimons as the girl student   Eric Matthews as Charlie Pitts
George Dockstader as the garbage collector   Rafer Johnson as Ed Blair
Jeff Cooper as Pete Phillips   Michael Beirne as Jim Thompson
Bob Bernard as the first student   and Brooke Hayward as Barbara Simms
Teleplay written for *The Alfred Hitchcock Hour* by James Bridges, based on a story by Robert Arthur.
Produced by Charles Russell. Directed by Alf Kjellin.
(twining ivy)   *Good evening. Welcome scholars to this evening's lecture. Because of the population explosion and the need for more and more institutions of higher learning, Universities seem to be springing up over night. Since everyone prefers to go to old established institutions, we have developed such products, as fast growing ivy. We can also in a matter of months, provide a campus with hundred year-old traditions, picked up at very reasonable prices from colleges that are sick of them. Aging the faculty has not yet presented any problems. In creating a new University, we first of all begin by granting several thousand honorary degrees. A process which we call, instant alumni. For those of you who long for days of beer and ivy, we have just the story. It is about two young men, Doc and Skip, and of a not-so practical joke. The school bell will ring in just one minute. When it does, remember. It tolls for thee.*

Story: College student Doc Carroll has a penchant for practical jokes. His roommate, Skip Baxter, has a huge drinking problem, a handicap Doc decides to use at his advantage. With the medical student on one binge after another, Doc, cooks up the perfect practical joke. "Borrowing" a corpse from the medical school (since Doc has access to them), one that looks much like a local waitress named Ruby, places it in bed next to an unconscious Skip. When the boy wakes up the next morning, he believes he killed the waitress in a drunken stupor, and in desperation he ditches the body. The joke is blown later that afternoon when Doc gets in trouble for stealing the cadaver, and asks Skip to return the body. Skip agrees but at the next anatomy class, Professor Dawson is shocked to find the cadaver replaced with the body of Doc, more fresh than alive.

(mid-line) *I can't say when we shall break this case. But we will break our stations – now. After which, we shall continue our play.*

Brother Alfred seems to have disappeared. We have a great deal of difficulty with our faculty that way. (caught by the ivy, Hitchcock with moustache is watering the ivy) *As for Skip Baxter the authorities took a dim view of his prankish nature and he is in another institution now and I don't mean the state University. One week from tonight we shall present another play, scenes of which will be on display in a few moments. First however, here is our companioned feature.*

Trivia, etc. Ruth McDevitt played Mrs. Fister in almost exactly the same manner that she played Mrs. MacGruder in Davidson's Pet Shop in *The Birds* (1963), one year earlier. Just three months later she appeared in the episode "The Gentleman Caller." Charles Russell also produced the television series *The Untouchables*, *Adventures in Paradise*, *The Crimebusters* and *The Murder Men*.

EPISODE #47 **"BEYOND THE SEA OF DEATH"** Broadcast on January 24, 1964
Starring: Mildred Dunnock as Minnie Briggs Diana Hyland as Grace Renford
Jeremy Slate as Keith Holloway (alias Harold Drummond)
Co-Starring: Abraham Sofaer as Dr. Shankara
Ann Ayars as Lucy Barrington Orville Sherman as Charles
Francis De Sales as Lieutenant Farrell Vince Williams as the hotel clerk
Ollie O'Toole as the second hotel clerk Jim Barringer as the messenger boy
Teleplay written for *The Alfred Hitchcock Hour* by Alfred Hayes and William D. Gordon, based on the short story of same name by Miriam Allen de Ford, originally published in May 1949 issue of *Ellery Queen's Mystery Magazine*. Subsequently collected in *The Quintessence of Queen* (Random House, 1962), and *The Theme is Murder* (Abelard-Schuman, 1967).
Produced by Joan Harrison. Directed by Alf Kjellin.
(in a love seat) *Good evening. Welcome to another session of group therapy. Television has done much for psychiatry. By spreading information about it, as well as contributing to the need point. This is a prop from one of the new psychiatry shows. It is for psychiatrists whose patients are well enough to sit up. By large, most psychiatrists prefer the conventional couch. They say this is fine, except that they don't find as much change left in the cushions. Actually this is called a love seat and in my opinion whoever named it that was a very sick man. This evening's drama is called "Beyond The Sea Of Death." It is about Grace Renford, a distant admirer and a message from beyond the sea of death.*

Story: Grace Renford, both pretty and wealthy, is fed up with men who are only interested in her money. Answering an advertisement in a spiritualist magazine, she begins writing to a young man named Keith, from Bolivia. When he travels to the United States to meet her, Grace rents an inexpensive apartment so he won't know about her wealth. The two fall in love and become engaged, over the objections of Grace's surrogate mother, Minnie.

Grace reveals her affluence to Keith, who declares he loves her for who she is, not for what she has. He returns to South America, planning to have her join him later. Days pass by till Grace receives the heart-breaking telegram that Keith has been killed in an accident. Out of desperation, she contacts Dr. Shankara, an expert in the mystic arts, who promises to put her in contact with Keith. Falling victim to the fake spiritualist, Grace decides to give away millions to his foundation, just as the mystic and a very alive Keith have planned all along. When Minnie discovers the plot, she calls for Lieutenant Farrell who explains that Keith Holloway is a con man, and "his real name is Harold Dummond." After Farrell has left, Grace promptly murders Minnie for attempting to destroy her fantasies.

(mid-line) *There are certain words one hesitates to use on television. I refer once again to that nasty word, 'reality.' It is here again. This time in the form of a station break, after which we shall return once again to our world of make believe.*

It is my duty to report that Miss Renford eventually paid for her crime. But the sympathetic jury recognized that there were mitigating circumstances. (shows sign with blood stains) *This will be used in the titles of a new medical show we are planning. That is not ink by the way, it is blood. We plan to call the show "The Bleeding Point." Next week we shall return with another story and if you wish to see scenes from that production, please keep your eyes glued to this spot. Good night.*

EPISODE #48   **"NIGHT CALLER"**   Broadcast on January 31, 1964

Starring: Felicia Farr as Marcia Fowler   Bruce Dern as Roy Bullock
David White as Jack Fowler   Leslie Barringer as Stevey Fowler
Will J. White as the first policeman   Diane Sayer as Nancy Willis
Elizabeth Harrower as Mrs. Masters   Frances Morris as the woman shopper
and Angela Greene as Lucy Phillips

Teleplay written for *The Alfred Hitchcock Hour* by Robert Westerby and Gabrielle Upton, based on a story by Gabrielle Upton.

Produced by Robert Douglas. Directed by Alf Kjellin.

(with a sword)   *Good evening. This interesting object was found at the site of an ancient Hittite civilization. Fortunately it was very clearly labeled. It's a plough-share. It was made during the period when the Hittites had signed a disarmament pact with their neighbors. I can see other uses for it, but of course I'm rather imaginative and my mind sometimes moves in disturbing directions. You see, I have been challenged to a duel, with my sponsor, and being allowed to choose the weapons, I selected this for him. For myself, I've chosen a hand grenade. I have dispensed with a second, however my opponent has 60 of them, during which he shall state his case. Following that we bring you tonight's play. It is the story of a modern day Lady Godiva and her Peeping Tom.*

Story: A well-proportioned young lady named Marcia Fowler, sunbathes in her backyard when she notices a neighborhood boy, Roy Bullock, perversely watching her. She isn't amused and when Marcia's husband Jack, confronts him later about the situation, Roy denies the incident – the first of many. When obscene phone calls begin, Marcia is certain Roy is behind it, which creates another confrontation between Roy and her husband. When Jack goes away on a business trip Roy pays a visit to see Marcia, hoping to straighten things out. Sure he is planning to harm or kill her, Marcia pulls out a gun and shoots him dead - just as the phone rings with the mysterious obscene phone caller on the line.

(mid-line) *As the gentleman said who was in the process of administering the coup de grâce, we are half-way through. In television, we hesitate at this point, in order to savor the moment and indulge in a station break. Granted the victim suffers a bit, but rules are rules. We shall continue after the following.*

That concludes our story. At least it concludes Mr. Roy Bullock. It was not the end of Mrs. Fowler, however, the jury recommended mercy. As for the anonymous caller, he was permitted one more call . . . to his attorney. You see a policeman happened to be waiting to use the pay phone at the time of that last call. I have traded my sword for a much more practical instrument. (shows a very big fork) *I feel much better. This is more my style. Now it is time to hear from my worthy opponent. He seems to have forgotten about our duel, so I imagine I can relax now.* (sword hanging above Hitchcock's head)

Trivia, etc. This episode was based on an original story idea by screen-writer Gabrielle Upton, and scripted with the help of Robert Westerby. Upton wrote scripts for television's *Alcoa Presents, The Big Valley,* and *The High Chaparral.* Westerby wrote teleplays on many popular books and novels, including Walt Disney's *The Scarecrow of Romney Marsh,* and *War and Peace* (1956). Bruce Dern, who would perform in two of Hitchcock's motion pictures, *Marnie* (1964) and *Family Plot* (1976), made his first of two appearances on the Hitchcock program. When asked about Hitchcock's popularity with the television series, he commented: "The whole thing of him [Hitchcock] being the host, the people loved. Because he was cute and I think that exposed Hitchcock to the mass media. They had already seen the movies and everything, but that [*Alfred Hitchcock Presents* and *The Alfred Hitchcock Hour*] did it on a weekly basis. That made him part of their home."
This was also the third episode in a row directed by Alf Kjellin.

EPISODE #49   **"THE EVIL OF ADELAIDE WINTERS"**   Broadcast February 7, 1964
Starring: Kim Hunter as Adelaide Winters
Co-starring: John Larkin as Edward Porter   Gene Lyons as Robert McBain
Sheila Bromley as Mrs. Thompson   Bartlett Robinson as Mr. Thompson
Teleplay written for *The Alfred Hitchcock Hour* by Arthur Ross, from his 1951 *Suspense* radio play of the same name.
Produced by Herbert Coleman. Directed by Laslo Benedek.
(by streetlight on stilts)   *Good evening. How do you do ladies and gentlemen and peeping Toms the world over. I think you deserve an explanation of my new tall, slim look. This is not entirely the result of vertical stripes. I had my face lifted and neglected to say 'when.' Seriously, I innocently stepped into a pair of elevator shoes . . . and pressed the wrong button. However there is nothing to worry about, I shall simply take the next pair going down. This evening, in addition to our sideshow, we are bringing you a bizarre little drama called "The Evil Of Adelaide Winters." It is about a woman with a strange talent which she use to bring happiness to people. Particularly herself. I would tell you more about the story, but it might frighten you off and then you would miss all the commercials. This little gem for example.*

Story: A few years after the second World War, Adelaide Winters began her unusual occupation of joining together family relatives with their loved ones, reported "missing in action." Establishing her trade and reputation as a successful medium, Adelaide makes a tidy sum of money, from rich prospects. In truth, she's a fake, but the dice roll her way when Edward Porter, millionaire, emotionally expresses the loss of his son. Adelaide uses her talents to convince a skeptical Porter that with her, his son can be reunited. Eager to give her what she wants, and blind with faith, Edward Porter invites the medium to come live with him in his grand estate. He even proposes marriage to her, believing that the three of them can be together forever. Little does Adelaide realize that the man means exactly what he says when during the evening of their honeymoon, he pulls out a gun and points it toward her.

(mid-line) *There can be serious disadvantages to being ten feet tall. For one thing, I just dropped a quarter on the sidewalk. We shall continue our story, after our local stations advise you, who is bringing our show.*

I finally had to come down. I became tired telling people how the weather was up there. Next week I shall remain the proper height. Scenes of next week's commercials will be shown in a moment, small segments of our next story follow that.

Trivia, etc. This story was originally written by Arthur Ross for the CBS radio anthology series *Suspense*. Ross, the same man who wrote the screenplay to *Creature From the Black Lagoon* (1954), wrote this teleplay based on his original radio script, broadcast on September 10, 1951. Originally, the radio script was not titled, until hours before broadcast. Here, Ross borrowed the same title given to the radio production, for his Hitchcock teleplay. Agnes Moorehead starred in the original role in the 1951 production.

EPISODE #50 **"THE JAR"** Broadcast on February 14, 1964
        Starring: Pat Buttram as Charlie Hill
        Co-starring: Collin Wilcox as Thedy Sue Hill

William Marshall as Jahdoo	Jane Darwell as Granny Carnation
Carl Benton Reid as Gramps Medknowe	James Best as Tom Carmody
George Lindsey as Juke Marmer	Jocelyn Brando as Emma Jane
Slim Pickens as Clem Carter	Alice Backes as Mrs. Tridden
Sam 'Sammy' Reese as Milt Marshall	Marlene DeLamater as Eva Ann
and Billy Barty as the Barker	

        Teleplay written for *The Alfred Hitchcock Hour* by James Bridges, based on the short story of the same name by Ray Bradbury, originally published in the November 1944 issue of *Weird Tales*. Subsequently collected in *Dark Carnival* (Arkham House, 1947), *The October Country* (Ballantine, 1955). and *The Stories of Ray Bradbury* (Knopf, 1980).
        Produced and directed by Norman Lloyd.
        Music composed and conducted by Bernard Herrmann.
        (in a bottle)   *Good evening. Welcome to the Alfred Hitchcock tale hour. The next time I buy a ship model kit I intend to read the directions more closely. I have one consolation to being unceremoniusly bottled like this. That is, wine connoisseurs will say this will be considered a good year. However, I feel I have aged enough. I only hope I'm let out while I still have some fizz. During my absence you'll be entertained by "The Jar," a story about some people who found a very strange source of fascination. It begins sixty seconds from now.*

        Story: At the Heron Swamp, country bumpkin farmer Charlie Hill becomes mesmerized by a strange-looking thing, on display at a travelling circus. Sealed inside the clear jar is a strange concoction that defies everyone's description and eager to impress his neighbors, Charlie offers to buy the jar. With all sales final, Charlie takes it home and invites his friends and neighbors to see it. No one can figure out what is in the jar, and every night they gather to sit and watch. Some envision pure horror while others envision romance. Charlie's young cheating wife, Thedy Sue, hates the evil-looking thing and expresses her desire to have it out of the house. When she has an attempt made on the jar, Charlie succeeds in saving the priceless object at the nick of time. People come from miles around to see the jar and it has won him his neighbors' respect. Jealous over her husband's new toy, Thedy Sue gets into a fight that turns physical. In a fit of rage, Thedy Sue opens the container and destroys the contents, resulting in Charlie taking drastic steps to refill the unusual jar . . . using Thedy Sue's head, still with the ribbon in her hair that spells her name.

        (mid-line) *We have come to the station break. And speaking of break, I wish this bottle would. I've been hearing the disturbing rumor that this is a no deposit, no return bottle, and that I may end up in the trash. All this will be continued after we hear from our local station.*

I wish to make one thing clear at once: Any resemblance between "The Jar" and any other type of home entertainment is purely coincidental. There is just no comparison. However, we are working every day to lift the level of television. Someday, who knows? Getting out of the bottle proved to be easier than I imagined. However, I had the help of an angry genie, who claimed I had invaded his home. That is all I have to offer this evening. Until next week then, good night.

Trivia, etc. Horror author Stephen King has, on more than one occasion, admitted that this episode was one of his favorite horror films of all time. "I don't think that, until I put him in 'The Jar,' Pat Buttram had ever done a straight play or straight dialogue. He'd always been a stand-up performer," producer/director Norman Lloyd recalled. "We were noted, if I may say so, for the excellence of our casting - in those days, we used to bring people out from New York. But not Pat, Pat was right here. And I think I had Slim Pickens in it, too, didn't I? Oh, these guys were marvelous. Pat, he was so wonderful in 'The Jar' that I didn't know where the part started and he left off, or vice versa! In one scene when he got into bed with Collin Wilcox (who was a tasty dip), he'd say [imitating Buttram], 'Mmmmm...my Albert is misbehaving!' [Laughs] Collin was, shall I say, a very sophisticated lady, and she handled it very well. But, oh, Pat was a funny man, oh, God! And he loved doing legitimate work, because it gave work to his Albert, I guess [laughs]! He was just so wonderful in it that I put him in another one with Teresa Wright."

"He [Hitchcock] was shooting *Marnie* (1964) at the time," continued Lloyd, "and I called him and said, 'If you have time, I'd love to run it for you.' Even when he was doing pictures, he would stop for an hour or so to look at the rough cut that we had to bring him, because we had to get 'em on the air. We would never dare go on the air without his approval. So you'd call him and he'd find time in the course of shooting that day, perhaps in his lunch hour or whatever. I remember running 'The Jar' with him and then going back on the set of *Marnie* with him, and he was telling people, 'I have just seen a wonderful picture' - which I thought was rare for Hitch. I don't think he ever came out and said, 'This is the best,' but I know he always really liked 'The Jar'."

And what was in the jar? Interviewer and author Tom Weaver interviewed Norman Lloyd: "A couple of bedsprings; some foam rubber; we made a head for Collin Wilcox and a ribbon with her name on it, a silly sort of 'Maisie Sue' name. But the original jar, before Collin Wilcox was beheaded and her head put in it, just had foam rubber, bedsprings . . . and there was another element in it, something that floated. It could have been a piece of fruit [laughs]!" (Tom: And water?) "Oh, yes, that's right. But, you see, it was just nothingness, and that was what was so wonderful about it - because everybody saw his life in it." *

EPISODE #51 **"FINAL ESCAPE"** Broadcast on February 21, 1964
     Starring: Stephen McNally as Captain Tollman
     Robert Keith as Doc   Guest Star: Edd Byrnes as John Perry
     Co-starring: Nicholas Colasanto as the work partner
     John Kellogg as the first guard   Ray Kellogg as the convict blacksmith
     Bernie Hamilton as the second convict Stacy Harris as the lawyer
     Hinton Pope as the second guard   Betsy Hale as Elissa
     and John Alderson as the third guard
     Teleplay written for *The Alfred Hitchcock Hour* by John Resko, based on a story by Thomas H. Cannan, Jr. and Randall Hood.
     Produced by Robert Douglas. Directed by William Witney.
     (stomping grapes in a wine cask)   *Good evening. How do you do? I find myself here as the result of a misunderstanding. I thought I was going to bathe in*

* In the story, Thedy Sue goes through it thoroughly: "Here's a piece of paper and here's the cotton and more cotton and wire and yarn and here's a piece of inner tube and here's a great big piece of clay."

champagne, but find myself stomping grapes instead. I did have a partner working with me but a short time ago he sank without trace. There is one consolation to drowning in wine. He had a smile on his face as he went under. However I'm not complaining. I've always wanted to have my tennis shoes dyed, though I didn't plan on having burgundy colored feet as well. But life must go on. Tonight's story is about a man called Perry and begins after a minute called tedious.

Story: John Perry, a bank robber sentenced to a state prison lumber camp, has no intention of serving out his eleven-year sentence. Becoming friends with an alcoholic inmate named Doc, who handles the burials of prisoners, John comes up with the idea of talking the old man into helping him escape in return for Perry financing an operation for Doc's granddaughter. The old man agrees to let Perry hide in a coffin on top of the next prisoner who dies, to be buried alive. The men would unknowingly be carrying out two bodies, behind the prison walls. Hours later, Perry will be secretly dug back up by Doc when no one is around - allowing him the perfect escape. Days later, a prisoner dies and all alone that evening, an eager Perry sneaks into the coffin and goes to sleep. The guards come to nail the coffin closed and the burial goes off without a hitch. But hours later, Doc never shows to dig him up, and Perry starts getting scared. The convict eventually realizes why when he lights a match and meets his host - the deceased is none other than Doc himself, who suffered a heart attack the night before.

(mid-line) *Our story will continue, after this friendly interruption from your local station.*

That concludes this evening's story. Next week I hope to bring you another one. Previews of which follow the next commercial, which I hope . . . (bubbles from the wine cask)

Trivia, etc. Director William Witney is considered the Hitchcock of the action film and the Spielberg of his generation. With absolutely no training he began directing at an early age during a crisis in the filming of the Republic Pictures cliffhanger series *The Painted Stallion* in 1937. He directed or co-directed more than two dozen subsequent Republic serials including such classics as *The Lone Ranger* (1938), *Daredevils of the Red Circle* (1939) and *Zorro's Fighting Legion* (1939) – considered by fans as the best Zorro serial of them all. In the fifties and sixties, most of his work was for TV series but he also did some spectacular uncredited second unit direction. Hitchcock hired Witney to direct the fox-hunt sequence in *Marnie* (1964), which Witney shot from a helicopter and which Hitchcock ruined in the editing room by intercutting close-ups of Tippi Hedren riding a bucking barrel. The fact that Witney got to film this episode of *The Alfred Hitchcock Hour* is sufficient evidence that Hitchcock must have admired his work. The superb helicopter footage of the hunt scene in *Marnie* – which Hitchcock clearly based on the hunt scene in the Academy Award-winning *Tom Jones* (1963).

Nicholas Colasanto also appeared as Mr. Constantine in Hitchcock's last movie, *Family Plot* (1976). On February 28, 1964, *The Alfred Hitchcock Hour* was not broadcast. Instead, a repeat performance of the music/comedy show *Carol and Company*, starring Robert Preston and Carol Burnett, was featured in the time slot.

EPISODE #52 **"MURDER CASE"** Broadcast on March 6, 1964

Starring: Gena Rowlands as Diana Justin   John Cassavetes as Lee Griffin
Co-starring: Murray Matheson as Charles Justin Ben Wright as Tony Niles
Brendan Dillon as Collins   David Frankham as Peter
John Bauner as the Dutch customs man   Richard Lupino as the author
Richard Peel as Sergeant Elliott   Ina Victor as the young Ingenue

Noel Drayton as the bar steward and Hedley Mattingly as Blackie

Teleplay written for *The Alfred Hitchcock Hour* by James Bridges, William Link and Richard Levinson, based on the short story of the same name by Max Marquis, originally published in the September 1955 issue of *London Mystery Magazine.*

Produced by Robert Douglas. Directed by John Brahm.

(leaking dam) *Good evening. I hope you will excuse me, but I seem to be immobilized. A small Dutch boy asked me to keep my finger in a hole in the dyke, while he went for help. That was a week ago, but of course help is very hard to get these days. I wonder if it might not be wiser if they simply turned this into a fountain. By the way, this is not the extent of tonight's entertainment. Later we plan to present a story called "Murder Case." It concerns a man who assumed a very strange identity for a very practical reason. It will follow hard upon this one-minute leak in the dyke of television.*

Story: London. A talented young American actor named Lee Griffin meets his old flame, a girl named Diana, who is now married to a wealthy older gentleman. It seems Lee just got hired by Diana's husband for the main part in a new stage play, and it doesn't take long for Lee and Diana to rekindle their relationship. Then they scheme to get make Diana a wealthy widow. After their first attempt at murdering Charles fails, the old man arranges for the play to close early, so he and Diana can run off to Paris and Monte Carlo for a second honeymoon. Overhearing their plans on the phone, Charles kills Diana and stashes her dead body in his car. Planning a more complicated act, Lee has a fake passport made up, sneaks on board the ferry to France, and shoots Charles. Switching identities, Lee pushes the body out the window, tied to heavy weights, feeding the corpse to the fishes. When Lee arrives in Paris, the fake passport fools the customs officer, but the inspector asks to check the luggage . . . and the automobile.

(mid-line) *I trust you found our first half interesting. For myself, my enjoyment was somewhat diminished by the discovery that my fingers are stuck. I can't get away. This is particularly annoying because I just remembered. . . I left the water running at home. My predicament and that of the hero of tonight's story will continue after this station break.*

You will be pleased to know that the little boy who went for help finally returned. Unfortunately, our little hero seemed to have forgotten what he was supposed to do. He was much more interested in going through my pockets for money. I'm quite distressed really. I don't mind losing the money or my illusions about our young hero, it's standing here in public with my pockets out. It's all too unseemly. Next week when I present another story, I trust that I shall be more presentable.

EPISODE #53 **"ANYONE FOR MURDER?"** Broadcast on March 13, 1964

Starring: Barry Nelson as James Parkerson
Patricia Breslin as Doris Parkerson Dick Dawson as Robert Johnson
Guest Star: Edward Andrews as Bingham Richard X. Slattery as Detective Barker
Robert Jacquin as Mr. Conelley, the editor
Grant Lockwood as the man at the bar David Fresco as the waiter

Teleplay written for *The Alfred Hitchcock Hour* by Arthur Ross, based on the short story of the same name by Jack Ritchie, originally published in the January 1964 issue of *Alfred Hitchcock's Mystery Magazine.* Subsequently collected in *Little Boxes of Bewilderment* (St. Martin's Press, 1989).

Produced by Herbert Coleman. Directed by Leo Penn.

(bow in hand, arrow in head) *Good evening. I shot an arrow into the air. It fell to Earth, I know not where. I think the bow and arrow has long been underrated as a weapon. Esthetically, it is far superior to the revolver, and can be just as effective without any unseemly powder burns. There is no danger of the victim suffering from lead poisoning and it requires no silencer. In fact, if it is used properly the entire weapon is a silencer. Of course one must be careful, the bow and arrow can be very dangerous when in the wrong hands. Cupid's for example. This type of weapon does not figure in tonight's story. Our tale is about a college professor engaged in a most unusual research project. It combines love, marriage, psychology and murder. All in one tidy package. A package which we shall open in just sixty seconds.*

Story: When professor James Parkerson places an advertisement in the paper, offering advice on how to kill a spouse, he promptly receives a visit from the police, asking questions. Parkerson explains that he's only gathering research for a project, so the officers leave. Parkerson then receives another visit, that of Robert Johnson and a hit man named Bingham. Johnson explains that he wants to bump off his girlfriend's husband, not realizing that the professor is her beloved spouse. Having accidentally discovered his wife's true intentions, Professor Parkerson pays the hit man to eliminate Johnson. Near the last minute, the professor kills the hit man, revealing his turnabout. Johnson suggests to Doris that they eliminate her husband swiftly, so they can blame the killing on the hit man. Doris agrees, and picking up a gun, surprises her husband.

(mid-line) *I still don't seem to be able to find my arrow. It's too bad, because I was planning to use it to break our stations. Now they shall have to do that themselves. After they are broken, we shall continue with our story of life among the intellectuals.*

I shot a second arrow into the air, hoping it would lead me to the first. Now I've lost the second one too. I think I shall abandon the sport, it's giving me a headache. One final word about our play. The authorities were finally able to determine precisely who did what to whom, and to meet up punishment accordingly. Speaking of authorities . . . here is another word from our sponsor.

EPISODE #54 **"BEAST IN VIEW"** Broadcast on March 20, 1964
 Starring: Joan Hackett as Helen Clarvoe   Kevin McCarthy as Paul Blackshear
 Guest Star: Kathleen Nolan as Dorothy Johnson
 George Furth as Jack Terola   Brenda Forbes as Brenda Clarvoe
 Curt Conway as Lieutenant Bromley   Peggy Moffitt as Robin Rath
 Anthony McBride as Tommy Tompson   Len Hendry as Mr. Horner
 William Boyett as the young policeman   Bruce Anderson as the father
 Jimmy Joyce as the cab driver
 Teleplay written for *The Alfred Hitchcock Hour* by James Bridges, based on the novel of the same name by Margaret Millar (Random House, 1955).
 Produced by Herbert Coleman. Directed by Joseph Newman.
 (powder box) *Good evening. The prevalence of mashers in our streets and parks has brought about this charming device. It looks like a lady's compact but it is really much more than that. When my lady is accosted by some undesirable party she simply takes this out, as though to powder her nose, however when she opens it. . . (pssss) Before you can say Jack-the-Ripper, a cloud of teargas is sprayed in the villain's face. Perhaps this lacks some of the excitement that went with wielding the old fashioned hatpin, but it is most effective. Furthermore, it actually contained a mirror and powder so that you can freshen up before the police arrive. That's odd. I should be weeping by now. (turns box) No wonder, it wasn't teargas after all. This one uses mustard gas. While we wait for developments, you may pass the time by watching tonight's narrative. It is about a young woman named Helen Clarvoe, who is the object of some mysterious threats. But first we have another device which can bring tears to the eyes of the more fastidious. A television commercial.*

Story: Paul Blackshear, attorney-at-law, is hired by Helen Clarvoe to prevent a murder. It seems a woman named Dorothy is making numerous phone calls, threatening her life. A few years ago, Dorothy was set to marry Helen's brother, but the wedding was called off when Helen brought to her father's attention, the theft of a large sum from the family. Now that the old man has passed on, it was Helen who inherited the family fortune, and Helen considers Dorothy to be a violent individual. When Paul begins investigating, he finds a dead photographer, who recently took publicity stills of Dorothy. One afternoon, Helen phones Paul to break the bad news. Dorothy has paid her a visit and is holding her captive inside her apartment. With the police surrounding the building, Paul orders the mad woman to surrender. Only, as it turns out, Helen's real adversary is far more sinister than anyone realized. The real Dorothy shows up, not knowing what is going on, until Helen shows signs of schizophrenia.

(mid-line) *A few of our viewers wrote in, telling us that they feel the station break is the high point of the evening. We shall now hear from one of those viewers.*

Our story is finished but I am most anxious for you to see scenes from our next production. They follow in a few moments. Our new compacts have been taken off the market. In the test areas, Los Angeles, Pittsburgh and London, the gas did not prove to be a deterrent. In fact the muggers, long accustomed to the atmosphere in these cities, regarded the gas as a distinct improvement. Perhaps next week, when I return, I shall have another device. Until then, I'm sure that heaven will protect the working girl.

Trivia, etc. As deserving the recognition of being one of the few original episodes of *The Alfred Hitchcock Hour* to be re-filmed during the 1980s series, 'Beast in View' suffered some problems with the leading lady. "That was one of my favorites and I'll never forget that one," Kevin McCarthy recalled. "We filmed that production in just a few days but Joan Hackett – she was a pain. She wouldn't let anyone watch her while she performed. Kept part of the crew outside, because she wanted everyone to clear out of the room when she was performing every scene. Stage hands, lights, anyone who couldn't be necessary to filming. She wanted to be alone and to herself - sincere. As for Newman, you couldn't have asked for better and perhaps he was on our side of things, but that Joan, what a problem. That drove everyone crazy."

Norman Lloyd recalled similar trouble with this episode: "Well, there was one actress, who I think was as fine an actress as there was in America: Joan Hackett. She had a [hang-up] about people seeing her while she worked. So we used to have to encase the show in flats, so that people walking onto the stage from outside wouldn't walk right into the scene, so to speak - they wouldn't be able to walk onto the stage and see her work. We had to protect her against that. That was purely her own . . . 'psyche,' so to speak - she was an extraordinarily sensitive person. Brilliant, brilliant actress. And a very attractive lady. But she just had this 'thing,' and so we just went with it."

EPISODE #55   **"BEHIND THE LOCKED DOOR"**   Broadcast on March 27, 1964
Starring: Gloria Swanson as Mrs. Daniels
James MacArthur as Dave Snowden
Co-starring: Lynn Loring as Bonnie Snowden
and Whit Bissell as Adam Driscott
Teleplay written for *The Alfred Hitchcock Hour* by Henry Slesar and Joel Murcott, based on the short story of the same name by Henry Slesar, originally published in the January 1961 issue of *Alfred Hitchcock's Mystery Magazine* (under the pen name of O.H. Leslie). Subsequently collected in *Death on Television* (Southern Illinois University Press, 1989).
Produced and directed by Robert Douglas.
Music composed and conducted by Bernard Herrmann.

(two doors) *Good evening. As you see, I'm devising a new parlor game. It is based on the story of the young man who had to choose between two doors. He was told that behind one was a beautiful lady, behind the other, a ferocious tiger. Of course my personal theory is: that he knew which door each was behind, but was still in a dilemma. You see, he couldn't remember whether they had said the lady was beautiful and the tiger ferocious, or that the lady was ferocious and the tiger beautiful. It was a very confused young man. Just as I am at this moment. This should make a perfect party game. It is the best way I've found to thin out a guest list without hurting anyone's feelings. Our main attraction this evening is not about tigers but we do have two ladies and one very interesting door. It is at the other end of this dismal one-minute corridor.*

Story: Dave Snowden and his new bride Bonnie, find themselves less than welcome when they visit her late father's estate. Mrs. Daniels, Bonnie's mother, believes Dave is only after the family inheritance and tries to buy him off, annulling the marriage, but to no avail. Although Bonnie will eventually inherit her parent's fortune, Dave wants money immediately, so he and Bonnie plan an elaborate scare. Bonnie takes a few sleeping pills, faking a suicide, hoping the old woman will come around to their way of thinking. Sadly, however, Bonnie dies as a result. After the funeral, the elderly woman agrees to turn over the estate to Dave, which satisfies the young man one-hundred percent, since it was what he wanted all along. Mrs. Daniels also requests that he check out what is behind the locked door in the grand, old estate. He does so, very impatiently, unlocking the door expecting to find a fortune . . . but instead steps inside the dark room only to discover it is the upper level of an abandoned elevator shaft.

Since you didn't seem to mind that two of our principals were disposed of during the course of the play, I'm certain you shall be able to bear up under the news that Mrs. Daniels did not live happily ever after. Justice triumphed and now she is behind a locked door. This concludes my portion of the program. You may think I've made this test too easy by putting signs on the doors. I don't think so. There's a tiger in here and in here. . . lady tigers.

EPISODE #56   **"A MATTER OF MURDER"**   Broadcast on April 3, 1964
> Starring: Darren McGavin as Sheridan Westcott
> Patricia Crowley as Enid Bentley   Patrick McVey as the police lieutenant
> Guest Star: Telly Savalas as Philadelphia Harry
> Howard Wendell as Mr. Flagstone   Than Wyenn as the general delivery
> Lewis Charles as Lopez   Jordan Grant as Al
> Paul Potash as Vinnie   Tyler McVey as the chief of police
> Marc Rambeau as Weldon   Calvin Bartlett as Harv
> An original teleplay written for *The Alfred Hitchcock Hour* by Boris Sobelman.
> Produced and directed by David Lowell Rich.
> (holds up big signs)   *Good evening. Welcome and a special greeting to all you television engineers who can't read.* (upside down This End Up) *Thank you. Now I look a trifle foolish.* (turns sign Do Not Bend) *I should like to make one thing clear at the outset.* (close-up) *This does not refer to me personally. Transmission has been faulty in some areas and viewers have been complaining about the condition our picture has been in, when delivered. We also have difficulty with friends of mine, of a suspicious nature. Anything I send them is immediately submerged in a bucket of water, it becomes rather messy. This evening we are sending you a surprise package. It is entitled "A Matter Of Murder," and is about a gentleman named Sheridan Westcott, who is surprised by the theft of a possession he*

holds dear. It is also about some thieves who are in for a surprise of their own, but first there is some postage due. A kind friend has volunteered to accept this obligation. He asks only one small favor in return. That he'll be allowed to insert this small, personal message.

Story: Fed up with his annoying wife, Sheridan Westcott kills her, stuffs her body in his Rolls Royce, and drives off to dump her in a local lake. But while Sheridan is checking the water for depth, the car is stolen by a notorious car thief named Philadelphia Harry. This gives Sheridan an idea. Over the evening news broadcast, Sheridan pleads with the thief to please return his car. claiming his wife was alive and well when the car disappeared. When Harry realizes that he's being framed for murder, he sneaks the automobile back to Sheridan's garage, and phones the police. Sheridan, however, finds the car beforehand, repaints the auto, and stashes it along the side of the road. Once again, Sheridan is clear, and the car is stolen by a gang of car thieves . . . run by Philadelphia Harry. Angry, Harry has the car plunged into the lake, and phones the police. This time the officers intend to drag the lake, which will give Sheridan some explaining to do.

(mid-line, Hitchcock addressing a larger than life envelope)   *I am adding your code number to the address, so that our program can be zipped to you as quickly as possible. There is only one difficulty. The numbers are so long, that by the time I finish addressing the envelopes, the show is over. Just now, that eager courier, who has delivered that first half, wishes to identify himself.*

Darren McGavin guest stars in "A Matter of Murder"
(Photo courtesy of Ronald V. Borst / Hollywood Movie Posters.)

There is little I can add. We did want you to hear what Mr. Westcott said when the police found his beloved's body, however we aren't allowed to send it through the mails. It was not his finest hour. By the way. we have a new complaint. Certain parties are claiming that the picture is coming through excellently, but that I look distorted. (Fragile sign) *Now I shall be handled in a more suitable manner and not tossed so wrecklessly about in transit. I'm sure that next week I shall arrive completely free of any unsightly bulges or wrinkles.*

EPISODE #57   **"THE GENTLEMAN CALLER"**   Broadcast on April 10, 1964
    Starring: Roddy McDowall as Gerald Musgrove

Ruth McDevitt as Miss Emmy Rice	Diane Sayer as Millie Musgrove
Naomi Stevens as Mrs. Goldy	Juanita Moore as Mrs. Jones
Frank Maxwell as Officer Petrie	Marjorie Bennett as the plump lady
William Fawcett as the junk collector	Norman Leavitt as the gas company man
Lew Brown as the first policeman	John Alonzo as the intern
Len Hendry as the night watchman	Joe De Angelo as the pedestrian

Teleplay written for *The Alfred Hitchcock Hour* by James Bridges, based on the short story of the same name by Veronica Parker Johns, originally published in the May 1955 issue of *Ellery Queen's Mystery Magazine*. Subsequently reprinted in *The Queen's Awards, Tenth Series*, ed. Ellery Queen (Little Brown, 1955).
    Produced by Herbert Coleman. Directed by Joseph Newman.
    (Hitchcock look-alike contest)   *Good evening. This evening's play is about an elderly recluse, who found a friend. Just how good a friend I shall allow you to judge for yourselves. I do not believe in usurping an audience's prerogative. But before we have our play, it must be introduced. This will be done, not by me but by the three finalists in the Alfred Hitchcock look-a-like contest. The reason for my lack of enthusiasm for this contest will be apparent when I tell you that I entered, and was eliminated in the first round. I couldn't make the weight. I shall now turn you over to Miss Whiteleather who is in charge of the finals.* (Whiteleather: "And now for our first contestant") *Good evening ladies and gentlemen.* (second contestant) *Welcome to The Alfred Hitchcock Hour.* (third contestant) *This evening we shall present a story but first a word from our. . .* (Whiteleather: "sponsor") *sponsor.*

    Story: Gerald and Millie Musgrove manage to steal over $100,000 from a bank, but hadn't considered where to put the money until the police stop looking for it. Gerald gets an idea after he meets a friendly old pack-rat of a woman named Miss Rice. It seems that Miss Rice saves anything, so Gerald hides the money in her apartment, among a pile of magazines, and befriend her, even convincing her to put him in her will as a beneficiary. Once all this is done, Gerald and Millie plan to knock off the elderly woman and "inherit" the $100,000 of hidden loot. Unfortunately, the lady turns out to be a lot craftier than they believed and every attempt to kill her fails. When next they pay a visit to the old woman, the thieves find the police waiting for them. Miss Rice then has them arrested for attempting to murder her, and claims that due to her landlord's insistence, the trash was hauled away – including the magazines. With the distraught thieves being taken away, Miss Rice goes to her icebox and admires the $100,000 of cold, hard cash.

    (mid-line)   *The introduction of the station break is far too important a task, to be delegated to one of the contestants in the look-a-like contest.*

    Now you see how the term 'cold cash' originated. Unfortunately for our intrepid heroine, she was arrested the next day at a bank, where she attempted to deposit her frozen assets. Miss Emmy now resides in a prison for senior citizens, where she is on the mahjong team. As for the Alfred Hitchcock look-a-like contest, all of your votes are in and the results are surprising, but we shall abide by them nevertheless. Here then is the winner who will close my part of the program. (Miss Whiteleather: "And so until next week. Good night.")

Trivia, etc. "I was looking at a brochure the other day, issued by UCLA," Norman Lloyd commented. "They were going to honor James Bridges the writer-director. Now, James Bridges was a discovery of mine: I found him through a play that he had written and which was being done in Los Angeles, and I assigned him to individual Hitchcock shows as a writer. He did 16 for me. Later on, when I was producing *Hollywood Television Theatre*, we did an original work of Jean Renoir's called 'Carola' [1973], which Jean was too ill to direct so I directed it as well as produced it. With Leslie Caron and Mel Ferrer. I put Jim on to polish the dialogue and make some cuts. In this UCLA brochure, they said that Jim Bridges wrote for Alfred Hitchcock and Jean Renoir. Well [laughs], he never met Hitchcock! (At least, I don't think he did...maybe I took him up to meet Hitch.) I did take him to meet Jean. But the point I'm getting at: He wrote for me! I developed those [Hitchcock] scripts with Jim, and then they were delivered to Hitch!"

"The Gentleman Caller" was also dramatized on the television series *Star Tonight* on August 2, 1956 with Don Hanmer in the lead. Hanmer was the same actor who played Wormer in "Final Vow" and Vern Byers in "The Faith of Aaron Menefee."

EPISODE #58   **"THE ORDEAL OF MRS. SNOW"**   Broadcast on April 17, 1964
      Starring: Patricia Collinge as Mrs. Addy Snow
      Jessica Walter as Lorna Richmond   Don Chastain as Bruce Richmond
      Co-starring: George Macready as Hillary Prine
      Cal Bartlett as John Wilson   June Vincent as Ruth Prine
      Pamela Curran as Sally Wilson   Bartlett Robinson as Harvey Crane
      Edit Angold as Frieda   Danny Gardino as Mr. Arthur
      Teleplay written for *The Alfred Hitchcock Hour* by Alvin Sargent, based on the novelette of the same name by Q. Patrick (credited on the show as Patrick Quentin), published in *The Ordeal of Mrs. Snow and Other Stories*, as by Patrick Quentin (Gollancz 1961, Random House, 1962).
      Produced by Joan Harrison. Directed by Robert Stevens.
      (snow-woman in the snow)   *Good evening. I suppose you think this is snow. It's confetti refrigerated, for realism. This began as a simple little celebration, paper-hats and horns. Then a cold-front moved in. I became separated from my party and I've been lost for days. This is not the abominable snow-man. In fact it isn't even a snow-man, it's a snow-woman. It was getting terribly lonesome here.* (blows a whistle) *I've been using this to call for help, however no one seems to hear me, except a rather amorous moose. For those of you who are safe and warm in the bosom of your family, we have a play. It is entitled "The Ordeal of Mrs. Snow" and it tells of a woman's battle to survive a terrifying experience.*

      Story: In order to cover his debts, Bruce Richmond has resorted to writing bad checks, a fact he doesn't want his wife Lorna to know, and a fact her elderly cat-loving aunt, Mrs. Snow, plans to tell Lorna, the next time they meet. To hide his mis-deeds, Bruce locks the old woman in a bank vault located in her home, along with one of her cats. He hopes she will be found after Bruce and his wife return from a trip - dead from suffocation. During the trip, Lorna phones her aunt numerous times, but after getting no answer, expresses the desire to return home. When they do, against Bruce's insistence, he discovers that he made a fatal mistake. You see, much like Edgar Allan Poe's "The Black Cat," the mews and growls give away Mrs. Snow's hiding place, just in time to save the old woman.

      (mid-line) *We shall continue our story in a few moments. I believe I have wandered near a television station. Perhaps it will answer my call.* (Hitchcock blows in a party horn.)

Ladies and gentlemen. Tonight's program has been sent to you for an hour's free trial. At the end of this time, if you are not completely satisfied, you may return it. There are of course, a few minutes which are not returnable. Here is one of them.

Trivia, etc. No new episode of *The Alfred Hitchcock Hour* was broadcast on April 24, 1964. A rebroadcast of "Terror at Northfield," starring Dick York, aired instead.

EPISODE #59   **"TEN MINUTES FROM NOW"**   Broadcast on May 1, 1954
Starring: Donnelly Rhodes as James Bellington   Lou Jacobi as Dr. Clover
Lonny Chapman as Lieutenant Wymar
Co-starring: Neile Adams as Sergeant Louise Marklen

Ed Peck as the first policeman	Sandra Gould as the secretary
Betty Harford as the woman in the museum	Edward Mallory as the thief
Jess Kirkpatrick as Thomas Grindley	Tony Franke as the messenger
Syl Lamont as the guide	Vince Williams as the newscaster
Harold Ayer as the salesman	Hinton Pope as the first bomb squad man
John W. Ziegler as the first detective	

Teleplay written for *The Alfred Hitchcock Hour* by Arthur Ross, based on the short story of the same name by Jack Ritchie, originally published in the October 1963 issue of *Alfred Hitchcock's Mystery Magazine.*   Subsequently reprinted in *Stories to Stay Awake By*, ed. Alfred Hitchcock (Random House, 1971).
Produced by Gordon Hessler. Directed by Alf Kjellin.
(bell and old lantern)   *Good evening. I'm resorting to this device to attract attention to our program. I have no shame what so ever. The town crier was a seventeenth century American newspaper.   As newspapers go, it was rather primitive.   It had no contests, no crossword puzzles, no funnies.   And of course, the columnists couldn't wrap their garbage in the town crier.   They simply threw it at him when they disagreed with his editorials.   There was no advertising either.   The more I describe it, the more attractive it sounds.   Naturally this has nothing to do with this evening's play.   Our story is a modern one about a man who moves about a large city carrying a box which was both mysterious and disquieting.   It follows . . . (shrugs his shoulders) this advertisement.*

Story: James Bellington begins to make bomb threats and shows up at various places in town, with boxes that appear to contain bombs, but even after multiple arrests, they always turn out to be harmless. Bellington is finally forced to see a psychiatrist, whom he confesses he plans to finally explode a real bomb at the city's Memorial Museum. And, just as he threatened, he shows up at the museum with a suspicious-looking box. While the cops are clearing out the building, unknown to the police, Bellington has a partner who is robbing the museum. Later they discover that his bomb is fake again . . . as are the paintings that are being hung by his partner in place of the stolen real ones.

(mid-line, Hitchcock rings bell) *Hear ye, hear ye. I dislike breaking in at the middle of our story, but we have some late-breaking news. The station over which you are viewing our show, has just been tentatively identified.   Your local announcer will now provide you with the details. After which, we shall return to our story.*

Unfortunately our hero chose to celebrate a bit early. The paintings were traced and he is now helping to manufacture cardboard boxes for the state. Of course this program is not to be interpreted as an endorsement of bomb threats, even when used by collectors of modern art. As for what this program . . . does endorse, I shall leave that to the town crier I hear in the wings.

EPISODE #60 **"THE SIGN OF SATAN"** Broadcast on May 8, 1964

Starring: Christopher Lee as Karl Jorla   Gia Scala as Kitty
Gilbert Green as Max Rubini   Co-starring: Adam Roarke as Ed Walsh
Myron Healey as Dave Connor   Byron Keith as Captain Hartzell
Nicki Brick as the script girl   Saul Gorss as the studio policeman
Horst Ebers as the first Acolyte   Dieter Jacoby as the second Acolyte
Eric Forst as the third Acolyte
Walter Friedel as the fourth Acolyte

Teleplay written for *The Alfred Hitchcock Hour* by Barré Lyndon, based on the short story "Return to the Sabbath" by Robert Bloch, originally published in the July 1938 issue of *Weird Tales.*

Produced and directed by Robert Douglas.

(Mars broadcast)   *Good evening. Welcome to the planet Mars. My getting here were not as remarkable as our finding a wire long enough to reach back to Earth. This remote broadcast is a first, but since there is absolutely nothing up here to talk about, I'm not sure the trip was worth it. We found no trace of life. In fact no trace of anything . . . except this item.* (shows a sign "If you lived here you'd be home now!") *This may seem like irrefutable logic, but from what I can observe, if you actually did live here, you would have had moved away long ago, to some place with a better view, more prestige or some oxygen. That last item rules out the scene of tonight's drama: Hollywood, California. Our story concerns some doings which will be considered rather peculiar, even in that bizarre town. For purposes of contrast however, we first present one minute of sanity and solemnity.*

Story: A low-budget Hollywood studio has hired Karl Jorla, a strange European horror-movie star, to take a lead in their new movie. He signs to play the part of a Satanic cult leader, a role the producers feel he is perfect for, having seen the filmed demo. Jorla grows terribly scared when, after watching the demo film himself, theorizes that the real followers of the devil might come after him. Despite constant security protection, an attempt is made on the actor's life. Jorla convinces the producers to let him stay in a remote, unknown address of his choice, without the knowledge of anyone – including the producers or director. On the first day of filming, Jorla fails to show up for work, which concerns the entire crew. Later, Jorla makes a sudden appearance, moans an address, and disappears again. The police are phoned, and sent to the address where they find the murdered body of the star, which is very odd indeed since the corpse is in the exact same place where he apparently died three days earlier!

The killers of Karl Jorla, method actor and devil worshiper, were eventually brought to justice. By the way, the preceding was not an expose of American burial customs. At least I sincerely hope it wasn't. Next week we shall return to Earth and present another story. I cannot express the keen disappointment I felt, in not finding any life here on Mars. I would have liked nothing better, than to be the first to discover life here. Perhaps I shall have better luck, another time. (A Martian is coming from behind) *Good night.*

Trivia, etc. Christopher Lee, known primarily for his role as Dracula in numerous horror films released through Hammer Studios in England, came to Hollywood for the very first time to star in this Hitchcock teleplay. "Oh, Christopher—what a riot he is!" Norman Lloyd laughed. "In addition to working with him on Hitchcock, years later I also acted with him in a movie in Yugoslavia [*Journey of Honor* (1992)]. Maybe we brought the whole civil war on [laughs]! The thing about Christopher was, he was a true eccentric, as I've said about a couple of other guys. I cast him in this part and I became fascinated with him. First of all, he knew the name of every English executioner from the fifteenth or sixteenth century on. Now, that is the weirdest hobby I have ever encountered, but it absolutely fit him like a skintight suit! There was an actor I knew back when I was in the Mercury with Orson Welles, Martin Gabel, and he knew the name of every winner of the Kentucky Derby since the first Kentucky Derby. He rattled 'em off. Christopher could do that with the executioners of England! You see, this is why one loves the profession, you don't find that in the grocery store [laughs]!

"When the phone rang and I heard an English voice I knew. The actor Bob Douglas, who was often a heavy in remakes in the *Prisoner of Zenda* class. I was surprised. The last I'd seen of him was golfing at Sunningdale years before. He said we'd be seeing a lot of each other in the next two weeks. I was even more surprised. Then he explained, 'I'm directing the film.' 'Isn't Alfred Hitchcock directing it?' I asked. 'Good heavens, no!' laughed Bob, 'He's only the host. He tops and tails. He never directs. He has a staff of directors, and I'm one.' " *

"Christopher also collected swords, great big swords, and also instruments of execution," Lloyd continued. "And I believe he lived in an old brewery! He was married to a Tuborg beer heiress. Very strange man. He was not imaginative casting in the pictures that he made - I mean, he was Dracula! And therefore when we were in Yugoslavia and acting, I was surprised to see him with health food grains and oats and corn flakes and stuff that he carried from England into Yugoslavia in little packets, so he could have them every morning with his breakfast. It all seemed so healthy and normal, I thought it was out of character! He was very amusing and a very nice man . . . but there was something very dark about him too.

"It was surprising to me on that film that the Americans seemed to include all kinds of routine falls and flights as stunts," Lee concluded. "When I maintained that I saw nothing arduous in throwing a man over my head, or falling over a chair, Bob Douglas told me that I would have to make good my commitments. After I had obliged, my own double remarked that when I had thrown the chair at the window, it had actually gone through the glass!"

This was one of the few episodes of *The Alfred Hitchcock Hour* to not have any mid-line delivered by Hitchcock.

EPISODE #61   **"WHO NEEDS AN ENEMY?"**   Broadcast on May 15, 1964
    Starring: Steven Hill as Charlie Osgood   Joanna Moore as Danielle
    Richard Anderson as Eddie Turton   Dee Carroll as the woman
    Paul Baxley as the man   Wally Rose as the second man
    and Barney Phillips as the first detective
    Teleplay written for *The Alfred Hitchcock Hour* by Arthur Ross, based on the short story "Goodbye Charlie" by Henry Slesar, originally published in the January 1964 issue of *Alfred Hitchcock's Mystery Magazine*.
    Produced by Herbert Coleman. Directed by Harry Morgan.
    (with a horse and stage-coach)   *Good evening. I am not the driver of this quaint vehicle. I'm riding tourist-class. The first-class passengers ride inside. I'm sure I needn't tell you who is in there. They come as standard equipment. One school-ma'am, a minister, a lady of doubtful virtue, a man unjustly accused of murder and a drunken doctor who would die later in the picture. Actually, one shouldn't be too hard on the doctor. I'm sure it's clear now why I prefer riding on the outside. This evening's saga misses being a western, by some seventy years and 3,000 miles but the spirit is there, nonetheless. It takes place in the world of business, where men are men . . . and the women are secretaries. But I see that some varmints are about to stage a hold-up, a hold-up of exactly one minute.*

* Christopher Lee's recollections are reprinted with permission from Lee's autobiography, *Tall, Dark and Gruesome* (Midnight Marquee Press, 1999). The book is highly recommended for all film fans.

Story: Eddie Turton is shocked to learn that his business partner has been secretly ripping him off for years. He gives Charlie two choices, going to jail or returning the money. Charlie talks it over with his girlfriend, Danielle, and they decide to go another route. They fake his suicide and pack for South America. Charlie and Danielle pull off their plan without a hitch and everyone, including Eddie, believes he is dead. Eddie even delivers a tear-jerking eulogy at the funeral services. Picking up the money at his office, Charlie and Danielle have a celebration drink - a drink that has been laced with drugs, knocking Charlie out for the count. Awakening, he finds himself surrounded by Danielle and Eddie. It is obvious that they are more than friends, and that Charlie has been brilliantly set up as the fall guy for the "missing" money. Now all they need to do is to fake another suicide, but this time they'll use a real body . . .

(mid-line) *I trust you realize that this is merely a way station, and not our final destination. After a brief way station break, we shall proceed on our way.*

(now with a pumpkin) *I seem to be left with nothing but a pumpkin. Containing a rather squashed school-ma'am, a minister, a lady of doubtful virtue, a man unjustly accused of murder and a drunken doctor. I warned them they should get out of that coach before midnight, but they wouldn't listen. Apparently justice is as relentless in the east as in the west, for when bits of Charlie began washing up on the shore, Eddie and Danielle were both arrested. They were sentenced to life imprisonment, for murder, and fined 10 dollars for littering. And now if you wish to see scenes of our next production, please bear with us through the following commercial.*

EPISODE #62   **"BED OF ROSES"**   Broadcast on May 22, 1964
   Starring: Patrick O'Neal as George Maxwell
   Kathie Browne as Mavis Maxwell
   Co-starring: Torin Thatcher as Alva Hardwicke   George Lindsey as Sam Kirby
   Alice Backes as Miss Hinchley   Alice Frost as Eda Faye Hardwicke
   Bill Walker as Sam   Pauline Myers as Celeste
   Robert Reiner as the bartender   and Ethel Griffies as Lulu
   Teleplay written for *The Alfred Hitchcock Hour* by James Bridges, based on the short story of the same name by Emily Neff, which would later be reprinted in the March 1977 issue of *Alfred Hitchcock's Mystery Magazine*.
   Produced by Norman Lloyd. Directed by Philip Leacock.
   (tranquillizing gun) *Good evening. I have here the very latest in weapons. It shoots tranquilizing capsules. It's quite harmless really. When hit, the victim becomes dozile and can easily be captured. As you might expect this gun is quite popular among law enforcement officers, big game hunters and unprincipled bachelors. So much for the sporting life. Tonight's story is about a man who finds himself in trouble because of a past indiscretion. It begins in one agonizing minute.*

Story: George Maxwell thinks he has struck gold when he marries Mavis, his boss' not-too-sharp, but wealthy daughter. After getting a phone call from a former girlfriend, George leaves by taxi to give her some money, but finds her dead instead. The next day, the taxi driver who gave him that ride pays George a visit, and demands blackmail money for his silence. In desperation, George breaks the news to his wife, who promptly searches out the taxi driver herself, and kills him, burying his body under the rose garden. Shortly after the news of the missing taxi driver hits the news, George's secretary demands blackmail as well, having seen the same taxi driver the other day, or she'll phone the police. With no other choice, George phones his wife, a woman after his own heart, asking her to prepare the rose garden . . . he's bringing home some more roses.

(mid-line) *We have now arrived at the very heart and center of this hour. The station break. This is the moment when we part the curtain of television, and let the local stations shine through. After which, we shall continue.*

One always wonders what happens after the curtain falls on a play. In this case the police became intrigued by the way the Maxwells kept subtracting people and adding rose bushes. An investigator managed to dig up some rather damaging evidence, that sent the Maxwells away for life. One further footnote. At the next flower show the Kirby-rose won first place. In regard to the medical use of firearms, there have been some disturbing developments. For example some people have been playing Russian roulette, putting a bullet in one chamber and aspirin in the other five. Of course in either case it cures the headache and that's what really matters. And now a commercial and some scenes from our next production.

EPISODE #63 **"THE SECOND VERDICT"** Broadcast on May 29, 1964
Starring: Martin Landau as Ned Murray
Frank Gorshin as Lew Rydell
Co-starring: John Marley as Tony Hardeman
Harold J. Stone as Mr. Osterman
Michael Beirne as Tom Bailey
William Remick as the jury foreman

Sharon Farrell as Melanie Rydell
Nancy Kovack as Karen Osterman
Richard Hale as Judge Arthur
Richard F. Guizon as the bailiff
Helen Mayon as the maid

Teleplay written for *The Alfred Hitchcock Hour* by Henry Slesar and Alfred Hayes, based on the short story of the same name by Henry Slesar, originally published in the February 1964 issue of *Alfred Hitchcock's Mystery Magazine*.
Produced by Gordon Hessler. Directed by Lewis Teague.
(cemetery plot) *Good evening. I am now in the real estate business, selling cemetery plots. For our modern nomadic civilization, the old fashioned cemetery presents a difficulty. A plot bought in Maine is of little use when someone moves to California. However, we have now solved this problem with portable plots. Now, at last, you can take it with you. Thus, whether driving on the freeway, or on a vacation or a honeymoon, you'll be ready for any eventuality. Actually, we don't sell the plot . . . just the hole. Here for example is one model. Three by six by eight feet. You can see it would be quite easy to carry and would fit into any excavation in any part of the country. A final word about plots. Tonight's is about a young criminal lawyer whose sense of ethics gets him into a dangerous situation. But first our sponsor takes a moment to point out a few simple truths.*

Story: After clearing his client of a murder charge, attorney Ned Murray discovers to his horror that his client, Lew Rydell, was actually guilty. Since the law states you can't be tried twice for the same crime, Ned contacts a friend of his, a mobster named Tony Hardeman. Obsessed with making Rydell pay for his crime, Ned asks Tony to help frame Rydell with murder. Misunderstanding his wish, Tony sets out to murder Rydell. Ned, realizing his mistake, tries to stop the killing and finds the gangster dead instead of Rydell. Before he can do anything else, Ned suddenly realizes that he has accomplished his goal: Rydell will now be arrested for another crime, a second count of murder.

(mid-line) *We now observe the ritual of the station break. Following this will be the second half of the Alfred Hitchcock Hour.*

That concludes our story Scenes of next week's play will be on view in a few minutes. One last word in behalf of my cemeterian funeral business. I'm running a special this week. A combination ten-day Caribbean cruise and a burial at sea. It's quite popular. As we learned this evening, the law of double jeopardy protects the criminal from having to face the same charge more than once. No such mercy is shown the television viewer. In other words, here is another commercial.

Trivia. etc. Martin Landau was one of the few actors who appeared in both the original and remake series. On top of that, he also played the part of Leonard in Hitchcock's *North by Northwest* (1959).

**Hitchcock in his customary suit and bow tie, warning the audience.
(Photo courtesy of Ronald V. Borst / Hollywood Movie Posters.)**

EPISODE #64 **"ISABEL"** Broadcast on June 5, 1964

Starring: Bradford Dillman as Howard Clemens Barbara Barrie as Isabel Smith
Edmon Ryan as Lieutenant Huntley Les Tremayne as Mr. Selby
Dabney Coleman as Sergeant Lou Snyder Doris Lloyd as Martha
Ken Patterson as the warden Ricks Falk as Finley
Don Marshall as Officer Healy Forrest Lewis as the sailor
Walter Woolf King as the judge Lou Byrne as the librarian

Teleplay written for *The Alfred Hitchcock Hour* by William Fay and Henry Slesar, based on the novel "The Bronze Perseus" by S.B. Hough (Secker & Warburg, 1959; Walker, 1962).

Produced by Joan Harrison. Directed by Alf Kjellin.

(raw-hide bathing suit) *Good evening. How do you do and welcome to the Alfred Hitchcock Hour. Strange how old fashion ways are sometimes best. In a plastic age with its many new and different fabrics, I have suddenly realized the amazing properties of a material as old as civilization. Raw-hide. Here are two of our new raw-hide bathing suits. They are identical. This one is still wet. This, is the way it looks after you have been lying in the sun. Obviously, this is the answer to man's most urgent problem: how to reduce without exercising. Of course, this material has other more important uses. As a gift to a friend. Perhaps I can explain by telling you. . . I have just presented the sponsor with a vest. It's quite modern, there are no unsightly buttons. After he puts it on, it sticks together up the back. After all, I don't want him to change his mind when it begins to dry and be able to take it off. And now a word from the man with the incredible shrinking vest.*

Story: Howard Clemens spends two years in prison for a crime he didn't commit, that of assaulting an aging woman named Isabel Smith. Once out of prison, Howard steals $13,000, the equivalent of two years wages, and then opens a record shop in his old home town. Accidentally running into Isabel a few times, Howard creates some powerful acting performances to encourage a few dates. Soon the two become engaged and once married, Howard has plans to complete his revenge by committing on their honeymoon, the perfect murder of Isabel, who still suspects nothing. Tampering with the fuel line on a rented boat, Howard sends his wife out to meet her fiery doom. And the boat does explode. When he returns home, however, Howard is visited by a policeman who expresses his suspicion of murder. But surprisingly to both of them, Isabel comes back still alive and well.

(mid-line) *A few of our viewers wrote in, telling us that they feel the station break is the high point of the evening. We shall now hear from one of those viewers.*

And so Isabel and Howard lived happily ever after. Oh, Howard occasionally had unwholesome thoughts but the knowledge of what the consequences would be, proved a purifying influence. He is now a model husband. A miserable husband, but a model one. Next week we shall be back with another uplifting story. Scenes of which will be on view in a few moments.

Trivia, etc. The mid-line for this episode is the same used for "Beast in View," which aired months before.

SUMMER RERUNS

All summer reruns were episodes from season two of *The Alfred Hitchcock Hour*. On September 25, 1964 "The Entertainers," a variety special, was broadcast instead of *The Alfred Hitchcock Hour*, from 8:30 to 9:20 p.m., EST. This revue features Bob Newhart, Carol Burnett, Art Buchwald, Caterina Valente, and others. Bob Banner produced.

June 12, 1964
    "A Home Away from Home"
June 19, 1964 "A Nice Touch"
June 26, 1964
    "You'll Be the Death of Me"
July 3, 1964 "Body in the Barn"
July 10, 1964
    "How to Get Rid of Your Wife"
July 17, 1964 "The Magic Shop"
July 24, 1964
    "Nothing Ever Happens in Linvale"
July 31, 1964 "Three Wives Too Many"

August 7, 1964
    "The Evil of Adelaide Winters"
August 14, 1964 "The Jar"
August 21, 1964
    "The Gentleman Caller"
August 28, 1964 "Anyone For Murder?"
September 4, 1964
    "Ten Minutes From Now"
September 11, 1964 "Bed of Roses"
September 18, 1964
    "Who Needs an Enemy?"

SEASON THREE - (29 episodes)

SELECTED PRODUCTION CREDITS:
Art Director: Howard E. Johnson, Russell Kimball, Henry Larreco,
John J. Lloyd and Alexander A. Mayer
Assistant Director: Donald Baer, Les Berke, George Bisk, James H. Brown,
John Clarke Bowman, Chuck Colean, Edward K. Dodds, Charles S. Gould, Arthur Jacobson,
Henry Kline, Frank Losee, Ronnie Rondell, Ray Taylor, Jr. and Dolph M. Zimmer
Costumes: Helen Colvig and Burton Miller
Costume Supervisor: Vincent Dee
Director of Photography: Stanley Cortez, a.s.c., William Margulies, a.s.c., Ray Rennahan,
John L. Russell, Walter Strenge and John F. Warren, a.s.c.
Editorial Dept. Head: David J. O'Connell
Executive Producer: Norman Lloyd
Film Editor: Douglas Stewart and Edward W. Williams, a.c.e.
Hair Stylist: Virginia Darcy and Larry Germain
Makeup: Bud Westmore
Music Score and Theme: Bernard Herrmann and his Orchestra
Musical Supervision: Stanley Wilson
Set Decorators: H. Web Arrowsmith, Robert C. Bradfield, Ollie Emmert, Julia Heron,
John McCarthy, Perry Murdock, Clarence Steensen, Ralph Sylos and James M. Walters
Sound: Robert Bertrand, Lyle Cain, Earl Crain, Sr., Deal Gilmore, William Lynch,
Melvin M. Metcalfe, Sr., David H. Moriarty, B.F. Ryan, Ed Somers,
Richard Tyler, J. S. Westmoreland and Frank H. Wilkinson
Filmed at Revue Studios in Hollywood, California (Universal City), in association with
MCA-TV, executive distributor for Shamley Productions, Inc.
Broadcast Monday over NBC-TV, 10 – 11 p.m., EST. Multiple sponsors.

EPISODE #65 **"RETURN OF VERGE LIKENS"** Broadcast on October 5, 1964
Starring: Peter Fonda as Verge Likens   Robert Emhardt as Riley McGrath
Co-starring: George Lindsey as D. D. Martin

Jim Boles as Sheriff Reynolds	William Bramley as Fred Starcher
Robert H. Barrat as Stoney Likens	Charles Seel as Rush Sigafoose, the barber
Nydia Westman as Aunt Ida Maye	June Walker as Aunt Mary Jane
Cathie Merchant as Mary Masterson	and Sammy Reese as Wilford Likens

Teleplay written for *The Alfred Hitchcock Hour* by James Bridges, based on the short story of the same name by Davis Grubb, originally published in the July 15, 1950 issue of *Collier's*. Subsequently collected in *Twelve Tales of Suspense and the Supernatural* (Scribner, 1964) and in *You Never Believe Me and Other Stories* (St. Martin's Press, 1989).
Produced by Norman Lloyd. Directed by Arnold Laven.
(drum set) *Good evening.* (puts on a Beatles wig) *If you see three young men with electric guitars, please send them back. They seem to have wandered off. They can't be far, however, for they are still plugged in. All evident to the contrary. I'm convinced that music has charms to soothe the savage breast. For example, this set of drums was made by a tribe of aborigines. A people completely uncivilized, yet they built every one of these lovely instruments out of human skin. Of course, when it came to drumsticks they were rather unoriginal.* (holds up two bones) *They make these out of plastic, which we supply them at a modest profit. Unfortunately we keep running out of salesmen. This evening's program is not completely musical. We also bring you a play. It concerns violence and revenge in a small mountain town. The time? One minute from now.*

Story: A country farmer named Stoney Likens is killed by Riley McGrath, a powerful man who went on to become a crooked politician, a fact his son, Verge Likens, has never forgotten - and vows to avenge. The killing was labeled self-defense even though Stoney wasn't armed when Riley shot him to death. Verge suddenly decides to go to school in Charlestown, "The kinda school that's gonna teach me how to kill Mr. Riley McGrath the way I want." A few years later, when Riley McGrath goes to see the barber for a haircut and shave, he finds his regular barber has hired a new assistant. The barber steps out for a while and the assistant, young Verge, bolts the door. Lathering up Riley, Verge begins recalling the events of his past, and it doesn't take long for the politician to realize who Verge is. While the young man wields the deadly razor up and down the politician's neck, Riley is petrified with fear knowing that the man who swore to kill him can do so with the flip of a wrist - a hair raising situation for a man receiving a close shave. The barber, in the meantime, finds his occupancy locked and with the help of the Sheriff, breaks down the door, finding the politician quite dead. Verge explains that he isn't guilty of murder, for the large man must died of a heart attack, because there isn't a mark on him.

(mid-line) *We have not come to the end of our play. There is much more, but we thought it wise to stop here in order to ease tensions and break stations.*

By the way, I know the secret of these wigs. They are actually earmuffs so you don't have to listen to your own music. Next week we shall be back with another story and perhaps by then, my three companions will have returned. Until then, good night.

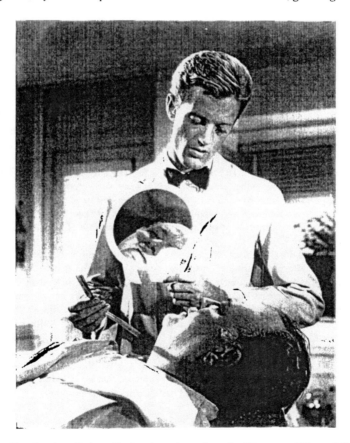

Peter Fonda gives Robert Emhardt a close shave in "Return of Verge Likens"
(Photo courtesy of Photofest)

Trivia, etc. *Variety* reviewed this episode: "The copycats come and go, but Alfred Hitchcock, in pro fashion, goes on forever, delivering suspense mellers that make for absorbing TV viewing. This marks the 10th successive season for the 'Alfred Hitchcock' show, which more recently went to the elongated hour form. This season, too, marks Hitchcock's return to NBC-TV after many years with CBS. The opener, starring Peter Fonda and Robert Emhardt, dealt with the revenge of a poor-white farmer against a crooked politician. The script neatly laid the ground work for the play of revenge, with motivations clear, characters well defined, and the spirit of surprise pervading the plot lines."

"Fonda, in the tradition of his family, underplayed his role to obtain greater conviction," *Variety* continued. "Emhardt, as the crooked politician who murdered Fonda's father in the teleplay, seemed to live his role. Sam Reese, portraying the weak. simpleminded brother of Fonda, added other dimensions to the story. The rest of the support cast lent strong support to the outing. In true Hitchcock style, the last few moments were sheer terror, ironic and satisfying in terms of the story. In the competitive three network race, the *Alfred Hitchcock Hour* is up against ABC-TV's formidable Nielsen sawbones *Ben Casey*. Hitchcock might come out second best to the Nielsens, but for what the series offers, he still sets the pace for suspense mellers on TV."

EPISODE #66 **"CHANGE OF ADDRESS"** Broadcast on October 12, 1964
  Starring: Arthur Kennedy as Keith Hollins Phyllis Thaxter as Elsa Hollins
  Co-starring: Royal Dano as Mr. John F. Miley Tisha Sterling as Rachel
  Robert Karnes as Sergeant Bryant Susan Davis as Reba, the secretary
  Arnold Lessing as Officer Raymo Mike Blodgett as Apollo, the dancer
  Teleplay written for *The Alfred Hitchcock Hour* by Morton Fine and David Friedkin, based on the short story of the same name by Andrew Benedict, originally published in the January 1952 issue of *The Mysterious Traveler*.
  Produced by Morton Fine and David Friedkin, and directed by David Friedkin.
  Music composed and conducted by Bernard Herrmann.
  (at the post office) *Good evening. Welcome to the dead letter office. I trust you have not come here to mail any letters that are still wiggling. We now have a firm policy from which we are not permitted to waver. All letters must be dead on arrival. I don't know why this was necessary, if any of the letters were not dead when they arrived. they certainly would be before we've finished with them.* (stamps "noisy" letters) *This evening we present "Change Of Address." It is about a woman who has definite reservations about the house she and her husband are renting. Doubts which are vague, but very disturbing. There is one person whose messages unfortunately, never find their way into our office. They are all too clearly addressed. That person . . . is our sponsor and an example of his work follows.*

Story: Despite the objections from his wife, Keith Hollins decides to rent a beach house, a place his wife feels "spooky," especially since she learns that he's been digging a hole in the basement, one that looks exactly like a grave. After learning that Keith has been seeing a younger girl, a beach bunny named Rachel, Elsa discovers her husband's plans on buying the house. Complaining about her situation, Elsa falls victim to her husband's brutality, and is murdered. After burying her body in the basement, Keith receives a visit from the police, all armed with shovels. Asking how they knew what he just did, the officers oblige. You see, Elsa was so insistent about Keith not buying the house, that she contacted the original owners, and discovered that the man's wife disappeared. After routine questioning, the original owner broke down and confessed that he killed his wife, and buried her body in the basement . . . just as Keith had done earlier this afternoon.

(mid-line) *It is now time to forward you, to our substations. But I shall clearly stamp you, to be returned in a few moments.* (Hitchcock stamps letters)

The preceding was a training-film, lent to us by husbands anonymous. That's a society of men who are determined to learn from the mistakes of others. I've decided to leave my position here. It's not that it was frightening being around all those dead letters, but some of them had been dead much too long. Now for another commercial, followed by a hint of things to come.

Trivia, etc. This was Royal Dano's third and final performance on the Hitchcock show. His first appearance was Martin Ross in "My Brother, Richard," broadcast at the same time Hitchcock's *The Trouble With Harry* was released in the theatres. In the movie, Dano had the important role of Calvin Wiggs. (His other appearance was in "Party Line.")

For some odd reason, this episode lists the author of the short story as Andrew Benedict, which was one of Robert Arthur's several pseudonyms. The original story was printed in *The Mysterious Traveler* under the byline "Robert Arthur." This same name credit was done in the episode "Completely Foolproof."

EPISODE #67 **"WATER'S EDGE"** Broadcast on October 19, 1964
Starring: Ann Sothern as Helen Krause
Guest Star: John Cassavetes as Rusty Connors

Rayford Barnes as Mike Krause	David Fresco as newsstand dealer
J.B. Brown as prison guard	Jimmy Joyce as prison orderly

Teleplay written for *The Alfred Hitchcock Hour* by Alfred Hayes, based on the short story of the same name by Robert Bloch, originally published in the September 1956 issue of *Mike Shayne Mystery Magazine*. Subsequently collected in *Terror in the Night and Other Stories* (Ace, 1958) and in *The King of Terrors* (Mysterious Press, 1977).
Produced by Herbert Coleman. Directed by Bernard Girard.
Music composed and conducted by Bernard Herrmann.
(on a train car)   *Good evening. Fellow citizens, I am now about to launch another campaign. My party chose this . . . as their platform. It is a very practical party. I have always thought it was much more dignified to stand for a seat, than to run for an office. But if it is necessary to run, then I'll say, be as comfortable as possible. By the way, I am not looking for an honest man. That would be rather absurd on a political campaign. In order to conserve funds, I'm also doubling as break man. During my absence, our players will present "Water's Edge." A story which is as far removed from politics as one could get. It begins in a prison, it concerns thieves and murderers. But most of all it concerns an uncontrollable lust for money. And money reminds me of this next item.*

Story: Having spent several years in prison, convict Rusty Connors made a lot of friends . . . one named Mike Krause. After being released, Rusty goes out in search of Helen, Mike's wife, hoping to get in good with her. Mike, you see, was convicted of murder and robbery, and since neither the money or his victim were ever found, both Rusty and Helen theorize that it's free for the taking. But Helen confesses that she doesn't know any more than he does. Piecing together clues they picked up from Rusty, the two find a deserted boat house, infested with large rats. Once Rusty finds the stolen loot, along with the rat-eaten body of the murdered partner, greed overpowers his better judgement and a fight breaks out. Helen gets the better hand, knocking Rusty out for the count. Waking up all tied and gagged, Rusty trips Helen as she tries to make her escape, causing the woman to be impaled on a large fishing hook. Now it is just him and the rats, who are moving in on him after smelling fresh blood.

(mid-line) *Please do not leave the train. This is just a whistle stop. Or as we say in television, a station break. We shall continue our journey in just a moment.*

And so we take leave of Rusty Connors. Lover, treasure hunter, pied-piper. Next week we shall return with another story and more campaign promises. Until then, good night. (puts his arms demonstratively high in the air, with "Titanic" on the back of the train car.)

Trivia, etc. Robert Bloch recounted the bitter irony relating to his short story, before and after it was broadcast on *The Alfred Hitchcock Hour.* "I'd written a story called 'Water's Edge' and submitted it for publication in the *Alfred Hitchcock Mystery Magazine*," Bloch recalled. "Somewhat to my surprise, it was rejected as 'unsuitable,' and subsequently I sold the yarn to another periodical. About a year later I was surprised again when the story was bought for reprint in an anthology entitled *Alfred Hitchcock Presents: Stories They Wouldn't Let Me Do on TV!* But that was not the end. Shortly thereafter this same

John Cassavetes and Ann Sothern in "Water's Edge"
(Photo courtesy of Photofest.)

story was purchased for television and appeared as a one-hour show, starring John Cassavetes and Ann Sothern – on *The Alfred Hitchcock Hour*! That's show-biz . . ."

EPISODE #68   **"THE LIFE WORK OF JUAN DIAZ"**   Broadcast on October 26, 1964
    Starring: Alejandro Rey as Juan Diaz
    Frank Silvera as Alejandro   Guest Star: Pina Pellicer as Maria Diaz
    Co-starring: Valentin De Vargas as Ricardo, the police chief
    Larry Donasin as Jorge   Alex Montoya as the coffin maker
    Hinton Pope as the man   Audrey Swanson as the second woman
    Gale Lindsey as the woman   Mark Miranda as the first boy
    Suzanne Barnes as the third woman   Concepcion Sandoval as the first child
    Yolanda Alonzo as the second child   Vincent Arias as the second boy
    Carmelita Acosta as the first girl
    Teleplay written for *The Alfred Hitchcock Hour* by Ray Bradbury, from his short story of the same name, originally published in the September 1963 issue of *Playboy.* Subsequently collected in *The Machineries of Joy* (Simon & Schuster, 1964).
    Produced and directed by Norman Lloyd.
    Music composed and conducted by Bernard Herrmann.

(in a large jack-in-the-box)   Good evening. (box opens) I trust I didn't frighten you unduly. I customarily pop up much more quickly, but my spring is bent. I also hope you will excuse this rather light-hearted opening, for our show. But tonight's story is somewhat different than usual. I thought that my usual gallows-humor might not be suitable. Our story takes place in Mexico. It concerns death and burial and tells of an eerie battle between a gravedigger and a courageous woman. It follows in sixty seconds.

Story: Upon learning that he is dying, a penniless farmer emotionally expresses the desire to perform one last task before he leaves the earth. In a tearful eulogy, his last wish is that his family would be provided for, something he was never fully able to do, and regrets whole-heartedly. Normally this would have been the end of the sad tale, but more was bound to come. Given the proper funeral. Juan Diaz is buried in the local cemetery and one year later, was dug up by an enterprising entrepreneur, who has large ideas. Juan's corpse is mummified and put on display in a large crypt, for tourists and passersby to view – for a price. When Maria, Juan's widow, finds out what is happening, she steals the mummy and puts it on display at her house. The income generated from the tourists keeps her three children fed and clothed. As a woman of principal, Maria's conscience eventually gets the better of her, and in private, she speaks to her husband, pleading to be forgiven . . . a call that Juan hears and answers with a twinkle in his eye.

(mid-line)   Due to circumstances beyond our control, we must interrupt to bring you the following station break. We shall continue in a few moments. Please bare with us.

That concludes our story. Previews of our next attraction will be shown in a few moments. First however, we come to the climax of this evening's entertainment. To be fully appreciated, this commercial must be seen from the beginning. Therefore no one will be seated after it starts.

Trivia, etc. As one of the finest of the *Alfred Hitchcock Hour*s, this episode marked the final episode written or adapted by Ray Bradbury. The producer and director, Norman Lloyd, recalled: "There was another Bradbury story I loved directing, 'The Life Work of Juan Diaz.' That was an *Alfred Hitchcock Hour* with Alejandro Rey and that great Mexican actress Pina Pellicer, who had been with Brando in *One-Eyed Jacks* (1961). And also Frank Silvera, one of the best American actors, who died trying to fix a plug - he got his finger in the plug and was electrocuted. This show, which Bradbury wrote himself from his own short story, was about a man who earned more money dead than alive. His body was put into the catacombs, but it happened to be in an area that preserved the bodies. The tourists would come through to look at these dead people, who were dressed up and standing there! So the guy's wife and the young son steal his body and put it back in their house, which is on the way to the catacombs, so that people stop off there first. So he earned much more dead than alive. Wonderful story! And Bernard Herrmann did the score - a wonderful score. Ray Bradbury said that someone tried to make an opera out of that story, but I don't think they succeeded."

Actress Pina Pellicer, who played the lead of Maria Diaz, also played the role of a young girl named "Maria" in the seventh episode of television's *The Fugitive*, broadcast almost a year before this *Alfred Hitchcock Hour* aired. Alejandro Rey, who played her dead husband in this episode, also made a guest appearance in the same *Fugitive* episode. Sadly, only thirty-nine days after this episode first initially over NBC, Pina Pellicer committed suicide in her birth town of Mexico City, Mexico. She was twenty-nine.

On November 2, 1964, *The Alfred Hitchcock Hour* was not broadcast. Instead, a political program was broadcast in the same time slot, sponsored by the Democratic National committee.

EPISODE #69   **"SEE THE MONKEY DANCE"**   Broadcast on November 9, 1964
        Starring: Efrem Zimbalist, Jr. as the stranger   Roddy McDowall as George
        Patricia Medina as the wife   George Pelling as the conductor
        Shari Lee Bernath as the little girl
        Teleplay written for *The Alfred Hitchcock Hour* by Lewis Davidson, based on a
script he wrote earlier for another television series (suspect a British TV series that never
made it to the major networks in the United States).
        Produced by Gordon Hessler. Directed by Joseph Newman.
        (marionette) *Good evening. I am attempting to assist my brother Alfred in
introducing this evening's chilling shocker. It is called "See The Monkey Dance."* (with an
Alfred doll) *There seems to be no end to the humiliations which I suffer in the name of art
and profit. See the monkey dance indeed. One of the disadvantages of show business is that
although it is sometimes possible to put the actors on strings, the audience is considerably
more difficult to manage. We are experimenting with a limited type of control using a single
string and tying them to their seats. Tonight's play is indeed entitled "See The Monkey
Dance." It is a story of a man who finds himself involved in a mad charade which he neither
understands nor can escape. It begins in a few moments.*

        Story: George is a young man on his way to visit his girlfriend, whom he already
knows is married. Picking up a stranger along the way, George makes conversation only to
discover that the stranger is none other than his girlfriend's husband. Both being practical
men, they logically agree that their meeting was no accident - the woman planned it that way.
If one was to wipe out the other, she would only have to contend with one man instead of two
– a method she apparently applied a long time ago – the stranger being the lone survivor.
Deciding to flip the coin the other way, her husband recommends that George sabotage her
car to get even, killing her in the process. George agrees, and the plan goes off without a
hitch. The woman dies, but only then does George realize that the stranger was not really her
husband, but another former boyfriend who was jilted and sought revenge - which he has just
obtained, at George's expense.

        (mid-line) *I would seem to be at the end of my rope but I still have a long way to
go. Our second half follows this announcement from your friendly neighborhood television
station.*

        *George was not the only one to go down to defeat. The authorities insisted that the
stranger go with him to prison. They have enough trouble coping with crime as it is, and
just didn't want to break up a losing team. That concludes tonight's episode in brother
Alfred's own theatre of the absurd. He plans to present some more buffoonery when he
returns next time.* (picks up the doll and puts it in a suitcase) *If he returns.*

EPISODE #70   **"LONELY PLACE"**   Broadcast on November 16, 1964
        Starring: Teresa Wright as Stella   Pat Buttram as Emory
        Bruce Dern as Jesse
        Teleplay written for *The Alfred Hitchcock Hour* by Francis Irby Gwaltney, based
on the short story of the same name by Douglas Farr (a pen name of C. B. Gilford), originally
published in the February 1960 issue of *Alfred Hitchcock's Mystery Magazine.*
        Produced by Herbert Coleman. Directed by Harvey Hart.
        Music composed and conducted by Lyn Murray.
        (wishing-well) *Good evening. This is a wishing-well. It is a very ancient,
romantic and profitable institution.* (drags up a bucket) *Naturally . . .* (holds up some small
coins) *we throw the smaller ones back. Into the water of course, it's the sporting thing to
do. It is very interesting how the wishing-well got its name. It seems a young man was
wishing he could find a way to make money, then he thought of this. You will find no*

wishing-well in tonight's story, but the setting is a bucolic one, where there is privacy and quiet and where help is far, far away. All this begins in just sixty seconds.

Pat Buttram makes his second appearance on *The Alfred Hitchcock Hour*
in "Lonely Place," as a peach farmer with low morals.
(Photo courtesy of Ronald V. Borst / Hollywood Movie Posters.)

Story: A pair of peach farmers, Emory and Stella, offer a drifter named Jesse three dollars a day, and some room and board, in exchange for his helping them out on the ranch. Jesse agrees, but his strange personality and preoccupation with a knife gives Stella the creeps. Call it female intuition, but Stella asks her husband to fire Jesse, but her husband won't listen. With a major concern for his work, Emory claims he'll be needing Jesse's help till the entire crop is harvested. As the days pass, Stella grows more and more scared, even finding her pet squirrel slashed by a knife, by the hands of Jesse. Listening to Emory complain about her cooking, and showing a lack of respect when Jesse is around, Stella packs her bags and sneaks out of the house. Jesse catches her and threatens to use his knife, ordering her to scream and wake Emory . . . clearly the boy is mad. But she fights him off, causing the knife to drop, and Jesse gets scared, leaving as fast as he can in Emory's truck. Back inside the house, Stella is infuriated when she learns that Emory knew a struggle was going on outside, but pretended to sleep so he wouldn't get involved. Angry, she stabs her husband to death with Jesse's knife, with the escaping lunatic providing the perfect scapegoat.

(mid-line) *I understand that many of you have been wishing to know the identification of the station which is bringing you this program. We shall now grant you that wish. After which, we shall continue our story.*

It grieves me to report that the sheriff was not taken in by Stella's story. He detected a domestic touch to her husband's demise and promptly arrested our heroine. You may be thinking that my wishing-well is gone, not so. Except . . . (walks towards oil-well) *that my wish obviously came through. Until next time then, good night.*

Trivia, etc. "Oh, he [Bruce Dern] was superb!" recalled Norman Lloyd. "Making 'Lonely Place,' I had a marvelous time with Pat, he was so funny, he had me laughing all the time. But Bruce Dern – very remote. A superb actor, and wonderful in the Hitchcocks, but he was rather remote, and one respected that. He sort of had his own "machinery" in his head, the way he worked, and one just hoped to have that flower and to aid and abet whatever he needed. He's a very interesting actor, and excellent to work with. We never had any contrary people. Never."

Teresa Wright, who played young Charlie Newton in one of Hitchcock's favorite movies, recalled her initial meeting in 1943 with Hitchcock: "He wanted to tell me the story of *Shadow of a Doubt*. I went to his office and sat opposite him. It was quite an amazing experience. He not only told me the story, he used any prop on his desk, anything possible to enhance the story. When I finally saw the film, I thought, 'I've seen this film before. I saw it right there in his office, sitting opposite him.' He was such a consummate storyteller."

"I was involved in seven of Hitch's movies * but he didn't direct or write any of those *The Alfred Hitchcock Hour* episodes. He didn't show much interest in doing television," recalled Herbert Coleman. "I worked with him for years until he wanted to do *Psycho*. I didn't like the idea and I put my foot down. I told Hitch it wouldn't work. I didn't like the way the film was turning out. But he did that so I left. Bruce Dern was perfect for the role. I think Hitch agreed with me, because he asked Bruce Dern for the part in *Marnie* (1964) and *Family Plot* (1976)."

EPISODE #71 **"THE McGREGOR AFFAIR"** Broadcast on November 23, 1964
    Starring: Andrew Duggan as John McGregor
    Guest Star: Elsa Lanchester as Aggie McGregor

Co-starring: Bill Smith as Tommy Lad	John Hoyt as Dr. Knox
Michael Pate as Hare	Arthur Malet as Burke
Betty Harford as Elsie	Michael Macready as Jarmley
William Beckley as Becker	Janine Gray as the wench
Barry Macollum as the vendor	Harriett Harper as Glynis
Iris Bristol as Rosie	Brendan Dillon as the bartender

    Teleplay written for *The Alfred Hitchcock Hour* by Morton Fine and David Friedkin, based on the short story of the same name by Sidney Rowland, originally published in the July 1953 issue of *Ellery Queen's Mystery Magazine*. Subsequently reprinted in *Butcher, Baker, Murder-Maker*, ed. George Harmon Coxe (Knopf, 1954).
    Produced by Morton Fine and David Friedkin, and directed by David Friedkin.
    Music composed and conducted by Bernard Herrmann.

    (bag-pipes) *Appearances to the contrary, this is not a hip flask for scotch whiskey, these are bag-pipes. I understand that the inventor of the bag-pipes was inspired when he saw a man carrying an indignant, asthmatic pig under his arm. Unfortunately the man-made music has never equaled the purity of sound achieved by the pig. Two of the characters in tonight's story are people who actually lived during the 19th century. These two made a large number of contributions to science. And science returned the favor. And now a word from a laddie who wants you to buy his product so that he can continue making trips to those bonny, bonny, banks.*

---

* *Rear Window* (1954), *To Catch a Thief* (1955), *The Trouble With Harry* (1955), *The Man Who Knew Too Much* (1956), *The Wrong Man* (1956), *Vertigo* (1958) and *North by Northwest* (1959).

468

Andrew Duggan as John McGregor in "The McGregor Affair."
(Photo courtesy of Ronald V. Borst / Hollywood Movie Posters.)

Story: Edinburgh, Scotland: 1827. John McGregor is upset over his life: that of having to care for his constantly drunk, alcoholic wife, who spends every cent he makes on whiskey. To help make ends meet, he hauls boxes of tanbark to a medical academy operated by Dr. Knox, where McGregor has heard stories about the school robbing graves to obtain bodies for medical studies. Noticing that the latest shipment of tanbark is much heavier than usual, McGregor pieces one and one together to discover that he is actually hauling the bodies of murder victims, people killed by a pair of unscrupulous body snatchers. Learning where the snatchers live, he decides to get rid of his drunken wife late one night by getting her intoxicated and dumping the body on the school doorstep - a plan that works, but one with repercussions when he himself become Burke and Hare's next victim.

(mid-line) *I do hope nothing untold happens to Aggie. She's such a bonny lass. But we shall find out after this wee interruption.*

Perhaps Robert Burns was anticipating McGregor when he wrote this epitaph.
"As father Adam first was fooled, a case that's still too common.
Here lies a man a woman ruled. The devil ruled the woman."
As you know Burke and Hare were brought to justice. Hare turned state's evidence but Burke was somewhat less fortunate. He ended up on the dissecting table after

he had been executed of course. (music) *I seem to have developed a leak. Music critics are a vindictive lot.* (more bag-pipe music) *Good night.*

Janine Gray as the wench in "The McGregor Affair" (Photo courtesy of Photofest.)

Trivia, etc. Morton Fine and David Friedkin were originally radio writers who scripted – literally – hundreds of scripts for mystery and horror anthologies, for both television and radio. In the summer of 1953, CBS radio featured a program entitled *Crime Classics*, featuring mystery dramas based on historical true-life crimes, from Jack the Ripper to Lizzie Borden. Fine and Friedkin wrote most of the scripts for the series. On December 2, 1953, an episode entitled "If A Body Need A Body, Just Call Burke and Hare" aired with a cast including Jeanette Nolan and Betty Harford. Harford played a small role in this teleplay, a television expansion on the similar radio version, but a different role than her radio counterpart. Although this episode was based on a story by Sidney Rowland, Fine and Friedkin did incorporate some of their earlier script into this one.

"She [Elsa Lanchester] was a delight to work with – nothing fazed her," recalled Michael Pate. "She did everything that she was asked for. It was quite incredible. This lady was a great talent and, as far as I ever knew, a delightful person to be with. Very definitive, very unique . . . maybe a little fey, but a giant of a talent, Elsa Lanchester."

Barry Macollum, who played the role of the vendor in this episode, also played the role of a tramp in Alfred Hitchcock's *The Trouble with Harry* (1955). Michael Macready is the son of actor George Macready. that appeared in three of the early episodes of *Alfred Hitchcock Presents* and one episode of *The Alfred Hitchcock Hour*. Elsa Lanchester's husband, actor Charles Laughton, appeared in two Hitchcock movies, *Jamaica Inn* (1939) and *The Paradine Case* (1947).

On November 30, 1964, *The Alfred Hitchcock Hour* was not telecast. Instead, on the occasion of his 90th birthday, NBC-TV presented a full-hour program in honor of Sir Winston Churchill entitled "The Other World of Winston Churchill." Based on the eminent statesman's book, *Painting as a Pastime*, this *Hallmark Hall of Fame* special explored Churchill's abiding interest in art, explaining how and why he started to paint and what his hobby meant to him. Paul Scofield narrated. Broadcast in color, from 10 to 11 p.m., EST.

EPISODE #72   **"MISADVENTURE"**   Broadcast on December 7, 1964
    Starring: Barry Nelson as Colin   Lola Albright as Eve Martin
    George Kennedy as George Martin   Michael Bregan as the boyfriend
    An original teleplay written for *The Alfred Hitchcock Hour* by Lewis Davidson.
    Produced by Gordon Hessler. Directed by Joseph Newman.
    Music composed and conducted by Bernard Herrmann.
    (kissing booth, $1) *Good evening. Welcome to the Hitchcock pavilion of the world's fair. The lack of activity at this stand is rather embarrassing. Especially when I tell you that I am buying kisses, not selling them. It all seemed like such a good idea. Buying some kisses for a dollar and then turning around and selling them for two. Unfortunately just after going into business, I discovered that several unscrupulous persons were giving them away. I shall probably lose my entire investment. This stand, a crate of lemons and a pound of alum. After all, with lips like mine puckering could be a problem. This evening's story concerns some rather bizarre events, which take place in a very ordinary home, in very ordinary surroundings . . . the suburbs of a large city. It is called "Misadventure" and begins just as quickly as we can run through this next commercial.*

    Story: Eve Martin is married to a wealthy businessman, but his thrifty style is not to her suiting and she often enjoys the company of other men. George is unaware of her flirtations and while at work one afternoon, she receives a visitor that will soon change George's life. A man named Colin, dresses up like the gas man and comes to check their meter, but the stranger eventually confesses to Eve that he isn't under the employment of the gas company at all, but someone who wants Eve's husband dead. For personal reasons he won't explain, he convinces Eve the benefits of bumping off a rich husband, and the greedy woman accepts. The two work out a plan to knock off George, but at the last minute, the stranger kills Eve instead, setting things up so perfectly that George will be incriminated. With his plan of revenge now completed, the stranger – in reality George's brother - is now vindicated against George's refusal to lend him money that would have saved his own wife's life.

    (mid-line) *We have reached the half-way point in our story. While you visit your local station for a moment, I shall act as an electric bookmark, so that you will know where you left off.*

    Colin was apprehended. I think it is worth mentioning that he was tried in a state that dispenses poetic justice. He went to the gas chamber. This concludes my portion of the program. I shall return next week with another story. (Hitchcock reveals the sign: "Kisses 50 cents")

EPISODE #73   **"TRIUMPH"**   Broadcast on December 14, 1964
    Starring: Ed Begley as Brother Thomas Fitzgibbons
    Jeanette Nolan as Mary Fitzgibbons
    Co-starring: Maggie Pierce as Mrs. Lucy Sprague
    Tom Simcox as Brother John Sprague
    Than Wyenn as Ramna   Tony Scott as the Indian employee

Teleplay written for *Hour* by Arthur Ross, based on the short story "Murder in Szechwan" by Robert Branson, originally published in the October 9, 1948 issue of *Collier's*. Subsequently reprinted in the May 1958 issue of *Ellery Queen's Mystery Magazine*, and *Happy Endings*, ed. Damon Knight (Bobbs-Merrill, 1974) as "The Red-Headed Murderess."

Produced by Herbert Coleman. Directed by Harvey Hart.

(butcher shop, saw)*Good evening. A palmist recommended that I opened a butcher shop. Actually she didn't read my palm, she got no further than my thumb. She felt I was well in doubt for the position. I have a chopping block and a cold room . . .* (knock, knock) *Are you decent? I want to be sure that all the meat is dressed.* (opens cold room and you see bodies hanging from the ceiling) *This evening's play takes place in the far east. However, it is the occidentals who prove inscrutable. The story also shatters another cliché when it demonstrates that a rectangle can be just as dramatic as a triangle. But first a word from a gentleman who is always welcome to enjoy the hospitality of my air-conditioned guestroom.* (points at the cold room) *Our sponsor.*

Story: Brother John Sprague and his wife Lucy arrive at the headquarters of missionary Thomas Fitzgibbons located in the wild jungles of India. Fitzgibbons turns out to be an incompetent quack with an unwarranted reputation for helping the poor natives. His power-hungry wife has accomplished most of what Fitzgibbons is credited for, and she realizes that their little empire, meager as it might be, will be destroyed by the newcomers when they learn the truth. Mary Fitzgibbons isn't about to let go of everything she has accomplished, and resorts to murder to keep things as they are.

(mid-line) *I believe they have something to confide in you. Following which we shall have the second half of our story.*

I have only a moment to tell you the rest of the story. Mr. Sprague was apprehended and punished, which seems to be precisely what is happening to me, although I don't understand why. I do know one thing. I shall never again make sausages out of python meat. This would appear to be the end of my part . . . of the program.

EPISODE #74 **"MEMO FROM PURGATORY"** Broadcast on December 21, 1964

Starring: James Caan as Jay Shaw / Phil Beldone

Lynn Loring as Filene	Walter Koenig as Tiger

Co-starring: Tony Musante as Emil 'Candle' Shaster

Zalman King as Fish	Simon Scott as the defender
Mark Slade as Slats	Michael Lamont as the trooper
Johnny Silver as Ben	Jacque Palmer as Cherry
Chuck Courtney as Ski	Jimmy Joyce as the proprietor
Will J. White as the guard	Leonard P. Geer as the derelict

Teleplay written for *The Alfred Hitchcock Hour* by Harlan Ellison, from his own autobiographical "Memos from Purgatory."

Produced by Joan Harrison. Directed by Joseph Pevney.

Music composed and conducted by Lalo Schifrin.

(ice-hockey goal) *Good evening. The game of hockey seems to combine all the best elements of ice-skating, polo and World War Two. However, we have found a method for reducing the fighting . . . and speeding up the game. We play over ten feet of water on melting ice. It keeps the players quite lively. There are dangers of course, occasionally a bobbing head is mistaken for the puck. This is most unfortunate because goals scored in this way are not counted. Tonight's tale is called "Memo From Purgatory" and is about a young man who wanted to learn about youth gangs by personal experience. He discovers that viewing juvenile delinquents at close range can be extremely dangerous. And now we are only a few seconds away from a commercial, which is as close as I care to get.*

Story: In an attempt to put together a book about street gangs, Jay Shaw assumes an alias and manages to pass an initiation to join a ruthless, youth street gang in Brooklyn called "The Barons." Their leader. Tiger, takes a liking to Jay and soon promotes him to second-hand man. Jay even begins spending time with Tiger's ex-girlfriend. Candle, now a former second-hand man, gets jealous and breaks into Jay's apartment, finding the preliminary notes about the gang, documented detail for detail. Furious when the truth comes out, Tiger sentences Jay to an execution. Putting a Baron jacket on Jay, the boys send him into the evening streets as target practice against their rival street gang, "The Flyers." But instead he is taken by the police. The Barons use Jay's money, stolen at the break-in, to bail him out just for the pleasure of killing him. The result, however, comes with horrifying consequences – as the girlfriend is stabbed by Tiger by mistake.

(mid-line) *We must now split to enjoy a station break. I shall remain here on our turf and watch for the fuzz. Our rumble will continue in a moment.*

This evening I am dispensing with the flippant remarks, which usually follow our plays. There are some stories which do not lend themselves to levity and "Memo From Purgatory" is certainly one of them. I regard juvenile delinquency as one of our nations most serious and pressing problems and tonight's story was produced with that thought up and most in our minds. Next week we shall present another story. Until then, good night.

Trivia, etc. "That was a gangster-type show with the teenagers. Goodness how I remember that one!" said Joseph Pevney. "It was I who got Koenig the job playing the Russian on *Star Trek*. Gene Roddenberry asked me one day to find someone who could play a young Russian. So I thought of Koenig, who was a very talented boy, and worked under me for that Hitchcock episode. Then he came in and read for the Russian with that accent. James Caan fancied himself as a horseman at that time. And he had a horse in the same stable where Caan kept his horse – I got him the horse from *Wagon Train* named Buck – it was an old wonderful animal – anyway, I used to bring both my kids over and this was in San Fernando Valley. And there was a horse barn and that's where my son kept his horse and that's where Caan kept his riding horse and he had an English saddle and he showed it off to my kids and he got onto the horse and he fell on his ass! [Laughs] My kids couldn't stop laughing. I introduced them to the stars like James Caan and boy did he hurt. But Koenig proved talent all the way through. That was where I first met Harlan too, and Harlan wrote a few of those *Star Trek* shows too."

Similar to "Bang! You're Dead," this episode featured a concern from Hitchcock about the problem of juvenile gangs, and their motives. In fact, the words "which do not lend themselves to levity" were the same words Hitchcock spoke in "Bang! You're Dead." The initiation tests Caan must go through in this episode are somewhat brutal in nature, one involving a strapping of belts, slapped against his body. But then again, his escape from the gang is no game either. For trivia fans, this was the first and only time they actually credited the name of the story source on the screen. Zalman King, who played one of the teenagers in this episode, would later write, produce and direct the critically acclaimed *Wild Orchid* in 1990. King also produced *Nine ½ Weeks* (1986).

EPISODE #75   **"CONSIDER HER WAYS"**   Broadcast on December 28, 1964
Starring: Barbara Barrie as Dr. Jane Waterleigh / Mother Orchid
Gladys Cooper as Laura
Co-starring: Robert H. Harris as Dr. Robert J. Perrigan

Gene Lyons as Max Wilding	Ellen Corby as the chief nurse
Virginia Gregg as the third doctor	Carmen Phillips as Mother Daisy
Diane Sayer as Mother Hazel	Dee J. Thompson as the first doctor
Alice Backes as the second doctor	Eve Bruce as the Amazon
Ivy Bethune as the nurse	Ginny Gan as the first worker

Stacy King as the female worker　　　Penny Zaferiou as the little servitor
and Leif Erickson as Dr. John S. Hellyer

Teleplay written for *The Alfred Hitchcock Hour* by Oscar Millard, based on the novelette of the same name by John Wyndham, first published with two other original novelettes by other authors in *Sometime, Never* (Ballantine, 1957). Later collected in *Consider Her Ways and Others* (Michael Joseph, 1961; U.S. title: *The Infinite Moment*, Ballantine, 1961).

Produced by Joan Harrison. Directed by Robert Stevens.

Music composed and conducted by Bernard Herrmann.

(telephone) *Good evening. Perhaps you have already heard of the latest in telephone services. Dial-analysis. It has been instituted in places suffering from a shortage of psycho-analysts or a shortage of money with which to pay them.* (makes a call) Voice: How do you do? This is dial-analysis. When you hear the signal begin telling dial-analysis your problem. Continue until you hear the second signal. The recording you will make will be monitored at a later time by one of our resident psychiatrists. *Dear Sir, gentlemen, mama.* I'm afraid that is the end of today's session. Please call tomorrow at the same time. Pleasant dreams. *Any problems or neurosis indicated by the preceding are my own and do not reflect those of the sponsor or of the management of the station to which you are listening. This evening's tale begins with a nightmare-like experience, but that is only a prelude to the terrifying events which follow. And now, speaking of terrifying events . . .*

Story: Mother Orchid awakens in a clinic with no memory of anything, other than her name and status. Even more strangely, she finds that she has gained a huge amount of weight, and is told that she produces wonderful babies – without the help of a man. In fact, no one around her knows what a man is. Believing she is in the middle of a delusion, Jane pleads with an old but respectable woman, for guidance. The old lady explains that Jane is in a future society with a single sex, the result of a genetic accident. It seems a scientist named Perrigan killed off all the males with a freak rat poison that unexpectedly mutated out of control. In our present-day reality. Mother Orchid is really Dr. Jane Waterleigh, who has used a mind-altering drug, and upon coming out of her drug-induced state, decides that the vision she had was real. After a little private eyeing, she discovers that a man named Dr. Perrigan really exists, and he's a professor of biotechnology. Questioning the doctor, she discovers his project, a form of disease that will wipe out all rats on the earth, is presently being worked on. Realizing what she must do, she kills him before he can destroy humanity's future. Only after she is arrested for murder does she find out from her attorney that it will be Dr. Perrigan's son - also a scientist - who will doom mankind, because now the son is intent on continuing his father's work and legacy.

(mid-line) *The last half of our drama will be seen in a moment. We pause now to place this station to station call.* (picks up phone and starts dialing)

I hope you have not been disturbed by our playlet. It is obviously just a hallucination of some over-enthusiastic feminist. (makes another call) *He keeps getting farther away.* Voice: Congratulations, you are our one-millionth customer and have been chosen for special analysis and experimentation under the direction of our own, Dr. Perrigan. *Until another week, or longer, good night.*

EPISODE #76　**"CRIMSON WITNESS"**　Broadcast on January 4, 1965
　　　Starring: Peter Lawford as Ernest 'Ernie' Mullett
　　　Martha Hyer as Judith Mullett　　　Joanna Moore as Madeline
　　　Guest Star: Julie London as Barbara
　　　Co-starring: Roger C. Carmel as Farnum Mullett

Alan Baxter as Mr. Baldwin
Larry Thor as Haskel
Nancy Hsueh as the secretary

Paul Comi as Modeer
Paul Micale as the waiter

Teleplay written for *The Alfred Hitchcock Hour* by Morton Fine and David Friedkin, based on the short story of the same name by Nigel Elliston, originally published in the December 1962 issue of *London Mystery Magazine*.

Produced by Morton Fine and David Friedkin, and directed by David Friedkin.

Music composed and conducted by Benny Carter.

(telescope)   *Good evening. I'm doing a bit of survey. We thought we would straighten out this channel. Some of the commercials have been scraping their sides as they go through. It would be dreadful if one of them were to become stuck. Since no one will hear of making the commercials smaller, we must make the channel larger. So much for television surveys. This evening we are presenting a story of the business world, and of an ingeniously planned crime. It is called "Crimson Witness." I have a target in my sight, that is most tempting, but I have no ammunition.* (turns the telescope) *You may see for yourselves.* (camera pulls up towards the telescope)

Story: Ernest Mullet thinks he has it all: a good home, a devoted wife, a beautiful girlfriend, and plenty of money. But things rapidly begin to fall apart. First his secretary/girlfriend brushes him off, then his boss calls him in to tell him that he is being replaced by Ernie's overachieving brother - who also just happens to have taken his girlfriend as well. Once at home, he gets into a fight with his brother, Farnum, who lives with him, and who soundly trounces Ernie then announces that not only is he moving out, but he is taking Ernie's wife with him. Ernie isn't about to take this lying down, so he reveals to the jealous secretary about Farnum and Judith, but that fails to get her upset. Finally, Farnum goes too far when he says he has discovered Ernie's habit of stealing money from the company and is holding the information to keep his brother in line, so Ernie makes plans to lock Farnum up in an air-tight safe, which should end all of his problems. Except, the police find a rose petal in the safe, that comes from Ernie's breast pocket decoration, proving he is the murderer.

(mid-line) *Just looking for the middle of the program. There seems to be a break here, which we plan to repair. In the meantime, why don't you detour by way of your local station. Then join us again for the second half.*

I have a confession to make. This surveying has nothing to do with television. We're putting a super highway through your living room and this was the only way we could do our preliminary work without facing all you angry home owners. The bulldozers should be along any day now. We shall try very hard not to allow to interfere with your enjoyment of next week's story. Scenes of which will be shown in a few moments.

EPISODE #77 **"WHERE THE WOODBINE TWINETH"**   Broadcast January 11, 1965
Starring: Margaret Leighton as Nell Snyder
Co-starring: Carl Benton Reid as Captain King Snyder
Juanita Moore as Suse, the maid
E. J. Andre as the preacher
and Eileen Baral as Eva Snyder

Joel Fluellen as Jessie
Lila Perry as Numa

Teleplay written for *The Alfred Hitchcock Hour* by James Bridges, based on the short story "You Never Believe Me" by Davis Grubb, originally published in the February 1964 issue of *Ellery Queen's Mystery Magazine*. Subsequently collected in *Twelve Tales of Suspense and the Supernatural* (Scribner, 1964) as "Where the Woodbine Twineth." Also collected as "You Never Believe Me" in *You Never Believe Me and Other Stories* (St. Martin's Press, 1989).

Produced by Norman Lloyd. Directed by Alf Kjellin.

Music composed and conducted by Bernard Herrmann.

(table with pies) *As you can see, I'm in training, for a pie-eating contest. I take all athletic matches seriously. I've been practicing for some weeks now, and have myself home to a razor-sharp edge. Furthermore, I do not expect to have any trouble making the weight. This evening, in addition to a pie-eating contest, we are presenting a story entitled, "Where the Woodbine Twineth."* (zoom-in) *Or, as our network insists on calling it, WT2. "Where the Woodbine Twineth," is about a little girl who had some imaginary playmates. This would not seem to be a very serious problem, but it was. It was. We now have a different kind of competition. An endurance contest. The question is, how many of you can endure the next sixty seconds?*

Story: Nell Snyder suddenly finds herself the parent of her orphaned niece, Eva, a little girl with decidedly strange behavior. It seems that every time Eva gets into trouble, she blames an imaginary playmate named Mr. Peppercorn. Nell is unable to comprehend the girl and their relationship becomes even worse after the arrival of Eva's grandfather, King Snyder, a riverboat captain who gives her a Creole voodoo doll. Within a short time, Nell is convinced that the doll is real and is trying to capture her soul - which she is determined to do something about. Following the child and the doll into the woods, Nell murders Numa, the doll, only to realize that she is too late. The child switched places and Eva's face is on the doll.

(mid-line) *How does one improve each shining hour? Some say by injecting a station break in the center of it. I shall allow you to judge for yourselves, before rejoining us for the second half of "Where The Woodbine Twineth."*

That concludes tonight's story. Next week we shall return with another. Until then, good night.

EPISODE #78 **"FINAL PERFORMANCE"** Broadcast on January 18, 1965
Starring: Franchot Tone as Rudolph Bitzner
Sharon Farrell as Rosie   Roger Perry as Cliff Allen
Co-starring: Kelly Thordsen as the sheriff   William Challee as Wint Davis
Teleplay written for *The Alfred Hitchcock Hour* by Clyde Ware and Lee Kalcheim, based on the short story of the same name by Robert Bloch, originally published in the September 1960 issue of *Shock.* Subsequently collected in *Blood Runs Cold* (Simon & Schuster, 1961) and in *Such Stuff as Screams Are Made Of* (Ballantine, 1979).
Produced by Gordon Hessler. Directed by John Brahm.
(with a blindfold) *Good evening.* (gunshots) *It seems to have been a bit of an uprising here by a group that is long on principle and short on marksmanship. If you're disturbed by what they did to the wall, just imagine what they did to my shirt . . . and my tie.* (tie is shot at) *It's completely ruined. The leader of a firing squad used to do this at parties, using a pair of scissors. It is comforting to know, he has not lost his sense of humor. Tonight's narrative is called "Final Performance." Although who's performance I shall let you discover for yourself. It begins in one minute.*

Story: A television writer wanna-be named Cliff Allen is driving to Hollywood to seek his fame, but finds himself picking up a pretty young hitchhiker named Rosie, instead. When Cliff is pulled over for a traffic violation he didn't commit, the girl suddenly claims she was kidnapped and the sheriff orders them to follow him to town. Thankfully for Cliff, his car conks out and they are all forced to stay overnight in a seedy motel. Once there, Cliff meets an over-the-hill vaudevillian named Rudolph Bitzner, who now runs the motel and is romantically involved with the young hitchhiker, Rosie. Cliff asks the connection and in private, Rosie explains that she's a virtual prisoner trying to escape from Rudolph's bizarre possession. Cliff agrees to help, but before the two can leave, Rosie disappears. Confronting Rudolph, Cliff is told that she has changed her mind, but Cliff says he'll only believe it from Rosie's own lips. Finding himself in Rudolph's stage hall, Rosie tells Cliff that she's changed her mind. Cliff decides to leave, not knowing that Rudolph's specialty is ventriloquism.

(mid-line) *Television has many ingenious devices to keep time from passing too quickly and pleasantly. One of them is the station break. After which, on with our story.*

Ventriloquism was of no avail to Rudolph when he faced the judge several months later. He is now talking to himself, in one of our larger prisons. I've run out of time, although there seems to be some left for others. One of these is a sponsor who is about to give his final performance . . . for this week.

Trivia, etc. "Gordon Hessler was the wonderful producer who worked under Norman Lloyd for that one. They were a great team and Gordon was pure British. I remember when they were talking about who they were going to get for the part, they talked about Ralph Richardson and other greats and they ended up with Franchot Tone, who was toward the end of his career," recalled Lee Kalcheim, the uncredited co-author of this script. "On the basis of my first script, I was asked to write another one. I never did any others because that was the last season for the show. We had a credit fight with that episode, too. 'Final Performance' was the second script I wrote, but the first broadcast. It was the second script I ever wrote for television, but being a playwright, I composed a magnificent piece and somebody put their bloody hands on it, which is the way of Hollywood, I guess. So I wrote this and I believe most of the stories originated from mystery magazines and I was just informed that this guy Clyde Ware was coming in so I read his script. It didn't change all that much so even today I still don't know why he got credit for it. But that's water over the dam now and not worth bothering about it."

On January 25, 1965, *The Alfred Hitchcock Hour* was not broadcast. Instead, an NBC-TV special color presentation entitled "The Stately Ghosts of England" was broadcast in the same time slot. Margaret Rutherford and her husband Stringer Davis, along with Tom Corbett, clairvoyant, took television viewers to three of England's traditional spirit rendezvous. Congleat, Salisbury Hall and Beaulieu that have reputations as haunted mansions, were the main attractions.

EPISODE #79   **"THANATOS PALACE HOTEL"**   Broadcast on February 1, 1965
    Starring: Angie Dickinson as Ariane Shaw
    Guest Star: Steven Hill as Robert Manners
    Co-starring: C. B. Atwater as Borchter, the manager
    Bartlett Robinson as Mr. J. Smith

Rex Comeaux as Devereau	Robert Reiner as the doctor
Charles Fredericks as the big man	Gail Bonney as the gray-haired woman
Pat Renella as the lean man	Adrianne Ellis as the young woman
Nancy Sanderson as the nurse	Len Hendry as the driver
Henry Wills as the first cowboy	Lew Brown as the second cowboy

    Teleplay written for *The Alfred Hitchcock Hour* by Arthur Ross, based on the 1938 short story "Suicide Hotel" by Andre Maurois, later reprinted in the February 1952 issue of *Ellery Queen's Mystery Magazine*.
    Produced by Herbert Coleman. Directed by Laslo Benedek.
    Music composed and conducted by Bernard Herrmann.
    (on horse-back) *Good evening. Has anyone seen a steeple run by here? Horseback riding is an exhausting sport. Actually the riding isn't tiring, it's getting up here. The ladder broke twice. As for getting down, everyone assures me that will be no problem. This horse has thrown its last five riders While I continue the steeple chase, you shall witness a*

story, about a very strange type of resort hotel. It offers a unique service to a very select clientele. But first we have another one-minute egg, laid by the golden goose of television.

Story: Facing the painful agony of a mis-calculation, Robert Manners carries out an ill-fated suicide attempt off a ledge near the top of a tall building. What he never counted on was a crew of firemen and a life-saving device, which saves him when he finally decides to go over the edge. Later that afternoon, Mr. J. Smith, who saw Manners jump off the ledge, introduces himself to Robert, representing an exclusive suicide club that operates from the Thanatos Palace Hotel, where members of the group are assigned to murder each other, after agreeing to do so. As a twist of fate, Robert falls in love with Ariane Shaw, another fellow member, and vice versa. "Love can't stop our deaths," Ariane explains, "love can't save our lives." Riding horseback in the hills, both decide to go on with their lives, but having already signed for the services, know they can't turn back – or escape. Upon discovering the method of operation used to kill the guests, Robert initiates a counter-plan, to over power and kill the guards. Employing the help of a few members of the hotel, Robert explains how they'll over power the guards, one-by-one, and kill them. But he discovers the horrifying truth that it was all a trap, and Ariane was in on it. A noose wraps around Robert's neck and one of the guards hangs him from a tree limb.

(mid-line) *We have come to the half-way point. Now we must turn around and go back. We shall proceed with the second half of our journey, after this word from our stations, local and otherwise.*

(Hitchcock is sitting on a chair, with a cast on his leg) *The operators of the Palace Hotel, were ultimately arrested and charged with homicide and failure to pay their gas-bill. They all received substantial sentences. There was an unhappy climax to my riding experience. My horse had an accident. He fell . . . on me. Broke my leg. There was a doctor present, but unfortunately he was the horse's, not mine. And his only recommendation was that they shoot me. Now, for those of you who are too busy to spend an hour, watching our next show, we shall give you a captful version. It follows this uncut commercial.*

Trivia, etc. C. B. Atwater also played the role of Mr. Bishop in Alfred Hitchcock's *The Wrong Man* (1956). Len Hendry also played a police lieutenant in *North by Northwest* (1959). Arthur Ross, who wrote the script for this episode, recalled the complications in adapting the original story for a teleplay: "I did one which was an adaptation of a short story by Andre Maurois, who was among the most famous of a whole generation of French writers and novelists. They'd tried to adapt it before, and no one could adapt it. I read it and I said, 'They can't adapt it because it's only half a story,' and I took it and added the other half to it. It was a thing called 'Thanatos Palace Hotel,' which was a resort where you went for the purpose of euthanasia. They would kill you painlessly . . . but, until then, you lived in a lovely room, you went to meals, and you never knew when the moment was coming. You wouldn't even be aware of the fact that it had taken place: there was no violence at all. What happens is that a man [Steven Hill] comes in total despair, and does so a woman [Angie Dickinson]. They fall in love and want to escape, but they're not allowed to. That was my half of the story - Maurois wrote of somebody coming there to die, and I wrote of somebody coming there and re-discovering life again and wanting to live. But the people who deal in death don't want that - you've made your commitment already. That was one that got quite a bit of attention."

Henry Wills, one of the horsemen in this episode, was also a stunt co-ordinator for television's *The High Chaparral*, *Bonanza*, and *The Magnificent Seven*. He supplied stunts for *The Beastmaster* (1982). In *The Phantom Rider* (1946), he was one of several stuntmen who took the Phantom Rider's place in the riding scenes.

EPISODE #80 **"ONE OF THE FAMILY"** Broadcast on February 8, 1965
Starring: Lilia Skala as Frieda
Jeremy Slate as Dexter Dailey   Kathryn Hays as Joyce Dailey
Co-starring: Olive Deering as Christine Callendar
Willis Bouchey as Dr. Bailey   Doris Lloyd as the maid
and Frances Reid as the mother

Teleplay written for *The Alfred Hitchcock Hour* by Oscar Millard, based on the short story of the same name by James Yaffe, originally published in the May 1956 issue of *Ellery Queen's Mystery Magazine.* Subsequently reprinted in *Ellery Queen's Awards, Eleventh Series,* ed. Ellery Queen (Simon & Schuster, 1956); and *Hitchcock in Prime Time,* ed. Francis M. Nevins and Martin H. Greenberg (Avon, 1985).

Produced by Joan Harrison. Directed by Joseph Pevney.

Music composed and conducted by Leonard Rosenman.

(boxes) *Good evening. Just trying out a new product. It's for people who are afraid to face reality. For the man who has everything and can't stand to look at it. We're doing a very brisk business. One of the appeals of the box is it's anonymity. But inside our boxes are some very important people. Several heads of state. At a very modest additional cost we have this popular attachment.* (picks up blind-fold) *You will observe there are no eye holes. It is for those people who buy one of these and then find they cannot face the reality of the inside of the box. As you can see, we have boxes to fit any size or shape of head, or problem. All this has nothing to do with tonight's story "One Of The Family" which begins after the following commercial and that is one minute of reality I intend to miss.*

Story: A nursemaid of German decent is hired by Dexter and Joyce Dailey to care for their newborn. After listening to a story on the radio about a German nurse wanted for questioning in San Francisco in connection with the death of a child under suspicious circumstances, Joyce becomes worried. Dexter insists Frieda is not the same woman, since he himself was raised by Frieda. Joyce, however, won't disregard female intuition and behind their backs, contacts the dead child's aunt for a description of the German nurse. When the information she is given sounds exactly like Frieda, Joyce again insists her child may become the next victim . . .

(mid-line; Hitchcock's voice is heard, and one of the boxes on the screen wiggles) *For the strong there is more to come. Our second half follows this word from a distant station.*

Our story ends happily for Frieda and the Dailey family. As for Christine, the authorities saw to it that she was placed in a sanitarium where she received psychiatric help. My own story has taken a turn for the better. I find I can face anything now. I have reached a new plateau of maturity. Next week we shall return with another story and more therapy. (moves children's lettered boxes)

Trivia, etc. "I remember being very pleased," James Yaffe recalled about the adaptation. "The TV version stuck to the original story line, and made the surprise ending more dramatic by bringing it onstage from offstage. This was my suggestion, when I sold them the story. And my characters always seem more interesting to me when I see them brought to life by good actors."

"Now when I directed *Star Trek* [television] a few years later," recalled Joseph Pevney, "I remember Lilia Skala working under me again. Skala I loved. I used her as the queen mother of Spock's home planet. She was a wonderful actress." Frances Reid, who played a supporting role in this episode, also played the uncredited role of Mrs. O'Connor in *The Wrong Man* (1956). Doris Lloyd, who played a supporting role in this (among many other Hitchcock episodes) played the role of Madame Kettisha in *Phantom Lady* (1944), also produced by Joan Harrison.

EPISODE #81   **"AN UNLOCKED WINDOW"**   Broadcast on February 15, 1965

Starring: Dana Wynter as Nurse Stella Crosson   T. C. Jones as Nurse Betty Ames
Co-starring: Louise Latham as Maude Isles   John Kerr as Glendon Baker
E. J. Andre as Sam Isles   Stephen Roberts as Boris Crispis
Cathie Merchant as Frieda Little   John Willis as the newscaster
Lew Brown as Al Ruben   Len Hendry as the man

Teleplay written for *The Alfred Hitchcock Hour* by James Bridges, based on the story of the same name by Ethel Lina White, published in *My Best Mystery Story* (Faber, 1939) and later *English Country House Murders*, ed. Thomas Godfrey (Mysterious Press, 1989).

Produced by Herbert Coleman. Directed by Joseph Newman.

Music composed and conducted by Bernard Herrmann.

(radio station Hitchcock)   *Good evening. We are broadcasting my portion of this evening's program by radio instead of television. I seem to have lost some weight and I don't wish to mar my image. I cannot reveal exactly how much weight. I can only say that had I lost ten more pounds I would have had to file a missing persons report. For the uninitiated I shall explain that radio is simply television with a tube burned out. In radio, sound is a rather important ingredient. When it does not exist, it is manufactured. For example, this cellophane simulates the sound of a crackling fire. This sound-effect is so authentic one can almost smell the smoke.* (smoke starts to show) *This evening's play tells of two nurses who spend one terrifying night in a large house in the country. But first, some sound and fury signifying our sponsor's product.* (fire alarm)

Story: A third murder in the last two weeks is reported over the television, and police confess they have a psychotic madman on the loose, preying only on live-in nurses. One dark stormy night, Nurse Stella Crosson and Nurse Betty Ames are tending to their employer, a man with a heart condition who needs constant attention. Their only company is an alcoholic housekeeper and her husband, the handyman. Shortly after the handyman goes out for a fresh oxygen tank for the patient, the power fails, the lights go out, and the women start feeling uneasy. Maude hears a man's voice and footsteps in the house, but the nurses don't believe her, since the woman has been known for taking one drink too many. A phone call from the murderer informs the women that he knows they're alone, and intends to pay them a visit before the night is over. Checking to make sure all the doors and windows are locked, Stella finds that she over-looked a basement window, a mistake that might prove all too costly. Nurse Betty Ames, however, is certain no one came through the basement window, as he reveals his true identity. During the struggle between nurses, Stella tears the man's wig off, to see that he's not a woman, but the evasive madman. "You're such a pretty nurse," says Betty, overpowering Stella . . .

(mid-line) *We shall return in a moment, but first we ask your local station to . . . take it away.*

Thus ends our story. Nothing more remains to be told. That is, unless you are interested in knowing more about Nurse Ames. You see, he later made a regrettable mistake and found himself attempting to throttle a nurse who turned out to be a policeman, in disguise. It was most embarrassing. Now I have another radio sound-effect to test. (creaking door) *Excellent. Until next week then. Good night.* (Goes out through the door and you hear knocking but there is no one there)

Trivia, etc. "It was great fun," recalled Dana Wynter. "Louise Latham and I were falling down laughing all the time. She had a mad sense of humor, and we just laughed our way through it. Poor T.C. Jones was not allowed to go to the commissary for lunch, 'cause

480

they didn't want to tip the ending. And every time he wanted to go to the loo, he'd stand there outside the men's room in his nurse's outfit and his false eyelashes, counting the men going in, waiting for them to come out and then making a dash for it and hoping to God nobody would walk in on him [laughs]. He was so good in it, the crew didn't refer to him as a man, they would say, referring to him, 'Tell her to move over to the left a little bit,' 'Put a little more light on her'."

Certainly one of the best Hitchcock thrillers, and photographed magnificently by Stanley Cortez, this episode concerned two nurses caring for an invalid in an isolated Victorian home, as a homicidal killer who preys on nurses is loose in the neighborhood. Director Joseph Newman, using Cortez's crepuscular camera angles to the hilt and Herrmann's fashioning a properly eerie orchestration, makes this episode a must to watch. For Hitchcock fans, this episode marked the appearance of the house built and filmed for Alfred Hitchcock's *Psycho*, but using only the outside view, not the inside. The front yard was purposely doctored up with tress and a front yard fence, and with the camera zooming in on the house from the front and not the all-too-familiar up-the-hillside shot, (and not to mention a lot of thunder, lightning and rain), even observant viewers didn't notice the similarity. The opening shot of the house, features a camera zoom toward the very window in which Norman Bates's mother was viewed from. As the character Glendon Baker said in this episode, "The real estate agent assured me there'd never been a murder, a suicide or any kind of violence within these walls. Belonged to a family, a little old lady finally, who died peacefully in a clinic at the age of 95. It's too bad a hideous old house like this has no hideous history to go along with it." He could be no farther from the truth.

"By the way, whenever we finally completed a script on the Hitchcock show," Norman Lloyd recalled, "they were always sent up to him for his reading and approval. There was no formal thing of his calling back and saying, 'I approve' - we'd never hear from him except if he had an idea of a creative nature. For example, in 'An Unlocked Window,' Hitch called back and said, 'Make sure, at the end, when the nurse's hat is ripped off him, that you also rip his shirt so that we see there are no breasts, and we know it's a man.' That kind of idea he would call down."

T.C. Jones was in real life, a Hollywood female impersonator, who performed his job so well, that the surprise ending almost goes unsuspected. As Dana Wynter recalled: "One evening he says to me, 'The car's broken down. You wouldn't give me a lift home, would you?' I said sure. So we're driving along, it's evening, Santa Monica Boulevard, and I notice people at a stoplight kind of . . . looking at us. I thought nothing of it. We went on, and it happened again. At that point, I turned around and I looked at him in the seat next to mine, and there he was in a T-shirt, with his little furry chest, lipstick, the eyelashes still on . . . and a bald head [laughs]! And this was in 1964, when these things weren't quite as 'taken for granted' as they are nowadays! I can't tell you how fast I drove that man home once I realized!"

Louise Latham played Marnie's mother in Hitchcock's *Marnie*, released in the theaters a year before.

EPISODE #82   **"THE TRAP"**   Broadcast on February 22, 1965

Anne Francis as Peg Beale	Donnelly Rhodes as John Cochran
Robert Strauss as Ted Beale	Patricia Manning as Jenifer Arnold
Mary Scott as the party guest	Walter Mathews as Glen Arnold
Emma Tyson as Rosemary Arnold	Pat Renella as the boyfriend
Gil Stuart as the butler	Harold Ayer as the servant
Murray Alper as the cabbie	Sandra Daro as the watusi dancer
Michael Blodgett as the watusi dancer	

Teleplay written for *The Alfred Hitchcock Hour* by Lee Kalcheim, based on the short story of the same name by Stanley Abbott, originally published in the November 1964 issue of *Alfred Hitchcock's Mystery Magazine*. Subsequently reprinted in *Anti-Social Register*, ed. Alfred Hitchcock (Dell, 1965).

Produced by Gordon Hessler. Directed by John Brahm.

(time-capsule)   *We seem to have a compulsion these days, to bury time capsules. In order to give those living in the next century or so, some idea of what we are like, I have prepared one of my own. In it I have placed some rather large samples of dynamite, gunpowder and nitroglycerine. My time capsule is set to go off in the year 3000. It will show them what we are really like. This evening's drama is about a different type of time capsule. It is called "The Trap." And it's set to go off in just sixty seconds.*

Story: John Cochran arrives at the home of Ted Beale, an eccentric but wealthy toy manufacturer, where he is interviewed for a job as Beale's secretary. Beale's wife, Peg, expresses a dislike toward Cochran, and makes sure she shares her feelings with Ted. Her husband gives him the job anyway, and before long John works himself into the confidence of Beale - and becomes involved with Peg, who by now has changed her mind. With Peg's money and John's ambitious influence, the pair decide to do away with the practical-joke pulling toy expert. Sadly, John moves too slowly for Peg and she decides to take matters into her own hands, and kill Ted herself. But after having committed the "perfect crime," she finds her husband very much alive . . . and John the victim of another practical joke.

(mid-line)   *One item which might as well go into a time capsule is the station break. In fact, I would love to enclose this next one, but they won't allow me to get my hands on it. However, you may examine it. after which, our story will continue.*

John was given a most fitting burial. He was lowered into the grave still in the elevator. It also saved everyone from the disagreeable chore of taking him out. As for the Beales, they eventually confessed to their part in the crime and received their just punishment. Next week I shall return with another story. While you await that event, you may listen to this plea, from our dear sponsor.

Trivia, etc. This episode showed a similar ending, with a man stuck and dying in an elevator, as in the Roald Dahl story "The Way Up To Heaven" dramatized on *Suspicion* (see *Suspicion* chapter). "I came out to Los Angeles on a Fellowship with Universal Studios," recalled Lee Kalcheim. They were trying to encourage young writers so they assigned you to a show, as they were looking after you, and I was assigned the Hitchcock show, and Gordon Hessler told me that he had read some of my one-act plays. I was totally unaware that he had, but he did and when I received my assignment, he said, 'You can write this stuff.' That got my foot in the door, and I wrote 'The Trap.' This was the first television script I had ever written and I was very excited. I wasn't there for the filming, but it was about a guy who was a toy manufacturer. You see, when I wrote the script, I invented these toys. And bless them at Universal – I forget what the toys was – they said, 'Do you know where you can get one of these things?' So you know, I ended up at F.A.O. Schwarz finding out if they even had anything I had invented, till I stopped and thought, 'you know, this is Universal we're talking about here. They made *The Birds*. They can make anything they want out there. Why am I tracing about F.A.O. Schwarz for this?' [laughs] I don't know if I ever found it or what they did. It has been a long time. Donnelly Rhodes was a Canadian actor who played the role of the toy manufacturer and he was okay. But Anne Francis, oh . . . she was wonderful! After *Hitchcock*, I wrote for other TV series like *NYPD* with Jack Warden and then I wrote comedy and won an Emmy for *All in the Family*!"

EPISODE #83   **"WALLY THE BEARD"**   Broadcast on March 1, 1965
     Starring: Larry Blyden as Walter 'Wally' Mills

Kathie Browne as Noreen Kimberly	Berkeley Harris as Curly
Katherine Squire as Mrs. Adams	George Mitchell as Keefer
Lee Bergere as the detective	Dave Willock as the salesman

Elizabeth Harrower as Mrs. Jones   Leslie Perkins as Lucy Jones
John Indrisano as the bartender

Teleplay written for *The Alfred Hitchcock Hour* by Arthur A. Ross, based on the short story "The Chinless Wonder" by Stanley Abbott, originally published in the January 1965 issue of *Alfred Hitchcock's Mystery Magazine*. Later reprinted in *Let It All Bleed Out*, ed. Alfred Hitchcock (Dell, 1973).

Produced by Gordon Hessler. Directed by James H. Brown.

Music composed and conducted by Bernard Herrmann.

(king for a day)   *Good evening. Have you ever wondered what it would be like, to be the absolute ruler of a nation? I am finding out. I am the winner on a television show called "King for a day." I'm a trifle disturbed however. I just learned how they are able to provide for a different winner each day. This country, like the earth, has one revolution every twenty-four hours. It is reassuring to know, however, that the state funerals are among the best. As usual, this prologue has absolutely nothing to do with tonight's play, which tells the story of a little man who becomes involved in a very odd charade. One of my first acts as king, was to ban from the country forever, all television commercials. They were deported to the United States. Here is one of them.*

Story: Walter Mills' fiancée breaks off her engagement with him, claiming that he is just "too boring." Deciding she may be right, he decides to make a drastic change in his self-image: he buys a wig and goatee and becomes playboy Philip Marshall. Walter's silly plan does gain the interest of a woman named Noreen, unaware that he's actually a fake. Sadly, this doesn't go all too well with Noreen's boyfriend, Curly. Wally soon finds himself in hot water when Curly discovers his true identity, and threatens to tell Noreen unless Wally agrees to help him to hide some stolen jewels. Wally reluctantly agrees to help, but when he discovers that the police are hot on the trail of the jewels, he finally reveals the truth to Noreen, who claims she loves him anyway, beard or no beard. Deciding to cut the bag of jewels loose from their boat, where Wally hid them, the police arrive. It's only then that Wally discovers that the bag contains not jewels, but the dead body of Noreen's husband. Wally is arrested for murder and only then does he realize that Curly and Noreen have set him up.

(mid-line)   *We shall have the second half of our story, after this word from the court jester.*

Curly and Noreen may have flown now, but they paid later. Sharing the sack with Mr. Kimberly was some very incriminating evidence and the pair was eventually brought to justice. By the way, I'll be staying on here for a while. We declared our independence from the producer of "King for a Day." He's now looking for another kingdom. We have already signaled out the target for our next revolution. We are granting him this next minute to plead his case.

Trivia, etc. Formerly an Assistant Director for episodes of *Alfred Hitchcock Presents* and *The Alfred Hitchcock Hour*, James H. Brown got his first and only opportunity to direct a Hitchcock production. This was also the only episode Arthur Ross was credited with a middle initial.

EPISODE #84   **"DEATH SCENE"**   Broadcast on March 8, 1965
Starring: Vera Miles as Nicky Revere / Monica Parrish
John Carradine as Gavin Revere   James Farentino as Leo Manfred
Buck Taylor as the dancer   Leonard Yorr as Bill Wagner
Virginia Aldridge as Susan 'Susu' Revere Captain Horace Brown as Harry
Nick Borgani as Sam Gread   Vince Williams as our hero

**Alfred Hitchcock describes the numerous ways to eliminate your opponent.
(Photo courtesy of Photofest.)**

Teleplay written for *The Alfred Hitchcock Hour* by James Bridges, based on Helen Nielsen's short story of the same name, originally published in the May 1963 issue of *Ellery Queen's Mystery Magazine*. Subsequently reprinted in *Ellery Queen's Double Dozen*, ed. Ellery Queen (Random House, 1964), and in *Hitchcock in Prime Time*, ed. Francis M. Nevins and Martin H. Grenberg (Avon, 1985).

Produced by Herbert Coleman. Directed by Harvey Hart.

Music composed and conducted by Bernard Herrmann.

(ticking clock in a bag)   *Good evening.   Someone seems to have left this interesting object at my door-step.   I don't believe it's a baby.   At least I've never before heard a baby ticking quite so loudly.* (takes clock from bag) *What a unique gift.   A clock that is powered by dynamite.   Tempus fugit, I wager it does.   I see the alarm is set to go off in a moment or two so I shall speak quickly.   I wouldn't want to be interrupted by any unseemly ringing.   Tonight we have a drama concerning some people who are in the motion picture business.   And speaking of business, we come to this item.*

Story: When an auto mechanic named Leo Manfred fixes a limousine owned by Gavin Revere, a famed but over-the-hill Hollywood director, he is invited to join the family for a couple days. It is here that Leo meets Nicky, Gavin's beautiful daughter, and the two youths fall in love. But when Gavin learns about their marriage plans, he fears Leo wanting only her money, and nothing more. To convince the director of his true intentions, Leo takes out a life-insurance policy for fifty thousand dollars, with the payoff going to Nicky. Gavin agrees and the marriage plans continue. Shortly before the wedding, however, Leo makes the fatal mistake of insulting one of Gavin's movies, entitled *Death Scene*, and the old man changes his mind. Not willing to give up Nicky over a quarrel, Leo takes the old man to a cliff, intending to push him off. Instead, a stranger who happens by, pushes Leo over the ledge instead. With the mechanic now dead, Nicky removes her make-up, turning out to be Gavin's real wife who is now $50,000 wealthier.

(mid-line) *That concludes the first half of our story. My new clock seems to have stopped. I suppose I shall have to buy fresh dynamite. Luckily our story is much more easily activated. It will resume after the following message from your friendly neighborhood station.*

On seeing that ending it occurs to me that we may inadvertently have given you the wrong impression. You see, Monica and her husband were caught and paid for their crime. I like to keep the records straight. As for my clock, I haven't been able to find a drug store that carries dynamite sticks. Oh, they had some but as you would expect, not the right size. (shakes clock, starts ticking) *Ah, there we are. And now we shall hear from our sponsor.* (bomb goes off)

Trivia, etc. Nick Borgani had an uncredited role in Alfred Hitchcock's *Rear Window* (1954). Helen Nielsen, whose story was adapted for this production, recalled: " 'Death Scene' was presented in the last season of the Hitchcock series. In order to go out with flying colors, top talent went into the production: a flawless cast, an ingenious adaptation, and an added twist-on-my-twist ending. I loved it!"

EPISODE #85 "THE PHOTOGRAPHER AND THE UNDERTAKER"
Broadcast March 15, 1965

Starring: Jack Cassidy as Arthur Mannix	Harry Townes as Hiram Price
Alfred Ryder as Mr. Rudolph	Jocelyn Lane as Sylvia

Co-starring: Philip Bourneuf as Mr. Sylvester
Jack Bernardi as the delicatessen man

Joan Swift as Miss Whiting, the secretary   Richard Jury as Willis
Clegg Hoyt as the man

Teleplay written for *The Alfred Hitchcock Hour* by Alfred Hayes, based on the short story of the same name by James Holding, originally published in the November 1962 issue of *Ellery Queen's Mystery Magazine*.

Produced by Gordon Hessler. Directed by Alex March.

(American football, gun) *Good evening. I have been asked to explain American football. Actually, in various forms, the game of football is played all over the world. In some countries such a game may be called, a soccer match. In others, a revolution. However, there are several differences between a football game and a revolution. For one thing, a football game usually lasts longer and the participants wear uniforms. Also, there are usually more casualties in a football game. The object of the game is to move this ball* (holds up the ball) *past the other team's goal-line. This counts as six points. No points are given for lacerations, contusions or abrasions, but then no points are deducted either. Kicking is very important in football. In fact, some of the more enthusiastic players even kick the ball occasionally. I trust that I have made everything perfectly clear. This evening's tale is not about football, it concerns another sport . . . murder. I might even add the word incorporated. You see, our hero is an organization man. But first, our sponsor has just sixty seconds left to play. Let's see if he can score.*

Story: Arthur Mannix is a man who loves his work. As a hit man willing to kill anyone, anywhere, for the right price, Arthur possesses the best of intentions. After murdering each of his victims, he always takes a photo of the deceased, evidence he provides to his employer to show that the job has been finished. After he polishes off his latest job, Arthur is told he will receive double his usual fee if he will kill a man named Hiram Price. The truth be known, Arthur has been recently getting too greedy and asking too many questions, as has Hiram, who turns out to be another assassin working for the same employer. Hiram has been given the assignment of eliminating Arthur, and now it is a matter of "survival of the fittest."

(mid-line) *This is the end of the first half. Please change sides. Before we begin the second half, your local couch wishes to give you a prep talk.*

Who says this program doesn't have a heart? Arthur and Sylvia lived happily ever after. She in San Diego and he in San Quentin. One of California's finest prisons. There his room-mate turned out to be Mr. Rudolph. It was rather sad to see Arthur's career cut short. By the time he was apprehended, he was only one heartbeat away from a vice-presidency. A further note about football. A gun shot usually signals the end of the game, which is where we are now. (bang) *Oh dear, we shall have to get a new referee next time. Good night.*

EPISODE #86 **"THOU STILL UNRAVISHED BRIDE"** Broadcast on March 22, 1965
Starring: Ron Randell as Tommy Bonn	David Carradine as Clarke
Sally Kellerman as Sally Benner	Co-starring: Michael Pate as Stephen Leslie
Kent Smith as Mr. Benner	Edith Atwater as Mrs. Benner
Virginia Gregg as Mrs. Setlin	Howard Caine as Mr. Setlin
Ben Wright as Mr. Sutherland	Richard Lupino as Guerny, Jr.
Betty Harford as the woman	Victor Rogers as Bobbie
George Pelling as the sergeant	Ted Bessell as Elliot Setlin
Brendan Dillon as the bartender	Doris Lloyd as the mother
Jana Lesley as Myrna	and Alan Napier as Guerny, Sr.

Teleplay written for *The Alfred Hitchcock Hour* by Morton Fine and David Friedkin, based on the short story of the same name by Avram Davidson, originally published in the October 1958 issue of *Ellery Queen's Mystery Magazine.* Subsequently reprinted in *Lost Ladies*, ed. Ellery Queen and Eleanor Sullivan (Davis Publications, 1983).

Produced by Morton Fine and David Friedkin. Directed by David Friedkin.

(with a large suggestion box) *The suggestion box is the mark of the enlightened company. We have had one for years. We offer prices to our workers for the best suggestions, but so far have been unable to make any awards since the suggestions are usually unsigned. We used to have a woman do this work, but some of the suggestions were improper. This first suggestion is directed at me.* (picks up a noose/rope) *I'm touched but I'll have to return it. I never accept gifts from employees. And now this evening's drama. It is about a disappearance, sudden, startling and frightening. It follows this suggestion, from our sponsor.*

Story: London. During a transatlantic cruise, a pretty American girl named Sally Benner falls head over heals for a British police officer named Tommy Bonn. Hours before the wedding, Sally has second thoughts about the commitment, and decides to go for a walk in the England fog to clear her head. Because of the recent murders detailed in the papers, and the possibility that a madman roams the streets at night, Tommy and his friend Stephen, start a manhunt. Unfortunately, they capture a man named Clarke who at first is suspect – till the stranger breaks down and confesses. He did kill a woman, earlier in the evening, fitting Sally's description, and dumping her body in the Thames. Tommy leaves to pay the Benner family a visit, intending to break the bad news to them, only to discover Sally is alive and well. She's cleared her head and without the use of cold feet, confesses that she's ready to marry Tommy now. As for the body the murderous Clarke stashed, it's promptly found and dragged on shore, with a resemblance to Sally, just as Clarke described. Thankfully, the body is not Sally.

I discovered that the suggestion box hadn't been opened for years and years. I wish we had taken the trouble for some of the oldest ones in the bottom of the box are quite good. This one for example: "Why not put wheels on a gasoline engine on the sled and call it a truck?" What is all the more remarkable is that when this suggestion was made, the wheel hadn't been invented yet. But he provides a drawing. Unfortunately we can not reward this man, he is no longer with us. I'm afraid this man isn't either: "Help, I am being held prisoner in the secretarial pool." Poor fellow, it's too late now. We must remember to look at these sooner. Next week we shall return with another story and of course, some commercials.

Trivia, etc. Edith Atwater would later play the role of Mrs. Clay in Hitchcock's final motion picture, *Family Plot* (1976).

EPISODE #87 **"COMPLETELY FOOLPROOF"** Broadcast on March 29, 1965
Starring: J. D. Cannon as Joe Brisson
Special Guest Star: Patricia Barry as Lisa Brisson
Co-starring: Geoffrey Horne as Bobby Davenport
Myron Healey as Foyle   Joyce Meadows as Anna
Lester Matthews as Walter Dunham   Robert P. Lieb as Baines
Jo de Winter as Betty Lawrence   Janet MacLachlan as the secretary
Teleplay written for *The Alfred Hitchcock Hour* by Anthony Terpiloff, based on the short story of the same name by Andrew Benedict, originally published in the March 1958 issue of *Alfred Hitchcock's Mystery Magazine*.
Produced by Herbert Coleman. Directed by Alf Kjellin.
(submarine periscope)   *Good evening.* (periscope up) *This is the latest in private yachts. I bought it in a war suppler store. It has many advantages over the normal yacht. I find that few of my friends free load and then of course the fact that my little craft came with torpedoes adds zest to yacht racing. I am not merely the first to cross the finish line, I am frequently the only one. Tonight's story is about the battle of the sexes. Actually in the case of this couple, open warfare would be a better phrase . . .* (periscope down) *I believe I'm directly on target. Suppose you take a look.*

Story: Joe Brisson, a crooked real estate developer known for holding back information for a price, finds he has little choice in the matter when his wife decides she wants a divorce.   As unscrupulous as she is, Lisa explains that she has plenty of documentation of everything he owns, and she intends to claim a three-quarter share of his holdings during the settlement.   Learning who Lisa's boyfriend is, Joe talks to Bobby, convincing him that money is sometimes better than the girl. Bobby, you see, has a huge debt resting on his shoulders and Joe is willing to overlook his past credentials, if Lisa is put out of the way. Bobby agrees and together, the two men plan the details. During a trip to Europe, via boat, Joe explains how he'll phone his wife at a specified time, whereas Bobby will take advantage of the distraction and bump off Mrs. Brisson. The plan goes off without a hitch and just as Joe hangs up the phone, a stranger enters the room and shoots the developer. It seems Lisa and Joe had more in common than they thought, for she too had a similar plan.

(mid-line; entire screen is upside down) *Most preculiar. I see nothing but mud. Perhaps that's because we're approaching a station break. Following this stop, we shall proceed with the second half of our journey.*

The sea of matrimony is not without its storms. Of course, the hired killers received their just deserts. Just as their victims had . . . (puts up an umbrella) *I realize that opening an umbrella indoors is considered bad luck, but I think this will be just the opposite. Some leaks have appeared. However, the umbrella should put a halt to that. Next week we shall return with another story. A few of the scenes have arrived a week ahead of time, so we might as well show them to you after this next commercial.*

Trivia, etc. For some odd reason, this episode lists the author of the short story as Andrew Benedict, which was one of Robert Arthur's several pseudonyms. The original story was printed in *The Mysterious Traveler* under the byline "Robert Arthur." This same name credit was done in the episode "Change of Address."

The master learns a few new tricks . . . Hitchcock is being locked into a magician's trunk, during the final moments of *The Alfred Hitchcock Hour*. This is an excellent example of how women appeared on stage with Alfred Hitchcock, during his hostings, but remained unbilled. The actress is unknown.

EPISODE #88   **"POWER OF ATTORNEY"**   Broadcast on April 5, 1965
Starring: Richard Johnson as James Jarvis   Geraldine Fitzgerald as Agatha
Special Guest Star: Fay Bainter as Mary Cawfield
Josie Lloyd as Eileen Caroll   Mary Scott Hardwicke as Sarah Norton
Jonathan Hole as the hotel clerk   Mark Sturges as Roger Reeves
George Sims as the policeman   Al Ruban as the clerk
Anthony Jochim as Thomas Barton

Teleplay written for *The Alfred Hitchcock Hour* by James Bridges, based on short story "Letter of the Law" by Selwyn Jepson, originally published in *The Evening Standard* (a newspaper) sometime in the early 1950s.   Subsequently reprinted in *The Evening Standard Detective Book, Second Series* (Gollancz, 1951) and the July 1952 issue of *Ellery Queen's Mystery Magazine.* *

Produced by Herbert Coleman.   Directed by Harvey Hart.

(harp and arrows) *Please do not be alarmed. This is not a remote broadcast. I am still very much with you. Actually, this is from my collection of ancient weapons. In the days of the bow and arrow, this could strike with the force of a machine gun. Furthermore, instead of the bothersome rattle of explosions, a burst of shots from this instrument was accompanied by sweet music. A feature which was undoubtedly appreciated by the victims. Actually you will find quite a number of these about today. Most of them are in our larger symphony orchestras. They help keep the conductors from becoming obstreperous. With that thought in my mind, I can't help to turn to our sponsor. That dear person would like to spend the next minute talking about himself. This will be followed by "Power of Attorney." A drama about a woman and her devoted companion, and about a man who helped her with her investments. And so in just one lamentable minute, "Power of Attorney."*

Story: Con artist James Jarvis works his way into the affections of a wealthy lady, Mary Cawfield, in order to gain control of her finances. Posing as an investment expert, James promises to invest her fortune, thus making her earnings grow within a relatively short period of time. Her live-in companion, Agatha, wants nothing to do with James, but Mary gives him a power of attorney to invest her fortune. Naturally, Jarvis pockets the money for himself and claims that the investment fails and Mary loses everything. Devastated by the news, Mary commits suicide, and Agatha finds her companion's body, stone cold dead. Knowing all too well what Jarvis was planning, Agatha puts a plan in motion to obtain revenge. Inviting him over to the house, she tricks him into placing his fingerprints on the murder weapon, and promptly locks him in the same room with the corpse. Phoning the police, Agatha watches as gunfire exchanges between the criminal and the law, and Jarvis is killed during the action.

(mid-line) *Into each life, some rain must fall. And in the center of every hour of television, we must have a station break. Afterwhich, we shall continue the story of Mary, Agatha, and their friend, Mr. Jarvis.*

Well, that's the way the body bounces. However, I feel compelled to say that the manor which Mary chose to leave this veil of tears, is not the one to solve one's problems. In short, we do not recommend suicide as a way of life. That is all the story we have for tonight. Some miscellaneous items follow. I've found a new use for my harp. If you like sliced homemade bread, just push the loafs through the harp before baking.

* This episode, "Power of Attorney," was based on a short story by Selwyn Jepson. Hitchcock's *Stage Fright* (1950) was based on two stories, both by Selwyn Jepson. They were called "Man Running" and "Outrun the Constable."

EPISODE #89 **"THE WORLD'S OLDEST MOTIVE"** Broadcast on April 12, 1965
Starring: Henry Jones as Alex Morrow   Linda Lawson as Fiona
Guest Star: Robert Loggia as Richard Schustak
Co-starring: Kathleen Freeman as Angela Morrow
Dee J. Thompson as Miss Rice   Joseph Mell as Jamieson
Susan French as the cleaning woman
Kai Hernandez as the hatcheck girl   Shawn Michaels as the drinker
Syl Lamont as the waiter   Tom Stears as the taxi driver
Teleplay written for *The Alfred Hitchcock Hour* by Lewis Davidson, based on the short story of the same name by Larry M. Harris, originally published in the December 1959 issue of *Alfred Hitchcock's Mystery Magazine*. Subsequently reprinted in *Noose Report*, ed. Alfred Hitchcock (Dell, 1966).
Produced by Gordon Hessler. Directed by Harry Morgan.
(ape at a typewriter) *Good evening. This is not one of our regular writers. We think it best if we keep them out of sight. This is one of our apprentices. You have of course heard the theory,* (close-up) *that if a room full of monkeys were allowed to type for a million years, they would eventually reproduce all the classics in the British Museum. This is not so. We have tried it and while the stories they wrote were quite good, and many of them publishable, they are not classics, yet.* (zoom-out) *This gentleman is one of our trainees. He types nothing but gibberish. But he is not to be faulted for this. His ideas are quite good and he has a flair for dialogue,* (close-up) *he just can't type. However he has made some progress. For example, he now knows that it is naughty to eat the paper. Before tonight's story, we would like to present a sample of our young student's work. Notice the skill with which he has captured the elusive banality of the television commercial.*

Story: Alex Morrow, attorney at law, is in love with a younger woman named Fiona, a beautiful model that makes any man's head swim. Fiona is in love with Alex, but the man cannot figure out a way to get rid of his current ball and chain. If he tries to divorce his wife, she will obtain his pride and joy, the stamp collection, of which Alex cannot think about parting with. So Alex hires a hit man named Richard Schustak to murder her, and the hit man works out a plan to kill her at home and make it look like an accident. All Alex needs to do is go out and establish an alibi at the set date and time. Near the last minute, Alex has second thoughts and tries to call the whole thing off. Richard agrees - but only if Alex will pay more money. Preventing a plan already set in motion is, as Richard explains, more complicated to prevent than to establish. Alex agrees to pay the fee, and the hit man promptly leaves town with his accomplice, Fiona, having fleeced another unhappily married husband. A plan that seems to work from state to state.

(mid-line; desk is empty with "Out to Lunch" sign) *While our talented young friend is out of the room, suppose we take a break, too. A station break. The second half of our program, will be shown when we return.*

My friend simply could not master the typewriter so we've made him the producer. Actually there wasn't much we could do about it. His uncle owns the studio. We will show you scenes from next week's story after the following commercial.

EPISODE #90 **"THE MONKEY'S PAW - A RETELLING"** Broadcast April 19, 1965
Starring: Leif Erickson as Paul White   Guest Star: Jane Wyatt as Anna White
Special Guest Star: Collin Wilcox as Celina
Co-starring: Lee Majors as Howard White
Janet MacLachlan as Gayle   Stuart Margolin as Robin Boyd
Zolya Talma as the gypsy woman   Dick Caruso as the gypsy boy

Gil Stuart as the British Man
Peter Howard as Curtis Welks
Michelle Marley as Joan Fanu
Pat Renella as Frank Corseli

Marusia Toumanoff as Natasha Gurlieff
Carmen Phillips as Mary Smith
Vincent Chase as Hume Ray

Teleplay written for *The Alfred Hitchcock Hour* by Morton Fine, David Friedkin and Anthony Terpiloff, based on the short story "The Monkey's Paw" by W.W. Jacobs, originally published in the September 1902 issue of *Harper's*, and collected in *The Lady of the Barge* (Harper, 1902; Dodd Mead, 1902).

Produced by Norman Lloyd. Directed by Robert Stevens.

(snake charmer) *Good evening. I'm sorry, I was under the impression this was to be a smoker. This jar was built in this shape especially for me. The jars come in one other shape. It is 76 inches, 38 inches and 75 inches. When he uses that jar he doesn't have to use his flute. He just whistles at it. This evening's story does not take place in India but it has its beginnings there. Before our friend, the snake charmer, would allow me to take part in this charade, he insisted that my venom be removed. Oh, I continue to strike out at the commercials, but my insults are no longer lethal . . . Here comes a commercial now. Boring, repetitive, noisy, tedious, soporific. You see, I'm completely harmless. Juvenile, dull, ridiculous . . .*

Story: Paul White and his wife Anna discover the hard way, the true meaning of "be careful what you wish for, you might just get it." When they travel to the Bahamas for a vacation, and to watch their only son race in a local Grand Prix, Paul keeps their financial problems a secret. Shortly before the race, Paul visits a gypsy woman out of desperation, in hopes that she might offer a solution to their financial crisis. She gives him a monkey's paw with magical properties: according to legend, it will bring the owner three wishes, but no more. And surprisingly it does when Paul wishes for a lot of money. The cash comes in the form of an insurance policy payoff when his son dies in a crash. Later, Anna suggests that they use the second wish to bring the long-buried Howard back to life. With the corpse outside wanting in, Paul realizes what will soon arrive at their home, and to his horror, decides it better to send the boy back to his grave. The couple agree and use their third and final wish to solve their problem.

That concludes the fictional portion of tonight's entertainment. Next week we shall return with another story. Our original plan called for me to make my exit by scrambling up this rope . . . and disappearing. The rope, however, seems to have other ideas. (reaches for the rope) *I don't intend to remain here and be insulted. I shall disappear in the conventional way. By the way, during this program our sponsor was granted three wishes, here is the last of them.*

Trivia, etc. The classic short story, from which this episode was *very* loosely based, described the ordeals set forth by two loving parents who wanted the same thing. Money and happiness. The W.W. Jacobs story was dramatized on television more faithfully in the past, but with the changing times, come a variation on an old theme, and with the help of Anthony Terpiloff, the Morton Fine/David Friedkin script received a revision, more modernized than a period piece. In the role of young Howard was Lee Majors, making his television debut – later best known for his role of Colonel Steve Austin on television's *The Six Million Dollar Man*. "Oh, I loved doing that, that was really fun," recalled Jane Wyatt. "And my son in that was Lee Majors – he had never been before the camera at all, and was he nervous! He was always holding his little Bible [laughs]!"

EPISODE #91 **"THE SECOND WIFE"** Broadcast on April 26, 1965

Starring: June Lockhart as Martha Hunter	John Anderson as Luke Smith
Alice Backes as Helen Fiske	Eve McVeagh as Sylvia Boggs
Jim Boles as Reverend Gilfoyle	Gertrude Flynn as Peggy Gilfoyle
David Fresco as Sam Ogle	Vincent Chase as the pawnbroker

Teleplay written for *The Alfred Hitchcock Hour* by Robert Bloch. based on the short story "The Lonely Heart" by Richard Deming, originally published in the December 1964 issue of *Alfred Hitchcock's Mystery Magazine*.

Produced by Herbert Coleman. Directed by Joseph Newman.

(family of robots)   *Good evening. The characters in television programs are becoming more and more unreal. We have robots, monsters, witches, Martians. In some cases, whole families are unreal. In one, for example, the leading lady is a witch and her husband is an advertising man. In a series which we are planning we have taken the next logical step. We have eliminated the actors and are using actual robots for all the parts. Other workers have been liberated by the machine age, why not the actor? Let him enjoy the benefits of automation, the relief from heavy labor, the added leisure time, the unemployment. Actually, only a few actors have objected and they, only on the grounds of this is type-casting. There are many advantages. For one thing, they never forget their lines. Providing, they are properly programmed. For example, here are a few lines from one of Hamlet's soliloquies:* (just tones) *Being method actors they are inclined to mumble a bit. Our play this evening will be acted by flesh and blood actors and follows in just one, long, minute.*

Story: A librarian named Martha Hunter decides to become a mail-order bride and soon arrives in a small northern town where she meets her husband-to-be, Luke Smith. Shortly after the wedding, she is a little dismayed to find there is no furnace, only a fireplace in their new house. With the weather so cold she asks her new husband to have a furnace put in, but he seems reluctant to do so because it would cost too much money. Not long after their marriage, Martha learns that she is not Luke's first mail-order bride. It seems he had married once before to a woman who died of poisoning just after she and Luke left on a vacation to visit his relatives. Martha becomes more and more suspicious as day after day she hears him digging in the basement at night. When she questions his motives, he stubbornly refuses to allow her in to see what he is doing. One day, Luke suddenly announces that he wants to take some time off to visit his relatives, but before they leave he asks her to visit the basement. Knowing full well what he plans to do, Martha pulls out a gun and shoots him dead in self-defense. In a fit of hysteria, Martha stumbles down the cellar steps in hopes of finding the body of his former wife, only to discover that he just installed a furnace – with a note on it: "Merry Christmas to my dear wife."

(mid-line) *The second half of our story will be visible in a moment. I don't like the way they're looking at me.*

(just tones from the robot with subtitles) "The Old Man died quickly. Martha will not get out. Ninety years became her sentence. How surprised she got."

Alternate narrative:

(just tones from the robot with subtitles, in prose) "The hubby's time was cut off short. Martha was the lucky sort. She was sentenced ninety years, by a jury of her peers."

EPISODE #92 **"NIGHT FEVER"** Broadcast on May 3, 1965

Starring: Colleen Dewhurst as Ellen Hatch	Tom Simcox as Jerry Walsh
Co-starring: Joe De Santis as Jake Martinez	Don Stewart as Gabe Greely
Don Marshall as Joe Chandler	Richard Bull as Dr. Michaels
Rayford Barnes as George Clark	Laurie Mitchell as Pinky

Carol Brewster as Mabel Cramm   and Peggy Lipton as Mary Winters

Teleplay written for *The Alfred Hitchcock Hour* by Gilbert Ralston, based on the short story "Night Work" by Clark Howard, originally publishes in the November 1962 issue of *Alfred Hitchcock's Mystery Magazine*.

Produced and directed by Herbert Coleman.

(pile of junk and camera)   *We have here all that remains of a television series. It succumbed not to the indifference of the viewers, but to a passion for reality. Everyone thought the idea would make a very amusing series. A family of cannibals moves in to the middle of a typical suburban community. The possibilities were endless. The clash of cultures would produce the laughter and underlining it all would be a subtle social criticism. Actually the cannibals weren't difficult as actors. They weren't temperamental, just hungry. And considering the food at the commissary, I'm not sure I blame them.*

Story: Jerry Walsh and a friend of his killed a cop in a shoot-out, making them wanted criminals. Although his partner got away, Jerry wasn't so lucky, having been shot by the officer's gun. At the city hospital, doctors remove the bullet and then place him into a quiet room to rest. When two detectives try to get Jerry to talk, a nurse by the name of Ellen Hatch objects to their torture and forces them to leave him alone. The detectives want to move him, but they can't because of his condition. The detectives finally leave, and the nurse shows a little pity for the murderer. Over a couple days, Jerry tries smooth talking the nurse into letting him go, but she won't break hospital rules. Seeing how she seems strangely kind to him, Jerry woos her into helping him to escape. With Ellen's assistance, Jerry gets free and makes for her home, all according to her instructions. But Walsh finds that his place of sanctuary holds a far worse fate than prison, when the nurse returns home with murderous vengeance on her mind. It seems she was married to the cop he shot, and she has now told the police where to pick him up . . .

(mid-line) *We shall resume our story in just a few moments. In order to prevent you from becoming bored, even for so short a time, we have asked your local announcer to entertain you.*

Next week I shall return with another story. Oh by the way, we just couldn't stand to see such a good comedy idea abandoned, so we have re-activated our series about the cannibal family. We're hoping to have better luck this time. (Sign: "Do not feed the actors.")

EPISODE #93 **"OFF SEASON"** Broadcast on May 10, 1965

Starring: John Gavin as Johnny Kendall
Co-starring: Richard Jaeckel as Milt Woodman

Tom Drake as Sheriff Dade	Indus Arthur as Sandy Evans
Dody Heath as Irma Dade	Frederick P. Draper as Dr. Hornbeck
Duncan McLeod as Bill, the bartender	Jimmy Joyce as Sergeant Racin
Harry Hines as the thief	Jim Drum as Al
and William O'Connell as Art Summers	

Teleplay written for *The Alfred Hitchcock Hour* by Robert Bloch, based on Edward D. Hoch's short story "Winter Run," originally published in the January 1965 issue of *Alfred Hitchcock's Mystery Magazine*. Subsequently collected in *The Night My Friend* (Ohio University Press, 1992).

Produced by Gordon Hessler. Directed by William Friedkin.

(with an axe in front of an Indian tent) *Good evening. I have made a rather interesting discovery. An Indian village in a remarkable state of preservation. Judging from the items I've found around here, this was the barber shop. I imagine it was originally part of a large shopping center which stood on this very spot. Actually this is a peace pipe. It was by far the most popular style of pipe because it was so handy in case the peace conference didn't work out. Tonight we shall show you a series of commercial messages and if you watch closely, a play.*

Story: After shooting an unarmed bum, Johnny Kendall is asked to resign from the police force, due to an excessive display of anger, and an itchy trigger finger. Deciding to leave town for a while, his girlfriend Sandy tags along faithfully, taking a waitress job. Johnny is assigned as a deputy watching over vacant summer vacation homes. People leave expensive possessions that need to be guarded, the sheriff explains, and this being a peaceful community, likes to keep it that way. Just when all appears okay, Johnny meets up with Milt Woodman, the former deputy, who was apparently fired for fooling around with a girl in one of the vacant homes. Milt express a dislike toward Johnny, and in retaliation, starts showing an interest in Sandy. Walking the beat one evening, Johnny finds a window ajar in one of the houses, and investigating, discovers evidence that Milt is carrying on again – this time with Sandy. The next evening, Johnny has his gun on him, and sneaking inside the vacant house, finds the two lovers humping away. Milt pulls out a gun in self-defense, and during the struggle, Johnny shoots Milt – and the woman, who turns out not to be Sandy at all. The body now lying on the floor is the sheriff's wife!

John Gavin is assigned as a deputy watching over vacant summer vacation homes in "Off Season," the final episode of the series.
(Photo courtesy of Photofest.)

(mid-line) *This second half of our story will be on view after we hear from your local station. But first I have some exciting news. I have just been informed that I have been selected for an honor which has been awarded only once before in our history. The previous winner was General George Custer.*

While enthusiasm for one's job is always to be admired, the sheriff thought that Johnny had outdone himself. He was given a life sentence for his unseemly conduct. I wish to welcome two new stations, who are receiving the program for the first time tonight. Fort Overland and Fort Maxwell. I hope the picture is coming through well. We had to send it by Pony Express. Next week we shall return with another story. Until then, good night.

Trivia, etc. " 'Winter Run,' televised under the title 'Off Season,' was the final new show to be done on *The Alfred Hitchcock Hour* before the series ended its run," recalled Edward D. Hoch. "It was the first of my stories ever to be adapted for television. I was so pleased by the prospect that I viewed it quite uncritically, not even minding a slight change in the story's final scene. The script, after all, was by Robert Bloch, one of the top writers in the business. I remember meeting Bloch at a party in New York a year or two later, however, and he told me his original script had been quite faithful to my story. He blamed the director for some last-minute changes in it. Whatever the circumstances, I was pleased by the final result."

The hotel lodge where Johnny and Sandy reside is the same Bates Motel set that was constructed and filmed in *Psycho*. Just like the Bates Mansion used in "The Schwartz-Metterklume Method" and "An Unlocked Window," employing the same sets was really a production convenience, not an homage to the movie.

SUMMER RERUNS

All summer reruns were from season three of *The Alfred Hitchcock Hour*. On August 2, 1965, *The Alfred Hitchcock Hour* was not broadcast. Instead, "Head for the Hills," a special NBC-TV presentation about a sun-filled tour of the vast vacation complex known as the catskills, was broadcast. Actor/comedian Dick Shaw narrated the hour-long special.

May 17, 1965 "See the Monkey Dance"
May 24, 1965 "Change of Address"
May 31, 1965
    "Where the Woodbine Twineth"
June 7, 1965 "Water's Edge"
June 14, 1965 "Crimson Witness"
June 21, 1965 "An Unlocked Window"
June 28, 1965 "Return of Verge Likens"
July 5, 1965 "Final Performance"
July 12, 1965 "Wally the Beard"

July 19, 1965 "Lonely Place"
July 26, 1965 "Thanatos Palace Hotel"
August 9, 1965
    "The Life Work of Juan Diaz"
August 16, 1965
    "The Photographer and the Undertaker"
August 23, 1965 "Power of Attorney"
August 30, 1965 "Night Fever"
September 6, 1965 "The Second Wife"

THE REVIVAL: HITCHCOCK IN THE EIGHTIES

In May of 1985, NBC-TV presented a feature-length movie, entitled appropriately enough, *Alfred Hitchcock Presents*. During the opening scene, which featured a camera panning the ever-familiar Hitchcock silhouette, the great director John Huston supplied the opening narration:

"Between the years of 1955 and 1965, the great motion picture director Alfred Hitchcock, presented more than three hundred and fifty television dramas to the American public. What follows are four, entirely new, contemporized renderings, of stories selected from that body of work. We are proud to again bring you ... Alfred Hitchcock Presents."

The acknowledged master of murder, mystery, and mayhem, was about to get a new turn in his career, hosting a variation on an old theme, five years after trade papers reported of his death. Produced through MCA/Universal, the two-hour movie was actually a compilation of four stories – all filmed previously on both *Alfred Hitchcock Presents* and *The Alfred Hitchcock Hour*.

A remake version of the original *Alfred Hitchcock Presents* series seemed inevitable, with TV networks' constant borrowing of older anthologies. *Twilight Zone: The Movie* was shown in theaters two years earlier, and received large box-office receipts. So with the popularity of Alfred Hitchcock, it was only a matter of time. In fact, when NBC later picked up the series for a regular run in September of 1985, CBS began broadcasting a revised version of *The Twilight Zone* the same month.

A lot of care went into the productions, and according to director Joel Oliansky, who directed the first of the four segments, "What Hitchcock did with those shows you couldn't do any better ... or you could do them with something different. We couldn't do any better than the Hitchcock shows with the money they had to spend and the resources in which you were allowed to do on television. Now things had opened up by the time we shot this so we had to expand rather than reproduce it. Anything we couldn't do then we were able to do now."

For the movie, story properties were tossed around, and the producers, Stephen Cragg and Alan Barnette, chose four they felt would best fit the thematic style. Then they hired four directors, each to film a different segment. "Somebody recommended me to one of the producers," recalled Oliansky, "a writer named William Sakheim. I worked with him on many projects including a film I wrote and directed called *The Competition* (1980)." Each director chose a story, the actors were hired, and the rest fell into place. NBC-TV agreed to broadcast the movie, as a Sunday night feature, under the stipulation that the movie be a proposed pilot. If the movie received enough attention and critical acclaim, and if the network saw potential, a regular half-hour series for a weekly time-slot would be commissioned.

For a film director whose roots began during the silent era, a time when Technicolor had not yet been developed, Alfred Hitchcock marked a return in style. It was obvious to the producers and viewers alike that without Hitchcock hosting the series, the show's format (not to mention the program's title) would have to be changed. The solution was obvious. Alfred Hitchcock would have to remain as host. By early 1985, news had spread through Hollywood, the film capitol of the world, about adding a splash of color to "those old pictures." Black and white movies were being colorized and, an example of a growing trend by syndicators, to add spice to their programming by colorizing the past. In March of 1985, an agreement was made between MGM and Color Systems Technology for the latter company to add color to 100 of the film studio's 700 black and white films. The order was made chiefly at the request of the studio's owner, Ted Turner.

There was another company, the Toronto-based "Colorization," 50%-owned by Hal Roach Studios, who also entered the business in 1985 with the transition of *Topper* (1937), the first black and white movie ever to be colorized. It was aired on pay cable networks, as well as some airlines. They were later responsible for colorizing a number of Laurel and Hardy movies and *Night of the Living Dead* (1968).

But it was Color Systems Technology (known as CST) who was responsible for Alfred Hitchcock's witty introductions for the series. CST was the same company that colorized sixteen Shirley Temple films for 20th Century Fox, and made the initial 100-film deal with MGM/Turner to apply their trade to *Casablanca* (1942), *Yankee Doodle Dandy* (1942), *Mutiny on the Bounty* (1935), *Camille* (1937) and many others.

According to both Colorization and CST, the cost of colorizing one minute of film began at $2,000. Some deals, however – and it was not said about the Hitchcock intros – were constructed for participation in gross or net revenues by the colorization studio, which altered the pricing scheme. The method of changing

Tippi Hedren and Ned Beatty pose for photographers.
(Photo by Ronald V. Borst / Hollywood Movie Posters.)

black and white into color was the result of a video process, involving a series of large computer systems, rather than a film process using chemical baths. Although original studio negatives were the primary source, the original masters remained untouched by the process. Only a copy of the original was used, so the initial quality print would remain in it's original historical integrity.

The films were colored scene-by-scene by personnel called "colorists." By freezing frames at the beginning, middle and end of a scene, they assigned colors to the various shades of gray. The scene was then completely colored using the computers. The entire process, with the research, the initial colorization and the complete run of the scene through the computer set-up, allowed them to color about ten minutes daily. At CST, 85 colorists were working three eight-hour shifts! Their training took about six months.

One of the problems confronting the crew at CST was that the computer could sometimes produce colors that were untrue. Gene Allen, former president of the Academy of Motion

Pictures Arts and Sciences, and an Oscar-winning art director, acted as quality consultant. For some occasions, color photos of various scenes were consulted on the conversion of the film. But coloring films as a profitable business for the studios in the long-term remained to be seen. In the eyes of many, it was sacrilegious to see *Casablanca* in color. Those in the business had one reply: Turn the color knob on the television set.

But an outcry was heard, and it did not remain as popular a fad as it was in 1985. As for Alfred Hitchcock himself, it will never be known his opinion towards coloring black and white films . . . even to see his own movies (or himself) colorized. His hosting chores, however, were slightly edited to fit the time, and to prevent comments by Hitchcock that would not have had any bearing on the newly-filmed story. A few of the colorized presentations included the "alternatives" filmed for the European market, so even die-hard fans of the program wouldn't always recognize the initial episode his narratives originated from. One consolation is that Hitchcock became historically known as the first dead man to host a television series, which to be sure, he would have admired. Or to paraphrase David Letterman, who remarked on his late-night NBC program, "it's tough these days for someone to get a job on television . . . especially when you're dead!"

Directors for the NBC episodes also included some of the production crew. Mario Di Leo, who was a cinematographer, directed "Road Hog." Supervising Producer Andrew Mirisch directed "Four O'Clock," the only non-original teleplay filmed that wasn't previously-filmed as an episode of the original Hitchcock series. (It was actually a remake of the Hitchcock-directed production of *Suspicion*.) Randy Roberts, who was the chief editor for the series, directed the episode "Happy Birthday." But there were a few notables among the list of directors. "As far as I know, during that opening season, each person did one episode," recalled director Jeff Kanew. "It was kind of like a guest director situation. John Byrum did one, Tim Burton did one, Burt Reynolds did one, I did one . . . You know, it was a short-term job they were trying to get feature directors." The revival of the series also created an interest to a younger generation, who never grew up watching the original series during the fifties and sixties. Nick-At-Nite (Nickelodeon), a cable network focusing on vintage television programs, presented the original series in their late-night line-up. The USA network began broadcasting episodes of *The Alfred Hitchcock Hour* during early mornings and on Sunday evenings, an hour after NBC had the remake series scheduled.

The teleplays usually gave credit to the author of the original story the episode was based on, and not the scriptwriter whose original scripts were sometimes consulted. "Man From the South," for example, utilized almost the same dialogue from the original episode, word for word, whereas "Incident From a Jail" varied considerably in dialogue, leaving only the plot to imitate the original production.

On May 5, 1985, from 9 to 11 p.m., EST, the television movie was on the air, and because it went over fairly-well with both fans and critics, a regular run of episodes was commissioned. While some of the best original episodes were re-filmed (such as "An Unlocked Window" and Ray Bradbury's "The Jar") the series still didn't catch on and was eventually cancelled by NBC.

The reasons for the cancellation are probably many, one of which being that NBC didn't quite give it a fair chance on a prime-time schedule. It was never faithfully on each week, often being pre-empted for another program, and even broadcast on an occasional Saturday and Tuesday evening, instead of the familiar Sunday night time-slot. It was also obvious that fans were somewhat less enthusiastic about up-dating episodes that were already considered "gems" of their own right. Only two were original stories, both fitting nicely within the

498

show's format and style. The others were remakes of previously filmed episodes, and the production values were either a hit or a miss. Then again, the possibility that the viewers were already familiar with the surprise twist endings, made the stories even less watchable, with no shock value whatsoever.

Shortly after the cancellation of *Alfred Hitchcock Presents* on NBC, the USA Network picked up the program, which was now produced by Paragon Motion Pictures, Inc. Production values plummeted in the new Canadian-made episodes (typical of many USA Network productions), and few "known" actors were used. The reason for producing the episodes in Canada instead of California was obvious – a cost factor. A standard half-hour episode cost only two-thirds to produce in Canada. Although a few of these new episodes were remakes of earlier episodes, the majority were originals, most of which lacked the same punch the originals had.

Throughout the USA network airings, reruns were aired, amidst the newly-filmed telecasts, first as an hour's worth of episodes, both an original and a rerun, eventually settling down to one half-hour episode per week. The USA Network had a method of showing many of its "resurrected" series (*Airwolf, The Hitchhiker, Ray Bradbury Theatre*, etc.) in no order whatsoever, so reruns were not shown in the order they initially aired.

But the program attempted to remain true to the original 1955-65 series, with an occasional stand-out episode such as the two-part "Hunted," the James Bond spoof "Diamonds Aren't Forever," the hysterical "Murder Party," the science-fiction "Romance Machine" or the Hitchcock spoof entitled "South by Southeast." (Most of the recommended viewing came during the program's last season, when the stories took a 180-degree turn, with offerings including a vampire rock-and-roll band, and a Sherlock Holmes mystery.) USA first aired all of the previously-made episodes from NBC, then began showing their own, squeezing them in between reruns of the original episodes. If this wasn't enough to make your head spin, they then started mixing in reruns of the new episodes with reruns of the original episodes with an occasional (*very* occasional) new episode! The broadcast dates listed in this book are the initial telecasts, not the reruns.

ALFRED HITCHCOCK PRESENTS: THE MOVIE

Casting: Jane Feinberg, c.s.a., Mike Fenton, c.s.a. and Troy Neighbors
Costume Designer: Julie Weiss
Costume Supervisor: Charles Velasco
Director of Photography: Mario Di Leo
Edited by Tom Finan and David Lloyd.
Executive Producer: Christopher Crowe
First Assistant Directors:
David L. Beanes, Jan DeWitt
Hairstylist: Bridget Cook
Make-up by John Elliott, Jr.
and Rodney Wilson.
Music Editor: Arnold Schwarzwald
Produced by Alan Barnette
and Stephen Cragg.

Production Designer:
Dean Edward Mitzner
Second Assistant Director: Jerry Ketcham
Set Decorator: Catherine Arnold
Sound by Jim Alexander, Bruce Bell
and Victor Dean Goode.
Supervising Film Editor:
Edward Abroms, a.c.e.
Supervising Producer: Andrew Mirisch
Unit Production Manager:
David Livingston
Titles and Optical Effects
by Universal Title.
Panaflex Camera and Lenses
by Panavision.
Color by Technicolor.

Some hotel accommodations and location sites were furnished by Desert Inn and Caesar's Palace.

EPISODE #1 **"INCIDENT IN A SMALL JAIL"**

    Starring: Ned Beatty as Larry Broome   Lee Ving as Curt Venner

    Tony Frank as Noakes, the sheriff   John Shearin as Roker

    Arthur Taxier as Skelly   Walter Klenhard as the Gas Station Attendant

    Richard Lineback as Billy   Gene Ross as Max Spaulding

    Jerry Curtin as the member of the mob   Cynthia Hartley as the young girl

    Based on the *Alfred Hitchcock Presents* teleplay by Henry Slesar (from his own short story), adapted for the movie by Joel Oliansky, originally broadcast March 23, 1961.

    Directed by Joel Oliansky.

    Music composed by John Goux.

    Opener taken from "Number Twenty-Two"

    (Hitchcock in line-up)   Voice: This is a police line-up. Here, desperate criminals who have been brought to bay appear before the detective force and are questioned by the chief detective. Listen. (Officer: "Take your hat off.") Name: Hitchcock, Alfred. Height: 5 foot six. Weight: prisoner refuses to make a statement. Here's his record: 1940 picked up on Suspicion, 1942 Spellbound, 1944 Notorious, 1955 Rear Window, 1956 The Man Who Knew too Much. Anything to say Hitchcock? *Well Sir, I admit it ain't a good record, but I'm trying to do better.* Better, do you call this latest charge doing better? Appearing on television. *I'm sorry Sir, but my family was hungry.* Take him away. *Wait a minute Sir, you've got the wrong man. Don't you want to see a sample of my work? O.K. Here is what we found on him when we picked him up.*

    Story: Traveling salesman Larry Broome gives a lift to a weird-looking hitchhiker, unaware that the stranger just came from the woods, where a young girl was raped and knifed. Picked up for failing to stop at a stop sign, Broome finds himself in the local police station trying to clear his innocence. At the same time, his travelling companion is imprisoned for the murder of the Spaulding girl, and Max Spaulding, the girl's father, gets half a dozen friends ready for a lynch mob. The odds are not in favor of the police, who are overpowered by the mob, when they attempt to move the prisoner to safety. Broome soon finds himself at the end of a rope, being mistaken for the hitch-hiker. He still claims his innocence, but the men hang him anyway. Just at the last second, reinforcements arrive and Broome is lowered to the ground. choking on air. Later that evening, with the entire misunderstanding straightened out, Broome phones his wife on the side of the road to tell her that he won't be home tonight – he'll explain his story when he gets there. Meanwhile, a tasty young dish finds herself stranded on the side of the road, and Broome pulls out his knife from the trunk of his car . . .

EPISODE #2 **"MAN FROM THE SOUTH"**

    Starring: John Huston as Carlos

    Melanie Griffith as the girl   Steven Bauer as the young man

    Special Appearance by: Tippi Hedren as the waitress

    Special Guest Star: Kim Novak as Mae Rosa

    Jack Thibeau as Bronson   Danny De La Paz as the bell hop

    Based on the *Alfred Hitchcock Presents* teleplay by William Fay (from a short story by Roald Dahl), adapted by Steve DeJarnatt, originally broadcast March 13, 1960.

    Directed by Steve DeJarnatt.

    Music composed by Basil Poledouris.

    Opener taken from "Salvage"

    (Hitchcock on the film set in director's chair)   *Hold it, hold it. Wait a minute, look, I object. I think you got much too much fill-light. I mean, look this is supposed to be a night scene. It's full of day-light. Quiet, quiet back there. Oh, I beg your pardon. Oh, oh good evening. We wanted to take you behind the scenes for a moment to show you how we make our films. The friendly co-operation of many, many people is needed to bring you these stories. Prop men, make-up men, electricians, cameramen.* (rises out of chair) *All* part of a team. *I'm very proud of them, and they in turn . . .* (spot light falls, crushing the chair) *You know, I sometimes consider getting out of this business. Now about tonight's show. Our story is entitled . . . oh well the title's unimportant. Tonight's story concerns, well . . . well small matter. I'm sure you'll . . . I'm sure you will enjoy our story, but first . . . but first, well, if you've been watching this program, I'm certain you always know when we have, but first. Here it is.*

Story: In the bar room of a Las Vegas casino, a young man without a penny to his name is offered a wager he'll never forget. An eccentric old Texan millionaire named Carlos, bets the young man that he couldn't light his lighter ten times in a row without missing. If the boy succeeds, he gets to keep the sports car outside, which the young man tries out for himself. If he misses just once . . . he loses one of his fingers – forfeit via a very sharp knife. Thinking it over, the young man agrees and accompanied by a couple of witnesses in search of action, the four people go up to Carlos' suite. The boy's hand is tied down to the counter-top, with one of his fingers protruding. One-by-one, the boy lights the lighter, and the referee counts with each light. At the count of ten, the lighter lights, the door opens and the flame goes out. Carlos swings and misses the finger by an inch. Mae Rosa, Carlos' wife, enters the room and takes the knife away. Scolding them for playing the foolish game, she explains that the car is actually hers, she won it herself. Pulling her glove off, they see that she only has one finger left!

EPISODE #3 **"BANG! YOU'RE DEAD"**

    Starring: Gail Youngs as Amanda's mother   Lyman Ward as Uncle Jack
    Special Appearance by: Bill Mumy as George Webster, the clerk
    Introducing: Bianca Rose as Amanda

Jonathan Goldsmith as Jensen, the manager	Kale Browne as Amanda's Dad
Mark L. Taylor as Darlene's Dad	Linda Hoy as the Big Brownie
David Held as Billy	Gregory Levinson as Stevie
Douglas Emerson as the kid soldier	Christina Lange as Darlene
Gail Barle as the Jiffy Snack Girl	Gigi Vorgan as the cashier

    Teleplay written for *Alfred Hitchcock Presents* by Harold Swanton and Christopher Crowe, from a story by Margery Vosper, originally broadcast on October 17, 1961.
    Directed by Randa Haines.
    Music composed by Craig Safan.
    Opener taken from "Bang! You're Dead"
    (movie box office) *The feature is about to commence. Please don't be alarmed, we are not charging admission. This is not pay-TV. As usual, all we ask is that on those occasions when you can't view our show that you let us know . . . so that we can send it to someone else. Please don't be a no-show.* (steps out of the booth) *This is not a hold up. I wish to dramatize the title of tonight's play. Tonight's story is called 'Bang! You're Dead'. Despite the fact that it has been introduced with my usual flippancy, it concerns a very serious subject, and I would be doing you a disservice if I led you to regard it lightly. Now I must hurry in to the theatre. For I don't want to miss the beginning. Fortunately I have a minute to find my seat before the feature starts, for it is preceded by an unselected short subject. It's the management's way of discouraging those who might stay through more than one show.*

Story: Six-year-old Amanda wants to play war games with her back yard friends, but the other children won't let her join them because she's a girl. Her uncle has just returned from Central America and going through his luggage, she finds a real gun with some real bullets. Exiting the house to join her friends, Amanda loads a single bullet into the gun, and then begins wandering through town. When her parents realize what has happened, they try to find her before she accidentally kills someone, but the little girl still manages to take a few shots at people – but failing to shoot a full cartridge. As the afternoon progresses, Amanda keeps loading the gun till it's fully loaded. Finding the boys playing another war game, Amanda is again told she can't join them, and she aims the gun. Just as the trigger is pulled, Amanda's mother knocks the gun out of her hand. The bullet just nearly misses Billy's ear. Everyone freezes in shock.

EPISODE #4 **"AN UNLOCKED WINDOW"**

Starring: Annette O'Toole as Stella	Owen Bush as Sam Ives
Helena Kallianiotes a Mrs. Maria Kyprianov	Ross Elliott as Glendon Baker
Nancy Burnett as the nurse	Bruce Davison as Betty Ames

Teleplay written by Fred Walton, based on the original teleplay by James Bridges (from a story by Ethel Lina White), originally broadcast on *The Alfred Hitchcock Hour* on February 15, 1965.

Directed by Fred Walton.

Music composed by Craig Safan.

Opener taken from "An Unlocked Window"

(radio station) *We are broadcasting my portion of this evening's program by radio instead of television. I seem to have lost some weight and I don't wish to mar my image. I cannot reveal exactly how much weight. I can only say, that had I lost ten more pounds I would have had to file a missing persons report. For the uninitiated I shall explain that radio is simply television with a tube burned out. In radio sound is a rather important ingredient. When it does not exist, it is manufactured. For example, this cellophane simulates the sound of a crackling fire. This sound-effect is so authentic one can almost smell the smoke.* (smoke starts to show) *This evening's play tells of two nurses who spend one terrifying night in a large house in the country. But first, some sound and fury signifying our sponsor's product.* (fire alarm)

Story: When the radio reports that the fourth hospital nurse in the past month was recently strangled to death, Stella and Betty Ames, two live-in nurses caring for an elderly patient, lock all the doors and windows. Sam, the caretaker, leaves to fetch an extra tank of oxygen for his employer, and Mrs. Kyprianov, an alcoholic housekeeper, begins hearing a man's voice in the hallways. After the nurses sedate Mrs. Kyprianov, the power goes out and the phone rings. It's the murderer who says he knows they're alone. Both nurses double-check the house, and Stella discovers to her horror that she forgot to lock a basement window. Hearing Betty scream for help, Stella runs down the hallway with a knife in hand, to find her companion in a corner. scared, claiming the killer is behind the door. Stella quietly sneaks over to the door, and stabs the stranger, only to find it's the corpse of Sam, who returned because his car broke down. Betty laughs madly and grabs Stella by the throat. During the struggle, Stella pulls off Betty's wig and tears the shirt, realizing she's really a man. "I told you I was coming. You're such a pretty nurse," the murderer says, as he strangles the life out of her.

Thus ends our story. Nothing more remains to be told. That is, unless you are interested in knowing more about Nurse Ames. You see, he later made a regrettable mistake and found himself attempting to throttle a nurse who turned out to be a policeman, in disguise. It was most embarrassing. Now I have another radio sound-effect to test. (squeaking door) *Excellent, until next week then. Good night.* (Goes out through the door and you hear knocking but there is no one there.)

Trivia, etc. *Variety* gave this movie a good review on May 8. "Re-creating four of the better *Alfred Hitchcock Presents* mellers in their half-hour form as a horror anthology analogous to an American *Dead of Night* and in color, to boot, doesn't hurt a bit - other than to bring to viewers' attention to how good those dramas were, compared to what's passing for entertainment on television today. Recast, redirected, the four entertainments do just that - entertain. What fun!"

"Purists will be driven up the wall by colorizing the wry appearances of the late Alfred Hitchcock," the review continued, "who doesn't seem to mind at all, and, because television addicts demand it, making the new versions of the dramas in color, too. What counts is that the acting is sound, the direction astute and often suspenseful, and the writing is superior. The four works are good enough to stand on their own without a star billing, but the producers have added some spark with unexpected performers showing up in surprise spots. In the second play, 'Man From the South,' Tippi Hedren and Kim Novak, both Hitchcock film veterans, appear as a waitress and as a dame with a surprise up her sleeve - and John Huston, who provides an introductory salute to the quartet, shows up as a gambling man. Bruce Davison appears in a dual role in 'An Unlocked Window,' and Annette O'Toole gets a surprise; Bill Mumy, who appeared in the original 'Bang! You're Dead' with Biff Elliott and Steve Dunne, reappears as a clerk in the new version . . . Colorizing Hitchcock, the host or his works, isn't painting the lily. Not at all. The master simply continues in his imperturbable way."

"I don't believe I ever read the original script, I just watched the episode," recalled director Joel Oliansky about the first segment. "There wasn't much point since you've got the story right there. When you direct for television, everybody has to agree on the same thing and especially with a good producer. I can't remember who suggested Ned Beatty, I think it was a terrific idea. We had six and a half days to film and I think we ran a little over. Because we were out on location and it was winter time, and you lose the sun a couple hours earlier than usual, which they didn't really plan on. We filmed a great deal of it in a valley, which is somewhat to the west of Los Angeles. The complication was fighting the sun going down. We had a lovely place to shoot, but a lot of what we filmed was day exterior and wouldn't have done any good at night. So you had to go out, and to get what we needed, shot by a certain time, was always a struggle. And then some of it in Griffith Park."

"The rest of it, the jail scenes, was filmed on the Universal lot," Oliansky continued. "That was a regular set and although I have no idea how long it took to build, I can't imagine that it took very long. That was very standard stuff. They probably took it out of stock and put it together because of the many sequences of jails Universal television used. They had to have a wall that matched the exterior we shot in the valley, with a door in it. I think it amused a lot of people and they enjoyed the colorization of Hitchcock. The casting gimmick such as Kim Novak and others who had been in the originals was a good idea. They had already picked the four stories to be filmed and "Incident in a Small Jail" was the only one remaining and they asked if I wanted to do it and I said sure."

The casting for "Man From the South," included Tippi Hedren, star of Alfred Hitchcock's *The Birds* (1963) and *Marnie* (1964). Hedren played the role of a waitress, serving the youngsters, one of whom was played by Hedren's real-life daughter, Melanie Griffith. * Alfred Hitchcock first discovered Tippi while viewing a commercial on NBC-TV's long-running morning program, *The Today Show*, and summoned her to Hollywood. In a *Look* magazine interview, Hitchcock remarked "Tippi Hedren is really remarkable. She's already reaching the lows and highs of terror." Hedren would later play roles in two more made-for-television pictures, a remake of *Shadow of a Doubt* (1991), and *The Birds II: Land's End* (1994).

Kim Novak, the star of Alfred Hitchcock's *Vertigo* (1958), entered this picture as Mae Rosa, wife of the eccentric Carlos. The hand that lacked all of its fingers during the final segment, was not Novak's of course. Another person who really had a disfigured hand, was hired to crouch below the actress and the bar, wearing the same color sleeve as Novak. When she moved her shoulder to imitate the movement of her arm, the double behind her

* Possible coincidence or inside influence? Hedren played Melanie Daniels in Hitchcock's *The Birds* (1963), the same first name as her daughter, Melanie Griffith, who was then only five-years old.

moved their arm onto the bar, a smooth yet unsuspected piece of trickery – far better than the original version that offered a real five-fingered woman wearing a two-fingered glove. (And yes, Novak is left-handed, which is why the duplicate arm was staged from her left side, not her right.)

Bill Mumy, child star of the original "Bang! You're Dead," makes a small appearance in the newly-filmed version as a grocer in the supermarket. The real star of this episode, however, was the seven-year-old Bianca Rose, making her screen debut and making a change from a male to a female lead. (This was not the only remake to make the sex change.) Later that summer, Bianca played a furry Ewok for many of the required stunts in *Ewoks: The Battle for Endor* (1985). In 1991, Bianca played the role of Midge Newton in another made-for-television movie, *Shadow of a Doubt*, a remake of the original Hitchcock movie. The objective of the story was to demonstrate the horrifying events and parental concern about young children having access to real handguns. Much like the original production, this episode remained true to the form, especially when Amanda's mother asks little Stevie if her daughter has a gun, he replies, "Most kids do."

The final segment, an abridged version of one of the most terrifying episodes of *The Alfred Hitchcock Hour*, was also filmed to perfection. The eerie atmosphere of the dark house was reproduced with wonderful cinematography, supplied by Mario Di Leo. In order not to spoil the ending for viewers not familiar with the original, actor Bruce Davison was not credited during the opening, unlike all the other actors in the movie. With the exception of "An Unlocked Window," there was no closer delivered by Hitchcock when each of the stories concluded, just a new presentation introducing the next story. For later syndication showings, in which the first three presentations were made into regular half-hour episodes, a copy of Hitchcock's closing remarks were then added. (When "An Unlocked Window" went into reruns, the episode retained the same closer from the movie.)

"An Unlocked Window" also contains a few errors. The character Mrs. Kyprianov in the play is spelled "Miss Kyprianov" in the closing credits. A horrifying goof at the end of the play shows Stella stab Sam in the chest, when she pulls the door back. Sam falls forward to land on his face, but then the viewers can clearly see the knife in his back. With a quick cut you can see his face, and somehow, Sam's body is now lying on his back!

NBC SERIES - ALFRED HITCHCOCK PRESENTS

Art Director: Anthony Brockliss
Associate Producer: Daniel Sackheim
Casting by Mark Malis, c.s.a.
Costume Supervisors and Designers : Sharon Day, Sheilla Hite,
Tom Johnson and Steven Sharp
Director of Photography: Mario Di Leo
Editors: Heather MacDougall and Randy Roberts
First Assistant Directors: Doug Metzger and Richard Peter Schroer
Music composed by Michael Colombier and Ernest Gold.
Music Editors: Robert Mayer and Dino A. Moriana
Production Designers: Bill Malley and Dean Edward Mitzner
Second Assistant Directors: Stephen Southard and Lonnie Steinberg
Set Decorators: Mary Ann Brienza, Victoria Hugo and Martin Price
Sound by Hank Garfield and Jim Alexander.
Sound Editors: Ian Macgregor-Scott and Burness J. Speakman
Story Editors: Stephen Bello and David Stenn
Unit Production Manager: David Livingston
Titles and Optical Effects by Universal Title.
Panaflex Camera and Lenses by Panavision. Color by Technicolor.

A total of twenty-two episodes were filmed and broadcast over the NBC network, and with the exception of Stephen Cragg, all of the producers from the pilot movie remained on board to supervise the new productions. The regular time-slot for these episodes was Sunday evenings, from 8:30 to 9 p.m. EST. Director Steven Spielberg was currently producing an anthology series of his own, in homage to *The Twilight Zone*, entitled *Amazing Stories*, and NBC decided to premiere both programs, back to back, for a full hour every Sunday evening, beginning September 29. This allowed audiences to tune into whimsical and often macabre stories, for a full hour.

EPISODE #5 **"REVENGE"** Broadcast on September 29, 1985

Starring: Linda Purl as Lisa Tate

David Clennon as Professor John Tate   Herbert Jefferson, Jr. as the policeman

Frances Lee McCain as Dr. Marianne Campbell

Beth Miller as Cindy   Victoria Ann-Lewis as the receptionist

Angela Moya as the nurse   Dennon Rawles as the male instructor

William 'Bill' Dearth as the mailman   Courtenay McWhinney as the bag lady

Fred Taylor as the biker   Loren Janes as the man (uncredited)

Nora Meerbaum as the female instructor (uncredited)

Teleplay written by David Stenn, based on the short story of the same name by Samuel Blas, and originally broadcast on October 2, 1955.

Directed by Roger E. Young.

Music composed by Michael Colombier.

Opener taken from "Festive Season"

(Hitchcock watching himself on TV) "Good evening and thank you for allowing me to come into your living room. The miracle of electronics makes many new pleasures possible." (Hitchcock now turns to the audience and says the same as the TV) *I frequently watch television, it takes my mind off my work. You aren't interrupting, however, for I seldom pay much attention to this part of the program. It's really quite superfluous. I find I can miss it entirely and still know what the commercial is all about. I must say I sometimes find myself fascinated by the amazing ego of this man. He speaks as though he were certain we were all sitting here with ears akimbo, listening to his every word. Let's listen to what he's saying now.* (Hitchcock turns back to the TV) "But first we have an important announcement. My sponsor . . ." *The way he bows and scrapes before the sponsor, it's disgusting. He's obviously a relative. Shhhhh.* ". . . and expensive message."

Story: Former ballet dancer Lisa Tate, is overcoming some emotional problems and her husband urges her to get out of the house and start taking dance lessons again. With his new job at Pepperdine University, in California, Lisa feels like a stranger at first, but thrilled after her first dancing class. When a man wearing jeans and cowboy boots follows her home, she rushes to lock the door, but it's too late. The stranger brutally rapes and beats her. John, her husband, rushes to the hospital when he hears the news, and the police officer explains that without any witnesses, they won't spend any more time than they need to. As a disgusted John drives Lisa home, she identifies her rapist on the street, which convinces John to pull the car over and follow the stranger through the streets. Catching up to the accused in a parking garage, John strangles him, getting revenge. Returning to the car, John starts driving down the road again when Lisa yells that she sees her attacker again . . . and again . . . and again . . .

". . . to keep you amused . . ." *This remote control device is second hand, but is in excellent condition. It belonged to a little old lady in Pasadena, a widow who only used it once.* ". . . please understand. . ." *Ah, there is that obnoxious fellow again.* ". . . until next week, good night." (boom!)

Trivia, etc. "Revenge" was not only the first episode broadcast for the series, but was also the same story featured in the premiere of the original series. David Stenn, who scripted this episode, was also one of the story editors for the series. Like a majority of the other episodes, this was adapted from the original production, but only credited the author of the original story, from which this episode was based on. Roger Young was hired to direct the pilot episode, because of his credentials at directing pilots for other television series, including: *Lou Grant, Magnum P.I., Hardcastle and McCormick, Legmen*, and later *Ohara* and *Hearts Are Wild*.

On October 9, 1985, *Variety* reviewed the premiere episode of the series. "The opening regular episode of NBC-TV's *Alfred Hitchcock Presents* feels a little short - for reasons that are not easily identifiable. The story seemed familiar and one knew what Clennon was going to do - but it's hard to know if it was obvious, or if the viewer unknowingly remembered the plot device from a 'Hitchcock' of yesteryear. Whatever the cause, the suspense was minimal and the hoped-for surprise non-existent. Like 'Amazing Stories' before it, 'Hitchcock' looked like it was padded a bit to fill out the half-hour running time. The thought persists that 'Amazing' and 'Hitchcock' (along with CBS-TV's *Twilight Zone*) may be on too early in the evening to permit the kind of reflection before bedtime, that the successful anthology series of the past generated."

EPISODE #6 **"NIGHT FEVER"** Broadcast on October 6, 1985
    Starring: Robert Carradine as Jerry Walsh   Lisa Pelikan as Ellen
    Basil Hoffman as Dr. Michaels   Debi Richter as Kathy
    Richard Foronjy as Detective Martinez   James David Hinton as Tom
    Eugene Butler as Detective Greeley   Roger Aaron Brown as Joe Chandler
    Jeanne Mori as the first physician   Christopher Crowe as the first surgeon
    Ken Foree as the orderly   Wendy Oates as the second anesthesiologist
    James Saito as the first anesthesiologist
    Jerry Boyd as the second ambulance attendant
    Charles Bazaldua as the first ambulance attendant
    Lisa Rafel as Emergency Room nurse
    Mo Malone as Mary Winters   Tim Cunningham as Phil
    Teleplay written for *Alfred Hitchcock Presents* by Jeff Kanew and Stephen Kronish, based on the short story "Night Work" by Clark Howard, and originally broadcast on May 3, 1965.
    Directed by Jeff Kanew.
    Music composed by Bob Ezrin and Kevin Savigar.
    Opener taken from "Mrs. Herman and Mrs. Fenimore"
(knife throwing board) *Good evening ladies and gentlemen. First of all I want to make it clear that we always appreciate constructive criticism. Any expression of your feeling is always welcome.* (knife) *We have a very warm feeling toward our viewers. We know they are intelligent, discerning and warmhearted.* (knife) *Present company excepted of course. Yes, I have an announcement to make.* (knife in the back of studio man) *Touché. Is Dr. Finchley in the audience?, he is wanted at home. And . . . if it's not too inconvenient, perhaps he could stop here on his way out. As for our knife throwing friend, here is something better to throw at.*

Story: Jerry Walsh talks his girlfriend into closing the convenience store early so they can go to a concert. When she goes to get her purse, she returns to find Jerry emptying the cash register. The police arrive and Jerry fires his gun. The law officer returns the shots, wounding Jerry. Both the policeman and the thief are rushed to the hospital, but Jerry is the lone survivor. It seems the officer died on the operation table, and now Jerry will be charged with murder and attempted robbery. Since the doctors say he cannot leave the hospital for a few days because of his wound, security tightens around the cop-killer. Knowing he'll need help to escape, Jerry befriends a nurse named Ellen, and it doesn't take long for the nurse to fall in love with him. Jerry, ever the smooth-talker, convinces her to plot an escape, which goes off undetected. After making it safely to her home, Jerry notices a picture on the dresser – that of the cop he killed. But now it's too late, as Ellen can exact revenge on the man who killed her husband.

By the way, that last commercial was one which was sent to Russia as part of the cultural exchange. I don't know what we received in return, we're afraid to open it. Now, until next week when we shall return with another story, good night.

Trivia, etc. "I was doing a film at Universal and the producers called and asked me if I would be interested in doing an episode," recalled director Jeff Kanew. "I thought it would be fun cause I always liked to watch the Hitchcock show as a viewer, and also Bobby Carradine and I, who had worked on *Revenge of the Nerds* together, had wanted to do something together and I thought this would be a good opportunity. Basically we watched the original episode and had a synopsis of it, so we never worked from the original script. We kind of tried to keep the same story theme, but the dialogue was all new. Steve [Kronish] probably did more of the dialogue than I did, but we both worked on it together."

On October 13, 1985, *Alfred Hitchcock Presents* was not broadcast over NBC, because of game four of the National League Championship Series. A pre-game baseball playoff for the game was broadcast in this time slot instead.

EPISODE #7 **"WAKE ME WHEN I'M DEAD"**   Broadcast on October 20, 1985
    Starring: Barbara Hershey as Jessie Dean   Brian Bedford as Stewart Dean
    Buck Henry as Prosecutor Walter Lang   Reid Shelton as Daniels
    George Innes as Charles Dean   Carolyn Seymour as Carla Robbins
    Lillian Lehman as Judge Branca   Gill Dennis as Dr. Leon Borofsky
    Michael J. London as the bailiff   Jennifer Nairn-Smith as the party guest
    Barry Pearl as the assistant D.A.

Teleplay written for *Alfred Hitchcock Presents* by Buck Henry and Irving Elman, based on the short story of the same name by Lawrence Treat, originally broadcast as "Murder Me Twice" on December 7, 1958.

Directed by Frank R. Pierson.

Music composed by Michael Colombier.

Opener taken from "Murder Me Twice"

(hypnotism)   Voice: "You are very sleepy, you can't seem to hold your eyes open. You're beginning to drift . . . you're drifting . . . you're sound asleep. Can you hear me?" Hitchcock: *Yes.* "Say, good evening ladies and gentlemen." *Good evening ladies and gentlemen.* "Thank you for tuning in." *Thank you for tuning in.* "You're now going back in time. Far back. Back years and years ago. You're drifting back through the years, back, back, back . . . When you speak next you will be 40 years old." *Forty!* (Hitch jumps up from sofa) I'm sorry, I mean 4. *That's better.*

Story: Jessie and Charles Dean are at a reception given in their honor by friend Carla Robbins at her mansion. Charles' younger brother, playwright Stewart Dean is there, along with District Attorney Walter Lang. Stewart claims he can hypnotize a person and bring out their former reincarnated self, and to prove his point, puts Jesse under. Jessie travels back in time and becomes Martine Saint-Pierre, a French woman suspecting her husband of having an affair with a slavegirl. While in the trance, Jessie/Martine stabs Charles to death with a steak knife. Walter, having witnessed the crime, takes on her case, prosecuting Jesse for murder. Stewart insists it was Martine who killed Charles, so during the trial, they decide to have her hypnotized again to establish her innocence - or guilt. Stewart once again puts her in a trance, and when she takes on the Martine personality – even speaking French - she ends up stabbing her brother-in-law to death with the same murder weapon. Carla talks with her friends weeks after the trial, relating how Jessie is doing in a Swiss rehabilitation clinic. Walter's career is ruined, with his two friends gone. But actually he's in Switzerland with Jessie, having taught her everything she needed to know in French.

(Hitchcock snaps his fingers)   *Since I can't wake you up, I can only leave you with this post-hypnotic suggestion. Next week when you awaken, you will feel compelled to tune in again when we promise to bring you another story and three less soporific commercials. Good night.*

Trivia, etc. Most of the television listings billed this episode as "Murder Me Twice," which was the title of the original production this episode was based on. The actual on-screen title was "Wake Me When I'm Dead." Buck Henry, who played the role of Walter in this episode, also co-wrote the script.

EPISODE #8   **"FINAL ESCAPE"**   Broadcast on October 27, 1985
        Starring: Season Hubley as Lena Trent   George DiCenzo as Richard Margolis
        Patrice Donnelly as Shirley   Jerry Hardin as the warden
        Davis Roberts as Doc   Linden Chiles as the judge
        Anne Seymour as Esther   Patricia Wilson as the trustee
        Eugene Lee as the guard   Don Maxwell as the bailiff (uncredited)
        Teleplay by Charles Grant Craig, based on a story by Thomas H. Cannan, Jr. and Randall Hood, originally broadcast on February 21, 1964.
        Directed by Thomas Carter.
        Music composed by Sylvester Levay.
        Opener from "Make My Death Bed" / close "Where the Woodbine Twineth."
        (lady experiment)   *Good evening fellow creatures. This evening we are making a daring experiment. We shall present a blank screen and let your imagination fill in the picture.* (lady) *Since I have no idea what you are thinking, I have no idea what you are seeing. I understand a good many men watch our show. Of course, I'm sure their wives occasionally peek in from the kitchen,* (lady disappears) *but when they see the show hasn't begun, they return to their work.* (lady comes back again) *I'm afraid our experiment may be getting out of hand.* (she starts taking her clothes off) *I shall ask our sponsor to fill the screen with his own wholesome, untroubled thoughts. This is especially designed for those of you with nothing at all on your mind.* (she takes her skirt off)

Story: Lena Trent is sentenced to life in prison for a murder she claims she didn't commit. Once at Mojave, a Maximum Security Prison, Lena shows no intimidation by another con, Shirley, who seems to run the prison. Willing to do anything to get out, Lena's first attempt to escape fails, caught while hiding in the laundry truck and put in solitary confinement. She meets an older man, Doc, who works in the infirmary and offers him the money he needs for a desperately needed eye exam, in exchange for helping her escape. Together they form a plan. When next time there is a death within the prison walls, a bell signal will sound and then she can slip into the coffin. After the burial (the graveyard is outside the prison walls) he will come and dig her up. Soon after their plans are made, news spreads that one of the inmates dies and eager to set the plan in motion, Lena hurries to hide in the coffin. Remaining as quiet and still as she can, the coffin is taken outside and given a respectable funeral. Hours pass and wondering where the old man is, Lena nervously lights a match to discover that her companion is none other than Doc himself.

That concludes tonight's story. Next week we shall return with another. Until then, good night.

Trivia, etc. "Final Escape" is an excellent example of how many of the original episodes of *The Alfred Hitchcock Hour* could have been dramatized under the half-hour format quite successfully. One of the many changes between this episode and the original version, is that the protagonist is a woman instead of a man. This wasn't the first episode to switch the sex of the characters. Hitchcock's closing remarks originate from the last season's episode "Where the Woodbine Twineth," and the same closer was used for four other episodes this season, including "Night Caller" and "Method Actor."

EPISODE #9   **"NIGHT CALLER"**   Broadcast on November 5, 1985
Starring: Linda Fiorentino as Betsy Van Kennon
Michael O'Keefe as Arthur C. 'Art' Toomey
Tony Bill as Steve   Stephen Davies as Detective Duane Calvin
Sandra Bernhard as Karen   Teri Fiorentino as the woman (uncredited)
Teleplay written for *Alfred Hitchcock Presents* by John Byrum, based on a story by Gabrielle Upton, originally broadcast on January 31, 1964.
Directed by John Byrum.
Opener from "A Secret Life," closer from "Where the Woodbine Twineth."
(diving boat)   *Good evening ladies and gentlemen.   Good evening ladies and gentlemen!* (tries second time during noise) *Good evening, ladies and gentlemen.   I hope you didn't mind that interruption.   This trip was my sponsor's suggestion.   He wanted to show off his diving prowess.   You see, he's the gentleman who just went over the side.   Now he's jerking on the line.   I intend to ignore him.   His messages are always the same, always just like this one coming up.*

Story: Betsy Van Kennon, a recent divorcee who just moved into an apartment complex in Marina Del Rey, tells everyone she enjoys her independence. In reality, she still suffers psychologically from her sexually abusive husband. Late one night, while she is changing for bed, Betsy notices a strange man watching her from across the courtyard. Quickly turning the light off and covering the window with a blanket, Betsy receives a phone call from the man, asking her to move the blanket – it's obstructing his view. Although she isn't certain who the stranger is, she suspects Art Toomey, her neighbor. As the days pass, the obscene phone calls continue, both at home and at work, and concerned for her well-being, she notifies the police. But when she explains her problem to a detective, he sadly explains that he is unable to do anything other than serve a verbal warning to Art. Finally Betsy becomes so distraught over the phone calls that she buys a gun and stays home from work one evening, waiting for a chance to rid herself of the pervert. When Art knocks on her door, asking to "talk about the mis-understanding," she takes advantage of the opportunity and shoots him . . . shortly before the phone rings again, with the same obscene voice tailing the other end.

That concludes tonight's story.   Next week we shall return with another.   Until then, good night.

Trivia, etc. On Sunday, November 3, 1985, *Alfred Hitchcock Presents* was not broadcast on NBC-TV. Instead, a special hour-long episode of *Amazing Stories* was broadcast from 8 to 9 p.m., EST. The broadcast was entitled "The Mission" and was directed by Steven Spielberg himself. Two days later, on Tuesday the 5th, NBC made up for the lack of Hitchcock by pushing the program *Riptide* ahead an hour, and presented an episode of *Amazing Stories* and *Alfred Hitchcock Presents* beginning 9 p.m. The above date is not a mistake. This episode was broadcast on Tuesday, Nov. 5 instead of Sunday, and from 9:30 instead of 8:30.

The John Carpenter TV movie, *Someone's Watching Me!* (1978) with Lauren Hutton and David Birney had a story very similar to this episode with hints of *Rear Window* thrown in. The Carpenter movie actually had another connection to *Alfred Hitchcock*

Presents as well. Len Lesser, who played the hoodlum in the episode "Heart of Gold," played the burly man in the Carpenter movie.

EPISODE #10 "METHOD ACTOR" Broadcast on November 10, 1985

Starring: Martin Sheen as Paul Dano   Robby Benson as Ed
Marilu Henner as Claire   Parker Stevenson as Lane Richards
Bernie Casey as Bernie   Whitney Kershaw as the girl
Ben Kronen as Max Goodman   Patti Negri as the assistant
Leila Hee Olsen as the waitress   Louis Silvers as the parking lot attendant

Teleplay written for *Alfred Hitchcock Presents* by Bill Kerby, based on the short story "The Geniuses" by Max Franklin, and the Robert Bloch teleplay originally broadcast as "Bad Actor" on January 9, 1962.

Directed by Burt Reynolds.

Music composed by Steve Dorff.

Opener taken from "Bad Actor," closer from "Where the Woodbine Twineth."

(woman and elephant) *Good evening. Before we begin our play, I would like to demonstrate the training method we use here at the Hitchcock Actor's Studio. You see, we give the students symbols or certain images to assist them in portraying character. Because of the type of character our Miss Schmeltz was to portray, we suggested that she think of herself as a tree.* (woman stands weird) *I think she projects it very well. Thank you, Miss Schmeltz. Our next student, Mr. Blackwood, was asked to portray a large jowlly captain of industry, and to help him we suggested that he think of himself as an elephant. Excellent.*

Story: Paul Dano, a successful but alcoholic actor, wants to take one last chance at screen immortality. His agent hears about a new script that would be perfect for Paul, and arranges a meeting with the producers. Confident that he'll land the role, Paul gets jealous when he hears that a newcomer, Lane Richards, is getting the part. Richards pays Paul a visit later that evening, asking him for professional advice. Paul, in a fit of anger. breaks Lane's neck and decides to rid himself of the body. Using sulfuric acid and a chain saw, he disposes of the corpse. As he sets out to clean up his mess in the bathroom, his girlfriend and agent pay a surprise visit, forcing the actor to play the role of innocence. But it seems they have some good news for Paul - the producer has changed his mind and he's getting the part after all. While waiting for Paul to get ready to leave, they find Lane's head in the ice bucket.

That concludes tonight's story. Next week we shall return with another. Until then, good night.

Trivia, etc. Burt Reynolds, who starred in the episode "Escape to Sonoita," that ended the fifth season of the original series, takes a turn directing an episode this time. Bill Kerby co-wrote the screenplay to *Hooper*, a movie starring Burt Reynolds in 1978. When watching this episode, keep an eye out among Paul Dano's memorabilia, because there is actually a signed photo of Hitchcock.

EPISODE #11 "THE HUMAN INTEREST STORY" Broadcast on Nov. 17, 1985

Starring: John Shea as Brian Whitman   Barbara Williams as Maggie Verona
James Callahan as William T. Everett   Richard Marcus as Levy
Albert Popwell as Nick   Grant Owens as the first man
Hardy Rawls as the second man   Michael Strasser as the first punk
Carlos Gary Cervantes as the second punk   Richard Camphuis as the sheriff
John Allen as the policeman   Wendy Oates as reporter #1
Floyd Foster, Jr. as reporter #2   Michael McCabe as reporter #3
Rhonda Dotson as Denise (uncredited)

Teleplay written by Karen Harris, based on the short story "The Last Martian" by Fredric Brown, originally broadcast as "Human Interest Story" on May 24, 1959.

Directed by Larry Gross.

Music composed by Thomas Newman.

Opener taken from "Human Interest Story"

(HiFi-equipment, jail)   *Good evening. Do you enjoy assembling your own high fidelity or stereophonic sound systems, with their complicated components and speakers on every wall? Then you'll be especially interested in what I'm about to show you. I have just developed what I consider the latest in sound reproduction. This is designed for those persons who desire simplicity rather than fidelity. As you can see there is only one speaker, nor is that the only improvement. We have also eliminated the old fashioned record changer. Now only two attachments are necessary, a small crank and a hearing aid. By the way, neither of those items is needed for our next number.*

Story: In a small neighborhood bar, a national football game is interrupted by an unknown transmission, featuring a man named Brian Whitman, who claims: "My name is Garo. I come from the solar system you people call Alpha Centauri. You must listen to what I'm about to say. Some of them are here already and others are close behind. They are going to colonize the Earth." Maggie Verona, a newspaper reporter, witnesses the broadcast and seeing a human interest story, seeks out Brian Whitman. Knowing her influence with the press, Brian (claiming he's Garo in Brian's body) asks her for help in putting his story out to the public before, he is killed by the Alpha Centaurians. If the aliens take over, all the Earth people will look the same, but act differently. They're possessing human bodies. Maggie hesitates at first, but when Brian insists on showing her proof, she goes along with the madman. After some bizarre obstacles, they reach their destination and Brian shows Maggie the proof she needs for her story. Returning to work, Maggies reports her story to Everett, the news director. Brian was telling the truth – there is an alien invasion commencing. He had the proof and she had to kill him. Maggie asks Everett if she can hide for a few days until the colonization is complete.

(first part taken out)   *My fellow Martians seemed to have taken umbrage of my letting the cat out of the bag. However I shall be allowed to return to Earth next week at the same time. We Martians have found that those not smart enough to be trusted, the ones with very low IQ's, are still perfectly suited to appear on television. Our institutions are full of them. Good night.*

Trivia, etc.   Director Larry Gross would later write the screenplay for the television movie *Rear Window*, in 1998, a remake of the 1954 Hitchcock classic. Gross also wrote the screenplay for *48 Hrs.* (1982) and *Another 48 Hrs.* (1990). On November 24, 1985, *Alfred Hitchcock Presents* was not broadcast. Instead, NBC-TV presented a three-hour movie entitled "Mussolini: The Untold Story." The name of Fredric Brown was mis-spelled as "Frederic" in the opening credits of this episode.

Albert Popwell also appeared in the first four "Dirty Harry" movies. As one of the robbers in *Dirty Harry* (1970), as Sidney in *Magnum Force* (1973), as Big Ed in *The Enforcer* (1976) and as Horace King in *Sudden Impact* (1983). This episode also featured a sex change. The role of the reporter was played by Steve McQueen in the original, but this episode featured a female reporter, instead. Strangely, the boss was called Everett in this episode, which was the reporter's name in the original!

EPISODE #12   **"BREAKDOWN"**   Broadcast on December 1, 1985

Starring: John Heard as William Callahan
Andy Garcia as Alejandro "Alex" Ramos
Stefan Gierasch as Karl Schuler   Al Israel as the coroner
Manuel Ojeda as General Vorteez   Wally Barron as the doctor

Patrick Welch as the executive

Rodrigo Puebla as Indio

Guillermo Rios as the coroner's assistant

Sebastian Ligarde as Tim

José Luis Cuevas as Roberto

Chava Godinez as the old man

Ramiro Ramirez as Mestizo

Paco Mauri as the white clad man

Pamela Gual as the secretary

Rául Chavero as the first boy

Teleplay written for *Alfred Hitchcock Presents* by Alfonse Ruggiero, Jr., based on the short story by Louis Pollock, originally broadcast on November 13, 1955.

Directed by Richard Pearce.

Music composed by Michael Colombier.

Opener taken from "Breakdown"

(reading a book)   *Oh, good evening. I've been reading a mystery story. I find them very relaxing. They take my mind off my work. These little books are quite nice of course, they can never replace hardcover books. They're just good for reading, but they make very poor doorstops. Tonight's story by Louis Pollock is one that appeared in this collection. I think you will find it properly terrifying, but like the other plays of our series, it is more than mere entertainment. In each of our stories we strive to teach a lesson or point a little moral. Advice like mother used to give: You know, walk softly but carry a big stick. Strike first and ask questions later, that sort of thing. Tonight's story tells about a business tycoon and will give you something to ponder, if you have ever given an employee the sack, or if you intend to. You'll see it, after the sponsor's story, which like ours, also strives to teach a little lesson or point a little moral.*

Story: William Callahan heads a multi-million dollar corporation and is a ruthless man who has just signed a very important drug contract. Flying out to Barrero, South America to meet with his contact, Alejandro Ramos and Karl Schuler, a German-American owner of a plantation, which is in reality a huge cocaine plant. Squaring the deal off, by setting up Ramos as the fall-guy, Callahan drives off but gets into a car accident. With the car pinned underneath a bulldozer, and everyone believing that he is dead, the road workers leave. Unbeknownst to them, Callahan is still alive, but paralyzed, unable to talk or move. Later that night he is taken to the morgue, and Callahan realizes that he must somehow let it be known that he is still alive before the coroner proceeds with the autopsy . . . and although being as ruthless as Callahan, a tear comes from his eye to let them know he's alive. But instead of being helped, he is just moved to the prison doctor, whom lets his new orderly, Ramos, take a look at him.

There now, that really held you in suspense, didn't it? For more of the same, I recommend you tune in next week at this time. I shall see you then. Bon Soir.

Trivia, etc. Stefan Gierasch also appeared on *The Alfred Hitchcock Hour* in the episode "Diagnosis: Danger."

EPISODE #13 **"PRISONERS"** Broadcast on December 8, 1985

Starring: Yaphet Kotto as Jack Worth

Christina Raines as Julie Nordstrom

Larry McCormick as the television anchorman

Walter Klenhard as the prison guard

Steve Eastin as the police captain

Doug Hale as the TV reporter

Chris Kriesa as the S.W.A.T. member

Teleplay written for *Alfred Hitchcock Presents* by John Byrum, based on a short story by Stanley Ralph Ross, originally broadcast as "You Got to Have Luck" on January 15, 1956.

Directed by Christopher Crowe.

Music composed by Miles Davis.

Opener taken from "You Got to Have Luck"

Good evening. The hour-glass is a wonderful invention but I'm afraid it will never replace the sun-dial - certainly not in my garden. This one doesn't even work. I sent it to a jewelist to be cleaned and he removed all the sand. Fortunately, the second hand still functions. Time is very important to the characters in tonight's story. One of them is doing it, for another time seems to be running out. Time is also very important in television. We buy it, we fill it, we must start on it, we must finish on it. And appropriately enough, we occasionally kill it. I refer of course to my own fumbling efforts. Certainly not to the vital announcement which follows.

Story: Julie Randall proceeds with her morning routine of cleaning the house, when the news reports the latest details about a local prison break, and the search for a wanted killer named Jack Worth, considered armed and dangerous. Julie never gives it one thought until she looks up to find Jack holding a gun on Julie, and insists on using her house as a hiding place until dark. Throughout the afternoon, Jack and Julie get to know each other by talking about their past and present lives, and through the help of the escaped prisoner, Julie discovers that she herself has been living in her own prison. "You're just as much a prisoner in this house, as I was yesterday," Jack explains. Julie, seeing reality hitting her in the face, makes a clean break from her boring life, while Jack is unable to escape his, being shot down by an armed patrol. Jack's mistake was made earlier in the evening - he shouldn't have forced her to answer the phone because Julie is deaf, and this led to a tip-off to the police.

This case is not without some merit, I grant you. I shall present my rebuttal next week at the same time. So not to miss it, I suggest you set your alarm clocks at once. Good night.

Trivia, etc. Christopher Crowe, executive producer for *Alfred Hitchcock Presents*, not only directed this episode, but also played the role of the first surgeon in the episode "Night Fever." The closing credits billed Christina Raines as Julie Randall, but her last name is Nordstrom in the drama.

EPISODE #14 **"GIGOLO"** Broadcast on December 15, 1985
      Starring: Sandy Dennis as Sylvia Locke   Brad Davis as Arthur Kreshner
      Virginia Capers as Ruth   Billy Ray Sharkey as Man
      Tina Challey as Molly   Tony Goodstone as Ted Crowley (uncredited)
      Teleplay written for *Alfred Hitchcock Presents* by Steve DeJarnatt, based on a short story by Arthur Williams, originally broadcast as "Arthur" on September 27, 1959.
      Directed by Thomas Carter.
      Music composed by Ernest Gold.
      Opener taken from "Apex"
(guard and tourist) *Good evening fellow tourists. The first item on today's schedule is a stop at Buckingham Palace for a view of the historic changing of the guard. The gentleman performing the gymnastics is a Mr. Wedgeley of Topper, Iowa. Mr. Wedgeley is engaging in one of the favorite tourist's sports. He's trying to make the stern-looking guardsman smile. In fact, Mr. Wedgeley has made a small wager with me . . .* (gun-shot, guard returns to his post) *I'm afraid that wasn't quite what Mr. Wedgeley had in mind. On second thought, I believe he did win his bet with me for I now see just the hint of a smile on the guardsman's face. Originally our tour-schedule provided for one minute of free time at this point. But because of this incident, I think a brief eulogy would be appropriate.*

Story: Gold digger Arthur Kreshner is heavily in debt, and has twenty-four hours to pay – or else. His solution comes in the form of a wealthy woman, Sylvia Locke, a pet lover who sings a mantra and grinds seafood in the kitchen every morning for her cats. Arthur woos the woman, and Sylvia marries him, against the warning of her maid. Arthur even tells Sylvia that he has promised a donation to the Society for Protection of Cats, which tricks Sylvia into revealing a secret door where she hides her loot. Smothering her with a pillow, he grinds her body in the grinder and feeds the meat to her pets. As Arthur searches the house, he discovers the hidden jewels. While relaxing in the tub enjoying the new wealth, one of the cats, Abendego, races into the bathroom and knocks the radio into the bathtub. Arthur is electrocuted and Abendego lets a growl. The maid enters, and praises her trained cat for giving her the perfect opportunity to acquire the loot, with Arthur taking the blame.

We shall be back with another story. Now I must bid you good night, until then.

Trivia, etc. Although this episode was billed as an adaptation of the Arthur Williams story "Being A Murderer Myself," originally directed by Alfred Hitchcock as the fifth season opener, under the title "Arthur." The plot bears little resemblance to the original broadcast. Instead, this episode appears more like a conduit of multiple *Alfred Hitchcock Presents* episodes. Arthur's wife Sylvia is the same name of the protagonist in "Sylvia" (broadcast January 19, 1958). His wife is a pet lover, like that of Barbara Baxley in "Anniversary Gift" (broadcast on November 1, 1959). Arthur suffocates his wife with a pillow, like that of Dennis Day in "Cheap is Cheap" (broadcast April 5, 1959). Last but not least, the climax of Arthur's downfall doesn't do "Post Mortem" any good (broadcast May 18, 1958). For those concerned, there really was no cat in the bag, dropped into the swimming pool by Arthur. The animal action was supervised by the American Humane Association. All of the cats were trained and supplied by Birds & Animals Unlimited, located in California.

On December 22, 1985, *Alfred Hitchcock Presents* was not broadcast on NBC-TV. Instead, an hour-long animated special was presented instead. Walt Disney's version of "Mickey's Christmas Carol," featuring the voice of Alan Young. On December 29, 1985, NBC-TV featured a rebroadcast of "Man From the South," starring John Huston, one of four stories featured on the pilot movie.

EPISODE #15   **"THE GLOATING PLACE"**   Broadcast on January 5, 1986
    Starring: Stephen Macht as Carl Cansino
    Isabelle Walker as Samantha 'Sam' Loomis *

Cindy Pickett as Marcia Loomis	Christie Houser as Debbie
Nicholas Hormann as Bruce Loomis	Bill Calvert as Peter Lake
Bill Gratton as the detective	Michael Zand as the teacher
Kristy Swanson as female student # 2	Lance Slaughter as male student # 1
Amy Sherman as female student # 1	Ron Jarvis as the sound man (uncredited)

    Teleplay written for *Alfred Hitchcock Presents* by David Stenn, based on the short story of the same name by Robert Bloch, originally broadcast on May 16, 1961.
    Directed by Christopher Leitch.
    Music composed by Peter Bernstein.
    Opener taken from "Touché," closer taken from "I'll Take Care of You."
    (as Zorro with sword)   *Good evening amigos. I fear the day of the illiterate swordsman has passed. They seem to be spending so much time writing that they are neglecting the really important work, scurrying opponents. It's a very unhealthy state of affairs. Take this gentleman for example, listen . . . he couldn't possibly win a duel, yet he can write sixty words a minute. Now, here is someone who can neither duel nor write, but can speak volumes, and insists on doing so.*

* Once again, the name of John Gavin's character in *Psycho*, Sam Loomis, is used, as in "Craig's Will," although this time for a girl.

Story: Carl Cansino of Action News takes his camera to the site of a brutal murder in the Forest Reserve Park, near a college campus, and reports the death. The next day, both students and teachers are talking about the murdered girl and one of her classmates, Samantha, becomes intrigued by the attention. Samantha, you see, is a loner and her parents are so busy with work that they neglect her. Coming up with a plan, Samantha fakes an attack on herself, which brings Carl to interview her, giving her instant notoriety. But a few days later, another girl is brutally attacked and survives through the ordeal, taking away Samantha's claim to fame. A few nights later, when Debbie is being chased by the murderer, Samantha answers her knock at the door, but Samantha won't help. She accuses Debbie of faking the attack to gain public sympathy, and as a result, Debbie is killed in front of Samantha's house. The raving reporter, Carl, arrives on the scene to search Samantha's house for the killer, and emotionally caught up in the excitement, reveals his true identity. He knows her secret about faking the attack, which only ruined his chances of reporting a new story . . . The next day, Carl reports that two more girls have been murdered, and he does so with tears in his eyes. Watching the heart-breaking report is another girl, looking just as thrilled . . .

By the way, those of you who witnessed tonight's crime will be glad to learn that the party who perpetrated it has been justly punished. (close-up) *Next week I shall be back with another story, until then, good night.*

EPISODE #16 "THE RIGHT KIND OF MEDICINE" Broadcast on January 12, 1986

Starring: Jack Thibeau as Joe Pugh

Robert Prosky as Dr. Vogel   Michael C. Gwynne as Hollingshead

Panchito Gomez as Vernon, the pharmacy clerk

Pamela Dunlap as Mrs. Farbor   Lyle Talbot as Fletcher, the pharmacist

Greg Finley as Sergeant Henry Monroe   Jill Hill as the stewardess

Maura Soden as the teller   Rif Hutton as the policeman

Ruben Moreno as the Hispanic man   Vaughn Armstrong as the Marine

Alma Beltran as Mrs. Mendez (uncredited)

Teleplay written for *Alfred Hitchcock Presents* by Michael Braverman, based on a short story by Henry Slesar, originally broadcast on December 19, 1961.

Directed by Jerrold Freedman.

Music composed by Elliot Kaplan.

Opener taken from "The Right Kind of Medicine"

(horse and blacksmith) *Good evening fellow villagers. I've been promised a chestnut tree, but it hasn't been delivered yet. The job came as a result of my answering an ad. I got it here somewhere, let's see, here we are. Wanted: man with large and sinewy hands. The muscles of his brawny arms strong as iron bands. Hair must be crisp black and long. His face must be quite tanned. No salary guaranteed. He earns whate'er he can. I found the job very interesting and not difficult at all. This case for example, he doesn't need new shoes. He needs arch supports. From this bucolic scene, we move to an urban setting for tonight's drama. Less the contrast be too jarring for your sensibilities, we present the following pleasantly incongruous transition.*

Story: Joe Pugh is just released from prison when he robs a bank, shoots a cop and gets shot in the leg exchanging gunfire with the police. He goes to Dr. Vogel's office, who reluctantly removes the bullet and prescribes a pain killer. Covering his tracks, Pugh shoots the doctor as well. At the pharmacy, Joe waits impatiently for the prescription to be filled by an old man. Constantly badgering the pharmacist to hurry up, Joe finally receives the medicine. Making it back to his apartment, Joe hears someone approaching up the steps. Suspecting the pharmacy clerk of recognizing him, Joe shoots the kid down. An hour later, as Joe is on his way out of town, taking the painkillers to ease his pain, the police call the pharmacist in to identify the body. The old man cries in his error. He made a mistake on the prescription, and sent Vernon over to inform Joe – before it was too late. The medicine is actually poison and if not treated immediately, Joe will surely die. The only action the police take is to smile. On the plane, Pugh takes some pills with his champagne.

I must say horseshoes are very cheap, yet sensible this year. Open-toed flats. Now until next week, good night.

EPISODE #17   **"BEAST IN VIEW"**   Broadcast on January 19, 1986
        Starring: Janet Eilber as Dr. Marion McGregor   Cliff Potts as Roger Harden
        Tom Atkins as Lieutenant Varner   Joseph Ruskin as Mr. X
        Mark Harris as the bookstore manager
        Michele Marsh as the woman in the bookstore
        Gerald Berns as Colin   Charles Stevenson as the minister
        Teleplay written for *Alfred Hitchcock Presents* by Robert Glass, based on the novel of the same name by Margaret Millar, originally broadcast on *The Alfred Hitchcock Hour* on March 20, 1964.
        Directed by Michael Toshiyuki Uno.
        Music composed by Steve Dorff.
        Opener taken from "Beast in View"
        (powder box)   *The prevalence of mashers in our streets and parks has brought about this charming device. It looks like a lady's compact but it is really much more than that. When my lady is accosted by some undesirable party she simply takes this out, as though to powder her nose, however when she opens it . . . (pssss) Before you can say Jack the Ripper, a cloud of teargas is sprayed in the villain's face. Perhaps this lacks some of the excitement that went with wielding the old fashioned hatpin, but it is most effective. Furthermore it actually contained a mirror and powder so that you can freshen up before the police arrive. That's odd, I should be weeping by now. (turns box) No wonder it wasn't teargas after all, this one uses mustard gas. While we wait for developments you may pass the time by watching tonight's narrative. It is about a young woman who is the object of some mysterious threats.*

        Story: Marion McGregor is an author of psychiatry, who comes home one evening to discover a life-threatening message on her answering machine. She tells her new husband, Roger, that the voice sounded like her dead husband, whose body was never found – but he dismisses her suspicions. After an autograph session some days later, Marion suspects someone followed her home. When she hears a man's voice again, she gets scared and runs down to the cellar to hide. Roger arrives home and from upstairs, he can hear the two arguing. Roger enters the cellar, looking for his wife, he finds Marion on the floor next to a rotting corpse – the body of her first husband. When Marion opens her eyes, the same threatening voice from the answering machine comes out of her mouth. Roger races up the stairs as Marion hunts him with a shovel. Following her wounded husband into the living room, Marion meets up with three policemen and the same man that followed her to the house. Madly making another attempt on Roger, the police are forced to shoot her down. It seems the man who was following her is her psychiatrist, Dr. Kaufman, who only wanted Marion to start her therapy again.

Our new compacts have been taken off the market. In the test areas, Los Angeles, Pittsburgh and London, the gas did not prove to be a deterrent. In fact the muggers, long accustomed to the atmosphere in these cities, regarded the gas as a distinct improvement. Perhaps next week, when I return, I shall have another device. Until then, I'm sure that heaven will protect the working girl.

516

Trivia, etc. "My agent had submitted a forward for a short film that I had received an Oscar nomination for," recalled director Michael Uno. "The executive producers, Chris Crowe and Andrew Mirisch had a more experienced director then, and they thought they'd like to give someone with less experience a shot, so they had me in and I got the job. My recollection is during the initial sit-down, there were these lists of people as there always are and they made some decisions and I made others and everything was all set . . . but there was a problem. You see, Cliff Potts was cast at the last minute. I really don't want to say the name of the actor who was originally cast, but we had to make a change the night before we started shooting. The actor who was originally set, I felt, was misbehaving and it would have been enough of a headache – and he looked weird – so it was quite a dilemma. We had to replace him. I said 'Look, this guy is a problem,' and the producers who made the casting initially backed me up and they said 'Well, if he's a problem we'll take him away from you.' I take my hat off to them because I was basically a first-time director at a network level and I think the actor would have taken advantage of me."

On January 26, 1986, *Alfred Hitchcock Presents* was not broadcast, due to the NFL's Super Bowl and Super Bowl Post Game. On February 2, 1986, NBC did not broadcast any episode of *Alfred Hitchcock Presents*, so they could feature a special episode of *The Cosby Show* at 8 o'clock, and an episode of *Amazing Stories* at 8:30, p.m., EST. On February 9, 1986, *Alfred Hitchcock Presents* was again not broadcast, because the network wanted to feature the television premiere of an original made-for-television movie entitled *Under Siege*, starring Peter Strauss, and directed by Roger Young (who had previously directed the episode "Revenge").

EPISODE #18 **"A VERY HAPPY ENDING"** Broadcast on February 16, 1986
Starring: Robert Loggia as Charley   Leaf Phoenix as Pagie Fisher
John Aprea as Fisher   Myrna White as Martha
Danny Dayton as Buzzy Carelli   Blackie Dammett as Doug
Mel Harris as the girlfriend   Michael Reed as the boyfriend
Sydne Squire as the stewardess   Ron Jarvis as the clown
Mercer Helms as the magician
Written and directed for *Alfred Hitchcock Presents* by Tom Rickman.
Music composed by Michael Colombier.
Opener taken from "Appointment at Eleven"
(as a bartender watching TV, but the noise is so loud, that you can't hear Hitchcock. He turns the volume down as the camera zooms for a close-up) . . . *from our sponsor.*

Story: Eleven-year-old Pagie Fisher II, son of a wealthy businessman, is both lonely and deaf. His father pays no attention to the boy, always promising to arrange for Pagie to hear again. Planning to go home for his twelfth birthday, Pagie witnesses a hit man bumping off another hit man in a phone booth at the airport. Later, on board the plane, Pagie meets up with the killer, whose name is Charley, and picks the sleeping man's pockets. When the hit man discovers that the boy holds the evidence, including his drivers license and the murder weapon, the boy makes a proposition. If Charley kills his father, he won't turn the evidence over to the police. But in New York, at the Fisher residence, Charley finds his property and attempts to leave, knowing full well that the boy, in the long run, will regret setting up his father's death. But before he can leave the house, Charley discovers that Mr. Fisher, is actually his employer, the same man who had him set-up for murder at the airport. When Mr. Fisher gives Pagie his birthday present, a hearing aid, Charley pulls out his gun. Seeing that the boy truly loves his father, the hit man decides it's time to settle a few differences between the three, in talk, not with force.

(Hitchcock watching an aquarium in a TV set) *Until next week, good night.*

Trivia, etc. The young actor who played the role of Pagie in this episode, went under the stage name of Leaf Phoenix. He was born Joaquin Raphael, but at the age of four, he decided that he wanted a more earthly name, like that of his elder brothers River and Rain, so he decided on Leaf. In the early 1990s, after establishing a more prominent film career, he took back his birth name, familiar to all as Joaquin Phoenix. Robert Loggia also played a murderer in "You'll Be the Death of Me" on the October 18, 1963 telecast of *The Alfred Hitchcock Hour*, in which he was "done-in" by the observations of a deaf girl named Ruby.

This episode was originally scheduled for February 2, 1986, but was pre-empted for this date instead. On February 23, 1986, *Alfred Hitchcock Presents* was not broadcast on NBC-TV so a special three-hour made-for-television movie, "The Fifth Missile" could be broadcast.

EPISODE #19 **"THE CANARY SEDAN"** Broadcast on March 1, 1986
>   Starring: Kathleen Quinlan as Anne Bowlby   Peter Haskell as Paul Bowlby
>   Adelle Lutz as Lin Chin   Arsenio 'Sonny' Trinidad as Feng Shui Man
>   Beulah Quo as the herbalist   Ping Wu as Victor
>   Michael Paul Chan as Denning   Ian Abercombie as the doctor (uncredited)
>   Teleplay written for *Alfred Hitchcock Presents* by Joan Tewkesbury, based on a
story by Ann Bridge, originally broadcast on June 15, 1958.
>   Directed by Joan Tewkesbury.
>   Music composed by Craig Huxley.
>   **Opener taken from "The Canary Sedan"**
>   (genie of the lamp)   *Good evening ladies and please don't adjust your sets. I
think the picture tube needs . . . little dusting.* (genie appears) "What is your wish O Master?" *Who are you?* "I'm Alfred, the genie of the lamp." *Wow, my name's Alfred too!* "Why is it Master, that when you can have any wish you desire, you prefer small talk?" *Any wish I desire!* "If you want me, rub the lamp." *How long have you been in that tube?* "Master, you have a mania for the unimportant. I have been there for years. No one ever dusts and whoever heard of a genie conjured up by a vacuum cleaner? And now master, the wish, and remember the words of Allah: think big." *But what I want is priceless.* "Nothing is too great, diamonds, rubies." *This would be too much to ask.* "Master, the wish, the wish!" *Give me a commercial, give me a commercial!*

Story: Anne Bowlby has arrived in China during the festival of Ta Chiu, a celebration to appease spirits caught in limbo, because living things refuse to let go of the past. She is picked up by Denning in an old black car, that she thinks is amazing, commenting that it should have been yellow. Denning thinks her remark is funny since the car was originally canary yellow. The more time Anne spends in the car, the more she is pursued by the spirit of her husband's mistress, Lin Chin. Entering a herbalist store, Anne meets Lin Chin face-to-face. In the shop, Lin mixes a special herbal tea and tells Anne that it will bring renewed passion into her marriage. Going home, Anne has Paul drink the tea and after enduring a tender moment, accuses his wife of going through his things. Lin later reveals to Anne how she was poisoned by her brother seven years ago, which is why she has come to Anne for help, asking to be released from her spiritual prison. Knowing she must get rid of the spirit of Lin Chin, so her marriage can be saved, Anne learns that to release Lin's spirit, she must burn Lin's bones, exhumed for the festival. Paul ends up buying the bones and without his knowledge, Anne steals them. Returning to Lin Chin, Anne helps burn them and Lin's soul is finally set free. When Anne returns to see her husband at the office, he is a totally different person, loving and receptive, something he hasn't been in years.

Genie: "I have already granted the little man his third wish, which was to leave you until next week. Granting wishes is easier two at a time. I save on overhead. Now that you know how to summon me, we shall probably be seeing more of each other. Well, don't just sit there, get a dust cloth."

Trivia, etc. One of Joan Tewkesbury's earliest exposures to Hollywood was playing the role of an Ostrich in the 1960 television production of *Peter Pan*, starring Mary Martin. Having written and directed her own movies, including *The Acorn People* (1981) and *Elysian Fields* (1989), Tewkesbury's rendition of the classic Hitchcock episode sheds a different ending than the original, but just as satisfying. This episode was broadcast on a special day and time, Saturday, March 1, 1986 from 9:30 to 10 p.m., EST, instead of Sunday, March 2, 1986 at 8:30.

EPISODE #20   **"ENOUGH ROPE FOR TWO"**   Broadcast on March 9, 1986
Starring: Jeff Fahey as Ray Lee Dick   Darlanne Fluegel as Zoe
Tim Daly as Scott Wexler   Charles Howerton as the highway patrolman
Jonathon Hugger as the gas station counterman
Teleplay written for *Alfred Hitchcock Presents* by David Chase, based on the short story of the same name by Clark Howard, originally broadcast on November 17, 1957.
Directed by David Chase.
Music composed by Mason Daring.
Opener taken from "Not the Running Type," closer from "Where the Woodbine Twineth."
(Hitchcock has a foreign translator) *You see, we are making an effort to reach the widest possible audience. Tonight* (translator speaks in three different languages) *the last was included in case this program reaches the moon. Tonight we present . . .* (translator talks again and Hitchcock shoots him) *Haven't you forgotten something?*

Story: Driving down to China Lake for a camping trip, Scott, his girlfriend Zoe, and her cousin Ray, stop at a gas station to fuel the vehicle. Inside the store, Ray buys a gun and then shoots a man. Although Scott wants to contact the police, Zoe suggests not to, since it won't look too good for him to be connected to the murder. Forced to ride along with the murderous pair, Scott learns Ray's true motives. He and Zoe are going to pick up a buried package, and then head to Mexico with the money. Driving through a closed Air Force base, the trio stops at an abandoned underground missile silo. Scott grabs a hatchet and runs after Ray, intending to end the nightmare, but the murderer shoots him in cold blood. Climbing down the silo to find the aluminum case, Ray sends the money up to the surface. But just as he climbs near the top, Zoe cuts the rope and Ray falls, breaking his leg. When the traitorous girl gets into the Jeep to drive off, she discovers that the keys are gone. Ray shouts up to her, laughing because he has the keys. With no water to drink, Zoe begins her long trek through the baking sand, knowing full well that there's no help within miles.

That concludes tonight's story. Next week we shall return with another. Until then, good night.

EPISODE #21   **"THE CREEPER"**   Broadcast on March 16, 1986
Starring: Karen Allen as Jackie Foster   Timothy Carhart as Rick
Clyde Kusatsu as the detective   Lori Butler as Carol
Danny De La Paz as the latino   Susan Peretz as the neighbor
Sam Vlahos as Griswald, the locksmith   Jack F. Crowe as the biker mechanic
Fred Taylor as the seedy guy   S.A. Griffin as the second policeman
Frank Sheppard as the black man   Kellyn Plasschaert as the receptionist
Tom Noga as the first policeman   John Hayden as the cashier
Sonny Klein as the hot dog vendor

Teleplay written for *Alfred Hitchcock Presents* by Steve Bello and Stephen Kronish, based on the teleplay by James Cavanagh and the story of the same name by Joseph Ruscoll, originally broadcast on June 17, 1956.

Directed by Christopher Crowe.

Music composed by Thomas Newman.

Opener taken from "The Creeper"

(keyhole, eye-test sign)   *Good evening and thank you for peeping in at me tonight. I shall try to make it worth your while. Now if you will look through the keyhole with your other eye.* (hangs up sign) *Excellent, thank you. Incidentally, those of you who think these letters don't spell anything, couldn't be more incorrect. The last line was copied from an old insurance policy. Now that we are all in focus, I should like to make a few prefatory remarks about tonight's liberate. It is called "The Creeper" and is about a person who had a very peculiar way of striking up an acquaintance with women. He killed them.*

Story: Fashion designer Jackie Foster lives in a converted apartment, and has to fly to Rome on business, leaving her keys with a friend, Carol. She is very concerned with all the press regarding "The Creeper," a mass murderer of young women. The trip is postponed and before she has a chance to leave, Jackie learns that Carol has been murdered and the keys to the apartment are missing. A man that she dated once, Rick, has been leaving weird messages on her machine, and scared of both parties, phones the locksmith to change the locks on her door. But the locksmith explains that he won't be able to finish the work until the next day. Spending the evening alone, worrying about whether the Creeper is outside or not, Jackie goes almost mad with fright. Surviving into the morning, the locksmith arrives to service her needs, and Rick phones to tell her the latest news. The Creeper is posing as a repairman. But it's too late, because she has already let him into the apartment and is strangled to death. Remembering Jackie's request for a locksmith the other day, Rick arrives in time and pulls out his gun. The Creeper is in his cab and runs over Rick, but not before our hero manages to shoot the Creeper.

Sorry, time is up. Pass in your papers at once. As for tonight's story, if you liked it, please write in. Perhaps we can give you a sequel to "The Creeper" called . . . "The Toddler."

Trivia, etc. Originally it was scheduled to be two back-to-back episodes of *Alfred Hitchcock Presents* for this evening. The second would have been an adaptation of Ray Bradbury's "The Jar." But instead, only this episode was broadcast over NBC, and "The Jar" was scheduled for a later date.

EPISODE #22   **"HAPPY BIRTHDAY"**   Broadcast on March 23, 1986

Starring: Lane Smith as Robert Warren	Lee de Broux as the plainclothes man
Bruce Gray as Mr. Pearson	Arsenio Hall as Cleavon
Sam Hennings as the patrolman	Nana Visitor as Doris
Sandy Ignon as Hartenstein	Noel Conlon as Tyler, Robert's Lawyer
Carolyn Carradine as Bev	James Boyce as the football stud

Written for *Alfred Hitchcock Presents* by Frisco Miller.

Directed by Randy Roberts.

Music composed by Nicholas Pike.

Opener taken from "The Case of M. J. H."

(microphone and hanging actors)   *Good evening ladies and gentlemen. Welcome to tonight's discussion program. Since we talk for hours without reaching any conclusion whatsoever, we call the program "Dead End." I have heard of anti-intellectualism, but this is a new high. Perhaps I should remove my microphone.* (close-up) *I see it can become rather lethal.* (blows in microphone) *This demonstrates that contrary to what I said previously, our participants can* (zoom-out) *reach conclusions . . . and all at the same time. It is very upsetting, however because we have a half-an-hour left. Too bad they couldn't wait. But I see our sponsor is already rushing to fill the void, and on his heels a story.*

Story: Newspaper reporter Robert Warren plans to spend his 50th birthday with a nice quiet evening at home, since his wife has business out of town. But the evening takes a turn for the worse when two men claiming to be detectives show up, arresting Robert for a 22-year-old murder. Robert knows there's been a mistake, but under the advice of his attorney, Robert must go along with them to straighten things out. He pleads his innocence with the officers, asking to let him go, and when talk fails, Robert makes an escape, vigorously running through the streets of town. The chase doesn't do Robert any good, as the detectives eventually catch up to him, and drag him to a hotel. Complaining about his sore arm in the elevator, the men won't listen, fearing another escape attempt. Dragging him into a hotel room where the lights turn on, Robert finds a loud surprise. His wife and all of their closest friends are gathered around for a surprise birthday party. But sadly, Mr. Birthday Boy has a cardiac arrest and falls to the floor, with mouth and eyes wide open - in disbelief and dead.

I may not be back with "Dead End" next week. You see, the producers prefer to be called intellectuals and they feel that my presence here tends to give credence to the epithet "egghead." It's absurd of course. Next week Alfred Hitchcock Presents will be seen in this spot. Until then, good night.

Trivia, etc. Randy Roberts was an assistant editor for the 1973 biographical documentary *Jimi Hendrix*, but his love for directing movies grew and soon eventually directed episodes for high-rated programs such as *Miami Vice, L.A. Law, Quantum Leap* and *Chicago Hope.* This was the only episode to be directed by Roberts, who was also an editor for the series, and used his talent to piece together a suspenseful – not to mention humorous – episode, worthy of the Hitchcock series. On March 30, 1986, *Alfred Hitchcock Presents* was not broadcast on NBC, so that the hour-long episode of *Amazing Stories.* entitled "The Mission," could be rebroadcast.

EPISODE #23   **"THE JAR"**   Broadcast on April 6, 1986

Starring: Griffin Dunne as Knoll	Fiona Lewis as Erica
Laraine Newman as Periwinkle	Stephen Shellen as Garson
Paul Bartel as the art critic	Paul Werner as the Nazi
Sunshine Parker as the Texan	Eileen Barnett as the Texan's wife
Peter D. Risch as Happy Kaufmann	Regina Richardson as the female art type
Susan Moore as the female fashion victim	
Nathan LeGrand as the male fashion victim	
Roy Fegan as the first person	Leah Kates as the second person
Lori Lynn Lively as the frail woman	Jeffrey Steven Kramer as the first guest
Nina Weintraub as the young woman chased by the Nazi (uncredited)	

Based on the story by Ray Bradbury, and adapted for *Alfred Hitchcock Presents* by Larry Wilson and Michael McDowell. Originally broadcast on February 14, 1964.
Directed by Tim Burton.
Music composed by Danny Elfman and Steve Bartek.
Opener taken from "The Jar"
(in a giant bottle)   *Welcome to the Alfred Hitchcock tale hour. The next time I buy a ship model kit I intend to read the directions more closely. I have one consolation to being unceremoniously bottled like this. That is, wine connoisseurs will say this will be considered a good year. However, I feel I have aged enough. I only hope I'm let out while I still have some fizz. During my absence you'll be entertained by "The Jar," a story about some people who found a very strange source of fascination.*

Story: Conceptual artist Knoll hasn't made one piece of work worthy of consideration.   An art critic writes a really bad review at Knoll's latest exhibit. While taking apart a 1938 Mercedes purchased at a junkyard, Knoll finds a jar with indescribable contents, and becomes entrapped within its spell. Putting the jar in the center of his exhibit, people come from all around to stare at the unusual thing, each seeing something different. One man leaves laughing in hysterics, while another woman claims it makes her sick to her stomach. One man says it's the most beautiful thing he's ever seen, while a pair of lovers feel sexual stimulant. Knoll becomes a huge success overnight and his other pieces sell for large sums. It seems everyone loves the jar except for his wife, Erica, who begs him to get rid of it. Out of jealousy, Erica knocks over the jar and the contents slither away. Grabbing a sharp knife, Erica intends to destroy it but instead she gets into a struggle with her husband and Knoll knows exactly what to do . . . During his next exhibit, Knoll has the jar back on display, now with a strange – but unsuspected - new ingredient: the head of Erica.

Any resemblance between "The Jar" and any other type of home entertainment is purely coincidental. There is just no comparison. However we are working every day to lift the level of television, someday, who knows? Getting out of the bottle proved to be easier than I imagined. However, I had the help of an angry genie, who claimed I had invaded his home. That is all I have to offer this evening. Until next week then, good night.

Trivia, etc. Actor Sunshine Parker plays a Texan in this episode, who looks a heck of a lot like Pat Buttram, the actor who starred in the original 1964 version of the Bradbury classic. In fact, as an in-joke, his wife during the program refers to him as "Charlie." Truly a bizarre episode for director Tim Burton, which marked his only directorial effort for the Hitchcock program.   Like the majority of Burton's movies, the music was specially composed for this episode by Danny Elfman and Steve Bartek. Elfman also composed music for numerous other Burton films including *Beetle Juice* (1988), *Batman* (1989) and *Edward Scissorhands* (1990).   Griffin Dunne, of course, was the dark-haired actor who gave the stomach-churning performance as a steadily decomposing lycanthrope victim in the horror comedy *An American Werewolf in London* (1981). Paul Bartel, director of the low-budget horror picture *Private Parts* (1972), played the character Mr. Walsh in Tim Burton's 1984 project, *Frankenweenie*.   Shortly after this episode aired, Paul Bartel got together with Griffin Dunne to film an episode of *Amazing Stories* entitled "Secret Cinema," directed by Bartel, and starring Dunne in the lead.

This also marked the only episode in which Hitchcock welcomes the viewers to *The Alfred Hitchcock Hour*, which is strange that they kept that line in, since this remake series was only a half-hour.   However, because this episode was originally scheduled as a double feature with "The Creeper," two weeks before, it would make sense that the producers kept that clause in.

EPISODE #24   **"DEADLY HONEYMOON"**   Broadcast on April 13, 1986
    Starring: Victoria Tennant as Carol Rigby
    David Dukes as Dr. Thomas 'Tom' Rigby
    Alan Fudge as Dr. Parker / Ed Wells   Nicholas Coster as Phil
    Lester C. Fletcher as the furniture salesman   Jerry Boyd as the doorman
    Helen Powell Nemir as the chief resident   David Clover as the policeman
    Arturo Bonilla as the parking attendant
    Teleplay written for *Alfred Hitchcock Presents* by Stephen Kronish, based on a story by Henry Slesar, originally broadcast as "First Class Honeymoon" on June 12, 1962.
    Directed by Don Medford.
    Music composed by Rick Conrad.
    Opener taken from "Maria"

(space monkey) *Good evening, ladies and gentlemen. I shall resist the temptation to make tiresome comparisons with my sponsor. After all, I have no desire to hurt anyone's feelings. And my friend here is about to become one of our nation's heroes. You must have learned the news, he's been selected to go to the moon. He's not very excited about it, either that or his trousers are too tight again. Before we launch our brave little explorer, we have a training film to show him. You may watch too.*

Story: Dr. Tom Rigby, Chief of Surgery at Cedars-Sinai, has been married twice before. Rumor has it that both of his wives died mysteriously. Only thirty-six hours after they meet, the two get hitched, and Tom gives his new wife Carol, a sparkling new Mercedes as a wedding present. Ed Wells, an investigator, catches up with Carol in private, and reveals his suspicions that Tom murdered one of his previous wives for the insurance money. When later approached by this odd fact, Tom explains that she died in a boating accident, confirmed in a police report. Carol remains skeptical until a phone message reveals that her husband just took out a $250,000 life insurance policy on her, which she was completely unaware of. Returning home the next day, Carol meets her husband's bookie, who wants to collect Tom's $200,000 debt, or the house. When Tom comes home, he finds his wife packing. Attempting to give his hysterical wife a sedative to calm her down, Carol pulls out a gun and shoots her husband. At the hospital the next day, the new Chief of Surgery, Dr. Parker, is commenting about Tom's unfortunate death . . . and it's uncanny how much Dr. Kenneth Parker closely resembles investigator Ed Wells.

I don't know how it happened. He simply outwitted me. I'm afraid to ask who's going to the moon now. So, until next week, or later, good night.

Trivia, etc. Don Medford was the only person to direct episodes from both the original Hitchcock series, and the remake. In fact, he holds the prestigious honor of directing the first episode filmed for the series, "Into Thin Air," starring Patricia Hitchcock. On April 20, 1986, *Alfred Hitchcock Presents* offered a rebroadcast of "Wake Me When I'm Dead." On April 27, 1986, *Alfred Hitchcock Presents* offered a rebroadcast of "Final Escape."

EPISODE #25 **"FOUR O'CLOCK"** Broadcast on May 4, 1986
　　　　Starring: Kenneth McMillan as Judge Paul Magrew
　　　　Ellen Tobie as Karen Magrew
　　　　Richard Cox as Ben　　　　　　　　Raymond Singer as the prosecutor
　　　　Nicholas Pryor as Ryan, the private detective
　　　　Robert Dryer as the first thief　　　Dennis C. Stewart as the second thief
　　　　Ernie Lively as the second policeman　James Ingersoll as the first policeman
　　　　Grant Owens as the defense attorney　Michael Yama as the Japanese gardener
　　　　Joe Colligan as the gas man　　　　Buzz Borelli as the paramedic
　　　　Teleplay written for *Alfred Hitchcock Presents* by Steve Bello, based on the short story by Cornell Woolrich, originally broadcast on *Suspicion* on September 30, 1957.
　　　　Directed by Andrew Mirisch.
　　　　Music composed by Michael Colombier.
　　　　Opener taken from "Safety For the Witness," closer from "Where the Woodbine Twineth."
　　　　(revolver duel, Hitchcock shoots a man in the back) *Well, as mother used to say, it's better to be safe than sorry. Actually, what you have just seen is not to be taken seriously. It was all make believe, all play acting. Of course the gun is genuine and was loaded, but the doctor isn't a real doctor, he's an actor. I think it's interesting that the duel is no longer considered good form, while cold-blooded murder is more popular than ever. There seems to be no way to stay the march of civilization.*

Story: Judge Paul Magrew, a jealous and obsessive old man, suspects his younger wife of having an affair. When he hires a private detective, who comes back with photographs of Karen meeting secretly with an ex-con named Ben, the judge's suspicions are confirmed. Presiding over a trial, the judge learns the details on how to make a homemade bomb and hurries home to set one up for his wife and her lover in the basement. Unbeknownst to the judge, two burglars break into the house and knock him unconscious, tying him up next to the explosive. When he regains consciousness, he finds himself with only twenty minutes to spare before the bomb is set to go off. Karen and Ben arrive, find the house ransacked, and Ben leaves before the police arrive. When Karen starts the microwave, a fuse is blown, causing the bomb to short circuit. Later, the police find the judge mad, having gone out of his mind from waiting for the explosion, and he has to be taken to a mental hospital for a little rest and relaxation. Ben returns shortly after, promising to take care of his little sister, while her husband recovers.

That concludes tonight's story. Next week we shall return with another. Until then, good night.

Trivia, etc. The choice to save the surprise of the stranger being her brother was a good idea for a surprise ending. That is, if you haven't seen the original hour-long *Suspicion* episode, in which Hitchcock went for a different approach. In the original, Hitchcock apparently felt that the twist of the bomb not going off was enough, and therefore, he let the viewers know early in the play that the man was her brother. The fact that the bomb never went off is a connection to the Hitchcock movie *Sabotage* (1936), in which a little boy is unaware that he is carrying a bomb around. The bomb finally went off and killed the boy, a fact Hitchcock regretted and explained in a 1964 interview: "I made a mistake. I let the bomb go off and kill someone. Bad technique, never repeated it."

EPISODE #26 **"ROAD HOG"** Broadcast on May 11, 1986
Starring: Burt Young as Ed Fratus　　　　Ronny Cox as Sam Medwick
Lee Bryant as Phyllis Medwick　　　　　David Cowgill as Mike Medwick
Vincent Barbour as Tom Medwick　　　　Doug Savant as Joey Medwick
Dennis Robertson as the emergency room doctor
Ed Hooks as the gas station attendant　　Vernon Weddle as the old wildcatter
Robert Covarrubias as the orderly　　　　Jeff Tyler as the young wildcatter
Teleplay written for *Alfred Hitchcock Presents* by Charles Grant Craig, Stephen Kronish and Steve Bello, based on a story by Harold Daniels, originally broadcast on December 6, 1959.
Directed by Mario Di Leo.
Music composed by John Goux.
Opener taken from "Man With a Problem"
(skeleton exercise)　　*1, 2, 3, 4 . . . 1, 2, 3, 4. Now raise your hands above your head. Higher. . . higher. I wish to take this opportunity to welcome you latecomers to Alfred Hitchcock Presents. Someone suggested I go to a slim and trim class and I decided to go even further and start one of my own. Here to encourage you beginners is an illustration of what hard work and determination can do. 1, 2, 3, 4 . . . 1, 2, 3, 4. This is Mr. Webster who I'm certain is the envy of all of you. When Mr. Webster first came to me, he weighed nearly 300 pounds. He was sluggish and run down and was the object of ridicule because of his obesity. Furthermore, his wife had threatened to walk out on him. Now all that has changed for the better. He has his old energy back. He's quite popular socially and his wife has left him. He also has a pleasant job, modelling in the anatomy department of one of our largest Universities. And in evenings, he's endman in a minstrel show. And now ladies and gentlemen, a special low calory story. However, first, for those of you who aren't dieting, we have this bit of treacle.*

Story: Arrogant and self-assured traveling salesman Ed Fratus likes to refer to himself as "King of the Highway" and is unreserved about his dislike for "hillbilly" customers. A serious oil-rig accident has Sam Medwick rushing his son to the hospital, which is in the nearby town. Racing down the mountain road, Sam gets behind Ed's Cadillac and honks his horn in urgency. But the stubborn salesman refuses to let him pass and even runs Sam's truck off the road. Having lost too much blood, Joey dies as a result. About a month later, Ed happens to be in the town's tavern where everyone treats him like dirt. They refuse to buy his wares, but the waitress, Phyllis, entices him with scotch, spiked with pills. Later, Sam and Phyllis confront Ed with the news that they are the parents of Joey Medwick, the boy who died by Ed's thoughtless driving. Believing they poisoned him, Ed runs out of the tavern, racing down the country road to the nearest hospital – the same road Joey died on. Tom and Mike, Joey's surviving brothers, renew the game of road hog with a panicking Ed on their tail. Becoming so hysterical with fright, Ed attempts to pass and runs off the road. When an unsuspecting county coroner investigates, he lists the cause of death as a heart attack. Ed's stomach only contained a lot of scotch and a couple of aspirin.

Mr. Webster seems to have disappeared again. This is one aspect of his life that is a bit tiresome. You see, the dogs keep carrying him off and burying him. I've had to dig him up at least three times. And now it's time for me to disappear. Until next week that is, I shall be back then with another story. Good night.

SUMMER RERUNS

May 18, 1986 *Alfred Hitchcock Presents* was not broadcast over NBC so a special three-hour movie entitled "On Wings of Angels: Part One," could be seen.

May 25, 1986 Rebroadcast of "Revenge"

June 1, 1986 Rebroadcast of "Night Fever"

June 8, 1986 *Alfred Hitchcock Presents* was not broadcast over NBC so *Bronco Billy* (1980), starring Clint Eastwood, could be presented (from 8:30 to 11 p.m., EST).

June 15, 1986 Rebroadcast of "Gigolo"

June 22, 1986 Rebroadcast of "The Gloating Place"

June 29, 1986 *Alfred Hitchcock Presents* was not broadcast over NBC so a premiere of an original made-for-television movie, *Poison Ivy* (1985), starring Michael J. Fox, could be presented.

The following dates are the last three NBC broadcasts of *Alfred Hitchcock Presents* before the USA network picked up the show. Each was a special hour-long double feature, with two half-hour episodes. The first was broadcast from 10 to 11 p.m., EST. The second two were featured from 8 to 9 p.m., EST.

July 6, 1986 "Prisoners" and "Night Caller"

July 13, 1986 "Method Actor" and "The Human Interest Story"

July 20, 1986 "A Very Happy Ending" and "Enough Rope for Two"

USA SERIES - ALFRED HITCHCOCK PRESENTS

By the time NBC ceased broadcasting the remake series in July of 1986, USA, a syndicated cable network, was already broadcasting reruns of the original episodes of *The Alfred Hitchcock Hour*, on Sunday evenings from 10 to 11 p.m., EST. If viewers couldn't get enough Hitchcock from the new series, they had the opportunity to tune to another channel an hour later, and watch the master at work hosting the originals. On October 26, 1986, USA presented their final hour-long presentation of the classic black-and-white series and the week after, November 5, USA began broadcasting reruns of the NBC series. "Man From the South," starring John Huston, was the first presentation. "Wake Me When I'm Dead," was broadcast on January 8, 1987. Two half-hour episodes of the remake series were presented, back-to-back, in the same 10 to 11 p.m. time-slot. During these airings, the episodes (both reruns and originals) were broadcast on other days of the week, from Saturday, Wednesday and Thursday evenings - not just Sunday. Near the end of the series in 1989, the program was seen on both Saturday and Sunday evenings, twice a weekend!

Beginning January 24, 1987, USA began featuring new episodes, filmed exclusively for the cable network. Still offering double features every Sunday night, the first presentation would be the new episode, the second being a rerun of an NBC broadcast. Example: After "The Mole," broadcast on February 21, a rerun of "An Unlocked Window" aired. This run of newly-filmed Canadian productions consisted of thirteen episodes. The only person to remain on board from the earlier NBC run was Andrew Mirisch, the supervising producer.

SEASON TWO – (13 EPISODES)

Art Director: David M. Davis
Casting: Maria Armstrong, c.d.c.
    and Ross Clydesdale, c.d.c.
Costume Designer: Delphine White
Director of Photography:
    Brian R.R. Hebb, c.s.s.
Editors: Tom Joerin and Ronald Sanders
Executive Producers: David Levinson
    and Jon Slan
First Assistant Director: Mac Bradden,
    Alan Goluboff, Bill Spahic
    and Erika Zborowsky
Gaffer: Christopher Porter
Hairdresser: G.E. Freddie Godden
Key Grip: Christopher Dean
Location Managers: Lin Gibson,
    Adam Shully and Steven Wakefield
Make-up Artist: Sandi Duncan
Music composed by Micky Erbe,
    Maribeth Solomon and Ken Wannberg

Music Supervisor: David Greene
Produced by Barbara Joy Laffey.
Production Managers: Mary Kahn
    and Michael McDonald
Production Sound: Bryan Day
Post Production-Coordinator:
    Catherine Hunt
Post Production Audio:
    Master's Workshop, Inc.
Post Production Video: The
    Magnetic North Corporation
Property Master: Doug Harlocker
Script Supervisor: Benu Bhandari
Second Assistant Directors: Karen
    Lee Hall and Wendy Ross
Set Decorators: Danielle Fleury
    and Elinor Rose Galbraith
Still Photographer: Ben Mark Holzberg
Story Editor: Jeremy Hole
Supervising Producer: Andrew Mirisch

U.S. Casting by Reuben Cannon & Associates
A Paragon Motion Pictures, Inc. Production, with MCA-TV as the exclusive distributor.
Broadcast Saturday over the USA network from 10 to 11 p.m., EST. (two episodes back-to-back). Various nationwide and local sponsors.

EPISODE #27   "THE INITIATION"   Broadcast on January 24, 1987
    Starring: Marion Ross as Margaret Sturdevant   Peter Spence as Andrew Spenser
    Dean Hamilton as John Mitchell   Albert Schultz as Greg Turner
    Jesse Collins as Rick Muldoon   Andrew Jackson as Parks
    Doug Lennox as the patrol man
    Teleplay written for *Alfred Hitchcock Presents* by James Norman Beaver, Jr., and
Rob Hedden, based on an original story idea by Rob Hedden.
    Directed by Robert Iscove.
    Opener taken from "The Morning After"
    (fan mail) *Good evening. I'm answering my correspondence. I receive some very interesting letters, threatening and otherwise. Dear Mr. Hitchcock, I'm a man of 60*
526

with a wife of 22. We have a handsome young man of 25 rooming with us. Yesterday I discovered ground glass in my sugar. Isn't this unusual? Anxious. Dear Anxious, Yes this is unusual. I believe arsenic is customary in cases of this kind. But your wife is young and I'm sure she'll learn. Dear Mr. Hitchcock, We have endured your snide and impertinent remarks about our commercials long enough. This to warn you that . . . (turns letter) *So much for fan mail. Now we come to that part of the program for which the sponsor has been waiting. I'm to prudent to describe it.*

Story: Beta Chi Omega is the typical fraternity house, full of young men, hard rocking music, empty beer cans and tons of dirty laundry. One of the boys, John Mitchell, constantly shames Margaret, their housekeeper, who until recently, was the victim of his practical jokes. When a new pledge arrives at the door, Andrew Spenser, John decides to turn his attention to the freshman. Andrew's initiation test will be to shoot Margaret with a gun, assuming it is filled with blanks. But when he pulls the trigger, Andrew is shocked to see the old woman grip her chest. Thinking her dead, the boys hide her body in the trunk of the car, until they can figure where to stash the corpse. What John doesn't know, is that Margaret is in on the joke and climbs out of the car unharmed. The boys go back to the house and try to sooth Andrew with some whiskey and reassurances. Next thing you know, Margaret enters the house dressed as a zombie and Andrew stares at her, and remarks, "Hi, Mom." The two were in cahoots to teach John a lesson. But when the other boys hear Margaret scream, they rush into the room. Andrew aims the gun at John, who turns and crashes through the third floor window. Rushing up to the broken glass, the survivors stare at the twisted body on the ground. It was supposed to be a joke.

I hope you liked our play. We now have a one minute soap opera which I'm sure you'll love. This is the story that asks the question: Can a poor, lonely advertising man from rural Madison Avenue, win customers for his sponsor and find happiness in the upper income brackets? (commercial break) *I'm afraid I may have done it again. However, if I'm sacked, moving up will be no great problem. I'm a clean desk man. This is the type of desk where everything is out of sight. The waste basket, the telephone and here is my secretary. That will be all, Miss Whiteleather. Suppose you tune in next week to see if I'm still on the job. I can at least promise you another story. Good night.*

Trivia, etc. "Jon Slan was the producer for Paragon as I believe he was doing the Hitchcocks," recalled director Robert Iscove. "I had done a series of Philip Marlowes for him [also broadcast over the USA network] so when they began doing the Alfred Hitchcock shows, he asked me to do them. We filmed that episode at a real fraternity house in downtown Toronto and took about eight days to film. I recall the hardest thing being story-telling in nineteen minutes because ultimately with commercials and credits, they cut down to about nineteen / twenty minutes. As for the climax, normally what was done was to have a dummy flying through the air and it was an actor on the ground. Simple camera tricks that didn't involve much thought, really."

EPISODE #28   **"CONVERSATION OVER A CORPSE"**   Broadcast on Jan. 31, 1987
Starring: Barbara Babcock as Cissie Enright   John Vernon as Mr. Brenner
Kate Reid as Johanna Enright
Teleplay written for *Alfred Hitchcock Presents* by Marian Cockrell and Norman Daniels, based on an original story idea by Norman Daniels, originally broadcast on November 18, 1956. (Marian Cockrell's name was mis-spelled in the credits of this episode as "Marion Cochrell.")
Directed by Robert Iscove.
Opener taken from "The Safe Place"
(as a surgeon with two other surgeons and a woman in a magician's box) *Good evening interns, patients and curiosity seekers. One of the marvels of television is its*

educational value. A few years ago, only a handful of people could have witnessed this rare and delicate operation. Now because of television, millions may witness this event, including the subject herself. For we are going to present her with a film of tonight's proceedings. Together with a projector, to say nothing of a beautiful charm bracelet. Each charm to represent a phase of the operation with replicas of each organ removed. Incidentally we call our program, "This is Your . . ." A sentence we don't finish until we see how the operation turns out. And now gentlemen, you may make the incision. (the two surgeons start sawing the box in half) *Stop. This is a dramatization.* (men continue) *Just a moment. Just a moment. We forgot the anaesthetic. However, I have something here that will put anyone to sleep in just sixty seconds.*

Story: When aggressive real estate agent Mr. Brenner talks Cissie and Johanna into selling their family home, the two offer him a cup of hot tea to celebrate. For ten years he has been trying to obtain their property, which will be worth some $75 million, once his shopping center goes up. But during the conversation, the women change their mind and only then does Mr. Brenner realize they poisoned his tea. Cissie couldn't bear to murder a man, so she didn't really put a fatal dose in the drink. Partially paralyzed as a result, Brenner watches as the women try several unsuccessful ways to kill him. Alone for a moment, Brenner begs Cissie to call the police. Johanna will kill him and blame the murder on her, he explains. When Cissie confronts Johanna in the kitchen, she denies it and heads to the living room to get rid of Mr. Brenner, once and for all. Slowly managing to grab a gun, Brenner shoots Johanna dead. As a consolation, Cissie offers him some whiskey (which contains poison) and he drinks it down without suspicion. Cissie gleefully smiles since the house is now hers, and the police will assume the two killed each other off.

I can now report that the operation was a huge success. Our patient now has what she wanted, perfect measurements. 36-0-36. So much for Operation: Operation. Now a word from you know who, after which I shall toddle back. (commercial break) *I'm sorry to say, that after further consideration, the girl on whom we operated became unhappy with the results. She learned that two cannot live as cheaply as one. For one thing she had to buy a sidecar for her motorcycle, things like that. So while she's pulling herself together, I would like to say that I shall be back next week with another play. Until then, good night.*

EPISODE #29   **"MAN ON THE EDGE"**   Broadcast on February 7, 1987
    Starring: Mark Hamill as Danny Carlyle
    Michael Ironside as Lieutenant Rick Muldoon

David B. Nichols as Captain Allard	Jessica Steen as Sally Carlyle
Clark Johnson as Officer Stoker	John Gilbert as Mr. Springer
Jack Jessop as Bristow, the bell man	James O'Regan as the TV cameraman
Sam Stone as the first cab driver	Warren Van Evera as the second cab driver

    Dick Callahan are the third cab driver
    Teleplay written for *Alfred Hitchcock Presents* by James Norman Beaver, Jr., based on a short story by Donald Honig, originally broadcast as "Man with a Problem" on November 16, 1958.
    Directed by Robert Iscove.
    Opener taken from "Don't Interrupt"
    (tied to the train-track)   *Good evening fellow tourists. I think this proves that in some areas the aeroplane can never replace the train. The gentleman who tied me here was most thoughtful. In order to keep the railroad ties from chapping my hips, he put me on an ant hill. And in the event I wanted to do some reading, he left me a railroad timetable. I have found it most useful.   You see my assailant was a railroad executive who took exceptions to some of my remarks about the promptness of trains.   I have the last laugh however, for I see by a footnote that the train he expected would trisect me, runs only on the*

Friday preceding Decoration Day and the Tuesday following Labor Day except on leap year. There isn't another train scheduled to pass for thirty minutes. That should give us just enough time to watch a half- hour television show. Keeping to the theme of tonight's program, I must warn you that before you get a look at the pleasant scenery, we must first pass through . . . one of those dismal tunnels.

Story: Danny Carlyle rents a room on the 28th floor of a hotel, climbs out on the ledge, and begins thinking about all the events that have led up to this night. How he and his young wife, Sally, lost their farm and moved to the city to live in a stuffy, cramped apartment. By the time people gather in the streets, police psychiatrist Lieutenant Muldoon arrives, to make an attempt of talking Danny out of it. Just as he gains Danny's trust, a rookie lets it slip that they are going to grab him, and the man moves away from Muldoon. Remembering when Sally left him for a man named Rick, Danny's heart fills with anger, especially when he recalls her voice on his answering machine saying how Rick would not leave his wife and children for her. When Danny rushed home to find Sally dead of an overdose, he knew then what he had to do. Outside the window, Danny tells Muldoon about the loss of his recently departed, how his wife died, and finally Muldoon convinces the man to put on a safety harness. Stepping out onto the ledge to help, Muldoon realizes who Danny is, and the suicidal man suspected that much. Danny quickly grabs Rick Muldoon and the two go over the ledge, leaving only Danny hanging on, with a strange and satisfied smile on his face.

(starting to snow) *I suppose you expect me to be discouraged but I'm not. I have faith that the railroad will not allow a man to lie here indefinitely. As a matter of fact, some passing workers have assured me that the train will be by in a few seconds.* (whistle) *There it is now. If you want to turn away. . . you may.* (commercial break, followed by the sound of a train crash) *Look, a complete loss. Fortunately no one was hurt. No one on the train that is. I seem to have sustained a very bad bruise on one finger. If you've enjoyed our story or any of this trivia, perhaps you'll be interested in tuning in next week, when we shall have more of the same. Until then, good night.*

Trivia, etc. "In all of those [episodes] there were a list of actors, you know, and we would talk about who would be right for the parts and we would then make offers to actors," recalled director Robert Iscove. "The difference from the original was with Hamill was in a safety harness and Gary Merrill was not. I think it was reflecting the times of the nature of how much violence you could do on television. The scenes on the ledge was a combination of two sets. Part of it was on a real building in downtown Toronto and part of it was green-screened in the studio. All of the close work was green-screened. On the set they were about three feet or four feet from the ground, something like that."

In this episode, Mark Hamill's character first says his name is Steve (before his real name is given to the lieutenant). Steve was actually the policeman's name in the original episode, "Man with a Problem."

EPISODE #30   **"IF THE SHOE FITS"**   Broadcast on February 14, 1987
    Starring: Ted Shackelford as Garret / Jason Cook
    Lawrence Dane as Mr. Adams   Lori Hallier as Samantha Cook
    Colin Fox as Victor Stouts   Cynthia Belliveau as Dana Besson
    Peter Laslow as Ralph   Denise Pidgeon as Margo
    William Colgate as Lieutenant Askew Lois Maxwell as Miss Golden
    An original teleplay written for *Alfred Hitchcock Presents* by Jonathan Glassner.
    Directed by Allan King.
    Opener taken from "The Kerry Blue"

(photographs and girl)   *Good evening, ladies and gentlemen. Welcome to "Candid Capers." This is the program which photographs people in amusing and embarrassing scenes and then shows them to the television audience. Our photographer is returning with a new set of pictures.* (lady hands photos) *Thank you. Allow me to explain how our program works. Our photographer goes into nightclubs, hotels or parked cars and snaps these candid pictures. We then show the photographs on television and everyone has a good laugh. This first picture was snapped in a dark corner of the New Vogue Pauvre Coffeehouse and shows Mr. Andrew Spearman and Miss Gertru . . .* (picture of Hitchcock) *Oh, there's something on this one, excuse me. It's from Mr. Spearman. I see . . .* (rips the photo) *Candid Capers loves a good laugh, but we certainly wouldn't want to cause any misunderstandings. Apparently all he could find on which to write his note, was a hundred dollar bill. While I go through these pictures, perhaps you'd like to look at the following, more formal photography. Thank you.*

Story: Successful businessman Garret Cook will do anything to get ahead in life, even if it means murdering his boss. But his troubles just began when his out-of-work twin brother named Jason, an actor, pays an unscheduled visit. Jason shoots Garret and buries the body in the back yard, planning to embark on his greatest role ever – Garret Cook. No one suspects any difference, even Samantha, Garret's wife, who originally left him over a quarrel. It seems Garret was known as a ladies man, having an affair with his secretary. and Samantha caught on. But with a changed Garret, the love affair rekindles. At the advertising agency where Garret works, Jason learns that he was supposed to present a new campaign for an "All Purpose Magic Cleaner," and now has minutes to create a good one, or be fired from the job. Looking at an X-rated movie marquee out the window that says "Talk Dirty to Me," Jason uses this catch-phrase in his ad campaign. The board of directors love it and just when Jason thinks he's now set for life, it all falls apart. Two policemen enter the office, arresting Jason for the murder of his boss, Charles Everly, because his fingerprints were found on the bottle of pills, which caused Everly's death. Jason can't protest too much about his innocence (or his brother's guilt) because if he does, they will find out about the murder of Garret.

(counting money) *Would you believe it? We don't have a single photograph to show you. I shall tell you more of this in just a moment.* (commercial break) *That concludes our show for tonight. As for Candid Capers, we have added a new feature. The Telephone Tapping Hour. We hope this will be even more entertaining and profitable. So until next week, good night.*

Trivia, etc. "That was the first script I ever sold for television and was quite proud of how the finished product looked," recalled Jonathan Glassner. "It's a funny thing because I had wanted to be a writer for many years and busted my butt to write for television. One day my agent called me and told me that the producer for the series was interested in meeting me. He didn't want any story ideas pitched to him – he just wanted to meet me and see if I could work on his writing staff. So in between the call and the visit I came up with a short story idea, not much really, about ten sentences long, just in case they wanted a story thrown at them. Well, when I got there they looked at me and said, 'Well, tell me what you've got for us.' So I used what I quickly came up with on the way there and they said, 'We'll take it.' And they gave me a contract and asked me to do two more episodes for them. It is amazing how they filmed my first draft word-for-word, without any revisions."

EPISODE #31   **"THE MOLE"**   Broadcast on February 21, 1987
      Starring: Edward Herrmann as Litton / "the fake" Dr. Maxwell Stoddard
      Don Francks as Sergeant Jim Willis   Tim Webber as Alan
      Ann Ward as Sally   Marilyn Boyle as Gladys
      Bernard Behrens as Dr. Parks   Richard Hardacre as Dr. Silver
      Michael Donaghue as the desk man   Eric Stine as the security guard

An original teleplay written for *Alfred Hitchcock Presents* by Rick Berger.
Directed by Richard Bugajski.
Opener taken from "The Baby-Blue Expression"
(at the piano)   *Good evening ladies and gentlemen. Before I begin tonight's concert, I would like to explain the structure of a symphony. All symphonies are composed of two parts, sounds and silences. It is very important that you know the difference between the two. Perhaps I shall give you an example: This is sound.* (finds a corpse in piano) *Good heavens, I don't like this a bit. I was told I would be the only one on the program. He's as stiff as a board, he must have been here some time. To continue our little chat about musical appreciation . . . For an example of sounds, I know nothing better than the next sixty seconds.*

Story: Fifteen years ago, a psychotic killer named Litton, went on a killing spree. Given the nickname "The Mole" because he was afraid of the daylight, and murdered people only at night, he was known for his cunning warfare, outsmarting the police before they could suspect. When he was finally captured and sentenced to life in a Mental Hospital, everyone forgot the horrors until this morning, when due to financial cutbacks, The Mole was released into society – a mistake protested by Dr. Maxwell Stoddard. When the good doctor informs the police that Litton is still very dangerous and has not yet recovered, the police sergeant goes to Litton's rented room where they find everything in shreds. Stoddard tells the sergeant that this type of behavior always precedes an attack. Later finding the body of a slashed security guard, they figure out that The Mole is hiding in the underground tunnels of a factory. Sergeant Willis calls for backup and Stoddard rushes into the tunnels. Over the walkie-talkie, a police call warns the sergeant that the real doctor was found murdered and torn to pieces several hours ago. When the sergeant turns around, it's too late, as he faces Litton holding a small, sharp gardening tool . . .

You have probably been wondering about our friend in the other piano. Rather than disturb him, we simply buried him in his piano. It was rather moving really. Like going down with one ship. And now I shall play the minute waltz. (commercial break) *That was the fastest I've ever played it. I suppose you've noticed that this piano has only one pedal. Because of my speed they had to put in an automatic transmission. Next week I shall be back with more music and further explanatory comments. Until then, good night.*

EPISODE #32   **"ANNIVERSARY GIFT"**   Broadcast on February 28, 1987
Starring: Pamela Sue Martin as Melinda Jensen
Peter Dvorsky as Mark Jensen   Paul Hubbard as Allen Farber
Sunny Besen-Thrasher as Peter Aquila   Robin White as the paramedic
Teleplay written for *Alfred Hitchcock Presents* by Rob Hedden, based on the short story by John Collier, originally broadcast on November 1, 1959.
Directed by Richard Bugajski.
Opener taken from "Anniversary Gift"
(meat-eating flower)   *Good evening ladies and gentlemen. I'm sending this beautiful plant to a dear friend. I believe it's feeding time. These carnivorous plants get quite hungry. This one has been quite useful around here as a garbage disposal. I shall hate to part with it, but I know my friend will love it and I'm sure it will love him too.*

Story: Melinda's husband Mark, a stockbroker, spends more time with his pets than he does with his wife. Forced to feed the snake, owl, tarantula, crocodile, fish, and other pets day after day, Melinda orders him to get rid of the animals or she'll leave. But Mark insists on keeping his pets, so Melinda gives up and turns to her friend Allen for support, whom she's been having an affair with for the past year. As it turns out, Melinda only married Mark for his money, hoping to one day collect a million-dollar life insurance policy. Her boyfriend, Allen, suggests she buy a deadly snake as an anniversary gift, from a friend of his who owns a pet store. Melinda does so, and later that evening, hands her husband his gift-wrapped box, excusing herself for a moment while she gets the anniversary cake. But when Melinda returns home, Mark is alive and well, and tells her that the snake escaped, slithering somewhere around the house. As Melinda goes into the bathroom to take a shower, the snake curls itself around her ankles. Mark hears his wife scream and when the police arrive on the scene, the coroner explains that she had a heart attack. Somehow she didn't know that king snakes, not coral snakes, are perfectly harmless.

I'm attempting to improve on nature by giving this flower a more inviting scent. I want my friend to get quite close. This perfume has such a suggestive name, I'm not even allowed to mention it on the air. The sales woman told me it's infallible in attracting men. This was the last bottle they had, their entire supply was bought up by the Army Recruiting office. I shall return next time with another story. Until then, good night. (continues spraying until he gets dragged down; commercial break; followed by Hitchcock being eaten by flower)

Trivia, etc. Pamela Sue Martin, who played the role of Melinda in this episode, is remembered for her role of Nancy Drew in the television series *The Hardy Boys 'Nancy Drew Mysteries*. Known for playing the first Fallon Carrington Colby in *Dynasty*, Martin recalled how she loves playing roles on both television and in movies, in which the female is in control over the male, just like her domineering role in this episode. "I enjoy the idea of playing a woman who is successful and strong, who is not one of these hideous nasty bitches that are so often portrayed in television. There have been too many of those cliche types where either a woman is weak and docile - a man's so-called 'dream woman' - or some real witch-like, awful demonic woman. I don't think either one of those types are realistic and this kind of role is a lot less black and white, more real and a better role model." This episode also featured a sex change in the plot, like previous episodes, but this was the first time that both main characters changed – the original episode featured actress Barbara Baxley as the pet lover, and actor Henry Morgan as the villain.

EPISODE #33   **"THE IMPATIENT PATIENT"**   Broadcast on March 7, 1987
          Starring: E. G. Marshall as Charlie Pitt
Patricia Hamilton as Mrs. Greysome   Patricia Collins as Dr. Winton
James Edmond as Philip Chase   Frances Hyland as Edith Ferris
William Webster as Mr. Prescott   Suzanne Cyr as Christine
Rod Wilson as Eddie   Irene Pauzer as Freda Smith
An original teleplay written for *Alfred Hitchcock Presents* by John Antrobus.
Directed by Allan King.
Opener taken from "What Frightened You, Fred?"
(following footsteps with a dog)   *Good evening, ladies and gentlemen. We have been trying to track down an escaped convict. But we seem to have lost him here. . . where he stopped to take some dancing lessons, obviously. What's worse, my friend the hound, now runs with a definite cha-cha-cha motion. It's rather embarrassing. He also insists that I lead and you can't track down anyone that way.* (close-up) *Of course it's fine while we're dancing. While I cope with the problem of a convict at large in a dance school and a hound who wants to learn the tango, suppose you take up the case of the sponsor, who merely wants to be liked.*

Story: When Charlie Pitt learns that he has terminal cancer, his only wish is to be left alone and die in peace. Even his doctor has given up, accepting Charlie's wish, since he gets no cooperation from the old man. One day, in the hospital, Charlie's gloomy routine changes when Mrs. Greysome shows up to volunteer her services twenty-four hours a day, seven days a week. She is so cheerful and boisterous, that she annoys all the sick patients in the hospital. When Mrs. Greysome notices the bread crumbs Charlie leaves for Jocko, his pet mouse, she gives him a lecture about the evils of mice. After a hectic search-and-destroy mission, Mrs. Greysome kills the mouse, throwing its little body in the garbage can. Charlie, saddened by the loss of his friend, retrieves the body and hides him in an empty Kleenex box. Seeking revenge, Charlie chloroforms the woman and places her in the bed of a female patient, due for exploratory surgery. The next day, Charlie's doctor arrives to explain the terrible mix-up which lead to Mrs. Greysome's death. But looking on the bright side, they do have some good news: Charlie is in remission and can go back home. Charlie says the credit for his recovery should go to Mrs. Greysome, who gave him a reason to live. Leaving the hospital with his tissue box, Charlie's first agenda is to give Jocko a decent burial.

(tuba) *This is all that is left of the dance school orchestra. They were playing the twist when it happened. When they began, this was a saxophone. I would say dancing the twist is like scratching your back on a post, without the post. Now, for those of you who wish to practice the twist, this would be an excellent time. In fact, if you twist around far enough, you might miss the next commercial, after which I shall waltz back.* (commercial break, footsteps lead up a wall) *We don't intend to turn our convict in, we just want him to show us, how he did it. We shall probably still be waiting here next week,* (close-up) *when we return with another story. Until then, good night.*

EPISODE #34 **"WHEN THIS MAN DIES"** Broadcast on March 14, 1987
  Starring: Adrian Zmed as Edgar Kraft   Brenda Bazinet as Maureen Kraft
  Frank Moore as James Stuyvesant   Frank Adamson as Lou Marks
  Cec Linder as the older doctor   Cheryl Wilson as the nurse
  Ray Paisley as Leon Dennison
  Teleplay written for *Alfred Hitchcock Presents* by Jeremy Hole, based on a story by Lawrence Block.
  Directed by Jim Purdy.
  Opener taken from "Flight to the East"
  (flying carpet) *Good evening earthlings. Now you housewives know what to do with your rugs when the moths get them. Put the moths to work. After all, if you can't lick them, join them. This could be the transportation of the future. I'm certain that the day is not far off, when the two-carpet family will be quite common. No special launching platform is needed. The well waxed hallway of your home will do. 10,000 feet up and yet I could swear I saw a billboard. Over there.*

Story: Maureen Kraft goes through the stack of overdue bills, trying to figure how to pay her creditor off. Her job at the beauty parlor doesn't pay much, and her husband, Edgar, is a compulsive gambler. Among the bills she finds a plain white envelope with a letter in it that reads: "When this man dies, you will receive $1,000. Joseph H. Neimann." Dismissing the letter as a prank, Maureen and Edgar laugh it off . . . until the papers report the death of Joseph H. Neimann, and they receive the money in cash, as promised. Edgar first pays back $500 to his loan shark, James Stuyvesant, with a promise to pay off the other half in a few days. Maureen wants to use the other half of the money to pay some bills, but Edgar grabs hold of it first, and gambles it away. Soon after, another letter arrives in the mail reading: "When this man dies, you will receive $5,000. Claude Pierce." A few days later, the man named Pierce is murdered during a house robbery and again, the money comes in the mail with a note: "As promised." Edgar tries to pay off the loan shark, but he still owes another $5,000. A third letter arrives, reading: "When this man dies, you will receive $10,000. Leon Dennison." This time Edgar decides to take care of the matter personally, bludgeoning Dennison to death. Returning home, he finds another envelope in the mail filled with money, and a note attached: "Thank you. How do you like your new job?"

I shall certainly never try that again. I learned too late that it was a three-stage carpet and I was the first stage. I did manage to take some pictures which I shall show you now. Here is how the earth people look to a Martian. (commercial break) *As you can see, the Martians have a rather distorted picture of our world.* (a carpet falls down) *It looks at though our flying carpet is falling earth-ward and disintegrating into throw rugs. This concludes tonight's space adventure. Next week I shall be back with more fiction, scientific or otherwise. Until then. Good night and a happy international geophysical year to all of you.*

EPISODE #35   **"THE SPECIALTY OF THE HOUSE"**   Broadcast on March 21, 1987

Starring: John Saxon as Garth December	Neil Munro as Russ Bennett
Jennifer Dale as Betty Jo Bennington	Larry Aubrey as Bernard
Derek Keurvorst as John Maxwell	Robert Morelli as Frank Keller
Peter Blais as the man	Patricia Idlette as the woman
Stella Sprowell as the bag lady	

Teleplay written for *Alfred Hitchcock Presents* by Jonathan Glassner, based on the short story by Stanley Ellin, originally broadcast as "Specialty of the House" on December 13, 1959.

Directed by Allan King.

Opener taken from "You Can't Trust A Man"

(waking up from a nightmare) *Oh, good evening, I just had a terrible nightmare. It lasted only a minute but it was a shattering experience. Let me tell you about it before we see tonight's play. It was like a motion picture and as I watched a voice kept shouting at me.*

Story: Garth December, an arrogant food critic of a large circulating newspaper, takes his friend Russ Bennett to a restaurant entitled "Where The Heart Is," and is given the "specialty of the house," known as lamb fritters. For once in his lifetime, Garth is unable to describe the ingredients, and asks Betty Jo, the owner (and chef) of the restaurant, if he could buy her recipe for inclusion in his latest book. But the woman turns his offer down and a furious Garth goes home to write a bad review about the dining club. Surprisingly, Betty Jo has a lot of avid supporters, who send hate mail to Garth, and the admission lines to her restaurant don't die down. In retaliation, Garth hires an actor to fake food poisoning outside the restaurant, but nothing can dissuade the customers once they've eaten her food. After many trials and errors, Garth sends in health inspectors and Betty Jo finally agrees to let him see her make the fritters. Alone together, she takes him into the kitchen, shows him everything, including her special ingredient, stashed away inside a large freezer. Holding a huge meat cleaver above his head, Betty Jo reveals her secret, remarking "we are what we eat."

I just learned that nightmare I had was a commercial. I suppose one can't expect to get pleasant dreams for nothing. but I never realized before, they that were sponsored. Now that you know, there is no escape in sleep, perhaps you'll watch the following electronic nightmare. Please do not be frightened. I shall be right here all the time. (commercial break) *That is all for tonight. Now you're on your own. So until next week at the same time, pleasant dreams.*

Trivia, etc. "That was the only episode I didn't write an original for," recalled Jonathan Glassner. "They had bought the rights to do this episode, taken from a short story by Stanley Ellin and asked me to write an adaptation for it. Apparently they had other writers attempt to make something out of it, but none were successful. The original, if you've ever read it, was inside personally, where the entire story concerned a man who did nothing but pay visits to the restaurant, and it was all in his head. I had to expand the story line a little and create outside characters. Of the three episodes I wrote for the program, this was the one that I liked the best. I think it was actually one of the best episodes of the series, too."

EPISODE #36 **"THE FINAL TWIST"** Broadcast on March 28, 1987
>   Starring: Martin Landau as Wallace Garrison   Robert Wisden as Mike Johnson
>   Ann-Marie MacDonald as Denise Tyler   Murray Cruchley as Lon Smith
>   Paul Soles as Moses Harper
>   Teleplay written for *Alfred Hitchcock Presents* by Jim Beaver, based on a story by
William Bankier.
>   Directed by Atom Egoyan.
>   **Opener taken from "Death Sentence"**
>   (in the bathtub)   *Good evening. No, this is not an effort on our part to add sex to the program. I'm dressed for the party . . . a come-as-you-are party. This is what one gets for having a telephone in the bathroom. Well it could have been worse. I feel a bit like Cinderella. For I've been warned that I must positively leave the ball before low tide, and I can't afford to take chances. After all, I was once arrested for indecent exposure when I removed a Halloween mask. All of you, of course, are invited to the party. But remember: don't drop what you're doing, bring it along. But first we must greet the man who throws these weekly soirées and who always manages to spoil the fun. Our dear host.*

Story: Special effects artists Mike Johnson and Denise Tyler, and account manager Lon Smith are fed up with their unscrupulous boss, Wallace Garrison. They all plan to quit their jobs at the post production film house, and uses Denise's new 3-D special effects process to bring in new business. Before they can do so, Garrison barges in and demands that Mike re-edit two day's worth of work in one day, fires his own public accountant, and orders Lon to fill out his personal income tax. If there are any late penalties for the deadline not being met, it will come out of Lon's salary. On top of all that, Garrison shows them the patent application for Denise's new special effects process - in his own name. Later that evening, Denise invites Garrison in to her office for a drink. Lon and Mike yell out "Fire!" and she runs to call the police while Garrison waits in her office. Over the phone, she tells the police to come right over because she's afraid Garrison will do something stupid, having drunk too much. Garrison, however, runs to the window and seeing a group of fire fighters holding a safety net, the unscrupulous boss climbs out on the ledge. Mike shouts for Garrison to jump and when the old man does, the cement pavement silences his screams. Denise turns off the projector, which uses an advanced mirror image, and the fire fighters vanish into thin air. Murder accomplished through special effects.

>   *This is not part of the festivities. I found this bottle with a message in it, floating in the tub. It could be a plea for help from some castaway, or even a last note from the hero of tonight's saga.* (reads the note) *This is certainly a sneaky way to get a message in. It's from big brother again. I'll just put some soap on the floor and slip back at the conclusion of his remarks.* (commercial break; now with bathrobe on) *Well, the evening wasn't a total loss. For I got my back washed and also received a very good job offer. An Italian actress needs a stuntman to take a bubble bath for her in her next picture. I was hired when it was discovered that the actress and I had the same measurements. In different places, of course. I shall be finished in time for next week's program. Until then, good night.*

Trivia, etc. In the pre-screening scene, there is a movie poster hanging on the wall of Alfred Hitchcock's *Vertigo* (1958). Martin Landau returned after appearing in *The Alfred*

Hitchcock Hour's "The Second Verdict." Landau also played the role of Leonard in *North by Northwest* (1959). Atom Egoyan, the Egyptian-born Canadian director, directed his first of two episodes, and was only 27 years old when he directed the feature *Family Viewing* the same year, which even impressed Wim Wenders. *The Sweet Hereafter* (1997), also directed by Egoyan, won the jury's special award at Cannes.

EPISODE #37 **"TRAGEDY TONIGHT"** Broadcast on April 4, 1987
        Starring: Catherine Mary Stewart as Rachel Jenkins

Isabelle Mejias as Kelly Jenkins	Denis Forest as Curt Slessinger
Robert Benson as Mr. Stein	Sean Hewitt as Ralph Elenson
Jeff Christensen as the student	Glynis Davies as the girl
Bob Collins as the masked man	

An original teleplay written for *Alfred Hitchcock Presents* by Jonathan Glassner. Directed by Sturla Gunnarsson.
Opener taken from "The Equalizer"
(as a golfer with no ball) *Good evening, and welcome to tee time. I'm taking up golf. I've learned to play by watching a demonstration on television. I'm convinced that it's very easy to make a hole-in-one. At least this one.* (starts to swing at man's head) *In the demonstration, a golfer knocked a ball off his friend's head. I'm not using a ball. Being a beginner, I feel I'm entitled to a larger target. Perhaps you'd better look the other way. I know I shall.*

        Story: Rachel Jenkins comes home to find her sister, Kelly, an actress, being attacked by a man. Rachel breaks his arm, only before Kelly introduces him as her acting partner, Curt. Apparently when Rachel injured Curt, she accidentally broke her architectural model that was for her presentation meeting in the morning. She has only one night to rebuild it, but keeps being interrupted by Kelly's assignments for her acting class. When Kelly tells Rachel about a man that has been following her recently, wearing a ski mask, and that he's in the building, Rachel dismisses her sister's actions as part of the acting course, and continues fixing her model. When the stranger with the mask enters the apartment, Rachel grabs a gun, but believing it's Curt under the mask, dismisses the firearm as a prop. Kelly screams to shoot but Rachel won't play their game. Still convinced that it's all an act, Rachel puts the gun to her face and pulls the trigger . . .

        So much for the high price of low fidelity. I'm quite angry with my friend. He ruined my club and he didn't land anywhere near the hole. As a matter of fact, I can't even find him. Now I have to buy a ball, it's quite distressing. Why don't you join me in the locker room after we pass one of those sand traps that dot the fairways of television. (commercial break) *I thought we'd never get out of that one. However, we seem to have completed the course in thirty minutes, which is par. Why don't you join us next week for another round? In the club house, of course. Good night.*

        Trivia, etc. "Nothing comes finer than 'Tragedy Tonight.' The inspiration came from some of my actor friends," recalled Jonathan Glassner. "One of them paid a visit to me once and began making characterizations and from that spawned this episode. I never went to the productions and of all the scripts I ever wrote, only on a few did I have production supervision, but this script came out quite good since I wasn't involved in the production."

EPISODE #38 **"WORLD'S OLDEST MOTIVE"** Broadcast on April 11, 1987

Starring: Dwight Schultz as David Powell	Diane D'Aquila as Ellen Powell
Cynthia Dale as Kelly	David B. Nichols as Mr. Smith
Toni Ellwand as Rosita	Gloria Reuben as Pam
George Buza as Cal	

Teleplay written for *Alfred Hitchcock Presents* by Richard Chapman, based on a short story by Larry M. Harris, originally broadcast on *The Alfred Hitchcock Hour* as "The World's Oldest Motive" on April 12, 1965. *

Directed by Allan King.

Opener taken from "The Door Without A Key"

(bicycle) *Good evening, ladies and gentlemen. I have just been competing in a six-day bicycle race. I'm quite proud to say I finished first. I quit after five minutes. Fortunately, the bicycle seems to have been invented by some realist who knew how often he would have to push it. For those of you who do not care to watch bicycling, we have a pageant presented by a group of travelling players. But first, this solo from a strolling troubadour.*

Story: David Powell is a real estate agent who has trouble keeping up with his bills because his critical wife, Ellen, spends money as fast as he makes it. At a bar, David meets his girlfriend Kelly, who listens impatiently to his story before walking out on him. In the next booth, a stranger named Mr. Smith introduces himself as a "problem contractor." David is dumbfounded by the hit man's offer, but finally agrees, seeing no other way out of his problem. The following day, David withdraws the money from his bank account and gives it to Mr. Smith. Squaring his relationship with Kelly, David gives her an expensive diamond necklace. Later that evening, Ellen cooks him a romantic dinner, apologizing for her recent behavior and the guilt-ridden David changes his mind. But when he tries to cancel the deal with Mr. Smith, the hit man turns blackmailer, and demands another $10,000. Frantic, David scrapes together the money and cancels the contract. Promising to take Ellen on a second honeymoon, David returns to Kelly's to retrieve the necklace, hoping it will pay for the trip. But when he gets there, Mr. Smith is relaxing on her sofa, and David realizes that he has been used. Returning home, David finds his wife changed back to her original self. With no money for the honeymoon, Ellen complains to no end.

I wan't to apologize for the lack of bloodshed on tonight's program. We should try to do better next time. However, if all you wishes something to make your blood run cold, we have commercials to do that. Here is one of them, after which I shall again peddle into view. (commercial break) *I have abandoned my bicycle. I find the job can be done much better by hand. Next week we shall be back again with another program. Based on authentic stories taken from the files of America's best television writers. Good night.* (Honk! Honk! Hitchcock drives off in golf cart)

EPISODE #39 **"DEATHMATE"** Broadcast on April 18, 1987

Starring: Samantha Eggar as Lisa Talbot   Wayne Best as Mark Taylor
John Colicos as Carter Talbot   Richard Monette as Brian Moss
Mary Beth Rubens as Beth

Teleplay written for *Alfred Hitchcock Presents* by Marlene Matthews, based on a story by James Causey, originally broadcast on April 18, 1961.

Directed by Allan King.

Opener taken from "Total Loss"

(in a steamcabinet) *Good evening, friends. . . and critics. Welcome to Alfred Hitchcock Presents. I say this for those of you who may be under the impression, you have tuned in to a production of Salome with me playing John the Baptist. I'm sure you are wondering why I, of all people would be in a steamcabinet. Actually, I'm having my suit pressed and was too modest to remove it.* (steam plus train whistle) *We had to hurry that a little. You see there's a certain party who wishes to press . . . his suit. A matter he will attend to at once.*

---

* Hitchcock's original opening to "The World's Oldest Motive" was used even for the remake series, but for a different episode.

Story: Carter Talbot is celebrating his 60th birthday and during his party, begins to show off so others won't get the impression that he's getting old. His beautiful (and younger) wife Lisa, flirts with her lover, Mark Taylor, but even a drunk Carter suspects. Lisa wants Mark to run away with her but he claims he cannot because of some financial trouble and needs $50,000. Against Mark's wishes, Lisa tells her husband about her love affair with Mark, which results in Carter beating his wife. Only by divorce or death will she inherit his fortune. Angry, Mark orders her to go and spend the evening with friends, and establish an alibi. Racing over to Carter's, Mark fights the gun out of the old man's hand and when Carter falls and hits his head, Mark drags the unconscious body to the bathroom and drowns him in the tub. Lisa arrives to find Mark in the act, informing him that she just phoned the police. You see, Lisa has another lover, a friend named Brian, who will vouch for her whereabouts, as they just arrived in time to catch Mark in the act of killing her husband. Only now does it dawn on Mark that he has been set up.

I can't seem to get out of here. The certain party I mentioned a short time ago locked me in and is now selling three baseballs for a dime to passers-by. I'm not sure what he has in mind, but I don't like the way they're looking at me. (baseballs thrown at Hitch) *Fortunately we had already planned to inject something at this time that may save my life a more inviting target, here it comes now. After which I shall try to rejoin you.* (commercial break) *As you see, I managed to escape. Next week, we shall be back with another story. Until then, . . .* (train sounds) *. . . plum pudding. Good night.*

SEASON THREE - (21 EPISODES)

Between seasons, the reruns continued as double features, with both the NBC and USA episodes. They were occasionally pre-empted due to tennis finals. On August 22, 1987, only one episode aired, from 7 to 7:30 p.m., EST, instead of two half-hour presentations later that evening, due to tennis Semi-Finals of Tennis. Less than a year after the new thirteen episodes were broadcast, a second production of episodes were broadcast over USA, all new stories, no remakes of originals. In fact, most of the scripts were written by either the producers or the story editors of the series. This second batch consisted of fourteen episodes. The opening episode, "VCR – Very Careful Rape," consisted of the specially-composed Hitchcock opener from "Mrs. Bixby and the Colonel's Coat," to open the new season.

Art Director: Katherine Mathewson
Associate Producer: Mary Kahn
Camera Operator: Ray Brounstein
Casting by Maria Armstrong,
    Ross Clydesdale, c.d.c.
    and Laela Weinzweig, c.d.c.
Costume Designers: Maureen Gurney
    and Delphine White
Director of Photography: Maris Jansons
    and Vic Sarin
Editors: Bill Goddard and Tom Joerin
Executive Producers: Jon Slan
    and Michael Sloan
First Assistant Directors: Alan Goluboff
    and Felix Gray
Gaffers: Eldie Benson
    and Michael McMurray
Hairdressers: Reg LeBlanc
    and Divyo Putney

Key Grips: Christopher Dean
    and Daniel Narduzzi
Line Producer: Mary Kahn
Make-up Artists: Sandi Duncan
    and Irma Parkkonen
MCA TV Production Executive:
    Nigel Watts
Music Composed by Micky Erbe,
    Milan Kymlicka, Maribeth
    Soloman and Ken Wannberg
Music Supervisor: David Greene
Post Production-Coordinator:
    Catherine Hunt
Post Production Audio: Filmhouse
Post Production Video: The
    Magnetic North Corporation
Produced by Barbara Joy Laffey.
Production Designer: David M. Davis
Production Manager: Len D'Agonstino

Production Sound: Bryan Day
and Clark McCarron
Property Masters: Doug Harlocker
and Byron Patchett
Script Supervisors: Benu Bhandari
and Kathryn Buck
Set Decorators: Enrico Campana
and Danielle Fleury

Still Photographer: Ben Mark Holzberg
Story Editors: Glenn Davis
and William Laurin
Supervising Producer:
Robert DeLaurentis
U.S. Casting by Donna Dockstader.

A Paragon Motion Pictures, Inc. Production
Michael Sloan Productions in association with MCA TV, exclusive distributor
Broadcast Saturday over the USA network from 10 to 11 p.m., EST. (two episodes back-to-back). Various nationwide and local sponsors.

EPISODE #40   "VCR - VERY CAREFUL RAPE"   Broadcast on February 6, 1988
Starring: Melissa Anderson as Laura Donovan   Cedric Smith as Paul Stevens
Cheryl S. Wilson as Molly Stevens   Laurie Paton as Kathy
Joe-Norman Shaw as Steve   Jim Bearden as Lieutenant Fraser
Barbara Budd as Detective Miller   David Walden as Phil Rossetti
An original teleplay written for *Alfred Hitchcock Presents* by Michael Sloan.
Directed by Zale Dalen.
Opener taken from "Mrs. Bixby and the Colonel's Coat"
Good evening ladies and gentlemen and welcome to a new season of Alfred Hitchcock Presents. As has been our custom, we shall present homey little stories of an unusual nature. We shall continue to give the little man, or woman, his due. When crime is occasionally dealt with, it will be crime as practiced by ordinary people, like the fellow next door. I think that by spring, a large number of you will be thinking of moving. There is one aspect of this program which has changed. If you have tuned in to hear me make snide remarks about an innocent sponsor, you are doomed to disappointment. I'm proud to say, I have resolved my antagonisms and have become completely sponsor oriented. I have met our new sponsor and find him (a halo appears above his head) *to be agreeable, charming, witty, honest, sincere, intelligent, dependable, trustworthy, loyal, brave, clean and reverent.*

Story: While reviewing her lines in front of a video camera, actress Laura Donovan is brutally attacked by a man who rips off her clothes and rapes her, unaware that the camera is still rolling. With the help of her friend Kathy, Laura turns to the police, and there, they discover that her attacker was Paul Stevens, a wealthy architect Laura knows only as a casual acquaintance. When Paul's wife hears the accusation, she claims her husband is innocent, stating that he was with her at the time of the rape. The following day, Paul meets up with Laura on the street, confessing she'll never be rid of him because deep down inside, he believes, she wants him. In acting class, Laura tells Kathy that she has proof of the rape, the video camera caught the whole thing, and needs a little assistance with a plan. Later that evening, Laura invites Paul to her apartment, and replays the tape. Paul insists it isn't him, but since he has Paul's coat, gloves and watch, Laura comments "That's right, but who's gonna believe it" and then she thrusts a pair of scissors into Paul's chest, whispering that she did it for Janice. You see, Paul raped her sister Janice a long time ago and now she's residing in a sanitarium with no chance of recovery. Having successfully murdered her sister's attacker, Laura thanks her friend, Steve, for helping arrange the performance, and packs her bags. She'll be leaving town for a while.

At least my sponsor doesn't seem to be taking any action as the result of my attitude. (rope with snare is let down) *Until next week . . . good night.*

EPISODE #41 **"ANIMAL LOVERS"** Broadcast on February 13, 1988

        Starring: Susan Anton as Diane Lewis

Ron White as Ray Tyler   Cec Linder as Dr. Alan Hoffman

Alec Willows as Detective Brown / Mr. Witherspoon

Tanja Jacobs as Marjorie   Francine Volker as the nurse

An original teleplay written for *Alfred Hitchcock Presents* by Robert DeLaurentis.
Directed by Sturla Gunnarsson.

Opener taken from "Craig's Will"

(with three dogs) *Good evening. I have some advice for those of you who want to be performers. Don't blindly answer an advertisement. How was I to know that they call themselves the Doheeny brothers. That is Shep, that's Talsa and this is Bounce. All right and I'm Spot. You have no idea what I've been through this week, jumping through hoops. They're jealous because I can stand on my hind legs better than they. It's the only trick I do well. Ours is a difficult act to follow. But I know someone who is just fool-hardy enough to try. After which, we shall have tonight's play.*

      Story: Animal lover Diane Lewis has a prized English sheepdog named Harry, and meeting a man named Ray Tyler in the park, takes his advice and sends the dog to a specialist, Dr. Alan Hoffman. In the waiting room, Diane meets Mr. Witherspoon and his bloodhound. Witherspoon kindly lets Diane see the doctor first, and by the next morning, learns from Hoffman that her pooch has a degenerative muscle disorder. She agrees to have Harry painlessly put to sleep, and later, puts the dog's ashes in an urn on her mantle. Inviting Ray over for a "thank you" dinner for being so kind about Harry, Diane surprises him when Dr. Hoffman shows up, also by invitation. Serving the two champagne, she tells them that she had Harry's ashes analyzed - it wasn't her dog. Then she recalls reading a magazine article about con men who supposedly put pets to sleep, but really sold them to a high bidder. With the champagne drugged, Dr. Hoffman and Ray Tyler fall to the floor. Diane explains how she locked all the windows and doors, and a ruptured gas line will kill them, the same way they intended to kill Harry. Outside, Diane meets Mr. Witherspoon who is really Detective Brown at the police precinct, and is reunited with Harry. Detective Brown thanks Diane for helping them apprehend Tyler and Hoffman.

      After the humiliations we've experienced this evening, I think it's time man reasserted his superiority over animals. Until next week, good night. (Hitchcock approaches four cats with a chair and whip)

EPISODE #42 **"PRISM"** Broadcast on February 20, 1988

        Starring: Lindsay Wagner as Susan Forrester

        Michael Sarrazin as Lieutenant Steven Rykker

Brent Strait as Jim Sweeny   Warren Davis as Jerry Katzman

Vivian Reiz as Dorothy Katzman   Susan Gattoni as Liddia

Terry Doyle as the coroner   Benjamin Barrett as the kid

Thomas Anderson-Baker as the redhead   Bruce McFee as Donovan

An original teleplay written for *Alfred Hitchcock Presents* by Michael Sloan.
Directed by Allan King.

Opener taken from "None Are So Blind"

(sitting in front of a mirror, with wigs) *Good evening. The entertainment industry is always crying for new faces. I've decided to give them one. Not that there is anything wrong with the old one. In fact I think it's rather good . . .* (mirror cracks) *Well it could have been worse, what if I had cracked? See here is the one . . .* (puts on a wig) *I've always wanted to be someone else . . .*

Story: Lieutenant Steven Rykker is assigned to investigate the murder of Jason Forrester. Forrester's wife, Susan, claims she saw an intruder running from the house. One of the neighbors across the street informs the detective that Jason was a ladies man, girls coming in and going out too many times for his wife not to suspect. Checking out the lead at an exclusive nightclub, Rykker meets a woman named Gypsy, who confesses that she once had an affair with Jason, but she didn't kill him. At an Aerobics Fitness Center, Steven questions Stella Freeman, who suggests they talk to a client named Susi Farmer, who also had an affair with Jason Forrester. At a playground late that evening, the detective sets a trap and apprehends Susi, who confesses that it was she who killed Jason. "He said to me 'I am tired of this sexual game. I want my wife back'," Susi cries. "He had to die. He used me." She confesses how she stabbed Jason and trashed the place, making it look like the act of an intruder. Now Steven knows which of Susan's multiple personalities is a murderous one. Sadly for Steven, she had a sixth personality, that of *his* lover, but with a little drink, he'll overcome that.

And now I shall remove myself, but soon I shall return with another story. Good night.

EPISODE #43 **"A STOLEN HEART"** Broadcast on February 27, 1988
Starring: William Katt as Dr. Burke   Bernard Behrens as Dr. Heller
Damir Andrei as Winters   Masha Grenon as Katherine Murphy
Sharry Flett as Judith Richardson   Kenner Ames as Zimmerman
T. J. Scott as Hardy   Patrick Rose as Dr. Stevenson
Marco Bianco as Jacobs   Johnny Goar as Bennet
Murray Ellis as Detective Lewis
An original teleplay written for *Alfred Hitchcock Presents* by Robert DeLaurentis. Directed by Rene Bonniere.
Opener taken from "Alibi Me"
(conducts orchestra) *Good evening. Some of our late viewers tuning in. One of the commonest questions that people ask our producer of mystery motion pictures is: Which is written first, the words or the music? In our case the background music always comes first. After it is written we sprinkle the score liberally with sound effects, and then hire an author to write appropriate scenes to accompany the music. Quiet scenes to coincide with the somber passages and scenes of violence, to synchronize with the noisier sections. Finally we garnish this pot-pourri with a title composed of from one to four words. Selected because they are eye catching and provocative and we arrange them in a manner designed to titillate and confuse. Let me show you what one of our stories sounds like, before it is written.* (conductor - music and then screams and noise) *How fortissimo can you get?*

Story: Dr. Burke is impatiently waiting on a heart donor for the beautiful Katherine, who has only days to live. Called to the Chief of Medicine's office, Burke is told by his superiors that a heart was made available, but will go to a wealthy patient Theodore Richardson, who promised two million dollars to the hospital who performs a successful heart transplant on him. Burke explains the situation to Katherine. Visiting his superior again, Burke is introduced to Judith Richardson, who knows the doctor disapproves of the methods her husband used to get the heart. As a faithful doctor to the end, he promises to do all he can. En route to the hospital with the heart in an ice cooler, the ambulance is stopped by masked gunmen, and the thieves demand $2 million in ransom for the return of the heart. When the money is exchanged, they find the heart rendered useless. Dr. Burke, however, isn't as stupid, and suspects Judith ransomed the heart to demand the money. Angry for what she has done, Burke tells Judith that she is the only donor left and shoots her, intending on disposing of the body. Days later, the transplant is successful and Katherine looks radiant, thanks to Dr. Burke. Although leading Burke on, now she has to tell him that she already has a boyfriend.

Next time we plan to bring you more music and sound effects and another story to accompany them, good night.

EPISODE #44   **"HOUDINI ON CHANNEL 4"**   Broadcast on March 5, 1988
        Starring: Nick Lewin as Jack Barton   Carolyn Dunn as Alicia Barton
        Barclay Hope as Oliver Craig   Neil Munro as David Barton
        Ray Paisley as Lieutenant Lansing   Jan Filips as Harry Houdini
        Charles Portanier as Maître d'   Rhonda D'Amour as the girl in the Magic Castle
        An original teleplay written for *Alfred Hitchcock Presents* by Michael Sloan.
        Directed by Timothy Bond.
        Opener taken from "Six People, No Music"
        (standing on the wall)   *Good evening ladies and gentlemen. In the television business it's extremely difficult to keep both feet on the ground. I'd be happy if I had just one foot down there. If you think this is easy, you should see me trying to get through a doorway. And yesterday I accidentally stepped through a window. If my arm hadn't caught in the sash I might still be going and that's not all. Twice I've been mistaken for a dirigible. They keep trying to deflate me. I'm certain by now, you have guessed that tonight's play is about gravity and people who resist the earth's pull. You're wrong.*

        Story: Magician Jack Barton has an obsession with the late Harry Houdini, considered the greatest escape artist of all time. One afternoon, while Jack is helping his assistant Alicia with her luggage, she is abducted by a man named Oliver Craig. A detective arrives at the Magic Castle, where Jack receives a call from Oliver, demanding $500,000 within twenty-four hours, or the girl gets it. Oliver is keeping Alicia locked in a tank of water with special locks that not even Houdini himself could not pick. Jack phones his brother David to help deliver the money. Returning home, Jack implores the spirit of Houdini to help him and after weighing the risk, which can mean death, the spirit of Houdini agrees to help. Learning where Alicia is being kept, Jack goes out to an old Flagship barge, while David makes the money drop. Using Houdini's magical lock-picks, Jack breaks open the water tank, but Alicia is not inside. When David enters, he finds Jack dead. At an abandoned warehouse, Alicia tells her accomplice Oliver to drop her off so she can hide the money. In a few months they will meet again. Hiding in the trunk of his car, Alicia is unaware of what is going on outside, as a black car circa 1926 pulls up. The license plate HHi blinds Craig, who is forced to drive off the barge and into the water. Oliver escapes just in time to see Jack and Houdini's face in the car. Alicia, however, is fighting the seeping water as the police arrive to find Oliver's crumpled body.

        That was short and sweet. Too sweet. Oh, that's a hopeful sign. Next week I shall return with another story. Perhaps by then I shall have settled down. Good night.

        Trivia, etc. Although the story is new, the idea might have partly come from "The Last Escape," although the escape artist was called Ferlini, not Houdini. Still, in both this episode and the other, someone died in a watery grave, as a result of not being able to escape from a locked trunk. Mistake: It says Jack Barton on a hanging poster in this episode, but the closing credits list the main character "as Jack Barclay."

EPISODE #45   **"KILLER TAKES ALL"**   Broadcast on March 12, 1988
        Starring: Van Johnson as Art Bellasco   Rory Calhoun as Jimmie Thurson
        Shelly Peterson as Barbara Maxwell, the nurse   Aaron Schwartz as Dr. Stern
        John Dee as Boots   Diane Fabian as Henrietta
        Nolan Jennings as Mr. Haverford   Susan Fletcher as Mrs. Haverford

An original teleplay written for *Alfred Hitchcock Presents* by Michael Sloan and Robert DeLaurentis.

Directed by Allan King.

Opener taken from "The World's Oldest Motive"

(ape at typewriter) *This is not one of our regular writers. We think it best if we keep them out of sight. This is one of our apprentices. You have of course heard the theory,* (close-up) *that if a room full of monkeys were allowed to type for a million years they would eventually reproduce all the classics in the British Museum. This is not so. We have tried it and while the stories they wrote were quite good, and many of them publishable, they are not classics, yet.* (zoom-out) *This gentleman is one of our trainees. He types nothing but gibberish. But he is not to be faulted for this. His ideas are quite good and he has a flair for dialogue.* (close-up) *He just can't type. However he has made some progress, for example he now knows that it is naughty to eat the paper. Before tonight's story we would like to present a sample of our young students' work. Notice the skill with which he has captured the elusive banality of the television commercial.*

Story: Jimmie Thurson, a former private detective and Art Bellasco, an ex-cop, live out their life at the Sunset Acres retirement home. Dr. Stern is constantly frustrated by the actions of his patients, over a stupid bet that the first to die signs over his estate to the surviving party. It's a killer-take-all-game. Later that night, Art sneaks into Jimmie's room and puts poison into his bottle of port. But when Art's mood lifts, looking through travel books of the French Riviera, Jimmie wakes from his deep sleep. It seems he caught on to Art's murder attempt, which was bungled. Dr. Stern, knowing how vile the two men are, orders nurse Barbara to keep them away from a prospective client, Mr. Haverford, who will be arriving in the afternoon. When the Haverfords arrive, they find Art accusing Jimmie of short-circuiting his electric blanket. Dr. Stern apologizes for his patients' behavior, and invites the Haverfords for dinner. Hearing the men fighting, later that evening, Barbara runs to Dr. Stern, but finds the bungalow gutted by a fire. A small, quiet funeral is held in memory of Jimmie and Art, and Dr. Stern waves goodbye to Barbara who remains executor of the men's estates. She joins the men in the limo, happy that their plan pulled off successfully, as it seems Mrs. Haverford knew Jimmie and gave him a generous donation. The three of them set out for the Riviera

My friend simply could not master the typewriter so we've made him the producer.

EPISODE #46 **"HIPPOCRITIC OATH"** Broadcast on March 19, 1988

Starring: Shaun Cassidy as Dale Thurston

Mavor Moore as Dean Jonathan Compton   Cynthia Belliveau as Mary Donovan

Eric Peterson as Hank Stewart   J. R. Zimmerman as McPherson

Lindsay Merrithew as Steve

Anthony Sherwood as Detective Simon David Rosser as the cop

An original teleplay written for *Alfred Hitchcock Presents* by Michael Colleary and Ray DeLaurentis.

Directed by Vic Sarin.

Opener taken from "Services Rendered"

(painted into a corner) *Oh, good evening. I have always been deathly afraid of painting myself into a corner, but my precautions have been useless, you see I now remembered that this door I've been backing toward is a closet.* (a skeleton falls out) *Of course, it's always comforting to learn that others have made the same mistake but I wish he hadn't done that. Its ruined my floor. Now I shall have to spend the next few minutes re-painting and miss the first commercial and the opening of the story. I don't mind about the story, I've seen that, but the commercials come in sets of three and if you miss one it might be difficult to learn who the sponsor is.*

Story: Medical student Dale Thurston is exposed by Dean Compton for selling copies of a final exam, but can't be expelled because Dale's grandfather will set up a trust of one million dollars for the school, when Dale gets his medical degree. When Dale decides to spend time studying with Hank Stewart, who works the night shift at the college morgue, he receives an offer he can't refuse. Hank will give Dale $100,000 and his BMW, if he will kill Dean Compton, an offer Dale accepts gleefully. Breaking into Compton's home to inject poison into his cough syrup, Dale accidentally drops the vial on the floor. The unsuspecting Compton returns home and slips on the vial, hitting his head on the tub. Dale, thinking him dead, puts the body in the back of the van in a large body bag and begins to put bricks in the bag. The Dean regains consciousness and tries to struggle him, but Dale hits him over the head with a brick, which finally kills him. Dumping his body into the river, Dale returns to Mary's place to study, thus creating an alibi. The next morning, Dale decides to borrow the BMW from the parking lot and detective Simon approaches the boy, showing him a blood-covered brick. Dale, now under arrest, goes to put his books in the trunk of his car where he finds the body of Dean Compton. It seems there is no night shift at the morgue, and Hank is now the new Dean of Brenner College. Mary enters the room and Hank tells her that she is to be the new Resident Surgeon at the college, and they'll discuss plans over a romantic dinner . . .

There are times when a loss of memory might be a good thing. (paints a door - and opens it) *Until next week at the same time, good night.*

EPISODE #47 **"PROSECUTOR"** Broadcast on March 26, 1988
    Starring: Parker Stevenson as Clark Taylor   Lawrence Dane as Joe Metcalf
    Robert Morelli as Rourke / Bob Fellows   Camilla Scott as Pamela Vance
    Roger Barnes as the reporter   Domenic Cuzzocrea as staff member # 1
    Carlton Watson as staff member # 2   Rod Heffernan as staff member #3
    Carla Charest as the anchor person   James O'Regan as the cop
    An original teleplay written for *Alfred Hitchcock Presents* by Glenn Davis and William Laurin.
    Directed by David Gelfand.
    Opener taken from "Outlaw in Town"
    (wanted poster) *Good evening ladies and gentlemen. This is one instance when two heads are not better than one. However I don't believe people realize what a happy lot we criminals have. What could be better than to be wanted? It gives one the inner security of knowing he has a place in society, that he is popular and sought after. No wonder criminals vie with each other to be among the top ten.*

Story: Attorney Clark Taylor is ecstatic after bringing in a guilty verdict on Robert Wenner, a cop killer who murdered Police Chief Charles Gambisto. Both Pamela Vance and Joe Metcalf of the District Attorney's office believe that Clark fixed the evidence, and that Wenner is actually innocent. After a victory celebration for Clark, the attorney is approached by a crazed-looking man who calls himself Rourke, and breaks the news that it was he who really murdered Gambisto. Clark gives Rourke a huge sum of money to keep his conscience and his mouth quiet. Soon after, Joe Metcalf announces that he will be leaving the D.A.'s office and Clark, will become his successor. When Rourke learns of Clark's advancement, he returns the money in exchange for part of his paycheck, and to live in his expensive condo. Angry, Clark tries to strangle Rourke. The front door opens and two marshals accompanied by Joe Metcalf, arrest Clark for tampering with state's evidence. The next day, Joe Metcalf congratulates Pamela Vance on her new job, that of District Attorney, and introduces her to Rourke, whose real name is Bob Fellows from Internal Affairs. But all is not what it seems. Apparently, Fellows did kill Gambisto and Vance have the proof and will make him, her first conviction.

544

I have just been reading some of the shocking things they have written about me. Age, weight . . . I assure you I'm not guilty. Why don't you tune in next week and see if I beat this wrap. Until then, good night.

Trivia, etc. Shades of repetition? This episode plays much like a combination of Hitchcock episodes. The attorney, Clark Taylor, had an innocent man found guilty of a crime he didn't commit, and like that of Courtney Price in "The Perfect Crime," purposely tried to cover up his deeds so he could continue hearing the cheers of praise, reaping the rewards of success. Joe Metcalf is similar to Peter Goodfellow in "The Derelicts," who used blackmail to gain not just money, but to live in his victim's expensive house. But the twist was yet to come, when Rourke turns out to be an undercover agent from Internal Affairs, similar to Dave Sumner in "Most Likely to Succeed."

EPISODE #48   **"IF LOOKS COULD KILL"**   Broadcast on April 23, 1988
Starring: Michelle Phillips as Katherine Clark
Duncan Regehr as David Harrison   Peter MacNeill as Dr. Austin
Lisa Schrage as Kelly   Andrea Roth as Anna
Sam Malkin as D'Angelo   Dale Wilson as Jason Clark
Teleplay written for *Alfred Hitchcock Presents* by Susan Woollen, based on a story by Michael Colleary and Ray DeLaurentis.
Directed by William Fruet.
Opener taken from "The Perfect Murder"
(knife in the back)   *Oh, good evening ladies and gentlemen and welcome to Hollywood. I think everyone enjoys a nice murder, provided he is not the victim. Well, tonight's little comedy of bad manners is concerned with that dream of all of us who harbor homicidal tendencies. The perfect murder. Of course, to be serious for a moment, there is no such thing as a nice murder or a perfect murder. It is always a sordid, despicable business, especially if you don't have a good lawyer.*

Story: Obsessed with looking young, forty-five year old Katherine Clark, an interior designer, is thrilled when she lands the lucrative David Harrison account, but when she finds him darkly handsome and thirty-six years old, Katherine falls in love. Returning to her office, her assistant, Kelly, advises Katherine to pursue David. After dinner at his house, Katherine makes love to David, only to discover his horrible secret. He too is fixated on a woman, Anna, whom he had the house built for. He was going to marry her when she suddenly disappeared. Over dinner at her home, Katherine's husband suggests she accompany him on a business trip, making it a second honeymoon. Katherine tells him she can't because of a new client and leaves. Searching through David's house, Katherine finds pictures of Anna and takes them to Dr. Austin, demanding that he make her into Anna's image. Six weeks later, Katherine looks exactly like the beautiful Anna. As David is taking a drink, holding a gun and contemplating suicide, he catches sight of Anna, and angrily accuses her of making a fool of him. David tracked Anna for years for one reason - to kill her. At Katherine's funeral, Jason and Kelly get into the car and passionately embrace. Kelly knew about David's obsession to kill Anna, and thanks to her idea, she now has what she wants. David is also at the funeral and when he is taken away by the police, he catches a glimpse of the real Anna.

We shall have our next performance of another play, one week from tonight. Oh yes, normally I detest sentimentality but I must leave you with this little thought for the day. Never turn your back on a friend. Good night.

EPISODE #49 "YOU'LL DIE LAUGHING" Broadcast on April 30, 1988
Starring: Anthony Newley as Phil Halloran
Gary Blumsack as Jed Salk Lorraine Landry as Elizabeth Salk
Barry Flatman as Lieutenant Jim Bishop J. Winston Carroll as Carl Gefsky
Murray Cruchley as Dr. Stevens Ronnie Edwards as Ted Rawley
An original teleplay written for *Alfred Hitchcock Presents* by Michael Sloan.
Directed by Zale Dalen.

Opener taken from "Forty Detectives Later"

(stone wheel and record) *Good evening. If you've been wondering where it all begun . . . here it is. In fact,* (close-up) *here is where the first flat tire was patched some 4,000 years ago. Patching was more practical since the spare tire weighed several thousand pounds. Of course, once the wheel was invented many things became possible. Things which before had been only dreams, things like the pancake, the pizza and the donut. Of course it took a long time for these things to catch on, since for hundreds of years, it was naturally assumed that they had to be made out of stone.*

Story: Jed Salk, a brilliant but arrogant comic, is informed by Lieutenant Bishop, that his wife Elizabeth is planning to leave him. She learned about his million-dollar life insurance policy, with she as beneficiary, in the event of a "violent death." When a letter is delivered to Jed containing pieces of his photograph covered with red nail polish, Elizabeth takes the children to his mother's for the night. At this point, it becomes obvious that Jed is writing the cryptic notes and cutting up his own photograph, to make it appear someone wants to murder him. Telling Bishop that someone broke into his house and stole his gun, the pieces fall into place. Jed is going to fake a death and collect. Later, after the body is found, Lieutenant Bishop returns to the comedy club and arrests an old vaudevillian named Halloran, for the murder of Jed. It seems the gun had blanks in it, true to a comic's form. But since Halloran didn't know that, Bishop loaded the gun with real bullets and shot Jed. With the comedians out of the picture, Elizabeth gazes lovingly at Bishop. Nothing can stop them from being together, the last laugh on her husband.

I seem to have been mistaken about this. It's not a wheel, it's a record. Long playing, of course. The title is "Ten Evenings with the Stonehenge Philharmonic." My their discjockeys must have been formidable men. While you are pondering my petty remarks, I must take leave. Next time we plan to show another story in two acts and of course your host making his two appearances in one. Until next time, good night.

EPISODE #50 **"MURDER PARTY"** Broadcast on May 7, 1988
Starring: David McCallum as Lieutenant Cavanaugh
Leigh Taylor-Young as Adelaide Walker David Hemblen as Andrew Walker
Michael J. Reynolds as Potter, the butler Christopher Bondy as Jack McCarthy
Colin Fox as Dr. Herman Vandenburg Malcolm Stewart as Frank Hamilton
An original teleplay written for *Alfred Hitchcock Presents* by Robert DeLaurentis.
Directed by Allan King.

Opener taken from "The Changing Heart"

(steps out of big cuckoo clock) *Present company excepted.* (close-up) *Good evening, fellow clock watchers and welcome to Alfred Hitchcock Presents. I shall never again lease an apartment on the strength of an advertisement. This one read: Quarters for rent for very slim gentleman who loves animals. The animals are that infernal bird you just heard and an idiotic mouse that runs up the pendulum every now and then. You know the nursery rhyme that goes, "when the clock struck one." Unfortunately, I'm the one it strikes, but enough of my problems. Now as is customary on this program, we shall have a word or two . . . from a dear friend: Listen.*

Story: When Andrew Walker dies at his fortieth birthday party, everyone in the room becomes a suspect of the murder investigation. These include Frank Hamilton, Walker's business partner; Dr. Vandenburg, Walker's psychiatrist; and Jack McCarthy, Walker's childhood friend. All of them claim their innocence to the police detective. Adelaide, Walker's wife, confesses to having had an affair with all three men, and Walker threatened suicide if she left him. She also points out that if Walker had been murdered, the estate would go to the twins – "Walker's two rats" – not her. To clear the matter up, Adelaide leaves to pay off the guests. They were rented from "Party People," since in reality, Walker didn't have any friends of his own. Later that evening, a laughing Andrew Walker appears. He informs a shocked Adelaide that the detective was also an actor, and the prank was a birthday present to himself. Pouring a glass of wine, Walker drinks it while Adelaide tells him how she knew all about the charade. She also reminds Walker that if he committed suicide, she *would* get the estate, and Walker promptly drops dead. The detective enters, and Adelaide passionately kisses him. But the joke is on her, when Walker gets up and the detective admits that he really is a police lieutenant, all a ruse to discover her true motives. As the two men share a drink, (one which Adelaide really poisoned), the men bend over in pain. The butler enters and kisses Adelaide, remarking that "the butler really did do it!"

That's all for tonight. Next week we shall be back with another story. Until then, good night. (clock strikes midnight)

EPISODE #51 **"TWIST"** Broadcast on May 14, 1988
Starring: Roberta Bizeau as Tirina Clark   Stella Stevens as Georgia Brooks
Clive Revill as Hector   Art Hindle as Alton Brooks
David Adamson as the pilot
An original teleplay written for *Alfred Hitchcock Presents* by Manny Coto.
Directed by Rene Bonniere.
Opener taken from "The Lonely Hours"
(hotel check-in)   *Good evening fellow traveler and welcome to Chez Hitchcock. We have had a rash of unexplained homicides lately.* (close-up) *I knew you would enjoy hearing that, but I'm terribly upset. You see, with all these people checking in and then not checking out, our books just don't balance. However, I'm sure our house detective will clear them all up, just as soon as he finds out who stole his seeing eye dog. I believe you'll be also interested in knowing that we have television in every room, television cameras that is. The receiving sets are in the dining room in the casino. I see the supper show will begin in a minute, just time enough for you to get settled.* (hits bell) *Front!*

Story: When Alton returns home one day, he finds his wheelchair ridden wife packing a bag containing three-quarters of a million dollars, and two airplane tickets. It seems she knows about his fling with a top model, Tirina, and the game is up. Finding the butler dead, Alton watches as Georgia points a gun at him. She orders him to take the money, and after he does, she shoots herself. In a panic, Alton sees no other recourse but to also shoot himself, believing the police are outside. The butler gets up, however, helps Georgia to her feet, and the two toast their plan. But Hector, wanting all the money for himself, laced the wine with cyanide, and the woman starts choking to death. Hector told Alton about her plan in advance and Alton recovers from his fake injury. But in a twist of fate, Georgia and Tirina were on to the two, let the initial plan go off without a hitch, and wait at the window for the two men to make their getaway. Pushing a remote control, the car erupts into flames, killing both men. Tirina and Georgia talk about their trip to Bolivia while the model leaves a poison cigarette for Georgia, guaranteed to kill her within minutes. As Tirina boards the private jet, the pilot assures her that Georgia left explicit instructions. Especially if Tirina boards the plane alone, he will make sure to follow his Aunt Georgia's specific instructions so she won't survive the trip.

I trust you have enjoyed your stay here. Please return next week for we plan to have another intriguing floorshow. As for your bill, someone else is taking care of that for you. I can't reveal his identity but, uh . . . he . . . he left this message for you.

EPISODE #52 **"USER DEADLY"** Broadcast on May 21, 1988

Starring: Peter Spence as Jerry
Geordie Johnson as Dave Lawrence
Eugene Clark as Captain Andy Wilson
Kim Nelles as Carrie Mansfield
Kirsten Kieferle as Ellen Fowler

Harry Guardino as Phil Mansfield
Sean Hewitt as Danny Mosely
Ted Wallace as Brendon Casey
Heather Clifford as Emmy
Rod Wilson as Paul

Teleplay written for *Alfred Hitchcock Presents* by William Laurin and Glenn Davis, based on a story by Brian Ross.

Directed by Allan King.

Opener taken from "Place of Shadows"

(two-way TV) *Good evening, and thank you for allowing me to come into your living rooms. Well, I'm not easily shocked but I did expect people to dress a bit more formally, before sitting in front of their sets. Now that two-way television is here.* (screams) *Apparently not everyone was aware of the incessant march of progress. The next improvement should be more to your liking. I understand that scientists will soon make it possible for any object thrown at the television screen to actually hit the performer. All of which reminds me of a story.*

Story: Phil Mansfield is about to retire in a week and his superior asks him to learn to work a computer, since all case files involving "the rainbow killer" have been eliminated. Meeting up with his partner, Dave Lawrence, Phil arrives on another murder scene, more work of the madman. While Phil is plugging away on the computer, documenting the details of the case, the screen fills with a message from the killer that gives Phil instructions to the next victim. Unable to break the code in time, another young woman dies. Captain Wilson tells Phil that he has thirty-six hours to find the killer, or hand the case over to his replacement, Casey. Phil enlists the help of his computer wizard nephew Jerry to help. When the screen again fills with numbers, Jerry tries to decipher the gibberish. Phil, realizing they are map coordinates, tracks them down, and surprisingly, they lead to his own house. Racing home he finds his daughter Carrie being attacked by the killer, whom he shoots to kill. When he pulls off the ski mask, they are shocked to see it is Lawrence, his partner. Captain Wilson congratulates Phil for solving the crime prior to his retirement. Meanwhile, Casey is working the graveyard shift when the computer screen displays the message that Lawrence was a copycat killer - the real one is still on the loose. We then see Jerry typing the message with a twisted smile on his face.

(sitting on desk) *For those of you who fail to grasp the point of that message, it was prepared by my sponsor who wishes you to buy his product. I don't think that's an unreasonable request to make. Next week my beloved sponsor and I, and all our actors who are not on the critical list, will be back to bring you another story. Until then, good night.*

Trivia, etc. During the shower scene, Carrie comments to herself, "Calm down Carrie, this isn't the Bates motel."

EPISODE #53 **"CAREER MOVE"** Broadcast on May 28, 1988

Starring: David Cassidy as Joey Mitchell
Mary Beth Rubens as Alison
Alar Aedma as Tommy

Robert Wisden as Marty Parks
Peter Virgile as Billy Gunn
Hal Johnson as Detective Stone

Teleplay written for *Alfred Hitchcock Presents* by Glenn Davis, William Laurin and Montgomery Burt, based on an original story idea by Montgomery Burt.

Directed by Timothy Bond.

Opener taken from "Cell 227"

(sitting behind bars) *Good evening ladies and gentlemen and why did it take you so long to get here? I've been sitting here for ten minutes. I don't know why everything is so heavily guarded. Even if I could get through this screen, I couldn't escape without breaking your picture tube. All this is to illustrate to you that while the television viewers lot may be difficult, the performers is even worse. Only one half-hour visit a week and in between nothing but work. There of course, my associates aren't the best, singers, comedians, news-analysts and the like. But perhaps we shall have our play, before I reduce all of you to tears.*

Story: After a bout with alcohol and a broken marriage, Joey Mitchell is making his comeback five years later as a rock and roll star. Going to the studio to lay down tracks, Joey grabs hold of a faulty amplifier, sparks fly, and the rock star dies from electrocution. After the funeral, Marty, Joey's manager and Alison, Joey's girlfriend, gain control over the estate with the assistance of Joey himself. Since his death, Joey's albums have been selling like never before. As the weeks pass, Marty releases memorial albums, and Joey records "lost sessions," puts out a biography, and has a number one hit on the Billboard chart, with a sold-out tribute concert being planned. Not able to stand being a virtual prisoner, Joey leaves the house and goes for a drive in his sports car. At full speed, he discovers that he has no brakes and the car flies off a cliff, exploding into flames. At the tribute concert, Joey walks on stage and begins performing. A detective arrests Marty backstage for tampering with the brakes. Tommy, a former band member, walks on stage accusing Joey of being an imposter and out of rage, shoots him dead. Visiting Tommy in jail, Alison reassures him that together, they'll keep Joey's legend alive. Alison wanted Joey dead, and told Tommy all about the fake death. But, unable to kill the real Joey, Tommy told the rock star about Alison's plan. The two boys "staged" the performance and with her confession just recorded, detectives surround Alison as she starts for her car.

I have a theory which would account for the immense popularity of revenge. Revenge is sweet without being fattening. (alarm) *I see the guard is signaling that our time is up. I hope you will visit me again next time. Until then, good night.*

EPISODE #54   **"FULL DISCLOSURE"**   Broadcast on June 18, 1988

Starring: Kevin Hicks as Jeff Wyatt   Robert Lansing as G. William Howe
Al Waxman as Dale Linseman   Donald Davis as Senator Thomas Powell
Eve Crawford as Sandy Howe   Gerry Mendicino as Lieutenant Jack Snyder
Ray Landry as Officer Gibbons   Ted Dillon as Bennett

An original teleplay written for *Alfred Hitchcock Presents* by Glenn Davis and William Laurin.

Directed by William Corcoran (credited as Bill Corcoran in this episode).

Opener taken from "Help Wanted"

(newspaper want ads) *Oh, good evening. How did you find me? I specifically asked for an unlisted channel. I'm taking the week off. I wanted a rest from television. If you're one of those critics who thinks that television is frightful, all I can say is, you should see it from this side. I've been reading the want ads. A man has a right to look around for a better job, hmm . . . Wanted: Host for television program, sounds like a job for me. Must be witty, charming, handsome . . . wow, this is perfect, gracious and must be willing to work every week. Apply: Alfred Hitchcock Presents. I think I better scamper back to the old job. I don't want to miss the show and don't you miss it either.*

Story: William Howe, a former reporter of Vietnam, is getting a divorce and in order to save his home, he will have to publish his memoirs, a book about politicians, scandals, and the betrayal of the American public. Dale Linseman, a friend from the Vietnam days, is now a publisher and offers Howe a contract. A Senator and Congressman both visit

Howe, trying to persuade him into forgetting about the book. On his private boat that evening, Howe's wife confesses that she still loves him and wants to reconcile. Handing her the keys to his car, she walks over to start the engine, and the automobile explodes. A police lieutenant named Snyder suspects Howe had a hand in his wife's death, and even shows the writer fake photographs that incriminate him. Howe, ordered by the Senator to give up the manuscript, has no other choice. Going home later that day, Howe is shot at by a mercenary, who in turn gets killed by a sniper. Returning to Linseman with the knowledge that Jeff Wyatt planted the bomb, the two break into Wyatt's house where they find all the ingredients in the basement. Linseman confesses that it was he who planted the bomb, and lieutenant Snyder, Jeff Wyatt and the police enter, overhearing the confession. It seems Linseman was afraid that if Howe and Sandy would get back together, there would be no book. With the guilty party under arrest, Howe goes to dine with the amused Senator, announcing that there never was any book, but he could write one.

And now please keep your eyes on this space for I shall return here next week to bring you another story. Good night.

EPISODE #55 **"KANDINSKY'S VAULT"** Broadcast on June 25, 1988
    Starring: Robin Ward as Adrian Gelthorpe Eli Wallach as Yosef Kandinsky
    Roberta Wallach as Charlotte Kandinsky Lisa Jakub as Missy
    David Eisner as Gordon Blake   Rex Hagon as Follet
    Marvin Karon as Paul Jones   Chris Benson as the policeman
    Michael Rothery as David Hackett Reg Dreger as detective Jamison
    An original teleplay written for *Alfred Hitchcock Presents* by Steven Hollander.
    Directed by René Bonnière.
Opener taken from "Wet Saturday"
(lying on shelf with sign: "moved to new location") *Oh, good evening. I'm so glad you found me. As you can see our new quarters are rather modest, but we like the location and thought the change might do us good, also.* (close-up) *And now, if you don't mind, I would like to indulge in an old American custom. No matter how busy they are or what the surroundings may be, Americans never omit this quaint ritual. If you don't care to join me, I think you'll find our play is about to begin on one of the lower shelves.*

  Story: Yosef Kandinsky. owner of a dusty old bookstore filled with many rare books, refuses millionaire Adrian Gelthorpe's offer of ten million for the storefront. Gelthorpe, you see, has promised his bank new capital to continue a development project, and he's running out of time. Employing the assistance of Gordon Blake, Gelthorpe uses Kandinsky's prospective son-in-law to con the old man into knowing why he won't sell. The truth be known, Kandinsky is actually holding back a fortune in gold bars, compliments of bootlegger Bugsy Stein, since the old days of prohibition. When Blake discovers an old map in a first edition of *Treasure Island*, he pays a young schoolgirl, Missy, into buying the book from the old man – which works without a hitch. But when Gelthorpe and Blake go underground and break through the wall, they find themselves under arrest. It seems they've been out-smarted, and just broke into his own bank vault. Down in the real vault, Kandinsky, along with his conspirators, which includes young Missy, laugh at the villain's foil. A twist in the tale for Bugsy Stein never really died . . . he's alive and well running a bookstore in Chicago.

  (Hitchcock drinks tea) *That was exceedingly dry. Next week we shall be back at the same old stand, please drop in again. Good night.*

  Trivia, etc. Eli Wallach's real-life daughter, Roberta Wallach, plays the role of his daughter in this episode.

EPISODE #56   **"THERE WAS A LITTLE GIRL . . . "**   Broadcast on July 2, 1988
Starring: Michael Tucker as Frank   Kate Vernon as Donna
Wanda Cannon as Martha   Wayne Robson as Chief Pickett
James Kee as Harry   David Christoffel as Randy
An original teleplay written for *Alfred Hitchcock Presents* by Charles Grant Craig.
Directed by Atom Egoyan.
Opener taken from "The Cuckoo Clock"

(shelf of cans)   *Good evening and thank you for your kind attention, erratic, though it may be. You have, of course, heard of canned laughter. The horror recorded laughter which accompanies some comedy shows. Naturally since this program is entirely serious in nature, we have never resorted to this means of audience stimulation. However, I have just been shipped a number of cans of fresh audience sounds which may be useful.* (opens a can and a scream lets out) *Most of these cans contains screams. There are some filled with shudders and some of them hold whimpers and gasps. Just now we do not intend to use these recordings. This is merely a warning. If you fail to react to our stories at the emotional level we feel they deserve, we'll turn these sounds loose. So much for blackmail. Now for our story.*

Story: Frank bails out his stepdaughter Donna, a beautiful, sensual young woman who continuously gets into trouble, only to gain her stepfather's attention. Upset by the latest disturbance, Donna overhears her mother, Martha, tell Frank that it is time for Donna to move out and settle down with her boyfriend Harry – even if it means losing the family inheritance. So the two children devise a plan . . . Alone together one night, Donna tells Frank that the temptation they both feel is very strong. If he wants her to stay, he should meet her at the beach shack. When Frank later bursts into the shack to see Donna, Harry hits him over the head. Donna begs Harry to shoot her father-in-law, but Harry won't, hitting Donna instead. The original plan was for Harry to see the chief of police, and tell him the story of how Martha followed Frank, hit her daughter, and then shot her husband in cold blood. But as Harry tries to leave, Donna fires the gun. When she approaches Chief Pickett, to tell the story herself, she finds a surprise. Martha and Harry are waiting for her, and Harry tells the truth. Running into the woods, Donna fires at Chief Pickett who returns the fire and kills her. That night Harry and Martha celebrate, as they can now begin their life in Tahiti. Their plan backfired, however, when Frank walks in, alive and well. Donna was a poor shot. It seems the chief of police was also in the act, collecting a payoff. Donna and Frank really had something going on between them, and knocking Harry over the head, Frank reminds Chief Pickett to put the real bullets back into his gun. After Donna and Frank leaves, Chief Pickett calls for back-up, to take them in.

Oh, this is from the section of quick frozen screams. They have to thaw out. A number of people have been asking, where we obtain these canned screams, gasps etc. They are of course authentic audience reactions recorded at a comedy show. I don't believe it's on the air any longer. (takes another can) *Good heavens, they forgot to remove the audience. Next time I shall return with another story laced together by my impertinent remarks. Until then, good night.*

EPISODE #57   **"TWISTED SISTERS"**   Broadcast on July 9, 1988
Starring: Mia Sara as Sara Fletcher   Carolyn Dunn as Candi Miller
Marianna Pascal as Denise Dutton   Yannick Bisson as Ty
Allison Mang as Amanda Hansen   Stan Coles as Detective Morrison
Clayton (Ed) McGibbon as the watchman   Lane White as the first policeman
Richard Gira as the second policeman
An original teleplay written for *Alfred Hitchcock Presents* by Ray DeLaurentis and Michael Colleary.

Directed by Timothy Bond.

Opener taken from "Beta Delta Gamma"

(fraternity paddle) *Good evening, brothers and sisters. This evening's story is concerned with higher education. Specifically with members of Greek letter fraternities. I presume there are fraternities for other nationalities as well. This is a fra . . .* (turns it around) *is a fraternity paddle. Apparently they have very small canoes. In keeping with tonight's theme we shall first see a short educational film and then a story. As the story opens you will find the students hard at work. Wrestling with the compact problems which face man in his never-ending quest for truth.*

Story: Sara Fletcher, a student at Wainwright College, is abducted outside her dormitory and taken to the Epsilon Delta Sorority House. The house president, Candi Miller, invites the pledges to enter the sisterhood if they pass "Hell Night." What Sara doesn't know is that Candi became jealous over her boyfriend showing affection for Sara, and believes the girl to pay for her flirtatious behavior by going through the House of Horrors. As Sara screams and tries to get herself out of a locked room, Denise tells Candi that they are playing a mean trick. Later on, when they let a very angry Sara out of the room, the girls find Ty's bloody body and the entrance to the room locked shut. Denise and Candi escape through a graveyard nearby and Amanda's ghost rises from a tombstone. Amanda accuses them of breaking her neck and dropping her down a hole. After they discover that the ghost is a projected image, Sara steps out with a gun and informs them that Amanda was her sister. The two practical jokers drop through a chute, only to discover the exit is sealed shut. Later that evening, the police question the night watchman as the bodies are carried out. Sara herself is helped out, and learns that Candi and Denise broke their necks falling down the chute. Back in her dorm room, Sara thanks Ty, who is alive and well, for helping to put right the wrong done to Amanda. Amanda always did say that Ty was a devoted boyfriend . . .

How he does go on. By the way, we would like it known that the foregoing story does not constitute a condemnation of fraternities or sororities or Greeks or Universities or young people or the sea shore or salt water or sand. I heel to no man in my affirm adherence to an uncompromising policy of offending no one. So, until next time, good night.

EPISODE #58 **"THE 13TH FLOOR"** Broadcast on July 16, 1988

Starring: Anthony Franciosa as Morris Conrad   Laura Robinson as Alyson Hanks
Hal Eisen as Doug Frazer   Ben Gordon as detective Harris
David Hughes as the elevator operator   Richard Comar as Williams
Robert King as the chauffeur   Irene Pauzer as Dora
John Curtis as the desk clerk

An original teleplay written for *Alfred Hitchcock Presents* by Naomi Janzen.
Directed by Mark Rosman.

Opener taken from "Out There – Darkness"

(elevator) *Good evening ladies and gentlemen and watch your step please. I'm certain that any of you who have wearily pushed rich maiden aunts in their wheelchairs, share my appreciation of elevator shafts. I also find the elevator quite easy to operate. It works just like a yo-yo. Well, not exactly but we do use the same grade of string. We are now about to have our first commercial. I want to assure you that it will only last 60 seconds. I have to tell everyone this because I understand it gives people the sensation of being trapped between floors, courage.*

Story: A greedy ambitious developer named Morris Conrad has documents falsified so he can demolish the grand old St. Sebastien Hotel. The public protests against the demolition, and one of them, Doug Frazer, claims the city needs to keep its history. Late one evening, the old elevator operator of the hotel explains to Conrad that he will remain on the thirteenth floor, despite demolition. The hotel has always been his home, and he has no intention of leaving. The following morning, Conrad signals for the explosion, knowing full well that the old man is inside, but the building doesn't explode. Doug Frazer, meanwhile, goes to the police with proof about Conrad's falsified report and asks for help. In the morning, waiting for the engineer to fix the tampered detonation wires, Conrad enters the hotel and calls out for Frazer to show himself. Stepping inside the elevator, Conrad finds himself stuck on the thirteenth floor. Outside, a police detective arrives to break the bad news to Frazer. There is no way to prove Conrad's guilt, even with the proof in hand. Inside the building, Conrad finally runs out of the elevator to the window, just in time to hear the countdown. The old building crumbles to the ground and in the distance, the old elevator operator meets up with his accomplices, after a job well done.

I hope you'll return next week, when we shall add another story. And now if you don't intend to climb aboard, please step back off the pad. Going up.

EPISODE #59 "HUNTED" (PART ONE) Broadcast on July 30, 1988

Starring: Edward Woodward as Drummond   Kate Trotter as Margaret Lord
Elizabeth Lennie as Jill Drummond   James Hobson as the father
Thor Bishopric as the teenage boy
An original teleplay written for *Alfred Hitchcock Presents* by Michael Sloan.
Directed by Timothy Bond.
Opener taken from "The Right Kind of House"
(as a real estate agent)   *Good evening, fellow realiters and clients. I'm very anxious to call your attention to the investment possibilities of our new subdivision. Pitted Hills. Naturally it lacks certain of the luxuries, but this is the price one pays for getting in on the ground floor. The sewer's are not yet in. However, there are enough craters to go around.* (close-up) *Like our prologue, tonight's story touches on real estate.*

Story: When real estate agent Margaret Lord shows a man named Drummond, a small third-story office for rent on Langham Street, she panics when he locks them in the office and pulls out a high-powered rifle. Drummond plans to start shooting people on the street below at noon, unless she can talk him out of it. Clearly disturbed, Drummond informs Margaret that as a young boy, his father would often take him hunting. That was, of course, at an early age when he came to realize that human beings don't have the animal awareness when life is in jeopardy, like animals do who can sense impending danger. His theory is that a sniper is just a hunter with human targets. Drummond tells her how his father was cleaning his own rifle, not realizing it was loaded, when it went off. Unable to cope with his father's death, Drummond wants to vent his anger through the third-story window. Margaret tries to grab the rifle, but he throws her on the floor. She pleads with him that it is not yet noon, to which he replies that she has seven minutes to persuade him out of it . . .

Trivia, etc. There were no closing remarks supplied by Alfred Hitchcock at the end of this episode. Both parts were later replayed back-to-back on July 16, 1989, from 5 to 6 p.m., EST.

EPISODE #60 "HUNTED" (PART TWO) Broadcast on August 6, 1988

Starring: Edward Woodward as Drummond
Kate Trotter as Margaret Lord   David Fox as Lieutenant Paul Hutchinson
Elizabeth Lennie as Jill Drummond
Stephen Makaj as Sergeant Matt Phillips   Carl Ritchie as policeman Jerry
Raymond Hunt and Mark Terene as the men on the stairs (uncredited)
Sunni McFadden as the woman on the stairs (uncredited)
An original teleplay written for *Alfred Hitchcock Presents* by Michael Sloan.
Directed by Timothy Bond.

Opener taken from "I Killed the Count" (part three)

(in knight's armor) *Good evening ladies and gentlemen. Those of you who have been sitting on the edge of your chairs since last time will be glad to know that tonight we shall definitely present the final chapter in our story. For those of you who have missed the earlier installments, or have lost your score-cards, I shall present a resume.*

Story: Drummond tells Margaret how his wife, Jill, left him with his three sons, for another man, and only then does Margaret realize that Jill and the same man are down in the park below. Angry, Drummond opens fire and Margaret screams. Panic erupts in the street below. Margaret begins to cry and Drummond assures the woman he would never harm her. People begin pounding outside the door and Drummond warns them that he has a hostage. Lieutenant Hutchinson and Sergeant Phillips ask Drummond to let Margaret go. The SWAT team have surrounded the building. Margaret runs for the door just as reality hits her. His rifle was filled with blanks. He never shot anyone, just created a panic. Then it becomes obvious what he really wants: the police to kill him. Forcing her out of the office, Drummond re-locks the door behind her. At the window he begins firing more blanks as the police return the rifle fire, which kills him. Later that evening, Jill Drummond and Detective Hutchinson celebrate with drinks. Jill is free of her husband, and no one will ever know that Drummond's rifle was filled with blanks – he'll take care of that. The story in the papers will read how a sniper was shooting at innocent people. In the next booth, Margaret raises her glass in Drummond's memory, promising she will never let them get away with it. She plans to pay a visit to the press herself.

Next time we shall resume our policy of telling a complete story on each program. I hope you will join us then. Good night.

SEASON FOUR - (20 episodes)

Art Director: Katherine Mathewson
Camera Operator: Ray Brounstein
Casting by Maria Armstrong, c.d.c,
   Ross Clydesdale, c.d.c.
   and Laela Weinzweig
Costume Designer: Maureen Gurney
   and Delphine White
Director of Photography: Maris Jansons
   and Vic Sarin
Edited by Bill Goddard and Tom Joerin.
Executive Producers: Jon Slan
   and Michael Sloan
First Assistant Director: Alan Goluboff
   and Felix Gray
Gaffer: Eldie Benson
   and Michael McMurray
Hairdresser: Reg LeBlanc, Divyo Putney
Key Grip: Christopher Dean
   and Daniel Narduzzi
Make-up Artist: Sandi Duncan
   and Irma Parkkonen
MCA TV Production Executive:
   Nigel Watts
Music Composed by Christopher
   Dedrick, Micky Erbe, Milan

Kymlicka, Maribeth Solomon
   and Kenneth Wannberg
Music Supervisor: David Greene
Post Production Audio: Filmhouse
Post Production Video: The
   Magnetic North Corporation
Post Production-Coordinator:
   Catherine Hunt
Produced by Mary Kahn
Production Designer: David M. Davis
Production Manager: Len D'Agonstino
Production Sound: Clark McCarron
   and Bryan Day
Property Master: Doug Harlocker
   and Byron Patchett
Script Supervisor: Benu Bhandari
   and Kathryn Buck
Set Decorator: Enrico Campana
   and Danielle Fleury
Still Photographer: Ben Mark Holzberg
Story Editors: Glenn Davis
   and William Laurin
Supervising Producer:
   Robert DeLaurentis
U.S. Casting by Donna Dockstader

A Paragon Motion Pictures, Inc. Production
Michael Sloane Productions in association with MCA TV, exclusive distributor
Broadcast Saturday over the USA network from 10 to 11 p.m., EST. (two episodes back-to-back) Various nationwide and local sponsors.

EPISODE #61 **"FOGBOUND"** Broadcast on October 8, 1988

Starring: Jonathan Crombie as Ricky	Kathleen Quinlan as Karen Wilson
Stephen Mendel as Simon Carter	Ric Sarabia as Manuel Sanchez
Jeremy Ratchford as Tom	Clifford Saunders as Ed
Michael Donaghue as Sheriff Geary	Lindsay Leese as the Intern / Foster

Written for *Alfred Hitchcock Presents* by Lee Erwin, based on his original teleplay "Forecast: Low Clouds and Coastal Fog," originally broadcast on *The Alfred Hitchcock Hour* on January 18, 1963.

Directed by Mark Sobel.

Opener taken from "Forecast: Low Clouds and Coastal Fog"

(with a surf board)   *Good evening ladies and gentlemen and fellow surfers. This evening's drama is only incidentally concerned with surfing. Actually it touches on many popular sports. Drinking, revenge, kidnapping, homicide . . . I first became attracted to surfing when I was told that it was possibly the only sport, which involved no competition, and where the participants did not throw or catch a ball or run and jump. It seemed to be a perfect way to relax from the strain of over-sleeping. I've become quite good at it really and I'm eager to see how it works in the water. You see, we're still looking for a wave, large enough to support me. Meanwhile, here is the sponsor who is supporting this portion of the program.*

Story: After her husband has left of the evening, a man named Manuel Sanchez begins beating on Karen Wilson's door. He asks to use the phone, claiming he is having problems with his car. Frightened and alone, Karen refuses entrance to the house, forcing him to go elsewhere for help. Later that evening, she is shocked to learn that while the stranger named Sanchez was walking to the nearest service station, his girlfriend was still waiting at the run-down car, and was brutally murdered. Karen's neighbor insists she did the best thing under the circumstances, but the opinion is not shared by Manuel, who seeks revenge. The next evening, Manuel sneaks into her house, as does her neighbor, who makes unwanted advances on her. Three college boys, friends of Karen's, comes to the rescue, and the neighbor is frightened off. The boys turn out the lights, confessing how they siphoned the gas from Manuel's car, a ploy that worked so they could get at his girlfriend. Now it's Karen's turn . . . Manuel, still in hiding, overhears the whole conversation, and shoots two of the boys while the other runs off. Apologizing for his actions, Manuel finds himself forgiven by Karen, who invites him into her home with welcome arms.

As for surfing, I've just discovered why one sees so many of these about. At the beach, on the highway, on top of automobiles etc. It's because they're so practical. (folds up an ironing-table) *Good night.*

Trivia, etc. Although a change in the title, the weather report in the play states: "Forecast calls for Low Cloud and Coastal Fog." The word sheriff is mis-spelled "sherriff" in the closing credits.

EPISODE #62 **"PEN PAL"** Broadcast on October 15, 1988

Starring: Geza Kovacs as Lieutenant Berger	
Jean Simmons as Margaret Lowen	
Page Fletcher as John Harris	April Banigan as Margie

Teleplay written for *Alfred Hitchcock Presents* by Hilary Murray, based on her teleplay of the same name, adapted from a story by Henry Slesar and Jay Folb, originally broadcast on November 1, 1960.

Directed by René Bonnière.

Opener taken from "Pen Pal"

(baseball)   *Baseball gets its name from the type of field on which it is played, a baseball field. There are 27 players on each team, however no more than 13 are allowed on the field at one time. Nine from one team and from one to four from the other. To make it a fair match, the team with the smaller number of players is allowed to carry clubs, the larger team has no weapons at all, except this pellet.* (baseball) *But it is hard enough to knock a man unconscious. Naturally both teams occasionally use their fists, but this is usually unnecessary. You see all players have ingeniously attached, sharply pointed metal cleats to their shoes. With these, the more experienced players can with grace and skill, badly lacerate an opponent, yet make it look quite accidental. As you can see, the game is an excellent means for building character and teaching young men good sportsmanship, fair play and first aid. So much for the finer points of the sport. I see our friend the umpire is signaling for time-out. The game will commence is just one minute.*

Story: A lonely spinster named Margaret receives a visit one evening from Lieutenant Berger, to break the news that her young niece, Margie, has been corresponding with John Harris, a prisoner serving a life sentence. Even worse, Harris just escaped prison and may be headed here to find Margie. But Margaret assures the officer that her niece is away for the weekend, safe and sound. Later that evening, Harris breaks into the house and demands to know where Margie is. The spinster tells him the truth, and serves him dinner. Harris confesses that he is in love with her niece and wants to run off with her. But Margaret begs him to leave her alone for she cannot live his kind of life. Still, he persists and she agrees to call Margie, but dials Berger's number instead, tipping off the police. Harris grabs the phone, hears a man's voice, and chases Margaret through the house. Hitting Harris over the head with a metal candleholder. he still keeps coming back, until she shoots him in the chest. A week later, Margaret sits down at her desk to reminisce with her old letters and photos from Harris.

I have an announcement to make which you will all be overjoyed to hear. There will be no more commercials. Positively no more commercials during the balance of this program, so until next week at this time, good night. (eats the ball)

Trivia, etc. The beginning of Hitchcock's original presentation for "Pen Pal" was not used for this broadcast, which concerned fictional letters that were written by viewers, with Hitchcock answering like an editor of a magazine or newspaper. Henry Slesar's name is mis-spelled as "Henry Sleasar" in this episode.

EPISODE #63   **"ANCIENT VOICES"**   Broadcast on November 12, 1988
Starring: Myron-Harvey Natwick as Adam Ouspensky
Richard Anderson as Tom Northcliff   Doug McClure as Clete Madden
John C. MacKenzie as Lieutenant Rick Hayden
Claire Cellucci as Cheryl Northcliff   Rob Stewart as Bradley
David Gardner as the Chief of Police   Denise Baillargeon as the young woman
Teleplay written for *Alfred Hitchcock Presents* by Glenn Davis and William Laurin, based on a story by Michael Sloan, Glenn Davis and William Laurin.

Directed by William Corcoran.

Opener taken from "Across the Threshold"

(TV seance)   *Good evening. So glad you could join us. We are holding a seance tonight. At our last session we managed to get in touch with the spirit of Marconi, the inventor of radio, but unfortunately it was impossible to understand what he was saying because of the static. Now, if all of you will place your hands palm down on the tops of your television sets, we shall attempt to speak to Alexander Graham Bell. Hallo, hallo* (knock, knock, knock) *I seem to have reached him already. Mr. Bell, do you?* (knock, knock, knock) *That's peculiar, it's a woman. She says Mr. Bell is not in.* (knock, knock) *No I'll call later. That was his answering service.*

Story: Tom Northcliff is upset that his wife Cheryl, a stunning soap opera actress, continues to have "channeling" sessions with her medium, Ouspensky. With the help of his junior law partner, Brad, Tom invents an elaborate murder scheme, using the phony medium as the accused. While Cheryl contacts Paul, her dead lover, and asks why he committed suicide, Tom turns on a video monitoring system, activated with a transmitter. Entering the dining room where Ouspensky and Paul are speaking, Tom breaks open a capsule under Ouspensky's nose, which knocks him out. He then strangles Cheryl using Ouspensky's scarf, and hurries back to the room just as the recording is ending. Lieutenant Rick Hayden comes to question Ouspensky, the prime suspect. As a last ray of hope to clear his name, the medium sets up a session where the spirit of Cheryl will identify her killer. Her apparition identifies Tom as her killer and angry, he fires a gun shot through the curtains. But all that is there is a tape recorder. The lieutenant arrests Tom, explaining the small clues that gave him away. Shooting the detective, Tom makes a getaway, falling into the hands of Clete Madden, Paul's cousin. Cheryl is alive and well, as a morgue worker noticed a faint heartbeat, but let everyone else think she was dead, in order to make her husband show his hand.

If you found this story amusing, you will be pleased to know that we have prepared another for our next presentation. So until then, good hyphened night.

EPISODE #64   **"SURVIVAL OF THE FITTEST"**   Broadcast on November 19, 1988
        Starring: Patrick Macnee as Thaddeus J. Russell
        Nigel Bennett as Griffin   Robert McKenna as the railroad clerk
        An original teleplay written for *Alfred Hitchcock Presents* by Michael Sloan.
        Directed by Allan King.
        Opener taken from "Safety For the Witness"
        (revolver duel, Hitchcock shoots a man in the back) *Well, as mother used to say, it's better to be safe than sorry. Actually what you have just seen is not to be taken seriously. It was all make believe, all play acting. Of course the gun is genuine and was loaded, but the doctor isn't a real doctor, he's an actor. I think it's interesting that the duel is no longer considered good form, while cold-blooded murder is more popular than ever. There seems to be no way to stay the march of civilization.*

Story: Mystery writer Thaddeus J. Russell is approached at a train station by a cab driver named Griffin, who drives the writer to his grand estate. Settling in his weekend home, Thaddeus admires his collection of antique weapons before eating a lovely meal with the company of a young lady (a photo of the lady - to be precise). Thaddeus soon learns that Griffin and six other well-armed men dressed in camouflage fatigues, are converging on the house. Resourceful in his methods of wounding his intruders, Thaddeus manages to live through the night. The next morning, the mailman delivers a letter stating he has survived the initiation into the Survivalist Society. Thaddeus laughs, clutching his heart, and drops to the floor. The mailman is really Griffin in disguise, who takes the money and diamonds from Thaddeus' pocket, and the picture of the mysterious woman. The woman, you see, had divorced Griffin and married Thaddeus. To Griffin's twisted mind, her death was due to some form of mistreatment. As Griffin turns around, he finds Thaddeus aiming a flintlock at him. The heart attack was faked because he saw through the mailman's disguise. Griffin takes the lead ball in the chest. Later that afternoon, a small card from the Survivalist Society arrives for Thaddeus. "No one destroys one of our own," it reads. Thaddeus looks up to see three Survivalists with high-powered rifles.

My worthy opponent has taken what I consider, an unfair advantage of my poor shooting, and insisted that we go through this again. Afterwards I should be back, next week with another story. Ready! (four guns point at Hitch) *Good night.*

Trivia, etc. This was the second episode of the remake series to use the opener of "Safety for the Witness." The other episode was NBC's "Four O'Clock," but that episode didn't use the same closer.

EPISODE #65 **"THE BIG SPIN"** Broadcast on January 7, 1989

Starring: Erik Estrada as Vinnie "The Price" Pacelli   Kathy Laskey as Sandy
Guylaine St. Onge as Tanya Verushka   Ida Carnevali as Mrs. Rodriquez
Maria Ricossa as Torre   Suzanne Coy as Rhonda
Marsha Nichols as Mrs. Gold   Dick Callahan as Sam
David Stein as Detective Bryant   Robert Bidaman as Detective Murphy

Teleplay written for *Alfred Hitchcock Presents* by Maxwell Pitt, based on an original story by Matthew Dearborn.

Directed by Al Waxman.

Opener taken from "Coming Home"

(body disposal unit) *Good evening ladies and gentlemen. Do you find it tiresome waiting for cement to dry before dropping it in the river? If so, you'll be interested in our new pre-fabricated body disposal units. At first glance this might appear to be a concrete telephone booth. It is far more useful. The body is placed in here. The two sides are bolted together. It is taken to the edge of the dock and then . . .* (pushes) *All very neat and tidy. You ladies will love it. No more messy mixing and pouring of concrete. No more complicated and expensive equipment. No more tell tale cement on the soles of your shoes. For details please consult your friendly neighborhood hood.* (close-up) *Now for a 60 second consultation with our sponsor. Definitely not a hood. This man's record is spotless. After all, boring people to death is not yet a criminal offense.*

Story: New York City cab driver Vinnie Pacelli picks up two unusual fares today. The first is supermodel Tanya Verushka, whom Vinnie arranges a date with; the second is Mrs. Rodriquez, a maid distraught over her employer's health. Shortly after the maid exits his cab, Vinnie finds two lottery tickets for the big game tonight, and pockets them. Regardless of the fact that he already has a girlfriend, an artist wanna-be named Sandy, Vinnie spends the evening with Tanya. When the model laughs because he can't keep his manhood up, Vinnie gets angry and kills her. Returning home with blood on his face and shirt, Vinnie makes up a story about three men attacking him, while Sandy cleans him up and puts him to bed. The next morning, Vinnie uses a chemical to clean off Tanya's address, which he wrote on the back of a lottery ticket, because, as it turns out, it had last night's winning number. When he tries to cash the ticket in, the police arrest him and tear the ticket in half, claiming it's a fake. You see, Sandy found the ticket last night when she went to clean his shirt, and with his employer asking about Mrs. Rodriquez's missing ticket, put one and one together. Making a fake ticket and tipping the police to check out the Big Spin office, her artistic talents paid off, to a tune of $250,000, courtesy of the maid. Sandy now has enough to go to art school in the mid-west.

Now I must show you our economy size. The only difference being that the victim must be allowed to stiffen, so that he can stand erect. Then his feet are placed in here and the concrete pieces bolted together. If you don't wish to be splashed, you just aim the gentleman toward the end of the dock and . . . roller skates. We think of everything. Until next week. Good night.

Trivia, etc. Director Al Waxman also played the role of Dale Linseman in the episode "Full Disclosure." Micky Erbe and Maribeth Solomon composed the music score for this episode, in a style of Geshwin's New York pieces. These same two musicians have worked together composing music scores for numerous movies and television shows, including *Earth: The Final Conflict* (1997) and *Blackjack* (1998).

EPISODE #66 **"DON'T SELL YOURSELF SHORT"**   Broadcast on January 14, 1989
Starring: Leon Pownall as Richard Martin   David Soul as Michael Dennison
Harvey Atkin as Sam Wickes   Susan Hogan as Joyce Martin
Erica Ehm as Sally   Terry Thomas as the customs captain
An original teleplay written for *Alfred Hitchcock Presents* by Douglas Steinberg.
Directed by René Bonnière.
Opener taken from "Cop for a Day"
(with a tea set)   *Good evening. So nice of you to come for tea. It's very pleasant to observe the amenities even in America. Unfortunately one of my other guests performed rather badly.* (dead man with broken cup) *He took one sip and fell to the floor like a common drunk. Not even a with your leave or a bye your leave. He just left, broke a piece of my good china, too. But what I shall never forgive him for, he took the cup of tea I had been saving for another guest. A dear friend of mine. Ah, here comes our guest now.*

Story: Michael talks his business partner into killing Joseph Caldwell, head of Caldwell Air. Once dead, they will be able to sell the stock short and make a killing on the market.   But when Caldwell Air's stock drops, Michael begins buying up stock of Dynagenics, a competing company, which only makes Richard furious. Joyce, his wife, knows about the game and is shocked to learn that her husband killed Caldwell, so she contacts Sam Wickes of the Securities Exchange Commission. When Richard asks Michael for $250,000 to leave the country, they meet on a bridge to exchange the payoff. Michael, of course, has no intention of paying and pushes Richard into the water. When Joyce learns of the news, she believes her husband committed suicide after learning of her affair with Michael, who promises her more money than she can imagine. The next day, Michael's secretary gives him a confidential report on Dynagenics, while he is packing a suitcase full of money. Sam Wickes shows up, asking questions, and stealing the suitcase for himself, pushes Michael down an empty elevator shaft. Sam then gives Joyce the suitcase and they toast their future – Sam is poisoned and drops dead. At the airport, Joyce gives her suitcase to customs and is promptly arrested. Customs had received an anonymous tip that she would be carrying counterfeit money, which they found in the x-ray machine. The secretary meets Richard in a hotel room, happy that he didn't die from the fall, with the suitcase full of money.

That exhausts our supply of commercials, to say nothing of our audience. Next week we shall all reassemble, renewed and refreshed. Until that happy day, good night.

EPISODE #67 **"FOR ART'S SAKE"**   Broadcast on January 21, 1989
Starring: Bruce Gray as Bryan Holland   Simon Williams as Arthur Hollister
Sheila McCarty as Sarah Hollister   Michele Scarabelli as Erica Fortune
Joan Heney as Mrs. Collier   Allen Stewart-Coates as Mr. Collier
An original teleplay written for *Alfred Hitchcock Presents* by Linda Chase.
Directed by William Corcoran.
Opener taken from "Portrait of Jocelyn"
(as a painter, a close-up of Hitchcock's thumb) *What an extraordinary thumb. It completely obscures the subject I'm painting. I used to paint along the roadside, but I had to quit. Motorists insisted on giving me rides. Hold that pose. Remain perfectly still for the next half-hour. Care to see my handy work. I have several canvases ready.* (shows signs, Post no bills, Kilroy was here) *Or if you like something more exotic,* (Pas de stationnement) *It's French. And of course. . .* (please stand by)

Story: Artist Arthur Hollister is very popular in the art scene of Manhattan. Everyone is buying up his work, which has a very striking and distinctive feature in it: his own face. This trademark is his wife Sarah's idea – but she also paints her own work, using Arthur's name. The gallery owner, Erica Fortune, also has a secret she keeps from the public – her affair with Arthur. When Erica asks Arthur to leave his wife, this poses a problem, since she doesn't know about his wife's talents. Certain his career would be destroyed, Arthur decides to kill Erica with an overdose of blood pressure pills. Returning home, Arthur finds his wife planning a new idea for his paintings, using his entire body. But first, she must cover him with a mixture. Sarah pours a drying compound into the mixture, covering his entire body, and just leaving a breathing tube in his mouth. As the predicament becomes obvious to Arthur, Erica arrives. She is supposed to be dead, but fate played a turn, for the two women have teamed together to finish off Arthur. Of course, once Arthur is dead, his pieces will soar in value and the two women will share the wealth, all due to the fact that the man they loved, gave his all to art.

Bravo, bravo. That was a real show stopper, in every sense of the word. Now I see there is just time enough for me to wish you pleasant dreams and a happy analysis. Good night.

EPISODE #68 **"MURDER IN MIND"** Broadcast on January 28, 1989
Starring: Ann-Marie MacDonald as Ellen Blanchard
Melissa Anderson as Julie Fenton
Noel Harrison as Charles Blanchard   Larry Lalonde as Donald Fenton
Teleplay written for *Alfred Hitchcock Presents* by Sarett Rudley, from her previous teleplay, based on a story by Emily Neff, originally broadcast as "Mr. Blanchard's Secret" on December 23, 1956.
Directed by Allan King.
Opener taken from "Mr. Blanchard's Secret"
(with umbrella) *Good evening, friends. Would you all please examine the tops of your television sets and see if one of you doesn't find a goldfish bowl with a crack in it?* (Holds out his hand to feel the rain) *Thank you. By the way, I have been asked to announce that some of you are missing this program unnecessarily. You have moved and not kept us informed of your address, so we don't know where to send the show to you. I hope you'll take care of that matter at once.*

Story: Julie Fenton likes to write murder scripts and keeps her ideas alive by imagining things about the people around her. One night in bed, she wonders about their new neighbors, the Blanchards. She talked with Mr. Blanchard, who was buying clothes for his wife, but when she expressed an interest in meeting his wife, he hurried off. Julie begins suspecting that Mr. Blanchard killed his wife. Investigating for herself, Julie gets caught spying and goes home to finish her story. Ellen Blanchard comes by and talks with Julie, proving to the writer that she has an over-active imagination. After Ellen leaves, Julie notices that her disfunctional lighter is missing, which leads her to believe that Ellen is a kleptomaniac, and that is why Mr. Blanchard is so over-protective for his wife. During the night, the police answer a phone call placed by Julie, again suspecting the worst of her neighbors, believing a dead body to be Ellen Blanchard. Later the police call back and ask Julie to come down to the morgue to identify the body. But Mr. and Mrs. Blanchard appear at the door with her fixed lighter in hand. For once, Julie is speechless. Going back to bed, her husband, being fed up with her constant talking, takes out a knife and stabs her.

Now if you will excuse me. I must hurry off to a little social affair. A dear friend is guest of honor. It's a stoning. I wouldn't miss it for the world. Good night.

Trivia, etc. This episode was actually a remake of an original *Alfred Hitchcock Presents* episode, "Mr. Blanchard's Secret." Not only is the plot almost exactly the same, but Hitchcock's opener and closer originate from the same episode. The main difference are that Mrs. Fenton's imaginative ideas are shown (a shower murder, among others) and of course the strange twist ending in bed.

EPISODE #69　**"MIRROR, MIRROR"**　Broadcast on February 4, 1989
   Starring:　Graham McPherson as Lieutenant Trevor Reed
   Elizabeth Ashley as Karen / Kate Lawson Robert Collins as Jimmy
   Brent Stait as Sergeant Jim Sweeney Robert McHeady as the pharmacist
   Steve Mousseau as the young man Danny Dion as the patrolman
   An original teleplay written for *Alfred Hitchcock Presents* by Jack Blum and Sharon Corder.
   Directed by Richard Lewis.
   Opener taken from "An Out for Oscar"
   (with a panda and hammer)　*Good evening ladies and gentlemen and show-offs the world over. I use this to test my strength. The panda bear that is. If I'm to lift it I feel that I'm keeping in good physical condition.* (close-up)　*Our story concerns a beautiful woman who looks as though she would be an asset but turns out to be a liability. But first we have something that manages to be both of these at the same time.*

   Story:　Leaving for the pharmacy to pick up a prescription, Karen is stopped by Lieutenant Reed. They question her about a vagrant that was stabbed in her apartment doorway earlier in the evening, but Karen insists it wasn't her. The apartment actually belongs to her sister Kate, who owns the disco downstairs. Returning from the pharmacy, Karen is ordered by her sister to fix the Mirror Image in the disco, and there, meets a young man named Jimmy, who followed her from the pharmacy. Karen returns to the dance club looking seductive, and invites him to come upstairs to see her. Moments later, Jimmy enters holding a butcher knife. He claims he found it in the club, then lays it on the counter. When he advances, she orders him to stay away and slaps him. The lieutenant enters, interrupts the struggle and sends the boy downstairs. When Karen tells him about the knife, the lieutenant observes that it disappeared. Searching for Jimmy in the disco, the cop is stabbed and drops to the floor. Karen tries to grab Jimmy, and the police barge in. But it is too late, for Jimmy has been stabbed to death. Karen stays on the floor, rocking back and forth like a child. At a window, Kate watches the police take her sister away. Mixing a drink, and undoing her hair, she explains to her boyfriend that her sister Karen was always two people. As she seductively approaches him, Kate hides the knife behind her back . . .

   As for this, I've developed a technique to master it. No hands. (steps on an amusement park sledgehammer machine)

   Trivia, etc. The opening for this episode is slightly different than the one used in "An Out for Oscar." The part about Oscar Blinney, that was in the original, was simply cut out for this episode.

EPISODE #70　**"SKELETON IN THE CLOSET"**　Broadcast on February 11, 1989
   Starring:　Mimi Kuzyk as Betty King Jeff Wincott as Tom King
   Elias Zarou as Larry Niles Bill Lake as Sheriff Sam McKay
   Elizabeth Hanna as Janice Forbes Michael Kirby as Al Gordon
   Sam Moses as the motel clerk　(uncredited)
   Teleplay written for *Alfred Hitchcock Presents* by Brian Clemens, Glenn Davis and William Laurin, based on an original story idea by Brian Clemens.
   Directed by George Mendeluk.

Opener taken from "Run for Doom"

(lockers, tar and feathers)   *Good evening and welcome to the grand opening of our new railway station. As one of the features of the celebration we are offering a prize to the person who can guess the number of bodies which will be found in these lockers during the first week of operation. Station lockers seem to be a favorite spot to check one's friends. It's much more tidy than having them lay around the house.*

Story: On the same evening Betty King's husband is elected captain of a prestigious country Club, she is confronted by Larry Niles, who was once a client of hers when she worked as a prostitute in college. Larry wants $10,000 or he will disrupt her life. Borrowing money against her life insurance policy, Betty goes to his hotel to pay the blackmailer off. But now he's not interested in money, and asks her to stay with him for the evening. As they struggle, Larry drops dead from a heart attack. The next morning, the sheriff visits with an old newspaper clipping in his possession, containing Betty's photo, and wants to know if Larry Niles came by to blackmail either of them. Betty makes up a few lies, which fools the sheriff, and after he leaves, she begins talking with her dead grandmother, Lizzie Borden. Following Lizzie's advice, Betty unlocks her husband's closet. removes the nice gleaming axe, and goes after her hubby when he comes home. Sheriff McKay returns for further questioning, finding the front door unlocked. When he opens the closet, Tom kills the officer and stashes his body next to Betty's (among other rotting corpses in the closet). Tom won't allow his crazy wife to jeopardize his position in the community anymore – especially by talking to her dead grandmother, after all, Lizzie only talks to him . . . But then as a final twist, Betty kills Tom with an axe, and then she becomes the new captain.

As for our modern terminal, for persons whose departure is being arranged by the entire community we have this: rather warm tar and . . . (feathers)

Trivia, etc. Although Hitchcock made an opening for "Services Rendered" with a skeleton in a closet, that presentation was not used for this episode. That opening had already been used for the episode "Hippocritic Oath." The premiere season's "The Older Sister" from the original series offered a different kind of Lizzie Borden story.

EPISODE #71   **"IN THE DRIVER'S SEAT"**   Broadcast on February 18, 1989
Starring: Greg Evigan as David Whitmore
Nadine Van Der Velde as Rebecca Whitmore
David Elliott as Ted   Judy Sloane as Ann
Bill Macdonald as Dr. Allan Gilmour   Mary Long as Alice, the nurse
Teleplay written for *Alfred Hitchcock Presents* by Glenn Davis and William Laurin, based on a story by Paul Monette and Alfred Sole.
Directed by Timothy Bond.
Opener taken from "The Blessington Method"
(in a wheelchair)   *Good evening ladies and gentlemen and welcome to Alfred Hitchcock Presents. I should explain. I came down with a cold. The broken leg was a later development. These nurses can become quite forceful at times. The National Safety Council has asked that I remind you that most accidents occur in the home. Therefore this might be a very good place to avoid . . .*
Story: When racecar driver David Whitmore lost his fame and fortune over a tragic accident on the track, he lost more than his pride. Filled with remorse, anger and paranoid, David remains confined in a wheel chair, suspecting his wife of having an affair. In order to discover her faithfulness, he pays his friend Ted to attempt to seduce her. Believing that Ted went farther than he was supposed to, David waits till his next therapy session at the swimming pool, and throws the electric barbecue starter into the water, electrocuting the Ted. When Ann. his sister, witnesses the crime, she helps bury the body, only on the condition that she leaves, never seeing David again. But after the body is stashed, David goes back on his

promise, claiming Ann is linked to the body. Angry, she pushes the wheelchair towards the pool . . . When David's wife returns, she finds Ann's lifeless body in the pool, and David walking on his two feet. It seems he's been able to walk for months, but kept it a secret in order to find out if his wife was remaining faithful to him. Chasing her through the house with a knife, a struggle ensues, resulting in David falling from the second story hallway, onto some living room furniture, now making him a cripple for life. Months later, after the police report is filed, David resides in a mental hospital recovering. When he becomes jealous over his nurse, David, still mentally unbalanced, stabs her to death.

(gets up with cast still in wheelchair) *Now until next time, good night.*

EPISODE #72 **"DRIVING UNDER THE INFLUENCE"** Broadcast on Feb. 25, 1989
Starring: Shirley Douglas as Monica Logan   Mike Connors as Robert Logan
John Novak as Jason Hathaway   Gwynyth Walsh as Anne Hathaway
David B. Nichols as Detective Frank Weston   Laurie Paton as Linda
James Hobson as Peter Taylor   John Gardiner as the bartender
Fay Dance as the television reporter   Doug Stratton as Ed
Written for *Alfred Hitchcock Presents* by Josephine Cummings and Richard Yalem. Directed by Bradley Silberling.
Opener taken from "Blood Bargain," closer taken from "Hangover."
(with car and sword) *Good evening.* (wiping windshield) *May I check to see if there's something loose under your bonnet?* (checks oil with sword) *I would suggest that you add a quart before it's too late. An automobile figures in tonight's play, which is the story of a man with an unpleasant job to perform. One which he did not wish to do, a situation which I understand perfectly, but duty is duty.*

Story: Advertising executive Robert Logan has a serious drinking problem, hitting a woman while driving under the influence. When he arrives home, his wife Monica is packing her bags, intent on leaving him. Logan watches the news report about the hit-and-run while he empties a decanter of Scotch. It seems that the victim, Alice Goodman, only suffered a concussion and may be able to identify the driver. The next day at work, Alice calls Logan and demands $250,000. Unsure of what to do, Logan seeks advice from Jason, his boss. Hathaway recommends a good lawyer and a full confession to the police. But Logan decides different, and pays his mechanic to fix the damage. This doesn't go unobserved to detective Weston, who notices the repair job. Logan tells his boss that this was his second accident, getting away with the first one by paying off the judge. When Logan goes to deliver the pay-off, instead of Alice Goodman, he meets up with his boss's wife. Alice Goodman is really a hired stuntwoman and it was Jason and Anne's daughter that Logan killed years ago. Logan pleads for them to take the money, but all they want is a confession as detective Weston steps forward to hear it. Logan attempts to flee from the scene, but frozen in the headlights of a car, is killed by a drunk driver – the bartender.

I customarily close on a light note but I feel that tonight's subject is an unsuitable one for humor. Alcoholism is being recognized as one of the most serious diseases of our society, and I hope this program has helped dramatize some of the frightening aspects of the problem. Good night.

EPISODE #73 **"IN THE NAME OF SCIENCE"** Broadcast on March 11, 1989
Starring: Dirk Benedict as Dr. Jeffrey Rush   Catherine Disher as Cindy Bertozzi
Sandey Grinn as Dr. Clifford   Joseph Ziegler as Dr. Hendricks
James B. Douglas as Dr. Bingham   Francois Klanfer as Herzog
Teleplay written for *Alfred Hitchcock Presents* by Alan Swyer, Glenn Davis and William Laurin, based on an original story idea by Alan Swyer.
Directed by Zale Dalen.

Opener taken from "Diagnosis: Danger"

(stethoscope-radio) *Oh, sorry. My transistor-radio, much more dignified looking than most models. People are terribly impressed. I understand these have become very popular in medical circles, in fact they are out-selling stethoscopes. They satisfy everyone. The patient is happy because he thinks the doctor is listening to his heartbeat, and the doctor is pleased because he's getting the latest ball-scores.*

Story: Dr. Jeffrey Rush has taken a high-paying job in an unknown controlled environment, where they will use his scientific knowledge for a project unnamed and unknown. His interest (other than his work) is his lab assistant, Cindy Bertozzi. Dr. Hendricks, a paranoid co-worker, thinks they should destroy their notes, believing the new drug they designed can either cure or kill an entire population. Feeling imprisoned, Hendricks wants to escape and Rush gives him a tranquilizer. When Hendricks keels over clutching at his chest, Rush takes his top secret computer disc. Trying to escape, Dr. Rush finds himself at the Berlin Wall with German guards, and forced to return to the compound. At a staff party in a hotel, the waiter approaches Rush and offers him five million and a safe passage in exchange for the formula. Rush takes the bait. Herzog pulls a gun and the doctor knocks him out and runs for his life. Outside, he finds that the hotel is connected to the lab, and runs into Cindy. She's been sent by the CIA to help him escape and escorts him to a safe house, where she tells him that they are still in America and the project was actually a loyalty test, of which he failed. Dr. Hendricks is alive and well and has been helping Cindy and Herzog with the testing. Only Hendricks is a traitor, shoots Rush, and tries to kill Cindy. Rush manages to shoot Hendricks, saving Cindy's life. Weeks later, Cindy relaxes on a beach and wondering what to do with the formula, throws the disc in the fire - not yet realizing that it wasn't the only copy.

This is the end of tonight's play. For those whose appetite for entertainment is not yet sated, we have another commercial. As for my transistor-radio it seems to have lost its enchantment, as far as the medical profession is concerned. The hospitals obtained their own transmitters and began cutting in on the broadcasts to page the doctors, sometimes right in the middle of a song or even a commercial. Something which will never happen on this program, I assure you. Observe!

EPISODE #74 **"ROMANCE MACHINE"** Broadcast on March 25, 1989
        Starring: Rich Hall as Edgar / Eddie   Diane Franklin as Paulette / Paula
        Art Hindle as Jack Gold   Barclay Hope as Harvey
        An original teleplay written for *Alfred Hitchcock Presents* by Robert DeLaurentis.
        Directed by René Bonnière.
Opener taken from "Ten O'Clock Tiger"
(someone standing on his shoulders) *Good evening ladies and gentlemen. Since you are accustomed to hearing my brother Alfred at this time, I shall allow him to make his usual announcement. You may carry on, Alfred.* (camera pans down to man on bottom, Hitchcock) *Thank you, kind Sir. I agreed to take part in this absurd charade only because I was assured it would get us a booking on a certain, Sunday night variety show. However, I'm not sure it's worth it, since watching us is rather a limited form of amusement. We have provided you with some alternate entertainment,* (lets go of one leg) (hey!) *Here it is.*

Story: In the far future: Jack Gold, president of Futurebase, Inc., a company that manufactures cyborgs – functional mechanical replicas of human beings – is invited to the house of Edgar Peckerman, an absent-minded professor under his payroll. Edgar reveals his feelings for Paulette, Jack's secretary, but being a pit of verbal paralysis, doesn't know what to say or do. So he's created a cyborg for the language of love, including physical chemistry, in the image of himself. Jack wants to market the cyborgs, but Edgar won't grant him the honor unless he can prove his invention is a success. So Jack authorizes a test, Paulette is wooed, and the experiment is a success. But there took some intervention on Jack's part. You see, Paulette faked it all, because she's really in love with her boss. Jack kills Edgar so he and Paulette can make the millions alone, only to discover to their horror that they killed the cyborg, not the real scientist. And if that wasn't enough, Edgar has another confession. Paulette – the real Paulette – is dead. What Jack saw with his own eyes is another cyborg. After all, as Eddie explains, if he can't improve his image, he had to improve the girl. And with that, Edgar kills his boss, shortly before a duplicate of Jack walks through the door to take his place.

Alfred has been strangely silent. Alfred, what are you up to? Nothing. Until next week . . . (lighted match to his shoe) *Good night.*

Trivia, etc. Although this was a new story, the idea must have been taken from "Design for Loving" that also dealt with cyborgs, although Ray Bradbury wrote "Marionettes, Inc." that "Design for Loving" was based on, and not credited for this episode. It does, however, play more like an *Outer Limits* episode than an *Alfred Hitchcock Presents*.

EPISODE #75   **"DIAMONDS AREN'T FOREVER"**   Broadcast on April 15, 1989
    Starring: George Lazenby as James . . .   Jack Blum as Mickey
    Eve Crawford as Rachel   Don Lake as A. C. Boone
    Peter Langley as the Colonel   Araby Lockhart as Mrs. Pickett
    Sam Malkin as Barney   Chris Moore as Honi
    Ian White as the agent on television
    An original teleplay written for *Alfred Hitchcock Presents* by Glenn Davis and William Laurin.
    Directed by Peter Crane.
    Opener taken from "Last Seen Wearing Blue Jeans"
    (as a border guard) *Good evening. Our country welcomes you, and may I search your luggage? I find the life of a border guard quite diverting. It's very much like working at the check-out stand of a giant super-market. I also have a very lucrative sideline. I retouch pass-port photographs for men.*

Story: When an aircraft lurches out of control, a British Secret-Service Agent parachutes to safety, landing in front of a small country inn. He receives his instructions to retrieve a priceless statue, the Golden Egret of Bishwara, hidden somewhere within the hotel. If he doesn't retrieve the statue soon, Bishwara will become under Soviet domination. Possible foreign agents within the hotel include a diverse group to choose from: psychiatrist Rachel and her patient Mickey; Producer A. C. Boone who does "nature" films; Honi who thinks that Boone is a porn producer; the inn-keeper Mrs. Pickett; the groundskeeper Tim; and the bartender named Barney. When the inn-keeper is found dead from a sickle, James narrows down the possible suspects and apprehends the murderer. As for the statue, James finds it and Mickey reveals his gun, and his true identity. He is the Russian courier. Before he can shoot the Secret Agent, Honi shoots Mickey, and unscrewing the base of the Egret, reveals a handful of diamonds, enough so the two can retire from this business and live "excessively" ever after.

By the way, you may proceed on through, I can now reveal that this is not actually the border of anything. Just a device to keep the audience until the play is over. Good night.

Trivia, etc. George Lazenby, star of *On Her Majesty's Secret Service* (1969), makes a guest appearance in this Hitchcock episode as a super-spy under the name of "James." Since the character of James Bond was already trademarked, the full name of the

British Intelligence Agent could not be given. Every time Lazenby (and another actor) gave out his name, some background noise purposely drowns out the word "Bond." Smashing plates on the floor or static on the television were two ways this trick was accomplished. The title of the script itself spoofs a James Bond film, *Diamonds Are Forever*, released in 1971 starring Sean Connery. Right down to ordering a martini (not stirred) and landing on the ground with a parachute in the image of England's national flag, James even makes reference about riding on a rocket sled! The music, of course, was specially composed by Christopher Dedrick - who supplied orchestral music for many movies - to recreate the same style music characterized in the Bond films. During the fight scene, one of the lamps is broken and as a last minute attempt to defend himself, James uses the live wire to shock a villain to death, and comments "shocking," much like Sean Connery did in 1964's *Goldfinger*. As a finishing touch, the credits listed Lazenby as "James . . ."

EPISODE #76 **"MY DEAR WATSON"** Broadcast on April 22, 1989
      Starring: Graeme Campbell as Mycroft Holmes

Brian Bedford as Sherlock Holmes	Patrick Monckton as Dr. Watson
John Colicos as Inspector Lestrade / Moriarty	Robert Nicholson as Grimes
Bunty Webb as Mrs. Hudson	Lori Lansens as Liz

      Teleplay written for *Alfred Hitchcock Presents* by Susan Woollen, based on the fictional characters created by Sir Arthur Conan Doyle.
      Directed by Jorge Montesi.
      Opener taken from "The Perfect Crime," closer taken from "Jonathan."
      (as Sherlock Holmes, blowing bubbles from a pipe) *Good evening ladies and gentlemen and Dr. Watson wherever you are.*

      Story: London, 1895. Inspector Lestrade, having suffered a mental collapse as a result of being out-witted once too many by Sherlock Holmes, spends the evening with the famed detective, and his sidekick, Dr. Watson. But when the guests take leave after dinner, Watson is kidnapped and held ransom. The kidnappers demand Lestrade visit them at Whitechapel with all of Holmes' case files, or the good doctor is no more. Employing the talents of his brother Mycroft, Holmes has some fake files made up and disguises his brother to look like Lestrade. The villains, however, are one step ahead of them and Mycroft is killed. Piecing the clues together, Holmes believes that Watson is held within a dungeon at the Tower of London. After Holmes and Watson reunite, Lestrade peels off his disguise to reveal that he is in actuality, the notorious Moriarty. But Holmes suspected that all along, and confesses that he staged his brother's death, so Moriarty will be apprehended. Holmes and Watson escape from the gas-ridden dungeon and reach the surface, barely in time for Mycroft and his men to go and fetch Moriarty's body. As Watson and Holmes climb into a cab, Watson congratulates Holmes on unmasking the vile professor. But all is not over, for we see that the smiling face of the cab driver is Moriarty's!

     This concludes tonight's divertissement. But please remain tuned to this channel. I am not familiar with the program which follows, nor the one after that, but I have seen the story we are presenting next time and I think it's worth waiting for. Good night.

      Trivia, etc. Susan Woollen, who wrote this script, also co-wrote three made-for-television movies with Michael Sloan: *Evening in Byzantium* (1978), *The Return of the Man from U.N.C.L.E.* (1983) and *The Return of the Six-Million Dollar Man and the Bionic Woman* (1987) – which were also produced by Sloan. Patrick Monckton would later play the role of Karparti in *Sherlock Holmes and the Leading Lady* in 1990.

EPISODE #77 **"NIGHT CREATURES"** Broadcast on April 29, 1989
      Starring: Jason Blicker as Freak   Ray James as Max Cantilever
      Brett Cullen as Cooper   Louise Vallance as Holly Sinclair

Michael Rhoades as Martin Lecross / Adam Lust
An original teleplay written for *Alfred Hitchcock Presents* by Michael Sloan.
Directed by Richard J. Lewis.
Opener taken from "The Ikon of Elijah"
(hammer in a tomb) *Oh good evening. I enjoy digging around in old tombs. They can be quite convenient too. If your assistance becomes as difficult as mine are you can always manage to . . . leave them inside. This one is typical, quiet, comfortable, attractive and roomy. Man has always provided better living conditions for the dead, than for the living. But that's enough persiflage badinage. Now for tonight's story.*

Story: Holly Sinclair, a San Francisco newspaper reporter, had a baffling vision about a horseman, dressed in a 17th Century outfit, riding out of the mist on a white horse. Instead of spending the evening with her fiancé, Cooper, she is assigned to go to Sacramento with a photographer named Freak, to cover a heavy metal rock group, "Adam Lust and the Vampyres." Arriving at Night Creatures, the nightclub where the band performs, the three enter, and Max Cantilever, owner of the club, welcomes Holly and her friends. Sticking her nose where it doesn't belong, the inquisitive reporter finds herself in the basement of the club, where bodies rest in coffins, and one of them bites her in the neck. When the group goes on stage, Cooper hunts for Holly. When Freak notices that Adam has no reflection in the stage mirror, he remembers all that he's read about vampires, and begins to attack the band. Cooper ends up plunging the stake into Adam's heart while the crowd cheers, believing it is all part of the stage show. Racing downstairs, Cooper finds Holly in a coffin while the bandleader's power dissipates, as does Holly's vampirism. Out in the alley, Holly runs from Cooper when she sees the same horseman from her vision, Cantilever, and rides off with him into the mist. Cooper makes a vow to find Holly as he too had a vision of her, being held by some unseen force.

So much for the Carpius caper. I'm sure it's very comforting to know where you are going to spend the rest of your life. (reads wall) *R. Montague loves J. Capulet. These teenagers, defacing property. Does it seem dark to you? I bet my assistant has accidentally shut the tomb door. I have a feeling it's time for me to say good night. Help.*

Trivia, etc. The rock band known as "Disaster Area" played the fictional satanic band called "The Vampyres" in this episode. Disaster Area band members included: Harvey Ray Lewis (guitar), Laurence Lee Langley (drums), Simon Anderson (guitar) and Steve White (bass). Disaster Area songs used in the show were "The Awakening." "Desirable Death" and "Bombshelter," all property of Disaster Music.

EPISODE #78 **"THE MAN WHO KNEW TOO LITTLE"** Broadcast on July 8, 1989
Starring: Lewis Collins as Bill Stewart

Cynthia Belliveau as Cassie Wilson	Richard Sali as Kovacs
Don Fenton as Hamilton	Chuck Shamat as Philip Bellamy
Frank Adamson as the bartender	Tommy Earlls as the bellhop
Kimball Fox as the driver	Jackie May as the maid

An original teleplay written for *Alfred Hitchcock Presents* by Pascal Bonniere, Glenn Davis and William Laurin.
Directed by Ray Austin.
Opener taken from "The Young One"
(with a gift collection) *Good evening and thank you for being so prompt. I detest being kept waiting. I thought you might be interested in this collection of gift selections. They range from conventional to rare. Here is the ever-popular revolver, it is an excellent means of establishing credit in a strange city. It is equally useful in the removal of unwanted or unsightly persons. Here is a jar of poison mushrooms for those smart alecks who know*

toadstools when they see them. (picks up an axe) *Here we have a weapon that is primitive but effective. It is guaranteed to be 50% painless. You see it takes two men to operate it and the one at this end doesn't feel a thing.*

Story: Waking up in a hotel room, Bill Stewart finds himself with a severe case of amnesia. All he can remember is the beautiful blonde he slept with, and when he meets her in the hotel lobby, her asks that she join him for a drink in the bar. Back in his suite, Bill is attacked and is forced to kill the stranger. Rushing downstairs, Bill witnesses the blonde being kidnapped. When the management of the hotel go up to his room, they find no body. At the bar, Paul tries to clear his head with a few drinks, and the bartender delivers a letter with Cassie's locket, and an address, ordering Bill to deliver the goods or the woman dies. Arriving at the address designated, a deserted movie theater, Bill discovers that the kidnapper is the owner of Chemtel Industries. They want a small vial of bacteria, enough to kill everyone in the theater, hidden inside Bill's pen. Switching the girl for the ransom, Bill throws the vial in the air, which turns out to be a fake. The contents were switched. Outside, Bill explains to Cassie that he's been working undercover at Chemtel, and just discovered that his employer is the real villain. He faked amnesia all along, knowing exactly how their method of operation works. As the two lovers relax on a bus getting out of town, a pair of hands presses a needle through the seat, into Bill's back. The hands belong to the bartender and when Bill wakes up, this time he really does have amnesia.

We have another play prepared to show you next week. I hope you'll join us then. Good night.

Trivia, etc, As in "Diamonds Aren't Forever," the title of this episode was a spoof. This time on Hitchcock's *The Man Who Knew Too Much* (1934 and 1956 versions).

EPISODE #79 **"REUNION"** Broadcast on July 15, 1989
Starring: Geraint Wyn Davies as Paul Stebbins
James Blendick as Colonel John Stacy   Patricia Collins as Laura Stacy
William Dunlop as Marvin Raggs   Wayne Best as Spindle Cook
Andrew Thomson as Tom Libowitz   Michael Dyson as James Hollister
Errol Slue as Jackson Forbes   Jim Murchison as J.J. Mahoney
An original teleplay written for *Alfred Hitchcock Presents* by Michael Sloan.
Directed by John Wood.
Opener taken from "A Crime for Mothers," with stills from other episodes.
(The Best of Hitchcock) *Good evening, and welcome to The Best of Hitchcock. In the absence of my vacationing brother Alfred, we are presenting clips from his past shows. I find it amusing, by the way, that television at last confirms what our family has known for years. That I, rather than Alfred am The Best of Hitchcock. And now for those clips:* (on the rails) *Alfred never looked better.* (skeleton in the closet) *The next sound you'll hear will be my sponsor.*

Story: Platoon leader Colonel John Stacy has a reunion every year to reenact a battle to discover who was responsible for the platoon's final demise. Vietnam vet Paul Stebbins is attending for the first time and looking at the photo of his comrades brings back unpleasant memories. Stacy's wife Laura leaves for the evening and one by one the members of the platoon arrive. After the dinner, the men go into the study to reenact the battle. When Stebbins and Stacy are the only two survivors, the Colonel is faced with the unpleasant fact that he split up his company. He couldn't call them back, having sent them into enemy territory by mistake. The Colonel has been plagued with guilt all these years and the reunions have been an obsession. Stebbins tells the Colonel that he did complete a heroic act by returning to be with the men and wants him to stop the reunions. "The men need to rest in peace."

Before taking leave, I would like to show you a few of my selections for The Best of Hitchcock. (dogs) *Now this is truly vintage Hitchcock.* (ape) *And without the violence my brother seems to admire. Next week we shall be back with another story. Until then, good night.*

EPISODE #80 **"SOUTH BY SOUTHEAST"** Broadcast on July 22, 1989

Starring: Patrick Wayne as Michael Roberts   Cedric Smith as Van Dorn
Pam Hyatt as Mary Conn   Bernard Behrens as Houseman
Arlene Mazerolle as Susan Sullivan   Shelley Young as Francesca
William Laurin as Laurin   Glenn Davis as Davis
Jim Millington as the auctioneer   Hamish McEwan as the bellhop
Michael Sloan as the executive movie producer (uncredited)

An original teleplay written for *Alfred Hitchcock Presents* by Michael Sloan and Robert DeLaurentis.

Directed by Timothy Bond.

Opener taken from "The Crystal Trench"

(mountain climbing)   *Good evening ladies and gentlemen. I thought I would cut this rope since it seems to be obstructing my path. I can't seem to find my partner. He was here a moment ago, then let out a cry and disappeared.* (Hitchcock cuts the rope and a man cries; close-up) *My, my. I seem to have made a faux pas. My friend was on the other end of that rope. Rotten luck. He was also my business partner, but the show must go on.*

Story: Actor Michael Roberts reluctantly goes to audition for a remake of Hitchcock's film *North by Northwest*, which is being filmed in Canada. His agent, Mary Conn, has him meet with the producers in a Toronto hotel. By mistaken identity, he is picked up by Francesca, assuming he's a man named Grant, and taken to meet sinister toy mogel Van Dorn. Meanwhile, in Washington, D.C., Houseman, the Director of the Agency, discovers that his men sent Agent Grant to St. Louis by mistake, rather than Toronto. Van Dorn, believing that Michael is an undercover agent, orders to have the actor killed. Michael goes into a model train store owned by Van Dorn's empire and meets an employee, Susan Sullivan, and the two fall in love. Later that day, Agents Laurin and Davis escort him out of an auction and they tell Michael that Van Dorn is the head of an international and lucrative film pirating operation. Van Dorn knows that Michael isn't the agent, which now puts the real agent, Susan, in danger. Michael later finds Susan and knocks Francesca out with an injection. Breaking open a Mount Rushmore statue that Van Dorn bought at the auction, they find inside a computer disc with all the worldwide pirate outlets, and a copy of Hitchcock's lost movie, *South by Southeast*. After the matter is all cleared up, Michael meets up with his agent and the executive producer. Mary confesses that she is also an agent for Houseman. Michael was brought in because she knew he could keep his head when in danger.

Next week I shall once again return with another story spiced together by commercials. Until then, good night.

Trivia, etc. For Hitchcock fans, this episode, the last original broadcast of the series, marked a salute to the great director by launching a spoof of *North by Northwest*. To list all the clichés would take pages, but to start, the famed theme music from the show, "Funeral March of A Marionette," was played for background accompaniment throughout key travel scenes. When Michael wakes from his sleep in Van Dorn's office, the television is playing a fictional episode of *Alfred Hitchcock Presents*.

As one of the few actors to claim this stake, Cedric Smith made more than one appearance on the remake series of *Alfred Hitchcock Presents*. This episode marked his second appearance. He also appeared in the third season's opener "VCR – Very Careful Rape." Cedric also dabbled in music, appearing on two albums by Loreena McKennitt, *Elemental* (1985) and *To Drive the Cold Winter Away* (1987) by Quinlan Road Productions.

The producers of the series had a large hand in the production as well. Not only did producers Robert DeLaurentis and Michael Sloan write the script, but story editors Glenn Davis and William Laurin played the shady characters named – respectfully – Davis and Laurin. Actress Pam Hyatt played Patrick Wayne's agent in the beginning and end of the episode, a woman named Mary Conn. (Mary Kahn was the producer of the series!) Michael Sloan, one of the executive producers of the Hitchcock series, plays himself, or rather an "unnamed" executive movie producer. After the closing credits finish rolling, when a portrait of Sloan hits the screen, the viewers can hear Sloan remarking "Don't you recognize his profile?"

The episode itself spoofed the Ernest Lehman script, first changing the title of the episode to "South by Southeast." Then many of the movie's scenes were re-enacted, including the famed auction house scene, and a walk in the park, where a red toy plane shoots and chases Michael, until it crashes in a fiery explosion. The statue purchased at the auction is that of Mount Rushmore, and in the toy store, a replica of the train on which Cary Grant and Eva Marie Saint went on their honeymoon, was staged by use of model trains. Not to mention the character of Michael Roberts, played by actor Patrick Wayne (the first names of the script writers Michael Sloan and Robert DeLaurentis), and the mistaken identity of an agent named Grant "no, not Cary," often exclaimed in the episode.

One last humorous side-light was near the end of the episode, when Michael Sloan suggested filming *The Birds II* . . . enough said.

APPENDIX A:
A SELECTION OF OTHER TELEVISION APPEARANCES

- HOLLYWOOD LEGENDS (a.k.a. "The Men Who Made the Movies") Produced, directed and written by Richard Schickel. Narrated by Cliff Robertson. (1973, 58 min)
- THE AMERICAN FILM INSTITUTE SALUTES ALFRED HITCHCOCK Hitchcock is presented with the Lifetime Achievement Award. (1979, 72 min)
- HITCHCOCK (BBC OMNIBUS) A Two Part series, both released in 1986. Part One was entitled: "It's only a Movie." (1986, 65 min)
- MUSIC FOR THE MOVIES: Bernard Herrmann . . . About the collaboration with Hitchcock and the killing of Gromek with Herrmann's score. (1992, 20 min)
- CINEMA EUROPE: The Other Hollywood Hitchcock in parts 5 and 6, with silent version of knife-scene in *Blackmail*. Narrated by Kenneth Branagh (1995, 12 min)
- VERTIGO (AMC Production) About the recent *Vertigo* restoration. (1996, 27 min)
- FAMILY PORTRAITS (AMC Production) Contained a lot of Hitchcock's home-movies. (1996, 27 min)
- CLOSE-UP ON HITCHCOCK (BBC) About 16 short items are available. (1997)
- BIOGRAPHY ON HITCHCOCK ON A & E Interviews with Alfred Hitchcock, Patricia Hitchcock, Peter Bogdanovich, Richard Schickel, Norman Lloyd, Janet Leigh, Doris Day, Ernest Lehman, James Stewart, Tippi Hedren and home movie clips. (46 min)
- HITCH - Alfred The Great & HITCH - Alfred the Auteur (BBC) Interviews and clips from *Marnie* screentest, a Sego commercial, and Kaleidoscope Frenzy. (1999, 100 min)

- DIAL H FOR HITCHCOCK: The Genius Behind the Showman (Universal)
  Written and directed by Ted Haimes. Interviews and clips from the set of *Frenzy* and home movies from 1939 trip to USA. (1999, 95 min)
- ALL ABOUT THE BIRDS . . . Produced, directed and written by Laurent Bouzereau. Interviews with Patricia Hitchcock, Tippi Hedren, Rod Taylor, Evan Hunter and Veronica Cartwright. (1999, 100 min)
- HITCHCOCK, SELZNICK AND THE END OF HOLLYWOOD (WNET)
  Produced, written and directed by Michael Epstein. (1998, 86 min)

INTERVIEWS

- DALI DOCUMENTARY
  Interview with Alfred Hitchcock about why he wanted Dali for *Spellbound*. (2 mins.)
- PATHE REPORTER MEETS
  Ingrid Bergman and Alfred Hitchcock at Heathrow (circa 1949?, 1 minute segment)
  > Hitchcock: "Is this your first time in England?"
  > Bergman: "No, no. You'll be happy to know I spent my honeymoon in England."
  > Hitchcock: "Tell me."
  > Bergman: "I think that the diet in England is gonna do you a lot of good."
  > Hitchcock: "Doesn't do me any good."
  > Bergman: "I'm not telling."
  > Hitchcock: "Is it gonna be good for you?"
  > Bergman: "Well I don't worry about it, but I worry about you."
  > Hitchcock: "Well, thank you very much and please go on worrying."
- PICTURE PARADE (BBC) Interview with Hitchcock by Robert Robinson. (1960, 5 minute segment)
- MONITOR (BBC) Interview with Hitchcock by Huw Wheldon. (1964, 14 mins)
- A TALK WITH HITCHCOCK (Telescope, Canada)
  Interview with Hitchcock by author and critic Fletcher Markle. (1964, 49 min)
- A FILM PROFILE (BBC) Interview with Hitchcock by Philip Jenkinson. (1966, 31 min)

TV SHOWS

- SHIP'S REPORTER
  Jack Mangan & Hitchcock talks about *Rope*, *Stage Fright* and coming to TV. (1950, 5 min)
- WHAT'S MY LINE ? (CBS, Sep 12, 1954)
  Hitchcock as the Mystery Celebrity.
  Miss Dorothy Kilgallan guesses Hitchcock's identity. (1954, 24 min)
- THE NEW RED SKELTON SHOW
  Hitchcock is presented the 1954 Look Award for Best Direction. (1954, 5 min)
- ART AND SCIENCE
  Two episodes with Hitchcock in Rome approx. 1960 and in Milan approx. 1966. (11 min)
- THE DICK CAVETT SHOW (1972, 90 min)
- TOMORROW WITH TOM SNYDER (1973, 60 min)
- CAMERA THREE: "THE ILLUSTRATED HITCHCOCK" (1972, 60 min)

APPENDIX B: THE BEST OF ALFRED HITCHCOCK PRESENTS

In 1981, a special twenty-six segment series of repeats began syndication on PBS stations across the United States. Known as "The Best of Alfred Hitchcock Presents," most of the episodes originated from the fifth season. The syndication package was shown at different times and dates, depending on what local PBS stations were able to accommodate. The following are all twenty-six in the order they were broadcast, on PBS affiliate WNEO-TV in Kent, Ohio. The WNEO showing weekly featured an afterward by Dr. William H. Zucchero of the Speech Department at Kent State University.

1. "Lamb to the Slaughter" (10/1/81) Stars Barbara Bel Geddes.
2. "The Baby-Blue Expression" (10/8/81) Stars Sarah Marshall.
3. "The Schartz-Metterklume Method" (10/15/81) Stars Elspeth March.
4. "Not the Running Type" (10/22/81) Stars Paul Hartman.
5. "Graduating Class" (10/29/81) Stars Gigi Perreau.
6. "Anniversary Gift" (11/5/81) Stars Barbara Baxley.
7. "Hitch Hike" (11/12/81) Stars Suzanne Pleshette.
8. "Road Hog" (11/19/81) Stars Richard Chamberlain.
9. "An Occurrence at Owl Creek Bridge" (11/26/81) Stars Ken Tobey.
10. "No Pain" (12/3/81) Stars Brian Keith and Joanna Moore.
11. "The Blessington Method" (12/10/81) Stars Dick York.
12. "Dry Run" (12/17/81) Stars Robert Vaughn and David White.
13. "Specialty of the House" (12/24/81) Stars Robert Morley.
14. "The Cure" (12/31/81) Stars Nehemiah Persoff.
15. "Special Delivery" (1/7/82) Stars Steve Dunne and Peter Lazer.
16. "Dead Weight" (1/14/82) Stars Joseph Cotten and Julie Adams.
17. "Across the Threshold" (1/21/82) Stars George Grizzard.
18. "The Cuckoo Clock" (1/28/82) Stars Beatrice Straight.
19. "Mother, May I Go Out to Swim?" (2/4/82) Stars William Shatner.
20. "Madame Mystery" (2/11/82) Stars Audrey Totter.
21. "Escape to Sonoita" (2/18/82) Stars Burt Reynolds.
22. "The Little Man Who Was There" (2/25/82) Stars Norman Lloyd.
23. "One Grave Too Many" (3/4/82) Stars Jeremy Slate.
24. "The Man Who Found the Money" (3/25/82) Stars Arthur Hill.
25. "Hooked" (4/1/82) Stars Anne Francis and Robert Horton.
26. "Make My Death Bed" (4/8/82) Stars Diana Van Der Vlis.

APPENDIX C: THE RATING SWEEP

So how popular was the Hitchcock program? The following is a season-by-season listing of the top-rated evening series, ranked by audience size. The American Nielsen rating is the percent of all TV-equipped homes tuned to the program on an average night, as measured by the A.C. Nielsen Company. Thus a rating of 33.9 for *Alfred Hitchcock Presents* means that on the average, 33.9 percent of all homes that had a TV were tuned to the show. A.C. Nielsen changed their system of computing ratings in 1960, so ratings prior to and after that date are not precisely comparable. It should also be noted that since the Nielsen system was basically a service for advertisers, only sponsored programs were measured.

The list on the following page shows the only four seasons of *Alfred Hitchcock Presents* that graced the top 25 highest-rating list.

* Source for this appendix was from *Television Drama Series Programming: A Comprehensive Chronicle, 1980-1982* by Larry James Gianakos. Published through The Scarecrow Press, Inc. Metuchen, NJ & Lonson, 1983.

October 1956 – April 1957 Season
1. I Love Lucy CBS 43.7
2. The Ed Sullivan CBS 38.4
3. General Electric Theater CBS 36.9
4. The $64,000 Question CBS 36.4
5. December Bride CBS 35.2
6. **Alfred Hitchcock** **CBS 33.9**
7. I've Got a Secret CBS 32.7
   Gunsmoke CBS 32.7
9. The Perry Como Show NBC 32.6
10. The Jack Benny Show CBS 32.3
11. Dragnet NBC 32.1
12. Arthur Godfrey's Talent Scouts
    CBS 31.9
13. The Millionaire CBS 31.8
    Disneyland CBS 31.8
15. The Red Skelton Show CBS 31.4
    The Lineup CBS 31.4
17. You Bet Your Life NBC 31.1
18. The Life and Legend of Wyatt Earp
    ABC 31.0
19 The Ford Show NBC 30.7
20. The Adventures of Robin Hood
    CBS 30.3
21. People Are Funny NBC 30.2
22. The $64,000 Challenge CBS 29.7
    The Phil Silvers Show CBS 29.7
24. Lassie CBS 29.5
25. Private Secretary CBS 29.0

October 1957 – April 1958 Season
1. Gunsmoke CBS 43.1
2. The Danny Thomas Show CBS 35.3
3. Tales of Wells Fargo NBC 35.2
4. Have Gun – Will Travel CBS 33.7
5. I've Got a Secret CBS 33.4
6. The Life and Legend of Wyatt Earp
   ABC 32.6
7. General Electric Theater CBS 31.5
8. The Restless Gun NBC 31.4
9. December Bride CBS 30.7
10. You Bet Your Life NBC 30.6
11. The Perry Como Show NBC 30.5
12. **Alfred Hitchcock** **CBS 30.3**
    Cheyenne CBS 30.3
14. The Ford Show NBC 29.7
15. The Red Skelton Show CBS 28.9
16. The Gale Storm Show CBS 28.8
17. The Millionaire CBS 28.5
18. The Lineup CBS 28.4
19. This Is Your Life NBC 28.1
    The $64,000 Question CBS 28.1
21. The Zane Grey Theater CBS 27.9
22. Lassie CBS 27.7

23. Wagon Train NBC 27.7
    Sugarfoot ABC 27.7
    Father Knows Best NBC 27.7

October 1958 – April 1959 Season
1. Gunsmoke CBS 39.6
2. Wagon Train NBC 36.1
3. Have Gun – Will Travel CBS 34.3
4. The Rifleman ABC 33.1
5. The Danny Thomas Show CBS 32.8
6. Maverick ABC 30.4
7. Tales of Wells Fargo NBC 30.2
8. The Real McCoys ABC 30.1
9. I've Got a Secret CBS 29.8
10. The Life and Legend of Wyatt Earp
    ABC 29.1
11. The Price Is Right NBC 28.6
12. The Red Skelton Show CBS 28.5
13. Zane Grey Theater CBS 28.3
    Father Knows Best CBS 28.3
15. The Texan CBS 28.2
16. Wanted: Dead or Alive CBS 28.0
    Peter Gunn NBC 28.0
18. Cheyenne ABC 27.9
19. Perry Mason CBS 27.5
20. The Ford Show NBC 27.2
21. Sugarfoot ABC 27.0
    The Ann Southern Show CBS 27.0
    The Perry Como Show NBC 27.0
24. **Alfred Hitchcock** **CBS 26.8**
25. Name That Tune CBS 26.7
    General Electric Theater CBS 26.7

October 1959 – April 1960 Season
1. Gunsmoke CBS 40.3
2. Wagon Train NBC 38.4
3. Have Gun – Will Travel CBS 34.7
4. The Danny Thomas Show CBS 31.1
5. The Red Skelton Show CBS 30.8
6. Father Knows Best CBS 29.7
   77 Sunset Strip ABC 29.7
8. The Price Is Right NBC 29.2
9. Wanted: Dead or Alive CBS 28.7
10. Perry Mason CBS 28.3
11. The Real McCoys ABC 28.2
12. The Ed Sullivan Show CBS 28.0
13. The Rifleman ABC 27.5
14. The Ford Show NBC 27.4
15. The Lawman ABC 26.2
16. Dennis the Menace CBS 26.0
17. Cheyenne ABC 25.9
18. Rawhide CBS 25.8
19. Maverick ABC 25.2

Alfred Hitchcock Presents and *The Alfred Hitchcock Hour* did not appear on the top 25 list during any other season, according to the Nielsens.

Alfred Hitchcock claims he has an itch in his back . . . wonder why?
(Photo courtesy of Ronald V. Borst / Hollywood Movie Posters.)

THE HITCHCOCK ANTHOLOGIES

One problem with documenting the Hitchcock anthologies is that, when Davis Publications bought *Alfred Hitchcock's Mystery Magazine* in 1976 from H.S.D., very few files were transferred, so there are virtually no records of the magazine's first twenty years, except by recollection from present-day employers, or what has already been written about them.

The history of the anthologies dates back to the first issue of *Alfred Hitchcock's Mystery Magazine*, which premiered – contrary to popular belief – a year and a half after the television series premiered. As already known, the first issue of *AHMM* was dated December 1956 (Vol. 1, No. 12). There were no numbers 1 through 11, probably because the staff wanted to start off as if it had begun in January of 1956.* The premiere publication hit the newsstands in November of 1956, in time for the Christmas buying season. There was a "message from Hitchcock" on the inside of the premiere issue. It gives a little account of the magazine's beginning, and weirdly, the same message was repeated in the second and third issues, verbatim.

It is definitely known that the early H.S.D. contracts with authors for stories, provided the magazine with a one-month first-refusal option for TV, movie, and radio rights – that is, one month after the story was published. (The performance rights thus remained with the author.) Hitchcock did prefer published stories over original teleplays, because he liked to work from what he could be certain already proved successful. Shortly after the premiere of the magazine, the producers of the series - Norman Lloyd and Joan Harrison - would scout the stories hoping to find one or two that would "meet the Hitchcock" style. From there, the authors would be contacted, financial arrangements would be made and the deal signed.

The Hitchcock magazine proved to be a perfect source for story material. Certainly the editors were attempting to buy and publish the same kind of stories that the television viewers were already familiar with, so in one fashion, both the producers of the series and the editors of the magazine, were profiting from this mutual arrangement.

The Hitchcock estate receives royalties from the publishers and magazines on the income they receive. Although *Alfred Hitchcock's Mystery Magazine* is currently a part of Dell Magazines, they have never been part of the Dell Books division, so there is no information access through files of the *AHMM*. For a few years *AHMM* was owned by Bantam Doubleday Dell (1992-96) as part of the magazine division (which was a lot of puzzle magazines, mostly). Then the entire magazine division was sold to Penny Press, where they presently reside. Many of the paperback and hardcover anthologies featured stories from both *AHMM* and *Ellery Queen's Mystery Magazine*. **

Many fans of the anthologies know or at the very least, guessed that the intros were of gentle fiction. Contrary to what has been said about the anthologies, Hitchcock did not write the introductions for any of the books. The actual editors of the anthologies were unbilled for the majority of the publications. Known as "ghost editors," these people simply compiled a selection of short stories (with an occasional novella), composed an introduction, and Hitchcock's trademark signature (and ocassional profile) was included. The rest was left to the reader's imagination. Among the ghost editors was Robert Arthur, whose stories were also adapted on *Alfred Hitchcock Presents*, and had a prolific career as an author.   ▬ ● ● ▬

* A magazine premiering on the newstands has a better chance of initial success if people buy what they think is already successful, and not leary on the first issue.
** Among the rival publications of *AHMM* was a magazine called *Suspense*, published in the U.K. by Fleetway Publications, Ltd., London. A particular Christmas issue, (Vol. 3, No. 12, December 1960) has an article by Hitchcock himself entitled "Murder Begins at Home." Stories by such authors as Julian Symons, Anthony Burgess and Georges Simenson were offered, and announced for the following issues were stories by John Masters and Victor Canning.

Robert Arthur – together with David Kogan, another writer – would write, produce and direct the long running (December 5, 1943 – September 16, 1952) radio horror anthology, *The Mysterious Traveler*. The stories featured on that series were mostly originals, not adaptations of previously published material, and they offered EC Comic-style horror and mystery tales with twists of fate providing the shock ending. The radio mystery series, *Murder by Experts*, was also produced and directed by Arthur and Kogan, and Alfred Hitchcock himself would host the gruesome murder tales near the end of the series' run in 1951. Together with David Kogan, Arthur also wrote scripts for *The Shadow*, *The Sealed Book* and a Mysterious Traveler spin-off, *The Strange Dr. Weird*. On television, Arthur wrote scripts for *Bonino*, *The Gulf Television Playhouse*, and *The Dark Room*. It can be said for certain that Robert Arthur was not only familiar with murder and mystery stories, but had plenty of experience as a writer.

In a few of the Hitchcock anthologies, there was a special dedication clause listed on the copyright page of mentioning that Alfred Hitchcock gratefully acknowledged "the invaluable assistance of Robert Arthur, in the preparation of this volume." No surprise since he was actually the ghost editor on several of these hardcover books.

"*Alfred Hitchcock Presents* has been my pleasure to dispose of several hundred victims in your living room. I trust the resultant gore hasn't made too much of a mess of your carpets. In case you didn't realize we had a philosophy, allow me to describe it for you. It consists of these principles:
1. Murder isn't nice.
2. Violence is a bore, unless there is a good reason for it.
3. Nobody is really squeamish.
4. Crime must not pay, but it can certainly entertain.
5. The play's the thing.
This last principle, while not entirely original, is perhaps the most important. On *Alfred Hitchcock Presents* we have continually endeavored to place the story above the Gory. Our rather large audience likes it that way, and our sponsors rather like our large audience."

If only this was true. The above quote was taken from one a 1960 printing of an anthology that bore Hitchcock's name below. Truth is, Hitchcock never wrote a word. The introductions themselves were made to give the appearance that Hitchcock himself wrote them, applying the same James Allardice-type of humor sprinkled throughout. What would have guessed?

In what is probably the first time Hitchcock ever lent his name to a mystery anthology dates back to 1941. The Pocket Book of Great Detectives was edited by Lee Wright, and featured an introduction by Alfred Hitchcock. Considered a very rare publication to find, it is not certain whether Hitchcock actually composed the introduction himself, but if he did, this publication would have been the *only* time during his career. Certainly the publishers would not have placed Hitchcock's name on the cover unless they felt his name alone would help sell copies. It can be fair to say that this was also the first publiation of its kind to attempt to commercially cash in on the "Hitchcock" name.

To best document the history of the anthologies, it is important to know that there were technically three series of publications. The first series of books began with Suspense Stories: Collected by Alfred Hitchcock. Published by Dell, this 192-page paperback made its appearance in bookstores around 1945. Also known as a "mapback" because it featured a picture of a map on the back cover, pointing out the locations where some of the individual stories occured. The book proved to be profitable for Dell, because they released four more anthologies using the Hitchcock name, for the next four years, until 1949 when they stopped issuing the publications.

By 1948, Dell decided to also release (as well as their yearly anthology) a small pocket-sized novelization of *Rope*, based on the movie of the same name, presently showing in the movie theaters. The title was billed as Alfred Hitchcock's Rope, labeled on the bottom of the front cover as "A Dell

Thriller." An artist's conception of James Stewart, the star of the movie, was featured on the front, against a red backdrop.

The second series of anthologies began in 1959, four years after *Alfred Hitchcock Presents* premiered on television. The purpose of this print run was to capture the commercial popularity of the television series, now airing over the networks. Simon and Schuster, Inc. released a hardcover entitled, Alfred Hitchcock Presents: Stories They Wouldn't Let Me Do on TV. This publication featured twenty-five short stories ranging from witchcraft to pure escapism.

The introduction, even though Hitchcock himself didn't write it, invited the readers to digest the tales as if they were watching the actual television episodes. "Being what is probably one of the most obtrusive producers on television has spoiled me," the introduction read. "I cannot conceive of giving people stories without adding my own comments. The publishers of this book, being far wiser than my television sponsors, have limited my interference to this short preface." The introduction continued: "This particular selection of tales is primarily aimed at those of you who find television far too bland. You may not care for some of these stories because you think them too shocking, macabre or grotesque, but I am confident that you will not find any of them bland or dull. The reason why some of these stories cannot be produced on the home screen will be obvious on reading." The title sort of missed its mark, however, because a few months after the book's publication, four of the stories were adapted for the program. The first story in the book, "Being a Murderer Myself," by Arthur Williams, was actually directed by Alfred Hitchcock as the fifth season's opener!

Months after the hardcover appeared in bookstores, two paperback editions featuring the same stories were made available. Alfred Hitchcock Presents: 12 Stories They Wouldn't Let Me Do on TV made its first appearance in May and June of 1958. In April of 1959, another paperback, this one consisting of the remaining stories from the above publication, also made its debut, Alfred Hitchcock Presents: 13 More Stories They Wouldn't Let Me Do on TV.

Advertisement for one of the *Alfred Hitchcock Presents* hardcovers from **Random House**.

In 1959, Random House began to put out their own hardcover *Alfred Hitchcock Presents* line. Neither H.S.D. Publications nor Davis Publications nor their agent, Scott Meredith Literary Agency, Inc., had any involvement with those volumes. The stories in the Random House books were reprinted from many sources, not just from the magazines. Dell made arrangements with Random House to release two paperback anthologies for each hardcover, each containing half of the stories from each harcdover.

With the success of these paperbacks, Dell made arrangements with H.S.D. Publications to publish 33 paperback books using stories from their magazines, not from the Random House hardcovers.* After the initial 33 paperback books, Dell then made arrangements with Davis Publications for an additional six books. All of these were licensed on behalf of H.S.D. and Davis by the Scott Meredith Literary Agency. Apparently Scott Meredith also packaged the books – that is, chose the stories. But of course Dell published a lot more than 39 titltes – the Random House anthologies, for instance.

Among these paperback books was the use of the Hitchcock humor, which has since become a tradition, evident among the introductions. In the hardcover (and paperback editions) of <u>Stories My Mother Never Told Me</u>, the intro read: "Permit me to observe that this is an absolutely accurate description of the contents. I am prepared to testify in any court of the land that none of these stories was ever recounted to me in any form by my mother. The reason for this is quite simple. None of them had been written at the time my mother was telling stories to me."

Another read: "I hope no one will construe the title of this tome as a challenge. It is - in case you were so eager to get to the stories that you didn't even notice – <u>Scream Along With Me: Stories That Scared Even Me</u>. This is meant as a simple statement of fact, not as a summons for you to cry in ringing tones that some of the stories didn't scare you. Why the word 'even' is in there I don't know. I proposed to call the book, in a simple and dignified manner, 'Scream Along With Me: Stories That Scared Me.' I was overruled. It seems that <u>Scream Along With Me: Stories That Scared Even Me</u> has more swing to it. And this is, obviously, the day of the swinger."

On the final page of the February 1973 edition of <u>Alfred Hitchcock Presents: 16 Skeletons From My Closet</u>, a second introduction featuring Hitchcock's name read: "Dear Readers. By now, I hope, you have read each and every one of the stories in this Dell Book Anthology, and your appetite for crime-mystery-fiction has been whetted to a keen edge as a result. There is always the possibility, of course, that you are one of those who start reading a book from the back instead of from the front. Psychologists have a name for this habit, which I shall not define further, since I have no wish to invade any other field of research. I am kept quite busy laboring in my own vineyard, to mix a metaphor. Others enjoys the fringe benefits of my labors. . ."

On a humorous note: In the introduction in one of the later Dell paperback publications, "Hitchcock" described how he was recently driving down a California road, and met up with some children. This is, of course, an obvious slip as everyone knows that with Hitchcock's fear of police, he never had a drivers license. Ooops!

A handful of these paperback anthologies were later reprinted during the mid-1980s. Obviously the publishers were attempting to cash in on the popularity of the revived Hitchcock series, broadcast over NBC-TV and the USA Cable Network.

The third and final anthology series, began in 1976. Published by Davis Publications in conjunction (for a while) with Dial Press, the first ten books were edited by Eleanor Sullivan, who was then the editor of *Alfred Hitchcock's Mystery Magazine*, as well as managing editor of *Ellery Queen's Mystery Magazine*. With three exceptions (see list), numbers 11 through 27 (the final volume) were edited by Cathleen Jordan. Cathleen had become the editor of *AHMM* in 1981 when Davis Publications decided to make *AHMM* and *EQMM* two editorially separate entities. As a rule, they

---

* The first two contracts are dated July 13, 1961.

put out two of those anthologies a year, using almost exclusively stories from the magazine's archives. Each anthology was published in both a hardcover (Dial Press) edition for bookstore sales and a simultaneous paperback edition (Davis) for newsstand sales. At first the hardcovers had titles of the usual sort, staring with "Alfred Hitchcock's Tales to ..."; the paperbacks – otherwise identitcal to the hardcovers – did not have such titles but instead were called "Alfred Hitchcock's Anthology, Volume 1," etc. That, however, ended after Volume 11, when subsequently, both hardcover and paperback began using the same title and the "Tales of..." was dropped in favor to just "Alfred Hitchcock's ..." Most of the first seven of these volumes had a brief introduction "by" Hitchcock (a.k.a. the editor Eleanor Sullivan); the seventh was published in 1980. With the passing of Alfred Hitchcock on April 29, 1980, the seventh anthology, labeled "Fall-Winter 1980" but must have been published in June of 1980 – records show that author copies were sent out on May 1, 1980, so it was too late, when Hitchcock died, to change the intro.

So except for that uncatchable one, H.S.D., Davis Publications, *AHMM*, did not release any books using Hitchcock's name at the bottom of the intros after he died. Nor, by the way, did they ever use *Alfred Hitchcock Presents* in their titles. Some of the later children's books featured Hitchcock's name below the introduction, but they were, obviously, ficticious.

After Davis Publications ceased publishing their own anthologies, the subsidiary rights department turned to packaging collections of stories with other publishing houses, sometimes with just *AHMM* stories, sometimes just *EQMM* stories, most often a mix.

Galahad Books produced three omnibus volumes, titled The Best of Mystery, Tales of Terror, and Portraits of Murder. These were amalgams of a number of the anthologies above, the earlier ones, anyway. Eleanor Sullivan was editor of The Best of Mystery, even though she received no author reference in the book. She also did Tales of Terror. As for Portraits of Murder, that included anthologies that both Eleanor Sullivan and Cathleen Jordan edited. In 1993 a paperback edition of Portraits came out from Bristol Park Books, a division of Budget Book Sevice, Inc., priced at $12.95. Boxed editions were also sold: one labeled "Library of Suspense" contained Best of and Terror; a second one labeled "Library of Mystery" contained Terror and Portraits. New printings of The Best of Mystery and Tales of Terror were published in 1999 by Galahad, a by-then division of Budget Book Service; no change except for redesigned covers. It isn't believed that there are paperback editions of the other two.

A series of British paperbacks printed and bound in Great Britain for Hodder and Stoughton Paperbacks, a division of Hodder and Stoughton Ltd., (Coronet Books), titled Alfred Hitchcock's Book of Horror Stories, ran for at least seven books, No. 1 to 7. These reprinted some of the "Tales of . . ." anthologies. The publication years suggest they did these paperbacks from the first dozen or so stories from a hardcover edition of the complete American editions.

Alfred Hitchcock's Book of Horror Stories Book 2, Hodder and Stoughton, Paperback, L1.75, 192 pgs., First published in Great Britain in 1982 by Max Reinhardt, Ltd. This Coronet edition 1984. (First appeared as the first half of the hardcover "Tales to Take Your Breath Away" edited by Eleanor Sullivan.)

"The Arrowsmith Prison Riddle" by Bill Pronzini, "End of the Line" by Edward D. Hoch, "The Dettweiler Solution" by Lawrence Block, "The Whitechapel Wantons" by Vincent McConnor, "Cora's Raid" by Isak Romun, "A Cup of Herbal Tea" by Robert S. Aldrich, "Albion, Perfidious Albion" by Everett Greenbaum, "Life or Breath" by Nelson DeMille, "The Silver Lining" by Mick Mahoney, "A Private Little War" by William Brittain, "Superscam" by Francis M. Nevins, "Have You Ever Seen This Woman?" by John Lutz, "Joe Cutter's Game" by Brian Garfield, and "A Cabin in the Woods" by John Coyne.

Alfred Hitchcock's Book of Horror Stories Book 4, Hodder and Stoughton, Paperback, L1.95, 192 pgs., First published in Great Britain in 1983 by Max Reinhardt, Ltd. This Coronet edition 1985. (First appeared as the first half of the hardcover "Tales to Make Your Blood Run Cold" edited by Eleanor Sullivan.)

"Searching the Crying Woman" by Harold R. Daniels, "Murder Between Friends" by Nedra Tyre, "Final Exam" by Allen Kim Lang, "The Tutor" by Michael Bruen, "Voice in the Night" by Robert Colby, "The Artist" by Al Nussbaum, "Undertaker, Please Drive Slow" by Ron Goulart, "The Girl Who Wouldn't Talk" by Paul W. Fairman, "Heir Presemptuous" by C.B. Gilford, "The Scar" by Donald Honig, "Spitting Image" by Mann Rubin, "Case of the Kind Waitress" by Henry Slesar, "Ghost of a Chance" by Carroll Mayers. "Storm's End" by Michael Zuroy, "The Picnic People" by Edward D. Hoch, "The Shunned House" by Robert Edmond Alter, and "The Welcome Mat" by Carl Marcus.

Alfred Hitchcock's Book of Horror Stories Book 5, Hodder and Stoughton, Paperback, L1.95, 208 pgs., First published in Great Britain in 1983 by Max Reinhardt, Ltd. This Coronet edition 1986. (First appeared as the second half of the hardcover "Tales to Make Your Blood Run Cold.")

"Career Man" by James Holding, "A Flower in her Hair" by Pauline C. Smith, "Proxy" by Talmage Powell, "The Intangible Threat" by Joseph Payne Brennan, "The Cost of Kent Castwell" by Avram Davidson, "My Unfair Lady" by Guy Cullingford, "Vacation" by Mike Brett, "A Flower for her Grave" by Hilda Cushing, "Another Beautiful Day" by Harold Dutch, "Incident at Mardi's" by Herbert Brean, "The Greatest Robbery on Earth" by Lloyd Biggle, Jr., "Damon and Pythias and Delilah Brown" by Rufus King, "Glory Hunter" by Richard M. Ellis, "Perfectly Timed Plot" by E.X. Ferrars, "#8" by Jack Ritchie, "All the Needless Killing" by Bryce Walton, "The Explosives Expert" by John Lutz, and "The 79 Murders of Martha Hill Gibbs" by Joseph Csida.

Alfred Hitchcock's Book of Horror Stories Book 6, Hodder and Stoughton, Paperback, L2.25, 192 pgs., First published in Great Britain in 1984 by Max Reinhardt, Ltd. This Coronet edition 1987. (First appeared as the first half of the hardcover "Tales to Make Your Hair Stand on End" edited by Eleanor Sullivan.)

"Hush, Dear Conscience" by C.B. Gilford, "Death by Misadventure" by Elijah Ellis, "The Death Desk" by S.S. Rafferty, "The Room at the End of the Hall" by Helen Nielsen, "Kisses and Chloroform" by Donald Olson, "A Left-Handed Profession" by Al Nussbaum, "Second Spring" by Theodore Mathieson, "Bank Night" by Arthur Porges, "The Contagious Killer" by Bryce Walton, "The Man Who Came Back" by Edward D. Hoch, "Bad Actor" by Gary Brandner, and "Pigeon in an Iron Lung" by Talmage Powell.

Alfred Hitchcock's Book of Horror Stories Book 7, Hodder and Stoughton, Paperback, L1.95, 166 pgs., First published in Great Britain in 1984 by Max Reinhardt, Ltd. This Coronet edition 1988. (First appeared as the second half of the hardcover "Tales to Make Your Hair Stand on End.")

"King of the World" by John Lutz, "Nice Shooting" by A.E. Eddenden, "Too Solid Mildred" by Jack Ritchie, "Free Advice, Incorporated" by Michael Brett, "Payoff Time" by Clark Howard, "The Way the World Spins" by Bill Pronzini, "The Real Criminal" by James M. Gilmore, "Bang! You're Dead!" by Margaret B. Maron, "The Hard Sell" by William Dolan, "The Prosperous Judds" by Bob Bristow, "The Dead Indian" by Robert W. Alexander, and "The China Cottage" by August Derleth.

Another British series was published by the New English Library under the imprint Four Square. The last four titles below were all published in 1967, all made up of H.S.D. stories. All original collections had been selected by Peter Haining from issues of *AHMM*, published during the last five years in the U.S.A.

NEL Books are published by The New English Library Limited, from Barnard's Inn, Holborn, London ECI. Made and printed in Great Britain by Ivor Nicholson & Watson Ltd., Redhill, Surrey. The collections were selected by Peter Haining (the editor of the books), and the stories originated from H.S.D. Publications, Inc. The New English Library / Four Square. Again, Hitchcock wasn't involved in the editing of these books. They all read "Presented by Alfred Hitchcock" except for the last book, which read "Edited by Alfred Hitchcock."

Guarenteed Rest in Peace, (late 1966) 224 pgs.

"The Awful Experiment" by Michael Zuroy, "A Hint of Henbane" by Frederick Pohl and C.M. Kornbluth, "Dig We Must" by Jeff Heller, "Guaranteed Rest in Peace" by Bryce Walton, "Top-Flight Acquarium" by William Link and Richard Levinson, "Deadly Shade of Blue" by Jack Sharkey, "Mr. Kang vs. the Demon" by Maxwell Trent, "A Change for the Better" by Arthur Porges, "The Thing in the Closet" by Don Tothe, "Countdown" by David Ely, "Ruby Martinson and the Great Coffin Caper" by Henry Slesar, "Walk Up to Death" by Andrew Benedict, "The Green Heart" by Jack Ritchie, "The Adventure of the Haunted Library" by August Derleth, "Bully Boy" by Leo R. Ellis, "The Egg Head" by Rog Phillips, "Prolonged Visit" by Hal Dresner, "Beauty and the Beasts" by Allen Kim Lang, "Requiem for Grandma" by Marvin Karp, and "The Crazy Wine" by Alex Austin.

Behind the Locked Door and Other Strange Tales, (March 1967) 160 pgs.

"The Crime Machine" by Jack Ritchie, "Perfect Pitcher" by Arthur Porges, "Diminishing Wife" by Michael Zuroy, "You Can't Blame Me" by Henry Slesar, "Behind the Locked Door" by O.H. Leslie, "All the Needless Killing" by Bryce Walton, "IQ-184" by Fletcher Flora. "Death Begins at Forty" by Richard Hardwick, "Adventures of the Sussex Arches" by August Derleth, "These Daisies Told" by Arthur Porges, "Antique" by Hal Ellison, "The Sweater" by Richard O. Lewis, "Upside Down World" by Jack Ritchie, and "Lady With a Hobby" by Raymond E. Banks.

Meet Death at Night and Other Tales of Terror, (May 1967) 160 pgs.

"Keeper of the Crypt" by Clark Howard, "The Nightmare" by D.A. Coleman, "Meet Death at Night" by C.B. Gilford, "Dead Giveaway" by Leo R. Ellis, "The Amateur Philologist" by August Derleth, "Mirror, Mirror" by Pauline K. Prilucik, "Death, the Black-Eyed Denominator" by Ed Lacy, "She Loved Funerals" by Hilda Cushing, "Avery's Ghost" by James M. Gilmore, "For Money Received" by Fletcher Flora, "Drawer 14" by Talmage Powell, and "The 79 Murders of Martha Hill Gibbs" by Joseph Csida.

Anyone for Murder? and Other Tales of Crime, (October 1967) 128 pgs.

"Anyone for Murder?" by Jack Ritchie, "Lovers' Quarrel" by Richard Hill Wilkinson, "The Widder Jackson" by Wenzell Brown, "The Glint" by Arthur Porges, "Another Chance for Sally" by James M. Ullman, "If This Be Madness" by Lawrence Block, "Second Verdict" by Henry Slesar, "Slow Motion Murder" by Richard Hardwick, "The Catbird Nest" by Hugh B. Cave, "Homicide Maybe" by Lawrence Treat, and "The Tool" by Fletcher Flora.

The Late Unlamented and Other Tales of Evil, (November 1967) 128 pgs.

"The Late Unlamented" by Jonathan Craig, "The Telltale Eye" by Arthur Porges, "Ghost of a Chance" by Carroll Mayers, "The Madness Machine" by Leo R. Ellis, "A Witch for the Burning" by C.B. Gilford, "Haunted Hall" by Donald Honig, "The End of an Era" by Richard Levinson and William Link, "Until Death Do Us Part" by Carroll Mayers, "The China Cottage" by August Derleth, "Death by Misadventure" by Wenzell Brown, "When This Man Dies" by Lawrence Block, and "Sheriff Peavy's Cosa Nostra Caper" by Richard Hardwick.

In order to fully document or list all of the Hitchcock books in easy format, they are numbered in chronological order, in which they were released. The first series from the 1940s is labeled A1, A2, etc. The second series consisted of only Random House hardcover releases, and two Dell paperbacks using the same stories. The Dell Paperbacks are numbered simply 1, 2, 3, etc. Hardcover books are listed as HC1, and HC2. The third and final anthology series is not numbered, since they were titled as "Anthology #1" and so on. A selected list of reprintings and later editions are listed below each entry.

SERIES ONE

A1. Suspense Stories: Collected by Alfred Hitchcock, Dell Publishing, Paperback, 192 pages, 25 cents, 1945

"Leiningen vs. the Ants" by Carl Stephenson, "The Liqueur Glass" by Phillis Bottome, "Flood on the Goodwins" by A.D. Divine, "R.M.S. Titanic" by Hanson Baldwin, "Blue Murder" by Wilbur Daniel Steele, "The House of Ecstasy" by Ralph Milne Farley, "Fire in the Galley Stove" by Captain William Outerson, "The Lady or the Tiger?" by Frank R. Stockton, "An Occurrence at Owl Creek Bridge" by Ambrose Bierce, "The Second Step" by Margery Sharp, "The Blue Paper" by Albert Payson Terhune, "The Baby in the Icebox" by James M. Cain, "The Room on the Fourth Floor" by Ralph Straus, and "Elementals" by Stephen Vincent Benet.

In 1949, Dell again reprinted Suspense Stories, featuring the same tales as the 1945 edition. Still at 192 pages, this reprint sold for a 50 cent cover price instead of 25 cents.

In January 1964, the same paperback was again reprinted, but under a different title. Alfred Hitchcock's 14 Suspense Stories to Play Russian Rouelette By. Published by Dell, it sold for 50 cents, and was actually 208 pages instead of 192. The reason for the different page numbers is obvious. The first story, "Leiningen vs. the Ants" by Carl Stephenson, was replaced with "Never Kill for Love" by C.B. Gilford.

A2. Alfred Hitchcock's Bar the Doors, Dell Publishing, Paperback, 192 pages, 25 cents, 1946
Cover artwork by Gerald Cregg.

"Pollock and the Porroh Man" by H.G. Wells, "The Storm" by McKnight Malmar, "Moonlight Sonata" by Alexander Woollcott, "The Half-Pint Flask" by DuBose Heyward, "The Kill" by Peter Fleming, "The Upper Berth" by F. Marion Crawford, "Midnight Express" by Alfred Noyes, "The Damned Thing" by Ambrose Bierce, "Metronome" by August Derleth, "The Pipe-Smoker" by Martin Armstrong, "The Corpse at the Table" by Samuel Hopkins Adams, "The Woman at Seven Brothers" by Wilbur Daniel Steele, and "The Book" by Margaret Irwin

The introduction explained: "A collection of stories of suspense which I edited for Dell Books having proved a success, the publishers asked me to bring together a group of tales which I admire because of their skillful handling of the element of terror." This leads credence to the belief that Suspense Stories: Collected by Alfred Hitchcock, was a financial success for Dell, and a logical reason why sequels were compiled and released. In January of 1962, the second printing of Alfred Hitchcock's Bar the Doors was released, now attempting to cash in on the television program by featuring a photo cover of Hitchcock attempting to saw his way through cell bars, and a new title: Alfred Hitchcock Presents: Bar the Doors.

Dell Publishing, 192 pages, 50 cents, January 1962 (new Dell edition, second printing)
Dell Publishing, Paperback, 192 pages, 50 cents, February 1963 (third printing)
Dell Publishing, Paperback, 192 pages, 50 cents, July 1965 (first printing of new edition)
U.K. edition: Mayflower Books, Ltd.: St. Albans, Paperback, 173 pages, 30 pence, 1972

A3. Alfred Hitchcock's Hold Your Breath, Dell Publishing, Paperback, 192 pages, 25 cents, 1947

"Taboo" by Geoffrey Household, "The Cone" by H.G. Wells, "Up Periscope" by Alec Hudson, "The Greatest Thing in the World" by Norman K. Mailer, "Footfalls" by Wilbur Daniel Steele, "Midnight Rendezvous" by Margaret Manners, "Action" by C.E. Montague, "Philomel Cottage" by Agatha Christie, and "Dygartsbush" by Walter D. Edmonds.

In July 1963, a second paperback printing appeared on bookshelves, again published by Dell, with the same number of pages, but the cover price was now 50 cents instead of 25. This second printing featured two changes from the original 1947 edition. First, "The Greatest Thing in the World" and "Action" was not featured in the 1963 printing. Second, the original introduction was reprinted with the exception of a whole paragraph, which happened to describe those very two stories. And yes, that is THE Norman Mailer.

HC1. Alfred Hitchcock's Fireside Book of Suspense, Simon and Schuster, Inc., Hardcover, 367 pages, 1947

"The Second-Class Passenger" by Perceval Gibbon, "The News in English" by Graham Greene, "Leiningen vs. the Ants" by Carl Stephenson, "If You Don't Get Excited--" by Edwin Corle, "Fire in the Galley Stove" by William Outerson, "The Liqueur Glass" by Phyllis Bottome, "The Alarm Bell" by Donald Henderson, "The Room on the Fourth Floor" by Ralph Straus, "With Bated Breath" by Ross Santee, "Flood on the Goodwins" by A.D. Divine, "Sunset" by Sidney Herschel Small, "The House of Ecstasy" by Ralph Milne Farley, "The Hangman Won't Wait" by John Dickson Carr, "The Second Step" by Margery Sharp, "After-Dinner Story" by William Irish, "The Tunnel" by John Metcalfe, "Triggers in Leash" by Allan Vaughn Elston, "The Blue Paper" by Albert Payson Terhune, "The Three Good Witnesses" by Harold Lamb, "R.M.S. Titanic" by Hanson Baldwin, "The Ringed Word" by T.O. Beachcroft, "Yours Truly, Jack the Ripper" by Robert Bloch, "The Baby in the Icebox" by James M. Cain, "Two Bottles of Relish" by Lord Dunsany, "Smee" by 'Ex-Private X', "His Brother's Keeper" by W.W. Jacobs, and "Elementals" by Stephen Vincent Benet.

This was the very first hardcover book to use Alfred Hitchcock's name in the title. Half of these stories were reprinted from the 1945 paperback anthology, Suspense Stories, while the other half were new ones, never before offered in any Hitchcock anthology. "Triggers in Leash," by Allan Vaughn Elston, was the basis for the third episode broadcast on *Alfred Hitchcock Presents*.

A4. Alfred Hitchcock's Fear and Trembling, Dell Publishing, Paperback, 192 pages, 25 cents, 1948

"Cassius" by Henry S. Whitehead, "The Tarn" by Hugh Walpole, "Little Memento" by John Collier, "Oh, Whistle, and I'll Come to You, My Lad" by M.R. James, "One Summer Night" by Ambrose Bierce, "Telling" by Elizabeth Bowen, "The Jar" by Ray Bradbury, "The Bad Lands" by John Metcalfe, "Ghost Hunt" by H.R. Wakefield, "Skule Skerry" by John Buchan, "The Red Room" by H.G. Wells, "The Sack of Emeralds" by Lord Dunsany, and "The Night Reveals" by William Irish.

Dell Publishing, Paperback, 192 pages, 50 cents, October 1963 (new Dell edition)

A5. Alfred Hitchcock's A Baker's Dozen of Suspense Stories, Dell Publishing, 25 cents, 192 pages, 1949

"The Mask" by F. Tennyson Jesse, "Accident" by Agatha Christie, "A Day Saved" by Graham Greene, "Roman Holiday" by Robert Lewis, "Revenge" by Samuel Lewis, "The Snake" by John Steinbeck, "Long Shadow on the Lawn" by Mary Deasy, "The Night" by Ray Bradbury, "The Rocking-Horse Winner" by D.H. Lawrence, "The Warden" by Georges Carousso, "Leviathan" by

Ellis St. Joseph, "Breakdown" by Louis Pollock, and "The Fool's Heart" by Eugene Manlove Rhodes.

Dell Publishing, Paperback, 192 pages, 50 cents, December 1963 (new Dell edition)

One printing of this book lists the Graham Greene story "The Case for the Defense" instead of "A Day Saved." Also note two stories from this anthology, "Revenge" and "Breakdown," both were filmed by Alfred Hitchcock during the premiere season of *Alfred Hitchcock Presents*. It is true that Hitchcock himself received complimentary copies of these books, so it is possible that this publication was the original source for Hitchcock's interest in filming teleplays based on these stories.

SERIES TWO

HC2. Alfred Hitchcock Presents: Stories They Wouldn't Let Me Do on TV, Simon & Schuster, Inc, Hardcover, $3.95 cover price, 373 pages, 1957 (Edited by Robert Arthur.)

"Being a Murderer Myself" by Arthur Williams, "Lukundoo" by Edward Lucas White, "A Woman Seldom Found" by William Sansom, "The Perfectionist" by Margaret St. Clair, "The Price of the Head" by John Russell, "Love Comes to Miss Lucy" by Q. Patrick, "Sredni Vashtar" by H.H. Munro (Saki), "Love Lies Bleeding" by Philip MacDonald, "The Dancing Partner" by Jerome K. Jerome, "Casting the Runes" by M.R. James, "The Voice in the Night" by William Hope Hodgson, "How Love Came to Professor Guildea" by Robert S. Hichens, "The Moment of Decision" by Stanley Ellin, "A Jungle Graduate" by James Francis Dwyer, "Recipe for Murder" by C.P. Donnel, Jr., "Nunc Dimittis" by Roald Dahl, "The Most Dangerous Game" by Richard Connell, "The Lady on the Grey" by John Collier, "The Waxwork" by A.M. Burrage, "The Dumb Wife" by Thomas Burke, "Couching at the Door" by D.K. Broster, "The October Game" by Ray Bradbury, "Water's Edge" by Robert Bloch, "The Jokester" by Robert Arthur, and "The Abyss" by Leonid Andreyev.

This hardcover book featured a white book jacket with a black silouette of the famous Hitchcock profile. "Nunc Dimittis" was originally published under the title "The Devious Bachelor" in a 1953 issue of *Collier's*. The short stories, "The Waxwork," "The Jokester," "Being a Murderer Myself" and "Water's Edge" was later filmed and broadcast on *Alfred Hitchcock Presents*. ("Being a Murderer Myself" underwent the title change to "Arthur.") "The Voice in the Night" was later filmed for *Suspicion*. This same book reprinted in Hardcover by Amereon, Ltd., June 2001.

Alfred Hitchcock Presents: 12 Stories They Wouldn't Let Me Do on TV, Dell Publishing, Paperback, 224 pages, 35 cents, June 1958

"Being a Murderer Myself" by Arthur Williams, "Lukundoo" by Edward Lucas White, "A Woman Seldom Found" by William Sansom, "The Perfectionist" by Margaret St. Clair, "The Price of the Head" by John Russell, "Love Comes to Miss Lucy" by Q. Patrick, "Sredni Vashtar" by H.H. Munro (Saki), "Love Lies Bleeding" by Philip MacDonald, "The Dancing Partner" by Jerome K. Jerome, "Casting the Runes" by M.R. James, "The Voice in the Night" by William Hope Hodgson, and "How Love Came to Professor Guildea" by Robert S. Hichens.

Dell Publishing, Paperback, 224 pages, 35 cents, August 1958 (second printing)
Dell Publishing, Paperback, 224 pages, 35 cents, October 1958 (third printing)
Dell Publishing, Paperback, 224 pages, 50 cents, September 1959 (fourth printing)
Dell Publishing, Paperback, 224 pages, 50 cents, February 1960 (fifth printing)
Dell Publishing, Paperback, 224 pages, 50 cents, May 1962 (sixth printing)
Dell Publishing, Paperback, 224 pages, 50 cents, November 1963 (seventh printing)
Dell Publishing, Paperback, 224 pages, 50 cents, June 1964 (eighth printing)
First U.K. edition was printed by Pan Books, Ltd.: London, in 1959 or 1960. The title of the U.K. edition was Alfred Hitchcock Presents: Stories They Wouldn't Let Me Do on TV.

<u>Alfred Hitchcock Presents: 13 More Stories They Wouldn't Let Me Do on TV</u>, Dell Publishing, Paperback, 224 pages, 35 cents, April 1959

"The Moment of Decision" by Stanley Ellin, "A Jungle Graduate" by James Francis Dwyer, "Recipe for Murder" by C.P. Donnel, Jr., "Nunc Dimittis" by Roald Dahl, "The Most Dangerous Game" by Richard Connell, "The Lady on the Grey" by John Collier, "The Waxwork" by A.M. Burrage, "The Dumb Wife" by Thomas Burke, "Couching at the Door" by D.K. Broster, "The October Game" by Ray Bradbury, "Water's Edge" by Robert Bloch, "The Jokester" by Robert Arthur, and "The Abyss" by Leonid Andreyev.

Dell Publishing, Paperback, 224 pages, 50 cents, May 1959 (second printing)
Dell Publishing, Paperback, 224 pages, 50 cents, February 1960 (third printing)
Dell Publishing, Paperback, 224 pages, 50 cents, October 1960 (fourth printing)
Dell Publishing, Paperback, 224 pages, 50 cents, March 1961 (fifth printing)
Dell Publishing, Paperback, 224 pages, 50 cents, December 1961 (sixth printing)
Dell Publishing, Paperback, 224 pages, 50 cents, May 1962 (seventh printing)
Dell Publishing, Paperback, 224 pages, $1.50, June 1978 (new Dell edition)
First U.K. edition was printed by Pan Books, Ltd.: London, in 1960. This 192 page paperback was reprinted *many* times, and by 1970, Pan released their 13th printing! The title of the U.K. edition was <u>Alfred Hitchcock Presents: Stories They Wouldn't Let Me Do on TV – Part Two</u>.

HC3. <u>Alfred Hitchcock Presents: My Favorites in Suspense</u>, Random House, Hardcover, 502 pages, 1959 (Edited by Robert Arthur.)

"The Birds" by Daphne Du Maurier, "Man With a Problem" by Donald Honig, "They Bite" by Anthony Boucher, "The Enemy" by Charlotte Armstrong, "The Inexperienced Ghost" by H.G. Wells, "Sentence of Death" by Thomas Walsh, "Spring Fever" by Dorothy Salisbury Davis, "The Crate at Outpost 1" by Matthew Gant, "My Unfair Lady" by Guy Cullingford, "New Murders for Old" by Carter Dickson, "Terrified" by C.B. Gilford, "The Duel" by Joan Vatsek, "Four O'Clock" by Price Day, "Too Many Coincidences" by Paul Eiden, "Of Missing Persons" by Jack Finney, "Island of Fear" by William Sambrot, "Getting Rid of George" by Robert Arthur, "Treasure Trove" by F. Tennyson Jesse, "The Body of the Crime" by Wilbur Daniel Steele, "A Nice Touch" by Mann Rubin, and "Composition for Four Hands" (novelette) by Hilda Lawrence.

This hardcover featured a dust jacket, but the book itself was printed in a variety of cloth/cardboard covers, a light bright blue, white, and even hot pink! "Man With a Problem" was dramatized during the fourth season of *Alfred Hitchcock Presents*, and "Getting Rid of George" and "A Nice Touch" were both filmed and broadcast during the second season of *The Alfred Hitchcock Hour*. It was the story "Four O'Clock," featured in this very publication, that caught the attention of playwrite Rod Serling, who wrote a teleplay adaptation for *The Twilight Zone*. During his interview with Francois Truffaut, Alfred Hitchcock recalled his discovery of the Daphne du Maurier story "The Birds" in one of the *Alfred Hitchcock Presents* books. Observe the first story in this anthology.

<u>Alfred Hitchcock Presents: 14 of My Favorites in Suspense</u>, Dell Publishing, Paperback, 50 cents, 286 pages, December 1960

"The Birds" by Daphne Du Maurier, "Man With a Problem" by Donald Honig, "They Bite" by Anthony Boucher, "The Enemy" by Charlotte Armstrong, "The Inexperienced Ghost" by H.G. Wells, "Sentence of Death" by Thomas Walsh, "Spring Fever" by Dorothy Salisbury Davis, "The Crate at Outpost 1" by Matthew Gant, "My Unfair Lady" by Guy Cullingford, "New Murders for Old" by Carter Dickson, "Terrified" by C.B. Gilford, "The Duel" by Joan Vatsek, "Four O'Clock" by Price Day, and "Too Many Coincidences" by Paul Eiden.

Dell Publishing, Paperback, 286 pages, 50 cents, March 1961 (second printing)
Dell Publishing, Paperback, 286 pages, 50 cents, November 1961 (third printing)
Dell Publishing, Paperback, 286 pages, 50 cents, July 1962 (fourth printing)
Dell Publishing, Paperback, 286 pages, 50 cents, April 1963 (fifth printing)
Dell Publishing, Paperback, 286 pages, 50 cents, June 1963 (sixth printing)
Dell Publishing, Paperback, 286 pages, October 1967 (eighth printing)
Dell Publishing, Paperback, 286 pages, $1.50, June 1976 (new Dell edition)
U.K. edition: Pan Books, Ltd.: London, Paperback, 269 pages, 3 shillings, 6 pence, 1963
The U.K. edition was retitled Alfred Hitchcock: My Favourites in Suspense – Part One, featuring the same stories as the U.S. edition but with one difference: "The Duel," "Four O'Clock," and "Too Many Coincidences" was substituted for "Composition for Four Hands" by Hilda Lawrence.

Alfred Hitchcock Presents: More of My Favorites in Suspense, Dell Publishing, Paperback, 287 pages, 50 cents, May 1961

"Of Missing Persons" by Jack Finney, "Island of Fear" by William Sambrot, "Getting Rid of George" by Robert Arthur, "Treasure Trove" by F. Tennyson Jesse, "The Body of the Crime" by Wilbur Daniel Steele, "A Nice Touch" by Mann Rubin, and "Composition for Four Hands" by Hilda Lawrence (novelette).

Dell Publishing, Paperback, 287 pages, 50 cents, April 1964 (second printing)
Third printing was retitled Alfred Hitchcock Presents: Don't Look a Gift Shark in the Mouth, now listed as "a new Dell edition." $1.25, 287 pages, November 1976 Featured the same stories as the May 1961 edition.
U.K. edition: Pan Books, Ltd.: London, Paperback, 269 pages, 3 shillings, 6 pence, 1963
The U.K. edition was retitled Alfred Hitchcock: My Favourites in Suspense – Part Two, featuring the same stories as the U.S. edition but with two differences: "The Duel," "Four O'Clock," and "Too Many Coincidences" was added, and "Composition for Four Hands" was substituted for "The Blank Wall" by Elisabeth Sanxay Holding.

HC4. Alfred Hitchcock Presents: Stories For Late at Night, Random House, Hardcover, 469 pages, 1961 (Edited by Robert Arthur.)

"Death Is a Dream" by Robert Arthur, "It's A Good Life" by Jerome Bixby, "The Whole Town's Sleeping" by Ray Bradbury, "Lady's Man" by Ruth Chatterton, "Evening Primrose" by John Collier, "The Sound Machine" by Roald Dahl, "The Cocoon" by John B.L. Goodwin, "Vintage Season" by C.L. Moore (novelette), "Pieces of Silver" by Brett Halliday, "The Whistling Room" by William Hope Hodgson, "Told for the Truth" by Cyril Hume, "The Ash Tree" by M.R. James, "Side Bet" by Will F. Jenkins, "Second Night Out" by Frank Belknap Long, "Our Feathered Friends" by Philip MacDonald, "The Fly" by George Langelaan (novelette), "Back There in the Grass" by Gouverneur Morris, "The Mugging" by Edward L. Perry, "Finger! Finger!" by Margaret Ronan, "A Cry from the Penthouse" by Henry Slesar, "The People Next Door" by Pauline C. Smith, "D-Day" by Robert Trout, "The Man Who Liked Dickens" by Evelyn Waugh, and "The Iron Gates" by Margaret Millar (novelette).

There was a special dedication listed on the copyright page of this book mentioning that Alfred Hitchcock gratefully acknowledged "the invaluable assistance of Robert Arthur, in the preparation of this volume," which is no surprise since he was actually the ghost editor on several of these hardcover books. The stories were compiled in the book alphabetically under the authors' last names. "Picked with an unerring flair for what will make your flesh creep. Wow!" reviewed the *San Francisco Chronicle*.

<u>Alfred Hitchcock Presents: 12 Stories for Late at Night</u>, Dell Publishing, Paperback, 223 pages, 50 cents, July 1962

"Death Is a Dream" by Robert Arthur, "The Whole Town's Sleeping" by Ray Bradbury, "Evening Primrose" by John Collier, "The Cocoon" by John B.L. Goodwin, "Vintage Season" by C.L. Moore (novelette), "The Ash Tree" by M.R. James, "Side Bet" by William F. Jenkins, "Second Night Out" by Frank Belknap Long, "Our Feathered Friends" by Philip MacDonald, "Back There in the Grass" by Gouverneur Morris, "D-Day" by Robert Trout, and "The Man Who Liked Dickens" by Evelyn Waugh.

Dell Publishing, Paperback, 223 pages. 75 cents, June 1966 (new Dell edition)
Dell Publishing, Paperback, 223 pages. 75 cents, October 1967 (second printing)
Dell Publishing, Paperback, 223 pages. 75 cents, December 1967 (third printing)
Dell Publishing, Paperback, 223 pages. 75 cents, October 1969 (fourth printing)
Dell Publishing, Paperback, 223 pages. 75 cents, January 1970 (fifth printing)
Dell Publishing, Paperback, 223 pages. 75 cents, May 1970 (sixth printing)
Dell Publishing, Paperback, 223 pages. 75 cents, December 1970 (seventh printing)
Dell Publishing, Paperback, 223 pages. 75 cents, November 1972 (eighth printing)

<u>Alfred Hitchcock Presents: More Stories for Late at Night</u>, Dell Publishing, Paperback, 208 pages, 50 cents, December 1962

"It's a Good Life" by Jerome Bixby, "Lady's Man" by Ruth Chatterton, "The Sound Machine" by Roald Dahl, "Pieces of Silver" by Brett Halliday, "The Whistling Room" by William Hope Hodgson, "Told for the Truth" by Cyril Hume, "The Fly" by George Langelaan (novelette), "The Mugging" by Edward L. Perry, "Finger! Finger!" by Margaret Ronan, "A Cry from the Penthouse" by Henry Slesar, and "The People Next Door" by Pauline C. Smith.

Dell Publishing, Paperback, 208 pages. 50 cents, August 1967 (new Dell edition/ second printing)
Dell Publishing, Paperback, 208 pages. 50 cents, February 1968 (third printing)
Dell Publishing, Paperback, 208 pages. 50 cents, April 1969 (fourth printing)
This same Dell Paperback was reprinted under a different title, <u>Alfred Hitchcock Presents: Skeleton Crew</u>, Dell Publishing, Paperback, $1.25, 207 pages, February 1977

There are two U.K. edition paperbacks from Pan Books, Ltd.: London. The first was titled <u>Alfred Hitchcock Presents: Stories for Late At Night – Part One</u>, printed in 1964, no price known. Contents included (in order of appearance) "Death is a Dream," "It's a Good Life," "The Whole Town's Sleeping," "Lady's Man," "Evening Primrose," "The Cocoon," "Vintage Season," "Pieces of Silver," "The Whistling Room," "Told for the Truth," "The Ash Tree," "Side Bet," "Second Night Out," "Our Feathered Friends," and "The Fly."

HC5. <u>Alfred Hitchcock Presents: Stories My Mother Never Told Me</u>, Random House, Hardcover, 401 pages, 1963 (Edited by Robert Arthur.)

"The Child Who Believed" by Grace Amundson, "Just a Dreamer" by Robert Arthur, "The Wall-to-Wall Grave" by Andrew Benedict, "The Wind" by Ray Bradbury, "Congo" by Stuart Cloete, "Witch's Money" by John Collier, "Dip in the Pool" by Roald Dahl, "The Secret of the Bottle" by Gerald Kersh, "I Do Not Hear You, Sir" by Avram Davidson, "The Arbutus Collar" by Jeremiah Digges, "A Short Trip Home" by F. Scott Fitzgerald, "An Invitation to Hunt" by George Hitchcock, "The Man Who Was Everywhere" by Edward D. Hoch, "The Summer People" by Shirley Jackson, "Adjustments" by George Mandel, "The Children of Noah" by Richard Matheson, "The Idol of Flies" by Jane Rice, "Courtesy of the Road" by Mack Morris, "Remains to Be Seen" by Jack Ritchie, "The Man Who Sold Rope to the Gnoles" by Idris Seabright, "Lost Dog" by Henry Slesar, "Hostage" by Don Stanford, "Natural Selection" by Gilbert Thomas, "Simone" by Joan Vastek, "Smart Sucker" by Richard Wormser, and "Some of Your Blood" by Theodore Sturgeon.

<u>Alfred Hitchcock Presents: Stories My Mother Never Told Me</u>, Dell Publishing, Paperback, 50 cents, 223 pages, March 1965

"The Child Who Believed" by Grace Amundson, "Just a Dreamer" by Robert Arthur, "The Wall-to-Wall Grave" by Andrew Benedict, "Witch's Money" by John Collier, "The Secret of the Bottle" by Gerald Kersh, "A Short Trip Home" by F. Scott Fitzgerald, "An Invitation to the Hunt" by George Hitchcock, "The Summer People" by Shirley Jackson, "Adjustments" by George Mandel, "The Children of Noah" by Richard Matheson, "The Idol of Flies" by Jane Rice, "Hostage" by Don Stanford, and "Smart Sucker" by Richard Wormser.

Dell Publishing, Paperback, 223 pages, $1.25, October 1976 (new Dell edition)

<u>Alfred Hitchcock Presents: More Stories My Mother Never Told Me</u>, Dell Publishing, Paperback, 50 cents, 190 pages, November 1965

"The Wind" by Ray Bradbury, "Congo" by Stuart Cloete, "Dip in the Pool" by Roald Dahl, "I Do Not Hear You, Sir" by Avram Davidson, "The Arbutus Collar" by Jeremiah Digges, "The Man Who Was Everywhere" by Edward D. Hoch, "Courtesy of the Road" by Mack Morriss, "Remains to Be Seen" by Jack Ritchie, "The Man Who Sold Rope to the Gnoles" by Idris Seabright, "Lost Dog" by Henry Slesar, "Slime" by Joseph Payne Brennan, "How Love Came to Professor Guildea" by Robert Hichens, "Natural Selection" by Gilbert Thomas, and "Simone" by Joan Vatsek.

Dell Publishing, Paperback, 190 pages, March 1977 (new Dell edition)

Note that the paperback edition did not include Theodore Sturgeon's "Some of Your Blood." Instead, Sturgeon's story was substituted with two short stories, "Slime" and "How Love Came to Professor Guildea." Henry Slesar's "Lost Dog" was previously dramatized on *The CBS Radio Mystery Theater* in January of 1974, with Kim Hunter in the lead. "Dip in the Pool" by Roald Dahl was directed by Alfred Hitchcock.

HC6. <u>Alfred Hitchcock Presents: Stories Not for the Nervous,</u> Random House, Hardcover, 363 pages, 1965 (Edited by Robert Arthur.)

"To the Future" by Ray Bradbury, "River of Riches" by Gerald Kersh, "Levitation" by Joseph Payne Brennan, "Miss Winters and the Wind" by Christine Noble Govan, "View from the Terrace" by Mike Marmer, "The Man With the Copper Fingers" by Dorothy L. Sayers (novelette), "The Twenty Friends of William Shaw" by Raymond E. Banks, "The Other Hangman" by Carter Dickson, "Don't Look Behind You" by Fredric Brown, "No Bath for the Browns" by Margot Bennet, "The Uninvited" by Michael Gilbert, "Dune Roller" by Julian May (novelette), "Something Short of Murder" by Henry Slesar, "The Golden Girl" by Ellis Peters, "The Boy Who Predicted Earthquakes" by Margaret St. Clair, "Walking Alone" by Miriam Allen deFord, "For All the Rude People" by Jack Ritchie, "The Dog Died First" by Bruno Fischer (novelette), "Room With a View" by Hal Dresner, "Lemmings" by Richard Matheson, "White Goddess" by Idris Seabright, "The Substance of Martyrs" by William Sambrot, "Call for Help" by Robert Arthur, and "Sorry, Wrong Number" by Lucille Fletcher and Allan Ullman (novelette).

"Sorry, Wrong Number" began as a radio play, initially broadcast on CBS-Radio's *Suspense*, in 1943, with Agnes Moorehead in the lead. It has since become a starring vehicle for Barabra Stanwyck and Burt Lancaster in a 1948 movie of the same name, and a made-for-TV movie in 1989 starring Loni Anderson. Lucille Fletcher originally wrote the radio script (and the 1948 screenplay) but Allan Ullman adapted the play into a short novelette, and Fletcher received co-credit.

<u>Alfred Hitchcock Presents: Stories Not for the Nervous</u>, Dell Publishing, Paperback, 50 cents, 188 pages, October 1966

"To the Future" by Ray Bradbury, "River of Riches" by Gerald Kersh, "The Man With the Copper Fingers" by Dorothy L. Sayers (novelette), "Levitation" by Joseph Payne Brennan, "Miss Winters and the Wind" by Christine Noble Govan, "The Dog Died First" by Bruno Fischer (novelette), "The Twenty Friends of William Shaw" by Raymond E. Banks, "The Other Hangman" by Carter Dickson, "Dune Roller" by Julian May (novelette), "No Bath for the Browns" by Margot Bennet, "The Uninvited" by Michael Gilbert, "The Substance of Martyrs" by William Sambrot, and "Don't Look Behind You" by Fredric Brown.

Dell Publishing, Paperback, 188 pages, 50 cents, May 1967 (second printing)
Dell Publishing, Paperback, 188 pages, 50 cents, March 1968 (third printing)
This paperback went at least as far as a sixth printing, in February 1970.
The U.K. edition was entitled Alfred Hitchcock: Stories Not for the Nervous – Part One. First published in 1968, second printing in 1969. Pan Books, Ltd.: London, Paperback, 187 pages, 5 shillings. The book included the same stories with the exception of the "The Substance of Martyrs" by William Sambrot.

Alfred Hitchcock Presents: More Stories Not for the Nervous, Dell Publishing, Paperback, 50 cents, 188 pages, March 1967

"Room With a View" by Hal Dresner, "Lemmings" by Richard Mathieson, "White Goddess" by Idris Seabright, "Call for Help" by Robert Arthur, "View From the Terrace" by Mike Marmer, "Something Short of Murder" by Henry Slesar, "The Golden Girl" by Ellis Peters, "The Boy Who Predicted Earthquakes" by Margaret St. Clair, "Walking Alone" by Miriam Allen deFord, "For All the Rude People" by Jack Ritchie, and "Sorry, Wrong Number" by Lucille Fletcher and Allan Ullman (novelette).

Dell Publishing, Paperback, 188 pages, 50 cents, October 1967 (second printing)
Dell Publishing, Paperback, 188 pages, 50 cents, November 1967 (third printing)
Dell Publishing, Paperback, 188 pages, May 1968 (fourth printing)
Dell Publishing, Paperback, 188 pages, October 1968 (fifth printing)
Dell Publishing, Paperback, 188 pages, June 1969 (sixth printing)
Dell Publishing, Paperback, 188 pages, 75 cents, September 1971 (seventh printing)
Dell Publishing, Paperback, 188 pages, 75 cents, March 1973 (new Dell edition)
On the cover of the March 1973 paperback, there is a portrait of Alfred Hitchcock reading a book in a private library. The book he is holding features the cover of the November 1972 Dell release, Alfred Hitchcock's A Hearse of a Different Color!

HC7. Alfred Hitchcock Presents: Stories That Scared Even Me, Random House, Hardcover, 463 pages, 1967 (Edited by Robert Arthur.)

"Fishhead" by Irvin S. Cobb, "Camera Obscura" by Basil Copper, "A Death in the Family" by Miriam Allen deFord, "Men Without Bones" by Gerald Kersh, "Not With a Bang" by Damon Knight, "Party Games" by John Burke, "X Marks the Pedwalk" by Fritz Leiber, "Curious Adventure of Mr. Bond" by Nugent Barker, "Two Spinsters" by E. Phillips Oppenheim, "The Knife" by Robert Arthur, "The Cage" by Ray Russell, "It" by Theodore Sturgeon (novelette), "Casablanca" by Thomas M. Disch, "The Road to Mictlantecutli" by Adobe James, "Guide to Doom" by Ellis Peters, "The Estuary" by Margaret St. Clair, "Tough Town" by William Sambrot, "The Troll" by T.H. White, "Evening at the Black House" by Robert Soerlott, "One of the Dead" by William Wood, "The Real Thing" by Robert Specht, "Master of the Hounds" by Algis Budrys, "The Candidate" by Henry Slesar, and "Out of the Deeps" by John Wyndham (novel).

Beginning with this hardcover, some the paperback books began using different titles, but they still contained the same stories. Most featured on the front cover, in small white or black words, "formerly titled: Alfred Hitchcock Presents: Stories That Scared Even Me" – or the hardcover they originated.

Alfred Hitchcock Presents: Scream Along With Me, Dell Publishing, Paperback, 224 pages, 75 cents, December 1970

"Fishhead" by Irvin S. Cobb, "Camera Obscura" by Basil Cooper, "A Death in the Family" by Miriam Allen deFord, "The Knife" by Robert Arthur, "Casablanca" by Thomas M. Disch, "The Road to Mictlantecutli" by Adobe James, "Guide to Doom" by Ellis Peters, "The Estuary" by Margaret St. Clair, "Tough Town" by William Sambrot, "The Troll" by T.H. White, "Evening at the Black House" by Robert Somerlott, "One of the Dead" by William Wood, "The Real Thing" by Robert Specht, "Journey to Death" by Donald E. Westlake, "The Master of the Hounds" by Algis Budrys, "The Candidate" by Henry Slesar, and "It" by Theodore Sturgeon (novelette).

Dell Publishing, Paperback, 224 pages. $1.25, September 1977 (second printing)

Alfred Hitchcock Presents: Slay Ride, Dell Publishing, Paperback, 75 cents, 240 pages, Feb. 1971

"Men Without Bones" by Gerald Kersh, "Not With a Bang" by Damon Knight, "Party Games" by John Burke, "X Marks the Pedwalk" by Fritz Leiber, "Two Spinsters" by E. Phillips Oppenheim, "The Cage" by Ray Russell, "Curious Adventure of Mr. Bond" by Nugent Barker, and "Out of the Deeps" by John Wyndham (novel).

Dell Publishing, Paperback, 240 pages. $1.50, December 1977 (new Dell edition)

HC8. Alfred Hitchcock Presents: A Month of Mystery, Random House, Hardcover, 403 pages, 1969 (Edited by Robert Arthur.)

"The Dusty Drawer" by Harry Muheim, "Drum Beat" by Stephen Marlowe, "South of Market" by Joe Gores, "The Uses of Intelligence" by Matthew Gant, "Love Will Find a Way" by David Alexander, "Retribution" by Michael Zuroy, "The Queen's Jewel" by James Holding, "Pool Party" by Andrew Benedict, "That Touch of Genious" by William Sambrot, "The Crooked Road" by Alex Gaby, "A Taste for Murder" by Jack Ritchie, "The Twelve-Hour Caper" by Mike Marmer, "The Amateur" by Michael Gilbert, "Death Wish" by Lawrence Block, "The Singing Pigeon" by Ross Macdonald, "Justice Magnifique" by Lawrence Treat, "The White Hat" by Sax Rohmer, "Hard Sell" by Craig Rice, "Greedy Night" by E.C. Bentley, "A Twilight Adventure" by Melville Davisson Post, "Murder Matinee" by Harold Q. Masur, "A Humorist" by Romain Gary, "The Oblong Room" by Edward D. Hoch, "Love Me, Love Me, Love Me" by M.S. Waddell, "Special Handling" by John Keefauver, "Dead Man's Story" by Howard Rigsby, "The Legend of Joe Lee" by John D. MacDonald, "Crooked Bone" by Gerald Kersh, "The Janissaries of Emilion" by Basil Cooper, "Chinoiserie" by Helene McCloy, "Soldier Key" by Sterling E. Lanier.

The eighth story in this anthology was written by Andrew Benedict, a pseudonym of Robert Arthur. "The Dusty Drawer," "The Twelve-Hour Caper" and "The Crooked Road" were all dramatized on *Alfred Hitchcock Presents*. Again, like the hardcover listed above, the paperback editions featured the same stories, but were retitled.

Alfred Hitchcock Presents: Dates With Death, Dell Publishing, 75 cents, 214 pages, January 1972

"The Dusty Drawer" by Harry Muheim, "Drum Beat" by Stephen Marlowe, "The Uses of Intelligence" by Matthew Gant, "The Queen's Jewel" by James Holding, "That Touch of Genius" by William Sambrot, "The Crooked Road" by Alex Gaby, "The Amateur" by Michael Gilbert, "The Singing Pigeon" by Ross Macdonald, "Justice Magnifique" by Lawrence Treat, "Greedy Night" by E.C. Bentley, "A Humanist" by Romain Gary, "The Oblong Room" by Edward D. Hoch, "Dead Man's Story" by Howard Rigsby, "The Janissaries of Emilion" by Basil Cooper, and "Chinoiserie" by Helen McCloy.

Dell Publications, Paperback, 214 pages, $1.25, December 1976 (new Dell edition)

Alfred Hitchcock Presents: Terror Time, Dell Publishing, 75 cents, 205 pages, February 1972

"South of Market" by Joe Gores, "Love Will Find a Way" by David Alexander, "Retribution" by Michael Zuroy, "Pool Party" by Andrew Benedict, "A Taste for Murder" by Jack Ritchie, "The Twelve-Hour Caper" by Mike Marmer, "Death Wish" by Lawrence Block, "The White Hat" by Sam Rohmer, "Hard Sell" by Craig Rice, "A Twilight Adventure" by Melville Davisson Post, "Murder Matinee" by Harold Q. Masur, "Love Me, Love Me, Love Me" by M.S. Waddell, "Special Handling" by John Keefauver, "The Legend of Joe Lee" by John D. MacDonald, "Crooked Bone" by Gerald Kersh, and "Soldier Key" by Sterling E. Lanier.

HC9. Alfred Hitchcock Presents: Stories to Stay Awake By, Random House, Hardcover, 464 pages, 1971 (Editor is unknown, but a possibility that this volume was edited by Jack Ritchie.)

"Success of a Mission" by William Arden, "The Splintered Monday" by Charlotte Armstrong, "Death by Judicial Hanging" by Francis Beeding, Floral Tribute" by Robert Bloch, "Red Wine" by Lawrence G. Blochman, "Canavan's Back Yard" by Joseph Payne Brennan, "A Murderous Slice" by Marguerite Dickinson, "The New Deal" by Charles Einstein, "Boomerang" by Guy Fleming, "Sleep Is the Enemy" by Anthony Gilbert, "The Second Coming" by Joe Gores, "From the Mouse to the Hawk" by Dion Henderson, "Letter to the Editor" by Morris Hershman, "The Spy Who Came to the Brink" by Edward D. Hoch, "Second Talent" by James Holding, "The Ohio Love Sculpture" by Adobe James, "The Great Three-Month Super Sonic Transport Stack-Up of 1999" by John Keefauver, "Homicide House" by Day Keene, "A Feline Felony" by Lael J. Littke, "The Devil-Dog" by Jack London, "The Homesick Buick" by John D. MacDonald, "Campaign Fever" by Patricia McGerr, "Run With the Wind" by James McKimmey, "Squeakie's Second Case" by Margaret Millar, "Ten Minutes from Now" by Jack Ritchie, "See and Tell" by Mary Linn Roby, "Fair's Fair" by Jane Speed, "The Doe and the Gantlet" by Pat Stadley, "The Last Day of All" by Fay Grissom Stanley, "The Nail and the Oracle" by Theodore Sturgeon, "Doctor's Orders" by John F. Suter, "The Man Who Laughs at Lions" by Bryce Walton, and "The Unsuspected" by Jay Wilson.

Alfred Hitchcock Presents: Stories to Stay Awake By, Dell Publishing, Paperback, 95 cents, 235 pages, September 1973

"Success of a Mission" by William Arden, "The Splintered Monday" by Charlotte Armstrong, "Death by Judicial Hanging" by Francis Beeding, "Floral Tribute" by Robert Bloch, "Red Wine" by Lawrence G. Blochman, "Canavan's Back Yard" by Joseph Payne Brennan, "A Murderous Slice" by Marguerite Dickinson, "The New Deal" by Charles Einstein, "Boomerang" by Guy Fleming, "Sleep Is the Enemy" by Anthony Gilbert, "The Second Coming" by Joe Gores, "From the Mouse to the Hawk" by Dion Henderson, "Letter to the Editor" by Morris Hershman, "The Spy Who Came to the Brink" by Edward D. Hoch, "Second Talent" by James Holding, "The Ohio Love Sculpture" by Adobe James, and "Homicide House" by Day Keene.

Alfred Hitchcock Presents: More Stories to Stay Awake By, Dell Publishing, Paperback, 95 cents, 235 pages, October 1973

"The Great Three-Month Super Supersonic Transport Stack-Up of 1999" by John Keefauver, "A Feline Felony" by Lael J. Littke, "The Devil-Dog" by Jack London, "The Homesick Buick" by John D. MacDonald, "Campaign Fever" by Patricia McGerr, "Run With the Wind" by James McKimmey, "Squeakie's Second Case" by Margaret Manners, "The Silent Butler" by Harold Q. Masur, "McGowney's Miracle" by Margaret Millar, "Ten Minutes From Now" by Jack Ritchie, "See and Tell" by Mary Linn Roby, "Fair's Fair" by Jane Speed, "The Doe and the Gantlet" by Pat Stadley, "The Last Day of All" by Fay Grissom Stanley, "The Nail and the Oracle" by Theodore Sturgeon, "Doctor's Orders" by John F. Suter, "The Man Who Laughs at Lions" by Bryce Walton, and "The Unsuspected" by Jay Wilson.

HC10. Alfred Hitchcock Presents: Stories to Be Read With the Lights On, Random House, Hardcover, 402 pages, 1973   (Editor is unknown, but there is a possibility that this volume was edited by Jack Ritchie.)

"Death Out of Season" by Mary Barrett, "Witness in the Dark" by Fredric Brown, "Shadows on the Road" by Robert Colby, "Mr. Mappin Forecloses" by Zena Collier, "Granny" by Ron Goulart, "The Landlady" by Roald Dahl, "Three Ways to Rob a Bank" by Harold R. Daniels, "No Loose Ends" by Miriam Allen deFord, "Goodbye, Pops" by Joe Gores, "Pin Money" by James Cross, "Social Climber" by Robert Higgins, "I'd Know You Anywhere" by Edward D. Hoch, "The Pile of Sand" by John Keefauver, "Payoff on Double Zero" by Warner Law, "The Bitter Years" by Dana Lyon, "Man's Best Friend" by Dee Stuart, "Killer on the Turnpike" by William P. McGivern, "Payments Received" by Robert L. McGrath, "Agony Column" by Barry Malzberg, "Guessing Game" by Rose Million Healey, "The $2,000,000 Defense" by Harold Q. Masur, "The Man in the Well" by Berkely Mather, "Crawfish" by Ardath F. Mayhar, "The Strange Case of Mr. Pruyn" by William F. Nolan, "Ludmila" by David Montross, "The One Who Got Away" by Al Nussbaum, "It's a Lousy World" by Bill Pronzini, "Only So Much to Reveal" by Joan Richter, "Who's Got the Lady?" by Jack Ritchie, "Hey, You Down There" by Harold Rolseth, "Too Many Sharks" by William Sambrot, "Christopher Frame" by Nancy C. Swoboda, "Obituary" by Paul Theridion, "Ransom Demand" by Jeffrey M. Wallmann, "The Mother Goose Madman" by Betty Ren Wright, "The Green Fly and the Box" by Waldo Carlton Wright, and "The Blue Rug" by Mitsu Yamamoto.

Two stories in this volume, "The Landlady" and "The $2,000,000 Defense" were previously dramatized on *Alfred Hitchcock Presents*.

Alfred Hitchcock Presents: Stories to Be Read With the Lights On (Volume One), Dell Publishing, $1.50, 256 pages, March 1976

"Death Out of Season" by Mary Barrett, "Witness in the Dark" by Fredric Brown, "Shadows on the Road" by Robert Colby, "Mr. Mappin Forecloses" by Zena Collier, "Granny" by Ron Goulart, "The Landlady" by Roald Dahl, "Three Ways to Rob a Bank" by Harold R. Daniels, "No Loose Ends" by Miriam Allen deFord, "Goodbye, Pops" by Joe Gores, "Pin Money" by James Cross, "Social Climber" by Robert J. Higgins, "I'd Know You Anywhere" by Edward D. Hoch, "The Pile of Sand" by John Keefauver, "Payoff on Double Zero" by Warner Law, "The Bitter Years" by Dana Lyon, "Man's Best Friend" by Dee Stuart, and "Killer on the Turnpike" by William P. McGivern.

Alfred Hitchcock Presents: Stories to Be Read With the Lights On (Volume Two), Dell Publishing, Paperback, $1.50, 220 pages, April 1976

"Payment Received" by Robert L. McGrath, "Agony Column" by Betsy Malzberg, "Guessing Game" by Rose Million Healey, "The $2,000,000 Defense" by Harold Q. Masur, "The Man in the Well" by Berkely Mather, "Crawfish" by Ardath F. Mayhar, "The Strange Case of Mr. Pruyn" by William F. Nolan, "Ludmila" by David Montross, "The One Who Got Away" by Al Nussbaum, "It's a Lousy World" by Bill Pronzini, "Only So Much to Reveal" by Joan Ritcher, "Who's Got the Lady?" by Jack Ritchie, "Hey, You Down There" by Harold Rolseth, "Too Many Sharks" by William Sambrot, "Christopher Frame" by Nancy C. Swoboda, "Obituary" by Paul Theridion, "Ransom Demand" by Jeffrey M. Wallmann, "The Mother Goose Madman" by Betty Ren Wright, "The Green Fly and the Box" by Waldo Carlton Wright and "The Blue Rug" by Mitsu Yamamoto.

In October of 1979, this same paperback was reprinted, but under a different title as a "new Dell edition."

Alfred Hitchcock: Breaking the Scream Barrier, Dell Publishing, Paperback, $1.95, 220 pages

HC11. Alfred Hitchcock Presents: Stories to be Read With the Door Locked, Random House, Hardcover, 368 pages, 1975 (Editor is unknown, but a possibility this was edited by Jack Ritchie.)

"Hijack" by Robert L. Fish, "Tomorrow and Tomorrow" by Adobe James, "Funeral in Another Town" by Jerry Jacobson, "A Case Of Quiet" by William Jeffrey*, "A Good Head for Murder" by Charles W. Runyon, "The Invisible Cat" by Betty Ren Wright, "Royal Jelly" by Roald Dahl, "Light Verse" by Isaac Asimov, "The Distributor" by Richard Matheson, "How Henry J. Littlefinger Licked the Hippies' Scheme to Take Over the Country by Tossing Pot in Postage Stamp Glue" by John Keefauver, "The Leak" by Jacques Futrelle, "All the Sounds of Fear" by Harlan Ellison, "Little Foxes Sleep Warm" by Waldo Carlton Wright, "The Graft Is Green" by Harold Q. Masur, "View by Moonlight" by Pat McGerr, "There Hangs Death!" by John D. MacDonald, "Lincoln's Doctor's Son's Dog' by Warner Law, "Coyote Street" by Gary Brandner, "Zombique" by Joseph Payne Brennan, "The Pattern" by Bill Pronzini, "Pipe Dream" by Alan Dean Foster, "Shottle Bop" by Theodore Sturgeon, "The Magnum" by Jack Ritchie, "Voices in the Dust" by Gerald Kersh, "The Odor of Melting" by Edward D. Hoch, "The Sound of Murder" by William P. McGivern, "The Income Tax Mystery" by Michael Gilbert, "Watch for It" by Joseph N. Gores, and "The Affair of the Twisted Scarf" by Rex Stout (novelette).

Alfred Hitchcock Presents: Stories to Be Read With the Door Locked (Vol. 1). Dell Publishing, Paperback, $1.25, 219 pages, January 1977

"Hijack" by Robert L. Fish, "Tomorrow and Tomorrow" by Adobe James, "Funeral in Another Town" by Jerry Jacobson, "A Case for Quiet" by William Jeffrey, "A Good Head for Murder" by Charles W. Runyon, "The Invisible Cat" by Betty Ren Wright, "Royal Jelly" by Roald Dahl (novelette), "Light Verse" by Isaac Asimov, "The Distributor" by Richard Matheson, "How Henry Littlefinger Licked the Hippies' Scheme to Take Over the Country by Tossing Pot in Postage Stamp Glue" by John Keefauver, "The Leak" by Jaques Futrelle, "All the Sounds of Fear" by Harlan Ellison, "Little Foxes Sleep Warm" by Waldo Carlton Wright, and "The Graft Is Green" by Harold Q. Masur.

Alfred Hitchcock's I Want My Mummy. Dell Publishing, Paperback, $1.25, 251 pages, July 1977

"View by Moonlight" by Pat McGerr, "There Hangs Death!" by John D. MacDonald, "Lincoln's Doctor's Son's Dog" by Warner Law, "Coyote Street" by Gary Brandner, "Zombique" by Joseph Payne Brennan, "The Pattern" by Bill Pronzini, "Pipe Dream" by Alan Dean Foster, "Shottle Bop" (novelette) by Theodore Sturgeon, "The Magnum" by Jack Ritchie, "Voices in the Dust" by Gerald Kersh, "The Odor of Melting" by Edward D. Hoch, "The Sound of Murder" by William P. McGivern, "The Income Tax Mystery" by Michael Gilbert, "Watch For It" by Joseph N. Gores, and "The Affair of the Twisted Scarf" by Rex Stout (novelette).

Dell Publishing, Paperback, 251 pages. $2.25, February 1981 (new Dell edition)

HC12. Alfred Hitchcock Presents: Stories That Go Bump in the Night, Random House, Hardcover, 307 pages, 1977 (Editor is unknown, but a possibility that this volume was edited by Jack Ritchie.)

"The Damned Thing" by Ambrose Bierce, "Edward the Conqueror" by Roald Dahl, "By the Scruff of the Soul" by Dorothy Salisbury Davis, "Murder on St. Valentine's Day" by Mignon G. Eberhart, "Hey, Look at Me!" by Jack Finney, "Muldoon and the Numbers Game" by Robert L. Fish, "The Capture" by James Hay, Jr., "The Guide's Story" by Dion Henderson, "Woodrow Wilson's Necktie" by Patricia Highsmith, "Something for the Dark" by Edward D. Hoch, "The Gray Shroud" by Antony Horner, "The Gentleman Caller" by Veronica Parker Johns, "The Coconut Trail" by Dan Knowlton, "Man in a Trap" by John D. MacDonald, "The Bearded Lady" by Ross Macdonald,

* William Jeffrey is a joint pseudonym of Bill Pronzini and Jeffrey M. Wallmann.

"Dead Game" by Harold Q. Masur, "No Such Thing as a Vampire" by Richard Matheson, "A Piece of the World" by Steve O'Connell, "Easy Mark" by Talmage Powell, "Proof of Guilt" by Bill Pronzini, "The Operator" by Jack Ritchie, "The Other Celia" by Theodore Sturgeon, "An Evening in Whitechapel" by Nancy Swoboda, and "Wile Versus Guile" by Arthur Train.

Hardcover number 12 and 13 are the only two hardcover books never to go into reprint in paperback editions. The story "A Piece of the World," was written by Steve O'Connell, a pseudonym of Jack Ritchie. "The Gentleman Caller" was previously dramatized on *The Alfred Hitchcock Hour*.

HC13. Alfred Hitchcock Presents: The Master's Choice, Random House, Inc., Hardcover, 358 pages, 1979 (Editor is unknown, but a possibility that this volume was edited by Jack Ritchie.)

"She Fell Among Thieves" by Robert Edmond Alter, "The Hills Beyond Furcy" by Robert G. Anderson, "A Gun Is a Nervous Thing" by Charlotte Armstrong, "See How They Run" by Robert Bloch, "Nothing Short of Highway Robbery" by Lawrence Block, "Puppet Show" by Fredric Brown, "De Mortuis" by John Collier. "Snowball" Ursula Curtiss, "Here, Daemos!" by August Derleth, "The Cookie Lady" by Philip K. Dick, "The Wager" by Robert L. Fish, "Scream in a Soundproof Room" by Michael Gilbert, "Return of Verge Likens" by Davis Grubb, "The Fair Chance" by James Hay, Jr., "Paste a Smile on a Wall" by John Keefauver, "The Alarming Letters from Scottsdale" by Warner Law, "My Last Book" by Clayre and Michel Lipman, "Homicidal Hiccup" by John D. MacDonald, "Gone Girl" by Ross Macdonald, "The Interceptor" by Barry N. Malzberg, "Doctor's Dilemma" by Harold Q. Masur, "Mother by Protest" by Richard Matheson, "Coincidence" by William F. Nolan, "The Same Old Grind" by Bill Pronzini, "Twenty-two Cents a Day" by Jack Ritchie, "Evil Star" by Ray Russell, and "A Woman's Help" by Henry Slesar.

"A Woman's Help" and "De Mortuis" were both previosuly dramatized on *Alfred Hitchcock Presents*. "Return of Verge Likens" was the third season opener for *The Alfred Hitchcock Hour*.

U.K. paperback edition: Alfred Hitchcock: Tales to Make Your Blood Run Cold, Published by Coronet-Hodder and Stoughton, 188 pages, 1.25 pounds, 1979

"She Fell Among Thieves" by Robert Edmond Alter, "The Hills Beyond Furcy" by Robert G. Anderson, "A Gun Is A Nervous Thing" by Charlotte Armstrong, "See How They Run" by Robert Bloch, "Nothing Short of Highway Robbery" by Lawrence Block, "Puppet Show" by Fredric Brown, "De Mortuis" by John Collier, "Snowball" by Ursual Curtiss, "Here, Daemos!" by August Derleth, "The Cookie Lady" by Philip K. Dick, "The Wager" by Robert L. Fish, "Scream in a Soundproofed Room" by Michael Gilbert, and "Return of Verge Likens" by Davis Grubb.

DELL PAPERBACK SERIES

All thirty-nine of the Dell Paperbacks printed in the United States are listed below in the order they were released. These are not the same paperbacks Dell continued to release over the years, with the same contents as the Random House hardcovers. All of the U.K. paperbacks seem to have the same stories as the U.S. editions, all published through Mayflower. (Pan published only paperback editions of the hardcovers.) Also enclosed is a selection of the additional printings, listed below each entry. While a few of these paperbacks never underwent second or third printings, other paperbacks feature multiple printings. The main problem documenting these is there are literally thousands of books floating about, and accurate records were not kept for historical documentation. Therefore, book number nine (for example) went through five different printings, but the fourth was elusive, so we didn't list the fourth.

The first story in book number fourteen, was written by the same Jack Webb of *Dragnet* and *Adam-12* fame. Webb wrote many short stories, and a few of his appeared within the pages of these Hitchcock anthologies. Book number nineteen is a unique mystery by itself. For some odd reason, the copyright page lists this publication, "© Copyright 1969" but there does not exist any previous printings or edition, either in hardcover or paperback. Could this have been a delayed publication? The cover of book number twenty-three has made this publication a collector's item for film fans, including horror fanatics and fans of the classic Universal Studios horror pictures. The artwork depicted on the front cover featured Bela Lugosi as Dracula, Lon Chaney as the Phantom of the Opera, and Lon Chaney, Jr. as the Wolf Man, drinking with Hitchcock at a bar.

In book one, Helen Nielsen's "Your Witness" and Jay Street's (pen name for Henry Slesar) "The Last Escape" were both previousuly dramatized on *Alfred Hitchcock Presents*. In book five, Stanley Abbott's "The Trap" was done on *The Alfred Hitchcock Hour*. In book six, Robert Bloch's "A Home Away From Home" starred Ray Milland. In book nineteen, Henry Slesar's "Sleep Is for the Innoncent" was dramatized with Dennis Weaver in the lead. In book thirty-one, another Slesar story, "Thicker Than Water," was dramatized on *Alfred Hitchcock Presents* as "The Test."

1. Alfred Hitchcock Presents: A Hangman's Dozen, 222 pages, 50 cents, December 1962

"Bomb #14" by Jack Ritchie, "The Forgiving Ghost" by C.B. Gilford, "The Children of Noah" by Richard Matheson, "An Attractive Family" by Robert Arthur, "Let the Sucker Beware" by Charles Einstein, "Fair Game" by John Cortez, "The Curious Facts Preceding My Execution" by Richard Stark, "Your Witness" by Helen Nielsen, "Blackout" by Richard Deming, "The October Game" by Ray Bradbury, "Stop Calling Me 'Mister' " by Jonathan Craig, "The Last Escape" by Jay Street, "Not a Laughing Matter" by Evan Hunter, "Most Agreeably Poisoned" by Fletcher Flora, and "The Best-Friend Murder" by Donald E. Westlake.

Dell Publishing, Paperback, 222 pages, 60 cents, April 1966 (new edition)
Dell Publishing, Paperback, 222 pages, 60 cents, June 1968 (second printing)
Dell Publishing, Paperback, 222 pages, 60 cents, May 1969 (third printing)
Dell Publishing, Paperback, 222 pages, $1.25, January 1976 (new Dell edition)
U.K. edition: Mayflower Books, Ltd.: St. Albans, Paperback, 189 pages, 30 pence, 1972

2. Alfred Hitchcock Presents: 16 Skeletons From My Closet, 222 pages, 50 cents, March 1963

"Ghost Story" by Henry Kane, "Where Is Thy Sting?" by James Holding, "The Butler Who Didn't Do It" by Craig Rice, "Christmas Gift" by Robert Turner, "The Man at the Table" by C.B. Gilford, "Death of Another Salesman" by Donald Honig, "Man With a Hobby" by Robert Bloch, ". . . Said Jack the Ripper" by Robert Arthur, "A Gun With a Heart" by William Logan, "Assassination" by Dion Henderson, "A Little Sororicide" by Richard Deming, "The Man Who Got Away With It" by Lawrence Treat, "Secret Recipe" by Charles Mergendahl, "Daddy-O" by David Alexander, "The Crime Machine" by Jack Ritchie, and "Homicide and Gentlemen" by Fletcher Flora.

Dell Publishing, Paperback, 222 pages, 50 cents, March 1964 (second printing)
Dell Publishing, Paperback, 222 pages, 75 cents, February 1973 (third printing)
Dell Publishing, Paperback, 222 pages, $1.25, February 1976 (new Dell edition)

3. Alfred Hitchcock's Once Upon a Dreadful Time, 192 pages, 50 cents, August 1964

"A Little Push from Cappy Fleers" by Gilbert Ralston, "The Safe Street" by Paul Eiden, "No One on the Line" by Robert Arthur, "Antique" by Hal Ellson, "Suspicion Is not Enough" by Richard Hardwick, "A Family Affair" by Talmage Powell, "Granny's Birthday" by Fredric Brown, "Third Party in the Case" by Philip Ketchum, "Hill Justice" by John Faulkner, "If This Be Madness" by Lawrence Block, "Anatomy of an Anatomy" by Donald E. Westlake, "A Cool Swim on a Hot Day" by Fletcher Flora, "By the Sea, by the Sea" by Hal Dresner, "Bodies Just Won't Stay Put" by Tom MacPherson, "The Dangerfield Saga" by C.B. Gilford, and "Number One Suspect" by Richard Deming.

4. Alfred Hitchcock's Witches' Brew, 192 pages, 50 cents, April 1965

"Premonition" by Charles Mergendahl, "A Shot from the Dark Night" by Avram Davidson, "I Had a Hunch, And . . ." by Talmage Powell, "A Killing in the Market" by Robert Bloch, "Gone as by Magic" by Richard Hardwick, "The Big Bajoor" by Borden Deal, "The Gentle Miss Bluebird" by Nedra Tyre, "The Guy What Laughs Last" by Philip Tremont, "Diet and Die" by Wenzell Brown, "Just for Kicks" by Richard Marsten, "Please Forgive Me" by Henry Kane, "A Crime Worthy of Me" by Hal Dresner, and "When Buying a Fine Murder" by Jack Ritchie.

Dell Publishing, Paperback, 192 pages, 95 cents, April 1975
Dell Publishing, Paperback, 192 pages, $1.25, February 1978 (new Dell edition)
In June 1989, Amereon, Ltd. Released a hardcover edition of this book.

5. Alfred Hitchcock's Anti-Social Register, 206 pages, 50 cents, October 1965

"Tune Me In" by Fletcher Flora, "A Question of Ethics" by James Holding, "The Trap" by Stanley Abbott, "A Habit for the Voyage" by Robert Edmond Alter, "The Empty Room" by Donald Honig, "I'll Go With You" by Hal Dresner, "The Watchdogs of Molicoti" by Richard Curtis, "The Affair Upstairs" by Helen Nielsen, "I'm Better Than You" by Henry Slesar, "A Simple Uncomplicated Murder" by C.B. Gilford, "Dead Drunk" by Arthur Porges, "The Last Autospy" by Bryce Walton, "One Man's Family" by Richard Hardwick, and "You Can't Trust Me" by Jack Ritchie.

Dell Publishing, Paperback, 206 pages, 95 cents, September 1975 (new edition – first edition)
Dell Publishing, Paperback, 206 pages, $1.50, May 1978 (new Dell edition)

6. Alfred Hitchcock's Noose Report, 191 pages, 50 cents, August 1966

"A Home Away From Home" by Robert Bloch, "High Tide" by Richard Hardwick, "The World's Oldest Motive" by Laurence M. Janifer, "A Very Cautious Boy" by Gilbert Ralston, "Something Very Special" by Fletcher Flora, "The Short and Simple Annals" by Dan J. Marlowe, "Others Deal in Death" by August Derleth, "The Promotion" by Richard Deming, "Contents: One Body" by C.B. Gilford, "The Trouble With Ruth" by Henry Slesar, "Make Your Pitch" by Borden Deal, "The Little Things" by Ed Lacy, "Holdout" by Jack Ritchie, and "The Late Unlamented" by Jonathan Craig.

Dell Publishing, Paperback, 191 pages, 50 cents, February 1968 (another printing)
Dell Publishing, Paperback, 191 pages, $1.50, August 1976 (new Dell edition)
Dell Publishing, Paperback, 192 pages, $1.50, July 1979 (another new Dell edition)
In June 1989, Amereon, Ltd. Released a hardcover edition of this book.

7. Alfred Hitchcock's Hard Day at the Scaffold, 175 pages, 50 cents, December 1967

"The Baby" by Jonathan Craig, "Don't Live in a Coffin" by Helen Nielsen, "A Hundred Times" by Sid Hoff, "Weep for the Guilty" by Henry Slesar, "Point the Man Out!" by Duane Decker, "Crooks, Satchels, and Selma" by Michael Brett, "Not Exactly Love" by Fletcher Flora, "The Swinging Sheriff" by Ed Lacy, "One on a Desert Island" by Donald E. Westlake, "Bite of Revenge" by James McKimmey, Jr., "Lily Bell" by Richard Deming, "Flora and Her Fauna" by C.B. Gilford, "The Pulque Vendor" by Hal Ellson, and "Prolonged Visit" by Hal Dresner.

Dell Publishing, Paperback, 175 pages, 50 cents, March 1968 (second printing)
Dell Publishing, Paperback, 175 pages, 50 cents, May 1968 (third printing)
Dell Publishing, Paperback, 175 pages, 50 cents, August 1968 (fourth printing)
Dell Publishing, Paperback, 175 pages, 50 cents, December 1968 (fifth printing)
Dell Publishing, Paperback, 175 pages, 50 cents, July 1969 (sixth printing)

8. Alfred Hitchcock Presents: Games Killers Play, 160 pages, 50 cents, April 1968

"The China Cottage" by August Derleth, "Killed by Kindness" by Nedra Tyre, "You Can't Be Too Careful" by James Holding, "Murder Delayed" by Henry Slesar, "Pattern of Guilt" by Helen Nielsen, "Weighty Problem" by Duane Decker, "Willie Betts, Banker" by Mike Brett, "Bus to Chattanooga" by Jonathan Craig, "The Feel of a Trigger" by Donald E. Westlake, "Captive Audience" by Jack Ritchie, "Room to Let" by Hal Ellson, "Double Trouble" by Robert Edmond Alter, "Heist in Pianissimo" by Talmage Powell, and "Wish You Were Here" by Richard Hardwick.

DELL | First Time in Paperback! 50c

ALFRED HITCHCOCK'S HARD DAY AT THE SCAFFOLD

Dell Publishing, Paperback, 160 pages, 50 cents, October 1968 (second printing)
Dell Publishing, Paperback, 160 pages, 50 cents, June 1969 (third printing)
Dell Publishing, Paperback, 160 pages, January 1970 (fourth printing)
Dell Publishing, Paperback, 160 pages, August 1970 (fifth printing)

On the right: A cover of book number seven, May 1968 edition. An excellent example of how later printings continued to say on the cover, "First Time in Paperback!" Some of the Dell paperback books featured only one or two-color covers, while others included full-color covers.

9. Alfred Hitchcock's Skull Session, 192 pages, 60 cents, October 1968

"A Degree of Innocence" by Helen Nielsen, "One Unnecessary Man" by Talmage Powell, "Kill Me, My Sweet" by C.B. Gilford, "Sam's Heart" by Henry Slesar, "The Incomplete Corpse" by Jack Webb, "Luck Is No Lady" by Robert Bloch, "Sweet Spirit" by Donald Honig, "The Only Bad Policeman" by Paul Eiden, "The Witness Was a Lady" by Fletcher Flora, "The Episode of the Telephone Number" by Charles Einstein, "Come Back, Come Back" by Donald E. Westlake, "Adventures of the Sussex Archers" by August Derleth, "Fat Jow" by Robert Alan Blair, and "Vacation" by Mike Brett.

Dell Publishing, Paperback, 192 pages, 60 cents, April 1969 (second printing)
Dell Publishing, Paperback, 192 pages, 60 cents, November 1969 (third printing)
Dell Publishing, Paperback, 192 pages, 75 cents, June 1971 (fifth printing)

10. Alfred Hitchcock's Death Bag, 160 pages, 60 cents, January 1969

"Dying a Thousand Deaths" by Hal Ellson, "Year-End Clearance" by Mary Linn Roby, "Ruby Martinson, Ex-Con" by Henry Slesar, "Beware: Dangerous Man" by C.B. Gilford, "Murder and Lonely Hearts" by Helen Nielsen, "To Avoid a Scandal" by Talmage Powell, "Revenge Is Bitter Sweet" by H.A. DeRosso, "Hospitality Most Serene" by Jack Ritchie, "The Tenth Part of a Million" by Robert Colby, "Horse-Collar Homicide" by Arthur Porges, "Schedule for an Assassination" by Robert Edmond Alter, "Ambition" by Michael Brett, "Successor" by Richard H. Hardwick, and "Stop Killing Me" by Hal Dresner.

Dell Publishing, Paperback, 160 pages, 60 cents, April 1969 (second printing)
Dell Publishing, Paperback, 160 pages, 60 cents, November 1969 (third printing)
Dell Publishing, Paperback, 160 pages, 60 cents, August 1970 (fourth printing)
Dell Publishing, Paperback, 160 pages, 60 cents, April 1971 (fifth printing)
Dell Publishing, Paperback, 159 pages, $1.50, July 1978 (new Dell edition)
U.K. edition: Mayflower Books, Ltd.: St. Albans, Paperback, 157 pages, 35 pence, 1974

11. Alfred Hitchcock's Happiness Is a Warm Corpse, 205 pages, 60 cents, May 1969

"Once Upon a Bank Floor. . ." by James Holding, Jr., "The Egg Head" by Rog Phillips, "Each Night He Pulled the Trigger" by Robert Edmond Alter, "The Waiting Game" by Pat Stadley, "Destruction Is Always Arranged" by Gilbert Ralston, "The Happy Death" by John Cortez, "The Sweater" by Robert O. Lewis, "IQ-184" by Fletcher Flora, "Kill, If You Want Me!" by Richard Deming, "Antique" by Hal Ellson, "Mrs. Gilly and the Gigolo" by Mary L. Roby, "This Day's Evil" by Jonathan Craig, "Private and Confidential" by Diane Frazer, and "Never Come Back" by Robert Colby.

Dell Publishing, Paperback, 205 pages, 60 cents, September 1969 (second printing)
Dell Publishing, Paperback, 205 pages, 60 cents, May 1970 (third printing)

12. Alfred Hitchcock: Murders I Fell in Love With, 207 pages, 75 cents, September 1969

"Lonely Place" by Jack Webb, "Triangular Weekend" by C.B. Gilford, "Job for an Amateur" by Henry Slesar, "Welcome to My Prison" by Jack Ritchie, "Perfect Pitcher" by Arthur Porges, "Home Free" by Ed Lacy, "Ebony Killer" by Robert C. Ackworth, "Of the Five Who Came. . ." by Fletcher Flora, "Single Jeopardy" by Poul and Karen Anderson, "Daisies Deceive" by Nedra Tyre, "Room With a View" by Hal Dresner, "The Running Man" by Bill Pronzini, "Rest Stop" by Frank Sisk, and "No Businessman" by Wenzell Brown.

Dell Publishing, Paperback, 207 pages, 75 cents, April 1970 (second printing)
Dell Publishing, Paperback, 207 pages, 75 cents, December 1970 (third printing)

13. Alfred Hitchcock's Coffin Corner, 220 pages, 60 cents, November 1969

"A Walk on the Mountain" by Richard Hardwick, "A Time for Rifles" by H.A. DeRosso, "The Last Gourmand" by Donald Honig, "Sudden, Sudden Death" by Talmage Powell, "Circle in the Dust" by Arthur Porges, "Joshua" by William Brittain, "The Amateur Philologist" by August Derleth, "Thieves' Honor" by John Lutz, "The Final Chapter" by Richard O. Lewis, "The Helpful Horticulturist" by Mary Linn Roby, "Dead Oak in a Dark Woods" by Hal Ellson, "A Recipe for Eggs" by Frank Sisk, "Not the Killer Type" by John Arre, and "Blood Kin" by Richard Deming.

Dell Publishing, Paperback, 220 pages, 95 cents, October 1975 (new Dell edition)

14. Alfred Hitchcock's Murders on the Half-Skull, 208 pages, 75 cents, April 1970

"One November Night" by Jack Webb, "The Already Dead" by C.B. Gilford, "#8" by Jack Ritchie, "The Day of the Execution" by Henry Slesar, "Who Has Been Sitting in my Chair?" by Helen Nielsen, "The Vapor Clue" by James Holding, Jr., "Wetback" by Murray Wolf, "Murder Between Friends" by Nedra Tyre, "Good for the Soul" by Lawrence Block, "Ace in the Hole" by Elijah Ellis, "Bad Noose" by Arthur Porges, "The Eyes of a Cop" by Edwin P. Hicks, "Cheers" by Richard Deming, and "Crime Doesn't Pay - Enough" by Ed Lacy.

Dell Publishing, Paperback, 208 pages, $1.50, June 1979 (new Dell edition)

15. Alfred Hitchcock's Get Me to the Wake on Time, 192 pages, 75 cents, September 1970

"Good-bye, Now" by Gil Brewer, "Woman Missing" by Helen Nielsen, "Murder Me Gently" by C.B. Gilford, "Be My Valentine" by Henry Slesar, "The Marquesa" by Ray Russell, "Highly Recommended" by Michael Brett, "Old Man Emmons" by Talmage Powell, "The Drum Major" by Arthur Porges, "Upside-Down World" by Jack Ritchie, "Nice Work If You Can Get It" by Donald Honig, "Bach in a Few Minutes" by Fletcher Flora, "Polka-Dot Blonde" by Richard Hardwick, "Experience Is Helpful" by Rog Phillips, and "Lucrezia" by H.A. DeRosso.

Dell Publishing, Paperback, 192 pages. 95 cents, June 1975 (second printing)
U.K. edition: Mayflower Books, Ltd.: St. Albans, Paperback, 192 pages, 35 pence, 1974

16. Alfred Hitchcock Presents: I Am Curious (Bloody), 208 pages, 75 cents, March 1971

"One-Armed Bandit" by Dan Sontup, "Never Kill for Love" by C.B. Gilford, "These Daisies Told" by Arthur Porges, "Canine Accomplice" by Grover Brinkman, "The Accidental Widow" by Robert Colby, "Twilight Thunder" by Edward D. Hoch, "Images" by Michael Brett, "The Skim" by Richard Deming, "One Way" by John Lutz, "That Guy What Laughs Last" by Phillip Tremont, "The Private Eye of Irving Anvil" by Richard Hardwick, "Holiday" by Hal Ellson, and "The Heir" by Talmage Powell.

Dell Publishing, Paperback, 208 pages. 95 cents, June 1974 (second printing)

17. Alfred Hitchcock Presents: This One Will Kill You, 205 pages, 75 cents, April 1971

"Six Skinny Coffins" by Jonathan Craig, "The Clock is Cuckoo" by Richard Deming, "Plan 19" by Jack Ritchie, "The Misopedist" by James Holding, "Fair Shake" by John Lutz, "Item" by Henry Slesar, "Curtain Speech" by Ed Lacy, "His Brother's Caper" by Richard Hardwick, "The Shunned House" by Robert Edmond Alter, "Don't Call it Murder" by C.B. Gilford, "Comfort, In a Land of Strangers" by Michael Brett, "Where Credit is Due" by Hal Ellson, "Variations on an Episode" by Fletcher Flora, and "Voice in the Night" by Robert Colby.

Dell Publishing, Paperback, 205 pages. $1.50, February 1979 (new Dell edition)

18. Alfred Hitchcock's Down by the Old Bloodstream, 195 pages, 75 cents, June 1971

"The Good Thief" by Hal Ellson, "The Happenstance Snatch" by Fletcher Flora, "Lone Witness" by Talmage Powell, "Monkey King" by James Holding, "Lucky Catch" by Ed Lacy. "Janie Zeroes In" by Arthur Porges. "A Fair Warning to Mystery Writers" by C.B. Gilford, "The Still Small Voice" by Richard Hardwick, "Haunted Hill" by Robert Edmond Alter, "The Monster Brain" by Richard Deming, "The Wrongo" by Michael Brett, "A Miracle Is Arranged" by Jack Webb, "Kurdistan Payload" by Pat Stadley, and "The Flat Male" by Frank Sisk.

Dell Publishing, Paperback, 195 pages. 75 cents, June 1974 (second printing)

19. Alfred Hitchcock's Rolling Gravestones, 209 pages, 75 cents, August 1971

"A Place to Visit" by Stephen Marlowe, "Call Me Nick" by Jonathan Craig, "Dead Stop on the Road South" by Robert Colby, "Rusty Rose" by Edward Hoch, "Henry Lowden Alias Henry Taylor" by Helen Nielsen, "The Enormous $10" by Jack Ritchie, "First Come, First Served" by Rog Phillips, "The Explosives Expert" by John Lutz, "I Hated the Hired Man" by H.A. DeRosso, "A Singular Quarry" by Ed Lacy, "Sleep Is for the Innocent" by Henry Slesar, "Sorry, Right Number" by Charles Einstein, "Free Advice, Inc." by Michael Brett, "A Sweet Young Thing" by Mary Linn Roby, and "The Price of Fame" by Richard Deming.

20. <u>Alfred Hitchcock: Death Can Be Beautiful</u>, 215 pages, 75 cents, May 1972

"Day of the Tiger" by Jack Webb, "The Fanatical Ford" by Arthur Porges, "The Sound of Murder" by Donald E. Westlake, "An Agent Named Riddle" by H.A. DeRosso, "Homicide En Route" by C.B. Gilford, "The Listening Cone" by Ed Lacy, "Cop Killer" by James Holding, "The Death of Autumn" by Hal Ellson, "Of Men and Vengeance" by Donald Honig, "Just Curious" by James H. Schmitz, "Beyond the Wall" by Nedra Tyre, "What If I Had Taken the Train?" by Robert Colby, "The Adventure of the Intarsia Box" by August Derleth, and "Beside a Flowering Wall" by Fletcher Flora.

Dell Publishing, Paperback, 213 pages, 95 cents, June 1974 (second printing)
Dell Publishing, Paperback, 213 pages, March 1982 (New Dell edition)

21. <u>Alfred Hitchcock's Happy Deathday!</u>, 212 pages, 75 cents, June 1972

"Settlement Out of Court" by Fletcher Flora, "Drawer 14" by Talmage Powell, "An Echo of Evil" by Mary E. Nutt, "The Hypothetical Plan" by Richard Deming (novelette), "With One Stone" by Jack Ritchie, "Obedience School" by John Lutz, "The Sound of Murder" by Robert Colby, "Journey With a Murderer" by Donald Honig, "Murder a la Davy Jones" by Richard Hardwick, "A Quiet Backwater" by Stanley Abbott, "The Return of Crazy Bill" by Frank Sisk, "Three Miles to Marleybone" by Henry Slesar (novelette), "The Sheriff's Rainy Day" by Elijah Ellis, and "Consult the Yellow Pages" by Phillip Tremont.

22. <u>Alfred Hitchcock's A Hearse of a Different Color</u>, 207 pages, 75 cents, November 1972

"Dream of a Murder" by C.B. Gilford, "The Missing Miles" by Arthur Porges, "Adventure of the Haunted Library" by August Derleth (novelette), "An Estimate of Rita" by Ed Lacy, "The Full Treatment" by Rog Phillips, "Another Day, Another Murder" by Lawrence Treat, "The Living Doll" by Richard O. Lewis, "The Flat Male" by Frank Sisk, "Chaviski's Christmas" by Edwin P. Hicks, "The Case of the Helpless Man" by Douglas Farr, "Fat Jow and the Sung Tusk" by Robert Alan Blair (novelette), "Echo of a Savage" by Robert Edmond Alter, "The Nonconformist" by William R. Coons, and "The Sapphire That Disappeared" by James Holding.

Dell Publishing, Paperback, 208 pages, $2.25, August 1980 (first printing – new Dell edition)

23. <u>Alfred Hitchcock's The Best of Fiends</u>, 208 pages, 75 cents, December 1972

"Sweet, Sweet Murder" by H.A. DeRosso, "Final Peformance" by Dick Ellis, "Say 'Cheese' " by Ed Lacy, "The Cemetery Man" by C.B. Gilford, "No Tears for Foster" by Fletcher Flora (novelette), "Code Brown" by Robert Colby, "Legacy of Office" by Rog Phillips, "Diary to Death" by Neil M. Clark, "Sing a Song for Tony" by Jack Ritchie (novelette), "The Remote Rattler" by Edwin P. Hicks, "Murder Most Convenient" by Gilbert Ralston, "Shakedown" by Richard O. Lewis, "False Alarm" by Richard Deming, and "Suitable for Framing" by Mary Linn Roby.

24. <u>Alfred Hitchcock's Death-Mate</u>, 224 pages, 75 cents, May 1973

"The Human Fly" by Syd Hoff, "Two Bits' Worth of Luck" by Fletcher Flora (novelette), "An Honest Man" by Elijah Ellis, "An Interrogation" by Talmage Powell, "Choice of Weapon" by C.B. Gilford, "Mr. D. and Death" by Henry Slesar, "Others Deal in Death" by August Derleth, "A Steal at the Price" by James Holding, "The Waiting Room" by Charles W. Runyon, "Everybody Should Have a Hobby" by Theodore Mathieson, "Beiner and Wife" by Michael Brett, "Select Bait" by Richard O. Lewis, "Punch Any Number" by Jack Ritchie (novelette), and "White Lie, or Black?" by Hal Ellson.

25. Alfred Hitchcock's Let It All Bleed Out, 221 pages, 75 cents, June 1973

"Cold Night on Lake Lenore" by Jonathan Craig, "The Attitude of Murder" by Nedra Tyre, "Hand" by William Brittain, "Sheriff Peavy's Double Dead Case" by Richard Hardwick (novelette), "Rich - or Dead" by David A. Heller, "Yellow Shoes" by Hal Ellson, "The Man Who Hated Turkey" by Elijah Ellis (novelette), "Coffee Break" by Arthur Porges, "A Padlock for Charlie Draper" by James Holding, "Mac Without a Knife" by Talmage Powell, "The Chinless Wonder" by Stanley Abbott, "No Tears for an Informer" by H.A. De Rosso, "A Rare Bird" by John Lutz, and "The Comic Opera" by Henry Woodfin.

Dell Publishing, Paperback, 221 pages, $1.95, June 1980 (new Dell edition)

26. Alfred Hitchcock's Boys and Ghouls Together, 253 pages, 95 cents, January 1974

"Homicide, Maybe" by Lawrence Treat, "Ebony Killer" by Robert C. Ackworth, "Sea of Troubles" by Henry Slesar, "Devil in Ambush" by C.B. Gilford (novelette), "The Adventure of the Red Leech" by August Derleth, "He Was Too Much" by Robert Colby, "Horn of Justice" by Ed Lacy, "The 'Backword' Sheriff" by Richard Hardwick, "Stung" by Arthur Porges, "Lock Your Door" by Donald E. Westlake, "To Stop a Fire" by Elijah Ellis, "A Lesson in Reciprocity" by Fletcher Flora (novelette), "The Ethical Assassination" by Frank Sisk, and "Fat Jow and the Manifestations" by Robert Alan Blair.

Henry Slesar's "Sea of Troubles" was dramatized on *The CBS Radio Mystery Theater* two months after this book appeared on the shelves in bookstores. In March of 1974, Bryan Raeburn and Staats Cotsworth starred in the dramatization, scripted by Henry Slesar himself.

27. Alfred Hitchcock's Coffin Break, 222 pages, 95 cents, May 1974

"A Girl Must Be Practical" by Richard Deming, "Trick" by Gil Brewer, "Older Than Springtime" by Syd Hoff, "Don't Sit Under the Apple Tree" by Helen Nielsen, "A Tale of 5 G's" by C.B. Gilford (novelette), "Blood Will Tell" by Arthur Porges, "The Ordeal of Ruby Martinson" by Henry Slesar, "Garcia's Bulls" by Hal Ellson, "The Midnight Train" by John Lutz, "Amen!" by Ed Lacy, "Conflict of Interest" by James Holding (novelette), "The Man on the Hook" by Dick Ellis, "Room With a View" by Hal Dresner, and "Last Night's Evil" by Jonathan Craig.

28. Alfred Hitchcock's Bleeding Hearts, 238 pages, 95 cents, August 1974

"The Play's the Thing" by Robert Bloch, "The Executioner" by H.A. DeRosso, "Man on a Leash" by Jack Ritchie, "The Deep Six" by Richard Hardwick (novelette), "Hidden Tiger" by Michael Brett, "The Sensitive Juror" by Richard Deming, "Fat Jow and Chance" by Robert Alan Blair, "Slay the Wicked" by Frank Sisk (novelette), "Into the Morgue" by Hal Ellson, "I'll Be Loving You" by Fletcher Flora, "Motive: Another Woman" by Donald Honig, "The Brotherhood" by Theodore Mathieson, "The Final Reel" by John Lutz, and "Chimps Ain't Chumps" by Talmage Powell.

29. Alfred Hitchcock's Behind the Death Ball, 176 pages, 95 cents, November 1974

"Perfect Shot" by Lawrence Treat, "The Amateur Philologist" by August Derleth, "The Glint" by Arthur Porges, "The Seventh Man" by Helen Nielsen (novelette), "Voodoo Doll" by Henry Slesar, "A Friendly Exorcise" by Talmage Powell, "Many Women Too Many" by C.B. Gilford, "Till Death" by Fletcher Flora (novelette), "The Hitchhikers" by Bruce Hunsberger, "Store Cop" by Ed Lacy, "Doom Signal" by John Lutz, "See What's in the Bag" by Hal Ellson, "Fat Jow and the Walking Woman" by Robert Alan Blair, and "The Ghost and Mr. Grebner" by Syd Hoff.

30. Alfred Hitchcock's Grave Business, 208 pages, 95 cents, February 1975

The Master's Choice!
First time in paperback!
Alfred Hitchcock's Happiness is a Warm Corpse
60c

"The Rich Get Richer" by Douglas Farr, "Just About Average" by William Brittain, "Between 4 and 12" by Jack Ritchie, "The Girl in Gold" by Jonathan Craig, "The Extra Watch" by Frank Sisk, "A Familiar Victory" by Elijah Ellis, "Jury of One" by Talmage Powell, "The Common Factor" by Richard Deming (novelette), "A Turn to the Right" by James Holding, "To Get an Inch" by Richard Hardwick, "The Master's Touch" by Helen Nielsen, "His Brother Baxter" by Thedore Mathieson, "A Killer in the Dark" by Robert Edmond Alter, and "An Important Kill" by Robert Colby.

Dell Publishing, Paperback, 208 pages, 95 cents, December 1985 (new Dell edition)

31. Alfred Hitchcock's Murderers' Row, 205 pages, 95 cents, May 1975

"Nice Guy" by Richard Deming, "The Bridge in Briganza" by Frank Sisk, "Thicker Than Water" by Henry Slesar, "The Artificial Liar" by William Brittain, "For Money Received" by Fletcher Flora (novelette), "The Compleat Secretary" by Theodore Mathieson, "The Hypothetical Arsonist" by Rog Phillips, "Who Will Miss Arthur?" by Ed Lacy, "Arbiter of Uncertainties" by Edward D. Hoch, "Slow Motion Murder" by Richard Hardwick (novelette), "Never Marry a Witch" by C.B. Gilford, "The Second Thief" by David A. Heller, "The Nice Young Man" by Richard O. Lewis, and "A Message for Aunt Lucy" by Arthur Porges.

32. Alfred Hitchcock's Murder Racquet, 176 pages, 95 cents, July 1975

"The Sawbuck Machine" by Frank Sisk, "Contraband" by James Holding, "For Every Evil" by Douglas Farr, "You Can't Win 'Em (at) All" by Ed Lacy, "Murder in Mind" by C.B. Gilford (novelette), "Charley's Charm" by Alice-Mary Schnirring, "Murder Door to Door" by Robert Colby, "Ransom Demand" by Jeffrey M. Wallman, "I'll Race You" by Fletcher Flora, "I Am Not a Thief, Mr. Kester" by Gilbert Ralston, "Mousetrap" by Edwin P. Hicks, "Mildly Murderous" by Elijah Ellis, "An Element of Risk" by Richard Deming (novelette), and "A Neighborly Observation" by Richard Hardwick.

33. Alfred Hitchcock's Speak of the Devil, 235 pages, $1.25, December 1975

"Yesterday's Evil" by Jonathan Craig, "Suspicion, Suspicion" by Richard O. Lewis, "Pep Talk" by Syd Hoff, "The Tool" by Fletcher Flora, "Who's Innocent?" by Lawrence Treat, "Heir to Murder" by Ed Lacy, "Beginner's Luck" by Richard Hardwick (novelette), "Two Days in Organville" by Edward D. Hoch, "The Sonic Boomer" by William Brittain, "No Escape" by C.B. Gilford (novelette), "The Chess Partner" by Theodore Mathieson, "Dr. Zinnkopf's Devilish Device" by Edwin P. Hicks, "Fat Jow and the Dragon Parade" by Robert Alan Blair, and "Calculated Alibi" by Richard Deming.

Dell Publishing, Paperback, 240 pages, $2.25, November 1980 (new Dell edition)

34. Alfred Hitchcock's Having a Wonderful Crime, 224 pages, $1.25, November 1977

"A Look at Mother Nature" by Frank Sisk, "The Moonlighter" by James Holding, "Honeymoon Cruise" by Richard Deming (novelette), "A Coffin for Bertha Stetterson" by Donald Honig, "The Jersey Devil" by Edward D. Hoch, "The Garage Apartment" by Joyce Harrington, "Attrition" by Clayton Matthews, "Another Way Out" by Robert Colby (novelette), "The Scientist and the Stolen Rembrandt" by Arthur Porges, "Murder on the Honeymoon" by C.B. Gilford, "A Gallon of Gas" by William Brittain, "The Deadly Telephone" by Henry Slesar, "Ego Boost" by Richard O. Lewis, and "Martha: In Memoriam" by Richard Hardwick.

Dell Publishing, Paperback, 224 pages. $2.95, December 1985 (new Dell edition)

35. Alfred Hitchcock's Murder-Go-Round, 204 pages, $1.50, January 1978

"Fat Jow and the Watchmaker" by Robert Alan Blair, "Doctor's Dilemma" by Harold Q. Masur, "A Nice Wholesome Girl" by Robert Colby, "Dinner Will Be Cold" by Fletcher Flora (novelette), "Poacher's Island" by Richard Hardwick, "Nobody to Play With" by Irwin Porges, "Gallivantin' Woman" by Wenzell Brown, "Hardheaded Cop" by D.S. Halacy, Jr., "Time to Kill" by Dick Ellis (novelette), "Murder Out of a Hat" by Henry Slesar, "The Electric Girl Caper" by Edward D. Hoch, "A Good Head for Murder" by Charles W. Runyon, "Roundhouse" by Frank Sisk, and "The Day of the Picnic" by John Lutz.

36. Alfred Hitchcock: Killers at Large, 223 pages, $1.50, August 1978

"System Player" by Richard Deming, "Loaded Guns Are Dangerous" by Richard O. Lewis, "Welcome Stranger" by Elijah Ellis, "Come Ride With Me" by Donald Honig, "Sheriff Peavy's Cosa Nostra Caper" by Richard Hardwick (novelette), "Yellowbelly" by William Brittain, "Because of Everything" by Glenn Canary, "Refuge" by Fletcher Flora, "The Ghost of Elliot Reedy" by Max Van Derveer (novelette), "A Long Trip for Jenny" by F.J. Smith, "The Double Corner" by Philip Ketchum, "The Scientist and the Exterminator" by Arthur Porges, "Border Crossing" by James Holding, and "Swamp Rat" by C.B. Gilford.

37. Alfred Hitchcock: Rogues' Gallery, 255 pages, $1.50, December 1978

"Tannenbaum" by Frank Sisk, "Hijack" by Max Van Derveer (novelette), "Blood Money" by Wenzell Brown, "Devious" by Irwin Porges, "Have You Ever Seen This Woman?" by John Lutz, "Captain Leopold Finds a Tiger" by Edward D. Hoch, "Elegy for a Songbird" by Clayton Matthews, "The Volcano Effect" by Elijah Ellis, "The Job" by Henry Slesar, "The Vital Element" by Talmage Powell, "A Possibility of Error" by Richard M. Ellis, "The 'Method' Sheriff" by Ed Lacy, "No Experience Necessary" by Robert Colby (novelette), and "The Perfectionist" by Helen Nielsen.

38. Alfred Hitchcock: Death on Arrival. 253 pages, $1.75, September 1979

"Gentle Bluebeard" by Richard Deming, "Cousin Kelly" by Fletcher Flora, "Fat Jow and the Reluctant Witness" by Robert Alan Blair, "The Long Way Down" by Edward D. Hoch (novelette), "The Fly Swatter" by Frank Sisk, "Double Zero" by Robert Colby, "You and the Music" by John Lutz, "The Impossible Footprint" by William Brittain, "First Principles" by Donald Honig, "The Sixth Mrs. Pendrake" by C.B. Gilford, "A Little Knowledge" by Arthur Porges, "Rope Enough" by Dick Ellis, "The Token" by Hal Ellson, and "Sheriff Peavy's Full Moon Caper" by Richard Hardwick (novelette).

39. Alfred Hitchcock's Alive and Screaming, 236 pages, $1.95, May 1980

"The Hand from the Past" by Christopher Anvil, "The Confident Killer" by Talmage Powell, "The Blue Man" by Wenzell Brown, "The Murderess" by Max Van Derveer (novelette), "Light O'Love" by Fletcher Flora, "Positive Print" by Richard Deming, "A Weighty Promotion" by Bruce Hunsberger, "Death, the Black-Eyed Denominator" by Ed Lacy (novelette), "Beware the Righteous Man" by Dick Ellis, "A Message From Marsha" by James Holding, "Seven Million Suspects" by Franklin M. Davis, Jr., "Heaven Is a Frame of Mind" by Richard Hardwick, "The Eye of the Pigeon" by Edward D. Hoch, and "The Tuesday Club" by C.B. Gilford.

ODDITIES

A. <u>Clean Crimes and Neat Murders</u>, Avon Publishing, Paperback, 170 pages, 1960

"Not the Running Type," "A Fist Full of Money," "Pen Pal," "Trust Me, Mr. Paschetti," "One Grave Too Many," "40 Detectives Later," "The Morning After," "The Deadly Telephone," "Something Short of Murder," "The Right Kind of House," "M Is for the Many," "The Last Escape," "The Man With Two Faces," "Case of the Kind Waitress," "Make Me an Offer," "Sleep Is for the Innocent," and "Day of the Execution."

Subtitled "Alfred Hitchcock hand-picks and introduces A Bouquet of Clean Crimes and Neat Murders," this Avon Publication featured seventeen short stories all written by Henry Slesar, who was the winner of the Mystery Writers of America Award for 1959. The Avon Book Division was part of the Hearst Corporation and was a means to deliberately cash in on the successful stories Henry Slesar had already translated and dramatized on *Alfred Hitchcock Presents*. Although most of the stories originated from *Alfred Hitchcock's Mystery Magazine*, a few did originate from *Ellery Queen's Mystery Magazine, Manhunt, Mike Shane Mystery Magazine, Playboy* and *Man's World*. A portrait of Alfred Hitchcock graced the cover. The U.K. edition featured the same stories, also published in paperback format, in 1963 under the title: <u>Alfred Hitchcock Introduces "A Bouquet of Clean Crimes and Neat Murders – Stories by Henry Slesar</u>. Arrow Books, Ltd., 192 pages, 3 shillings and 6 pence.

"I had no connection with the Hitchcock anthologies," recalled Slesar, "althought I suspect I had something to do with their origin. I put together two collections of my Hitchcock-aired fiction and asked Hitch's permission to include a forward, which I wrote them myself under his name. Both paperback collections sold very well, which may have led to the idea of a regular series [for Dell in 1962]. I met with Hitchcock to discuss one storyline. He was extremely courteous and had an excellent grasp of storytelling essentials."

B. <u>Alfred Hitchcock in Prime Time Television</u>, Avon Publishing, Paperback, 356 pages, August 1985   Edited by Francis M. Nevins, Jr., and Martin Harry Greenberg.

"And So Died Riabouchinska" by Ray Bradbury, "The Orderly World of Mr. Appleby" by Stanley Ellin, "Momentum" by Cornel Woolrich, "The Better Bargain" by Richard Deming, "The Hands of Mr. Ottermole" by Thomas Burke, "The Dangerous People" by Fredric Brown, "Enough Rope for Two" by Clark Howard, "Suburban Tigress" by Lawrence Treat, "The Day of the Execution" by Henry Slesar, "The $2,000,000 Defense" by Harold Q. Masur, "The Dusty Drawer" by Harry Muheim, "Backward, Turn Backward" by Dorothy Salisbury Davis, "Hangover" by John D. MacDonald, "Hangover" by Charles Runyon, "A Home Away from Home" by Robert Bloch, "Terror Town" by Ellery Queen, "Anyone for Murder?" by Jack Ritchie, "One of the Family" by James Yaffe, "Death Scene" by Helen Nielsen, and "Winter Run" by Edward D. Hoch.

In perfect timing of NBC's *Alfred Hitchcock Presents* revival, this book features twenty short stories, that were all previously adapted for *Alfred Hitchcock Presents*. The introduction was written by Henry Slesar. "In the 1980s, Marty Greenberg and I edited something like a dozen anthologies and collections of mystery fiction," recalled Francis Nevins. "For most of them the division of labor between us was very simple: I chose the stories and either wrote the introduction or had someone else like Bill Pronzini do it. Marty took care of rights, sales, royalties and all the boring stuff. Of all the Nevins & Greenberg titles the most successful commercially was 'Hitchcock in Prime Time,' which

Marty sold to Avon as a trade paperback and later to several overseas publishers. Once the contracts were signed, I chose one, two or three stories that were adapted for the Hitchcock show during each of its ten seasons and Marty got in touch with the authors or their agents to secure the rights. (As things turned out we were unable to include anything we liked that was used during the 1960-61 season but all the other nine seasons were represented.) The money Avon paid us to put the book together allowed us to offer a bonus to any living author who would write an afterword to his or her story. For those who were unwilling, like Ray Bradbury, or dead, like Cornell Woolrich, Fredric Brown and Ellery Queen, I did the honors. I'm staring at a copy of the first edition, dated August 1985. The paper has turned brownish like an old newspaper and so many of the contributors I knew who were alive then and wrote afterwords to their stories – Stanley Ellin, Richard Deming, Lawrence Treat, John D. MacDonald, Robert Bloch – are dead now. God, where do the years go?"

C. Death on Television: The Best of Henry Slesar's Alfred Hitchcock Stories,
Southern Illinois University Press, Hardcover, 259 pages, 1989
Edited by Francis M. Nevins, Jr., and Martin Harry Greenberg.

"Night of the Execution," "The Right Kind of House," "One Grave Too Many," "Party Line," "The Money," "A Crime for Mothers," "The Last Escape," "A Woman's Help," "Coming Home," "Cop for a Day," "The Case of M.J.H.," "The Test," "Burglar Proof," "Most Likely to Suceed," "Final Vow," "Blood Bargain," "Starring the Defense," "Behind the Locked Door" and "Second Verdict."

Just as the title refers, all of the stories in this collection were penned by Henry Slesar, and all of them were previously dramatized on *Alfred Hitchcock Presents*. The titles in this collection are the same as the episode titles, not the original publication titles.

D. Alfred Hitchcock: Tales of Terror, Galahad Books, Hardcover, 631 pages, 1986
Edited by Eleanor Sullivan.

"Killed by Kindness" by Nedra Tyre, "Just a Minor Offense" by John F. Suter, "A Home Away From Home" by Robert Bloch, "Death of a Derelict" by Joseph Payne Brennan, "The Arrowmont Prison Riddle" by Bill Pronzini, "The Dettweiler Solution" by Lawrence Block, "The Whitechapel Wantons" by Vincent McConnor, "Cora's Raid" by Isak Romun, "Life or Breath" by Nelson DeMille, "A Private Little War" by William Brittain, "Have You Ever Seen This Woman?" by John Lutz, "Joe Cutter's Game" by Brian Garfield, "A Cabin in the Woods" by John Coyne, "The Long Arm of El Jefe" by Edward Wellen, "Kid Cardula" by Jack Ritchie, "Career Man" by James Holding, "The Perfidy of Professor Blake" by Libby MacCall, "Sea Change" by Henry Slesar, "The Blue Tamborine" by Donald Olson, "Graveyard Shift" by William P. McGivern, "A Bottle of Wine" by Borden Deal, "Man Bites Dog" by Donald Honig, "Never Trust an Ancestor" by Michael Zuroy, "Another War" by Edward D. Hoch, "Sparrow on a String" by Alice Scanlan Reach, "The Missing Tattoo" by Clayton Matthews, "The Fall of Dr. Scourby" by Patricia Matthews, "The Loose End" by Stephen Wasylyk, "That So-Called Laugh" by Frank Sisk, "A Very Special Talent" by Margaret B. Maron, "The Joker" by Betty Ren Wright, "The Very Hard Sell" by Helen Nielsen, "The Tin Ear" by Ron Goulart, "The Time Before the Crime" by Charlotte Edwards, "After the Unfortunate Accident" by Barry N. Malzberg, "The Grateful Thief" by Patrick O'Keeffe, "The Inspiration" by Talmage Powell, "Death Is a Lonely Lover" by Robert Colby, "The Witness Was a Lady" by Fletcher Flora, "Scheme for Destruction" by Pauline C. Smith, "To the Manner Born" by Mary Braund, "Black Disaster" by Richard O. Lewis, "The Marrow of Justice" by Hal Ellson, "Innocent Witness" by Irving Schiffer, "We're Really Not That Kind of People" by Samuel W. Taylor, "Pocket Evidence" by Harold Q. Masur, "The Death Desk" by S.S. Rafferty, "A Left-Handed Profession" by Al Nussbaum, "Second Spring" by Theodore Mathieson, "Bank Night" by Arthur Porges, "The Contagious Killer" by Bryce Walton, "Bad Actor" by Gary Brandner, "Free Advice, Incorporated" by Michael Brett, "The Real Criminal" by James M. Gilmore, "The Hard Sell" by William Dolan, "The Prosperous Judds" by Bob Bristow, "The Dead Indian" by Robert W. Alexander, and "The China Cottage" by August Derleth.

This was the first of three hardcover books published by Galahad. Commercially packaged in two-volume sets, these three books used Alfred Hitchcock's name on the cover, but no photo or portraits. "A Home Away From Home" and "A Bottle of Wine" were both previously dramatized on the Hitchcock program.

E. Alfred Hitchcock: The Best of Mystery, Galahad Books, Hardcover, 636 pages, 1987

"Winter Run" by Edward D. Hoch, "You Can't Blame Me" by Henry Slesar, "A Flower in Her Hair" by Pauline C. Smith, "The Cost of Kent Castwell" by Avram Davidson, "Pseudo Identity" by Lawrence Block, "That Russian!" by Jack Ritchie, "Galton and the Yelling Boys" by Hillary Waugh, "Blind Date" by Charles Boeckman, "Pressure" by Roderick Wilkinson, "The Running Man" by Bill Pronzini, "The Vietnam Circle" by F.J. Kelly, "Sadie When She Died" by Ed McBain, "A Very Cautious Boy" by Gilbert Ralston, "A Try for the Big Prize" by Borden Deal, "Voice in the Night" by Robert Colby, "Undertaker, Please Drive Slow" by Ron Goulart, "Never Shake a Family Tree" by Donald E. Westlake, "Here Lies Another Blackmailer" by Bill Pronzini, "Dead Duck" by Lawrence Treat, "Games for Adults" by John Lutz, "Night of the Twister" by James Michael Ullman, "Variations on a Game" by Patricia Highsmith, "Child's Play" by William Link and Richard Levinson, "Just a Little Impractable Joke" by Richard Stark, "Murder #2" by Jean Potts, "The Third Call" by Jack Ritchie, "Damon and Pythias and Delilah Brown" by Rufus King, "Glory Hunter" by Richard M. Ellis, "Linda Is Gone" by Pauline C. Smith, "Frightened Lady" by C.B. Gilford, "Come Back, Come Back . . ." by Donald E. Westlake, "Once Upon a Bank Floor" by James Holding, "Warrior's Farewell" by Edward D. Hoch, "Death by Misadventure" by Wenzell Brown, "With a Smile for the Ending" by Lawrence Block, "Television Country" by Charlotte Edwards, "Art for Money's Sake" by Dan J. Marlowe, "Nothing but Human Nature" by Hillary Waugh, "Murder, 1900" by C.B. Gilford, "Panther, Panther in the Night" by Paul W. Fairman, "Perfectly Timed Plot" by X. Ferrars, "#8" by Jack Ritchie, "All the Needless Killing" by Bryce Walton, "A Melee of Diamonds" by Edward D. Hoch, "One for the Crow" by Mary Barrett, "Happiness Before Death" by Henry Slesar, "I Don't Understand It" by Bill Pronzini, "News From Nowhere" by Ron Goulart, "A Case of Desperation" by Kate Wilhem, "An Interlude for Murder" by Paul Tabori, "Death Overdue" by Eleanor Daly Boylan, "The Best-Friend Murder" by Donald E. Westlake, "Pattern of Guilt" by Helen Nielsen, "A Real, Live Murderer" by Donald Honig, "Doctor Apollo" by Bryce Walton, "The Pursuer" by Holly Roth, "Final Arrangements" by Lawrence Page, "Countdown" by David Ely, "Murder Between Friends" by Nedra Tyre, "Case of the Kind Waitress" by Henry Slesar, "Ghost of a Chance" by Carroll Mayers, "The Montevideo Squeeze" by James Holding, and "The White Moth" by Margaret Chenoweth.

Four stories in this anthology, "Winter Run," "You Can't Blame Me," "Final Arrangements" and "Case of the Kind Waitress" were previously dramatized on the Hitchcock program.
This publiation was reprinted in April of 1999.

F. Alfred Hitchcock's Portraits of Murder, Gallahad Books, Hardcover, 504 pages, 1988

"Shattered Rainbow" by Edward D. Hoch, "Wonderful, Wonderful Violence" by Donald Honig, "The Most Unusual Snatch" by Lawrence Block, "A Murder Is Arranged" by Nedra Tyre, "The Poisoned Pawn" by Henry Slesar, "The Lifesaver" by Don Tothe, "What Frightened You, Fred?" by Jack Ritchie, "Doctor's Dilemma" by Harold Q. Masur, "Money to Burn" by Clark Howard, "The House Guest" by Babs H. Deal, "The Man in the Lobby" by William Link and Richard Levinson, "Family Code" by Lawrence Treat, "To Kill an Angel" by William Bankier, "That Monday Night" by Pauline C. Smith, "The Waiting Room" by Charles W. Runyon, "The Keeper" by Clark Howard, "The Jade Figurine" by Bill Pronzini, "The Volunteers" by Reynolds Junker, "Arbiter of Uncertainties" by Edward D. Hoch, "Variations on an Episode" by Fletcher Flora, "Finders-Killers" by Ed Lacy, "The Pearls of Li Pong" by W.E. Dan Ross, "Who?" by Michael Collins, "A Quiet Backwater" by Stanley Abbott, "Murder, Anyone?" by Phil Davis, "The Island" by William Jeffrey, "Room to Let" by Hal Ellson, "The One Who Got Away" by Al Nussbaum, "Unidentified and Dead" by Bryce Walton, "The Lure and the Clue" by Edwin P. Hicks, "The Big Bajoor" by Borden

Deal, "The Operator" by Jack Ritchie, "The Souvenir" by Donald Olson, "Speak Well for the Dead" by Nancy Schachterle, "The Girl in Gold" by Jonathan Craig, "Minutes of Terror" by Donald Honig, "Puddle" by Arthur Porges, "When This Man Dies" by Lawrence Block, "Public Office" by Elijah Ellis, "The Beast Within" by Margaret B. Maron, "Murder in Mind" by C.B. Gilford, "The Invisible Tomb" by Arthur Porges, "Just Curious" by James H. Schmitz, "The Girl Who Found Things" by Henry Slesar, "Death Trance" by Clayton Matthews, "The Healer" by George C. Chesbro, and "Murder by Dream" by Patrick O'Keeffe.

The short story "What Frightened You Fred?" by Jack Ritchie, was previously dramatized on *Alfred Hitchcock Presents*. This same book was reprinted by Galahad, with 512 pages, in September 2000.

G. Alfred Hitchcock's Home Sweet Homicide: Stories From Alfred Hitchcock's Mystery Magazine, Walker and Company Publishers, Hardcover, 228 pages, $18.95, 1991. Edited by Cathleen Jordan.

"Deadly Fantasies" by Marcia Muller, "The Unlikely Demise of Cousin Claude" by Charolotte MacLeod, "Witness" by Nancy Pickard, "The Moonstone Earrings" by Herbert Resnicow, "The Owl in the Oak" by Joseph Hansen, "Domestic Intrigue" by Donald E. Westlake, "The Stone Man" by John F. Suter, "A Young Man Called Smith" by Patricia Moyes, "In the Bag" by Ralph McInerny, "Greektown" by Loren D. Estleman, "What You Don't Know Can Hurt You" by John Lutz, and "A Candle for the Bag Lady" by Lawrence Block.

ANTHOLOGIES

The following is a list of all the Davis-and-sometimes-Dial anthologies. The publisher of the hardcovers read "The Dial Press/Davis Publications." For the paperbacks, just "Davis Publications." Also you'll note that many have months and years of newsstand release. Here are all 27 anthologies, listed in the order they were published. The final story in number thirteen was actually an original, unlike all the other stories that were reprints.

A #1. Alfred Hitchcock's Tales to Keep You Spellbound, The Dial Press/Davis Publications, Inc., Hardcover, 384 pages, $8.95, 1976 (Edited by Eleanor Sullivan.)

"The Pursuer" by Holly Roth, "Final Arrangements" by Lawrence Page, "Countdown" by David Ely, "She Is Not My Mother" by Hilda Cushing, "Spook House" by Clark Howard, "Second Chance" by Robert Cenedella, "The Last Witness" by Robert Colby, "Death a'la Newburgh" by Libby MacCall, "A Cold Day in November" by Bill Pronzini, "A Degree of Innocence" by Helen Nielsen, "The Man We Found" by Donald Honig, "Night on the Beach" by Wenzell Brown, "Scott Free" by Miriam Lynch, "A Very Cautious Boy" by Gilbert Ralston, "A Try for the Big Prize" by Borden Deal, "Killed by Kindness" by Nedra Tyre, "Just a Minor Offense" by John Suter, "The Long Terrible Day" by Charlotte Edwards, "Cicero" by Edward Wellen, "Winter Run" by Edward D. Hoch, "You Can't Blame Me" by Henry Slesar, "Death of a Derelict" by Joseph Payne Brennan, "Present for Lona" by Avram Davidson, "Murderer #2" by Jean Potts, "The Third Call" by Jack Ritchie, "A Home Away From Home" by Robert Bloch, "The Handyman" by Clayton Matthews, "Nothing but Human Nature" by Hillary Waugh, "Murder, 1990" by C.B. Gilford, and "Panther, Panther in the Night" by Paul W. Fairman.

Paperback edition: ALFRED HITCHCOCK'S ANTHOLOGY Vol. 1, $2.25, November 1976 (Novemeber 1976 is definite, even though "1977 edition" was on the front cover and spine.)

A #2. Alfred Hitchcock's Tales to Take Your Breath Away, The Dial Press/Davis Publications, Inc., Hardcover, 384 pages, $8.95, 1977 (Edited by Eleanor Sullivan.)

"The Arrowmont Prison Riddle" by Bill Pronzini, "End of the Line" by Edward D. Hoch, "The Dettweiler Solution" by Lawrence Block, "The Whitechapel Wantons" by Vincent McConnor, "Cora's Raid" by Isak Romun, "A Cup of Herbal Tea" by Robert S. Aldrich, "Albion, Perfidious

Albion" by Everett Greenbaum, "Life or Breath" by Nelson DeMille, "The Silver Lining" by Mick Mahoney, "A Private Little War" by William Brittain, "Superscam" by Francis M. Nevins, "Have You Ever Seen This Woman?" by John Lutz, "Joe Cutter's Game" by Brian Garfield "A Cabin in the Woods" by John Coyne, "Crook of the Month" by Robert Bloch, "Death of a Peruke-Maker" by Clayton Matthews, "The Forever Duel" by James McKimmey, "The Challenge" by Carroll Mayers, "Extra Work" by Robert W. Wells, "The First Moon Tourist" by Duffy Carpenter, "The Long Arm of El Jefe" by Edward Wellen, "Death Sentence" by Stephen Wasylyk, "Kid Carcula" by Jack Ritchie, "Invisible Clue" by Jeffrey Scott, "Accidental Widow" by Nedra Tyre, "Element of Surprise" by Bruce M. Fisher, "Looking for Milliken Street" by Joyce Harrington, "Judgement Postponed" by Robert Edward Eckels, and "The Window" by William Bankier.

Paperback edition: ALFRED HITCHCOCK'S ANTHOLOGY Vol. 2, $2.25, December 1977 (December 1977 is definite, even though "Spring-Summer 1978 edition" was on the front cover and spine.)

A #3. Alfred Hitchcock's Tales to Make Your Blood Run Cold, The Dial Press/Davis Publications, Inc., Hardcover, 350 pages, $8.95, 1978 (Edited by Eleanor Sullivan.)

"Search the Crying Woman" by Harold R. Daniels, "Murder Between Friends" by Nedra Tyre, "Final Exam" by Allen Kim Lang, "The Tutor" by Michael Bruen, "Voice in the Night" by Robert Colby, "The Artist" by Al Nussbaum, "Undertaker, Please Drive Slow" by Ron Goulart, "The Girl Who Wouldn't Talk" by Paul W. Fairman, "Heir Presemptuous" by C.B. Gilford, "The Scar" by Donald Honig, "Spitting Image" by Mann Rubin, "Case of the Kind Waitress" by Henry Slesar, "Ghost of a Chance" by Carroll Mayers, "Storm's End" by Michael Zuroy, "The Picnic People" by Edward D. Hoch, "The Shunned House" by Robert Edmond Alter, "The Welcome Mat" by Carl Marcus, "Career Man" by James Holding, "A Flower in her Hair" by Pauline C. Smith, "Proxy" by Talmage Powell, "The Intangible Threat" by Joseph Payne Brennan, "The Cost of Kent Castwell" by Avram Davidson, "My Unfair Lady" by Guy Cullingford, "Vacation" by Mike Brett, "A Flower for her Grave" by Hilda Cushing, "Another Beautiful Day" by Harold Dutch, "Incident at Mardi's" by Herbert Brean, "The Greatest Robbery on Earth" by Lloyd Biggle, Jr., "Damon and Pythias and Delilah Brown" by Rufus King, "Glory Hunter" by Richard M. Ellis, "Perfectly Timed Plot" by E.X. Ferrars, "#8" by Jack Ritchie, "All the Needless Killing" by Bryce Walton, "The Explosives Expert" by John Lutz, and "The 79 Murders of Martha Hill Gibbs" by Joseph Csida.

Paperback edition: ALFRED HITCHCOCK'S ANTHOLOGY Vol. 3, $2.25, May 1978 (May 1978 is definite, even though "Fall-Winter 1978 edition" was on the front cover and spine.)

A #4. Alfred Hitchcock's Tales to Scare You Stiff, The Dial Press/Davis Publications, Inc., Hardcover, 348 pages, $8.95, November 6, 1978 (Edited by Eleanor Sullivan.)

"Come Back, Come Back" by Donald E. Westlake, "Once Upon a Bank Floor" by James Holding, "Warrior's Farewell" by Edward D. Hoch, "Adventures of the Sussex Archers" by August Derleth, "Don't Lose Your Cool" by Dan J. Marlowe, "Bus to Chattanooga" by Jonathan Craig, "The Perfidy of Professor Blake" by Libby MacCall, "I Don't Understand It" by Bill Pronzini, "News From Nowhere" by Ron Goulart, "A Case of Desperation" by Kate Wilhelm, "The Books Always Balance" by Lawrence Block, "The Second Debut" by Arthur Porges, "Sea Change" by Henry Slesar, "The Green Heart" by Jack Ritchie, "Supply and Demand" by James M. Ullman, "Bird Island" by Ross Brown, "Daisies Deceive" by Nedra Tyre, "Dead Duck" by Lawrence Treat, "Vengeance on the Subway" by Patrick O'Keeffe, "A Very Cold Gimlet" by Frank Sisk, "Games for Adults" by John Lutz, "Farewell, My Brothers" by Theodore Mathieson, "Object all Sublime" by Helen Kasson, "Galton and the Yelling Boys" by Hillary Waugh, "Blind Date" by Charles Boeckman, "The Blue Tambourine" by Donald Olson, and "Graveyard Shift" by William P. McGivern.

Paperback edition: <u>ALFRED HITCHCOCK'S ANTHOLOGY Vol. 4</u>, $2.25, Nov. 28, 1978 (Noevmber date is definite, even though "Spring-Summer 1979 edition" was on the front cover and spine.)

A #5. <u>Alfred Hitchcock's Tales to Send Chills Down Your Spine</u>, The Dial Press/Davis Publications, Inc., Hardcover, 348 pages, $8.95, 348 pages, May 1979 (Edited by Eleanor Sullivan.)

"A Bottle of Wine" by Borden Deal, "The Glass Bridge" by Robert Arthur, "Luck Is no Lady" by Robert Bloch, "The Exit Was a Wall" by Evans Harrington, "An Interlude for Murder" by Paul Tabori, "Peephole" by Henry Slesar, "Death Overdue" by Eleanor Daly Boylen, "The Best-Friend Murder" by Donald E. Westlake, "Man Bites Dog" by Donald Honig, "Go to Sleep, Darling" by James Holding, "Murder Is Dominant" by Glenn Andrews, "A Reform Movement" by Donald Martin, "Remote Control" by Jean Garris, "The Bond" by Bob Bristow, "The Seeing Eye" by Warren Donahue, "Never Trust an Ancestor" by Michael Zuray, "Anyone for Murder?" by Jack Ritchie, "Death by Misadventure" by Wenzell Brown, "With a Smile for the Ending" by Lawrence Block, "Don't Hang Up" by Michael Wilson, "Another War" by Edward D. Hoch, "Pressure" by Roderick Wilkinson, "The Running Man" by Bill Pronzini, "Sparrow on a String" by Alice Scanlan Reach, "The Clock Is Cuckoo" by Richard Deming, "Esther's Dress" by Donald Olson, "A Gallon of Gas" by William Brittain, "Night of the Twisters" by James Michael Ullman, and "Variations on a Game" by Patricia Highsmith.

Paperback edition: <u>ALFRED HITCHCOCK'S ANTHOLOGY Vol. 5</u>, $2.50, Fall-Winter 1979

A #6. <u>Alfred Hitchcock's Tales to Be Read With Caution</u>, The Dial Press/Davis Publications, Inc., Hardcover, $9.95, 350 pages, 1979 (Edited by Eleanor Sullivan.)

"A Melee of Diamonds" by Edward D. Hoch, "One for the Crow" by Mary Barrett, "Happiness Before Death" by Henry Slesar, "The Letters of Mme. de Carrere" by Oscar Schisgall, "Linda Is Gone" by Pauline C. Smith, "Which Is the Guilty One?" by Edward Wellen, "Frightened Lady" by C.B. Gilford, "The Followers" by Borden Deal, "Never Shake a Family Tree" by Donald E. Westlake, "Here Lies Another Blackmailer" by Bill Pronzini, "The Missing Tattoo" by Clayton Matthews, "The Fall of Dr. Scourby" by Patricia Matthews, "Within the Law" by John Lutz, "Act of Violence" by Arthur Gordon, "The Loose End" by Stephen Wasylyk, "That So-Called Laugh" by Frank Sisk, "A Very Special Talent" by Margaret B. Maron, "The Joker" by Betty Ren Wright, "The Man Who Took It With Him" by Donald Olson, "The Plural Mr. Grimaud" by Jacques Gillies, "Pseudo Identity" by Lawrence Block, "That Russian!" by Jack Ritchie, "The Very Hard Sell" by Helen Nielsen, "The Privileges of Crime" by Talmage Powell, "Comeback Performance" by Richard Deming, "The Tin Ear" by Ron Goulart, "Infinite License" by Dan J. Marlowe, "The Montevideo Squeeze" by James Holding, "The White Moth" by Margaret Chenoweth, and "The Time Before the Crime" by Charlotte Edwards.

Paperback edition: <u>ALFRED HITCHCOCK'S ANTHOLOGY Vol. 6</u>, $2.50, November 1979 (November 1979 is definite, even though "Spring-Summer 1980 edition" was on the front cover and spine.)

A #7. <u>Alfred Hitchcock's Tales to Fill You with Fear and Trembling</u>, The Dial Press/Davis Publications, Inc., Hardcover, $9.95, 350 pages, 1980 (Edited by Eleanor Sullivan.)

"The Ring With the Velvet Ropes" by Edward D. Hoch, "Pattern of Guilt" by Helen Nielsen, "The Grateful Thief" by Patrick O'Keeffe, "A Real, Live Murderer" by Donald Honig, "The Inspiration" by Talmage Powell, "Light Fingers" by Henry Slesar, "Doctor Apollo" by Bryce Walton, "Fair Grounds for Murder" by Donald Olson, "After the Unfortunate Accident" by Barry N. Malzberg, "A Professional" by Robert McKay, "Where the Finger Points" by Jack Ritchie, "Give Me Ten Days" by Theodore Pratt, "Death Is a Lonely Lover" by Robert Colby, "Television Country" by Charlotte Edwards, "Art for Money's Sake" by Dan J. Marlowe, "A Sound Investment" by James M. Ullman, "Lady With a Hobby" by Raymond E. Banks, "The Witness Was a Lady" by Fletcher Flora, "Scheme for Destruction" by Pauline C. Smith, "And Seven Makes Death" by Jeff Heller, "Child's Play" by William Link and Richard Levinson, "Just a Little Impractical Joke" by Richard Stark, "To the Manner Born" by Mary Braund, "Deadly Shade of Blue" by Jack Sharkey, "The Dead Past" by Al Nussbaum, "The Vietnam Circle" by F. J. Kelly, and "Sadie When She Died" by Ed McBain.

Paperback edition: ALFRED HITCHCOCK'S ANTHOLOGY Vol. 7, $2.50, May 1980
(May 1980 is definitie, even though "Fall-Winter 1980 edition" was on the front cover and spine.)

A #8. Alfred Hitchcock's Tales to Make Your Teeth Chatter, The Dial Press/Davis Publications, Inc., Hardcover, $9.95, 350 pages, 1980 (Edited by Eleanor Sullivan.)

"Black Disaster" by Richard O. Lewis, "Memory Game" by William Link and Richard Levinson, "A Place to Hide" by Richard Deming. "Kasch for Your Clothes" by Fred S. Tobey, "One Way Out" by Clark Howard, "Sweet Tranquility" by Leo P. Kelley, "Deathbed" by Frank Sisk, "The Choker" by Edward D. Hoch, "Not an Enemy in the World" by Charlotte Edwards, "What Difference Now?" by Clayton Matthews, "All of a Sudden" by John Lutz, "The Lipstick Explosion" by James Holding, "The Deadly Guest" by Helen Nielsen, "That Kind of a Day" by Lawrence Block, "The Slave" by Henry Slesar, "Teeth in the Case" by Carl Henry Rathjen, "The Marrow of Justice" by Hal Ellson, "Favor" by Stephen Wasylyk, "That Year's Victim" by Jack Ritchie, "Innocent Witness" by Irving Schiffer, "Dead Stop on the Road South" by Robert Colby, "We're Really Not That Kind of People" by Samuel W. Taylor, "Weighty Problem" by Duane Decker, "There's Something Funny Here" by James Michael Ullman, "The Ultimate Prey" by Talmage Powell, "Vienna Sausage" by Joyce Harrington, "Sniff" by Donald E. Westlake, and "Pocket Evidence" by Harold Q. Masur.

Paperback edition: ALFRED HITCHCOCK'S ANTHOLOGY Vol. 8, $2.50, October 1980
(October 1980 is definite, even though "Spring-Summer 1981 edition" was on the front cover and spine.)

A #9. Alfred Hitchcock's Tales to Make Your Hair Stand on End, The Dial Press/Davis Publications, Inc., Hardcover, $9.95, 350 pages, April 1981 (Edited by Eleanor Sullivan.)

"Hush, Dear Conscience" by C.B. Gilford, "Death by Misadventure" by Elijah Ellis, "The Death Desk" by S.S. Rafferty, "The Room at the End of the Hall" by Helen Nielsen, "Kisses and Chloroform" by Donald Olson, "A Left-Handed Profession" by Al Nussbaum, "Second Spring" by Theodore Mathieson, "Bank Night" by Arthur Porges, "The Contagious Killer" by Bryce Walton, "The Man Who Came Back" by Edward D. Hoch, "Bad Actor" by Gary Brandner, "Pigeon in an Iron Lung" by Talmage Powell, "Alfred Hitchcock Photoquiz" by Peter Christian *, "King of the World" by John Lutz, "Nice Shooting" by A.E. Eddenden, "Too Solid Mildred" by Jack Ritchie, "Free Advice, Incorporated" by Michael Brett, "Payoff Time" by Clark Howard, "The Way the World Spins" by Bill Pronzini, "The Real Criminal" by James M. Gilmore, "Bang! You're Dead!" by Margaret B. Maron, "The Hard Sell" by William Dolan, "The Prosperous Judds" by Bob Bristow, "The Dead Indian" by Robert W. Alexander, and "The China Cottage" by August Derleth.

Paperback edition: ALFRED HITCHCOCK'S ANTHOLOGY Vol. 9, $2.50, Fall-Winter 1981

A #10. Alfred Hitchcock's Tales to Make You Weak in the Knees, The Dial Press/Davis Publications, Inc., Hardcover, $10.95, 350 pgs., November 1981 (Edited by Eleanor Sullivan.)

* This was not a short story, but rather a compilation of photos from Hitch's various movies with trivia questions regarding each movie. The answers were given on the last two pages of the trivia quiz.

"Shattered Rainbow" by Edward D. Hoch, "The Shoe Freak" by Stephen Wasylyk, "The House Guest" by Babs H. Deal, "Our Man in Office 52" by Stewart Pierce Brown, "Wonderful, Wonderful Violence" by Donald Honig, "Find Artie Smerz – Dead or Alive" by Irwin Porges, "The Most Unusual Snatch" by Lawrence Block, "A Murder is Arranged" by Nedra Tyre, "Persistent Image" by Jules Archer, "The Clean Platter" by Frank Sisk, "The Poisoned Pawn" by Henry Slesar, "The Lifesaver" by Don To the, "What Frighted You, Fred?" by Jack Ritchie, "Loyalty" by Patrick O'Keeffe, "A Place to Visit" by Stephen Marlowe, "The Man in the Lobby" by William Link and Richard Levinson, "A Message From Andrea" by Robert Colby, "Suggestion of Murder" by Clayton Matthews, "That'll Never Happen No More" by Ron Goulart, "Family Code" by Lawrence Treat, "The Art of Deduction" by Richard Deming, "Living All Alone" by John Lutz, "Doctor's Dilemma" by Harold Q. Masur, "Miranda's Lucky Punch" by James Holding, "Money to Burn" by Clark Howard, and "To Kill an Angel" by William Bankier.

Paperback edition: ALFRED HITCHCOCK'S ANTHOLOGY Vol. 10, $2.50, Spring-Summer 1982

A #11. Alfred Hitchcock's Tales to Make You Quake and Quiver, The Dial Press/Davis Publications, Inc., Hardcover, $12.95, 348 pgs., May 1982 (Edited by Cathleen Jordan.)

"That Monday Night" by Pauline C. Smith, "Big Tony" by Jack Ritchie, "Martin for the Defense" by Jamie Sandaval, "The Waiting Room" by Charles W. Runyon, "Scream All the Way" by Michael Collins, "Thieves' Bazaar" by W.L. Heath, "The Keeper" by Clark Howard, "Nice Guy" by Richard Deming, "A Funny Place to Park" by James Holding, "The Jade Figurine" by Bill Pronzini, "A Small Down Payment" by Stephen Wasylyk, "Coffee Break" by Arthur Porges, "The Volunteers" by Reynold Junker, "Death at Stonehenge" by Norma Schier, "Call Me Nick" by Jonathan Craig, "One November Night" by Douglas Farr, "Arbiter of Uncertainties" by Edward D. Hoch, "Witness" by Lee Chisholm, "Breakfast in Bed" by Maeva Park, "Summer in Pokochobee County" by Elijah Ellis, "Variations on an Episode" by Fletcher Flora, "Finders-Killers" by Ed Lacy, "The Pin-Up Boss" by Georges Carousso, "Rainy Wednesday" by Thomasina Weber, "The Short and Simple Annals" by Dan J. Marlowe, "Bite of Revenge" by James McKimmey, Jr., and "The Pearls of Li Pong" by W.E. Dan Ross.

Paperback edition: ALFRED HITCHCOCK'S ANTHOLOGY Vol. 11, $2.95, April 1982 (April 1982 is definite, even though "Fall-Winter 1982 edition" was on the front cover and spine.)

From this point on, the paperback editions were given actual names like the hardcovers, instead of just "Alfred Hitchcock's Anthology." Also note that #12 had a varied title, unlike the rest.

A #12. Alfred Hitchcock's Your Share of Fear, The Dial Press/Davis Publications, Inc., Hardcover, $12.95, 348 pgs., July 1982 (Edited by Cathleen Jordan.)

"Haunted Hall" by Donald Honig, "Chinoiserie" by Helen McCloy, "The Billiard Ball" by Isaac Asimov, "The Bitter End" by Randall Garrett, "The Strange Children" by Elisabeth Sanxay Holding, "A Year in a Day" by Erle Stanley Gardner, "The Mezzotint" by M. R. James, "The Peregrine" by Clark Howard, "Anachron" by Damon Knight, "Change for a Dollar" by Elijah Ellis, "Rest in Pieces" by W.T. Quick, "Lot No. 249" by Arthur Conan Doyle, "Play a Game of Cyanide" by Jack Ritchie, "A Kind of Murder" by Larry Niven, "Confession" by Algernon Blackwood, "The Adventure of the Intarsia Box" by August Derleth, "A Question of Ethics" by James Holding, "A Hint of Henbane" by Frederick Pohl and C.M. Kornbluth, and "The Cold Equations" by Tom Godwin.

Paperback edition: ALFRED HITCHCOCK'S FEAR, (Anthology #12), $2.95, September 1982 (September 1982 is definite, even though "Winter 1982 edition" was on the front cover and spine.)

A #13. Alfred Hitchcock's Death-Reach, The Dial Press/Davis Publications, Inc., Hardcover, $12.95, 348 pgs., November 11, 1982 (Edited by Cathleen Jordan.)

"Who?" by Michael Collins, "A Quiet Backwater" by Stanley Abbott, "Murder, Anyone?" by Phil Davis, "The Island" by William Jeffrey, "T'ang of the Suffering Dragon" by James Holding, "The Hung-Up Juror" by George Antonich, "Room to Let" by Hal Ellson, "Mexico, With Lettuce" by Allen Lang, "The Five-Minute Millionaire" by James Cross, "Christmas Gift" by Robert Turner, "The One Who Got Away" by Al Nussbaum, "Not Exactly Love" by Fletcher Flora, "Unidentified and Dead" by Bryce Walton, "The Lure and the Clue" by Edwin P. Hicks, "The Big Bajoor" by Borden Deal, "Henry Lowden Alias Henry Taylor" by Helen Nielsen, "The Girl With the Dragon Kite" by Edward D. Hoch, "Fat Jow and the Demon" by Robert Alan Blair, "All the Same" by Bill Pronzini, "Two Women - Two Victims" by Donald Honig, "Heaven Is a Frame of Mind" by Richard Hardwick, "The Operator" by Jack Ritchie, "Death by Calculation" by Donald Martin, "Fiesta Time" by Douglas Campbell, "A Man Called Cuervo" by George Grover Kipp, "Occupational Hazard" by John Crowe, and "A Moment, One Night" by Michael Van De Ven.

Paperback edition: ALFRED HITCHCOCK'S DEATH-REACH, (Anthology #13), $2.95, Nov. 19, 1982 (November 1982 is definite, even though "Spring 1983 edition" was listed on the front cover and spine.)

A #14. Alfred Hitchcock's Fatal Attractions, The Dial Press/Davis Publications, Inc., Hardcover, $12.95, 348 pgs., April 1983 (Edited by Elana Loe.)

"The Knight's Cross Signal Problem" by Ernest Bramah, "Murder in Mind" by C.B. Gilford, "The Invisible Tomb" by Arthur Porges, "The Avenging of Ann Leete" by Marjorie Bowen, "Just Curious" by James H. Schmitz, "The Vultures of Malabar" by Edward D. Hoch, "A Matter of Gravity" by Randall Garrett, "August Heat" by W.F. Harvey, "The Girl Who Found Things" by Henry Slesar, "The Return of Max Kearny" by Ron Goulart, "Death Trance" by Clayton Matthews, "The Healer" by George C. Chesbro, "The Monkey's Paw" by W.W. Jacobs, "Rowena's Brooch" by Donald Olson, "Fat Jow and the Manifestations" by Robert Alan Blair, "Murder by Dream" by Patick O'Keeffe, "The Clairvoyant Countess" by Dorothy Gilman, "The Oracle of the Dog" by G.K. Chesterton, "The Dream-Woman" by Wilkie Collins, "The Stolen Rubens" by Jacques Futrelle, and "The Story of the Bagman's Uncle" by Charles Dickens.

Paperback edition: ALFRED HITCHCOCK'S FATAL ATTRACTIONS, (Anthology #14), $2.95, June 1983 (June 1983 is definite, even though "Summer 1983 edition" was on the front cover and spine.)

A #15. Alfred Hitchcock's Borrowers of the Night, The Dial Press/Davis Publications, Inc., Hardcover, $12.95, 348 pgs., July 1, 1982 (Edited by Cathleen Jordan.)

"The Souvenir" by Donald Olson, "Speak Well for the Dead" by Nancy Schachterle, "The Girl in Gold" by Jonathan Craig, "Four on an Alibi" by Jack Ritchie, "The Bag" by Patrick O'Keeffe, "The Long Curve" by George Grover Kipp, "The Green Fly and the Box" by Waldo Carlton Wright, "Minutes of Terror" by Donald Honig, "Long Shot" by Michael Collins, "Puddle" by Arthur Porges, "A Bum Rap" by Marilyn Granbeck, "The Snatch" by Bill Pronzini, "Night Storm" by Max Van Derveer, "The Right Move" by Al Nussbaum, "When This Man Dies" by Lawrence Block, "Busman's Holiday" by James Holding, "The Feel of the Trigger" by Donald E. Westlake, "Public Office" by Elijah Ellis, "The Beat Within" by Margaret B. Maron, "Where Have You Been, Ross Ivy?" by Pauline C. Smith, "Bronze Resting" by Arthur Moore, "Dead End" by Stephen Wasylyk, "The Trouble Was" by Ron Goulart, "The Grapevine Harvest" by Ed Dumonte, "Final Acquittal" by Edward Wellen, "Mousetrap" by Edwin P. Hicks, and "The Adventures of the Haunted Library" by August Derleth.

Paperback edition: <u>ALFRED HITCHCOCK'S BORROWERS OF THE NIGHT</u>, (Anthology #15), $2.95, July 7, 1983 (July date is definite, even though "Fall 1983 edition" was on the front cover and spine.)

A #16. <u>Alfred Hitchcock's A Choice of Evils</u>, The Dial Press/Davis Publications, Inc., Hardcover, $12.95, 348 pgs., October 25, 1983 (Edited Elana Lore.)

"The Battered Mailbox" by Stanley Cohen, "Center of Attention" by Dan J. Marlowe, "Lesson for a Pro" by Stephen Wasylyk, "Aftermath of Death" by Talmage Powell, "Enough Rope for Two" by Clark Howard, "A Change for the Better" by Arthur Porges, "A Killing in the Market" by Robert Bloch, "Do it Yourself" by Charles Mergendahl, "Lost and Found" by James Michael Ullman, "Passport in Order" by Lawrence Block, "Moonlight Gardener" by Robert L. Fish, "Courtesy Call" by Sonora Morrow, "Restored Evidence" by Patrick O'Keeffe, "The Standoff" by Frank Sisk, "A Fine and Private Place" by Virginia Long, "Dead, You Know" by John Lutz, "A Certain Power" by Edward D. Hoch, "Hunters" by Borden Deal, "The Driver" by William Brittain, "Class Reunion" by Charles Boeckman, "Mean Cop" by W. Sherwood Hartman, "Kill, If You Want Me! by Richard Deming, "Welcome to My Prison" by Jack Ritchie, "Come Into My Parlor" by Gloria Amoury, "Lend Me Your Ears" by Edward Wellen, "Killer Scent" by Joe E. Hensley, "Dear Corpus Delicti" by William Link and Richard Levinson, "Knight of the Road" by Thomasina Weber, "The Truth That Kills" by Donald Olson, "Where Is Thy Sting?" by John F. Suter, "Anatomy of an Anatomy" by Donald E. Westlake, "Murder Me Twice" by Lawrence Treat, "Not a Laughing Matter" by Evan Hunter, and "The Graft Is Green" by Harold Q. Masur.

Paperback edition: <u>ALFRED HITCHCOCK'S A CHOICE OF EVILS</u>, (Anthology #16), $2.95, October 25, 1983 (October date is definite, even though "Winter 1983 edition" was on the front cover and spine.)

A #17. <u>Alfred Hitchcock's Mortal Errors</u>, The Dial Press/Davis Publications, Inc., Hardcover, $12.95, 348 pgs., January 6, 1984 (Edited by Cathleen Jordan.)

"Where's Milo?" by Fletcher Flora, "The Wastebasket" by Jack Ritchie, "Dead Game" by Harold Q. masur, "Poltergeist" by W. Sherwood Hartman, "Blood Relatives" by Donald Olson, "A Choice of Witnesses" by Henry Slesar, "One Bad Winter's Day" by William Link and Richard Levinson, "Beyond the Wall" by Nedra Tyre, "Hungry Lion" by Isabel Field, "A Matter of Experience" by Wye Toole, "An Easy Score" by Al Nussbaum, "The Quiet Investigation" by Max Van Derveer, "The Great Rodeo Fix" by Leo R. Ellis, "Fool's Gold" by Gil Brewer, "Voices in Dead Man's Well" by Donald Honig, "The Artificial Liar" by Wlliam Brittain, "The Last Revival" by Clark Howard, "A Padlock for Charlie Draper" by James Holding, "The Late Unlamented" by Jonathan Craig, "The Very Best" by John Lutz, "Give-and-Take" by Dan J. Marlowe, "If a Body" by Stephen Wasylyk, "The Web" by Bill Pronzini, "One Step to Murder" by Jamie Ellis, "The Choice" by Mark Sadler, "Dreaming Is a Lonely Thing" by Edward D. Hoch, "Scents in the Dark" by Edward Wellen, "Lessons from a Pro" by George Kipp, "The Night Helen Was Killed" by Pauline C. Smith, and "A Case for Quiet" by William Jeffrey.

Paperback edition: <u>ALFRED HITCHCOCK'S MORTAL ERRORS</u>, (Anthology #17), $2.95, January 10, 1984 (January date is definite, even though "Spring 1984 edition" was on the front cover and spine.)

A #18. <u>Alfred Hitchcock's Crime Watch</u>, The Dial Press/Davis Publications, Inc., Hardcover, $12.95, 348 pgs., June 7, 1984 (Edited by Cathleen Jordan.)

"Who's Innocent?" by Lawrence Treat, "Item" by Henry Slesar, "I Had a Hunch, and . . ." by Talmage Powell, "The Fly Swatter" by Frank Sisk, "The Patchwork Quilt" by Pauline C. Smith, "Farewell Gesture" by George Grover Kipp, "The Plum Point Ladies" by Henry T. Parry, "The Wells Plan" by Thomasina Weber, "A Debt to Doc" by Carl Henry Rathjen, "Footprints in a Ghost

Town" by Donald Martin, "No Small Problem" by John Lutz, "Water Witch" by William M. Stephens, "You Can't Win 'Em (at) All" by Ed Lacy, "My Escaped Convict" by Donald Honig, "A Husband is Missing" by Fletcher Flora, "Sam's Conscience" by Douglas Farr, "Sweet Smell of Murder" by Allen Lang, "The Donor" by Dan J. Marlowe, "You Can't Get Away with Murder" by Charles Boeckman, "The Invisible Cat" by Betty Ren Wright, "A Woman Is Missing" by Helen Nielsen, "A Good Kid" by James Holding, "Enter the Stranger" by Donald Olson, "The Crime Machine" by Jack Ritchie, and "The Greatest Cook in Christendom" by S.S. Rafferty.

Paperback edition: ALFRED HITCHCOCK'S CRIME WATCH, (Anthology #18), $3.50, June 7, 1984 (even though "Summer 1984 edition" was on the front cover and spine.)

A #19. Alfred Hitchcock's Grave Suspicions, The Dial Press/Davis Publications, Inc., Hardcover, $12.95, 348 pgs., October 1984 (Edited by Cathleen Jordan.)

"The Night of the Sea Serpent" by Thomasina Weber, "The State Against Sam Tucker" by William M. Stephens, "To Catch a Big One" by Robert Edmond Alter, "Never Trust a Woman" by Helen Nielsen, "Piggy Bank Killer" by Jack Ritchie, "No Fish for the Cat" by Neil M. Clark, "The First Crime of Ruby Martinson" by Henry Slesar, "Till Death Do Not Us Part" by Talmage Powell, "Mr. Reed Goes to Dinner" by Ed Dumonte, "The Return of Crazy Bill" by Frank Sisk, "A Dash of Murder" by Jack Morrison, "Strange Prey" by George C. Chesbro, "Sweet Remembrance" by Betty Ren Wright, "A Voice from the Leaves" by Donald Olson, "This Day's Evil" by Jonathan Craig, "The Forgiving Ghost" by C.B. Gilford, "The Crazy" by Pauline C. Smith, "Police Calls" by Carroll Mayers, "Funeral in a Small Town" by Stephen Wasylyk, "Hit or Miss" by Edward Wellen, "Murder in Miniature" by Nora Caplan. "Smuggler's Island" by Bill Pronzini, "Monkey King" by James Holding, "Nice Work If You Can Get It" by Donald Honig, "The Weapon" by John Lutz, "Dead Drunk" by Arthur Porges, "Jurisprudence" by Leo P. Kelley, and "My Daughter, the Murderer" by Eleanor Boylan.

Paperback edition: ALFRED HITCHCOCK'S GRAVE SUSPICONS, (Anthology #19), $3.50, October 1984 (October date is definite, even though "Winter 1984 edition" was on the front cover and spine.)

A #20. Alfred Hitchcock's No Harm Done, Longmeadow Press/Davis Publications, Inc., Hardcover, $7.95, 288 pgs., 1985 (Edited by Cathleen Jordan.)

"Goodbye, Memory" by Jack Ritchie, "The Episode of the Telephone Number" by Charles Einstein, "You Can't Win" by Michael Zuroy, "In the Proper Order" by Ed Dumonte, "Cop Goes the Weasel" by Lawrence Treat, "Put Together a Man" by Steve O'Connell, "The Doll" by Pauline C. Smith, "Ruby Martinson, Cat Burglar" by Henry Slesar, "The Broken Pipe" by Stephen Wasylyk, "Nor Any Drop to Drink" by James R. Berry, "The Alectryomancer" by Charles Willeford, "One Deadly Sin" by Anthony Marsh, "A Good Head for Murder" by Charles W. Runyon, "Of Snow and Death" by Earl Fultz, "By the Sea, by the Sea" by Hal Dresner, "Double Entry" by Kris Giles, "Relative to Murder" by Nora and Lee Caplan, "A Friendly Exorcise" by Talmage Powell, "Aloha, Jenny Swire" by Ernest Savage, "The Blonde and the Bogeyman" by Marshall Schuon, "The Penny-Ante Murders" by Allen Lang, "Seven Story Dream" R.A. Lafferty, "Two for the Moose" by Fred S. Tobey, and "For Whom the Wedding Bell Tolls" by Alex Austin.

Grave Suspicions was the last Dial/Davis title. No Dial hardcovers from here on. This hardcover was "Published exclusively for Longmeadow Press by Davis Publications, Inc." It was shorter by six stories than the paperback couter-part, and bore the Longmeadow Press logo on the spine.

Paperback edition: Alfred Hitchcock's No Harm Done, (Anthology #20), $3.50, 352 pgs., June 1985 The six additional stories was featured between "Two for the Moose" and "For Whom the Wedding Bell Tolls": "Babysitter" by Dion Henderson, "They Sent You" by Donald Olson, "The

Carpenter Ant" by Frank Sisk, "The Scientist and the Stolen Rembrandt" by Arthur Porges, "Manhunt – Indiana Style" by Robert Edward Eckels, and "Rough Justice" by P.A.T. Wilde.

A #21. Alfred Hitchcock's Words of Prey, Hardcover, $3.50, 352 pgs., April 1986 (Edited by Lois Adams and Gail Hayden.)

"Ruby Martinson's Poisoned Pen" by Henry Slesar, "The Desperate Theft" by Stephen Wasylyk, "The Girl From Ishikawa" by Ann F. Woodward, "The Gun Law" by Brian Garfield, "Requiem for Three Sharks" by T.M. Adams, "When the Sheriff Walked" by Jack Ritchie, "Korda" by Al Nussbaum, "Silver Spectre" by Jon L. Breen, "The Prodigal Brother" by William Bankier, "Alternate" by Kevin O'Donnell, Jr., "Faithful Viewer" by Miel Tanburn, "A Bully's Downfall" by John H. Dircks, "Dead Man" by John Lutz, "A Matter of Arson" by Lawrence Treat, "Nemesis" by Jeffry Scott, "Colloquies in Quad" by Frank Sisk, "Death in the Barrio" by Kenneth Gavrell, "Murder Strikes Out" by Richard M. Ellis, "The Seventh Son" by Jean Darling, "Killing Time" by Gary Alexander, "Stranger's Gift" by Talmage Powell, "The Scientist and the Time Bomb" by Arthur Porges, "Safe Delivery" by Tonita S. Gardner, "Inspector Saito and the Shogun" by Seiko Legru, "True Friends" by Patrick O'Keeffe, "Life Sentence" by Kathryn Gottlieb, "It's Called Living" by Max Van Derveer, "Yellow Shoes" by Hal Ellison, and "The Answer" by Bruce M. Fisher.

Paperback edition: Alfred Hitchcock's Words of Prey, (Anthology #21), $3.50, 352 pgs., April 1986. (April 1986 is definite, even though "Summer 1986" was printed on the front cover and spine.)

A #22. Alfred Hitchcock's A Mystery by the Tale, Hardcover, 350 pages, 1986 (Edited by Cathleen Jordan.)

"Stately Ruins" by Frank Sisk, "The Small Hours" by Ernest Savage, "Drawer 14" by Talmage Powell, "The Unstained Code" by George Grover Kipp, "Next in Line" by Jack Ritchie, "A Little Time Off" by Stephen Wasylyk, "Understanding Electricity" by John Lutz, "False Alarm" by Anne Morice, "Flight of the Sparrow" by Gerald Tomlinson, "Martha Myers, Movie Star" by Raymond Mason, "Happy as a Harp Song" by Pauline C. Smith, "Meditations Upon Murder" by Donald Martin, "You Can Die Laughing" by Robert Arthur, "Beware: Dangerous Man" by C.B. Gilford, "The Fanatical Ford" by Arthur Porges, "A Grave on the Indragiri" by Alvin S. Fick, "It Started Most Innocently" by O.H. Leslie, "Last of the Big-Time Spenders" by Duffy Carpenter, "Parlor Game" by Gary Brandner, "Albert and the Amateurs" by Len Gray, "Thin Air" by Bill Pronzini, "Typed for Murder" by Nedra Tyre, "Make My Death Bed" by Babs H. Deal, "Murder on the Edinburgh-London Express" by John H. Dirckx, "A Woman's Work Is Never Done" by Helen Fislar Brooks, "Home Ground" by A.F. Oreshnik, "The Letter Carrier" by Kathryn Gottlieb, and "The World According to Uncle Albert" by Penelope Wallace.

Paperback edition: Alfred Hitchcock's A Mystery by the Tale, (Anthology #22), $3.50, 352 pgs., July 1986. (July date is definite, even though "Fall 1986" was printed on the front cover and spine.)

A #23. Alfred Hitchcock's A Brief Darkness, Hardcover, $3.50, 352 pgs., June 1987 (Edited by Cathleen Jordan.)

"Ley de Fuga" by Brad Williams, "A Piece of the World" by Jack Ritchie, "A Murderous Slice" by Marguerite Dickinson, "High Tide" by Richard Hardwick, "Number One Suspect" by Richard Deming, "Some Lucky License" by Charles Willeford, "A Habit for the Voyage" by Robert Edmond Alter, "Diminishing Wife" by Michael Zuroy, "Jambalaya" by Douglas Craig, "Tight Fix" by Harold Rolseth, "Homicide, Maybe" by Lawrence Treat, "The Sunburned Fisherman" by James Holding, "The Sheriff's Rainy Day" by Elijah Ellis, "Hijack" by Max Van Derveer, "Dream of a Murder" by C.B. Gilford, "Blood Will Tell" by Arthur Porges, "The Mark of Cain" by Allen Lang, "A.C. from E.B." by Lee Millar and Wayne Hamilton, "Crime Buff" by James H. Schmitz, "Small

Town Justice" by Leo R. Ellis, "Man With a Hobby" by Carroll Mayers, "Obligations" by Beatrice S. Smith, "$16,940.00" by Larry Niven, "Bertillon's Odds' by Talmage Powell, "The Zigzag Line" by Don Tothe, "Something for the Club" by Pat Stadley, "The Park Plaza Thefts" by Ernest Savage, and "Waiting for the Coroner" by Gary Brandner.

Paperback edition: Alfred Hitchcock's A Brief Darkness, (Anthology #23), $3.50, 352 pgs., June 1987 (June date is definite, even though "Spring/Summer 1986" was printed on the front cover and spine.)

A #24. Alfred Hitchcock's The Shadow of Silence, Hardcover, $3.50, 352 pgs., December 1987 (Edited by Cathleen Jordan.)

"Nature Morte" by Wincent McConnor, "Too Many Sheriffs" by Richard Hardwick, "Bone of Contention" by Thomas M. Disch, "The Trophy" by Stephen Wasylyk, "The Happenstance Snatch" by Fletcher Flora, "The Return of Sam Lipkin" by Michael Zuroy, "One in a Million" by Charles Einstein, "The Electronic Brain" by Leo R. Ellis, "The Dream-Destruction Syndrome" by James Holding, "The Super Salesman" by Charles McIntosh, "A Perfect Cop Story" by Miel Tanburn, "The Displaced Spirit" by Bryce Walton, "Twice Fifteen" by Anthony Marsh, "Off Trail" by Ray T. Davis, "A Gun Is to Shoot" by Pauline C. Smith, "The Man in the Chair" by Clayton Matthews, "The Sheriff's Christmas Gift" by Elijah Ellis, "Day of the Tiger" by Jack Webb, "Opportunity" by Bill Pronzini, "The Magic Tree" by James McKimmey, "The Creator of Spud Moran" by John Lutz, "See and Tell" by Mary Linn Roby, "The Adventure of the Red Leech" by August Derleth, "Delay En Route" by Dick Ellis, "Process of Elimination" by Max Van Derveer, "Plan 19" by Jack Ritchie, "The Method" by Donald E. Westlake, and "Never Marry a Witch" by C.B. Gilford.

Paperback edition: Alfred Hitchcock's The Shadow of Silence, (Anthology #24), $3.50, 352 pgs., December 1987. (December date is definite, even though "Fall/Winter 1987" was printed on the front cover and spine.)

A #25. Alfred Hitchcock's Most Wanted: The First Lineup, Hardcover, $3.95, 400 pgs., June 1988 (Edited by Cathleen Jordan.)

"The Attache Case" by Ernest Savage, "Auction at McKay's Corners" by Alan K. Young, "Bottomed Out" by Robert Twohy, "Hit and Run" by Clark Howard, "The Incomplete Salmagundi" by S.S. Rafferty, "China Trader" by James Holding, "Going to Meet Terry" by Rick Hills, "The Blushing Bride" by Barbara Ninde Byfield, "A Matter of Chances" by Ron Butler, "The Marley Case" by Linda Haldeman, "To Catch a Wizard" by Walter Sattertwait, "The Right to Sing the Blues" by John Lutz, "The Roughneck and the Dead Guy" by Brent Haywood, "Greektown" by Loren D. Estleman, "Poor Dumb Mouths" by Bill Crenshaw, "The Last Day" by Rob Kantner, "St. Anne Mystery" by Tonda Barrett, "The Mystery of the Lion Window" by Jane Rice, "The Sweetiepie Caper" by Dan A. Sproul, "Stork Trek" by Edward Wellen and Josh Pachter, and "An American Visit" by F.M. Maupin.

Paperback edition: Alfred Hitchcock's Most Wanted: The First Lineup, (Anthology #25), $3.95, 400 pgs., June 1988. (June date is definite, even though "Summer 1988" was printed on the cover and spine.) The cover illustration was created by Jan Glinski, after Andy Warhol.

A #26. Alfred Hitchcock's Shrouds and Pockets, Hardcover, $3.50, 348 pgs., Nov. 1988 (Edited by Cathleen Jordan.)

"A Matter of Kicks" by Lawrence Treat and Richard Plotz, "Caveat Emptor" by Kay Nolte Smith, "The Monster Brain" by Richard Deming, "The Maundering Syndrome" by Dana Lyon, "Jigsaw Puzzle" by Stephen Wasylyk, "Not Worth Flypaper" by Ernest Savage, "The Fake" by Isabel Langis Cusack, "The Revenooer" by Janet Biery, "Meeting Kathleen Casey" by Barbara Callahan, "The Return of Bridget" by Jack Ritchie, "Trial by Fury" by Caryl Brahms and Ned Sherrin, "Theft by Hanko" by Ron Butler, "The Day We Killed the Madman" by Edward D. Hoch, "Where Is Harry Beal?" by John Lutz, "Deep Water" by John C. Boland, "Twang!" by Robert Twohy, "Driscoll's Box Score" by Dick Stodghill, "The Jack in the Sack" by Arthur Moore, "The Experts" by Michael Zuroy, "Murder on Tape" by Herscel Cozine, "Lost Gun" by Arthur Porges, "Vintage Murder" by Vincent McConnor, "Time Waits for No Man" by Kevin O'Donnell, Jr., "Where Have You Gone, Sam Spade?" by Bill Pronzini, "Self-Protection" by James Micahel Ullman, "Slay the Wicked" by Frank Sisk, "I" by Edward Wellen, "Trial Tactics" by Joe L. Hensley, and "A Shroud for the Railroad Man" by Alvin S. Fisk.

Paperback edition: Alfred Hitchcock's Shrouds and Pockets, (Anthology #26), $3.50, 348 pgs., November 1988. (November date is definite, even though "Winter 1988" was printed on the front cover and spine.)

A #27. Alfred Hitchcock's Murder and Other Mishaps, Hardcover, 320 pgs., June 1989 (Edited by Cathleen Jordan.)

"The Intruder" by Henry Slesar, "And Two Bodies Make Four" by C.B. Gilford, "The Minnow" by Bruce M. Fisher, "The Hanging Tree" by Jack Ritchie, "Conspiracy" by William Campbell Gault, "Work for Idol Hands" by Charles Peterson, "A Gross Mscarriage of Justice" by Joyce Porter *, "Shima Maru" by James Holding, "...Said Jack the Ripper" by Robert Arthur, "Just Like a Dog" by Bryce Walton, "Deep Water Double Cross" by Gary Brander, "After Jamie" by Pauline C. Smith, "Sudden, Sudden Death" by Talmage Powell, "Inspector Saito's Simple Solution" by Janwillem Van de Wetering, "Murphy's Day" by Ernest Savage, "A Killing in Real Estate" by Tom Parsons, "A Garden Full of Snow" by T.M. Adams, "Dead Soldier" by Loren D. Estleman, "Anything for a Laugh" by Mann Rubin, "The Frightening Frammis" by Jim Thompson, and "The Curse of Istvan Kodaly" by Alec Ross.

Paperback edition: Alfred Hitchcock's Murder and Other Mishaps, (Anthology #27), $3.50, 320 pgs., June 1989.

TWO HARDCOVERS
Alfred Hitchcock's Mystery by the Tale. Castle, Hardcover, 374 pages, June 1988
Two years after anthology #22 appeared in bookstores, another hardcover printing of this book was published, this time by Castle, a division of Book Sales, Inc. Stated copyright 1986 by Davis Publications, (since the anthology was published in 1986, this makes sense). The book also has the same lineup of stories as the Davis Publication including six additional stories (from Words of Prey):

"Requiem for Three Sharks" by T.M. Adams, "When the Sheriff Walked" by Jack Ritchie, "Korda" by Al Nussbaum, "Silver Spectre" by Jon L. Breen, "The Prodigal Brother" by William Bankier, and "Death in the Barrio" by Kenneth Gavrell.

Alfred Hitchcock's A Brief Darkness, Castle Publishers (a division of Book Sales, Inc.), Hardcover, 379 pages, 1988

One year after anthology #23 premiered on bookshelves, this hardcover edition, again printed by Castle, featured the same stories as the anthology, including eight additional stories, (from Words of Prey):

"Ruby Martinson's Poisoned Pen" by Henry Slesar, "The Desperate Theft" by Stephen Wasylyk, "The Girl From Ishikawa" by Ann F. Woodward, "The Gun Law" by Brian Garfield, "A Bully's Downfall" by John H. Dirckx, "A Matter of Arson" by Lawrence Treat, "Faithful Viewer" by Miel Tanburn, and "Alternate" by Kevin O'Donnell.

* "A Gross Mscarriage of Justice" is not spelled incorrectly, that is the actual way the title of the story is spelled.

CHILDREN'S BOOKS

Since young children were also part of the television viewing audience, it was without a doubt that children's books would also be issued. Twelve different books would be published over a thirty-year period. A series of nine released through Random House would start off the dozen. The stories, of course, were more oriented toward young adults and children, using contemporary and classic tales instead of modern adult-type stories. (Thus no husband-committing-adultry-type stories). All nine of the Random House books were originally published in hardback format and then reprinted in paperback formats throughout the later years by Random House and other subsidiary publishers. During the late 1980s and early 1990s, three more books came into print, released through other publishing houses.

In the U.K., Max Reinhardt Publishers released all of the children's books in hardcover format except for the last three. Sinister Spies was not on their list of being published through them but the rest were.

The first, Alfred Hitchcock's Solve-Them-Yourself Mysteries was published by Random House. Many Three Investigator fans/collectors believe this book to be the seeds to Robert Arthur's eventual creation of the Three Investigators series. One of the Three Investigators' books, #8 "The Mystery of the Silver Spider" featured a mention in the actual story about AH's Solve-Them-Yourself-Mysteries. Specifically, it is the last of the five mysteries called "The Mystery of the Four Quarters." (As a side note: there are no authors listed next to any of the five stories in "Solve-Them-Yourself" but Robert Arthur did pen the last one.) The reference appears on page 133 of the Three Investigators #8 Random House hardbound edition.

Daring Detectives featured stories by the best mystery writers of the twentieth century. Fictional detectives Hercule Poirot, Perry Mason, Ellery Queen, Hildegarde Withers, and The Saint all made an appearance. Virginia Kirkus, an established literary critic, reviewed Haunted Houseful as "a collection of whodunits including selections from Conan Doyle, Mark Twain, Elizabeth Coatsworth, Manly Wade Wellman, John Kendrick Bangs and Donald and Louise Peattie. Nine in all, some are real thrillers, others are exercises in the logic of sleuthing, all are decidedly engrossing." Boy's Life Magazine reviewed Ghostly Gallery: "These are cool creepies from the master of the wacky ghastly . . . Some of the greatest story tellers present their best ghosts in this volume: Robert Louis Stevenson, H.G. Wells, Lord Dunsany." The Chicago American reviewed Sinister Spies: "An especially good collection. Adults will find the stories as interesting as their teen-agers will."

1. Alfred Hitchcock's Solve-Them-Yourself-Mysteries, Random House, Hardcover, 206 pages, 1963 Illustrated by Fred Banbery. Later reprinted in 1986. (Edited by Robert Arthur.)

The five mysteries included were titled: "The Mystery of the Five Sinister Thefts," "The Mystery of the Seven Wrong Clocks," "The Mystery of the Three Blind Mice," "The Mystery of the Man Who Evaporated," and "The Mystery of the Four Quarters."

2. Alfred Hitchcock's Haunted Houseful, Random House, Hardcover, 208 pages, May 1961 Illustrated by Fred Banbery. (Edited by Robert Arthur.)

"Let's Haunt a House" by Manly Wade Wellman, "The Wastwych Secret" by Constance Savery, "Jimmy Takes Vanishing Lessons" by Walter R. Brooks*, "The Mystery of Rabbit Run" by Jack Bechdolt, "The Forgotten Island" by Elizabeth Coatsworth, "The Water Ghost of Harrowby Hall" by John Kendrick Bangs, "The Red Headed League" by Sir Arthur Conan Doyle, "The Treasure in the Cave" by Mark Twain, and "The Mystery in Four-and-a-Half Street" by Donald and Louise Peattie.

* This story was adapted for the Wonderland Record release, Alfred Hitchcock Presents: Ghost Stories for Young People.

3. <u>Alfred Hitchcock's Ghostly Gallery</u>, Random House, Hardcover, 206 pages, 1962
Illustrated by Fred Banbery. (Edited by Robert Arthur.)

"Miss Emeline Takes Off" by Walter Brooks, "The Valley of the Beast" by Algernon Blackwood, "The Haunted Trailer" by Robert Arthur, "The Upper Berth" by F. Marion Crawford, "The Wonderful Day" by Robert Arthur, "The Truth About Pyecroft" by H.G. Wells, "Housing Problem" by Henry Kutter, "In a Dim Room" by Lord Dunsay, "Obstinate Uncle Otis" by Robert Arthur, "The Waxwork" by A.M. Burrage, and "The Isle of Voices" by Robert Louis Stevenson.

4. <u>Alfred Hitchcock's Monster Museum</u>, Random House, Hardcover, 207 pages, 1965
Illustrated by Earl E. Mayan. (Edited by Robert Arthur.)

"The Day of the Dragon" by Guy Endore, "The King of the Cats" by Stephen Vincent Benet, "Slime" by Joseph Payne Brennan, "The Man Who Sold Rope to the Gnoles" by Idris Seabright, "Henry Martindale, Great Dane" by Miriam Alen deFord, "The Microscopic Giants" by Paul Ernst, "The Young One" by Jerome Bixby, "Doomsday Deferred" by William F. Jenkins, "Shadow, Shadow on the Wall" by Theodore Sturgeon, "The Desrick on Yandro" by Manly Wade Wellman, "The Wheelbarrow Boy" by Richard Parker, and "Homecoming" by Ray Bradbury.

The U.K. Edition, released through Max Reinhardt, Ltd., was hardcover, cost 4.5 pounds, and released in 1971. The U.K. edition differed from the U.S. edition in one way. The title of Mirian Allen-de Ford's story "Henry Martindale, Great Dane," was changed to "Gone to the Dogs."
<u>Monster Museum</u> underwent at least two reprints, the third in 1979.

5. <u>Alfred Hitchcock's Sinister Spies</u>, Random House, Hardcover, 206 pages, 1966
Illustrations by Paul Spina. (Edited by Robert Arthur.)

"The Strange Drug of Dr. Caber" by Lord Dunsany, "The Army of the Shadows" by Eric Ambler, "The Adventure of the Bruce Partington Plans" by Sir Arthur Conan Doyle, "Somewhere in France" by Richard Harding Davis, "The Traitor" by W. Somerset Maugham, "Code No. 2" by Edgar Wallace, "The Problem Solver and the Spy" by Christopher Anvil, "The Uninvited" by Michael Gilbert, "QL696.c9" by Anthony Boucher, "Legacy of Danger" by Patricia McGerr, and "Citizen in Space" by Robert Sheckley.

Reprinted in 1982 by Random House.
U.K. Edition: Puffin Books / Penguin Books, Ltd.: Harmondsworth, Paperback, 25 pence, 1971

6. <u>Alfred Hitchcock's Spellbinders in Suspense</u>, Random House, Hardcover, 206 pages, 1967
Illustrated by Harold Isen. (Edited by Robert Arthur.)

"The Chinese Puzzle Box" by Agatha Christie, "The Most Dangerous Game" by Richard Connell, "The Birds" by Daphne du Maurier, "Puzzle for Poppy" by Patrick Quentin, "Eyewitness" by Robert Arthur, "Man From the South" by Roald Dahl, "Black Magic" by Sax Rohmer, "Treasure Trove" by F. Tennyson Jesse, "Yours Truly, Jack the Ripper" by Robert Bloch, "The Treasure Hunt" by Edgar Wallace, "The Man Who Knew How" by Dorothy L. Sayers, "The Dilemma of Grampa DuBois" by Clayre and Michel Lipman, and "P. Moran, Diamond-Hunter" by Percival Wilde.

7. <u>Alfred Hitchcock's Daring Detectives</u>, Random House, Hardcover, 208 pages, 1969
Illustrated by Arthur Shilstone.

"The Day the Children Vanished" by Hugh Pentecost, "Through a Dead Man's Eye" by Cornell Woolrich, "The Disappearance of Mr. Davenheim" by Agatha Christie, "Green Ice" by Stuart

Palmer, "The Grave Grass Quivers" by MacKinlay Kantor, "The Case of the Irate Witness" by Erle Stanley Gardner, "The Adventure of the Grice-Paterson Curse" by August Derleth, "The Headmaster" by Michael Gilbert, "The Adventure of the Seven Black Cats" by Ellery Queen, "The Wicked Cousin" by Leslie Charteris, and "The Footprint in the Sky" by John Dickson Carr.

8. Alfred Hitchcock's Supernatural Tales of Terror and Suspense, Random House, Hardcover, 172 pages, 1973   Illustrated by Robert Shore.

"The Triumph of Death" by H. Russell Wakefield, "The Strange Valley" by T.V. Olsen, "The Christmas Spirit" by Dorothy Bennett, "The Bronze Door" by Raymond Chandler, "Slip Stream" by Sheila Hodgson, "The Quest for 'Blank Claveringi'" by Patricia Highsmith, "Miss Pinkerton's Apocalypse" by Muriel Spark, "The Reunion After Three Hundred Years" by Alexis Tolstoy, "The Attic Express" by Alex Hamilton, "The Pram" by A.W. Bennett, and "Mr. Ash's Studio" by H. Russell Wakefield.

9. Alfred Hitchcock's Witch's Brew, Random House, Hardcover, 171 pages, 1977 Illustrated by Stephen Marchesi.

"The Wishing Well" by E.F. Benson, "That Hell-Bound Train" by Robert Bloch, "As Gay as Cheese" by Joan Aiken, "Madame Mim" by T.H. White, "Blood Money" by M. Timothy O'Keefe, "His Coat so Gay" by Sterling Lanier, "They'll Never Find You Now" by Doreen Dugdale, "The Widow Flynn's Apple Tree" by Lord Dunsany, "In the Cards" by John Collier, "Strangers in Town" by Shirley Jackson, "The Proof" by John Moore.

10. Tales from Alfred Hitchcock's Mystery Magazine, Morrow Junior Books/Davis Publications, Hardcover, 312 pages, $12.95, 1988.   (Edited by Cathleen Jordan and Cynthia Manson.)

"Mysterious Ways" by Richard F. McGonegal, "Going to Meet Terry" by Rick Hills, "Upon Reflection" by Elliott Capon, "Bridey's Caller" by Judith O'Neill, "Love Always, Mama" by Maggie Wagner-Hankins, "The Batman of Blytheville" by Robert Loy, "The Girl in the Orange Beret" by Lee Russell, "The Eye Went By" by Rob Kantner, "Western Wind" by Janet O'Daniel, "Our Little Red Shovels" by David Holmstrom, "Double Substitution" by Colleen M. Kobe, "The Terrible Three" by Thomasina Weber, "A Specialist in Dragons" by Al and Mary Kuhfeld, "The Matchbook Detective" by E.E. Aydelotte, "Appointment with Yesterday" by Hugh B. Cave, "No One Ever Listens" by Stephanie Kay Bendel, "The Marley Case" by Linda Haldeman, "The Poison Flowers" by Anita McBride, "Hunting the Tiger's Eye" by Ruthven Earle-Patrick, and "The Dear Departed" by Dan Crawford.

11. Alfred Hitchcock's Tales of the Supernatual and the Fantastic, Smithmark Publishers, Inc./Bantom Doubleay Dell Direct, Inc., Hardcover, 472 pages, 1993. (Edited by Cathleen Jordan.)

"The Time Between" by J.A. Paul, "Work for Idol Hands" by Charles Peterson, "Second Nature" by William T. Lowe, "The Balancing Man" by Charles Ardai, "Enter the Stranger" by Donald Olson, "The Griffin and the Minor Canon" by Frank Stockton, "Roughin It" by Michael Beres, "Life After Life" by Lawrence Block, "The Last Day" by Rob Kanter, "Don't Make Waves" by George Ingersoll, "An American Visit" by F.M. Maupin, "The Man Who Could Work Miracles" by H.G. Wells, "Spectre in Blue Doubleknit" by Bruce Bethke, "Poltergeist" by W. Sherwood Hartman, "Magic Nights" by Jas R. Petrin, "Strange Prey" by George C. Chesbro, "Love at Second Sight" by Patricia Moyes, "The Misfits" by Jane Rice, "The Masque of the Red Death" by Edgar Allan Poe, "Catechism for Granma" by Charles M. Saplak, "Separate Vacations" by Maggie Wagner-Hankins, "The Bottle Imp" by Robert Louis Stevenson, "Extra Cheese, and I Have Your Coupon" by Dan Crawford, "It Ain't Necessarily So" by Terry Black, "The Undertaker's Wedding" by Chet Williamson, "Ash" by Charles Garvie, "The Horror of the Heights" by Arthur Conan Doyle, "Going Buggy" by J.P. McLaughlin, "Old Flame" by Taylor McCafferty, "There Are Fantasies in the Park" by Marion M. Markham, "The Ronnie" by K.D. Wentworth, "The Canterville Ghost" by Oscar Wilde, and "The Last Crime Story" by Robert Loy.

12. <u>Fun and Games at the Whacks Museum and Other Horror Stories</u>, Simon & Schuster Books for Young Readers/Bantam Doubleday Dell Direct, Inc., Hardcover, Book Design by Paul Zakris, September 1994 (Subtitled: "From Alfred Hitchcock's Mystery Magazine and Ellery Queen's Mystery Magazine." Edited by Cathleen Jordan.)

"Pouring the Foundations of a Nightmare" by Nina Kiriki Hoffman, "Sitter" by Theodore H. Hoffman, "The Three D's" by Ogden Nash, "The Witch, the Child, and the U.P.S. Fellow" by Alan Ryan, "Puddle" by Arthur Porges, "Witch and Cousin" by Maggie Wagner-Hankins, "I Can't Help Saying Goodbye" by Ann MacKenzie, "Fun and Games at the Whacks Museum" by Elliott Capon, "The Undertaker's Wedding" by Chet Williamson, "Old Flame" by Taylor McCafferty, "A Tale Told at Dusk" by Jack Kelly, "The Black Cat" by Lee Somerville, and "The Balancing Man" by Charles Ardai.

Alfred Hitchcock and the Three Investigators

The original Three Investigators Series consists of forty-three different titles. Alfred Hitchcock appears only on the first thirty titles. The publishers/editors then replaced him with a fellow named Hector Sebastian for titles 31 to 43. Only the first thirty, the titles featuring Hitchcock, are listed below. The first 28 were originally published by Random House in hardback format and then reprinted in paperback formats in later years by Random House and other subsidiary publishers. Books #29 and #30 were originally published in paperback format and were not initially published in a hardback trade edition. All titles (including #29 and #30) were also available in Gibralter Library Bindings (hardcover format) for libraries.

All thirty of the original books were revised in paperback between the years of 1982 and 1985 to feature Hector Sebastian instead of Hitchcock as the publisher's supply of the Hitchcock variety were sold. From 1991 to 1993, those same thirty were later reprinted in paperback format by Knopf/Bullseye Books, featuring Hector Sebastian.

Scholastic printings are tricky. Only books one and four have a definitive Scholastic edition date printed in them (included in the info below). The size of these two books are also larger than all the rest. All other known Scholastic editions simply contain the original Random House publishing date inside, but were not necessarily printed by Scholastic in that year. The following contains all known Scholastic titles. #1, #3, #4, #6 - 9, #11, #12, #14, #15, #18 - 21, #25, and #30. Note: The reprintings were slightly abridged, not the full lengths the originals were.

#1 "The Secret of Terror Castle" written by Robert Arthur.
      First published by Random House, hardcover, 1964, 179 pages
      Published by Scholastic, paperback, 1971
      First Windward Silverback Edition, paperback, October 1972
      Reprinted by Random House, paperback, 1978

#2 "The Mystery of the Stuttering Parrot" written by Robert Arthur.
      First published by Random House, hardcover, 1964, 182 pages
      First Windward Silverback Edition, paperback, 1973
      Reprinted by Random House, paperback, 1978

#3 "The Mystery of the Whispering Mummy" written by Robert Arthur.
      First published by Random House, hardcover, 1965, 185 pages
      Reprinted by Random House, paperback, 1978
      Reprinted by Random House, paperback, June 1998, 180 pages

#4 "The Mystery of the Green Ghost" written by Robert Arthur.
    First published by Random House, hardcover, 1965, 181 pages
    Published by Scholastic, paperback, 1971
    Reprinted by Random House, paperback, 1981
    Reprinted by Random House, paperback, June 1998, 179 pages

#5 "The Mystery of the Vanishing Treasure" written by Robert Arthur.
    First published by Random House, hardcover, 1966, 159 pages
    Reprinted by Random House, paperback, 1980
    Reprinted by Random House, paperback, November 1998, 152 pages

#6 "The Secret of Skeleton Island" written by Robert Arthur.
    First published by Random House, hardcover, 1966, 158 pages
    Reprinted by Random House, paperback, 1978
    Reprinted by Random House, paperback, November 1998, 152 pages

#7 "The Mystery of the Fiery Eye" written by Robert Arthur.
    First published by Random House, hardcover, 1967, 180 pages
    Reprinted by Random House, paperback, 1978

#8 "The Mystery of the Silver Spider" written by Robert Arthur.
    First published by Random House, hardcover, 1967, 184 pages
    Reprinted by Random House, paperback, 1978

#9 "The Mystery of the Screaming Clock" written by Robert Arthur.
    First published by Random House, hardcover, 1968, 184 pages
    Published by Random House, paperback, 1978

#10 "The Mystery of the Moaning Cave" written by William Arden (Dennis Lynds).
    First published by Random House, hardcover, 1968, 176 pages
    Reprinted by Random House, paperback, 1978

#11 "The Mystery of the Talking Skull" written by Robert Arthur.
    First published by Random House, hardcover, 1969, 179 pages
    Reprinted by Scholastic, paperback, September 1974
    Reprinted by Random House, paperback, 1978

#12 "The Mystery of the Laughing Shadow" written by William Arden (Dennis Lynds).
    First published by Random House, hardcover, 1969, 178 pages
    Reprinted by Random House, paperback, 1978

#13 "The Secret of the Crooked Cat" written by William Arden (Dennis Lynds).
    First published by Random House, hardcover, 1970, 182 pages
    Reprinted by Random House, paperback, 1981

#14 "The Mystery of the Coughing Dragon" written by Nick West.
    First published by Random House, hardcover, 1970, 181 pages
    Reprinted by Random House, paperback, 1981

#15 "The Mystery of the Flaming Footprints" by M.V. Carey (Mary Carey).
    First published by Random House, hardcover, 1971, 182 pages
    Reprinted by Random House, paperback, 1978

#16 "The Mystery of the Nervous Lion" written by Nick West.
First published by Random House, hardcover, 1971, 150 pages
Reprinted by Random House, paperback, 1981

#17 "The Mystery of the Singing Serpent" written by M.V. Carey (Mary Carey).
First published by Random House, hardcover, 1972, 152 pages
First paperback edition was printed in 1981 by Random House.

#18 "The Mystery of the Shrinking House" written by William Arden (Dennis Lynds).
First published by Random House, hardcover, 1972, 153 pages
Reprinted by Random House, paperback, 1978

#19 "The Secret of the Phantom Lake" written by William Arden (Dennis Lynds).
First published by Random House, hardcover, 1973, 148 pages
Reprinted by Random House, paperback, 1979

#20 "The Mystery of Monster Mountain" written by M.V. Carey (Mary Carey).
First published by Random House, hardcover, 1973, 149 pages
Reprinted by Random House, paperback, 1979

#21 "The Secret of the Haunted Mirror" written by M.V. Carey (Mary Carey).
First published by Random House, hardcover, 1974, 152 pages
Reprinted by Random House, paperback, 1980

#22 "The Mystery of the Dead Man's Riddle" by William Arden (Dennis Lynds).
First published by Random House, hardcover, 1974, 152 pages
Reprinted by Random House, paperback, 1980

#23 "The Mystery of the Invisible Dog" written by M.V. Carey (Mary Carey).
First published by Random House, hardcover, 1975, 152 pages
Reprinted by Random House, paperback, 1981

#24 "The Mystery of Death Trap Mine" written by M.V. Carey (Mary Carey).
First published by Random House, hardcover, 1976, 152 pages.
Reprinted by Random House, paperback, 1980

#25 "The Mystery of the Dancing Devil" written by William Arden (Dennis Lynds).
First published by Random House, hardcover, 1976, 141 pages
Reprinted by Random House, paperback, 1981

#26 "The Mystery of the Headless Horse" written by William Arden (Dennis Lynds).
First published by Random House, hardcover, 1977, 151 pages
Reprinted by Random House, paperback, 1981
Reprinted by A.A. Knopf, paperback, March 1992

#27 "The Mystery of the Magic Circle" written by M.V. Carey (Mary Carey).
First published by Random House, hardcover, 1978, 150 pages
Reprinted by Random House, paperback, 1981

#28 "The Mystery of the Deadly Double" written by William Arden (Dennis Lynds).
First published by Random House, hardcover, 1978, 147 pages
Reprinted by Random House, paperback, 1981

#29 "The Mystery of the Sinister Scarecrow" written by M.V. Carey (Mary Carey).
First published by Random House, paperback, 1979, 151 pages

#30 "The Secret of Shark Reef" written by William Arden (Dennis Lynds).
First published by Random House, paperback, 1979, 181 pages

INDEX

The titles of the Hitchcock episodes are listed in alphabetical order. Episodes broadcast on *Suspicion, Ford Startime,* and *Alcoa Premiere* are listed (in brackets). **Episodes in bold are from the 1980s remake series broadcast over NBC and USA.** *Titles of movies and television programs are listed in italics.* Due to the enormous wealth of author names among the anthology chapter, this index covers the entire book – except – for the table of contents in the anthology chapter.

SELECTED BIBLIOGRAPHY

Books:

Bouzereau, Laurent, The Alfred Hitchcock Quote Book, Citadel Press, 1993.
Brooks, Tim and Marsh, Earle, The Complete Directory to Prime Time Network and Cable
    TV Shows, 1946 – Present, New York, Ballantine Books, 1995 edition.
Brown, Gene, Movie Time, New York, MacMillan, 1995.
Dunning, John, On the Air: The Encyclopedia of Old Time Radio, New York,
    Oxford University Press, 1998.
Gianakos, Larry J., Television Drama Series Programming (numerous editions),
    New Jersey, Scarecrow Press, Inc., 1987.
Grams, Jr., Martin, Radio Drama: American Programs, 1932 – 1962, North Carolina,
    McFarland & Company, Inc., 2000.
Grams, Jr., Martin, Suspense: Twenty Years of Thrills and Chills, Nebraska,
    Morris Publishing, 1998.
Hunter, Evan, Me and Hitch, London, England, Faber and Faber Limited, 1997.
Katz, Ephraim, The Film Encyclopedia, New York, Harper & Row, 1979.
LaValley, Albert, Focus on Hitchcock, Englewood Cliffs, New Jersey, Prentice-Hall, 1972.
McCarthy, Brian and Kelleher, Brian, Alfred Hitchcock Presents, St. Martin's Press, 1984
Mogg, Ken, The Alfred Hitchcock Story, London, England, Titan Books, 1999
Bogdanovich, Peter, The Cinema of Alfred Hitchcock, New York, Doubleday, 1963.
Naremore, James, Filmguide to Psycho, Bloomington, Indiana University Press, 1973.
Nevins, Jr., Francis and Greenberg, Martin Harry, Hitchcock in Prime Time,
    New York, Avon Books, 1985.
Phillips, Gene D., Alfred Hitchcock, Boston, Mass., Twayne Publishers, 1984.
Prouty, Howard H., The Alfred Hitchcock Teleguide, West Hollywood, California
    (unpublished manuscript), 1984.
Rothman, William, Hitchcock – The Murderous Gaze, Cambridge,
    Harvard University Press, 1982.
Schatz, Thomas, The Genius of the System: Hollywood Filmmaking in the Studio Era,
    New York, New York, Metropolitan Books, 1988.
Spoto, Donald, The Dark Side of Genius: The Life of Alfred Hitchcock, New York,
    Ballantine Books, June 1993.
Taylor, John Russell, Hitch: The Life and Times of Alfred Hitchcock, New York,
    Pantheon Books, 1978.
Truffaut, Francois, Hitchcock (revised edition), New York, Simon and Schuster, 1983.
Weaver, Tom, It Came From Weaver Five, 1996.
Weaver, Tom, Monsters, Mutants and Heavenly Creatures, Baltimore,
    Midnight Marquee Press, 1996.
Weaver, Tom, Science Fiction Stars and Horror Heroes, 1991.
Weaver, Tom, Interviews with B Science Fiction and Horror Movie Makers, 1988.
Weaver, Tom, Return of the B Science fiction and Horror Heroes, 2000.
Weaver, Tom, Science Fiction and Fantasy Film Flashbacks, 1998.
Zicree, Marc Scott, The Twilight Zone Companion, Los Angeles,
    Silman-James Press, 1989.

Periodicals:

The New York Post, May 7, 1942, "Screen News and Views" by Irene Thirer.
Coronet, September 7, 1955, "My Five Favorite Mysteries" pp. 74 – 77.
The Herald Tribune, November 16, 1955, "Macabre Merriment"
Daily Variety, December 29, 1955, "TV Can't Compare with Theatrical Pix for Quality"
New York Times, February 12, 1956, "Hitchcock: Violence With Quips"
McCalls, March 1956, "The Woman Who Knows Too Much" p. 12.
Catholic World, March 1956, "Film and TV" p. 465.
Newsweek, June 11, 1956, "Alfred Hitchcock, Director" pp. 105 – 108.

Theatre Arts, September 1956, "We Present Alfred Hitchcock" pp. 27 – 28.
Reader's Digest, September 8, 1956, "His Pleasure is Scaring People" pp. 165 – 168.
Cosmopolitan, October 7, 1956, "Hitchcock Speaking" pp. 66 – 67.
TV Guide, October 27, 1956, "Hitchcock's Observations Concerning Horror,
       Humor and McGuffins" 00. 17 – 19.
House and Garden, December 3, 1956, "How to Harrass a Hitchcock" pp. 42 – 43.
Time, December 26, 1956, "Fat Silhouette" p. 46.
New York Times Magazine, March 3, 1957, "Murder, with English On It" pp. 17 and 42.
New York Times Magazine, July 21, 1957, "Harrison Horror Story" p. 44.
Saturday Evening Post, July 27, 1957, "I Call on Alfred Hitchcock" pp. 36 – 37, 71 – 73.
Theatre Arts, September 1957, "Hush Mush" p. 14.
Look, November 26, 1957, "Hitchcock's World" pp. 51 – 54.
TV Guide, November 30, 1957, "No Problem for Alfred Hitchcock" pp. 17 – 19.
Look, December 24, 1957, "Hitchcock Solves a Murder" p. 129.
TV Guide, March 8, 1958, "Specialty: Murder" pp. 17 – 19.
McCalls, April 1958, "Alfred Hitchcock in the Hundred-Pound Murder" p. 58.
Family Circle, June 1958, "My Husband Hates Suspense" written by Alma Hitchcock.
TV Guide, February 14, 1959, "An Old Master Opposes Sink-to-Sink TV" pp. 17 – 19.
Life, July 13, 1959, "The Master of Suspense Explains his Art" p. 72.
The New Republic, August 10, 1959, "Movies" p. 23.
The New Republic, September 14, 1959, "Reply with Rejoiner" p. 3.
Cosmopolitan, October 5, 1959, "Master of Mayhem" pp. 22 – 25.
The Herald Tribune, June 1, 1960, "Honors for Hitchcock"
Arts: Lettres, Spectacles, June 1 – 7, 1960, "Why I Am Afraid of the Dark" by Hitchcock.
Life, July 11, 1960, "Phantom Face in the Foliage" p. 54.
Coronet, September 1960, "My Recipe for Murder" pp. 49 – 61.
TV Guide, March 25, 1961, "Alfred, The Great Shocker" pp. 17 – 19.
Esquire, July 1961, "Violence" pp. 107 – 112.
Time, May 18, 1962, "Alfred, Squeeze Me a Grape" p. 54.
The Newark New Jersey Evening News, August 26, 1962, "Suspense Shows a Problem."
Senior Scholarship (Teacher edition), November 14, 1962, "Violence Bores Me" p. 23.
Saturday Evening Post, December 15, 1962, "Alfred Hitchcock Resents" pp. 62 – 64.
Milwaukee Journal, March 3, 1963, "Hitchcock Views the Stars"
Redbook, April 1963, "Redbook Dialogue: Alfred Hitchcock and Dr. Fredric Vertham"
Saturday Review, April 20, 1963, "Screens and Screams" p. 44.
TV Guide, May 16, 1964, "The Chairman of the Board" pp. 10 – 13.
Holiday, September 1964, "The Man Behind the Body" pp. 85 – 86.
Variety, October 14, 1964, "Director of Arts: Norman Lloyd"
TV Guide, May 29, 1965, "The Elderly Cherub That is Hitchcock" pp. 14 – 18.
Film Fan Monthly, June 1968, "Hitchcock's TV Films" pp. 3 – 6.
The Los Angeles Times, September 7, 1969, "Hitchcock Abhors Violence
       and Prefers Suspense"
Cinema, Fall 1971, "The Television Films of Alfred Hitchcock" pp. 2 – 7.
Oui, February 1973, "A Conversation with Alfred Hitchcock"
The Jersey Journal, December 7, 1974, "PBS Dramas Rival BBC's" p. A-17.
Emmy, Summer 1979, "Hitchcock: Video Noir" pp. 51 – 53 and 85 – 86.
Cinefantastique, Fall 1980, "The Making of Alfred Hitchcock's The Birds"
Fangoria, May 1986, "An AIP Director Screams Again" pp. 24 – 27, 67.
New York Daily News, June 29, 1986, "Norman Lloyd's Fall to Stardom"
Performing Arts, January 1990, "Actor, Director, Professional" pp. 17 – 22.
Scarlet Street, Winter 1996, "Family Plot: Interview with Patricia Hitchcock" pp. 58 – 60.
SPERDVAC, July 2000, Article about Alfred Hitchcock and "The Lodger"
The Nostalgia Digest, June/July 2000, "Alfred Hitchcock and the Golden Days of Radio"
       pp. 34 – 37.

ABOUT THE AUTHORS

My first exposure to *Alfred Hitchcock Presents* was about a decade ago, when a cable network, Nick-at-Nite, regularly featured the original series, five-times-a-week. Although I myself didn't have cable or satellite at the time, I was always pestering friends who had access, to record copies for me. Like *The Twilight Zone*, (which is one of my other favorite horror/mystery television anthologies), *Alfred Hitchcock Presents* gave me haunting images that to this day, I still recall with vivid imagination.

A few years ago I began writing books on network programs, such as *Suspense* and *The CBS Radio Mystery Theater*. Both programs featured stories also dramatized on the Hitchcock program, and somewhere in the back of my mind, there settled a notion that perhaps one day, with a little inspiration, I would write a book on *Alfred Hitchcock Presents* – both the original and remake. Over the years I made lots of friends, many of whom I consider, some of the greatest scholars on Alfred Hitchcock and his movies. Turning to their expertise, I slowly but surely began gathering information, trivia, interviews, and so on, about the television series, until one day, the dream became a reality.

To be honest, I cannot recall how I first met Patrik, but I can say for certain, that he was the inspiration for making this project a reality. A dedicated fan all-around, Patrik knew each episode by heart, and by coincidence, also had the same idea brewing in the back of his mind. Our collaboration is the final product you hold in your hands, and a labor of love. As of the time this book is being completed, construction is beginning on my other dream, a beautiful two-story log home. During my spare time – of which I seem to have less and less as the years pass by – I work on my stamp collection, read numerous magazines, and further research for future book projects, including co-authoring with Francis M. Nevins, a book documenting the history of *The Radio Adventures of Ellery Queen*.

Martin Grams, Jr., United States, March 2001

Martin Grams, Jr, is the winner of the 1999 Ray Stanich Award.
Martin is also the author of
Suspense: Twenty Years of Thrills and Chills, Morris Publishing, 1998
The History of the Cavalcade of America, Morris Publishing, 1998
The CBS Radio Mystery Theater: An Episode Guide and Handbook, 1974 - 1982,
     (co-authored with Gordon Payton) McFarland & Company, Inc., 1999
Radio Drama, American Programs, 1932 - 62, McFarland & Company, Inc., 2000
The Have Gun – Will Travel Companion, (co-authored with Les Rayburn)
     OTR Publishing, 2000
Martin also contributed chapters for the following:
Vincent Price, (edited by Gary and Susan Svehla) Midnight Marquee Press, 1998
The Alfred Hitchcock Story, (edited by Ken Mogg) Titan Books, 1999

ABOUT THE AUTHORS

I first got in contact with Alfred Hitchcock through re-runs of the TV series on Swedish television in the early 70s, when I was only about seven years old (born 1964). The first episode I remember seeing together with my father was a *Suspicion* episode entitled, "Voice in the Night." I finally got hold of a copy of that episode in October 1999.

Sadly, I wasn't old enough to see the final Hitchcock movie *Family Plot* when it was showing in the cinemas. Instead, I started to collect every film on video but it wasn't until 1985, when I moved from my birthplace, Hoting (a small village in northern Sweden), down to the capital Stockholm, that I started to collect seriously. I bought films on several trips to England and the USA, on which I also visited "Hitchcock" places like London, Mount Rushmore, San Francisco, Santa Rosa and Bodega Bay, to name a few.

My first real involvement was attending the 1996 Hitchcock Convention in Austin, Texas. There I met a lot of Hitchcock scholars and authors, and then the idea for a book started to grow. In February 1998, I started a web page about Hitchcock, which got me in contact with even more Hitchcock collectors and scholars. Through all this I got in touch with Martin Grams, Jr. and instead of doing two separate books that individually would have lacked certain aspects, we decided to write the book together.

On August 13, 1999, I attended the Hitchcock Centennial in Beverly Hills which I felt was the least I could do for a man that has given me so much joy. This book is another thing that I felt was needed. There is so much written about Hitchcock but almost nothing about the TV series.

Other time-consuming hobbies include genealogy, darts, discgolf, music and travel. I got married at Pukulani Falls at Waimanalo Bay, Hawaii, January 6, 2000.

Patrik Wikstrom, Sweden, March 2001

The Alfred Hitchcock Presents Companion
Written by Martin Grams, Jr. and Patrik Wikstrom.

- Did you borrow this book from your local library?

- Has your friend been looking for a copy of this book?

- Looking for that perfect gift for a Hitchcock fan in your family?

- Did you borrow your friend's and find that you won't part with it?

ORDERING INFORMATION:

Please provide the following information:

5. Your name, mailing address, city, state and zip, and a phone number in case we need to contact you.

6. Enclose a check or money order for $35.00 for each copy. Please include ample postage per book. (Check your local post master.)

7. For credit card orders, please list what kind of card you are using (Visa or Mastercard), the card number, expiration date, and the name as it appears on the card.

8. Mail to:
   OTR Publishing,
   Po Box 252
   Churchville, Maryland 21028

Please allow 2 – 3 weeks for delivery. Wholesale prices are available, dealer inquiries are welcome.

The Alfred Hitchcock Presents Companion
Written by Martin Grams, Jr. and Patrik Wikstrom.

- Did you borrow this book from your local library?

- Has your friend been looking for a copy of this book?

- Looking for that perfect gift for a Hitchcock fan in your family?

- Did you borrow your friend's and find that you won't part with it?

ORDERING INFORMATION:

Please provide the following information:

5. Your name, mailing address, city, state and zip, and a phone number in case we need to contact you.

6. Enclose a check or money order for $35.00 for each copy. Please include ample postage per book. (Check your local post master.)

7. For credit card orders, please list what kind of card you are using (Visa or Mastercard), the card number, expiration date, and the name as it appears on the card.

8. Mail to:
   OTR Publishing,
   Po Box 252
   Churchville, Maryland 21028

Please allow 2 – 3 weeks for delivery. Wholesale prices are available, dealer inquiries are welcome.

LaVergne, TN USA
06 February 2010
172268LV00003B/1/P